KU-749-813

HOMERIC DICTIONARY

PHOEBE HAWKES

20/2.   DATH.

HOMERIC DICTIONARY

GEORG AUTENRIETH

Translated by
Robert Keep

DUCKWORTH

This impression 2009
This edition first published in 1984 by
Gerald Duckworth & Co. Ltd.
90-93 Cowcross Street, London EC1M 6BF
Tel: 020 7490 7300
Fax: 020 7490 0080
info@duckworth-publishers.co.uk
www.ducknet.co.uk

A catalogue record for this book is available
from the British Library

All rights reserved. No part of this publication
may be reproduced, stored in a retrieval system, or
transmitted, in any form or by any means, electronic,
mechanical, photocopying, recording or otherwise,
without the prior permission of the publisher.

A catalogue record for this book is available
from the British Library

ISBN 978 0 7156 1773 1

Printed in USA by
IBT Global, Troy, NY

PREFACE.

Dr. Georg Autenrieth, the compiler of the "Wörterbuch zu den Homerischen Gedichten," of which the present volume is a translation, is the Director of the Gymnasium at Zweibrücken, in the Bavarian Palatinate. A favorite scholar and intimate personal friend of that admirable man, Von Nägelsbach, of Erlangen, there devolved upon him, on the death of the latter, the editorial charge of his works, and Autenrieth's editions of the "Gymnasial Päda-gogik," the "Homerische Theologie," and the "Commentary on the First Three Books of Homer's Iliad" gained him the repute of a thorough and judicious scholar, and led to his appointment, at an unusually early age, to the important position which he now holds.

In 1868, at the request of the publishing house of Teubner & Co., of Leipzig, he undertook the preparation of a school dictionary of the Iliad and Odyssey, which appeared in 1873. This work met with favorable criticism in Germany, was translated, within a year from its publication, into Dutch, and has passed to its second German edition. Of Autenrieth's special fitness for the task of compiling such a dictionary, his experience as a practical educator, his devotion for many years to the study of Homer, his numer-ous contributions to the admirable Commentary of Ameis, and the frequent citation of his name in Crusius's Homeric Lexicon (the last edition, that of Seiler and Capelle) furnish sufficient proof. Autenrieth's aim has been not only to convey, in the compactest form consistent with clearness, the results of Homeric study and criticism up to the present time, but also to communicate such col-lateral information as may serve to render the study of Homer in-teresting and attractive. Passages of doubtful or difficult interpre-tation are translated, and the derivations of words receive from the author, who has made the science of comparative philology a special study, particular attention. A novel feature of the work is the introduction into the text of nearly one hundred and fifty small wood-cuts—mainly representations of veritable antiques—which are designed to give to the student a vivid conception of the things mentioned by Homer, by placing before his eyes the warfare, navigation, costume, and sacrificial rites of the Homeric age.

It was the test of actual use which suggested to the editor the idea of translating this book. With it in his hand he read, first the Odyssey, then the Iliad. Tried by this test, it seemed to combine so many excellences that the wish arose in his mind that the work might be made generally accessible to students in America and in England. From the time when he decided to undertake the translation to the present date he has been in frequent correspondence with the author, calling his attention to articles which seemed obscure, and receiving from him the corrections and changes which have been incorporated into the second German edition. The number of additions made by the editor himself is considerable, and many articles have been entirely rewritten, as a comparison of the present with the German edition will show.

Autenrieth's dictionary rests especially upon the labors of three distinguished Homeric scholars—Von Nägelsbach, Döderlein, and Ameis. The frequent references which, in the original edition, are made to these commentators, have been omitted in the translation.

Autenrieth frequently employs a Latin to define a Greek word. The practice commends itself from its conciseness and its precision, and the translator has accordingly in most cases continued it; yet he has not felt that he could presuppose, in the case of American students, such an acquaintance with a large Latin vocabulary as would justify him in omitting to add (in most cases) an English translation.

The present dictionary was intended to be primarily one of Homeric forms. Hence the plan of the work requires that, in the definitions of words which are inflected, the first inflexional form actually occurring in Homer should begin the article, and not, in all cases, the first person singular present indicative active or the nominative singular. Whenever, in rare cases, a non-Homeric form occupies the first place, this is printed in thin-faced type. Occasionally, moreover, a verb which occurs only in a historical tense, and is therefore augmented, will be found in that place which the first person singular of its present indicative active would properly occupy : e. g., ἐξ-έφθιτο, a ἅπαξ λεγόμενον, will be printed but once (to save space), and will be found where (if it occurred in Homer) the present, ἐκ-φθίνω, would stand ; so, likewise, ἐξ-ήρπαξε will occupy the place properly belonging to ἐξ-αρπάζω.

The necessity for extreme conciseness and the restriction of the work to Homeric usage cause some articles to lack that full account of the various meanings of a word, as developed one from the other, which is to be found in a general lexicon like that of Liddell & Scott. A certain baldness and inadequateness in the treatment of many words must, indeed, be a characteristic of such a dictionary. The test of the book, however, is its practical adaptation to the ends it is intended to serve. The writer's own experience has led him to believe that it is well adapted to meet the wants of the young student, as well as to be a companion in the reading of those professional men who have unwillingly let their acquaintance with Homer drop because of the inconvenience of carrying with them on a journey or to the seashore a cumbrous lexicon. It is his earnest hope that this book —so attractive in form, and procurable at so low a price—will render possible, alike in our secondary schools and in our colleges, the reading of a considerably larger portion of Homer than has heretofore been attempted.

The following suggestions as to the use of the book may be found serviceable :

Let the beginning be made by grounding the student carefully and thoroughly upon the forms and peculiarities of the Homeric dialect, with the necessary constant comparison of Homeric and Attic forms. During this stage, the use of the larger lexicon in connection with the present volume will be necessary. Two Books read in this way would suffice. This done, the second step would be to proceed much more rapidly, requiring of the students in recitation only an accurate and intelligent translation of the text and such knowledge as to the meaning and history of the words as this dictionary furnishes.

The editor's own experience leads him to believe that a pupil with this dictionary in his hands will easily read two pages of Homer in the time which, with the large lexicon, would be required for one page. The dictionary also supplies, in a good degree, the place of a commentary, and will be found equally full upon all parts of the two poems. The translator even ventures to hope that the present volume, while offering only legitimate help to the student, may operate to remove the temptation to resort to translations. He is aware of the feeling of dislike with which many teachers regard all special lexicons. That there are grave objections to their use when they cover only a part of the works of an author seems perfectly clear; for then the vocabulary becomes so brief and the range of meaning of the definitions so narrow that translation is rendered for the scholar a merely mechanical exercise. These objections, however, have little force as respects a special lexicon for the Homeric Poems. These poems represent to us every thing, in a connected form, which survives of Epic Greek literature. Not only do their forms differ so widely from those of Attic usage as to constitute a separate dialect, but their vocabulary is an extremely copious one,* and contains a great multitude of words which are used only once, or but a very few times. This latter class of words, it is evident. if occurring in Homer alone, can receive no better elucidation from a large dictionary than from a small one, while the outlay of time required in seeking them in a volume of 1600 pages is very great. The requirements of a scheme of liberal study in our times are so extensive that the necessity of economizing labor, whenever it can be done without detriment to mental discipline, is self-evident. It may be, indeed, that Greek and Latin will only be able to hold their place in our courses of higher education by welcoming and encouraging every legitimate help

---

* The Iliad and the Odyssey contain about 9000 different words.

by which the labor necessary for acquiring a knowledge of the two chief ancient languages, and gaining an acquaintance with their literatures, may be abridged.

There remains for the translator the pleasant duty of mentioning that the proofs of the dictionary have passed under the eye of Dr. Autenrieth, of Zweibrücken, and Prof. John H. Wright, late of Columbus, Ohio. The references have all been twice verified by himself. It will thus be seen that great pains have been taken to secure that accuracy which is at once so indispensable and, in a work like the present, so difficult to attain.

ROBERT PORTER KEEP.

WILLISTON SEMINARY, EASTHAMPTON, MASS., *Sept.* 1, 1876.

The editor avails himself of the opportunity afforded by a new issue of the Dictionary to incorporate the corrections which have accumulated since its first publication. He wishes to express his thanks to Dr. Drisler, Professors F. D. Allen and T. D. Seymour, and to Mr. Irving G. Stanton, an undergraduate student in Harvard College, for the valuable corrections which they have furnished, and to request similar favors in the future from all who may use the book.

R. P. K.

Sept. 1, 1878.

The issue of a new edition of the Dictionary again gives opportunity for the insertion of corrections, and for some additions which suggest a word of introduction.

On pp. xv., xvi. will be found a new Index, in which the attempt is made to enumerate, in connection with each cut, all the important objects which it illustrates. This Index, which forms an almost necessary supplement to that upon pp. xiii., xiv., was prepared and furnished to the editor by Professor John Williams White, of Harvard College.

Pp. xvii.–xxi. are occupied by an outline of the Peculiarities of the Homeric Dialect, based, in contents and arrangement, upon the excellent sketch which forms the first appendix to Koch's *Griechische Schulgrammatik*, 2d ed., Leipzig: B. G. Teubner, 1871. Such an outline seemed likely to be of especial service to those friends of the Dictionary—men in professional life—who wish to read Homer cursorily and from a text-edition, and who look to the Dictionary to furnish all the aid they require.

The editor would renew his suggestion that the Dictionary yields its best results if scholars are not encouraged to use it much until they have mastered, by the aid of Liddell and Scott, at least one book of Homer. Now that the amount of Xenophon required for admission to college is generally read by the aid of special vocabularies, the student comes to Homer, in most cases, without having used a general dictionary. This is the point at which the purchase of a Liddell and Scott should be insisted upon. The thorough study of the Homeric forms involves at every step their comparison with the corresponding Attic forms, and cannot be satisfactorily prosecuted by the aid of the Autenrieth alone.

When three books of the Iliad have been mastered, the scholar will be well prepared for the rapid reading of the Odyssey. Passages especially suited for such reading are Bk. V. (Odysseus's departure from Calypso's island); Bks. VI. and VII. (his meeting with Nausicaa and his reception by Alcinous); Bks. IX. and X. (his account of his adventures with Cyclops, and on Circe's island). Any of these passages can be read by ordinary pupils, with the use of the Dictionary alone, at the rate of fifty to seventy-five lines per hour. And the result of a few weeks of such reading will be to develop the confidence of the student in his own power to translate (a prerequisite to reading at sight with any success) and to greatly increase his interest in Homer.

In addition to the obligations already acknowledged, the editor has to thank for corrections the following friends: Professor J. W. White, Professor O. M. Fernald, and Professor J. H. Wright.

R. P. K.

EASTHAMPTON, MASS., *July* 1, 1879.

IN sending out the Fourth Edition of the Dictionary, the editor desires to express his thanks for the continuance of the favor with which, from the first, the book has been received. Acknowledgments of corrections and suggestions are due to Messrs. F. D. Allen, H. Drisler, A. C. Merriam, L. R. Packard, A. S. Pattengill, E. D. Perry, T. D. Seymour, J. H. Wright, E. G. Coy, T. D. Goodell. The editor has also had before him, in this revision, the third edition of the original work (Leipzig, 1881), containing much new matter. Perhaps the most noticeable changes will be found in the etymologies: these have been carefully revised, and some have been dropped as not supported by sufficient authority.

It is possible that not all teachers and scholars realize what can be done in the way of rapid reading by the use of the Dictionary, and attention is therefore called to the following extract from a letter from one of the professors in Greek in an important Western college:

"In view of your aim in making the book an aid to rapid translation, I think perhaps you will be interested in learning that my class of seventy-five freshmen have read ten books of the Odyssey, and one half of the class have read eleven books. As we do not require any Homer in preparation for college, they had to learn the Epic dialect to begin with. They have almost universally used your book."

With reference to this same matter, the account given by Professor A. C. Merriam, of Columbia College, of the results of his experiments in rapid reading (*Transactions of the American Philological Association*, Vol. XI., 1880), will be found suggestive.

For changes and corrections in this issue of the Homeric Dictionary, the editor acknowledges obligation to Messrs. B. Perrin, G. F. Nicolassen, and W. B. Richards.

R. P. K.

FREE ACADEMY, Norwich, Conn., *July*, 1886.

EXPLANATION OF REFERENCES.

References are made to the several books of the Iliad and the Odyssey respectively, according to the usage of the ancient commentators, by the large and small letters of the Greek alphabet. Thus A 10 signifies Iliad, Bk. I., line 10; and ω 8 signifies Odyssey, Bk. XXIV., line 8; or, in detail:

A.....	Iliad....	I.	....Odyssey....	α	N.....	Iliad....	XIII.	....Odyssey....	ν
B.....	"	....II.	"	....β	Ξ....	"	....XIV.	"	....ξ
Γ.....	"	....III.	"	....γ	O.....	"	....XV.	"	....ο
Δ....	"	....IV.	"	....δ	Π.....	"	....XVI.	"	....π
E.....	"	....V.	"	....ε	P.....	"	....XVII.	"	....ρ
Z.....	"	....VI.	"	....ζ	Σ.....	"	....XVIII.	"	....σ
H....	"	....VII.	"	....η	T.....	"	....XIX.	"	....τ
Θ....	"	....VIII.	"	....Ꝍ	Υ.....	"	....XX.	"	....υ
I.....	"	....IX.	"	....ι	Φ....	"	....XXI.	"	....φ
K....	"	....X.	"	....κ	X.....	"	....XXII.	"	....χ
Λ.....	"	....XI.	"	....λ	Ψ.....	"	....XXIII.	"	....ψ
M....	"	....XII.	"	....μ	Ω.....	"	....XXIV.	"	....ω

The character † designates Homeric ἅπαξ λεγόμενα.

Two references connected by the word *and* designate δὶς λεγόμενα.

Il. or Od. affixed to a definition denotes that the word defined occurs only in the Iliad or only in the Odyssey.

The references in general are to be understood as explanatory, and not as exhaustive: they are uniformly made to the small Teubner edition of the Iliad and Odyssey, edited by Dindorf.

To aid the eye, the first word of each article, or, if that chance not to occur in Homer, the first Homeric form, is printed in full-faced type.

LIST OF ABBREVIATIONS.

acc.	signifies	accusative.
act.	"	active.
adj.	"	adjective.
adv.	"	adverb.
aor.	"	aorist.
cf.	"	confer, compare.
cogn.	"	cognate.
coll.	"	collective.
coll. forms	"	collateral forms.
comm.	"	{ commonly; common gender.
comp.	"	comparative.
compd.	"	compound.
conj.	"	conjunction.
constr.	"	construction.
dat.	"	dative.
dep.	"	deponent.
d., du.	"	dual.
epith.	"	epithet.
esp.	"	especially.
euphem.	"	euphemistically.
exc.	"	except.
fem.	"	feminine.
follg.	"	following.
foreg.	"	foregoing.
freq.	"	frequent.
fut.	"	future.
gen.	"	genitive.
imp.	"	imperative.
indic.	"	indicative.
inf.	"	infinitive.
instr.	"	instrumental.
intrans.	"	intransitive.
ipf.	"	imperfect.
irreg.	"	irregular.
iter.	"	iterative.
κ. τ. λ.	"	καὶ τὰ λοιπά, etc.
lit.	"	literally.
masc., msc.	"	masculine.
met.	"	metaphorical.

mid.	signifies	middle.
nom.	"	nominative.
neut., ntr.	"	neuter.
opp.	"	opposed to.
opt.	"	optative.
orig.	"	originally.
part.	"	participle.
pass.	"	passive.
pf., perf.	"	perfect.
pers.	"	person, personal.
plupf.	"	pluperfect.
pl.	"	plural.
pr., pres.	"	present.
prob.	"	probably.
q. v.	"	quod vide, see.
red.	"	reduplicated.
reg.	"	regular.
sc.	"	scilicet, supply.
signif.	"	signification.
sing., s., sg.	"	singular.
sq., sqq.	"	{ sequens, sequentia.
subj.	"	subject, subjunctive.
subst.	"	substantive.
sup.	"	superlative.
sync.	"	syncopated.
trans.	"	transitive.
verb.	"	verbal adjective.
v.	"	vide, see.
v. l.	"	{ varia lectio, different reading.
w.	"	with.
in tmesi tm. tmesis	"	{ separation of preposition from verb in a compound.
in arsi	"	{ in the arsis (the accented syllable of the foot).
1, 2, 3	"	{ adjectives of one, two, or three terminations.

INDEX OF ILLUSTRATIONS.

PLATES, AT END OF THE VOLUME.

* Plates II., IV., and V. have been added by the translator.

INDEX OF OBJECTS ILLUSTRATED BY EACH CUT.

THE CHIEF PECULIARITIES

OF THE

HOMERIC DIALECT.

IN GENERAL.

A. VOWELS.

1. η is regularly found when, in Attic, ā only would be admissible, e. g. ἀγορή, ὀμοίη, πειρήσομαι.
2. Similarly, ει is sometimes found for ε, ου for υ, e. g. ξεῖνος, χρύσειος, πουλύς, μοῦνος.
3. More rarely οι is found for ο, αι for α, η for ε, e. g. πνοιή, αἰετός, τιθήμενος.
4. By what is called metathesis quantitatis, αο becomes εω (for ἄω). Similarly, we have ἕως and εἷος, ἀπερείσιος and ἀπειρέσιος κ. τ. λ.

B. CONTRACTION OF VOWELS.

1. Contraction, when it occurs, follows the ordinary rules, except that εο and εου form ευ, e. g. θάρσευς, βάλλευ.
2. But the contraction often does not take place, e. g. ἀέκων; and a few unusual contractions occur, e. g. ἱρός (ἱερός), βώσας (βοήσας), εὑρρεῖος instead of εὑρρέους from εὑρρέ-εος.
3. Two vowels which do not form a diphthong are often blended in pronunciation (synizesis), e. g. Ἀτρειδέω, δὴ αὖ, ἐπεὶ οὐ, ἢ οὐ.

C. HIATUS.

Hiatus is allowed :
1. After the vowels ι and υ.
2. When the two words are separated by cæsura or a mark of punctuation.
3. When the final (preceding) vowel is long and in arsis.
4. When the final (preceding) vowel, though naturally long, stands in thesis and has been shortened before the following short vowel.
5. When the final vowel of the preceding word has been lost by elision, e. g.:
    1. παιδὶ ὄπασσεν, − ∪ ∪ | − ∪.
    2. Ὀλύμπιε, οὐ νύ τ' Ὀδυσσεύς, ∪ | − ∪ ∪ | − ∪ ∪ | − ∪ ∪ | − −.
    3. ἀντιθέῳ Ὀδυσῆι, − ∪ ∪ | − ∪ ∪ | − ∪.
    4. πλάγχθη ἐπεί, − ∪ ∪ | −.
    5. ἄλγε' ἔδωκεν, − ∪ ∪ | − ∪.

Remark.—Many apparent cases of hiatus result from the loss of a digamma or other consonant, e. g. τὸν δ' ἡμείβετ' ἔπειτα Ϝἄναξ ἀνδρῶν Ἀγαμέμνων.

D. ELISION.

Elision is much more frequent than in prose. α, ε, ι, ο are elided in declension and conjugation ; αι in the endings μαι, σαι, ται, σθαι ; οι in μοι ; ι in ὅτι.

E. APOCOPE.

Before a consonant, the final short vowel of ἄρα, and of the preps. ἀνά, παρά, κατά, may be cut off (apocope).

Remark.—The accent in this case recedes to the first syllable, and the consonant (now final) is assimilated to the following consonant, e. g. κὰδ δύναμιν, κάλλιπε, ἀμ πεδίον.

F. CONSONANT-CHANGES.

1. Single consonants, esp. λ, μ, ν, ρ, and σ, at the beginning of a word, after a vowel, are frequently doubled, e. g. ἔλλαβον, τόσσος. So also a short final vowel before a follg. liquid is often lengthened by doubling (in pronunciation, though not in writing) the liquid, e. g. ἐνὶ μεγάροισι.
2. Metathesis of vowel and liquid is common, e. g. κραδίη and καρδίη, θάρσος and θράσος.

DECLENSION.

G. SPECIAL CASE-ENDINGS.

1. The termination φι(ν) serves for the ending of the gen. and dat. sing. and pl., e. g. ἐξ εὐνῆ-φι, βίη-φι, ὀστεόφι θίς, σὺν ἵπποισιν καὶ ὄχεσφι.
2. The three local suffixes θι, θεν, δε answer the questions where ? whence ? whither ? e. g. οἴκοθι, οὐρανόθεν, ὄνδε δόμονδε.

H. FIRST DECLENSION.

1. For ᾱ we find always η, e. g. θύρη, νεηνίης, except θεά.
2. The nom. sing. of some masculines in -ης is shortened to -ᾰ, e. g. ἱππότα, νεφεληγερέτα.
3. The gen. sing. of masculines ends in -αο or -εω, e. g. Ἀτρείδαο and Ἀτρείδεω.
4. The gen. pl. of masculines ends in -άων or -έων (rarely contracted, as in Attic, into -ῶν), e. g. θεάων, ναυτέων, παρειῶν.
5. The dat. pl. ends in -ησι or -ης, rarely in -αις, e. g. πύλῃσι, σχίζῃς, but θεαῖς.

I. SECOND DECLENSION.

1. The gen. sing. has retained the old ending in -ιο, which, added to the stem, gives the termination -οιο. Rarely occurs the termination -οο—more commonly the Attic ending -ου. Cf. H. 39 Rem. a, 32 d. Cf. also G. 9, 2.
2. The gen. and dat. dual end in -οιιν.
3. The dat. pl. ends in -οισι or -οις.

K. THIRD DECLENSION.

1. The gen. and dat. dual end in -οιιν, e. g. ποδοῖιν.
2. Dat. pl. -σι, -σσι, usually joined to a consonant stem by a connecting vowel ε, e. g. πόδ-ε-σσιν and ποσσί, βελέεσσι, βέλεσσι, βέλεσι.
3. Stems ending in -σ are generally uncontracted in declension, but -εος often contracts into -ευς.
4. Words in -ις generally retain the ι in all their cases, e. g. μάντις, μάντιος.
   Remark.—For the various forms of πόλις, vid. sub voc. in Lex.
5. Stems in -ευ generally lengthen ε to η in compensation for the omitted υ (Ϝ), e. g. βασιλῆος, βασιλῆι. But proper names may retain the ε, e. g. Τυδέα.

L. ADJECTIVES.

1. The feminine of adjs. of the 1st and 2d declensions is always formed in η, e. g. ὁμοίη, αἰσχρή, exc. δῖα.
2. The Attic rule, that compd. adjs. have only two terminations, is not strictly observed, and, vice versâ, some adjs. which in Attic have three terminations have only two in Homer.
3. Adjs. in -υς are often of only two terminations, and often change the fem. -εια to -εα or -εη. For the various declensional forms of πολύς, vid. sub voc. in Lex.
4. The comp. and superl. endings -ίων and -ιστος are much more extensively used in the Homeric than in the Attic dialect.

M. PRONOUNS.

1. For special forms of pers. prons., vid. sub vocc. ἐγώ, νῶι, ἡμεῖς. σύ, σφῶι, ὑμεῖς. οὗ, σφωέ, σφέων.
2. ὁ, ἡ, τό, in Homer, is dem. pron. In nom. pl. the forms τοί and ταί occur by the side of οἱ and αἱ. The forms beginning with τ have often relative signif., vid. sub voc. in Lex. τοίσδεσσι and τοίσδεσι are forms of ὅδε. κεῖνος is another form for ἐκεῖνος.
3. For peculiar forms of rel. pron., as well as for demonstr. meaning of some of these forms, vid. sub voc. ὅς.
4. For peculiar forms of interrog., indef., and indef. rel. prons., vid. sub vocc. τίς, τις, and ὅστις.

CONJUGATION.

N. AUGMENT AND REDUPLICATION.

1. The augment may be omitted; in this case the accent is thrown back as far as possible toward the beginning of the word. Monosyllabic forms with a long vowel take the circumflex, e. g. λῦσε (ἔλυσε), βῆ (ἔβη).
2. The 2d aor. act. and midd. is often formed in Homer by a reduplication. The only examples of a similar formation in Attic are ἤγαγον, ἤνεγκον (ην-ενεκ-ο-ν), and εἶπον (ἐϜεϜεπον). Among the examples of reduplicated aorists may be mentioned: ἐπέφραδον (φράζω), ἐκέκλετο and κέκλετο (κέλομαι), πιφιδέσθαι (φείδομαι), πεπίθομεν (πείθω), πεπύθοιτο (πυνθάνομαι), ἀμπεπαλών (ἀναπάλλω). Examples of a very peculiar reduplication are ἐνίπ-απ-ον (ἐνίπτω) and ἐρύκ-ακ-ον (ἐρύκω). Here the last consonant of the stem is repeated after a connecting α.
3. There are a few examples of a reduplicated fut. of similar formation with the reduplicated aor., e. g. πεφιδήσομαι, πεπιθήσω.

O. ENDINGS.

1. The older endings of the sing. number μι, σθα, σι, are common in Homer: ἐθέλωμι (subj.), ἐθέλησι (also written ἐθέλῃσι).
2. The ending of the 3d pers. dual in the historical tenses is -τον as well as -την in the act., -σθον as well as -σθην in the midd., voice. In 1st pers. pl., μεσθα is used for μεθα, and μεσθον for 1st pers. dual.
3. The 2d sing. midd. and pass. often loses σ and remains uncontracted, e. g. ἔχηαι, βάλλεο, ἔπλεο (also ἔπλευ), ὠδύσαο. In perf. midd., βέβληαι occurs for βέβλησαι.

4. For the 3d pl. endings -νται and -ντο, -αται and -ατο are often substituted, e. g. δεδαίαται, γενοίατο. Before these endings (-αται and -ατο) smooth or middle labial or palatal mutes are changed to rough, e. g. τετράφαται (τρέπω).

5. The inf. act. frequently ends in -μεναι, also shortened to -μεν, e. g. ἀκουέμεναι, τεθνάμεν·(αι). The 2d aor. inf. appears also in the form -έειν, e. g. θανέειν. There are one or two examples of a pres. inf. in -ήμεναι and -ῆναι from verbs in -άω and -εω, e. g. φορῆναι (.= φορεῖν).

6. The endings -σκον and -σκόμην express repetition of the action, and are called iterative endings. They have the inflection of the ipf. of verbs in -ω, and are rarely augmented. They are attached to the ipf. and 2d aor. of verbs in -ω by the connecting vowel ε, rarely α, e. g. ἔχ-ε-σκον, ῥίπτ-α-σκον, φύγ-ε-σκε. When joined to the 1st aor., these endings follow directly after the connecting vowel of the aor., e. g. ἐλάσα-σκε, μνησά-σκετο. Verbs in -μι append the iterative endings directly to the stem: ἔφα-σκον, στά-σκον, κέ-σκετο (κεῖ-μαι), ἔσ-κον (= εσ-σκον from εἰμί).

The long mood-vowels of the subj. are frequently shortened to ε and ο, e. g. ἴομεν for ἴωμεν, θωρήξομεν for θωρήξωμεν, εὔξεαι for εὔξηαι (= εὔξῃ). This shortening is especially common in 1st aor. subj., which might, in that case, easily be confounded with fut. indic.

1. Verbs in -αω appear in open, contracted, and expanded (assimilated) forms. The expansion consists in prefixing to the long contracted vowel a like-sounding, short, accented vowel, e. g. ὁρόω, ὁράᾳ, ἱλόωσι, ἱλάαν. Cf. G. 120, b.

  Remark.—Sometimes, for the sake of the requirements of metre, a long vowel is prefixed ; or the short vowel is affixed, instead of prefixed, to the long, contracted vowel, e. g. ἡβώωσα, ἡβώοντες.

2. Verbs in -εω are generally uncontracted, but sometimes form ει from εε and εει, η from εε, ευ from εο or εου. In uncontracted forms the stem-vowel ε is sometimes lengthened to ει.

3. Verbs in -όω are generally contracted ; in open forms the stem-vowel ο is generally lengthened into ω. Resolved forms are : ἀρόωσι for ἀροῦσι, δηιόῳεν for δηιοῖεν.

1. Many presents in -ζω are formed from stems ending in γ, e. g. πολεμίζω (fut. πολεμίξομεν), μαστίζω (aor. μάστιξεν). The stem of πλάζω ends in -γγ, e. g. aor. pass. πλάγχθην.

2. Several presents in -σσω are formed from lingual stems, e. g. κορύσσω (perf. pass. ptc. κεκορυθμένος), λίσσομαι (aor. ἐλλισάμην).

3. νίζω shows a stem νιβ, e. g. νίψασθαι.

4. Several other vowel stems, additional to καίω and κλαίω, form the present stem by the addition of ι, e. g. μαίομαι (perf. μέμαμεν).

1. Such pure verbs as do not lengthen the final stem-vowel, in the formation of their tenses, before a single consonant, often double σ in the fut. and 1st aor. act. and midd., e. g. αἰδέσσομαι, νείκεσσε, ἐτάνυσσε. Sometimes the stems in -δ show a similar doubling of σ, e. g. κομίσσατο.

2. The fut. of liquid verbs is generally uncontracted, e. g. μενέω, ἀγγελέω. A few liquid stems take the tense-sign σ, e. g. ἐκέλσαμεν (κέλλω), κένσαι (κεντέω), ὦρσε (ὄρ-νυμι).

3. A few verbs form the 1st aor. act. and midd. without σ, e. g. ἔχευα and χεῦα (χέω=χεύω), ἔσσευα (σεύω), ἠλεύατο, ἀλέασθαι (ἀλεύομαι), ἔκηα, subj. κήομεν, inf. κῆαι (καίω).

4. ο and ε sometimes take the place of α as connecting vowels of the 1st aor., e. g. ἷξον, ἷξες (ἱκνέομαι), δύσετο (δύω). Similarly, the imvs. βήσεο (βαίνω), ὄρσεο and ὄρσεν (ὄρ-νυμι), ἄξετε (ἄγω), οἶσε (φέρω), and the infins. ἀξέμεναι, σαώσεμεν, κελευσέμεναι, occur; and a single example of an aor. ptc. with connecting vowel ο is seen in δυσόμενος (α 24).

5. A 2d aor. act. and midd. is often formed, similarly to the aor. of verbs in -μι, without a connecting vowel. Of this formation there are many instances, e. g. ἔκτα, ἔκτᾶν, ἔκτᾶτο (stem κτᾶ=κτεν), σύτο (σεύω), ἔχυτο (χέω), λῦτο (λύω), opts. φθίμην, φθῖτο—inf. φθίσθαι—ptc. φθίμενος (φθί-ν-ω), ἔβλητο, βλῆσθαι (βάλλω), ἆλτο (ἅλλομαι), δέκτο (δέχομαι), ἔμικτο and μίκτο (μίγνυμι). The imvs. κέκλυθι and κέκλυτε are similarly formed from a reduplicated stem.

T. FORMATION OF PERFECT AND PLUPERFECT.

1. In the forms ἔμμορα (μείρομαι) and ἔσσυμαι (σεύω) we see the same doubling of the initial consonant of the stem after the augment (reduplication), as if the stem began with ρ. The reduplication has been lost in δέχαται (=δεδεγμένοι εἰσί), and is irregular in δείδεγμαι (δέχομαι) and δείδοικα or δείδια.

2. The 1st perf. is formed from vowel-stems alone. The 2d perf. is very common, but always without aspiration, e. g. κέκοπα (κόπτω). There occur frequently forms from vowel-stems which have lost the tense-sign κ, esp. perf. ptcs., e. g. πεφύασι (=πεφύκασι), βεβαρηότες (βαρέω), κεκμηῶτα (κάμνω), τεθνηῶτος and τεθνηότος (θνήσκω).

3. In the plupf. the older endings -εᾰ, -εᾰς, -εε(ν) contracted ει(ν) or η appear, e. g. ἐτεθήπεα, ᾔδεα κ. τ. λ. (cf. ᾔδεα=ᾔδεσαμ, with Lat. videram; ᾔδεας =ᾔδεσας, with Lat. videras; ᾔδεσαν=ᾔδεσαντ, with Lat. viderant).

U. AORIST PASSIVE.

1. The 3d pl. indic. often ends in -εν instead of -ησαν, e. g. ἐμίχθεν, φόβηθεν, τράφεν.

2. The subj. remains uncontracted, the ε of the pass. sign is often lengthened to ει or η, and the follg. mood sign shortened to ε or ο, e. g. δαείω (stem δα), δαμείῃς or δαμήῃς (δάμνημι).

Remark.—A very peculiar form is τραπείομεν, by metathesis, for ταρπείομεν (=ταρπῶμεν, 2d aor. pass. from τέρπω) (Ξ 314).

V. VERBS IN -μι.

1. Forms of the pres. indic. of verbs in -μι occur as if from verbs in -εω and -οω.

2. As the ending of the 3d pl. of the ipf. and 2d aor. act., ν often takes the place of σαν, e. g. ἵεν (ἵεσαν), ἔσταν and στάν (ἔστησαν), ἔβαν and βάν (ἔβησαν), ἔφαν and φάν (ἔφασαν), ἔφυν (ἔφυσαν).

3. In the 2d aor. subj. act., to meet the requirements of the verse, the mood sign is sometimes shortened and the stem-vowel lengthened. Thus arise such forms as θείω, θείῃς, and θήῃς; στήῃς, γνώω, δώῃσι, and δώῃ. Sometimes the α of the stem is weakened to ε, and this again protracted to ει. Thus arise the forms στέωμεν and στείομεν (=στῶμεν), βείομεν (=βῶμεν).

4. For peculiar Homeric forms from the verbs ἵστημι, τίθημι, ἵημι, δίδωμι, εἶμι, εἰμί, οἶδα, ἧμαι, and κεῖμαι, vid. sub vocc. in Lex.

Α- in composition—(1) so-called α privativum, see ἀν-.—(2) α copulativum, orig. *σα (cf. ἅ-μα, English same), then ἀ-, ἁ-, ὁ- contains the idea of union or likeness, Lat. idem or unâ, e. g. ἅπας, ἀολλής, ἄξυλος, ἀθρόος, ἀτάλαντος, ὅτριχες (in words like ἀθρόος cf. ἁμαρτῆ, the existence of an α intensivum was formerly, but incorrectly, assumed).—(3) α protheticum, simple euphonic prefix (like ἰ and ε in Low Latin istatus, ispero; Italian esperanza; French espérance, état), e. g. ἀλείφω, ἀμάω, ἀείρω, ἀμέλγω, ἀμύνω, ἀνεψιός, ἄποινα, ἀσπαίρω, ἄσταχυς, ἀστεμφής, ἀστήρ.

ἆ, interjection expressive of pity or horror, freq. with δειλέ, δειλοί, δειλώ, ξ 361, Λ 816, Ρ 443.

ἀ-άατον [‿-◡◡]. acc. masc. and ntr. (ἀ-, ἀϜάτη), involving harm, ruinous, destructive; Στυγὸς ὕδωρ, Ξ 271, as banishing faithless mortals and perjured deities to the lower world; ἀεθλον, φ 91.

ἀ-αγές (ἀϜαγές, ἄγνυμι), not to be broken, stout, λ 575†. [‿-‿]

ἄ-απτοι, ους, (ΣΑΠ, ἔπω), intractabiles, unapproachable; χεῖρες, χεῖρας; esp. freq. in Il.. e. g. A 567, λ 502, χ 70, 248.

ἀάσχετος, lengthened from ἄσχετος.

ἀάω, (1) injure; (a) τῷδ ἄτῃ ἄασας 2 sing. aor. Θ 237; κ 68, ἄασαν (‿ - -); (b) esp. of injury to understanding, mislead, delude; ἄασε (- ◡ ‿), φ 296; ἄσε, λ 61; with φρένας, φ 297, pass. Τ 136; μίγ' ἀάσθη, Π 685; πολλὸν ἀάσθη, Τ 113; cf. φ 301.—(2) mid. (a) commit a folly, ἀασάμην (- ‿ ‿ -); ἀάσατο (‿ - ◡ ◡)

δὲ μέγα θυμῷ, deceived himself greatly in his thought; Τ 95, Ζεὺς ἄσατο (- ◡ ◡) (v. l. Ζῆν' ἄσατο, see no. 1); (b) trans. dupe, beguile, "Ατη ἢ πάντας ἀᾶται, Τ 91, 129. [aor. 1, act. and mid. ‿ ‿ ‿ and ‿ ‿ ‿ -; pass. ‿ - -.]

ἀβάκησαν, ὃ 249† [‿ ‿ - ‿], of doubtful deriv. (βάζω? ἀϜαω?), and meaning, were befooled, suspected nothing.

Ἄβαντες, inhabitants of Euboia, Β 536. [‿ - ‿]

Ἀβαρβαρέη, Trojan fountain-nymph, Ζ 22. [‿ ‿ ‿ ‿ -]

Ἄβας, αντα, son of dream-reader Eurydamas; slain by Diomedes, Ε 148. [‿ - ‿]

Ἄβιοι, δικαιότατοι ἀνθρώπων, Ν 6, fabulous tribe of the North. [‿ ‿ ‿]

Ἄβληρος, a Trojan, Ζ 32. [- - ‿]

ἀ-βλῆτα (from ἀβλής, βάλλω), ἰὸν, non missum, not discharged, new, Δ 117†. [- - ‿]

ἀ-βλητος, not hit, Δ 540†. [- - ‿]

ἀ-βληχρός, 3, v. l. ἀμβληχρός, (ἀ prothetic, μαλακὸς), only at beginning of verse.—(1) weak, feeble, Ε 337, Θ 178.—(2) θάνατος, gentle, λ 135, ψ 282. [- - ‿]

ἀ-βρομοι (ἀ prothetic, βρέμω), loud-roaring, clamorous, Ν 41. [‿ ‿ ‿]

ἀβροτάξομεν, from ἀβροτεῖν, i. e. ἀμβροτεῖν, ἀμαρτεῖν, aor. subj. fail of, miss; τινός, Κ 65†. [‿ ‿ ‿ ‿ ‿]

ἀ-βρότη νύξ, divine night, Ξ 78†, δ 429. [‿ ‿ -]

Ἄβυδος [‿ - ‿]. town on S. shore of Hellespont, Β 836. Hence Ἀβυδόθεν, Δ 500; Ἀβυδόθι, Ρ 584.

ἀγα-, prefix, exceedingly, mirum in modum, mirum quantum.

ἀγάασθαι, ἀγάασθε, see ἄγαμαι, miror.

ἀγαγεῖν,-ἄγαγον, etc., see ἄγω.

ἀγάζομαι, see ἄγαμαι, miror.

ἀγαθός, 3, (ἄγαμαι), strictly = admirabilis, good, capable, in widest signif.—(1) of persons, valiant, brave, Δ 181, I 341; efficient, B 732, Γ 179; freq. with acc. of specification, πύξ, βοήν; common in signif. noble (cf. optimates, Ξ 113, Φ 109, (opp. χέρηες, o 324); bold, daring, N 238, 284, 314, Φ 280 (opp. κακός, N 279, P 632).—(2) of things and circumstances, excellent, Z 478, ι 27, ν 246; advantageous, B 204, A 793, ρ 347; noble, Ω 632, δ 611; ἀγαθόν τε κακόν τε, blessing and curse, δ 237, 392, θ 63; ἀγαθοῖσι γεραίρειν, do honor, ξ 441; ἀγαθὰ φρονεῖν, bene velle, wish one well, α 43; sana mente uti, think rightly, Z 162; εἰς ἀγαθόν or ἀγαθὰ εἰπεῖν, advise with friendly intent; εἰς ἀγ. πείθεσθαι, follow good counsel. [∪∪∪]

Ἀγάθων, son of Priamos, Ω 249. [∪∪∪]

ἀγαιομένου, parallel form to ἀγαμένου, viewing with indignation, υ 16, κακὰ ἔργα, indignantis scelera; cf. β 67. [∪∪∪∪∪]

ἀγα-κλεής, ες, (from κλέος), only gen. and voc., greatly renowned. [∪∪∪∪] Ἀγακλεής, -κλῆος, Π 571, a Myrmidon.

ἀγα-κλειτός, 3, praeclarus, illustrious, glorious, epith. of men, of a Nereid, Σ 45, and of hecatombs. [∪∪∪∪]

ἀγα-κλυτός, 3, praeclarus, illustrious. of men; δώματα. [∪∪∪∪]

ἀγάλλομαι, only pres., have joy in (τινί), plume one's self upon, P 473, Σ 132, Υ 222; exult, make display, B 462; νῆες, ε 176, speeding gladly forward under Zeus's fair wind.

ἄγαλμα (ἀγάλλομαι), any thing splendid, beautiful, or precious, Δ 144; votive offerings, γ 274, θ 509, μ 347; applied to sacrificial victim, γ 438; to horses, δ 602; personal adornments, σ 3 0, τ 257. [∪∪∪]

ἄγαμαι (ἄγη), aor. ἠγασάμην, ἠγασσάμην (also unaugmented); and from parallel form, ἀγάομαι; ἀγάασθε, ἀγάασθαι, ipf. ἠγάασθε; the form ἄγαμαι, only in signif. 1.—(1) admirari, admire, H 41, 404, Θ 29, and mirari, demirari, gaze at with amazement, σ 71; in π 203, θαυμάζειν, behold with wonder, joined with ἀγάασθαι, be astonished.—(2) in bad sense, (a) indignari, be indignant, outraged at, with acc., β 67; with dat., θ 565; be vexed, annoyed, Ψ 639; with κότῳ, Ξ 111; (b) invidere, envy. grudge, δ 181, with inf., ε 129; esp. freq. of envy of the gods, δ 181, ψ 211, θ 565, H 442. [∪∪−]

Ἀγαμεμνονίδης, son of Agamemnon, Orestes, α 30.

Ἀγαμέμνων, ονος. His grandfather was Tantalos, whose sons were Atreus and Thyestes (father of Aigisthos); Atreus's sons, Agamemnon and Menelaos; Agamemnon's children, Orestes, Chrysothemis, Laodike, Iphianassa; cf. B 104, I 287; his wife, Klytaimnestra. King in Mykenai, but at the same time πολλῇσιν νήσοισι καὶ Ἄργεῖ παντὶ ἀνάσσειν, B 108; his wealth in ships, B 576, 610–14; commander-in-chief of Grecian host before Troy; εὐρυκρείων and ἄναξ ἀνδρῶν, A 172; κρείων, ποιμὴν λαῶν, δῖος; his bodily size, Γ 166, 178; B 477–83; ἀριστεία, exploits, Λ 91–661; honor accorded him, Ψ 887; sceptre, B 104; return from Troia, γ 143 sqq., 156, 193 sqq., 234 sq.; is murdered, γ 248 sqq., δ 91, 512–37, 584, λ 387–463, ω 20–97 [∪∪ −−]. Hence fem. adj. Ἀγαμεμνονέη.

Ἀγαμήδη (cf. Μήδεια), daughter of Augeias, granddaughter of Sun-god, Λ 740. [∪∪−∪]

ἄ-γαμος, 2, (from γάμος), unmarried, Γ 40†. [∪∪∪]

ἀγά-ννιφον Ὄλυμπον (ἀγα-σνιφ., see νίφω), A 420, Σ 186; nivosum, covered with deep snow, snow-capped. [∪∪∪∪]

ἀγανός, 3, (from γάνυμαι), lenis, pleasant, gentle, ἔπεα, δῶρα; kind, friendly, εὐχωλαί, βασιλεύς (opp. χαλεπός), β 230; common phrase, οἷς ἀγανοῖς βελέεσσι, with his (or her) gentle missiles, describing a (natural) sudden, painless death dealt by Apollo upon men, by Artemis upon women, γ 280.

ἀγανο-φροσύνη, ἡ, comitas, gentleness, friendliness, λ 203, cf. β 230. [∪∪∪−∪∪∪]

ἀγανό-φρων, comis, gentle, friendly, Υ 467†. [∪∪−−]

ἀγάομαι, see ἄγαμαι, miror.

ἀγαπάζω (parallel form of ἀγαπάω) and -ομαι, only prs., τινά, receive kindly, π 17, η 33; espouse the cause of, Ω 464. [‿‿–‿]

ἀγαπάω, ἀγάπησα, ψ 214, I lovingly received; and φ 289, art thou not therewith content? [‿–‿–]

ἀγαπ-ήνωρ, ος, loving - manliness, manly, Ο 392. [‿‿––]

Ἀγαπήνωρ, Ἀγκαίοιο πᾶϊς, Β 609, king of Arkadians, vassal of Agamemnon, to whom he brought the equipment of sixty ships.

ἀγαπητός (ἀγαπάω), beloved, dear, always with παῖς, son, which is to be supplied in β 365. [‿–‿‿]

ἀγά-ρροος (ἀγα-σρόϝος, ῥέω), strong-flowing; Ἑλλήσποντος, Β 845, acc. Μ 30.

Ἀγασθένης (σθένος), son of Augeias, king in Elis, Β 624.

ἀγά-στονος (στένω), fremens, boisterous, epith. of Ἀμφιτρίτη, μ 97†. [‿–‿‿]

Ἀγάστροφος, a Trojan, Λ 338. [‿–‿‿]

Ἀγαύη, a Nereid, Σ 42. [‿––]

ἀγανός, 3, (from ἄγαμαι), admirabilis; illustrious (cf. clarissimus), an epithet applied, honoris causâ, to rulers, nations (Phaiakians, Trojans, ν 272 to Phoinikes, Ν 5 to Hippemolgoi); also freq. to suitors; ν 71 to the noble πομπῆες; ε 1 to Tithonos; and thrice to Persephoneia. [‿‿‿]

ἀγγελίη, ἡ, (ἄγγελος), tidings, message, report, Η 416, Ι 422, Ξ 355, Ο 174; ἀλεγεινή, λυγρή; πατρός, de patre, α 408, cf. β 30; command, ε 150, η 263; as causal gen., Γ 206, he came (because of) on a mission respecting thee; ἀγγελίην ἐλθόντα, Λ 140; cf. also ἀγγελίης in Ν 252. Ο 640, Γ 206; see also ἀγγελίης. ὁ. [‿‿‿–]

ἀγγελίης, ὁ, (ἄγγελος), nuntius, messenger, handed down by old grammarians as nom. masc., like ταμίης and νεηνίης; thus we may explain Γ 206, Ν 252, Ο 640, Δ 384, Λ 140; also such passages as α 414, β 92, ν 381. [‿–‿‿‿]

ἀγγέλλων (ἄγγελος), fut. ἀγγελέω, aor. ἤγγειλα, inf. Ο 159; nuntiare, report, announce; τί, also τινά. ξ 120, 123; with inf., bid, π 350, Θ 517.

ἄγγελος, ὁ and ἡ, (cf. German gellen, English yell, nightin-gale), nuntius, nuntia, messenger; common phrase, ἦλθέ τινι, Λ 715; Ὄσσα Διὸς ἄγγ., Β 94; also of birds, ο 526.

ἄγγος, εος, τό, vas, vase, bowl; for victuals, β 289, and drink.

ἄγε, ἄγετε, (ἄγω), particle like age, agedum; quick! come! after ἀλλά, or before δή; with subj. or imp., cf. French allons! ἄγε often occurs with pl., e. g. γ 475; see also εἰ δ᾽ ἄγε.

ἀγείρω (cf. gerere?), aor. ἤγειρα; pass. pf. ἀγήγερμαι, aor. ἠγέρθην, 3 pl ἄγερθεν; mid. aor. ἀγερόμην, inf. ἀγείρεσθαι (written by ancient grammarians as pres. ἀγέρεσθαι), part. ἀγρόμενος. —(1) act. colligere, congregare, collect, call together, assemble, τ 197, ἀγορήν, concionem advocare; pass. and aor. mid. gather together; ἐς φρένα θυμὸς ἠγέρθη, consciousness (Δ 152, courage, presence of mind), came back again.

ἀγελαίη (ἀγέλη), βοῦς, βύες, βόας, gregaria, belonging to a herd, feeding at large. [‿‿––]

Ἀγέλαος (ἄγω, λαός), (1) son of Damastor, suitor, χ 131, 247, Ἀγέλεως.— (2) son of Phradmon, a Trojan, Θ 257. —(3) Greek, Λ 302. [‿‿‿‿]

ἀγελείη (ἄγουσα λείαν), praedatrix, bestower of spoil; cf. ληῖτις, epith. of Athene, only at end of verse, ν 359. [‿‿––]

ἀγέλη, ης, (ἄγω), grex, herd of cattle, exc. Τ 281, where it is a drove of horses; ἀγέληφι, Π 487, with the herd. [‿‿–]

ἀγεληδόν, gregatim, in herds, Π 160. [‿‿–‿]

ἀγέμεν = ἄγειν.

ἄγεν = ἰάγησαν, from ἄγνυμι.

ἀ-γέραστος (γέρας), inhonoratus, without a gift of honor, Α 119†. [‿‿–‿]

ἄγερθεν, see ἀγείρω, congregati sunt.

ἀγέρωχοι, ων, (ἄγα, ἐρωή), impetuous, brave in combat; epith. of Trojans, Mysians, Rhodians, and of Periklymenos, λ 286; formerly explained, very honorable, as if from α copul. and γερα-οχος. [‿‿‿‿]

ἄγη μ᾽ ἔχει (de)miror, I am astonished, Φ 221. [‿–]

ἀγηγέραθ' (ατο), sec ἀγείρω, congregati erant.

ἀγ-ηνορίη, ης, ἡ, (ἀγήνωρ), virtus, manliness, courage, M 46 ; X 457, of the courage which will not let Hektor rest; Ι 700, pride.

ἀγ-ήνωρ (ἄγα, ἀνήρ), ferox, very manly.—(1) brave, bold, σ 43, a 106; high-hearted, θυμός, δ 658 ; high-beating life, Υ 406 ; also, μ 414, of helmsman ; elsewh. with θυμός, freq. = noble, generous mind.—(2) haughty, Ι 699, Φ 443. [∪ − −]

Ἀγήνωρ, ορος, son of Trojan Antenor and Theano, Λ 59, Φ 579, Υ 474, Ο 340.

ἀ-γήραος, ἀγήρως, 2, (γῆρας), aeternus, ageless, of undecaying vigor, always with ἀθάνατος, Θ 539 ; αἰγίς, Β 447. [∪ − ∪ ∪]

ἀγητός (ἄγαμαι), admirabilis (with εἶδος, acc. of respect); surpassingly beautiful, X 370, ξ 177. [∪ − ∪]

ἀγινέω (ἄγω), inf. -έμεναι, ipf. ἠγίνεον and ἠγίνευν, Σ 493; iter. ἀγίνεσκον, agere, lead, bring, sc. animals more comm. ; also, conduct, sc. a bride, Σ 492; haul wood, Ω 784. [∪ − ∪ ∪]

ἀγκάζομαι, ipf. ἀγκάζοντο (ἀγκάς), were raising in their arms the body from the earth, P 722†.

Ἀγκαῖος, (1) son of Lykurgos, chief of Arkadians, B 609.—(2) wrestler from Pleuron, vanquished by Nestor, Ψ 635.

(ἀγκαλίς, from ἀγκάλη) ἐν ἀγκαλίδεσσι, in complexu, in the arms, only X 503, Σ 555.

ἀγκάς, adv., brachiis, complexu, into or in the arms, with ἔχε, ἑλών, λαβέτην, ἐλάζετο, ἐμάρπτε, η 252. [− ∪]

ἀγκίστροισι, ntr., (ἄγκος, uncus), hamis, with fish-hooks, μ 332. (Od.)

ἀγ-κλίνας = ἀνακλίνας, aor. part.

ἀγκοίνῃσι (ἀγκών), Διὸς ἐν, Jovis in complexu, in Zeus's embrace, λ 261.

ἄγκεα, τὰ, (cf. ad-uncus), crooked winding valley, gorge.

ἀγ-κρεμάσασα, aor. part. from ἀνακρεμάννυμι.

ἀγκυλο-μήτης, εω, (μῆτις), versutus, crooked in counsel, epith. of Kronos, occurs in nom. only, Δ 59. [− ∪ ∪ − −]

ἄγκυλον, α, (ἄγκος), only ntr., cur-

vus, bent, curved, epith. of bow and of chariot, φ 264. [− ∪ ∪]

ἀγκυλό-τοξοι, ους, (τόξον), bearing the bent bow, B 848 ; epith. of Paionians. [− ∪ ∪ − ∪ ∪]

ἀγκυλο-χείλης, ου, (χεῖλος), adunco rostro praeditus, with hooked beak, nom. sing. only τ 538, elsewh. pl., epith. of birds of prey. [− ∪ ∪ − ∪]

ἀγκών, ῶνος, ὁ, (ἄγκος), cubitus, elbow, ξ 494, K 80; Λ 252, in the middle of the arm, below the elbow; Π 702, τείχεος, corner of the wall.

ἀγλαΐεῖσθαι (ἀγλαΐζω), fut. splendere, take delight in, K 331†. [− ∪ ∪]

ἀγλαΐη, ης, ἡ, (ἀγλαός), splendor, beauty, ο 78 ; dazzling beauty, of Penelope, σ 180; of dogs; display, ρ 310; scatter the fine things which you now have, ρ 244; Epic dat. ἀγλαίηφι, Z 510.

Ἀγλαΐη, wife of Χάροψ, mother of Νιρεύς, ὃς κάλλιστος ἀνὴρ ὑπὸ Ἴλιον ἦλθεν, B 672.

ἀγλαό-καρποι, μηλέαι, apple-trees with shining fruit, η 115, λ 589. [− ∪ ∪ − ∪]

ἀγλαός, όν, (ἀ-γαλ-Fός), only masc. and ntr., splendidus, shining, bright, brilliant.—(1) epith. of clear water; of polished gifts, esp. of gold or other metal; of ransom ; of fame, H 203 ; so also in reproach, κέραι ἀγλαέ, famous with thy bow (and little else), = ἀγλαϊζόμενος, Λ 385.—(2) in wider signif. : illustrious, υἱός, υἱόν, δ 188 (always at end of verse), τέκνα ; stately, Τ 385 ; ἄλσος, sunny grove, ζ 291, B 506. [− ∪ ∪]

(ἀ-γνοέω), sync. aor. iter. ἀγνώσασκε, for ἀγνοήσασκε, ψ 95 ; from ἀγνοιέω, only aor. ind. ἠγνοίησεν, subj. ἀγνοιῇσι, ω 218, part. ἀγνοιήσασα, υ 15 ; (ἀγνώς), ignorare, fail to recognize, A 537, neque cum conspicata Juno ignoravit, knew right well; so also N 28, ε 78.

ἀγνή (ἄζομαι), only fem., intaminata, holy; Artemis, Persephone ; ἑορτή, φ 259. [− −]

ἄγνυμι (Fάγνυμι), ἀγνυμενάων, fut. ἄξω, aor. ἔαξα, ἦξα, inf. ἆξαι, pass. aor. ἐάγην (ᾰ, exc. Λ 559), Fάγη, Fάγεν (= ἐάγησαν), frango, break, shiver, shatter.—(1) act., spears, yoke, chariot (at end of pole), Z 40, Π 371 ; shoots

of trees, M 148, Π 769; ships, mast.—
(2) pass., spear, sword, Γ 367; cudgel,
Λ 559; barbs of arrow, Δ 214; neck of
Elpenor, κ 560; *suffer shipwreck*, κ 123.

ἀ-γνῶτες (γιγνώσκω, ἀγνώς), igno-
ti, *unknown*, ε 79†.

ἀγνώσασκε, see ἀγνοίω, ignora-
bat.

ἄ-γνωστον (γνωστός), ignotum,
unrecognized (with τεύξω, reddam);
unrecognizable, ν 191. (Od.)

ἄ-γονος (γόνος), *unborn*, Γ 40†.
[‿‿‿]

ἀγοράομαι (ἀγορή), pres. **ἀγορά-
ασθε**, B 337; ipf. ἠγοράασθε, ἠγορόωντο, aor. only 3 sing. ἀγορήσατο,
usually at end of verse with καί με-
τέειπεν, and following oratio di-
recta, β 160, σ 412; concionari,
*speak publicly, harangue in the assem-
bly;* Δ 1, ἠγορόωντο, *held assembly.*
[‿‿‿]

ἀγορεύω (ἀγορή), fut. ἀγορεύσω, aor.
ind. only ἀγόρευσεν, Θ 29, inf. and imp.
more common; concionari, loqui,
dicere, *speak, say;* freq. ἔπεα πτερόεντα, ἐνί or μετά τισι; μή μοι ἀγόρευε,
with acc., *speak* to me not of, Φ 99, X
261; ἢν ἀγ., quam dico, which I *mean,*
β 318; freq. declare, θεοπροπίας, and
with part. θεοπροπίων, *prophesy;* διη-
νεκέως τι, relate at length, η 241, μ 56;
speak (joined with idea of action of
contrary import, ρ 66, σ 15), παρα-
βλήδην, speaking maliciously, Δ 6; peculiar phrase, B 788, ἀγορᾶς ἀγόρευ-
ον, were discussing in the assembly, cf.
B 796, σ 380; ὀνειδίζων ἀγορεύοις, thou
shouldst not insultingly *mention* my
hungry belly (cf. also πρόφερε, Γ 64).
[‿‿––]

ἀγορή, ῆς, ἡ, (ἀγείρω), concio.—
(1) *convoked assembly of people* or
army (cf. ἄγυρις, βουλή), ἀγορήνδε
καλεῖν (through the heralds), καθίζειν,
ποιεῖσθαι, τίθεσθαι; ἐς δ᾽ ἀγορὴν ἀγί-
ροντο, εἰς ἀγορὴν κίον ἀθρόοι, π 361;
εἰν ἀγορῇ ἕσαν ἀθρόοι, Σ 497.—(2) *public speech,* B 275; *discussion* in assembly, B 788, Ο 283, δ 818, Ι 441, B 370,
Δ 400, Σ 106; *debate before tribunal,*
Π 387.—(3) *place of meeting, market,*
β 150, ζ 266, η 44, θ 503, π 377, υ 362;
ἀγοραί, *meeting-places,* θ 16; *place of
assembly,* H 382; *time* (afternoon), μ
439 [‿‿–]; hence

ἀγορῆθεν, c concione, *from the assembly,* B 264.

ἀγορήνδε, ad concionem, *to the
assembly,* καλέσσαι, κιόντες, A 54.

ἀγορήτης (ἀγορή), concionator,
haranguer, speaker (opp. βουληφόρος,
H 126); λιγύς, loud speaking, powerful; ἐσθλός.

ἀγορητύν, τήν, (ἀγορητής), facun-
dia, *gift of speaking, eloquence,* θ 168†.
[‿‿‿‿]

ἀγός, οῖ, (ἄγω), dux, *chief,* Δ 519,
Γ 231. [‿‿]

ἀγοστῷ, ἕλε γαῖαν —, palmâ, *with
flat, outstretched hand,* Λ 425, N 508,
520, Ξ 452, P 315, of mortally wounded. [‿––]

ἄγραυλος, only **ἀγραύλοιο βοός**,
ἄγραυλοι ποιμένες, Σ 162; πόριες, κ
410 (ἀγρός, αὐλή), *belonging to the
farm enclosure,* epith. of domestic cow,
as distinguished from the cows driven
to or roaming in remote pasture; epith.
also of herd of cattle, of calves.

ἄγρει and υ 149 ἀγρεῖτε, imp. from
ἀγρέω (ἄγρη, ἄγω), *quick! forwards!*
used alone or with μάν, δή, νῦν, followed by imp., or inf. used as imp.
(literally *seize! lay hand upon!*).

ἄγρη, ἡ, (ἄγω), venatio, *hunt, ἐφέ-
πεσκον,* were following the *chase,* μ
330. (Od.)

ἄγριος, 2, yet shows fem. termination
in ι 119 (ἀγρός), agrestis, *wild.*—(1)
of beasts. *fierce,* τὰ ἄγρια, ferae.—(2) of
men, *ferocious;* of combatants, *savage,*
α 199, ζ 120, θ 575, ι 215; of Polyphemos, Skylla, μ 119; Gigantes, η 206.
—(3) *horrible, dreadful,* of tumult of
conflict, ἄτη, χόλος, θυμός; Ω 41, rages
grimly like a lion. [‿‿‿]

Ἄγριος, son of Portheus in Kalydon, Ξ 117.

ἀγριο-φώνους μετά Σίντιας, θ 294†,
to the *harsh-voiced* Sintians.

ἀγρόθεν (ἀγρός), rure, *from the
field,* κατιέναι, ἔρχεσθαι, go home, ν
268. (Od.)

ἀγροιῶται, οἱ, ruricolae, *peasants;* also adj. *rustic,* Ο 272.

ἀγρόμενος, part. aor. mid. from ἀγείρω.

ἀγρόνδε, rus, *to the country, coun-
try-house,* ο 379.

ἀγρο-νόμοι (νέμω) νύμφαι, ζ 106†,
ruricolae, *rural.* [‿‿‿‿]

ἀγρός, οὖ, ὁ, ager, rus, *field, land;* ἀγροῦ ἐπ' ἐσχατιῆς, *far out in the country; κατ' ἀγρούς,* ruri, *in the country* (for term opp. to ἀγρός, cf. π 383, ρ 182); villa, *country-seat,* λ 188, ο 428, π 330, ψ 139. [‒◡]

ἀγρότερος, 3, ferus, *wild, σῦς κά-πριος, αἶγες, ἔλαφοι,* Φ 471; Ἄρτεμις, *ranging through the fields, the huntress.* [‒◡◡◡]

ἀγρόται, οἱ, ruricolae, *peasants,* π 218†.

ἀγρώσσων (ἄγρα), ἰχθῦς, ε 53†, piscans, *ever catching* fish; of sea-gull.

ἄγρωστιν (ἀγρός), μελιηδέα, ζ 90†, honey-sweet *field grass,* on which mules feed; identified by some with *dog's tooth,* by others with *panic.*

ἄγυια, ἡ, (ἄγω), does not occur in nom. sing., via publica, *wagon road; σκιόωντο δὲ πᾶσαι ἀγυιαί,* and darkness overshadowed all ways, i. e. everything; also of the *streets* and *public squares* in cities, plateae, E 642, Z 391; *μέσην εἰς ἄγυιαν* [◡‒◡] *ἰοῦσαι,* in publicum progressae, on the open street, Υ 254. [◡‒‒]

ἀγύρει, ιν, fem. (ἀγορά), coetus, *chance gathering* (cf. ἀγορή), *company, host; νεκύων, νηῶν* (fleet, laid up on the shore), Πυλίων. [◡◡‒]

ἀγυρτάζειν (ἀγύρτης, ἀγείρω), τ 284, colligere, *collect by begging.*

ἀγχί-μαχοι (ἄγχι, μάχῃ), cominus proeliantes, *fighting hand to hand* (opp. τοξόται); otherwise explained as *fighting in close array,* P 165. [‒◡◡‒]

ἄγχι (cogn. with ἄγχω), prope, iuxta, *near, close to, hard by, τινός;* freq. with *παρίστασθαι, στῆναι, ἐλθεῖν; ἄγχι μάλα,* sc. ἐστί, τ 301; Υ 283, οι, is dat. of disadvantage, *ἄγχι* being used absolutely, because the missile had struck and remained fixed so near him. [‒◡]

ἀγχί-αλον (ἅλς), acc., maritimam, *near the sea;* epith. of Χαλκίς and Ἀν-τρών. [‒◡◡◡]

ἀγχι-βαθής (βάθος) θάλασσα, ε 413†, *deep near the shore.* [‒◡◡‒]

ἀγχί-θεοι (θεός), diis propinqui, *related to the gods;* of Phaiakians. [‒◡◡◡]

ἀγχι-μαχηταί (μαχητής), cominus proeliantes, *fighting hand to hand =* ἀγχέμαχοι, B 604, ἀνέρες; *also of whole* tribes. [‒◡◡◡‒]

ἀγχί-μολον (μολεῖν), ntr. acc. with adverbial force, prope, *near;* usually with dat. with ἐλθεῖν, ἔρχεσθαι, ρ 260; ἐπὶ ἦλθεῖν, χ 205, ω 502; only in Ω 352, ἐξ ἀγχιμόλοιο ἰδών, e propinquo conspicatus; ρ 336, *close after him* Odysseus entered the house.

ἀγχί-νοος (νόος), *quick of apprehension,* ν 332†; *self-possessed.* [‒◡◡◡]

Ἀγχίσης, (1) son of Κάπυς, father of Αἰνείας, ἄναξ ἀνδρῶν, E 268.—(2) father of Ἐχέπωλος, from Σικυών, Ψ 296. [‒◡◡‒]

Ἀγχισιάδης, (1) Αἰνείας, P 754.—(2) Ἐχέπωλος. [‒‒◡◡‒]

ἄγχιστα, see ἄγχιστος, proximum.

ἀγχιστῖνοι, αι, (ἄγχιστος), conferti, *close together, one after another,* P 361, χ 118.

ἄγχιστον (ἄγχι), proximum, *very near, close by;* proxime aberat, *least distant,* ε 280; pl. *nearest,* with gen.; ἄγχιστα ἐοικώς and ἐΐσκω, *nearest resembling,* I compare (him) first with.

ἀγχόθι (ἀγχοῦ), with gen., prope a, *hard by,* ν 103. [‒◡◡]

ἀγχοῦ (ἄγχι), prope, *near,* with *ἵστασθαι, ναιέιν, ξυμβαλέσθαι,* ζ 5.

ἄγχε (from ἄγχω, ipf.), *was choking,* Γ 371†.

ἄγω (ago), ἄξω, aor. ἦξα (imp. ἄξετε, inf. ἀξέμεν, ἀξέμεναι), mid. ἠξάμην (ἄξε-σθε, ἄξοντο); comm. form ἤγαγον, subj. ἀγάγωμι, mid. ἠγαγόμην (also unaugmented); agere, *lead, bring, drive;* I. act. (1) *lead, conduct, bring,* Λ 842, Ω 564 (in ρ 218 ὡς is prep., *brings* like *to* like), ρ 243, η 248, δ 312; *βοῦν, ἵππους, put to; ἐκατόμβην,* A 431; of lioness's cubs, P 134; bones of the fallen, H 335; (a) *bring* or *carry with one,* Γ 401, I 664, Λ 650, A 390, 184, δ 601; of persons and things; (b) *plunder, carry off, make away with;* prisoners and booty, beside Ω 764, cf. I 594, Υ 194, E 484, Ψ 512; Λ 332, the goddesses of dark death were carrying away, cf. E 614 and N 602.—(2) *transport, remove,* vehere, persons and things as subj. *ναῦται,* α 172; also freq. *νῆες,* even *ἄξων,* E 839; (a) *carry away, νεκρόν, κόπρον,* cf. Λ 598, Λ 338, κ 551; *recover,* κ 268;

(b) *fetch*, things living or without life,
A 184, Γ 105, Θ 368, Ψ 613, 50, Ω 778,
β 326, γ 424, ξ 27, φ 266.—(3) *bring
to pass, occasion*, Ω 547; *sport*, σ 37,
tempest.—(4) κλέος, *spread abroad* renown, ε 311; cf. παιήονα ἄγ., Χ 392,
raise a song of exultation.—(5) *guide,
control*, combat, Λ 721; *water*, Φ 262;
esp. the army, *steer* ships, B 580, 631,
557; λόχον, ξ 469, insidias struere.
The part. ἄγων is often added to verbs
of motion, where it is not necessary to
the sense, for the sake of greater vividness, a 130, δ 525, o 47, cf. γ 118.—
II. mid. (1) *take with one* one's effects,
or what one regards as one's own,
clothes, ζ 58, cf. Γ 72, Δ 19, Χ 116;
booty, κ 35, 40, cf. H 363; prizes, Ψ
263; captives, Z 455.—(2) γυναῖκα,
bring home as wife; of bridegroom, *take
to wife*, I 146, Π 190, Χ 471; of father,
who brings to his son in marriage, κού-
ρην δ 10; of brother, to brother, o 238;
of master, to his slave, φ 214; of those
who accompany the bride, ζ 58.

ἀγών, ῶνος, ὁ, (ἄγω), comitium,
place of meeting.—(1) *assembly*, ἴζανεν,
Ψ 258; λῦτο, Ω 1.—(2) *place where assembly meets*: (a) θεῖος, H 298, *area before the temple, temple enclosure*; Σ 376,
hall of the gods, yet cf. θ 264; νεῶν,
space behind the ships, i. e. between the
ships and the shore, *the encampment at
the ships*; νεῶν ἐν ἀγῶνι, Π 500, differs
in meaning from O 428; (b) *place scene of combat, arena*, including the
space reserved for spectators, Ψ 531.
[ᴗ–]

ἀ·δαημονίη (ἀδαήμων), inscitia,
inexperience, ω 244†. [ᴗᴗ–ᴗᴗ–]

ἀ·δαήμων, ον, gen. ονος, (δαήμων),
imperitus, *unacquainted with*, τινός,
ρ 283. [ᴗᴗ––]

ἀ·δάκρυτος (δακρύω), lacrimis carens, *tearless, dry*, δ 186. [ᴗ–ᴗᴗ]

Ἄδαμας, αντος, son of Ἄσιος from
Troja, N 771, 759.

ἀ·δάμαστος (δαμάζω). inflexibi-
lis. *inflexible*, Ἀίδης, I 158†. [ᴗ––ᴗ]

ἀδδεές, see ἀδειής, impudens,
shameless.

ἀδδηκώς, ἀδδήσειε, see ἀδέω, pertaesus.

ἄδδην, see ἄδην, *to satiety*.

ἀ·δειής (δέος), intrepidus, *undis-
mayed*, H 117, but κύον ἀδδεές, impu-

dens, *shameless* hound, as abusive epithet; later form ἀδεές. [–ᴗᴗ; H 117,
ᴗᴗ–.]

ἀ·δελφειοῦ, ἀδελφεός, οἱ, όν, (ἁ
copul. and δελφύς, uterus), frater,
own-brother.

ἀ·δευκεῖ, έα, (δεῦκος, decus), in-
dignus, *disgraceful*; φῆμις, ζ 273,
slanderous gossip.

ἀ·δεψήτῳ, ον, (δέψω), crudus, *untanned*, υ 2 and 142.

(ἀδέω) only opt. aor. **ἀδδήσειε,** perf.
part. **ἀδηκότες,** also written ἀδήσειε,
ἀδηκότες, and ἀδηκότες, (sat-ur) sa-
tiatum fastidire, *be satiated, loathe
from excess*, τινί, δείπνῳ; καμάτῳ,
ὕπνῳ, *be overwhelmed with*.

ἄδην, ἅδην, (ἀδέω, orig. ἄδδην=σάδ-
jην). *to satiety*, ἕδμεναι, and *to excess*;
esp. ἐλάαν τινὰ κακότητος, πολέμοιο,
etc., *drive one into misery* (war), *until
he has had enough of it*. [ᴗ–; E 203,
––.]

ἀ·δήριτος (δῆρις), non depugna-
tus, *uncontested*, P 42†. [ᴗ–––]

ἀδινάων Σειρήνων, ψ 326, seems to
mean *sweet - singing, seducing* Sirens
(Ϝαδινάων, from ἡδύς, ἕαδα). [ᴗᴗ––]

ἀ·δινοῦ, ά, όν, (δίω), commotus,
Π 481, *moved, agitated*.—I. epith. (1)
of κῆρ, *throbbing with anxiety*, τ 516.—
(2) μέλισσαι, B 87, μυῖαι, B 469, *buzzing;* μῆλα, oves trepidantes, *restless, flurried*, α 92, δ 320.—(3) γόος,
sobbing, *whimpering lament*, Σ 316, Ψ
17, etc. (Σειρῆνες, see foreg.)—II. adverbial, ἀδινόν, ἀδινά, *vehemently, with
utterance broken by sobs*, with στενάχω,
στοναχέω, στεναχίζω, κλαίω (ἀδινώτε-
ρον, *more dolefully*, π 216), γοάω, μυ-
κᾶσθαι, κ 413.—III. adv. **ἀδινῶς** ἀνενείκατο, flebiliter suspiravit, T 314,
cf. 338. [ᴗᴗ–]

ἀ·δμής, ῆτες, (δάμνημι), indomi-
tus.—(1) *untamed;* of mules, δ 637,
cf. ἀδμήτην.—(2) *unmarried;* of a virgin. (Od.)

ἀ·δμήτην (δάμνημι), indomitam,
unbroken, not yet brought under the
yoke; of beasts of draught, K 293, Ψ
266, 655.

Ἄδμητος, father of Εὔμηλος, B 713,
Ψ 289, 391, 532; husband of Ἀλκήστις,
B 714.

ἄδον, aor. 2 from ἀνδάνω, placui.

ἄδος (see ἀδέω), μιν ἵκετο θυμόν,

disgust (with toil) entered his soul, Λ 88†. [- ᴗ]

'Αδρήστεια, town on the Propontis, in what was afterward Mysia, B 828.

'Αδρήστη, handmaid of 'Ελένη, δ 123.

'Αδρηστίνη, daughter of "Αδρηστος, Αἰγιάλεια, Ε 412†.

"Αδρηστος, (1) from "Αργος, fugitive to Σικυών, succeeds Πόλυβος there as king; becomes also king in Argos, harbors Τυδεύς, and gives him his daughter in marriage, cf. Ξ 121; his swift steed 'Αρείων, Ψ 347.—(2) son of Μέροψ, from Περκώτη, founder of 'Αδρήστεια, leader of Trojan allies from thence, B 830, Λ 328.—(3) Trojan slain by Menelaos, Z 37, 51 et sq.—(4) Trojan slain by Patroklos, Π 694.

άδροτῆτα (άδρός), acc. from άδροτής, coupled with ἥβην and μένος, *full bodily maturity*, ll. (Cf. άνδροτῆτα.)

. **ἄ-δυτον** (δύω, *not to be entered*), fa-num, *shrine*, only Ε 448, 512.

ἀ-εθλεύειν (ἄεθλον), c e r t a r e, *institute, or contend in, a gymnastic contest; ἐπί τινι*, in honor of some one, Ψ 274; Ω 734, *toiling for* a merciless master. [ᴗ - - -]

ἀέθλιον, τό, (ἄεθλον).—(1) c e r t a-m e n, *contest for a prize*, θ 108, Π 590. —(2) *implements of combat, weapons*, φ 4, 117.—(3) *prizes in contest*, ἀρέσθαι, carry off; ἀνελεῖν, ἀνελέσθαι, win; φέρεσθαι, bring in, I 127. [ᴗ - ᴗ ᴗ]

ἄ-εθλον, τό, (ἄϜεθλον, v a d a r i; German wetten, English bet).—(1) pl. c e r t a m i n a,*prize contests*, θ 160, ω 89. —(2) sing. and pl. *prize;* for such a prize, λ 548; having come, entered, for the prize, Λ 700. [ᴗ - ᴗ]

ἄ-εθλος (ἄθλων, θ 160), ὁ, (ἄεθλον), (1) c e r t a m e n, *prize contest*, distinguished from πόλεμος, Π 590; varieties, θ 103, Ψ 646, 753; καταθήσω, τ 572; ἐκτελέειν, φ 135. χ 5.—(2) *combat* (in war), Γ 126; τελεῖν, γ 262; μογεῖν, δ 241; *hardships* of every sort, ψ 248, 350, esp. Εὑρυσθῆος, those imposed by Eurystheus upon Herakles.

ἀέθλο-φόρος (ἀθλοφόρος), prac-mium certaminis ferens, *bearing away the prize, victorious;* only of horses, X 22.

ἀεί, αἰεί (at close of verse), **αἰέν** (cogn. with αἰϜών, a e v u m), s e m p e r,

always; often strengthened by ἀσκελέως, ἀσφαλές, διαμπερές, ἐμμενές, μάλα, νωλεμές, συνεχές; also αἰεὶ ἤμα-τα πάντα.

ἀείδω (ἀϜείδω), fut. ἀείσομαι, aor. ind. ἄεισε, imp. ἄεισον, inf. ἀεῖσαι, c a n t a r e, *sing.*—(1) trans. *sing, παιήονα, κλέα ἀνδρῶν*, minstrels' lays, heroic songs; of something, μῆνιν (cf. "sing and say," Nibelungen Lied), *relate in song*, 'Αχαιῶν νόστον, α 326, Δαναῶν κακὸν οἶτον, α 350, 'Αχαιῶν, θ 489 (λίην κατὰ κόσμον, very becomingly, altogether in order); ἵππου κόσμον, 492, with ὡς, 514, and with acc. and inf. 516.—(2) intrans. *sing; μάλ' ἀεῖσαι*, sing merrily; with adj. used adverbially, *καλόν*, α 155 and often, so probably A 473, Σ 570; λίγ', loud, κ 254; also of nightingale (ἀϜηδών); of bow string, it *sang*, i. e. *twanged* under the touch, φ 411. [ᴗ - - , exc. ρ 519.]

ἀ-εικείην, ας, fem. (ἀϜεικείη, *ἤϊοικεν*), strictly d e d e c u s.—(1) d e f o r m i t a s, *disfigurement*, Ω 19.—(2) ἀεικείας φαίνειν, ν 308; behave *unseemly*, pro-terve agere. [ᴗ - - -]

ἀ-εικέλιος, 2 and 3, (ἀϜεικέλιος, from ἤϊκελος), i n d e c o r u s, t u r p i s, *unseemly, shameful*, ἀλαωτύς, πληγαί; *wretched*, Ξ 84, τ 341; *ill-favored, filthy*, ζ 242, ν 402, υ 259, ρ 357, ω 228 [ᴗ - - ᴗ -]; adv. *ἀεικελίως, ignominiously*, π 109, υ 319; *wretchedly*, θ 231.

ἀ-εικής, ές, (ἤϊοικε), i n d i g n u s, *un-becoming, unseemly.*—(1) *νόος οὐδὲν ἀεικές*, mind altogether faultless; οὔ τοι ἀεικές, nec vero dedecet.—(2) *dis-graceful, ignominious; ἔργον*, indig-num facinus; λοιγός, πότμος, στόνος, Κ 483, λώβη.—(3) turpis, *mean, poor; ἀεικέα ἕσσαι*, thou art vilely clad, πήρη. —(4) v i l i s, *small, mean, μισθός*, Μ 435, ἀρωγα. [ᴗ - -]

ἀ-εικίζει (ἀεικής), ipf. ἀείκιζεν, fut. ἀεικιῶ, aor. subj. ἀεικ.σσωσι, mid. ἀει-κισσαίμεθα, ἀεικίσσασθαι, pass. ἀεικι-σθήμεναι, f o e d a r e, *maltreat, insult*, Π 545, σ 222, Ω 54; *disfigure*, Τ 26; for *yea* (δή), he even insults in his wrath the lifeless clay (κωφήν), Ω 54. [ᴗ - - -]

ἀείρων (ἀϜείρω), pl. αἴροντας, aor. ἤειρα and ἄειρα, mid. I. ἀειράμην, pass. ἀέρθην (ἀερθείς, ἀρθείς), plupf. ἄωρτο, *tollere, raise up*, (1) in strict sense (from ground and otherwise), I 465; stones, Ξ 411, H 268; corpses, Π 678, P 724; the wounded, Ξ 429; *swing on ᾗigh* the lash, Ψ 362; *brandish* a spear, Υ 373, Θ 424; freq. with ὑψόσε, c. g. Υ 325; hence also ὑψόσ' ἀειρόμενος, *raising one's self* on high, *rising*, Φ 307. Also pass. ε 393, μ 249, 255, and ὑψόσ' ἀερθείς, μ 432, θ 375; of horses, ὑψόσ' ἀειρέσθην, Ψ 501; of birds, ἀρθείς, Ν 63, τ 540, ἀέρθη; the fortunes of the Trojans rose aloft, Θ 74. Part. ἀείρας, for greater vividness, with verbs of bearing, placing, e. g. Τ 380, α 141, β 425, ρ 335. Of ships (γ 312, ἄειραν), *carry*, ἄχθος.—(2) promere, *bring forth*, *produce*; οἶνον, Ζ 264, esp. mid. (out of one's store), Ζ 293, ο 106, ρ 335.

ἀ-εκαζόμενος, η, (ἀέκων), invitus, *unwillingly*, σ 135, τ 133; also with πολλά, quite against one's will. [˘˘-˘˘˘]

ἀ-εκήλια (ἔκηλος), ἔργα παθέειν, Σ 77†, literally *unwished-for things*, suffer doleful woes, cf. sq.

ἀ-έκητι (ἔκητι), contra voluntatem, *against the will of*, with gen., ζ 287; esp. freq. with θεῶν, Μ 8, γ 28. [˘˘˘˘˘]

ἀ-έκων, ουσ(α), (ἀϜέκων, from ἑκών), invitus, *unwilling*.—(1) *without design*, Π 264.—(2) *reluctant*, *against one's will*; οὐκ ἄκοντε, gladly; ἀέκοντος ἐμεῖο, me invito, *in spite of* me; against their wish, to their annoyance, Θ 487, cf. Π 369; vi me invitum retinebit, Ο 186; notice also σε βίῃ ἀέκοντος ἀπηύρα, with acc., vi nolentem privavit, robbed thee by force, against thy will; Α 430, cf. δ 646. [˘-˘]

ἄελλα, ἡ, (ἄημι), procella, *gust of wind*, *stormy wind*, χειμέριαι, Β 293; παντοίων ἀνέμων; also in simile, to describe onset of heroes, Λ 297, Μ 40, Ν 795. [˘-˘]

ἀ-ελλής κονίσαλος ὤρνυτο, turbidus pulvis surrexit, *a thick cloud of* dust rose, Γ 13†. [˘-˘]

ἀελλό-πος Ἰρις, *storm-footed*, i. e. *swift-footed* Iris (Il.); cf. πυϜήνεμος. [˘-˘˘]

ἀ-ελπέα, insperatam, Zeus has given me to see land which I *never expected to behold*, ε 408†.

ἀ-ελπτέοντες (ἔλπω), desperantes

eum salvum esse, *despairing* of his safety, H 310†. [˘-÷-]

ἀ-νάοντα (from αἰὲν νάοντα) ὕδατα, juges aquae, *never-failing* springs, ν 109† (v. l. αἰενάοντα). [˘˘˘-˘]

ἀ-έξω (ἀϜέξω, cogn. with augeo, German wachsen, English wax), only pres. and ipf., *increase*, Ζ 261, ι 111; *nourish*, *let grow up*, υἱόν, ν 360; μέγα πένθος, cherish great grief; ἀέξεσθαι, *come to manhood*, of Telemachos, χ 426; *prosper*, ἔργον, ξ 66; ἀέξετο ἱερὸν ἦμαρ, the sacred day *advanced*, Θ 66, ι 56.

ἀ-εργίης (Ϝέργον) ἕνεκα, pigritiae causa, *out of sloth*, ω 251†. [˘---]

ἀ-εργός, όν, (Ϝέργον), piger, *idle*, *lazy*. [˘-˘]

ἀερθείς, ἄερθεν, part. and 3 pl. aor. pass. from ἀείρω, sublatus.

ἀερσί-ποδες, ων, (ἀείρω), ἵπποι, tolutarii equi, *quick-trotting*, *high-stepping* horses, cf. Ψ 501 (Il.). [˘-˘˘-]

ἄεσα, ἀέσαμεν, aor. from ἰαύω, dormivi.

ἀεσι-φροσύνησιν (ἀεσίφρων), dat. pl. temere, *thoughtlessly*, ο 470.

ἀεσί-φρων, ονος, (ἀάω, φρένες), amens, *thoughtless*. *light-headed*, φ 302, Ψ 603, Υ 183. [˘˘--]

ἀζαλέοιο, ης, ην, ας, (ἄζομαι), aridus, *dry*, *parched*, *withered*; of trees; ox-hide shield, H 239; ὄρος, Υ 491. [˘˘-]

Ἀζείδαο, Ἄκτορος, *the son of Azeus*, B 513. [˘-˘˘-]

ἄζη, τῇ, (ἄζω), situ inquinatum, covered with dust, *dirt*, χ 184†. [--]

ἀ-ζηχής, ές, (διέχω), penetrans, continuus, *unceasing*, of pain; *penetrating*, of sound of combat; adverbial, ἀζηχές, perpetuo, *incessantly*, Δ 435, Ο 658, σ 3. [--˘]

ἄζομαι (ἅγιος), only pres. and ipf., vereri, *dread*, *shrink from*; esp. before the gods, τινά; religioni habere, with inf., Ζ 267, ι 478; with μή, Ξ 261. [˘-˘]

ἀζομένη (ἄζω), arescens, *becoming dry*, Δ 487†. [-˘˘-]

ἀηδών (ἀϜείδω) χλωρηίς, luscinia, the *songstress* in green foliage, τ 518; Ἀηδών, the daughter of Pandareos, is meant, the wife of Ζῆθος of Thebai, mother of Itylos, whom she slew by mistake while intending, out of jealousy, to kill the son of Niobe, her sister-in-law; after this deed, transformed into a nightingale, she ever sadly repeated the name of her murdered son, Ἴτυ, Ἴτυ.

ἀ-ήθεσσον (ἀ-ηθεσ-jω, ἦθος) αὐτῶν, insucti erant, (the horses) *were as yet unaccustomed* to the sight of corpses, Κ 493†. [∪–––∪]

ἄημι (ἄϜημι, cf. ventus, English wind), 3 du. **ἄητον**, inf. ἀῆναι, ἀήμεναι, part. ἀέντες, ipf. ἄη, ἄει, pass. ἀήμενος. (1) *blow*, of wind, always act.; ἀήμενος, ventis exagitatus.—(2) Φ 386, δίχα δέ σφιν ἐνὶ φρεσὶ θυμὸς ἄητο, their minds *wavered* to and fro. [∪–∪]

ἀήρ, fem., *gloom*, E 864, ι 144; *fog*, η 143; see also ἠήρ.

ἀήσυλα (=ἀ-ίσυλα) ἔργα, facinora violenta, *deeds of violence*, E 876†. [∪–∪∪]

ἀήτης, ου, ὁ, (ἄϜημι), ventus, *wind*, only Ξ 254; elsewh. with ἀνέμοιο, ζεφύροιο, ἀνέμων, flatus, *blast, gusts*.

ἄητο, see ἄημι.

ἄητον θάρσος ἔχουσα, with *stormy courage*, impetuoso animo, Φ 395†. (Of uncertain derivation; cf. θυμὸς ἄητο and ἀήσυλα, E 876; scarcely related to αἴητος.)

ἀθάνατος, 3, (θάνατος), *immortal;* also subst., e.g. Α 503, Ω 61, Α 265; freq. with θεοί; in phrase ἀθάνατος καὶ ἀγήραος; also predicated of bodily members, Α 530, Ν 19, and of *imperishable* possessions (δ 79, Β 447) of the gods; opp. βροτοί, Λ 2, ε 2; θνητοί, Ξ 199; ἄνδρες, π 265; ἀθ. κακόν, Charybdis, μ 118. [–∪∪–]

ἄθαπτος, only masc. (θάπτω), inhumatus, *unburied*. [∪––]

ἀθεεί, οὐκ ἀθ., (θεός), non sine numine, *not without divine guidance*=it is really a *special providence* that—, σ 353†. [∪∪–]

ἀθεμίστιος, οι, α, (θέμις), nefarius, *criminal;* ἀθεμίστια εἰδέναι, *live impiously, godlessly.* [∪∪∪–∪]

ἀθέμιστος, ων, (θέμις), ferus, *lawless, ι* 106; nefarius, *wicked;* opp. ἐναίσιμοι, ρ 363. [∪–∪∪]

ἀθερίζω, ipf. ἀθέριζον, (ἀθερές), contemno, *despise*, always with negation, Α 261, θ 212, ψ 174. [∪∪–∪]

ἀθέσφατος, 2, (ἀ, θεός, φημί), immensus, *immeasurable, boundless;*

γαῖα, θάλασσα, ὄμβρος, νύξ; also joined hyperbolically with οἶνος and σῖτος. [∪–∪∪]

Ἀθῆναι, *Athens*, capital of Attika, Β 546, 549, γ 278, 307; also sing. εὐρυάγυιαν Ἀθήνην, η 80.

Ἀθηναίη, ης, the goddess *Athene*, Διὸς ἐκγεγανῖα, ἀγελείη, γλαυκῶπις, ἠΰκομος, κούρη Διός (αἰγιόχοιο), λαοσσόος, ληΐτις, ἐρυσίπτολις, cf. Ἀτρυτώνη, Τριτογένεια, esp. Παλλάς; fosters the arts, ζ 232, ψ 160, esp. domestic and feminine accomplishments, Ι 390, β 116; as goddess of war, Ἀλαλκομενηΐς, she protects cities, and is the especial patron of wary warriors like Odysseus; see Ἀθήνη.

Ἀθηναῖοι, *Athenians*, Β 551, 558, Δ 328, Ν 196, 689, Ο 337.

Ἀθήνη, parallel form of Ἀθηναίη; Ἀλαλκομενηΐς, γλαυκῶπις, ἐυπλόκαμος, πολύβουλος, etc.; η 80, the city *Athens*.

ἀθηρ-ηλοιγός (ἀθήρ, λοιγός), lit. *chaff-destroyer*, designation of winnowing-shovel in Teiresias's prophecy to Odysseus, λ 128†.

ἀθλήσαντε and **ἀθλήσαντα** (part. aor. from ἀθλέω), laboribus exerceri, *toil, drudge*, Η 453, Ο 30.

ἀθλητῆρι, οὐδ᾽ — ἔοικας, neque enim certatoris similis es, nor dost thou resemble *one who takes his part in manly contests*, θ 164†.

ἆθλος, see ἄεθλος.

ἀθλοφόροι, see ἀεθλοφόρος.

Ἀθόω, ἐξ —, *from Athos* (nom. sing. Ἀθόως), Ξ 229†, the well-known rocky promontory of Akte in Chalkidike, now Monte Santo.

ἀθρέω, only aor. ἀθρήσειε, ἀθρῆσαι, intueri, cernere, *gaze*, εἰς; *perceive*, τινά; *comprehend*, τ 478. [–––∪]

ἀ-θρόος, 3, only pl., cuncti, (*all*) *together, in crowds*, Ξ 38, Σ 497; ἠγερέθοντο, β 392; freq. ἀθρόα πάντα; also written ἀθρόοι. [–∪∪]

ἀ-θυμοι (θυμός), animo destituti, *faint-hearted, despondent*, κ 463†. [∪–∪]

ἀθύρματα, τὰ, (ἀθύρω), ludicra, *playthings*, Ο 363; elegantiae minutulae, *child's toys*, σ 323; ornaments, *trinkets*, ο 416. [∪–∪∪]

ἀθύρων, part. from ἀθύρω, Ο 364†, per lusum, *in sport*. [∪––]

αἰ (perh. old case-form of relative; cf.

παραί, ὑπαί, as also εἰ; this relative force may be traced in λ 348, αἴ κεν ἔγωγε ἀνάσσω, as true as that I reign; so sure as I reign) never stands alone, but I. expressing a wish, optative use. —(1) αἰ γάρ, utinam, would that, always with opt., (a) where fulfillment of wish is regarded as possible, Θ 538, N 825, Π 97, Σ 464, X 454, γ 205, ζ 244, θ 339, ι 523, ο 156, 536, ρ 163, 251, σ 235, τ 309, ν 236, φ 200, 372 (αἰ γὰρ δή, Δ 189, K 536, Σ 272, X 346, δ 697, τ 22, ν 169, ρ 513); (b) where fulfillment of wish is regarded as impossible, π 99: the formula, αἰ γάρ, Ζεῦ τε πάτερ καὶ Ἀθηναίη καὶ Ἄπολλον, is followed by opt. in sense of (a) above, B 371, Δ 288, Π 97, σ 235; in sense of (b) above, H 132, δ 341=ρ 132; by inf. in sense of (a), η 311; in sense of (b), ω 376.—(2) αἴθε (cf. εἴθε), utinam, oh that! would that! (a) where fulfillment of wish is conceived as possible, with opt. Δ 178, X 41, η 331, ξ 440, ρ 494, σ 202, υ 61; (b) where fulfillment is conceived as impossible, with opt. Π 722; with ipf. ὤφελλε, Ξ 84, σ 401; with aor. ὄφελον, Α 415, Γ 40, Σ 86, Ω 253, ν 204.—II. interrogative use, αἴ κε (never separated by intervening word), si, whether, with subj. ξ 118, εἰπέ μοι, αἴ κέ ποθι γνώω τοιοῦτον ἐόντα, Ζεὺς γάρ που τόγε οἶδε, εἴ κέ μιν ἀγγείλαιμι ἰδών; so also after ὄφρ' ἴδητε, Δ 249; πειρήσομαι, E 279, ω 217; and freq. without a preceding verbum tentandi, A 66, Z 94, H 243, K 55, Λ 797, 799, Ω 301, α 379, β 144, γ 92, ν 182, δ 34, αἴ κέ ποθι Ζεὺς; so also α 379, β 144, μ 215, χ 252, ρ 51, 60, αἴ κέ ποθι, strictly=si qua, if, if in any case; the opt. occurs only in oratio obliqua, αἴ κε γένοιτο, H 387, yet see A 207.—III. conditional use, αἴ κε (never separated by intervening word), si, if, perhaps, (1) with subj., (a) where fut. follows in principal sentence, θ 496, ρ 230; (b) where opt. follows in principal sentence, Ω 688; (c) where inf. follows in principal sentence, E 260.—(2) with opt. (where a wish is involved) where opt. follows in principal sentence, ν 389.—(3) in a period, where there is an ellipsis of one of its members, αἴ κ' ἐθέλῃσθα, Σ 457, δ 322, μ 49, υ 233; after

ὄψεαι, Θ 471, N 260, T 147, δ 391, ω 511 (to be distinguished from αἰ ἐθέλεις, π 82, ρ 277), Δ 353 ἦν ἐθέλῃσθα καὶ αἱ κέν τοι τὰ μεμήλῃ.

αἰ- has been sometimes regarded by some as a strengthening prefix=very, exceedingly, cf. αἴζηλος.

αἶα, αἴης, αἶαν, (probably from γαια), terra, earth, land, φυσίζοος; πατρίδος αἴης; Ἀχαιΐδος αἴης; πᾶσαν ἐπ' αἶαν, over the whole earth; Θρηκῶν αἶαν.

Αἰαίη, (1) νῆσος, island Aeaea, home of Kirke, κ 135, λ 70, ὅθι τ' Ἠοῦς ἠριγενείης οἰκία καὶ χοροί εἰσι καὶ ἀντολαὶ Ἠελίοιο, μ 3 sq., a fabulous region far in N. W. (the Romans located it at Circeii); hence (2) δολόεσσα, the goddess Kirke herself, ι 32; μ 268, 273, sister of Aietes.

Αἰακίδης, descendant of Aiakos, (1) son, Peleus, Π 15, Σ 433, Φ 189.—(2) grandson, Achilleus.

Αἰακός, son of Zeus, father of Peleus, grandfather of Achilleus, Φ 189.

Αἴας, αντος, (Αἴϝας), (1) Τελαμώνιος, Τελαμωνιάδης, μέγας, son of Telamon from Salamis, half-brother of Teukros, ἕρκος Ἀχαιῶν, bulwark of the Achaians ("a tower in battle"), φέρων σάκος ἠΰτε πύργον, Λ 485; πελώριος, Γ 229; λ 550, ὃς πέρι μὲν εἶδος πέρι δ' ἔργα τέτυκτο τῶν ἄλλων Δαναῶν μετ' ἀμύνονα Πηλείωνα; ὅπλων κρίσις, λ 543 sqq.—(2) Ὀιλῆος ταχὺς (cf. Ψ 793) Αἴας, μείων, Ὀιλιάδης, Oileus's son, leader of Lokrians; for his presumption swallowed up in the sea near the Γυραὶ πέτραι, δ 499.—(3) the two heroes often coupled in dual or pl., e. g. Αἴαντε δύω, θεράποντες Ἄρηος, θοῦριν ἐπιειμένοι ἀλκήν, πολέμου ἀκορέστω; H 175, Αἴαντε = Aias and Teukros.

Αἰγαί, lit. "wave city," in Αἰγιάλεια, Ἀχαϊκαί; a town in Achaia, seat of worship, Θ 203, and favorite haunt, of Poseidon, N 21, ε 381.

Αἰγαίων, acc. lit. "wave-demon," popul. epith. of sea-giant Βριάρεως (the "mighty," the "crusher"), only A 404.

αἰγανέης, gen. ἐγσιν, ἐας, (αἶξ), venabulum, hunting-spear, ι 156, also thrown for amusement. [‿‿‿‿‿]

Αἰγείδην, Θησέα τ', in interpolated verse, A 265, Aigeus's son.

αἴγειος, 3, (αἶξ), caprinus, of or belonging to a goat.—(1) τυρός, cheese of goat's milk, Λ 639.—(2) ἀσκός, goat-skin bottle, see ἀσκός; κυνέη, goatskin cap. ω 231.

αἴγειρος, ἡ, populus nigra, *black poplar*; as tree in lower world, κ 510.

αἴγεον (= αἴγειον) ἀσκόν, *goatskin* bottle, ι 196†.

Αἰγιάλεια, daughter of Adrestos, wife of Diomedes, E 412†. [‑‿‿ ‑‿]

αἰγιαλός, ῷ, όν, litus, *shore, beach*, μεγάλῳ, πολυηχέι, κοῖλον. [‑‿‿‿]

Αἰγιαλός (ora maritima, coast-line), (1) division in N. Peloponnesos, afterward Achaia, B 575†.—(2) town in Paphlagonia, B 855†.

αἰγίβοτος (βόσκω), capras alens, *abounding in goats*, δ 606; *goat pasture*, ν 246. [‑‿‿‿]

αἰγίλιπος, κατ' — πέτρης, I 15, II 4, of doubtful deriv. and signif.; the second part is perhaps from λίπτομαι, *loved and haunted by goats* alone, for men too steep. [‑‿‿‿]

Αἰγίλιπα τρηχεῖαν, name of village in, or island near, Ithaka, B 633†.

Αἴγιναν, acc., island in Saronic gulf, opposite Peiraieus, still bearing its ancient name, B 562†. [‑ ‑ ‑]

Αἴγιον (cf. Αἰγιαλός), afterward chief city of the Achaian league, B 574†. [‑‿‿]

αἰγί‑οχος (αἰγίς), *Aigis-holding*, epith. only of Zeus, though it might also be with propriety applied to Athene and Apollon, ω 164. [‑‿‿‿]

αἰγίς, ίδος, ἡ, (strictly *storm-cloud*, cf. ἐπαιγίζω), *Aigis*, represented as a *ponderous shield* with a hundred golden tassels, B 448; hence ἐρίτιμος; the handiwork of Hephaistos, O 309; the means in Zeus's hands, P 593, Δ 166; or at his command, in the hands of Apollon, of exciting tempests and of spreading dismay among men, O 229; described, E 738, B 448; serves esp. in battle, seconded by ἔρις, ἀλκή, ἰωκή, as means of spreading terror and flight; above all when borne by Athene, B 448, χ 297; in E 738 and Σ 204, it would at first sight appear as if the later conception, which regards the Aigis as the movable breast armor of the goddess, and with which she is uniformly represented in sculpture (cf. cut No. 17), might be traced,

but ἀμφιβάλετο refers as often rather to the τελαμών by which the shield was suspended over the shoulder; cf. also θυσανόεσσαν.

Αἴγισθος, son of Thyestes, seducer of Klytaimnestra; despite the warning of Zeus, α 35, he murdered her returning husband, ὥς τίς τε κατέκτανε βοῦν ἐπὶ φάτνῃ, γ 196, λ 409, δ 512 sqq.; wherefore eight years later Orestes slew him and his own mother Klytaimnestra, λ 410, α 30, γ 196.

αἴγλη, ἡ, (cogn. with γαλήνη), splendor, radiance; λευκή, gleaming brightness of sky, of daylight, ζ 45; also of sun and moon; of weapons, B 458, Τ 362, οὐρανὸν ἷκε.

αἰγλήεντος (αἴγλη), ἀπ'—Ὀλύμπου, de splendido Olympo, from re-splendent Olympos, A 532.

αἰ‑γυπιός, ὁ, (ἀίσσω, γύψ), vulture, lammergeyer, Π 428, χ 302, ἀγκυλο-χεῖλαι, γαμψώνυχες; with ὄρνις, Η 59. [‑‿‿‿]

Αἰγύπτιος (when ultima is long, Αἰγυπτῆς to be read with synizesis), Aegyptius.—(1) an *Egyptian*, δ 83.—(2) *Egyptian*, ξ 263, ρ 432.

Αἰγύπτιος, name of an aged Ithakan, β 15.

Αἴγυπτος, ἡ, Aegyptus.—(1) river Nile, ἐυρρείτην, ξ 257.—(2) Aegypt, the land of (magic) herbs, δ 355; Αἰγυπ-τόνδε, in Aegyptum.

αἰδεῖο = αἰδέεο, imp. from αἰδέομαι, verere, *respect, reverence*, ι 269.

αἰδέομαι (αἰδώς), pr. imp. αἴδεο, ipf. αἴδετο, fut. αἰδέσ(σ)ομαι, aor. mid. ᾐδέσάμην and αἰδεσσάμην, pass. ᾐδέσθην, αἰδέσθην, 3 pl. αἴδεσθεν, vereri, *feel shame*.—(1) τινά, *reverence* or *stand in awe of*, A 23, Z 442, X 124, γ 96, φ 28, I 640; also joined with δείδια; *was ashamed of his tears in the presence of the Phaiakians*, θ 86.—(2) with inf., vereri, *shrink from*, by reason of religious or other scruples, ξ 146, π 75, υ 343, χ 312, X 82, out of regard to propriety, ζ 221, σ 184, where εἰσιέναι is to be supplied.

ἀδηλος, ον, (of doubtful derivation; ἀι‑, δαΐω, cf. δαΐς, δαυλός, or δήιος, δη-λεῖσθαι).—(1) perniciosus, *destroying*, πῦρ.—(2) protervus, *violent, insolent*, of Ares, E 897, θ 309; Athene, E 880; suitors, π 29, ψ 303; Melan-

thios, χ 165. **ἀιδήλως**, *with reckless violence*, Φ 220. [‿‿‿—]
Ἀίδης, Ἀιδωνεύς, gen. Ἀίδαο [‿‿ —‿], Ἀίδεω [‿‿—]. and Ἀιδος [≐‿‿], dat. Ἀιδι [‿‿≐], Ἀιδωνῆι, acc. Ἀίδην, *Aides, Hades*, god of lower world, ἐνέροισιν ἀνάσσων, ἄναξ ἐνέρων, Ζεὺς καταχθόνιος, 1 457, cf. Ο 188, πελώριος, κλυτόπωλος, ἴφθιμος, κρατερός, πυλάρτης, also στυγερός: freq. Ἀιδος δόμον εἴσω, or εἰς δόμον, ἐν δόμοις, etc.; often also only Ἀιδόσδε (sc. δύμονδε), or simply prep. ἐν, εἰς, followed by gen. Ἀιδος, without proper case of δόμος.
ἀιδοίων τε μεσηγὺ καὶ ὀμφαλοῦ, between *privy parts* and navel, N 568†.
ἀιδοῖος, 3, (αἰδώς).—(1) verecundus, ἀλήτης, *shamefaced, bashful*, ρ 578.
—(2) venerandus, *revered, venerated, august*, applied to all persons connected with one by ties of relationship or obligation: of the ταμίη, α 139; of kings, gods; of friends, guests, suppliants; often joined with φίλος or δεινός; ο 373, αἰδοιοῖσιν ἔδωκα=have given to the *needy*; in λ 360, αἰδοιότερος καὶ φίλτερος, more *respected* and beloved. **αἰδοίως** τ᾽ ἀπέπεμπον, τ 243, *with due regard to the claims of a guest, with fit escort.*
αἴδομαι, see αἰδέομαι.
Ἀιδος, Ἀιδόσδε, see Ἀίδης.
ἀιδρείη, ῃσι,(ἄιδρις), inscitia, *folly*, Η 198, μ 41; αἰδρείῃσι νόοιο, κ 231, 257, λ 272. [‿—‿—]
ἄιδρις, ει, (ἀϝιδρις, from ϝίδμεναι), ignarus, *unacquainted with, χώρου stupid*, Γ 219. [‿—‿]
αἰδώς, οῦς, ἡ, pudor.—(1) subj. *sense of shame*; υ 171, οὐδ᾽ αἰδοῦς μοῖραν ἔχουσιν, not a spark of shame; scruple, ἐν φρεσὶ θέσθε αἰδῶ καὶ νέμεσιν, Ν 122, cf. Ο 561, with δέος, Ο 657; reverentia, *regard*, with φιλότης, Ω 111, ξ 505; with τιμή, θ 480; *diffidence*, γ 14.—(2) obj. *disgrace, dishonor*, used elliptically sc. ἔστω, Π 22, or ἐστίν, γ 24; with acc. and inf., Ε 787; *privy parts*= αἰδοῖον, Χ 75; Β 262, hide thy nakedness.
αἰεί, αἰέν, see ἀεί.
αἰει-γενετάων, θεῶν, and θεοῖς αἰειγενέτῃσιν (regular formula for closing the verse), *born to unending life, eternal, immortal*, ω 373.
αἰει-νάοντα, see ἀενάοντα, *ever flowing, never failing.*

αἰετός (cogn. with οἰωνός, avis), aquila, *eagle*, τελειότατος πετεηνῶν, favorite of Zeus, Jovis ales, Ω 311; bird of omen; μορφνὸς θηρητήρ, dusky bird of prey; high-soaring, Μ 201, Χ 308; hook-beaked, τ 538. [—‿‿]
ἄιζηλον (ἀι, ζῆλος=δῆλος), τὸν μὲν ἀίζηλον θῆκεν θεός, Β 318, eum deus perillustre fecit exemplar, the god made it a *conspicuous* omen.
αἰζήιος ἀνήρ (=ἀιζηός), vegetus homo, *vigorous* man, only Ρ 520, μ 83.
αἰζηός (ἀι, cf. ἥβη?), vegetus, robustus, *vigorous, robust*, with ἀνήρ, and as subst. with θαλεροί, ἀρηίθοοι, κρατερός; used as equivalent to man, μ 440.
Αἰήτης, son of Ἥλιος and Πέρση, brother of Κίρκη; robbed by Jason of the golden fleece, μ 70; ὀλοόφρων, κ 137. [—‿—]
αἴητον, πέλωρ, Σ 410, epith. of Ἥφαιστος, of doubtful origin and meaning, perhaps best explained as from ἄημι, with intensive prefix ἀι, *breathing strongly, hard-puffing*. [—‿‿]
αἰθαλόεις, εσσα, εν, (αἴθω), fumosus, fuliginosus, *smoky, black with smoke or soot*, μέλαθρον, μέγαρον, Β 414, χ 239; κόνις, of ashes that have burnt out and lost their glow, pulvis niger.
αἴθε, utinam, see αἴ, I. 2.
Αἴθη, name of mare, lit. *fiery, Sorrel*, Ψ 295.
αἰθήρ, έρος, ἡ, (αἴθω), aether, *space filled by light of day* (αἴθρη), situated under the heaven, οὐρανός, to which it is considered to belong, and separated by the clouds from the ἀήρ, which belongs to the earth; αἰθέρι ναίων, as dat. of place (locative), dwelling in aether. In Ο 20, Here hangs from a cord made fast in οὐρανός, and swings ἐν αἰθέρι καὶ νεφέλῃσιν; Π 365, as when a cloud rises from Olympos, out of the gleaming *light of day*, and mounts into heaven, i. e. the cloud seems to be generated out of the transparent aether, and then rising perpendicularly, subsequently spreads over the sky. See Ὄλυμπος.
Αἰθίκεσσι, dat. pl., to the *Aithikes*, a tribe west of Mount Pindos, Β 744†. [—‿‿‿]
Αἰθίοπες, ων, εσσιν, ας and ῆας,

τηλόθ' ἰόντας and ἰσχάτους ἀνδρῶν, ἀμύμονας, *Aethiopians*, "burnt faces," dwelling on Okeanos' stream, in two divisions, east and west, a pious folk whom the gods loved and often visited. It is nowise unreasonable to suppose that some tidings of the existence of a black race may have found its way to the Greeks of the Homeric age.

αἰθόμενος (αἴθω), flagrans, ardens, *burning*, πῦρ, etc., ἄστυ, Φ 523.

αἴθουσα, ης, porticus, *hall, porch*; epithets; polished (smoothly planked), resounding. We distinguish two αἴθουσαι, see Table II. at end of volume. —(1) on either side of vestibule, after passing the entrance door; αἴθ. αὐλῆς, φ 390, ν 176, χ 449.—(2) after traversing the αὐλή, just before entering into the banqueting-hall, μέγαρον; this latter, αἴθουσα δώματος, served as sleeping-room for guests, γ 399, δ 297, and was roofed.

αἴθοπα, ι, (αἴθω), acc. and dat. fulgidus, coruscus, radians, *sparkling*, χαλκός, οἶνος; *red*, of smoke mixed with flame, κ 152. [‒ ◡ ◡]

αἴθρη, ην, (αἴθω), aether, *light of day, clear sky*, ἀνέφελος, ζ 44, P 646, μ 75. [‒ ‒]

Αἴθρη, mother of Theseus, follows Helene as captive to Troja, Γ 144.

αἰθρη-γενέτης, Βορέης, *sprung from aether*, ε 296†.

αἰθρη-γενέος, ὑπὸ ῥιπῆς —Βορέαο, under the blast of *aether-born* Boreas, Ο 171.

αἴθρῳ δεδμημένος, frigore confectus, *overcome by cold*, ξ 318†.

αἰθυίῃ, fem., *water-hen*, ε 337 and 353.

αἴθων, ωνος, fulgens, fulvus, *shining, tawny;* of horses, see Αἴθων; also of cattle, eagle, lion, and metal implements, σ 372, B 839.

Αἴθων, ωνος, name (1) assumed by Odysseus, τ 183.—(2) of horse, Θ 185, which we should best describe as *Sorrel*.

αἴκ', see αἴ(κε).

ἀικάς, τὰς, (ἀίσσω), τόξων, telorum impetus, *storm* or *hail* of arrows, Ο 709†. [‒ ‒ ‒]

ἀικῶς (ἀϊκῶς, ἠϊκῶς) = ἀεικῶς, turpiter, *ignominiously*, Χ 336†. [‒ ◡ ◡ ‒]

αἷμα, ατος, τό, sanguis, *blood*, (1) in the veins, Ψ 717, also of gods,

E 339, 870.—(2) cruor, *carnage*, K 298; in sausage, σ 119.—(3) of descent, *blood relationship, kin*, joined with γενεή.

αἱμασιάς λέγειν, septa colligere, *plant out* a *thorn-hedge*. [‒ ◡ ◡ ‒]

αἱματόεις, εσσα, εν, *bloody*.—(1) sanguineus, σμῶδιξ *bloody* wales, ψιάδες drops *of blood*.—(2) cruentatus, *blood-besprinkled*.—(3) sanguinarius, *murderous*, ἤματα. [‒ ◡ ◡ ‒]

Αἱμονίδης, Λαέρκης, P 467†.

Αἱμονίδης, Μαίων, from Thebes, Δ 394†.

αἱμο-φόρυκτα (φορύσσω), δὲ δὴ κρέα ἤσθιον, and were eating pieces of flesh *all bloody* (crudas), υ 348†.

αἵμονα, θήρης (cogn. with amans?), *skilled in* the chase, E 49†.

αἱμυλίοισι λόγοισι θέλγει, *persuasive, persistent*, α 56†.

Αἵμων, ονος, κρείων; ἕταρος Νέστορος, Δ 296†.

αἰν-αρέτη (αἰνός), voc. *terribly-brave* (contains at once recognition of bravery and censure for the faults which attend it), Π 31†.

Αἰνείας, gen. Αἰνείαο, Αἰνείω, ἰὺς πάϊς Ἀγχίσαο and of Aphrodite; ascending pedigree as follows: Anchises, Kapys, Assarakos, Tros, Erichthonios, Dardanos, Zeus; represented as in feud with Priamos the great-grandson of Tros, N 460, Υ 180, 307; favorite of the gods, E 344, Υ 291.

αἰνέω (αἶνος), prs., -ήσω, -ησα, comprobare, *approve, praise;* opp. νείκει, K 249; esp. of oracle, αἰνεῖ, π 403.

αἰνίζο(μαι), with περί and ἔξοχα Βροτῶν ἀπάντων, prae omnibus te mortalibus praedīco, *praise* thee above all other mortals, N 374 and θ 487.

Αἴνιον, a Paionian, slain by Achilleus, Φ 210†.

αἰνόθεν αἰνῶς = αἰνοῦ αἰνότερον, non ferendum in modum, *horribly*, H 97†.

Αἰνόθεν, *from Αἶνος* (in Thrake), Δ 520†.

αἰνό-μορος (μόρος), infortunatus, *child of misfortune*.

αἰνο-παθέα (πάθος), acc. with μάλα, me perquam infortunatam, ah me, *poor sufferer!* σ 201†.

αἶνος, laudatio, laus, *praise*, Ψ 795.

αἰνός, ή, όν, terribilis, formido-
losus, *frightful*, dreadful, horrible, in
different grades of intensity; αἰνότατε
Κρονίδη, dread son of Kronos; as we
sometimes use dreadfully = extremely,
exceedingly, very; αἰνότατον περιδείδια,
N 52, α 208; freq. αἰνὸν ἄχος, dire woe;
often with δηϊοτῆτι, φύλοπις, κάματος,
κότος, etc.; αἰνά, adverbial, τεκοῦσα =
wretched mother that I am, A 414;
with ὀλοφύρομαι παθοῦσα, having en-
countered such sorrow, X 431; αἰνῶς,
adv. esp. with δείδια, ἐοικέναι; intens-
ively with κακά, ρ 24, cf. τ 324.

αἴνυμαι, αἴνυται, αἴνυτο, and part.
prs. comprehendere, take, Λ 374,
580, N 550, O 459, Φ 490, ι 225, 232,
429, φ 53; seize, ξ 144, χ 500.

αἴξ, αἰγός, ή, ὁ, dat. pl. αἴγεσιν, ca-
pra, caper, goat.

ἀίξασκον, iter. aor., from ἀίσσω.

Αἰολίδης, son of Αἴολος, see Κρηθεύς, Σίσυφος.

Αἰολίην, νῆσον, island of Αἴολος,
with surrounding wall of bronze, κ 1
sqq.; identified by the ancients with
Strongyle or Lipara.

αἰόλλη (αἰ-, Ϝολ-, volvo), ὅτε γαστέρα ἔνθα καὶ ἔνθα—, as when one
turns this way and that a paunch full
of fat and blood, υ 27†.

αἰολο-θώρηξ, splendida lorica
armatus, with glancing mail, Γ 83.

αἰολο-μίτρης (μίτρη), with glancing
(because plated with metal) girdle, E
707†.

αἰολό-πωλος, with glancing (with
metal trappings) steeds, Γ 185†.

αἰόλος, ον, οι, (αἰ-Ϝολ-, volvo), mi-
cans.—(1) of movement; quick-moving, swift-footed, T 404; wriggling, X
509; buzzing, χ 300; μέσον αἰόλοι,
of wasps, pliant in the middle, because
their body in the middle is so slender.
—(2) of the impression which rays of
light falling upon smooth, moving
surfaces make; shimmering, glancing,
gleaming; of weapons, of snakes, M 208.

Αἴολος, (1) Ἱπποτάδης, son of Hippotes, lord of winds, κ 2 (36, 60, – – –,
for Αἰόλοο).—(2) father of Sisyphos,
Z 154.

Αἴπειαν, καλήν, town on Messenian
gulf, I 152, 294.

αἰπεινός (αἰπύς), arduus, precipitous, steep, of localities; cf. ζ 123.

αἰπήεσσαν, montuosam, high-lying, mountainous, Φ 87†.

αἰπήν and ά, (αἰπύς), only with πόλιν, and in Il. with ῥέεθρα, high-lying,
plunging sheer down.

αἰπόλιον, properly, belonging to the
αἰπόλος; caprarum grex, herd of
goats; αἰπόλια πλατέ᾽ αἰγῶν, wide-
grazing (dispersed widely) herds of
goats, ξ 101.

αἰ-πόλος (for αἰγπ., πέλομαι, versari), goatherd, also with ἀνήρ and
with αἰγῶν.

Αἰπύ, town subject to Nestor, B
592†.

αἰπύς, εῖα, ύ, praeceps, arduus,
precipitous, sheer.—(1) of localities:
Olympos, mountains, towns, islands,
lofty; of noose, hung high aloft, λ 278.
—(2) bursting headlong in, sudden,
utter, ὄλεθρος, φόνος, χόλος.—(3) arduus, hard, πόνος, toil of combat; N
317, he shall find it hard.

Αἰπύτιον παρὰ τύμβον, at funeral
mound of Αἴπυτος (progenitor of royal
line) in Arkadia, B 604†.

αἱρεῖ, εἴτω, -ήσω, aor. εἷλον, ἕλον
(Ϝέλον), iter. ἕλεσκον; mid. αἱρεύμενοι,
αἱρήσομαι, εἱλόμην, ἑλόμην, prehendere, take.—I. act. (1) seize, lay hold
of, χεῖρά τινος, σ 258, Ω 361; τινὰ
χειρός, by the hand; by the hair, Φ
242; also with acc., Θ 319, K 335, M
397, Σ 416. Φ 242; δουρός, grasp the
spear, Π 406; ὀδὰξ οὔδας, mordicus
humum (of mortally wounded); ἐπὶ
μάστακά τινα χερσί, lay one's hands
upon some one's mouth, hold the mouth
shut with the hands; τινὰ προτὶ οἷ =
(ἀγκὰς) ἑλεῖν, embrace, η 252, λ 210;
overtake in running, θ 330; win prizes,
Ψ 779, κῦδος; χροΐ εἵματα, put on garments (also ἑλέσθαι, ψ 132).—(2) metaphorically, take possession of, ἄλγος,
ἄτη, Π 805; so of various emotions,
joy, grief, courage, astonishment, longing, fear; ἔνθεν ἑλών, taking up the story
where, θ 500.—(3) tollere, take away
from, Ω 579; rob, A 356; capture, B
37, N 42; take captive, Φ 102; slay, II
306, Δ 457, and freq.—II. mid. (1), take
one's own, or for one's self; also with
ἀπό, E 210; τεύχεα ἀπ᾽ ὤμων, lay off,
H 122; cf. O 125, Z 472, also spoliare, strip off, P 206.—(2) take to one's
self, as food, δόρπον, δεῖπνον, πιέειν,

take with one, φ 40, K 501; *receive*, ξ 297, o 367, Σ 500; *enjoy*, H 482; *attain, reach a decision*, Σ 501; *take an oath of*, ὅρκον τινί and τινός.—(3) *choose, select*, K 235, B 127, ε 121.—(4) *rob*, μ 246, Σ 445.

Ἄ-ιρος, *No Iros, unhappy Iros*, σ 73†.

αἴρω, see ἀείρω.

Ἄις, see Ἀΐδης.

αἶσα, ἡ, (ἴσος), portio, *allotted share*.—(1) pars, *part*, τ 84, Σ 327; τίω δέ μιν ἐν καρὸς αἴσῃ (cf. Attic phrase, ἐν οὐδενὸς μέρει τίθεσθαι).—(2) *propriety*, κατ᾽ αἶσαν, suitably; opp. ὑπὲρ αἶσαν, Z 333.—(3) *length of life*, vitae portio, A 416.—(4) *destiny*, sors; ἰῇ αἴσῃ, to one destiny; κακῇ α., to misfortune; θανάτοιο α., to death; αἶσά μοι ἔστι, I am destined, ε 206, ψ 315.—(5) *destiny*, as controlling power, Υ 127, η 197; ὑπὲρ αἶσαν, Z 487, contrary to fate's decree; Διὸς δαίμονος α., decree pronounced by Zeus, by divinity; ὑπὲρ Διὸς αἶσαν, in disregard of Zeus's fateful decree, P 321; κακὴ Διὸς α. παρέστη ἡμῖν, the ill destiny sent by Zeus reached us; πεπρωμένος αἴσῃ, handed over to fate.

Αἴσηπον, acc., son of Abarbaree and Bukolion, Z 21†.

Αἴσηπος, river on Mount Ida.

ἄισθε, ἀΐσθων, ipf. and part. (ἄϜω), always with θυμόν, animam efflans, exspirans, *breathing out* one's life, Π 468. [∪–∪]

αἴσιμον, η, α, (αἶσα).—(1) fatalis, *decreed by fate*.—(2) decorus, *becoming*, idoneus, *suitable*; aequus, *just*; αἴσιμα εἰδέναι, think justly, be right-minded.

αἴσιος (αἶσα), auspicious, propitius, *opportune*, Ω 376†.

ἀΐσσουσι, -ων, aor. ἤϊξα, (ἀΐξω, ἀῖξαι, ἀΐξας), ἀΐξασκον; mid. ἀΐξασθαι; aor. ἤϊχθην, (ἀιχθήτην), impetu ferri, *move with eager haste*.—I. act. (1) *hasten*, Ω 711, o 183, ω 488; ἤϊξε πέτεσθαι, flew rapidly; ἀΐξας, in haste; πρόσσω, φόβονδε, ἀπό τινος, *fly*, of birds; of arrows (*speed*); of chariot (*sped over the ground*), Ψ 369; of thoughts (*rove*, O 80); τοὶ δὲ σκιαὶ ἀΐσσουσι, but they *flit about* like shadows, trepidant, κ 495.—(2) *charge, come rushing on*, ἀντίοι, δοχμώ, λικριφίς, esp. in hostile signif., φασγάνῳ, ἔγχεϊ,

charge upon (*strike, thrust*, etc.); Σ 506, with these they rose quickly up, —II. dep. = act. signif., X 195, Ψ 773, Z 510; Π 404, the reins *slipped from his hands*.

ἄ-ιστος (Ϝίδμεναι, ἰδεῖν), ignotus, *of which nothing is known or seen; disappeared without leaving a trace, vanished, lost*; Ξ 258, and he would have cast me out of the upper air, and submerged me *out of sight* in the sea. [∪–∪]

ἀιστώσειαν, from ἀιστόω, (ἄιστος), *cause to disappear*, υ 79, annihilate; ἀιστώθησαν, vanished, κ 259.

αἰσυμνητῆρι, v. l. for αἰσυμνητῆρι, Ω 347†, princely.

Αἰσυήταο, (1) γέροντος τύμβος, Trojan, father of Antenor, B 793†.—(2) διοτρεφέος υἱόν, Alkathoos, N 427†.

αἰσυλό-εργος (Ϝέργον), v. l. for αἴσυλα ῥέζων, or ὀβριμοέργος, E 403†, nefarius, *high-handed, wicked*.

ἀίσυλα (ἄ-ισος), only with ῥέζειν and μυθήσασθαι; nefaria, turpia, do or speak *evil*. [∪–∪]

Αἰσύμηθεν, Θ 304†, *from Aisyme*, in Thrake. [———∪]

αἰσυμνητῆρι κούρῳ, *princely youth*, Ω 347†.

αἰσυ-μνήτης, msc. (αἶσα, μνῆμα), cf. ἱερομνήμων, *umpire, unprejudiced referee*, θ 258†.

Αἴσυμνον, acc., *Grecian chief, slain by Hektor*, Λ 303†.

αἶσχος, ntr. (αἰδέομαι), ignominia, dedecus, *disgrace*, λ 433, σ 225; pl. *spoken insults*, Z 351, 524, if I must listen to *words of* contumely for thy sake; α 229, *outrageous acts*.

αἰσχρός, turpis, *disgraceful*. (1) B 216, *ugly*.—(2) *injurious, insulting*, ἔπεα; adv., αἰσχρῶς ἐνένιπεν, *ignominiously* reproved.

αἰσχύνω (αἶσχος), aor. ᾔσχυνε, foedare.—(1) *disfigure*, Σ 24, 180, Ω 418.—(2) *insult*, Σ 209, β 86; Ψ 571, *tarnish* my fame.—(3) mid. verecundari, *have scruple, hesitation*.

Αἴσονα, acc., *Aison*, son of Kreteus and Tyro, father of Jason, king in Iaolkos, λ 259.

αἴτει, imp. prs., fut. -ήσω, rogare; *ask*, τινά τι, some one for something; *beg, sue for*, Ω 292, τινί τι; *seek as wife*, N 365.

αἰτιάασθαι, see αἰτιάομαι.

αἰτιάασθαι (αἰτία), only pres. and ipf., usually resolved, i n c u s a r e, *accuse of; α* 32, what charges the mortals bring against the gods!

αἰτίζειν (αἰτέω), only pres., only Od., r o g a r e.—(1) *ask, δ* 650.—(2) *beg, importune.*

αἴτιος, οι, (αἰτία), c u l p a n d u s, r e u s, *guilty of* something (in bad sense), T 86, 'tis no fault of mine; σοὶ δ' οὔτι μνηστῆρες αἴτιοι εἰσίν, the suitors are nowise responsible for that, β 87.

αἰτιόωνται, 3 pl. pres., αἰτιόῳο, -ῳτο, 2 and 3 sing. opt. from αἰτιάομαι.

Αἰτώλιος, *Aitolian.*

Αἰτωλός, Ψ 471, ξ 379; -οί, the *Aitolians* in Hellas, I 531, 549, 597.

αἰχμάσσουσι, fut. from αἰχμάζω, *αἰχμάς*, youths *should hurl the spears*, Δ 324†.

αἰχμή, ἡ, (ἀκίς, a c u t u s), c u s p i s, *point, ἔγχεος, δουρός*; then *the whole spear*, O 542.

αἰχμητά and αἰχμητής, ὁ, *spearman, warrior*, Γ 179; also adj., *fighting with spear, warlike*, B 543.

αἶψα (=αἰπέσα, from αἰπύς), e x t e m p l o, *forthwith; αἶψα δ' ἔπειτα*, immediately after; *μάλ' αἶψα, αἶψα μάλα*, very quickly; *αἶψα καὶ ὀτραλέως*, at once and quickly.

αἰψηρός, ή, (αἶψα), c i t u s, T 276, he dissolved the *quickly dispersing* (prolepsis) assembly, β 257, δ 103, *soon comes a surfeit* of the chilling lament for the dead.

ἄιον (ἀῆναι), ἐπεὶ φίλον—ἦτορ, when I *was breathing out* my life, O 252†.

ἀίων (ἀΓίω), only pres. and ipf. ἄιον, s e n t i o, *perceive.*—(1) by senses, πληγῆς.—(2) by mind, σ 11.—(3) *learn of*, by hearsay: οὐκ ἀίεις, knowest thou not? by sense of hearing, κτύπον, ὄπα, voice, usually with gen. φθογγῆς, exc. ω 48; *regard*, O 378, Ψ 199.

αἰών, ῶνος, ὁ, (ἡ, X 58), (αἰΓών, a e v u m), *lifetime*, Δ 478, Ι 415; *life*, a n i m a, Τ 27, X 58; with ψυχή, Π 453, ι 523.

ἀ-κάκητα, masc. (ἀ priv., κακός), *deliverer*, applied to Hermes, ω 10.

ἀκαλα-ρρείταο (ἦκα, ῥέω), ἐξ — βαθυρρόου Ὠκεανοῖο, from the *smoothly*

---

flowing, deep-streaming Okeanos, H 422, τ 434.

ἀ-κάμαντι, α, (κάμνω), i n d e f e s s u s, *untiring*, Π 823.

Ἀκάμας, αντος, (1) son of Antenor and Theano, leader of Dardanians, Ξ 478.—(2) son of Eussoros, leader of Thrakians, Z 8.

ἀ-κάματον (κάματος), i n d e f e s s u s, πῦρ, *untiring, smouldering* fire. [- ᴗ ᴗ -]

ἀκάνθας (ἀκή), acc. pl. from ἄκανθα, c a r d u o s, *thistles*, ε 328†. [ᴗ - -]

Ἄκαστος, king of Dulichion, ξ 336†.

ἀκαχείατο, 3 pl. plupf., ἀκαχεῖν; ἀκαχήσω, ἀκαχημένος, see ἀκαχίζω.

ἀκ-αχίζω, aor. ἤκαχε, ἀκαχεῖν, and ἀκάχησε; mid. ἀκαχίζομαι, pf. ἀκάχημαι, 3 pl. ἀκηχέδαται, part. also ἀκηχεμένη, αι, inf. ἀκαχῆσθαι, plupf. 3 pl. ἀκαχείατο, aor. ἀκάχοντο, -οιτο (ἄχος); *distress, afflict*, π 432, Ψ 223; mid. *distress one's self*, pf. *grieve*, θυμῷ, -όν, ἦτορ, in heart; because of something, τινός τινι; with part., λ 486; πυκινῶς, υ 84; λίην, Z 486; μάλα, Π 16 (cf. ἄχνυμαι).

ἀκαχμένος, 3, (ἀκή), a c u t u s, *sharpened, pointed*; ἔγχος ἀκ. (ὀξέι χαλκῷ), lance *tipped* (with sharp bronze point); πελεκὺς ἀμφοτέρωθεν ἀκ., double-edged axe, ε 235.

ἀκάχοιτο, see ἄχνυμαι.

ἀκέομαι, ἀκειόμενον, οι, aor. ἠκεσάμην (imp. ἄκεσσαι), s e d a r e, a s s u a g e.—(1) *heal, repair*, ξ 383; *make good*, κ 69, N 115.—(2) *slake* thirst.

ἀ-κερσε-κόμης (κείρω), *with unshorn, flowing* hair, Phoibos, Υ 39†.

ἀκέσματα (ἀκέομαι), pl., as *means of alleviating* pain, O 394†.

Ἀκεσσαμενοῖο, gen., a king of Thrake, father of Periboia, Φ 142†.

ἀκεσταί (ἀκέομαι) φρένες, *tractable*, N 115†.

ἀκέων, οντε, ουσα, (ἀκαλός), s e d a t u s, t a c i t u s, *silent*, A 34; ἀκέων is generally used adverbially; a neuter form, ἄκεων (cf. ἀκήν), may have once existed, which was afterward confounded in common use with the part. ἀκέων.

ἀ-κήδεστοι, *unburied*, Z 60; ἀκηδέστως, *pitilessly*, X 465.

ἀ-κήδεις and ἀκήδεσεν, from ἀκηδέω (κηδέω), n e g l i g e r e, *disregard, slight*, esp. tl e dead, wounded; always with negative, Ψ 70.

ά-κηδής, ές, (κῆδος), incuriosus.— (1) act. *unfeeling*, Φ 123, ρ 319; *without sorrow*, Ω 526.—(2) pass. *neglected*, ζ 2ſ τ 18; *unburied*, ω 187, Ω 554.

ά-κήλητος (κηλέω), νόος, *inflexible* purpose, κ 329†.

άκήν, ancient acc., cf. ἄκων, placide, tacite, *silent*, with ἴσαν, ἔσαν; also common phrase, ἀκὴν ἐγένοντο σιωπῇ, *became hushed in silence*, π 393. [‿ ‿]

ά-κηράσιον (κήρ), intactum, *not meddled with*, pure, οἶνον, ι 205†. [‿ ‿ ‿ ‿]

ά-κήρατος, ον, (κήρ), integer, *untouched*, pure, Ω 303.

1. ά-κήριοι (κήρ), incolumes, *uninjured*, ψ 328.

2. ά-κήριον and οι, (κῆρ).—(1) inanimus, *dead*.—(2) ignavus, *spiritless*, cowardly, δέος, Ε 812.

άκηχέδαται, άκηχέαται, άκηχεμένη, see ἀκαχίζω.

άκιδνότερος, 3, (κιδνός?), neglectus, miser, *more insignificant*, in figure; *more wretched*, σ 130.

ά-κικυς (κικύς), imbecillus. *feeble;* only in Od. [‿ ‿ ‿]

ά-κίχητα (κιχάων), διώκων, negata persequens, pursuing *the unattainable*, Ρ 75†. [‿ ‿ ‿ ‿]

ά-κλαυτος (κλαίω), illacrimabilis, (1) *unwept.*—(2) δ 494, *tearless*.

ά-κλεής (κλέος), acc. sing. ἀκλέα, better ἀκλεᾶ, pl. ἀκλεεῖς, *inglorious;* adv. ἀκλειῶς.

ά-κλήρῳ (κλῆρος), sine patrimonio, *portionless, needy*, λ 490†.

άκμής (ἄκρος), ἐπὶ ξυροῦ ἵσταται, in discrimine res est, *stands on the razor's edge*, Κ 173†.

άκμηνός (ἀκμή), θάμνος ἐλαίης, *full-grown olive-tree*, ψ 191†.

άκμηνος (ἄκμη, ieiunia), famelicus, *unsatisfied, hungry*, with gen. (only Τ).

ά-κμῆτες, pl. (κάμνω). indefatigati, *fresh, unwearied* (only Il.).

άκμό-θετον (ἄκμων). *anvil-block*.

άκμονα, -ας, incudem, es, anvil (ἄκμων).

άκνηστιν, κατ', in spina dorsi, in the *backbone*, κ 161†.

άκοίτης, ὁ, ἄκοιτις, ἡ, coniux, *husband, wife*, ε 120, Ι 397, and freq.

άκόλους, frusta, *morsels*, ρ 222†. [‿ ‿ ‿]

ά-κομιστίη, *lack of care, neglect*, φ 284.

άκοντίζω (ἀκόντιον), aor. ἀκόντι(σ)σα, iaculari, *hurl javelin*, τινός, ἐπί τινι, εἴς τινα; αἰχμάς, δοῦρα, ἐγχεῖ, δουρί.

άκοντισταί, άς, iaculatores, *spearmen, lancers*, σ 262.

άκοντιστύν, acc. fem., *game of the dart, spear contest*, Ψ 622†. [ΰ]

ά-κόρητος (κορέννυμι), insatiabilis, *insatiate*, with gen., Υ 2.

άκος, τό, (ἀκέομαι), remedium, *cure, remedy*, χ 481.

ά-κοσμα (κόσμος), ἔπεα, indecentia, *unbecoming*, Β 213†.

άκοστήσας (ἀκοστή), ἐπὶ φάτνῃ, *having fed abundantly* (on barley) at the manger (Il.).

άκουάζεσθε, ονται, ωνται, (ἀκούω), ausculto, *listen, hearken;* τινός, Δ 343, ye are they who *are first invited* to the feast.

άκονή, ἡ, (ἀκούω), auditus.—(1) *sound*, Π 634, one hears it from far away. —(2) fama, *tidings, report* (hearsay).

ά-κουρον (κοῦρος), filio carentem, *without male heir*, η 64†.

άκούω, -σομαι, ἤκουσα, audio, *hear*, (1) Μ 442, Ο 129, β 423; *listen*, Τ 79, α 370. ἀοιδοῦ; *hear*, with acc., κ 221; ὄπα, φθόγγον, στόνον, ὑλαγμόν, or with gen. μυκηθμοῦ, μ 265, αὐτῆς (mid., Δ 331), φθογγῆς, κωκύτου οἰμωγῆς, στοναχῆς κτύπου (φ 291, μύθων καὶ ῥήσιος); τινός τι; or with gen. of participle στενάχοντος, θ 95, ι 497. —(2) comperire, *learn of by hearsay*, κλέος, Ω 543; with inf., Ζ 386; with gen. of partic. in Il., only Ω 490; λ 458, ρ 115, α 289; with gen. alone, δ 114; περί τινος; ὑπέρ σέθεν, Ζ 524; ex aliquo audire, τινός, μ 389, ἐκ τινός τι, ο 374.—(3) exaudire, *give ear to*, with gen. and dat., also with part.; audientem esse, *obey*, Τ 256, η 11, ὑμοκλητῆρος; pres. used with signif. of perf., ξ 375.

ά-κράαντος (κραιαίνω), irritus, *unaccomplished, vain*. [‿ ‿ ‿]

άκραεῖ and αέα, (ἄκρος, ἄημι), impetuosus, *blowing strongly, fresh*, β 421. [‿ ‿ ‿ ‿]

ἄκρη (ἄκρος), summa pars, summit, promontory; κατ' ἄκρης, a vertice, from the summit; then, from top to bottom, i. e. utterly, N 772.

ἄκρηθεν, in κατάκρηθεν, see κάρ.

ἄ-κρητος, 2, (κεράννυμι), merus, unmixed, pure, ω 73.

ἀκρίδες, αἱ, locusts, Φ 12†.

ἄκριας (ἄκρις, from ἄκρη), δι', amid the windy mountain-tops, ι 400. (Od.)

Ἀκρισιώνη, daughter of Akrisios, Δανάη, Ξ 319†.

ἀ-κρῖτό-μῦθος (ἄκριτα, μῦθος), senseless babbler, B 246; useless are the confused dreams, τ 560.

ἄ-κρῖτος, 2, (κρίνω).—(1) undistinguished, common, τύμβος.—(2) endless, beyond measure, also with πολλά; adverbially ἄκριτον, unceasingly.

ἀ-κρῖτό-φυλλον ὄρος, thickly overgrown (with foliage), B 868†.

ἀκρο-κελαινιόων, growing black on surface, with troubled surface, Φ 249†.

ἀκρό-κομοι (κόμη), with hair tied up on the crown of head, Δ 533†.

ἄκρον (ἄκρος), summum, point, summit, promontory.

Ἀκρόνεως, name of a Phaiakian, θ 111.

ἀκρό-πολις, citadel of Troja, only θ 494, 504.

ἀκρο-πόλοισιν (πέλομαι), ἐν—ὄρεσσιν, on lofty mountains, E 523.

ἀκρο-πόρους (πείρω), acumine transfigens, ὀβελούς, with penetrating points, sharp-pointed, γ 463†.

ἄκρος, 3, (ἀκή, acies), extremus, summus, at the point or end or top, outermost, topmost, highest, the extremity of; tail, Ψ 519; hand, foot, Π 640, shoulder, rudder; πόλις ἄκρη, ἄκρη πόλις, upper city; edge, surface, etc.; κατ' ἄκρης, see ἄκρη; adverbially ἄκρον, Υ 229, along the top.

Ἀκταίη, a Nereid, Σ 41†.

1. ἀκτή (ἄγνυμι), mola, always with ἀλφίτου (or Δημήτερος), barley meal; in opposition to the whole kernels, οὐλαί, ξ 429.

2. ἀκτή, litus, coast, often προβλῆτες ἀκταί, tongues of land, promontories, κ 89.

ἀ-κτήμων (κτῆμα), carens, not possessing, with gen., I 126.

ἀκτίνεσσι, ἀκτῖσιν, fem., (ἀκτίς), Ἠελίοιο, radiis, beams of Helios.

Ἀκτορίδαο, gen., descendant of Aktor, Echekles, Π 189†.

Ἀκτορίς, attendant of Penelope, ψ 228†.

Ἀκτορίων, name for either of the sons of Aktor; the two were called Ἀκτορίωνε, and also Μολίονε, after their mother Molione, Λ 750.

Ἄκτωρ, (1) Ἀζείδης, son of Azeus, B 513.—(2) father of Μενοίτιος, Λ 785, Π 14.—(3) father of the Ἀκτορίωνε, son of Φόρβας, brother of Αὐγείας.—(4) father of Ἐχεκλῆς.

ἄκυλος, ἡ, edible acorn, κ 242†. [∪∪∪]

ἀκωκή (ἀκή), cuspis. point, of missiles, χ 16.

ἄκων, οντος, ὁ, (ἀκή), iaculum, dart, K 335, Δ 137, ξ 531.

ἄκων=ἀέκων, invitus, unwillingly.

ἅλαδ(ε) (ἅλς), in mare versus, seaward, A 308, also with εἰς. [∪∪∪]

ἀλάλημαι, see ἀλάομαι, vagari.

ἀλαλητός, ῷ, masc. (ἀλαλά), clamor, shout, war-cry; also cry of fear, and, ω 463, of joy.

ἄλαλκε, -εῖν, -ών, see ἀλέξω.

Ἀλαλκομενηίς, epithet of Ἀθήνη, from the Boiotian city Ἀλαλκομεναί, near the lake Triton (see Τριτογένεια), Δ 8, E 908. [∪–∪∪–∪]

ἀλάομαι, ἀλᾶσθε, imp. ἀλόω, ipf. ἠλώμην, aor. ἀλήθην, pf. ἀλάλημαι, -ησθε, ἀλάλησθαι, ἀλαλήμενος, vagari, wander, rove, δ 368, ο 276, 492, γ 302, ε 377; ἀλώμενος, vagatus, errans.

ἀλαός, οῦ, caccus, blind [∪∪∪; κ 493. μάντιος ἀλαοῦ, or v. l. μάντηος ἀλάοῦ].

ἀλαο-σκοπιήν (σκοπιή), οὐδ'—εἶχε, nor did he keep a blind, i. e. a careless watch. [∪∪–∪∪–]

ἀλάωσεν (ἀλαόω, from ἀλαός), ὀφθαλμοῦ, caccavit, blinded, (Od.). [∪–∪∪]

ἀλαπαδνός, 3, infirmatus, feeble, σθένος, στίχες, etc.

ἀλαπάζω, ει, ipf. ἀλάπαζε, fut. -ξω, aor. ἀλάπαξα (ἀλαπαδνός), infirmare, esp. with πόλιν, sack; φάλαγγας, rout, also slay.

ἀλαστέω (ἄλαστος), only ipf. ἠλάστεον, nor. part. ἀλαστήσας, aegre fero, be indignant.

Ἀλαστορίδην, Tros, Υ 463,

ἄλαστος, ον, (λαθέσθαι), horrendus, never to be forgotten, dreadful, ἄχος, πένθος, ἄλιαστον ὀδύρομαι.

'Αλάστωρ, ορος.—(1) a Lykian, E 677.—(2) leader of the Pylians, Δ 295.—(3) father of Tros.

ἀλᾰωτύν, τήν, (ἀλαός), ὀφθαλμοῦ, excaecationem, blinding, ι 503†.

ἀλγέω, aor. subj. ἀλγήσετε, part. ἀλγήσας, (ἄλγος), dolere, feel pain; in Il. of bodily pain; Od., μ 27, in more general sense.

ἄλγιον (comp. from ἀλγ-ος), peius, worse; in exclamations : cf. French, tant pis, so much the worse; with dat. in threats, that shall be the worse for him; also ἀλγίστη δαμάσασθαι, difficillima domitu, very hard to tame, break.

ἄλγος, dolor, pain, grief, distress, only of mind, esp. πάθεν ἄλγεα θυμῷ, κρατέρ' ἄλγεα πάσχων, ἅ. θεῖναι, δοῦναι, τεύχειν, κάλλιπ' ὀπίσσω, etc.

ἀλδαίνω (ἀλ-δ-, alo), only aor. μέλε' ἤλδανε ποιμένι λαῶν (Od.), aluit, she filled out his limbs.

ἀλδήσκοντος (ἀλ-, alo), ληΐου, crescentis, growing, Ψ 599†.

ἀλέασθαι, see ἀλέομαι.

ἀλεγεινός, 3 (ἄλγος), dolore afficiens, painful.—(1) of bodily pain, αἰχμή, ἰδύνη.—(2) in wider signif., molestus, aerumnosus, grievous, mournful, ἀγγελίη, Ἄρης, ἀγηνορίη.—(3) difficilis, hard, πυγμαχίη, μάχη, πνοιή, κύματα, hard to struggle with; ἵπποι ἀ. δαμήμεναι, hard to break, cf. Ψ 655; hard to endure, σ 224. [⌣ ⌣ – ⌣]

'Αλεγηνορίδαο, Προμάχοιο, son of Alegenor, Ξ 503†.

ἀλεγίζω (ἄλγος), always with οὐ, contemno, not to concern one's self about, τινός.

ἀλεγύνειν (ἄλγος), only with δαῖτα, δαῖτας, parare cenam, give (strictly, prepare), a banquet, entertain (Od.).

ἀλέγω (ἄλγος), trouble one's self, heed; I 504, who follow, troubled, behind Ate ; usually with negation : contemno, despise, τινός ; hence οὐκ ἀλέγουσαι, shameless, insolent ; ζ 268 = ἀλεγύνουσι, they attend to the rigging.

ἀλεείνω (ἀλέη), only pr. and ipf., avoid, shun, τινά, τί ; also with inf. [⌣ ⌣ – –]

1. ἀλέη (ἀλέϜ-ομαι), escape, Χ 301†.
2. ἀλέη (sol?), warmth of sun, ρ 23†.

ἀλείατα (ἄλειαρ, ἀλέω), farina triticea, wheaten flour, v 108†.

ἀλείς, εἶσα, ἐν, aor. pass. part., from εἴλω.

'Αλείσιον, town in Elis, B 617, Λ 757.

ἄλεισον, τό, drinking goblet, usually costly, cf. ο 469 ; with handles, χ 9. [⌣ – ⌣]

ἀλείτης, ον, (ἀλιταίνω), sceleratus homo, reckless offender, Γ 28, ν 121. [⌣ – –]

ἀλείφαρ, ατος, (ἀλείφω), only gen. and dat., unguentum, ointment; fat, for anointing corpses; γ 408, shining with fat. [⌣ – ⌣]

ἀλείφω (λίπα), ἤλειψαν, -άμην, only aor., and usually with λίπ' ἐλαίῳ, ungere, anoint; oblinere, smear with wax, μ 200. [⌣ – ⌣]

'Αλεκτρυόνος, υἱός, i. e. Λήιτος, an Argonaut, P 602†.

ἄλεν, ἀλέν, see aor. from εἴλω.

ἀλεξάμενος, ἀλέξασθαι, aor. mid. from ἀλέξω.

'Αλέξ-ανδρος, name given by Greeks to Πάρις ; epithets, δῖος . . . 'Ελένης πόσις ἠυκόμοιο, θεοειδής, βασιλεύς, Δ 96 ; not characterized by Homer as so effeminate and feeble as in later representations (Γ 16, 39, 59), yet usually represented with the bow (Λ 369, 507, 581), and as betraying a sensual character ; cf. also Γ 442, Ζ 290, Γ 39, Ω 28, 763, Δ 94.

ἀλεξ-άνεμον (ἄνεμος), χλαῖναν, ventum arcentem, protecting against the wind, ξ 529. [⌣ – ⌣ ⌣ ⌣]

ἀλεξητῆρα μάχης, defensor pugnae, stemmer of battle, one who bears the brunt in the fight, Υ 396†.

ἀλεξί-κακος (κακόν), mala arcens, warding off ill or evil, protecting, Κ 20†.

ἀλέξω (ἀλκή), inf. ἀλεξέμεν(αι), fut. ἀλεξήσω, red. aor. ἄλαλκε, subj. ἀλάλκῃσι, inf. ἀλαλκεῖν, -έμεναι, -έμεν, aor. opt. ἀλεξήσειε, and subj. mid. ἀλεξώμεσθα, arceo, ward off, τί, τινί, dat. commodi, τινί τι ; mid. keep off from one's self (τινά), se defendere (ab aliquo).

ἀλεώμεθα and -εύεται, -όμενος, aor. ἠλεύατο, ἀλεύατο, -ντο, opt. ἀλέαιτο, imp. ἄλευαι, ἀλέασθε, inf. ἀλέασθαι, part. ἀλευάμενος (subj. ἀλέFηται, ἀλε-Fώμεθα, aor. or pres.), evitare, avoid, escape, τί, esp. the weapons, the wrath of any one, esp. of the gods, E 444, Π 711, ι 277; hence, secondly, (vereri), stand in dread of, be on one's guard before, ι 274, with inf.

ἄλεται (aor. subj. from ἄλλομαι), insilierit.

ἀλετρεύουσι (ἀλετρίς), grind, η 104†.

ἀλετρίς (ἀλέω), γυνή, female slave who grinds corn, υ 105†.

ἀλεύεται = ἀλέFεται, see ἀλεώμεθα.

ἀλέω, see καταλέω.

ἀλεωρή (ἀλεFωρή, ἀλέομαι), munimentum, defense, τινός, against some one; but Ω 216, flight. [⌣⌣ ‒ ‒]

ἄλη, ή, (ἀλάομαι), oberrationes, roaming without knowledge whither, nor hope of rest, ceaseless wandering of Odysseus and his companions, o 345. (Od.) [⌣‒]

ἀληθείη, ή, (λήθω), veritas, truth, ἀποείποι, παιδὸς (de filio) πᾶσαν μυθήσομαι, καταλέξω. [⌣‒‒‒]

ἀληθείς (aor. part. from ἀλάομαι), vagatus.

ἀληθής, ές, (λήθω), verus, ἀληθὲς ἔνισπε, γ 247; elsewh. ἀληθέα μυθήσασθαι, εἰπέ, πάντ' ἀγορεύσω, verum loqui, speak the truth, tell truly; only M 433 ἀληθής, proba, honest. [⌣‒‒]

'Αλήιον, πεδίον τὸ, Aleïan plain in Asia Minor (v. sq.=plain where no harvest grows—barren waste), Z 201†.

ἀ-λήιος (λήιον), sine arvis, without corn land, poor, cf. ἄκληρος. [⌣‒ ⌣‒]

ἄ-ληκτος (λήγω), unceasing; adverbially ἀλληκτον, unceasingly.

ἀλήμεναι, ἀλῆναι (inf. 2 aor. pass. from εἴλω), congregari.

ἀλήμονες (ἀλήμων, ἄλη), errabundi, roving, ρ 376.

ἄληται (aor. subj. from ἄλλομαι), saliat.

ἀλητεύειν (ἀλήτης), vagari, roam about, σ 114, (Od.)

ἀλήτης, γ, ην, masc. (ἀλάομαι) erro, tramp, beggar, ρ 576. (Od.)

'Αλθαίη, wife of Οἰνεύς in Καλυδών, mother of Μελέαγρος, I 555†.

ἄλθετο (from ἄλθομαι), χείρ, was healing, E 417†.

ἀλι-αέες (ἅλς, ἄφημι) οὖροι, venti maritimi, blowing on the sea, good sea-winds, δ 361†. [⌣⌣⌣⌣]

'Αλίαρτον, ποιήεντα, Haliartos, in Boiotia, with its rich meadows, B 503†.

ἀ-λίαστος (λιάζομαι), obstinatus, stubborn, unceasing (only Il.). [⌣⌣‒⌣]

ἀλίγκιος, like, with which it seems to be etymologically connected.

ἁλιεύς, ἧος, (ἅλς), maritimus, π 349; elsewh. piscator. fisher. [⌣⌣‒‒]

'Αλιζώνες, tribe of Trojan allies from Pontos led by 'Οδίος.

'Αλίη βοῶπις, a Nereid, Σ 40†. [⌣‒⌣]

'Αλι-θέρσης, son of Mestor, friend of Odysseus, Ithakan, β 157, ρ 78. (Od.)

ἁλι-μυρήεντα, των, (μύρω), maris aestu oppletus, reached by salt water, briny, ε 460, Φ 190.

1. ἅλιος, ίοιο, 3, (ἅλς), maritimus, belonging to the sea; of old man of the sea, δ 365, etc.; ἅλιαι = Nereids, ω 47.

2. ἅλιος — (ἅημι? vâ-nus?), fruitless; of missiles, words, speeches, e. g. E 715, Ω 92. [⌣⌣⌣]

'Αλιος, a Lykian, E 678.—(2, son of Alkinoos, θ 119, 370. [⌣⌣⌣]

ἁλιο-τρεφέων (ἅλς), φωκάων, in mari nutritarum, the seals which find their food in the sea, δ 442†. [⌣⌣‒⌣⌣]

ἁλίωσε, -ῶσαι (aor. from ἁλιόω, ἅλιος), render fruitless, baffle, ε 104; hurl in vain, Π 737. [⌣⌣‒ ⌣]

ἁλι-πόρφυρα (σαλι-πορφύρα), ntr. pl. purpurata, sea-purple (Od.).

ἅλις (Fάλις; ἐFάλην), confertim, in heaps, in swarms, in crowds, in quantities, B 90, Γ 384, Ξ 122, Φ 236; abunde, abundantly, I 137, P 54, Φ 352; ἅλις δέ οἱ, I 376, he has done it enough (already); enough and more than enough, ἤ οὐχ ἅλις ὅτι (ὡς), is it not enough (that)? [⌣‒]

ἁλίσκομαι (ἐFάλην), aor. ἥλω, subj. ἁλώω, opt. ἁλώην, ἁλοίην, inf. ἁλῶναι, part. ἁλούς, capi, be taken captive, be seized, of men, towns; θανάτῳ, overtaken by death; be slain, fall in battle, X 253, ο 300; E 487, lest ye, as if caught in the meshes of a net, become a prey.

ἀλιταίνω (ἀλάομαι?), aor. ἀλιτόμην (I 375, ἤλιτον); part. pf. ἀλιτόμενος, violare, sin against, τινά, τί, Ω 586; with part., T 265; θεοῖς ἀλιτήμενος, *transgressor* in the sight of the gods, δ 807.

ἀλιτήμων, ονος,(ἀλιταίνω), violentus. *transgressor*, Ω 157.

ἀλιτρός (ἀλιταίνω), nefarius, offender, sinner; δαίμοσιν, against the gods; also in milder signif., *rogue, rascal*, ε 182. [∪∪∪]

Ἀλκά-θοος, Αἰσυήτao υἱός, son-in-law of Ἀγχίσης, N 428. [∪∪∪∪]

Ἀλκ-άνδρη, Πολύβοιo δάμαρ, in Thebes, δ 126†.

Ἄλκ-ανδρος (=Ἀλέξανδρος), a Lykian, E 678.

ἄλκαρ (ἀλκή), only nom. and acc., protection, defense, safety, τινί, τινός, E 644 and Λ 823.

ἀλκή, ῆς, ἀλκί,(ἀλκῇ, ω 509),(arceo, ἀλέξω), fortis defensio, *defense, power of defense, prowess*; common phrase, θούριδος ἀλκῆς, δ 527, impetuous defense, i. e. *self-defense*, cf. N 330; with μένος, fury; with σθένος, steadfastness, χ 237; with ἠνορέη, manly endurance, ω 509; freq. ἀλκὶ πεποιθώς, ζ 130; ἐπιειμένος ἀλκήν. As divinity, E 740.

Ἄλκι_στις, Πελίαo θυγατρῶν εἶδος ἀρίστη, wife of Ἄδμητος of Pherai in Thessaly, mother of Εὔμηλος, B 715† sq. [– – ∪]

ἀλκὶ πεποιθώς, see ἀλκή.

Ἀλκι-μέδων, Λαέρκεος υἱός, chief of Myrmidons, P 481, Π 197. [∪∪∪–]

Ἀλκιμίδης (Ἀλκίμου υἱός), i. e., Μέντης, χ 235†. [∪∪∪–]

ἄλκιμος, ον, (ἀλκή), defendens, *capable of self-defense, brave, bold*, opp. δειλός, N 278; applied also as epithet to ἔγχος, υ 127, also to δοῦρε.

Ἄλκιμος, (1) father of Mentor.—(2) charioteer of Achilleus.

Ἀλκί-νοος, son of Ναυσίθοος, king of Φαίηκες in Σχερίη, husband of Ἀρήτη; his daughter Ναυσικάα, and his sons Λαοδάμας, Ἅλιος, Κλυτόνηος; Ἀλκινόου ἀπόλογοι, tale of Odysseus at the court of Alkinoos, ι—μ. [∪∪∪∪∪∪]

Ἀλκ-ίππη, slave of Ἑλένη, δ 124†.

Ἀλκ-μαίων, son of Ἀμφιάραος and Ἐριφύλη, brother of Ἀμφίλοχος, o 248†.

Ἀλκμάων, Θεστορίδης, Greek, M 394†.

Ἀλκμήνη, wife of Ἀμφιτρύων in Thebes, mother of Ἡρακλέης by Zeus, and of Ἰφικλέης by Amphitryon.

ἀλκτῆρα, ες, masc., (ἀλκή), defender, ξ 531, safeguard. [– – ∪]

Ἀλκυόνη, name given to Κλεοπάτρη, wife of Μελέαγρος, daughter of Μάρπησσα, I 562.

ἀλκυόνος, πολυπενθέος οἶτος, alcedinis, kingfisher, I 563†.

ἀλλ'=(1) ἄλλο.—(2) ἀλλά.

ἀλλά, ἀλλ', (from ἄλλα), orig. adv., then adversative conj., in contrasted clauses, (1) *but, on the contrary*, A 25, α 190; freq. after negation, μ 404, Φ 276, θ 312.—(2) subjoining additional circumstance, immo, *nay, but, rather*, A 94, 165; after question expecting a negative answer, α 68.—(3) corresponding to a concession, expressed or understood, *but, yet*, A 24, β 107; in apodosis, after a condition expressed or implied, A 281, Θ 154; μέν or εἰ may be omitted, A 287, α 42; also εἴπερ τε —ἀλλά τε; ἀλλὰ καὶ ὧς, but even thus; ἀλλ' οὐδ' ὧς, but not even thus.—(4) beginning anew, changing subject, *but, yet, then*, A 135, 233, 281, Γ 433, α 6, 16, 22, 195.—(5) breaking off, *but, yet*, α 169, 267; ἀλλ' ἦτοι, sed vero, *but yet*, A 140.—(6) repelling an ungrounded assumption (καί νύ κε), ι 79.—(7) after ἄλλος, ἕτερος, with negative, *than*, Φ 275, θ 311, μ 403, φ 70, γ 377.—(8) in appeal, A 32, 259, 274, ι 269, κ 69; freq. phrases, ἀλλ' ἄγε, ἀλλ' ἄγετε, with subj., β 404; ἀλλὰ μάλα, ε 342.—(9) with other particles, ἀλλ' ἄρα, see ἄρα, ἀλλὰ γάρ, ξ 355; ἀλλὰ τε, *but still*, A 81; ἀλλ' ἤτοι, see no. 5.

ἄλ-λεγον, ἀλ-λέξαι, ipf. and aor., from ἀναλέγω, colligere, *gather*.

ἄλλη (ἄλλος), (1) aliâ, alibi, *elsewhere*; ἄλλον ἄλλῃ, alium alibi, *one in one direction, another in another*.—(2) aliorsum, ἄλλυδις ἄλλῃ, alias alio, *every one in a different direction*; A 120, (distinction) the honor (due to me) comes to naught; O 51, mean very differently.

ἄ-λληκτος =ἄληκτος, *unceasing, unwearied*.

ἀλλ-ήλοιιν, gen. du., pl. -ων, -οις, -ῃσι, -ους, -ας, inter sc, *of one another, to one another, one another, mutually*; also with prepositions (avoided by a periphrasis, ι 47); μ 101, near *to each other* are they (the rocks).

ἀλλο - γνώτῳ (γνῶναι), ἐνὶ δήμῳ,

apud exteros, in a *foreign* land, β
366†.

ἀλλοδαπός, 3, (ἄλλος), exterus,
extraneus, *strange, foreign;* also
subst., *stranger.* [‿ ‿ ‿ ‿]

ἀλλοειδέα [‿ ‿ ⏒ ⏒], see ἀλλοίδεα.

ἄλλοθεν (ἄλλος), aliunde, *from
elsewhere,* B 75; γ 318, *from abroad;
ἄ. ἄλλος,* alius aliunde, *one from
one side, another from another* = undique. [‿ ‿ ‿]

ἄλλοθι (ἄλλος), alibi, *elsewhere,
abroad;* γαίης, β 131, but in ρ 318 =
procul a patria. (Od.) [‿ ‿ ‿]

ἀλλο-θρόων, -ους, gen. acc. pl. (θρόος), always with ἀνδρῶν or ἀνθρώπους
(Od.), aliter sonantium, *talking
otherwise* from one's own people, *speaking a strange tongue.*

ἀλλο-ϊδέα (i. c. ἀλλοϝιδέα, ‿ ‿ ‿ ⏒ ⏒),
transformia, *looking differently,* ν
194† (cf. π 181).

ἀλλοῖος, -ῳ, -ον, (ἄλλος), alius spe-
ciei, *of another sort;* π 181, *different
looking;* τ 265, *inferior, commonplace.*

ἅλλομαι (salio), aor. 2 and 3 pers.
sing. ἆλσο, ἆλτο, subj. ἅληται, ἅλεται,
part. ἅλμενος, salio, *leap, spring;* ἐξ
ἵππων χαμάζε; hasten, θύραζε; *start
up,* Υ 62; *fly,* Δ 125; *hasten to,* ἐπί τινα;
charge upon, ἐπί τινι.

ἀλλο-πρόσ-αλλον, -ε, acc. voc., applied to Ares, E 831 and 889; desul-
torius, *inconstant, changeable* (cf. ἑτερ-
αλκής. [‿ ‿ ‿ ‿ ‿]

ἄλλος, η, o, (alius), (1) *another,* adj.
and subst., with gen., with τίς, οὔ τις
ἄλλος εἰ μή (ἀλλά, Σ 403, Φ 275), non
alius nisi; ἄλλον instead of ἐμέ, etc.,
B 360, 200; and freq. in antithetical
clauses, ἄλλος (or ὁ, cf. Ι 594, or ἕτερος)
μὲν—ἄλλοι δέ, without μὲν—δέ, Μ 267,
Σ 536; μέν τ' ἀλλ'—αὐτὰρ ἐπ' ἄλλα,
Ν 799; ἄλλο δέ τοι ἐρέω, κ. τ. λ., verse
marking, in Homer, a transition, π 299;
(a) *other, additional,* reliquus, Γ 223;
ἄλλο, *besides,* Ξ 249; ἄλλο τόσον, as
much *more;* (οἱ) ἄλλοι, *the rest;* ἔξοχον
(ὑπείροχον) ἄλλων, ε 105; (b) used
when it can with difficulty be translated into English = *besides, moreover,
as for the rest* (cf. nous autres Fran-
çais), Θ 211, Β 191, α 132, β 412, ο 407,
Ν 622, α 157, Β 665, etc.; (c) for emphasis, in apposition with compar., O
569, X 106; and πλησίος, Δ 81 and

often; (d) with other forms or cases of
ἄλλος, cf. alius alium, B 75, see ἄλλυδις, ἄλλοθεν, δ 236.—(2) alieni,
strangers, intruders, υ 213.—(3) *untrue,*
δ 348.

ἄλλοσε (ἄλλος), *to* or *in another place,*
ψ 184 and 204. [‿ ‿ ‿]

ἄλλοτε (ἄλλος), alias, *at another
time, formerly;* often doubled with or
without μέν—δέ; in first member, ὅτε
μὲν often substituted for ἄλλοτε μέν;
in second member, often ἄλλοτε δ' αὖτε,
now—then, now—now, Φ 464, Λ 65, Σ
159; ἄλλοτε ἄλλῳ, modo huic,
modo illi; ἄλλοτ' ἐπ' ἄλλον, modo
in hunc, modo in illum. [‿ ‿ ‿]

ἀλλότριος, 3, (ἄλλος), *strange, belonging to another.*—(1) alienus, ἀλλό-
τρια, *others' goods,* cf. α 160; υ 347 (cf.
ἀλλοιδέα and π 181), with *distorted*
cheeks they were laughing, laughed
with strange grimaces.—(2) exterus,
φώς, *stranger,* hence *enemy,* π 102; γαίη,
foreign land.

ἄ-λλοφος (λόφος), non cristatus,
without crest; κυνέη, K 258†. (See cut,
under κυνέη.)

ἀλλο-φρονέων, -ντος, see φρονέω.

ἄλλυδις (ἄλλος), alio, *to another
place,* always with ἄλλος, alius alio,
or with ἄλλῃ, now *in one way, now in
another;* N 279, the coward changes,
from moment to moment, i. e. *every moment,* his color. [‿ ‿ ‿]

ἀλ-λύεσκον, εν, iter. ipf. from ἀνα-
λύω, retexebat, *unravel,* β 105, τ 150.
(Od.).

ἄλλως (ἄλλος), aliter, *otherwise,*
(1) in strict signification, ε 286, φ 429;
besides, ε 267; *for some other reason,*
ρ 577; *already, without this,* φ 87.—(2)
melius, *better,* θ 176, ν 211, ω 107, Ε
218, Ξ 53, Τ 401.—(3) incassum, *in
vain,* ξ 124, Ψ 144.—(4) alioquin, *in
other circumstances,* o 513.

ἅλμα, ατι, ασι, (ἅλλομαι), saltus,
leaping, as a game, θ 103 and 128.

ἅλμη, ἡ, (ἅλς), aqua marina, *sea-
water, brine,* ε 53. (Od.)

ἁλμυρόν (ἅλμη) ὕδωρ, aqua marina, *salt water,* δ 511. (Od.)

ἀ-λογήσει (λεγ-, cf. ἀλέγω), con-
temnere, *disregard, despise,* O 162,
178.

ἀλόθεν (ἅλς), ἐξ—, c mari, *from the
sea,* Φ 335†. [‿ ‿ ‿]

ἀλοία (ἀλωή), ipf. from ἀλοιάω, contudit, she *smote;* γαῖαν χερσίν, Ι 568†.
[‿ – –]

ἀλοιφή, ή, (ἀλείφω), adeps, *fat,* Ι
208, P 390, Ψ 32; for rubbing in, to
render pliant, φ 179; unguentum,
ointment, ζ 220, σ 179.

Ἄλον, acc., Ἀλόπην, acc., *towns in*
domain of Achilleus, B 682†.

ἀλο-σύδνης (ἅλς, Gothic sunus,
son), gen. mari natae, *daughter of
the sea,* Υ 207, δ 404.

ἄ-λοφος, see ἄλλοφος.

ἄ-λοχος (λέχος), uxor, *she who
shares the bed, wife,* Z 299, γ 264; also
the *concubine* is called ἄλοχος; adjectives, μνηστή, αἰδοίη, κυδρή, καλλικρή-
δεμνοι, κεδνή, πολύδωρος.

ἀλόω, ἀλόωνται, see ἀλάομαι, vagari.

ἅλς, ἁλός, ὁ, sal, *grain of salt,* ρ
455=ne hilum quidem; — ἡ, *the
briny deep, sea* (near the shore), A 308.
[‿‿]

ἄλσο, 2 sing. aor. from ἅλλομαι,
saliisti.

ἄλσος, εἰ, εα, έων, ntr. (alere), lu-
cus, *grove,* usually with altar, and sacred to a divinity, B 506, ζ 321.

Ἄλτης, king of the Λέλεγες, father
of Λαοθόη, Φ 85.

ἆλτο, 3 sing. aor. from ἅλλομαι,
saluit.

Ἀλύβαντος, ἐξ —, *out of Wandering,*
ω 304†, word formed by a pun out of
ἀλάομαι.

Ἀλύβης, τηλόθεν ἐξ —, *from Alybe,*
whence silver comes, B 857†.

ἀλυσκάζω (ἀλύσκω), only pres. and
ipf., evitare, *avoid,* τι, Z 443, ρ 581.

ἀλύσκανε (ἀλύσκω), effugiebat,
was seeking how to escape, χ 330†.
[‿ – ‿ ‿]

ἀλύσκων (ἀλεύομαι), ἀλύξω, ἤλυξα,
effugio, *avoid, escape,* κῆρας, ὄλεθρον; μ 335, clam me subduxi
sociis, χ 363, 382.

ἀλύσσοντες (from ἀλύσσω, see ἀλύ-
ων), *confused,* X 70, *maddened in spirit;*
ἀλαλύκτημαι, K 94, *I am beside myself.* [‿ – ‿ – ‿]

ἄ-λυτον, 2, (λύω), insolubilis, *not
to be loosed,* N 360. [‿ ‿ ‿]

ἀλύων, ουσ(α), ἀλάομαι, perturba-
ta mente esse, furere, *be beside
one's self*—(1) with joy, σ 333, 393.—(2)

with pain; ι 398, he dashed it with his
hands wildly from him. [‿ ‿ –]

Ἀλφειός, river in Ἤλις; then the
river-god, γ 489.

ἀλφεσί-βοιος (ἀλφεῖν, βοῦς), boves
comparans, *bringing in cattle,* i. e.
making wealthy, see ἕδνα, Σ 593†.

ἀλφηστάων, -ῇσιν, -άς, (ἀλφεῖν),
victum quaerentes, ζ 8, ν 261,
hard-working, contrasted with ῥεῖα ζώοντες; others translate *flour-eating,
fruit-eating.* (Od.)

ἀλφίτου (albus), ἀκτή, β 355, *bar-
ley-meal;* elsewh. ἄλφιτα, *barley-groats*
or *meal* (the porridge made of them),
β 290, etc.; μυελὸς ἀνδρῶν, λευκά, ἐπι-
παλύνειν. [‿ ‿]

(ἀλφεῖν), aor. ἦλφον, opt. ἄλφοι, 3
pl. ἄλφοιν, ν 383, so Ameis, (German
arbeit), parere, *bring in, yield,* ὦνον,
βίοτον, ο 452, ρ 250. (Od.)

Ἀλωῆος, *of Aloeus,* the father of
Ὦτος and Ἐφιάλτης, husband of Ἰφι-
μέδεια. [‿ – – –]

ἀλωή (ἀλοιάω), area, *threshing-floor,*
Υ 496; also *orchard* and *vineyard;* Σ
561, *corn-field;* see γουνός.

ἀλωῆ, ἀλώῃ, ἀλώμενος, from ἁλίσκομαι, capi.

ἀλώμενος, from ἀλάομαι, errans.

ἀλώω, from ἁλίσκομαι, aor. subj.
captus sim.

ἀμ, ἀμ, instead of ἀνά before labials.

ἅμα (from σάμα, cf. Σαμοκλῆς, ὁμός),
una, simul, *at once, at the same time.*
—(1) adv., A 343; ἅμ' ἄμφω, H 255;
often with τὲ—καί, B 281; with following δέ, Τ 242.—(2) prep. with dat.,
simul, *at same time with,* ἅμ' ἠελίῳ
ἀνιόντι, καταδύντι; una, *beside, with,*
A 348, α 428; ἕπεσθαι, go with, attend.
so, τροχόωντα, θέουσα, *run after;* α 98,
Π 149, *swift as the wind.* [‿‿]

Ἀμαζόνες ἀντιάνειραι, Γ 189, dwelt
on the river Thermodon in Pontos;
made a plundering foray into Phrygia,
B 814, Z 186. [ᾰ]

Ἀμάθεια, a Nereid, Σ 48†. [‿ – – ‿]

ἀμάθοιο (ψάμαθος) βαθείης, E 587†,
he fell into deep sand. [‿ ‿ – ‿]

ἀμαθύνει, πῦρ, solo aequat, *destroys,* Ι 593†. [‿ ‿ – –]

ἀ-μαιμάκετος, 3, (μαιμάσσω), saevi-
ens, *furious,* Z 179, Π 230; ξ 311, the
mast *tossed to and fro* by the waves,
like a man reeling in drunkenness.

ἀμαλδύνω (σμερδ-, mordeo?), only aor. ἀμαλδῦναι, -ύνας, and pass. ἀμαλδύνηται, contercre, destroy; only with τεῖχος. (Il.)

ἀμαλλο-δετήρ, ὁ, (ἄμαλλα, δέω), binder of sheaves. (Il., Σ.)

ἀμαλήν, -ῆσι, (mollis), teneram, tender; of lamb, dog.

ἄμ-αξα, ἡ, (ἅμα, ἄξων), parallel form ἄμαξα, plaustrum, four-wheeled freight wagon, ι 241; also the constellation of the Great Bear, Σ 487, ε 273; cf. ἅρμα, ἀπήνη. [ă]

ἀμαξ-ιτόν (ἄμαξα, εἶμι, κατ᾽ —, viâ publicâ, wagon-road, X 146.

ἀμάρης (μύρω? mare?), ιξ —, canal for irrigation, Φ 259†. [⌣⌣—]

ἀμαρτάνω (ἀ-, μέρος), ἁμαρτήσομαι, aor. ἥμαρτον and ἤμβροτον—(1) impertem fieri esse, lose, φ 155, ι 512; then (2) in general, fail of; miss, τινός; λ 511, mistook not the word, spoke the right word; Ω 68, failed not to bring gifts; η 292, let not presence of mind fail her.—(3) peccare, fail, err; with ὑπερβήῃ, l 501; χ 154, I myself have overlooked this.

ἁμαρτῇ (ἅμα, ἄραρον), simul, simultaneously, χ 81. [ă]

ἀμαρτο-επές (ἔπος), temere locutus, speaking thoughtlessly, N 824†. [ă]

'Αμάρυγκείδης Διώρης, B 622, Δ 517. [ă]

'Αμαρυγκέα θάπτον 'Επειοὶ Βουπρασίῳ, his burial in Messene, with funeral games, described, Ψ 630†.

ἁμα-τροχόωντα se τροχόωντα, running about after me.

ἁμα-τροχιάς (τροχός), acc. pl., concursus impactarum rotarum, running together, clash of chariots, Ψ 422†. [⌣—⌣⌣—]

ἀ-μαυρὸν (ἀ-, μάρμαρος) εἴδωλον, pale, dim, lurid, δ 824 and 835. (Od.) [ă]

ἀ-μάχητί (μάχη), sine pugna, without contest, Φ 437†. [ῑ]

ἀμάω (Ger. mähen, Eng. mow), ipf. ἤμων, aor. ἀμήσαντες, -σάμενος, manu colligere, gather together, collect, ι 247; mow. [≃ — —]

ἀμβ-, see ἀναβ-.

ἀμ-βατός (ἀνα-βαίνω), aditum praebens, that may be scaled, Z 434.

ἀμ-βλήδην (ἀναβάλλομαι), adv. exorsa, as prelude, at first, X 476†.

ἀμ-βολάδην (ἀναβάλλω), adv., bubbling up, Φ 364†.

ἀμ-βροσίη (ἀμβρόσιος), ambrosia, adj. used as subs., strictly signifies immortal and conferring immortality; used by the gods as food; as ointment, for embalming, for perfume; also as food for horses of the gods.

ἀμ-βρόσιος (ἄμβροτος), divinus, immortal, divine, E 369.—(1) that which the gods send, νύξ, ὕπνος, or (2) belongs to them; πλοκάμους, χαῖται, κάλλεϊ, ἑανόν, πέπλου, even of their horses, εἶδαρ and κάπῃσιν. [⌣⌣⌣⌣]

ἄμ-βροτος, ο, (βροτός), immortal, Υ 358, θ 365, θεός; then like ἀμβρόσιος, divine.—(1) νύξ.—(2) αἶμα, εἵματα, τεύχεα, ἐλαίῳ, ἱστόν, ἵπποι.

ἀ-μέγαρτος (μεγαίρω), only sing., invisus, unenviable, doleful, dreadful (proleptically of battle, B 420); mighty blast, λ 400; miserable, ρ 219. [ă]

ἀμείβω (moveo), fut. ἀμείψω, -ομαι, aor. ἠμείψατο, alternare, alternate, change.—I. act., exchange, τί, τινός, for something, πρός τινα, with some one; ὀλίγον γόνυ γουνὸς ἀμ., pedetentim cedendo; οἱ ἀμείβοντες, rafters.—II. mid., (1) change with each other, ἀμειβόμενος, alternans, A 604, relieving one another; θ 379, in quick alternation (of dance); α 375, passing from one house to another; θρώσκων ἀμείβεται, O 684, leaps in turn.—(2) answer, δ 382; μύθῳ, κ 71; (μυθῷ, -οισι, ἐπέεσσι) τινά, some one; εὖ δώροις τινά, make beautiful gifts in return.—(3) pass over, I 409, κ 328.

ἀ-μείλικτον (μειλίσσω) ὄπα, implacabilem, harsh, inexorable words. (Il.) [ă]

ἀ-μείλιχος, 2, (μειλίσσω), inexorabilis, implacable, relentless. [ă]

ἀ-μείνων, ον (Old Lat. mānus= bonus), melior, better, more excellent, superior, more favorable, more advantageous (opposed in signif. to χέρηα, Δ 400); μέγ᾽ ἀμείνων, multo praestantior; α 376, more profitable and better.

ἀ-μέλγω, only pr. and ipf., mulgeo, milk; pass., Δ 434, yielding white milk. [ă]

ἀ-μέλησε (μέλω), aor., always with negation; οὐκ ἀμ. τινός, curabat, he bethought himself of. [ă] ἄμεναι, inf. from ἄω, satiare.

ἀ-μενηνός, 2, (μένος), debilis, *feeble*, E 887; νεκύων ἀμ. κάρηνα, *feeble heads of the dead* (periphrasis)=the *feeble* dead ; ὀνείρων, *unsubstantial*. [ᾰ]

ἀ-μενήνωσεν (ἀμενηνός), debilitavit, *made ineffective*, N 562†. [ᾰ]

1. ἀ-μέρδω (μέρος), aor. ἄμερσε, -σαι; pass. pres. ἀμέρδεαι, aor. subj. ἀμερθῇς, privare, *deprive*, θ 64 ; pass., *lose, be deprived of*, X 58.

2. ἀ-μέρδω (μάρμαρος), only pres. and pf., *make lustreless, blind*, ρ 18 ; *dazzle, blind* by excess of light, N 340.

ἀ-μέτρητος, 2, (μετρέω), immensus, *immeasurable*, ρ 512 and ψ 249. [ᾰ ‒ ‒ ‿]

ἀ-μετρο-επής (μέτρον, Ϝέπος), immoderate loquax, *immoderate talker*, B 212†.

ἀμητῆρες (ἀμάω), messores, *reapers*, Λ 67†. [≃ ‒ ‒ ‿]

ἄμητος (ἀμάω), messis, *reaping, harvest;* metaph. for *slaughter*, Τ 223†. [≃ ‒ ‿]

ἀ-μηχανίη (ἀμήχανος), desperatio, *helplessness, despair*, ι 295†. [ᾰ]

ἀ-μήχανος, 2, (μῆχος), *helpless.*—(1) act., miser, *wretched*, ρ 363.—(2) pass., difficilis, *impossible*, Ξ 262; Θ 130, *irremediable mischief*; ρ 560, *useless* dreams; *unyielding*, Ο 14, Τ 273; *stubborn, hard-hearted*, Π 29 ; N 726, *thou canst not* (for thou art too obstinate) *yield to*, etc.

Ἀμίσωδάρου υἷες (Ἀτύμνιος, Μάρις), in Karia, Π 328†. [ᾰ]

ἀ-μιτρο-χίτωνες (μίτρη, χιτών), *wearing coat of mail without girdle*, or the word may mean *wearing both coat of mail and girdle*, χιτών in this cmpd. =θώρηξ, Π 419†. [‿ ‒ ‿ ‿ ‒ ‿]

ἀμιχθαλόεσσαν (ὀμίχλη), Λῆμνον, vapore obductam, *foggy, misty, smoky*, since Lemnos is a volcanic island, Ω 753†. [ᾰ]

ἄμμε, ἄμμες, ἄμμι, see ἡμεῖς.

ἀμ-μίξας, aor. part. from ἀναμίγνυμι, admiscens.

ἀμ-μορίην (μόρος), *misfortune*, υ 76†.

ἄμ-μορος, 2, (μέρος), expers, ε 275, Σ 489, *deprived of* the bath of the ocean, of the Great Bear, which never sinks below the horizon in Greece; elsewh. *unfortunate*.

ἀμνίον, ntr., *basin in which the blood of victims was caught*, γ 444‡. (See cut.)

Ἀμνίσῳ, ἐπ', at *Amnisos*, harbor of Knosos, τ 188†. [ῐ]

ἀ-μογητί (μογέω), sine labore, *without trouble*, Λ 637†. [ῐ]

ἀμόθεν (ἀμός), τῶν, alicunde (orsa), *from any point soever; beginning with any point whatever*, relate to us, α 10†. [ᾰ]

ἀμοιβάς (ἀμείβω), χλαίνη, mutatoria, *for a change*, ξ 521†. [ᾰ]

ἀμοιβή, ἡ, (ἀμείβομαι), retributio, *recompense, gift in return, restitution*. (Od.) [ᾰ]

ἀμοιβηδίς, *in turn*, Σ 506 and σ 310.

ἀμοιβοί (ἀμείβω), succedanci, as *substitutes* (in exchange for former aid furnished by Priam), N 793†. [ᾰ]

ἀμολγῷ (ἐν), νυκτός, *in darkness*, of night. [ᾰ]

Ἀμοπάονα, Πολυαιμονίδην, slain by Τεῦκρος, Θ 276†. [‿ ‿ ‒ ‿ ‿]

ἀμός, 3, (also ἁμός)=ἡμέτερος. [ᾰ]

ἄμοτον (μέμαα, moveo), vehementer, *insatiably, unceasingly, eagerly;* esp. with μέμαα, κλαίω, κεχολωμένος, τανύοντο. [ᾰ]

ἀμπ-, see ἀναπ-.

ἀμπελόεντ(α), -εσσαν, (ἀμπελό-εις), B 561, Γ 184, vitibus abundans, *full of vines, abounding in vines;* of districts and towns. (Il.)

ἄμπελος, ἡ, *grape-vine*, vine. (Od.)

ἀμ-πεπαλών, aor. part. from ἀναπάλλω, vibrans.

ἀμ-περές (ἀνά, περάω), always διὰ δ' ἀμπερές, penitus, *through and through*.

ἄμπ-εχεν, ἅλμη ὤμους, circumdabat, *covered, lay thick upon*, ζ 225†.

ἀμ-πήδησε, aor. from ἀναπηδάω, exsiluit.

ἀμ-πνεῦσαι, ἄμ-πνυε, ἀμ-πνύνθη, ἄμ-πνυτο, see ἀνα-πνέω.

ἄμπ-ῠκα (ἀμπέχω), head-band, fillet, ornament of woman's head, χ 469. (See cut.)

ἀμῠδίς (Aeolic instrumental case, from ἁμός; parallel form, ἄμυδις), una, simul, at once, (1) together, καθίζειν, κικλήσκειν, etc., πάντ' ἄμυδις, all together, μ 413, M 385.—(2) at once, immediately, Ι 6, Ν 336, Ψ 217, ξ 305. [ă]

Ἀμῠδῶνος, ἲξ —, Amydon, city of Παίονες, on the river Ἀξιός, in Makedonia, Β 849 and Π 288. [ă]

Ἀμῠθάονα, acc., son of Κρηθεύς and Τυρώ, father of Βίας and Μελάμπους, λ 259†. [∪∪−∪∪]

Ἀμύκλαι, ας, city in Lakonia, near the Eurotas, twenty stadia S.E. of Sparta, residence of Tyndareos, Β 584†. [ă].

ἀ-μύμων, ονος, [μῶμος], irreprehensus, faultless, used esp. of external appearance, but also in a more general sense, excellent, glorious (fortunate, ᴈ 232, μ 261). [∪−−]

ἀμύντωρ, -ορα, -ας, (ἀμύνω), acc., defensor, defender, protector. [ă]

Ἀμύντορος, Ὀρμενίδαο, gen., father of Φοῖνιξ, Ι 448. [ă]

ἀμύνω (μύνη, munio), arcere, propulsare, ward off, (1) act., N 814, τινί τι, Ι 674, Ι1 835 ; τινός, from some one, τι, M 402, Ο 731; ἀπό, ρ 538; help, defend, τινί, Ε 486, Λ 674, λ 500 ; τινός,

Ν 109 ; περί τινος, Ρ 182; ἀπό τινος, Π 75, 80.—(2) mid., defend one's self, β 62, χ 106, 116; ward off, τί, Ν 514, Ρ 510; protect, τινός, Μ 155, Ι 531; ναῦφι, Ν 700; περί τινος, Μ 170, 243. [∪−−]

ἄμυσσεν, ἀμύξεις, (ἀμύσσω, mucro), ipf., fut. lacerare, scratch, tear, Τ 284, out of grief; Α 243, θυμόν, thou shalt gnaw thy soul with vexation. [ă]

ἀμφ-ἀγάπαζον, -όμενος, (ἀγαπάζω), ipf. act. and pres. mid., amplecti, receive hospitably, Π 192, ξ 381.

ἀμφ-ἀγέροντο (ἀγείρω), ipf., μιν —, circa eam conveniebant, were grouping themselves about her, Σ 37†.

ἀμ-φάδιον, adj. (φάος), γάμον, open, publicly declared, ζ 288; esp. ἀμφαδίην, adv. palam, openly, Η 196. [ă]

ἀμ-φάδὰ γένοιτο, detegeretur, that the thing should come to light; ἀμφαδόν, palam, openly, undisguisedly (opp. κρυφηδόν, ξ 330; δόλῳ, α 296), publicly.

ἀμφὶ δ' ἀίσσονται (ἀίσσω), undique concitantur, spring upon it from all sides, Λ 417; ὤμοις, float round his shoulders, Z 510, O 267. [ă]

ἀμφὶ τ' ἀλείψαι (ἀλείφω), aor. inf., perungere, anoint thoroughly, Ω 582†.

ἀμφ-ἀράβησε (ἀραβέω), aor., his armor crashed around him, Φ 408†.

ἀμ-φᾰσίη (φάναι), μιν—ἐπέων λάβε, speechlessness took possession of him, Ρ 695, δ 704.

ἀμφ' αὐον ἀὔτευν (ἀϋτέω), ipf. aridum circa sonabant, gave a dull sound, M 160†. [ῠ]

ἀμφ-ἀφάω (ἅπτω), part. ἀμφ-αφόων, -όωσα, mid. inf. -άασθαι, ipf. -όωντο, contrectare manibus, feel of all around, touch, grasp; also with χερσί, handle, θ 215.

ἀμφ-εποτᾶτο, ipf. from ἀμφιποτάομαι, circumvolitabat, Β 315†.

ἀμφ-έπω, see ἀμφιέπω.

(ἀμφέρχομαι), only aor. ἀμφ-ήλυθε, versabatur circa, sounds about me, ζ 122; rose about me, μ 369. (Od.)

ἀμφ-έχανε, devoravit, see ἀμφιχαίνω.

ἀμφ-έχυτ', circumfundebatur, see ἀμφιχέω.

ἄμφ-ηκες (ἀκή), utrimque acutus, two-edged, of sword, π 80.

ἀμφ-ήλυθε, circumiit, from ἀμφ-έρχομαι.

ἄμφ-ημαι, only ἀμφὶ δ' εἵατο, circumversabantur, O 9†.

ἀμφ-ηρεφέα (ἐρέφω), utrimque contectaṁ, close-covered, A 45†.

ἀμφ-ήριστον (ἐρίζω), ambiguum (victorem), doubtful (his victory doubtful), Ψ 382†.

ἀμφί (see ἀμφίς), utrimque, on both sides, often synonymous with περί.
—I. adv., utrimque, β 153, 427, σ 173; round about, γ 32, 429, φ 122; exchanged with περί, Σ 564, O 647; ἀμφὶ περί (sometimes wrongly written as one word), Φ 10, Ψ 191, λ 609; περί τ' ἀμφί τε, with acc., P 760; so περί, κ 262.—II. prep., (1) with gen., de, about, concerning, Π 825, θ 267.—(2) with dat., (a) local, circa, around, among, B 388, Γ 328, Σ 231, M 396, Δ 493; ὀβελοῖσιν ἔπειραν, proleptically, pierced the meat so that it was around the spit, A 465, cf. Ψ 30; ἀμφὶ πυρί, on the fire, θ 426; with, λ 423, I 470; (b) causal, because of=for, Γ 70, 157, α 48, δ 153, λ 546, Λ 672; de, with respect to, ρ 555, δ 151, H 408.—(3) with acc., local; circa, about, Ω 588, B 461, A 409; within, Λ 706; ἀμφί τινα, any one in company with those about him, χ 281, Γ 146.

Ἀμφί-αλος, a Phaiakian, θ 114. [ῐ]

ἀμφί-άλῳ, ἐν Ἰθάκῃ, mari cinctā, sea-girt. (Od.)

Ἀμφί-άραος, son of Ὀικλῆς, great-grandson of Μελάμπους, pious and brave; seer, and king of Argos; he participated in the Argonautic expedition and in the Kalydonian boar-hunt, and finally, through the treachery of Eriphyle, in the expedition of the Seven against Thebes, o 244. [ἄ]

ἀμφί-αχυῖαν (ἄχος), as she flew shrieking about, B 316†.

ἀμφι-βαίνω, ipf., pf., plupf.; only ipf. (aor. P 359) in tmesi; surround, cingere, τι, μ 74; τινί, Π 66; Ζ 355, θ 541, occupies the thought, heart; μέσον οὐ-

ρανόν, stand at zenith; τί, tenere, possess, protect, esp. of perf. and plupf. with dat.

ἀμφι-βάλλει, fut. -βαλεῦμαι, cast about, (1) amicire, induere, put on, of garments, weapons, etc., always in tmesi τινά τι, also without acc. of the person (also mid., clad one's self), τί, τινί (dat. of pers., ξ 342; of thing, E 722, N 36) τι; ἀμφιβαλόντες, P 742, putting on strength; fut. only mid., I will equip myself.—(2) circum ponere, ψ 192, building upon this (as foundation); χεῖρας, χεῖρε—δειρῇ Ὀδυσῆι, ψ 208, or τινί, τινά, embrace; γούνασί τινος, amplecti genua; δ 454, seize; ρ 344, as much as his hands could hold in their clasp; K 535, encompass, resound about.

ἀμφί-βάσῑν, resistance, E 623†.

ἀμφι-βρότης, -ην, (βροτός), hominem undique tegentis, covering the entire man, ἀσπίδος, B 389, Λ 32. (Il.)

Ἀμφί-γένεια, town subject to Nestor, B 593†.

ἀμφί-γυήεις (γυῖα), ambidexter, strong-armed, only at close of verse, usually subst. work-master, with περι-κλυτός, of Ἥφαιστος, θ 300.

ἀμφί-γύοισιν (γυῖον), ἐγχεσιν, almost always at close of verse, utrimque acutis, sharp at both ends, π 474; see οὐρίαχος. (See annexed cuts.) [ῐ]

ἀμφι-δαίω, only -δέδηε, -δεδήει, (δαίω), perf. plupf., circa exarsit, rages round about, τι, Z 329. (Il.)

Ἀμφι-δάμας, -αντος, (1) from Κύθηρα, K 268.—(2) from Ὀπόεις, Ψ 87.

ἀμφΐ-δάσειαν (δασύς), αἰγίδα, circa villosam, shaggy all around, with shaggy border, O 309†.

ἀμφΐ-δῑνέω, -δεδίνηται, pf. pass., Ψ 562, round whose edge goes a border (casting) of tin; θ 405, encloses it.

ἀμφι-δρΰφής (δρύπτω), quae genas lacerat, with both cheeks torn from grief, B 700†.

ἀμφί-δρύφοι (παρειαί), circa laceratae, (both) torn from grief, Λ 393†.

ἀμφί-δῦμοι, duplices, double (outer and inner harbor), δ 847†.

ἀμφΐ-ελίσσης, -αι, -ας, (ἑλίσσω), gen. sing., nom. and acc. pl., utrimque curvatae, curved at both ends, only of ships at rest, γ 162. [−⌣⌣−−] (The cut represents a Phoenician ship, as represented on an Egyptian monument.)

ἀμφι-έννῡμι (ἕννῡμι), fut. ἀμφϊ-έσω, aor. -εσ(σ)α, and mid. -άμην, (no pres. or ipf.), amicire, put on, don, τινά τι, Τ 393, ξ 23; mid., induere sibi, dress one's self in, ψ 131, K 23.

ἀμφι-έπων, only pr. (imp. and part.) and ipf., ἄμφεπε, also in tmesi, circa versari, to be busy about; τινά, Λ 473, surround (mid.); πῦρ, envelop in flame; apparare, dress, θ 61; arrange, B 525; ἀμφιέποντες, seduli, busily, γ 118.

ἀμφι-εῦσε (εὔω), ambussit, singed round about, ι 389†.

ἀμφ-ίξανε (ἱζάνω), circa adhaerebat, hung upon, Σ 25†.

ἀμφϊ-θαλής (θάλος), undique affluens, rich; others interpret, having father and mother still alive, X 496†.

Ἀμφι-θέη, wife of Αὐτόλυκος, grandmother of Ὀδυσσεύς, τ 416†.

ἀμφί-θετος φιάλη, reversible cup, i. e. with double bowl and base, which may stand upon or be drunk from either end, the base serving also as bowl (cf. ἀμφϊ-κύπελλον δέπας), Ψ 270. (Ψ.)

ἀμφϊ-θέουσιν (θέω), circumsiliunt, run about, κ 413†.

Ἀμφιθόη, a Nereid, Σ 42†.

ἀμφϊ-κᾰλύπτει (also in tmesi), with fut. and aor. (calim, occulo, Ger. hüllen, Eng. hull, of grain), obvolvo, wrap around, veil, B 262; shelter, enclose, Ψ 91, δ 618, θ 511; becloud, of swoon, Υ 417; of sleep, υ 86; θανάτου μέλαν νέφος, Π 350, cf. M 116, E 68, δ 180; ἔρως με φρένας, love engrossed my heart; τινί τι, surround, Ξ 343, N 420, P 132, θ 569, E 507.

ἀμφι-καρῆ, double-headed, v. l., ρ 231.

ἀμφϊ-κεάσσας (κεάζω), having hewed off all around (the bark), ξ 12†.

Ἀμφι-κλος, a Trojan, Π 313†.

ἀμφι-κόμῳ (κόμη), frondoso, shady, P 677†.

ἀμφϊ-κύπελλον, δέπας, double-cupped goblet, whose base is bowl-shaped, and may be drunk from, γ 63. [ῠ]

ἀμφϊ-λάχαινεν, sarriebat, was digging about, ω 242†.

Ἀμφί-λοχος, son of Ἀμφιάραος, from Ἄργος, a seer, ο 248†.

ἀμφϊ-λύκη (lucere), νύξ, diluculum, gray of early dawn, H 433†. [ῠ]

ἀμφϊ-μάσασθε, 1 aor. imp. mid., σπόγγοισι, wipe off all over, υ 152†.

ἀμφϊ-μάχονται, fight around, (1) τί, besiege, Z 461.—(2) τινός, fight for (as a prize), of defenders and assailants, Π 496; cf. ἀμφί νέκυι, Π 526. (Il.)

Ἀμφί-μαχος, (1) son of Κτέατος, leader of Ἐπειοί, N 203.—(2) son of Νομίων, leader of Κᾶρες, B 870.

Ἀμφί-μεδων, son of Μελανεύς, a suitor, χ 242.

ἀμφϊ-μέλαιναι, -ας, φρένες, dark on both sides, darkened (lit. diaphragm, dark on both sides), metaph. of soul, darkened by rage or grief, of instantaneous effect of strong feeling. (Il.)

ἀμφϊ-μέμῡκεν (μυκάομαι), circumsonavit, re-echoed, κ 227; in tmesi, aor. -μύκε, -ον, resounded, Υ 260, M 460.

Ἀμφι-νόμη, a Nereid, Σ 44.

Ἀμφί-νομος, son of Νῖσος, from Δουλίχιον, a suitor, χ 89.

ἀμφι-ξέω, only ἀμφίξεσα, dolavi, *I hewed round about*, ψ 196†.

Ἄμφιος, (1) son of Σέλαγος, from Παισός, ally of the Trojans, E 612.— (2) son of Μέροψ, a Trojan chief, B 830.

ἀμφι-πέληται, circumsonet, *resounds*, α 352†.

ἀμφι-πένονται, and ἀμφεπένοντο, ipf., curant, *attended*, o 467; *take up, tend* (the wounded); *assail*, Φ 203, Ψ 184.

ἀμφι-περί, see ἀμφί.

ἀμφι-περι-στρέφεται, see περιστρέφ.

ἀμφι-περι-στρώφα, see περιστρώφα.

ἀμφι-πεσοῦσα (πίπτω), amplexata, *embracing, clinging to* (her lifeless husband), θ 523†.

ἀμφι-πολεύειν (ἀμφίπολος), only pr., curare, *till*, ὀρχατον; βίον, *watch over*; υ 78, *attend, serve* (ironical). (Od.)

ἀμφί-πολος, ἡ, (πέλομαι), comes, *female attendant* (not a slave), without whom the noble dame of the heroic age never appears in public, α 331.

ἀμφι-πονέομαι, only ipf. -επονεῖτο and fut. -πονησόμεθα, curare, *attend* (so also ἀμφιπένονται), Ψ 681; *superintend*, Ψ 159, υ 307.

ἀμφι-ποτάομαι, only ἀμφ-εποτᾶτο, circumvolitabat, *was fluttering about*, B 315†.

ἀμφι-ρύτη (ῥέω), νήσῳ ἐν —, circumflua, *sea-girt*, α 50. (Od.) [ῡ]

ἀμφίς (from ἄμφω, old instr. case, Φ 162; weakened to ἀμφί, which orig. stood before σέκαστον [ἕκαστον], Λ 634, 748, τ 46; and in composition, ἀμφι-σέχω, α 54, γ 486, θ 340; replaced at close of verse by ἀμφίς; η 4, ζ 266, E 723, Φ 442), utrimque, *on both sides*. —I. adv., (1) Σ 519; Φ 162, hurl the spears *from both hands at once*; ἔχειν, have on both sides, carry; α 54, hold asunder; *round about*, H 342, Γ 115.— (2) *apart*, N 706; *singly*, χ 57, cf. X 117; εἶναι, π 267, with gen., *be far from*, τ 221, O 709.—(3) *differently*, φράζεσθαι, φρονεῖν, B 13, N 345.—II. prep. (always following the word it governs, except ἀμφὶ before (σ)έκαστος), (1) with gen., *far away from*, ξ 352, π 267, Θ 444; *on one side of*, Ψ 393; *in all its parts, narrowly*, B 384.—(2) with dat., *on either end*, E 723.—(3) with acc., *about, around*, Ξ 274, ζ 266, Λ 635, 748, τ 46.

ἀμφίσταμαι, only ipf. and aor. ἀμφέσταν, ἀμφ-έστησαν, circumstare,

obsidere, Σ 233; in tmesi, η 4, ι 380, ω 58.

ἀμφὶ-(νέφος) ἔστεφε, cinxit, *crowned with*, Σ 205†.

ἀμφ-εστρᾰτόωντο, τὴν, obsidebant, *were besieging*, Λ 713†.

ἀμφι-στρεφέες (στρέφω), flexiles, *turning all ways*, Λ 40†.

ἀμφι-τίθημι, induere, *put on*, τινί τί; in tmesi, yet ἀμφιτεθεῖσα, *placed upon*, K 271; mid. ἀμφέθετο, *girded on*, φ 431; in tmesi, θ 416, K 149.

ἀμφὶ-(ἑανὸς) τρέμε, circa tremebat, *trembled round about*, Φ 507†.

Ἀμφι-τρίτη, sea-goddess (not represented in Homer as wife of Poseidon), ε 422, μ 97, 60.

ἀμφι-τρομέω, τοῦ δ᾽— καὶ δείδια, *tremble for*, and *fear lest*, δ 820†.

Ἀμφι-τρύων, ωνος, only with παῖς, υἱός (Ἡρακλέης), and ἄκοιτιν (Ἀλκμήνην), king of Τίρυνς, E 392, γ 266.

ἀμφί-φᾰλον (φάλος) κυνέην, *double-plumed*, strictly, *double-ridged*; helmet *with double* or *divided crest*. (See cut, *a* and *b*.)

ἀμφι-φοβέω, only -εφόβηθεν, aor. pass. μιν, *were put to flight around* him, Π 290†.

ἀμφί-φορεύς, ὁ, (ἀμφίς, φέρω), *two-handled vase* or *jar for wine*; also, ω 74, *for ashes of the dead*. (See the following cuts, the first two from Egyptian, the others from Greek, originals.)

ἀμφί (μάλα) φράζεσθε, weigh carefully, Σ 254†.

ἀμφ-έχᾰνε, aor. (χαίνω), devoravit, yawns on every side, Ψ 79†.

ἀμφι-χέω, aor. χεῦε, χέε, circumfundo.—(1) in tmesi, τί τινι, circumdare, shed about, P 270, θ 278.—(2) aor. mid. ἰχυντο, thronged about, χ 498; were laid round them, θ 297 (tmesis); τινά, sound in one's hearing, B 41; encompass (tmesis), τινί, N 544, Π 414; also aor. pass. -εχύθη, δ 716, Ξ 253, Ψ 63; embrace, π 214; Ψ 764, before the dust-cloud rose.

ἀμφι-χὔθείς, -ῆναι, see ἀμφι-χέω, amplexus.

ἀμφί-χὔτον (χέω), circumfusum, encompassing (earthen wall), Υ 145†.

Ἀμφίων, ονος, (1) son of Ἰάσιος and Χλῶρις, king of Ὀρχομενός, λ 283.—(2) son of Zeus and Ἀντιόπη, brother of Ζῆθος, founder of Θῆβαι, λ 262.—(3) leader of the Ἐπειοί, N 692. [ῑ]

ἀμφότερος, η, ον, ambo, both; ἀμφότερον—τε—τε (καί), utrumque et—et; ἀμφοτέρῃσι (χερσί), κ 264 (E 416), ambabus (manibus); χεῖρε ἀμφοτέρας, ω 398.

Ἀμφοτερός, a Lykian, Π 415†.

ἀμφοτέρωθεν, utrimque, from or on both sides, at both ends, κ 167.

ἀμφοτέρωσε, in utramque partem, in both directions, Θ 223. (Il.)

ἀμφ-ουδίς (οὖδας), humi, on the ground, at his feet, ρ 237†.

ἀμ-φράσσαιτο, aor. from ἀναφράζομαι, agnosceret.

ἄμφω (ambo), ambo, utrique, both (sides), A 363 (B 124); the two pieces, μ 424.

ἄμφ-ωτον (οὖς), two-handled, χ 10†.

ἀμφῶεν, opt. pres. from ἀμάω, metent.

ἀ-μωμήτοιο (μῶμος), irreprehensus, irreproachable, M 109†.

1. ἄν (possibly from ἀμός, strictly, aliquâ), somehow, similar in its use to κέ; hence, I., with opt., mere (subjective) supposition, sumtio ficti; P 711, οὐ γάρ πως ἄν Τρώεσσι μάχοιτο, non enim Troes impugnaverit, he would (could) not, unarmed, attack the Trojans; in hypothetical periods, sumtio ficti, conclusion of expressed or implied supposition made without regard to fact, ἥ τ' ἄν ἀμυναίμην (εἰ μοι δύναμίς γε παρείη), ego vero me defenderim, I would defend myself, β 62; in relative periods, ὅς νῦν γε καί ἄν Διί πατρί μάχοιτο, who now at least would fight even with father Zeus, E 362; also with assumption contrary to fact, sumtio falsi, A 232.—(2) in interrogations, α 65, πῶς ἄν ἔπειτ' Ὀδυσῆος ἐγώ θείοιο λαθοίμην; how should (could) I forget? in requests, ζ 57, οὐκ ἄν δή μοι ἐφοπλίσσειας ἀπήνην, couldst (wouldst) thou not?—(3) in dependent relation after past tenses, προΐεις (με) ὄφρ' ἄν ἐλοίμην, ut acciperem, didst send me that I might receive, ω 334; hypothetically, in oratione obliqua, στεῦτο νικησέμεν εἴπερ ἄν—ἀείδοιεν (oratio recta would be ἰάνπερ ἀείδωσι), he stood and boasted that he would conquer even though (as he said) the Muses should sing, B 597.—II. with indic., (1) past tense (supposition contrary to fact), sumtio falsi, οὐκ ἄν τόσσα θεοπροπέων ἀγόρευες, non tam multa vaticinatus loquereris, wouldst not be talking so much, disclosing (forsooth) the will of the gods, β 184; hypothetically, ε 39, quae—ne ex Troia quidem abstulisset, si incolumis rediisset, as he would not have brought away from Troy, had he returned home without mishap.—(2) with future, seldom, X 66, αὐτόν δ' ἄν πύματόν με—ἐρύουσι, me ipsum postremo dilacera verint, me last of all shall the dogs rend.—III. with subj., denoting that which is soon to take place, scarcely different from simple future.—(1) in principal sentences, τάχ' ἄν ποτε θυμόν ὀλέσσῃ, soon shall he lose his life; thus esp. freq. with aor. subj., also (2) in dependent sen-

tence, ὃν δ' ἂν ἐγὼν—νοήσω, quem
conspicatus ero, whomsoever I
shall have perceived, Θ 10 (yet subj.
pres., ἐῃ, τ 332); ὡς ἂν ἐγὼ εἴπω,
quomodo ego locutus ero? how
shall I speak? A 510, ὄφρ' ἂν—τίσωσι,
quoad honorabunt, until *they shall
honor.*—Ἄν and κέ in one sentence,
ζ 259, ε 361. [◡; but – by position before Γερύσαιτ', Θ 21; σϜῷ, Θ 406, where
òrig. initial consonants have disappeared.]
    2. ἄν by apocope for ἀνά, before ν,
K 298; before τ, E 167; before στόμα,
ε 456; and in ἂν δέ, sc. ὤρνυτο, Γ 268,
Ψ 755 (cf. 812, 709, and θ 110–118).
    3. ἀν-, negative prefix, cf. Lat. in-,
Eng. in-, un- (cogn. with ἄνευ, possibly
with ἀνά), shortened before consonants
to so-called ἀ privativum, which
also (as ἀνα-) appears before vowels
when in the ancient form a spirant, σ,
Ϝ, or j, was heard : ἀνάϜεδνος, ἀϜαγής.

ἀνά, ἄν, before labials ἀμ (opp. κατά),
up, aloft.— I. adv., ἀλλ' ἄνα, but up!
quick! Σ 178, σ 13; thereon, Σ 562; upon,
β 416; mixed, pouring in (upon the
water) the wine, γ 390; often separated
by tmesis from the verb to which it
belongs.—II. prep., (1) with gen., ἀνὰ
νηὸς (νεῶν) βαίνειν, embark, α 210.—
(2) with dat., aloft on, upon, A 15, O 152,
ψ 275, Σ 177; ω 8, to each other.—(3)
with acc., strictly per, along a line
(contrast successively with κατά, on
different points of a surface, passim
per—; ἐν, with dat., at one point within
a given boundary; εἰς, with acc., to such
a point.—(1) of space, aloft to, or in,
ἀναβαίνειν, χ 132 ; τιθέναι, Κ 466; in
my breast, and rose to my mouth, ἀνὰ
στόμα, X 452; ῥῖνας, ω 318; along, K
339; ἀν' ἰθύν, straight forward; (a)
throughout, along, with verbs of motion,
E 74, K 362, 298, O 657, 101, N 270, P
257, Σ 546, Υ 319, Ψ 321, Ω 166, ψ 136,
also figuratively, Ψ 716; (b) with other
verbs, throughout the confines of, over,
amid, ἀν' Ἑλλάδα, N 117, B 575, β 291,
ξ 286; ἀνὰ στόμ' ἔχειν, having (their
names) in their mouth, B 250: ἀνὰ θυμὸν φρονεῖν, judge in one's soul; also,
ὁρμαίνειν, θαμβεῖν, ὀίεσθαι; follg. the
governed word, νειὸν ἀνά, ν 32.—(2)
temporal, ἀνὰ νύκτα, per noctem, all
night through, Ξ 80. [◡ ◡]

1. ἄνα, see ἀνά, I.
2. ἄνα, voc. from ἄναξ.
ἀνα-βαινέμεν, ἀμ-βαίνειν, -βήσομαι,
-έβην, often in tmesi, go up, μ 77; with
acc., ascend (to), οὐρανόν, ὑπερώια, ἅρματα; ζ 29, permeat homines,
goes abroad among men; ἀνά τι, χ 132,
143; εἴς τι, Ξ 287, Π 184, χ 143, ε 470;
with dat., K 493, per corpora in-
gredientes; ἐν δίφροισι, Ψ 132; ἐς
δίφρον, Π 657, X 399; with gen., νηός
(νεῶν), embark upon; also absolute (before taking ship for Troy), α 210, cf. A
611; also trans. in tmesis, A 143, τινά,
put on board; cf. ο 475, ἀναβησάμενοι,
having taken us into their ship.
ἀνά-βαλλε, ἀμ-βαλλώμεθα, (1) pro-
crastinare, postpone, τ 584; tmesis, ρ
262; mid., B 436.—(2) mid., ordiri,
make a prelude, ἀείδειν, α 155, ρ 262.
ἀνα-βέβρυχεν (βρέχω) ὕδωρ, scaturivit, bubbled up, P 54† (v. l. ἀνα-
βέβροχεν).
Ἀνα-βησί-νεως, a Phaiakian, θ 113†.
ἀνά-βλησις (ἀναβάλλω), dilatio,
postponement, B 380. (II.)
(ἀνα-βραχεῖν), aor. ἀν-έβράχε, rattled
aloud, T 13; creaked aloud, φ 48.
(ἀνα-βρόχω), only ἀνα-βρόξειε, μ
240, as often as she gulped down; and
ἀναβροχέν, λ 586, vanished as if sucked
up.
ἀνα-βρύζω, -βρύχω, see ἀναβέβρυχε,
scaturivit.
(ἀνα-γιγνώσκω), only aor. ἔγνων, etc.,
agnoscere, know again, δ 250, τ 250;
N 734, maxime vero ipse sentit,
the fortunate possessor knows it best
of all; λ 144, quomodo talem me
agnoscat, recognize me for such as
I am.
ἀναγκαίη (= ἀνάγκη), necessitas,
necessity, want, Z 85; dat., perforce, Δ
300; ἀναγκαίηφι δαμέντες, Υ 143.
ἀναγκαῖος, η, ον, (ἀνάγκη), (1) violentus, constraining; ἦμαρ, day of
constraint, servitus; μύθῳ, word of
force, χρειοῖ, dira necessitate.—(2)
coactus, perforce, δμῶες (captivi),
πολεμισταί, inviti.
ἀνάγκη, necessitas, constraint, necessity, κρατερή; τινί ἐστι (with inf.),
necesse est, K 418, Ω 667 (E 633, Υ
251); ἀνάγκῃ, vi, of necessity, κ 434, vel
coacti; ὑπ' ἀνάγκης, out of compul-
sion. [◡ – –]

ἀνα-γνάμπτω, only ἀν-έγναμψαν, retro curvabant, *unloosed*, and· ἀνεγνάμφθη, *was bent back*, P 44.

ἀν-άγουσι, -άξω, aor. -ήγαγον, *bring up, conduct, carry to* a place.—(1) on land, δ 534, ξ 272, ρ 441 (to the interior), cf. Θ 203; producere, *bring forth*, σ 89.—(2) by water, on shipboard, τινά, τί, *carry away* (home, γ 272), Ν 627, Γ 48, Ζ 292; *despatch*, σ 115; *bring back*, Ο 29; *guide hither*, Ι 338; ἀνάγοντο (opp. κατάγοντο), *put to sea*, τ 202.

ἀνα-δέδρομε, imminebat, see ἀνατρέχω.

(ἀνα-δέρκω), ἀν-έδρᾰκεν ὀφθαλμοῖσιν, aperuit oculos, *opened again* his eyes, Ξ 436†.

ἀνα-δέσμην (δέω) πλεκτήν, (twisted or plaited) *head-band*, Χ 469†. (See cut.)

(ἀνα-δέχομαι),only ἀνεδέξατο, excepit, *received*, Ε 619; and ipf. ἀνιδέγμεθα, suscepimus, *have undergone*, ρ 563.

(ἀνα-δύομαι), only in the forms ἀνδύεται, -εδύσετο, and 2 aor. -έδυ, -δύη, -δῦναι, emergere, *emerge*, ε 322; with gen., Α 359, ε 337; with acc., *arose to* the wave (surface) of the sea, Α 496; recedere, *draw back*, ι 377; εἰς, Η 217; and acc. without prep., Ν 225, cf. 214, *out of* the combat.

ἀν-ά-εδνον (ἀ-έεδνα), *without bridal gifts*, Ι 146. (Il.) [⏑⏑–⏑–⏑]

ἀν-αείρω, imp. -άειρε, aor. ind. -άειρε, opt. -αείραι, inf. -αεῖραι, part. -αείρας— tollere, *lift up* (tmesis, Η 130, Χ 399, χεῖρας, τεύχεα); limbs, θ 298; the opponent in wrestling, *carry off* a prize. (Il. Ψ.)

ἀνα-θηλήσει (θηλέω), revirescet, *shall bloom again*, Α 236†.

ἀνα-θήματα (τίθημι), δαιτός, additamenta cenae, *ornaments, delights* of the banquet, α 152, φ 430. (Od.)

·ἀνα-θρώσκων, exsultans, *bounding*, Ν 140†.

ἀν-αιδείης (ἀναιδής), gen. ἐπέβησαν, trod the path of *insolence*, χ 424; -ίην ἐπιειμένος, Ι 372, clad in *impudence*.

ἀν-αιδής, ές, (αἰδώς), impudens, *insolent, shameless*, ρ 449, of the suitors;

applied to inanimate objects, κυδοιμός, πέτρη, Ν 139, and λᾶας, λ 598.

ἀν-αίμονες (αἷμα), sanguine carentes, *bloodless*, i. e. without mortal blood, Ε 342†. [⏑ – ⏑ ⏑]

ἀν-αιμωτί (αἷμα), sine caede, *without bloodshed*, σ 149. [ῑ]

ἀναίνομαι, ipf. ἀναίνετο, aor. ἀνήνατο, ἠνήνατο, etc. (αἴνυμαι)—negare, *deny*, Σ 500, ξ 149, Ι 116; recusare, *refuse*, Σ 450, Ψ 204, Ι 585; spernere, *repel, reject* (opp. ὑποδέχεσθαι), Η 93, σ 287, Ι 510, 679; γ 265, *spurn*.

ἀν-αιρέω, -ήσεσθαι, aor. -εῖλον, -ειλόμην, tollere, *take up*.—(1) *lift from* the ground, γ 453; mid., *take up for* one's self, οὐλοχύτας; *take up in* one's arms, Π 8; *lift up* and *sweep away*, υ 66. —(2) comprehendere, *lay hold of*, Α 301, σ 16; mid., capere, *take*, arms, Ν 296; cloak, ξ 530; goblet, χ 9; *come to reason*, τ 22.—(3) accipere, *bear off*, prizes, Ψ 736; mid., 823, φ 117 (or in signification 2).—(4) conducere, *to take into one's service*, σ 357.

ἀν-ᾱΐσσουσι, aor. ἀν-ήιξα, *spring up, rise suddenly* from a sitting posture, Α 584, σ 40, for combat, etc., Η 106, Ψ 203; *gush forth* (pr. only in this sense), Χ 148; with acc., *leap upon*, Ω 440.

ἀν-αίτιος (αἰτία), insons, *innocent*, Υ 297, υ 135.

ἀνα-καίω, always with πῦρ, only ἀνέκαιε (and -ον), accendit, *kindled*, ι 251 (υ 123). (Od.)

ἀνα-κεράννυμι, only ἀνά-κέρασσεν, aor., *filled and mixed*, γ 390†.

ἀνα-κηκίει, ipf. -κήκιε, *gush forth*. (Il.)

ἀνα-κλίνω, only 1 aor. act. (part. ἀγκλίνας) and pass. part., ἀνα-κλινθείς, reclino, *make to lean upon*.—(1) τινὰ πρός τι, σ 103; τόξον ποτὶ γαίῃ, *bracing* against the ground, Δ 113, cf. τ 577; *open*, doors (opp. ἐπιθεῖναι), λ 525, χ 156, Θ 395; ἀνακλινθείς, supinus, *leaning back*, ν 78, ι 371, δ 794.

ἀν-ακοντίζω, only ipf. ἀνηκόντιζε, *shot forth*, αἷμα, Ε 113†.

ἀνα-κύπτω, ipf. ἀν-έκοπτε, *shoved back*, φ 47†; see ὀχεύς.

ἀνα-κράζω, aor. ἀν-έκρᾰγον, *since I have once for all broken silence*, ξ 467†.

ἀνα-κρεμάννυμι, aor. part. ἀγ-κρεμάσασα, *after she had hung it up*, α 440†.

ἀνακτορίῃσι (ἄναξ) ὕεσσιν, *belonging to the master*, ο 397†.

ἀνα-κυμβαλιάζω, ἀν-εκυμβἄλίαζον, *fell rattling over*, Π 379†. [ῐ]
ἀνα-λέγω, ipf. ἄλ-λεγον, aor. inf. ἀλλέξαι, colligere, *gather*, Φ 321. (Il.)
ἀν-αλκείῃσι δαμέντες, overmastered *by fear*, Z 74. (Il.)
ἄν-αλκις, ιδος, acc. -ιδα (-ιν, γ 375), ignavus, *defenseless, cowardly*, O 62.
ἄν-αλτον (alere), insatiabilem, *insatiable*, σ 114. (Od.)
ἀνα-λύω, ipf. iter. -ἀλ-λύεσκεν, part. ἀλ-λύουσαν, aor. ἀν-έλυσαν, solvere, *untie*, ι 178 (in tmesi); retexere, *unravel*, β 105. (Od.)
ἀνἄ-μαιμάει πῦρ ἄγκεα, grassatur per, *rages through*, Υ 490†.
ἀνἄ-μάξεις, fut. (μάσσω) σῇ κεφαλῇ, *shalt wipe off* on thy own head, *expiate with* thy life, τ 92†.
ἀνα-μένω, aor. ἀν-έμεινα, exspectavi, *was awaiting*, τ 342†.
ἀνα-μετρήσαιμι (μετρέω), aor., emetirer, *remeasure the road to*, μ 428†.
ἀνα-μίγνυμι, see ἀναμίσγω.
ἀνα-μιμνήσκω, ἀν-έμνησας, aor., commonuisti, *hast reminded*, ταῦτα, γ 211†.
ἀνα-μίμνω, only ipf., manere, *await*, Λ 171; *stand fast*, Π 363. (Il.)
ἀνα-μίσγω, ipf. and aor. (tmesis), ἀμμίξας, admiscere, *to mix with*, *mix together*, κ 235, δ 41, Ω 529.
ἀνα-μορμύρω, ipf. iter. ἀν-εμορμύρεσκε, efferbuit, *seethed up*, μ 238†.
ἀνα-νέομαι, ἀν-νεῖται, oritur, *rises*, κ 192†.
ἀνα-νεύω, only ipf. and aor., abnuere, *deny, refuse*, Z 311; with inf., Π 252; ὄφρυσι, vetare, *forbid*, ι 468; without inf., φ 129; καρήατι, X 205.
ἄν-αντα, sursum, *up-hill*, Ψ 116†.
ἄναξ, κτος, (Ϝάναξ), voc. ὦ ἄνα, of gods; dat. pl. ἀνάκτεσι, ο 557, tutor, dominus, *master*, *ruler*.—(1) as *possessor*, δ 87.—(2) as *ruler*, (a) of gods, Ζεῦ ἄνα, Διῒ Κρονίωνι ἄνακτι, etc.; Apollo, H 23; κλῦθι ἄναξ, Π 514; Poseidon, Hephaistos, ἀν. ἐνέρων Ἀιδωνεύς; (b) of men, e.g., Λ 164; common phrase, ἄναξ ἀνδρῶν, A 172, A 7.
ἀνα-ξηραίνω, ἀγ-ξηράνῃ, aor. subj., exsiccat, *dry up*, Φ 347†.
ἀν-οίγεσκον, see ἀνοίγνυμι, aperiebant.
ἀνα-πάλλω, only (1) aor. part. ἀμ-

πεπάλών, vibratam, *having poised and drawn back*, Γ 355.—(2) mid. ἀνα-πάλλεται, Ψ 692, aor. ἀν-έπαλτο, exsiluit, *sprang up*, Θ 85.
ἀνα-παύω, aor. ἀν-έπαυσε, τινά τινος, arcuit, *hinders from*, P 550†.
ἀνα-πείρω, aor. part. ἀμ-πείραντες, transfixa, *having spitted*, B 426†.
ἀνα-πεπταμένας, see ἀναπετάννυμι, apertas.
ἀνα-πετάννυμι, expando, *spread out*; only (1) ἀνὰ δ' ἱστία—πέτασσαν, unfurled, shook out the sails, A 480, etc.—(2) ἀνα-πεπταμένας, apertas, open (opp. ἐπικεκλιμένας, M 121), θύρας.
ἀνα-πηδάω, aor. ἀμ-πήδησε, exsiluit, *sprang up out of*, Λ 379†.
ἀνα-πίμπλημι, only fut. -πλήσειν and 1 aor., explere, *fill up, accomplish* (one's fate), Θ 34, Λ 263, Δ 170; *endure woes*, ε 207, 302, O 132.
ἀνα-πλέω, fut. -πλεύσεσθαι and ipf., *sail up*, στεινωπόν, ad fretum, μ 234; ἐς Τροίην.
ἀνά-πνευσις (πνέω) πολέμοιο *recovering of breath, respite from battle*, Λ 801. (Il.)
ἀνα-πνέω, ipf. and aor. -έπνευσα and ἄμ-πνυε, pass. ἀμ-πνύνθη, and plupf. mid. ἄμ-πνυτο, respirare, *respire, take breath, come to one's senses*, Π 42; τινός, *receive from* (only 1 aor. act.).
ἀν-άποινον (ἄποινα), non redemptam, *without ransom*, A 99†. [ᾰ]
ἀνα-πρήσας (πρήθω) δάκρυ, lacrimas exprimens, *letting tears flow*, β 81.
ἀν-άπτω, religare, *attach*, of cables, μ 162; ἀν-ήφθω imp. aor. pass., religantor ad malum, μ 51; suspendere, *hang up*, γ 274; μῶμον, *impute fault*, β 86.
ἀνά-πυστα (πεύθομαι), nota, *notorious*, λ 274†. [ᾰ]
ἀνα-ροιβδέω, see ἀναρροιβδέω.
ἀν-αρπάζω, only aor. -ήρπασε, -αρπάξας, eripere, *snatch out*, X 276; *carry off*, Ι 564; *snatch away*, Π 437, esp. of sudden gusts of wind, δ 515.
ἀνα-ρ-ρήξας, and -ρήξειε (ῥήγνυμι), lacerare, *tear open*; evertere, *destroy*, H 461. (Il.)
ἀνα-ρ-ριπτέω, only pres. and ipf. (ἀν-ερρίπτουν, ν 78), aor. -ἐρριψαν—ἅλα (πηδῷ, κ 130, is to be supplied), *turn up* with oar-blades; cf. torquent

spumas et caerula verrunt.
(Od.)
ἀνα-(ρ)-ροιββέω, - εροίβδησε, devorare, *swallows up*, μ 104. (Od.)
ἀν-άρσϊοι (ἄρω), alienati, *not fitting, incongruous*, hence *hostile* (opp.
θυμήρης), (Od., Ω 365).
ἄν-αρχοι (ἀρχός), sine duce, *without leader*, B 703, 726.
ἀνα-σείω, ἀνέσσυτο, 2 aor. mid., exsiluit, *sprang forth*, Λ 458†.
ἀνα-σπάω, ἀν-εσπάσατο, ἔγχος, *drew
his spear forth*, N 574†.
ἄνασσα, ης, (ἄναξ), domina, *mistress, queen* (only ζ 149 of a mortal).
ἀνάσσω (ἄναξ), fut. -άξω, aor. mid.
-άξασθαι (ipf. ἄνασσε), tueri, A 7,
dominari, *be sovereign, rule, reign
over.*—(1) persons ; comm. with dat., A
180, also with μετά, Δ 61, ἐν, η 62 ; with
gen., Κ 33 ; with acc. (duration of time),
ἀνάξασθαι γένεα, *ruled* through three
generations of men, γ 245.—(2) *country
and city* ; with gen., A 452, ρ 443 ; with
dat., B 108 ; with ἐν, Π 572, λ 276.—(3)
κτήμασιν, α 117, cf. δ 93 ; τιμῆς, Υ 181 ;
be master of Priam's sovereignty over
the Trojans, ω 30 ; pass., *be ruled*, τινί,
δ 177.
ἀνα-σταδόν, adv. (cf. σταδίῃ), assur-
gendo, *standing upright*, Ψ 469. (Il.)
ἀνα-στεναχίζω, ἀν-εστενάχιζε, ipf.,
ingemuit, *wailed aloud*, Κ 9†.
ἀνα-στενάχουσι, and ipf. ἐστενάχον-
το, lamentari, *bemoan, bewail aloud;
τινά*, Ψ 211. (Il.)
ἀνα-στοναχίζω, v. l. for ἀνα-στεναχίζω.
ἀνα-στρέφω, only aor. opt. ἀν-στρέψειαν, everterent, *overturn*, Ψ 436;
and -στρέφομαι, γαῖαν, peragro, *wander through*, ν 326.
ἀνα-στρωφῶν(-στρωφάω), versans,
turning it over and over, φ 394†.
ἀνα-σχέμεν, ἀνά-σχεο, see ἀνέχω,
perferre.
ἀνασχόμενος, -σχέσθαι, -σχών, tollens, see ἀνέχω.
ἀνα-τέλλω, aor. ἀνέτειλε, emisit,
caused to spring up (as food), E 777†.
ἀνα-τίθημι, fut. ἀναθήσει, ἐλεγχείην,
ignominia afficiet, *will heap insult
upon me*, X 100†.
ἀνα-τλάς, part. of aor. ἀνέτλην, endure, *withstand* (poison), κ 327. (Od.)
ἀνα-τρέπομαι, aor. ἀνετράπετο,

eversus est, *fell backward*, Z 64.
(Il.)
ἀνα-τρέχω, only pf. -δέδρομε, and aor.
-έδραμεν, -ον.—(1) *run up, spout up*,
P 297 ;, wales *started up* under the
blows, Ψ 717 ; Σ 437, *shot up; ε 412,
up rises* the sheer rock.—(2) *run back;*
Λ 354, cito immensum.
ἄν-αυδος (αὐδή), mutus, *speechless*,
ε 456. (Od.)
ἀνα-φαίνω, only pres. act. and mid.,
and aor. act. -φῆναι, monstrare.—(1)
were feeding by turns *the flame* (to give
light), σ 310.—(2) *disclose*, A 87 ; *displaying*, Υ 411; *show* loquacity, δ 159;
betray, δ 254.—(3) mid., *appear.*
ἀνᾰ-φανδόν (-φαίνω), Π 178†, and
-φανδά (Od.), openly, *before the eyes of
all.*
ἀνα-φέρω, only aor. 1 ἀν-ένεικα,
brought up, λ 625, and -ινείκατο, *drew
a long-drawn sigh*, T 314.
ἀνα-φλύω, ipf. ἀνὰ δ᾽ ἔφλυε, ebul-
liebat, *waves were boiling up*, Φ 361†.
ἀνα-φράζομαι, aor. opt. ἀμφράσσαιτο, agnosceret, *should recognize*, τ
391†.
ἀνα-χάζομαι, pres., ipf., part. aor.
-χασσάμενος, recedo, *was retiring*, E
600 ; also with ἄψ, ὀπίσω, τυτθόν, πολλόν.
ἀνα-χέω, ἀνὰ-χεῦε, aor., infudit,
poured therein, ι 209†.
ἀνα-χωρέιτω, pres., fut. aor. 1, recedo, *withdraw*, χ 270 ; also with ἄψ,
ρ 461, Κ 210.
ἀνα-ψύχειν (ψῦχος), pres. ipf., and Κ
575 -έψυχθεν, 3 sing. aor. pass., refri-
gerare, *cool*, δ 568 ; E 795, assuage,
alleviate. [⏑ – – –]
ἀνδάνει (Ϝανδάνω, (σϜ)ἁδύς, suavis), ipf. ἐήνδανε (ἐϜήνδανε), ἥνδανε,
pf. ἑαδότα (ϜεϜαδότα), aor. εὔαδε (for
ἔϜαδε) and ἅδε, placere, *please, delight*, gratify; esp. with θυμῷ, κ 373 ;
with two datives, A 24, O 674 (π 398,
by speech) ; σ422, gratum, *acceptable.*
ἄν-δῐχᾰ, asunder, Π 412 ; *in twain.*
(Il.)
ἀνδρ-άγρια (ἄγρη), spolia, *spoils
of arms*, Ξ 509†.
Ἀνδρ-αιμονίδης, i. e. Θόας, Η 168†.
Ἀνδρ-αίμων, ονος, king of Αἰτωλοί
in Καλυδών, B 638, ξ 499.
ἀνδρακάς, viritim, *man by man,
each*, ν 14†. (v. l. ἄνδρα κάθ᾽.)

ἀνδρα-πόδεσσι, mancipiis, slaves, Η 475†.

ἀνδρ-αχθέσι (ἄχθος), ingentibus, with man-burdening stones, κ 121†.

ἀνδρεϊ-φόντῃ (φένω), homicidae, man-slaying, Ἐνναλίῳ, Β 651. (Il.)

ἄνδρεσσι, dat. pl. from ἀνήρ.

ἀνδρο-κμήτῳ (κάμνω), manibus facto, wrought by men's hands, Λ 371†.

ἀνδρο-κτἄσίη (κτείνω), only gen. sing. pl., nom. pl., caedes, slaughter of men (in battle). (λ 612, Il.)

Ἀνδρο-μάχη, daughter of Ἠετίων in Θήβῃ ὑποπλακίη; wife of Hektor, ἄλοχος πολύδωρος, λευκώλενος, Ζ 371, 395, Χ 460, etc. (Il.)

ἀνδρόμεος, ον, (ἀνήρ), humanus, human flesh, ι 297; pieces of human flesh, ι 374; blood, χ 19; body, Ρ 571; ὅμιλος, tumult of men, tumultuous crowd, Λ 538.

ἀνδροτῆτα (ἀνδροτής), valor (better reading, as regards sense, than ἀδροτῆτα, vigor, but unmetrical).

ἀνδρο-φάγοιο (φαγεῖν), Κύκλωπος, homines devorans, eating man's flesh, κ 200. [ἄ]

ἀνδρο-φόνος, ον, (φένω), viros occidens, man-slaying, Ἄρης, Ἕκτωρ, χεῖρες, Achilleus, Ω 479, vegetable poison, α 261.

ἀν-δύεται, see ἀναδύω, shun.

ἀν-εγείρεις, pres., and 1 aor. ἀνέγειρα, excitare, wake up, ἐξ ὕπνου, ἐκ λεχέων, δ 730; κ 172, encouraged.

ἀν-έγνω, aor. from ἀναγιγνώσκω, agnovi.

ἀν-εδέγμεθα, ipf. from ἀναδέχομαι, suscepimus, we have sustained.

ἀν-έδραμον, aor. from ἀνατρέχω, exortae sunt, started up.

ἀν-έεδνος, see ἀνάεδνος, sine dote.

ἀν-έεργω, ipf. ἀνέεργον (for ἀνέϜεργον), cohibebat, was holding back, Γ 77; also ὀπίσσω, Ρ 752. (Il.)

ἀν-έζω, only 1 aor. part. ἀν-έσαντες, having placed him upon, Ν 657; opt. ἀνέσαιμι, should bring upon the nuptial bed, Ξ 209. (Il.)

ἄν-ειμι, -εισι, (ἰέναι), subire, (1) go up, κ 146, 274; ἅμ' ἠελίῳ ἀνιόντι, oriente, with the dawn, ψ 362.—(2) redire, return, Χ 499, Ζ 480; σὺν νηΐ, κ 332; ἄψ, Τ 290.—(3) adire ad, Χ 492.

ἀν-είμονος (εἷμα), gen., veste carentis, destitute of bedclothing, γ 348†.

ἀν-είρεαι (ἔρομαι), ipf. ἀνείρετο, interrogo, inquire, δ 420, τινά τι; with μεταλλᾶν, α 231; τί, ask respecting, ν 238.

ἀν-εκτός, -όν, (ἔχω), tolerabilis, endurable, ν 83; usually with οὐκέτ', also ἀνεκτῶς, ι 350, in a fashion no longer to be endured.

ἀν-ελθών, aor. part. from ἀνέρχομαι, reversus.

ἀν-έλκων, ipf. ἄν-ελκε, attrahere, draw up, draw, Μ 434, φ 128, 150; draw back, Λ 375; mid., draw out and recover (one's spear), χ 97; tear out (one's hair), Χ 77.

ἀν-ελών, see ἀναιρέω.

ἄνεμος, ου, ventus, wind; ζαής, λιγέων, δυσαήων; ἀνέμου ἴς, hurricane, τ 186, θύελλα, ἄελλα, πνοιαί, ἀήτης, ἰωή, βία, ἀυτμένα; as symbol of swiftness, Μ 207, Ω 342, Κ 437; ταμίης, Αἴολος, κ 21. Chief winds, νότος, εὖρος; see also Ψ 195, ε 383.

ἀνεμο-σκεπέων (σκέπας, ε 443), sheltering against the wind, Π 224†.

ἀνεμο-τρεφές (τρέφω), ventis auctus, swollen by the wind, Ο 625, Λ 256; made from a tree toughened by exposure to wind.

ἀνεμώλιος, ον, (for ἀνεμώνιος), futilis, useless, Υ 123; vanus, vain, Ε 216; -ια βάζειν, Δ 355; adv. -ιον, Φ 474.

Ἀνεμώρεια, ἡ, town in Φωκίς, Β 521†.

ἀνενείκατο, see ἀναφέρω, respiravit.

ἀν-έπαλτο, see ἀναπάλλω, vibravit.

ἀν-ερείπομαι, only aor. ἀν-ηρείψαντο, abripuerunt, snatched away, α 241.

ἀν-ερύω, aor. ἀνά θ' ἱστία λεῦκ' ἐρύσαντες, hoist, μ 402. (Od.)

ἀν-ερχόμενον, aor. -ελθών, (1) go up, cf. ἄνειμι, κ 97; shoot up, ζ 163.—(2) return, ἄψ, Δ 392, Ζ 187.

ἀν-ερωτάω, ipf. ἀνειρώτων, questioned repeatedly, δ 251†.

ἀν-έσαιμι, ἀνέσαντες, imponerem, see ἀνέζω.

ἄν-εσαν, aor., ἀν-έσει fut., from ἀνίημι.

ἀν-έσσυτο, aor. from ἀνασύω, exsiluit.

ἀν-έστιος (ἑστία), hearthless, home-
less, I 63†.

ἄνευ (ἀν- privative, in-, un-), with
gen., sine, without; θεοῦ, invito deo,
β 372, cf. O 213 ; δηΐων, procul ab
hostibus, N 556.

ἄνευθεν, -θε,—(1) procul, far away,
B 27, Δ 277, X 300 (opp. ἐγγύθι), Ψ
241; κιών, A 35 ; ἐόντος, Ψ 452.—(2)
sine, with gen., without, X 39, π 239 ;
θεοῦ, invito deo, E 185, cf. Π 89 ;
procul a, far from, κ 554 ; μέγα ἄν.
νῶϊν, remotissimum a nobis, X 88.

ἀ-νέφελος αἴθρη, innubilus aether, cloudless blue sky, ζ 45†. [ᾱ-
σνεφ.]

ἀν-έχω, aor. ἀνέσχον (inf. ἀνασχέμεν)
and ἀνέσχεθον (inf. ἀνσχεθέειν), mid.
fut. ἀνέξομαι (inf. ἀνσχήσεσθαι), aor.
ἀνεσχόμην (imp. ἀνάσχεο, ἄνσχεο),
sustinere, hold up. I. act. τί, Ξ 499,
X 80, χ 297, ρ 291 ; χεῖρας, in combat
(boxing), σ 89 ; in prayer, θεοῖς, A
450 ; σκῆπτρον, in making oath, H
412; maintain, τ 111; hold back, Ψ 426;
jut forth, emerge, ε 320, P 310.—II.
mid. (1) hold one's self up, bear up, endure, E 285, π 277 with part.; A 586, Ψ
587, forbear ; λ 375, stay awake.—(2)
hold up before one, σκῆπτρον, K 321 ;
χεῖρας, σ 100; δούρατα, often ἀνασχόμενος, exsurgens, lifting up arm for
striking, Γ 362.—(3) perferre, endure,
tolerate, τί, χ 423, η 32 ; entertain, ρ 13;
τινὰ ἄλγε' ἔχοντα, E 895 ; with part.,
would gladly sit, δ 595.

ἀ-νεψιός, ὁ, (nepos), sister's son,
nephew, O 422.

ἄν-εω (ἄφημι), mutus, speechless.—
(1) pl. from ἄνεως ; muti, ἐγένεσθε,
etc., B 323, I 30, β 240.—(2) adv., ψ
93, ἧστο.

ἀν-ήγαγον, aor. from ἀνάγω.

ἀν-ήῃ, 3 sing. aor. subj. from ἀνίημι.

ἀν-ήϊον, see ἄνειμι.

ἀν-ήκεστος, ον, (ἀκέομαι), insana-
bilis, inappeasable, E 394. (Il.)

ἀν-ηκούστησε (ἀκούω), οὐδ' — πατρός, obsequium detrectavit, was
rebellious, O 236. (Il.)

ἀν-ήμελκτοι (ἀμέλγω), unmilked, ι
439†.

ἀν-ήνοθεν (ἄνθος), perf., ebullivit,
gushed forth, Λ 26⁶ ⁷. See ἐνήνοθε.

ἀν-ηνύστῳ (ἀνύω) ἐπὶ ἔργῳ, endless,
aimless, π 111†.

ἀν-ήνορα (ἀνήρ), acc., non viri-
lem, unmanly, κ 301. (Od.)

ἀνήρ, ἔρος, ἀνδρός, dat. pl. ἀνδράσι,
ἄνδρεσσι (perhaps Ϝανήρ, P 65, Λ 371;
cognate with Sabine word nero).—(1)
vir, man; (a) as distinguished from
γυνή, ο 163 ; (b) in age, λ 449 ; (c)
emphatically, man indeed, hero, E 529,
I 189 ; cf. in combat, Δ 472 ; (d) of
occupation and nationality; with ἰητρός,
Λ 514, ἐλαφηβόλους, Σ 319 ; νομῆες, αἰ-
πόλοι, χαλκῆες, ἐπακτῆρες ; Σίντιες ;
δήμου, unus e plebe, B 198.—(2)
maritus, husband, λ 327, ω 196, α 292, ζ
181.—(3) homo, human being, often with
βροτοί, θνητοί, among mortals, ρ 354 ;
πατὴρ ἀνδρῶν τε θεῶν τε, A 544 ; opp.
gods, ε 119 ; opp. giants, φ 303, κ 120.
[ᾱ in arsi, and in trisyllable forms.]

ἀν-ήροτος (ἀρόω), non culta, un-
ploughed, ι 109. (Od.)

ἀν-ήφθω, perf. pass. imp. from ἀν-
άπτω, alligantor.

Ἄνθεια, town in Μεσσήνη, I 151.
(Il.)

Ἀνθεμίδης, Σιμοείσιος, son of Αν-
θεμίων, Δ 488†. [‿‿‿—]

Ἀνθεμίων, ωνος, father of Σιμοείσιος
in Troia, Δ 473†.

ἀνθεμόεντος, ι, (ἄνθος), floridus,
flowery, B 467 ; adorned with flowers,
λέβης, γ 440 ; κρητῆρα, ω 275; cf. cut
No. 98.

ἀνθερεῶνος, ῶνα, masc. (ἄνθος),
mentum, chin; to take by the chin in
token of supplication, A 501.

ἀνθερίκων, gen. pl. (ὁ ἀνθέριξ), ἐπ'—,
per aristas, over the ears of grain, Υ
227†.

ἀνθέω, ἀνθῆσαι, aor., bloom, λ 320†.

Ἀνθηδών, όνος, town in Βοιωτία, B
508†.

ἄνθινον (ἄνθος) εἶδαρ, floridum
cibum, food of flowers, flowers as food,
ι 84†. [‿‿‿]

ἀνθ-ίσταντο, ipf., aor. ἀντ-έστη, re-
sistere, resist, Π 305, Υ 70. (Il.)

ἄνθος, εος, (ad-or), flos, blossom,
flower, I 542 ; fig., N 484 ; young shoots,
youthful herbage, ι 449.

ἀνθρακιήν, τήν, (ἀνθρακιή), prunae,
heap of glowing coals, I 213†. [‿‿‿
—]

ἄνθρωπος, ου, (Ϝαν. ἀνήρ, β 65, λ
365, Σ 288), homo, man, (opp. to gods,
Σ 107, γ 48 ; to animals, ζ 125, Π 315);

homines, *mankind, the world*, ρ 354, I
340, ☲ 361, Ω 535, ψ 125, α 95, cf. ν
123 and θ 29; quisquam, *any one*, ν
400.

ἀνιάζω (ἀνίη), ipf. ἀνίαζον, pertaesum esse, *be disgusted with, weary of*,
δ 460, 598, Σ 300 : θυμῷ, indignari,
indignant, grieved in heart, Φ 270, χ
87 ; trans. *annoy, distress*, Ψ 721, τ 323.
[ῐ]

ἀνιάω (ἀνίη), ἀνιήσω, pass. ἀνιᾶται,
ἀνιηθείς, act., taedio afficere, *incommode*, υ 178, τ 66 ; pass., *be annoyed,
wearied*, γ 117 ; τινί, α 133, ο 335 ; Β
291, 'tis indeed hard to *return out of
weariness*. [‿ − − −]

ἀν-ιδρωτί, sine sudore, *without
sweat*, Ο 228†. [‿ − − −]

ἀνίη, ης, molestia, *burden, weariness*, ο 394, υ 52 ; μ 223, *unendurable
bane; trouble, plague*, η 192, ρ 446.
(Od.) [ῐ]

ἀνιηθείς, aor. pass. from ἀνιάω, pertaesus.

ἀν-ίημι, 2 sing. -ίεις, 2 sing. opt.
-ιείης, fut. -ήσω, aor. 1. -ῆκα, -ίηκεν, 2
-εσαν, subj. 3 sing. -ίῃ (conjectural
false reading, εσει, σ 265), -ῄη, mittere.
—(1) *send forth*, δ 568 ; μ 105, *vomit
forth.*—(2) *loose, δεσμόν; open, πύλας*
(mid. κόλπον, *laying bare her bosom*, Χ
80 ; αἴγας, *skin*, β 300) ; *let go*, σ 265,
ὕπνος, Β 34 ; ω 440, *forsake; give reins
to*, Ε 880.—(3) *loose upon, urge on*, incitare, Υ 118, β 185 ; ἐπί τινι, *against*,
Ε 405, 882 ; *with inf.*, ☲ 362 ; excitare, *stir up against, impel*, Ρ 705, esp.
θυμός τινα, also with inf., Χ 252, ξ 465.
[ἀνίει, ἀνιέμενος ; elsewh. ῐ.]

ἀνιηρός (ἀνίη), molestus, *troublesome*, ρ 220, 377 ; ἀνιηρέστερον, *the
more troublous for him*, β 190. (Od.)

ἀ-νιπτό-ποδες, Σελλοί, illotis pedibus, *with unwashed feet*, Π 235†.

ἀ-νίπτοισι (νίπτω), illotis, *unwashed*, Ζ 266†.

ἀν-ίστημι, I. ipf. -ίστη, fut. ἀν(α)-
στήσω, aor. 1. -έστησε, imp. ἄνστησον,
part. ἀναστήσασα, exciere, *bid or make
stand up*, η 163 ; χειρός, *supporting with
his hand*, ξ 319 ; *disperse*, Α 191 ; *wake
up*, Κ 32 ; *call to life* the dead, Ω 756 ;
deport, transfer, ζ 7 ; excitare, *stir
up to battle*, Ο 64, Σ 358.—II. ἀνίστα
μαι, fut. -στήσεσθαι, aor. -έστην (du.
ἀνστήτην, 3 pl. -έσταν, part. -στάς ἀν-

στᾶσα, inf. ἀνστήμεναι, for imp. see ἄνα
under ἀνά-, I.), surgere, *rise up.*—(1)
from seat (of whatever sort), Ι 195, ε
195, Σ 410, or from bed, ☲ 336, υ 124.
—(2) for *action* (of whatever sort), θ
258, μ 439, with inf., incipere, υ 380 ;
to speak, τοῖσι δ' ἀνέστη, *rose up* (before
or among them), cf. τοῖσι δ' ἀνιστάμε
νος μετέφη, Α 58 ; for combat, battle, δ
343, Β 694 ; τινί, σ 334 ; ἄν repeated, Ψ
709 ; freq. in tmesi, e. g. θ 118.— (3)
from sick-bed, Ο 287 ; from grave, Φ
56.

ἀν-ίσχων, ἴσχοντες, part., tollens,
raising, Ε 798, Ο 369 ; ἀνὰ δ' ἴσχεο=
ἀνάσχεο, *hold thyself erect*, i. e. *be of
good courage.*

ἀν-ιχνεύων (ἴχνος), investigans,
tracking back, Χ 192.

ἀν-νεῖται, see ἀνανέομαι, oritur.

ἀ-νοήμων, imprudens, *unreflecting*,
β 270. (Od.)

ἀν-οίγω, ἀνέῳγε, ἀνῷγε, ipf., and
iter. ἀναοίγεσκον, aperio, *open*, κ 389,
☲ 168, Ω 228.

ἀν-όλεθρους (ὄλεθρος), incolumes,
untouched by destruction, Ν 761†.

ἄνομαι, see ἄνω.

ἄ-νοον, κραδίην, quam excors fuisti, *silly, foolish heart*, Φ 441†.

ἀνόπαϊα, see ὀπαῖα.

ἀν-όρνυμι, see ἀνῶρτο.

ἀν-ορούω, only aor. -όρουσεν, -σαν,
-σας, exsilio, *spring up, ἐκ θρόνων,
-σας, exsilio, *spring up, ἐκ θρόνων*,
ὕπνου, ἐς δίφρον, Ρ 130 ; Ἥλιος,
climbed swiftly up the sky, γ 1.

ἀ-νόστιμον (νόστος), reditu interclusum, ἔθηκαν, reddiderunt, *cut
off his return*, δ 182†.

ἀ-νόστους (νόστος), reditu carentes, ἔθηκαν, *made void their return*, ω
528†.

ἄ-νουσοι (νοῦσος), sine morbo,
without disease, ξ 255†.

ἀν-ούτατος (οὐτάω), non cominus
vulneratus, *unwounded*, Δ 540†.

ἀν-ουτητί, nor did any one draw
near *without inflicting a wound*, Χ
371†. [ῐ]

ἀν-στάς, -στᾶσα, -στησον, -στήτην,
στήσεσθαι, etc., see ἀνίστημι.

ἀν-στρέψειαν, see ἀναστρέφω.

ἀν-σχεθέειν, -σχεο, -σχήσεσθαι, etc.,
see ἀνέχω.

ἀν-σχετά (ἀνέχω), οὐκ, intolerabilia, *unendurable*, β 63†.

ἄντ' = ἄντᾰ (old instr. case, ἀντί,
German prefix ant, ent), adversum,
opposite; adv., and prep. with gen.,
(1) e regione, *in the vicinity of,* Β
626; coram, *in presence of, before,* ζ
141, she remained standing *before* him,
χ 232; α 334, holding the veil *before*
her cheeks; *straight forward,* ἰδεῖν,
τιτύσκεσθαι; ἄντα ἐῴκει, properly ore
(instr.) similis fuit, was like him *in
countenance.*—(2) in hostile sense, adversus, contra, *against,* ἰέναι, Υ 75,
355; ἐλθεῖν, πολεμίζειν, στῆῃς, ἔγχος
ἀεῖραι; ἀνασχομένω, having drawn back
their hands (to strike); δ 159, *before
thee, to thy face.*

ἀντ-άξιος, ον, aequi pretii, *equivalent to,* with gen., I 401, Λ 514. (Il.)

ἀντάω (ἄντα), ipf. ἤντεον, fut. ἀντή-
σω, aor. ἤντησα, occurrere, *meet,* Δ
375, δ 201; τινί, Η 423, Ζ 399; τινός,
encounter, ὀπωπῆς, δ 327; Η 158, then
might he soon *take part in battle,* i. e.
*find an opponent; meet in hostile en-
counter,* π 254.

Ἄντεια, δῖα, wife of Προῖτος, Ζ
160†.

ἄντην (ἄντα), strictly, *the face,* εἰσιδέ-
ειν, Τ 15, Ω 223, cf. ε 77; acc. of specification, *in respect to countenance,* with
ἐναλίγκιος, εἰκέλη; acc. of direction,
face to face, openly, co-oram, palam,
Α 187, Κ 158, Ο 247, Ω 464, γ 120, ζ
221, θ 213, 158; *in battle,* Λ 590, Σ
307, Χ 109; *forward,* Θ 399; *in front,*
Μ 152.

Ἀντηνορίδης, son of Ἀντήνωρ, Ἐλι-
κάων, Γ 123; pl. Λ 59, sons of Antenor.

Ἀντήνωρ, ορος, son of Αἰσυήτης, husband of Θεανώ, Γ 262, Λ 59, 262.

ἄντηστιν (ἀντάω), κατ'—, *at the
junction* of the men's and women's
apartments, *opposite the entrance of the
house* (see table III. at end of volume),
ex adverso, υ 387†.

ἀντί (locative from ἄντα), prep. with
gen., strictly (1) *in the face of,* adversum, Ο 415, Φ 481; δ 115, *before the
eyes.* — (2) placed over against as
equivalent, loco, *instead of;* I 116, θ
546, υ 307, χ 290.

ἀντί, ἀντία, see ἀντίος.

ἀντι-άνειραι, -ανείρας, *matching-
men,* of Amazons, Γ 189. (Il.)

ἀντιάω, ἀντιόω (ἀντί), fut. ἀντιάσω,

ἀντιόω; aor. ἀντιάσαιμεν, etc., occurrere, *meet,* η 293, μ 88, ν 312, Κ 551,
encounter, Ο 297 (with dat., Ζ 127, Φ
431, σ 147), with gen., Η 231; Ν 290,
strike; have or take part, share, with
acc., only Α 31; elsewh. with gen., Α
67, Μ 356, Ν 215, Υ 125, Ψ 643 (mid.
Ω 62), α 25; φ 402, would that he
might *enjoy* just as much good luck as
—, χ 28; ω 56, *participate in* the funeral ceremonies of her son.

ἀντῐ-βίοις, dat. pl. (βία), adversis,
hostile, ἐπέεσσι, Α 304, σ 415; ἀντίβιον,
adv., with verbs of combating, Γ 20,
435, Λ 386; so also ἀντιβίην, Α 278,
Ε 220, Φ 226. (Both advs. only Il.)

ἀντι-βολέω (ἀντί, βάλλω), -ήσω, aor.
ἀντῐ-βόλησε, *come in the way of,* cf.
ἀντιάω, occurrere.—(1) *meet acci-
dentally, encounter,* Π 790, Ω 375, ζ 275,
η 16; with gen., only δ 547, σ 272
shall be my lot, φ 306; elsewh. with
dat., c. g. Η 114.—(2) *meet intentionally*
(a) as friend, Κ 546, η 19, κ 277; (b)
as foe, Λ 365, Μ 465; τινί, Π 847, ν
229.—(3) *intercesse, have part in,*
μάχης, Δ 342; φόνῳ, τάφῳ.

ἀντί-θεος, 3, *godlike,* distinguished
in rank, might, size, beauty; common
epithet of kings, Ε 663; heroes, I 623,
Ω 257, α 21, o 90; Odysseus's companions, δ 571; nations, ζ 241, Μ 408;
suitors, ξ 18; Penelope, λ 117; Polyphemos, α 70. [ῐ]

ἀντί-θυρον (θύρη), κατ'—, *opposite
the entrance* (out of doors), π 159†.
[ῐ]

Ἀντί-κλεια, daughter of Αὐτόλυκος,
wife of Λαέρτης, λ 85, ο 358.

Ἄντι-κλος, name of a Greek warrior in the wooden horse, δ 286.

ἀντι-κρύς, ἀντικρύ, ex adverso,
opposite.—(1) coram, *face to face
with,* Ε 130, 819, Η 362; Ἕκτορος, Θ
310. — (2) *straightforward,* Ν 137;
outright, utterly, Π 116, 380, Ψ 673,
867, κ 162; often joined with foll.
prep., e. g. παραί, διά, κατά, ἀνά; also
in compounds, e. g. διέσχε, Ε 100; δι-
ῆλθε, Ψ 876, cf. Δ 481. [– – ‿, Ε 130,
819.] [ῡ]

Ἀντί-λοχος, son of Νέστωρ, Δ 457,
Ν 554, Π 320, Ν 93, Ο 569, Ε 565, γ
452, δ 187.

Ἀντί-μαχος, a Trojan, Λ 123, 132.
138, Μ 188.

Ἀντί-νοος, Εὐπείθεος υἱός, α 383 ; the most insolent of the suitors, β 84, π 418, χ 22, ω 424.

ἀντίον, see ἀντίος.

Ἀντί-όπη, daughter of Ἀσωπός, mother of Ἀμφίων and Ζῆθος, λ 260.

ἀντίος, 3, (ἀντί), advcrsus, against, towards.—(1) ἤλυθε, Υ 463 ; τινός, Χ 113 ; π 160, ἰδεῖν, look up.—(2) with friendly intent, obviam (ire), (go) to meet, Ζ 54, Ρ 257 ; τινί, Η 20 ; τινός, Β 185, Λ 594, Φ 539, π 14 ; ἔσταν, Α 535.—(3) with hostile intent, contra, ἵστασθαι, ἐλθεῖν, ἔγχε' ἄειραν, ἐείσατο, ἀίξας, τ 445, Λ 94, 216, (ἀίσσουσι, Λ 553, Ρ 662) ; τινί, Ο 584, Υ 422 ; elsewh. τινός, e. g. Η 98, Ο 694, Ρ 8, 31, χ 90. ἀντίον, adv., in opposition, against.—(1) in friendly signif., coram, before, in presence of, ρ 529 ; answer, ηὔδα τινά, Γ 203, β 208, α 213 ; ἵζεν, etc., ε 198, ψ 165, τινός, Ι 218 ; π 160, look up ; κατέθηκε, ρ 334 ; ἀίξασθαι πυλάων, Χ 195.—(2) in unfriendly signif., contra, τινός, εἴπῃ, Α 230 ; ἰέναι, Ε 256 ; ἐλθεῖν, Η 160.   Similar significations has ἀντία, (1) coram, τινός, Γ 425, ο 377.—(2) contra, against, with verbs of combating, Υ 88, 80, 113, 333, Χ 253, α 78. [ῐ]

ἀντιόω, see ἀντιάω.

ἀντι-πέραια (πέραν), advcrsa, the lands lying over against, Β 635†.

ἀντ-ίσχω, ἀντ-ίσχεσθε, contra opponite, oppose, interpose (tables against arrows), gen., χ 74†.

ἀντι-τορέω, aor. τορήσας, perforare, only δόμον, break into—, Κ 267 ; pierce, χροός, Ε 337.

ἄν-τῐτα (τίω), ἔργα, talio, requital, vengeance, ρ 51 ; cf. β 76.

Ἀντί-φάτης, ᾱο, (1) a Trojan, Μ 191.—(2) son of Μελάμπους, ο 242.—(3) king of the Λαιστρυγόνες, acc. -ῆα, κ 114. [ᾰ]

ἀντι-φερίζεις, ειν ; τινί, (τι), match one's self against, Φ 411. (Φ)

ἀντι-φέρεσθαι, measure one's self with, μάχῃ, Ε 701 ; with acc. of respect, Φ 482.

Ἀντί-φονος, son of Priam, Ω 250†.

Ἄντι-φος, (1) a son of Priam, Δ 489, Λ 109.—(2) son of Αἰγύπτιος, β 19.—(3) Ἰθακήσιος, ρ 68.—(4) son of Ταλαιμένης, Β 864 : leader of Μῄονες.

—(5) son of Θεσσαλός, leader of Greek islanders, Β 678, Ἡρακλείδης.

ἄντλος, ου, ὁ, sentina, bilge-water, hold, μ 411. (Od.)

ἀν-τολαί (τέλλω), ortus, Ἡελίοιο, rising-places of the sun, μ 4†.

ἄντεσθαι, ὁμίνη, αι, (ἄντα), only pres., ipf., occurro, encounter, Β 595, Θ 412 ; τινί, Χ 203 ; join, τινί, Δ 133 ; come together with hostile purpose, Ο 698, Π 788.

ἄντρον, antrum, cave, ι 216, ω 6. (Od.)

Ἀντρών, ῶνος, town in Thessaly, Β 697†.

ἄν-τυξ, γος, ἡ, (τέγος).—(1) metal rim of shield, Ζ 118 ; serving to bind together the layers of metal or leather, of which the shield was composed (see the cut).—(2) rim of chariot ; rim surrounding (περίδρομος) the body (διchariot, sometimes double, E 728; it served also as place of attachment for the reins. (See the cut.)

ἄνυμι (ἀνύω), ἤνῠτο, ipf., cito ei successit opus, *was progressing*, ε 243†.

ἄνῠσις, -ιν, ἡ, (ἀνύω), *accomplishment*, successus; B 347, they will accomplish nothing; δ 544.

ἀνύω (ἄνω), fut. -ύσω, -ύσ(σ)εσθαι, conficere.—(1) τινά, *consume*, ω 71.—(2) δ 357, ο 294, *traverse*; proficere, *effect* (nothing), Δ 56; mid., π 373. [⌣⌣−]

1. ἄνω, ipf. ἤνον, conficere.—(1) *were completing*, γ 496.—(2) pass. ἄνεται, ἄνοιτο, *draw to a close*, K 251, Σ 473. [⌣−; K 251, −⌣⌣]

2. ἄνω (ἀνά), sursum, *upwards*, λ 596; porro, from down south *upwards*, i. e. *to the northward*, Ω 544. [⌣−]

ἄνωγα (ἄγχω?), pf. (imp. ἄνωχθι, -ώχθω and -ωγέτω, -ωχθε and -ώχετε, inf. -ωγέμεν); plupf. ἠνώγεα (3 sing. ἠνώγει and -ειν, ἀνώγει), also forms like pres. ipf. ἀνώγει, -ιτον; ἤνωγον, ἄνωγον; fut. ἀνώξω, aor. ἤνωξα, iubere, *command*, constr. like κελεύω, β 113, ρ 508 (τινί, only ν 139); θυμός (ἐποτρύνει κε ἀνώγει, Z 439, T 102, Θ 522, σ 409, etc.

ἀνῷγεν, ipf. from ἀνοίγω, aperiebat.

ἀνῷγω, see ἄνωγα, iussi.

ἀν-ωθέω only ἀν-ώσαντες, ο 553†, *having shoved off* from land.

ἀν-ωιστί (ὀίω), necopinato, *unexpectedly*, δ 92†. [ῐ]

ἀν-ώιστον (ὀίω), inopinatum, *unimagined*, Φ 39†.

ἀν-ώνῠμος (ὄνομα), sine nomine, *nameless*, θ 552†.

ἀν' ὦρτο (ὄρνυμι), aor. in tmesi, surrexit, *arose*, Ψ 812, θ 3.

ἄνωχθε, -θι, -θω, imp. from ἄνωγα, iubete, etc.

ἄξαντος, -ασθε, -έμεν, -έμεναι, -ετε, from ἄγω.

ἀξίνη, ησι, ἡ, bipennis, *double battle-axe* of Trojans, Ο 711. (See cut.)

ἄξιος, 3, (ἄγω), *counterbalancing, equivalent*, τινός, Ο 719, Ψ 562; *worth a gift in return*, τινός, α 318; *equal in strength*, Θ 234; *corresponding to one's station or requirements, suitable*, I 261, Z 46, N 446, υ 383; *worth*, Ψ 885; βοός, θ 405, πολέος.

Ἀξιός, river in Paionia, Φ 141, B 849.

ἀ-ξύλῳ (σα-, ξύλον), lignis abundante, *dense forest*, Λ 155†. [⌣⌣−]

Ἄξυλος, son of Τεύθρας in Ἀρίσβη, Z 12†.

ἄξων, ονος, (axis), *axle*, E 838, Λ 534. (Il.)

ἀοιδή, ῆς, (ἀϝοιδή, from ἀείδω).—(1) cantus, *singing, the power to sing*, B 595, N 731, θ 44, 253; *song*, α 328, 159, 421; ἀοιδῆς ὕμνον, θ 429, *strains of the bard*.—(2) carmen, *song, ballad, story; that song* men hear most willingly, α 351; *mournful song*, α 340; *funeral lament, elegy*, Ω 721; with pregnant signif. *song, subject for song*, ω 197, 200, γ 204, (v. l. πυθέσθαι), θ 580.

ἀοιδιάει, -ουσα, (ἀοιδή), καλόν, ὀπὶ καλῇ, sweetly *sings*, only κ 227, ε 61. [ᾰ]

ἀοίδιμοι, cantabiles, *subject for song, notorious*, (infames), Z 358†. [ᾰ]

ἀ-οιδός, οὖ, (ἀϜείδω), cantor, *singer* (of funeral ode), Ω 720; elsewh. *singer and poet*, regarded with special favor by the gods (θ 43, 479, 487, ρ 518, αὐτοδίδακτος, χ 347; e. g. Φήμιος, Δημόδοκος), hence θείυς, ρ 385, θ 479, sqq., and highly honored.

ἀ-ολλέες, έα, (σα-, Ϝολλ, εἰλέω), conferti, *crowded together*, in throngs, Ε 498, O 306; cuncti, N 39, γ 165,412; ἅπασαι, *all together*, χ 446.

ἀολλίζω, only aor. ἀόλλισαν, -σσασα, and pass. ἀολλίσθησαν, -θήμεναι (ἀολλέες), congregare, *collect*, Z 270, O 588. (Il.)

ἄορ, ορος, τὸ, (ἀείρω, ἄσϜορ, English sword), gladius, *sword*, in form =ξίφος, θ 403, 406, κ 294, 321; acc. pl., ἄορας, ρ 222. [⏑⏑; ⏑⏑⏑, in arsi –⏑⏑.] (See cut.)

ἀορτήρ, ῆρα, etc., masc. (ἀείρω, ἄσϜορτ.), balteus, *sword-belt* = τελαμών (see cut), λ 609; Λ 31, ἀορτήρεσσιν, *with hooks* or *handles; of strap* on wallet, ν 438.

ἀ-οσσητήρ, ῆρα, ες, ας, masc. (socius, ἀ-σοκịητήρ), defensor, *companion in battle*, O 254; *helper*, δ 165, ψ 119.

ἄ-ουτον (οὐτάω), non percussum, *unwounded*, Σ 536†.

ἀπ-αγγέλλω, only ipf. ἀπαγγέλλεσκε, and 1 aor., renuntio, *report*, τί, I 626; *bring tidings*, τινί, P 640, o 210.

ἀπ-άγχων, strangulans, *throttling*, τ 230†.

ἀπ-άγουσιν, fut. -άξω, aor. -ήγαγον, abducere, *lead away;* always with pers. obj., exc. σ 278, *bring with them from their own estates;* always with pers. subj., exc. O 706.

ἀπ-ἀειρόμενον, πόλιος πεδίονδε, campum petentem, withdrawing from the city, and *seeking* the plain, Φ 563†.

ἀπ-αίνυτο, ipf., also (ἀποϜαίνυται, -το, cf. μ 419) only pres. and ipf., adimere, *take away, rob*, Λ 582, O 595, μ 419; τί τινος, ρ 322 (v. l. ἀπαμείρεται), N 262.

Ἀπαισός, Trojan town, B 828†; see Παισός.

ἀπ-αίξας (ἀίσσω), κρημνοῦ, desiliens, *springing down from* a crag, Φ 234†.

ἀπ-αιτίζοντες, res repetentes, *reclaiming*, β 78†.

ἀπ-άλαλκε, -οι, (ἀλκή), imp. and opt. 2 aor., arcere, *ward off*, δ 766, X 348, τί τινος. [ᾰ]

ἀ-πάλαμνος (παλάμη), sine palmis, *not knowing how to swim, helpless*, Ε 597†. [ᾰ]

ἀπ-αλέξήσειν, -ήσαιμι, fut. and aor. opt., arcere, *keep off*, τινά τινος, Ω 371; ρ 364, but not even thus could she *keep some one from* maliciously insulting him, cf. ρ 462.

ἀπ-αλθήσεσθον, 3 du. fut., ἕλκεα, *shall they be healed* of their wounds, Θ 405, 419.

ἀπ-αλοιάω, ἀπ-ηλοίησεν, ἄχρις, contudit penitus, *crushed* utterly, Δ 522†.

ἀπαλός, 3, tener, *tender*, δειρή, αὐχένος, ἦτορ, παρειάων (πόδες, Τ 92, of Ἄτη, as ἠεροφοῖτις, like the Ἐρινύς), χεῖρας, φ 151; ἁπαλὸν γελάσαι, *heartily*, ξ 465.

ἀπαλο-τρεφέος, σιάλοιο, bene saginatae, *well-fed*, Φ 363†.

ἀπ' ἀμήσαντες (ἀμάω), *after having cut* (hacked) *off*, φ 301†.

ἀπ-αμβροτεῖν, see ἀφαμαρτάνω.

ἀπ-αμειβόμενος, and ipf. -ετο (former with προσέφη, latter with φώνησέν τε), respondens, *answering*, A 84, δ 824, θ 400, λ 347.

ἀπ-αμείρεται, v. l. for ἀποαίνυται, ρ 322†.

ἀπ-αμύνω, only aor. (in tmesi ἀμῦναι, A 67, β 59), act. and mid.; and ipf.

ἀπήμυνεν, arcere, *ward off*, mid. *defend one's self*, λ 579, O 738 ; τινά, *defend one's self against*, Ω 369, π 72.

ἀπ-αναίνομαι, only aor. -ηνήναντο, -ανήνασθαι, recusare, *decline, refuse*, only H 185, κ 297.

ἀπ-άνευθε(ν), (1) procul, *far away*, K 434 ; κιών, A 35 ; *out from it*, T 374.—(2) separatim, *apart*, κ 524, K 425.—(3) with gen., sine, *without the knowledge*, A 549 ; *far from*, A 48, ι 36 ; follg. its gen., μάχης, Λ 283.

ἀπάντη (ἅπας), quoquoversus, *on every side*, Il. and θ 278.

ἀπ-ήνυσαν (ἀνύω), pervenerunt, *accomplished the journey home again*, η 326†.

ἅ-παξ (σα-, παγῆναι), semel, *once*, μ 22 ; *once for all*, 350. (Od.)

ἀπ-αράσσω, only aor. ἀπήραξεν, and in tmesi ἄραξεν, detruncare, *smote to the earth*, Ξ 497. (Il.)

ἀπ-αρέσσασθαι (ἀρέσκω), reconciliare sibi, that a king should *conciliate* a man, T 183†.

ἀπ-άρχομαι, -αρξάμενος, sacra ordiri, *to begin the sacred rites* by cutting off hair from the forehead of the victim, γ 446.

ἅ-πᾶς, -πᾶσα, -πᾶν, universus, *entire, all*; pl., cuncti, *all together*; ο 158, *nothing but kindness*; δ 616, argento solidum, *of massive silver*; ξ 196, *in a year and a day*. (The trisyllabic forms scarcely found, exc. at end of line.)

ἅ-παστος (πασσάμενος), non pastus, *not having eaten, fasting*, with ἐδη-τύος, carens, *without food*, cf. δ 788.

ἀπ-ατάω, fut. -ατήσω, aor. ἀπάτησε(ν) (ἠπ-), fallo, *deceive*, δ 348. [ἄ]

ἀπ-άτερθε, seorsim, *apart*, B 587 ; *far from*, E 445. [ἄ]

ἀπάτη, ης, dolus, *deceit*, Δ 168 ; pl. fallaciae, *tricks*, O 31. [ἄ]

ἀπατήλια, ntr. fallacia, only ξ 127, βάζει, *speaks falsely* to her, and 288, skilled in *deceit*.

ἀπατηλόν, fallax, *deceitful*, A 526†. [ἄ]

ἀπ-ητίμησε (ἀτϊμάω), prorsus contempsit, *greatly insulted*, N 113†.

ἀπ-αυράω (cogn. with Fερύω ?), only ipf. ἀπηύρων, ας, α, fut. -ουρήσουσι, q. v., aor. part. ἀπούρας, eripere, *wrest away*, A 356 ; τί, I 107 ; τινί τι,

ν 132, γ 192, (θυμόν, P 236, Φ 296) ; τινά τι, P 125, Ψ 291, 560, (θυμόν, Υ 290) ; not τινός τι, A 430 (but gen. absol.), T 88, σ 273, I 107 ; see also ἀέκων.

ἀπάφίσκει, and 2 aor. ἤπαφε, mid. ἀπάφοιτο, ludificari, *delude, beguile*, only λ 217, ψ 216. [ἀπ]

ἀπ-έειπε, see ἀπ-εῖπον.

ἀπ-έεργε, see ἀπο-έργω.

ἀπειλεῖς, εῖτε, fut. -ήσω, ipf. ἀπειλήτην. — (1) minari, *threaten*, τινι, ἀπειλάς, N 220, Π 201 ; μῦθον, A 388 ; with inf., A 161, Θ 415, O 179.—(2) gloriari, *boast*, Θ 150 ; with inf., θ 383.—(3) vovere, *utter a vow*, τινί, Ψ 863, 872. [⌣–]

ἀπειλαί, άων, άς, minae, *threats*, I 244, N 219 ; then iactantia, *boasting*, Ξ 479, Π 200.

ἀπειλητῆρες, iactatores, *boasters*, H 96†.

1. ἀπ-ειμι, subj. -έῃσι, ipf. -έην, -εσαν, fut. -έσσεται, -εσσεῖται ; often in tmesi, abesse, *be far from*, τινός, τ 169 ; τόσσον, as far away, ε 400 ; δουρηνεκές, as far as a spear is cast ; *be absent, wanting*, Υ 7, ο 146.

2. ἀπ-ειμι, imp. -ιθι, part. -ιών, ipf. ἤιε, abire, *go away*, ρ 478 ; ἄψ, K 289.

ἀπ-εῖπον (Fείπω, voco), ind. also ἀπέ-Fειπε, -Fείπω (subj.), -Fείποιμι (opt.), -Fειπ(ε) (imp.), -Fειπεῖν (inf.), -Fειπών (part.), and without F ; ἀπ- ειπών, etc. —(1) *speak out* (fully), *deliver*, an errand, π 340 ; a mission, H 416 ; the truth, Ψ 361 ; μῦθον ἀπηλεγέως, *speak out regardless of feelings*, α 373.—(2) negare, *say no*, A 515, I 431, 510, 675.— (3) renuntiare, *give solemn warning*, τινί, α 91 ; μῆνιν, T 35, 75, *renounce*.

Ἀπειραίη, she who *springs from Apeira*, Ἀπείρηθεν (Ἤπειρος ?), η 8, 9†.

ἀ-πειρεσίην, οι, αι, and ἀ-περείσια, ntr. pl. (πέρας, πείρατα), infinitus, *boundless, infinite, vast*, πολλοί, τ 174 ; γαῖαν, ὀιζύν, ἄποινα, ἕδνα.

ἀ-πείρητος (πειράομαι), imperitus, *unskillful*, opp. ἐὺ εἰδώς, β 170 ; non tentatus, *untried*, P 41.

ἀ-πείρῐτος (πείρατα), infinitus, *boundless*, κ 195†.

ἀ-πείρων, -ονος, (πείρατα), infinitus, *immeasurable*, Ω 545 ; *endless*, η

286; δεσμοί, in which the end can not be found, indissoluble, θ 340.

ἀπ-εκ-λελάθεσθε (λήθω), imp., obliti sitis. forget altogether, ω 394†.

ἀ-πέλεθρον (πλῆθος?), immensam, immeasurable, ἵν', vim, E 245; and immensum quantum, sprang back enormously far, Λ 354.

ἀπ-έμεσσεν (ἐμέω), aor., evomuit, spat out, Ξ 437†.

ἀπ-εμνήσαντο, see ἀπο-μιμνήσκομαι, meminerunt.

ἐνάριζον (ἔναρα), ἀπ' ἔντεα, ipf., spoliabant, were despoiling, τινά, only M 195, O 343.

ἀπ-ένεικας, αν, aor. from ἀποφέρω, abstulisti.

ἀπ-έπλω, ipf. from ἀποπλώω, naves solvit.

ἀπερείσιος, see ἀπειρεσίην, infinitus.

ἀπ-ερύκω, -ξω, arcere, ward off, scare away, τινά; also in tmesi, Ω 156.

ἀπ' ἐρύσαι (ἐρύω), tmesis; detrahere, tear off, ξ 134†. [ῠ]

ἀπ-έρχομαι, -ήλθε, -ελήλυθα, abire, go away, τινός, β 136, Ω 766; leave, Ω 514 (tmesis).

ἀπ-ερωεύς (ἐρωή), exstinctor, thwarter, annihilator, ἐμῶν μενέων, Θ 361†.

ἀπ-ερωήσειας (ἐρωέω), opt. aor. πολέμου, decederes, wouldst thou miserably withdraw from battle, Π 723†.

ἄπ-εσαν, see ἄπειμι, aberant.

ἀ-πευθής (πεύθομαι), (1) ignarus, ignorant, only γ 184.—(2) ignotus, unknown, only γ 88.

ἀπ-εχθαίρει, only δ 105, μοι ὕπνον, makes hateful; and aor. subj. ἀπεχθήρω, oderim, hate, Γ 415.

ἀπ-εχθάνεαι, 2 sing., aor. -ήχθετο, inf. -έχθεσθαι (ἔχθος), odisse, hate, π 114, cf. 96; elsewh. odio esse, be hated, τινί, Δ 53, Ζ 140, I 614, Φ 83. [∪ – ∪ ∪]

ἀπ-έχω, -ομαι, fut. ἀφίξω, -ομαι, ἀποσχήσει, aor. -σχῃ, -σχωνται, ipf. ἔχοντο, prohibere, keep away, hold off, τί, τινά τινος (τινί, Ω 19), τ 572; an enemy, Z 96; X 324 (tmesi), χεῖρας (so also mid. tmesi, χ 316), A 97, ʋ 263; ἑκὰς νηῶν, ο 33; mid., hold one's self aloof from, τινός, M 248, Θ 35, Ξ 78, 206; abstinere, abstain, ι 211; parcere, spare, μ 321, τ 489.

ἀπ-ηλεγέως (ἀλέγω), ἀποειπεῖν μῦθον, speak out without scruple, only α 373, I 309.

ἀ-πήμαντον (πημαίνω), incolumem, uninjured, τ 282†.

ἀπ-ήμβροτον, aor. from ἀφαμαρτάνω, decerravi.

ἀ-πήμων, ονος, (πῆμα), sine damno.—(1) fortunatus, safe, unharmed, A 415, ε 40, δ 519, ν 39, N 744.—(2) prosper, favoring, kindly, οὖρος, η 266; speech, escort, healthful, Ξ 164.

ἀπήνη, ης, plaustrum, freight wagon, four wheeled, Ω 324; with tentlike cover, ζ 70; not unlike the Roman rheda. (See cut.)

ἀπ-ηνήναντο, aor. from ἀπαναίνομαι, recusabant, refused.

ἀπ-ηνής, έος, unfriendly, harsh, A 340; θυμός, O 94; νόος, Π 35; μῦθος, O 202.

ἀπ-ήραξεν, aor. from ἀπαράσσω, detruncavit, struck off.

ἀπ-ήυρων, aor. from ἀπαυράω, eripui.

ἀπ-ήωροι (ἀείρω), procul pendentes, high-hanging (Odysseus hangs upon one of the roots which project from the land), μ 435†.

ἀ-πιθέω, only fut., and aor. 1 ἀπίθησε, σαν (πείθω), adversari, disobey, only with οὐκ and οὐδ', χ 492.

ἀ-πινύσσειν, and -ων, (πινυτός), amentem esse, lack understanding, ε 342; κῆρ (acc.), be unconscious, O 10.

ἀπίης, ἐξ — γαίης, from a remote land, A 270, π 18. [∪ ∪ -]

'Απισάων, ονος.—(1) Ἱππασίδης, a Greek, P 348.—(2) Φαυσιάδης, a Trojan, Λ 582.

ἀ-πίστεον, ipf. (ἄπιστος), οὔ ποτ'—, desperavi, was doubting, ν 339†.

ἄ-πιστος (πιστός), sine fide, (1) faithless, Γ 106.—(2) incredulous, ξ 150.

ἀπ-ισχε = ἄπεχε, hold away, λ 95†.

ἀπλοΐδας, acc. pl. (ἀπλόος), χλαίνας, single cloak or mantle, i. e. to be wrapped only once around the body, only Ω 230, ω 276.

ἄ-πνευστος (πνέω), sine spiritu, breathless, ε 456†.

ἀπό, ab, prep. with gen., after its case ἄπο, ξ 525; freq. with words to which the (orig. instr.) suffix -φι is appended, Λ 374, 351, 44, Θ 300, O 313, K 347, Π 246, Ω 268; also with words having suffix -θιν; very freq. in tmesi, in which case the compound word must be sought (e. g. Π 82 under ἀφαιρεῖν).—(1) from starting-point, out, away, O 610, 714, Z 472, E 13, Λ 645; ἀπ' οὐδεος, M 448, cf. Ψ 730; fight, etc., from, i. e. on, ἀφ' ἵππων, ἀπὸ νεῶν, O 386, ι 49; fasten to (cf. pendere a), λ 278; ἀπ' αἰῶνος νέος ὤλεο, depart from life (cf. recens a), Ω 725; ἀπὸ δ' αὐτοῦ, from the meal to something else, immediately after, Θ 54 (no other examples of temporal use).—(2) separation, away from, from, Ω 514, I 437, Δ 535, Υ 278, K 465, 575, N 640, Π 436, 733; after ἀπ', φ 364; after ἐκτός, K 151, outside of; νόσφιν, E 322; τῆλε, ε 315.—(3) remoteness; far from, ξ 525; ἀπ' Ἄργεος, N 227; ἀπ' οὔατος, X 454; out of my hearing, ἀπ' ὀφθαλμῶν, e conspectu, Ψ 53; ἀπὸ σκοποῦ οὐδ' ά. δόξης, contrary to our intention and meaning, λ 344; ά. θυμοῦ εἶναι, odio esse; θυμὸς ὤχετ' ἀπὸ μελέων, N 672, cf. H 131. Π 861, P 17, ο 354.—(4) origin : out of, from, M 97; τ 163, for thou didst not spring from an ancient oak nor from a rock, so also converse speaking from a tree or a rock (as shepherd with shepherdess), X 126; κάλλος ἀπὸ χαρίτων, from the Graces (as source); μ 187, ἀπὸ στομάτων ὄπα, out of our mouth; M 306,

from his swift hand; Θ 279, sending destruction from his strong bow; ἀπὸ σπουδῆς, in earnest, H 359. [∪ ∪; ∪ — before σνευρῆς, Γρίου.]

ἀπο-αίνυμαι = ἀπαίνυμαι, adimere.

ἀπο-αιρέομαι (Ϝαιρέω?) = ἀφαιρέομαι, adimere.

ἀπο-βαίνω, fut. -βήσομαι, aor. -έβην, 3 sing. -εβήσατο and -σετο, abire, go away, πρὸς μακρὸν Ὄλυμπον, Ω 468, etc.; dismount, ἐξ ἵππων ἐπὶ χθόνα, Γ 265, cf. Λ 619; ἐπὶ χθονί, Ω 459; ἵππων, P 480; disembark, νηός, ν 281; forsake, σχεδίης, ε 357.

ἀπο-βάλλω, aor. inf. -βαλέειν, only in tmesi, abicere, throw off, τί, B 183, ζ 100; χαμαί, Φ 51; χαμάδις, τ 63; Π 793, cast down from his (τοῦ) head (κρατός) the helmet; δάκρυ παρειῶν, let tears fall from his cheeks, δ 198; νῆας ἐς πόντον, push off to sea, δ 359.

ἀπό-βλητον, -α, (βάλλω), contemnendus, only found with οὔτοι, not to be despised, B 361 and Γ 65.

ἀπο-βλύζων, ebulliens, letting spirt out of the mouth, οἴνου, I 491†.

ἀπο-βρίξαντες (βρίζω, βαρύς), conniventes, having fallen asleep, ι 151 and μ 7.

ἀπο-γυιώσῃς, aor. subj., (γυῖα), debilites, shouldst unnerve, Z 265†.

ἀπο-γυμνωθέντα (γυμνόω), nudatum armis, disarmed, κ 301†.

ἀπο-δαίω, only fut. ἀποδάσσομαι, and aor. inf. -δάσσασθαί τινί τινος, only X 118, Ω 595, and P 231, ἥμισυ τῷ ἐνάρων, partiri, share.

ἀπὸ δειδίσσεο, deterruit, frightened back, M 52†.

ἀπο-δειρο-τομήσω, fut., aor. -εδειροτόμησα (τέμνω), iugulare, slaughter, men, Σ 336, Ψ 22; sheep, λ 35.

ἀπ-εδέξατο, aor. from -δέχομαι, recepit, accept, A 95†.

ἀπο-διδράσκω, ἀπο-δράς, aor. part. (διδράσκω), qui aufugit, escape by stealth, (ἐκ) νηός, only (π 65) ρ 516.

ἀπο-δίδωμι, fut. -δώσομεν, aor. -έδωχ' (= κε), 3 sing. subj. -δῷσι, opt. -δοῖτε, inf. -δοῦναι (tmesis -δόμεναι), opt. aor. pass. -δοθείη, reddere, deliver up, Γ 285, E 651, Π 84, χ 58, 61; restore, Λ 98, Σ 499, β 78, θ 318; τοκεῦσι θρέπτρα, requite parents for one's nurture.

ἀπο-δίωμαι (δίω), subj., exturbem, drive out of, E 763†. [ῑ]

ἀπο-δοχμώσας (δοχμόω), aor. part., inflexam ponere, αὐχένα, bend to one side, ι 372†.

ἀπο-δράς, see ἀποδιδράσκω, qui aufugit.

ἀπο-δρύφοι, opt., aor. 3 sing. -δρύψε, subj. δρύψωσι, aor. pass. -δρύφθη, 3 pl. -ἐδρυφθεν, cutem lacerare, stripped the muscles from the shoulder, Π 324; τινά, ρ 480; ε 426, then would his skin (acc. of respect) have been stripped off, cf. 435. [ῠ]

ἀπο-δύνω, ipf. -έδυνε, exuit, threw off, χ 364; so also 2 aor. part. ἀπο-δύς; but fut. -δύσω and aor. -ἔδυσα, τινά, nudare, strip off, B 261; spoliare, despoil of, Δ 532, Σ 83; also in tmesi.

ἀπο-δυσάμενος, ε 349, better reading -λυσάμενος.

ἀπο-δῷσι, aor. subj. from ἀποδίδωμι, reddat.

ἀπό-εικε (Ϝείκω), imp., recede, retire from, κελεύθου, Γ 406†.

ἀπο-είπον, see ἀπ-εῖπον.

ἀπο-έργαθε, and -έργαθε ipf., (Ϝέργω), separavit, held aloof from, τινός, Φ 599; removed from, φ 221; also in tmesi.

ἀπο-έργω, ipf. -έεργε, (Ϝέργω), also in tmesi, separare, keep away from; τινός, Θ 325, λ 503; drive away, Ω 238.

ἀπό-ερσε, aor., subj.-έρσῃ, opt. -έρσειε, (Ϝέρσε, Ϝέρρω), abripuit, had washed one away, Ζ 348. (Il.)

ἀπ-εθαύμασε, aor., (θαυμάζω), demirata est, wondered at, with acc., ζ 49†.

ἀπό-θεστος (θέσσασθαι), spretus, despised, ρ 296†.

ἀπο-θνήσκων, part., pf. -τεθνηῶτος, moribundus, expiring, λ 424; X 432, defuncti.

ἀπο-θρώσκων, part., in tmesi, 3 pl. ipf. θρῶσκον, part. aor. θορόντες, θορούσα, exsilio, spring up, ψ 32; spring down from, νηός, Β 702; νευρῆφι, fly from the string, O 314; rise, α 58.

ἀπο-θύμια (θυμός), ntr., ingrata, things displeasing, offense, Ξ 261†. [ῠ]

ἀπ-οικίζω, only aor. ἀπῴκισε, deduxit, transferred, μ 135†.

ἄ-ποινα, ων, (ποινή), poenae, mulcta, fine, recompense, satisfaction,

T 138; esp. ransom, A 13; τινός, for any one, A 111, Ω 137. (Il.)

ἀπ-οίσω, see ἀποφέρω, auferam.

ἀπ-οίχομαι, only prs., go away; τινός, deserere, abandon, Λ 408, T 342; -οιχόμενος, digressus, absens, ξ 8, φ 70.

ἀπ-εκαίνυτο, ipf., superavit, excelled, only θ 127, 219.

ἀπο-καίω, only 3 sing. opt. aor. κῆαι (in tmesi), comburat, consume, Φ 336†.

ἀπὸ ἐκάπυσσεν, aor. from καπύω, efflavit, gasped forth her life (swooned), X 467†. [ᾰ]

ἀπο-κείρω, only aor. (ἐ)κέρσε (in tmesi), and -εκείρατο, dissecuit, cut through, N 546; totondit, sheared his hair, Ψ 141. (Il.)

ἀπο-κηδήσαντε, du. part. aor.,(κηδέω), negligentes, through your negligence, Ψ 413†.

ἀπο-κῑνέω, only aor. iter. -κινήσασκε, subj. -κινήσωσι, amovebat, moved away, Λ 636 and χ 107, dislodge, τινά τινος.

ἀπο-κλίναντα, aor. part., (κλίνω), ἄλλῃ, deflectentem, turn off, interpreting differently, τ 556†. [ῑ]

ἀπο-κόψειν, fut., and aor. -έκοψα, also in tmesi, abscindo, cut off, Λ 146, Φ 455, ι 325; Π 474, cut loose the out-running horse, i. e. cut the reins by which he drew.

ἀπ-εκόσμεον, ipf., auferebant, clear off, η 232†.

ἀπ-εκρέμασε, aor., (κρεμάννυμι), inflexuit, let droop, Ψ 879†.

ἀπο-κρινθέντε, du. part. aor. pass., (κρίνω), separati, i. e. parted from the throng, E 12†.

ἀπ-έκρυψεν, aor., inf. -κρύψαι, occultare, hide, Λ 718; deny, conceal, ρ 286; shelter, save, Σ 465.

ἀπο-κτάμεν(αι), aor. inf., see following word.

ἀπο-κτείνω, 1 aor. -έκτεινε, usually 2 aor. -έκτανε, -έκταμεν, -έκτανον, subj. -κτάνῃ, inf. -κτάμεν(αι), interimo, kill, ξ 271; slaughter, μ 301; with pass. signif. 2 aor. mid. -έκτατο, -κτάμενος, interemtus, P 472, Δ 494, Ψ 775.

ἀπ-έλαμπε, -ετο, ipf., resplendebat, shone forth resplendent, Z 295, σ 298, T 381; X 319, flashed back (the splendor from the spear-point).

ἀπο-λείβεται (λείβω), destillat,

trickles off (from the closely woven linen), η 107†.

ἀπο-λείπουσιν, ipf. -έλειπεν, relinquere (with οὐδέ), *quit*, M 169; *leave over*, ι 292, (I 437, tmesis, *remain behind*).

ἀπο-λεψέμεν, fut. inf., (λέπω), detruncare, lit. *peel off, cut off*, v. l. ἀποκοψέμεν, Φ 455†.

ἀπ-ολέσκετο, aor. iter., from ἀπόλλυμι, peribat.

ἀπο-λήγω, ipf. -έληγε, fut. -(λ)λήξεις, aor. subj. -(λ)λήξῃς, -ωσι, opt. -(λ)λήξειαν (λήγω), desistere, *abandon, cease*, τινός, H 263, ν 151, μ 224; with part., τ 166; *vanishes*, Z 149.

ἀπο-λιχμήσονται, fut. mid., (λιχμάω, lig-urio), delambent, *lick off* (blood from wound), Φ 123†.

ἀπο-λλήξεις, see ἀπολήγω, desistes.

ἀπ-όλλυμι, fut. -ολέσσω, aor. -ώλεσα, I. perdere.—(1) *lose*, πατέρα, πόσιν, θυμόν, βίοτον, β 46, δ 814, Κ 452, β 49. —(2) *annihilate, kill, destroy*, E 758, 648. II. -όλλυμαι, aor. -ωλόμην (-όλοντο), iter. -ολέσκετο, pf. -όλωλεν, perire. —(1) *be lost, disappear*, δ 62, λ 586, 556, ρ 253.—(2) *perish* (opp. σαωθῆναι, Ο 502), I 230, Ψ 81; ὀλέθρῳ, ὄλεθρον, μόρον, γ 87, ι 303.

'Απόλλων, ωνος, son of Ζεύς and Λητώ, brother of 'Άρτεμις, like her, bringing death, see ἀγανός; god of the sun and of light, Φοῖβος, Λυκηγενής; of prophecy (his oracle in Πυθώ, θ 79), A 72, θ 488; of music, A 603 (yet not known to Homer as μουσαγέτης, leader of the Muses); of poesy; of youth, τ 86; guardian of flocks and herds; epithets, ἀκερσεκόμης, ἀφήτορος, διϊφιλος, ἑκατηβόλος, ἕκατος, ἑκηβόλος, ἑκάεργος, ἤϊος, λαοσσόος, παιήων, χρυσαόρου, Σμινθεύς, Φοῖβος.

ἀπο-λούσῃ, aor. subj., opt. -λούσειαν, (λούω), abluere, *wash off*, Ξ 7; τινά τι, Σ 345; mid. fut. -λούσομαι, aor. -σασθαι, τι, *wash from off one's self*, ὤμοϊϊν, ζ 219.

ἀπο-λυμαίνεσθαι, ipf. -ελυμαίνοντο, (λυμαίνω), sordes abluere, *cleanse one's self by bathing*, A 313 sq. (Il.)

ἀπο-λῡμαντῆρα, acc., -ες nom. pl., (λυμαίνω), δαιτῶν, purgator, *one who clears off* the tables by devouring the fragments, *plate-licker*, ρ 220 and 377.

ἀπο-λύσομεν, fut., aor. -έλυσε (λῦσε), mid. fut. -λυσόμεθα, aor. -λυσάμενος (λύω), solvere. — (1) *undo*, γ 392; τινός, *loose from*, φ 46, μ 421.—(2) *release*, A 95, for ransom (Il.).—(3) mid. τινὰ χρυσοῦ, *ransom* with gold, X 50; *loosen from one's self, untie*, ε 349. [ῦ]

ἀπο-μηνίσει, fut., aor. part. -μηνίσας, (μηνίω), succensere, *be angry*, π 378; τινί, B 772. [ῑ]

ἀπ-εμνήσαντο, aor., (μιμνήσκω), therefore *they have remembered* (repaid) him, Ω 428†.

ἀπ-ώμνυ and -νε, -νον, ipf., aor. ὤμοσα, (ὄμνυμι), iureiurando renuntiare, *swear not to do*; ὅρκον, κ 381. (Od.)

ἀπ' ὀμόργνυ, ipf., and -ομόρξατο,-ξαμένω, aor. mid., (ὀμόργνυμι), abstergere, *wipe off*, E 798; τινός, E 416; *wipe clean*, Σ 414; mid. *wipe any thing off from one's self*, B 269, Ψ 739; *wipe one's self clean of* any thing, σ 200.

ἀπ-εμῡθεόμην, ipf., (μῡθέομαι), dissuasi, (earnestly) *dissuaded*, I 109†.

ἀπ-όναιο, -οναιατο, see ἀπονίνημι.

ἀπο-ναίω, only aor. subj. -νάσσωσι, and aor. mid. -ενάσσατο; II 86, remittant domum, *send away;* mid. demigraverat, *withdraw to*, ο 254.

ἀπο-νέονται, pres. subj., inf. -νέεσθαι [-᷉᷉-], ipf. -νέοντο, redire, *return*, *go home*, π 467; with προτί, ἐπί (ἐς) with acc., -δε, παλιμπετές, ἄψορροι (-ον).

ἀπ-όνηθ᾽ (-όνητο), -ονήμενος, see ἀπονίνημι, frui.

ἀπο-νίζοντες, -ουσα, part. pres., ipf. -ενίζομεν, and aor. imp. -νίψατε, part. -νίψαντες, -νιψαμένη, -οι, from pres. -νίπτεσθαι, abluere, *wash off*, τινά, τ 317; τί, H 425, ω 189; *wash clean*, ψ 75; mid. *wash off from one's self*, K 572; *wash one's self clean*, σ 172, 179, χ 478.

ἀπ-ονίνημι, only fut. mid., -ονήσεται, aor. -άνητο (opt. -όναιο, part. -ονήμενος), perfrui, *have enjoyment, profit, advantage*, π 120; τινός, ω 30, Ω 556; οὐδ᾽, nihil profecit.

ἀπο-νίπτεσθαι, -νίψατε, etc., see ἀπο-νίζοντες, abluere.

ἀπο-νοστήσειν, fut.,(νοστέω), always after ἄψ, rediturum esse, *return*, A 60, ω 471.

ἀπό or ἄπο νόσφι(ν) (should always be written separately), (1) separatim, *apart*, B 233; procul, *away*, Λ 555, O 548, σ 268, ε 350.—(2) after its object, τινός, procul, A 541, ε 113, μ 33 (o 529); cf. νόσφιν ἀπύ, K 416, O 244.

ἀπὸ ἔξεσε (ξέω), aor., abscîdit, *cut* (lit. *shaved*) *off*, E 81†.

ἀπ-οξύνουσι, and aor. inf. -οξῦναι, pracacuere, *bring to a point, make taper*, ζ 269, ι 326 (v. l. ἀπο-ξῦσαι, *smooth off*).

ἀπο-ξύσας (ξύω), aor. part., expoliens, *smoothing off* (wrinkles), I 446†. (inf. -ξῦσαι v. l., ι 326.) [ῡ]

ἀπο-παπτάνέουσι, fut., (παπταίνω), terga dabunt, *will turn in flight*, Ξ 101†.

ἀπό-παυε, imp., fut. -παύσει, aor. -έπαυσας, -ε, -αν, reprimo, *keep off*, τινά, Σ 267; τί, *check, hinder*, Τ 119; τινός, *repress*, Λ 323; *from any thing*, Φ 340; with acc. and inf., μ 126, σ 114; mid. -παύεαι, imp. -εο, fut. -σομαι, desisto, *desist*, Φ 372, E 288; τινός, *from something*, α 340, A 422, Π 721, Θ 473.

ἀπο-πέμπω, inf. -πεμπέμεν, ipf., fut. ἀπ- and ἀπο-πέμψει, etc., 1 aor. -έπεμψα, dimittere, *send away*, ξ 108, ρ 76; *send off*, Φ 452, o 83, ψ 23, β 113; *dismiss*, ε 146, 161; *strangers with escort*, κ 65, 73, ω 285.

ἀπο-πέσῃσι, aor. subj., from -πίπτω, deciderit.

ἀπο-πέτομαι, only follg. forms from 2 aor. -επτάμην: ἀπὸ ἔπτατο, -πτάμενος, η, avolavit, *flew away*, arrow, dream; life, θυμός, (of animals), Π 469, κ 163, τ 454; ψυχή, (of men), λ 222.

ἀπ-έπιπτον, ipf.,-πέσῃσι, subj. 2 aor., (πίπτω), decĭdo, *fall down*, only Ξ 351, ξ 129.

ἀπὸ πλάζει, in tmesi, pres. only α 75, πατρίδος, *keeps him away from*; elsewh. only aor. pass. -επλάγχθης, etc., *be driven from one's course*, θ 573; with gen. o 382, ι 259 (-θεν), μ 285; *rebound*, X 291, N 578, 592.

ἀπο-πλείειν, inf., ipf. -έπλειον, (πλέϝω), navibus proficisci, *sail away*, I 418, θ 501.

ἀπο-πλήξας, aor. part., (πλήσσω), detruncare, *strike off*, κ 440†.

ἀπο-πλύνεσκε, ipf. iter., (πλύνω), diluebat, *was washing clean*, ζ 95†. [ῡ]

ἀπ-έπλω (πλώω, πλέϝω), ipf., a vec-

ta est, *had sailed away from*, γαίης, ξ 339†.

ἀπο-πνείων, ουσα(αι), part., (πνέϝω), exhalans, *breathing forth*, life, fire, smell, δ 406.

ἀπο-πρό, πολλὸν, Π 660, *far away*; τυτθὸν ἀ. νεῶν, H 334, *not far from*.

ἀπο-προ-αιρέω, only -ελών, *take away from what lies before*, ρ 457†.

ἀπο-προ-έηκε, aor. from ἀπο-προ-ίημι, delegavit.

ἀπό-προθεν, procul, (*from*) *far away*, στῆτε, ζ 218; ρ 408, the house would hold him *aloof*.

ἀπό-προθι, procul, *far away*, Ψ 832.

ἀπο-προ-ίημι, part. -ιείς and aor. -έηκε, delegavit, *sent away*, ξ 26; *shot forth*, χ 82; *let fall*, χ 327. [‿‿‿—]

ἀπο-προ-τέμνω, only aor. part. -ταμών, desecans, *cut off from*, with gen., θ 475†.

ἀπο-πτάμενος, aor. part. from πέτομαι, avolans.

ἀπο-πτύει, 3 sing. and part. pres., (πτύω), exsputare, *spit forth*, Ψ 781; *dash forth*, Δ 426. [ῡ]

ἀ-πόρθητος (πορθέω), non excisa, *not destroyed*, M 11†.

ἀπ-ορνύμενον, part., profectum, *having set out from*, Λυκίηθεν, E 105†. [ῡ]

ἀπ' ὄρουσε, -σαν, aor., (ὀρούω), also in tmesi, desiliit, *sprang away*, E 297, P 483; *rebounded*, Φ 593; *sprang down*, E 20.

ἀπο-ρραίσει and -ρραῖσαι, fut. and inf. aor., (ῥαίω), eripere, *wrest away from*, α 404.

ἀπὸ ῥῆξε, -ρρήξας, aor. ind. and part., (ῥήγνυμι), abrupit, *break off, shatter*, Z 507, Π 587; *hinges*, M 459.

ἀπ-ερρίγασι, for ϝεϝρίγασι, pf., (ῥιγέω), perhorrent, *shrink from*, β 52†.

ἀπὸ ἔρριψε, ἀπο-ρρῖψαι, -ρρίψαντα 1 aor., (ῥίπτω), excutere, *put off, lay aside* (anger), I 517; *veil*, X 406.

ἀπο-ρρώξ (ϝέϝρωγα, ῥήγνυμι), *branch* (of the Styx), κ 514; *morsel* (of Nectar), ι 359; as adj. -ρρῶγες, *steep*, ν 98†.

ἀπ-έσσυτο, -εσσύμεθα, aor. mid., (σεύω), se proripuit, *hurried away*, ι 396; ὤματος, Z 390.

ἀπ-εσκίδασεν, -σκίδασον, tmesis,

indic. and imp. aor., (σκιδάννυμι), p r o-
p u l i t, *scattered*, λ 385 ; *dismissed*, Τ
309. [◡ – ◡ ◡ ◡]
ἀπο-σκίδνασθαι (σκίδνημι), d i g r e-
d i, *disperse*, Ψ 4†.
ἀπο-σκύδμαινε, imp., (σκυδμαίνω),
be indignant at, τινί, Ω 65†.
ἀπο-σπένδων, part., (σπένδω), l i-
b a n s, *pouring out a libation*, γ 394. (Od.)
ἀπο-στᾰδόν and -ά, adv.. (σταδίη),
only Ο 556, ζ 143, *standing far away*.
ἀπο-στείχων, part. pres., and aor.
-έστιχε, imp. ἀπόστιχε, a b s c e d e r e,
go away, λ 132, Α 522.
ἀπο-στίλβοντες, pres. part., n i t e n-
t e s, *gleaming* with oil, with gen., γ 408†.
ἀπο-στρέψοντας, fut. part., -στρέ-
ψασκε, aor. iter., -ψῃσι, -ψαντε(ς),
(στρέφω), a v e r t o, *twist back*, hands and
feet, χ 173 ; *turning about*, γ 162 ; *turn
back in flight*, Ο 62 ; *roll back*, λ 597 ;
recall, Κ 355.
ἀπ-εστῠφέλιξεν, -ξαν, aor., (στυφε-
λίζω), r e t u d i t, *forced back*, Π 703 ; Σ
158, τινός.
ἀπο-σφήλωσι, aor. subj., -σφήλειε,
opt., (σφάλλω), aberrare faciat,
cause to drift away, γ 320 ; lead them
astray from object of their labor, cause
them to fail of the result of their toil
(through the death of Menelaos), Ε 567.
ἀπο-σχέσθαι, aor. inf., see ἀπέχω,
a b s t i n e r e.
ἀπὸ ἔσχισεν (σχίζω), d i s c i d i t, *split
off, split in sunder*, δ 507†.
ἀπο-τάμνω, ipf. -έταμνε (in tmesi :·
τάμνε, 1 aor. τάμε, subj. τάμῃσι, opt.
τάμοι), pres. mid. -ταμνόμενον, d e c i-
d e r e, *cut off, cut open*; throats, Γ 292,
Χ 328 ; thread, Ψ 867 ; reins, halter,
Ο 87 ; *cut off for one's self*, Χ 347.
ἀπο-τηλοῦ, p r o c u l, *far away*, ι
117†.
ἀπο-τίθημι, only aor. -έθηκα (also in
tmesis), and aor. mid. θέτο (tmesis), and
inf. -θέσθαι, d e p o n e r e, *put away, lay
off*, garments and weapons, esp. freq. in
mid., habit of fault-finding, Ε 492.
ἀπο-τῑνύμενοι, part. pres., ipf. -ετί-
νυτο, (τίνω), τινά τινος, u l c i s c i p r o,
take vengeance for, β 73, Π 398. [ῠ]
ἀπο-τίνειν, -έμεν ; -ετον, imp., -τί-
νων ; fut. -τίσεις, aor. -έτισε, etc., inf.
-τῖσαι, s o l v e r e, *pay back*, τιμήν, m u l c-
t a m, a fine, Γ 286 ; *pay*, Ψ 487 ; *atone
for*, Χ 271, Φ 399, γ 195, σὺν μεγάλῳ

Δ 161, Ι 512, χ 168, ν 193 ; Σ 93, *atone
for* slaying and despoiling Patroklos ; *make good*, Α 128, Ι 634, β 132 ;
recompense, Θ 186, χ 235 ; mid. -τί-
σομαι, etc. fut., aor. -ετίσατο, *avenge
one's self upon, punish*, u l c i s c i, τί, λ
118, ν 386 ; ποινὴν ἑτάρων, exact satisfaction for his companions, ψ 312.
[ῑ]
ἀπο-τμήγουσι, aor. opt. -τμήξειε,
part. -τμήξας, a b s c i n d e r e, *cut off*,
sever, Σ 34, Λ 146, κ 440 ; fig. *cut off*,
intercept, Κ 364, Λ 468 ; *plough, tear*
(hill-sides), Π 390.
ἄ-ποτμος, infortunatus, *ill-
starred*, Ω 388 ; sup. -ότατος, α 219.
ἀπο-τρεπέτω, imp. prs., fut. -τρέψεις,
ἀπο-έτραπε, a v e r t e r e, *turn away from*,
τινά τινος, Μ 249, Υ 256, 109 ; r e d u-
c e r e, *turn back*, Λ 758 ; *scare back*, Ο
276 ; mid. aor. -ετράπετο, etc., *turn
one's self away*, Μ 329 ; ἀπὸ νόσφι,
turn away the face, ε 350 ; *turn about*,
Κ 200.
ἀπο-τρίψουσι, fut., (τρίβω), d e t e-
r e n t u r, many footstools, thrown from
both sides about his head, as he is made
a target of throughout the house (gen.
absol. of part.), (as they slip down)
shall rub off his ribs ; *coarse jest* of
goatherd Melantheυs, ρ 232†.
ἀπό-τροπος (τρέπω), r e m o t u s,
(live) *retired*, ξ 372†.
ἀπο-τρωπῶσι, subj. -ῶμεν (-τρωπάω),
a v e r t e r e, *drive back*, Υ 119 ; *forbid*,
π 405 ; mid. -τρωπᾶσθε, imp., -ετρω-
πῶντο, ipf., τινός, t e r g i v e r s a m i n i,
turn the back upon, delay about; with
inf., *shrink from*, Σ 585.
ἀπ-ούρας, aor. part. from ἀπαυράω,
e r i p e r e.
ἀπ-ουρήσουσι, fut., e r i p i e n t (-αυ-
ράω), or ἀπ-ουρίσσουσι, a m o v e b u n t
t e r m i n o s (οὖρος), *remove the boundary
stones* = intrude upon his fields, Χ 489†
ἀπο-φέρω, only fut. -οίσετον, -οίσειν,
aor. -ένεικας, -αν, a u f e r o, *carry home*,
π 360 ; *bear back*, Ε 257 ; *drive away*
(at sea), Ξ 255 ; *bring back*, Κ 337.
ἀπό-φημι, and aor. mid. imp. -φασθε,
pronuntio, ἀντικρύ, *I say it to thy
face*, Η 362 ; *deliver* this message, Ι 422.
ἀπ-έφθιθεν, 3 pl. aor. pass., (φθίω),
p e r i e r u n t, only in interpolated verses
of Od., ε 110.
ἀπο-φθΐνύθουσι (φθίω), p e r e u n t, Ε

643; θυμόν, Π 540, perdunt, lose life.
[ῠ]

ἀπο-φθίω, perdo, prs. pass. opt. -φθίμην, imp. -φθίσθω, part. -φθιμένου, -οιο, -ον, -η; mid. aor. with pass. signif. -ἐφθιτο, aor. pass. 3 pl. -(ἐ)φθίθεν, ψ 331 (and interpolation, ε 110); perire, perish, ὀλέθρῳ, in destruction, o 268, T 322, ω 88; mortua, o 357; occisi, Σ 499.

ἀπο-φώλιος, -οι, -α, (φύω, φώς), sine fetu, not unblessed with offspring is intercourse with the gods, λ 249; =ἀφυής (non-Homeric), unfruitful, i. e. aimless, foolish, ε 182 ; unseemly, ξ 212; vile, θ 177.

ἀπο-χάζεο, imp. prs., (χάζομαι), recede a, go away from, τινός, λ 95.

ἀπὸ χεῦεν, for ἔχεFεν, aor., (from χέω), excussit, threw down from the table, only χ 20, 85.

ἀπο-ψύχοντα (ψύχω), part., exspirantem, fainting, ω 348; elsewh. ἱδρῶ, with ipf. mid. -εψύχοντο, were letting the sweat dry off from their garments, and pass. -ψυχθείς, having cooled off. [ῠ]

ἀπ-πέμψει, fut. from ἀποπέμπω, dimittet.

ἄ-πρηκτον, -ους, acc., (πρήσσω), irritum, endless, B 121, 376 ; with or against which nothing can be done, hopeless, incurable, μ 223, β 79 ; active, unsuccessful, Ξ 221.

ἀ-πρίάτην (πρίαμαι), adv., gratis, without money, for nothing, ξ 317 ; without ransom, A 99. [ᾰ]

ἀ-προτί-μαστος (-μαίομαι), intacta, undefiled, T 263†.

ἄ-πτερος (πέτομαι), ἔπλετο μῦθος, τινί, non excidit, nor did the word escape her, she perceived its sense, ρ 57. (Od.)

ἀ-πτῆσι, dat. pl., (-πτήν), implumibus, unfledged, I 323†.

ἀ-πτο-επές (ἐπτοίηθεν, ἔπος), audacter loquens, rash-speaking, Θ 209†.

ἀ-πτόλεμος, -ον, -ους, imbellis, unwarlike, B 201. (Il.)

ἅπτω, only aor. part. ἅψας, aptans, making fast, φ 408 ; ἀψαμένη ἀπό, suspending a noose on high upon, λ 278 ; elsewh. only mid. prs. ἅπτεσθαι, ipf. ἥπτετο, fut. ἅψεσθαι, aor. ἥψατο, ἀψάσθην, etc., cling to, τινός, Π 9; hit,

strike, Θ 67, P 631 ; touch, clasp, τινός, τ 344 (also with double gen., τ 348); esp. with γούνων, γενείου (supplicare), A 512, 500, Ω 357; lay hold of, Θ 339, B 152; clasp, δ 522 ; lay hands on, τινός, β 423 ; lay hold of in eating, δ 60, κ 379 ; τ 28=sits at my table ; sc. πυρός, take fire, ι 379 ; aor. pass. ἑάφθη, ἐπὶ, fell after, sank upon him, N 543.

ἀ-πυργωτόν (πύργος), immunitam, unfortified, λ 264†.

ἄ-πῡρον, -ους, (πῦρ), kettle or tripod, not yet placed over the fire, Ψ 267, I 122. (Il.)

ἀ-πύρωτον (πῦρ), ignis expertem, untouched by fire=ἄπυρον, Ψ 270†. [ῠ]

ἄ-πυστος (πυθόμενος), (1) ignotus, unknown, α 242.—(2) ignarus, uninformed of, τινός, δ 675. (Od.)

ἀπ-ωθέω, only fut. -ώσω (inf. -σέμεν), aor. -ῶσε, etc., mid. fut. -ώσεαι, etc., aor. -ώσατο, repellere, push back, Ω 446, χ 76 ; cast off, o 280, β 130, Υ 489; drive from one's course (at sea), ι 81, cf. ν 276 ; tear away, E 308 ; τινός, drive away from, Θ 96 ; mid. drive away from one's self (enemies), Θ 206, O 503 ; dislodge, push aside, α 270, Θ 533, Ω 508.

ἄρα, before consonants ἄρ, enclitic ῥα, always postpositive, (ἀραρεῖν), orig. adv. containing the idea of being firmly fixed, denotes, as conjunction, a natural inference from what precedes, now, now then, no doubt, exactly, therefore, then.— (1) of what is fixed by decree of fate, esp. in phrase οὐδ' ἄρ' ἔμελλεν, δ 107, λ 553, ν 293, ι 475, K 336, M 3 ; B 419, λ 139 ; Ψ 670, δ 605.—(2) of what experience has taught us to regard as fixed, ν 209, π 420, E 532.—(3) often joined with causal conjs., γάρ ῥα, A 113, 236; ἐπεί ῥα, o 390, α 263 ; ὅτι ῥα, because you know, A 56.—(4) εἴτ' ἄρα, if namely, A 65 ; εἰ μὴ ἄρα, unless indeed, Z 75, ψ 242.—(5) recapitulating, with demonstratives, precisely, to wit, B 482, Γ 153, A 405; ὥς ἄρα, φ 163, A 428, 584, Γ 13, H 7 ; with τοὔνεκα, ἔνθεν, τότε, τῆμος, etc.; with relatives, H 182 just the one which, ξ 449, υ 106, Z 131 ; ὅς ῥα, who, you see = since he. — (6) with weakened force, without doubt, naturally, of course, surely, A 46, 56 ; εἴτ' ἄρα, A 65, cf. 93 ; in questions, τίς τ' ἄρ, α 346, A 8; κατ' ἄρ' ἕζετο, A 68;

in first member of antithetical period, followed by δέ : μέν ῥα, B 1 ; δ᾽ ἄρα, then in due course, A 471 ; οὐδ᾽ ἄρα, A 330 ; αὐτὰρ ἄρα, B 103.—(7) denoting a subtle, inherent sequence of thought, often untranslatable, H 360, B 433.—(8) ἄρα, ῥα, following participles, θ 458, ν 380; sometimes doubled, π 213. [ᴗ ᴗ]

ἀράβησε (ἀραβέω), aor., δὲ τεύχε᾽ ἐπ᾽ αὐτῷ, his armor rang around him, ω 525. [ᾰ]

ἄράβος ὀδόντων, chattering of teeth, K 375†.

Ἀραιθυρέη, town in Argos, B 571†.

ἀραιή, etc., adj. fem., tenuis, thin, slender, κ 90, Π 161 ; legs of Hephaistos, Σ 411; delicate, E 425. [ᾰ]

ἀράται, etc., prs. (-άομαι), inf. ἀρήμεναι, χ 322; inf. ἠρώμην, ἆτο, fut. -ήσεται, aor. ἠρήσατο, -αντο, etc., precari.—(1) pray, η 1 ; πολλά, fervently, δαίμοσιν, ἀθανάτοισι, πάντεσσι θεοῖσι (see cut, for attitude); εὐχομένη, imploring, supplicating, Z 304, I 567; grieving sore, with inf., Ψ 209; with acc. and inf., δ 827.—(2) wish, long for, with inf., N 286, Δ 143, α 366; call down upon, Ἐρινῦς, curse, β 135; with acc. and inf., r 533.

ἀράρισκε, I. ipf., 1 aor. ἄρσε (with imp., inf., part.), 2 aor. ἤραρε, ἄραρον, (artare), coniungo, fit together, rafters, Ψ 712 ; fit upon, τί τινι, ξ 23 ; close, β 353 ; β 289, seal up in jars ; M 105, formed themselves in close array with their shields ; build (put together) a wall with stones, Π 212; parare (ἀρτύω) γέρας, A 136; θάνατον καὶ κῆρα, π 169 ; θυμὸν ἐδωδῇ, satisfy.—II. pf. ἄρηρε, (part. ἀρηρώς, ἀράρυῖα, etc.), plupf. ἀρήρει, (2 aor. ἤραρεν, ἄραρον, but only Π 214, δ 777), and 3 pl. aor. pass. ἄρθεν, and part. aor. mid. ἄρμενος, artari, be closely joined together, of ranks, O 618, Η 211; of jars standing close together against wall, β 342 ; close tightly, I 475, ψ 42, Σ 275 ; with dat.: joined together with or of (metal plates, Ο 530; palisades, M 56; paved with

flags, ζ 267); lie close upon, fit, Γ 338, Σ 600, ε 234 (also with prep., σ 378); please, δ 777 ; hold fast to, ε 361 ; fitted to, ε 254 ; K 265, with ἐν ; be provided with, Λ 31, E 744, Ξ 181, ζ 70, κ 553.

ἄραρον, aor., ἀραρυῖα, pf. part., see ἀράρισκε.

ἄρασσεν, ipf., compegit, drove home and made fast, ε 248†.

ἀράχνϊα, τά, aranea, spider's web, only θ 280, π 35.

ἀργαλέος, η, ον, (ῥίγιον?), arduus, impossible, difficult, A 589, M 63, β 244; also in pers. constr., A 589, δ 397; difficilis, difficult to manage, shocking, violent, K 107, P 385, O 10, Λ 812, λ 400.

Ἀργεάδης, Πολύμηλος, Π 417†.

Ἀργεῖος, η, ον, inhabitant of Ἄργος; freq. in pl. as collective designation of Greeks, B 159, A 79, Γ 286, 99.

Ἀργεϊ-φόντης (ἀργει instr., φαν, clear-shining), epith. of Ἑρμῆς, swift messenger, a popular (mistaken) etymology seems to have been the origin of the myth of the Argos-slayer, B 103.

ἀργεννάων,-ῶν,-ῇσι,-ῇς, (from ἀργεσινάων), candidus, white, Γ 198, 141.

ἀργεστᾶο Νότοιο, only Λ 306, Φ 334, rapidi, rapid.

ἀργής, ῆτος, (also -ἔτι, ἔτα, dat. acc.), dazzling white, bright; of linen, fat, lightning, Γ 419.

ἀργι-κέραυνε, voc., (κεραυνός), fulmen coruscum gerens, wielder of the dazzling thunderbolt, T 121 ; fulminator, thunderer, Υ 16. (Il.)

ἀργινόεντα, acc., candidum, gleaming; epith. of town in Kreta, because of chalk cliffs near it, only B 647, 656.

ἀργϊ-όδοντος, etc., (-όδους), white-toothed, epith. of dogs and swine.

ἀργί-ποδᾰς (πούς), acc., swift-footed, Ω 211†. [ῐ]

Ἄργισσα, town in Θεσσαλία, B 738‡.

ἐργμᾰτᾰ, τά, (ἄρχεσθαι), consecrated pieces of flesh burned at beginning of sacrifice, ξ 446†.

Ἄργος, ὁ, name of the faithful hound of Odysseus, ρ 292†.

Ἄργος, εος, ntr.—(1) town on river Inachos in Argolis, domain of Diomedes, ο 224, φ 108, Z 224, Ξ 119, γ 180, B 559; ἱππόβοτον, ο 239, 274.—(2) in wider sense, realm of Agamemnon, who dwelt in Mykene, B 108, 115, A 30, I 22, O 30, N 379, γ 263, Δ 171.—(3) probably, the entire Peloponnesos, δ 174; Ἀχαιικοῦ, γ 251; ἱπποβότοιο, Ζ 152; so often joined with Ἑλλάδα, which latter word then designates Northern Greece; cf. Ἴασον, σ 246.— (4) Πελασγικόν, domain of Achilleus, B 681, Ω 437, ω 37, Ζ 456, valley and plain of river Pencios.—(5) in widest sense, the whole of Greece, M 70, N 227, Ξ 70; also Ἀχαιικόν, ἱπποβότοιο, B 287, I 246, δ 99; πολυπύρῳ, O 372. Not all passages admit of satisfactory explanation, e. g. H 363, δ 562.

ἀργήν, οἱ, οὕς, *white*, ο 161, Ψ 30; *swift* (with and without πόδας), κύνες, β 11.

Ἄργοσδε = εἰς Ἄργος.

ἀργύρεος, ἐη, εον, (ἄργυρος), argenteus, *of silver*, δ 615; *inlaid* or *adorned with silver*, E 727, A 219. [ῠ]

ἀργυρο-δίνης, (δίνη), *silver-eddying*, of rivers, B 753. (Il.) [ῑ]

ἀργυρό-ηλος, ηλον, ον, (ἧλος), *adorned with silver studs* or *knobs, silver-studded;* ξίφος, θρόνος, φάσγανον, B 45, η 162, Ξ 405.

ἀργυρό-πεζα (-πεδjα), *silver-* (in whiteness) *footed*, Θέτις, A 538. (Il.)

ἄργυρος, ου, ὁ, (ἀργός), argentum, *silver*, B 857, ψ 200.

ἀργυρό-τοξος, *bearing the silver bow*, Ἀπόλλων; also subst., A 37.

ἀργύ-φεον (ἀργός, φα-), ntr., *dazzling-white*, ε 230. [ῠ]

ἄργυ-φον, α = ἀργύφεον, ntr. Σ 50, κ 85.

Ἀργώ (lit. *swift*), ship of Argonauts, μ 70.

ἀρδμός, -οί, aquatio, *watering-place*, ν 247.

ἀρειῇ (ἀρά), minis, *by threats*, P 431. (Il.)

Ἀρεθούση, κρήνη in Ithaka, ν 408†.

ἄρειον, τεῖχος, see follg. word.

ἀρείων, acc. sing. -είω and -είονα, nom. pl. -είους, -είονες, ntr. ἄρειον, (ἀραρεῖν), compact, τεῖχος, Δ 407, T 33; fortis, ι 48; then, *surpassing*, praestans, Ψ 588, β 277; β 277, opp. κακίους, ν 130, opp. χείρονα. [ᾰ]

Ἀρείων, name of horse of Ἄδρηστος at siege of Θήβη, Ψ 346.

ἄ-ρεκτον (ῥέζω), infectum, *unaccomplished*, T 150†.

ἀρές, voc., (from ἀρής, ἀρε-ίων), *Oh brave one*, restore in E 31, 455.

ἀρέσαι, -έσασθαι, see ἀρέσκω.

ἀρέσθαι, inf. aor. from ἄρνυμαι, comparare.

ἀρέσκω, only ἀρέσαι, inf. 1 aor., *make amends;* also fut. mid. ἀρεσσόμεθα, and aor. ἀρεσσάσθω, -σσασθαι, *appease*, τινά; reconciliare, δώροις, etc.

ἀρετᾷ, -ῶσι, *thrive*, only Θ 329, τ 114.

Ἀρετάων, a Trojan, Ζ 31†.

ἀρετή, ῆς, (ἀρείων), praestantia, *excellence*, of whatever sort, Υ 411, Ψ 276; *superiority, accomplishment*, δ 725, σ 251, O 642, Υ 242; *capacity, prowess*, ξ 212, Ψ 571; virtus, Θ 535, N 237, Θ 239; *skill*, ρ 322; *success*, ν 45, σ 133; *prosperity*, ξ 402.

ἀρετῆτα, conjecture for ἀδροτῆτα.

ἀρή, ῆς, preces, (1) *prayer*, δ 767. —(2) imprecatio, *curse* (ἀρέων, I 566), ρ 496; *destruction*, M 334; with λοιγόν, Ω 489; calamity, χ 208. [◡◡—; in arsi —]

ἄρηαι, aor. subj. from ἄρνυμαι, compares.

ἀρήγω, fut. -ξω, (ἄρκιον, ἀλκή), opitulari, τινί, aid, A 77. (Il.) [ᾰ]

ἀρηγών, -όνες, fem., (ἀρήγω), *helper*, E 511 and Δ 7. [ᾰ]

ἀρηΐ-θόων (ἄρης, θούς), *swift in battle, valiant*, Θ 298. (Il.)

Ἀρηΐ-θοος, (1) κορυνήτης, son of Μενέσθιος from Βοιωτία, H 10, 137.— (2) θεράπων of Ῥίγμος, Υ 487.

ἀρηϊ-κτάμένῳ, in pugna caeso, *slain in battle*, X 72.

Ἀρηΐ-λυκος, (1) father of Προθοήνωρ, Ξ 451.—(2) a Trojan, Π 308.

ἀρήϊος (ἄρης), *warlike, martial*, B 698, ψ 220; τεύχεα, ἔντεα, *of weapons*, armor, Ζ 340, K 407.

ἀρηΐ-φάτοι, ους, (φένω), in pugna caesi, *slain*, λ 41, T 31. [ῑ]

ἀρηΐ-φιλος, -ον,-οι, Marti gratus, *loved by Ares, valiant*, ο 169. (Il.) [ῑ]

ἀρήμεναι, inf. from ἀράομαι, precatus esse.

ἀρημένος, -ον, *overcome, burdened*, Σ 435, σ 53.

ἀρήν, see ἀρνός.

ἀρηρομένος, pf. pass. from ἀρόω, aratus.

Ἀρήνη, town subject to Νέστωρ, B 591, Λ 723.

Ἄρης, -ηος, -ῆϊ, -ηα, -ην (also -εος, -εϊ, and -ει), voc. Ἄρες (see ἀρές), god of war and of the tumult of conflict, E 890 sqq.; son of Ζεύς and Ἥρη, brother of Ἔρις, father of Δεῖμος and Φόβος; common epithets, ἀλλοπρόσαλλος, ἆτος πολέμοιο, βροτολοιγός, δεινὸς ἐννάλιος, θοῷ, θοῦρος, μιαιφόνος, ὄβριμος, ταλαυρινὸν πολεμιστήν, χάλκεος, etc.; his favorite abode, N 301 sqq., θ 361; his size, E 860; cf. E 385, θ 267 sqq.; brave heroes are called ὄζος or θεράποντες Ἄρηος; cf. follg.

ἄρης (ἔρις?), orig. the god Ἄρης (cf. Ἥφαιστος), then his element, the tumult of battle, ὀξὺν ἄρηα ἐγείρειν, B 440; ξυνάγειν, B 381; φέρειν πολύδακρυν, Γ 132; ἔριδα, etc.

ἄρησθε, subj. aor. from ἄρνυμαι, comparetis.

Ἀρήτη, daughter of Ῥηξήνωρ, wife of Ἀλκίνοος, η 54, ν 66. (Od.) [ᾱ]

ἀρητήρ, ῆρος, α, (ἀράομαι), one who prays, a priest, A 11. [ᾱ]

Ἀρητιάδης, Νῖσος, π 395. [ᾱ]

ἄ-ρητον (perh. from ἄϜρητον = ἄρρητον, cf. εἴρηκα, from ἔ-Ϝρηκα), infandum, unspeakable, P 37, Ω 741; others interpret, accursed, shocking, from ἀράομαι.

Ἄρητος, (1) son of Νέστωρ, γ 414. —(2) son of Πρίαμος, P 535.

ἄρθεν, conferti sunt, 3 pl. aor. pass. from ἀράρισκε.

ἀρθμήσαντε, part. aor. (ἀρθμέω), ἐν φιλότητι, having been brought together (in combat), separated in friendship, H 302†.

ἄρθμιοι (ἀραρίσκω), coniuncti, allied, π 427†.

ἀρῐ- (ἀρείων), intensive, inseparable prefix, exceedingly, very. [ᾰ]

Ἀρι-άδνη, κούρη Μίνωος, λ 321, Σ 592.

ἀρί-γνωτος, η, ον, recognizable, N 72, δ 207; famose, = infamous, ρ 375 (where – – –˘).

ἀρι-δείκετος, illustrious, λ 540; usually with gen. part. ἀνδρῶν, λαῶν, θ 382.

ἀρί-ζηλος, η, (δῆλος), valde clarus, conspicuous, Σ 519; clear, shrill, Σ 219 (B 318, αἴζηλον). ˘– – –˘ adv. -ζήλως, clearly, μ 453†.

ἀριθμήσω, fut. (ἀριθμέω), aor. -ήσας, pass. -ηθήμεναι, numerare, count,

reckon up; δίχα, divide into two companies, κ 204.

ἀριθμῷ, -όν, numero, number, λ 449. [ᾱ]

Ἀρίμοις, ἐιν—, name of a region in Κιλικία, B 783†. [ᾰ ῐ]

ἀρι-πρεπής, -ές, conspicuous, distinguished; Z 477, Τρώεσσιν, among the Trojans.

Ἀρίσβας, αντος, father of Λειώκριτος, P 345†. [ᾰ]

Ἀρίσβη, town in Troia; Ἀρίσβηθεν, from Arisbe, B 838. [ᾰ]

ἀριστερός, όν, sinister, left, ἐπ' ἀριστερά (-όφιν, N 309), sinistrorsum, ε 277; foreboding ill, ν 242. [ᾰ]

ἀριστῆος, gen., pl. -ῆες, nobilis, optimates, chiefs, O 489, H 73, ο 28.

ἀριστεύειν, ipf. iter. ἀριστεύεσκε, excellere, be the best or bravest, usually with inf. μάχεσθαι, Λ 746; with gen. τ.νός, (μεθ' ἡμέας, δ 652); with both gen. and inf., Z 460.

ἄριστον (ἦρι), breakfast, π 2, Ω 124. [ᾰ]

ἄριστος, η, ον, (ἀρείων, ἀρι-), and ὤριστος = ὁ ἄρ., optimus, the best, most excellent, most capable, bravest, first; of things animate and inanimate; among, with gen. part., A 69; with ἐν (with verbs), Z 7, O 296; with dat. of manner (or respect), I 54, θ 247, π 419, ν 297; with acc. of respect, Γ 39, Ψ 483, λ 469, γ 370, also followed by inf., θ 123; often intensified by advs., μέγ', ὄχ', ἔξοχ', διακριδόν (M 103, O 108), decidedly; Ζεύς, Ξ 213, Τ 95, τ 303, N 154; princeps, e. g. Γ 274, K 214, Z 209, I 3, (by birth, rank, or other title to honor); advantageous, I 103, Γ 110, ν 154; Z 56, σοὶ—πεποίηται, honorable (indeed) has been their conduct toward thee! [ᾰ]

ἀρι-σφαλέα, acc., (σφάλλομαι), lubricum, slippery, the ground, ρ 196†.

ἀρι-φραδές and -έα, ntr., (φράζομαι), very plain, easy to recognize, σῆμα, ὀστέα, Ψ 240; adv. φραδέως = ἀριζήλως, v. l. ψ 225†.

Ἀρκάδες, inhabitants of Ἀρκαδίη, B 611, 603, in the Peloponnesos. (Il.) [ᾰ]

Ἀρκείσιος, son of Ζεύς, father of Ἀρκεισιάδης, i. e. Λαέρτης, π 118, ω 270. (Od.)

Ἀρκεσί-λαος, leader of the Βοιωτοί, B 495, O 329. [ῐ]

ἀρκέω, only ipf. ἤρκει, fut. ἀρκέσει, aor. ἤρκεσε (ἀλκή), arcere, keep off, τινί τι, Z 16; ἀπό τινός τι, N 440; patrocinari, protect, τινί, π 261, Φ 131.

ἄρκιος, -ον, (ἀρκέω), sufficient, K 304; B 393, ei non erit opportunitas, shall have no further opportunity to; certum, O 502.

ἄρκτος, ὁ and ἡ, ursus, bear, λ 611; ἡ, constellation of the Great Bear, or Wain, Σ 487, ε 273; septem triones.

ἅρμα, ατος, τό, (ἀραρίσκω), chariot, ἀγκύλον, εὔξοον, εὔτροχον, θοόν, καμπύλον; usually in pl., δαιδαλέοισιν, ποικίλα χαλκῷ (adorned with gold and silver, K 438), κολλητοῖσιν; esp. war chariot, drawn by horses, hence these often named with it, E 199, 237, Δ 366; the Homeric chariot differed in no essential respect from that in use centuries earlier by the Egyptians and by the Asiatics; for description of separate parts, cf. ἄντυξ, ἄξων, ῥυμός, ἕστωρ, ἴτυς, ἐπίσσωτρα, πλῆμναι, κνήμη, δίφρος, ζυγόν (see cut No. 10, and tables I. and II.).

Ἅρμα, village in Βοιωτία, B 499†.

ἁρμᾰτο-πηγός (πήγνυμι), ἀνήρ, chariot-builder, Δ 485†.

ἁρμα-τροχίή (τρόχος), wheel-rut, Ψ 505†.

ἄρμενος, fitting, part. aor. mid. (ἀράρισκε).

ἁρμόζεο, imp. pres. mid., aor. act. ἥρμοσε, from ἁρμόζω, strictly, fit together, Γ 333, the cuirass fitted him; fit together, beams, ε 247; 162, unite them together into a raft.

Ἁρμονίδης, ship-builder in Troy, (ἁρμόζω), E 60†. [ῐ]

ἁρμονῐάων, ῃσι, gen. dat. pl., (ἁρμόζω), bands, slabs, one side flat, the other curved; serving to bind together the raft: see d, in cut; also k, in cut No. 35. Also fig., bond, compact, χ 225.

ἀρνειός, ὁ, aries, ram, Γ 197, ι 444; with ὄιν, κ 527, 572.

ἀρνεῖται, etc., ipf. ἠρνεῖτο, aor. ἀρνήσασθαι, (ἀρνέομαι), negare, recusare, στερεῶς, Ψ 42; withhold, φ 345.

ἀρνευτῆρι, dat., (ἐρευνᾶν), diver, μ 413; cf. Π 747 sq.

Ἄρνη, town in Βοιωτία, H 9, B 507. With initial F, B 507 ?

ἄρνα, acc. sing., du. -ε, pl. regular, dat. only -εσσιν, gender comm. (Ϝαρν-, Γ 310), sheep, lamb, δ 85, Δ 102.

ἄρνυμαι, pres. ipf., aor. ἤρατο, -άμεθα and ἀρόμην, etc., comparare, procure for one's self, μισθόν; gain, κλέος, κῦδος, εὖχος, νίκην, ἀέθλια (also gain for another, τινί, A 159, I 303, Δ 95, Π 84); also carry off as share of booty, Ψ 592, I 188; ἀνδράγρια, Ξ 510; receive, Ξ 130; experiri, take upon one's self, δ 107, a 390; carry, as burden, νηῦς, Υ 247; seeking to gain, a 5, X 160. [‒ ◡ ◡; ◡ ‒ ◡]

ἀροίμην, etc., aor. opt. from ἄρνυμαι.

ἄροσις, ἡ, (ἀρόω), arva, arable land, ι 134; ψιλήν, unwooded. [ᾰ]

ἀροτήρ, ῆρες, arator, plough-man, Σ 542. [ᾰ]

ἀρότοισιν, arationibus, by cultivation, ι 122†. [ᾰ]

ἄροτρον, τό, (ἀρόω), aratrum, plough, πηκτόν, firmly put together, N 703.

ἄρουρα, ης, (earth), plough-land, Z 195, M 422, N 707; field, K 7, Ψ 599; ground, Γ 115; ζείδωρος, corn-bearing earth, δ 229 (used in altogether general sense, cf. also r 593=upon the earth). As goddess=Γαῖα, B 548. [ᾰ]

ἀρόωσι (ἀρόω, cf. obsolete Eng. ear, to plough), arant, plough, ι 108; ἀρηρομένη, perf. pass., aratae, Σ 548. [ᾰ]

ἁρπάζω, fut. -ξω, aor. ἥρπαξα, ἥρπασε, etc., rapio, rob, carry off, Σ 319, N 528; draw out, Π 814; carry off, ο 250; sweep away, ε 416.

ἁρπακτῆρες (ἁρπάζω), robbers, Ω 262†.

ἁρπαλέων, eagerly sought (gains), θ 164; ἁρπαλέως, greedily, ξ 110. (Od.)

Ἁρπάλίων, son of Πυλαιμένης, N 644.

ἄρπη, unknown bird of prey, perh. falcon, Τ 350†.

ἅρπυιαι, rapaces, snatchers, personified storm-winds, by whom those who have mysteriously disappeared are conceived of as *borne away* (not the Harpies, Monsters, of later myths), *a* 241.

ἄ-ρρηκτος (-Ϝρηκτος, Ϝρήγνυμι), *indissoluble, firm,* with ἄλυτος, Ν 360; θ 275, *indestructible.*

ἄ-ρρητος (Ϝρητός, ver-bum, Eng. word), *unspoken,* ξ 466; *unspeakable,* see ἄρητον.

ἄρσην, ενος, masculus, *masculine, male,* Θ 7, ι 425.

Ἀρσί-νοος, father of Ἐκαμήδη, of island Τένεδος, Λ 626†. [ι]

Ἀρτάκίη, name of fountain in country of Λαιστρυγόνες, κ 108†. [ῐ]

ἀρτεμέα, -έεσσι, acc. sing., dat. pl., incolumis, *safe and sound,* Ε 515, ν 43.

Ἄρτεμις, ἀγνή, ἰοχέαιρα, χρυσηλάκατος, χρυσήνιος, χρυσόθρονος, ἀγροτέρη, κελαδεινή, daughter of Ζεύς and Λητώ, sister of Ἀπόλλων, death-goddess (cf. ἀγανός), intaminata venatrix, ε 123, ρ 37 ; as huntress, haunting the mountains of Peloponnesos, ζ 102.

ἀρτῑ, prefix, *suitable, excellent.*

ἀρτῐ-επής (Ϝέπος), *speaking excellently;* μύθων, glib-tongued, Χ 281†.

ἄρτια (ἀράρισκε), *suitable things,* θ 240 ; *friendly,* τ 248.

ἀρτῐ-πος (πούς), pedibus valens, *strong* or *swift of foot,* Ι 505, θ 310.

ἀρτί-φρων, mente valens, *intelligent* (*friendly*), ω 261†.

ἄρτον, ους, acc., *wheaten bread,* ρ 343, σ 120. (Od.)

ἀρτύνω (ἄρτιος), fut. -υνέουσι, aor. part. -ύνας, mid. ipf. aor. ἠρτύνατο, pass. aor. ἀρτύνθη, compono, paro, *put in order, form in close array,* Μ 43, 86, Ο 303 ; *prepare, a* 277, ξ 469, ω 153; *devise,* λ 366 ; pass., Λ 216, *the battle began;* mid., *put in order for one's self, arrange,* δ 782 ; *place,* Β 55.

ἀρτύει, prs., ipf. ἤρτῡε, (cf. ἀρτύνω), parare, δ 771, υ 242; *make ready,* Σ 379. [ῠ]

Ἀρύβας, a native of Sidon, ο 426†. [ῠ]

ἀρχε-κάκους, *beginning mischief,* Ε 63†.

Ἀρχέ-λοχος, son of Ἀντήνωρ, Ξ 464.

Ἀρχε-πτόλεμος, Ἰφιτίδης, charioteer of Ἕκτωρ, Θ 128.

ἄρχευε, -ειν, pres., (ἀρχός), τινί, ducere, command. (Il.)

ἀρχή (ἄρχω), initium, *beginning,* ἐξ ἀρχῆς, *of old,* α 188 ; τινός, φ 4, Ι' 100, Λ 604 ; *occasion,* Χ 116.

ἀρχός, dux, *leader,* Β 493, Ε 39, θ 162, δ 653, χ 48.

ἄρχω (and mid., but without pf., plupf., and pass.), I. active : praeire, (1) *precede,* Α 495, Γ 420 ; *lead the way,* ε 237 ; τινί, ω 9.—(2) ducere, *lead,* Ρ 262 ; τινί, Β 805, Ε 592, ξ 230 ; τινός, Β 494, Μ 93, κ 205 ; νηῶν, Β 576 ; τινὶ μάχεσθαι, Π 65.—(3) regnare, *rule,* only ζ 12.—II. act. (and mid.*), incipere, inire, commence, begin.—(1) with inf., Β 84, θ 90*, Η 324, Φ 437, Ν 329 ; with dat. of interest, τινί, Η 324*, Ι 93* ; esp. τοῖσι δὲ ... ἦρχ' ἀγορεύειν, Α 571, β 15 (also Β 378 sc. μαχήσασθαι ; ξ 428* sc. ὠμοθετεῖν).— (2) with gen., *make a beginning with, begin,* Ι 97, Δ 335, φ 142* (ἔκ τινος, ψ 199*).—(3) τινί τινος, Ο 95, ζ 101* ; common phrase, τοῖς ἄρα μύθων ἦρχε, Β 433, a 28, and τοῖσιν δ' ... ἤρχετο μύθων. (Od.)

ἀρωγή, ἡ, (ἀρήγω), auxilium, *help, aid,* in battle or combat ; Φ 360, why should I concern myself with *giving succor?* (Il.) [ᾰ]

ἀρωγός, -οί, -ούς, opitulator, *helper, advocate,* in battle and before tribunal, σ 232. [ᾰ]

ἆσαι, (1) aor. from ἄω, satiare.

—(2) aor. from ἀάω, obcaecare.

ἄσαιμι, opt. aor. from ἄω, satiarem.

Ἀσαῖος, a Greek, Λ 301†.

ἄσαμεν, aor. from ἰαύω, dormivimus.

ἀσάμινθος, ἡ, labrum, *bathing-tub,* δ 48. [ᾰ]

ἄσασθαι, aor. inf. from ἄω, satiare.

ἄσατο, aor. of ἀάω, obcaecare, *blind.*

ἄ-σβεστος, 3, (σβέννυμι), *unextinguishable,* fire, laughter ; *unceasing,* βοή, κλέος, η 333.

ἄσεσθαι, fut. mid. from ἄω, satiare.

ἀ-σημάντοισιν (σημαίνω), sine ductore, *without a shepherd or leader,* Κ 485†. [ᾰ]

---

* Denotes that the form referred to is in mid. voice.

ἄσθμα, -ατι, (ἀίσθω), *short - drawn breath, panting,* O 10. (Il.)

ἀσθμαίνων (ἄσθμα), anhelans, *panting, gasping,* Φ 182. (Il.)

Ἀσιάδης, son of Ἄσιος, Ἀδάμας, Φαῖνοψ.

Ἀσίνη, in Ἀργολίς, Β 560†. [ă ĭ]

ἀ-σινέας, acc. pl. from -ής,(σίνομαι), illaesas, *unmolested,* λ 110. (Od.) [‿‿⏓]

Ἄσιος, ον, (1) son of Δύμας, a Phrygian; brother of Ἑκάβη, Π 717. — (2) son of Ὕρτακος from Ἀρίσβη, ally of Trojans, Μ 95.

ἄσῑν, τόσσην, situm, *slime,* Φ 321†. [ă]

ἄ-σῑτος, sine cibo, *without food,* δ 788†. [ă]

Ἀσίῳ ἐν λειμῶνι, *in the Asian* meadow; from Asia, a district in Lydia, from which the name was gradually extended to the whole continent, Β 461. [ā ĭ]

Ἀσκάλαφος, son of Ἄρης, leader of Βοιωτοί, Β 512.

Ἀσκᾰνίη, a town in Bithynia, on lake of same name, Β 863, Ν 793. [ĭ]

Ἀσκάνιος, (1) son of Ἱπποτίων, Ν 792.—(2) leader of the Φρύγες, Β 862. [ĭ]

ἀ-σκελέες, -ές, (σκέλλω), tabe confecti, *wasted,* κ 463; ntr. and adv. ἀσκελέως with αἰεί, *unceasingly,* Τ 68.

ἀσκέω, 3 sing. ipf. ἤσκειν, aor. ἤσκησε, etc., pf. pass. ἤσκηται, *work out with skill and care,* Κ 438 ; *smooth out,* α 439.

ἀ-σκηθής, -ές, (σκάζω), incolumis, *uninjured, unscathed,* ξ 255.

ἀσκητόν, ntr., (ἀσκέω), *curiously wrought,* δ 134. (Od.)

Ἀσκληπῐάδης = Μαχάων, Δ 204. (Il.) [ă]

Ἀσκληπιός, Thessalian prince, a famous physician, father of Ποδαλείριος and Μαχάων, Δ 194. (Il.) [‿‿⏑‿]

ἄ-σκοπος, temerarius, *thoughtless,* Ω 157.

ἀσκός, ὁ, uter, *leather bottle,* usually a goat skin (see cut, after a Pompeian painting), Γ 247 ; elsewh., corium, *hide,* κ 19.

ἄσμενος, ῳ, οι, (ἔαδα, σϜαδ-), lubens, *glad,* ι 63; Ξ 108, *it would please me.*

ἀ-σπάζομαι, only ipf. ἠσπάζοντο, (σπάω), amplectebantur, *were making welcome* (by reaching out hands to draw toward one), χερσί ; cf. Κ 542.

ἀ-σπαίρων, part. ipf., *move convulsively, quiver,* Κ 521 ; πόδεσσι, χ 473, τ 231.

ἄ-σπαρτα (σπείρω), non sata, *unsown,* ι 109†.

ἀ-σπάσιος, 3 and 2, (ἀσπάζομαι).— (1) acceptus, *welcome,* Θ 488.—(2)

lubens, *joyful*, ε 397, *to his joy* the gods have delivered him; so also **ἀσπασίως**, adv. [ᾰ]

ἀσπαστός, όν, acceptus, *welcome*, ψ 239; ε 398, *a grateful thing*.

ἄ-σπερμος (σπέρμα), sine prole, *without offspring*, Υ 303†.

ἀ-σπερχές (σπέρχομαι), ntr., studiose, *eagerly*, Σ 556; μενεαίνω, be *vehemently* enraged with.

ἄ-σπετος, 2, (ἐ-σπετε), infandus, *unutterable*, P 332; with πολλά, Λ 704, δ 75; *enormously great*, Τ 61, Π 157; *countless, unlimited*, χ 407, Λ 245; *endless supplies* for his needs, ν 424.

ἀσπιδιώτας (ἀσπιδιώτης), scutatos, *shield-bearing*, Β 554 and Π 167.

ἀσπίς, ίδος, ἡ, *shield*, (1) *the great oval shield* (see cut); epithets, ἀμφιβρότη, ποδηνεκής; more than 2 ft. broad, 4½ ft. high, and weighing about 40 lbs.; Agamemnon's shield described, Λ 32–40; it was carried over the left shoulder, sustained by the τελαμών and by the πόρπαξ, or ring within the shield.—(2) *smaller circular shield*, πάντοσ' ἐίση (see cut), with only two handles; or with one central handle for

the arm and several for the hand (see cut No. 12): it was of about half the size and weight of the larger ἀσπίς; cf. description of Sarpedon's shield, M 294 sqq. The shield consisted generally of 4 to 7 layers of ox-hide (ῥινοί, Ν 804); these were covered by a metal plate, and the whole was firmly united

by rivets, which projected on the outer convex side of the shield; the head of the central rivet, larger than the rest, was the ὀμφαλός, and was usually fashioned into the form of a head; instead of the plate above mentioned, concentric metal rings (δινωτήν, ἐύκυκλος) were sometimes substituted. The rim of the shield was called ἄντυξ, and the convex surface bore some device analogous to our coat of arms, Ε 182, Λ 36, cf. Ε 739. The shield of Achilleus, Σ 478–608, which was large and round, does not exactly correspond to either of the two ἀσπίδες above described.

ἀσπιστάων, gen. pl., (-τής), scutatorum, *shield-bearing*, Δ 90. (Il.) [ᾰ]

Ἀσπληδών, όνος, a town in Βοιωτία, Β 511†.

ἀ-σπουδί (σπουδή), μὴ μὰν — γε, *may I at least not perish without combat*, Χ 304. (Il.) [ῑ]

ἄσσα=ἅ τινα.

ἄσσα, ὁπποῖ', *what sort of*, τ 218†.

Ἀσσάρᾰκος, son of Τρώς, Υ 232, 239 (supreme deity of Assyrians). [ᾰ]

ἆσσον, comp. from ἄγχι, propius, *nearer*, τινός, ρ 303; with twofold comparative termination, **ἀσσοτέρω**, ρ 572; τινός, τ 506.

ἀ-στᾰχύεσσιν (from ἄσταχυς), aristis, *with its ears of grain*, Β 148†. [ᾰ̆]

ἀ-στεμφέα, ές, acc., *firm, persistent, unyielding*, Γ 219; adv. **-ές**, δ 419, 459.

Ἀστέριον, τό, a town in Θεσσαλία, Β 735†.

Ἀστερίς, an imaginary island S. of Ithaka, δ 846†.

ἀστερόεντος, ι, α, (nom. -όεις; ἀστήρ), stellatus, *starry*, ι 527; *spangled* (for ornament), Π 134 and Σ 370. (See cut on follg. page, also No. 22.)

Ἀστεροπαῖος, son of Πελάγων, leader of Λύκιοι, Μ 102, Φ 179.

ἀστεροπή, ἡ, *lightning*. (Il.)

ἀστεροπητής, Ὀλύμπιος, fulminator, *sender of lightning*, Α 580. (Il.)

ἀστήρ, -έρος, ἀστράσι, dat. pl., stella, star, e. g. Sirius, E 5, X 26; ἕσπερος, X 317, ν 93; stella cadens, falling star, Δ 75.

ἀστοί (ἄστυ), citizens, Λ 242 and ν 192.

ἀστράγαλον, acc., -ων, -οισι, (strangulare?), neck-vertebra, κ 560; pl., game of dice, cf. our jack-stones, Ψ 88. (See cut, after an ancient painting in Resina.) [ă]

ἀστράπτει, aor. part. -άψας, (ἀστεροπή), fulgurat, gleams, lightens, B 353. (Il.)

ἄστρα, τά, astra, constellations, μ 312; sank toward the horizon, K 252.

ἄστυ, εος, (Fάστυ), habitations, α 3; city, e. g. Ἴμβρου; ἄστυδε, in urbem, κ 104; P 144, civitatem et urbem.

Ἀστύαλος, a Trojan, Z 29†. [ŭ]

Ἀστυ-άναξ, epithet conferred by Trojans, in honor of Hektor, upon Σκαμάνδριος, his son, Z 403.

ἀστῠ-βοώτην, acc., (βοάω), calling throughout the city, Ω 701†.

Ἀστύ-νοος, (1) son of Προτιάων, a Trojan, O 455†.—(2) a Trojan leader, E 144†. [ŭ]

Ἀστῠ-όχεια, mother of Τληπόλεμος, B 658†.

Ἀστῠ-όχη, mother of Ἀσκάλαφος and Ἰάλμενος, B 513†.

Ἀστύ-πῠλος, a Paionian, Φ 209†. [ŭ]

ἀ-σύφηλον, ntr., insulting, I 647 and Ω 767. [ŭ]

ἀ-σφᾰλές (σφάλλω) αἰεί, immutable, ζ 42, = ἀσφαλέως, P 436; θ 171, steadily, without faltering.

Ἀσφᾰλίων, servant of Μενέλαος, δ 216†. [ῐ]

ἀ-σφάρᾰγον, τόν, (φάρυγξ?), windpipe, X 328†. [ă]

ἀ-σφοδελὸν λειμῶνα, acc., asphodel-meadow, λ 539. (The asphodel is a plant of the lily kind.) (Od.)

ἀ-σχᾰλάᾳ, -όωσι, 3 sing. pl., -άαν inf., -όων prs. part., (σχολή), be impatient, B 297; τινός, at —, τ 159, 534; to be beside one's self (with grief), X 412. [ă]

ἄ-σχετος, ον, (and ἀάσχετον), irresistible, E 892; μένος, in courage, β 85; overpowering grief, Π 549, Ω 708.

Ἀσωπός, a river in Βοιωτία, Δ 383.

ἀ-τάλαντος (σα-, τάλαντα), balancing, equal, τινί (θεόφιν, γ 110, 409); μῆτιν, in counsel. (Il.) [ă]

ἀ-τᾰλά-φρονα, acc., harmless, tender, Z 400†.

ἄταλλε, ipf., skip, gambol (cf. Psalm 104, 26), N 27†. [ă]

ἀτᾰλαί, -ῇσι, and -ὰ φρονέοντες, frisking; λ 39, Σ 567, light hearted. [⏑⏑⏑]

ἀτάρ (from αὖ, τε, ἀρ? ἀτάρ, ε 108, τ 273), sed, but, however, α τ, but, yet.—(1) after μέν, A 166, Z 86, 125; also ἀτὰρ αὖτε, K 420; attamen, and yet, after ἦ μήν, vero, verily, I 58.—(2) without μέν, introducing a new thought. δ 236, A 506, B 313; after μάψ, B 214; after voc. not easily translatable, for indeed, Z 429 (in contrast with 413–28), X 331.—(3) after ἐπεί, in apodosis, M 144; following a wish, φ 404. [⏑⏑]

ἀ-ταρβής (τάρβος), impavidus, fearless, N 299†. [ă]

ἀ-τάρβητος (ταρβέω), impavidus, fearless, intrepid, Γ 63†. [ἄ]

ἀ-ταρπῑτός, ἡ, (ἀταρπός), path, Σ 565 and ρ 234. [ᾰ]

ἀ-ταρπόν, τήν, (τραπῆναι?), semita, path, footway, P 743 and ξ 1. [ᾰ]

ἀ-ταρτηρέ, -οῖς, (τάρταρος?), infernal, horrible, A 223. [ᾰ]

ἀτασθᾰλίαι, αἱ, (ἀτάσθαλα), scelus, wantonness (sin), μ 300. [ᾰ ῐ]

ἀτασθάλλων, -ουσα, prs. part., (ἀτάσθαλα), acting wantonly, σ 57 and τ 88. [ᾰ]

ἀτάσθᾰλος, ον, (ἄτη), scelestus, wanton, presumptuous, wicked, ῥίζειν, ἑώργει; esp. μηχανάασθαι ἀτάσθαλα, practice wickedness, X 418, π 86. [ᾰ] ἅ τε, never as in Attic=tanquam, see ὅς τε.

ἀ-τειρής, -έα, -έας, (τείρω), not to be worn out, (1) hard, χαλκός.—(2) unyielding, enduring, Γ 60, Ο 697. [ᾰ]

ἀ-τέλεστος, -ον, -α, (τέλος), without purpose, without result, unaccomplished; π 111, without ceasing. [ᾰ]

ἀ-τελεύτητον, -ῳ, (τελευτάω), unfulfilled, Δ 175 (cf. π 111), unfinished.

ἀ-τελής (τέλος), unaccomplished, ρ 546†.

ἀτέμβω (ἀτέων), only pres., act. and pass., vex, deceive, pass. carere, be deprived of, be without, τινός, ι 42, Ψ 445, 834.

ἄτερ, with gen., sine, without, E 473; Ζηνός (cf. β 372), invito Jove; procul, apart from, A 498.

ἀ-τέραμνον (τείρω), hard, ψ 167†. [ᾰ]

ἀ-τερπής, -έα, (τέρπω), joyless region, η 279; T 354, tormenting. [ᾰ]

ἀ-τέρπου, gen., (τέρπω), doleful, Z 285†. [ᾰ]

ἀτέοντα, acc. part. from ἀτέω (ἄτη), temerarius, foolhardy, Υ 332†. [‿ ‿‿ ‿]

ἄτη, ης, (ἀάω), noxa, bane, hurt, μ 372; folly, infatuation, B 111, Θ 237; euphemistically for sin, crime, Z 356, δ 261, T 270. [ᾰ]

ἀ-τίζων, part. from ἀτίζω (τίω), contemnens, unheeding, Υ 166†. [ᾰ]

ἀ-τῑμάζω, ipf. iter. ἀτιμάζεσκε, aor. ἠτίμασε,(ἀτιμάω),despicere,treat with disrespect, dishonor, φ 332, σ 144, A 11. [ᾰ]

ἀ-τῑμάω, ipf. ἀτίμα, fut. and aor. ἠτίμησα (τιμάω), despicere, treat with contempt, Ξ 127; maltreat, A 356, ξ 57. [ᾰ]

ἀ-τίμητον (τιμή), contemtum, despised, μετανάστην, I 648 and Π 59. [ᾰ]

ἀ-τίμησιν (ἄτιμος), assail with insults, ν 142†. [ᾰ]

ἀ-τῑμος (τιμή), inhonoratus, despised; comp. -ότερον, sup. -οτάτη; π 431, without making return. [ᾰ]

ἀ-τῑτάλλω, inf. ἀτιταλλέμεναι, ipf. ἀτίταλλεν, aor. ἀτίτηλα; pass. part. prs. ἀτιταλλομένην, rear, of gods, Ω 60; of men, λ 250; of animals, ο 174. [ᾰ]

ἀ-τῑτος (τίω), unpaid (penalty for), Ξ 484; unavenged, N 414.

Ἄτλας, αντος, father of Καλυψώ, η 245, α 52.

ἄ-τλητον, -ῳ, (τλῆναι), unendurable, I 3 and T 367.

ἄτος (ἄ-ατος, ἄμεναι), insatiabilis, insatiable, τινός, ν 293. (Il.)

ἀ-τρᾰπῑτοί = ἀταρπιτοί, paths, ν 195†.

Ἀτρεΐδης, ου, son of Atreus, title of Ἀγαμέμνων and of Μενέλαος; also in pl. and du., ω 24, λ 397, A 16, 17, Γ 182.

Ἀτρεΐων, ωνος, son of Ἀτρεύς, Ἀγαμέμνων, A 387, B 192. (Il.)

ἀ-τρεκές (ἄτρακτος), ntr. as adv., undistorted, real, true, E 208; adv. -έως, truly, ρ 154.

ἀ-τρέμα and before vowels (exc. O 318) ἀτρέμας (τρέμω), motionless, τ 212; calm, B 200.

Ἀτρεύς, father of Ἀγαμέμνων and of Μενέλαος; his sceptre, B 105.

ἀ-τρίπτους (τρίβω), not hardened, tender, φ 151†.

ἄ-τρομος, ον,(τρόμος),intrepidus, fearless, E 126. (Il.)

ἀ-τρῠγέτοιο, ον, gen. acc., (τρύω), unwasting, restless, unresting, epith. of the sea, and P 425, of αἰθήρ, glimmering; the ancients derived the word from τρυγᾶν, unfruitful; opp. γαίην πολυφόρβην, A 316.

Ἀτρῠτώνη, Διὸς τέκος—, (ὀτρύνω), Ἀθηναίη, δ 762.

ἄττᾰ (cf. in Swiss dialect Aetti), term of endearment used in addressing elders=father, π 31.

ἀτυζομένω, ω, part. pres., and aor.

ἀτυχθείς, from ἀτύζω (ἄτη?), strictly, *blinded*, *dazed*, *frightened*; *fleeing bewildered* over the plain, Z 38; *terrified at*, Z 468; *amazed*, ψ 42. [ă]

Ἀτυμνιάδης, son of Ἀτύμνιος, Μύδων, E 581†. [ă]

Ἀτύμνιος, son of Ἀμισώδαρος, Π 317, 328.

αὖ, rursus, *again*, *on the contrary*, adversative conjunction, (1) nearly equals δέ, B 493; after μέν, Λ 109; νῦν αὖ, but now, ν 149; εἰ δ' αὖ, σ 371; but if *on the contrary*; *again*, *moreover*, B 671, 678, 681, Γ 200.—(2) *on the other hand*, Γ 323, Δ 240; δ' αὖ, but *again*, Δ 17, Z 229; esp. freq., τὸν δ' αὖ ἀντίον ηὔδα, α 213, 230.—(3) denuo, *also*, *again*, A 540, υ 88; αὖ νῦν, ε 129, δεύτερον αὖ.

ἀυαίνω, **ἀυανθέν**, aor. pass. part., (αὔω), siccatum, *when it was dry*, ι 321†.

αὐγάζομαι (αὐγή), *discern*, Ψ 458†.

Αὔγειαι, town, (1) of Λάκωνες, B 583†.—(2) of Λοκροί, B 532†.

Αὐγείας, ao, father of Ἀγαμήδη, Λ 701, 739.

αὐγή, ῆς, *bright light, radiance*, N 341, ζ 305; pl., *beams*, of sun, of light of day, Διός, N 837.

Αὐγηιάδης, son of Αὐγείας, Ἀγασθένης, B 624†.

αὐδάω, imp. **αὔδα**, ipf. ηὔδα, aor. (iter. αὐδήσασκε), part. αὐδήσας, *speak*, ἔπος, Z 54, ν 199; ἀντίον—τινά, alloqui, *address*, Γ 203; ἔπος, E 170; μεγάλα, *boast* loudly, δ 505.

αὐδή, ῆς, *voice*, A 249, Σ 419, T 418; φ 411 (of the swallow).

αὐδήεις, εσσα, *speaking with human voice*, T 407, ε 334; v. l. οὐδήεσσα, *earthly*.

αὐ-έρυον, ipf., aor. αὐ-έρυσαν (ἀν-Fερύω), *draw out*, M 261; *bend back* (head of victim), A 459.

αὔη, **αὔῃ**, see αὖοι, accenderet.

αὖθ', (1) = αὖτε.—(2) Λ 48, M 85, β 369, σ 48 = αὖθι.

αὖθι, (1) eodem loco, *on the spot*, *here*, *there*, A 492; with following determination of place by prep., ι 29.— (2) illico, *at once*, σ 339.

αὐίαχοι, pl., (ἀ-Fίαχοι), *speechless*, N 41†. (Others interpret, *shouting loudly*.)

αὐλείου, γσι, (αὔλειος, αὐλή), *belonging to the* αὐλή, *of the court*, α 104. (Od.)

αὐλή, ῆς, (FΑΣ), *court enclosure*, (1) before the house; with gate, gate-way, portico, stables, slave-quarters, altar, and θόλος; see table III.—(2) before the cave of Πολύφημος, ι 239; before the tent of Ἀχιλλεύς, Ω 452; round the palace of Αἴολος, κ 10. αὐλῃ, v. l. instead of αὐλῇ, κ 10.

αὐλιζομενάων, pres. part. from αὐλίζομαι (αὐλή), *penned in*, μ 265. (Od.)

αὖλιν, acc., (ἰαύω), *place of repose*, χ 470.

Αὐλίς, ίδος, rendezvous of Greeks before sailing for Troja, town in Βοιωτία, B 303.

αὐλός, οῦ, (ἀFῆναι), (1) *wind instrument*, *flute*, Σ 495, K 13.—(2) *socket* in which point of lance was fitted, P 297; *holes* or *eyes*, receiving the tongue of a buckle, τ 227.—(3) *stream of blood*, χ 18.

αὐλῶπις, ιδι, (αὐλός), *with upright socket* to receive the plume, E 182. (Il.) (See *b* in cut; see also cuts 17, 18, 122.)

αὖος, 3, (εὔω), siccus, *dry*, P 493, αὖον, of sound, *dull*, *hollow*, *grating*, M 160, N 441.

ἄ-υπνος, -ους, (ὕπνος), *sleepless*, (1) of persons, ι 404, κ 84.—(2) νύκτας, ι 325. [ă]

αὔρη (ἄFημι), aura, *breeze*, ε 469†.

αὔριον (ἦρι), *to-morrow morning*, θ 535, η 318.

ἀυσταλέος (αὖος), squalidus, *unanointed*, *unkempt*, τ 327†. [ă]

αὐτ-άγρετα, ntr. pl., (ἀγρεῖν), *self-chosen*, *attainable*, π 148†.

αὐτάρ (αὖτε, ἄρα), but, *however*, adversative conj., differing from δέ chief-

ly in marking a contrast more strongly, (1) after μέν, A 127, B 103, a 215;
also αὐτὰρ ὁ αὖτε, B 107, and αὐτὰρ
ἄρα, B 103; after εἰ —, Γ 290; after
a wish, φ 404.—(2) at beginning of
sentence, but, yet, now, A 118, 348;
αὐτὰρ ὁ, Γ 18; in transitions esp. with
ἐπεί, ἐπήν, A 458, 464, 467, ω 467.
[-- ~, the first syllable always in arsi.]
αὖτε (αὖ, -τε), lit. on that occasion;
then, further, moreover, but, (1) adversative, with νῦν, A 237; τότε, B 221;
ἔνθα, Z 234; Γ 180, also; further, B
407, and δεύτερον αὖτε; on the other
hand, H 345; with δέ, Γ 76, 121, β 203,
331; like δὲ in apodosis, A 137, Δ 321.
—(2) hereafter, A 340, B 225, 370;
again (in disapproval), A 202; cf. also
Z 73, 81, H 335.

ἀϋτέω (2 αὖω), only ipf. 3 sing. and
pl. ἀϋτει, ἀϋτευν, call aloud, Υ 50, Φ
582; call upon, Λ 258; of things, ring,
resound, M 160. [ᾰ]

ἀϋτή, ῆς, (2 αὖω), cry, ζ 122, B 153;
esp. battle-cry, Δ 331, Ξ 96; battle, O
718.

αὐτ-ῆμαρ (ἦμαρ), on the same day, γ
311; A 81, to-day.

αὐτίκα (cf. ἡνίκα, πόκα), forthwith,
straightway, ξ 403, Δ 160, A 199; often
with νῦν, Z 308; ἐπεί, M 393; ἔπειτα,
T 242; μάλα, κ 111.

αὖτις (αὖ, τέ), again, rursus, back
again, A 425, B 208; with ἄψ, φ 139;
πάλιν, E 257; once more, again, A 513,
522, H 462, Δ 15, κ 461, see ἐξαῦτις;
on the other hand, in turn, H 170, o 439;
another time, in future, Γ 440, a 317.

ἀϋτμή, -ήν, (German Athem; ἀϜῆ-
ναι?), breath, Ι 609, Ξ 174; μ 369,
scent; scorching heat, ι 389; blast, λ 400,
Σ 471. [ᾰ]

ἀϋτμένα, acc. from ἀϋτμήν, masc.,
(ἀϋτμή), breath, Ψ 765; blast, γ 289.

αὐτο-δίδακτος (διδάσκω), self-taught,
χ 347†.

αὐτόδιον (αὐτοῦ), e vestigio,
straightway, θ 449†.

αὐτό-ετες (ἔτος), in the same year, γ
322†.

αὐτόθ' = αὐτόθι.

αὐτόθεν (αὐτ-οῦ), from the very spot,
Υ 120; elsewh. with ἐξ—. from one's
seat, chair, T 77, ν 56, φ 420.

αὐτόθι (= αὐτοῦ), on the spot, K 443;
often with more definite limitation fol-

lowing: e.g. ἀγρῷ, ruri, λ 187; or ἐν,
with dat., ι 29; κατ', K 273.

αὐτο-κᾱσιγνήτη, soror germana,
own sister, κ 137†.

αὐτο-κᾱσίγνητος, ον, frater ger-
manus, Γ 238; see κασίγνητος. (Il.)

Αὐτό-λυκος, ον, father of Ἀντίκλεια,
mother of Ὀδυσσεύς, τ 394 to 466, K 267.

αὐτό-μᾱτος, 3, (μέμαα), sponta-
neus, of one's own accord, B 408. (Il.)

Αὐτο-μέδων, οντος, son of Διώρης,
charioteer of Ἀχιλλεύς, P 536, Π 145.

Αὐτο-νόη, handmaid of Πηνελόπεια,
σ 182†.

Αὐτό-νοος, (1) a Greek, Λ 301†.—
(2) a Trojan, Π 694†.

αὐτο-νυχί (νύξ), this very night, Θ 197†.

αὐ-τός, ή, ό, lit. again he, (1) idem,
same, pron. of identity, preceding subst.,
θ 107, M 225; with demonstr. (τόν), Z
391, δ 654, A 338, η 55.—(2) ipse,
pron. of emphasis, opposition, A 47, 51,
112, 161, Γ 301, A 4, λ 602; immediately under, N 615; middle of the
road, κ 158; dat. (with and without
σύν), together with, Ι 194, θ 186, ν 118;
of one's own free will, β 168, θ 218;
alone, Θ 99, N 729; often with preceding pers. pron., τ 93, γ 49, ξ 331, Ψ
312, a 279, K 389, Ω 292; pers. pron.
must sometimes be supplied, χ 38, Ω
430, B 263; with enclitic pron. forms
preceding, ε 179, 190, K 242, β 33, λ
134, δ 66; following, E 459, χ 345, X
346, δ 244; in reflexive sense, φ 249, ξ
51, θ 68, κ 416, β 125, δ 247, H 338;
with possessive prons., a 409, χ 218, π
197, K 204, o 262, δ 643, O 39, β 138.
—(3) as pron. 3 pers. (only in oblique
cases), Λ 633, κ 302, β 154, P 546, B 347.

αὐτο-στᾰδίη, ἐν—, (ἵστασθαι), hand-
to-hand fight, N 325†.

αὐτο-σχεδίη, -ην, (σχεδόν), close
combat, O 510; acc. cominus.

αὐτο-σχεδόν, -ά, (σχεδόν), cominus,
hand to hand, O 386, Π 319.

αὐτοῦ (αὐτός), eodem loco, on the
spot, usually more closely defined by
following preposition, θ 68; illico, β
250. Φ 114; hic, ibi.

αὐτόφι(ν) = αὐτῷ, T 255; = αὐτῶν,
Λ 44; = αὐτοῖς, N 42; always with
prep.

Αὐτό-φονος, father of Πολυφόντης
of Θήβη, Δ 395†.

αὐτο-χόωνον, acc., (χόανος) τύλον,

of mass of stone in its natural rough shape, *massive* quoit, Ψ 826†.

αὔ-τως (αὐτός), (1) eodem modo, *just so*, X 125 ; esp. ὡς δ' αὔτως, *so in this very way*, ζ 166.—(2) sponte, *even without this*, A 520 ; *utterly, simply*, B 138, v 379, Γ 220, Z 400, Ψ 268 ; just as you are, Σ 198. — (3) sic (temere), *thus*, with ellipsis, as you propose, as he was, A 133, v 130 ; *in vain*, B 342. (Reading often doubtful between αὔτως and οὔτως.)

αὐχενίους, acc. pl., (αὐχήν), τένοντας, *neck* sinews, γ 450†.

αὐχήν, ένος, ὁ, cervices, *neck*, of men and animals, Z 117, κ 559.

αὐχμεῖς, 2 sing. prs. from αὐχμέω (αὐχμός), *be dry*, i.e. *unanointed, squalid*, ω 250†.

1. αὔοι (αὔω, εὔω), accenderet, where *he could not obtain fire* from other source, v.l. αὔῃ, that *he may not be forced to seek fire* from elsewhere, ε 490†.

2. αὔω, only ipf. **αὖε**, and 1 aor. **ἤϋσε** and ἄϋσε (ἀϋσαι, ἀϋσας, etc.), *call aloud*, (1) vocare, *call upon*, τινά, Λ 461, N 477, ι 65.—(2) clamare, *call aloud*, of things, *ring*, with μέγα, δεινόν, καρφαλέον ; αὖον, of harsh, dry sound (cf. aridum) ; διαπρύσιον, piercingly ; (ἐπὶ) μακρόν, so as to be heard a great distance, aloud (E 347, Θ 160), Γ 81, ζ 117.

ἀφ-αιρέω, fut. mid. -αιρήσεσθαι; aor. -εῖλον, etc., also ἀπο-αίρεω, pres. imp., (Ϝαίρεω?), -εῖσθαι, ἀπο-Ϝεῖλε(το), often in tmesi, adimere, (1) act., *take away*, ι 313 ; τί τινος, Ε 127, ι 416 ; τί τινι, ξ 455.—(2) *take away to hold for one's self*, Γ 294, Π 54, I 336 ; τινά τι, Θ 108, X 18, A 182 ; *remove from one's self*, μ 199 ; *take away*, A 299, ζ 91 ; θυμόν (life) τινος, and τινά ; *frustrate*, νόστον, νόστιμον ἦμάρ τινι, βίας τινός ; *take off* armor, ὤμων, Η 122 ; ὤμοϊιν, Π 560.

ἀ-**φάλον** (φάλος), *without crest*, ταυρείην—τε καὶ ἄλλοφον, K 258†. [ᾰ]

ἀφ-ἄμαρτεν, -ών, -ούσῃ, and **ἀπ-ήμβροτεν**, aor. from ἀμαρτάνω—τινός, (1) *miss*, deerrare a, Θ 302.—(2) *lose*, orbari, Z 411. (Il.)

ἀφ-ἄμαρτο-επής, *missing the point, rambling speaker*, Γ 215†.

ἀφ-ανδάνει (ἀνδάνω), *displeases*, π 387†.

ἄ-φαντος, -οι, (φαίνω), *unseen, leaving no trace behind*, Z 60†. (II.)

ἄφαρ, statim, *at once, instantly*, Φ 528. When joined with δέ (exc. Ψ 593, θ 409) it begins the sentence ; when used alone, it follows one or more words. [◡◡]

Ἀφάρεύς, ῆος, Καλητορίδης, name of a Greek leader, N 541.

ἀφ-αρπάξαι, aor. inf., (ἁρπάζω), deripere, τι τινός, *wrench away from*, N 189†.

ἀφάρ-τεροι, celeriores, *swifter*, Ψ 311†.

ἀφαυροῦ, -ότερος, -ον, -ότατος, -η, (φάϝος), *insignificant*, debilis, *weakly*, Η 235, v 110.

ἀφάω, **ἀφόωντα**, (ἅπτω), tractantem, *busy with handling*, τι, Z 322†. [ᾰ]

Ἀφείδας, αντος, Πολυπημονίδης, fictitious, assumed name, ω 305†.

ἀφείη, aor. opt. from ἀφίημι, iacularetur.

ἄφενος (opes), *possessions*, esp. in cattle, ξ 99, A 171. [ᾰ]

ἀφ-έξω, -ξομαι, fut. from ἀπέχω, prohibebo.

ἀφ-ήμενος (ἧμαι), seorsum sedens, *sitting apart*, O 106†. [ᾰ]

ἀφ-ήτορος, gen. (ἀφίημι), sagittarii, *of the archer*=ἑκηβόλου, I 404†. [ᾰ]

ἄ-φθῖτος, 2, (φθίω), aeternus, *unwasting, imperishable*, only of possessions, exc. I 413, Ω 88.

ἀφ-ίημι, reg., collat. forms of ipf. ἀφίει, ἠφίει, aor. ἀφέηκε, subj. -ίῃ, -ῇσ, opt. -είη (ἵημι), dimittere, (1) *send away*, A 25 ; *drive away*, B 263, Λ 642 ; *shed blossom*, η 126 ; *let fall*, M 221 ; μένος, *slackened* its force, N 444 ; *release*, Υ 464 ; mid. ψ 240 ; pass., *are emitted from*, Δ 77.—iaculari, *hurl* weapons, lightning, etc., K 372, Ψ 432, P 631, χ 251, ω 539, Θ 133. [◡◡–◡ ; χ 251 ◡–◡◡.]

ἀφ-ικάνω (ἱκάνω), pervenio, *come to, reach*, πρός τι, Z 388 ; δεῦρο, huc, Ξ 43 (Od. only with acc.).

ἀφ-ίκομαι, only fut. -ίξεαι, perf. inf. -ῖχθαι, aor. -ικόμην, etc. (tmesis, μ 2), pervenio, with acc., *come to* (a person), *arrive at* (a place), φ 25, a 332, φ 42, o 489, also with εἰς, ἐπί, ποτί,

-ίστημι 63 Ἀχαιοί

κατά, ὑπό ; reach, Ω 329, θ 202 ; Σ 395,
trouble came upon me.
ἀφ-ίστημι, I. trans., only mid. ἀποστήσωνται, demand pay for themselves for,
N 745.—II. intr., -ίσταμαι, pf. -έστατε,
-έστᾶσιν, -έσταίη, -έσταύτες, plupf.
-έστασαν, aor. -έστη, stand away, stand
off, Ψ 517, N 738 ; νόσφιν, λ 544 ;
τινός, from a person, ψ 101 ; from a
thing, Δ 340.
ἄ-φλαστον, aplustre, ornamental
knob on stern of ship, figure-head, O 717†.
[᷍ ᷍ ᷍ — ᷍] (See cut, also No. 41.)

ἀ-φλοισμός (φλοῖσβος), spuma,
foam, O 607†.
ἀφνειός, 2, -ότεροι, -ότατος, (ἄφενος),
opulentus, wealthy, rich in, τινός
(means of subsistence, gold, etc.);
flourishing house, α 232 ; coupled with
μέγα δυναμένοιο, λ 414.
ἀφ-ωπλίζοντο (ὁπλίζω), ipf., ἔντεα,
laid off their armor, Ψ 26†.
ἀφ-ορμηθεῖεν, opt., and -θέντες, aor.
pass. part., (ὁρμάω), proficisci, ναύ-
φιν, set out from the ships ; depart, β
375.
ἀφόωντα, sec ἀφάω, tractantem.
ἀ-φραδέουσι, pres. indic., -έοντι,
part. (ἀ-φραδής), amentem esse, be
foolish, η 294, I 32.
ἀ-φραδέες, έων, (φράζομαι), senseless,
λ 476 ; foolish, β 282 ; adv. -έως, foolishly, Γ 436.

ἀ-φραδίη, dat. sing., (φράζομαι), ig-
norance, B 368 ; elsewh. dat. pl. -ίῃσι,
folly, Π 354, ξ 481 ; νόοιο, K 122.
ἀ-φραίνω (φρήν), be mad, H 109, v
360.
ἄφρεον, ipf. (ἀφρός), spumabant.
breasts were covered with foam, Λ 282†.
[᷍ ᷍᷍ = ἄφρευν.]
ἀ-φρήτωρ (φρήτρη), no respecter of
race, I 63†.
Ἀφροδίτη, ης, daughter of Ζεύς, Γ
374, Υ 105 ; and of Διώνη, E 370 ; also
Κυθέρεια, Κύπρις, from her seats of
worship ; δῖα, ἐυστεφάνου, φιλομμειδής,
χρυσέη ; wife of Ἥφαιστος, θ 267 sq. ;
goddess of love, E 429, δ 261, Γ 54 ; and
of beauty, Τ 282 ; of love's charms, Ξ
214 (see κεστός) ; attended by Χάριτες,
σ 192 ; mother of Αἰνείας. As common
noun = hot passion, χ 444.
ἀ-φρονέοντες, pres. part., (ἄφρων),
foolish, O 104†.
ἀφρός, οῦ, spuma, foam of waves,
of lion, Υ 168. (Il.)
ἀφροσύνης, -άων, gen., (ἄφρων),
folly, H 110 ; pl., foolish behavior, π
278, ω 457.
ἄ-φρων, -ονι, -ονα, (φρήν), thoughtless, Δ 104, E 875, Λ 389 ; Ω 157,
foolish.
ἀ-φύλλοισιν, dat. pl., (φύλλον), leaf-
less, stripped of leaves, B 425†. [ἄ]
ἀφύξειν, fut. from ἀφύσσω.
ἀ-φυσγετόν, acc., slime, Λ 495†. [ᾱ]
ἀφύσσων, ipf. ἄφυσσεν, -ον, fut. ἀφύξειν, aor. ἠφύσαμεν, part. ἀφύσσας, mid.
ipf. ἠφύσσετο, aor. ἠφυσάμην, ἀφυσσά-
μεθα, ἀφυσσάμενος, fundere, draw,
pour into (mid. for one's self), wine or
water, ι 9, 85 ; with ἀπὸ, ἐκ, ἐν, or with
simple gen., ψ 305 ; η 286, I was scattering the leaves over myself ; Α 171,
do I intend to acquire for thee, σοί.
Ἀχαιαί, Achaian women (with beautifully braided hair). (Od.) [ᾰ]
Ἀχαιάδες, ων, E 422, Achaian
women, E 424 (with beautiful mantles).
[ᾰ]
Ἀχαϊκόν, acc. msc. and ntr. nom.,
Achaian, I 521, 141, γ 251. [ᾰ]
Ἀχαΐς, ίδος, land of Ἀχαιοί, Achaia
Northern Greece, Γ 75, λ 166, ν 249, Α
254, φ 107 ; pl. as subst., Achaian women
I 395 ; contemptuously, B 235. [ᾰ]
Ἀχαιοί, ῶν, chief tribe of Greeks in
Θεσσαλία, Μεσσήνη, Ἄργος, Ἰθάκη ;

collective appellation of the Greeks, A 2, a 90 ; epithets, ἀρηϊφίλων, δῖοι, ἑλίκωπες, ἐυκνήμιδες, κάρη κομόωντες (κοῦροι), μεγάθυμοι, μένεα πνείοντες, χαλκοχιτώνων. [ᾰ]

ἀ-χᾰρίστερον (ἄχαρι.., ingratins, more unwelcome, υ 392†. [ᾰ]

ἀ-χάριστα, ntr. pl., (χάρις), ingrata, unpleasing, θ 236†. [ᾰ]

Ἀχελώϊος, river-god, (1) in Greece (Αἰτωλία), Φ 194†.—(2) in Φρυγία, Ω 616†.

ἀχέρδῳ (ἡ ἄχερδος), wild pear-tree, ξ 10†. [ᾰ]

ἀχερωΐς, white poplar, N 389. (Il.) [ᾰ]

Ἀχέροντα, acc., (Ἀχέρων, ἀ-χέρων, cuncta abripiens), the chasm, abyss (not river), of lower world, κ 513†. [ᾰ]

ἀχεύων, prs. part., (ἄχος), troubled for, τινός, ξ 40 ; εἴνεκα, φ 318 ; θυμόν, grieved at heart. [ᾰ]

ἀχέων, ουσα, part. prs. (ἄχος), grieving, τινός, B 694 ; κῆρ, at heart. [ᾰ]

ἄχθομαι, ipf. ἤχθετο (ἄχθος), (1) be laden, ο 457.—(2) moleste fero, take ill, be pained or afflicted with, τί, N 352, E 361 ; ὀδύνῃσι, tormented with pains ; κῆρ, vexed at heart.

ἄχθος, τό, (ἄχος), onus, burden, Υ 247 ; ἀρούρης, dead weight upon the earth, of idle, useless man, υ 379.

Ἀχιλεύς, Ἀχιλλεύς, ῆος, (Πηλείδης), son of Πηλεύς and Θέτις, Αἰακίδης, king of Μυρμιδόνες, foster-child of Φοῖνιξ, pupil of Χείρων, hero of the Iliad : his destiny, I 410 sq. ; expedition against Troy, B 681 ; forays, I 328, A 392, B 690, see Βρισηΐς ; μῆνις, A ; πρεσβεία, I ; death of his friend Πάτροκλος, Π 827 ; μηνίδος ἀπόρρησις, T 56 ; Ἕκτορος ἀναίρεσις, X ; Ἕκτορος λύτρα, Ω ; his death, ε 310, ω 37 sq. ; epithets, δαΐφρων, δῖος, διΐφιλος, θεοῖς ἐπιείκελ(ε), θεοείκελ(ε), πελώριον, ποδάρκης δῖος, ποδώκης, πτολιπόρθῳ, ῥηξήνορος, πόδας ταχύν, (πόδας) ὠκύς. (See cut, in next column, from Panathenaic Amphora.)

ἀχλύς, ύος, ἡ, caligo, mist, E 127, Υ 321 ; of death, Π 344 ; swoon, E 696 ; grief, Υ 421. [-⌣⌣, nom. and acc. -⌣.]

ἤχλῦσε, aor. from ἀχλύω, grew dark, μ 406. (Od.)

ἄχνη, ῃ, ην, foam of water, Λ 307 ; chaff, E 499, pl.

ἄχνῦμαι, pres., ἄχνυτο, ipf., (ἀκαχίζω, ἄχος), dolere, grieve, mourn, θυμός (ἐνὶ στήθεσσι, Ξ 38), κῆρ ἄχνυται (ἐν θυμῷ, Z 524), ἀχνυμένῃ κραδίῃ, Ω 584 ; ἀχνυσθαι κῆρ, in heart, ω 420 ; τινός, λ 558, for some one ; with part., Σ 320.

ἄ-χολον, dissipating-wrath, others translate mild, soothing, δ 221†. [ᾰ]

ἄχομαι (ἄχος), only σ 256, τ 129, I mourn. [ᾰ]

ἄχος, εος, τό, also pl., (ἄγχω), grief, pain, τινός, over some one, for something, Θ 124, N 417, ο 358 ; περί, φ 249 ; sorrow seizes, θυμὸν ἵκανεν, ἀμφεχύθη τινά, γένετό τινι (κατὰ θυμόν) ; ἀπὸ πραπίδων ἔλθοι, roll a stone from one's heart ; cf. Υ 282, K 145 ; εἷλε, ἔλλαβε, τύψε τινά (θυμόν), N 581, Ξ 475, T 125 ; τινί ἐστι, I 249 ; ἄχεος νεφέλη, P 591. [ᾰ]

ἀ-χρεῖον, ntr. = adv., (χρεῖος), B 269, looked foolishly about, as one who has no χρεῖος, i. e. knows not what he shall do ; σ 163, constrainedly (a forced laugh without cause) (164, οὔτι πάρος γε).

ἀ-χρημοσύνη (χρήματα), i..opia, *want*, ρ 502†.

ἄχρῐ(ς) (κατ' ἄκρης), prorsus, *altogether*; σ 370, perhaps *until*.

ἀχῠρμῑαί (ἄχυρον), *heaps of chaff*, E 502†. [ᾰ]

ἄψ (ἀπύ), *back, back again*, ἀπονοστήσειν, Θ 499; ἀπιών, Κ 289; with gen. *back from*, Μ 420; ἀπό, Μ 390; ἀποφέρω, Κ 337; and freq. with cmpds. of ἀπό-; with πάλιν, *back again*, Σ 280; αὖτις, Θ 335.

'Α-ψευδής, a Nereid, Σ 46†.

ἀψῐδες, αἱ, (ἄψος), maculae, *meshes*, E 487†.

ἀψο-ρρόου (ῥέω) 'Ωκεανοῖο, of the Okeanos stream which *flows back into itself*, i. e. *encircling*, Σ 399.

ἄψο-ρροι, -ον, (ῥέω, -σροος), reduces, *back*, with verbs of motion; usually ntr., retro, κ 558.

ἄψεα (ἅπτω), artus, *joints, limbs*, δ 794 and σ 189.

ἄω, inf. ἄμεναι, fut. ἄσειν, aor. subj. ἄσῃ, opt. ἄσαιμι, inf. ἄσαι, mid. fut. or aor. imp. ἄσισθε, aor. inf. ἄσασθαι (aveo), (1) satiari, Φ 70, *eager to sate itself* with human flesh; γόοιο ἄσαι, Ψ 157, cf. κλαυθμοῖο ἄσεσθε. — (2) satiare, τινά τινος, E 289; τινί, Λ 817.

ἄωροι (ἀείρω) = μετ-έωροι, penduli, *dangling*, i. e. *formless, useless, misshapen*, μ 89†. [ᾰ]

ἄωρτο, plupf. pass. from ἀείρω, pendebat.

ἀωτεῖς, εἶτε, (from ἀωτίω, ἄημι), dormire, with acc. ὕπνον, Κ 159 and κ 548. [ᾰ]

ἀώτου, ψ, ον, (ἄημι, αϜϜτος), floccus, *lock of wool*, οἰός, α 443; *nap of linen*, Ι 661; *fleece, sheep's wool*, ι 434; on sheep's back; spun, Ν 599. [ᾰ]

B.

βάδην (βαίνω), pedetentim, *step by step, slowly*, Ν 516†.

βάζω, pres., ipf., and perf. pass. βέβακται, loqui, *speak*, esp. with ntr. adjs., e. g. ἄρτια, fit things, Ξ 92; cf. Ι 58, Δ 355, σ 392, δ 32, ξ 127; ἔπος, θ 408.

βᾰθῠ-δῑνήεις, δῑνήεντος, -α, *full of deep eddies*, Φ 15.

βᾰθῠ-δίνης (δῖναι), *deep'-eddying*, Υ 73; always of rivers, exc. κ 511.

βᾰθῠ-ζώνους, acc., (ζώνη), *deep-girdled*, i. e. with girdle low down over the hips, Ι 594. (See cut.)

Βᾰθῠ-κλῆς, ῆα, son of Χάλκων, a Μυρμιδών, Π 594†.

βᾰθῠ-κόλποι, ων, (κόλπος), *with deep folds* or *bellies in garment*, i. e. with garment falling low or in deep folds over and below the girdle, which its folds hid from sight; the word may be translated *deep-girdled*; epithet of Trojan women, Σ 122. (Il.) (See cut.)

βᾰθῠ-λειμον, acc. comm., (λειμών), *with rich meadows*, i. e. *with deep soil*, Ἄνθειαν, Ι 151. (Il.)

βᾰθῠ-λήϊον, *with deep-*, i. e. *high-waving grain, fruitful*, Σ 550†.

βαθύνω, only ipf. βάθυνε, *deepen, hollow out*, Ψ 421†.

βᾰθῠ-ρρείταο (-σρειταο, ῥέω), *deep-flowing* Okeanos, Φ 195†.

βᾰθῠ-ρρόου, όον, (-σροος), *with deep current, deep-streaming* Okeanos, and Φ 8, river.

βᾰθύς, εῖα, (-έης, -έην), ύ, sup. -ιστον, (1) vertically: altus, *high, deep,* Τάρταρος; *low lying,* of court, chasm, plowed land, sandy shore, forest, storm, and fog, Τ 125, *deep* in the heart.—(2) horizontally : *deep, stretching far into* the land; of bay, B 560; of shore pierced by numerous inlets, B 92; to the limits of the *broad* plough-land, Σ 547.

βᾰθύ-σχοινον (σχοῖνος), *deeply overgrown with rushes,* Δ 383†.

βαίνω, ipf., fut., 1 aor. ἔβησα, trans.; 2 aor. ἔβην (βάτην, ἔβαν, subj. βείω, -ῃ or βήῃ, βείομεν, βήμεναι), pf. βέβηκα, *stand, tread* (βεβάασιν, inf. βεβάμεν, part. βεβαώς), fut. mid. βήσομαι, also aor. (ἐ)βήσετο, -σατο, *go, πάλιν, redire;* νόσφι, secedere; B 134, βεβάασι, praeterierunt; *set out,* θ 49; hence often with inf., βῆ (βάν, βεβήκει) δ' ἰέναι, ῥ' ἴμεν, etc., σ 428; with pres. part., B 302, 665, ξ 207; fut., Λ 101; cf. α 424; aor., ω 488, N 582. —(1) *go* (whither?), πῆ, Ζ 377 (B 339, Θ 229, what *is become of?*); χαμᾶζε, with -δε Οὐλυμπόνδε, οἴκαδε, Ἀϊδόσδε, cf. also λ 277, 627; (a) with acc., *go and take one's place by the side of,* Γ 262; with ἀνά, Δ 209; διά, Θ 343; εἴς, ἐς (Ὀδυσῆα, χ 202); κατά, *stalks* over the heads of men, Τ 93; throughout, B 47; go for, δ 701, Α 424; μετά, sequi, β 406; adire, Δ 292, λ 563; aggredi, Π 864; παρά, Τ 40; πρός, Ζ 313; ὑπέρ, χ 182.—(b) with gen. διά, ρ 26; διέκ, σ 185; ἐπί, Ι 589 (χέρσου, ἠπείρου, ἵππων, Ι 589); ὑπέρ, ρ 575; ἰθύς, Ε 849.—(c) with dat. ἀμφί, tueri, *guard,* Α 37; ἐν, N 618; ἐπί, accedere, *draw near,* P 574; aggredi, Λ 460, Π 751.—(2) (where?), ἐπὶ χθονί, incedere, *walk,* Δ 443; ἐν νηυσί, avehi, *sail away,* α 210.—(3)(whence?), ἀπὸ πύργου, κατ' Ἰδαίων ὀρέων; 1 aor. ἀφ' (ἐξ) ἵππων, *cause to dismount, dash down, shoot down;* ἐπὶ Βουπρασίου ἵππους, *bring* horses to Bouprasion.

βάλᾰνον, τήν, glandem, *acorn,* ν 409, and ἄκυλον, edible acorn, κ 242.

Βᾰλίος, one of the horses of Ἀχιλλεύς. Τ 400. (Il.)

βάλλω, reg. as in Attic, exc. fut. βαλέω, aor. subj. βάλῃσθα, opt. βάλοι-

σθα, plupf. 3 sing. βεβλήκειν, pf. pass., 3 pl. βεβλήαται, plupf. -ήατο (the forms βεβολημένος, and plupf. βεβόλητο and 3 pl. -ήατο only of inward [mental] feelings) ; aor. mid. with pass. signif., βλῆτο, subj. βλήεται, opt. βλεῖο, part. βλήμενος, mitto, iacio.—(1) *throw,* Ι 588, *was struck;* esp. tela mittere, *discharge missiles* (opp. ἐλαύνω, ρ 279 ; τύπτειν, Υ 378, Ο 495; οὐτάσαι, Ξ 424); *shoot,* Θ 282, Γ 82; also lapides coicere, *hurl stones.*—(2) *strike, hit,* Φ 591, Λ 380 (and *wound*) ; τόν ῥ' ἔβαλεν κεφαλήν, in the head, etc., Ο 433, Ν 411 ; also κατὰ (ἀσπίδα δουρί, Ε 537), Λ 108, Μ 189, and πρὸς στῆθος, Λ 144; βλῆσθαι, pass., χ 253; ἕλκος, vulnus infligere, *inflict wound;* ἐν κονίῃσι, deicere, *lay low in,* cf. προτὶ γαίῃ, *sink* to the earth, λ 423 ; χαμαί, χ 188; fig., *wounded* (ἦτορ or κῆρ), ἄχεϊ, πένθεϊ; reaih, οὖατα, ἀκτῖσιν, ε 479 ; conspergere, bespatter, ἄντυγα, ἡνίοχον.—(3) in wider signif., mittere, fundere, *send, pour,* ὕπνον ἐπὶ βλεφάροισι, δάκρυ (χαμάδις, δ 114), *let fall,* λ 424, sc. χεῖρας; *shake off,* Ρ 457 (βάλλεσθαι, *discharge, εἰς* ἅλα) ; εἰς κακόν τινα, *plunge, μετὰ* νείκεα, *involve in,* φιλότητα μετά τισιν, *conclude* friendship; ὄμματα ἑτέρωσε, *turn* (περὶ τέρμα, mid. of horses, drive round the turning-post), ἵππους πρόσθε, *drive by;* Ψ 639, πρόσθε, superare, *be superior;* ponere, *place,* esp. *throw* the arms *about* some one, *embrace* (ἀμφί, περί, πρός τινι) (mid. ἐν θυμῷ, φρεσί, animo volvo, *turn over* in mind, Ι 435, μ 218, Α 297; *take* to heart, Ο 566).—(4) amicire, *put on* garments or weapons, also mid., Γ 334 and freq.; *put* wheels *on* axle, ἀμφ' ὀχέεσσιν ; *make fast, ἐφ'* ἱστῷ, μ 423 ; pass., *were spread,* λ 194.

βαμβαίνων (βαίνω, cf. παμφαίνων), trepidans, *quivering* (with terror), Κ 375†.

βάν = ἔβαν (ἔβησαν).

βάπτῃ, subj. from βάπτω, *dips,* ι 392†.

βαρβάρο-φώνων, gen. pl., *harshspeaking,* B 867†.

βάρδιστοι = βράδιστοι, from βραδύς, tardissimi, *slowest.*

βαρέω, only βεβαρηότα, ότες, (βαρύς), gravati, *weighed down with,* οἴνῳ (φρένας, τ 122); γ 139, *drunken.*

βαρύθει (βαρύθω, βαρύς), grave-
scit, pains (me), Π 519†. [‿‿–]
βαρύνω, only ipf. (ἐ)βαρῦνε, pres.
pass. βᾰρύνεται and aor. part. βᾰρυν-
θείς, -θέν (βαρύς), gravare, disable,
χεῖρα; oppress by weight, Θ 308.

βᾰρύς, ύν, ι 257, εῖα,ύ, gravis, heavy
woe, Κ 71; grievous pains, Ε 417; strong
delusion, Β 111; harsh voice, ι 257;
χεῖρες, mighty arms; κῆρες, dread, inexorable; βαρὺ and βαρέα στενάχειν,
moaning loudly, sobbing heavily, ε 420;
esp. βαρὺ στενάχων, θ 95.

βᾰρυ-στενάχων, better βαρὺ στενάχων, see βαρύς.

βᾰσίλεια, ης, αν, fem. of follg., re-
gina, queen; γυναικῶν, queenly dame,
λ 258; princess, ζ 115.

βᾰσῐ-λεύς, ῆος, ὁ, (βάσις, λαός),
leader of people, princeps, (1) subst.,
prince, king, exercising functions of
commander-in-chief, priest, and judge;
nobles, a 394; Σ 556, master, lord.—(2)
used adjectively with ἄναξ, υ 194;
ἀνήρ, Γ 170; comp. βασιλεύτερος, ον,
more kingly; super. -τατος, Ι 69, most
princely.

βᾰσῐλεύεμεν, prs., ipf., fut., regnare, be king (Ζ 425, queen), τισί, Β
206; ἐν τισι, β 47; κατὰ δῆμον, χ 52;
Πύλου, ἐν Ἰθάκῃ.

βᾰσῐληῖδος τιμῆς, regiae digni-
tatis, royal honor, Ζ 193†.

βᾰσῐλήῐον γένος, regium genus,
scion of the royal stock, π 401†.

βάσκ᾽ ἴθι, imp. from βάσκω (βαίνω),
haste and go, Β 8. (Il.)

βαστάζοντα, pres. part., and aor.
ἐβάστασε, grasp, raise, λ 594. (Od.)

βάτην = ἐβήτην, 3 du. aor. from
βαίνω.

Βατίεια, height on the plain of Troy
before the city, Β 813†.

βάτων, gen. pl. from ἡ βάτος, sen-
tis, thorn-bushes, thorns, ω 230†.

βεβάασι, βεβάμεν inf., βέβασαν
plupf., βεβαώς perf. part. from
βαίνω.

βεβαρηότα, see βαρέω, gravatum.

βεβίηκε, pf. from βιάω, coegit.

βεβλήαται, -το, pf. and plupf. pass.
from βάλλω, ictus est, erat.

βεβολήατο, plupf. pass., -ημένος, pf.
pass. part. from βάλλω, ictus.

βεβρώθοις, intensive form of pf.
opt., (βιβρώσκω), devorares, Δ 35†.

βεβρωκώς, βεβρώσεται, pf. part., 3
fut. with pass. signif., from βιβρώσκω.

βέη, βείομαι, see βέομαι.

βείω, aor. subj. = βῶ, see βαίνω.

βέλεμνα, τά, acc., (βάλλω), tela
missiles, flying wide, Ο 484; Χ 206,
sharp.

Βελλερο-φόντης, ῃ, ην, son of Γλαῦκος, Ζ 155, 220. His true name, according to the Scholiast,was Ἱππόνοος.
(Z.)

βέλος, εος, τό, (βάλλω), telum, missile, in widest sense, spear, arrow, stone,
even the foot-stool, ρ 464; and the
rocky mountain-summit, ι 495; Apollo's missiles, see ἀγανός; missiles of
the Εἰλείθυιαι, Λ 269; ἐκ (ὑπὲκ, Σ 232)
βελέων, out of shot, outside of battle;
joined with verbs, Μ 159, Δ 498, Ε 174,
Ε 106, 278, ρ 464, Θ 67, Λ 576.

βέλτερον (Ϝελέσθαι), preferable, better,
more advantageous, with inf., Ο 511;
praestat aut—aut—, quam (cf.
Hor. Sat. 1, 1, 8), Ο 197; with εἰ, ζ
282, if she herself had gone abroad and
found.

βένθος, εος, τό, also pl., (βάθος),
profundum, depth, esp. of the sea,
βένθεα, a 53 (βένθοσδε, δ 780); of the
forest, ρ 316.

βέομαι, βείομαι, (βήομαι), 2 sing.
βέῃ, fut., (βίος), vivam, Ο 194, will not
live, i. e. order my life according to the
will of Zeus. (Il.)

βέρεθρον, ου, τό, (βιβρώσκω), vorago,
abyss, chasm, μ 94.

βῆ = ἔβη.

βηλοῦ, ῷ, masc., (βαίνω), liminis,
threshold, Α 591, Ψ 202. (Il.)

βῆμεν = ἔβημεν, βήμεναι = βῆναι
(βήσαμεν, βῆσε, βήσατο, βήσετο unaugmented forms), see βαίνω.

Βῆσα, town in Lokris, Β 532†.

βήσσης, gen., ῃ, αν, etc., (βαθύς),
glade, glen, valley, ravine, Γ 34, Χ 190,
κ 210.

βητ-άρμονες (βῆναι, ἀρμονία), dancers, θ 250 and 383.

βιάζετε, 2 pl.; elsewh. only prs. ipf.
mid., (βιάζω), domo, vim affero,
constrain, μ 297; mid. also with pass.
signif., Ο 727, Λ 576.

βίαια ἔργα (βία), deeds of violence, β
236†; adv. -αίως, per vim. (Od.)

Βίας, αντος, (1) father of Λαόγονος
and of Δάρδανος, Υ 460†.—(2) leader

of Ἀθηναῖοι, Ν 691†.—(3) from Πύλος,
Δ 296†.

βιάω=βιάζω, pf. βεβίηκε, mid. prs.,
3 pl. ind. βιόωνται, opt. -ῷατο, ipf.
βιόωντο, fut. -βιήσεται, aor. -ατο, beset, Π 22; maltreat, ψ 9; overreach,
Ψ 576; withhold, τινά τι, Φ 451; Λ
558, overmasters.

βίβημι, βιβάσθω, βιβάω, assumed
pres. of βιβάς,-άντα,βιβάσθων(Il.),and
of βιβῶντα acc. masc., βιβῶσα fem.,
stride along, usually with μακρά (βι-
βάσθων so always), Η 213, Ν 809, Γ
22; ι 450, with mighty strides. [‿—]

βιβρώσκω, only βεβρωκώς, χ 403,
βοός, having eaten of; τι, Χ 94; and
βεβρώσεται, β 203, comedetur, shall
be devoured.

βίη, ης, dat. with instr. suffix βίηφιν,
vis, robur, force, strength, Λ 561, Η
288, φ 185, Ο 165, Ρ 569; in periphrasis, e. g. Πριάμοιο, Ἡρακληείη = the
mighty Priamos, Herakles, Γ 105, Β
658; βίηφιν, βίῃ, ο 231, per vim;
οὐκ ἐθέλοντα, Ν 572; ἀέκοντα, Ο 186, α
403; with κάρτος, σ 139, δ 415, ζ 197;
pl. violence, Ψ 713, γ 216; sing., ψ 31;
βίῃ ἀέκοντος (gen. absol.), δ 646, Α
430.

Βι-ήνωρ, ορος, a Trojan, Λ 92†.

βίον, τόν, vitam, life, ο 491. (Od.)

βιός, οἶο, ὁ, arcus, bow, Α 49, Δ
125.

βίοτος, οιο, ὁ, sing., vita, Η 104, α
287; victus, provisions, bona, substance, Ξ 122, γ 301, λ 116, 490, ο 446.

βιόω, only aor. imp. βιώτω, vivat,
let him live, Θ 429; inf. βιῶναι, ξ 359;
mid. ἐβιώσαο, servavisti, hast saved
me, θ 468.

βιῶατο, -ώονται, -ώοντο, see βιάω.

βλάβω (μαλακός), only pass. βλάβεται, pf. βεβλαμμένον, aor. ἐβλάβεν,
βλάβεν = ἐβλάβησαν and βλαφθείς,
etc., act. (ἐ)βλαψας, etc. (see βλάπτω,
debilitare, weaken, injure, physically,
Τ 166, Η 271, Ψ 774; mentally, Χ 15;
φρένας, ξ 178; Ι 512, baffle; impedire, pass., is confused, Τ 82; impede,
Π 331; 660, wounded in the heart (see
also βλάπτω).

βλάπτω, only prs. ipf., (see βλάβω),
impedio, incommode, hinder, ν 22;
τινός, α 195; delude, infatuate (φρένας,
Ο 724), Ι 507, φ 294; τῇ ἐνὶ, entangled
in which, Ο 647; cf. Ζ 39, ὄζῳ ἔνι.

βλεῖο, opt. aor. mid. from βάλλω,
ferireris.

βλεμεαίνει, -ων, prs., (βάλλω?), se
iactare, exult in, always with σθένεϊ,
only θυμός . . . περὶ σθένεϊ βλεμεαίνει,
heart beats high in its strength, Ρ 22†.

βλεφάροϋν, and pl., (τὸ βλέφαρον,
βλέπω), palpebra, eyelid (conceived
of as the seat of sleep), Κ 26, Ξ 165, α
364, μ 366, ι 389.

βλήεται, βλήμενος, aor. mid. from
βάλλω, feriatur.

βλήτροισι, ntr., (βάλλω?), rivets, or
perh. better, rings, bands, Ο 678†.

βληχήν, τήν, (blacterare), bleating,
ὀϊῶν, μ 266†.

βλοσυροῖσι, -ῇσι, (voltuosus),
horridis, horrible, dreadful, Η 212, Ο
608. (Il.)

βλοσυρ-ῶπῐς, ἡ, horrido voltu,
with awful countenance, Λ 36†.

βλωθρή, ήν, procera, tall, Ν 390, ω
234.

βλώσκω, only pf. μέμβλωκε, ρ 190,
and 2 aor. subj. μόλῃ and part., come,
also of time, Ω 781, ρ 190.

βο-άγρια, τά, shields of ox-hide, Μ 22
and π 296.

Βο-άγριος, ον, river of Λοκροί, Β 533.

βοάᾳ, pl. βοόωσι, part. acc. βοόωντα,
pl. -όωντες, aor. ἐβόησα, etc., clamare,
shout, Β 198; resound, Ρ 265; call aloud,
Ι 12, ε 400; with acc. of kindred meaning, μέγα, μακρά, σμερδνόν, ὀξύ.

βόειος, βοείην, ον, etc., (masc. wanting), and βοέον, έη (ntr. wanting), of an
ox or oxen, bubulus, ox- (dung, Ψ
777), esp. of ox-leather, Ε 452, Δ 122 (Ρ
492, shields); freq. as subst. (sc. δορή),
ox-hide, Ρ 389, υ 142 (χ 364 and Σ 582,
with βοός).

βοεύς, dat. pl. βοεῦσι, thongs of ox-
hide, on sails, β 426, ο 291.

βοή, ῆς, ἡ, clamor, cry, esp. cry of
alarm, χ 77, κ 118, ξ 266; and battle-
cry, Λ 50, 500, 530; βοὴν ἀγαθός, good
at the battle-cry, i. e. brave in battle,
hero, γ 311 and freq.; also cry of pain,
of distress, Ζ 465, ω 48, ι 401; βοὴν
ἔχον, sonabant, resounded, Σ 495.

Βοηθοΐδης, Ἐτεωνεύς, ο 95. (Od.)

βοη-θόον (βοῇ θοόν), swift in battle,
warlike, bellicum, Ρ 481; bellico-
sum, Ν 477.

βο-ηλᾰσίη (ἐλαύνω), cattle-lifting, Λ
672.

βοητύς, ἡ, (βοᾶν), vociferatio, clamor, α 369†.

βόθρου, gen. etc., masc., scrobs, hole in the ground, for planting trees, for sacrificial blood, P 58 ; natural trough for washing clothes, λ 25.

Βοίβη, name of town in Θεσσαλίη. Hence Βοιβηὶς λίμνη, Β 712, 711†.

Βοιώτιος, subst., Βοιωτοί, Boiotians, Β 494 and freq. (ll.)

βολαί, άων, ῆσι, fem., (βάλλω), iactus, ictus; ὀφθαλμῶν, glance, δ 150. (Od.)

βόλεται, etc., see βούλομαι.

βομβέω, only aor. βόμβησε, σαν, rang ; θ 190, hummed, whizzed ; μ 204, rushed roaring through the water.

βοόων, -όωντα, -όωντες, see βοάω, clamans.

βορέης, έαο, ὁ, (ὄρος), aquilo, north wind. Personified, Boreas, Ψ 195.

βόσιν, acc. fem., pastum, food, Τ 268†.

βόσκει, prs., ipf. act. and pass. (iter. βοσκέσκοντο), fut. act., pasco, βοῦς, αἶγας, αἰπόλια, κήτεα, μ 97 ; ξ 325, give subsistence; feed, nourish, σ 364; mid., pasci, feed, graze, δ 338, φ 49.

βοτάνης, τῆς, (βόσκω), herba, fodder, grass, Ν 493 and κ 411. [⏑⏑–]

βοτῆρας, τούς, (βόσκω), pastores, shepherds, ο 504†.

βοτοῖσι, τοῖς, ntr., (βόσκω), pecoribus, flocks, Σ 521†.

βοτρυδόν, adv., (βότρυς), like a bunch of grapes, in a swarm, Β 89†.

βότρυες, οἱ, uvae, grape-clusters, Σ 562†.

βού-βοτος, ἡ, (βοτός), cattle-pasture, ν 246†.

βού-βρωστις, ἡ, ravenous hunger, Ω 532†.

βουβῶνα, τόν, inguen, groin, Δ 492†.

βου-γάϊος, ε, braggart, usually derived from βοῦς and γαίω, perh. better, βοῦς, γέγαα, big and awkward as an ox, abusive epithet, applied to a big but cowardly fellow, Ν 824, σ 79.

Βούδειον, town in Φθίη, Π 572†.

βου-κολέων, part. prs., ipf. iter. -κολέεσκες (βου-κόλος), pascere (boves), pasture, E 313 ; but Υ 221, ἵπποι βουκολέοντο, equae pascebantur, graze.

Βου-κολίδης, αο, Σφήλος, Ο 338†.

Βου-κολίων, ωνι, son of Λαομέδων, Ζ 22†.

βου-κόλος, ῳ, ον, οι, ὁ, (-πόλος), cattle-herd, ἄνδρες, Ν 571 ; ἀγροιῶται, λ 293.

βουλευτῆσι (βουλευτής, from βουλεύω), γέρουσι, old men of the council, Ζ 114†.

βουλεύουσιν, inf. -ευέμεν, fut. (inf. βουλευσέμεν), 1 aor. ; mid. prs., Ι 99, 1 aor.,(βουλῇ), take counsel, deliberate, Β 347 ; with βουλήν, -άς, Ι 75, Κ 147 ; discuss, discourse with one another, Α 531, ν 439 ; ἐς μίαν (βουλήν), Β 379, harmoniously ; meditari, meditate, τί, Κ 311 ; devise, ε 179 (mid., Β 114); suggested this plan, ε 23 ; bethink one's self, ὅπως, ι 420 ; think of, with inf., ι 299.

βουλή, ῆς, ἡ, consilium, (βούλομαι), (1) will, Διός, Α 5, Μ 241 ; and decree, Ζηνός, (θεῶν), Η 45, Ρ 469 ; plan, β 372 ; designs, counsels, Διός, Ν 524, θ 82 ; θεῶν, λ 276 ; cf. 437.—(2) proposal, counsel, κ 46, ξ 337, μ 339, Κ 43 ; ἀρίστη φαίνετο, freq. πυκινὴν ἠρτύνετο, callidum struebat consilium, Β 55 ; pl. plans, μητιόωντες, Υ 154, Β 340.— (3) discernment, shrewdness, Λ 627, Ν 728, Ι 54, λ 177, μ 211.—(4) council of nobles, cf. senatus; opp. ἀγορά, concio, γ 127, Β 53, 194, 202.

βουλη-φόρος, οι, (φέρω), giving counsel, advising, ἀγοραί, ι 112 ; ἀνήρ, Α 144 ; ἄναξ, Μ 414 ; also subst. counsellor, Ε 180, Η 126.

βούλομαι, (also βόλεται, -εσθε, ἐβόλοντο, α 234), only pres. and ipf., (βουλή), velle, (1) decernere, τινί τι, grant, accord, Η 21, Θ 204, Ρ 331.— (2) wish, with inf. (and acc.), τό, λ 358 ; βούλεται, Α 67, is subjunctive; μέγα, desire greatly.—(3) malle, prefer, ρ 187 (ι 96) ; with and without following ἤ, ρ 228 ; with πολύ, Α 112.

βου-λῦτόν-δε (λύω), the sun began to decline toward eventide, lit. toward the time of unyoking plough-cattle, ι 58.

βου-πλῆγι, from -πλήξ, (πλήσσω), with the ox-goad, Ζ 135†.

Βου-πράσιον, οιο (περᾶν, cf. Oxford), Λ 756, 760. (Il.)

βοῦς, ἡ, ὁ, dat. pl. βόεσσι, acc. βόας, βοῦς, bos, usually fem., cow, the cows of Helios, μ 379 ; yet also masc., bullock, ox, in which case another word is often added to make the gender more clear, ἄρσενα(ς), ταύροιο ; pl. *cattle, kine*, βοῶν ἔργα = ἄροσις, ploughed lands ; slaughter cattle, ἱερεύειν (cf. Ο 633, γ 450) ; adjectives ἀγελαίη, ἀγραύλοιο, εἰλίποδες, ἕλικες, ἐριμύκων, ὀρθοκραιράων ; as symbol of flight, pecorum ritu, Λ 172. Βοῶν ἀγέλαι, herds of cattle, constitute the chief wealth, cf. ἀλφεσίβοια ; hence βοῶν ἴφθιμα, perh. costly (usually explained as mighty), κάρηνα, Ψ 260; as means of exchange and measure of value, Ψ 885, see ἐννεαβοίων; bestowed as prizes in athletic contests ; κέρας, μ 253, horn guard just above hook, to prevent fish from biting off the line; ῥινὸς βοός (cf. βοὸς βοείην, Σ 582), oxhide, Υ 276 ; shield of ox-hide, Κ 155. Also as fem. subst., (acc. βῶν), ox-hide, Η 474, untanned ; the *shield* made from the same, ἀζαλέην, Η 238 ; αὔας, Μ 137 ; ἐυποιητάων, τυκτῇσι.

βου-φόνεον, 3 pl. ipf., (φονή), *were slaughtering cattle*, Η 466†.

βο-ῶπις, usually πότνια Ἥρη, voc. ῑ, Α 551, *ox-eyed, with large, calm eyes*; otherwise applied, Η 10, Σ 40.

Βοώτης, ὁ, lit. *Herdsman*, the constellation Arcturus, α 272†.

βρᾰδύς, έες, comp. βράσσων, sup. βάρδιστοι, t a r d u s, *slow*; with inf. θείειν, Ψ 310; νόος, Κ 226 ; in proverb, θ 329.

βρᾰδῡτῆτι, τῇ, (βραδύς), t a r d i t a t e, *slowness*, Τ 411†.

βρᾰχίονος, α, ες, (ὁ βραχίων), b r a-c h i u m, *arm*, πρυμνοῖο, *shoulder*, στιβαροί, firm. [‿ ‿ ‿ ‿]

βρᾰχε, ἔβρᾰχε, ipf., *creak*, μέγα, loud, Ε 838; *rattled*, δεινόν, *roared*, Φ 9; *shrieked aloud*, of Ares, Ε 859; of wounded horse, Π 468.

βρέμει, -εται, (fremo), *roar*, Β 210, Ξ 399. (Il.)

βρέφος, τό, acc. ἡμίονον, mule *foal*, yet in the womb, Ψ 266†.

βρεχμόν, τόν, *forehead*, Ε 586†.

Βρῐάρεως = Αἰγαίων, name of hundred-armed water-giant, Α 403†.

βριαρῆ, ἥν, (βριαρός, βρί-θω), g r a-v i s, *heavy*, only of helmet, Λ 375, Τ 381. (Il.)

βρῐζοντα (βαρύς), *drowsy*, Δ 223†.

βρῐ-ήπυος, *loud shouting, roaring* (cf. Ξ 398 sqq.), Ν 521†.

βρῑθοσύνῃ ⟨βρίθω⟩, *with the weight*, Ε 839 and Μ 460.

βρῑθύ, adj. ntr., *ponderous*, only with ἔγχος—μέγα στιβαρόν, α 100.

βρῑθῃ, prs., ipf. βρῖθον, aor. ἔβρισα, pass. only pres. part., Θ 307; also perf. act. βέβρῑθε, and plupf. βεβρίθει (βαρύς), g r a v a r e, *weigh down*, Θ 307; t u r g e r e, *be full of*, Σ 561 ; τινί, π 474, τ 112; τινός, ι 219 ; *be drenched with* water, Π 384; u r g e r e, *charge*, Μ 346; *be superior through gifts*, ζ 159; βεβρῑθυῖα, *heavy*, only Φ 385.

Βρῑσεύς, ῆος, king and priest in Λυρνησσός, Α 392, Ι 132, 274; father of follg.

Βρῑσηΐς, ΐδος, daughter of Βρισεύς, the occasion of the μῆνις Πηληιάδεω, Α 184. (Il.) (See cut, after a Panathenaic Amphora.)

βρομέωσι, subj., (βρόμος), *buzz*, Π 642†.

βρόμος (βρέμω), *roar, crackling*, Ξ 396†.

βροντάω, only aor. (ἐ)βρόντησε, only of Ζεύς, *thunder*; μεγάλ', δεινόν, loud, terribly ; ἄμυδις, peal on peal.

βροντῆς, ῇ, ήν, fem., (βροντή, βρόμος), t o n i t r u, δεινήν, dread *thunder*, Φ 199.

βροτέη (βροτός) φωνῇ, humana voce, τ 545†.

βροτόεντα, ntr. pl., (βρότος), cruentata, bloody, ἔναρα, Ξ 509. (Il.)

βροτο-λοιγός, only sing. masc., of *Αρης and of heroes, man-destroying, E 31. (Il. and Θ 115.)

βροτός, οῦ, (orig. μροτός from μόρος, mors), mortalis, mortal, adj. ἀνήρ, E 361, and subst. T 2, θνητοῖσι, γ 3; δειλοῖσι, ὀιζυροῖσι, μερόπεσσι, ἐπιχθόνιος; Ψ 331, κατατεθνηῶτος, hominis mortui; Υ 248.

βρότον, τόν, μέλανα, ω 189, clsewh. (Il.) αἱματόεντα, blood from a wound, gore.

βροτόω, only βεβροτωμένα, cruentata, gory, τεύχεα, λ 41†.

βρόχον, τόν, and pl. -οι, laqueum, noose, λ 278 and χ 472.

Βρυσειαί, town in Λακονική, B 583†.

βρυχάομαι, only pf. βέβρυχε, ὡς, ἐβεβρύχειν, 3 sing., roar; shriek, falling with death wound, N 393, Π 486.

βρύει (βλύω), efflorescit, ἄνθεϊ λευκῷ, swells with white bloom, P 56†.

βρώμης, τῆς and -ην, (βιβρώσκω), cibi, food, κ 379. (Od.)

βρῶσις, -ιν, ἡ, (βιβρώσκω), cibus, food, always with πόσις, potus, drink. (Od., and T 210.)

βρωτύν, τήν, (βιβρώσκω), cibum, food, T 205 and σ 407.

βύβλινον, τό, ὅπλον, lit. made of papyrus = braided, twisted, φ 391†.

βυκτάων, τῶν, whistling, howling, κ 20†.

βυσσο-δομεύων, pres. part., and pl. ipf. βυσσοδόμευον (βυσσός, δέμω), always with κακά (φρεσί), ρ 66, secretly devise. (Od.)

βυσσόν, τόν (βύθος), profundum, deep, depths, Ω 80†.

βύω, only βεβυσμένον, τόν, confertum, stuffed full of, δ 134†.

βῶλος, ὁ, gleba, clod, σ 374†.

βωμός, ὁ, (βαίνω), gradus, step, η 100; stand, rack, Θ 441; esp. altar, θυήεις, smoking, fragrant with incense, Θ 48; εὔδμητον, A 448. (See cut.)

Βῶρος, (1) Maionian, father of Φαῖστος, E 44†.—(2) son of Περιήρης, husband of Πολυδώρη, daughter of Πηλεύς, Π 177†.

βῶν, acc. from βοῦς, scutum, shield.

βώσαντι, aor. part. from βοάω.

βωστρεῖν, inf. = imp., call loudly upon μ 124†.

βωτι-άνειρη, man-nourishing, fruitful, A 155†.

βώτορες, ας, (βόσκω), ἄνδρες, pastores, shepherds, M 302†.

Γ.

γαῖα, ης, ἡ, terra, *earth*, (1) as division of universe, ρ 386; opp. heaven, Ξ 174, Θ 16, Υ 58, ε 184, α 54; opp. sea, ε 408, μ 242, 282, 315; *world*, Ρ 447, Ω 351, σ 130.—(2) *country*, *land*, Ο 81, Θ 284, 555, ζ 119; *particular land*, Α 254, Η 124, ε 280; *native country*, Ι 244, α 21, ν 188.—(3) *surface of earth*, *ground*, Ν 508, Α 245, Θ 65, Φ 168; ὑπὸ γαῖαν, Τ 259; fruitful, τ 111; *place of burial=grave*, γ 16, λ 549, ν 427; pulvis, Η 99.

Γαῖα, as deity, Tellus, *Earth*, Ο 36.

Γαιήϊον υἱόν, son of Γαῖα, *earth-born*, Τιτυός, η 324†; cf. λ 576.

γαιή-οχος (ἔχω), *earth-possessing*, *earth-surrounding*, epithet of Ποσειδάων, Ι 183, α 68.

γαίων, pres. part., (γαίω, gaudeo), κύδεϊ, *exulting in* his glory, Α 405.

γάλα, ακτος, τό, lac, *milk*, Ε 902.

γαλα-θηνούς, τούς, (θῆσθαι), *sucking*, *tender*, δ 336 and ρ 127.

Γαλάτεια, name of a Nereid, Σ 45†.
[‿ ‿ ‿ ‿]

γαλήνη, ην, ἡ, (γάλα, γελᾶν), *smooth surface of water*, *calm of the sea*, μ 168. (Od.)

γαλόῳ, ων, dat. sing., nom. gen. pl., glos, *husband's sister*, Γ 122. (Il.)

γαμβρός, ὁ, (1) gener, *son-in-law*, Ζ 249.—(2) *brother-in-law*, Ν 464 and Ε 474.

γαμέω, aor. ἔγημε, γῆμε, uxorem ducere, *marry*=θέσθαι γυναῖκα, φ 72; mid. γαμέεσθαι, aor. γήμασθαι, *to give one's self in marriage*, of the woman, τινί, nubere; but in Ι 394, fut. γαμίσσεται, of the parents, *to get a wife for their son*; α 36, *took as his wife*.

γάμος, ὁ, *marriage*, ρ 476; *marriage-feast*, Τ 299, α 226.

γαμφηλῇσι, dat. pl., (γόμφος), maxillae, *jaws*, Ν 200. (Il.)

γαμψ-ώνυχες (γναμπτός? ὄνυξ), αἰγυπιοί, *with crooked claws*, π 217.

γανόωντες, ὁωσαι, (γαίω), *gleaming*, *bright*, *luxuriant*.

γάνυται, -νται, fut. -νύσσεται.(γάνος), gaudere; φρένα, *glad* at heart, Ν 493.

Γανυμήδης, son of Τρώς, *cup-bearer* of Zeus, Ε 266 and Υ 232.

γάρ (γέ, ἄρα, γᾶρ, Β 39, λ 580), always second word in its clause, apparent exc., like ρ 317, explained by considering that the two preceding words make but one idea; particle denoting immediate, indisputable certainty, *yes*, *yes doubtless*, *namely*, *for*.—I. independently, without relation to another clause, (1) in declaration, Λ 408, ρ 78; ἦ γάρ, Α 293, 342, 355; ἀλλὰ γάρ, but yet, Η 242, κ 202.—(2) after relatives, Κ 127 (τ᾽ ἄρ?); and in a question, after the interrogative word, e. g. πῶς γάρ, etc., e. g. κ 337, 383, 501; emphasizing (cf. δή), Κ 424, Σ 182.—(3) in wishes, with opt., εἰ γάρ, Ν 825, ρ 513; αἲ γὰρ (δή), Β 371, ζ 244 (Δ 189, ι 523).—II. with relation to another sentence, (1) which may be co-ordinate, and connected by a pron. (τῷ, then, therefore, τῶν), or by a conj., Ρ 227, Η 73, ξ 496, ν 273.—(2) which may inclose, as a parenthesis, the clause with γάρ, Μ 326, α 301; thus esp. freq. after vocs., Ψ 156, κ 174; and after ἀλλά, ξ 355, cf. Η 328 sq.—(3) which has its truth confirmed, *for*, Α 9, 55, 78, 120, 177; γὰρ may even be transferred to the preceding, instead of remaining in the following sentence, e. g. Α 81, Β 123.—(4) which thus receives explanation of its meaning, *to wit*, *namely*, Α 195, δ 86. Joined with other particles: ἀλλὰ γάρ, but *really*; γὰρ δή, for indeed; γάρ ῥα, for certainly; γάρ τε, namque; γάρ τοι, *for* surely. [‿; in arsi ā.]

Γάργἄρον, τό, south peak of Ἴδη in Τροίη, Ξ 292. (Il.)

γαστήρ, έρος, ἡ, (and sync. forms, -στρός, -στρί), venter, (1) *pit of belly*, Δ 531, Ε 539; *womb*, Ζ 58.—(2) *belly*, *paunch*, Π 163; *hunger*, ζ 133; *fasting*, Τ 225.—(3) *paunch* stuffed with minced meat, *blood sausage*, σ 44.

γάστρην, τήν, *belly*, of a caldron, Θ 437.

γαυλοί, οἱ, *milk-pails*, ι 223†.

γδουπέω, see δουπέω.

γέ, enclitic particle, Lat. quidem, used with great variety of meaning, often untranslatable, (1) restrictive; *at all events, at least*, A 60, 81, β 62, α 229; γὲ μέν, *but yet*, B 703; often to emphasize a relation subsisting between two parties, also doubled, e. g. σέ γε, θ 488, Γ 143; cf. πρίν γε, A 97.—(2) causal, A 352.—(3) emphatic with voc., τ 215; esp. with pron., A 173, 216, 261, 525, α 46, 47, 163, 226, 403; with pron. in second member of the period, Γ 409. —(4) γέ often seems to be used only to give greater force of sound to a word, e. g. ὅ γε, cf. h i-c e, h i c, in Latin, α 222, β 132.

γεγάασι, -ἄῶτα(ς), pf. indic. and part., from γίγνομαι, n a t i s u n t, B 866, ζ 62, ω 84; usually = εἰσίν, ἐόντες, ε 35.

γέγηθε, ει, pf. and plupf., from γηθέω, g a v i s u s e s t.

γέγωνε, pf. with pres. signif., inf. -εῖν and -έμεν, part. -ώς, plupf. 1 sing. ἐγε-γώνευν, 3 sing. -ει, also 1 sing. and 3 pl. γεγώνευν, *make one's self heard* (by a call, as is often specified, M 337, Θ 227; ε 400, ὅσσον τε γέγωνε βοήσας, as far as one shouting *can be heard*), τινί, *cry out to*, Ξ 469, ρ 161; in distress, μ 370; Ω 703, shouted throughout the whole city.

γεγωνέω, see γέγωνε.

γείνεαι, ὁμένῳ, ipf. -όμεθα, aor. ἐγείναο, ατο, γείνατο, -ασθαι, (γένος), prs. ipf., n a s c i, *to be born*, X 477, to a like fate; aor., g i g n o and p a r i o, *beget, bring forth*; λ 299, brought forth to Tyndareos.

γείτονες (nom. γείτων), v i c i n i, *neighbors*, δ 16. (Od.)

γελαστά, ntr. pl.,(γελάω), r i d i c u l a, θ 307†.

(γελάω), prs. γελόω, part. γελόωντες and -ώοντες (false reading -οίωντες, v 390), ipf. 3 pl. γελώων, aor. (ἐ)γέλασ-σε(ν), 3 pl. γέλασσαν, part. γελάσσας, also forms with one σ, (γέλος), r i d e r e, *laugh, ἡδύ, ἀχρεῖον; ἐπί(τι), laugh at, laugh over, ἐπ' αὐτῷ, at him, B 270; my heart laughed within me, ι 413; χείλεσι, of feigned, forced laughter, Ο 101; γναθμοῖς ἀλλοτρίοισιν, v 347, with distorted grin; χθών, Τ 362, *was smiling*.

γελοίων, incorrect reading for γε-λώων, see γελάω, r i d e b a n t, v 347.

γελοίιον, ntr., (γέλως), r i d i c u l u m, B 215†.

γελοίωντες,false reading for γελώον-τες, see γελάω, r i d e n t e s, v 390.

γελόω, -όωντες, -ώοντες, see γελάω.

γέλως (dat. -ῳ), acc. -ω; and γέλος, dat. -ῳ, acc. -ον, r i s u s, ἄσβεστος, un-extinguishable=uncontrollable *laugh;* ἔχει τινά, indulge in, be overcome by laughter; σ 100, laughed themselves almost to death.

γενεή, ῆς, ἡ, (γένος), g e n u s, (1) *de-scent, origin, race*, Φ 157; of animals, E 265; *home*, α 407; *family*, Z 145; joined with τόκος, ο 175, *birthplace* and its young; g e n s, *house*, α 222, Υ 306; *descendants*, Φ 191, δ 27; *rank*, Λ 786.—(2) *generation*, Z 149; plur. only A 250; a e t a s, *age, γενεῆφι ὁπλότερος*, etc., B 707, O 166.

γενέθλη, ης, ἡ, only sing., (γένος), o r i g o, *race, stock*, εἶναι (ἐκ) γενέθλης τινός, a l i q u o o r i u n d u m e s s e; τῶν γενέθλης ἐγένοντο, there were born to him six of their stock, E 270; cf. T 111; B 857, *home* of silver.

γενειάδες, αἱ, *beard*, π 176†.

γενειάω, aor. part. γενειήσαντα, *be-ginning to grow a beard*, σ 176 and 269.

γένειον, ου, ῳ, m e n t u m, *chin*, ἁψα-μένη Ὀδυσῆα γενείου, τ 473, as sign of homage, elsewh. as s u p p l i c a n t i u m g e s t u s, attitude of suppliants, A 501. (See cut under γουνοῦμαι.)

γένεσις, ἡ, (γένος), o r i g o, *source*, θεῶν, πάντεσσι, Ὠκεανός. (Ξ.)

γενετῆς, τῆς, (γενέσθαι), only ἐκ, i n d e e n a t u, *from the hour of birth*, σ 6.

γενναῖον, ntr., (γέννα), οὔ μοι, n o n e x i n d o l e m e a e s t, *suitable to one's birth*, or *descent*, E 253†.

γένος, ευς, εὸ, (γίγνομαι), g e n u s, cf. γενεή; (1) *family*, ζ 35; *race*, as a whole, ἀνδρῶν, ἡμιθέων ἀνδρῶν, βοῶν.—(2) *generation*, γ 245; a e t a s, *age*, Γ 215. —(3) *scion*, Z 180.—(4) *extraction, γένος εἰμί (ἐκ) τινος*, a l i q u o o r t u s s u m; also of the *home*, ο 267, B 852.

γέντο, 3 sing. aor., p r e h e n d i t = λάζετο, with acc. Σ 476, N 241. (Il.)

γένυς, ἡ, pl. -ύων, acc. ῦς, m a x i l l a, *under jaw;* also of jaw of boar, Λ 416.

γεραιός, έ; αἱ, άς, s e n e x, *old, aged*, with ἄττα and παλαιγενές; P 561;

freq. ὁ γ., A 35; fem., Z 87; comp. -αίτερος, ον, senior(em).

γεραίρεις, -ειν, prs., ipf. γέραιρεν (γέρας), honorare, show honor, H 321, ξ 437.

Γεραιστός, οὗ, promontory of Εὔβοια; now Geresto, γ 177†.

γερᾰνων, gen. pl., gruum, from ἡ γέρανος, crane, Γ 3. (Il.)

γερᾰρόν, acc. masc., comp. -ώτερος, Γ 170 and 211, stately.

γέρας, τό, pl. **γέρα**, honor, Δ 323; precedence, prerogative, λ 175; gift of honor, A 118; rendered to the gods, Δ 49; gift, υ 297; θανόντων, last honors of the dead, viz., burial, the thrice-repeated call, the funeral mound, and a column, Ψ 9, ω 190.

Γερήνιος (ἱππότα), Νέστωρ, from Γερηνός in Ἦλις, B 336.

γερούσιον, acc. masc., (γέρων), senatorium, belonging to the old men of the council, of wine, ν 8; of oath, X 119.

γέρων, οντος, (1) senex, adj., aged, A 358, Θ 100, Φ 85; σάκος γέρον, vetustum, old, χ 184; subst., old man, opp. νέοι, I 36, παῖδας, Θ 518; ἀλίοιο =Νηρέως, Πρωτέως, Φόρκυνος, old man of the sea; honorable title of Λαέρτης, β 227.—(2) elder, member of the council or βουλή, cf. Lat., senator.

γεύσεται, -σόμεθα, -σισθαί, fut., aor. inf. γεύσασθαι, (γεύω), gustare, taste, ρ 413, προικός; elsewh. fig. ironical, φ 98, Υ 258; temptemus inter nos, try.

γεφύρῃ, αι, ας, agger, dam, dike, E 88; πτολέμοιο, ordines, rows of combat, i. e. of combating hosts, Δ 371, Θ 378, 553. (Il.) [‿ – –]

γεφύρωσε, aor. from γεφυρόω, exaggeravit, dammed it up, Φ 245; made a causeway, O 357. [ῠ]

γῆ, ἡ, terra, earth, ν 233, ψ 233, Φ 63.

Γῆ, Γῇ, dat., Tellus, Earth, as goddess, Τ 259, Γ 104.

γηθεῖ, prs., ipf. ἐγήθεεν, etc., also fut., aor. γήθησε, etc., pf. γέγηθε, plupf. -θει (γηθέω), gaudeo, rejoice, θυμῷ, H 189; κατὰ θυμόν, N 416; φρένα, Θ 559, in his heart; so also with ἦτορ, κῆρ, θυμός τινι (τινος), N 494; at any thing, τι, or with ὅτι, οὕνεκα, and follg. clause.

γηθοσύνῃ, τῇ, (γηθέω), for joy, N 29 and Φ 390. [ῠ]

γηθόσυνος, η, -οι, laetus, κῆρ, glad at heart; because of something, τινί, N 82, ε 269.

γηράς, see γηράσκω.

γῆρας, αος, αϊ and αι, τό, (γέρων), senectus, Ξ 86; λυγρῷ, in a wretched old age (opp. τ 368), χαλεπόν, στυγερῷ; ἐς γῆρ., up to old age; ἔχειν γῆρ., ω 249; ἔχει τινά, Σ 515; ἱκάνει, ἔπεισι; ἐπὶ γήραος οὐδῷ, on the threshold of hoary old age, o 348.

γηράσκει, prs., ipf. γήρασκε, aor. ἔγηρα (ἐγήρα), part. γηράς, (γῆρας), senesco, grow old, P 197; of hale old age, δ 210; maturescit, ripen, η 120.

γῆρυς, ἡ, speech, Δ 437†.

Γίγαντες, dat. ἐσσι, Giant-race in Θρινακίη, η 59, 206, and κ 120.

γίγνομαι, fut. etc. reg. as in Attic, aor. iter. γενέσκετο, pf. γέγονε, see also γεγάασι, plupf. γεγόνει, (γένος), (1) nasci, be born, δ 418, ζ 201, κ 350, μ 130; crescere, grow, ν 245, ν 211; arise, Π 634, Σ 212, Ξ 415, O 607, μ 326; fieri, arise, begin, A 49, K 375, N 283, Ψ 505, δ 417; obtingere, fall to one's lot, happen, [N 659], γ 228, A 188, Ω 45; ε 299, what now last of all shall come upon me?—(2)=εἶναι, β 320, μ 87, ξ 157, O 490, T 386; exstare, Δ 245; come to be, Z 82, H 99; ἐπὶ πῆμα, come to ruin; Δ 382, ὁδοῦ, and ὁδοῖο πρὸ γένοντο, profecerunt, progressed on the way.

γιγνώσκω (not γινώσκω), reg., but aor. subj. γνώω, ομεν, ωσι, inf. γνώμεναι, fut. mid. γνώσεαι, (- gnosco), (1) sentio, intelligo, perceive, understand, τ 160, π 136, N 223, Π 658; with ὅτι, Θ 175, E 331; ὅτ’, P 623, γ 166; ὡς, X 10; with εἰ, si, Φ 266; with obj. attracted from follg. clause, E 85; with part., recognize, o 532; nosse, know, X 356; τινός, know, φ 36; learn to know, Σ 270.—(2) agnosco (of senses), recognize, Λ 651, O 241, υ 94; by his shield, E 182.—(3) callere, understand, β 159.

γίνομαι, un-Homeric, see γίγνομαι.
γινώσκω, un-Homeric, see γιγνώσκω.
γλάγος, τό, (γάλα), lac, milk, B 471 and Π 643.

γλακτο-φάγων, gen. pl., (γάλα, φαγεῖν), lacte vescentium, living on milk, N 6†.

Γλαύκη, Νηρηίς, Σ 39†

γλαυκιόων, pres. part. from γλαυκιάω, *with glaring eyes*, Υ 172†.

γλαυκή, θάλασσα, *gleaming*, Π 34†.

Γλαῦκος, (1) 'Ιππολόχοιο πάις, Λυκίων ἀγός, Η 13; Ζ 119, guest-friend *of Διομήδης.*—(2) son of Σίσυφος, father of Βελλεροφόντης, Ζ 154 sqq.

γλαυκ-ῶπις, ιδος, (acc. also -ιν, a 156), voc. ῖ, only of 'Αθήνη, *with gleaming eyes, bright-, glaring-eyed*, a 44, A 206. The type of expression recognizable in Attic tetradrachm. (See cut No. 43.)

Γλάφυραι, town in Θεσσαλίη, Β 712†.

γλαφυρός, ή, όν, (nom. masc. wanting), cavus, *hollow*, esp. of ships, B 454; of grotto, Σ 402, β 20, a 15; rock, Β 88; φόρμιγξ, θ 257; *deep, spacious*, μ 305.

γλήνη, ης, ην, (γαλήνη), pupilla, *pupil of eye*, ι 390; Θ 164, then, perh. because figures are reflected in miniature in the eye, contemptuous epithet, *timid coward!*

γλήνεα, τά, (radical syllable ΓΑΛ), (gleaming) *jewelry*, Ω 192†.

Γλῖσας, αντος, town of Βοιωτοί, B 504†.

γλουτόν, ούς, acc., clunem, *rump, buttocks*, Ε 66, Θ 340. (Il.)

γλυκερός, ή, όν, comp. -ώτερον, (γλυκύς), dulcis, gratus, *sweet, dear*, Λ 89, ξ 194; φάος, dear to me as the light, π 23.

γλυκύ-θυμος, mitis animi, *of mild temper*, Υ 467†.

γλυκύς, ύ; fem. γλυκερή, comp. -ίων, -ιον, dulcis, *sweet*, A 598, 249; gratus, *grateful*, ὕπνος, ἵμερος; acceptus, *dear*, ε 152, Β 453.

γλυφίδᾶς, τάς, (γλύφω), *notches on the arrow*, φ 419. (See cuts Nos. 96, 97.)

γλῶσσα, ης, ἡ, lingua, (1) *tongue*, Ε 292, Ρ 618, Β 489, Π 161; τάμνειν, cut out the *tongues of victims*, γ 332.— (2) *language*, Β 804, Δ 438.

γλωχῖνα, τήν, (γλῶσσα), *end of the strap* or *thong* of the yoke, Ω 274†. (See cut under ζυγόν, letter b, No. 49.)

γναθμοῖο, όν, and pl. masc., (γένυς, gena), maxilla, Ν 671, π 175; σ 29, I would beat all the teeth out of his *jaws* upon the ground; υ 347, with distorted jaws, disfigured countenance.

γναμπτόν, ntr., and masc. fem. and ntr. pl., (γνάμπτω), (1) curvus, *curved*,

δ 369.—(2) *flexible, pliant*, of limbs of living beings, ν 398; metaph. *placable*, νόημα, Ω 41.

γνάμψε, aor., (γνάμπτω), ἐν—, suplantavit, *bent* in his knee, tripped up, Ψ 731; ὑπό—, bent under, passed under, Ω 274. (See cut under ζυγόν.)

γνήσιον, acc. masc., -τοι, (γενέσθαι), legitimum, *genuine*, υἱόν; opp. νόθον, ξ 202.

γνύξ (γόνυ) ἔριπε, -ών, fell *upon the knee*, E 309. (Il.)

γνῷ, γνώμεναι, γνώομεν, aor. from γιγνώσκω.

γνώριμος, notus, *acquaintance*, π 9†.

γνωτός, όν, fem. -αί, (1) notus, *evident*, Η 401, ω 182.—(2) cognatus, *relative*, Ο 350, Γ 174; *brother*, Ρ 35.

(γοάω) γοῶν, -ντες, (γοῶντες), -ντας, -όωσα, part. pres., opt. γοάοιμεν, -άοιεν, inf. γοήμεναι, 3 pl. ipf. γόον, γόων, iter. γοάασκεν, fut. γοήσεται, (γόος), lamentari, *sob*, θ 92; esp. in lamentation for dead, *wail*, τινά, Ζ 502, Ζ 500, Φ 124; πότμον, Π 857.

γόμφοισι, masc., *with nails, with pins*, ε 248†.

γονή, ήν, (γέγονα), proles, *offspring*, Ω 539 and δ 755.

γόνος, οιο, ον, masc., (γέγονα), origo, *origin*, a 216; proles, *offspring*, δ 12; commonly = filius, σ 218, Ζ 191, Ν 449, Ω 59; *young*, of cattle, μ 130.

Γονόεσσα, ἡ, town near Πελλήνη, Β 573†.

γόνυ, τό, all other forms with lengthening of first syllable, gen. γούνατος, γουνός, pl. γούνατα, γοῦνα, gen. γούνων, dat. -ασι, -εσσι, genu, *knee*, κάμπτειν, rest, ἐπὶ γοῦνα ἕζεσθαι, sit down; γοῦνα βλάβεται, tremble; πήγνυνται, are stiff; ἐπὶ and ποτὶ γούνασι, X 500; Ε 408, in gremio, cf. also ἐν γούνασι πίπτε, E 370; θεῖναί τι ἐπὶ γούνασι θεοῦ, as gift, Ζ 92; θεῶν ἐν γούνασι κεῖται, *lies at the disposal of the gods*, α 267.—(2) genua, as seat of *pity*, in phrases like the follg., ἅψασθαι, ἑλεῖν, λαβεῖν, ἀντίον ἐλθεῖν, λίσσεσθαι γούνων, etc., A 500; cf. Eurip. Iph. T. 361 sqq., 1069 sq.; Plin. Historia Naturalis, XI., 45, (103). —(3) as seat of *physical power, strength*, λύειν τινὸς γούνατα=slay any one, and λύεται γούνατά τινος, knees sink under him; γ. ὀρώρῃ, as long as I can move my limbs.

γόον, ipf. from γοάω.

γόος, ου, and οιο, ον, pl. ους, masc., (βοή?), lamentatio, δ 758; πατρός, lament for one's father, Ω 507; esp. of the sobbing (ἀδινοῦ) lamentation for the dead, Σ 316; κρυεροῖο, chilling weeping; δακρυόεντος, tearful lamentation; γόον δ' ὤιετο θυμός, his soul foreboded death.

Γοργείη, ην, with κεφαλή, head of the Γοργώ, Ε 741.

Γοργύθίων, ωνα, son of Πρίαμος and of Καστιάνειρα, Θ 302†.

Γοργώ, οὖς, ἡ, a dread-inspiring monster, Λ 36.

Γόρτυν, ὑνος, city in Κρήτη, γ 294 and Β 646.

γοῦν, i. e. γ' οὖν, in εἰ γ' οὖν, if however; ἐμέ γ' οὖν, me quidem certe.

γουνάζομαι, prs., and fut. άσομαι, (γόνυ), supplico, beseech, implore, τινά, (ὑπέρ, πρός), τινος, for the sake of, by; γούνων, τοκήων, by my knees, by (my) parents, Χ 345.

γούνατα, ασι, εσσι, see γόνυ.

Γουνεύς, leader of two tribes of Πελασγοί, Β 748†.

γουνοῦμαι, only pres., and ipf. γουνούμην, λ 29, (γόνυ), supplico, τινά, with inf., supplicando vovere, supplicate and vow to offer, κ 521. (See the cut, from ancient gem, representing Dolon and Ulysses.)

γουνός, ῷ, όν, masc., (γόνυ), strictly curve, winding (applied by Herodotos to

Attica, because of its irregular form), corner, α 193; ἀλωῆς, garden-plot, Σ 57.

γραίης, τῆς, (γρῆυς), vetulae, old woman, α 438†.

Γραῖα, town in Βοιωτία, Β 498†.

γραπτῦς, τάς, nom. ἡ γραπτύς, (γράφω), scratches, ω 229†.

γράφω, (en-grave), only aor. **γράψεν**, part. γράψας, scratch, engrave, Ζ 169; penetrate to, Ρ 599.

Γρήνικος, river Granicus, rising in Mount Ἴδη, Μ 21†.

γρήυς and γρηῦς (τ 346), dat. γρηί, voc. γρῆυ and γρηῦ, (γεραιός), old woman, also with παλαιγενέϊ, παλαιή.

γύαλον, οιο, οισι, ntr., only θώρηκος (q. v.), convexity, Ν 507; γυάλοισιν ἀρηρότα, fitted together of convex (metal) plates, Ο 530. (Il.)

Γυγαίη, λίμνη, lake in Μῃονίη, Υ 391. Nymph of this lake, Β 865.

γυῖα, ων, τά, artus, joints, only of arms and feet, Ψ 627, Ε 811, κ 363; λύονται γυῖα (see γόνυ), are wearied, Ν 85; in death, Η 16.

γυιόω, only fut. **γυιώσω**, σειν, lame, Ο 402 and 416.

γυμνός, οῦ, όν, nudus, naked, ζ 136; uncovered, τόξον (i. e. taken out of the γωρυτός); usually unarmed, defenseless, Φ 50, Ρ 122, Χ 124.

γυμνόω, **γυμνοῦσθαι**, aor. (ἐ)γυμνώθη, -θείη, -θέντα (γυμνός), nudari, lay off one's clothes, ζ 222, κ 341; with gen., χ 1; unprotected, unarmed, Μ 389, 428; unprotected against attack, Μ 399.

γυναικείας, διὰ βουλάς, mulicbribus dolis, woman's designs, λ 437†.

γυναι-μανές, voc., (μαίνομαι), mad after women, Ἀλέξανδρος, Γ 39. (Il.)

γυναίων, δώρων, gifts to a woman, λ 521 and ο 247.

γυνή, γυναικός, etc., (quean, queen), woman.—(1) as designating sex, woman, female, Ο 683, Ω 708, Τ 110, Λ 269; θηλύτεραι, Θ 502; as contemptuous epithet, Θ 163, Χ 125; often with distinguishing title, to mark occupation, χερνῆτις, ταμίη; in general signif., mulieres, Τ 301, Ω 722; δῖα γυναικῶν, Γ 171; γ. δμωαί, also without δμωαί=maid-servants, ρ 75, υ 6.— (2) uxor, wife, Ζ 160, Ι 394, Ζ 516, Κ 422, Δ 162, θ 523; χήρη, vidua, widow, Ζ 432; concubine, Ω 497.—(3)

hera, *mistress*, ξ 123, X 48; *queen*, π 334.—(4) opp. θεά, Π 176; θνητάων, Υ 305; Ω 58, has sucked the breast of a woman (mortal).

Γῦραι πέτραι, Γῦραίην πέτρην, and Γῦρῇσι, name of rocky cliffs near Νάξος, δ 500, 507.

γῦρὸς ἐν ὤμοισιν, *round*-shouldered, τ 246†.

Γυρτιάδης = Ὕρτιος, Ξ 512†.

Γυρτώνη, town in Πελασγιῶτις, on the river Πηνειός, Β 738†.

γύψ, only γῦπε, γῦπες, εσσι, vultures, λ 578, X 42, χ 30.

γωρῦτῷ, τῷ, *bow-case, quiver,* φ 54†.

(See cuts, from ancient Greek and Assyrian representations.)

Δ.

δ᾽ = (1) δέ, (2) δή, in δ᾽ αὖ, δ᾽ αὖτε, also in δ᾽ οὕτως and εἰ δ᾽ ἄγε, see δή ad. fin.

ΔΑ; pres. δι-δά-σκω (q. v.), aor. δέδαεν, d o c u i t; τινά τι, ζ 233, θ 448; with inf., ν 72. In pass. signif. pf. δεδάηκας, ε,-ότες, and δεδαώς, novisse, *have been taught,* i. e. *know,* β 61, ρ 519; aor. pass. ἐδάην, cognovi, Γ 208; subj. δαείω, ῶμεν, discam; inf. δαῆναι, cognoscere, δ 493, and δαήμεναι, nosse, Ζ 150; comperire, *learn,* ν 335; τινός, *understand* any thing, Φ 487; aor. mid. δεδάασθαι, e x p e r i r i, *test, try,* π 316; fut. δαήσεαι, noveris, *thou shalt know,* γ 187; τινός, τ 325.

δαήμονος, ι, α; ε; ες (δαήμων, δέδαα), τινός, p e r i t u s, *skilled in,* θ 159; Ψ 671, πάντεσσ᾽ ἔργοισι.

δαῆναι, δαήσεαι, δαώμεν, see ΔΑ.

δαήρ, έρα, voc. δᾶερ, pl. -έρων [ᴗᴗ _], (δαϝηρ, Lat. l e v i r), f r a t e r m a r i t i, *brother-in-law,* Z 344, Ω 762. (Il.)

δάηται, see δαίω.

δαί, after τίς: q u i s - n a m, *what pray,* α 225; v. l. τίς δέ.

δαΐ, dat. from δαΐς.

δαιδάλεος, 3, (δαίδαλα), *skillfully wrought, delicate, graceful,* I 187, κ 315, α 131.

δαιδάλλων, pres. part., (d o l a r e), *elaborate skillfully, decorate,* Σ 479 and ψ 200.

δαίδαλον, τό, only τ 227; elsewh. pl., (d o l a r e), *piece of skillful workmanship* (in metal), *ornament,* Ξ 179, Ε 60.

Δαίδαλος, famous artist and artisan from Κνωσός, Σ 592†.

δαΐζω, fut. ξω, etc., pf. pass. δεδαϊγμένος, (δαΐω), l a c e r a r e, *cleave, tear in sunder, wound,* by a cut or thrust, *pierce, cut through,* with or without mention of the weapon; and so generally, *cut down, slay,* Β 416, Η 247, Φ 147; ξ 434, *divide;* δεδαϊγμ. ἦτορ, Ρ 535 and Σ 236, c o n f o s s u m, *wounded* in the heart, *transfixed* (ὀξέϊ χαλκῷ). Distinguish fig. heart *rent* (by grief), ν 320; mind *confused* or *divided* (in perplexity or in doubt), I 8, Ξ 20.

δάϊ-κταμένων, gen. pl., (δαΐς), *fallen in battle,* Φ 146 and 301.

δαιμόνιος, ίη, of person *standing under influence of a god* (δαίμων), this influence may be friendly or unfriendly, hence the word has opposite significations; either *admirable,* or more commonly, *wretch, luckless wight,* '*strange being*' (Bryant), ξ 443.

δαίμων, ονος, ὁ, *divinity,* (1) = θεός, A 222, ο 261, φ 196, 201; of specified divinity, Γ 420.—(2) n u m e n d i v i n u m, *divine power,* P 98; as unfriendly, with κακός, στυγερός, etc., ω 149; Θ 166, *death;* in general, *the divinity,* in its influence upon human life, hence δαίμονος αἶσα, etc.

δαίνυ(ο), aor. mid. from δαίνυμι, epulabaris, Ω 63.

δαίνυμι, δαινύντα, with pres. mid.; ipf. (δαίνυ'=ἐδαίνυε), aor. ἔδαισα, and mid. δαίνυντο, opt. δαινῦτο, pl. -ύατο, fut. δαίσειν, aor. mid. δαισάμενοι,(δαίω), dispertio, *divide, distribute*, a portion of food, δαῖτα; g've a *marriage-* or *funeral-feast*, δ 3, Ψ 29; mid., epulari, *feast*, Ω 665, σ 408, τ 425; *consume, feed upon*, κρέα καὶ μέθυ, ι 162; ἑκατόμβας, μῆρα; *hold a banquet*, εἱλαπίνην, δαῖτα, δαίτην.

δαΐς,(1) δαΐδες, ων, ας,(δα-ϝίδες, δέδηα), faces, *pine splinters*, σ 310; *torches consisting of a number of such splinters bound together*, α 428, Σ 492. (See cut.)—(2) ἐν δαΐ (δαϝί, δεδήϝειν, Υ 18), λυγρῇ, λευγαλέῃ, *heat of combat*, Ν 286. (Il.)

δαίς, τός, ἡ, also pl. δαῖτες, ας, (δαίω, δαίνυμι), *portion, share; εἴση, due share*; then, convivium, *meal, banquet*, α 225, κ 124, Ι 487, Λ 424; Ψ 48, let us now comply with the *invitation to the banquet*, odious though the feast be; =cibus, β 245; ἔντεα δαιτός, *table utensils*. (The root syllable always stands in arsi.)

δαίτη, δαίτης, ην, ῶν, ῃσι, (δαίς), convivium, *banquet*, ρ 220; -ηθεν, de convivio, κ 216.

δαιτρεύειν, inf., ipf. δαίτρευον, fut. -εύσων, aor. -εῦσαι, (δαιτρός), *distribute*, Λ 687; esp. food, ξ 433.

δαιτρόν, τό, (δαίω), *portion*, Δ 262†.

δαιτρός, ὁ, (δαίω), structor, *carver, distributor*, α 141. (See cut.)

δαιτροσύνης, τῆς, (δαιτρός), *art of carving and distributing*, π 253†.

δαιτυμόνες, οἱ, dat. -εσσι, (δαιτύς),

convivae, *banqueters*, also with ἀνδρῶν, ο 467, χ 12. (Od.)

δαιτύος, τῆς, (δαίω), ἐκ, de cena, from the *feast*, Χ 496†. [–◡◡]

Δαίτωρ, ορα, a Trojan, Θ 275†.

δαΐ-φρων, ονος, only sing., (δαῆναι), expertus, *skillful, tried*, of heroes, e.g., Β 23, Σ 18, Λ 791, Ζ 162; in works of art or skill, θ 373; in women's accomplishments, ἔργα γυναικῶν, ο 356.

δαίω, (1) prs. δαίωσι, ipf. δαῖε, pl. δαῖον, iu pass. sense : pf. δέδηεν, plupf. δεδήει, pass. part. δαιόμενον, η, ων, ipf. δαίετο, and aor. subj. mid. δάηται, (δαϝ-ίς), incendere, *kindle, set in a blaze*, of fire, cities, etc., Σ 227; pass. ardere, *blaze*, ἔρις; μάχη, Υ 18; ὄσσε, *sparkle*, ζ 132 (πυρί, Μ 466).

—(2) δαίεται,-ύμενος, ipf. δαίετο, and perf. 3 pl. δεδαίαται, (δαίς), dividitur, *is divided*, in mid. signif. *distribute* o, 140 and ρ 332; ἦτορ, laceratur, α 48.

δάκνω, only aor. 3 sing. δάκε, inf. δακέειν, mordeo, *bite*, Σ 585; *sting*, Ρ 572; stung Hektor's heart, Ε 493. (Il.)

δάκρυ, ύ, pl. ὕα,·ύσιν, and δάκρυον, -οισι, and gen. of separation, -όφιν, (δάκ-νω, Lat. dacruma, Goth. tagr, Eng. tear), lacrima, *tear*, esp. common phrases, δάκρυ (χέων, -ουσα, etc., β 24; πλώειν, ἀναπρήσας), where sing. is collective=δάκρυα, β 81; εἴβειν, (κατα) βάλλειν, ἧκε and χύτο ἀπ' ὀφθαλμῶν, ἔκπεσε, ῥέε; ὁμόρξασθαι, τέρσοντο.

δακρυόεις, εσσα, εν, lacrimosus, (1) *weeping*, Φ 493; *tearful*, δ 801; -ύεν γελάσασα, laughing *through tears*.—(2) *tear-bringing*, μάχη, ἰῶκα, Λ 601.

δάκρυον=δάκρυ.

δάκρυ πλώω, not one word, but two, swim in *tears* (δάκρυ), τ 122†.

δάκρυ χέων, ουσα, etc., see each word.

δακρύω, aor. δάκρυσα, σ(ε), part. δακρύσας, pass. pf. δεδάκρυσαι, νται (δάκρυ), lacrimare, *shed tears*, pf. pass., *be tearful*, Π 7.

δᾱλός, ῷ, όν, masc., (δαϝίω), *firebrand*, αἰθόμενος, *blazing torch*, Ν 320.

ΔΑΜ, to this root belong, (1) prs. δαμάᾳ, όωσι.—(2) δαμνᾷ, 3 sing. prs., ipf. (ἐ)δάμνα. — (3) δάμνημι, ῃσι, prs., mid. δαμνᾷ (-άσαι), αται, ασθαι, part. δαμναμένους, ipf. mid. δάμνατο, pf. pass. δεδμημένος, plupf. δεδμήμην, ητο,

-ήμεσθα, 3 pl. -ηντο, γ 305, -ήατο, fut.
act. δαμάσσομεν (mid. -σσεται); aor.
δάμασσεν (mid. -άσσατο, opt. -ασαίατο);
pass. 1 aor. δαμάσθη, σθείς, and imp.
δμηθήτω; 2 aor. ἐδάμην, δάμεν (=ἐδά-
μησαν), subj. δαμείω, ἥῃς, ἥῃ, ἥετε, opt.
-είη, inf. -ήμεναι, (domare, Eng.
tame), (1) tame, P 77, δ 637.—(2) give
as wife, τινί, Σ 432, Γ 301.—(3) overpower, βίηφι, ἀνάγκῃ, ἶφι; weaken, exhaust, θ 231; χεῖμα, ξ 488; στίβῃ, ρ
24; αἴθρῃ, καμάτῳ, ξ 318, Φ 52; ἁλί,
ε 454; reduce to subjection (Ζ 159),
pass., be subject to, Γ 183, Ε 878, γ 304,
λ 622; overcome, δεσμός, μοῖρα, χ 413;
(φρένας) οἴνῳ; τινὰ ἐπέεσσι, πληγῇσι
(δ 244, foedare, disfigure) Διὸς μά-
στιγι; π 105; λοιμός, ἔρος θυμόν, Ξ
316; succumb, Ξ 353, γ 269; give over
into any one's power in battle, τινά τινι,
ὑπό τινι, ὑπό τινος, Π 434; χερσί τινος,
ὑπὸ χερσί (δουρί) τινος, ὑπὸ σκήπτρῳ
τινί, Ζ 159; deicere, slay, δουρί, βέλεϊ,
δεδμημένος εὕδει ἔγχει ἐμῷ, Ξ 482;
pass., be slain, fall by hand of, τινί,
τινὸς δουρί (χερσι), ὑπὸ δουρί, ὑπό τινος,
κηρί; slay, of arrows, Α 478, Ε 278;
θυμόν, Ξ 439, held unconscious (elsewh.
with θυμόν, overcome, control, Σ 113, λ
562), conterere, shatter, Υ 266, Φ
401; mid., subject one's self, used like
active, yet the following forms in pass.
signif., δαμναμένους, and inf. δάμνα-
σθαι, Θ 244, and ipf. δάμνατο, Λ 309.

δάμαρ, τι, τα, ἡ, (δμηθεῖσα, Σ 432),
uxor, wife, τινός, υ 290. [∪–, Ξ 503.]

Δάμασος, a Trojan, Μ 183. [∪∪∪]

Δᾰμαστορίδης, (1) Τληπόλεμος, Π
416.—(2) Ἀγέλαος. a suitor, υ 321.

δαμάω, δαμείω, δάμεν, δαμήῃ, δαμήμεναι, δαμνάω, δάμνημι, δαμόωσι, see
ΔΑΜ.

Δᾰνάη Ἀκρισιώνη, daughter of
Ἀκρίσιος, mother of Περσεύς, Ξ 319†.

Δᾰνᾰοί, ῶν, collective
designation of the Greeks
who shared in the ex-
pedition against Troy.

δᾱνά, ntr. pl., (δανός,
δαϜίω), arida, dry, ο 322†.

δᾱλός, τό, (δαϜός, δαϜίω),
facem, torch, firebrand,
μετὰ χερσὶν ἔχουσα(ι) (Od.
and Ω 647). [∪–] (See
cut.)

δά-πεδον, -ῳ, τό, (πέδον), ground,

λ 577; esp. pavimentum, pavement,
floor beaten until it was hard, esp. in
houses, δ 627; λ 420, floor of men's
apartment.

δάπτει, ουσι, ἔμεν, fut. δάψει, aor.
ἔδαψας, ε, (δαίω, dapes), lacerare,
rend, Ν 831; consume, Ψ 183. (Il.)

Δαρδᾰνίδης, son of Δάρδανος; Πρίαμος, Ἶλος.

Δαρδᾰνίη, ἡ, city founded by Δάρδανος, Υ 216†.

Δαρδᾰνίαι πυλαί, of Troy, Ε 789, Χ
194, 413.

Δαρδάνιοι = Δάρδᾰνοι = Δαρδᾰνίω-
νες (fem. Δαρδανίδες, Σ 122, 339), inhabitants of Δαρδανίη, of same race as
Ἴλιοι, called also Τρῶες, in connection
with whom they are often named as
representatives of the ἐπίκουροι, Β 819,
839, Γ 456.

Δάρδᾰνος, (1) son of Ζεύς, father of
Ἶλος and Ἐριχθόνιος, progenitor of
Τρῶες (Δαρδάνιοι), founder of Δαρ-
δανίη, Υ 215, 219, 304.—(2) son of
Βίας, Υ 460†.

δαρδάπτουσι (δάπτω), only 3 pl.
prs., devorant, devour, Λ 479, ϛ 92.

Δάρης, ητος, priest of Ἥφαιστος, Ε
9 and 27.

δαρθάνω, ἔδρᾰθε, aor., dormivit,
slept, υ 143†.

δασάσκετο, δάσασθαι, see δατέομαι.

δά-σκιος, ον, fem.,(σκιά), umbrosa,
thick-shaded, Ο 273 and ε 470.

δασμός, ὁ, (δατέομαι), distributio
(praedae), division (of the booty), Α
166†.

δάσονται, δάσσατο, ασθαι, see δατέομαι.

δα-σ-πλῆτις, hard-smiting, dread, ο
234; derivation unknown.

δᾰσύ-μαλλοι (μαλλός), thick-fleeced,
ι 425†.

δᾰσείας, ύ, densas, shaggy, ξ 49
and 51.

δᾰτέομαι, prs. and ipf., (3 pl. δᾰ-
τεῦντο, έοντο), fut. δάσονται, aor. δασ-
σάμεθα, αντο, ασθαι and ἐδάσαντο, δάσασθαι and δατέασθαι, iter. δασάσκετο,
perf. pass. 3 sing. δέδασται, (δαίω), di-
videre, divide among themselves, πα-
τρώια, μοίρας, ληίδα, κρέα, κατὰ μοῖραν
ἐφ᾽ ἡμᾶς, ἄνδιχα, τριχθά, ξ 208, ζ 10, ρ
80, Σ 511; dissecabant, cut in sunder, Υ 394; conculcabant, were
treading (to dust), and in this sense

dividing, Ψ 121; Σ 264, *share with each other* the fury of combat, fight on both sides with equal fury.

Δαυλίς, ίδος, ή, town of Φωκῆες, Β 520†.

δάφνῃσι, dat. pl., (δάφνη), lauris arboribus, *with laurel* or *bay trees*, ι 183†.

δα-φοινός, όν, οί, and **δα-φοινεόν**, Σ 538†, *blood-red*, Β 308; *tawny*, Λ 474.

δέ, particle serving to continue the narrative, usually untranslatable, *and*, *further, again, but, also*, (1) introducing additional or corresponding circumstances, A 3, 5, 10, 16, α 3, 4, 28, 44; in contrast, A 4, 20, 29, 57, α 19, 20, 26; after μέν, A 126, 141, α 13, 24, 66, the two uses often hard to distinguish; after interrogatives, A 540; second member of antithesis often precedes instead of following, Ζ 46, μ 220, π 130.—(2) introducing an apodosis (cf. αὖ), correlative, Ζ 146, λ 592; hypothetical, A 137, M 246, μ 54; in period consisting of two members, M 10–17, γ 470–74; cf. A 57, 137, 193, H 148; δ᾽ ἄρα, ζ 100, η 142.—(3) adversative, in sentence inserted between the two members of the period, υ 227; after negative sentence, ι 145; to mark a fact, in opposition to a mere assumption (esp. νῦν δέ), A 354, 417, B 82, α 166, β 79; the true in opposition to the false (τὸ δέ, τὰ δέ), χ 32, ψ 152.—(4) continuative, with causal force, apparently instead of γάρ, A 259, B 26; continuative, apparently supplying the place of a relative, A 162, B 209 sq., Δ 541, α 3, 52 sq.; instead of subordinative conjunction, Ζ 148, β 313, ι 292.—(5) recapitulating, after a parenthesis, μ 356; after vocative, γ 247; δ᾽ αὖτε, but again, σ 48; δέ τε, A 403, B 90; δέ as third word instead of second in the clause, θ 540, φ 299.

-δε, remnant of ancient pron., (1) τοίςδεσσι, *to those there*, otherwise indecl., e. g. ὅ-δε, *the one there*, so with other pronouns.—(2) *towards, -ward*, κλισίηνδε, οἰκόνδε, ὄνδε δόμονδε.

δέατο, ipf., (δίFατο), and **δοάσσατο** (δF-ασσατο), aor. subj. δοάσσεται, Ψ 339. (ΔΙF δῆλος), videbatur, *appeared*, ζ 242; *seemed*, ο 204.

δέγμενος, see δέχομαι, opperiens, *awaiting*.

δέδαα, άασι, άηκα, αήμενος, αώς, see ΔΑ.

δεδαίαται, δέδασται, see δατέομαι, divisa sunt.

δεδαϊγμένος, pf. pass., (δαΐζω), laceratus.

δέδηε, ἦει, see δαίω 1, exarsit.

δεδίασι, see δείδω, veriti sunt, *feared*.

δεδισκόμενος, ο 150 = **δειδισκόμενος**, γ 41, ipf. δειδίσκετο, (δείκνυμι), salutare, *bid welcome* (by gesture), δέπαϊ, δεξιτερῇ χειρί. (Od.)

δεδμήατο, δεδμημένος, see ΔΑΜ.

δεδοκημένος, see δοκάω.

δέδορκε, ώς, see δέρκομαι.

δεδραγμένος, see δράσσομαι.

δέελον = δῆλον, conspicuum, Κ 466†.

δεῖ, opus est, *it behooves*, I 337†.

δείδεκτο, -δέχαται, -το, plupf. and pf. from δείκνυμι.

δειδήμονες (δείδω), timidi, Γ 56†.

δείδια, ιθι, ιμεν, ίμεν, see δείδω.

δειδισκόμενος, see δεδισκόμενος.

δειδίσσεο, εσθω, imp., εσθαι, inf. prs., fut. δειδίξεσθαι, aor. -ασθαι, (δείδω, δίω), territare, *terrify*; only B 190, pass., trepidare, *fear*. (Il.)

δείδοικα, see δείδω.

δείδω (always in first foot of verse), fut. δείσεται, -εσθαι, aor. ἔδδεισας, ε, and δείσε, σαν, etc., pf. δείδοικα, ας, ε, other form δείδια, ίε, ίμεν, ίασι, imp. ἴθι, ἴτε, inf. -ίμεν, part. -ιότες, plupf. ἐδείδιμεν, ἴσαν, (δέος), metuo, timeo, *fear*; revereri, *stand in awe of*, ξ 389, π 306; μή, with indic., ε 300; with prs. or aor. subj. (after principal tenses), with opt. (after hist. tenses); with inf. when subject remains the same; (ἰνί) θυμῷ, κῆρι, κατὰ φρένα, in one's heart, in one's thought; περὶ τινος, τινῶν πέρι (ἀμφί); (μάλ᾽) αἰνῶς; E 827, fear not so much Ares; revereri, ξ 389, *revering* Zeus Xenios, and taking pity on thee, π 306.

δειελιήσας, aor. part., (δείελος), qui coenavit, *having supped*, or *toward evening*, ρ 599†.

δείελον (δείλη), vespertinum, ἦμαρ, ρ 606, late in the afternoon; δείελος, vespera, *evening*, Φ 232.

δεικανόωντο, ipf., from -νάομαι, (δεικνύμενος, δ 59), consalutabant = *extend hospitable welcome*, by motion of cups, O 86; or with words, ω 410.

δείκνυμι, prs., only δεικνύς and -νύμενος, fut. δείξω, etc., aor. δεῖξε; mid. pf. 3 pl. δειδέχαται, plupf. 3 sing. δείδεκτο, 3 pl. δειδέχατο, (δίκη), monstrare, show, point out, act. and mid., Ψ 701; σῆμα, τέρας, give a sign or portent, teach; mid., consaluto, make welcome (by gesture, or with words), κυπέλλοις, δεπάεσσι, μύθοις, Ι 196, δ 59, Ι 224, 671, Δ 4, Χ 435, η 72.

δείλη, afternoon, Φ 111†.

δείλω, only δείλετο, declined toward setting; v. l. of Aristarchus for δύσετο, η 289†.

δειλός, ή, όν, (δεῖσαι), ignavus, cowardly, Ν 278, Α 293; wretched, miserable, θ 351; miser, P 38, X 431, Ψ 223; esp. in phrase δειλοῖσι βροτοῖσι, λ 19, and ἆ δειλ' (δειλέ), δειλώ, -ώ, heu te miserum, etc.

δεῖμα, τό, (δεῖσαι), terrorem, Ε 682†.

δείματο, ομεν, see δέμω.

Δεῖμος, ον, (δείδω), Terror, terror of combat personified, Δ 440. (Il.)

δεινός, ή, όν, (δέος), horrendus, dread, terrible, Β 321, 755; δεινὸν δέρκεσθαι, Γ 342, and δεινὰ ἰδών, Ο 13, λ 608 and elsewh.=adv. Η 566, Ε 439, Δ 420, Θ 133; vast, great, Η 346, Ο 309, Ξ 385; mighty, Ε 839; venerandus, venerated, θ 22. (Orig. form δϜεινός, cf. Γ 172.)

δείους, τοῦ, gen. from δέος, timoris, cf. the form σπείους.

δειπνέω, ipf. ἐδείπνεε, plupf. δεδειπνήκει, also aor., (δεῖπνον), coenare, take a meal, ξ 111.

δείπν-ηστος, ὁ, (δειπνέω), meal-time (afternoon), ρ 170†.

δειπνίσσας, aor. part. from -ίζω, (δεῖπνον), after having entertained him at his table, δ 535 and λ 411.

δεῖπνον, ον, τό, (δάπτω, dapes), cena, chief meal (in the afternoon, see δόρπον, v 392), repast, Β 381, Κ 578; ἑλέσθαι, ρ 176; food, o 316; fodder, Β 383.

δείρας, αντος, aor. part. from δέρω.

δειρῆς, ῇ, ήν, αἱ, ῇσι, collum, cervices, neck, throat, Γ 371, Τ 285, μ 90.

δειρο-τομήσεις, ει, fut., and -ῆσαι, σας, aor. from δειροτομέω, (τέμνω), iu-

gulare, cut the throat, behead, Ψ 174, χ 349.

Δεισ-ήνωρ, ορα, a Lykian, P 217†.

δέκα, decem, ten; as a round number, η 253, Β 489; δεκάκις, decies; δεκάς, άδος, Eng. decade; δέκατος, decimus, as a round number, ξ 325; δεκάχῖλοι, centum milia.

δέκτῃ, τῷ, (δέχομαι), mendico, beggar.

δέκτο, aor. from δέχομαι, excepit.

δελφῖνος, τοῦ, and -ῖνας, τούς, delphini, dolphin, Φ 22 and μ 96.

δέμας, τό, (δέμω), frame, build of body, Α 115; joined with εἶδος, φυή, αὐδή; freq. δέμας, as acc. of specification, in figure, also with gen., like, cf. instar, Λ 596.

δέμνια, τά, (δέω), wooden bedstead (with cords), τ 318, λ 189.

δέμω, ipf. 1 sing. δέμον, aor. ἔδειμε, (and mid. -ατο), subj. δείμομεν, pass. pf. δεδμημένοι, plupf. (ἐ)δέδμητο, (domus), build, Ι 349, Η 337.

δενδίλλων, pres. part., of doubtful origin, address one's self in turn to, ἐς, Ι 180†.

δένδρεον, ἐῳ, τό, (δένδρον), arbor, tree. [Γ 152, τ 520; ‿⌢.]

δενδρήεντι, dat. masc., nom. fem. -εσσα, (δενδρήεις), woody, ι 200, a 51.

Δεξαμένη, daughter of Νηρεύς, Σ 44†.

Δεξιάδης, i. e. Ἰφίνοος, Η 15.

δεξιός, όν, (δέχομαι), (1) dexter, on the right hand or side, ἐπὶ δεξιά and δεξιόφιν, Ν 308; esp. δεξιῇ [Κ 542, ‿⌢], αἱ, dextra (manus); also fides interposita, pledges of faith, Β 341.—(2) faustus, propitious, o 160.

δεξιτεροῖο, όν, ῆς, ῇ, ήν, ῇφι=δεξιτοῖο, etc., dextri, A 501, Λ 377.

δέξο, aor. imp. from δέχομαι.

δεόντων, imp. from δέω, false reading for διδέντων.

δέος, τό, δείους, gen., (δείδω), timor, fear, Α 515; nihil tibi timendum; with inf., Μ 246.

δέπας, τό, αἵ and αι, pl. α, άων, άεσσι and άων, (δάπτω?), vase or cup for drinking; only Λ 632, as mixing-bowl. (See cut.)

δέρκεσθαι, prs., ipf. iter. δέρκεσκετο, pf. δέδορκεν, ὥς, aor.

ἔδρακον, tueri, look, δεινόν, σμερδαλέον, πῦρ, with fiery glance, ἐπὶ χθονί; joined with ζῆν, live and "see the light of the sun;" behold, N 86.

δέρμα, τό, ατι, ατα, ασι, (δέρω), hide, stripped off, pellis; skin, on human body, cutis; hide dressed for shield, Z 117; skin prepared for bottle, β 291.

δερμάτῐνοισιν (δέρμα), leathern (row-locks), δ 782 and θ 53.

δέρον, ipf. from δέρω.

δέρτρον, τό, membrane which contains the bowels; penetrating into the intestines, λ 579†.

δέρω, ipf. ἔδερον, δίρον, aor. ἔδειραν, δείραντας, strip off the hide, flay, A 459, τ 421.

δέσμᾰτα, τά, (δέω), vincula, X 468, head-band. (See cut No. 8.)

δεσμός, οἷο, ὁ, (δέω), vinculum, band, κρατερός, ἀργαλέος, θυμαλγέϊ, νηλέϊ, ὀλοῷ; χαλεπός, fetter; halter, Z 507; rivets for securing handles to tripod, Σ 379; hawser, ν 100; knot, ξ 348; latch-string, φ 241.

δέσποινα, ης, ἡ, (δεσπότης), mistress, also with ἄλοχος and γυνή, γ 403 (cf. πότνια).

δεταί (δέω) καιόμεναι, burning fagots, Λ 554 and P 663.

δενήσεσθαι, see δεύω.

Δευκᾰλίδης, Ἰδομενεύς, M 117. [ῐ]

Δευκᾰλίων, ωνος, (1) son of Μίνως, king of Κρήτη, N 451 sq., τ 180 sq.—(2) a Trojan, Υ 478.

δεῦρο, δεῦτε (possibly δί-Ϝρω-θι, δέ-Ϝρ-ιτε), huc i, come here, θ 292; allons! hither, δεῦρ' ἴθι, ἄγε δεῦρο, δεῦτ' ἄγετε; often with subj. of exhortation.

δεύτατος, ον, (δεύτερος), ultimus, last, T 51.

δεῦτε, see δεῦρο.

δεύτερος, ῳ, ον, οι, (δύω), alter, secundus, Ψ 265; with gen. of compar., Ψ 248; -ον, iterum, with αὖ, αὖτις, αὖτε; τὰ δεύτερα, second prize, Ψ 538.

1. δεύει, prs. 3 sing., ipf. ἔδευε and δεῦε, iter. δεύεσκον, pass. -εται, -ετο, -οντο, drench, moisten, N 655, B 471.

2. δεύω, only prs. δεύεαι, -ῃ, opt. 3 pl. δευοίατο, etc., ipf. ἐδεύεο, fut. δευήσεαι, -ήσεσθαι, aor. ἐδεύησε, egere, miss, want, τινός; θυμοῦ, vita privatos, Γ 294; οὐ δεύεσθαι οὕτω, will not be so wanting (in battle) (πολέμου); P 142, be deficient in—, (τινός); be inferior to,

(τινός); ἐδεύησε, with infin., ι 540, it just missed hitting the rudder.

δέχαται, δέχθαι, see δέχομαι.

δέχομαι, 3 pl. δέχαται, fut. and 1 aor. reg., 2 aor. ἐδέγμην, δέκτο, imp. δέξο, inf. δέχθαι, part. δέγμενος, pf. δέδεξο, imp. δεδέγμένος, 3 fut. δεδέξομαι, (δέκα), exciperc, accipere, receive, παρά τινος (ἐμεῦ πάρα, Ω 429), τινός τι, τινί τι, receive at hand of, υ 271; accept, κῆρα, death; await attack of, Υ 377; ἔγχεϊ, etc.; esp. 2 aor. await, with part., Δ 107; τινὰ ὁπότε λήξειε, I 191; εἰσόκεν ἔλθῃς, K 62 (δεδεγμένος, Λ 124, nactus, having received at the hands of), stand one's ground against in combat. Intrans. only T 290, sic mihi semper malum excipit malum, succeeds.

δεψήσας, aor. part. from δέψω, knead, μ 48†.

1. δέω, aor. δῆσεν, caruit, stood in need of, Σ 100† (δεῖ, see separately).

2. δέω, prs. imp. δεόντων, ipf. mid. δέοντο, aor. δῆσε, -σαν, imp. -σάντων, mid. aor. iter. δησάσκετο, plupf. pass. δέδετο, -ντο, ligare, vincire, tie, bind, men, ☒ 73, Φ 30; cattle, βίη, N 572; (ἐν) δεσμῷ; ἔκ τινος, to something, κ 96, X 398; Ψ 854 (ποδός, by the foot); ὅπλα ἀνὰ νῆα, make fast tackle throughout the ship, β 430; ἐρετμὰ ἐπὶ κληΐσιν, to the thole-pins; παρ' ἅρμασιν, to the chariot, Θ 544; τινὰ κελεύθου, hinder one's journey.

δή (cognate with jam, Eng. yea, yes?), particle marking a conclusion; cf. in meaning, jam, with various signif., according to the words with which it is connected.—(1) in general, evidently, and of time, now, already, τὰ δή, just that; νῦν δή, at this very moment, B 284; now finally; δὴ τότε, then indeed, ν 92; γὰρ δή, for surely; οὕτω δή, just so; it strengthens superlatives, confessedly the best, A 266; ἄλλοι δή, others, be they who they may; after interrogative words gives greater definiteness, τίς δή, quis tandem, who pray; πῇ δή, B 339; in commands, strengthens the command, yet, only, A 295, 514, 545; common phrases, ἄγε δή, agedum; ἴθι δή, μὴ δή, only do not, A 131; so also with expressions of wish, αἴ γὰρ δή, if only.—(2) in dependent clauses, ὡς δή, that without doubt, A 110; οὕνεκα δή, because *indeed;* ἐπεὶ δή, since *now;* in relative clauses, ἐξ οὗ δή, when *once for all*, A 6; in temporal clause, ὅτε δή, when *now*, as soon as; in conditional clause, εἰ δή (ἦν δή), if *now*, if *really*, if *at all events*, expressing a supposition which can not be contradicted; in interrogative clause, εἰ δή, whether *really*, a 207; in final clause, ἢ ἵνα δή, is it *perhaps* that thou mayest give *as is to be expected?* H 26; δὴ αὖτε, actually again; δ', better δὴ αὖ, αὖτε, οὕτως, pronounced with synizesis, A 131, 338, 540, δ 400; δή is often merged by synizesis with following word, Λ 138, 386, μ 330; yet never so, δὴ ἔπειτα. δή always follows the emphatic word, exc. in δὴ τότε, γάρ, πάμπαν.

δηθά, δήθ', diu, *long,* B 435, a 49. [‒ ⏑]

δηθύνειν, subj. δηθύνῃσθα, ipf. δήθῡνεν, (δηθά), cunctari, *linger,* A 27, Z 503.

Δηϊ-κόων, ωντος, (hostes speculans), a Trojan, E 533 sqq.

1. **δήϊοιο,** ον, (δέδηε, δαίω, 1), *blazing,* πῦρ, B 415; πόλεμος, *hot* combat, Δ 281.

2. **δήϊος,** ον, hostilis, ἄνδρα, Z 481, and hostis, B 544.

Δηϊοπῐτης, ην, son of Πρίαμος, Λ 420†.

δηϊοτῆτος, ι, α, nom. δηιοτής, ἡ, (δήϊος), caedes, *slaughter,* usually with αἰνῆς, H 174.

Δηΐ-οχος, ον, a Greek, O 341†.

δηϊόω, only pres. forms, e. g., Λ 153, Ψ 176, δ 226, and ipf. pass., N 675; all other forms, prs. ipf. fut. aor. also pass. from **δηόω,** pres. part. δῃῶν, more commonly δηϊόων, (δήϊος), caedere, concidere, *slay, cut in pieces,* χαλκῷ, Θ 534; lacerare, *rend,* P 65; Σ 195, *fighting* with the spear for—.

Δηΐ-πυλος, ῳ, companion at arms of Σθένελος, E 325†.

Δηΐ-πυρος, ον, a Greek, N 576.

Δηΐ-φοβος, οιο, son of Πρίαμος, M 94, δ 276.

δηλέομαι, only fut. and aor., (δαλός, deleo), laedere, *hurt,* χαλκῷ, χ 368; violare (ὑπὲρ, Δ 67), ὅρκια; *harm,* Ξ 102; by theft, θ 444, ν 124.

δηλήματα, τά, (δηλέομαι), *destroyers,* μ 286†.

δηλήμονα, ες, nom. δηλήμων, (δηλέ-

ομαι), infestus, *baneful,* Ω 33; βροτῶν, *destroyer,* σ 85.

Δῆλος, ῳ, ἡ, a famous island, sacred to Apollo and Artemis, ζ 162†.

δῆλον (δέελον), manifestum, ν 333†.

Δημήτηρ, τερος, τερα, (τρος, τρα), prob. = Γῆ μήτηρ, Demeter; ἀνάσσης, Ξ 326, ε 125, B 696; ἀκτή, barley meal.

δημιο-Fεργοί, *workers for the community, handicraftsmen,* e. g. seers, physicians, carpenters, bards, heralds, ρ 383.

δήμιος, ον, *belonging to the people;* publicus; δήμιον, *public affair;* δήμια πίνειν, publice, at public expense.

δημο-βόρος, *devourer of the people,* of grinding, avaricious βασιλεύς, A 231†.

δημο-γέροντος, ες, (γέρων), *elder of the people,* Γ 14. (Il.)

Δημό-δοκος, ου, name of blind bard in Σχερίη, θ 44. (Od.)

δημόθεν (δῆμος) ἀγείρας, publice collectum, having levied *from among the people,* ρ 197†.

Δημο-κόων, ωντα, son of Πρίαμος, Δ 499†.

Δημο-λέων, οντα, son of Ἀντήνωρ, Υ 395†.

Δημο-πτόλεμος, ον, a suitor of Πηνελόπεια, χ 266. (Od.)

δῆμος, ου and οιο, ὁ, commons, community, (1) civitas, *body of citizens,* opp. βουλὴ γερόντων and βασιλεύς, θ 157; with πόλις, Γ 50, town and *people;* so often = *people, the public,* e. g. M 213 = δήμου ἀνήρ, unus ex plebe.— (2) *country-district* with its inhabitants, Z 158, Ι 634, Ω 481; Ὀνείρων δῆμος, land of Dreams.

δημῷ, όν, dat. acc., from δημός, *fat,* of man and beasts, ἀργέτι, Λ 818; πίονα, X 501, exuberant fat; Ψ 243.

Δημ-οῦχος, ον, Φιλητορίδην, Υ 457†.

δήν (orig. δϜήν), diu, *long;* οὔτι μάλα δήν, N 573; οὐδ' ἄρ (οὗτοι) ἔτι δήν, β 36, ζ 33; οἰχομένοιο, β 215.

δηναιός (δήν) μάλ' οὔ, minime longaevus, by no means *long lived,* E 407†.

δήνεα, τά, (δαῆναι), consilia, *counsels, arts,* ψ 82, Δ 361.

δηῶν, δῃόω, see δηϊόω.

δηρῐάασθον, 3 du. indic., δηρῐάασθαι

inf., -άάσθων imp. prs., ipf. δηρύωντο; also from δηρίομαι; aor. δηρίσαντο, also aor. pass. in act. signif. δηρινθήτην, (δῆρις), contend, P 734 (with words, only θ 76, 78, M 421).

δῆριν, τήν, rivalry, ω 515; battle, P 158.

δηρινθήτην (=δῆριν ἐθέσθην, P 158), see δηρίάασθον.

δηρόν, acc. masc. and neut., (δήν), diuturnum, long, χρόνον, Ξ 206; elsewh. =diu, B 298.

δησάσκετο, aor. from δέω, vinciebat.

δῆσε, from δέω, (1) caruit.—(2) ligavit.

δήω, δήεις, ομεν, ετε, invenies, N 260; find out, attain, I 418.

Δία=Ζῆνα, see Ζεύς.

διά, prep., I. with gen., per, through, Λ 398, Γ 61, 357, λ 581; κυνέης διὰ χαλκοπαρῄου, M 183, P 294; στήθεσφιν, E 57; ὄρεπφι, K 185; ἔπρεπε δ. πάντων, was conspicuous even among all, M 104; throughout, amid, ι 298, Δ 495, Z 226, I 468, N 755.—II. with acc. (1) per, through, throughout, A 600, K 375, M 62, X 190, ι 447, ρ 72; διὰ στόμα ἄγειν, in ore habere, to have in one's mouth, upon one's lips; trans, across, H 247, θ 343, K 298; of time, during, per, δ. νύκτα, B 57, θ 510, ι 143; νύκτα δι' ὀρφναίην, K 83, 142, 297, 386, Ω 363.—(2) propter, because of, A 72, ψ 67; ope, by means of, θ 520, O 41, 71, K 497, θ 82, λ 276; auxilio, Ἀθήνης, θ 520. [∪∪, –∪ at beginning of verse.]

δια-βαινέμεν, inf. prs., -βήμεναι aor., traicere, cross over, εὖ διαβάς, placing his legs far apart, i. e. planting himself firmly, M 458.

δια-γιγνώσκω, inf. aor. -γνῶναι, agnoscere, recognize, H 424; dignoscere, distinguish. (Il.)

δια-γλάψασα (γλάφω), excavans, scoop out, δ 438†.

δι-άγω, δι-ήγαγον aor., transportaverunt, carry over, v 187†.

διὰ δᾰσάσκετο, διὰ δατέοντο, dispertiebat, distributed, see δατέομαι.

διὰ ἔδαψας, ε, see δάπτει, laceravisti.

διὰ-δέρκ-μαι, aor. opt. δια-δράκοι, look through at, pierce through, Ξ 344†.

δι-εδηλήσαντο (δηλέομαι), laceravissent, ξ 37†.

δι-άει, see δι-άημι, perflat.

δια-είδεται (ιδον), prs. pass., cernitur, is discerned, N 277; fut. mid. -είσεται, prae se feret, display, θ 535.

δια-ειπέμεν, inf., imp. δίειπε (Ϝεῖπε), δ 215 and K 425, talk over fully, relate precisely.

δι-άημι, only 3 sing. ipf. δι-άη, better reading δι-άει, prs., perflare, blow through, ε 478. (Od.)

δι-εθείωσε, aor., (θειόω, θέειον), fumigate (with sulphur), χ 494†.

δια-θρύπτω, aor. pass. δῐᾰ-τρῠφέν, confractum, shivered, Γ 363†.

διαίνω, ipf. δίαινε, pass. διαίνετο, aor. ἐδίηνε, humectare, moisten, X 495. (Il.)

δι-αιρέω, aor. διὰ ἕλε, dissecuit, cut through, Υ 280†.

δια-κεάζω, aor. inf. διὰ κεάσσαι, discindere, split, ο 322†.

δια-κείρω, aor. inf. διακέρσαι, interrumpere, frustrate, θ 8†.

δια-κλάσσας, aor. part., (κλάω), diffringens, breaking in twain, E 216†.

δια-κοσμέω, ipf. -εκόσμεον, aor. mid., -εκοσμήσαντο, aor. pass. opt. -κοσμηθεῖμεν, part. -θέντες, (κόσμος), dispertio, dispose; χ 457, put in order.

δια-κρῐδόν (κρίνω) ἄριστος, decidedly the best, M 103 and O 108.

δια-κρίνω, reg., fut. 3 sing. -κρῐνέει, mid. -κρῐνέεσθαι (also in pass. signif.); aor. pass. 3 pl. -ἐκρῖθεν, opt. -κρινθεῖτε, inf. -κρινθήμεναι, pf. part. -κεκρῐμέναι, (κρίνω), separare, separate, B 475; B 387, shall part the fury of the men, i. e. the furious combatants; cf. H 292; pass., be parted, separate peacefully, Ι 98, ω 532; dignoscere, distinguish, θ 195.

δῐ-άκτορος, ου, ὁ, (δίάγω), guide, conductor, Ἀργεϊφόντης, α 84; epith. of Hermes as messenger of the gods, and guide of Priamos, Ω; of Odysseus, κ; of souls of departed, ω.

δια-λέγομαι, aor. δι-ελέξατο, ἀλλὰ τί ἦ μοι ταῦτα φίλος—θυμός, why does my heart thus converse with me? Λ 407, and freq.

δι-άμησε, aor. -αμάω, dissecuit, cut through, Γ 359 and H 253.

δια-μελεϊστί, see μελεϊστί.

διε-μέτρεον, ipf., (-μετρέω), metabantur, were measuring off, Γ 315†.

δια-μετρητῷ, metato, laid off, Γ 344†.

δῐ-έμοιρᾶτο, ipf., -άομαι, (μοῖρα), lispertiit, portioned out, ξ 434†.

δῐ-αμ-περές, also διὰ δ' ἀμπερές, (πείρω), piercing through, (1) through and through, penitus; successively, deinceps, H 171, χ 190, ξ 11.—(2) perpetuo, forever, constantly, λ 558, ν 59; ἤματα πάντα, ὁ 209.

δῐ-άν-δῐχᾰ (δίχα), bifariam; μερμηρίζω, hesitated between two resolves; I 37, gave them but one of two things.

δῐ-ήνῦσεν, aor., (ἀνύω), οὔπω—ἀγορεύων, finished narrating, ρ 517†.

διὰ πείρεν, aor. from πείρω, transfixit, Π 405†.

δια-πέρθω, fut. 1 aor., and 2 aor. -επράθομεν, ον, έειν, evertere, overthrow, but διεπράθετο, ο 384, eversa est.

δια-πέτομαι, see δι-ίπταμαι.

δια-πλήσσοντες, part. from -πλήσσω, splitting, Ψ 120; aor. inf. πλήξαι, θ 507.

δια-πορθήσας, aor. part. from -πορθέω, diripere, sack, B 691†.

δια-πρᾰθέειν, aor. from δια-πέρθω, evertere.

δια-πρήσσω, prs. ipf., (πέρας), emetiri, pass over, accomplish, κέλευθον, πεδίοιο; spend, ἤματα, with part. I 326; λέγων, finish narrating, ξ 197, cf. ρ 517.

δῐα-πρό, penitus, right through, with gen. after verbs of motion, E 281; without gen., E 66, M 184, 404.

δῐα-πρύσῐον (διαπρό), penetrans, reaching far and wide, P 748; piercingly, ἤϋσεν.

δῐ-επτοίησε, aor. from -πτοιέω, conterruit, startle and scatter, σ 340†.

δῐ-αρπάζουσι, auferunt, carry off, Π 355†.

δια-ρ-ραίουσι, and fut., aor. -ρᾶίσαι, fut. mid. -ραίσεσθαι, percellere, shatter, μ 290; evertere, overthrow, πόλιν; perdere, destroy, α 251; dilacerare, P 727.

διὰ ῥήξασθαι, aor. from ῥήγνυμι, dirumpere, break through, M 308†.

δια-ρ-ρίπτασκεν (Fρίπτω), iter. aor., traiciebat, shot through, τ 575†.

δια-σεύομαι, only aor. διέσσυτο, pervolavit, flew (charged, hastened) through, with acc. and with gen., O 542, δ 37.

δια-σκεδάννυμι, aor. -εσκέδᾰσε, ειε, disiecit, scatter, ε 369; comminuit, shatter, η 275; ρ 244, would he scatter to the winds all thy fine things=insolence.

δια-σκιδνᾶσι, from -σκίδνημι, dispellunt, E 526†.

δια-σκοπιᾶσθαι, from -σκοπιάομαι, speculari, spy out, K 388 and P 252.

δια-σχίζω, aor. -έσχισε, pass. -εσχίσθη, discindere, part, cleave asunder, ι 71 and Π 316.

διὰ τάμε, 3 sing. 1 aor., subj. -τάμῃ, (τέμνω), dissecuit, P 522 and 618.

διὰ τελευτᾷ, from τελευτάω, perficit, bring fully to pass, T 90†.

δια-τινάξῃ, aor. subj. from -τινάσσω, discusserit, shatter, ε 363†.

δια-τμήγω, aor. -τμῆξαι, ας, 2 aor. -έτμαγεν, aor. pass. 3 pl. -έτμαγεν, (έταμον), cleave, ε 409, μ 174; traiciens, crossing, according to others, parting, Φ 3; pass., have become dispersed, Π 354; part, separate; M 461, were shattered, flew asunder.

δια-τρέσσω, aor. -έδραμον, run over (the sea), γ 177 and ε 100.

δι-έτρεσαν, aor. from -τρέω (P 729, tmesis), diffugerunt, scattered, Λ 481. (Il.)

δια-τρίβειν, only pres., and aor. -τρίψας, conterere, rub, Λ 846; tempus terere, T 150, morari, delay; lose time on the road, ὁδοῖο, β 404; τινὰ ὅν γάμον, put off one with her wedding, β 204.

δια-τρύγιος, bearing in succession, ω 342†.

δια-τρύφέν, see διαθρύπτω, comminutum, shivered.

δι-εφαίνετο, ipf., was visible through, νεκύων, Θ 491; glowed through, ι 379.

δια-φθείρω, fut. -φθέρσει, pf. -έφθορας, evertet, destroy, N 625; O 128, periisti, thou art doomed (threat).

διὰ φορέουσι, from φορέω, divulgant, spread abroad, τ 333†.

δια-φράζω, only redup. nor. -επέφρᾰδε, indicate, Υ 340; tell, Σ 9; admonish, ζ 47.

δῐ-αφύσσω, ipf. ἄφυσσε (tmesis), aor. -ήφῦσε, pass. prs. -αφυσσόμενον, draw off, consume, π 110; tear away,

τ 450; *cut through* and *let gush forth*,
ἔντερα.

δια-χέω, only aor. -ἔχευαν, (ἔχεϜαν),
dissecuerunt, *cut up*, γ 456.

διδάσκω, prs., inf. σκέμεναι, aor. 3
sing. δίδαξε, pass. pres., part., and
δεδιδάχθαι, pf. inf., (ΔΑ), doceo, *teach*,
τινά τι, θ 481, χ 422; pass., discere,
learn, πρός τινος, of one, Λ 831; part.
with gen., modo edoctus, one who
has just begun to learn, *tyro*, Π 811.

δίδημι, only imp. **διδέντων**, and ipf.
3 sing. δίδη, (δέω), vincire, *bind*, Λ
105 and μ 54.

δίδυμάονε, du.,-οσι,dat.pl.,(δίδυμοι),
gemini, *twins*, Π 672, also παῖδε.

δίδῡμοι, οισι, (δύω), gemini, *twins*,
Ψ 641; duplicibus, *twofold*, τ 227.

δίδωμι, collat. form διδόω; irreg.
forms, διδοῖς, διδοῖσθα, inf. διδόμεν,
διδοῦναι,imp.δίδωθι,δίδου,ipf.(ἐ)δίδου,
3 pl. δίδοσαν, δίδον, fut. διδώσομεν,
ώσειν, δωσέμεναι; aor. 3 pl. δόσαν,
subj.δώῃ,δώομεν,δώωσιν,inf.δόμεν(αι),
aor. iter. δόσκον, εν, ον, (dare), *give,
present*, Χ 470, ι 197, freq. with inf., χ
253; with inf. of purpose, Λ 20; *bestow, accord*, of gods (opp. ἀνένευσε, Π
250; ἰάσει, ξ 444), Η 288, Ι 37, 255;
with inf., Σ 293, Γ 322; ὁδόν, *prosperous journey*, οὖρον, Η 4; also of evils,
decree, inflict, ἄτην, δ 262, etc. ; tra-
dere, τινά κυσί; ἀχέεσσι, *deliver over
to*, Ψ 390, ω 219, Ψ 512, abducen-
dam; collocare filiam,*give* daughter *in marriage*, δ 7; ἀνέρι μητέρα, β
223 ; *offer*, ν 378 ; *pay*, Φ 42, α 431.

δίε, see δίω, persecutus est, *pursue*.

δι-έδραμον, see διατρέχω.

δι-έεργον (ἔϜεργον), ipf., *separated,
parted*, Μ 424†.

δια - Ϝειπέμεν, inf., imp. δίειπε,
(Ϝεῖπον), δ 215 and Κ 425, *tell fully,
converse of*.

δι-είρεαι, 2 sing. indic., -είρεο, imp.,
(εἴρομαι), perquirere,*question*, Α 550,
δ 492.

δῖ-έκ, with gen., *out through*, προ-
θύρου, μεγάροιο, σ 101, 185.

δι-ελαύνω, aor. **διὰ ἔλασσεν** (imp.
-σσον), and **διήλασεν**, plupf. pass. ἐλήλατο, *drive through*, with gen., Κ 564;
of spear, *thrust through* (with gen.), Ν
595; also διαπρό—ἐλάσσαι, Ν 647.

δι-ελθέμεν, see δι-έρχομαι.

δίενται, ισθαι, prs., (δίω), *speed* across
the plain, Ψ 475 ; *be frightened off from*,
with gen., Μ 304. [◡ – –]

δῖ-εξ-ίμεναι, inf., (εἶμι), *go out through*,
Ζ 393.

δι-εξ-ερέεσθε (ἐρέομαι), inquiritis,
question, Κ 432†.

δι-επέφρᾰδε, see διαφράζω, expli-
cuit.

δι-έπρᾰθον, see διαπέρθω, evertit.

δι-έπτᾰτο, see διίπταμαι, pervolavit.

δι - έπουσιν, ipf. δίειπε, διείπομεν,
(ἔπω), exsequi, *perform*, Α 166, μ 16;
persequi, *chase away*, Ω 247 ; *pass
through*, Β 207.

δι-ήρεσα, aor. from -ερέσσω, *paddled
hard*, μ 444 and ξ 351.

διερός, ψ, *living*, ζ 201 ; *quick*, ι 43.

δι-έρχεται, etc., pres. fut. aor.,
transire per,*pass through*, with acc.,
Γ 198; with gen., Υ 100, ζ 304 ; διαπρὸ
ἤλυθεν, Ν 260.

δι-έσσυτο, aor. from -σεύομαι, pervolavit.

δι-έτμᾰγεν, aor. from -τμήγω, discesserunt, disiecti sunt.

δι-έχω, aor. **διάσχε** and δι'—ἔσχεν,
prominebat,*project out*, Ε 100 ; with
gen., Ν 519.

δί-ζηαι, pres. 2 sing., etc., (δι-ζῆ-
ianus? strictly, *go, go to seek*, cf. Italian, cercare), quaerere, *seek*, Ἄσιον
εἴ που (si qua) ἐφεύροι, Ν 760; *seek
to win*, woo, τινί τι, π 391.

δί-ζύγες (ζυγῆναι), biiugi, *yoked
two abreast*, Ε 195 and Κ 473.

δίζε, ipf., (δίζω, from δϜίς, δύο), du-
bitabat, *debated*, Π 713†.

Δίη, ῃ, an island =Νάξος, λ 325.

διη-κόσιοι, ων, ducenti, Ι 383,
Θ 233.

δι-ηνεκέα, acc. masc., ἑς, ἑεσσι,
-έσσι, adv.-έως,(ἤνεγκον),continuus,
continuous, unbroken, long; adv., *at
length, minutely*, δ 836.

δι-ήρεσα, aor. from -ερέσσω.

δίηται, see δίω.

δι-ίημι, διὰ δ' ἧκε, with gen., *shot
through*, φ 328, ω 177.

δί-ικεο, aor., fut. -ίξομαι, (ἱκνέομαι),
go through, recensere, *review*, Ι 61,
Τ 186.

δῖι-πετέος, gen., (ΔιϜί, πετ-ής), *fallen
from Zeus*, i. e. *from heaven*, of rivers,
Π 174.

δι-ίπταμαι, aor. δι-έπτᾶτο, E 99, O 83, pervolavit, *flew through*.

δι-ίσταμαι, reg., (pf. -ίσταμεν), *separate*; Π 470, *parted from each other*; A 6, *quarrel*; Φ 436, *stand aloof*.

δῐκάζέμεν, inf. prs., 3 pl. ipf. δίκαζον, 3 pl. aor. δίκασαν, imp. δικάσσατε; prs. mid., (δίκη), *pass sentence upon, τισί*; between two persons, ἐς μέσον τισί, Ψ 574; mid., *seek justice*, μ 440.

δῐκαιον, ῳ, οι, comp. -ότερος, sup. ότατος, ων, adv. αἴως, (δίκη), iustus, aequus, *just, equitable*, γ 52; οὐδὲ δίκαιον, *nor is it right*, υ 294; *in due form*, ξ 90; σ 414, *upon a thing rightly* said, a just request.

δῐκασ-πόλον, -οι, (πέλω), *lawgiver*, A 238; ἄνδρα, λ 186.

δίκη, ης, ἡ, (δείκνυμι), *usage, custom*; τ 168, for such is *the way*; *right*, ius, Π 388, pervert *justice*; εἰπεῖν, *give judgment*; pl., *decisions*; δίκῃ, iure, *duly, rightly*.

δι-κλῐδες (κλίνω), *double-folding*, of door and gates, M 455. (See cut, representing ancient Egyptian doors.)

δικτύῳ, nir., reti, *in* or *with the net*, χ 386†.

δινεύοι, etc., prs. ipf., (iter. δινεύεσκε), versari, *move about*, Δ 541; *turn about*, τί, Σ 543; *fly in circles*, Ψ 875; Σ 606, *turn somersaults*; oberrare, *wander about*, Ω 12.

δινέω, ipf. δινέομεν, (ἐ)δίνεον, also mid. 3 du. δινείσθην, (δίνη), *whirl*, Ψ 840; *turn around*, ι 384, 388; mid. (and act., Σ 494), *whirl about*; oberrare, *roam*, ι 153 (δινηθῆναι, π 63).

δίνη, ης, and pl., vortex, *eddy*. (Il. Φ.)

δινήεις, εντος, *eddying*, Φ 125.

δινωτοῖσι, τήν, (δινόω), *inlaid*, τ 56.

δῖο-γενής, voc. -ές, (Ζεύς, divo), *sprung from Zeus*, A 337.

Διόθεν, Jovis iussu, O 489, Ω 194, 561.

δῐ-οϊστεύω, aor. -οϊστεύσῃ, εύσειας, εῦσαι, (ὀϊστός), *pierce with arrow*, with gen., τ 578. (Od.)

Δῖο-κλῆς, ῆος, son of Orsilochos of Pherai, γ 488.

δι-όλλῡμι, pf. δῐ-όλωλε, *be plundered*, β 64†.

Δῖο-μήδη, daughter of Phorbas of Lesbos, slave of Achilleus, I 665†.

Δῖο-μήδης, εος, Τυδέος υἱός, Ψ 472 (H 163), husband of Aigialeia, E 412; king of Argos, B 567; his exploits, ἀριστεία, E; dealings with Glaukos, Z 232–236.

Δίον, ον, town in Euboia, B 538†.

Διονύσου, λ 325†, see Διώνυσος.

δι-οπτεύσων, fut., speculaturus, *to spy about*, K 451†.

δι-οπτῆρα, τόν, (διοπτέω), speculatorem, *scout*, K 562†.

διὰ δρύξας, aor. part. from ὀρύσσω, *digging a long straight trench*, φ 120†.

δῖος, α, ον, (δῖϜος), illustris, *illustrious, divine, noble*, of gods, men, horses, elements; also of Λακεδαίμονα.

Δῖος, ον, son of Priamos, Ω 251†.

δῖο-τρεφέος, ές and pl., -ής, (Διός, τρέφω), *nourished, cherished by Zeus*, A 176.

δί-πλἄκι, α, dat. acc., *double mantle*, Γ 126.

δι-πλόος, duplex, Δ 133; διπλῆν χλαῖναν, *double* mantle, see δίπλακι.

δί-πτὔχα, acc., from -πτύξ, (πτύσσω), *double, folded in two layers*, κνίσην, A 461, γ 458.

δί-πτὔχον, acc., from -πτύχος, *thrown twice around his shoulders*, ν 224†.

δίς (δϜίς), bis, τόσσον, *twice as far*, ι 491†.

δισ-θᾰνέες, bis mortales, μ 22†.

δισκέω, ipf. ἐδίσκεον, *hurled the discus*, θ 188†.

δίσκου, ῳ, ον, οισι, from δίσκος, ὁ, (δικεῖν), *quoit, discus*, of metal, stone, wood; κατωμαδίοιο (cf. Statius, Thebais, VI., 646–721), attitude illustrated by the cut, see follg. page, after Myron's famous statue the discus-thrower (Discobolos); δίσκου οὖρα, τά = δίσκουρα, *a quoit's cast*, Ψ 431, 523.

διφῶν, part. from διφάω, diving (for oysters), Π 747†.

δίφρος, ου, οιο, ὁ, etc., (1) seat or stool, without back or arms, τ 97 (see cut No. 79).—(2) seat or box of chariot, Ε 728, esp. of war-chariot, Γ 262; word also designates the chariot itself, or in γ 324, a traveling chariot. (See cut No. 10.)

δῐχᾰ (δΕίς), bifariam, diverse, in two parts, twofold, in doubt, at variance, Σ 510, γ 127; o 412, in halves.

διχθά (δίχα), twofold, α 23; my heart was divided, Π 435.

διχθάδῐας, α, acc. pl., (διχθά), duplices, twofold, Ι 411; Ξ 21=δίχα.

δίψα, γ, αν, sitis, thirst, Φ 541. (Il.)

διψάων, part. from διψάω, sitiens, thirsting, λ 584†.

δίω, only aor. **δίον**, ε, mid., pres. subj. inf., flee, Χ 251; be anxious for, τινί; mid., aspellere, drive away, φ 370, υ 343; repel from, ἀπό τινος, Π 246.

δί-ωσε, aor. from ὠθέω, dirupit, tore away, Φ 244†.

διώκω, prs., ipf. 3 du. διώκετον, Κ 364; act., ipf. mid., pres. pass., drive, of ship and horses; insequi, pursue, Ε 65 (also consequi, overtake, Χ 199); ποσὶν ταχέεσσι, Χ 173; drive away, σ 409; also gallop, speed, with like signif. in act. and mid., μ 182, ν 162; δόμοιο, domo pellere; πεδίοιο, per campum, through the plain.

Διώνη, ης, Ε 381; mother of Ἀφροδίτη, Ε 370.

Διώνῡσος, οιο, (and Διονύσου, λ 325), Ζ 132, 135, Ξ 325, ω 74.

Δίώρης, εος, (1) Ἀμαρυγκείδης, chief of Ἐπειοί, Δ 517.—(2) father of Αὐτομέδων, Ρ 429.

δμηθείς, -θήτω, see ΔΑΜ, domitus.

δμῆσιν, τήν, (δάμνημι), domationem, taming, Ρ 476†.

δμήτειρα, victrix, Ξ 259†, = sq.

Δμήτωρ, ορι, victor, Tamer, ρ 443†.

δμωαί, άων, (ῶν), ῇσι, αἰ, (δμώς), female slaves, η 103; often captives in war, ζ 307; freq. with γυναῖκες, Ζ 323, χ 421.

δμώς, ωός, pl. δμῶες, ώων, (ΔΑΜ), slaves, often captives in war, δ 644, π 140; with ἄνδρες, μ 230. (Od. and Τ 333.)

δνοπαλίζω, ipf. **ἐδνοπάλιζεν**, fut. -ίξεις, (δινύω, πάλλω ?), wrap around, ξ 512; grapple with, overthrow, deicere, Δ 472.

δνοφερή, ήν, όν, (δνόφος), dark, dusky, Π 4, ν 269.

δοάσσατο, see δίατο, videbatur.

δοιῇ, ἐν, in dubio, in perplexity, Ι 230; also **δοιώ**, οἱ, αἱ, ά, duplices, twofold, β 46, Ω 527, τ 562; duo, Μ 455, Χ 148.

δοκάω, only mid. **δεδοκημένος**; also prs. 3 sing. **δοκεύει**, and aor. part. -εύσας, observe sharply, watch, τινά, Ο 730, Ψ 325, ε 274.

δοκέω, έεις, έει, (εῖ), aor. δόκησε, intend, with inf., Η 192; videri, seem, pers., Ζ 90, Ψ 459, and impers., Μ 215, α 376; δόκησέ σφισι θυμὸς ὡς ἔμεν ὡς εἰ, their heart felt as if; ὡς ἐμῷ θυμῷ δοκεῖ εἶναι ἄριστα=ἐμοί, ν 154; δόκησέ οἱ κατὰ θυμόν, υ 93.

δοκόν, τήν, and pl. οἱ, οἷσιν, (δέκτο), beam, esp. in roof, χ 176.

δόλιος, ίης, etc., (δόλος), fallax, deceitful, δ 455. (Od.)

Δόλιος, οιο, (ου), slave of Πηνελόπεια, ω 397. (Od.)

δολῐχ-αύλους (αὐλός) αἰγανέας, spears with long socket, ι 156†.

δολῐχ-εγχέας, adj. acc. pl. from -ής, (ἔγχος), having long spears, Φ 155†.

δολῐχ-ηρέτμοιο, οι, οισι, (ἐρετμός), long-oared, using long oars, of ships and Phaiakians, θ 191. (Od.)

δολῐχόν, ή, ήν, long, longus, Ο 474; dinturnus, ψ 243 (ntr., diu, Κ 52); of distance, ὁδόν, πλόον.

δολῐχό-σκιον (σκιά), casting long shadows, Γ 346; or perh. -σκίον from κίων, long-shafted?

δολόεντα, όεσσα, (δόλος), dolosus, artful, η 245. (Od.)

δολόμητις, ιν, voc. -μῆτα, from -μήτης, (μῆτις), wily; Αἴγισθος, Κλυταιμνήστρη (Ζεῦ, Α 540).

Δολοπίων, ονος, father of Ὑψήνωρ, Ε 77†.

δόλος, ου, ὁ, dolus, trick; δύλῳ, per dolum; λάθρη ἀνωϊστί, γ 235, δ 453, κ 232; opp. ἀμφαδόν, α 296; κράτεϊ, Η 142; βίηφι, ι 406; plot, θ 276 (the wooden horse, θ 494; bait, μ 252); ὑφαίνειν, ε 356.

δολο-φρονέων, έουσα, (φρονέω), wily-minded, l' 405, κ 339.

δολο-φροσύνην, τήν, pl. -ῃσι, wile, Τ 97 and 112.

Δόλοψ, οπος, (1) tribe on river Ἐνιπεύς in Thessaly, Ι 484, Λ 302.— (2) name of son of Λάμπος, Ο 525.

Δόλων, ωνος, Εὐμήδεος υἱός, Κ 314, spy, from whom Bk. 10, Il., receives its name. (See cut No. 26.)

δόμος, οιο, ου, ὁ, (δέμω), building, house, δ 618; pl., designating the complex of rooms which make up the house, ρ 85; also rooms, ζ 303, θ 57; dwelling of gods, η 81, λ 627, δ 834; of men, α 380, η 88; of animals, Μ 301, 169; in restricted signif., hall, α 126; in wider signif., home, habitation (ὅνδε) δόμονδε, ω 220.

δονᾰκῆα, τόν, acc., nom. -εύς, thicket of reeds, Σ 576†.

δόναξ, ᾰκος, ὁ, (δονέω), arundo, reed, Κ 467; shaft of arrow, Λ 584.

δονέουσι, 3 pl. prs., aor. ἐδόνησε and part., agitare, shake, Ρ 55; drive, Μ 157.

δόξης, gen., (δόξα), οὐδ' ἀπὸ—, nec praeter opinionem, not disappointing expectation, Κ 324 and λ 344.

δοροῖσι, nom. ὁ δορός, (δέρω), leather bag, β 354 and 380.

δορπέομεν, prs., ipf. (δορπείτην), also fut. aor, (δόρπον), cenare, sup, ο 302, Ψ 11.

δόρπον, cenam, evening meal, chief meal of day; ἑλέσθαι, Λ 86, prepare one's supper.

δόρυ, τό, -ατα, also (cf. γόνυ) parallel forms, δούρατος, ατι, ατα, ασι, and δουρός, ί ; ε ; α, ων, εσσι, (1) lignum, wood, ἐλάτης, Ω 450; τάμνετο, ε 243; trabs, beam, Γ 61; ship-timber, Ο 410, cf. μ 441 ; θ 507, hollow belly (of wood-

en horse).—(2) shaft of spear, Θ 494; μείλινον, Ε 666; spear, chief weapon of heroes, Β 382, Ε 73; Γ 78, grasping the spear by the middle; χάλκεον, ΙΙ 608; χαλκοβαρές, λ 532; κεκορυθμένον χαλκῷ, χ 125.

Δόρυ-κλος, ον, Πριαμίδην, νόθον υἱόν, Λ 489†.

δόσις, ἡ, -σιν, (δίδωμι), gift; ζ 208, though small (to thee) dear (to me); ἀνήνασθαι, refuse a gift, σ 287.

δόσκον, aor. iter., see δίδωμι.

δοτῆρες, οἱ, (δίδωμι), dispensers, Τ 44 and θ 325.

δούλειον (δοῦλος) εἶδος, servilis habitus, ω 252†.

δούλη, ης, (δοῦλος), female slave, Γ 409, δ 12.

δούλιον ἧμαρ, servitutis dies, bondage, ξ 340.

Δουλίχιον, island S. E. of Ithaka, inhabited by Ἐπειοί, Β 625, α 246; Δουλιχιόν-δε, to D., Β 629; Δουλιχιεύς, inhabitant of D., σ 424.

δουλιχο-δείρων, gen. pl., (δειρά), long-necked, Β 460 and Ο 692.

δουλοσύνην, τήν, (δοῦλος), servitutem, χ 423†.

δουπέω, prop. γδουπέω (κτύπος), aor. ἐγδούπησαν, Λ 45; δούπησεν δὲ πεσών, he fell with a crash; fall, Ν 426; δεδουπότος ἐς τάφον, sunk into his grave, Ψ 679.

δοῦπος, ου, ὁ, (κτύπος), fremitus, strepitus (cf. French, le bruit), any dull, heavy sound, din, Ι 573; noise, tread, Κ 354, π 10; clash of spears, Λ 364; roar, Δ 455, ε 401; hum of javelins, Π 361.

δουρᾰτέου, ον, (δουράτεος, δόρυ), lignei; θ 493 and 512.

δουρ-ηνεκές (δόρυ, ἤνεγκον), a spear's throw, Κ 357†.

δουρὶ κλειτός = δουρι-κλυτός, όν, hasta inclutus, renowned in the use of the spear, Ε 55, ο 52, ρ 71.

δουρῑ-κτητήν, acc., (κτητός, κτάομαι), captured in battle, I 343†.

δοῦρα, δούρατος, see δόρυ.

δουρο-δόκης, της, (δέχομαι), case or stand for spears, perh. a ring on a column in the vestibule, α 128†.

δόχμια, obliqua, obliquely, Ψ 116; and δοχμώ, sideways, Μ 148.

δράγματα, τά, (δράσσομαι), manipuli, handfuls of grain gathered by the reaper, and cut by a single stroke of the sickle, Λ 69 and Σ 552.

δραγμεύοντες, *g⸱therers of the handfuls,* as they fall from the sickle, into bundles for the binders, Σ 555†.

δραίνεις, prs., (δρᾶν), moliris, *undertake,* K 96†.

Δρακίος, leader of Ἐπειοί, N 692†.

δράκων, οντα, οντες, ὁ, (δρακεῖν), anguis, *snake,* X 93; *dragon,* Z 181, M 202.

δράσσομαι, pf. part. **δεδραγμένος,** *grasping* (with hand), N 393 and Π 486.

δρᾰτά (δαρτά, δέρω), excoriata, *flayed,* Ψ 169†.

δράω, opt. **δρώοιμι,** exsequerer, *execute as servant,* (δρηστήρ), ο 317†.

δρεπάνας, τάς, (δρεπάνη), falces, *sickles,* Σ 551†.

δρέπᾰνον, τό, *sickle, reaping-hook,* σ 368†.

δρέπω, aor. **δρεψάμενοι,** *plucking, culling,* μ 357†.

Δρῆσος, ον, a Trojan, Z 20†.

δρηστῆρες, οἱ, (δράω), famuli, *slaves, workmen,* π 248; **δρήστειραι,** αἱ, famulae, *female slaves, work-women,* κ 349. (Od.)

δρηστοσύνῃ, τῇ, (δρηστήρ), *in service,* ο 321†.

δρῖμύς, εῖα, ύ, *piercing, sharp;* Λ 270, piercing missile overcomes; ω 319, *keen,* irresistible wish.

δρίος, masc., (δρῦς), arbustum, *thicket,* ξ 353†.

δρόμος, ὁ, -ου, -ον, -οι, (δραμεῖν), cursus, *running,* θ 121; of horses, Ψ 300; *home-stretch,* Ψ 373; *race-courses* (catt'e-runs, Gladstone), δ 605.

Δρύας, αντος, (1) king of Λαπίθαι, A 263†.—(2) father of Λυκόοργος, Z 130†.

δρύϊνον, acc. masc., (δρῦς), *oaken,* φ 43†.

δρῠμά, τά, (δρῦς), *oak-thicket, πυκνά,* κ 150.

δρῠ-όχους, τούς, (δρῦς, ἔχω), *ribs* of ship or boat, τ 574†. (See cut.) Later the same word designates the keelson, as holding fast the ribs, the lower ends of which are inserted into it. (See cut, where *f e* designates the *stem; b g, keelson; i h, mast; o, o, o, ribs.*)

Δρύοψ, οπος, son of Πρίαμος, Υ 455.

δρῦς, υός, ἡ, (δόρυ), arbor, *tree,* Λ 494, N 389; quercus, *oak,* ξ 328; οὐκ ἀπὸ δρυὸς οὐδ' ἀπὸ πέτρης, X 126, 'tis no time now to talk, at ease, from *oak* or *rock* with this one; τ 163, thou art not, as the ancient proverb says, from *oak* or *rock*; cf. non es e saxo sculptus aut e robore dolatus (Cic. Acad. Posteriora, 31, 100), where the sense is slightly different.

δρῠ-τόμος, ων, ὁ, (τέμνω), lignator, *wood-chopper,* Ψ 315; with ἀνήρ, A 86.

δρύφθη, see ἀπο-δρύφω.

δρύφω, 3 sing. aor. **δρύψε,** mid. aor. **δρυψαμένω,** Π 324, *tear away;* β 153, *tearing each other's* cheeks and necks.

δρώοιμι, ώωσι, see δράω.

δῦ=ἔδυ (δύομαι).

δύωσι, 3 pl. prs. from δύω, (δήιος), *alter the appearance of for the worse, disfigure,* υ 195†.

δύη, ης, η, γς, fem., (δυς-), miseria, *misery, want,* ξ 338, σ 53. (Od.) [‿ ‿]

Δύμας, αντος, (1) father of Ἑκάβη, Π 718†.—(2) one of the Φαίηκες, ζ 22†.

δύμεναι, inf. aor. from δύω.

δύναμαι, ασαι, etc., ipf., (also δύναο, ἄμεσθα), fut. reg., 2 sing. also δυνήσεαι, aor. δυνήσατο and (ἐ)δυνάσθη, posse, *be able,* in every sense, physically, φ 247; valere, *avail, dare,* a 78; λ 414, μέγα δυναμένοιο, of a rich and potent man; is sum qui, δ 644; δύναται γὰρ ἅπαντα, ξ 445; θεοὶ δέ τε πάντα δύνανται, κ 306; often with negative (οὔ τι, α 78).

Δυναμένη, ης, a Nereid, Σ 43†.

δύναμις, ει, ιν, ἡ, (δύναμαι), *power,* κ 69; robur, *strength,* υ 237, N 786, 787; πὰρ δύναμιν, *beyond one's* strength; δ. πάρεστιν, *as far as* strength reaches.

δύνω, part. δύων, δύομαι, ipf. δῦνε, δίοντο, iter. δύσκε, fut. δύσομαι, εαι, aor. ἔδυν, 3 sing. δῦ, δύη, part. δύντα, aor. mid. ἐδύσατο, δύσετο, opt. δυσαίατο, pf. δέδῦκε, intrare, enter, make one's way into, στρατόν, (καθ') ὅμιλον, πόλεμον (-οιο στόμα), οὐλαμόν; imbibitur, sinks in, P 392; induere, put on, χιτῶνα, (ἐς)τεύχεα, ἔντεα, θώρηκα; also with ἐν and dat.; intrare, πόλιν, πύλας, τεῖχος, δόμον, σπέος, (ὑπὸ, ἐς) πόντον, θαλάσσης κόλπον, sink, go under the earth, χθόνα, γαῖαν (of dead); of sun, sink into the sea, set, of evening, Φ 232, Θ 487; of stars, ε 272, Λ 63. — With prepositions, εἰς, Θ 271; εἴσω, Π 340 (οἱ —, Φ 118); δέρτρον ἔσω, λ 579, burrowing into; δόμον εἴσω, Λ 263; of passions and emotions, δύνει, δύεταί τινα, enter, come upon, take possession of, χόλος, Ἄρης; ἄχος ἦτορ, Τ 367; ὀδύναι μένος, Λ 268; λύσσα ἐ, Ι 239; κάματος γυῖα, Ε 811. [ῠ̆ in prs. ipf. act. and mid., elsewh. and in δύνω only ῡ, e. g. subj. aor. δύω.]

δύο, δύω, duo, two, with du. and pl., Γ 116; K 224, when two go in company, one thinks for the other.

δυοκαίδεκα, duodecim, twelve.

δυόωσι, see δυάω.

δυς-, insep. prefix, opp. εὖ, like our un-, miss- (cf. un-rest, mis-chance), conveys idea of hard, bad, evil, untoward. (See δύη.)

δυσ-αής, άεος, άήων, (άημι), male flans, ill-blowing, stormy, μ 289.

δύσ-άμ-μορος, ε, οι, (μόρος), per-quam infortunatus, most miserable, X 428. (Il.)

δύσ-άριστο-τόκεια (τόκος), unhappy mother of a hero, Σ 54†.

δύσεο, ετο, aor. mid. from δύνω.

δύσ-ζηλοι (ζῆλος), exceeding jealous, suspicious, η 307†.

δύσ-ηλεγέος, έα, (ἀλέγω), painful, doleful, Υ 154 and χ 325.

δύσ-ηχέος, gen. from -ηχής, (ἠχέω), loud roaring, πόλεμος, also θανάτοιο, ill-boding death, Π 442. (Il.)

δυσ-θαλπέος, gen. from -θαλπής, (θάλπος), ill-warming, chilly, P 549†.

δυσ-κελάδου, gen., (κέλαδος), ill-sounding, shrieking (fear), Π 357†.

δυσ-κηδέα, acc. from -κηδής, (κῆδος), dreadful, ε 466†.

δυσ-κλέα, acc. from -κλεής, (κλέος), infamem, inglorious, B 115 and I 22.

δύσκον, 3 sing. δύσκε, ipf. from δύνω.

δυσ-μενέων, ἐοντες, (μένος), malignus, bearing ill-will, β 72. (Od.)

δυσ-μενέες, ἐεσσι, (μένος), infesti, hostiles, enemies, K 100, π 121.

δύσ-μητερ, voc., my mother, yet no mother, ψ 97†.

δύσ-μορος, ῳ, ον, (μόρος), infortunatus, ill-fated, α 49.

Δύσ-πάρι, voc., hateful Paris, Γ 39 and N 769.

δυσ-πέμφελος, stormy, Π 748†.

δυσ-πονέος, gen. from -πονής, (πόνος), toilsome, ε 493†.

δύστηνος, οιο, etc., pl. ων, infelix, miser, wretched, miserable, λ 76, X 59.

δυσ-χειμέρου, ον, (χεῖμα), hiemalis, wintry; of Dodona, B 750 and Π 234.

δύσ-ώνυμος, οι, (ὄνομα), infamis, ill-omened, hateful, Z 255, τ 571.

δύσ-ωρήσωσι, aor. from -ωρέω, (ὥρα), keep wearisome watch, K 183†.

δύω = δύο.

δύων, see δύνω.

δυώδεκ(α) = δυοκαίδεκα, K 488, B 637; δυώδέκατος, η = δωδέκατος, A 493.

δυωδεκά-βοιον, worth twelve oxen, Ψ 703†.

δυω-και-εικοσί-μετρον, holding twenty-two measures, Ψ 264†.

δυω-και-εικοσί-πηχυ, twenty-two cubits long, O 678†.

δῶ, τό (=δῶμα), A 426.

δώδεκα, duodecim, Z 248; with πάντες, πᾶσαι, twelve in all; δωδέκατος, η, duodecimus, β 374.

Δωδωναῖος, Dodonaian, epithet of Zeus, see follg.

Δωδώνη, ης, in Ἤπειρος, oldest oracle of Zeus, ξ 327.

δώῃ, τό and δώῃσι, 3 sing. subj. aor. from δίδωμι.

δῶμα, ατος, τό, (δέμω), house; also palace, κ 398; δώματα ναίειν, dwell, live, yet in ο 227 with adj.; δώματα, rooms=aedes, house, ο 109; largest apartment of house, meeting-place of men, χ 494; δῶμ' Ἀΐδαο=Ἀΐδαο δόμον, inferos, lower world.

δωρήσαιτο, opt. aor. from δωρίομαι,

δωρητοί 92 ἐγείρω

(δῶρον), donaret, *would give*, K 557†.

δωρητοί (δωρεῖσθαι), *open to gifts, reconcilable*, I 526†.

Δωριέες, tribe in Κρήτη, τ 177†.

Δώριον, town, subject to Νέστωρ, B 594†.

Δωρίς, a Nereid, Σ 45†.

δῶρον, ῳ, ων, οις, οισι, (δίδωμι), donum, *gift;* ὕπνου, Ἀφροδίτης,

θεῶν ; *present,* περίκλυτα, κάλλιμα, ἐρικύδεα.

δωτῆρες, pl., (δίδωμι) ἐάων, *givers* of good, θ 325†.

δωτίνην, τήν, pl. -ῃσι, (δίδωμι), *gift, present,* λ 352. [ῑ]

Δωτώ, a Nereid, Σ 43†.

δῶτορ, voc. from δώτωρ, ἐάων, *giver* of good, θ 335†.

δώωσι, aor. subj. from δίδωμι.

E.

ἔ', ξ 222, false reading for ἔᾰ=ἦν.

ἔ, enclitic, and ἐέ, see οὗ.

ἔα=(1) ipf. sing. ἦν, eram. [⏑≃] —(2) imp. prs. and 3 sing. ipf. from ἐάω. [⏑–]

ἐάγη, aor. pass. from ἄγνυμι, rupit.

ἐαδότα, perf. part. from ἀνδάνω, gratum.

ἐάλη, aor. pass. from εἰλέω.

ἐανοῦ, ῳ, όν, (Ϝεσθής), *enveloping*, E 734; *pliant*, Σ 613.

ἐανός, οῦ, ὁ, (Ϝεσθής), vestis, *garment*, Φ 507, Γ 419.

ἔαξε, αν, aor. from ἄγνυμι, discidit.

ἔαρος, τοῦ, (Ϝέαρος), veris, *spring*, Z 148.

ἔασιν=εἰσίν.

ἔαται, το, see ἧμαι.

ἐάφθη, aor. pass. from ἅπτω, (ἕπω), *sank after* him.

ἐάω, ἐῶ, 3 sing. ἐᾷ, pl. εἰῶσι, subj. εἰῶ, ἐᾷς, ἐᾷ, εἰῶμεν, εἰῶσι, opt. 3 sing. ἐῷ, imp. ἔα, inf. ἐάαν, ipf. (3 sing. also ἔα, iter. εἴασκον, ες, ε, εἴασχ', Λ 125, and ἔασκες, εν), fut. reg., so also aor. εἴασα (also ἔασας, ε, subj. ἐάσω), *let, permit,* (οὐκ—, impedire, *prevent*); with inf., e. g. κεῖσθαι, T 8; κατακεῖσθαι, Ω 523; ζώειν, χ 222; κάρη ἕλκεσθαι, X 398, K 344; T 65, *let us dismiss*= obliviscamur; *leave, say no more of,* ξ 171, 183 (τινά, τί); omittere, *let alone. let be,* Π 731, P 13, Υ 456, δ 212; *withhold*, i. e. *let alone giving,* ξ 444; relinquo, Δ 226, κ 166. [ᾰ in prs. and ipf.; ἐᾷ, ἔα, ἐῶμεν, ἐάουσιν, often pronounced with synizesis.]

ἐάων (ἐύς), bonorum, Ω 528 ; with θεοὶ δωτῆρες, θ 325 (possibly from fem. ἔη, *good*).

ἑβδομάτῃ and ἕβδομος, septimac, -us.

ἔβλητο, aor. mid. from βάλλω, ictus est.

ἐγεγάᾱσι, pf. from ἐγγίγνομαι.

ἐγ-γείνωνται, subj. prs., ingignant, *engender*, T 26†.

ἐγ-γίγνομαι, only pf. ἐγ-γεγάᾱσι Ἰλίῳ, Troiae nati sunt, Z 493 and P 145.

ἐγ-γνάμπτω, see γνάμπτω.

ἐγ-γυαλίξει, fut. ξω, aor. ἐγγυάλιξε, (γύαλον), *put into the hand*, θ 319; *hand over,* π 66 ; confer, κάρτος, etc.

ἐγ-γύαι, ἐγ-γυάασθαι, from ἐγγύη, (γυῖα), δειλαί τοι δειλῶν γε καὶ, *worthless to receive* are the *pledges* of the worthless, θ 351†. (ἐγγυάω, *give pledge.*)

ἐγγύθεν, (ἐγγύς), ex propinquo= *near*, Α 723; temporal, T 409; and εἶναί τινι, propinquum esse, *related,* η 205.

ἐγγύθι, prope, of space, H 341; with gen., *near to,* I 76, ν 156 ; *of time,* K 251; with dat., X 300.

ἐγγύς (ἄγχι), adv., prope, *near,* Γ 344 ; with στῆναι, ἰέναι, εἶναι ; with gen., N 247, P 484; temporal, with dat., X 453.

ἐγδούπησε, see δουπέω.

ἐγείρω, aor. ἤγειρα, ἔγειρε, excitare, *wake up,* Ψ 234; ο 8, anxiety for his father *kept him awake;* ἐξ ὕπνου, ο 44;

arouse, to combat, P 544; *stir* the fight, Υ 31, Ε 496, Ν 357; Ἄρηα, Β 440; τινά, Ε 208; ἕκαστον, quemque ex urbibus excitavi, P 222; μένος, *fire* courage.—Mid. prs. ἐγειρομένων, aor. ἔγρετο, οιτο, ἔγρεσθαι, ὁμενος, pf. ἐγρήγορθε, -όρθασι, inf. -όρθαι, whence part. pres. **ἐγρηγορόων**, *watch*; υ 100, as they wake; ἔγρεο, wake up, Κ 159.

ἔγκατα, τά, dat. ἄσι, viscera, *entrails*, P 64.

ἐγ-κατ-έπηξα, ε, (in tmesi, Η 441), aor. from πήγνυμι, *thrust into*; κουλεῷ, the scabbard, λ 98.

ἐγ-κατα-τίθημι, mid. aor. 3 sing. **ἐγκάτθετο**, imp. -θεο, imposuit; λ 614, let not the craftsman who *conceived* this belt by (lit. in) his art, hereafter attempt any thing further, i. e. he would only injure his reputation; ψ 223.

ἔγ-κειμαι (ἐνὶ **κείμην**, ξ 501, δ 127), fut. **ἐγ-κείσεαι**, with dat., in iis iacebis, *shalt* not *sleep in* them, Χ 513.

ἐγ-κεράννυμι and -κεράω, ipf. **ἐν κε-ρόωντο**, and aor. **ἐγκεράσᾶσα**, with dat., *mix in* or *with*, κρητῆρσιν, υ 253 (Θ 189).

ἐγ-κέφᾰλος, οιο, ὁ, cerebrum, *brain*, Γ 300, ι 290.

ἐγ-κλάω, see ἐνι-κλᾶν.

ἐγ-κλίνω, pf. **ἐγκέκλιται**, *lies upon* you, Ζ 78.

ἐγ-κονέουσαι, prs. part.,(διά-κονος?), *in haste*, η 340 and ψ 291.

ἐγ-κοσμεῖτε, imp. prs., disponite, *put in order* (within), ο 218†.

ἐγ-κρύπτω, aor. **ἐν-έκρυψε**, with dat., *bury in* ashes, ε 488†.

ἐγ-κυκάω, see κυκάω.

ἐγ-κυρέω, aor. **ἐνέκυρσε**, with dat., incidit in, *met*, Ν 145†.

ἔγρεο, ετο, εσθαι, ἐγρήγορθε, θασι, θαι, ὁων, see ἐγείρω.

ἐγρηγορτί (ἐγρήγορα), adv., *awake*, Κ 182†.

ἐγρήσσεις, οντα, οντες, (ἐγείρω), indic. and part. pres., vigilare, *keep watch*, Λ 551, υ 33.

ἐγχείη, ης, ἡ = ἔγχος, *lance*, Ν 339.

ἐγ-χείῃ, subj. from ἐγχέω.

ἐγχέλὔες, αἱ, anguillae, *eels*, Φ 203.

ἐγχεσί-μωρος, ων, ους, *mighty with the spear*, γ 188.

ἐγχέσ-πᾰλος, οι, (πάλλω), *spearbrandishing*, Β 131.

ἐγ-χέω, aor. **ἔχευε** = ἔχεϜε, ἔχεαν, subj. ἐγχείῃσι, also in tmesi, (χέω), infundere, *pour in*, with dat., γ 40, and with ἐν, ζ 77; mid. ἐνεχεύατο, *poured in for herself*, τ 387.

ἔγχος, εος, τό, *spear, lance*, for hurling and thrusting, the most honorable weapon : the shaft, δόρυ, was of ash, μείλινον, Χ 293, about 7 ft. long, δολιχόσκιον ; the upper end, καυλός, was fitted with a bronze socket, αὐλός, into which the point, ἀκωκή, αἰχμή, was inserted, Π 802, being held fast by the πόρκης ; the lower end, οὐρίαχος, was furnished with a ferule or spike, σαυρωτήρ, for sticking into the earth. The warrior carried two spears—for hurling (at distance of about 12 paces), and for thrusting from above. Hektor's spear was 16 ft. long, Ζ 319. (See also σῦριγξ, and cut No. 22.)

ἐγ-χρίμπτω, only aor. **ἐγχρίμψας**, *let graze*, Ψ 334; mid. ipf. -χρίμπτοντο, pass. aor. imp. and part. ἐγ-χριμφθείς, ἐνιχριμφθέντα, (χρίω), *almost touch* the stake, Ψ 338; P 405, *press forward to* the gates; Η 272, ἀσπίδι, *dashed flat against* his shield ; P 413, *were crowding* constantly *forward*; Ν 146, *approach closely*.

ἐγών, ἐγώ, ego, forms as in Attic, but gen. ἐμεῖο, ἐμεῦ, ἐμέο, μευ, ἐμέθεν.

ἐδάην, cognovi, see ΔΑ.

ἐδάνῳ, dat., (Ϝιδ-, σϜήδύς), *sweet*, Ξ 172†.

ἐδάσατο, -σσατο, see δατέομαι, distribuit, *distributed*.

ἔδαφος, τό, (ὑδός), *floor of ship*, ε 249†. (See next page.) *a*, μεσόδμη, *mast-box; b*, beams *running parallel to*, *c*; ἐπηγκενίδες, *gunwale; d*, κληῗδες, *rowlock*, *thole-pin; e*, σκαλμοί, part of the gunwale on which the oar rests, *bed of the oar; f*, ζυγά, *cross-p'anks; g*, θρῆνυς, *braces* for the feet of the oarsmen ; *h*, ἴκρια, *ribs; i*, τρόπις, *keel; k*, ἁρμονιαί, *slabs*, sustaining the floor ; *l*, ἔδαφος, *floor; m*, *keelson*, was probably not distinguished from *i*, *keel*. (See also plate No. IV., at end of vol.)

ἔδδεισε, ἐδείδιμεν, etc., δείδω, timuit.

ἐδέδμητο, plupf. from δέμω, aedificatum erat.

ἔδεκτο, aor. from δέχομαι, excepit, received.

ἐδητύος, τῆς, gen. from -τύς, (ἔδμεναι), cibi, food, Λ 469, κ 384.

ἔδμεναι, inf. from ἔδω, edere.

ἔδνα, ἔεδνα, τά, (ἐFεδνα, (σF)ἡδύς), bridal gifts, chiefly cattle, (1) suitor's presents to bride.—(2) to her father and relatives, σ 276 sqq.—(3) dowry of bride, portion given her by her father, α 277.

ἔδομαι, fut. of ἐσθίω, comedam, ι 369.

ἔδος, τό, gen. pl. -έων, (ἔζομαι), sedes, (1) act of sitting, time or reason for it, οὐχ ἕ., non vacat (mihi) sedere, Λ 648.—(2) sitting place, seat, Α 534.—(3) seat, abode, Θ 456, ζ 42; situation, ν 344.

ἔδράθον, aor. from δαρθάνω, dormivit.

ἕδρη, ης, ἡ, (ἔζομαι), (1) seat, stool (see cut; also No. 79), Τ 77. —(2) rows of seats, e. g. stone benches in the ἀγορά, θ 16; and elsewh., e. g. γ 7; τίειν ἕδρῃ, honor with a seat, i. e. show to a place of honor.

ἐδριάασθαι, inf., ipf. ἑδριόωντο, (ἕδρη), sit down, γ 35; take seats in council, Κ 198, η 98.

ἔδυν, aor. from δύνω, δύομαι.

ἔδω, inf. ἔδμεναι, ipf. ἔδον, iter. ἔδεσκεν, fut. ἔδομαι, εαι, ονται, pf. part. ἐδηδώς, pass. ἐδήδοται (ΕΔ, edo), eat, devour, of men and animals; σῖτον ἔδοντες= ἀλφησταί, bread-eating; θυμόν, κ 379, and κραδίην, Ω 129, metaph. consume one's soul with toil and pain; ι 75, devour, οἶκον (νήποινον, impune); ν 419, βίοτον; ξ 417, the fruit of the sweat of our brow.

ἐδωδή, ῆς, ἡ, only sing., (ἔδω), food, meat, fodder, Τ 167; ἤραρε θυμόν ἐδωδῇ, strengthened his soul with meat, ξ 111.

ἐέ, see οὖ.

ἔεδνα=ἔδνα.

ἐεδνώσαιτο, aor. opt., (ἐδνόω, ἔεδνα 3), that he may portion off his daughter, β 53†.

ἐεδνωταί (ἔεδνα 3), κακοί, stingy givers (of dowry), Ν 382†.

ἐεικοσά-βοιον, α, (βοῦς), worth twenty cattle, α 431 and χ 57.

ἐείκοσϊν=εἴκοσιν.

ἐεικοσ-όροιο (ἐρέσσω), twenty-oared, ι 322†.

ἐεικοστόν=εἰκοστόν, Ω 765

ἐείλεον, see εἰλέω.   [and Od.

ἐεισάμενος, etc., see εἴδω II. and εἶμι.

ἐεισάσθην, from εἶμι.

ἐέλδομαι, see ἔλδομαι.

ἐέλδωρ, τό, nom. and acc., (ἐFέλδωρ, velle), desiderium, wish, desire, Α 41, ψ 54.

ἐέλμεθα, μενος, σαι, see εἰλέω.

ἐέλπομαι=ἔλπομαι.

ἐεργάθω=ἐργάθω.

ἔεργε, γμένος, from ἔργω.

ἐέργνυμι, see κατείργνυμι.

ἱερμένον and -μέναι, σ 296, pf. pass., and ἔερτο, plupf. from

O P E Ϟ Ϟ T E Υ

stem ΣΕΡ,(σειρά,ὅρμος,series),necklace on which were strung alternately gold and amber beads, or a golden necklace strung (at intervals) with amber beads, o 460 ; E 89,*firmly united.*

ἑέρση, -ήεις, see ἑρσ-.

ἔερτο, see ἱερμένον.

ἑέρχατο, see ἔργω.

ἑέσσατο, στο, see ἕννυμι.

ἑέσσατο, see following word.

ἕζω, aor. εἶσα, imp. εἶσον, part. ἕσας, ἕσασα, *set down, place,* ξ 280; λόχον, *lay an ambush*; ἐν κλισμοῖσι, κατὰ κλισμούς τε θρόνους τε; ἐπὶ θρόνου, *bid to be seated*; υ 210, ἐπὶ—, *set over*; δῆμον Σχερίῃ, *settled* in Scheria; here belongs also aor. mid. ἑέσσατο, imposuit, *take on board* (ship), ξ 295.—Mid. pres.

ἕζομαι, -εαι, ipf., considere, *take a seat*; subsedit, *crouched down,* X 275, du. ἱζέσθην ; with (inanimate) pl. subject, κῆρες, Θ 74, *settled down upon,* touched the surface of the earth ; ἐπὶ δίφρῳ, ἐπὶ γοῦνα, ἐν λέκτρῳ, ἐν κλισμῷ, ἐπὶ δίφρου, ἀνὰ μέλαθρον, κατὰ κλισμούς τε θρόνους τε, ἐς θρόνους, ποτὶ βωμόν, ἐπ᾽ ἐρετμά, *took their places at the oars.*

ἕη=ᾗ, subj. from εἰμί.

ἕηκε=ἧκε, aor. from ἵημι.

ἕην=ἦν.

ἑήνδανε=ἥνδανε from ἁνδάνω.

ἑῆος (ἑῆος), see ἑύς.

ἕης=ἧς, rel. pron. from ὅς.

ἑῆς, poss. pron. gen. from ἑύς.

ἕησθα, 2 sing. ipf., ἕησι, 2 sing. prs. subj. from εἰμί.

ἑθ᾽=ἔτι.

ἕθειραι, αἱ, -ας, *horse-hair,* of mane, tail, plume of helmet, Θ 42, Π 795.

ἐθείρῃ, subj. prs., colat, *till,* Φ 347†.

ἐθελοντῆρας, τούς, (ἐθέλω), *volunteers,* β 292†.

ἐθέλω (θέλοιεν, only o 317), subj. ἐθέλωμι, ipf. ἔθελον, ἠθέλετον, την, etc., iter. ἐθέλεσκες, ε, ον, fut. ἐθελήσεις, etc., aor. ἐθέλησα, *be resolved,* B 391; *be ready,* T 187 ; οὐκ—, recuso, A 112; *I've no thought,*θ 223; ἐθέλων,lubens; οὐκ ἐθέλων, invitus, o 280; πολλὰ μάλ᾽ οὐκ—, sorely against his will; μηδ᾽ ἔθελε, *venture not, attempt not,* B 247 ; *wish,* Δ 37, I 397, ι 262 ; μάλα, *would gladly,* Δ 318; θυμός, κῆρ (μοι) ἐθέλει ; also ᾧ θυμῷ τις ἐθέλει, ἐκπάγλως, *desire exceedingly* ; *be able,* γ 120 ; *desire,*

ζ 64, ν 40, σ 113, H 182. In A 133, ὄφρα=in order that.

ἔθεν=οὗ, reflexive pron., see οὗ.

ἐθηεύμεθα, ipf. from θηέομαι.

ἔθνος, τό, -εα, (Ϝέθνος), *company, band, host,* ἑτάρων, λαῶν, νεκρῶν; *swarm, flock,* μελισσάων, ὀρνίθων, μυιάων; *herd,* χοίρων, ξ 73.

ἔθορε, aor. from θρώσκω, saluit, *sprang.*

ἔθρεψε, aor. from τρέφω, nutrivit.

ἔθων, part. prs., pf. εἴωθε (ἔωθε) -ώς, (σϜέθω, σϜέο, ἔο), suctus, consuevit, Θ 408 ; I 540, *laying waste continually;* Π 260, *provoke in their wanton way;* but in E 231, solitus.

εἰ (from pron. ὅς, as also αἰ), orig. *as;* this signif. recognizable in Δ 321. —I. optative use : cf. utinam, with opt., K 111, O 571, Π 559, Ω 74, δ 388 ; esp. with γάρ, α 255, P 561 ; with κέν, o 545.—II. interrogative use : si, *if, whether* (in MSS. often confounded with ἤ, ν 415), with indic., B 300, E 183, τ 325 ; fut., A 83, Z 367 ; subj., O 16, π 138 ; opt. and subj., Ξ 163; tentative use : freq. after such verbs as πειρήθη, T 385 ; γνώμεναι, Φ 266 ; μενοίνεον, M 59 ; also after other verbs when an ellipsis is to be supplied, e. g. *to see,* followed by opt. or indic., K 206, 19, M 122, Ψ 40. O 571.—III. conditional use : si, *if,* (εἴ ποτ᾽ ἔην γε, see under I. ἤ), εἰ μή, nisi, *unless,* without verb, after negations, μ 326; other combinations, e. g. εἰ δέ, εἰ δ᾽ ἄγε, etc., see under special heads.—(1) when the condition is formal rather than real, i. e. the sentence is not really hypothetical; indic. pres., M 233, A 178, 280 ; εἰ ἐθέλεις, with follg. inf., o 80; ipf., Δ 321; aor., A 290, E 104, Σ 305 (εἴ ποτε, A 39, γ 98); pf., A 173, Z 128, I 42, γ 93 ; the principal sentence is entirely uninfluenced in form by the condition, M 233, Π 452, 494, Z 142, A 290, Σ 305, Z 128, X 390. — (2) with condition likely to be realized, seldom indic., Σ 427 ; more often fut., A 135, 137, N 375, β 115, O 163, A 294 (principal sentence is free to take any form, A 135, Υ 26, 130) ; usually subj., E 258, A 340, ε 221 ; often with κέν, Φ 553, α 288, A 324, I 135, Γ 281, 284, I 412, 414, Λ 315 ; rarely with ἄν, Φ 556, Γ 290 ; the principal sentence unaffected by the conditional clause, M 71, A 324, I 277, H 77, E 212, I 363, Δ 415.—(3) condition wholly uncertain, with no expectation of being realized; here the optative (never in iterative sense), Δ 34, P 102, I 379, Ξ 209, Π 73; also with κέν, I 141, 283, A 60 ; after negations οὐδ' εἰ, Θ 22, χ 61 (κεν, I 445, K 381); ὡς εἴ τε, as if, κ 420, ι 314 ; in the principal sentence, opt. with κέν (ἄν, Θ 22, I 445).—(4) condition contrary to reality; indic. ipf. for present time, the verb of the principal sentence, instead of following in indic. ipf, is often potential, Ω 220; indic. aor. for past time, (also Λ 310, ipf. joined with aor.), Λ 750, δ 363, Ο 460, Π 686, 700, Ψ 527 ; plupf., δ 363; in principal sentence we expect aor. indic. with κέν; yet we also find in principal sentence κέν with opt., E 311, 388, B 81, α 236, P 70; irreg., B 488, Γ 453. Irregularities in the hypoth. period are common, e. g. the conclusion (principal sentence) begins often with τῷ, ἤτοι, ἦ τ'.—IV. concessive use : εἰ καί (yet not in every case, e. g. B 367), if also, and καὶ εἰ, even if, with indic., O 51; with opt., χ 13, I 318; with subj., E 351 ; εἰ περ, see this word.

εἰάμενῇ, τῇ, (ἧμαι ?), depression, Δ 483 and O 631.

εἰανοῦ=ἑ.ίνοῦ, Π 9†.

εἰάρινή, ῇσι, οἶσι, (ϝέαρ), ὥρῃ, springtime; ἄνθεσι, spring blossoms, B 89.

εἴασε, aor. εἴασκε, ipf. iter. from ἑάω.

εἴαται, **το**, see ἧμαι, εἴατο=ἦσαν.

εἴβεις, etc., ipf. εἶβον, ε, (λείβω), δάκρυον, θ 531, shed tears; often with κατά, Π 11.

εἰ γάρ, see εἰ I.

εἰ γε, siquidem, if at least, since, usually separated as εἰ ἐτεόν γε, ι 529 ; except εἴ γε μέν, ε 206, and εἴ γ' οὖν— γε, E 258 (see γοῦν).

εἰδάλίμας, acc., (εἶδος), venustas, comely, ω 279†.

εἰδάρ, τύ, -ᾰτᾰ, (ἔδω), cibus, λ 123, α 140; ἄνθινον, flowery food; fodder, E 369.

εἰ δέ, (1) but if, π 387 and freq.—(2) **εἰ δ' ἄγε** (ἄγετε), usually explained by ellipsis of βούλει ; perh. better as an old imp. from εἶμι, instead of ἴθι δή (cf. τί δέ, εἰ δέ, I 262), vade age! come

go! P 685, 'Αντίλοχ', εἰ δ' ἄγε δεῦρο, διοτρεφές, ὄφρα πύθηαι; later, its signif. having been forgotten, it is joined with ἄγετ', X 381 ; and with pl. verbs, Z 376, Θ 18 ; often with vocatives, the verb following in imp. (yet sometimes fut., φ 217. A 524, I 167, Ψ 579; or subj., ι 37, ω 336), A 302 (μήν, vero), Π 667, T 108 ; or subj. of exhortation, X 381.

εἰ δή, if now, seeing that, expressing conviction; also in indirect questions, whether now. (See δή 2.)

Εἰδοθέη, daughter of Proteus, a sea-goddess, δ 366.

εἰδ-, I. prs., (εἴδημι), subj. εἰδέω, opt. εἰδείην, classed with οἶδα; mid. **εἴδεται** (stem ϜΙΔ, video, Eng. wit), -όμενος, -η, videor, seem, A 228; with inf.,Ω 197,ι 11; part.,similis—,δέμας, like in bodily shape; lucere, Θ 559, N 98.—II. aor. **εἰσάμην**, ἐείσατο, (ἐ)εισάμενος, η, videbar, M 103 ; appeared, Ω 319; ὡς ὅτε, ε 281; seemed, with inf., Θ 295, β 320, B 215; was like, φθογγήν, in voice, B 791; part., similis, τινί, N 45, 216, ζ 24.—III. fut. **εἴσομαι**, cognoscam, recognize, K 88; sciam, know, β 40, π 246 ; experiar, find out, Θ 532, χ 7 ; αἴ κε, with subj., Θ 111, Π 243,ῆ; also **εἰδήσεις**, ειν, ἐμεν, sciam, η 327, ζ 257, cogniturum esse. — IV. perf. **οἶδα**, novi, I know, with which are classed follg. forms, 2 sing. οἶδας, 3 pl. ἴσασι, ξ 89 ; ἰδέω, Ξ 235, and εἰδέω, ομεν, ετε, inf. ἴδμεναι, ἴδμεν, part. ἰδυίῃσι, plupf. ᾔδεα, 2 sing. ἠείδης, ἠείδεις, ᾔδησθα, 3 sing. ᾔείδη, ει, ᾔδειν, η, 3 pl. ἴσαν—ἐκ τινος, ex aliquo, from some one, X 280; (μάλ') εὖ, ψ 175, (οὐ)σάφα, (not) accurately, certainly ; περὶ κείνου, de illo, concerning him, ρ 563; παλαιά τε πολλά τε, have been through much, η 157 ; πλείονα, more experienced, T 219 ; with gen., peritum esse, M 229, O 412, P 5, nondum peperisse; with follg. ὅ, δ 771; ὅττι, Λ 408; ὅτ' ἄν, Θ 406; ὡς, ε 423; εἰ, δ 712; εἴ κε, β 332; with indirect question, Λ 653, ι 348, λ 463; with attraction, B 409, N 275, ρ 373 ; part., P 402; calleo, know how, with inf., H 238, 358; with acc., understand, ἔργα, M 236, B 832, θ 134; esp. with ntr. adj., be versed in, practice, ἤπια, τ 329, 332, B 213, ι 189, 428 ; χάριν τινί, gratiam habere, thank; εὖ εἰδώς,

with gen., peritissimus; σάφα—,
with inf., Ο 632; with acc., Ν 665, δ
534; fem., Α 365, and ἰδυίῃσι πραπίδεσσι, of Ἥφαιστος, with inventive
mind, η 92.—V. aor. εἶδον (ἔϝιδον),
also ἴδον, subj. ἴδω(μι), mid. ἰδόμην,
subj. ἴδηαι, opt. ἰδοίατο, vidi, Δ 275, Χ
25, ξ 29; opp. πυθύμην, ψ 40; νοῆσαι,
Ε 475; ὀφθαλμοῖσιν (without ἐν), very
often; intelligo, perceive, Δ 249,
with subj.; with acc. part., Τ 283, 292,
γ 221, Δ 223, 232; spectare, behold,
λ 94; visitare, α 3; look, εἴς τινα, τι
(ὀφθαλμοῖσι, π 477), πρός, ἄντα, Ν 184;
ἐσάντα, λ 143; ἀντίον, π 160; κατέ-
νωπα, Ο 320, straight forward, into
one's countenance, ἀχρεῖον, ὑπόδρα;
mid., videre, see, with part., Δ 374,
516, (ἐν) ὀφθαλμοῖσι (Σ 135), Ο 600;
ἐνὶ φρεσί, in thought; cognoscere,
Φ 61, φ 159; ἰδέσθαι, to look upon, Γ
194; θαῦμα, θ 366; εἰς ὦπα, τ 383.

εἶδος, dat. εἴ, ntr., (εἴδον), species,
outward form or appearance, esp. of
countenance; often joined as acc. of
specification with adjs., in form, beauty,
Γ 124; often coupled with μέγεθος,
φυήν, always of human beings, exc. ρ
308, to judge from his (such an) appearance.

εἴδωλον, τό, φ, α, ων, (εἶδος),
species, illusive image, Ε 449; phan-
tom, δ 796; esp. (καμόντων), shades of
the dead who flit about in the lower
world, κ 476.

εἴθᾰρ, statim, immediately, Λ 579.

εἴθε (see αἴθε, εἰ, I.), utinam, oh that!
with opt., β 33, ξ 468, Δ 313: εἴθ᾽, γ
90=εἴτε, sive.

εἰ καί, si etiam, even if, Υ 371;
etiamsi, although, Ψ 832. (Β 367,
see ἦ καί.)

εἴ κεν, see εἰ, III., 2, 3.

εἶκε, ipf., (1) from εἴκω, yield.—(2)
from εἴκω, appear.

εἴκελος (also ἴκελος), η, ον, (II. εἴκω), similis, like, τινί, λ 207; αὐδήν, in voice.

εἰκοσάκις, vicies, twenty times, I 379.

εἴκοσι, ἐείκοσι, viginti, twenty.

εἰκοσίν-ήρῐτα (cf. ἐριήρης). joined
twenty times, twenty-fold, X 349†.

(ἐ)εικοστόν, ῷ, vicesimum, o. (Ω
765.)

ἔικτο, τον, την, ἐικυῖα, see II. εἴκω.

I. **εἴκω, εἴκετε,** imp., εἴκων, ipf. εἶκε,
1 aor., iter. εἴξασκε, (ϝεικ-), retire before

any one, τινί, Ρ 230 (χάρμης, withdraw
from battle; τὸ ὄν μένος, be inferior in
courage); θυμῷ εἴκων, from impulse,
ν 143; θυμῷ εἴξας, in consequence of
impulse; τινός, retire from, σ 10, χ 91;
be inferior in, τινί (πόδεσσι, ξ 221); Χ
321, where he might most easily be
wounded; Ψ 337, give him the reins
with thy hands, i. e. give him free rein.

II. **εἴκω** (JIK?) ipf. **εἶκε** (ἴϊκε), pf.
ἔοικα (ϝέϝοικα), 3 du. ἔϊκτον, part. ἐοικώς
and εἰκώς, ἐοικυῖα and ἐικυῖα, plupf.
ἐᾐκειν, εἰς, εἰ(ν), ἐίκτην, ἐοίκεσαν, mid.
plupf. ἔϊκτο, ἤϊκτο, (1) similem esse,
resemble, τινί τι, in any thing, Υ 371,
Ψ 379, α 208, τ 380; ἄντα, Ω 630;
εἰς ὦπα, in countenance, Γ 158; ἄγχιστα, maxime, πάντα, in all respects.
—(2) decēre, beseem, ἔοικέ τοι οὔτοι
ἀεικές, Ι 70; οὐδὲ μὲν οὐδὲ ἔοικε, nec
vero decet (personal, χ 348, decet
me); Κ 440, with acc. and inf., Β 190,
233, α 278 (χ 196, sc. καταλέχθαι, ω
273, sc. πορεῖν).—(3) convenit, suit,
Σ 520, Ι 399. **ἐοικώς** (εἰκώς), (1)
similis, τινί, Α 47, Ψ 430, γ 124 sq.
—(2) meritus, deserved, α 46.—(3)
what is becoming, suitable, δ 239.

εἰλᾰπῐνάζων, ουσι, part. and 3 pl. prs.,
(εἰλαπίνη), epulans, feasting, β 57.

εἰλᾰπῐναστής, ὁ, conviva, guest,
Ρ 577†

εἰλᾰπῐνη, ἡ, compotatio, drinking
bout, α 226.

εἰλᾰρ, τό, (ϝεῖλαρ, εἰλέω), munimentum, defense, Η 338, ε 257.

εἰλᾰτῐνος, ον, οισι, αι, of pine, β 424,
Ξ 289.

εἶλε, aor. from αἱρέω.

Εἰλείθυια, ἡ, Eileithyia, daughter of
Hera, τ 188; usually pl. as sister-
goddesses who preside over childbirth,
Τ 119, Λ 270.

Εἰλέσιον, town in Βοιωτία, Β 499†.

εἰλέω, aor. ἔλσαν, 3 pl. inf. ἔλσαι and
ἐέλσαι, part. -σας; pass. pf. ἐέλμεθα,
μένος, aor. ἐάλη [ᾰ], 3 pl. ἄλεν, inf.
ἀλήμεναι, ἧναι, part. ἀλείς, (ϝΕΛ),
crowd together, confine, Ν 524; esp.
force back enemy, Φ 295; game, λ
573; shut in, μ 210, Σ 447; hold back,
Β 294; smite with lightning, shatter and
sink in the sea, η 250; pass.. in close
array, Ε 782; obsideri, shut up in
siege, Ε 203; includi. crowded together, Μ 38, Σ 287; collect themselves

in one body, E 823, Π 714, Φ 534, Ψ 420; contrahi, cower, crouch (gather strength for a bound, onset), Π 403, Υ 168, Φ 571, X 308.

εἰλήλουθα, μεν, ει, pf. and plupf. = εἰλήλυθα, ει, see ἔρχομαι.

εἰλι-πόδεσσιν, ποδας, (πούς), bringing the feet close together, of oxen or cows, which plait their hind-legs as they go, each describing, alternately, an arc of a circle about the other, and occasioning a rolling gait; others translate trailing-footed, and explain of the hind-feet, which approach successively the fore-feet on the opposite side, α 92 and freq.

εἷλον, ὁμην, aor. from αἱρέω.

εἰλῦᾶται, pf. pass. from εἰλύω.

εἴλῦμα, τό,(velamen,Fειλ.,English, veil), wrapper, ζ 179†.

εἰλῦφάζει, 3 sing. and part. **εἰλῦφόων**, whirl about, Υ 492, Λ 156†.

εἰλύω, fut. **εἰλύσω**, pass. pf. εἴλῡμαι, 3 pl. -ύαται, part. -μένος, plupf. εἴλῡτο, obvolvere, wrap, envelop, E 186, υ 352; cover, ξ 479, Π 640.

εἷμα, τό, -τι, -τα, -σι,(Fέσμα, ἕννυμι), vestimentum, garment; ζ 214, as clothing.

εἷμαι = Fέσμαι, pf. pass. from ἕννυμι.

εἵμαρται, το. pf. and plupf. from μέρω.

εἱμένος = Fεσμένος, ἕννυμι, indutus.

εἰ μή, nisi, also after ἄλλος, μ 326.

εἰμί (ἐσμί, esse), 2 sing. ἐσσί (never εἶ), 1 pl. εἰμέν, 3 pl. ἔασι, subj. ἔω, εἴω, 3 ἔῃσι, ᾖσι, 3 pl. ἔωσι, ὦσι, opt. 2 ἔοις, 3 ἔοι, inf. ἔ(μ)μεν(αι), part. ἐών, ἐοῦσα, ἐόν; ipf. 1 ἔα, ᾖα, ἔον (ἔην, Λ 762 ἦην? O 82, τ 283), 2 ἔησθα, ἦσθα, 3 ἔην, ἤην, ἦεν, du. ἤστην, pl. ἔσαν (mid. εἴατο, correct to εἴατο, υ 106), iter. ἔσκον, ε; fut. ἔσσομαι, -σεαι, -σεῖται, -σόμεθα, -σονται, also ἔσεαι, ἐσόμεθα.—Pres. indic. is enclitic; excs. 2 sing., epic 3 pl. ἔασιν, and forms in signif. exist; esse, suppetere, be, be at hand, ξ 496; ἔνδον ἐόντων, of her store; with inf. of purpose or obj., δ 215, Ω 610; ἠώς, ο 50; μῦθοι, δ 214, to-morrow also we shall be ab!e to converse with each other; B 393, surely he shall find no means; cf. β 355, σ 371, Δ 271, Ψ 412; ἔστι τί μοι, habeo aliquid, have any —, ο 336, σ 3; ὄνομ'

ἐστί (τινι, with nom. of name, σ 5); ἔστι δέ τις, ἔσκε δέ, introductory formula, γ 293, ο 417; originate with, α 33; spring from, τινός, α 215; cf. Υ 106 sq., β 274, γ 123, ξ 204, ν 130, Z 211, T 111, Ψ 347; be in life, exist, ω 263, β 119, ω 351, ζ 201; οὐ δήν, Ζ 131; οὐκέτ' ἐόντος, mortui, X 384, α 289; take place, ὅπως ἔσται τάδε ἔργα, what turn these things will take; ὡς ἔσεταί περ, as it will also come to pass; εἴη κεν καὶ τοῦτο, this might well come to pass, ο 435; τίσις, α 40; ἐσσόμενοι, posteri; ἐόντα—ἐσσόμενα πρό τ' ἐόντα, praesentia futura praeterita; be, as verb copula, αἶσα=αἴσιμον, is fated, with inf. (A 416); ἦ ποτ' ἔην γε, alas! it was he; παρήιον ἔμμεναι, to be an ornament, Δ 142; ἀπὸ θυμοῦ μοι, mihi odio eris; οὐχ ἕδος ἐστί, non vacat sedere; impersonal, ὧδε, Σ 266; οὕτω, λ 348, π 31; ἐμοὶ ἀσμένῳ, mihi gaudio, would be grateful to me, Ξ 108; ἔστι, it is possible, with inf., οὐκ ἔστι, M 327 = οὔπως, nullo modo, δ 193; with acc. and inf., ε 103, οὐ —μῆχος (expedient, remedy); ἦ θέμις ἐστί, sicut fas est; οὐ θέμις, Ξ 386, nefas est. (Ellipsis of ἐστί is frequent, in various forms, e. g. ἔῃ, Ξ 376; ἔστω, O 502.)

εἰμι, 2 sing. εἶσθα, subj. ἴησθα, ἴῃς, ἴῃσι, ἴομεν, ἴωσι, opt. εἴην, εἴη, Τ 209, ἰείη, inf. ἴ(μ)μεν(αι), ipf. ἤιον ᾖα, ἤιες ἴες, ἤιεν ἠ̈ ἴε, ἤομεν, ἤισαν ἴσαν ἤιον, aor. mid. (ἐ)είσατο, ire, go, in widest range of meaning; usually with fut. signif., ξ 526 (yet not so in comparisons, e. g. δ 401); with fut. part., Γ 383, Ξ 200, O 136, P 147; ὁδόν, go by a road; ἄγγελος, as messenger for, τινί, Λ 652, K 286, examples of different constructions:—δῶ, χορόν, σ 194; πεδίοιο, through the plain, ἄστυ-, Οὐλυμπόν-, Αἴγυπτόν-, πόλεμόν-, ἠπειρόνδέ, πρὸς Ὄλυμπον, παρά τινα; μετά τινα, seek for, go to fetch, N 247, ψ 83; ἐς δαῖτα, ἐπὶ δόρπον, ἐπὶ δεξιά, ὑπὸ γαῖαν=εἰς Ἄιδος, ἄντα θεῶν, ἐπὶ νηός ἐν νηΐ, sail,—pass, ἔτος, β 89; return, δ 670, γ 257, Α 169, Γ 305; incedere, walk (majestic), ζ 102, H 213; rise to go, go away, then as exhortation (βάσκ', ἀλλ', δεῦρ'), ἴθι; fly, B 87, M 239, X 309; plough the waves, A 482; penetrate, Γ 61, Δ 138; of stars, pursue their course, X 27, Ψ 226 ; φάτις, go abroad, ψ 362; advance (of enemy). Γ 2, 8, M 88, P 759, χ 7 ; ἐπί τινι, ἀντί τινος, ἰθύς τινος, straight upon, ἀντίος, H 98, χ 89. [ῐ-, ἴομεν.]

εἰν=ἐν.

εἰνά-ετες (ἔτος), adv., nine years, γ 118.

εἰνάκῐς, novies, nine times, ξ 230†.

εἰν-ἀλίη, αι, (ἅλς), adj., marina, of the sea, sea-, ο 479 and ε 67.

εἰνά-νῠχες (-νύχ-), adj. pl., nine nights long, I 470†.

εἰνάτερες, ων, αἱ, janitrices, brothers' wives, Z 378.

εἴνᾰτος, nonus, ninth, B 295.

εἵνεκα=ἕνεκα.

εἰνί=ἐν.

εἰν-οδίοις, adj., (ὁδός), in the way, Π 260†.

εἰν-οσί-γαιος=ἐννοσίγαιος.

εἰν-οσί-φυλλον, acc., (φύλλον), leaf-shaking, with quivering foliage, ι 22.

εἴξασκε, iter. aor. from εἴκω, cedebat.

εἷο=οὗ, χ 19, Δ 400, sibi inferiorem, inferior to himself.

εἰοικυῖαι, pf. part. from ἔοικα, II. εἴκω.

εἷος=ἕως.

εἷπα, -έμεν(αι), see εἶπον.

εἴπερ, if only, if for once, as sure as, contains often an emphatic assertion ; the leading idea or important word often precedes, θ 408 ; with indic. preterit, ζ 282 ; fut., K 115, M 223, Π 263 ; subj. pres., M 245 ; aor., K 225, Φ 576, X 86, 191 ; opt., N 288 (apodosis, οὐκ ἂν πέσοι), Υ 100 (οὐ μὲ νικήσει) ; additional examples with past tense of indic., Π 618 (τάχα κεν κατέπαυσε), Π 847 (πάντες κ' ὄλοντο).

εἶπον (ἔϝειπον, ϝέπος), aor., parallel form iter. εἴπεσκεν, subj. εἴπωμι, ῃσθα, indic. 1 sing. εἶπα, 2 pl. εἴπατε (ἔσπετε, see this word), say, speak, τινί or πρός τινα ; τί τινι, bid one execute something γ 427 ; τινά, (1) address, B 59.—(2) call, tell, τ 334, Θ 373 (attraction, τ 219), ω 337.—(3) (εὖ) τινὰ, speak (well) of one, α 302 ; περί τινος, ἀμφί τινι, de aliquo ; ἐν (μετά) τισι, before, in presence of ; ἔπος, A 108, 543 (σ 166, say something) ; μῦθον, T 85 ; ἀγγελίην, θεοπρόπιον, θέσφατα ; δίκην, give judgment ; ὑπέροπλον, speak arro-

gantly ; σάφα, clearly, accurately ; καί ποτέ τις εἴπῃσι, olim dicturus sit aliquis.

εἴ ποτε, si quando, if ever ; εἰ ποτ' ἔην γε, see I. ἤ.

εἴ που, sicubi, if any where, γ 93, **εἴ πως**, si qua, if in any way, serve to state more mildly an assertion or suspicion, K 206, Ο 571, δ 388, π 148, Δ 17.

εἰράων, τῶν, meeting-places, Σ 531†. εἴργω, un-Homeric, Ψ 72, see ἔργω.

εἴρερον, τόν, (σειρά, servus), servitutem, slavery, θ 529†.

εἰρεσίη, ης, ἡ, (ἐρέσσω), remigium, rowing, μ 225. (Od.)

Εἰρέτρια, αν, town in Εὔβοια, B 537†.

εἴρηαι, see ἔρω III.

εἴρημαι, see (1) εἴρω, say.—(2) ἔρω, ask.

εἰρήνη, ης, ἡ, (εἴρημαι), peace, ἐπ' εἰρήνης, in pace.

εἴρια, τά, (ἔριον, ἀρνός), vellera, wool ; εἴ. ξαίνειν, card wool, χ 423.

εἰρο-κόμῳ, τῇ, (κομ-έω), lanas curanti, dressing wool, spinning, Γ 387†.

εἴρομαι, see ἔρω III.

εἰρο-πόκων, οις, gen. and dat. pl. from -πόκος, (πέκω), wool-fleeced, woolly, ι 443 and E 137.

εἷρος, τό, (εἴρια), vellus. fleece, δ 135 and ι 426.

εἴρῠαται, see ἐρύομαι and ἐρύουσι.

εἴρω (FEP, ver-bum), fut. ἐρέω, ἔει, ἔουσι, ἔων, ἔουσα, pass. pf. εἴρηται, ἡμένα, plupf. εἴρητο (fut. εἰρήσεται), aor. ῥηθέντι,—say, A 297 ; announce, ἔπος, ἀγγελίην, φόως ; παρέξ, falso, ψ 16.

εἴρω, see ἐερμένον.

εἰρωτᾷς, prs., ipf. εἰρώτα, ἠρώτα ; (εἴρομαι), interrogare, ask, ο 423. (Od.)

εἰς, before vowels and βαίνω, **ἐς** (εἰν, ἐν, in), prep. with acc., (cf. in with acc. in Latin).—(1) of place, into, to, εἰς ἅλα (δῖαν, δ 577), ἅλαδε, κ 351 ; λαύρην, χ 128 ; with κατέθηκεν, ν 96 ; with designations of place, also names of cities, to, Θ 203 ; τρέπεσθαι, turning themselves toward, α 421 ; elsewh. of object or aim, e. g. ἐς θήρην, μάχην, πόλεμον ; apparently with gen., sc. δόμον, κ 512, Ζ 378, Ω 160, 482, ν 23, esp. with Ἀΐδαο ; δ 581, sc. ῥοάς ; yet εἰσ-   100   εἴσεται

cf. ξ 258; ἐς δίσκουρα, at a discus-throw; look upon, Ω 484, θ 170, π 477; εἰς ὦπα, a 411; εἰς ἄντα, ε 217, in the face; distributive, B 126, in decurias distribueremur, by˙ tens, ι 135;—of end or purpose: εἰπεῖν (μυθεῖσθαι, Ψ 305) εἰς ἀγαθόν, I 102, advise one for his good; εἰς ἄτην, to my ruin, μ 372; E 737, for the combat;—of result : B 379, come to one conclusion.—(2) of time, up to, for, ἐνιαυτόν, δ 595, λ 356; ἐς τί, quousque, how long; εἰς ὅτε κεν, until when, with subj., β 99.

εἰσ-, in compounds, see ἐσ-.

εἶς (εἵς) = ἔεσσι, (εἶμι), es, only before vowels, exc. ρ 388.

εἶς, μία, ἕν, unus, a, um; Δ 397, ἕνα οἶον, μία μούνη, μι᾿ οἴη, β 412, one single one; so εἷς, only one, a single one, ν 313, χ 138; idem, same, N 487, O 511, once for all; o 106=nearly aliquem, some one; ἕνα αἰεί, i. e. one after another, χ 117.

εἶσα, see ἕζω.

ἐς ἀγείρομεν, ipf. ἐσαγείρετο, aor. -ατο, collect into, A 142 (v. l. ἐν δ᾽—); ξ 248, collected itself into ; O 240, was just coming back to life.

εἰσ-άγω, reg., aor. freq. in tmesi, ἐς δ᾽ ἄγαγε, introducere, lead in; Z 252, ἐσάγουσα, bringing with her (by chance); elsewh. with design, e. g. Λ 778; Ω 447, bid come forward, be seated; προτέρω, δ 36; Κρήτην ἑταίρους, brought safely to Krete, γ 191; δόμον, into the house; bring in, ξ 419, τ 420.

εἰσάμενος, ατο, (1) from εἴδομαι, similis. — (2) from εἶμι = ἐείσατο, ivit.

εἰσ-ανα-βαίνοι, opt. prs., ipf. -έβαινον, aor. -έβην, mount, Θ 291; go back to, Z 74; go up to, Ω 700; Ω 97, Σ 68, went up the shore, π 449 (tmesis, τ 602).

εἰσ-αν-άγουσι, carry off into bondage, with acc., θ 529†.

εἰσ-αν-ιδών, intuitus, looking up into, with acc., Π 232 and Ω 307.

εἰσ-αν-ιών (εἶμι), with acc., climbing the sky, H 423†.

εἰσ-άντα (εἰς ἄντα), in the face, straightforward, o 532, also ἐσάντα.

εἴσατο, aor., see εἶμι and εἶδον.

εἰσ-αφ-ίκανεν, ipf., came to, χ 99.

εἰσ-αφ-ικόμην, only subordinate

modes, pervenire ad, arrive at, with acc., μ 84, ψ 66, Υ 336.

εἰσ-βαίνω, ipf. and aor., embark upon, enter, τι, ι 103, δ 48, θ 314 ; M 59, come in ; ἐς δ᾽ βῆσε, drove in, A 310.

εἰσ-εῖδον, ε, see εἰσοράω.

εἴσ-ειμι, ipf. ἐς δ᾽ ἤιεν, ἴτην, go in; μετ᾽ ἀνέρας, among the men; enter, χ 470; Ω 463, in conspectum veniam.

εἰσ-ελθών, drive in, κ 83 ; εἰσ-ἤλασαν, ran in the ship, ν 113; drive into battle, O 385.

εἰσ-ερύσαντες (ἐρύω), aor. part., having dragged it into the cave, μ 317†.

εἰσ-έρχεο, fut. ἐσελεύσομαι, aor. εἰσ-ῆλθε, ἐς δ᾽ ἦλθε, ἔσελθε, etc., also ἐσ-έρχεται, intrare, enter, τί, ρ 275; ἐς τι, δ 802 ; εὐνήν, δ 338; incessere, enter into, come upon, P 157, o 407 ; B 798, very often have I been present in battles; ingredi, Φρυγίην.

ἴσῃ, ης, ῃ, ην, αι, (ἐFισFη, fem. from ἐFισος=ἶσος), aequus, like, proportionate, epithet of (1) δαιτός (δαῖτας, λ 185), fitting share, A 468; equal, i. e. equally divided, feast.—(2) νῆες, νῆας, νηός, symmetrical, well-proportioned, ε 175.—(3) ἀσπίδα παντόσ᾽ ἴσην, uniform on every side, circular.—(4) φρένας ἔνδον (nearly = ἐναίσιμοι, σ 220), well-balanced, thoughtful, reasonable.

εἶσθα = εἶς, from εἶμι.

εἰσ-ιέμεναι, prs. part. mid. from εἰσίημι, seeking to enter, χ 470.

εἰσ-ίθμη, ἡ, (εἶμι), entrance, ζ 264†.

ἴσκω, prs. indic., ipf. ἤισκε, ομεν, ἐίσκομεν (ἴκελος), liken, (1) with reflexive pron. and dat., assume form (appearance) of any one, ν 313.—(2) discern resemblance, τινά τινι, ἄγχιστα, πάντα altogether, ἐνωπαδίως, ψ 94; compare, Γ 197; ι 321, judged it as large as.—(3) censere, hold, with acc. and inf., N 446, may we think it an equivalent ?

εἰσ-νοέω, only aor. εἰσενόησα, ε, discern, Ω 700†.

εἴσ-οδος, ἡ, entrance, κ 90†.

εἰσ-οιχνεῦσι, εὖσαν, 3 pl. indic. and part., (οἴχομαι), with acc., enter, ζ 157 the choral dance.

εἰσόκε(ν) = εἰς ὅ κε, dum, with subj., (1) until, Γ 409, θ 318.—(2) as long as, I 609.

εἴσεται, fut., (1) from εἶμι, ibit.—(2) from οἶδα, sciet, see ΕΙΔ, IV.

εἰσ-οράω, prs. εἰσορόωσι, opt. -ορόψτε, part. -ορόων and -ῶν, mid. pres. imp. -οράασθε, inf. -άασθαι, ipf. -ορόωντο; aor. εἰσεῖδον εἴσιδον, iter. ἐσίδεσκεν (ψ 94), mid. -ίδοντο, ἰδέσθην, ἰδηται, (often in tmesi, σ 219, 320), intueri, look upon, ὀφθαλμοῖσιν, π 477; ἐνωπαδίως=ἀντην, gazed into his eyes; ψ 94, ἐσίδεσκεν, instead of usual reading ἠίσκεν (ἤισκεν); behold, H 214, with part. Σ 235, θ 526; π 277, endure the sight; θεὸν ὥς, dei instar suspicere, gaze upon one as a god; spectare, behold (mid.), Ψ 448; the infin. is often used after verbs of comparing where it seems superfluous, ι 324, γ 246, ζ 230; Ξ 345, whose rays are the most piercing to the sight.

ἴσος, see ἴση.

εἰσ-πέτομαι, only aor. εἰσέπτατο, with acc., involavit, fly into, Φ 494†.

εἴσω, ἔσω, (εἰς), introrsum, within, freq. after acc., Π 364, ο 40, Ζ 284, sc. δόμον; with gen., η 135, θ 290; with pregnant signif., seeming to have partially the force of a prep., N 553, κ 91; η 13, and carried in to her the evening meal.

εἰσωποὶ ἐγένοντο νεῶν, they arrived just opposite (εἰς ὦπα) the ships, O 653†.

εἶται = Fέσται, vestitus est, ἔννυμι.

εἴ τε—εἴ τε, sive—sive, either—or, with indic., A 65; and subj., M 239.

εἶτε = εἴητε, opt. from εἰμί.

εἰῶ = ἐάω.

εἰῶ = ὦ, subj. from εἰμί.

εἴωθα, pf. of ἔθω.

εἴων, ipf. from ἐάω.

αἴως = ἕως.

ἐκ, before vowels ἐξ, prep. with gen., ex, (1) local: out of, forth from, I 344, K 13, Λ 239, σ 29; ὕπνον, E 413; K 107, turn his heart from wrath; ζ 224, washed himself in the river; partitive, Δ 96, O 680, Ω 397; ἐκ παντων, prac omnibus, β 433; from, ε 283, Ζ 257, N 493, Π 365, Υ 377; ἵππων, ἕδρης, θρόνου, θυμοῦ from the heart; on the part of, η 70, α 313; from—to, Π 640, X 397; ἄρχεσθαι, begin with; away from, Γ 273, Σ 107, ζ 226; Λ 163, βελέων, out of shot; = ἐκτὸς ἀπό, away from, i. e. from elsewhere than, λ 134; translated by, to, or upon, with many verbs, e. g. κρεμάσας, θ 67, Θ 19; ἦκα,

O 18; τείνας, E 322; ἦν, Λ 38; ἀνήφθω, μ 51; δῆσε, Ψ 853; so also with προσφυἱα, τ 58, and ω 8; cf. Σ 480.— (2) temporal: from—to, Υ 290, one misfortune after another, Ω 535, Ξ 86; ἐξ οὗ, ex quo, since, A 6, Θ 295 sq.; ἐκ τοῦδε, λ 168; ἐκ τοῖο, henceforth, A 493; ἐξ ἔτι πατρῶν, since the days of our ancestors.—(3) causal: springing from, (γένος, Ψ 347), εἶναι ἐκ τινος, Υ 106, a 207; γενέσθαι, E 897, 548, Ζ 206, κ 350; γενεή, Φ 157, cf. A 63; γαίης, α 406, cf. ο 425; ἐκ νυκτῶν, μ 286, β 136; in consequence of, I 566, Λ 308, ψ 224; ἔριδος, H 111; denoting the prime mover, α 33, π 447, B 669, ἐκ Διός; κλύειν ἐκ, from one's mouth, τ 93; from some other country, Π 13. Examples of anastrophe, E 865, Ξ 472, Ω 743, ρ 518.

Ἑκάβη, ης, Δύμαντος θυγάτηρ, wife of Πρίαμος, Ζ 293, Π 718. (Il.)

ἑκά-εργος, ον, ε, (σε-κα-Fεργ-ος, from ἔέργω, not from ἔργον), as god of death, he who banishes, he who shuts up far away (in the grave or in the lower world), I 564. (Il. and θ 323.)

ἐκάη, aor. pass. from καίω, combustus est.

ἔκαθεν (ἑκάς), e longinquo, far, far away (usually from stand-point of speaker), ρ 25; far and wide, B 456.

Ἑκα-μήδη, ης, daughter of Ἀρσίνοος, maid-servant of Νέστωρ, Λ 624.

ἑκάς (σFε=Lat. se+κάς), adj., for one's self, alone, Υ 422; usually adv., remote, ἀπό, Σ 256; freq. used as prep. with gen., far from, N 263, γ 354, ξ 496.

ἑκαστέρω, farther than, gen., η 321†; and ἑκαστάτω, farthest off, K 113†.

ἑκάστοθι, in each division, γ 8†.

ἕκαστος, η, ον, (ϝ-Fε—κα=unusque), unusquisque, each one; in apposition often in pl., where we should expect the sing., ν 76; sing. distributive apposition, κ 397; with demonstratives, τά, ταῦτα, μ 16; ξ 436, one to each.

ἑκάτερθε(ν), utrimque, on both sides, ὁμίλου, = the two armies, Γ 340, α 335, ζ 19.

ἑκάτη-βελέτάω, gen. from -έτης, sender of missiles, A 75†.

ἑκάτη-βόλος, ον, (ϝἑκατος, βέλη), sender of missiles, epith. of Ἀπόλλων, A 370, θ 339, O 231.

ἑκατόγ-χειρον, acc., (χείρ), centimanum, *hundred-handed*, A 402†.

ἑκατό(ν)-ζῠγος (ζυγόν), *with hundred rowers'-benches*, Υ 247† (hyperbolically).

ἑκατόμ-βης, τῆς, -η, -ας, (βόες), hecatomb, *great public sacrifice*, etymologically *of a hundred oxen*, but, in fact, of far less, Ζ 93, 115; often part or all of the victims are rams; pl. used of a single sacrifice, B 321.

ἑκᾰτόμ-βοιος, ον, α, *worth a hundred oxen*, B 449; *a hundred oxen*, Φ 79. (Il.)

ἑκᾰτόμ-πεδον, better **-ποδον**, *a hundred feet* (each way), Ψ 164†.

ἑκᾰτόμ-πολις, *hundred-citied*, of Κρήτη, B 649†. (Yet see τ 174.)

ἑκᾰτόμ-πυλοι, *with hundred gates*, Θῆβαι Αἰγύπτιοι, Ι 383†.

ἑκᾰτόν, centum, *hundred*, Ι 85; freq. as large round number, B 448, Ξ 181; so also in compounds, e. g. with -βης, -πολις, -πυλοι.

ἑκάτοιο (ϳέκατος, ἵημι), missor, *shooter*, A 385. (Il.)

ἐκ-βαίνοντα, prs. part. ipf., aor. often in tmesi, ἐκ δ᾽ ἔβαν, Γ 113, (βαίνω), exire, *go out*, A 437, 439; descendo, *descend*, πέτρης; 1 aor., *set on land*, A 438, ω 301.

ἐκ-βάλλων, prs. part., ipf. aor. usually in tmesi, ejicere, *cast forth*, Φ 237; dejicere, *hurl down from*, E 39; excutere e manibus alicuius, β 396; fundere, *let fall*, δάκρυα; emittere, *utter*, ἔπος; excidere, *hew out*, ε 244.

ἔκ-βᾰσις, ἡ, *landing-place*, ε 410†.

ἐκ-βλώσκω, only aor. **ἐκμολεν**, processit ex, *went forth*, Λ 604†.

ἐκ-γεγάμεν, άτην, αώς, άονται, see ἐκγίγνομαι.

ἐκ-γελάσας, aor. part., (γελάω), *laugh out*; ἡδύ, heartily, π 354, σ 35; but Ζ 471, ἐκ δέ, thereat laughed.

ἐκ-γίγνομαι, aor. **ἐξεγένοντο**, pf. γεγάτην, άασι, inf. άμεν, part. -άωτι, ἀυῖα, often in tmesi, *spring from*, τινός, Φ 185, Ο 641, ζ 229.

ἔκ-γονος, ον, ὁ and ἡ, filius, filia, *child*, *offspring*, E 813, λ 236.

ἐκ-δέρω, only aor. part. **ἐκδείρας**, detractam, *having flayed*, κ 19†.

ἐξ-εδέχοντο, (τινί τι), *received from* him, Ν 710†.

ἐκ-δέω, ipf. **ἐξέδεον**, aor. inf. ἐκδῆσαι,

bind upon, with gen., Ψ 121 and χ 174.

ἐκ-δηλος, conspicuus, μετὰ πᾶσιν, E 2†.

ἐκ-δια-βάντες (βαίνω), τι, *having passed quite over*, Κ 198†.

ἐκ-δοτε, aor. imp., (δίδωμι), tradite, *deliver over*, ι' 459†.

ἐκ-δυνε, ipf., exuit, *put off*, α 437; -εδύοντο, exuerunt sua, Γ 114; aor. -δύς, ξ 460, but μεγάροιο, *escaping from*; so Π 99, opt. -δῦμεν, with acc., *may we escape*; ξ 341, ἔδυσαν, *stripped from* my body.

ἐκεῖθι, ibi, ρ 10†.

ἐκεῖνος and **κεῖνος**, η, ο, illc, μέν τοι ὅδ᾽ αὐτὸς ἐγώ, in truth I who am here am *he*, ω 321, cf. Τ 344; κεῖνος ἀνήρ, δ 145, ρ 243; freq. with follg. rel. sentence, e. g., ξ 156; κάκεῖνος = καὶ ἐκεῖνος, now usually replaced by the reading καὶ κεῖνος.—**κείνῃ**, illâ, *there*, ν 111†.

ἐκέκαστο, plupf. from καίνυμαι, superabat.

ἐκέκλετο, see κέλομαι; **ἐκέκλιτο**, plupf. from κλίνω; **ἔκηα**, see καίω.

ἐκη-βολίαι, *skill in shooting missiles*, E 54†.

ἐκη-βόλος, ου, (ϳέκη, jacula, βάλλω). *shooting*; also subst.. A 96. (Il.)

ἔκηλος, ον, οι, and **εὔκηλος**, οι, (Ϳέκηλος, ἐϳέκηλ. ἐκών), *of good cheer*, *at ease*, *unmolested*, E 805, Ζ 70, β 311, λ 184, φ 289, ξ 479.

ἔκητι (ϳέκητι), favore, *by grace or aid* (of a god), with gen., τ 86. (Od.)

ἐκ-θνήσκω, only aor. 3 pl. **ἔκθᾰνον** γέλῳ, risu emoriebantur, (nearly) *died of laughter*, *laughed themselves* (almost) *to death*, σ 100†.

ἐκ-θρώσκει, aor. **ἐξέθορε**, **ἔκθορε**, freq. ἐκ θόρε, exsilire, *spring forth*, Η 182; with gen., desiluit, Θ 320; prosiluit, Ο 573; with gen., εὐνῆφι, Ο 580, Κ 95, *leaps from my breast* (from throbbing).

ἐξ-εκάθαιρον, ipf., purgabant, *cleanse*, B 153†.

ἐκ-και-δεκά-δωρα, ntr. pl., *sixteen palms* (δῶρα) *long* (of horns of wild goat), Δ 109†.

ἐκ-καλέω, only aor. part. act. and aor. mid. **ἐξεκαλεῖτο**, καλεσσάμενος, *summon*, mid., *for one's self*, τ 15, ω 1.

ἐκ-καλυψάμενοι, mid., (καλύπτω),

(capita) revelantes, *unveiling their heads* (which they had previously covered in token of grief), κ 179†.

ἐκ-κατέ-παλτο, better οὐρανοῦ ἐκ κατ., (πάλλομαι), *sprang down from* heaven, Τ 351†.

ἐκ-κατ-ιδών, better Περγάμου ἐκ κατ., *looking down from* Pergamos, Δ 508 and Η 21.

ἐκ-κίεν, ipf. from κίω, *came forth*, ω 492†.

ἐξ-έκλεψεν, aor., (κλέπτω), *stole away* (from his chains), Ε 390†.

ἐξ-εκυλίσθη, aor. pass., (κυλίω), *rolled headlong down from*, Ζ 42 and Ψ 394.

ἐκ-λανθάνω, only -λέλαθον, *made quite forget*, κιθαριστύν, Β 600 ; mid. aor. -λελάθοιτο, οιντο, ἐσθαι, with gen., -λάθετο, οντο, with gen., Π 602 ; with inf., κ 557, *forget utterly*.

ἔκλε΄, ipf. pass. = ἐκλέετο, from κλείω, *thou wast celebrating*.

ἐκ δέ με πάντων ληθάνει, *makes— forget* all my sufferings, η 221†.

ἔκ-λησιν, τήν, (λήθω), *forgetting and forgiving* (bring about), ω 485†.

ἐκ-λύσομαι, fut. from -λύω, exsolvam, *set free from*, with gen., κ 286 ; ἐξελύθη, better ἐξεσύθη, Ε 293.

ἔκ-μολεν, aor. from -βλώσκω, *went forth*.

ἐκ-μυζήσας, aor. part. from -μυζάω, (μύξα), exsugere, *suck out*, Δ 218†.

ἐκ-νοστήσαντι, see νοστῆσαι.

ἔκ-παγλος, ον, α, οις, sup. -όταт', adv. -ως, (πάγος, cf. ῥιγεδανής and καταρριγηλά), strictly, *fro ty*, ξ 522 ; horridus, *horrible, dreadful*, Φ 589, Α 146, κ 448 ; ntr. εἷος, adverbially, Ν 413, Χ 256 ; so also ntr. pl. used like adv. ἐκπάγλως, only with verbs of hating and loving, and always in signif. *exceedingly, beyond measure* (exc. Α 268, Β 357).

ἐκ-παιφάσσειν, (φάος), emicare, *rush madly into the fray*, Ε 803†.

ἔκ-παλτο, aor. mid., (πάλλω), with gen., excussa est, (*spirted out*, Υ 483†.

ἐκ-πεπᾰταγμένος (πατάσσω) φρένας, lit. with senses *beaten out of* one, *stricken in* mind, σ 327†.

ἐκ-πέμπεις, ipf. fut. 1 aor., (also mid.), freq. in tmesi, emittere, *send forth*, Ω 381, π 3 ; Μ 28, *wash away* ;

conduct forth, Ω 681 ; *cast out*, with gen.

ἐκ-πέποται, pf. from -πίνω, epotatum est, *has been drunk up.*

ἐκ-περάω, 3 sing. -περάᾳ, pl. -όωσι, aor. -ησεν—ἀντικρύ, *pierced through* on the opposite side ; μέγα λαῖτμα (ἁλός, θ 561), *traverse the mighty deep.*

ἐκ-πέρθω, only fut. and aor. 1 (and 2 ἐξεπράθομεν), evertere, *destroy, only of cities* ; Α 125, πολίων, *we have pillaged* from the cities. (II.)

ἐκ-πεσέειν = -πεσεῖν, aor. from πίπτω, casurum esse ex—.

ἐκ-πεφυυῖαι, pf. from -φύω, enatae.

ἐκ-πίνω, aor. ἔκπιε, ebibit, *drank up* ; perf. pass. -πέποται, quantum epotatum est, χ 56. (Od.)

ἐκ-πίπτον 3 pl. ipf., fut. -πεσέειν, aor. ἔκπεσε, ον, also in tmesi, excIdere, *fall out*, Φ 492, Ψ 467 ; with gen., Λ 179 ; τινί, *escaped from* her hand, Χ 448 ; δάκρυ, *streamed from* his eyes ; χειρός, from the hand ; η 283, having given clear of the water *I sank down* (on the shore).

ἐκ-πλήσσουσι, aor. pass. -πλήγη, 3 pl. ἔκπληγεν, perturbare, *confuse* (Ν 394. φρένας, in mind) ; Σ 225, *were terrified.*

ἐκ-ποτέονται, 3 pl. prs., (πίπτω), deeIdunt (ex aëre), *fall down from* Zeus = from the sky, Τ 357†.

ἐκ-πρεπέα, acc., nom. -ής, (πρέπω) ἐν πολλοῖσι, *conspicuous* among many, Β 483†.

ἐκ-προ-καλεσσαμένη, aor. mid. from -καλέω, with gen., *having called him forth to herself*, β 400†.

ἐκ-προ-λιπόντες, aor. from λείπω, egressi ex, *having gone out of*, with acc., θ 515†.

ἐξ-έπτυσεν, aor. from -πτύω, exspuit, *spat forth*, with gen., ε 322†.

ἐκ-πεύσεται, fut., aor. πύθεσθαι, explorare, *search out*, Κ 308 and 320 (better θεῶν ἐκ, Υ 129).

ἐκρέμω, 2 sing. ipf. from κρέμαμαι, suspensa eras.

ἐκ δ' ῥέε, ipf. from ῥέω = ἔσρεϜε, effusum est, *flowed forth*, Ν 655.

ἐξ-έρρηξε, aor. from Ῥήγνυμι, scidit, *snapped*, Ο 469 ; ὁδοῖο, *carried away* a part of the road.

ἐξ-εσάωσε, aor. from -σάωω, servavit, δ 501, from the sea, with gen.

ἐκ δὲ ἰσσεύοντο, ipf., aor. ἐξέσσῦτο (B 809, Θ 58, tmesis), pass. -ἐσύθη, *rush forth* (of enemy); πυλῶν, *from the gates*; *hurried forth*, ι 438; μ 366, *fled away from my eyes*; ι 373, *streamed from his throat*; E 293, *burst out.*

ἐκ δὲ σπάσεν = ἐξέσπάσε, mid. -σπάσ(σ)ατο, -σσαμένω, aor. from σπάω, extrahere, evellere, *wrench forth*, always of spear, with gen. of part of body whence it is drawn out, στέρνοιο, etc., Δ 530. (Il.)

ἐξ-έστρεψε, aor. from -στρέφω, with gen., *root up out of*, P 58†.

ἔκτα, aor. act., ἔκταθεν, aor. pass. 3 pl. from κτείνω.

ἐκ-τᾰδίην, acc. fem., (τείνω), extensam, *broad, with ample folds*, K 134†.

ἐκ-τάμνῃσι, subj., -τάμνοντε part., aor. -έταμον (ἔκταμε, imp.), *cut out the thigh-bones or thigh pieces of victims; arrows from wound*, Λ 515; *hew out, hew off*, trees, ι 320; *breaking off the low growth* (of wild boars), M 149.

ἔκταν = ἔκτασαν, aor. from κτείνω.

ἐκ-τανύω, only aor. ἐτάνυσσα, -τανύσας part., pass. -ετανύσθη, *stretch out*, Ω 18; *fall one's length, prone* (pass.), H 271; *lay low*, P 58; *stretched out within it*, ψ 201.

ἐκ-τελέω, τελέει, ipf. -ετέλειον, fut. ἔσω, aor. -εσσε, subj. -έσωσι, pf. pass. τετέλεσται, fut. τελέεσθαι, perficere, *bring to fulfillment, finish, achieve*, B 286, δ 7; γόνον, *present with offspring*; *bring to pass*, Σ 79; χ 5, *has come to a close.*

ἐκ-τίθημι, only aor. ἐκ θῆκε and ἐκθεῖσαι, extra ponere, υ 97, ψ 179.

ἐκ δ' ἐτίναχθεν = -ησαν, pass. aor. from τινάσσω, *were dashed out*, Π 348†.

ἔκτοθεν (ἐκτός, ἐκ), extra, with gen., *separate from*; ι 239, the MSS. have ἔκτοθεν, but Ameis reads ἐντοθεν. (Od.)

ἔκτοθι (ἐκτός), extra, *outside of, far from*, νηῶν, Ο 391; πυλάων, Χ 439.

Ἑκτόρεος, Hectoreus, *of Hektor*, B 416; Ἑκτορίδης = Ἀστυάναξ, Z 401.

ἐκτός (ἐκ), extra, *outside*, Δ 151; with gen., *outside of*, Ψ 424; and with ἀπό, K 151, *apart from.*

ἔκτος, ον, sextus, um, *sixth.*

ἔκτοσε (ἐκτός), *out of*, with gen., ξ 277†.

ἔκτοσθε(ν) (ἐκτός), *outside*, H 341;

with gen., *outside of, before*, I 552, η 112.

ἔκτῠπε, aor. from κτυπέω, tonabat, *thundered.*

Ἕκτωρ, ος, son of Πρίαμος (Ω) and of Ἑκάβη, X 80, 405, 430, Ω 747; husband of Ἀνδρομάχη, Z 390, Ω 723; "fighting for his household gods, he fell as preserver," Schiller, Siegesfest; οἷος γὰρ ἐρύετο Ἴλιον Ἕκτωρ, Z 403; slain by Achilleus in revenge for slaughter of Patroklos, Σ 115, X 326, 331, 361.

ἑκῠρή, ῆς, socrus, *mother-in-law*, X 451; ἑκῠρός, ἑ, socer, *father-in-law*, Γ 172 (σΓεκυρ, svocr, Ger. schwieger).

ἐκ-φαίνω, fut. ἐκφανεῖ, *shall bring to light*; aor. ἐξεφάνη, 3 pl. ἐκ ἔφανεν and ἐξεφάανθη, apparuit, *appeared*, Σ 248, Θ 557; emicuit, *is revealed*, N 278; -φάανθεν, *sparkled*, T 17.

ἔκ-φασθαι (ἐκφημι), *utter*, κ 246 and ν 308.

ἐκ-φέροι, -έμεν (inf.), ipf. also ἔκφερε, ον, efferre mortuum, *carry out the dead*, Ω 786; surripere, *abstract*, o 19; reportare, *carry off*, Ψ 785; πολέμοιο, *carry off out of the fight*; Φ 450, *brought about the end of our service; spring to the front, take the lead* (of horses), Ψ 376 sq.

ἐκ-φεύγω, aor. also ἔκφυγε, ομεν and in tmesi, inf. -έειν, effugere, ἁλός, *escape from the sea*; βέλος (χειρός, *slip from the hand*); τί, *avoid.*

ἐκ-φθέγξατο, see φθέγγομαι.

ἐξ-εφθῖτο, aor. from -φθί-ίνω, νηός, *had been consumed out of the ships*, ι 163 and μ 329.

ἐκ-φόρεον, ipf. 3 pl., (φέρω), *were carrying forth from*, οἴκων; ἐκφορέοντο, *were moving forth from*, νηῶν.

ἔκ-φυγε, aor. from ἐκφεύγω.

ἐκ-φύομαι, only pf. ἐκπεφυῖαι; Λ 40, *growing out of*, αὐχένος.

ἐκ-χέω, ipf. ἔκχεον, effundere, aor. mid. ἐκχεύατο, *poured forth his arrows*; pass. ipf. χέοντο, plupf. -ἐκέχυντο, aor. -εχύθη, and aor. mid. -έχυτο (ἔκχυτο, ὑμένοι, μένοιο), *stream out*; θ 279, *hung from.*

ἑκών (old part. Ϝεκών), volens, *willingly*, Γ 66; sponte, Δ 43, *of free will, yet reluctantly; intentionally*, Z 523, K 372.

ἐλάαν, inf. from ἐλάω.

ἐλαίη, ης, ἡ, olea, *olive-tree, ν* 102.

ἐλάϊνος, ῳ, ον, and ἐλάϊνέῳ, εον, *of o'ive-wood,* ι 320, ε 236, Ν 612.

ἔλαιον, ῳ, τό, oleum, *olive-oil,* Ψ 281; λίπ(α) ἐλαίῳ, *fat,* i. e. abundantly with olive-oil, γ 466; ἐν ληκύθῳ, ζ 79; η 107, from the firmly woven stuff, the oil trickles off.

ἔλασ(α), ἔλασσε, ἐλάσασκε, see ἐλάω.

Ἔλᾱσος, ον, a Trojan, Π 696†.

ἔλασσον, minus, *less,* Κ 357†.

ἐλάστρεον, ipf. 3 pl., (ἐλάω), *were driving* (plough-cattle), Σ 543†.

ἐλάτης, ην, *pine;* pl., *oars,* Η 5, μ 172.

ἐλᾰτῆρι, τῷ, -α, -ες, (ἐλάω), auri-gae, *charioteer,* Δ 145. (Il.)

Ἔλᾰτος, ον, (1) ally of the Trojans, Ζ 33.—(2) suitor of Πηνελόπεια, χ 267.

Ἐλᾰτρεύς, one of the Φαίηκες, θ 111, 129.

ἐλαύνω, see ἐλάω.

ἐλάφη-βόλος (ἀνήρ), *deer-hunter,* Σ 319†.

ἔλαφος, ἡ, -οιο, -οισιν, -ους, cerva, *hind,* Γ 24; symbol of cowardice, Α 225.

ἐλαφρός, αἱ, όν, ά; -ότερος, οι; -ότατος, οι, ην; adv. -ῶς, ε 240; levis, agilis, *nimble,* πόδας, θείειν; *swift,* Τ 416.

ἔλᾰχε, -ον, aor. from λαγχάνω.

ἐλάχεια, fem. from ἐλαχύς, ι 116, κ 509. *small* (ἐλάσσων), v. l. λάχεια.

ἐλάω, ἐλάαν, inf., ἐλαύνω, prs., ipf. ἔλων, fut. ἐλόωσι, aor. ἤλασσε, ἔλασσε, ἔλασε, iter. ἐλάσασκε, plupf. pass. ἠλή-λατο, ἐλήλατο, 3 pl. ἐληλέδατο, *drive,* Δ 279, 299, Τ 281; *beset, discipline, exercise,* Ν 315; ἄδην κακότητος, in satietatem mali adigere, persecute him until he has had enough, ε 290; *drive away,* Ζ 158, Ω 532; *drive off,* Α 154, ι 405, 465, ο 235; ῥύσι' ἐλαυνόμενος, driving away cattle for himself in reprisal, Λ 674; ἅρμα, ἵππους, Ψ 334, Ω 696; νῆα, *sail* a ship, Ν 27, μ 47, 109; *row, sail,* ν 22, Η 6, η 319; *draw, lay out* in a given direction, Ι 349, Σ 564, ζ 9, η 86; *strike, hew, thrust,* with weapons, sceptre, Ε 80, Υ 475; οὐλήν. so as to leave a scar, φ 219; with whip, Ρ 614, γ 484, swung the lash to drive them forward; drive in (stakes), ξ 11;

χθόνα μετώπῳ, strike the earth with the forehead; πρὸς γῆν κάρη τινός, strike off some one's head and dash it against the earth; *forge,* Μ 296; κολῳόν, prolong the brawl; ὄγμον, make one's way down a swath, in reaping or mowing; Π 518, my arm is pierced with sharp pains.

ἔλδεαι, εται, όμεναι, also ἔλδομαι, etc., prs. ipf., desidero, *long for,* τινός, Ξ 276; also τι, *desire,* α 409; the part. construed like ἄσμενος, φ 209, Η 4; pass., Π 494. (Ϝελέσθαι, velle.)

ἕλε = εἷλε, aor. from αἱρέω.

ἐλεαίρω, prs., ipf. ἐλέαιρεν, iter. ἐλεαίρεσκον, (ἔλεος), misereri, *pity,* τινά, with part., Η 27, Ι 302; οὐκ ἐλ., with inf., thou involvest without compassion, υ 202.

ἐλεγχέες, *despicable;* ἐλέγχιστος, ον, ε, *most infamous,* Β 285.

ἐλεγχείη, ην, (ἔλεγχος), *reproach, disgrace;* τινὶ ἀναθήσει, κατέχευας, inflict upon, cover with, Χ 100, ξ 38.

ἔλεγχος, τό, -εα, probrum, *disgrace;* φ 333, why do ye reckon this (what people will say of ye), as disgrace? pl., miscreants, cowards, Β 235, Ω 260.

ἐλέγχει, prs. 3 sing., aor. subj. ἐλέγξῃς, *dishonor;* φ 424, *bring disgrace upon;* Ι 522, despise neither their words nor their mission.

ἐλέειν = ἑλεῖν, aor. from αἱρέω.

ἐλεεινός, όν, ά, -ότερος, -οτάτῳ, (ἔλεος), miserandus, *pitiable,* Φ 273; ntr., flebiliter, *pitifully,* θ 531; esp. pl., Χ 37, Β 314.

ἐλεέω, only fut. ἐλεήσει, aor. ἐλέησε, αἵ κ' ἐλεήσῃ, and part., (ἔλεος), misereri, *have pity upon,* τινά, Π 431, and τι, Ζ 94; with part., Ο 44, Ρ 346, ε 336.

ἐλεήμων, misericors, *compassionate,* ε 191†.

ἐλεητύς, ύν, ἡ, (ἔλεος), misericordia, *compassion,* ξ 82 and ρ 451.

ἔλεκτο, aor., see stem ΛΕΧ.

ἐλελίζω, aor. ἐλέλιξε, aor. mid. ἐλελιξάμενος, plupf. ἐλέλικτο, aor. pass. ἐλελίχθη, 3 pl. ἐλέλιχθεν, *shake,* Α 530, Χ 448; *rally,* Ρ 278; mid., *twist one's self,* Λ 39; *brandish* quivering sword, Ν 558; *whirl round and round,* μ 416, Ζ 109.

Ἑλένη, ης, wife of Μενέλαος; daughter of Ζεύς, Γ 199, 426, and of Λήδα;

sister of Κάστωρ and of Πολυδεύκης, Γ 238; 'Αργείη, Β 161, δ 184; Γ 91, 121, Ω 761, δ 12, 219, 279.

"Ελενος, ου, (1) son of Πρίαμος; the best seer of the Trojans, Ζ 76, Ν 576, Ω 249.—(2) a Greek, Οἰνοπίδης, Ε 707†.

ἐλεό-θρεπτον, growing in marshes, Β 776†.

ἔλεον, τόν, misericordiam, pity, Ω 44†.

ἐλεοῖσι, τοῖς, dressers, I 215 and ξ 432.

ἔλεσκον, ε, aor. iter. from αἱρέω.

ἐλετή, capienda, to be caught, neither plunder nor choice can make the breath of man return when once it has passed the barrier of the teeth, I 409†.

ἐλεῦ, imp. aor. mid. = ἑλοῦ, take thy spear, Ν 294.

ἐλεύθερον κρητῆρα, mixing-bowl of freedom, i. e. celebrating its recovery, Ζ 528; ἦμαρ, day of freedom=freedom, Ζ 455.

ἐλεφαίρονται, 3 pl., part. aor. ἐλεφηράμενος, decipere, delude, overreach, τ 565 and Ψ 388.

ἐλέφαντος, τοῦ, -ι, -α, ivory, Δ 141, Ε 583, δ 73, θ 404; symbol of whiteness, σ 196, ψ 200.

Ἑλεφ-ήνωρ, ορος, Χαλκωδοντιάδης, ἀρχὸς Ἀβάντων, Β 540, Δ 467.

Ἑλεών, ῶνος, town in Βοιωτία, Β 500.

ἐληλάδᾰτο, ἐλήλᾰται, ᾰτο, ἐληλέδᾰτο, etc., see ἐλάω.

ἐληλουθώς, ἐλθέμεν(αι), see ἔρχομαι.

Ἑλῐκάων, ονος, son of Ἀντήνωρ, husband of Λαοδίκη, Γ 123.

Ἑλίκη, a town in Ἀχαιία, Β 575, Θ 203, with shrine of Ποσειδάων.

Ἑλῐκώνιον ἄνακτα = Ποσειδῶνα, Υ 404.

ἑλῐκ-ῶπες, ας, -ῶπιδα, shining-eyed, Α 98.

ἕλῐκες, ας, (usually digammated, Fέλικες, Fελίσσω), (1) adj. camurae, crooked-horned, βόες, never ταῦροι (explained by Ameis as for σέλικες, cf. σέλας, shining, sleek).—(2) subst. ἕλικες γναμπταί, Σ 401, arm-bands bent into a spiral. (See cut No. 12.)

ἑλισσέμεν, inf., aor. part. ἑλίξας, also mid., pres. ipf. εἱλίσσετο, ἑλίσσετο, aor. ἑλιξάμενος, pass. aor. ἑλιχθέντων (Fελισσ.), turn, Ψ 466, 309; pass., whirled

around in the eddies, Φ 11; turn one's self (from flight), rally, Μ 74; mid., go eagerly about, Μ 49, Σ 372; turning at bay, Ρ 283; turn round (the goal), Ψ 309, Μ 408; turned himself this way and that, υ 28; coiling himself within his hole, Χ 95; roll, Ν 204.

ἑλκεσί-πέπλους, Τρωάδας, wearing long, trailing robes. (Il.)

ἑλκε-χίτωνες, Ἰάονες, trailing the tunic, wearing long tunic, Ν 685†.

ἕλκεον, ipf., fut. ἑλκήσουσι, aor. ἥλκησε, aor. pass. ἑλκηθείσας, (ἕλκω), were dragging this way and that, Ρ 395, Χ 336; carried off, as captives, Χ 62; maltreat, λ 580.

ἑλκηθμοῖο, τοῦ, carrying into captivity, Ζ 465†.

ἕλκος, τό, -εος, -εϊ, -αε, vulnus, wound, Τ 49; ὕδρου, from the Hydra, Β 723.

ἑλκυστάζων, part. pres., dragging, Ψ 187 and Ω 21.

ἕλκει, etc., (ἑλκέμεν(αι), inf., only prs. ipf. (unaugmented), act. mid. and pass. (cf. ἕλκεον), draw, Β 165, Κ 353, Υ 405; drag, Ω 52; Χ 401, from him as he was dragged along; ποδός, drag by the foot, σ 10; Π 406, drew him over the chariot-rim; drew the bow-string, Δ 122, φ 419; Θ 486, drawing after it, Μ 398, tugged at it; raise, hoist, of balance, sails, Χ 212, ο 291; vehere, draw along, Ψ 518; pass., Ε 665, trailing along; Ψ 715, wrenched; mid., drew his sword; tore his hair, Κ 15; draws down the skin over his forehead, Ρ 136; drew his seat nearer, τ 506.

ἔλλαβε=ἔλαβε, aor. from λαμβάνω.

Ἑλλάς, άδος, ἡ, Hellas, the ancients understood as a Thessalian city and district in Φθιῶτις, under the sway of Ἀχιλλεύς, Β 684; now more correctly described as the tract between the Asopos and Enipeus; coupled with Phthia, I 395; λ 496, the realm of Peleus; καὶ μέσον Ἄργος=the whole of Greece, see Ἄργος; epithets, εὐρυχόροιο, I 478; καλλιγύναικα, Β 683, I 447.

ἐλλεδανοῖσι, τοῖς, straw bands for bundles of grain, Σ 553†.

Ἕλληνες, οἱ, inhabitants of Ἑλλάς, primarily in Φθιῶτις; Β 684, in Northern Greece (β 530, Πανέλληνας).

Ἑλλήσ-ποντος, ῳ, ον, Hellespont, with adjacent bodies of water, ω 82.

ἐλλισάμην, σσετο, aor. from λίσσομαι.

ἐλλιτάνευε, ipf. from λιτανεύω.

ἐλλόν, τύν, young deer, τ 228†.

ἕλοιμι, ἐλών, etc., aor. from αἱρέω.

ἕλος, εος, τό, (Fέλος), meadow-land,
marsh, Δ 483, ξ 474.

"Ἑλος (Fέλος, V eliac), (1) in Λακω-
νική, Β 584, maritime city, named from
its marshes.—(2) town of the Πύλιοι,
Β 594.

ἐλόωσι, see ἐλάω.

Ἐλπ-ήνωρ, ορος, companion of
Ὀδυσσεύς, κ 552, λ 51, 57.

ἐλπίδος, τῆς, spei; τ 84, there is
still a portion of hope, a gleam of hope.

ἔλπει, mid. ἔλπομαι, ipf. ἔλπετο
(ἐFέλπεται, το), pf. FέFoλπα, ε=ἔολπα,
ε, plupf. ἐώλπει, (volupe), give hopes,
β 91, ν 380; mid., expect, P 406, γ 218,
η 293, ζ 297; think, λ 40, N 309, Τ 328,
ι 419, φ 314; fear, Ο 110; hope, ἐνὶ
φρεσί, κατὰ θυμόν, θυμῷ, but also Τρω-
σὶν Fέλπετο θυμὸς ἐνὶ στήθεσσιν ἑκάστου, Ο 701, 288, Ρ 395; parenthetically, Σ 194; with acc. and inf., γ 375;
inf. fut. prs. aor. pf.

ἐλπωρή τοι ἔπειτα, tum tibi spes
est, ψ 287. (Od.)

ἕλσαι, σας, aor. from εἱλέω.

ἐλύω, aor. pass. ἐλύσθη, εἱς (Fελυ-
volv-), bent itself, i. e. sank upon the
ground, Ψ 393, Ω 510; ι 433, drawing
one's self together.

ἔλχ'=ἔλκε, from ἕλκω.

ἕλων, ipf. from ἐλάω.

ἕλωρ, α, (Fέλωρ, Fελεῖν), praeda,
spoil, prey (of enemies, wild-beasts,
birds); Σ 93, pay the penalty for slaying and stripping Patroklos.

ἐλώρια, τά=ἕλωρα, Α 4, gave them
to dogs and birds to prey upon, lit. as
prey.

ἐμβαδόν, on foot (over the sea), Ο
505†.

ἐμ-βαίνων, part. prs., ipf. ἔμβαινον,
aor., (also in tmesi), ἔμβη, ητον, subj.
ἐμβήῃ, pf. ἐμβεβαῶτα, -υἶα, plupf.
βέβασαν, ἐν νηΐ, vehi navibus, embark for, α 210; ἅρμασιν ἐμβεβαῶτα,
currui insistentem, vehentem,
step into, mount, step upon, Ζ 65, κ 164;
Ψ 403, allons! hasten! forward! but
Α 311 and freq. ἐν δέ=eorum in numero, e. g. δ 653; Π 94, enter the combat; λ 4, μῆλα ἐβήσαμεν, got on board.

ἐμβάλλω, prs., ipf., aor. act. mid,
τί τινι, injicere, cast in, lay in, imponere, Ω 645, δ 298; thrust, Ε 317·
εὐνήν, prepare; Τ 394, put in; hand
over to, Η 188 (also οἱ—χειρί, ἐν χερσί,
take in the hand, give over into the hand
of, Φ 47, 104); infuse, P 451, N 82,
courage, strength, flight, fear, longing;
μοι — φρεσὶν ἄτην, blind the mind;
βάλλεσθαι ἐνὶ φρ., lay to heart; θυμῷ
τι, think upon something; νηΐ ἐμβάλλειν τινά, embark; κεραυνόν, hurl
upon; κώπῃς, lay one's self to the oar;
Σ 85, gave thee to share the bed of a
mortal.

ἐμ-βάσίλευεν, ipf., with dat., in them
ruled, ο 413.

ἐμ-βεβάσαν, βεβάώς, βήῃ, βη, see
ἐμβαίνων.

ἐμ-βρέμεται, ἱστίῳ, roars in the sail,
Ο 627†.

ἔμβρυον, τό, new-born lamb, (ι).

ἐμέθεν, ἐμεῖο, ἐμέο, ἐμεῦ, = ἐμοῦ.

ἐμέμηκον, see μηκάομαι.

ἔμεν(αι)=εἶναι.

ἔμεν(αι)=εἶναι, aor. inf. from ἵημι.

ἐμέων (Fεμ-), vomens, spitting out,
Ο 11†.

ἔμικτο, aor. from μίγνυμι.

ἔμμαθε, aor. from μανθάνω.

ἐμ-μάπέως (μαπέειν, μάρπτω), con-
tinuo, instantly, Ε 836 and ξ 485.

ἐμ-μεμαώς, -υἶα, part. from μίμαα,
eager, persistent. (Il.)

ἔμμεν(αι)=εἶναι.

ἐμ-μενὲς αἰεί (μένω), only at close
of verse, persistently, always, N 517.

ἔμμορε, pf. from μέρω.

ἔμ-μοροι (μόρος), participes,
sharers in, τιμῆς, θ 480†.

ἐμός, ή, όν, meus, a, um, no voc.,
β 96, τ 406; usually without article
(yet Ψ 585, σ 254, Λ 608, and elsewhere οὑμός, Θ 360=ὁ ἐμός; ἐμός ἐσσι
=my son, π 300 (τῷμῷ τῆμῷ, by crasis
with article; better τῷ ἐμῷ τῇ ἐμῇ,
pronounced with synizesis).

ἐμ-πάζομαι, prs., and ipf. ἐμπάζετο,
respicere, care for, τινός (acc., π
422), usually with negative, exc. imp.,
α 271, 305.

ἔμ-παιος, ον, particeps, peritus,
conversant with, υ 378, φ 400. (Od.)

ἐν-έπασσε, ipf., (πάσσω), intexe-
bat, was weaving in, Γ 126 and Χ 441.

ἔμ-πεδος, ον (ἐν πέδῳ), firmly stand-

ing, ψ 203, N 512; τ 113, produces un-
failing sheep, i. e. never fails to produce; enduring, Δ 314; so also ἴς,
μένος; firm, immovable, νόος; κ 493,
unimpaired, φρένες; thoughtful mind,
discretion, σ 215, Z 352; cf. ἔμπ. οὐδ'
ἀεσίφρων, Υ 183; cf. illico, speedy,
θ 30; certus, sure, τ 250; ntr. ἔμπε-
δον μένειν, await, remaining in one's
place (αὖθι, αὐτόθι, there), ἐστάθη; without wavering, constantly (θέει); στηρίξαι,
support myself firmly.

ἐμ-πεσεῖν, aor. from ἐμ-πίπτω.

ἐν πήξεις, fut., and aor., (πήγνυμι),
τινί μεταφρένῳ (ἥπατι) δόρυ (βέλος),
fix or plant in (the back liver), E 40.
(χ 83.)

ἔμπης (ἔμπεδα? not from πᾶς),
prorsus, at any rate, by all means, (1)
affirmative: P 632, Zeus doubtless
guides them all; οὔ τινα ἔμπ., no one
whatever; ἔμπης δ' οὐκ, not at all (cf.
οὐ πάνυ); τ 302, yet I must give thee
oath; in doubt and surprise; yet (however it may seem to you), σ 354, τ 37.
—(2) concessive: quidem, yet, although, Ξ 98, T 308; without περ, δ
100, cf. 104; still, cf. French, toute-
fois, γ 2.9; tamen, nevertheless, Ξ
174, σ 12, A 562, B 297, Θ 33, P 229;
ἀλλ' ἔμπ., ἀλλὰ καὶ ἔμπ., υ 311, T 422;
Ω 214; ἔμπης—ἀχνύμενοί περ, Ω 522
sq.; freq. phrase περ ἔμπης, which always stands at end of the verse, I 518,
Ξ 1, σ 165, τ 356.

ἐμ-πίπληθι, imp. prs., -πίμπλαντο,
ipf. mid., other forms from -πλήθω;
fut. inf. ἐμ-πλησέμεν, aor., (3 pl. also
-πλῆσαν), fill full, of something, τινός,
Σ 351, X 312, τ 117; aor. mid. ἐμ-
πλήσατο, ἐνιπλήσασθαι, fill one's self, η
221; X 312, one's heart; one's belly,
ι 296; X 504, having satisfied his
heart with dainties; pass. aor. 3 pl.
ἐν-ἐπλήσθεν, ἐνιπλησθῆναι, and aor.
mid. ἐμ-πλῆντο, -πλῆτο, be full of; λ
452, sate myself with looking at my
son.

ἐμ-πίπτει, ων, prs., ipf. -πῖπτε, fut.
-πεσέεσθαι, aor. -έπεσε, etc., usually in
tmesis, with dat., incιdere, fall into,
ε 318, ο 375, τ 469; incessit, come
upon, Φ 385, χόλος, δέος; impetu
ferri in, charge upon, ω 526, Η 81;
irrumpo, irruo, burst into, rush upon,
O 624, Λ 297, 311, 325, Φ 9; penetrate,

Δ 134, O 451, χ 259; break in upon, β
45; cast themselves into, B 175, Λ 824;
μοι—θυμῷ, the words came to my mind,
μ 266.

ἐμ-πλείην and ἐνί-πλειος, ον, im-
pletus, filled with, with gen., σ 119,
τ 580. (Od.)

ἐμ-πλήγδην (πλήσσω), temere, at
random, υ 132†.

ἔμ-πλην (πέλας), iuxta, hard by,
with gen., B 526†.

ἐμ-πλήσατο, -ηντο, -ητο, see ἐμ-
πίπληθι.

ἐμ-πλήσσω, see ἐνι-πλήξωμεν.

ἐμ-πνείοντε, part. prs., aor. ἔμπνευσε,
ἐνέπνευσε, also in tmesi, subj. -πνεύσῃσι,
τινί, afflare, breathe upon; τινί τι
(μένος, θάρσος), inspirare, suggest a
thought, τ 138; pass. ἐμ-πνύνθη, recovered his senses, E 697.

ἐμ-ποιέω, only ipf. ἐν-εποίεον, fitted
into, H 438; tmesis, ποίησε ἐνὶ φρεσί,
put into his heart.

ἐμ-πολόωντο, ipf., (πολάω), gained
for themselves by trading, ο 456†.

ἔμ-πορος, ὁ, one who goes on shipboard as passenger, β 319 and ω 300.

ἐμ-πρήθω, see ἐνι-πρήθω.

ἐμ-πύρι-βήτην, τρίποδα, standing
over the fire, Ψ 702†.

ἐμ-φορέοντο, ipf., κύμασιν, innata-
bant, were borne about in the waves, μ
419 and ξ 309.

ἔμ-φῦλον, τόν, of the same tribe, ο
273†.

ἐμ-φύομαι, ipf., -φύοντο ἐν χείρεσσι,
ω 410; so also ἔν τ' ἄρα οἱ φῦ (aor.)
χειρί, he grew to his hand=grasped
heartily his hand, β 302; cf. κ 397;
ἔφυν, ὀδὰξ ἐν χείλεσι φύντες, biting hard
the lips, α 381; ἐμπεφυῖα, clinging
closely; ἐμπεφύᾶσι, innati sunt, grow
upon; ἐνέφυσε, insevit, implant.

ἐν (εἰνί, ἐνί, εἰν), I. as adv., in eo
numero, among them, δ 653; intus,
therein, ρ 270, Ω 472; sc. ἐστι, εἰσί, ἢν,
δ 358, η 95, E 740 sq.—II. preposition,
with dat., freq. in anastrophe, or separated from verb by tmesis, e. g. ἐστί
Σ 419, ἔασι, ν 105 = Lat. in, προθύροισι,
νεῶν ἐν ἀγῶνι; upon, on, οὔρεσι, ἵπποισι, καὶ ὄχεσιν, νηῦσιν ἔβη, went on
shipboard; inter, among, Γ 31, K
127, N 689, 829, Η 166; ἀνθρώποισι,
Τρώεσσι, τοῖσι, among these, E 395, Υ
55, Ω 62, (μῦθον) ἔειπεν, ἐρέω; in the

midst of, N 555, δηίοισι; coram, in presence of, A 109, I 121, πᾶσιν; ὀφθαλμοῖσι, before her eyes, θ 459 ; οἴνῳ ἐν, sprinkling them with wine, ω 73 ; in the shaft, N 608; of my bow, O 463; upon his limbs, Ω 359, ν 398 ; at the mouth, προχοῇς, λ 242. Apparently =εἰς, with acc., with πεσεῖν, βαλεῖν, βῆναι, ἔδυνον, θῆκε (ἐν χερσί—, βαλεῖν, λαβεῖν, O 229), κάθιζον, εἶσε, δῆσαν. ἐν, with gen., sc. δόμοις, cf. in French, chez, Z 47, η 132, κ 282.—Of states and conditions, πολέμῳ, δηιοτῆτι, φιλότητι, amicc, πένθεϊ, θαλίῃ, θυμῷ, ὀνείρῳ, δοιῇ, in dubio, μοίρῃ, iure, rightly; αἴσῃ, X 61, divâ fortunâ; ἐν καρὸς αἴσῃ, I 378, I regard him not a whit.—Temporal, ὥρῃ ἐν εἰαρινῇ, in spring-time ; penes, in possession of, H 102, κ 69.

ἐν-αίρω, inf. -έμεν, mid. -αιρόμενος, aor. ἐνήρατο (Ἄρης), interimerc, kill in battle, slay, murder, game, Φ 485; fig., τ 263, disfigure.

ἐν-αίσιμος, ον, οι, α, (ἐν αἴσῃ), fitting, proper, seemly, just, Ω 40, 425, ε 190, κ 383, ρ 363 ; ominous, β 182, B 353; the future, β 159.

ἐνᾰ-λίγκιος, ον, οι, α, like, τινί τι, to some one, in something, α 371 ; ἄντην, in countenance.

ἐνάλιος, see εἰν-αλίῳ.

ἐν-άμελγεν, ipf., milked therein, ι 223†.

ἔν-αντᾰ (ἐν ἄντῃ) τινός, coram, ex adverso, over against, Υ 67†.

ἐν-αντῐ-βῐον, (stand, advance), with hostile front against, ξ 270, ρ 439, Υ 130.

ἐν-αντίος, ον, ω, οι, η, (ἀντί), adversus, opposite, στῆναι, ἐλθεῖν ; visib'y, ζ 329 ; lying opposite, κ 89 ; esp. ntr. ἐναντίον, against, Λ 129 ; opposed to, N 106 ; τινί, against, O 304 ; νεικεῖν, Υ 252 ; straightway, ρ 544 ; face to face, χ 65, ψ 107 ; τινός, before, A 534, Υ 97. [ῐ]

ἔναξε, aor. from νάσσω.

ἔν-ἀρᾰ, τά, -ων, (ἀρηρώς), spolia, armor of slain foe: usually βροτόεντα, O 347; praeda, booty, I 188.

ἐν-αργής, ές, εἶς, (ἀργός, argutus), clear, in real form, δ 841, η 201 ; Υ 131, the gods are dangerous when they appear in their real forms.

ἐν-άρηρός (AP), well fitted in, ε 236†.

ἐνᾰρίζων, opt. ἐναρίζοι, ipf. ἐνάριζε, ον, aor. ἐνάριξα, ε, (ἔναρα), spoliarc, strip off, τινά τι, P 187; also slay, A 191.

ἐν-ἀρίθμιος, ον, (ἐν ἀριθμῷ), of account, B 202; filling up the number, μ 65.

ἔνασσαν, aor. from ναίω.

ἐνάτη, εἰνάτος, nona, us, ninth, B 313, 295.

ἔν-αυλος, οι, ους, ὁ, (αὐλός), torrens, perh. denotes the ragged bed of the (in summer dry) water-courses in the Trojan plain ; Π 71, fossa, ditch.

ἐν-δείξομαι, fut., (δείκνυμι), indicabo, I will declare it, T 83†.

ἔν-δεκᾰ, undecim, eleven, ξ 103, Φ 45 (round number).

ἐνδεκά-πηχυ, eleven cubits long, Z 319 and Θ 494.

ἐνδεκάτῳ, η, ῳ, undecimus, a, ae, eleventh, δ 588 (round number).

ἐν-δέξιᾰ (ἐν δεξιᾷ), dextra, favorable, σήματα, I 236; also adv., from left to right, ρ 365, A 597.

ἐν-δεόντων, imp. prs., aor. ἐνέδησε (-δῆσε), pass. plupf. -δέδετο, entangle, with dat. (in bonds; B 111, I 18, in delusion) ; fasten upon, ἐν-, ε 260.

ἐν-δίεσαν, aor., (δίημι), were only (αὔτως) setting on the dogs, Σ 584† (prob. for ἐδίεσαν, sought to terrify).

ἐνδίνων, τῶν, (ἔνδον), intestinorum, entrails, Ψ 806†.

ἔν-δῐος, οι, meridianus, i, at midday, δ 450 and Λ 726.

ἔνδοθεν (ἔνδον), intus, from within, also within, δ 293, 283, 467 ; with gen., Z 247, intra.

ἔνδοθῐ (ἔνδον), intus, within, Z 498 ; with gen., intra, Σ 287 ; within = ἐν φρεσί, when joined with θυμός, μῆτις, νόος; opp. θύρηφιν, χ 220.

ἔνδον (ἐν), intus, in the house, tent, etc., Σ 394 ; ἔνδον ἐόντων, of household store ; with gen. = French chez, Υ 13, Ψ 200; so freq. = chez moi, toi, etc., at home, π 355, 462, φ 207, ψ 2.

ἐν-δούπησα, ε, aor. from δουπέω, dropped like a plummet into the water, μ 443 and ο 479.

ἐν-δῠκέως (δεῦκος, decus), decenter, duly, Ω 158, κ 65 ; suitably, gallantly, κομίζειν, attend, wait upon, φιλεῖν ; busily, i. e. greedily, ξ 109.

ἔν-δῠνε (=δῦν'), ον, ipf. aor. -εδύτην,

imp. -δύτω, part. -δῦσα, and mid. -εδύσατο, induere, *put on*, arma, τὶ περὶ στήθεσσι, K 131; in tmesi with dat., *clothe* in armor, K 254, Ξ 377, Ψ 131; Τ 367, unendurable woe *entered* his soul.

ἐν ἔηκε, aor. from ἐν-ίημι; **ἐνεῖκαι**, aor. inf. from φέρω.

ἔν-εστι, -ειμεν, prs., opt. -είη, ipf. -έην = -ῆεν, 3 sing., -εσαν, 3 pl., in esse, τινί, *be within*, A 593 (ἔνδον ἐν φρεσί); in tmesi, Σ 419 (not so however in follg. examples, but simple verb εἶναι, β 345, η 291, μ 320, ν 438, σ 293; nor do we have compound verb in follg. examples, ἔνι sc. εἰσί, Σ 53, Υ 248, ι 126, 132, φ 288; ἐν sc. ἐστί, Φ 569, ι 134).

ἕνεκα, ἕνεκεν, εἵνεκα, causâ, *on account of*, with gen., placed before and after its case; cf. οὕνεκα.

ἐν-έκυρσε, see ἐγκυρέω, incidit in, met.

ἐνενήκοντα, nonaginta, *ninety*, B 602.

ἐνένῑπεν, aor. from ἐνίπτω.

ἐν-έπω (for ἐν-σέπω), **ἐν-έποιμι**, imp. **ἔννεπε** (insece), part. ἐνέποντα, ἐς, -έπουσα, fut. ἐνίψω, ἐνισπήσω; aor. ἐνίσπες, ε = ἔννεπε, 3 sing., subj. ἐνίσπω, ῃ, opt. ἐνίσποις, οι, inf. ἐνισπεῖν, imp. ἐνίσπες, γ 101 = ἔνισπε, *report, inform*, τινί τι; Λ 643 = ψ 301, referentes, *relating*.

ἐν-έρεισαν, aor. 3 pl. from ἐρείδω, infixerunt, *thrust into*, τινί τι, ι 383†.

ἔνερθεν, ἔνερθε, νέρθεν, νέρθε, (ἔνεροι), *from below*, Υ 57; usually *below*, N 75, Ξ 274, ι 385, H 212, Υ 500, υ 352; esp. in reference to the feet; with gen., infra, *below*, Ξ 204, λ 302, Θ 16, Λ 252.

ἔνεροι, ων, οισι, οί, (ἐνί), inferi, *those beneath the earth*, Ο 188; comp. **ἐνέρτερος** Οὐρανιώνων, *lower* than the gods = in the lower world, E 898; pl. θεοί, Ο 225, Τιτῆνες.

ἔν-εσαν = ἐνῆσαν, ipf. from εἰμί.

ἐν-εστήρικτο, plupf. from ἐν-στηρίζω, infixa erat.

ἐν-ετῇσι, ταῖς, (ἐνίημι), fibulis, *with clasps* = (a variety of περόναι, σ 293), Ξ 180†.

Ἐνετοί, ῶν, a tribe τῶν Παφλαγόνων, B 852†.

ἐν-εύδειν, ipf. ἔνευδεν, *sleep in* or *on*, γ 350. (Od.)

ἐν-ευναίων, gen. pl., (εὐνή), incubantium, *people to sleep in it*, π 35; but ἐνεύναιον, *place to sleep in*, ξ 51.

ἐν-ηείης, gen. (sec follg.), *gentleness, amiability*, P 670†.

ἐν-ηής, έος, έα, (aveo?), comis, *gentle, amiable*, Ψ 252, θ 200.

ἐν-ῆμαι, -ήμεθα, insidebamus, *sit within*, δ 272†.

ἐνήρατο, aor. mid. from ἐναίρω.

ἐνήνοθε (ἄνθος), strictly, *has blossomed forth, streams forth*, ρ 270†.

ἔνθᾰ, *there*, γ 120.—(1) local: ζ 266; with following explanatory clause, γ 365; ἄρα, just *where*, χ 335; ἢ ἔνθα, to or *fro*, κ 574; καὶ ἔνθα, *this way* and *that*, *long* and *broad*; περ, exactly *where*, ν 284; τε, for ἔνθα δὲ, θ 363; *thither*, ο 415.—(2) temporal: *thereupon*, ξ 345, B 308; as introduction of a tale, α 11; continuative, Δ 293, E 155; αὖ, E 1; introducing apodosis, B 308; ἔπειτα, κ 297.

ἔνθάδε, (1) eo, huc, *thither*, Z 256.— (2) hic, *here*, A 171, B 203. [- ‿ ‿]

ἔνθεν, (1) inde, *thence*, Δ 58, κ 108; ab illa (altera) parte, μ 230 (59, 211); ex iis, ξ 74.—(2) unde, *whence*, H 472, Ω 597, δ 220, τ 62.—(3) dein, *then*, N 741.

ἔνθένδε, inde, hinc, Θ 527.

ἐν-θρώσκω, only aor. **ἔ/ορε** (tmesi, E 161, Υ 381), insiluit, *sprung upon*, usually with dat.; λάξ, *gave a thrust* with the heel.

ἐν-θύμιος (θῡμός), *taken to heart, subject of anxiety*, ν 421†.

ἐνί, see ἐν; ἔνι = ἔνεστι.

ἐνιαύσιον (ἐνιαυτός) σῦν, *yearling*, π 454†.

ἐνιαυτός, etc., annus; περιπλομένων -ῶν, *as the seasons rolled on, the year came*, α 16.

ἐν-ίαυε, ipf., *therein slept*, ι 187. (Od.)

ἐν-ίημι, ἵησι, etc., prs., ipf., fut., aor. (freq. in tmesi), immitto, *send in* or *into*, Ξ 131; Ψ 177, *cast in* the fire's might; τινί τι, Π 729; Φ 338, τινὰ πυρί, *set on* fire; *put to* (in harness), Π 152; ο 198, *lead to* concord; πόντῳ νῆα, *launch*; injicere, τινί τι, κ 317, M 441; πόνοις, *plunge into* hardships; inserere, *insert*, key, ear-rings, Ξ 182; inspirare, *courage, wrath*.

Ἐνιῆνες, B· 749† (Αἰνιᾶνες), tribe dwelling about Dodona.

ἐνι-κλᾶν, *frustrate*, only Θ 408, 422.

Ἐνῑπεύς, ῆος, a river-god, λ 238†.

ἐν-ῑπή, ῆς, ῇ, ἤν, άς, (ἵπτομαι), *reprimand*, E 492.

ἐνί-πλειος, ον, see ἔμπλειος.

ἐνι-πλησθῆναι, πλήσωσι, see ἐμ-πίπλημι.

ἐνι-πλήξωμεν, ωσι, αντες, aor., from -πλήσσω, *rush into*, τινί, into the noose, χ 469. (Il.)

ἐνι-πρήθω, ipf. -έπρηθον, fut. πρήσω, aor. -έπρησεν, etc., lit. *fly forth in sparks*, (1) *inflate*, β 427, ἔμπρησιν.—(2) *kindle*, I 589; usually with πυρί, Θ 182; πυρός, Π 82.

ἐν-ίπτω (ἰάπτω), opt., increpet, *scold, upbraid*, μέ, Ω 768; μὲ θυμὸν ὀνείδεσι, Γ 438; τινὰ μύθῳ (κακῷ, etc.), B 245; aor. ἐνένῑπε, αἰσχρῶς, Ψ 473, and ἠνίπαπε μύθῳ, at close of verse, υ 17.

ἐνι-σκίμψαντε, aor. part., and -σκίμφθη, aor. pass. from σκίμπτω, (σκήπτω), always with οὔδει; *lean upon* the ground, *bury in* the ground, P 437, 528. (Il.)

Ἐνίσπη, town in Arkadia, B 606.

ἐνι-σπήσω, ἐνί-σπον, ες, see ἐν-έπω.

ἐνισσέμεν, ων, ὁμένος, ipf. ἐνίσσομεν, (ἐνίπτω), exc. X 497, always with ἐπέεσσιν, or like word, *upbraid*.

ἐνι-χριμφθέντα, *pressing forward*, see ἐγ-χρίμπτω.

ἐν-ίψω, fut. from ἐν-έπω.

ἐννέα, novem, *nine*, Π 785.

ἐννεά-βοίων, gen. pl. ntr., *worth nine cattle*, Z 236†.

ἐννεα-καί-δεκα, *nineteen*, Ω 496†.

ἐννεά-πηχυ and -πηχέες, *nine cubits long*, λ 311.

ἐννεά-χιλοι, *nine thousand*, E 860.

ἔννεον, ipf. from 1. νέω.

ἐννε-όργυιοι, pronounce ἐννῃόργυιοι, *nine fathoms long*, λ 312†.

ἐνν-εσίῃσιν, dat. pl., (ἐνίημι), *at the command; κείνης ἐνν.*, E 894†.

ἐννέ-ωρος, οιο, οι, οισι, *nine years old*, κ 19. [Pronounce ἐννῆωρ.]

ἐννήκοντα, *ninety*, τ 174†.

ἐνν-ῆμαρ, *nine days long*, η 253.

Ἔννομος, (1) οἰωνιστής, chief of Mysians, slain by Achilleus, B 858, P 218.—(2) a Trojan slain by Odysseus, Λ 422.

ἐνν-οσί-γαιος, ῳ, ον, ε, (ὠθέω, γαῖα), *earth-shaker* (also joined with γαιήοχος, I 183), epithet of Poseidon as causer of earthquakes, ε 423. [ῑ]

ἕννυμι (Ϝέσνυμι, Ϝεσθής, vestis), fut. ἕσσω, aor. ἕσσε (imp. ἕσσον), mid. ἕσσατο, ἑέσσατο, pass. prs. ipf., pf. ἕσσαι, εἶται, εἱμένος, plupf. sing. ἕσσο, ἕστο, du. ἕσθην, pl. εἵατο, induere, *put on*, εἵματα, τινά τι, η 265, π 457; mid., *clothe one's self;* pass., *wear*, τί, K 334, Ξ 350; εἵματα, or simply adj., κακά, ἀεικία, καλά, *be well or ill clad;* (περὶ) χροΐ, on the body; ἀμφ' ὤμοισι, and ὤμοῖϊν νεφέλην, O 308; εἱμένα χαλκῷ, *clad in brass;* Γ 57, hadst been clad in coat of stone=stoned to death.

ἐν-νύχιος, οι, αι, *in the night-time*, Φ 37=ἐν-νυχος (νύξ), Λ 715†.

ἐν-οινο-χοεῦντες = χοέοντες (οἰνοχόος), *pouring in*, γ 472†.

ἐν-οπή, only sing., (ὄψ), (1) voces, *voices;* κ 147, *shout.*—(2) *tumult*, Π 782; joined with μάχη.

Ἐνόπην, acc., town in Messenia, subject to Agamemnon, I 150, 292.

ἐν-όρνυμι, only aor. ἐν-ῶρσας, ε, -ῦρσῃ, τινί (Αἴαντι, Λ 544) τι, *excite in one*, fear, flight, courage, longing; ἐν-ῶρτο, aor. mid. γέλως θεοῖσι, *began among the gods*, θ 343 (also in tmesi).

ἐν-ορούω, only aor. -όρουσε, σαν, σας, σῃ, irruit, *broke in upon* (of hostile charge), τινί, Λ 149; Φ 182, *stepping upon.*

ἐν-ορχα, *uncastrated*, Ψ 147†.

ἐν-οσί-χθων = ἐνν-οσί-γαιος, with (εὐρὺ)κρείων, Λ 751, N 10.

ἐν-οσκίμπτω, see ἐνι-σκίμπτω.

ἐν-έστακται, pf. pass. from -στάζω, instillatum est, *has been infused in* thy veins, β 271†.

ἐν-εστήρικτο, plupf. pass. from -στηρίζω, *remained sticking fast*, Φ 168†.

ἐν-στρέφεται ἰσχίῳ, *plays in* the hipjoint, E 306†.

ἐν-τάνύουσιν, fut. -τανύειν, φ 97; aor. ἐντάνυσε, ἐτάνυσσε, *stretch out within*, ψ 201; elsewh. always with νευρίην, *stretch tight*=*string*, or with τόξον, βιόν, *bend, string the bow*, τ 577. (Cf. the cut on follg. page, from antique gem.)

ἐν-ταῦθα, huc, *hither*, I 601†.

ἐν-ταυθοῖ, huc, ἧσο; hic, *here*, κεῖσο, Φ 122.

ἔντεᾰ 112 ἐξ-αιρέω

ἔντεᾰ, εσι, ntr., strictly *cattle-gear*; then δαιτός, *table-furniture*; usually armor, esp. *breast-plate*, Γ 339 ; ἀρήϊα, fighting-gear, ψ 368, K 407.

ἐν-τείνω, only pass. pf. plupf. ἐντέ-τᾰται, το, *was lined with tightly stretched* straps, K 263 ; the front of the chariot *is ornamented (plaited) with* gold and silver straps, E 728 ; cf. Ψ 335, 436.

ἔντερον, α, intestina, (1) *gut*, φ 408.—(2) *bowels.*

ἐντεσί-έργους (ἔντεα, Ϝεργ.), *working in harness*, Ω 277†.

ἐντεῦθεν, inde, *thence*, τ 568†.

ἐν-τίθημι, ipf. ἐν-ἐτίθει, also fut. and aor. 1, 2 (-θέμεναι), mid. only 2 aor. (freq. in tmesi), inponere, *put* or *place, in, into*, or *upon, τινά τινι*, on fire, bed, anvil-block ; *thrust* sword *into* the sheath, κ 333 ; ἐνὶ φρεσί, *suggest, infuse into* the mind, courage, etc., γ 77 ; *put* strength *into* the shoulders, P 569; χερσί, *put into* the hand; ξ 312, *give into* the hand ; o 357, *plunge into* premature old age; Δ 410, *place in* like honor, mid. also θυμῷ, *store up* wrath, etc., *in one's* heart ; μῦθον θυμῷ, *take to* heart ; ἐν σήθεσσι θυμόν.

ἔντο, 2 aor. from ἐξ-ίημι.

ἐντός, intus, with gen., intra, M 374.

ἔντοσθε(ν) (ἔντοθεν, ι 239, 338, conjectural v. l.) = ἐντός, M 296, Z 364, κ 92.

ἐν-τρέπεται, pass., *is* not (thy heart) *moved*, O 554 and α 60.

ἐν-τρέχοι γυῖα, if his limbs *played freely in* the armor, T 385†.

ἐν-τροπᾰλιζόμενος, η, ην, *turning frequently about*, Ζ 496, Λ 547. (Il.)

ἔντῡνον, ipf., and 1 aor. imp., (see ἐντύω), with aor. part., mid. pr. ipf. aor. (subj. ἐντύνεαι, pronounce ἐντῡνῃαι),

parare, *adorn one's self, ἑαυτήν*, and mid. ; *get ready*, δέπας ; *prepare one's meal*, o 5C0, Ω 124 ; *raise the strain*, μ 183 ; *get ready*, ζ 33.

ἐν-τῡπάς (τύπτω), *prostrate*, or better *closely wrapped in* his mantle, Ω 163†.

ἐντύω, ipf. **ἔντῡεν**, ον, (ἔντεα), *harnessed*, E 720 ; *made ready*, ψ 289.

Ἐνῡάλιος, sing., ('Ενῡώ), Ares as raging god of battle, P 211 ; elsewh. subst. *Enyalios.* [By synizesis, -ῠᾰλῐῳ ᾿νδρεϊφόντῃ.] (Il.)

Ἐνῡεύς, ῆος, king of Skyros, slain by Achilleus, I 668†.

ἐν-ύπνιον (ὕπνος), ntr. as adv., *in sleep*, B 56.

Ἐνῡώ, ἡ, *Enyo*, tumult of battle, personified companion of Ares, E 333, 592.

ἐν-ωπᾰδίως (ἐν-ῶπα), *face to face, clearly*, ψ 94†.

ἐν-ωπῇ, dat., (ὄψ), *openly*, E 374. (Il.)

ἐν-ωπῐᾰ (ὄψ, cf. façade), παμφανό-ωντα, the bright shining *side walls* of the vestibule, see plate III. A and B.

ἔξ, sex, *six*, μ 90.

ἐξ-αγγέλλω, only -ήγγειλεν, aor., detulisset ad, *report to*, E 390†.

ἐξ-άγνυμι, only -έαξεν, and άξῃ, confregit, *break*, Λ 175.

ἐξ-αγόρευεν, ipf., *related*, λ 234†.

ἐξ-άγε, pr., ipf., aor., often in tmesi : educere, *lead out*, A 337; τινά (also τινός, from a place, Σκυρόθεν), ξ 264, N 379; *drag out, θύραζε* ; exstruere, *raise* a mound, τύμβον, H 336.

Ἐξάδιος, one of the Lapithai, A 264†. [- ‿ ‿ ‿]

ἐξ-ετες (ἔτος), ntr., *six years*, γ 115†.

ἐξ-αίνῦτο, ipf., (αἴνυμαι), tmesis, Δ 531, θυμόν, *took away* his life ; o 206, *took out from* the chariot and placed in the vessel's stern.

ἐξαίρετοι (αἱρεῖσθαι), eximii, ae, *chosen, choice*, δ 643, B 227.

ἐξ-αιρεύμην, ipf. mid., see follg.

ἐξ-αιρέω, only ipf. and aor. act. and mid., also in tmesi, (1) act., eximere, *take out*, Ω 229 ; eligere, ι 160, γέρας. —(2) mid., *select for one's self* (one's own use), arrows, sheep, birds, *choose for one's self* from booty, I 130, Λ 696, μ 123 ; *took away his* sense, τινός or τινί, Z 234 ; take away fear, fatigue from the limbs, γυίων; take away life, θυμόν, M 150; λ 201, μελέων; τινά, Π 58; τινί, υ 61, Λ 381; τινός, Φ 112; τινί ρι, π 218.

ἐξ-αίρω, only aor. ἐξήρᾰτο, *carry off as booty from*, Τροίης, ε 39.

ἐξ-αίσιον, acc., (αἶσα), *unbecoming, undue*, δ 690, ρ 577; *presumptuous*, Ο 598.

ἐξ-αίσσω, only ἀΐξαντε, *rushing forth from; ἤϊχθη, has flown from* my hands, Γ 368.

ἔξ-αιτον, ους, (αἴνυμαι?), *choice, chosen*, wine, Μ 320; of oarsmen, hecatombs.

ἐξ-αίφνης (αἰπύς), *on a sudden.* (Il.)

ἐξ-ἀκέονται, placant, *soothe*, aor. -ακέσαιο, Δ 36.

ἐξ-ἀλἄωσας, σε, aor., (ἀλαόω), *thou hast utterly blinded*, τινά, ὀφθαλμόν. (Od.)

ἐξ-ἀλᾰπάξειν, fut. and aor. -αλαπάξαι, (ἀλαπάζω), evertere urbes, *sack, storm*; only Ν 813, delere naves.

ἐκ ἀλέοντο, vitabant, *were shrinking from*, Σ 586†. [‿‿–‿]

ἐξ-ἅλλεται, and aor. part. -άλμενος, (ἅλλομαι), prosiliens, ex aula, *leaps out from* the enclosure, Ε 142; τινῶν, prae—, *springing to the lead*, Ψ 399.

ἐξ-ἀνἄ-βᾶσαι, part. aor., (βαίνω), escendentes in, *climbing up upon*, Ω 97†.

ἐξ-ἀνἄ-δῦσαι, 1 aor. part., 2 aor. part. -δύς, (δύνω), *emerge from*, τινός, δ 405. (Od.)

ἐξ-ἀνἄ-λῦσαι, aor., (λύω), *release*, θανάτοιο, from death, Π 442. (Il.)

ἐξ-ἀνἄ φανδόν (φαίνω), *openly*, υ 48†.

ἐξ-ἀν-ῖεῖσαι, part., (ἵημι), emittentes, *sending forth*, Σ 471†.

ἐξ-ἀνὕω, fut., aor. -ήνυσε, (ἀνύω), perfecit, Θ 370; conficere aliquem, *kill*, Λ 365. (Il.)

ἐξ-ἀπᾰτήσειν, fut., and aor. -ησε, (ἀπατάω), decipere, *deceive utterly*, Χ 299.

ἐξ-ἀπ-ἀφίσκω, aor. -ήπᾰφε, subj. -φω, aor. mid. -απάφοιτο, decipere, Ι 376.

ἐξ-ἀπίνης (αἰπύς), *suddenly*, ξ 29, Ε 91.

ἐξ-ἀπ-έβησαν (βαίνω), *stepped down out of* the ship, (νηός), μ 306†.

ἐξ-ᾶποδίωμαι, subj., (δίω), *after* μάχης, *hunt out of* the combat, Ε 763†.

ἐξ-ἄπ-έδῦνε, ipf., exuit, *put off*, ε 372†.

ἐξ-ἄπ-όλλυμι, pf. -όλωλε, deperiit, τινός, *disappeared from*; aor. -ολοίατο, pereant, *may they perish*, Ζ 60.

ἐξ-ἀπο-νέεσθαι μάχης (better ἐξ ἀπο-), *return out of*—, Ι 252. (Il.)

ἐξ-ἀπ-ένιζε, ipf., *with which she usually washed*, τ 387†.

ἐξ-ἀπο-τίνοις, *satisfy in full*, Φ 412†.

ἐξ-ἅπτων, ipf. -ῆπτε, aor. part. ἅψας, (ἅπτω), *bind to*, τινός; mid., Θ 20, *hang ye all to it.*

ἐκ ἄραξε, aor., (ἀράσσω), *dashed* the mast *out of* the keel, μ 422†.

ἐξ-ήρπαξε, aor. -ξασα, (ἁρπάζω), *snatched away*, μ 100; in Il. in good sense, *save*; in which case the subject is always a goddess.

ἐξ-άρχους (ἄρχω), *leaders* of the dirges, Ω 721†.

ἐξ-άρχων, ipf. -ῆρχε and -ῆρχετο, (ἄρχω), βουλάς, *be author of* counsel, Β 273; mid., μ 339, τινός, *begin something*; a game, a dirge. Χ 430.

ἐξ-αυδᾶ, imp., (αὐδάω), proloquere, *speak out*, Π 19. (Il.)

ἐξ-αῦτις, rursus, *again*, Ε 134, δ 213.

ἐξ-ἄφ-αιρέω, mid. subj. aor. -έλησθε ψυχάς, *have taken the life from* them all (ἐκ μελέων), χ 444†.

ἐξ-ἀφύοντες, part., *drawing out*, ξ 95†.

ἐξ-ῖδεν, aor., *looked out far, saw clearly*, Υ 342†.

ἐξείης (ἔχω), adv., deinceps, *in order*, Ο 137; *one after another*, Χ 240.

ἐξ-ειμι, -εισθα, inf. also -ίμεναι, ipf. ἤϊον, (ἰέναι), exire, *go out*, θύραζε; τινός, β 139.

ἐξ-είπω, ῃς, ῃ, subj. -οι, aor. opt. ἐξ-ερέω, fut., esp. ὧδε γάρ, φ 337, and ἐκ (μέν, δ 376; γάρ, ο 318, ω 265, 324) τοι ἐρέω, *speak out*, Α 204.

ἐξ-ειοθα, 2 sing. ἐξ-ειμι.

ἐξ-εκυλίσθη, aor. pass. from ἐκκυλίω.

ἐξ-ελαύνω, only ipf. -ήλαυνε, and aor. -ήλᾰσε, -έλᾰσε, etc., *drive out*; τινός, Λ 562; *drive away from*, π 381; drive out, λ 292; *driving out* (his flocks), κ 83; sc. ἵππους, ἅρμα, *drive out*, seemingly intrans., Ω 323; *dash out* (teeth), σ 29.

ἐξ-ελεῖν, aor. from -αιρέω.

ἐξ-έλκουσα, part., ipf. -έλκεν, pass. pr. -ελκομένοιο, extrahere, draw out, the thread of the woof through the warp, Ψ 762; a polypus from his hole, ε 432.

ἐξ-έμεν = ἐξ-έμεναι, inf. aor. from -ίημι.

ἐξέμεν, inf. fut. from ἔχω.

ἐξ-εμέσειε, opt. aor. from -εμέω, evomeret, disgorge, μ 437. (Od.)

ἐξ-έμμορε, better θεῶν ἐξ ἔμμορε, ε 335, from μέρω, particeps factus est, has obtained from the gods dominion amid the waves of the sea.

ἐξ-εναρίζεις, ων, fut. -ίξεις, aor. -ενάριξε, etc., (ἔναρα), spoliare, strip or spoil a foe, τινά, E 151; τεύχεα, P 537. (Il. and λ 273, χ 264.)

ἐξ-ερεείνοι, prs., ipf. -ερέεινε, (ἐρέω), make inquiry, absolutely, K 543; τί, μ 34; τινά, ψ 86; mid., K 81.

ἐξ-ερέεσθαι, pres., ipf. -είρετο, -ερέοντο, (ἐρέω), sciscitari, inquire into, of, τί, Υ 15; τινά, γ 24.

ἐξ-ερείπω, only aor. subj. -ερίπῃ, part. -ριπούσα, fall down, P 440. (Il.)

1. ἐξ-ερέω, fut. from -εἴπον.

2. ἐξ-ερέω, -ερέουσι, pr. subj. -έῃσι, opt. -έοις, part. ἐόντες, -έουσα, mid. prs. ipf. ἐρέοντο, (ἐρέω), (1) ask, I 671, γ 116, η 17; question, τινά, γ 24; explore, κνημούς.—(2) mid., interrogate, α 416, E 756.

ἐξ-ερύοι, opt. prs., aor. -έρυσε, είρυσε, είρυσσαν, iter. -ερύσασκεν, (ἐρύω), evellere, draw out or away, σ 86, χ 476; τί τινος, spear out of shield, Υ 323; laying hold of was dragging away by the foot, K 490; by the pole, K 505.

ἐξ-έρχομαι, only aor. -ήλυθε, ἦλθε, etc., egredi ex, go out of, with gen., φ 190, X 237; march forth, I 576.

ἐξ-ερωέω, only aor. -ηρώησαν, (ruere), have run away, Ψ 468†.

ἐξ-εσίην, acc., (ἵημι), ἐλθεῖν, going on an embassy, Ω 235 and φ 20.

ἐξ-έτεα, acc., (-έτης, ἔτος), sexennem, six years old, Ψ 266. (Il.)

ἐξ-έτι, with gen., inde, ex, ever since, I 106; a patrum memoria, θ 245.

ἐξ-εύροι, aor. opt., (εὑρίσκω), if he may any where light upon them, Σ 322†.

ἐξ-ηγείσθω, imp. with gen., (ἡγέομαι), educat, let him lead out, B 806†.

ἐξήκοντα, sexaginta, sixty, ξ 20.

ἐξ-ήλασε, ασσαν, aor. -ελαύνω.

ἐξ-ήλατον, acc., (ἐλαύνω), beaten out, M 295†.

ἐξ-ῆμαρ, for six days, ξ 249. (Od.)

ἐξ-ημοιβά (ἀμείβω), ntr., for change, changes of raiment, θ 249†.

ἐξ-ήπαφε, aor.. (-απαφίσκω), deceive.

ἐξηράνθη, aor. pass. from ξηραίνω.

ἐξ-ήρατο, aor. from -αίρω.

ἐξ-ηρώησαν, aor. from -ερωέω.

ἐξῆς = ἐξείης, one after another, μ 147. (Od.)

ἐξ-ίημι, only aor., emittere, (1) act. inf. -ίεμεν(αι), τινά, send forth, release; remove the desire for any thing; τινὸς ἔρον (εἵην, εἶναι), satiate one's self with, N 638, Ω 227; freq. πόσιος καὶ ἐδητύος ἐξ ἔρον ἔντο, got rid of their desire for food and drink—driven away from themselves hunger and thirst, A 469, α 150.

ἐξ-ιθύνει (ἰθύνω), straightens, O 410†.

ἐξ-ικόμην, -ίκετο, aor., (ἱκνέομαι), with acc., reach, a place, a person, ν 206; gain, μ 166.

ἐξ-ίμεναι, λ 530, exire; better ἐξ-ίμεναι, from ἐξ-ίημι.

ἐξ-ίσχει, extends, μ 94†.

ἐξ-οίσουσι, fut. from φέρω.

ἐξ-οιχνεῦσι (οἰχνέω), exeunt, I 384†.

ἐξ-οίχεται, exiit, Z 379; tmesi, δ 665.

ἐξ ὤλεσαν, ὀλέσειε, aor., (ὄλλυμι), τινά, pessumdare, utterly destroy; τινὶ φρένας, rob of reason, H 360.

ἐκ τ' ὀνόμαζεν (from ὄνομα, hence pronounce a name, the name usually follows), always after ἔπος τ' ἔφατ', spoke the word and uttered it aloud, proclaimed, A 361, β 302, and freq.

ἐξ-ονομήνῃς, subj. and -ονομῆναι, inf. aor., (ὀνομαίνω), mention by name, Γ 166; speak out, ζ 66.

ἐξ-ονομακλήδην, adv.,(ὄνομα,καλέω), mentioning by name, X 415; call upon, μ 250.

ἐξ-όπιθε(ν), adv., (ὄπισθεν), a tergo, Δ 298; κεράων, behind the horns.

ἐξ-οπίσω, adv., (1) backwards, P 108; νεκροῦ, back from the corpse. (Il.)—(2) hereafter, in future. (Od.)

ἐξ-ορμήσασα, part. aor., (ὁρμάω), λά-

θῇσι (νηῦς), without thy intention
swerve from its course, μ 221†.

ἐκ ὄρουσε, σαν, aor., (ὀροΰω), pro-
ruerunt, rushed furth; Γ 325, ex-
siliit, sprang forth.

ἐξ-οφέλλω, only ipf. -ώφελλεν, large
auxit, greatly augment, ο 18†.

ἔξ-οχος, οι; ον, α, (ἔχω), eximius,
excellens inter, distinguished among,
with gen., Ξ 118; with dat., φ 266,
B 483; ntr., egregie, ι 551, by way
of preference; ἄλλων, above the others;
ἔξοχα ἄριστοι, longe optimi, far
the best.

ἐξ-ὑπ-ᾰν-έστη, aor., (ἵσταμαι), μετα-
φρένου, started up from under the skin
of the back, B 267†.

ἔξω, adv., foras, forth, ξ 526; with
gen., ex, out of, χ 378; foris, extra,
without, P 265.

ἔξω, fut. from ἔχω. ἔο, ἐοῖ, see οὗ.
ἔοι=εἴη. ἔοικα, see II. εἴκω. ἐοῖο=
ἐοῦ, see ἑός. ἔοις=εἴης. ἔολπα, see
ἔλπω. ἔον=ἦν. ἔοργας, ε, ὡς, from
ἔργω.

ἑορτή, festival; ἁγνή, holy, φ 258.
(Od.)

ἑός, οῦ, οἷο, ᾧ, ὅν; ἑοί, ὧν, οἷσι, ούς.
ἑή, ἧς, ᾖ, ἥν; ᾗσι. ἑύν, ἑά, (=ὅς, σϜός),
suus, his, her, own, αὐτοῦ, K 204, δ
643; with pron., τόν, Ψ 295; τό, K
256.

ἐπ-ἀγαλλόμενος, exulting in, Π 91†.
ἐπ-αγγείλῃσι (ἀγγέλλω), aor., de-
ferat, announce, δ 775†.
ἐπ-αγείρειν, bring together, A 126;
mid., λ 632, crowded to the spot.
ἐπάγη, aor. pass. from πήγνυμι.
ἐπ-αγλαϊεῖσθαι (ἀγλαΐζω), super-
biturum esse, will glory in, Σ 133†.
ἐπ-άγω, pres., and aor. adducere,
bring upon, Λ 480; induce, ξ 392; incitare, sc. κύνας, setting on the dogs,
τ 445; τινί τι, Ψ 188, spread out over.
ἐπ-άειραν (ἀείρω), only aor., tollere;
τί τινος, lift and place upon, H 426.
(Il.)
ἐπὶ ἀέξῃ (ἀέξω), subj., prospers, ξ
65†.
ἔπᾰθες, ον, aor. from πάσχω.
ἐπ-αιγίζων (αἰγίς), rushing on, B 148,
ο 293.
ἐπ-αινέομεν (αἰνέω), prs. ipf. fut. aor.,
agree, η 226, Δ 380; approving, B 335;
τινί, assentiri; often in tmesi, Γ 461.
ἐπ-αινή (αἰνός), only sing., always

of Περσεφόνεια, sacra, dread, I 457,
κ 491.
ἐπ-αΐσσω, pr., ipf., fut., aor. -ἀῖξαι,
adorior, rush upon, absol., χ 187, B
146, N 687; τινός, νεῶν, ἵππων (Il.);
τινί, κ 295, Ψ 64; with dat. of instr.,
δουρί, ἔγχει, μοι μελίῃσι, ξ 281 (Od.);
τινά, τί, invadere, attack; also with
κατά, Σ 159 (Il.); mid. χεῖρες ὤμων
-αΐσσονται, move lightly in the shoulders; αἴξασθαί τι, rush at, seize.
ἐπ-αιτήσειας, opt. aor., (αἰτέω), insuper postulaveris, ask besides, Ψ
593†.
ἐπ-αίτιοι (αἰτία), blameworthy, A
335†.
ἐπ-ἀκούει, prs., aor. hearken to, ἔπος,
πάντα, βουλήν; with indirect question, Σ 63; βουλῆς, interfuerant,
participate in, B 143.
ἐπ-ακτῆρες (ἄγω), venatores, τ
435, P 135.
ἐπὶ ἀλήθην (ἀλάομαι), only aor.,
(part. at end of verse), wander about,
πολλά, long, δ 81; over, to, with acc.,
δ 83, in tmesi, ξ 120, 380. [ᾰ]
ἐπ-ἀλαστήσασα (ἀλαστέω), indig-
nabunda, indignant, α 252†.
ἐπὶ ἄλειψα (ἀλείφω), only aor., oblinere, besmear, μ 47, 177. [ᾰ]
ἐπ-ἀλεξήσων (ἀλέξω), only fut.,
adesse, assist in battle, τινί; ward off,
τινί τι, Υ 315, tmesis. (Il.)
ἐπ-ἀληθείς, see ἐπὶ ἀλήθην, vagatus.
ἐπ-ἀλλάξαντες (ἀλλάσσω), entwining
in each other, connecting (the ends of the
cord of war), i. e. prolonging the contest; others translate, drawing the cord
of war now this way, now that, N 359†.
ἐπ-ἄλμενος, see ἐφάλλομαι.
ἔπ-αλξις, ή, -άλξιος, ιν, ιες, εσιν, εις,
(ἀλέξω), breastwork, battlement, M 263.
(Il.)
Ἐπάλτην, a Lykian, slain by Patroklos, Π 415†.
ἐπ-ᾶλτο, aor. from ἐφ-άλλομαι.
ἐπ-ἀμήσατο (ἀμάω), sibi corrasit,
heaped up for himself, ε 482†.
ἐπὶ - ἀμείψομεν, fut., (ἀμείβω), exchange, ἀλλήλοις; πρός τινα; mid.,
ἄνδρας, come in turn to, Z 339. (Il.)
ἐπ-ἀμοιβᾰδίς (see preceding), invi-
cem; ἀλλήλοισιν ἔφυν, had grown
each into the other, i. e. had intertwined
their branches, ε 481†.

ἐπ-ἀμύντορα, acc., (see follg.), defender, π 263†.
ἐπ-ἀμύνειν, only pres. and imp. aor. -ἀμῦνον, aid in battle, absol., E 685; τινί, Θ 414. (Il.)
ἐπ-αν-θέμεναι (τίθημι), better reading, ἐπ᾽ ἄψ θ., rursus claudere, shut again, Φ 535†.
ἐπ-ἀν-ίσταμαι, -έστησαν, aor., simul assurrexerunt, stood up also, Β 85†.
ἐπ-ἀοιδῇ, dat. fem., (ἀείδω), incantatione, by a spell, τ 457†.
ἐπ-ἀπειλέω, only aor. -ηπείλησε, and part., minari, τί, menace, ν 127, Ν 582.
ἐπ-αραρίσκω, aor. -ῆρσε, fit to, τινί; -αρήρει, plupf., fitted exactly=made fast the gates, Μ 456.
ἐπ-ἀράς, acc. pl. fem., (ἀρά), curses, Ι 456†.
ἐπ-ἀρήγειν, only pres., and (in tmesi) aor. inf., succor, Α 408; τινί, Ψ 783.
ἐπ-ἀρήρει, -αρηρώς, see ἐπ-αραρίσκω.
ἐπ-αρκέω, only -ήρκεσε, aor., ward off, τινί τι, ρ 568.
ἐπ-ἀρουρος (ἄρουρα), serf, λ 489†.
ἐπ-αρτέες, έας, (-αρτύω), instructi, parati, equipped, ready, τ 289. (Od.)
ἐπ-αρτύω, only ipf. -ήρτυε, fitted on, θ 447; added, γ 152. (Od.)
ἐπ-αρξάμενος, οι, ἄσθω, part. and imp. aor., (ἄρχω), δεπάεσσι, having performed the dedicatory rites with the cups, i. e. having filled the cups for the libation, Α 471, γ 340.
ἐπ-ἀρωγός (ἀρήγειν), helper, λ 498†.
ἐπ-ασκέω, only pf. pass. -ήσκηται, the walled and turreted court is skillfully joined to it, ρ 266†.
ἐπ-ἀσσύτεροι, ους, αι, ntr. ον, (ἄσσον), closer and closer, close together, Δ 423; in quick succession, Α 383, π 366.
ἐπ-αύλους (αὐλή), cattle-pens, stabula, ψ 358†.
ἐπ-αυρίσκω, only aor. act., -αύρη, εῖν, έμεν, mid. -ηαι, ωνται, and mid. prs. -ίσκονται, fut. -ήσεσθαι, attingere, consequi, (1) touch, τινός, Λ 573; impingi, strike, Ψ 340; κακόν (σε), befall, σ 107.—(2) (usually mid.) partake of, enjoy, reap fruit of, τινός, ρ 81; ironically, Ο 17, Ζ 353.
ἐπὶ ἄυσε (ἀύω), aor., hailed, E 101. (Il.)

ἐπ-ήφῦσε (ἀφύσσω), aor., poured upon, τ 388†.
ἐπ-έγειρε, imp. pr., and (tmesis) ipf.; aor. mid. -έγρετο, waken, χ 431; excitare, arouse, Ο 567; mid., expergisci, wake up.
ἐπ-έδραμεν, aor. from ἐπι-τρέχω.
ἐπ-έην, ipf. from ἔπ-ειμι.
ἐπ-εί, conjunction, after that, after, when, (1) temporal: (a) with indic. pret., of facts, A 57, Γ 99, κ 414; πρῶτα, A 235, ρ 573; τὰ πρῶτα, Ζ 489, θ 553; τὸ πρῶτον, δ 13.—(b) with subj., of uncertainty, υ 86, Ο 363; with expectation of realization, with κέν, Τ 402, Χ 125; with ἄν, Ζ 412, Ν 285 (see also ἐπήν); iterative with κέν, Β 475.—(c) with opt., iterative, ω 254, Ω 14, and freq.; with ἄν in simple assumption, Ι 304.—(2) causal: since, with indic., Ζ 333, A 352, Β 171, Ν 1; with preterit indic. in conditional sentence, Ο 228; after suppressed principal sentence, A 231, γ 103, ι 352.—(3) joined with other particles, αὐτὰρ ἐπεί, but when; ἐπεὶ ἄρ, -ρα, since then; -γε, since at least; ἐπεὶ δή, since, now that; ἐπεὶ ἦ, since in truth, ι 276 [⏑–⏑– ἐπήῃ]; ἐπεὶ οὖν, when then, well then when; ἐπεί περ, seeing that; ἐπεί τοι, since of a truth; αὐτίκ᾽ -τε, simul atque, as soon as. [At beginning of verse, pronounce – – ἐπῄει; ἐπεὶ οὐ, synizesis ἐπῄου, exc. ε 364, θ 585.]
Ἐπειγεύς, son of Agakles, a Myrmidon, slain by Hektor, Π 571.
ἐπείγω, only pres. and ipf. (no aug.) act. pass. mid., (1) premere, oppress, Μ 452; urgeo, beset, Ζ 85, Ψ 623, Λ 157, E 622; propellere, drive forward, Ο 382, μ 167; pass., ο 297; pursue (subj.), Κ 361; agitare, ply, μ 205; exigere, hurry on the sale, ο 445; mid., urge on in one's interest, γάμον.; pass., incitari, hasten; part. ἐπειγόμενος, citatus, eager, ε 399, Ξ 519, Ψ 119; desiderans, desirous, with inf., ν 30; τινός, appetens, Τ 142; ὁδοῖο, longing for the departure; περὶ νίκης.
ἐπειδάν (ἐπεὶ δὴ ἄν), doubtful reading, Ν 285†.
ἐπειδή, see ἐπεί 3.
ἐπειή, see ἐπεί 3.
ἐπ-είη, see 1. ἐπ-ειμι.

1. **ἔπ-ειμι** (cf. ἐπί I., ἔπι), εἴη, opt., ipf. 3 sing. -ἐην = -ῆεν, 3 pl. -εσαν, fut. -ἐσσεται, be upon, B 259 ; β 344, be found, remain.

2. **ἔπ-ειμι** (ἰέναι), prs. with part., ipf. ἤιεν, ἤισαν, ἦσαν, fut. ἐπιείσομαι, aor. mid. ἐπιεισαμένη, Φ 424, accedere ad, come upon; τινά, Α 29; τί, count over, visit, ψ 359, δ 411 ; ὁρυμαγδός τινι, drew near, P 741 ; aggredi (usually in tmesi), τινά, go against, Υ 454 ; with dat., Γ 15, Υ 176.

Ἐπειοί, tribe in north Elis, Λ 732, Ν 686, Δ 537.

Ἐπειός, υἱὸς Πανοπῆος, Ψ 665, 838, builder of wooden horse, λ 523.

ἐπεί-περ, see ἐπεί 3.

ἔπειτα (ἐπί, εἶτα), postea, then, afterward, (1) in general, of mere sequence, Α 35, 48, 121, 387, 440, α 80, 84. 106 ; αὐτίκ' ἔπειτα, immediately after; καὶ ἔπ., θ 520 ; αὐτὰρ ἔπ., often after πρῶτον μέν.—(2) in apodosis δὴ ἔπ., α 84 and freq.—(3) referring back to what has been already stated, so then, for, α 106, γ 62.—(4) of futurity, hereafter, β 60, Ψ 551.—(5) of sequence in thought, then, therefore, γ 62, O 49, Σ 357 ; in questions, α 65, I 437 ; and yet, α 65, φ 29.

ἐπ-εκέκλετο, aor. from -κέλομαι.

ἐπ-έκερσε, aor. from -κείρω.

ἐπ-ελαύνω, aor. ἐπὶ ἤλασε, welded on (as eighth layer); -ελήλατο, plupf. pass., Ν 804. (Il.)

ἐπ-έλησε, aor. from -λήθω.

ἐπ-εμ-βεβαώς, pf., (βαίνω) οὐδοῦ, standing on the threshold, I 582†.

ἐπ-ενείκαι, inf. aor. from -φέρω.

ἐπ-ένειμε, aor. from -νέμω.

ἐπ-ενήνοθε, pf., (ἄνθος), strictly bloomed upon=grew thereon, B 219, K 134 : yet θ 365, θεοὶς ἐπενήνοθεν must be translated surrounds, i. e. such as bathes and exhales from the gods.

ἐπ-εν-τανύσας, part. aor. from τανύω, χ 467†; supra intendens, stretching the rope high over the θόλος (to hang each one in a noose upon it). [ῠ]

ἐπ-εντύνονται, subj., [ῠ], se accingant ad—, τι, ω 89 ; ἐπ-έντυε, ipf., (ἔντεα), harnessed, Θ 382. (Il.)

ἐπ-έοικεν, pf., and -εῴκει, plupf., (ϝεικω), decet, it is seemly, υ 293 ; usu-ally with acc. with inf., λ 186, A 126; τινί τι, befits, Ω 595 ; libet, I 392.

ἐπέπιθμεν, 1 pl. plupf. from πείθω.

ἐπέπληγον, 3 pl. red. aor. from πλήσσω.

ἐπ-έπλως, 2 sing. aor. from -πλώω.

ἐπεποίθει, plupf. from πείθω.

ἐπεπόνθει, plupf. from πάσχω.

ἐπ-έπτάρε, aor. from -πταίρω.

ἐπ-έπτάτο, aor. from -πέτομαι.

ἐπέπυστο, plupf. from πυνθάνομαι.

ἐπ-έρεισε, aor., (ἐρείδω), put to it vast strength, ι 538; drove against, E 856 ; also in tmesi, Λ 235.

ἐπὶ ἔρεψα (ἐρέφω), roof over = build, A 39†.

ἐπ-ερρώσαντο, aor. -ρώω.

ἐπ-έρυσσε, aor. from -ἐρύω, drew to, α 441 ; tmes. ἐρύσαντες, having dragged thither, μ 14 ; ἠπείροιο, draw toward the mainland, Α 485. [ῠ]

ἐπ-έρχεαι, 2 sing., (-έρχομαι), pres., fut. -ελεύσομαι, aor. -ήλυθε, -ῆλθε, with subj., part. ; pf. -ελήλυθα, often in tmesi.—(1) adoriri, attack, O 406.— (2) ἐς τι, come to, η 280 ; τι, permeare, traverse, δ 268, Σ 321, Ψ 251 ; adire, approach, π 27; redire, ρ 170; advenire, ω 354, of seasons and hours of day, arrive, come on, νύξ, κνέφας ; of advance of enemies, τμήδην, struck and grazed; come over, ὕπνος.—(3) τινί, draw near, Δ 251, Υ 91, O 84; adoriri, E 219, K 485 ; surprise, ὕπνος, νοῦσος, νύξ.

ἐπεσβολίας, acc. pl., (see follg.). forward talk, δ 159†.

ἐπεσ-βόλον, acc. masc., (βάλλω), scurrilous, impudent, B 275†.

ἔπεσον, aor. from πίπτω.

ἐπ-έσσεται, fut. from 1. ἔπειμι.

ἐπ-έσσυται, pf. pass. from -σεύω.

ἐπ-έστη, aor. from ἐφ-ίστημι.

ἐπ-έσχον, aor. from -ἔχω.

ἐπ-ετήσιος (ἔτος), throughout all the year, η 118†.

ἔπευ, imp. from ἔπομαι.

ἐπ-ευφήμησαν, 3 pl. aor., (-ευϝημίω), reverently approved, A 22, 376.

ἐπ-εύχεται, pres., also fut. aor. (εὔχομαι), (1) precari, pray, τινί, κ 533; φ 203, with inf. ; adding a petition thereto, ξ 436.—(2) gloriari, exult, abso... χ 286, Φ 427 ; τινί, Λ 431, Π 829, Ξ 478.

ἔπεφνον, aor. from Φεν-.

ἐπέφρᾰδον, aor. from φράζω.

ἐπ-έχεις (ἔχω), pres., ipf. -εῖχε, -εχε, aor. -έσχον, praebeo, *offer* (wine, the breast), X 83 ; τινί, impono, *place upon*, ρ 410; instarc, *attack*, τ 71 (tmesis, χ 75); τι, occupare, *extend over*, Φ 407, Ψ 190, 238; *check*, Φ 244, ν 266; *restrain* the mind from ; sc. ἑαυτόν, *kept aloof*, φ 186. (See ἐπώχατο.)

ἐπ-ήβολος, particeps, *possessing*, β 319†.

ἐπ-ηγκενίδεσσιν, dat. pl., *uppermost streaks*, or *planks of ship*, forming the gunwale, ε 253†. (See cut No. 35, letter c.)

ἐπ-ῆεν, see 1. ἔπ-ειμι.

ἐπ-ηετανός, οἱ, οὐς, όν, (αἰεί), *lasting constantly*, neut. *always, abundantly*, κ 427. (Od.)

ἐπ-ήιεν, from 2. ἔπ-ειμι.

ἐπ-ήλυθον, redierunt, aor. from -έρχομαι.

ἐπ-ημοιβοί (ἀμείβω), *serving for a change*, ξ 513 ; ὀχῆες, *cross-bars*, *shutting one over the other in opposite directions*. (See cut No. 32.)

ἐπί τ᾽ ἠμύει, *nods to* (the wind) with its ears, i. e. dips its heads to the wind, B 148†.

ἐπήν = ἐπεὶ ἄν, *when, after*, (1) with subj., (a) of fut. expectation, δ 414, Ο 147, α 293, Π 96, M 369, δ 412, χ 254 ; (b) general supposition, θ 553, ξ 130, Τ 223.—(2) with opt., (a) dependent upon clause containing a wish, and thus attracted into opt., Ω 227 ; (b) iter., δ 222. (ἐπεὶ ἄν=ἐπεί-ήν=ἐπήν.)

ἐπ-ήνεον, -ησαν, see ἐπ-αινέομεν.

ἐπήιξεν, aor. from πήγνυμι.

ἐπ-ήπῦον, ipf., (ἠπύω), ἀμφοτέροισι, utrisque acclamabant, *applaud*, Σ 502†.

ἐπ-ήρᾰτος, ον, ον, α, (ἐρατός), *lovely, pleasing*, δ 606, X 121.

ἐπ-ήρετμοι (ἐρετμός), *fitted with oars*; but β 403, *at the oar*. (Od.)

ἐπ-ηρεφέες, έας, (ἐρέφω), *overhanging*, *steep*, M 54, μ 59.

Ἐπήριτος, name coined by Odysseus, ω 306†.

ἐπ-ῆρσε, aor. from -αραρίσκω.

ἐπ-ῆσαν, see 2. ἔπ-ειμι.

ἐπ-ητής, ῇ, *discreet*, ν 332, σ 128. (Od.)

ἐπ-ήτριμοι, α, crebri, a, *numerous*, Σ 211. (Il.)

ἐπ-ητύος, gen., (-ητύς, -ητής), benevolentiae, φ 306†. [∪−∪∪]

ἐπί, I. adv., *thereto*, Ο 321, Ψ 840, Θ 507, K 466 ; *thereupon*, γ 9, Λ 630; *on the upper part of it*, Π 612 ; *moreover*, ε 443, Σ 529 ; *thereon*, I 187. So naturally ἔπι=ἔπεστι, adest, θ 563; est, λ 367, Γ 45, E 178, N 104 ; imminet, *hangs over*, Φ 110.—II. prep. A. with acc., (1) of the point or goal (a) aimed at : *toward*, *to*, B 218, α 149, χείρας ἴαλλον, ἄλτο, ἰών, Γ 154, M 375 ; νῆας, θῖνα, Λ 440 ; in hostile sense, *upon*, *against*, E 590, Λ 343, M 375, 443, N 101, P 504, K 85, Φ 248, ρ 295 ; *over*, α 146 ; *upon*, ε 84, N 682 ; ψ 76, =stopped my mouth ; *upon*, ἕζετο ; *at*, μ 171 ; (b) attained : *to*, ἷξε, K 470, θ 226 ; *upon*, e. g. descend from chariot upon, fall upon, K 541, χθόνα, Ψ 393, λ 18 ; sit upon, Ξ 437 ; (c) esp. with neut. pl., ἡμέτερα, *to* our house, ο 88 ; ἀριστερά, sinistrorsum, a sinistra, δεξιά.—(2) of purpose, (a) with verbs of motion, θ 395 ; cenatum ire, ω 394 ; cubitum, ξ 455; ἔργα ; ω 466, ad arma concurrere, hastened to arm themselves; στίχας, *to*, i. e. *in* or *by* ranks ; (b) with verbs of seeking, go *for*, fetch, γ 421, cf. φ 17, N 459.—(3) of extension (a) *over* a space, λ 577 ; πόντον, γαῖαν, νῶτα θαλάσσης, σ 131; ἄρουραν, χθόνα, Ω 532 ; ἄστεα, νῶτα, B 308 ; (πάντας) ἀνθρώπους, *throughout* the whole world ; ὅσσον, how far ; τόσσον, so far, so large ; ἥμισυ, as far as the middle; πολλά, far and wide ; (b) in time : δηρόν, *for* a long time, P 41 ; χρόνον, *for* a time, until, η 288.—(4) secundum, according *to* ; ἶσα, uniformly ; στάθμην, by the rule, straight. —B. with dat., (1) local : *upon*, *at*, βωμοῖς, cf. δ 134; χθονί, humi, in terris, πύργῳ, ἐσχάρῃ and ἐσχαρόφιν, γούνασι ; amid, α 218 ; κτεάτεσσι, νηυσί, σταθμοῖσι, φάτνῃ, αὐτόφι, ν 221 ; *on*, *at*, cf. French sur, on the river, Λ 712 ; ῥηγμῖνι, θῖνι, κρήνῃ, ὀδῷ, κόλπῳ, μαζῷ, *upon* ; over the corpse of, Λ 261 ; *in the place of*, Π 649, P 400 ; βαίνειν ἐπὶ νηυσί, go to the ships, freq. with verbs of motion, esp. πίπτω, χέω, τίθημι (ἐπὶ φρεσί, enjoin upon), ἕζομαι, also κ 375. —(2) temporal : ἤματι, cf. French un jour ; *after*, H 163 sqq., Ψ 401, 514. —(3) attending circumstance : *with* this intention, τῷδ' ἐπὶ θυμῷ, π 111, *with* work unaccomplished, Δ 235.—(4) approach: *upon, at* or *near, a* 103, K 568, Γ 23, O 743, P 574, νηυσί; εἶναι, *succor;* πέλομαι, come upon, ν 60; *at* or *against,* δ 822, χ 8, A 382, Γ 15, Θ 327.—(5) additional circumstance: *over and above, besides,* η 216, ρ 454, χ 264, I 639.—(6) causal: *for,* δόρπῳ; motive: *because of,* π 19, Υ 35; *in honor of,* ἀεθλεύειν; with hostile intent, *against,* K 185; *upon* clear right, σ 414; *for,* A 162, K 304, Ψ 574; condition: *upon,* Φ 445.—C. with gen., (1) local: *upon, in, on,* νηός, ἠπείρου, ἀγροῦ, νευρῆφιν, ἰκριόφιν, ἵππων, πύργου, *over* the battle-field, P 368; *against,* η 278; with verbs of motion, βαίνω, ἵζω, ἕζομαι, τίθημι, ἐρύω, νηός, *upon* the ship; ἰκριόφιν, γ 353; δεξιόφιν, ἀριστερόφιν; ε 238, *to* the verge of the island, Λ 546, Ψ 374.—(2) temporal: εἰρήνης, p a c e, *in time of* peace, Ψ 332.—(3) of goal: make *for* Psyria, γ 171.—(4) ἐπὶ παιδὸς ἕπεσθαι, accompany a daughter, α 278; ἐφ' ὑμείων, *by* yourselves, H 195.

ἐπὶ ἰάλλοντα, ipf. ἴαλλε, aor. -ιηλε, -ιῆλαι, injicere, τινί τι, *lay upon* (handfetters); immittere, *send upon,* β 316, ο 475; χ 49, *brought to pass.* [ῐ, with augm. ῑ.]

ἐπι-άλμενος, aor. part. from ἐφάλλομαι.

ἐπι-ανδάνει, see ἐφανδάνω.

ἐπ-ίαχον, tmesi, ἴαχε, ipf., (ἰάχω), a c - clamabant, H 403; conclamabant, P 723.

ἐπί-βαθρον (ἐπι-βατήριον), *fare, passage-money,* ο 449†.

ἐπι-βαινέμεν -ειν, pr. ipf., fut. -βήσομαι, aor. -έβην, subj. εἴομεν, βήμεναι, mid. -εβήσετο, imp. -βήσεο; freq. in tmesi, *get a footing, stand,* I. absol., μ 434, E 666; βίβηκε, Π 69, has advanced, *has marched forth.*—(1) with gen., *set foot on, tread,* of country, city, etc.—(2) fig. *tread* (the path of insolence, χ 424; of mirth, ψ 52).—(3) *mount, go on board,* chariot, bed, scaffold, ship, Δ 99; *climb,* πύργων, M 444.—(4) with acc. Πιερίην, *traverse.*—II. trans. fut. act. ἐπιβήσετε, and 1 aor. -έβησε, (1) *set upon,* η 223.—(2) *bring to* great glory, Θ 285; bring to reason, ψ 13.—(3) *cause to mount,* Θ 129, 197; *bring upon,* I 546.

ἐπὶ βάλλον, ipf., aor. act. mid., freq. in tmesi, *throw, cast upon,* act. τινί τι, ξ 520; ζ 320, *ply* the whip; (νηῦς) Φεάς, *steered for,* nid., s e i n j i c e r e i n, ἐνάρων; *cast lots with each other for,* ξ 209; pass. ipf., *lay over it,* τ 58.

ἐπι-βασκέμεν (see ἐπιβαινέμεν, II., 2), τινὰ κακῶν, *bring into* misfortune, B 234†.

ἐπι-βήμεναι, aor. from ἐπι-βαινέμεν.

ἐπι-βήτορα, ας, acc., (-βήτωρ), ἵππων, *mounted warrior;* συῶν, *boar.*

ἐπι-βλής, ὁ, (βάλλω), o b e x, *bar,* Ω 453†. (See cut No. 60, and the adjacent representation of Egyptian doors; see also No. 32.)

ἐπι-βοάω, only mid. fut. -βώσομαι, *call upon,* for help, as witnesses, θεούς, α 378, K 463 (v. l. δωσόμεθα).

ἐπι-βου-κόλος (κέλομαι), βοῶν— ἀνήρ, *cattle - herd, herdsman,* γ 422. (Od.)

ἐπι-βρέμει, *set roaring,* P 739†.

ἐπι-βρίθω, only aor. -έβρῖσαν, with subj. and opt., *fall heavily upon, full heavily,* E 91; *make* the vines *heavy* (with fruit), ω 344.

ἐπι-βωσόμεθα, fut. from -βοάω.

ἐπι-βώτορι, dat., (-βώτωρ), μήλων, *shepherd,* ν 222†.

ἐπὶ ἐγδούπησαν (γδουπέω), *thundered approval,* Λ 45†.

ἐπι-γίγνεται, a p p e t i t, *approaches,* Z 148†. (O 358, read ὅσον τ' ἔπι, as far as.)

ἐπι-γιγνώσκω, only aor. subj. -γνώῃ, ώωσι, *recognizes,* ω 217; *look upon,* us fighting, σ 30.

ἐπι-γνάμπτει, aor. -έγναμψε, flectit, *changes,* τινά, νόον τινός; *bending,* Φ 178; κῆρ, *bowing* her will.

ἐπι-γνώῃ, see -γιγνώσκω.

ἐπι-γουνίδα, τήν, (γόνυ), f e m u r,

θεῖτο, would grow a stout *thigh*, ρ 225. (Od.)

ἐπι-γράβδην, adv., (-γράφω), βάλε, struck *scratching*, i. e. grazed, Φ 166†.

ἐπι-γράφω, only aor. -έγραψε, *graze*, χρόα, Ν 553; κλῆρον, *scratch*, *mark*.

Ἐπίδαυρος, ή, town in Argolis, Β 561†.

ἐπι-δέδρομε, pf. from -τρέχω.

ἐπι-δέξια, ntr. pl., dextrorsum, *toward the right* (*auspicious*, Β 353).

ἐπι-δευής, pl. -έες, εῖς, (δέομαι), egemus, we are *in need of*; οὐκ ἐπιδευεῖς (ἐσμεν), with gen., non egemus; βίης—, robore inferior; ω 171, sc. βίης, far too *weak*; ἐπιδευὲς ἔχρσθα, with gen., *mayst fail* in nothing *of* thy right.

ἐπι-δεύομαι, ipf. -εδεύετο (δεῖ), egeo, *lack*; with gen., inferior sum, Ε 636; esp. μάχης, pugnando, in battle; but Ω 385, non sibi defuit in pugna contra Ach.; desiderantes, Σ 77.

ἐπι-δημεύεις (δῆμος), *stayest at home* (ἐν δήμῳ), π 28†.

ἐπι-δήμιος, ον, ον, οι, (δῆμος), *at home*; Ω 262, *domestic*; Ι 64, civilis.

ἐπι-δίδωμι, only fut. aor. act., *give besides*, Ψ 559; *give with her*, Ι 147; mid. fut. -δωσόμεθα (better βωσόμεθα), *bestow gifts upon*; and aor. subj. -δώμεθα, testes nobis adhibeamus, *take as witness*, Χ 254.

ἐπι-δινέω (δίνη), aor. -δινήσας, *having whirled it*, mid. -δινεῖται, secum volvit, *weighs* (in thought), υ 218; pass. -δινηθέντε, *wheeling* (in the air), β 151.

ἐπι-διφριάδος, τῆς, (δίφρος), *rim of body* or *box of chariot*, Κ 475†. (See cut No. 10, under ἄντυξ.)

ἐπι-δίφρια, ntr., (δίφρος), θεῖναι= ἐπὶ δίφρῳ, place *in the chariot*, ο 51 and 75.

ἐπ-ιδόντα, aor. from ἐφ-οράω, Χ 61.

ἐπι-δραμέτην, εῖν, aor. see -τρέχω.

ἐπί-δρομον (δρόμος), ntr., *that may be scaled*, Ζ 434†.

ἐπὶ δῦναι, aor. inf. expressing a wish; may the sun *set*, utinamne occidat, Β 413†.

ἐπι-δωσόμεθα, see -βοάω.

ἐπι-δώμεθα, see -δίδωμι.

ἐπι-είκελος, ον, ε, (ἴκελος), consimilis, *like*, θεοῖς, ἀθανάτοισι, Α 265.

ἐπι-εικία, acc. and -ές, ntr., (-εικής, ἔοικε), *becoming*, *suitable*; Ψ 246, thus *of suitable size*; with ntr. (freq. with ὡς, as), ἐστίν is always to be supplied =decet.

ἐπι-εικτόν, ά, ntr., (εἴκω), concedendus, always with οὐκ, unendurable (unheard of), θ 307; elsewh., *intincible*, *unceasing*. (Il.)

ἐπι-ειμένος, pf. pass. part. from ἐπι-έννυμι.

ἐπι-είσομαι, fut. from 2. ἐπ-ειμι.

ἐπι-έλπεο, imp. pres., -εται (tmesis), -όμενος, *have hope of*, Α 545.

ἐπι-έννυμι, aor. act. -έσσαμεν, pf. pass. -ειμένος, οι, super induere, *put on over*, υ 143; pass., praeditus; with acc., Η 164, Α 149.

ἐπι-ζά-φελος (φαλ-, Eng. swell), *raging*, *furious*, χόλος; adv., *rehemently*, with χαλεπαίνοι, μενέαινε.

ἐπι-ήλε, see ἐπι-ιάλλω.

ἐπι-ήνδανε, see ἐφ-ανδάνω.

ἐπί-ηρα, see ἦρα.

ἐπι-ήρᾰνα, ntr. pl., (ἐπίηρα), θυμῷ, *corresponding to the wish*, *desired*, τ 343†.

ἐπι-θαρσύνων, part., (θάρσος), *encouraging*, Δ 183†. [ῠ]

ἐπι-θεῖτε, 2 aor. opt., -τίθημι.

ἐπι-θήματα, ntr. pl., (τίθημι), *lids*, Ω 228†.

ἐπι-θρέξαντος, aor. from -τρέχω.

ἐπι-θρώσκουσι, and part., aor. always in tmesi, -θόρον, (τόσσον ἔπι, so far, Ε 772), insilire, *spring on board*, νηός; insultare, *leap upon* (in contempt), τύμβῳ; aggredi, *attack*, τινί, Θ 252, χ 303.

ἐπ-ιθύουσι, pres., aor. -ιθύσαντες, (ἰθύς), irruentes, *rush upon*, π 297; also Σ 175.

ἐπι-ίστορα, acc., (οἶδα), conscium, *privy to*, i. e. *accomplice in*, heinous deeds; others, *performer of great labors*, φ 26†.

ἐπι-καίω, only ipf. ἐπὶ μηρί' ἔκαιον, comburebant, *were burning*, γ 9, and aor. ἔκηε, αν.

ἐπί-καρ, see III. κάρ.

ἐπι-κάρσιαι, pl. adj., (ἐπὶ κάρ), *head-foremost*, ι 70†.

Ἐπικάστη, mother of Oidipus, λ 271†.

ἐπ-έκειντο, ipf., fut. -κείσεται, (κεῖμαι), *lay thereon*, i. e. *were closed*, ζ 19; instabit, *beset*, Ζ 458.

ἐπὶ κείρει, ipf. -κεῖρεν, aor. -κερσε, accĭdo, maim, baffle, μήδεα; mow down, Π 394.

ἐπὶ κελάδησαν, aor., ⟨κελαδέω⟩, shouted applause, Θ 542. (Il.)

ἐπι-κέλλω, only aor. -έκελσεν, etc., beach, let take the land, νῆας, ι 148. (Od.)

ἐπι-κέλομαι, only aor. -εκέκλετο, invocabat, call upon, I 454†.

ἐπι-κεράννυμι, inf. aor. -κρῆσαι, admiscere, mix in addition, η 164†.

ἐπι-κερτομέων, part., ⟨κέρτομος⟩, τινά, irridens, mocking, only Ω 649, iocatus, laughingly.

ἐπί-κευθε, imp. pres., fut. -κεύσω, aor. subj. -κεύσῃς, celare, conceal, always with negative; with dat. and after other verbs, Ε 816, ε 143, σ 171; δ 744, rem te non celabo.

ἐπι-κίδναται (σκεδάννυμι), dispergitur, diffuses itself over, Β 850, Η 451. (Il.)

ἐπι-κλείουσι ⟨κλέος⟩, collaudant, praise the more, α 351†.

Ἐπικλῆς, ῆα, companion at arms of Sarpedon, slain by Aias, Μ 379†.

ἐπί-κλησιν, acc., (-κλησις), cognomine, καλεῖν τινα; Π 177, according to report.

ἐπι-κεκλιμένας, pf. pass. part., (κλίνω), closed (doors), Μ 121†.

ἐπί-κλοπος, ον, (κλέπτω), καὶ ἐ., and, no doubt, a sly fox (who will steal the bow if he can), φ 397.

ἐπ-έκλυε, ipf., (κλύω), audiebat, τί, τινός, ε 150.

ἐπι-κλώθω, only aor. -έκλωσε, σαν, σαντο, σωνται, spin to, allot; subj. always some deity; obj. either ὀϊζύν, ὄλβον, or inf. after ὥς. (Od. and Ω 525.)

ἐπι-κόψων ⟨κόπτω⟩, caesurus, to strike, to fell, γ 443†.

ἐπι-κουρήσοντα, fut., (ἐπίκουρος), auxiliaturum, to aid, Ε 614†.

ἐπί-κουρος, οι, ων, ους, adiutor, aider in battle, Ε 478; adiutrix, Φ 431; esp. pl., auxilia (Troianorum), allies of Trojans.

ἐπι-κραίνω, aor. -κρήνειε, and imp. -κρήηνον, ipf. -εκραίαινε, (κρανίον), accomplish; τινί τι, fulfill, ἐέλδωρ, Α 455. (Il.)

ἐπι-κρατέουσι, indic. and part. only pres., (κράτος), have the upper hand, Ξ 98; elsewh. hold power, rule over.

ἐπι-κράτέως (κράτος), mightily, victoriously, Π 67. (Il.)

ἐπι-κρήηνον, -κρήνειε, see -κραίνω.

ἐπι-κρῆσαι, aor. inf. from -κεράννυμι.

ἐπ-ίκριον, antenna, yard, only ε 254 and 318.

ἐπὶ κῦρε, aor. -κύρσας, (κυρέω), encounter (in hostile signif. kept always aiming at, Ψ 821).

ἐπ-έλαμψε, aor., (λάμπω), shone in, Ρ 650†.

ἐπι-λανθάνω, see -λήθω.

ἐπι-λέγεσθε (λέγω), collect in addition, Θ 507†.

ἐπὶ ἔλειβε, ον, and aor. λεῖψαι, (λείβω), pour a libation over, ἱεροῖσι, μ 362.

ἐπὶ λεύσσει, after τόσσον τίς τ', better separated; one sees as far as, Γ 12†.

ἐπί-ληθον, ntr., (-λήθω), κακῶν, causing forgetfulness of ills, δ 221†.

ἐπι-λήθω, only aor. -έλησεν, made forget, τινός, ν 85; fut. mid. -λήσομαι, aor. -ελήθετο, oblivisci, τινός (also tmesis, -λάθωνται).

ἐπ-ελήκεον, ipf., beat time, θ 379†.

ἐπι-λίγδην βλῆτο ὦμον, received a stroke grazing his shoulder, Ρ 599†.

ἐπ-ιλλίζουσί μοι, wink to me, σ 11†.

ἐπ-ελώβευον, ipf., (λώβη), mock at, β 323†.

ἐπι-μαίνομαι, aor. -εμήνατο, τῷ, was madly in love with him (or τῷ may be construed with μιγήμεναι), Ζ 160†.

1. ἐπι-μαίεο, imp. prs., ipf., (μίμαα), τινός, seek to gain, make for, Κ 401, μ 220.

2. ἐπι-μαίομαι, ipf. -εμαίετο and aor. -εμάσσατο, (ΜΑ), lay hold of, grasp; τί χείρ' = χειρί, ι 302; contrectare, touch, λ 591; touch with sceptre, ν 429; Ε 748, strike with whip; was reaching after, λ 531.

ἐπι-μάρτυρος, οι, testis (deus), Η 76.

ἐπι-μάσσεται, etc., see 2. ἐπι-μαίομαι.

ἐπί-μαστον (-μαίομαι), contrectatum, one who has been passed through many hands, filthy, ν 377†.

ἐπι-μειδήσας (μειδάω), smiling at or upon, Δ 356; with scornful smile, Κ 400.

ἐπι-μέμφεαι, εται, find fault with,

τινί, π 97; τινός, B 225, what art thou coveting? A 65, 93, be dissatisfied with.

ἐπι-μένω, only imp. aor. -μεινον, stay, a 309; wait (ὄφρα, δ 587), with subj., Z 340.

ἐπ-εμήδετο, ipf., πατρί, she devised a trick against her father, ὃ 437†.

ἐπι-μῆνις, reading of Aristarchus, E 178†, wrath thereat.

ἐπ-εμήνῖε (μηνίω) τινί, succcensebat, was at feud with, N 460†.

ἐπι-μιμνήσκομαι, only aor. mid. -μνησαίμεθα, and pass. -μνησθείς, recordari, call to mind, A 65, δ 191.

ἐπι-μίμνω, wait upon, superintend, ᾧ, ξ 66. (Od.)

ἐπι-μίξ, adv., promiscue, indiscriminately, Ψ 242.

ἐπι-μίσγομαι, only pres., have to do with, τινί, ζ 205; accedere, draw nigh to, ζ 241 ; manus conserere cum, contend with.

ἐπι-μνησαίμεθα, aor., see -μιμνήσκομαι.

ἐπι-μύζω, only aor. -έμυξαν, murmured at, Δ 20. (Il.)

ἐπι-νέμω, aor. -ένειμε τινί τι, dispertiit, distributed to, I 216.

ἐπι-νεύω, ipf. ἔνευε, aor. -ένευσα, ε, annuit, he nodded with his helmet, i. e. its plumes nodded, X 314 ; nod assent, κάρητι, ὀφρύσι (tmesis), A 528, φ 431, as promise, or as sign previously agreed upon.

ἐπι-νεφρίδιον, adj. acc., (νεφρός), over the kidneys, Φ 204†.

ἐπι-νέω, only aor. -ένησε, Destiny spun to him at his birth with her thread, Υ 128, Ω 210.

ἐπ-ενήνεον, ipf., (νέω, νηέω), νεκρούς πυρκαϊῆς, were heaping up the corpses upon the funeral pile, H 428.

ἐπι-ξύνῳ (ξυνός), communi, common, where several have rights, M 422†.

ἐπι-ορκήσω, fut., (-ορκέω), peierabo, swear falsely; πρὸς δαίμονος, per deum, T 188†.

ἐπί-ορκον, neut., (ὅρκος), periurum. false, T 264 ; subst. periurium, false oath, Γ 279 (vainly, K 332).

ἐπὶ ὅρονται, το, pres. ipf., (οὖρος), watch over them, ξ 104 ; were serving, γ 471.

ἐπι-οσσομένω, part. du., tuentes, τι; having before their eyes, avoiding, P 381†.

ἐπί-ουρα, see -ουρον.

ἐπί-ουρος, ον, (οὖρος), Κρήτῃ, ruler in Kreta (Il.); ὑῶν, chief swine-herd. (Od.)

ἐπι-όψομαι, see ἐφ-οράω.

ἐπι-πάσσειν, ων, and ipf. πάσσε (tmesis), φάρμακα, sprinkle healing drugs (powder made of roots) upon, Δ 219. (Il.)

ἐπι-πείθεται, εο, ipf. -ετο, fut. -σεται, obey, τινι (ἐπέεσσι, O 162), μύθῳ ; subj. θυμός τινι. (Od.)

ἐπὶ πελεμίχθη, simul vibrabatur, quivered as it struck, Π 612. (Il.)

ἐπὶ πέλεται, ονται, aor. -πλόμενον, coming, η 261 ; τινὶ θάνατος, comes upon; so also γῆρας, νοῦσος. (Od.)

ἐπ-έπτατο, -πτέσθαι, aor., (πέτομαι), advolavit, fly toward, N 821.

ἐπι-πίλναται (πέλομαι), is there there, ζ 44†.

ἐπι-πλάζω, only aor. pass. -πλαγχθεὶς πόντον, driven about over—, θ 14†.

ἐπὶ πλέων = πλείων, πλεῖν, ipf. -έπλεον, sail over, the sea, the waves, A 312, δ 474 in tmesi.

ἐπι-πλήσσεις, ων, fut. πλήξειν, vituperare, rebuke, M 211, Ψ 580; striking, lashing, K 500.

ἐπι-πλώσας, aor. part., aor. sync. -έπλως, part. -πλώς, (from ἐπιπλέων), sail upon, πόντον, γ 15.

ἐπι-πνείησι, subj., πνείουσα part., aor. subj. πνεύσωσι, cf. adflare navi, νηΐ, breathe or blow upon, δ 357.

ἐπι-ποιμένες, shepherdesses, μ 131†.

ἐπι-πρέπει, τοι, is manifest, ω 252†.

ἐπι-προ-έμεν, inf. aor. -ίημι.

ἐπι-προ-ίηλε, aor., (ἰάλλω), set before them, (σφῶϊν), Λ 628†. [ῑ]

ἐπι-προ-έηκα, aor., and inf. -έμεν, send forth to Troy, Σ 439; νηυσί, embark for ; Δ 94, shoot at Menelaos ; made for, o 299. [ῑ]

ἐπι-πτάρε, aor., (πταίρω), μοὶ πᾶσιν ἔπεσσιν, has been sneezing all the while I spoke, ρ 545†.

ἐπι-πτέσθαι, inf. aor., see -έπτατο.

ἐπι-πωλεῖται (πόλος), obit, inspect, Δ 231; -επωλεῖτο στίχας, was scouring to find a combatant, Λ 264. (Il.)

ἐπι-ρρέζεσκον (ῥέζω), were accustomed to sacrifice, ρ 211†.

ἐπι-ρρέῃ, subj., (ῥρεπ.), ἡμῖν, settle down upon us, Ξ 99†.

ἐπι-ρρέει (σρεει, ῥέω), flow upon (surface); -έρρεεν, were streaming toward us, Λ 724. (Il.)

ἐπι-ρρήσσεσκον, ipf. iter., (ῥήσσω), drove to, pushed home, Ω 454, 456.

ἐπι-ἔρριψαν (Ϝρίπτω) μοι, in me conieccrant, cast upon me, ε 310†.

ἐπί-ρροθος (ῥέθος?), adiutor, -trix, helper, Δ 390. (Il.)

ἐπι-ρώομαι (ruo), only ipf. -ερρώοντο, υ 107, τῇσιν, at which were busy, were toiling night and day, aor. -ερρώσαντο, flowed waving down, A 529.

ἐπι-σσείων, -σσείῃ, (σϜἰω), brandish over, against, τινί, Δ 167. (Il.)

ἐπι-σεύῃ, ipf. -έσευε, (freq. σσ, from σϜ), send upon, let loose upon, (τινί), dogs, monsters; met. ill-luck, dreams ; pass. prs. ipf., pf. -έσσυται, -εσσύμενος, plupf. -έσσῦτο, rush up, upon, χ 310 ; τί, ζ 20 ; ἔς τινα, N 757 ; τινί, O 347 ; -δε, ν 19 ; freq. in tmesi, often in hostile signification, charge upon, τινί, τί, Π 511, with gen. ; raging through the plain, πεδίοιο ; bursting forth, P 737 : was hastening to follow, Φ 601 ; so also with subject, θυμός.

ἐπί-σκοπος, ον, οι, (σκέπτομαι), lookout, watch (K 38, 342 ?), for something, τινός, θ 163 ; guardian, Ω 729, X 255.

ἐπι-σκύζωνται, subj., aor. opt. -σκύσσαιτο, indignari, be indignant at, τινί, η 306.

ἐπι-σκύνιον (scu-tum, cu-tis), skin over the brows, knitted in frowning, P 136†. [ῠ]

ἐπι-σμυγερῶς, misere, sadly, γ 195. (Od.)

ἐπί-σπαστον (σπάω), of his own seeking, σ 73. (Od.)

ἐπι-σπεῖν, inf. aor. from ἐφ-έπω.

ἐπι-σπέρχουσι, 3 pl. and part. -ων, incitans ; ε 304, rush to the spot.

ἐπι-σπέσθαι, -σπών, see ἐφ-έπω.

ἐπι-σσείῃς, etc., see ἐπι-σείων.

ἐπι-σσεύῃ, see -σεύῃ.

ἐπί-σσωτρα, ων, οις, sing., Ψ 519, (σϜω, σεύω), tire. (Il.)

ἐπι-στᾰδόν, adv., (ἵσταμαι), stepping up to in turn; π 453, were making ready (standing) on the spot.

ἐπ-ίσταμαι, prs. ipf., and fut. -ιστήσονται, know how, understand, with inf., B 611 ; ᾖσι φρεσί, of intellectual comprehension, in one's thought, ἔργα, η 111 ; be skillful, an adept in, etc. (in this sense, part. very common); φόρμιγγος, φ 406; with skillful feet, Σ 599 ; ἄκοντι, in throwing the spear, also of

animals; though knowing well in your hearts, δ 730.

ἐπ-ισταμένως (-ίσταμαι), skilfully, H 317 ; εὖ καί—, ψ 197.

ἐπι-στάτῃ, dat., (ἵσταμαι), a cccdenti, beggar, ρ 455†. [ᾰ]

ἐπὶ δὲ στενάχοντο (στενάχω), wailed in reply, T 301. (Il.) [ᾰ]

ἐπὶ δ' ἔστενε (στένω), groaned in answer, Ω 776†.

ἐπι-στεφέας (στέφω) οἴνοιο, filled to the brim with wine, Θ 232.

ἐπι-στέφομαι, only aor. -εστέψαντο ποτοῖο, filled to the brim with drink, A 470.

ἐπ-ιστήμων (ἐπίσταμαι), discreet, through thought and instinct, π 374†.

ἐπί-στιον (ἵσταμαι), place where the ships stand when drawn up, ζ 265†.

ἐπ-εστονάχησε, aor., billows roared as they closed upon her, Ω 79†. [ᾰ]

ἐπὶ ἱστόρεσεν, aor., (στορέννυμι), spread over, ξ 50†.

ἐπι-στρέψας, part. aor., (στρέφω), having turned him toward the Achaians, Γ 370†.

ἐπι-στροφάδην, adv., (στρέφω), turning in every direction, on every side, K 483. [ᾰ]

ἐπί-στροφος (στρέφω) ἀνθρώπων, conversant with (in his wanderings), α 177†.

Ἐπί-στροφος, (1) leader of the Halizonians, B 856†.—(2) son of Euênos, slain by Achilleus, B 692†.—(3) son of Iphitos, chief of Phokians, B 517†.

ἐπι-στρωφῶσι (=άουσι) πόληας, circumeunt urbes, haunt, ρ 486†.

Ἐπίστωρ, a Trojan, slain by Patroklos, Π 695†.

ἐπι-σφυρίοις, dat. pl., (σφυρόν), ἀραρυίας, furnished with clasps around the ankles, Γ 331. (Il.) (See cut on next page.)

ἐπι-σχερώ, adv., (σχερός), in a row, close together, Ψ 125. (Il.)

ἐπι-σχεσίην, acc., (ἐπέχω), μύθον, pretext, φ 71†.

ἐπί-σχεσις, ἡ, (ἐπέχω), restraint, with inf., δ 451.

ἐπ-ίσχειν (ἔχω), (1) hold to their course, P 465.—(2) τινί, impono, Ξ 241 ; θυμόν τινος, restrain one's thoughts from—; mid. part. aiming at, χ 15.

ἐπὶ τάνυσσε, σαν, (also σσ), only aor., extend, stretch out over, extend over, N μᾰτα, names are given, θ 554 ; mid. aor. χεῖράς τινι, lay his hands upon.

ἐπι - τῑμήτωρ, ultor, guardian, ι 270†.

ἐπι-τλήτω, imp. aor., (-τλῆναι), be patient, Ψ 591 ; μύθοισιν, hearken patiently to—.

ἐπι-τολμάτω, imp. prs., aor. -ετόλμησε, (τολμάω), endure to listen, α 353 ; ρ 238, hold out.

ἐπί-τονος [ῐ] (τείνω), back-stay, μ 423†. (See cut, representing an Assyrian war-ship.)

359, Π 567 ; laid it down upon, ο 283 ; drew forward by, α 442.

ἐπι-τάρροθος, ον, ω, οι, (ῥέθος), springing to aid ; adiutor, helper. (Il. and ω 182.)

ἐπι - τείνω, only pass. pf. -τέτᾰται, plupf. -τέτᾰτο—τινί, is spread over, λ 19.

ἐπι - τέλλω, pr. ipf. aor. act. and mid., lay upon, mandare, τινὶ τάδε, μῦθον (κρατερόν), ἐφετμάς, Ε 818, συνθεσίας ; ὧδε, ὥς, πολλά, earnestly, εὖ, sharply ; mid. also μύθῳ—ἠδὲ κελεύεις, Κ 61 ; impose, λ 622, α 327 ; give orders, ρ 21 ; pass. plupf. ἐτέταλτο, commands had been given. [ἐπῑ, ψ 361.]

ἐπι-τέρπεται ἔργοις, takes pleasure in, ξ 228†.

ἐπι-τέτραπται, -τετράφαται, see -τρέπω.

ἐπι-τηδές (τείνω), intente, intently, ο 28 ; quickly, Α 142.

ἐπι-τίθημι, prs. ipf. fut., aor. 3 pl. -έθηκαν, subj. -θείω, opt. -θεῖτε, inf. -θεῖναι, -θέμεναι, aor. mid. -έθετο, -θέμενος (freq. in tmesi), put to, add, τινί τι, Η 364 ; confer, Ψ 400 ; φρεσί, put into the mind ; devising trouble, Ε 384 ; place upon, κ 355 ; τινὶ γούνασι, τ 401 ; pi!e Ossa on Olympos, λ 315 ; lay upon (wound, altar), Δ 190, φ 267 ; λεχέων, Ω 589 ; put on, Π 137 ; also of veil, arrow on string, τινί τι, Θ 324 ; impose, θ 245, also punishment, destiny ; ἄτην, send delusion into the mind ; φρένα τινί, animum advertere ad, apply the mind to, place before, τινί ; close door, also of stone serving as door, χ 157, 201, Φ 535, [λ 525]; pass. πᾶσι ὀνό-

ἐπ-ετοξάζοντο, ipf., (τοξάζω), were shooting arrows at—, τῷ, Γ 79†.

ἐπι-τρᾰπέουσι, prs., (ἐτράπην), Τρωσί, intrust the watch to the Trojans, Κ 421†.

ἐπι-τρέπω, ipf. -έτρεπε, aor. 1 (-έτρεψεν), aor. 2 (-ετράπομεν), pass. pf. (-τέτραπται, -τετράφαται), cedere, give over to, τί ; with inf., the victory, (Κ 79, γήραϊ, yield to) ; leave behind him, η 149 ; intrust, ο 24, Ε 750, Β 25 ; νεκρόν (defendendum); charge with, Κ 59 ; θεοῖσι (μῦθον), commit in confidence ; σοὶ θυμός, with inf., ι 12, thy heart is inclined.

ἐπι-τρέχω, ipf. -έτρεχον, aor. 1 -θρίξαντος, aor. 2 -έδραμον, etc. ; pf. -δέδρομεν, accurro, run up, Δ 524, ξ 3''; strike upon, graze, Ν 409 ; roll after, Ψ 504 ; is spread over, ζ 45, υ 357.

ἐπι-τροχάδην, adv., (τροχός), glibly, Γ 213, σ 26.

ἐπι-φέρειν, prs. act. and mid., fut. -οίσει, aor. -ένεικα (freq. in tmesi), inferre, bring upon, τινὶ Ἄρηα, bellum ; κῆρα, perniciem ; χεῖρας, lay hands upon, π 438 ; = have intercourse with, Τ 261.

ἐπι-φθονέοις, opt. prs., τινί τι, refuse, deny, λ 149†.

ἐπι-φλέγει, y, pres., (φλέγω), comburit, consumes, Β 455. (Il.)

ἐπι-φράζω, only aor. -έφραδε, etc., act. (1) *point out*, κ 111; (2) *declare*, Λ 795; (3) *show how*, θ 68; mid. aor. -ἐφράσατο, subj. ἐπῑφράσσεται, opt. φρασσαίατο, and pass. aor. -εφράσθης; *perceive* (by mind), σ 94; sentire, by senses, θ 94, νόησεν, took note (of the sound), *think thereon*, E 665; *meditate*, βουλήν; *devise*, τινὶ ὄλεθρον; ε 183, that thou hast thought of speaking this.

ἐπι-φρονέουσα, part. prs., (-φρων), *justly*, τ 385†.

ἐπι-φροσύνην, ας, acc., (-φρων), *thoughtfulness* (presence of mind), τ 22, assume *discretion*. (Od.)

ἐπί-φρων, φρονι, α, (φρήν), *discreet*; βουλήν, in counsel, ψ 12. (Od.)

ἐπ-εχείρεον, ipf., fut. -ήσειν, (χειρέω), τινί, *lay hand upon, partake of*, ω 386, 395.

ἐπι-χεῦαι, inf. aor., v. sq.

ἐπι-χέω (freq. tmesis), aor. 1 -έχευα (χεϝ), -χεε, inf. -χεῦαι, mid. ipf. -χέοντο, aor. -εχεύατο, 2 aor. -έχυντο, pass. pf. κέχυται, aor. opt. χῡθείη, *pour upon*, τινί τι, δ 214; *pour out*, Μ 284; met. (sleep) *over*, τινί, βλεφάροισιν; τινὶ βέλεα, *showering over* them missiles, Θ 159; *heap up*, earth, funeral mound, bed of boughs, material of whatever sort (mid., *raise for one's self*), ε 257.

ἐπι-χθόνιος, masc. plur., (χθών), *earthly* (opp. οὐρανίωνες), A 266; also as subst., Ω 220; =*men*, ρ 115.

ἐπι-χράω, aor. -έχραον, *fall upon*, τινί, Π 352; *annoy, distress (by wooing)*, β 50; *do harm to*, κ 64.

ἐπι-χρίοντες, aor. part. -χρίσασα, mid. prs. *besmear* (mid., *one's self*), ἀλοιφῇ, σ 172. (Od.)

ἐπι-ψαύῃ, subj. prs., (ψαύω), ὀλίγον πραπίδεσσι, *touches* the matter only a little with his mind, uses only a little his reason, θ 547†.

ἐπ-ιωγαί, pl., *places of shelter against* wind and wave, *roadstead*, ε 404†.

ἐπι-ιών, see 2. ἐπ-ειμι. ἔπλε, aor. from πέλω. ἔπλεο, ευ, ετο, aor. from πέλομαι.

ἔπληντο, aor. from πελάζω. ἐπ-οίσει, fut. from -φέρω.

ἐπ-οίχεσθαι, ὁμενος, ipf. -ῴχετο, tmesis, Ξ 381.—(1) obire, *go to and fro, back and forth*, παντόσε, ἀνά, Λ 383; ζ 282, if she herself should *go abroad* and look for a husband there.

—(2) τινά, accedere ad, *approach*, ρ 346, α 324; invadere, *attack*, Ε 330, Α 50.—(3) τί, permeare, Ο 676; obire, ἱστόν, *ply* the loom (*going up and down* before it); ν 34, *go to* evening meal; ρ 227, σ 363, *attend to* work in the field.—(4) τινί, accedere ad, α 143.

ἐπόμεσθα, see ἕπω.

ἐπ-όμνυμι, fut. -ομοῦμαι, aor. ὄμοσσεν (tmesis), *swear in addition*, Ι 274.

ἐπ-ομφάλιον, ntr., (ὀμφᾰλός), the shield, *on the boss*, Η 267†.

ἐπ-οπίζεο, imp. pr., (ὄπις), revere, reverence, *stand in awe of*, ε 146†.

ἐπ-οπτάω, only ipf. -ώπτων, *broiled over* (the blazing wood), μ 363†.

ἐπ-οπτεύεσκε, ipf. iter., (ὀπτεύω), *superintended*, π 140†.

ἐπ-ορέγω, aor. act. only in tmesi, ὀρέξῃ, *reach to, confer upon*, E 225; mid. aor. part. -ορεξάμενος, *stretching one's self out towards, lunging at*, E 335.

ἐπ-ορνύω, ipf. -ώρνυε, aor. -ῶρσε, imp. ἔπορσον; freq. in tmesi, incitare contra, *excite* (courage, Υ 93) against, τινά τινι, Μ 253, ε 366; (in hostile signif.) *send* (against, τινί) warrior, storm, wild beast, waves, sleep (day of death, Ο 613).—Mid. ipf. ὤρνυτο, aor. -ῶρτο, plupf. ὀρώρει, surgere, *rise*; Ψ 112, τινί, *rise up against* (for combat).

ἐπ-όρομαι, see ἐπὶ ὄρονται.

ἔπορον, aor. see πόρον.

ἐπ-ορούω, only aor. -όρουσε, *charge upon, rush to*, (a) with dat., usually in hostile signif., Γ 379; τινὶ δουρί, Π 320; in friendly signif., E 793.—(b) with acc., P 481, *spring upon* the chariot.

ἔπος, ntr. (gen. sing. wanting), ἐπεϊ, only E 879, (ϝεπ, voc), vox, *that which is spoken, word*, A 108, Σ 384, α 64; *prophetic utterance*, μ 266; in general signif. cf. vox, *promise, decree*; διακέρσαι, *baffle*, Θ 8; *threat*, τελεῖν, fulfill, Ξ 44; sententia, I 100; plur., recital, δ 597; *legend*, Υ 204; *desire*, Ξ 212; ἔπεσιν καὶ χερσίν, with *word* and *deed*; ἔργον τε ἔπος τε, β 272; ἔπος often is nearly equal to *fact, thing*, Λ 652, γ 243; λ 146, usually with verb of saying; it is to be distinguished from μῦθος, δ 597.

ἐπ-οτρύνω, prs. ipf., aor. -ώτρῡνας,

etc., impellere, (1) *drive on, excite,*
encourage, Z 439, ι 488, 561; τινά,
with inf. (τινί, only κ 531; II 524, dat.
depends on κεκλόμενος, in other parallel examples on κελεύω); πολλά, eagerly; *stir up (irritate,* τινά, θ 185), *πό-*
λεμόν τινι, against any one; ἀγγελίας,
send quickly tidings, ω 355; make haste
with, mid., furnish quickly, our cus-
tomary escort (πομπήν), θ 31.

ἐπ-ουράνιος, also dat. pl., (οὐρανός),
caelestis, *heavenly,* with θεός, Z 129;
opp. ἐπιχθόνιοι ἄνθρωποι.

ἐπ-οχήσεται, fut., (ὀχέομαι), *be car-*
ried upon, ride upon, ἵπποις, P 449.
(Il.)

ἐπ-όψεαι, -όμενος, fut. from ἐφ-οράω.
ἔπραθον, aor. from πέρθω.

ἑπτά [ᾰ], septem. ἑπτα-βόειον, *of*
seven folds of hide, septemplex, H
266. (Il.) ἑπτά-ετες, *seven years,* γ
305. (Od.) ἑπτα-καί-δεκα, septem-
decim, ε 278. ἑπτᾰ-πόδην, *seven feet*
long, O 729†. 'Επτά-πορος, river in
Mysia, flowing from Mount Ida, M 20.
ἑπτᾰ-πύλοιο, *of seven gated* (Thebes,
Δ 406).

ἔπταρεν, aor. from πταίρω. ἔπτατο,
aor. from πέτομαι.

ἑπτᾰχᾰ (διεμοιρᾶτο, divided), *into*
seven parts, ξ 434†.

ἔπω, I. act. pres. and ipf. ἔπον, *were*
making ready, μ 209; *be busy* (about,
περί, O 555); τί, Z 321, *occupied with;*
μετά τινα, *going after,* K 516.—II. mid.
prs. ipf. εἵπετο, usually without augm.
ἑπόμην, etc., fut. ἕψομαι, aor. ἕσπετο,
etc., (orig. redup. form σε-ΣΕΠ, sequi), προτέρω, accede, *draw near,* Σ
387; comitor, attend, A 424; τινί, ζ
276; ἅμα, Γ 447 (τινί, M 87, β 11).
μετά τινι, Σ 234; σύν τινι, η 304; τινά,
N 492; praesto esse, *be at hand,* Θ
140; τινί, B 675, O 204, δ 643; *what*
my strength is, and *with* what sort of
arms *I am furnished,* υ 237; πομπῆς,
πομπόν, *conduct;* with ntr. subj., *go*
with, sail after, γ 165, Γ 376,
Π 504, M 398 (*belong to,* I 513, Δ 415;
accompany, Γ 255, α 278); *correspond*
in strength, Δ 314; *follow,* with hostile
intent, τινά, Λ 154; ἀμφί τινα, Λ 474,
565. [μ 209, v. l. ἔπι instead of ἔπει.]

ἐπ-ώνυμον (ὄνομα), *by name,* I 562;
ὄνομα, was *given to him.* (Od.)

ἐπ-ῶρτο, aor. mid. from -ορνύω.

ἐπ-ώχατο, 3 pl. plupf. pass., (ἔχω),
clausae erant, *had been shut,* M
340†.

ἔρα-ζε (ἔρα), *on the ground,* P 619,
χ 20.

ἔρᾰμαι, ται, ipf. ἠράασθε, aor. ἠρά-
σάμην, (σ)σατο, ἐράσσατο, (ἔρω), τινός
(πολέμου, I 64), amans sum, *be in*
love with.

ἐραννῆς, ήν, fem., (ἐρατός), *charming,*
I 531, η 18.

ἔρᾰνος, φ, masc., *picnic,* α 226. (Od.)
ἐρά(σ)σατο, aor. from ἔραμαι.

ἐρᾰτεινός, ῆς, ήν, άς, ά, (ἐρατός),
lovely, charming, Γ 239, T 347, Γ 175,
δ 13; *pleasing* (prowess), Z 156; *wel-*
come, ι 230.

ἐρᾰτίζων, part., (ἐρατός), κρειῶν,
craving (flesh), Λ 551. (Il.)

ἐρᾰτά, ntr. pl., (ἔραμαι), *charming,*
Γ 64†.

ἐργάζεσθαι, only prs., and ipf. εἰργά-
ζετο, ἐργάζοντο, (Fέργον), *work, labor,*
τινί; *perform, bring to pass,* ἔργα; ρ
321, do what is proper; ω 210, did
what it pleased him to command;
wrought, γ 435.

ἔργαθεν and ἐέργαθεν, ipf., (Fέργω),
τὶ ἀπό τινος, *cut off,* E 147. (Il.)

ἔργον, sing. and pl., (Fέργον, Α 395,
Eng. work), (1) facinus, *deed,* M
366, I 443, α 338; *shocking deed,* γ 265,
275, π 346, φ 26, ω 426; *work,* opera,
M 412; *action,* B 436; *task,* Z 324,
492, α 356 (T 133, unseemly toil = bondage); *action,* opp. deliberation, 1 374;
opp. word, A 395, 504; opp. discussion,
T 242; *state of the case,* τ 391.—(2)
opus, tasks, ι 250, ξ 228; φιλοτήσια,
love affairs; ἔργα τέτυκται τινός, opus
est re.—(3) *work in field, husbandry,*
π 140, 144; ἀνδρῶν βοῶν, κ 98, i. e.
neither plough-*land* nor vineyard;
ἀνθρώπων, αἰζηῶν, = rura, *fields,* B
751; (paterna), β 127, cf. 22, paternal estates; bona, ἀέξεται, *property* in-
creases which is in my charge, ξ 66.
—(4) *severe combat,* Δ 470, M 271;
μέγα ἄρηος, Λ 734; μάχης, Z 522.—
(5) opera, *what is wrought or made,*
works of skill, N 432, I 128, 390, ζ 234;
women's *works,* Σ 289; of Hephaistos,
ο 117; *accomplishments,* θ 245.—(6)
res, A 294, Σ 77, Φ 19, δ 663; *matter,*
B 252, Λ 573, X 450, Γ 321; ἀμήχανα,
evil without remedy.

ἔργω (Fέργω), act. prs. εἴργουσι, aor. ἔρξαν, pass. prs. ἐργομένη, aor. ἐρχθέντα, pf. ἔρχαται, plupf. ἔρχατο, also act. prs. ἐέργει, ουσι, ων, ipf. ἔεργε, ον, pass. pres. ἐεργόμενοι, part., plupf. ἐέρχατο, press, (1) shut in, ἐντός (with gen.), τι, ξ 411, Φ 282, κ 283; ἐκ, outside of, Θ 213 ; were covered, P 354.—(2) hold off, ἀμφίς,utroque; τῆλε,procul; τινός, ἀπό τινος, ἐκτός, keep away from; μ 219, separate; τινός, Ν 525 ; cutting off, parting, Μ 201 ; force back, Π 395. (Ε 89, better reading ἐερμέναι.)

ἔρδω (Fέργͮω), prs. ipf. ἔρδομεν, ον, iter. -δεσκες, ε, pf. ἐοργώς, plupf. ἐώργει, fut. ἔρξω, ἔμεν, aor. ἔρξαν, imp. ἔρξον, inf. ἔρξαι, perform, sacrifice, deeds, β 236 ; treat well, o 360; joined with τελευτᾶν, λ 80, α 293; τί τινι, o 360, υ 314 ; κακόν τινα, Ε 175.

ἐρεβεννή, ῇ, ῶν, (ἔρεβος), ater,black, Ι 474. (Il.)

ἐρέβινθοι, pl., chickpeas, Ν 589†.

ἔρεβος, gen. ἐρέβευς, ἐρέβεσφι, realm of darkness (of the lower world), ἐρεβόσδε, to Erebos, υ 356, Π 327.

ἐρεείνεις, ε, prs., and ipf. ἐρέεινεν, (ἔρω),ask, absol., Γ 191,η 31 ; (ἐπέεσσι) τινά, ε 85 ; τινά τι ; ἀμφί τινι, asked after—, ω 262; ipf. mid. μύθῳ,ρ 305.

ἐρεθίζω, only prs., ipf. ἐρέθιζον, (ἔρις), irritate, Α 32, Ω 560.

ἐρέθω (ἔρις), only prs., excite; δ 813, disquiet.

ἐρείδοντες, prs., ipf. ἔρειδε, aor. ἔρεισε, mid. -σατο, -σάμενος, and pass.—(1) press against, support firmly, lean upon, τὶ πρός (περί) τι, (ἐπί) τινι ; pass. pf. ἐρήρεισται, have been rammed down upon; Ψ 284, rest upon (the ground, οὔδει); plupf. ἐρηρέδατο, were set (firmly); ἠρήρειστο, stuck fast.—(2) press upon, Ν 131 ; τινά, beset (with missiles); crowd thickly together, ἀλλήλοισιν.—(3) mid., support one's self on one's spear, τινί ; χειρὶ γαίῃ, lean with the hand on the earth ; ἐρισθείς, supporting one's self; struggle against each other, Ψ 735 ; ἐρισάμενος, having planted himself firmly.

ἐρεικόμενος, prs. part. pass., and aor. ἤρικε, rend (frangi), περὶ δουρί, pierced by the spear, Ν 441. (Il.)

ἔρειο, ἐρείομεν, see ἔρω II.

ἐρείπω (ripa?), fall, tumble, (1) trans. prs. and ipf. ἔρειπε, tear down, Ο 361 ; pass. plupf. ἐρέριπτο ; (2) intr. aor. ἤριπε, ἐρίπῃσι, ἐριπούσα πρηνής, forwards, ἐξοπίσω, backwards, γνύξ, on the knee, Υ 417.

Ἐρεμβοί, a fabled folk, δ 84†.

ἐρεμνή, ήν, (ἔρεβος), atrae, dark, black, Μ 375, ω 106.

ἔρεξα, aor. from ῥέζω.

ἐρέοντο, see ἔρω II.

ἐρεπτόμενοι, ους, depascentes, feeding upon; of lotus-eaters, ι 97.

ἐρέριπτο, plupf. pass. from ἐρείπω.

ἐρέσσαι, see ἔρω I.

ἐρεσσέμεναι, inf. pr., and ipf. ἔρεσσον, (ἐρετμός), remigare, row, I 361.

ἐρέται, pl., ἐρέτης, nom. ὁ (ἐρετμός), remiges, rowers, A 142.

Ἐρετμεύς, a Phaiakian, θ 112.

ἐρετμόν, pl. ά, οῖς, (remus, Eng. rudder), oar, λ 77. (The cut, from drawing on antique vase, represents a

different way of working the oars from that of the Homeric age; see cut 126.)

ἐρεύγομαι, prs., ipf. ἐρεύγετο, aor. ἤρυγε, (ructare), evomere, Π 162; ι 374, belched forth ; roar (of sea, cattle).

Ἐρευθαλίων, leader of the Arkadians, slain by Nestor, H 136.

ἐρεύθων, part., aor. ἐρεῦσαι, (ἐρυθρός, rutilus), redden, dye, with blood, Λ 394. (Il.)

ἐρευνάω (-άων), prs., ipf. ἐρεύνα, track, Σ 321 ; seek, χ 180.

Ἐρεχθεύς, Erechtheus, a national hero of the Athenians, Β 547, η 81.

ἐρέχθων, part., pass. ἐρεχθομένην, rack, waste, ε 83; buffet about, Ψ 317.

ἐρέω, see (1) εἴρω, say.—(2) ἔρω, ask.

ἔρημον, η, ην, α, abandoned; Ε 140, desolate.

ἐρηρέδαται, το, pf. and plupf. from ἐρείδω;

ἐρητύειν, ipf. ἐρήτὕε, pass. ἐρητὕεται, το, [elsewh. ὔ], aor. ἐρητύσειε, iter. ἐρητύσασκε, pass. ἐρήτυθεν, 3 pl., hold back, check, Λ 567, Β 164 ; mid. and aor. pass. restrain one's self, Ν 280 ; remain, Β 99 ; allow itself to be controlled, I 462 ; trans. only Ο 723.

ἐρι-, like ἀρι-, and περ-, strengthening prefix, very, much.

ἐρι-αύχενες, ας, with high-arching necks, Λ 159. (Il.)

ἐρι-βρεμέτεω, gen. from -έτης, (βρέμω), loud thundering, Ν 624†.

ἐρι-βῶλᾶκος, ι, α = ἐρι-βῶλου, ον, no nom., (βῶλος), with large, thick clods, epithet of fertile, fruitful regions, ν 235, ε 34. (Il.)

ἐρί-γδουπος, ου, οιο, οι = ἐρι-δούπου, ῳ, ων, (δοῦπος), loud thundering, roaring, of river, shore ; resounding, of vaulted porch ; echoing, of horses' tread, Λ 152.

ἐρῐδαινέμεν, only prs. and aor. ἐριδήσασθαι, Ψ 792, (ἔρις), certare, quarrel, contend, τινί, ἀντία πάντων, over, about something ; ἕνεκά τινος, περὶ πτωχῶν, with words or by deeds, in rivalry, β 206, Π 765.

ἐριδμαίνωσι, subj., (ἔρις), irritate, Π 260†.

ἐρι-δούπου, etc., see ἐρί-γδουπος.

ἐριζέμεν, prs., ipf. ἔριζε, iter. ἐρίζεσκον, aor. ἐρίσωσιν, ἐρί(σ)σειε, ειαν, ἐρίσαντε, also mid. aor. ἐρίσσεται, (ἔρις), certare, contend with, vie with, some one, τινί, in respect to something, τί, Ι 389, ε 213 ; τινί, δ 80, ο 321 ; περὶ τινος, e. g. concerning eloquence, with inf., σ 38 ; wrangle, contend for fair division of property, Μ 423 ; be wroth with, τινί, Ν 109.

ἐρί-ηρος, ον, pl. -ες, ας, (ἀρηρώς), strongly attached, trusty, ἑταῖρος, ἀοιδόν, α 346.

ἐρι-θηλές, έων, έας, (θάλλω), luxuriant (blooming, verdant), Ε 90. (Il.)

ἔρϊθοι, οισιν, reapers, Σ 550, 560.

ἐρι-κυδέος, έα, fem. acc., (κῦδος), famous, glorious, of gods ; then θεῶν ὥρα, ἥβης, δαῖτα, κ 182.

ἐρι-μύκων, ους, gen. acc., (μυκάομαι), loud bellowing, βοῦς, Ψ 775.

ἐρινεός, όν, caprificus, wi'd fig-tree, μ 103 ; Il. the great wild fig-tree, near the sources of the Skamandros, Ζ 433.

ἐρινόν, τό = ἐρινεός, reading of Aristarchus in ε 281†.

Ἐρινύς, pl. ύες, ύσιν, ύας = ῦς, the Erinyes, subterranean powers or goddesses, who fulfill curses and punish crimes, Ι 571. (See cut.)

ἔριον, see εἴρια.

ἐρι-ούνης and -ούνιος, ον, (ὀνίνημι), helpful, epithet of Hermes ; also subst. Helper, Ω 440.

ἔρις, ῐδος, ῐδι, ῐδα, and ἔρῑν, pl. ἔρῐδας, —(1) strife, quarrel, certamen, iurgium, rixa, pugna, Ε 732; ἔριδος νεῖκος, Ρ 384 ; Α 8, ἔριδι ξυν. μάχ., bring together in strife, cf. Υ 134, Υ 251 ; Υ 55, let loose dire strife among them ; enmity (heart-consuming, Η 210).—(2) rivalry, προφέρουσαι, displaying rivalry = in emulation ; θ 210, reveals to his host his longing for contests ; ἐξ ἔριδος, in combat.—(3) Eris or Discord personified, Δ 440, Λ 73.

ἐρι-σθενέος, gen., (σθένος), mighty, all-powerful, Zeus, Τ 355.

ἔρισμα (ἐρίζω), occasion of variance, Δ 38†.

ἐρι-στάφὔλον, acc., (σταφυλή), large-clustered, epithet of wine, ι 111, 358.

ἐρι-τίμοιο, ον, (τῑμή), highly prized, precious, Β 447 (Il.)

ἐρίφων, gen. pl.. οισι, ους, haedorum, kids. ι 220. [ι]

Ἐρι-φύλη, wife and betrayer of Amphiaraos, λ 326†. [ῡ]

Ἐρι-χθόνιος, son of Dardanos, father of Tros, Υ 219, 230.

Ἐριῶπις, wife of Oileus, step-mother of Medon, Ν 697.

ἑρκείου, gen., (ἕρκος), protector of the enclosure or court, (epithet of Zeus, whose altar stood in court ; see plate III., at end of volume), χ 335†.

ἑρκίον (ἕρκος) αὐλῆς, wall or hedge of court, Ι 476, σ 102. [ι]

ἕρκος, sing., and pl. ἕρκεα, εσι, (1) enclosure, hedge, railing or wall, around fields, gardens, or court-yard of house, π 341, υ 164; ὀδόντων, barrier, line of the teeth, Δ 350, κ 328; χαλκείψ = armatorum, Ο 567. — (2) safeguard, defense (against, gen.), also as epithet of heroes, Α 284, Δ 299.

I. ἕρμα, pl. ατα, (ὅρμος, σειρά, series), pendants, ear-rings, prob. strings of beads, pl. (see cut to the left, an Athenian tetradrachm; see cut to the right, Sicilian dekadrachm); ὀδυνάων, chain = succession of sharp pangs, Δ 117.

II. ἕρμα, pl. ατα, (of doubtful connection with preceding; columen, (1) props, set in a row, on which the ship was supported when drawn up on shore, Α 486.—(2) πύληος. pillar, prop of the city, Π 549.

Ἕρμαιος λόφος, hill of Hermes, offshoot of Mount Neion in Ithaka, π 471†.

Ἑρμῆς, acc. ῆν, and Ἑρμείας, είαο =είω, ἑᾳ, είαν, εία, Hermes, the messenger of the gods, διάκτορος; (in Od.), son of Maia, ξ 435; guide of Priamos, Ω 457; also escort of the dead, ω 1; cf. ἐριούνιος, σῶκος, ἀκάκητα, χρυσόρραπις, ἐύσκοπον.

Ἑρμιόνη, (1) daughter of Menelaos and of Helene, δ 14.—(2) city in Argolis, Β 560.

ἑρμῖνα, acc., pl. -ῖσιν, (II. ἕρμα), bed-posts, θ 278. (Od.)

Ἕρμος, river in Aiolis, Υ 392.

ἔρνος, dat. ει, ntr., (ὄρνυμι), sprig, shoot, germen, ἐριθηλές, blooming, Ρ 53 (ξ 175, ζ 163, Σ 56, symbol of youthful grace and beauty).

ἕρξω, fut. from ἔρδω.

ἔρομαι, see εἴρω.

ἔρος, ψ, ον, nom. also ἔρως, Γ 442, Ξ 294, love, passion, τινός; desiderium, appetitus, Α 469; ἐξ ἔρον εἶναι, take away, the wish for—, satiate with—, τινός.

ἑρπετά (ἕρπω), moving, living beings, δ 418†.

ἑρπύζων, οντα, part., (ἕρπω), creeping, crawling, Ψ 225; from grief or age.

ἕρπω, only prs., and ipf. εἷρπον, (serpo), walk, move, ρ 158, Ρ 447.

ἑρράδαται, pf. pass. from ῥαίνω.

ἔρριγα, ῃσε, see ῥιγέω.

ἔρρε, έτω, ετε, imp., and ἔρρων, οντι, (ῥέρρω), go, δ 367; hobble about, Σ 421; sail, Θ 239; imp. begone! off with thee! abi in malam rem.

ἔρση, αι, and ἑέρση, αι, ας, ros, pl. dew-drops, stained with blood, Λ 53; ι 222, new-born lambs.

ἑρσήεις, εντα, (ἔρση), dewy, fresh, recens, of lotus, Ξ 348; of Hektor's corpse, Ω.

ἐρύγμηλον, acc., (ἐρεύγομαι), mugientem, bellowing, Σ 580†.

ἐρυγόντα, aor. from ἐρεύγομαι.

ἐρύθαίνετο, ipf. pass., (ἐρυθρός), was reddened, Κ 484. (Il.)

Ἐρυθῖνοι, place in Paphlagonia, Β 855.

Ἐρύθραι, town in Boiotia, Β 499.

ἐρυθρός, όν, άς, (rutilus, Eng. ruddy), red, ruddy, Ι 365.

ἐρυκακέειν, -κακον, see ἐρύκω.

ἐρύκανε, κ 429, better ἐρύκακε.

ἐρῡκανόωσι, subj. prs. from ἐρυκανάω, (ἐρύκω), retinebunt, detain, α 199†.

ἐρύκω, pres., ipf. ἔρυκε, fut. ἐρύξω, aor. ἔρυξε, and red. ἠρύκακε, ἐρύκακε, ετε, κάκοι, κακέειν, retinere, restrain, detain, Ζ 217, λ 105; hold fast, Θ 317; check, Υ 268; hold back, ο 68, γ 144; detain, ἵππους, Ε 262, 321; Γ 113, held, i. e. placed them in ranks; arcere, keep away, τ 16, Θ 178, Π 369, Η 342, τινὰ μάχης, from the battle; τινί τι, keep off, ε 166, Ο 450; separare, Κ 161; mid. pres. cessare, tarry, δ 466, Ψ 443; in Μ 285 = act. restrains = melts.

Ἐρύλαος, a Trojan, slain by Patroklos, Π 411†.

ἐρύμα (ῥύομαι) χροός, protection for his body, Δ 137†.

Ἐρύμανθος, mountain in Arkadia, ζ 103†.

Ἐρύμας, αντος, a Trojan, (1) slain by Idomeneus, Π 345; (2) by Patroklos, Π 415.

ἐρύομαι (σρυ, σερϜ, servo, Ω 430, ξ 107, ο 35), ἐρύεσθαι, (sync. ἐρῦσθαι, εἰρῦσθαι, as also ipf. ἔρυσο, το, and εἴρυτο, ντο), pr. ipf., fut. and aor. (σ and σσ); equally common also, parallel forms εἰρυ-, servare, preserve, shield, (1) τινά, P 327; watch, κ 444, ρ 429, ψ 229, 151, (against outbreak of indignation, Ω 584); watch over, γ 268; observare, respect, A 216; lie in wait for, π 463.—(2) ward off, τι, B 859, E 538, Ψ 819; defend one's self against, Θ 143; τινί, protect [ῡ in fut. and aor. (exc. ξ 279) on acc. of σσ; in sync. forms, by contraction].

ἐρῦσ-άρματες, ταις, (ἐρύω, ἅρμα), chariot-drawing, O 354. (Il.)

ἐρυσί-πτολι, see ῥυσί-πτολι.

ἐρύω, ἐρύουσι, (Ϝερύω, verro, the Ϝ often disregarded, augm. εἰ); act. prs. ipf., fut. (σσ, also without σ, Λ 454), aor., pass. pf. εἰρύαται, -ὑμεναι, plupf. εἴρῦτο, υντο; mid. prs. fut. (also ἐρύεσθαι), aor., vellere, trahere, draw; ἔθεν ἄσσον, nearer to him; αὖ, lift up; πάλιν, draw back, E 836; hoist aloft, χ 176; drag off, νεκρόν; drag behind chariot, Ω 16; draw the bow string, O 464 (αὖ, Θ 325); evellere, Φ 175, E 110; convellere, M 258, 261; lacerare, O 351; τινὰ χλαίνης, by the mantle. — Mid. reflexive, Ξ 79, nostras; χ 90, suum; Ξ 422, to their side; φ 125, toward one's self (see cut No. 37); κ 165, to me; νεκρόν, μάχης, drag out of the combat after having slain, E 456, P 161. [ῡ even in fut. and aor., exc. Θ 21, Π 863, X 351, β 389; only through σσ; also pf. plupf. pass. ῡ, exc. Δ 248.]

ἔρχαται, το, pf. plupf. pass. from ἔργω.

ἐρχατόωντο, ipf. pass., (ἐρχατάω, ἔρχαται), were penned up, ξ 15†.

ἐρχθέντα, see ἔργω.

ἔρχομαι, prs., imp. also ἔρχευ, fut. ἐλεύσομαι, aor. ἤλθον (indic. also ἤλυθον, inf. also ἐλθέμεν, μεναι), pf. εἰλήλουθα, θας, θεν, θας (O 81, εἰληλουθώς), plupf. εἰληλούθει, Δ 520, (1) go, vado, ι 448, εἰς ἀγορήν, ἀγορήνδε; march, B

457; ἐπὶ πολλὴν γαῖαν, journey far; incedere, move, H 208; χαμαί, on the ground; fly, P 755, Π 478; sink, Ω 82; πεδίοιο, through the plain; μετ᾽ ἄεθλα, to the games; μετά (τι, for something; τινα, to some one, sectari) ἅμα τινί, comitari; πρός τι, ἐπί τινα, accedere; ὁδόν, A 151; ἐξεσίην, go on an embassy, Ω 235; imp. ἔρχεο, also agedum, ψ 254, ρ 529, 544.—(2) come, K 540, α 408; παρά, ἀπό, ἔκ τινος, ὑπὸ Ἴλιον, ἄντην, forward; ἀγχί(μολόν τινι), σχεδόν, ἐγγύθεν, σχεδόθεν, near; ἄντιον, ἄντα τινός, obviam, to meet; ἄντιος, adversus; ἄγγελος = ἀγγελίης, as messenger; ἀμοιβοί, in exchange; ἐπίρροθος, ἐπίκουρος, as helper; φάος, succor; πεζός, on foot; ἐναργής, visibly, in bodily form; μόρσιμος, destined for her; ὑποχείριος, in the power of; ἐς ὁρμὴν ἔγχεος, within spear-throw; ἐκ βελέων, out of reach of weapons; θέων, ουσα, quickly; φθάμενος, before. ἐλθών, often used pictorially to render the description more vivid, B 147, Π 521.—Of inanimate objects, summer, λ 192; dawn, μ 142; night, Ξ 77; star, ν 94; death, λ 135; age, ν 60; marriage, ζ 288; dream, B 56; storm, μ 288; stream of blood, χ 18, σ 97.—(3) go forth, P 741, Φ 62, Ψ 737, ρ 599; ἄλλῃ(η), away=is lost, λ 120; proficisci, set out, E 150, 198; redire, return (ἀὖ, O 550, K 211; πάλιν, I 408, τ 533), Γ 428, Θ 12, M 225, π 23, 131, 206, = referri, be brought back, Σ 180; ἄλγος, depart from, X 43.—Also with simple acc., A 322, δ 82, ξ 167; or -δε, ξ 373, κ 320; λέχοσδε, to bed; χορόνδε=εἰς χορόν, to the dance; with part. fut. denoting intention or purpose, α 281, κ 284, cf. Ξ 304, Ω 240.

ἘΡΩ, I. mid. aor. subj. ἐρώμεθα, opt. ἔροιτο, imp. ἔρειο; inf. ἐρέσθαι. — II. pres. ἐρέων, subj. ἐρείομεν, opt. ἐρέοιμι, μεν; mid. pres. subj. ἐρώμαι, ἐρέεσθαι, ipf. ἐρέοντο.—III. mid. prs. εἴρομαι, εαι, subj. εἴρωμαι, ηται, ὥμεθα, imp. εἴρεο, inf. εἴρεσθαι, part. εἰρόμενος, α, γ, αι, ipf. εἴρετο, οντο, fut. εἰρήσομαι, εἴρηαι, α 188, quaerere, seek, φ 31; elsewh. ask, τινά, A 553, α 284, τί, after something, H 128; τινὰ ἔπος ἄλλο, something else of one, γ 243; τινὰ δίκας, seek justice at one's hands; ask

one *after*, τινά τινα, Κ 416, Ω 390;
περί τι, ρ 571; περί τινος, a 405;
ἀμφὶ πόσει, τ 95; Α 513, *pray, implore.*

ἔρῳ, see ἔρος.

ἐρῳδιόν, acc., ardeam, *heron*, Κ 274†.

1. **ἐρωέω** (1. ἐρωή), fut. ἤσει, fluere, *flow*, Α 303 and π 441.

2. **ἐρωέω** (2. ἐρωή), imp. **ἐρώει**, εἴτω, fut. ἤσουσι, aor. inf. ἦσαι, *cease*, τινός, Τ 170; with ὀπίσσω, Ψ 433, fall back; but Ν 57, trans. *you would drive back.*

1. **ἐρωή**, ῇ, ἤν, (ῥώομαι, ῥέω, ruo), impetus, *sweep*, Ν 590 ; *power*, Γ 62; shower of weapons, Δ 542 (as measure of distance, flight of a spear, Ψ 529).

2. **ἐρωή** (ἐρωϜή, Old Ger. ruowa), πολέμου, *cessation, pause*, Π 302, Ρ 761.

ἔρως, see ἔρος.

ἐρωτάω, see εἰρωτᾷς.

ἐσ-, see also εἰσ-.

ἐσ-αθρέω, aor. **ἐσ-αθρήσειεν**, conspiceret, *descry*, Γ 450†.

ἐσ-ακούω, aor. **ἐσάκουσε**, *give ear*, Θ 97.

ἐσ-άλλομαι, aor. -ήλατο, Π 558, and 2 aor. -ᾶλτο, -αλλόμενοι, irrumpere, *burst into*, τεῖχος, πύλας.

ἔσβην, εσεν, see σβέννυμι.

ἐσ-δέρκομαι, only aor. -έδρακον, εν, conspexit, adspexit, Ω 223 and (Od.).

ἐσ-δύνω, only ipf. ἐς τεύχεα **ἔδυνον**, and aor. δύντε, induere, *put on*, also fut. **ἐσδύσεαι**, te immiscebis, *take a part in*, ἀκοντιστύν, Ψ 622.

ἐσ-έρχεο, see εἰσ-έρχεο.

ἐσ-ήλατο, aor. from ἐσ-άλλομαι.

ἔσθην, aor. pass. from ἕννυμι.

ἐσθής, ῆτος, ῆτι, ῆτα, (Ϝεσθ., vestis), *clothing, clothes*, α 165, ζ 74 ; *garments* given by the Nereids, ω 67 ; *bed-clothing*, ψ 290. (Od.)

ἔσθος, τό = foreg., *garment*, Ω 94†.

ἐσθίω, prs., ipf. **ἤσθιον**, ε, (fut. see ἔδω), aor. ἔφαγον (φάγον), inf. φαγέμεν, ἔειν, etc.. pass. ἐσθίεται, edere, *eat*, τί ; e t of, τινός, ι 102 ; *consume*, also of fire ; *devour*, μ 310 ; *partake of food*, ω 254, ρ 478 ; δ 318, is being devoured.

ἐσθλός, ή, όν, etc., (ἐστί, ἐύ), *excellent, glorious*, κλέος ; *valiant*, Δ 458, Ζ 443, Ι 319, Ν 733; *brave*, Π 837, Ω 167; *noble, good*, Ι 514, Ο 203, ζ 182, η 73,

Α 108, Ζ 489, θ 553 ; ntr., *good, ble-sing*, Ω 530, ο 488; *costly*, Κ 213; κ 523, ἐσθλά, *valuables.*

ἔσ-θορε, aor., (θρώσκω), *sprung in*, Μ 462, Φ 18.

ἔσθω, inf. **ἐσθέμεναι**, ipf. ἦσθε = ἐσθίω, *eat, partake of food*, ε 94, Θ 231, Ω 476 ; *consume*, β 75 ; *devour*, ι 479.

ἐσ-ιδέσθην, ἰδέσκεν, ἴδηται, etc., see εἰσ-οράω.

ἐσ-ιέμεναι, prs. part. mid., (ἵημι), *hurrying into*, χ 470†.

ἐσ-ίζηται, subj., (ἵζομαι), *places himself in* the ambuscade, Ν 285†.

ἐς ἐκάλέσσατο, aor., (καλέω), *called in his* wife, Ω 193†.

ἐσ-κατά-βαίνων, permeans, *traverse*, ω 222†.

ἔσκον, εν, see εἰμί.

ἐσ-εμάσσατο, aor., (μαίομαι), θυμόν, *distressed* my heart, Ρ 564, Υ 425.

ἐσ-όψομαι, εται, fut. from εἰσ-οράω.

ἐσπέριος, οι, ων, ους, (ἕσπερος), vespertinus, *in the evening*, Φ 560; *of the west*, θ 29. (Od.)

ἕσπερος, ον, (vesper), *evening;* ἀστήρ, evening star; ποτὶ ἕσπερα (ntr. pl.), sub vesperam, *toward evening*, ρ 191.

ἔσπετε, imp. red. aor., see ἔσπω.

ἐσπόμεθα, etc., red. aor., see ἕπομαι.

ἔσσα, αι, ἄμενος, etc., aor. from ἕννυμι.

ἔσσαι, aor. inf. from ἕζω. **ἔσσεαι**, εῖται, ἐσσί, ἐσσ' = ἔσσο, see εἰμί. **ἐσσεύοντο**, see σεύω. **ἔσσο**, aor. mid. from ἕννυμι. **ἔσσυνται**, etc., pf. pass. from σεύω.

ἐσσυμένως (σεύω), raptim, *hastily*, Ψ 55, ξ 347.

ἔστάμεν, 1 pl., ἔστἄν, 3 pl. aor., **ἔστἄμεν**, 1 pl. ἐστάμεν, inf. pf., **ἔστατον**, du. pf. plupf., **ἔστασαν**, 3 pl. plupf. from ἵσταμαι. **ἔστο**, plupf. pass. from ἕννυμι. **ἔστρωμαι**, το, pf. plupf. pass. from στορέννυμι.

ἔστορι, dat., *bolt at end of pole of chariot, yoke-pin*, Ω 272†. (See cut in follg. page, at centre ; cf. also No. 49.)

ἐσ-φέρεται, prs. mid., ipf. act. **ἔσφε-ρον**, *were carrying in*, η 6 ; *draws into its current*, Λ 495.

ἐσ-φόρεον, ipf., (φορέω), inferebant, *were carrying in*, τ 32 ; ὕδωρ, in aquam, into the water. (Od.)

ἔσχ', β 346 = ἔσκε, see εἰμί; elsewh. (Il.) aor. from ἔχω.

ἐσχάρη, dat., αι, ὄφιν, *portable hearth*

or *basin of coals*, ε 59, ζ 305, υ 123; in Odysseus's house *stationary fire-place*, yet portable fire-basins were doubtless common then as now in the East. (See cut No. 90; cf. also Pompeian warming-pan and water-warmer represented in the adjoining cut.) πυρὸς ἐσχάραι, *watch-fires*, K 418.

ἐσχατιῆς, ῦ, ήν, (ἔσχατος), or ac, *border, edge, remotest part ; subst.* ξ 104, *remotest estate.*

ἔσχατον, acc., ἔσχατοι, (ἐξ), extremi; ἄλλων, ceteris exteriores, *outside of* the others, K 434; ἔσχατα, *at the outside.*

ἐσχατόωντα, ὅωσα, αν, (ἔσχατος), extrema, of cities, B 508, 616. *frontier town ;* K 206, extra vagantem, *straggler.*

ἰσ-χέω, only aor. mid. ἐσ-έχυντο, *poured, rushed in at,* M 470. (Il.)

ἔσχον, εν, ετο, etc., see ἔχω.

ἔσω = εἴσω.

ἐταίρη, ην, and ἐτάρη, (ἔτᾱρος), socia, *companion,* attendant, I 2, Δ 441, ρ 271.

ἐταιρίσσαι, aor. act., -σσαιτο, mid., (ἐταιρίζω), τινί, comitari, *attend ;* mid. τινά, *take as one's companion,* N 456. (Il.)

ἑταῖρος, no voc., and ἔτᾰρος, οιο, etc., du. ω, pl. adj., (ἐτης), sociatus, ἀνήρ, λαοί; Ἕκτορι; subst. socius, *companion ; comrade,* Σ 80 : in battle, danger, journey, esp. of followers of Odysseus in Od.

ἐτεθήπεα, plupf., see ταφών.

Ἐτεοκλείης, βίης = Eteoclis, Δ 386†; cf. 375 sqq., *Eteokles, son* of Oidipus and Epikaste.

Ἐτεό-κρητες, *genuine, primitive Kretans,* τ 176†.

ἐτεόν, ntr., (ἐστί), verum, *the truth,* B 300, O 53; ὡς ἐ. περ, these things ye must have heard, that they are in fact *true,* Ξ 125; ἐτεὰ νεικεῖν, utter many *just reproaches ;* εἰ ἐτεόν (also with γέ, δή), if 'tis (really indeed) *true,* E 104 (M 217, γ 122, H 359) ; always at beginning or end of verse.

ἐτερ-αλκέα, acc., (ἕτερος, ἀλκή), νίκην, χ 236 (elsewh. Il.), *decisive; δῆμον, able to change the fortune of the fight,* O 738.

ἐτερ-ήμεροι (ἡμέρα), diebus alternantes, *on alternate days,* Λ 303†.

ἕτερος, η, ον, etc., (1) alter, plur. alteri, *other party,* Λ 71 (Υ 210, one set of parents); ἑτέρηφι = ἑτέρῃ, altera manu, γ 441, Π 734; doubled =unus—alter, *one—the other,* Γ 103; corresponds freq. to ἄλλος, N 731, I 313; joined with pron. ὁ, X 151, cf. υ 132 ; elliptically, Ω 528, H 420.—(2) secundus, M 93, κ 354, ν 69.—(3) alius, ι 302, I 302; ρ 266, *one part is* joined to another.

ἑτέρσετο, see τερσαίνω.

ἑτέρωθεν, ex altera parte, *from the other side ; on the other side,* H 311, Γ 230.

ἑτέρωθΐ, *on the other side ; elsewhere,* δ 531, O 348; corresponds to ἔνθεν, μ 235; = *from far away,* E 351.

ἑτέρως, aliter, *otherwise,* α 234†.

ἑτέρωσε, *in the other direction,* Δ 492, τ 470; *to one side,* Θ 306, 308 ; *in another direction=away,* Ψ 231; π 179, looked away.

ἐτέταλτο, see ἐπι-τέλλω. ἐτετεύχατο, plupf. pass., see τεύχω. ἔτετμεν, see τέτμον. ἐτέτυκτο, see τεύχω.

Ἐτεωνεύς Βοηθοΐδης, companion-at-arms of Menelaos, δ 22. (Od.)

Ἐτεωνός, town in Boiotia, B 497†.

ἔται, ῃσι, ας, pl., (Fέται = σΓέται, sui), *friends, retainers,* δ 3.

ἐτήτῦμος, ον, (ἔτυμος), *truthful,* messenger, speech, words, ν 232; *real,* γ 241; ntr.=profecto, *actually, really,* A 558, Σ 128, εἰ δὴ καὶ πάμπαν ἐ., but if now even quite without doubt, N 111.

ἔτι (et, etiam), *still, yet*, (1) temporal continuance, B 344 sq., υ 12; ἔτι τυτθὸν ἰόντα; ἔτι καὶ νῦν, *even now once more*, A 455; *still*, B 344; οὐ–ἔτι, non iam, *no longer*, see οὐκέτι.—(2) strengthening, ἔτι καί, *even, still more*, B 229; πρὸς δ' ἔτι καὶ τόδε μεῖζον ἐνὶ φρεσί, π 291; with comparatives, μᾶλλον, ἄλλος, Z 411; ἕτερον, ξ 325. [⏑⏑; ⏑– before δήν, δηρόν; see these words.]

ἔτλην, ης, η, ητε, see τλῆναι.

ἑτοιμάζω, only aor. imp. ἑτοιμάσατε, άτω, and mid. 1 aor. -ἄσαντο, and opt. -άσαιντο =-ασαίατο, *make ready, prepare, provide*, A 118, ν 184.

ἑτοῖμος, η, α, adj., praesto, (1) *ready, at hand*, ὀνείατα; *feasible*, μῆτις. —(2) *evident, certain*, Ξ 53, Σ 96, θ 384.

ἔτορε, see τορέω.

ἔτος, εος, εῖ, ει; εα, ἑων, (Fέτος, vetus), annus, *year*; ἐπιπλόμενον, coming; περιτελλομένου, *as the year came round*; προτέρων, *in by-gone years*, Λ 691.

ἔτραπε, etc., see τρέπω.

ἔτραφεν, aor. pass. -ἐτην, aor act. from τρέφω.

ἔτυμον, α, οισι, ntr., (ἐτεός), verum (dicere, K 534), pl., *truth*, τ 203; 567; bring *accomplishment; ἔτυμον, really*, ψ 26; οὐ ἔτ., falso, Ψ 440.

ἐτώσιον, α, (Fετώσ.), vanum, *fruitless*, ἔγχος, βέλεα.

εὖ, ἐΰ, (for ἐσύ, ntr. from ἐΰς), and ἠΰ, *good* (in widest signif.), (1) adv., *well, skilfully, carefully*, ν 20; joined with κατὰ κόσμον, *fitly*, in due form; καὶ ἐπισταμένως, εἰδέναι, γνῶναι, etc.; εὖφρονεῖν, *well advising, intelligent*, A 73.—(2) *morally well*, βάζουσι, φρονεῖν, bene velle, η 74; ἔρδειν τινά, bene facere.—(3) feliciter, *prosperously*, A 19, B 253.—(4) with ναιόμενος, *well inhabited, habitable*, so also ναιετάωσα; strengthening = *quite*, before πάντες, μάλα.—(5) in composition, before two consonants or a double consonant, usually ἐϋ-, elsewh. εὐ-.

εὖ = οὗ, sui.

εὐ-αγγέλιον (ἄγγελος), *reward for good tidings*, ξ 152, 166.

εὔαδε = ἐϜαδε, aor. from ἀνδάνω, placuit, *pleased*.

Εὐ-αιμονίδης, son of Εὐαίμων, Eurypylos, grandson of Ormenos, E 76, H 167. (Il.)

εὐ-ανθέι, dat., nom. -ανθής, (ἄνθος), λάχνῃ, with *luxuriant, abundant* down, λ 320†.

Εὐ-άνθης, father of Maron, ι 197†.

Εὔ-βοια, island of the Abantes, B 536, γ 174, η 321.

εὔ-βοτος, *abounding in fine cattle*, ο 406†.

εὔγματα, pl., (εὔχομαι), κενά, *empty boastings*, χ 249.

ἐυ-γνάμπτοις, dat. pl., (γνάμπτω), *gracefully bent*, σ 294†.

εὐ-δείελος, ον, ον, (δέελος, δῆλος), *clearly-*, or *far-seen;* epithet of islands, esp. of Ithaka, β 167. (Od.)

ἐυ-δικίας, acc., (δίκη), ἀνέχῃσι, *maintains justice*, τ 111†.

ἐυ-δμήτου, οιο, ῳ, ον, ων, ους, (δέμω), *well built, well fashioned;* wall, altar, A 448, η 100.

εὔδω, pres. subj. 2 sing. εὔδῃσθα, ipf. εὗδον, iter. εὕδεσκε, *sleep*, sweet sleep, *sleep of death*, Ξ 482; be still, E 524.

Εὔ-δωρος, son of Hermes and of Polymele; chief of Myrmidons, Π 186, 179.

εὐ-ειδέα, acc., (εἶδος), *well shaped beautiful*, Γ 48†.

εὐ-εργεσίη, ας, (ἔργον), *well-doing, kindness*, χ 235, 374†.

εὐ-εργής, έος, έα, έες, έων, (ἔργον), *well made, well* or *firmly wrought* (ship, chariot, seat); pl., bene factorum, χ 319.

εὐ-εργός, fem., (ἔργον), *excellent*, λ 434. (Od.)

εὐ-ερκής, gen. from -ερκής, (ἕρκος), αὐλῆς, *well fenced, well enclosed;* ρ 267 (v. l. εὐεργέες), *with strong posts*.

ἐΰ-ζυγον, gen., pl. -οι, (ζυγόν), *firmly built, well bound together* (with strong cross-beams), ν 116.

ἐΰ-ζωνος, οιο, ους, (ζώνη), *beautifully girdled,* the girdle giving a graceful form to the garment, Z 467, A 429. (Il.) (See cut.)

εὐ-ηγενέος, έων, (γένος), *well* or *nobly born*, Λ 427. (Il.)

εὐ-ηγεσίη (ἡγεῖσθαι), ἐξ-, *in consequence of good government* (v. l. εὐεργεσίης), τ 114†.

εὐ-ηκέος, gen., -ής, (ἄκων), *well-pointed, sharp, piercing*, X 319†.

Εὐηνίνη, *daughter of Euenos,* Marpessa, I 557†.

Εὐηνορίδης, *son of Euenor,* Leiokritos, β 242. (Od.)

Εὐηνός, Evenus, (1) son of Selepios, B 693.—(2) father of Marpessa.

εὐ-ήνορα, acc. from -ωρ, (ἀνήρ), *manly, glorious, famous,* δ 622. (Od.)

Εὐήνωρ, ορος, father of Leiokritos.

εὐ-ῆρες, εα, ntr.,(ἀρηρώς), *well poised, handy,* epithet of oars, λ 121. (Od.)

ἐϋ-θριξ only **ἐΰ-τριχας,** *with flowing mane,* Ψ 13. [ῐ]

ἐϋ-θρονος, ον, (θρόνος) Ἡώς, *with beautiful throne, well throned,* Θ 565. (Od.)

εὐθύ, see εὐθύς.

εὐ-θῡμος, *well disposed, kindly,* ξ 63†.

Εὔ-ιππος, a Trojan, slain by Patroklos, Π 417†.

εὐ-καμπέα, ές, (κάμπτω), *well bent, curved,* sickle, key, φ 6. (Od.)

εὐ-κεάτοιο, gen., (κείω), *easily cleft or split,* ε 60†. [ᾰ]

εὔκηλος, οι, (ἕκηλος, ε-Ϝεκ.), *quiet, unmolested,* A 554, γ 263.

ἐϋ-κλεής, masc. pl. acc. **-κλείας,** ntr. sing. **-κλεές,** (κλέος), adv. **ἐϋκλειῶς,** gloriosus, famous, K 281, φ 331.

ἐϋ-κλείη, ης, *good reputation, fame,* Θ 285, ξ 402.

ἐϋ-κλῆϊς (κληΐς), *close shutting,* Ω 318†

ἐϋ-κνήμιδες, ας,(κνημίς),*well greaved*

(Achaians, companions), A 17, β 402. (See cut under ἀμφι-βρότης.)

εὐ-κόσμως, *well disposed, well arranged,* φ 123†.

ἐϋ-κτίμενον, η, ης, ην, (κτίω), bene cultus, *well tilled, laid out, appointed, built,* B 501, ι 130, Φ 77, ω 336. [ῑ]

ἐϋ-κτῑτον (κτίω), *firmly built,* B 593†.

εὐκτά (εὔχομαι) γένηται, *occasion for triumph* (εὖχος, εὖγμα), Ξ 98†.

εὔ-κυκλον, ον, ους, (κύκλος), *well rounded, well rimmed* (Il.); *well wheeled,* ζ 58.

εὐ-λείμων (λειμών), *abounding in meadows, adapted for* (cattle) *pasturing,* δ 607†.

εὐλαί, άς, fem. pl., maggots, X 509. (Il.)

εὔληρα (ἐϜλ. Ϝελίσσω?), *reins,* Ψ 481†.

Εὔ-μαιος, son of Ktesios, Ormenides, o 414; the illustrious swine-herd, π 461; faithful to his master Odysseus, cf. ξ 17–190, χ 267.

εὐ-μενέτῃσιν (μένος), *those who think rightly, the well disposed,* ζ 185.

Εὐ-μήδης, father of Dolon, Trojan herald, K 314, 412.

εὔ-μηλος (μῆλα), *abounding in sheep,* o 406†.

Εὔ-μηλος, son of Admetos, Ψ 288. (Il.)

ἐϋ-μμελίης, ου, and ω. ην, αι, (also with single μ, σμελ.), *skillful with the spear,* γ 400. (Il.)

εὐνάζω, fut. εὐνάσω [ᾰ], mid. pr. εὐνάζεσθαι, ipf., (εὐνή), *put in ambush,* δ 408; mid., *lay one's self down, sleep,* υ 1. (Od.)

εὐ-ναιετάοντες, ας, (ναιετάω), *pleasant to dwell in, comfortable,* B 648, β 400. [ᾰ]

εὐ-ναιόμενον, ψ, η, ην, (ναίω), *well inhabited, thickly peopled; of* cities, esp. Troia, A 164.

εὐνάω, aor. act. **εὔνησε,** pass. εὐνηθῆναι, (εὐνή), plice (in ambush), δ 440; *still, quiet* (lament, wind); pass., *lay one's self to rest,* (ἐν)φιλότητι, of sexual intercourse, Γ 441.

εὐνή (no gen. dat. pl., but the form εὐνῆφι, bed, *couch,* of individual, I 618; of army, K 408; of wild animals, cattle; also *marriage bed, cohabitation; bedding,* τ 317, Κ 75, ψ 179; *bedstead,* ᾰ 427, β 2, θ 2. Plur., freq. *mooring stones*, which served as anchors, having cables (πρυμνήσια) attached to them, and being cast upon the land or on the bottom, A 436, 476.—εὐνῆθεν ἀνίστατο, arose *from his couch*, υ 124†.

Εὔ-νηος, son of Jason, king of Lemnos, H 468. (Il.)

εὔ-νητον, οι, ους, (ἐύ-ννητ., νέω), *well, firmly woven*, Σ 596.

εὐνῆφι, see εὐνή.

εὖνιν, acc., (Gothic, vans), *lacking;* ἔθηκεν, ποιήσας, o r b a v i t, X 44, ι 524.

εὐ-νομίην (νόμος), *good order, obedience to laws*, ρ 487†.

ἐύ-ξεστον, ον, φ, οι, φ, ην, ας, (ξέω), *well scraped, smooth, polished*, Ω 275, 290, 271.

ἐύ-ξοον, ον, K 373, ἐύξου, (ξέω), *well planed, polished;* only ε 237, *polishing smoothly.*

εὔ-ορμος, ου, (ὅρμος), *affording good moorage* or *anchorage*, Φ 23. (Od.)

εὐ-πατερείη, ειαν, (πατήρ), *sprung from noble father, high-born*, epithet of Helene and of Tyro, Z 292, λ 235.

Εὐ-πείθης, εος, εα, father of Antinoos, slain by Telemachos, ω 523.

εὐ-πέπλω, ον, ων, fem., (πέπλος), *with beautiful mantle, beautifully robed*, E 424, ζ 49.

ἐυ-πηγής (πήγνυμι), *strongly built*, φ 334†.

ἐυ-πήκτου, φ, ων, (πήγνυμι), *firmly joined together, well built*, of ship, tent, apartment, B 661, ψ 41.

ἐυ-πλείην (πλεῖος), *well filled*, ρ 467†.

ἐυ-πλεκέες, έας, and ἐυ-πλέκτῳ, ους, *well plaited*, of body of chariot, tassels, cord, etc., Ψ 335, B 449, Ψ 115.

ἐυ-πλοίην, acc., (πλόος), *prosperous voyage*, I 362†.

ἐυ-πλοκάμῖδες and ἐυ-πλόκᾰμος, φ, ον, οι, οισι, (πλόκαμος), *adorned with beautiful tresses, fair-haired*, epithet of goddesses, ε 125, 390; of women, Z 380, β 119, X 442. (See cut No. 47.)

ἐυ-πλῦνές (πλύνω) φᾶρος, *well washed* (fair-shining), θ 392. (Od.)

εὐ-ποίητον, οιο, οισι, α, ἀων, ῃσι, ⟨ποιέω⟩, *well made, well wrought*, of works of skill, E 466, II 106, 636.

εὔ-πρηστον (πρήθω) ἀυτμήν, *sparkling, fiery* breath, or *strong blowing*, Σ 471†.

ἐύ-πρυμνοι (πρυμνή), *with well-rounded sterns*, Δ 248†.

ἐύ-πυργον (πύργος), *well towered*, H 71†.

ἐύ-πωλον, acc., (πῶλος), *abounding in horses*, Ἴλιον, E 551, β 18.

εὐρᾱξ, *on one side*, Λ 251, O 541.

εὐ-ρεῄς, see ἐυρρεῖος.

εὑρίσκω, only aor. εὖρον, etc., mid. prs. imp. εὕρεο, opt.-οίμην, aor. εὕρετο, i n v e n i r e, r e p e r i r e. *find out, discover;* mid. τέκμωρ, goal, end, remedy; *invent* a name; *draw down upon one's self*, φ 304.

ἐύ-ρροος, ον, (ὁρο-, ῥέω), *beautifully flowing*, H 329, Φ 130.

Εὖρος, E u r u s, *S.E. wind*, stormy, B 145; but warm, τ 206.

εὖρος, acc., τό, (εὐρύς), *in breadth*, λ 312†.

ἐυ-ρρεῖος, gen. and (Il.) ἐυ-ρρείταο, ην, (ὀρει-, ῥέω), *fair flowing*, Z 508, ξ 257.

ἐυ-ρραφέεσσι (ῥάπτω), *firmly sewed*, β 354, 380.

εὐρύ-ἄγυια, αν, (ἀγυιά), *broad-streeted*, epithet of cities, Τροία, δ 246, B 141.

Εὐρυ-άδης, suitor, slain by Telemachos, χ 267†.

Εὐρύ-ᾰλος, (1) son of Mekistos, companion of Diomedes, Z 20, Ψ 677.—(2) a Phaiakian, θ 115, 396.

Εὐρυ-βάτης, herald (1) of Agamemnon, A 320.—(2) of Odysseus, B 184, τ 247.

Εὐρυ-δᾰμας, (1) father of Abas and of Polyeidos, E 149.—(2) suitor, slain by Odysseus, χ 283.

Εὐρυ-δίκη, daughter of Klymenos, wife of Nestor, γ 452.

Εὐρύ-κλεια, daughter of Ops, α 429; nurse of Odysseus, and faithful housekeeper in his palace, τ 357, β 361.

εὐρυ-κρείων, *far-ruling*, Agamemnon, A 102; Poseidon, Λ 751.

Εὐρύ-λοχος, companion and cousin of Odysseus, κ 232, λ 23, μ 195, 339. (Od.)

Εὐρύ-μαχος, son of Polybos, α 399; suitor, slain by Odysseus, χ 82. (Od.)

Εὐρὔ-μέδουσα, attendant of Arete, η 8†.

Εὐρὔ-μέδων, (1) son of Ptolemaios, Agamemnon's charioteer, Δ 228.—(2) Nestor's servant, Θ 114, Λ 620.—(3)

king of the giants, father of Periboia, η 58.

εὐρυ-μέτωπον, οι, ων, ους, broad-browed, K 292, λ 289.

Εὐρυμίδης, Eurymos's son, Telemos, seer among the Kyklops, ι 509†.

Εὐρὔ-νόμη, (1) Okeanos's daughter, Σ 398.—(2) Penelope's stewardess, ρ 495, τ 97.

Εὐρὔ-νομος, son of Aigyptios in Ithaka, β 22. (Od.)

εὔρῦναν, aor. from εὐρύνω, enlarged (the arena of combat), θ 260†.

εὐρὔ-οδείης, gen., (ὁδός), with broad ways (ways open to all), Π 635, γ 453.

εὐρὔ-οπᾰ, voc., also old nom. for -όπης ; acc. from -οψ, (ὄψ, vox), far-thundering, Ξ 203, Θ 206.

εὐρυ-πόροιο (πόρος) θαλάσσης, traversable far and wide, with broad ways, Ο 381. (Od.)

εὐρυ-πυλὲς (πύλη) ᾿Αϊδος δῶ, wide-gated, Ψ 74, λ 571.

Εὐρὔ-πυλος, (1) son of Euaimon, from Thessaly, Β 736, Ε 76, Ζ 36, Λ 580, 809.—(2) (son of Poseidon and of Astypalaia) from Kos, Β 677.—(3) son of Telephos, slain by Neoptolemos, λ 520.

εὐρὔ-ρέεθρος, broad-flowing, Φ 141†.

εὐρὺ ῥέων, broad-streaming, Β 849. (Il.)

εὐρύς, έος, έϊ, έα, ύν ; fem. εὐρεῖα, ntr. εὐρύ, etc., broad, wide, applied to heavens, earth, sea, countries, (only Β 575, to city and surroundings) ; elsewh. broad ; comp. εὐρύτερος, γ, Γ 194.

εὐρυ-σθενές, voc., with far-reaching might, epithet of Poseidon, ν 140. (Il.)

Εὐρυσθεύς, ῆος, son of Sthenelos, king of Mykenai, Τ 103 sqq. ; imposes labors upon Herakles, Ο 639, Θ 363, λ 620.

Εὐρὔτίδης, son of Eurytos, Iphitos, Odysseus's guest-friend, φ 14, 37. (Od.)

Εὐρὔτίων, ωνα, Κένταυρον, φ 295†.

Εὔ-ρυτος, (1) son of Aktor, Epeian, with his brother Kteatos, ally of Augeias, Β 621 ; Μολίονε, Λ 709.—(2) son of Melaneus, king of Oichalia, Β 730, φ 32 ; slain by Apollo, θ 224.

εὐρὔ-φυές (φύω), wide growing, i. e. with its two rows of kernels far apart, epithet of barley, ὃ 604†.

εὐρὔ-χόροιο, ῳ, οιο, (χορός), with broad dancing-places, with broad squares, δ 635.

εὐρώεντα, acc., (εὐρώς), mouldy, dank, ψ 322.

Εὐρώπη, **Φοίνικος θυγάτηρ**, mother of Minos and Rhadamanthys, Ξ 321†.

ἐύς, ἐῆος, ἰύν, also **ἠΰς**, ἠύν, ntr., ἠύ, (=ἰσύς, ἐσθλός), bonus, good, excellent, brave, Β 653. (ἰύ and εὐ, also ἰάων, q. v.)

εὖσε, αν, aor. from εὔω, singed.

ἐϋ-σκάρθμοι (σκαίρω), lightly bounding, Ν 31†.

ἐΰ-σκοπος, ῳ, ον, (σκοπή), ἀργεϊφόντης, far, sharply seeing (Hermes) ; but λ 198, of Artemis.

ἐϋ-σσέλμου, οιο, ῳ, and pl., (σΓέλμα, solum), well decked, of ships ; with good deck (only at bow and stern), Β 170, β 390. The Egyptian ships seem to have had a kind of caboose. (See cut.)

Ἐΰ-σσωρος, father of Akamas, a Thrakian, Ζ 8†.

ἐϋ-σταθέος, gen. from -ής, (ἵστημι), well based, firmly built, Σ 374 ; apartment, ψ 178.

ἐϋ-στέφανος, ον, ῳ, (στεφάνη, ος), (1) with beautiful fillet or head-band, of Artemis and Aphrodite (see cut No. 47).—(2) strongly walled, of Thebes, Τ 99.

ἐϋ-στρέπτοισι, dat. pl., (στρέφω), tightly plaited or twisted, β 426 ; so also **ἐϋ-στρεφέϊ**, έα, ές, έεσσι, Ο 463 ; and **ἐϋ-στρόφῳ**, Ν 599, of cords, ropes, string of bow and sling.

εὖτε (ὅτε), (1) quom, when, disjunctive : the sentence in which its clause stands connected with what precedes by another conjunction in the apodosis, γ 9 ; with subj. with (Β 34), or without ἄν (η 202), to express general expectation, B 228.—(2) quasi, as= ἡ̃ντε, Γ 10.

εὐ-τείχεα, fem. acc., and -τείχεον, as fem., (τεῖχος), strongly walled, Π 57, A 129.

ἐυ-τμήτοισι, ους, (τέμνω), well cut, of straps, Ψ 684. (Il.)

ἐυ-τρεφέος, ές, έες, from -τρεφής, (τρέφω), well nourished, fat, ι 425. (Od.)

Εὔτρησις, village in Boiotia, B 502.

ἐυ-τρήτοισι (τιτράω), well pierced, Ξ 182†.

ἐύ-τριχας, nom. εὔθριξ, with flowing mane.

ἐύ-τροχον (τροχός), well wheeled, Θ 438.

εὔ-τυκτον (τεύχω), well wrought, Γ 336, δ 123.

εὐ-φημῆσαι, aor., -φημίω, (φήμη), bona verba loqui, favere linguis, shun unlucky words, keep silence, at sacrifice, I 171†.

Εὔ-φημος, son of Troizenos, chief of Kikones, B 846†.

Εὐ-φήτης, ruler over Ephyra in Elis, O 532†.

Εὔ-φορβος, Panthoos's son, Trojan, who having wounded 'Patroklos, Π 806, is slain by Menelaos, P 59.

ἐυ-φραδέως (φράζεσθαι), thoughtfully, wisely, τ 352†.

εὐ-φραίνοιμι, fut. -ανέω, ἀνέϊιν, aor. εὐφρηνε, ἦναι, (φρένες), exhilarare, delight, gladden; mid., β 311, take one's pleasure.

ἐὺ φρονέων, well meaning and well judging, with kind and wise thought, A 73, β 160.

ἐυ-φροσύνη, sing., and pl. -γσιν, laetitia, mirth, gladness, ζ 156.

ἐύ-φρων, ονα, (φρένες), laetus, Γ 246, rejoicing the heart.

εὐ-φυέα, acc. sing., pl. έες, well grown, stately, shapely, Δ 147. (Il.)

ἐυ-χάλκου, ον, ων, wrought of fine brass, well mounted with brass, Ψ 322.

εὐχετάομαι, opt. εὐχετοῴμην, οὗτο, inf. -τάασθαι, ipf. εὐχετόωντο,(εὔχομαι), wish, (1) pray to, τινί, X 394.—(2) boast, M 391; μεγάλα, loudly; ἐπί τινι, χ 412.

'Εὐχήνωρ, son of Polyeidos, N 663.

εὔχησι, nom. εὐχή, by prayers, κ 526†.

εὔχομαι, prs., ipf. εὔχοντο, fut., aor. (subj. εὔξεαι), declare a wish, ξ 463.— (1) precari, pray, θεῷ, Γ 296, Σ 75; μέγα, aloud; πολλά, devoutly; ὑπέρ

τινος and τινί, in behalf of.—(2) vovere, implore, ο 353, τινί τι; inf.—(3) asseverare, avow, Σ 499; de se praedicare, avouch myse'f, esp. with εἶναι, a 180, usually of just pride.—(4) gloriari, boast, N 447.

εὖχος, τό, gloria, fame, E 654.

ἐυ-χροές, ntr., (χρώς), bright-colored, ξ 24†.

εὐχωλή, ῆς, ήν, αί, ῇσι, (εὔχομαι), preces, prayer, ν 357; votum, vow, A 65; gloriatio, triumph, Δ 450, Θ 229, B 160; my pride, X 433.

εὔω, prs. act. and pass. aor. εὖσε, σαν, singe, bristles of swine, I 468; eyelids of Kyklops, ι 379.

εὐ-ώδης, εἴ, ες, (ὄδωδα), fragrant, β 339.

εὐ-ώπιδα, acc. from -ῶπις. fair-faced, ζ 113. (Od.)

ἔφαγον, see φαγεῖν.

ἐφ-άλλομαι, aor. ἐπᾶλτο, ἐπ(ι)άλμενος, (ἄλλομαι, salio), insilio, spring upon (in hostile signif.), charge upon, τινί, N 643; ἵππων, leap upon; ω 320, spring toward.

ἔφ-αλον (ἐπὶ ἁλός), maritimus, B 538. (Il.)

ἔφαν, see φημί.

ἐφ-ανδάνω, ἐπι-ανδάνει, ipf. -ήνδανε (and ἐφήνδ., H 45), placere, please.

ἐφάνη, aor. pass. from φαίνω.

ἐφ-άπτω, pf. pass. ἐφῆπται, plupf. -ῆπτο, aor. mid. subj. ἐφάψεαι, (1) hang over, τινί, Φ 513.—(2) mid., attigeris, touch, ἠπείροιο, ε 348.

ἐφ-αρμόσσειε (ἀρμόζω) εἰ οἱ, whether they fitted him, T 385†.

ἐφ-εζόμενος, η, part., inf. prs., ipf. ἐφείζετο, pf. ἐφήμενος, aor. imp. ἔφεσσαι, inf. ἐφέσσαι, mid. -εσσάμενος (tmesis, ξ 295), insido, sit upon, τινί, δ 509; pf., ζ 309; aor. act., take on board; π 443, set me on his knee.

ἐφ-έηκα, ε, -είην, see ἐφ-ίημι.

ἐφ-έλκεται, with part., ipf. ἐφέλκετο, mid., draw to one's self, attract; pass., trailing, dragging after, Ψ 696.

ἐφ-έννυμι, see ἐπι-έννυμι.

ἐφ-έπων, I. act. prs., ipf. ἔφεπε, iter. -έπεσκον, fut. -έψεις, aor. -έσπον, ἐπι-σπεῖν, (ἔπω, sequor), (1) persequi, pursue, τινά, Λ 177.—(2) instigare contra, turn against, τινί, Π 732.—(3) percurrere, rush through, over, τί, τινάς, Ψ 494, ι 121.—(4) follow up (occupation), τί, μ 330, ξ 195.—(5) fut. aor., assequi, draw down upon one's self, πότμον, etc., γ 134, Τ 294, Φ 100.—II. mid. fut. and aor., sequi, τινί, Δ 63, Ν 495; obsequi, comply with, γ 215, ξ 262.

ἐφ-έσσαι, ἐσσεσθαι, etc., see ἐφ-εζόμενος.

ἐφ-έστιος, ον, οι, (1) = ἐφ' ἑστίᾳ, at one's own hearth, γ 234; native, Β 125. —(2) = ἐφ' ἑστίαν, to one's hearth, ψ 55, η 248.

ἐφ-ετμή, ἤν, ἑων, άς,(ἵημι), iussum, command, behest, Ξ 249.

ἐφ-εύρομεν, etc., aor., (εὑρίσκω), invenire, come upon and find, surprise, β 109, Δ 88.

ἐφ-εψιόωνται, το, prs. ipf., (ἐψιάομαι), illudunt, mock, τινί, τ 331, 370.

ἐφ-ηγέομαι, see ἐπὶ στίχας.

ἐφ-ῆμαι, see ἐφ-έζω.

ἐφ-ημέριος, α, (ἡμέρα), the day through, δ 223; but φ 85, every day, trivial thoughts.

ἐφ-ημοσύνης, ην, gen. acc., (ἵημι), iussum, π 540.

ἔφησθα, aiebas, see φημί. ἔφθης, η, see φθάνω. ἐφθίαθ' (-ίατο), see φθίω.

Ἐφιάλτης, son of Aloeus (Poseidon), brother of Otos, giant, Ε 385, λ 308.

ἐφ-ίζανε, etc., ipf., (ἵζω), insIdebat, ὕπνος; assidebant, δείπνῳ, Κ 578.

ἐφ-ῖζε, ipf., iter. -ίζεσκε, insidebat, sit upon, τινί, γ 411, τ 55.

ἐφ-ίημι, ipf. -ίει, fut. -ήσω, aor. -ῆκε, ἑηκε, subj. -είω, opt. -είην, imp. ἔφες, immitto, send to, τινά τινι, Ω 117; launch at, τί τινι, Α 382, Ο 444, τ 550; imponere, place upon, τινί τι; χείρας, lay hands upon; νόστον, decree; impellere, constrain, with inf., ξ 464, Σ 108; mandare, propose, τ 576; so also mid. -ιέμενος, and fut. -ήσομαι τινί τι, Ψ 82. [ῑ, but ἱεμενος, ἵεις, ἵει, exc. ω 180.]

ἐφ-ίκοντο, aor., (ἱκνέομαι), ἀλλήλων, fe'l upon one another, Ν 613†.

ἐφίληθεν, aor. pass. from φιλέω.

ἐφ-ίστατο, (1) ipf. and 2 aor. -έστη, approached, drew near, τινί, Κ 496, Ψ 201, Λ 644.—(2) pf. -εστᾶσι, inf. -εστάμεν(αι), part. -εστᾶότες, plupf. -εστήκει, -έστασαν, stand by (near), upon, at, τινί, Ν 133, Ζ 373, α 120, Σ 554, 515.

ἐφ-όλκαιον (ἕλκω), rudder, ξ 350†.

ἐφ-ομαρτεῖτον, ε, imp. prs., follow close upon, Θ 191. (Il.)

ἐφ-οπλίζοιμεν, prs., fut. -οπλίσσουσι, aor. with σσ (inf. ἱ(σ)σαι), get ready, repast, chariot, ship; mid. fut. -ισόμεσθα, get ready our supper, Ι 66.

ἐφ-ορᾷς, etc., prs., fut. ἐπιόψομαι, ἐπόψεαι, aor. ἐπιδόντα, ἰδεῖν, intueri, behold, watch over; visere, τινά, τί; select, Ι 167.

ἐφ-ορμάω, aor. -ώρμησαν, excitaverunt contra me, stir up against, Γ 165; elsewh. mid. -ορμᾶται, and aor. -ωρμήθην, irruere, adoriri, attack, τινά (τινί, tmesis, κ 214); cupere, desire, with inf., Ν 74; captabam, strive, λ 206.

ἐφ-ορμή, aditus, entrance, approach, χ 130† (only from the interior into the ὁδὸς ἐς λαύρην).

ἐφ-υβρίζων, insultans, Ι 368†.

ἐφ-υδρος (ὕδωρ), pluviosus, wet, ξ 458†.

ἐφ-ύπερθε(ν), desuper, supra, above, Ω 645, ι 383.

Ἐφύρη, (1) ancient name of Korinth, Ζ 152, 210.—(2) Pelasgic city in northern Elis, on the river Selleïs, residence of Augeias, Β 659, Ο 531, Λ 739.—(3) town in Thesprotia in Epeiros, α 259, β 328.—(4) town of the Ἔφυροι, in Thessaly, afterward Krannon, Ν 301.

ἔχαδε, aor. from χανδάνω, held.

ἔχεε, αν, aor. from χέω, fudit, pour.

ἐχέ-θυμος, cohibens cupiditatem; οὐκ ἐ., libidinosa, lustful, θ 320†.

Ἐχε-κλῆς, ῆος, son of Aktor, a Myrmidon, Π 189.

Ἔχε-κλος, (1) Agenor's son, slain by Achilleus, Ὑ 474†.—(2) a Trojan, slain by Patroklos, Π 694†.

Ἐχέμμων, ονα, Priamos's son, slain by Diomedes, Ε 160†.

Ἐχένηος, an aged Phaiakian, λ 342. (Od.)

Ἐχε-πευκές (πεῦκος), pointed, Α 51. (Il.)

Ἐχέ-πωλος, (1) descendant of Anchises, dwelling in Sikyon, Ψ 296.—(2) son of Thalysios, a Trojan, slain by Antilochos, Δ 458.

ἔχεσκον, ipf. iter. from ἔχω.

Ἔχετος, fabled king, βροτῶν δηλήμονα πάντων, φ 308. (Od.)

ἔχενα, ε, ατο, aor. from χέω, fudi.

ἐχέ-φρων, ονι, ονα, thoughtful, prudent, 1 341. (Od.)

Ἐχέ-φρων, son of Nestor, γ 413.

ἔχησθα, subj. pres. from ἔχω.

ἐχθαίρουσι, pr. and ipf., aor. ἤχθηρε, (ἔχθος), oderunt, hate, γ 215.

ἔχθιστος (ἔχθος), most hateful, most odious, E 890. (Il.)

ἐχθοδοπῆσαι, aor., "Ἥρῃ, enter into hostilities against Hera, A 518†.

ἔχθεσθαι, prs., ipf. ἤχθετο, (ἔχθος), odio esse, be odious, δ 756. (Od.)

ἔχθος, pl. εα, hate, wrath, ι 277.

ἐχθρός, fem. ῆς, αί, ntr. όν, hateful, ι 312.

Ἐχῖναι, a group of islands in the Ionian Sea, near Dulichion, B 625†.

Ἐχίος (ῑ), (1) father of Mekisteus, Θ 333.—(2) a Lykian, slain by Patroklos, Π 416.—(3) a Lykian, slain by Polites, O 339.

ἔχματα, pl., (ἔχω), prop, support (earth under mass of rock), Ξ 410, N 139 ; bearers of the towers, M 260; Φ 259, mud, rubbish from canal (as holding back the flow of water).

ἔχω, ipf. εἶχον and ἔχεν, iter. ἔχεσκον, ες, ε, fut. ἕξω, σχήσω, aor. ἔσχον, inf. σχέμεν, fut. mid. ἕξεται, σχήσεσθε, αι, aor. mid. ἐσχόμην, imp. σχέο, parallel forms, aor. ἐσχέθον, inf. σχεθέειν, Ψ 466. —I. trans. (1) tenere, hold, τί, ὑψοῦ, Ζ 509 ; (μετὰ) χερσί (Ω 724), Υ 420 ; πρόσθεν, Δ 113; ἀπὸ ἕο, out before him, N 163; ὄπιθεν, Ψ 136 ; τινά, ζ 281, τ 228, Σ 580 ; τινὰ ποδός, etc., Π 763, Δ 154, by the foot, hand, etc. ; (ἐν) φρεσί (ο 445), B 33 ; πένθος, σ 324 ; possess, ρ 81; H 102, cords of victory are held ; hold together, λ 219 ; close, M 456, χ 128 ; enclose, X 324 ; shut out, ι 301 ; hold back, τί τινι, Λ 96 ; τί τινος, δ 758; τινά, Λ 820, N 51, 687, Υ 27 ; τί τινι, withhold, ο 230 ; ἀμφίς, keep apart, α 54 ; restrain, T 119, X 412; tears, π 191 ; choke, T 418, τ 458; let rest, θ 537; sustineo, hold ground, stand, M 433, K 264 ; tenere, guide, steer, νῆα, ι 279; ἵππους, N 326 ; ἐπί τινι, χ 75, E 240 ; -δέ, Γ 263, Θ 139.— (2) habere, have, in widest signif., ἕλκος, πόνον, ποθήν, νόον; periphrasis with part., ξ 416, A 356 ; ἐπιδευὲς δίκης, have less, be lacking in what is right; occupy, ψ 46 ; understand, P 476 ; possideo, α 402, Γ 282 ; inhabit, rest upon,

E 890, ζ 177, 183, μ 76, ν 245 ; have as wife, δ 569, pass., Z 398 ; be lord over, care for, dispense, α 53, δ 737, Λ 272 ; manage, T 43 ; be heavy upon, compel, κ 160, ξ 239 ; abide with, I 609 ; of mental states, etc., θάμβος ἔχει τινά, seize, cf. α 95, Φ 543 ; ὕπνος, ο 7 ; οἶνος, σ 391 ; ω 249, no kindly care awaits thee ; pass., be absorbed by, X 409, ν 2 ; gestare, wear, carry, ρ 24, T 18, B 872 ; indu'ge, ὕβριν, δ 627 ; practice, χ 445 ; make, Π 105, Σ 495; keep, σκοπιήν, θ 302 ; be able, Π 110, μ 433. —II. intr. persist, Ω 27 ; ω 245, goes on well ; rise, ὑψόσι, τ 38.—III. mid. hold one's self fast, cling closely, μ 433 ; to, τινός, ε 429 ; hold ground, stand, Π 501, I 235, P 639 ; control one's self, ρ 238 ; abstinere, cease, τινός, B 98, ν 151, N 630 ; στῆ σχομένη, stood still, ζ 141 ; haerere, stick in the throat, δ 705 ; ἄχϊι, held fast by, not being able to get rid of, λ 279 ; πρὸς ἀλλήλοισιν, sticking to one another, ε 329 ; pendere de, ἐκ, λ 346 ; let be, my friends, cessare, β 70 ; gestare, wear.

ἐψιάασθων, imp., and -ασθαι, inf. prs., (ἐψία), make merry, ρ 530 ; with dat., φ 429.

ἐῶ, ἐῷ, indic. and subj. prs. from ἐάω.

ἔωθεν, pf. from ἔθων. ἐώκει, see εἴκω II.

ἐώλπει, plupf. from ἔλπω.

ἔωμεν, neither in form nor meaning understood, T 402†; we should perh. read χέωμεν (from Χλάσκω, χῆρος, cf. στέωμεν, φθέωμεν), aor. subj., when we separate, withdraw ourselves (with gen.) from battle.

ἐών, part. from εἰμί. ἐῳνοχόει, ipf. from οἰνοχοέω. ἐῴργει, plupf. from ἔρδω.

ἕως [‿ ‿, only β 78; elsewh. pronounced with synizesis, P 727, ε 123], εἴως, ν 315, and εἷος (should perh. be written ἦος), δ 90, ν 315, ο 153, etc.— I. quamdiu, as long as, ρ 358, followed in apodosis by τέως, τόφρα, δέ ; quoad, until, with indic., ε 123 ; with subj. and κέ final, P 622, Ω 154 ; with opt. after past tenses, ε 386, with κέ, β 78 ; purely final=ut, δ 800, ι 376.—II. aliquamdiu (μέν), β 148.

ἕωσι, subj. prs. from εἰμί. ἐῶσι, from ἐάω.

Ἑωσ-φόρος, Lucifer, morning star, Ψ 226†.

Z.

ζα-, intensive prefix (from διά)= per-, very.

ζαής, acc. ζαῆν, (ἄημι), strongly blowing, tempestuous, μ 313.

ζα-θέοισι, ην, ας, very divine, sacred, of localities favored by the gods, O 432. (Il.)

ζά-κοτον, acc., (κότος), surly, morose, Γ 220†.

Ζάκυνθος, woody island in realm of Odysseus ; now Zante, α 246, B 634. [ᾰ]

ζα-τρεφέων, έας, pl., (τρέφω), sleek, ξ 19.

ζα-φλεγέες, pl., (φλέγω), full of fire, Φ 465†.

ζα-χρηεῖς, ειῶν, (χράω), impetuosi, raging, bold, M 360. (Il.)

ζάω, see ζώω.

ζειαί, άς, a coarse kind of barley, spelt, δ 41, 604.

ζεί-δωρος, ον, (ζειή, δῶρον), grain-giving (plough-land, ἄρουρα), μ 386.

Ζέλεια, town at the base of Mount Ida in Troas, B 824. (Il.)

ζέσσεν, aor. from ζέω.

ζεύγλης, gen., (ζευγνύναι), cushion between the neck and the yoke, P 440. (Il.) (See cut No. 77, also 49, letter d.)

ζευγνύμεναι, ῦμεν, inf. prs., Π 145 ; aor. ἔζευξαν, ζεῦξε, iungo, put to, yoke, ὑπ' ὄχεσφιν, ὑφ' ἅρματα, ὑφ' ἅρμασιν ; only Υ 495, couple together ; also mid., put to for one's self. Pass. σανίδες ἐζευγμέναι, Σ 276, joined, i. c. barred gates. (See cut under δικλίδες.)

ζεύγεα, pl., from τὸ ζεῦγος, a yoke, a pair (of draught animals), Σ 543†.

Ζεύς, Διός, Διόθεν, Διί, Δία, and Ζήν, Ζηνός, Ζηνί, Ζῆνα, and Ζῆν' (not Ζῆν), Zeus, the father of gods and of men ; also simply Ζεῦ πάτερ, (Diespiter), ὑψίζυγος ; αἰθέρι ναίων, hence god of time ; B 134, god of weather and of the clouds ; Διὸς ὄμβρος, εὐρύοπα, ἐρίγδουπος πόσις Ἥρης, αἰγίοχος, ὑψιβρεμέτης, νεφεληγερέτα, κελαινεφέα, στεροπηγερέτα, τερπικέραυνος, ἀστεροπητῇ, ἀργικέραυνε, ἐριβρεμέτεω ; hence sender of portents, τέραα, πανομφαίῳ ;

shaper of destiny, Διὸς τάλαντα, Π 658 ; βουλή, αἶσα, ὅσσα, α 282 ; θέμιστες, μητίετα, δοιοὶ πίθοι, Ω 527 ; protector of kings, διοτρεφέων, and διογενής ; of beggars and suppliants, ξείνιος, ἱκετήσιος ; of house and court, ἑρκείου ; presides over fulfillment of oaths ; ταμίης πολέμοιο.—Διὸς υἱός, esp. Herakles ; κούρη, Athena ; κοῦραι, the Λιταί and the Nymphs ; Zeus himself is the son of Kronos, Κρονίδης, Κρονίων. His majestic person described, A 530 ; chief seat of his worship, Dodona, Π 233. The orig. meaning of the root of the word is the brightness of the sky, afterward personified ; cf. δῖος, Lat. sub divo, under the clear sky.

Ζεφύρίη πνείουσα, the western breeze, η 119†, adj. from

ζέφυρος, only sing., (ζόφος), the rough west wind, the swiftest, bringing (to Asia Minor) rain and snow, only in fable land is it soft and balmy, η 119, δ 567 ; personified, Π 150, Ψ 200.

ζέω, ζεῖ, ipf. ζέεν, aor. ζέσσεν, fervet, boil, ὕδωρ ; a caldron, Φ 362.

Ζῆθος, son of Zeus and of Antiope ; with Amphion, founder of Thebes, λ 262 ; father of Itylos, τ 523.

ζηλήμονες, pl., grudging, jealous, ε 118†.

Ζήν, Ζῆν', see Ζεύς.

ζήτει, ipf. from ζητέω, requirebat, seek, Ξ 258†.

ζόφου, ον, (ζόφος, δνόφος), darkness, (1) darkness of evening into which the light of day (and fig. every thing living into death, υ 356, Ψ 51) subsides, γ 335 ; evening as region, the setting sun, west, ι 26, μ 81.—(2) the realm of shadows, O 191.

ζυγό-δεσμον, acc., yoke-band, cord or strap for fastening the yoke to the pole, Ω 270. (See cut under ζυγόν, b ; and cut No. 45.)

ζυγόν, οῦ, ὄφιν, ῷ, ά, (jugum), (1) yoke or cross-bar by which beasts of draught were attached to whatever was to be drawn. (See adjacent cut, combined from several antique repre-

and greaves (see cut under ἀστερόεντος; also cut No. 12, the figure of Αἰνείας). — (2) *broad girdle* around the middle of boxers, like that of the tumbler in adjoining cut, Ψ 683.

sentations.) *a*, ὀμφαλός ; *b*, ζυγόδεσμος ; *c*, κρίκος ; *d*, ζεῦγλαι ; *e*, straps to fasten in place the ζεύγλαι ; *f*, λέπαδνα ; *g* and *h*, οἴηκες, points of attachment for the collars, and rings through which the reins pass ; *i*, ζυγόν; *k*, projections to hold, e. g. the reins of the παρήορος. (Cf. also the Assyrian yoke on the chariot on board a ship, represented in adjoining cut.)—(2) *cross-*

bar of lyre (see φόρμιγξ), to which the strings were attached, I 187.—(3) pl., *cross-beams of ship* (see cut No. 35, under ἔδαφος).

ζω-άγρια, τά, (ζωός, ἄγρα), *reward for saving life*, Σ 407, θ 462.

ζώγρει, εἴτε, imp., (ζωός, ἀγρέω), *take alive*, i. e. *grant quarter*, τινά, K 378 ; only E 698, ipf. ζώγρει (ἐγείρω ?), *revived, reanimated*.

ζωή, ήν, (ζάω), v i c t u s, *substance*, ξ 208. (Od.)

ζῶμα, ntr., (ζώννυμι), (1) *apron* of leather or of felt, extending from the flank to the uppᵉʳ part of the thigh, and serving to protect the part of the body left exposed between the cuirass

and greaves (see cut under ἀστερόεντος; also cut No. 12, the figure of Αἰνείας).

ζώνην, acc., (ζώννυμι), (1) *woman's girdle* (see cut, also Nos. 47 and 65).— (2) *the waist*, B 479, Λ 234.

ζώννυσθαι, ipf. ζώννυτο and iter. ζωννύσκετο, aor. act. ζώσαντες, c i n g e r e, *put a girdle round the loins*, σ 76; elsewh. mid. s e a c c i n g e r e, *gird one's self* (for combat), σ 30 ; *gird one's self with, gird on*, τί, Ψ 130; τινί, K 78; ζώννυνται, ω 89. is subjunctive.

ζωός, masc. (exc. λ 86, Σ 418), and **ζώς**, E 887 ; acc. ζών, Π 445, v i v u s, *living*.

ζωρότερον (ζωρός) κέραιε, make the mixture *stronger*, I 203†.

ζωστήρ, ῆρος, ὁ, (ζώννυμι), (1) *warrior's body-girdle*, of leather strengthened with metal plates, which covered the lower part of the θώρηξ, and the upper part of the μίτρη and of the ζῶμα (see cuts Nos. 78 [where the ζωστήρ is very broad], 3, and 85). (Il.) —(2) *girdle worn over the tunic*, ξ 72. (See cut No. 79.)

ζῶστρα, pl., (ζωστήρ), *girdles, belts* (that could be washed), ζ 38†.

ζώω, inf. ζωέμεν(αι) and -ειν, part. ζώοντος (and ζῶντος, A 88, from ζάω), ipf. ἔζωον, v i v o, *live*, joined with ὁρᾶν φάος ἠελίοιο, δ 833 and freq.; with ἔστιν, ω 263; ῥεῖα ζώοντες, who live at ease.

H.

I. ἤ, particle of asseveration (διαβε-
βαιωτικός), always at beginning of sentence (ἀρκτικός), confirms an assertion
(expressing subjective certainty); *in
truth, certainly, to be sure* (usually with
other particles), A 78, 229, 240, 254,
255; with particles expressing objective certainty: γάρ, yes to be sure, A
293; δή, evidently to be sure, A 518, a
384; with particles expressing subjective certainty: μάν, μέν, A 77, 140,
211; μήν (καί), nimirum (etiam),
verily, B 291; μάλα (δή), most certainly
indeed, Γ 204, ι 507, σ 201; ἤ τοι, q.v.;
που, surely methinks; ἄρα, T 56, μ 280;
ἤ ῥά νυ, M 164; θήν, νυ, τε, κάρτα,
μάλα, β 325, ν 304.—Here belongs also
ἤ ποτ' ἔην γε (acc. to G. Curtius instead of εἰ), yes (=alas!), it was he.
—ἤ is also joined with other particles:
ἐπεί ἤ (not so good ἐπειή) πολὺ φέρτερος (μάλα), *since in truth*, ι 276, A 156,
169, κ 465 [always ‿ ‿ –]; and τί ἤ,
why then, A 365, Z 55.

II. ἤ or ἦε (accent of ancient grammarians), interrogative particle, (1)
[ἐρωτηματικός] (a) in simple direct
question, ἤ καί μοι νεμεσήσεαι, α 158,
A 133, 203; (b) in double direct question, utrum, β 30, 32.—(2) [διαπο-
ρητικός, ἀπορηματικός] in second member of a double question, cf. Lat. an
(also ἤ, ἠέ); the double question may
be: (a) direct, β 30, 32, ν 130; or (b)
indirect, α 175, λ 493, 495; common
phrase, ἠε καί οὐκί, or also not, δ 80.

ἤ or ἠέ (accent of ancient grammarians), A. simply interrogative, (1)
=εἰ, *whether*, in indir. single question,
πευσόμενος ἤ που ἔτ' εἴης, ν 415; (2)
utrum, in indir. double question (εἰ,
B 367), οὐκ οἶδ' ἤ τις—ἠὲ καί, δ 712, α
408.—B. [διαζευκτικός] (1) disjunctive,
(a) aut, vel, sive, only in second or
subsequent member of sentence, separating single ideas (vel, A 62) or
clauses (aut, A 515); (b) ἤ may be
several times repeated, cf. aut—aut,
A 138; sive—sive, β 29, Σ 308, ξ
183, I 701, X 253, ο 300.—(2) in ques-

tions: (a) simple question marking
opposition, α 391, or, dost thou hold?
also α 298; (b) to continue an inquiry: or is it that? β 32; or indeed, ν
167 (in both these last cases it is better
to read ἤ, an, and also in ι 253, φ 197).
Many modern grammarians accent as
oxytone (ἤ) the ἤ, an, of the previous
article, II., ἤ, 2.—(3) ἤ comparative,
quam, *than;* after comparatives, Λ
162; after ἄλλος, ἕτερος, βούλεσθαι,
malle, A 112 (sc. ἤ ἄποινα δέχεσθαι);
ἔφθης, λ 58. [ἤ οὐκ are usually pronounced as one syllable by synizesis.]

III. ἤ, aor. of defective verb (ait),
always following a passage in oratio
recta, and succeeded by (ῥα) καί, *he
said*, and, β 321; σ 356, ἤ ῥ' ἄμα τε.

ἤ, qua, corresponds to τῇ, ea, N 53.
ἤ θέμις ἐστίν, sicut fas est, *as is
right*, relative, B 73, γ 45, and freq.;
demonstrative only ω 286.

ἦα=ἔα=ἦν, eram. ἦα=ἤια only
ε 266, ι 212, at end of verse.

ἠβαιόν, αί, always at end of verse
after οὐδ', ne paululum (parvae)
quidem, not even a (*very*) *little;* without neg. and in middle of verse, only ι
462, paulum, *a little way*.

ἠβάω, ἡβώμι, -ώοιμι opt., -ῶν, -ώον-
τες, -ώωσα part. prs., ἡβήσας, ῃ aor.,
be in youth's prime; ε 69, *luxuriant*.

ἥβη, only sing., pubertas, *youth;*
ἥβης μέτρον, youthful prime; also vigor, *youthful strength*, Λ 857.

Ἥβη, *Hebe*, daughter of Zeus and
of Hera, wife of Herakles, λ 603; in
Iliad she always appears as goddess
performing some manual service for
other divinities.

ἡβώμι, ἡβώοιμι, see ἡβάω. ἠγάασθε, see ἄγαμαι. ἤγαγον, -όμην, see
ἄγω.

ἠγά-θεον, ἐῃ, ἐῃν, (ἄγαν, θεός? or
perh. from θέα=*beautiful?*), *sacred,
very divine*, of localities, Ζ 133, δ 702.

ἤγειρα, aor. (1) from ἀγείρω, col-
legi.—(2) from ἐγείρω, excitavi.

ἠγάσσατο, aor. from ἄγαμαι, admi-
ratus est.

ἡγεμονεύειν, prs., ipf., fut., (ἡγέμων), *lead the way for*; τινί, *conduct*; πρόσθεν, go in advance; ὁδόν, point out the way; τινί, ῥόον ὕδατι.—(2) (Il.) d u c e r e exercitum, *lead* (the army), Π 92; τινῶν, B 527; τισίν, only B 816.

ἡγεμών, no dat. sing., dat. pl. -μόνεσσιν, (ἡγέομαι), *leader, guide* (Od.); *commander, chief*, opp. λαοί, B 365. (Il.)

ἡγέομαι, ἡγείσθω, imp., ipf. fut. 1 aor., in signif. and construction = ἡγεμονεύειν, (1) *guide, lead the way for*, opp. (ἅμ᾽) ἕπεσθαι (M 251), θ 46, cf. β 405; πρόσθεν, Ω 96; craftily, X 247; in his folly, foolishly, ω 469.—(2) d u c e r e, τισίν (τινῶν), aliquos, might *lead* them to their ranks, B 687; but E 211, Τρώεσσιν, dat. advantage.

ἡγερέθονται, εσθαι, ipf. -οντο, (ἀγείρω), *assemble themselves* (gradually one by one), Γ 231.

ἤγερθεν, aor. pass. from ἀγείρω = congregati sunt.

ἡγηλάζεις, ει, prs., (ἡγέομαι), *guide, lead*, ρ 217; λ 618, leadest some such wretched life as I.

ἡγήτορι, α, ι, ες, (ἡγήτωρ, ἡγεῖσθαι), d u c i, *leader*, λαῶν; freq. with μέδοντες, *chiefs in war* and leaders in council; principi, α 105.

ἡγοράασθε, ἠγορόωντο, ipf. from ἀγοράομαι, *sit in council, hold assembly*.

ἠδέ (orig. following ἠμέν), et, *and, also,* B 27, 79; with ἔτι, B 118; joined with καί, *and* also, A 334; O 663, ἠδὲ—καί—ἠδέ; with τέ, Z 446; ἠδὲ—καί, A 400; καί, Z 429 sq. See also ἰδέ.

ᾔδεα, ἤδη, plupf. from οἶδα.

ἤδη (ἠ, δή), i a m, *now*, in contrast (1) with what heretofore had no existence : *already*, A 250, β 89; καὶ ἄλλοτε, i a m alias quoque; with part. B 663.—(2) contrasting the present moment with other time: *now*, A 456; *at once*, υ 315; with fut., α 303; with aor., Γ 98; freq. before or after νῦν : now at length, A 456; ξ 213, now already.

ἤδομαι, aor. ἥσατο, gavisus est, *rejoice*, ι 353†.

ἦδος, τέ, (ἡδύς), c o m m o d u m, *profit, advantage*, always in negative sense, μίνυνθα, οὐδέ τι, τί μοι (ἐστιν, ἔσσεται τινος); paullum, neque quidquam, quid expediet? A 576, Λ 318, ω 95.

ἡδῠ-επής, *sweet-speaking*, suaviloquens, A 248†.

ἡδῠ-πότοιο (ποτόν), *sweet to drink*, β 340. (Od.)

ἡδύς, εἶα, ύ, έος, ἐι, ὑν, εῖαν, (σϝαδ-, εὖαδε, suavis, Eng. sweet), *sweet*; ἡδὺ γέλασσαν, dulce (heartily) riserunt; κνώσσουσα, softly slumbering, δ 809. ἦε, ἠέ, see II. ἤ, ἤ. ἦε, erat, from εἰμί.

ἤείδεις, ης, ει, ειν, noverat, see ΕΙΔ IV.

ἠέλιος, only sing., [θ 271, Ἠλιος], (Lat. Ausēlius), s o l, *sun;* sunrise, Λ 735, γ 1, τ 433; ἀντολαί, μ 4; midday, Θ 68; afternoon, Π 779, η 289; sunset, A 605, 475, Θ 485, β 388, κ 191; τροπαί, ο 404; πύλας, ω 12; his curved path in the heavens, (ὑπερίονος, α 8), λ 16, H 421, Θ 68; phrases signifying to shine, Λ 735, ἐπέλαμψε, ἀκτῖσιν ἔβαλλε, ἐπιδέρκεται ἀκτίνεσσιν, φάος (as figure of life, Λ 19, Σ 11, 61, ὁ 540), αὐγή, ὑπ᾽ αὐγάς, αἴγλη; μένος, vis, heat, Ψ 190, κ 160; epithets, ἀκάμαντα, (λαμπρός, τ 234; λευκός, Ξ 185), παμφανόωντα, φαεσίμβροτος; expressions for east, ν 240, M 239, (and west, κ 191).—*Sun* as god, cf. Lat. S o l, observing all things, Γ 277, Ξ 344, θ 271, (yet not so, μ 375); father of Kirke, κ 138; of Phaethusa and Lampetie, μ 133; propitiated by sacrifice, Γ 104, T 197; oath by the sun, T 259; his βόες καὶ μῆλα, μ 128, 322, τ 276, ψ 329.

ἦεν, erat. ἤἐπερ, see ἤπερ.

ἠερέθονται, prs., ντο ipf., (ἀείρω), *float, flutter*, Φ 12; Γ 108, *be unsteady*.

Ἠερίβοια, μητρυιά of the Aloidae, second wife of Aloeus, E 389.

ἠέριοι, η, αι, (ἀήρ), matutini, *at early morn*, Λ 497, ι 52.

ἠερο-ειδεῖ, έα, ές, (-ειδής), *cloudygray*, πόντον, σπέος, πέτρην; but E 770, quantum acrium prospicit =as far as one sees *in the dim distance*, i. e. *through the haze*.

ἠερόεντος, τα, (ἀήρ), *cloudy, dark*, ζόφου; only Θ 13, Τάρταρον, and υ 64, κέλευθα.

ἠέρος, see ἀήρ.

ἠερο-φοῖτις (φοιτᾶν) Ἐρινύς, *walking in darkness*, I 571. (Il.)

ἠερο-φώνων (ἀείρω, φωνή), vocem tollentium, *loud-voiced*, Σ 505†.

Ἠετίων, ωνος, α, (1) *father of An-*

dromache, king of Thebe in Troas, Z 396, A 366.—(2) of Imbros, guestfriend of Priamos, Φ 43.—(3) a Trojan, P 590.

ἤην, erat, see εἰμί.

ἠήρ (see ἀήρ), **ἠέρος,** ι, α, fem., *fog, mist,* λ 15; esp. as means of rendering invisible, Γ 381; *darkness,* η 15 (41), 143; πουλύν, masc., from necessity of the verse, E 776.

ἠθεῖον, acc., **ἠθεῖε** voc., fem. εἴη, (ἦθος, suetus), carus, *beloved, dear,* ξ 147.

ἤθεα, pl. from ἦθος, (suetus), *accustomed places, haunts,* Z 511; ξ 411, *pens.*

ἤια, τά, (ἰέναι), pronounced with synizesis at end of verse, ἦja, viaticum, *provisions, food,* N 103. (Od.)
ἤϊων, τῶν, (ἄημι?), synizesis ἤjων, *chaff,* ε 368†.

ἤϊε, ibat, from εἶμι.
ἤϊθεος, ον, οι, (viduus), *unmarried youth,* Σ 567. [ῐ]
ἤϊκτο, *resembled,* see II. εἴκω.
ἤϊξε, *sprang,* aor. from ἀΐσσω.
ἠϊόεντι, dat., (ἠϊών), *with changing banks,* E 36†; since rivers, like the Skamander, in warm countries, and with sources in near mountains, have in consequence of rains a broad, ragged bed out of all proportion to the ordinary size of the stream, and banks ragged and often high.

ἤϊον, iverunt, from εἶμι.
Ἠϊόνες, sea-port in Argolis, B 561†.
Ἠϊονεύς, (1) father of Thrakian king Rhesos, K 435.—(2) a Greek, slain by Hektor, H 11†.

ἤϊε Φοῖβε, apostrophized, O 365, Υ 152, *gleaming* [?]. (αὔως.)
ἤϊσαν, iverunt, see εἶμι. **ἤϊχθη,** aor. pass. from ἀΐσσω.
ἠϊών, **ἠϊόνος,** α, ες, εσσι, ας, fem., *shore, strand,* M 31, ζ 138.
ἦκα (Fῆκα), placide, *softly, gently, slightly,* Γ 155.
ἦκα, ες, αν, etc., misi, from ἵημι.
ἤκαχε, *troubled,* aor. from ἀκαχίζω.
ἠκέσατο, sanavit, *healed,* aor. from ἀκέομαι.
ἠ-κέστας, acc. pl., (κεντέω), *having nev r felt the lash, untamed,* Z 94. (Il.)
ἤκιστος (Fῆκα), *slowest, most sluggish,* Ψ 531†.

ἤκω, ειν, adveni, *come,* E 478, ν 325.
ἠλάκατα, τά, *wool,* or *woolen thread on distaff;* στρωφῶσα, στροφαλίζετε, *ply the distaff,* σ 315. (Od.) (See the first of the cuts below.) [ᾰ ᾰ]
ἠλᾰκάτη, ην, (ἀράχνη), *spindle,* Z 491. (Od.) (See the cuts, representing distaff and spindles.)

ἤλασα, εν, αν, ἀμεσθα, aor. act. and mid. from ἐλάω.
ἠλασκάζει, prs., ων, (ἠλάσκω), vagans, *wander;* ι 457, vagando effugiat.
ἠλάσκουσι, pres., and part. -ουσαι, (ἀλάομαι), *prowl about, swarm about,* B 470. (Il.)
ἠλᾶτο, vagabatur, from ἀλάομαι.
ἤλδανε, aluit, from ἀλδαίνω.
ἠλέ, see ἠλεός.
Ἠλεῖοι, *inhabitants of Elis,* Λ 671†.
ἠλέκτρου, οισιν, (ἠλίκτωρ), *amber,* δ 73. (Od.)
ἠλέκτωρ, splendens, *beaming* (sun), with and without Ὑπερίων, T 398, Z 513. (Il.)
ἠλεός, voc. ἠ and ἠλέ, *infatuated, crazed.* φρένας, in mind=*mad;* ξ 464, *confusing, maddening.*
ἠλήλατο, penetraverat, plupf. pass. from ἐλάω.
ἠλίβατος, ον, οι, *steep, lofty,* ι 243, Ο 273.
ἤλιθα πολλή(ν), satis multum, *very much,* A 677.
ἠλῐκίην (ἦλιξ), aetatem, *equals in age, fellows,* Π 808. (Il.)
ἤλῐκες, pl. from ἦλιξ, adultae, *full-grown,* σ 373†.
ἤλιος, see ἠέλιος.
Ἦλις, ιδος, *Elis,* division of Peloponnesos on west coast, inhabited in the north by Epeioi, in the south by Achaioi, B 615, ὃ 635.

ἥλιτε, aor. from ἀλιταίνω, pecca-
vit.

ἠλῑτό-μηνον (ἀλιτεῖν, μήν), untimely
born, T 118†.

ἥλκησε, aor., vim attulerat, from
ἑλκέω.

ἧλοι, οισι, nails, studs, Λ 29. (Il.)

ἤλυθον, ες, aor. from ἔρχομαι.

Ἠλύσιον πεδίον, Elysian fields, abode
of the blest, δ 563 sqq.† [ῠ]

ἦλφον, aor., (ἀλφεῖν), have gained.

ἥλω, capta est, aor. from ἁλίσκομαι.

ἠλώμην, vagabar, from ἀλάομαι.

Ἠλώνη, a city in Phthiotis, B
739†.

ἤμασιν, dat. pl., (ἵημι), at javelin
throwing, Ψ 891†.

Ἠμαθίη, ancient name of Makedonia, Ξ 226†.

ἠμαθόεντος, ι, α, comm., (ἄμαθος),
arenosa, sandy, epithet of Pylos, α
93.

ἦμαι, σαι, σται, 3 pl. (ἧνται), ἕαται,
εἵαται, imp. ἧσο, inf. ἧσθαι, part. ἥμενος,
ipf. ἥμην, στο, σθην, 3 pl. ἥντο, ἕατο,
εἵατο, sedeo, sit, ἥμενος ἤ ἕρπων, ρ
158; often with collateral meaning
supplied by part. with which it is joined, A 134, B 137, Δ 412.

ἦμαρ, ατος, ατι, ατα, day, (a) as opposed to night, E 490; (b) division of
the year, season, χειμέριον, etc.; (c)
periphrastically with adj., e. g. ἐλεύθερον ἦμαρ, condition of freedom; δούλιον—, servitus; νόστιμον—, redi-
tus, Z 455, σ 137; ἥματα πάντα, always, forever; ἐπ' ἥματι, in one day, but
Τ 229, one whole day; ἥματι τῷ ὅτε,
tum quum, B 351.

ἠμάτίη, αι, adj., (ἦμαρ), (1) diurna,
die, by day, β 104.—(2) quotidianae,
daily, I 72.

ἤμβροτον, ες=ἥμαρτον, ες, missed.

ἡμεῖς and ἄμμες, ἡμείων, -έων ; ἀμ-
μῖ(ν), ἡμῖν, encl. ἡμιν ; ἄμμε, ἡμέας
(ἡμῖας), ἡμᾶς only π 372, we.

ἠμέν, usually corresponding to ἠδέ
(καί), δέ, τέ, καί ; both, as well, Π 664.

ἡμέρη, pl. αι, (other forms from
ἦμαρ), dies, day.

ἡμερίς, ἡ, (ἥμερος), cultivated vin°,
ε 69†.

ἥμερον, acc., cicurem, tame, ο
162†.

ἡμέτερος, η, ον, etc., (ἡμεῖς), noster,

our; ntr. subst. with εἰς-, -δε and ἰφ
ἡμέτερα=home, β 55.

ἡμῐ- = semi-, half-.

ἡμῐ-δᾰής (δαίω), semiusta, half-
burnt, Π 294†.

ἡμῐ-θέων, semi-deorum, demigods;
M 23†.

ἡμῐ-όνειον, ην, adj., (ἡμί-ονος), belonging to a mule, mule-, of chariot, yoke,
Ω 268.

ἡμῐ-ονον, acc., etc., (nom. and dat.
sing. wanting), comm., mulus, mule,
Ψ 266, 655.

ἡμῐ-πέλεκκα, half axes, one-edged
axes, Ψ 851. (Il.)

ἡμῐσεες, εων, ntr., v, semis, γ 155;
ntr. usually subst., half, ρ 322.

ἡμῐ-τάλαντον, half a pound (gold),
Ψ 751, 796.

ἡμῐ-τελής, half complete, desolate,
B 701†.

ἦμος, quum (temporal), when, always at beginning of verse, exc. μ 439;
followed in apodosis by τῆμος (ἄρα),
δή τότε, δή or καί τότ' ἔπειτα, or (δή)
ἄρα with indic. of histor. tenses; with
subj. (=pres.), only δ 400.

ἤμυσε, prs., aor. ἤμυσε, σειε, (κάρη,
καρήατι, with head), nod; B 148, it, the
ploughed field, nods (to the breeze),
with its heads of grain.

ἤμονες, pl., (ἵημι), ἄνδρες, darters,
Ψ 886†.

ἤν (εἰ ἄν), si, if, when, (1) with subj.
of pres. expectation, the verb of the
principal clause standing in; (α) imp.,
φ 237, π 274; (β) fut., I 394, Δ 353;
(γ) opt., μ 288; (δ) prs. subj., μ 121,
Θ 482.—(2) with subj. of repeated
action, verb of principal clause being
pres., A 166, λ 159; often with πέρ, σ
318. — (3) = whether, with subj., α
282. (εἰ ἄν, ἐάν, ἤν.)

ἡναίνετο, negabat, from ἀναίνομαι.

ἤνεικε, καντο, tulit, aor. from
φέρω.

ἡνεμόεντα, acc., -όεσσα, αν, ας, (ἄνεμος), windy, breezy, airy, (of towns,
mountains, trees), πτύχας, τ 432.

ἡνία, τά, frena, reins, often adorned
with gold or ivory, σιγαλόεντα, E 226.
[ι]

ἡνίκα, when, with indic., χ 198†.
[ι]

Ἠνιοπεύς, ἦα, son of Thebaios,

charioteer of Hektor, slain by Diomedes, Θ 120†.

ἠνί-οχεύς, ἠνίοχῆα, ες, ας, (Il.), = ἡνίοχος.

ἡνιόχευεν, ipf., (ἡνίοχος), held the reins, guided, drove, Ψ 642.

ἡνίοχος, οιο, ῳ, ον, οι, οισι, ους, (ἡνία, ἔχω), charioteer, θεράπων, E 580, etc. The charioteer stood usually left of the πρόμαχος; among the Assyrians, the warrior (armed with bow) had also a second attendant, shield-bearer, with himself on the chariot (see cut); the Egyptian monuments represent only one warrior or triumphing king upon the war-chariot.

ἦντο, sedebant, from ἦμαι.

ἤνυτο, successit, from ἄνυμι.

ἠνώγεα, ει, iussit, from ἄνωγα.

ἦξε, fregit, from ἄγνυμι.

ἠοῖον, acc., οι, ων, fem. ῃ, ην, (ἠώς), matutinus; subst. morning, dawn, δ 447; elsewh. orientalis, eastern.

ἦος, see ἕως.

ἦπαρ, ατι, dat., jecur, liver, ι 301.

ἤπαφε, ludificatus est, see παραπαφίσκω.

ἠπεδανός, feeble, weakly, Θ 311, Θ 104.

ἤπειρος, ἠπείροιο, ον, ῳ, ον, fem., (ἀ - πείρω ?), mainland, terra firma, opp. sea and islands, cf. esp., B 635;

ἠνίπαπε, compellavit, hail, see ἐνίπτω.

ἠνῖν, acc. pl. ἠνῖς, (AN), sleek, shining, γ 382.

Ἠνοπίδης, Satnios, Ξ 444†. [ῑ]

ἠνορέῃ, ἐηφι, ἐην, (ἀνήρ), prowess, manhood, Z 156.

ἤνοπι, dat., (ἤνοψ, AN), gleaming, dazzling, of naked metal, always with χαλκῷ, Π 408.

Ἦνοψ, (1) father of Satnios of Mysia, Ξ 445†.—(2) father of Klytomedes from Aitolia, Ψ 634.—(3) father of Thestor, of Troja, Π 401.

ἤντεον, obviam facti sunt, meet, from ἀντέω.

interior, opp. sea (coast), ι 49; yet used even of island, ε 56; ἠπειρόνδε, toward the land.

ἤπερ = ἠέπερ, quam, than, Ξ 468.

ἤπερ (ὅσπερ), eadem qua, just there (thither), where, μ 81, Φ 4; just as, I 310.

ἠπεροπῆα, acc. from ἠπεροπεύς, λ 364†, and ἠπεροπευτά, voc. from -τής, deceiver, seducer, Γ 39 and N 769.

ἠπερ-οπεύεις, ει, ειν, prs., ipf. ἠπερόπευον, aor. -εύσῃς, (Ger. afterreden, ϝοπ), deceive, cajole, seduce, Γ 399.

ἠπἴό-δωρος (ἤπια), kind'y giving, bountiful, Z 251†.

ἤπιος, ου, ον, η, α, *mild*, of persons, of remedies, Δ 218 ; of counsels, Δ 361.

ἠπύτα (ἠπύω), *loud voiced*, H 384†.

Ἡπῦτίδης, Periphas of Troja, P 324†.

ἠπύει, ipf. ἤπυε, *hail; ρ 271, sound shrill ; Ξ 399, roar*.

ἦρα φέρειν τινί, also ἐπὶ ... ἦρα, *do a favor*, gratify, humor, γ 164, Α 578 (Ϝῆρα, βούλομαι).

Ἡρακλείδης, (1) Tlepolemos, Β 653. —(2) Thessalos, Β 679.

Ἡρακλῆος, ηι, ῆα, often replaced in nom., as in other cases, by periphrasis, βίη Ἡρακληείη, voc. wanting, *Herakles*, son of Zeus and of Alkmene; his birth, Τ 98 ; ἄεθλοι, Θ 362, λ 623, φ 26 ; destroys Laomedon's Troja, Ῐ 145, Ε 642; makes conquest of Pylos, Λ 689 sqq., cf. also Ε 392, 397 ; death, Σ 117 ; his shade, λ 601 ; his wife (on earth) Megara (see Thessalos and Tlepolemos), in Olympos, Hebe. National hero. celebrated in popular songs before Homer's time, λ 602, 267. Épithets, θείοιο, θρασυμέμνονα, κρατερόφρονα ; cf. φ 25.

Ἡρακληείη, ης, ῃ, ην, always with βίη, periphrasis for Herakles, Λ 690.

ἠράμεθα, see ἄρνυμι, *gain*.

ἤραρε, aor. from ἀραρίσκω.

ἤρατο, aor. mid. from αἴρω.

ἠρᾶτο, from ἀράομαι, *precari*.

Ἥρη, *Hera*, daughter of Kronos and of Rhea, sister and wife of Zeus; her education, Ξ 201 sqq.; relation to Zeus, Α 568, Ο 13, Ξ 153; hostile to Trojans; to Herakles; patron of Greeks; her children : Ares, Hephaistos, Hebe, Eileithyia; her favorite haunts, Argos, Mykenai, Sparta, Δ 51, 52. Epithets, Ἀργείη, βοῶπις πότνια, πρέσβα θεά, Διὸς κυδρὴ παράκοιτις ; ἠυκόμοιο, λευκώλενος, χρυσόθρονος, χρυσοπεδίλου, Zeus gives her yet other (dishonorable) names, Ο 14 ; likewise Poseidon, Θ 209 ; *δολοφρονέουσα*.

ἠρήρει, plupf. from ἀραρίσκω.

ἠρήρειστο, plupf. pass. from ἐρείδω.

ἦρῑ, loc., (ἠέρι), mane, *at early morn*, Ι 360 ; with ἠῶθεν, τ 320.

ἠρῐ-γένεια, ης, αν, *early born*, epithet of ἠώς, δ 195. As substantive=Eos, *Child of dawn*, χ 197.

ἤρῐκε, fracta est, *break*, from ἐρείκω.

ἠρῐον, τό, *sepulchral mound*, Ψ 126†.

ἤριπε, lapsus est, *slip*, from ἐρείπω.

ἤρυγε, vomuit, from ἐρεύγομαι. ἠρῶ, precabaris, from ἀράομαι. ἠρώσαν, cesserunt, *retire*, from ἐρωέω.

ἥρως, ωος, ωϊ (ψ, Η 453, θ 483), ωα (ζ 303 [- ‿ ‿], ω᾿ before vowels); pl. ωες, ώων, ώεσσι, ωας, *hero, warrior*, title of honor for the free and brave ; standing alone as subst., Α 4, Κ 179 ; in address, Ῐ 104, Κ 416 ; with Δαναοί, Ἀχαιοί, likewise with single names, Δ 200, β 15, Φ 163; joined with θεράποντες Ἄρηος, Β 110; γέρων, η 155. (Never=demigod.)

ἦσ᾿ = (1) ἦσαι, Ο 245, sēdes.—(2) ἦσο, π 44, conside.

ἦσαι, σται, sedes, sedet. ἥσατο, gavisus est, from ἥδομαι. ἥσειν, fut. from ἵημι. ἦσθα, eras.

ἤσκειν, wrought, ipf. from ἀσκέω.

ἦσο, conside, imp. from ἦμαι.

ἥσσων, pl. ονας, ntr. ον, deterior, ο 365 ; ὀλίγον ἧσσον, paullo minus, *little less*.

ἧσται, sedet. ἥστην, erant ambo.

ἡσυχίη, ἡ, quies, *peace, quiet*, σ 22†.

ἥσυχιον, acc. masc., tutum, *uninjured*, Φ 598†.

ᾐσχυμμένος, pf. pass. from αἰσχύνω.

ἤ τ=ἤ τε, Γ 366.

ἤ τε—ἤ τε, sive—sive, *either—or*.

ᾐτιάσθε, ὀωντο, ipf. from αἰτιάομαι.

ἦ τοι (I. ἤ, and III. τοι), marks (1) calm assurance, *surely :* in address, Η 406, α 307, Η 191; in narration, Α 140, Ζ 201; after ἤ, ρ 372.—(2) marks antithesis=μέν, α 68, ο 6, Η 188, Λ 487; quamquam, *and yet*, Χ 280 ; ἀλλ᾿ ἤ τοι, but *by all means*, Α 211, Ω 48, ο 488, π 278 ; -μέν, sed vero, but Α 140; with imp., *yet*, δ 238, κ 271 ; after ὡς, ε 24, and ὄφρα, γ 419 ; μέν before δέ, *by all means*, Γ 168 ; (ι 339 read ἤ τι ; τοι, τ 599, is dat.).

ἦτορ, τό, *heart*, not as bodily organ, though used as synonymous with κραδίῃ, Κ 93 ; κῆρ, Ρ 535 ; likewise with θυμός ; also with ἐνὶ φρεσί, Π 242, Τ 169,θ 413, ν 320, cf. Ρ 490; ἐν κραδίῳ, Ῐ 169 ; synonymous with anima, Ν 84, Φ 201; *life*, Ε 250; *power of thought, mind*, Α 188 ; *heart, feelings*, Ι 497, 572; seat of astonishment, ρ 514 ; of joy, Ψ 647 ; of grief, Ε 364; of hope, π 92; of fear, Γ 31; of courage, Π 209; of desire, E 670; of wrath, Ξ 367; of appetite, T 307, I 705.

ἠϋ-γένειος (γένειον), with λίς at end of verse (Il.), δ 456, with λέων, *strong-bearded*, from the long hairs ("feelers") around the lion's jaws.

ηὔδα, locutus est, ipf. from αὐδάω.

ἠΰ-κομος, οιο, (κόμη), *beautiful-, fair-haired*, A 36.

ἠΰς, ύν, ύ, see ἐΰς.

ἤυσε, clamavit, from ἀύω.

ἠΰτε (ἠϜέ τε), *as also*, (1) quam, *as, comparable to*, Δ 277.—(2) tanquam, quasi, *as it were*, A 359. — (3) ceu cum, *as when, like*, B 87.

Ἥφαιστος, no dat., (σϜη-, per se, φαινων?), son of Zeus and of Hera, god of fire, and of arts which need the aid of fire; his wife, Charis, Σ 382 sqq.; but in Odyssey, the faithless Aphrodite; from childhood on, ἀμφιγυήεις, κυλλοποδίων, Σ 395 sqq.; his favorite abode, A 593, θ 283; chief works: armor of Achilleus; net in which he entrapped Ares and Aphrodite, θ 274; brazen houses of gods on Olympos and their outfit; sceptre and aegis of Zeus; his titles, χαλκεύς, κλυτοτέχνης,

κλυτόεργον, κλυτόμητιν, πολύφρονος, περίκλυτος, πολυμήτιος. Hephaistos is orig. nothing else than the element of fire, as may be recognized in I 468, and esp. in B 426.

ἧφι (σϜῆφι, see ὅς) βίηφι, sua (v i), X 107†.

ἠχή, ῇ, (ἠχώ), *noise, roar, hum*, B 209, Π 769.

ἠχήεντα, ntr., ἠεσσα, fem., (ἠχή), *echoing*, δ 72; *roaring*, A 157.

ἤχθετο, ipf. from ἄχθομαι and ἔχθομαι.

ἧχι, ubi, *where*, A 607.

ἠῶθεν (ἠώς), mane, *early; cras mane, to-morrow at dawn*, Σ 136; with μάλ' ἦρι, cras multo mane.

ἠῶθι πρό, *before daybreak*, Λ 50.

ἠώς, οὖς, οῖ, ῶ, (aurora), *daybreak*, Φ 111, π 2; *dawn*, ε 390; cras mane, Θ 470, λ 375; *day*, Ω 31; *east*, ι 26. Personified, Ἡώς, Eos, *Aurora;* her son Memnon, δ 188; husband, Tithonos, Λ 1, but cf. ε 121, o 250; abode, μ 3, Λ 1, T 1, χ 197; Ἑωσφόρος, Ψ 226, precedes her as she drives her chariot aloft, ψ 246; epithets, ἠριγένεια, ῥοδοδάκτυλος, δῖα, εὔθρονος, κροκόπεπλος, χρυσόθρονος.

Θ.

θαάσσεις, ἔμεν, ipf. θάασσε, sedere, *sit*, O 124.

θαιρούς, acc. pl., (θύρα), *hinges* of door or gate, M 459†. (See cuts from Egyptian originals; also under ἐπιβλῆς, No. 38.)

θἄλά, ;ης, gen., *bed, hole*, ε 432†.

θἄλἄμη-πόλος, ή, (πέλεσθαι, cole-re), *woman of the bedchamber, chambermaid*, η 8. (Od.)

θάλαμος, ὁ, no dat. pl., (θέλυμνον), *room* (opp. large hall, μέγαρον δῶμα), hence the rooms of the rear portion of the house [see table III., at end of volume], e.g. *women's chamber* (δ 121), *room for weapons* (τ 17), *store-room* (β 337), *bedchamber*, Γ 42·.

θάλασσα, ή, (ταράς·.·, orig. form ταραχ̓ϳα, Curtius), no pl., the *sea*, as element; when used of any particular sea it means the Mediterranean, B 294.

θαλάσσια (θάλασσα) ἔργα, maritima (negotia), *belonging to the sea*, B 614, ε 67.

θαλέθων, οντες, part., (θάλλω), *blooming*, ζ 63; ἀλοιφῇ, *teeming* with fat.

θάλεια, ῃ, αν, (θάλος), always with
δαίς, abounding, goodly feast, θ 76.

Θάλεια, name of a Nereid, Σ 39†.

θαλερός, οῖο, όν, ώ, οί, ῶν, ούς, ή,
ήν, (θάλλω), blooming, (1) fresh, strong,
thick, μηρώ, χαίτη.—(2) manly voice
was mute, φωνή; shedding big tears,
δάκρυ; rich, reeking, ἀλοιφή; thick and
frequent sob, γόος; entered into in the
prime of youthful freshness, blooming,
γάμος.

θάλέων, gen. pl. from τὸ θάλος,
(θάλλω), good cheer, X 504†.

θαλίῃ, dat. pl. -ῃς, from ἡ θαλίη,
(θάλλω), abundance, λ 603.

θαλλόν, acc. masc., (θάλλω), foliage
(as fodder for goats), ρ 224†.

θάλλω, only pf. part. τεθηλώς, τεθαλυῖα, ῃ, αν, plupf. τεθήλει, cf. θηλέω,
abound in, teem with, dat. ; part., abundant, fresh, ἕρση, ν 245, cf. ε 467.

θάλος, acc., τό, (θάλλω), shoot, scion,
X 87, ζ 157; see θαλέων.

θαλπιόων, part., (θάλπος), warm, τ
319†.

Θάλπιος, son of Eurytos, chief of
the Epeians, B 620†.

θάλπων, οντες, part., (Od.), calefa-
ciens, warming, φ 246.

θαλπωρή (θάλπω), warming, metaph.
comfort, Z 412.

θαλύσια, τά, (θάλος), offering of first-
fruits, harvest offering, I 534†. [ῠ]

Θαλϋσιάδης, Ἐχέπωλος, son of Thalysios, Δ 458†.

θαμά, frequenter, often, α 143,209.

θαμβέω, only pl. ipf. ἐθάμβεον, aor.
θάμβησεν, σαν, part. θαμβήσαντε, σασα,
(θάμβος), be struck with astonishment, Γ
398, α 360; gaze upon with wonder, Ω
483.

θάμβος, ευς, ntr., wonder, bewilder-
ment, ω 394.

θἄμέες, έσι, έας, ειαί, ειάς, frequen-
tes, crowded, thick, frequent, ε 252, Λ
552.

θαμίζεις, 2 sing. ind., and -ίζων part.
prs., ipf. θάμιζε, frequentare, come
frequently, resort; with part. = frequenter, θ 451.

θάμνος, ῳ, and pl., frondes, bush,
shrub, thicket, ψ 190, Λ 156.

Θάμυρις, Thrakian bard, vanquished
and blinded by the Muses, B 595†. [ᾰ]

θάνατος, sing., and οι μ 341, mors,
nex, mortes; θανατόνδε, to death, Π

693. Personified, Death, twin-brother
of Sleep, Ξ 231. [ᾰ ᾱ]

θάομαι, only 3 pl. 1 aor. θησαίατο,
admirarentur, admire, σ 191†.

θάπτω, prs. ipf., 3 pl. aor. θάψαν,
plupf. pass. ἐτέθαπτο, sepelire, bury,
ὑπὸ χθονός, λ 52.

θαρσᾰλέος, ον, οι, η, ntr. comp.
-εώτερον, adv. -έως, (θάρσος), ferox,
courageous, daring; ρ 449, impudent.
θαρσέω, prs., pf. τεθαρσήκασι, also 1
aor., (θάρσος), be bold, also in bad signif. be impudent; part. confident; θ 197,
with acc., be of good courage as regards
the contest.

θάρσος, ους, ευς, (Eng. dare), audacia, boldness, also = impudence, P 570.

θαρσῦνος, adj., (θάρσος), confident,
relying upon, οἰωνῷ, N 823.

θαρσύνω (subj.), prs., ipf. 1 sing.
θάρσυνον, iter. θαρσύνεσκε, 2 sing. aor.
θάρσυνας, (θάρσος), confirmare, encourage, Δ 233.

θάσσων, etc., comp. from ταχύς.

θαῦμα, τό, (θάομαι), miraculum,
res mira, wonder, also with ἰδέσθαι,
as exclamation, ρ 306; only κ 326,
miratio, surprise.

θαυμάζω, prs., ipf. θαύμαζε, iter.
-ξεσκον, mid. θαυμαζόμην, fut. θαυμάσ-
σεται, aor. θαυμάσωσι, (θαῦμα), mirari, wonder (at), B 320, γ 373; τινά, E
601, σ 411; τί, N 11, η 43; τό, on account
of; with dependent sentence, B 320, Ω
629 sq.; with acc. and inf., E 601.

θαυμάνέοντες, fut. part. from θαυ-
μαίνω, admiraturi, θ 108†.

Θαυμᾰκίη, town in Magnesia, under
rule of Philoktetes, B 716†.

θάω, only mid. prs. inf. θῆσθαι, aor.
θήσατο, suck (the breast of a mortal),
Ω 58; milk, δ 89.

θεά, ᾶς, άν, αί, (θέαιναι), άων, ῇσι,
ῇς, άς, dea, goddess, (opp. γυνή), Ξ
315, appos. with μήτηρ, νύμφαι.

Θεανώ, Κισσηΐς ἄλοχος Ἀντήνορος,
Z 302, priestess of Athena in Ilios.

θέειον, only sing., sulfur, sulphur,
as sacred instrument of purification;
κακῶν ἄκος, χ 481; with fumes of sulphur, μ 417. (θέιον = θέϜιον, cf. θύω.)

θεειοῦσαι, fut., and pres. mid. θειοῦ-
ται, fumigate and purify with brimstone
(one's house), ψ 50.

θεῖεν, opt. aor. from τίθημι.

θειλό-πεδον (θ' εἱλόπεδον?), drying-

place, a sunny spot in vineyard where grapes were dried, η 123†.

θεῖμεν, opt., θεῖναι inf. aor. from τίθημι.

θεινέμεν, inf., θείνῃ subj. prs., ipf. θεῖνε ἔθεινε, part. aor. θείνας and part. pres. pass., (fendo), *strike, τινά τινι,* with (the bow behind the ears), Φ 491.

θείομεν, subj. aor. from τίθημι.

θεῖος, ον, οιο, ον, ων, η, ης, ην, divinus, *divine,* B 41; also = *glorious,* β 341; sacer, H 298.

θείω, (1) = θέω, curro.—(2) = θέω, θῶ, aor. subj. from τίθημι.

θέλγω, prs., ipf. **θέλγε,** iter. θέλγεσκε, γ 264; fut. θέλξαι, aor. 1; pass. prs. opt. θέλγοιτο, aor. ἐθέλχθης, and 3 pl. ἔθελχθεν, *charm, cajole, bewitch,* Φ 276; *delude, deceive, τινά, τινός,* and *τινὶ* θυμόν, O 322, 594; *blind,* N 435.

θελκτήριον, α, τό, (θέλγω)= deliciae, *charm* ; θ 509, *means of appeasing the gods.*

θέμεθλα and **θεμείλια,** τά, (θεῖναι), fundamenta, M 28; the first, fig. *bed* (roots) of the eye, Ξ 493; *lower part* of throat, near the jugulum, P 47.

θέμεν(αι)=θεῖναι, inf. aor. from τίθημι.

θέμις, ιστος, ιστι, ιστα, ι, ιστες, (θεῖναι), *custom, usage,* that which is laid down or established not by written law, but by old law, E 761, ι 112, 115; ἐστί, fas iusque est; with inf. ἦ θ. ἐ., sicut fas est, as is right, B 73; also with gen., ξείνων, with dat., Ξ 386; fatum, Διὸς θέμιστες; *decisions,* Π 387; *prerogatives,* joined with σκῆπτρον; τελεῖν, pay *dues, taxes.* Personified, *Themis,* β 68, Υ 4, O 87, 93.

θεμιστεύει, οντα, (θέμις), *give law, τινί* ; τινός, *govern,* ι 114.

θέμωσε, aor. (θεμόω), coegit, *forced,* with inf., ι 486 and 542.

-θεν, suffix (cf. Lat. -tus). I. in general, (1) local, answering question whence, πεδόθεν, funditus; Τροίη-, οὐρανό-, οἰκό-; also with ἐξ, ἀπό; with verba movendi, φέρειν, ἄγειν; sentiendi, Ἰδηθεν μεδέων.—(2) denoting source, ε 477, Υ 305, cf. αἰνό-, οἰό-.—(3) specifying originator, O 489, π 447.—(4) temporal, ἠῶθεν, ὄπισθεν, postmodo. II. with designations of persons, θεό-, divinitus; πατρό-, Διό-, δημό-, ἐμέ- (with ἄνευ, O 213), σέ-, ἕ- ;

---

(1) with ablative force, audire ex, B 26, ζ 289; de, Ω 490; obedire, obey, O 199; after comparatives, A 114, ξ 56, Ψ 312; ὑπερίχω, I 419; also with ἐξ, ἀπό, πρό, E 96; πρόσθεν, E 56.—(2) with verba recordandi, θ 431, Δ 127; εἵνεκα, ἀέκητι, γ 213; ὑπέρ, Ζ 524; ἄνευ, P 407.—(3) joined with word in gen., υ 42, A 180, π 94, Σ 337; with ἄντα, ἀντίον, ἀντιᾶν, πειράζειν, ψ 114.—(4) instead of gen., δ 393, υ 232, π 439; but never instead of gen. partitive.

θέναρος, gen. from τὸ θέναρ, *flat of the hand,* E 339†.

θέο, imp. aor. act. from τίθημι.

θεο-δμήτων, gen. pl., (δέμω), a diis constructorum, *god-built,* Θ 519†.

θεο-ειδής, έα, acc., (εἶδος), *godlike, beautiful as the gods,* B 623, o 271.

θεο-είκελος, ον, (ε), (ἴκελος), *like the gods,* in exterior, A 131.

θεόθεν, divinitus, *from the gods,* π 447†.

Θεο-κλύμενος, seer in Ithaka, son of Polypheides, o 256, υ 350.

θεο-προπέων, part., vaticinans, *prophesying,* A 109.

θεο-προπίης, gen., ην, ας, and **-πρό-πιον,** gen. pl. ίων, (θεοπρόπος)=θεό-φαντον, vaticinatio, vaticinium, *prophecy, oracle,* A 385.

θεο-πρόπος, acc. ον, (cf. ἀρι-πρε-πής)=θεοφάντωρ, *one who discloses the will of gods;* vates, *seer* (N 70, οἰωνιστής), α 416.

θεός, οῦ, οἷς, ῷ, ὄφιν, όν, οἱ, ῶν, οἷσι, οἷς, οὕς, comm., deus (dea), *god* (*goddess*) ; of individual deities, Δ 514, Σ 394; then like numen, *the deity,* σὺν θεῷ, ἄνευ(θε) θεοῦ, ὑπὲρ θεὸν, ἐκ θεόφιν. [Often pronounced by synizesis, e. g. ξ 251, *l'j.*]

θεουδής, έα, (θεο-Fαδής ?), *pleasing the gods, pious,* τ 364. (Od.)

θεράπευον, 1 sing. ipf., (θεράπων), serviebam, *serve,* ν 265†. [ᾰ]

θεράπων, οντι, οντα, ε, ες, ας, *comrade, comrade at arms* (esquire, not *servant*), cf. λ 255, B 110, δ 23.

θερέω, see θέρομαι.

θερμαίνω, only subj. aor. **θερμήνῃ,** calefaceret, *warm, heat,* Ξ 7; opt. prs. pass. θερμαίνοιτο, calefieret.

θερμόν, ntr. ά, fervidum, a, *hot, warm,* ι 388.

θέρμετε, imp. prs., calefacite;

pass. ipf. 3 sing. θέρμετο, calefiebat, Ψ 381.

θέρος, εος, ει, (fornax, fur-nus), aestas, *summer*, η 118.

Θερσί-λοχος, a Paionian, slain by Achilleus, Φ 209, P 216.

Θερσίτης, slanderous demagogue in Greek camp, B 212–69.

θέρεσθαι, prs., fut. mid. θερσόμενος, τ 507, pass. aor. subj. θερέω, fervescere, *be warm, warm one's self*, so also pass., ρ 23; πυρός, incendi, Z 331.

θές, imp. aor. from τίθημι.

θέσ-κελον, α, (κέλω), *wondrous, ἔργα*; ntr. adv., mirum in modum, Ψ 107.

θεσμόν, acc., (θεῖναι), *site*, ψ 296†.

Θέσπεια, town in Boiotia, B 498†.

θεσπεσίοιο, gen., ῳ, ον, η, ῳ, ην, άων, adv. -ως, O 637 (θεός and πέτομαι?), *astonishing, tremendous*, in good and bad sense; θεσπεσίῃ, *by providential ordering*, B 367.

θεσπι-δαές (δαίω), πῦρ, *fiercely blazing*, M 177.

θέσπῐν, acc., (σεπ-, sequi?), *following, attending the deity; pious* or *divine, glorious*, ἀοιδόν, ρ 385; ἀοιδήν, α 328. (Od.)

Θεσπρωτοί, tribe dwelling about Dodona in Epeiros, π 427; their king Pheidon, ξ 316. (Od.)

Θεσσαλός, son of Herakles, father of Pheidippos and Antiphos, B 679†.

Θεστορίδης, son of Thestor, (1) Kalchas, A 69.—(2) Alkmaon, M 394.

Θέστωρ, (1) father of Kalchas.—(2) of Alkmaon.—(3) son of Enops, slain by Patroklos, Π 401†.

θέσ-φατος, ον, α, θέσφαθ' before rough breathing, (θεός, φάναι, φαίνειν), cf. fatum, ntr., *decrees of fate;* with ἀήρ, η 143 = *thick*.

Θέτῐς, ιδος, ῑ, ῐν, ῑ, a Nereid, mother of Achilleus by Peleus, Σ 431 sqq., Ω 62, cf. A 502 sqq., 397 sqq.; epithets, ἀλοσύδνη, ἀργυρόπεζα, ἠϋκόμοιο, καλλιπλοκάμου, τανύπεπλε.

θέω, θέεις, etc., prs., (inf. also θείειν), ipf. (iter. θέεσκον), fut. θεύσεαι, σθαι, curro, *run;* of men and animals; past. joined with other verbs = ocius, *quickly, in haste*, M 343, Z 394, χ 106; also of ships, potter's wheel, vein, and in gen. of round or quick-moving things.

θεώτεραι, θύραι, divinae, ν 111†.

Θήβη and Θήβῃσι, ας, name of a city, (1) in Troas, at foot of Mount Plakos, residence of Eetion, A 366, Z 397; destroyed by Achilleus. — (2) ἑπταπύλοιο, ἐϋστεφάνῳ, πολυηράτῳ, ἱερὰ τείχεα, in Boiotia, orig. founded by Kadmos; Θήβασδε, *to Thebes.*

Θῆβαι, only pl., ἑκατόμπυλοι, city in Egypt on Nile (Διὸς πόλις), δ 126, I 381.

Θηβαῖος, (1) a *Theban;* but (2) as proper name, father of Eniopeus, Θ 120.

θήγει, ων, prs., *whet* (the teeth); imp. aor. mid. θηξάσθω, let each one *sharpen* well his spear, B 382.

θηέομαι, only opt. θηοῖο, ipf. θηεῖτο, ἐθηεύμεσθα, θηεῦντο, aor. θηήσατο, αντο, αιο, and θησαίατο, 3 pl., (θέα), mirari, contemplari, *gaze at, admire*, Ω 418, η 133; τινά, σ 191; with part., ρ 64; τί, K 524, ο 132; θυμῷ, ε 76; joined with synonymous verb, Ψ 728, θ 265.

θήης, 2 sing. subj. aor. from τίθημι.

θηητήρ (θηέομαι), *beholder*, i. e. *fancier, connoisseur*, φ 397† (v. l. θηρητήρ).

θήϊον, θέειον, sulfur, *brimstone*, χ 493†.

θήλεας, see θῆλυς.

θήλεον, ipf., (θηλέω θάλλω), (the meadows) *bloomed* (with violet blossoms, ἴου), ε 73†.

θῆλυς (also with fem. substs.), νν, fem. εια, αι, ας, and θήλεας, E 269, and θηλύτεραι, άων, ῳσι, λ 386, *gentler, feebler*, cf. gentle sex; femininus, muliebris, *female.*—(2) *fresh, refreshing* (dew, ε 467).

θημῶνα, τόν, (θεῖναι), congeriem, *heap*, ε 368†.

θήν, = in prose, δήπου, allied perh. to δή, *then, so then;* also ἦ-, οὐ- (δή).

θηοῖο, mirareris, opt. from θηέομαι.

θηρί, θῆρε, du., and θῆρες, εσσιν, ας, (Eng. deer), fera, *wild beast*, ε 473.

θηρευτῆσι, dat. pl., (θήρη), venatoribus, *hunters*, joined adjectively with ἀνδράσιν and κύνεσσιν, M 41. (Il.)

θηρεύοντα, part., (θήρη), venantem, *hunting*, τ 465†.

θήρη, ης, ην, (θήρ), venatio, *chase*, ι 158.

θηρητήρ, α, ες, ας, and θηρήτορας, I 544, (θήρη), venator, *hunter ; φ* 397, better reading θηητήρ.

θηρίον, τό, (θήρ), *beast, κ* 171 and 180.

θῆτες, pl., (θεῖναι, conditio), *laborer on fixed terms, hired laborer, day laborer* (opp. δμῶες, vanquished serfs, slaves), δ 644†.

θησαίατο, 3 pl. opt. aor. from θηίομαι, mirarentur. θήσατο, *he sucked*, see θάω.

Θησεύς, acc. έα, λ 631, *Theseus ;* national hero of Athens and Attika, A 265.

θῆσθαι, see θάω.

θητενέμεν, inf., -εύσαμεν, 1 pl. aor., (θητεύω, θῆτες), *work for hire, be a day laborer,* λ 489.

-θι (cf. Lat. -bi), suffix added to subst. and pron. stems to mark place *in which.*

θίς, θινί, θῖνα, masc., (θῖναι ?), (1) acervus, *heap, μ* 45. — (2) elsewh. *strand.*

Θίσβη, town in Boiotia, πολυτρήρωνα, B 502†.

θλάω, only aor. ἔθλᾰσε, θλάσσε, *shattered,* E 307.

θλίβω, only fut. θλίψεται ὤμους, *will rub his shoulders, ρ* 221†.

θνήσκων, prs., aor. ἔθανεν, etc., inf. θανέειν, fut. θανέεσθαι, pf. τέθνηκα, part. τεθνηώς, ὥτος (and ότος, ότα, ότας), etc., τεθνηκυῖαν ; pf. sync. τεθνᾶσι, αίην, ης, η ; τεθνάμεν(αι), τέθναθι, άτω, mori, *die, ὑπὸ χειρσίν τινος ;* joined with πότμον ἐπισπεῖν, H 52 ; οἰκτίστῳ θανάτῳ, λ 412. τεθνηῶτες and θανόντες, mortui, *the dead.*

θνητός, ή, etc., (no ntr.), mortalis, Y 41 ; βροτόν, π 212.

Θόας, αντος, (1) son of Andraimon, B 638 ; in Aitolia, Δ 527.—(2) θεῖος, son of Dionysos and of Ariadne, of Lemnos, Ξ 230.—(3) a Trojan, slain by Menelaos, Π 311.

Θόη, name of a Nereid, Σ 40†.

θοινηθῆναι, aor. pass., (θοινάω), *to be entertained, δ* 36†.

θόλου, οιο, only gen. sing., *building of circular form, with vaulted roof,* in court-yard of Odysseus. (See plate III., k.)

θοός (no gen. sing.), only gen. dat. and acc. pl. θοή, άων, ῇσ(ιν), adv. θοῶς,

(θέω), citus, *quick,* with δαῖτα, θ 38, proleptically ; νύξ, *swift-descending,* because night, in the countries on the Mediterranean, follows more speedily than with us the setting of the sun (cf. β 388) ; νῆσοι, *swiftly flitting by,* and sinking in the horizon, ο 299.

θοόω, only aor. ἐθόωσα, (ἄκρον, prae), acui, *brought to a point, ι* 327†.

θόρε, aor. from θρώσκω.

θοῦρος, ον, fem. θούριδος, ῖν, (θρώσκω), impetuosus, *rushing, raging, impetuous ;* Ares, E 30 ; ἀλκῆς, ἀσπίδα, αἰγίδα.

θόωκος, οι = θῶκος, οι.

Θόων, ωνος, (1) a Phaiakian, θ 113. —(2) son of Phainops, slain by Diomedes, E 152.—(3) a Trojan, slain by Odysseus, Λ 422.—(4) a Trojan, comrade of Asios, slain by Antilochos, M 140, N 545.

Θόωσα, a nymph, daughter of Phorkys, mother of Polyphemos, α 71.

Θοώτης, herald of Menestheus, M 342.

Θράσιος, a Paionian, slain by Achilleus, Φ 210. [ᾰ]

θράσος, τό, Ξ 416 [ᾰ]=θάρσος, audacia, *boldness, courage.*

θρᾰσύ-δημος, v. l. see Θρασύμηλος.

θρᾰσύ-κάρδιος, *stout-hearted,* K 41. (Il.)

θρᾰσύ-μέμνονα (μίμνω), *bravely steadfast ;* Herakles, E 639.

Θρᾰσύ-μήδης, son of Nestor, Π 321, K 255.

Θρᾰσύ-μηλος, Sarpedon's charioteer, Π 463†.

θρασύς, ύν, ειάων, audax, *bold, daring, rash,* Λ 553.

θρέξασκον, aor. iter. from τρέχω.

θρέπτρα, τά, (=θρεπτήρια from τρέφω), praemia educationis, *return for bringing up, οὐδὲ τοκεῦσιν θρέπτρα φίλοις ἀπέδωκεν,* Δ 478 and P 302, nor did he recompense his parents for (their care in) bringing him up.

θρέψα, aor. from τρέφω.

Θρήκη, Θρήκηνδε, Θρήκηθεν, *Thrake,* a region in northern Greece beyond the Peneios, inhabited by Kikones and Paiones, B 845, Υ 485, Λ 222 ; traversed by river Αξιος ; hence adj. Θρηΐκιον, ῳ, οι, ης, *Thralian ;* sea, Ψ 230 ; Σάμου = island *Samothrake,* N 13 ; the inhabitants of Thrake are called **Θρῆκες**, ῶν, (sing. Θρῄικα), also Θρήικες ἀκρόκομοι, Δ 533.

θρήνεον, ἐθρήνεον, ipf., (θρηνέω), *were raising the funeral song* (**θρῆνος**, Ω 721), Ω 722, ω 61.

θρῆνυς, υϊ, υν, *footstool*, (1) of the helmsman running athwart the ship, Ο 729.—(2) elsewh. *footstool*, either as in cut No. 113, from Assyrian original, attached to the chair, or usually standing free. (See cuts Nos. 73, 74, 113.)

θρῄξ, see Θρῄκη.

θριγκός, οῖσι, *coping, cornice*, pl. *battlements*, ρ 267. (Od.)
θριγκόω, only aor. **ἐθρίγκωσεν**, *crowned the top* of the wall, to make it impassable, with bramble-bushes, ξ 10†.

Θρῐνᾰκῐη, fable-island, pasture of the cattle of Helios, μ 135; the ancients identified it and located it in Sicily.

θρίξ, **τρίχα**, ες, ας, θριξίν, c a p i l l u s, pilus, *hair*, also spoken of wool, and of bristles, Ψ 135.

θρόνα, τά, *flowers*, X 441†.

Θρόνῐον, town of the Lokrians, B 533†.

θρόνος, ου, etc., *arm-chair*, with high back and footstool; cushions were laid upon the seat, and over both seat and back carpets were spread. (See cut, under ἄμπυκα; cf. also No. 113, where two chairs, from Assyrian and from Greek originals, are represented.)

θρόος, ὁ, *speech, tongue*, Δ 437†.

θρυλίχθη, aor. pass., (θρυλίσσω), *was crushed*, Ψ 396†.

θρύον, τό, coll., *rushes*, Φ 351†. [ῠ]

Θρύον, τό, (lit. reedy), and **Θρυόεσσα πόλις** (lit. reed-town), a town on a ford of the Alpheios, B 592, Λ 711.

θρώσκωσι, ων, prs., ipf., aor. θόρε, θορών, etc., s a l i r e, *leap, ἐπί (ἐν) τινι*, i n v a d e r e, *attack*.

θρωσμῷ, dat., (θρώσκω), πεδίοιο, *rising* or *rise* of the plain (on Skamandros), K 160. (Il.)

θῦγάτηρ, ἐρος, ὁς, ἐρι, ἐρα, ἐρες, ἐρεσσιν; sync. θυγατρός, ι, θύγατρα, τρες, τρῶν, f i l i a, *daughter*, Ο 197. [ῠ in forms of four and five syllables.]

ἐνέεσσιν, see θύος.

θύελλα, ῃ, αν, αι, ας, (θύω), *tempest* (of wind or of fire); also of *sudden gust* which, like the Harpies, snatches away

those who suddenly and irrecoverably disappear, υ 63, δ 515. [ῠ]

Θυέστης, brother of Ἀτρευς, δ 517, B 107; father of Aigisthos, who is hence called **Θυεστιάδης**, δ 518.

θυήεις (θύος), *smoking with incense, fragrant*, Θ 48.

θῦηλάς, τάς, (θύω), *part of the victim to be burned*, I 220†.

θῡμ-αλγέος, έι, έα, ές, (ἄλγος), *heart-paining, grieving*, π 69.

ἐῦμ-ᾰρέα, ές, *dear, welcome*, ρ 199, I 336.

Θυμβραῖος, a Trojan, slain by Diomedes, Λ 320†.

Θύμβρη, plain bordering on the Thymbrios, a branch of the Skamandros, K 430†.

θῦμ-ηγερέων (ἀγείρω), *scarcely still rallying the life* in one, *tired out*, η 283†.

θῦμ-ηδέα, ntr. pl., (ἀδεῖν), *delighting the heart, agreeable*, π 389†.

θῦμ-ήρες (ἐρί-ηρες), *pleasantly*, κ 362†.

θῡμο-βόρου, οιο, ῳ, (βορά), ἔριδος, *heart-gnawing*, H 301. (Il.)

θῡμο-δᾰκής (δακεῖν), *stinging to the heart*, θ 185†.

Θύμοίτης, a Trojan chief, Γ 146†.

ἐῦμο-λέοντα, acc., *lion-hearted*, E 639.

ἐῦμο-ραῖστής, έων, (ῥαίω), *life-destroying*, N 544. (Il.)

θῦμός, οῦ, ῷ, όν, (θύω), strictly, *that which is in constant motion* (blood as the vehicle of the a n i m a), (1) *life, vital strength*, ἐλέσθαι, ἀποπνείων, etc.—(2) *heart*, as seat of emotions, courage; also *wrath*, ἀπὸ θυμοῦ = ἀπο-θύμιος; as feeling desire, *appetite* (even for food and drink).—(3) as *seat of reason; mind, thought*, ἐν θυμῷ βαλέσθαι, lay to heart.—(4) in general signif. *disposition, nature, heart*,—ἐν στήθεσσι, ψ 215; (ἐν) θυμῷ, locat., *in* (his) *heart, soul*, ν 145, υ 301, 304 ; *from the heart, seriously*, ε 212, Ω 778 ; κατὰ θυμόν, m e n t e a n i m o q u e, in mind and in soul, in the inmost heart ; θυμός, used as equivalent to *one's own self*, ε 298, o 202, X 122.

θῦμο-φθόρος, ον, α, (φθείρω), *destroying life, fraught with death, fatal* ; Z 169, *inciting to murder* ; *at risk of his life, wanton*, τ 323 ; δ 716, *consuming* (grief).

θύνων, part. prs., imp. θῦνε, besides these forms, ipf. θῦνε, ον, (θύω), *rush* or *dart along, charge,* Λ 342.

θὔόεν, ntr., (θύος), *odorous,* O 153†.

θύου, gen., *arbor-vitae,* with fragrant wood, ε 60†.

θύεα, θὔέων, ntr., *burnt-offerings,* Z 270.

θὔο-σκόος, οι, (σκοϜεῖν), *one who, from the smoke rising from the burnt-offering, draws an omen,* Ω 221, φ 145.

θυόω, only pf. part. **τεθυωμένον,** (θύος), *fragrant,* Ξ 172†.

θύραζε, foras, *to the door, forth, out,* E 694, ε 410.

θὔρα-ώρους, acc. pl., (ὥρα), *guarding the doors,* X 69†.

θὔρεόν, τόν, *door-stone,* placed by Polyphemos at mouth of his den, ι 240. (Od.)

θύρετρα, τά, (θύρη), *wings of a door, door,* B 415; αὐλῆς, χ 137, *near to the στόμα λαύρης* (see plate III., o). [ῠ]

θύρη, no gen. and dat. sing., pl. gen. άων, dat. ῃσι, *door, folding doors, gate,* α 441, φ 47; *entrance,* ν 370; B 788, ἐπὶ θύρῃσι, =*at the court* (cf. our phrase ' Sublime Porte,' as designation of Sultan, also [Xen.] βασιλέως θύραι).

θύρηθι, ξ 352 = **θύρηφι,** foris, *forth.* θύραζε, foras. [ῠ]

θὔσἄνόεσσαν (θύσαιοι), *richly tasseled, many-tasseled,* E 738. (Il.)

θύσᾰνοι, οις, (θύω), *tufts, tassels,* B 448. (Il.) [ῠ]

θύσθλα, τά, (θύω), *implements employed at orgies of Dionysos, Thyrsi,* Z 134†. (See cuts.)

I. θύων, prs., ipf. θῦε, (θέω), (1) *heave, surge;* of water, Φ 234, rushing with swollen stream; αἵματι, *swam* in blood. —(2) saevire, Λ 342, *raged;* περὶ πρὸ ἐγχέϊ, raged charging around and in front with his spear, Π 699.

II. θύοντα, part. prs., ipf. θῦε, aor.

θῦσε, σαμεν, σαι, (θύος, tus), offer by throwing or pouring upon the fire to be *burnt* a part of, the first-fruits of, a meal, ξ 446, o 260. (See adjoining cut.)

θὔ-ώδεος, εα, (ὑδω-δα), *fragrant,* δ 121. (Od.)

θωήν, τήν, multam, *penalty,* β 192, N 669.

(θῶκος) **θόωκος,** οι, **ϐῶκον,** ῳ, ους, (1) sedes, *seat,* β 14.—(2) consessus, *assembly,* β 26; θῶκόνδε, ε 3, *to the assembly.*

Θῶν, ῶνος, a noble Egyptian, δ 228†.

θωρηκτάων, οἷσι, from θωρηκτής, (θώρηξ), *cuirassed,* Φ 429. (Il.)

θώρηξ, no dat. pl., *breastplate, cuirass, corselet,* Λ 19 sqq.; usually of bronze, consisting of two plates (γύαλα). (See adjacent cut, also cuts Nos. 36 and 78.)

The cuirass fitted closely to the body, and was cut square off at the waist; the shoulder pieces (see cut) were drawn down by small chains and fastened to buttons (see cut No. 78); the metal plates were united by clasps (see cut No. 22); the upper part of the thighs was protected by the μίτρη, worn over the apron, ζῶμα, of leather 'or felt, by its metal flaps, πτέρυγες (Nos. 12, 36, 85), or plates (Nos. 3, 36, 78); over th ɩ

θώρηξ, μίτρη, and ζῶμα was bound the ζωστήρ (Nos. 3, 78), below which projected the lower end of the χιτών (Nos. 3, 22, 36, 78; cf. λινοθώρηξ and χιτών).
θωρήσσω, pr., ipf. mid. 3 du. θωρήσ-

σεσθον, N 301; fut. aor. act. and mid., (θώρηξ), arm with breastplate, or cuirass, mid. arm one's self, H 101; aor. pass. θωρήχθησαν, θῆναι, θέντες, Γ 340, Α 226, Θ 530, (σὺν) τεύχεσιν, Θ (530) 376.
θῶες, θώων, οἱ, jackals, Λ 474. (Il.)

I.

ἴα, ἴης, see ἴος. ἰά, see ἰός.
ἰαίνει, ομαι, εται, prs., ipf. ἰαίνετο, aor. ἰήνατε, ἰήνῃ, aor. pass. ἰάνθης, η, subj. ῄς, ῇ, calefacere, warm, pass., calefieri, κ 359; cheer, lighten, δ 549; pass. σφίν, iis gaudeo, take delight in them, freq. with θυμόν, φρένας. [ῐ]
Ἴαιρα, a Nereid, Σ 42†.
ἰάλλειν, prs., ipf. ἴαλλον, εν, aor. ἴηλα, ε, ον, ἰήλαι, (ἐλθεῖν), mitto, send forth, usually with ἐπί, followed by dat. or acc.; ν 142, ἀτιμίῃσι, assail with insults. [ῐ]
Ἰάλμενος, son of Ares, chief of Boiotians, B 512. (Il.)
Ἰαμενός, Trojan chief, M 139†. [ῐ]
Ἰάνασσα, Ἰάνειρα, Nereids, Σ 47†. [ῐ]
ἰάνθη, aor. pass. from ἰαίνω.
ἰᾶτο, ipf., fut. ἰήσεται, aor. ἰήσασθαι, curare, tend, τινά, τί; heal, Μ 2, ι 525. [ῐ]
Ἰάονες, Ionians, N 685†. [⏑–⏑–]
Ἰάπετός, a Titan, Θ 479†.
Ἰάρδανος, river (1) in Kreta, γ 292. —(2) in Elis, near Pheiai, H 135.
ἴασι (εἰμί), eunt.
Ἰασίδης, son of Jasos, (1) Amphion, λ 283.—(2) Dmetor, ρ 443. [ῐ]
Ἰασίων, ωνος, beloved by Demeter, slain by thunderbolt of Zeus, ε 125†. [ῐ]
Ἴασον Ἄργος, σ 246†=the entire Peloponnesos. [ῐ]
Ἴασος, (1) son of Sphalos, leader of Athenians, slain by Aineias, Ο 332. —(2) father of Amphion.—(3) father of Dmetor.
ἰαύειν, prs., ipf. ἴαυον, iter. ἰαύεσκον, -εν, aor. ἰαῦσαι, λ 261, and ἄεσα, σαμεν, σαν, ἀέσαι, ἄσαμεν, π 367, (ΓΑΣ), per-

noctare, pass the night, sleep, also with νύκτα, νύκτας, I 325, τ 340. [ῐ; ᾱ when augmented.]
ἰαχή, ῆς, ῇ, (ϝιαχή), clamor, cry, shout; in field, hunt, or distress. [ῐ]
ἰάχων, ουσα, part. prs., ipf. ἴαχε, ον, (ϝιάχω, Ger. wiehern?), cry aloud, of single person or of many, B 333; of things, strepere, ring, roar, twang, hiss, resound, crackle, Ψ 216. [ῐ; though orig. having ϝ, it is often augmented, when ῐ becomes ῑ.]
Ἰάωλκός, town in Thessaly, εὐρυχόρῳ, λ 256, B 712.
ἰγνύην, τήν, (γόνυ), poplitem, inner part of the knee, hollow of the knee, N 212†. [ῠ]
Ἰδαῖος, (1) son of Dares, a Trojan, E 11.—(2) herald of Trojans, Γ 248; charioteer of Priamos, Ω 470. [ῑ]
Ἰδαῖος, of Mount Ida, Idaean, (1) Zeus, Π 605; Ω 291, Κρονίωνι.—(2) ὀρέων, Idaean mountains=Ida, Θ 170, Υ 189. [ῑ]
ἰδέ=ἠδέ, et, Γ 194, α 113.
ἴδε, ἰδέειν, ἴδεσκε, vidit, see ΕΙΔ V.
ἰδέω, sciam, see ΕΙΔ IV.
Ἴδη, ης, Ida, a mountain range, rich in springs, ravines, forests, and game, extending from Phrygia, through Mysia, toward the Hellespont, and subsiding into the plain near Troy, B 821, Λ 183; its summit, Γάργαρον; Zeus Ἴδηθεν, from Ida (as his seat), Θ 397, μεδέων, Γ 276.
ἴδηαι, cernas, see ΕΙΔ V.
Ἴδης, εω, father of Kleopatra, I 558†.
ἴδιον, ntr., ίη, (viduus), privatum, private, δ 314. (Od.) [⏑⏑]
ἴδιον, ipf., (σϝιδ-, Eng. sweat), I was sweating, ν 204†. [ῑ]

ἴδμεν(αι), scire, see ΕΙΔ IV.

ἰδνώθη, θείς, aor. pass. from ἰδνόω, (ὀπίσω), bent himself (backward), B 266.

ἰδοίατο, viderent, see ΕΙΔ V.

Ἰδομενεύς, ῆος and έος, son of Deukalion, grandson of Minos, chieftain in Kreta, Δ 265, M 117, B 645; σθένος Ἰδομενῆος, periphrasis=Idomeneus, N 248; his son Arsilochos, ν 259; comrade in arms Meriones, Ψ 113.

ἰδρείῃ, dat., (ἴδρις), by skill (in battle), Π 359. (Il.)

ἴδρις, ιες, (ἴδμεναι), peritus, skilled, skillful, with inf., η 108. (Od.)

ἰδρώοντα, ας, ουσα, ἰδρώωσι, part. prs., fut. ἰδρώσει, aor. ἴδρωσα, (ἴδρως), sudare, sweat, ἰδρῶ, Δ 27; be drenched with sweat, B 388.

ἴδρυε, imp. prs., aor. ἴδρῦσε, σασα, bid be seated, B 191; aor. pass. ἱδρύνθησαν, took their seats. [ῠ]

ἱδρώς, dat. ῷ, acc. ῶ, (ἴδιον), sudor, sweat, with ἰδρόω, Δ 27.

ἰδυῖα, sciens, see ΕΙΔ IV. ἴδω(μι), see ΕΙΔ V. ἴε, ἴεν, ibat. ἴει, mittebat.

ἰείη=ἴοι, iret. ἱέμενοι, mid., ἵεν, ipf. 3 pl. aor. from ἵημι.

ἵενται, χ 304, and ἵεσθε, M 274, variae lectiones for ἵε- from ἵημι.

ἱέρειαν, τήν,(ἱερεύς), priestess, Z 300†. [ῑ]

ἱερεύς, ῆα, ῆες, and ἱρεύς, (ἱερός), sacrificial priest of a single god, also soothsayer, A 23. [ῑ]

ἱερεύετε, prs., ipf. ἱέρευον, iter. ἱερεύεσκον, υ 3; fut. ἱρεύσομεν, σειν, etc., aor. ἱέρευσεν, mid. ἱρεύσασθαι, τ 198; pass. plupf. ἱέρευτο, Ω 125, (ἱερεύς); slaughter, Z 174; offer, sacrifice, θεῷ ξείνῳ, in the stranger's honor.

ἱερήιον, ἥια, (ἱερεύς), victima, victim, animal for sacrifice or slaughter, ξ 94.

ἱερός, ή, όν,(ἷς?), strong, mighty, fresh, K 56, Δ 378, P 464, joined, in this signif., with ἴς, μένος, ἰχθύς; holy, of day, darkness, rivers, barley; sacer, sacred, of altar, grove, house, hecatombs, cities, localities, φ 108, α 2; hallowed, of threshing-floor, olive-tree.

ἱερόν, ά, and ἱρόν, ά, subst.,sacrum, ῥέζειν, ἔρδειν=sacrificare, sacrifice, α 61; victimae, victim, A 147.

ἰζάνει, prs., ipf. ἵζανεν, ον, (ἵζω),

consido, sit; instituted a contest, or bade the broad assembly be seated, Ψ 258.

ἵζει, prs. act. and mid., ipf. ἷζον and mid., iter. ἵζεσκε, (σιέjω, sido), take one's seat, with gen. of place, I 218, cf. π 53; lie down, recline (also mid.), Γ 326, χ 335; bid be seated, τινά, Ω 553; βουλήν, hold a council.

ἵηλε, αι, ον, aor. from ἰάλλω.

Ἰηλυσός, town in Rhodos, B 656†.

ἵημι, peculiar forms: 3 pl. prs. ἱεῖσι, inf. ἱέμεναι, ipf. ἵει, ἵεν, aor. ἧκε, mitto, send (Π 152, harness, put to), cast, let fall, ἀπὸ ἔθεν, χαμᾶζε; φέρεσθαι, hurled headlong, esp. shoot (with and without obj.), τινός, ἐπί τινα; let flow forth (voice, a river its waters); let loose (hair), mid. cupio, endeavor, strive after, with gen., with inf. Ἐρεβόσδε, πρόσσω; hasten, ν 334; pres. part. mid. ἱέμενος, cupidus, eager. [ῑ in pres.; but freq., esp. in part. and ipf., ῑ.]

ἰήνατε, aor. from ἰαίνω, and ἰήσασθε, σθαι, from ἰάομαι. ἵησι, eat.

Ἰησονίδης, Euneos, son of Ἰήσων, leader of Argonauts, μ 72, H 469.

ἰητήρ, ῆρος, ῆρα, and ἰητρός, οί, οἷς, (ἰάομαι), medicus, healer, ρ 384, Π 28. [ῑ]

ἰθαι-γενέεσσι, dat. pl., (ἰθύς, -γενής), born in lawful wedlock, legitimate, ξ 203†. [ῑθ.]

Ἰθαι-μένης, father of Sthenelaos, Π 586†.

Ἰθάκη, native island of Odysseus; the ancients identified as Ithaka the present island Theaki, with mts. Νήριτος, Νήιος, Κόραξ; its harbor, Ῥείθρον; epithets, ἀμφίαλος, εὐδείελον, ἐυκτιμένης, κραναῆς, παιπαλόεσσαν, τρηχείης. Hence Ἰθάκηνδε, to Ithaka; the inhabitants, Ἰθακήσιοι. [ῑθᾰ.]

Ἴθακος, eponymous hero of island Ithaka, ρ 207†. [ῑθᾰ.]

ἴθι, imp. from εἶμι, often with ἄγε.

ἴθματα, τά, (ἰθύς), straight flight, E 778†.

ἰθύντατα, sup. from ἰθύς,

ἰθύνει, prs., ipf. ἴθυνεν, ον; prs. ipf. mid., aor. pass. ἰθυνθήτην, (ἰθύς), hew so as to be straight, φ 121; make straight, ρ 341; direct, guide (missiles, ship), in a given direction, with acc., E 290, also ἐπί τινι; Π 475, pass., placed themselves in line, i. e. parallel to the pole; mid. re-

flexive, *was directing his* arrow, etc.,
χ 8.
ἰθΰ-πτίωνα, acc., (πέτομαι, Υ 99),
straight-flying (lance), Φ 169†. [— —
— ⌣]
I. **ἰθύς,** εἷα, ύ, *straightforward,
straight, just,* Ψ 580 ; ἰθύντατα, *most
fairly.*
II. **ἰθύς** and **ἰθύ,** adv., *straight at,
straight for,* with gen., E 849 ; with
verbs of motion, φέρειν, *bring against*
(in hostile signif.).
III. **ἰθΰν,** τήν, (ἵμεν), *undertaking, expedition,* δ 434, Ζ 79 ; *tendency, course,*
π 304, *upright or faithless disposition ;*
ἀν' ἰθύν, straight upward. [ῑ]
ἰθύω, only aor. **ἴθϋσε,** σαν, (ἰθύς), *go
straight forward, advance, attack* (of
lion and warriors), Μ 48 ; with gen.,
Ο 693, νεύς ; with inf., *desire.*
Ἰθώμη, town in Thessaly, Β 729†.
ἰκάνω, prs., ipf. aor. and prs. mid.,
(ἵκω), *arrive at, reach,* τινά, τι, with
designations of place and names of
persons ; less freq. with prep. ; γοῦνά
τινος, supplicare alicui, come as
suppliant ; τόδ', come hither ; noun denoting mental condition (e. g. grief,
pain), is sometimes found as subj. ; ἱκάνει τινὰ κραδίην (τινὶ ἦτορ), υ 228.
[ῑ]
Ἰκάριος, father of Penelope, brother of Tyndareos, α 276, 329, δ 797.
[ῑκᾰ.]
Ἰκάριος πόντος, S.W. of Asia Minor, Β 145†. [ῑκᾰ.]
ἴκελος, ψ, ον, οι, η, (jῑκ, ἔοικα), similis, *like,* τινί, Ν 53. (See εἴκελος.)
Ἰκεταονίδης, *son of Hiketaon,* Melanippos, Ο 546†. [ῑ]
Ἰκετάων, (1) 'scion of Ares,' son of
Laomedon, Priamos's brother, Γ 147,
Υ 238.—(2) father of Melanippos, Ο
576. [ῑ]
ἱκέτευον, ipf., aor. ἱκέτευσα, etc., (ἱκέτης), supplicare, *approach as suppliant,* (εἰς) τινά (Π 574), η 292 ; with acc.
and inf., λ 530. (Od.) [ῑ]
ἱκέτης, αο, εω, αι, άων, ῃσι, no dat.
sing. or accus. pl., (ἵκω), supplex,
suppliant, for protection, and esp. in
search of purification from homicide
(cf. Tlepolemos, Lykophron, Patroklos), ι 269, Φ 75. [ῑ]
ἱκετήσιος Ζεύς, *protector of suppliants,* υ 213†. [ῑ]

ἵκηαι, see ἱκνέομαι.
Ἰκμάλιος, τέκτων in Ithaka, τ 57†.
[ᾰ]
ἰκμάς, ή, humor, *moisture,* Ρ 392†.
ἴκμενον (ϝίκω) οὖρον, *fair* following
wind, Α 479. (Od.)
ἱκνεύμεναι, prs. part., ἱκνεύμεσθα,
ipf., (ἵκω), *arrive,* ι 128. (Od.)
ἴκρια, ἰκριόφιν, (ic o), *deck,* which in
the Homeric ship was partial, only fore
and aft (see plate IV., at end of vol.) ;
ε 252, *ribs of ship.* (See cuts Nos. 15
and 35.)
ἵκω, ipf. ἷκε, aor. ἷξον, ες, ε, mid. prs.
ἵκομαι, subj. 2 sing. ἵκηαι, opt. 3 pl.
ἱκοίατο, aor. ἱκόμην, fut. ἵξεται, σθαι,
(ϝίκω), consequi, *reach,* τινά, τί ;
τέκμωρ, the goal ; τέλος μύθων, substance of discourse, end proposed ;
ἥβης μέτρον, full strength of youth,
arrive at dawn, old age ; also with
πρός, ἐπί, εἰς, μετά τι (τινα), οἴκαδε,
δεῦρο (τόδ', ρ 524, 444, thither), so
generally *come ;* ὑπότροπον, reducem,
come back, return ; an abstract noun is
freq. the subj., e. g. wrath, grief, longing, ἵκει τινά (φρένας) ; whom wandering (exile) and distress and grief *befall,*
ο 345 ; *characterizes,* ν 228 ; δασμός,
division (of spoils) arrives, Α 166 ; χείρας, *fall into* hands of ; also=suppli-
care, τινά, π 424, δ 516 ; cf. τὰ σὰ
γοῦνα, ι 267. [ῑ, but ἵκετο.]
ἰλαδόν (ἴλη), adv., catervatim, *in
troops,* Β 93†.
ἴλαος, ον, (ἰλάω), placabilis, *propitious, gentle,* Ι 639. (Il.) [ῑ]
ἰλάονται, Β 550. ἰλάσκονται, εσθαι,
ipf. ἰλάσκοντο, fut. ἰλάσσομαι, σσεαι,
ἰλασόμεσθα, and aor. ἰλασσάμενοι, (ἵλαος), placare, *reconcile one's self to, make
propitious, appease ;* θεὸν ταύροισι καὶ
ἀρνειοῖς, μολπῇ, Α 472. [ῑ]
Ἰλήιον πεδίον, plain *of Ilion,* Φ
558†. [ῑ]
ἰλήκῃσι, subj., opt. ἰλήκοι, imp.
ἵληθι, (ἵλαος), *be gracious,* φ 365. (Od.)
Ἰλιόθεν, *from Ilios.* **Ἰλιόθι** πρό, *before Ilios.* **Ἰλιόφι**=Ἰλίου.
Ἴλιον, τό, Ο 71, elsewh. **Ἴλιος,** ή,
(1) *Ilios* or *Ilion,* the residence of Priamos, and capital city of the Trojan plain
(see plate V., at end of vol.) ; epithets,
αἰπεινή, αἰπύ, ἐραΤεινήν, εὐτείχεον, ἠνε-
μόεσσαν, ἱερήν, ὀφρυόεσσα, πύργον.—
(2) in wider signif., *the region about*

Troy, Ἴλιον εἴσω, Α 71, τ 182; Ἴλιον εἰσανέβαινον, β 172.

ἰλλάσι, ταῖς, (εἰλέω), *with twisted cords,* Ν 572†.

Ἶλος, (1) son of Tros, father of Laomedon, Υ 232; Ἴλου σῆμα, Κ 415; τύμβος, Λ 372; παλαιοῦ Δαρδανίδαο, Λ 166.—(2) son of Mermeros of Ephyra, α 259.

ἰλύος, τῆς, (lutum), *mud, slime,* Φ 318†. [ῑλῡ.]

ἱμάς, άντι, α, ων, εσσι, ας, masc., *leather strap* or *thong,* (1) in connection with the chariot, (a) *straps* in which chariot-box was hung, or, perh. more likely, the *network of plaited straps* enclosing the body of the chariot, Ε 727; (b) *the reins,* Ψ 324, 363; (c) *the halter,* Θ 544.—(2) *chin-strap of helmet,* Γ 371. —(3) *cestus* of boxers, see πυγμάχοι.— (4) *the leash* or *latch-string* by which doors were fastened and unfastened. See adjacent cut, in four divisions:

above, the closed, below the unfastened door; on the left, as seen from the inner side, on the right as seen from the outside. To close, now, the door from the outside, the string, hanging loosely in fig. 1, was pulled until it drew the bolt from the position of fig. 2 to that of fig. 3, when it was made fast by a knot difficult to untie to the ring, κορώνη, e, fig. 4. To open, from the outside, the string was first untied,

and then the κληΐς, not unlike a hook (fig. 4, *f*), was introduced through the key-hole, *c,* and by means of a crook (*g,* fig. 3) at the end of it the bolt was pushed back from the position of fig. 3 to that of fig. 2 and the door opened, α 442.—(5) *bed-cord.*—(6) *magic girdle* of Aphrodite, Ξ 214, 219.—(7) *thong which makes the drill revolve.* (See cut No. 127.) [ῑ]

ἱμάσθλης, ην, gen. and acc. ἡ, (ἱμάς), *lash, whip,* Ψ 582.

ἱμάσσω, subj. ῃ, aor. ἵμασε, (ἱμάς), *lash,* Ε 589; *beat,* Β 782, Ο 17.

Ἰμβρασίδης, son of Imbrasos, Peiroos, Δ 520†.

Ἴμβριος, *inhabitant of Imbros,* Φ 43; but proper name in Ν 171, 197; son of Mentor, son-in-law of Priamos, slain by Teukros.

Ἴμβρος, island on coast of Thrake, with capital city of same name, Ξ 281, Ν 33.

ἱμείρετε, ων, mid. -εαι, εται, όμενος, αιτο, (ἵμερος), desiderare, *yearn after,* with gen. or inf., ε 209, Ξ 163. [ῑ]

ἵμεν(αι)=ἰέναι, ire.

ἱμερόεις, όεντος, τα, όεσσαν, όεν, (ἵμερος), *charming;* γόος, *fond, passionate* lament; ntr. as adv., Σ 570.

ἵμερος, ον, (ἵσμαρος), desiderium, *longing,* τινός; *passionate longing, love;* πατρὸς γόοιο, *yearning after tears=*to weep for his father. [ῑ]

ἱμερτόν, masc., amoenum, *lovely,* Β 751. ἴμμεναι=ἰέναι, ire.

ἵνα, pronominal adverb, quâ (viâ or ratione), *where, wherewith, therewith,* Γ 252; ἵνα περ, Ω 382, ν 364, ubi maneant; ζ 58, quo (plaustro) aveham.—(1) ubi, *where,* Β 558, Ε 360, ι 136, δ 821, Κ 127 (τ' ἄρ?); *in circumstances in which* he would not be able to obtain fire from any other source, or ἵνα may be taken as final, *in order that* he may not need to kindle, ε 490.—(2) u t, *that, in order that,* never repeated (γ 78, not a genuine line), (a) with subj., after principal tenses, Ξ 484, Ψ 207, Γ 252, Α 203, β 307, (joined with κι, μ 156), with imp., α 302, Α 363, η 165 (also Α 410); sometimes with subj. even after historical tenses, Η 26, Ι 99, 495; (b) with opt. after historical tenses, γ 2, 77; after opt., ξ 408, even after principal tense, ρ 250 ; (c) subj. and opt. interchanged (text corrupt), O 598, cf. Ω 584 and 586. [⏑⏑, in arsi ⏑–.]

ἰνδάλλεται, το, (εἶδος), apparct, videtur, τίς τινι, with part., but τ 224, *it appears to me*, in my mind, *floats before me* in recollection.

ἴνεσι, dat. pl. from ἴς.

ἰνίον, ου, (Ϝίν-), *bone of the back of the head, back of head*, E 73. (Il.)

Ἰνώ, see Λευκοθέα.

ἰξάλου αἰγὸς ἀγρίου, Δ 105†, apparently designates a species of wild goat=perh. *chamois*.

Ἰξιονίη = Ἰξίωνος, Ξ 317, mother of Peirithoos.

ἴξον, see ἵκω.

ἰξυῖ, τῇ, *waist*, ε 231. (Od.)

ἰο-δνεφές (ἴον, κνέφας), *violet, dark, violet blue*, of wool, δ 135. (Od.) [ῐ]

ἰο-δόκος, ον, (ἰός, δεκ, δέχομαι), *arrow-receiving*, φ 12, of quiver. [ῐ]

ἰο-ειδέος, gen., ἐα, (ἴον), *violet-colored, dark blue*, ε 56. [ῐ]

ἰόεντα (ἰός) σίδηρον, *rusty iron*; others interpret, *violet-colored, dark*, from ἴον, Ψ 850†. [ῐ]

ἰό-μωροι, adj. applied to Ἀργεῖοι, Δ 242, Ξ 479 (ἰό-της ?), of doubtful deriv. and signif., *skilled in arrow-shooting*= *cowardly*; or *strong in wishing* and worthless in action.

ἴον, gen. from Ϝίον, (vio-lae), collective noun, *violets*, ε 72†.

ἰονθάδος, τῆς, barbatae, *shaggy*, ξ 50†. [ῐ]

ἰός, ῷ, όν, pl. ἰοί, (ἰά, Υ 68), ὦν, οἶσι, οὑς, sagitta, *arrow*, Λ 515.

(ἰος) ἰῷ, ἴα, ἰῆς, ἰῇ, unus, a, *one*, N 354, Δ 437. (Il. and ξ 435.) [ῐ]

ἰότητι, τα, (ἵμερος), τινός, *will, moving*, O 41.

ἰούλους, τούς, (οὖλος), *first growth of the beard, downy hair*, λ 319†. [ῐ]

ἰο-χέαιρα, αν, (ἰός, χέω), *arrow-shooting*, E 53.

ἱππάζεαι, 2 sing. prs., *thou art driving* (thy steeds), Ψ 426†.

Ἱππασίδης, son of Hippasos, (1) Apisaon. — (2) Hypsenor. — (3) Charops, and his brother Sokos, Λ 431.

ἱππείου, ον, εἴων, ῃ, ῃσι, (ἵππος), *of* or *for horses, horse*— ; λόφον, *horse-hair plume*, O 537.

ἱππεύς, ἱππῆες, ἥων, εὖσι, ἧας, (ἵππος), *hero fighting from chariot, contest-*

ant *for prize in chariot-race*, Δ 297, Ψ 262.

ἱππ-ηλασίη (ἐλαύνω) ὁδός, *road where chariots may be driven*, H 340 and 439.

ἱππ-ηλάτᾰ, ὁ, (ἐλαύνω), *driver of horses, fighter from chariot, knight*, H 125, γ 436.

ἱππ-ήλᾰτος, *passable with chariots*; δ 607, *adapted to driving horses*.

Ἱππ-ημολγοί (ἀμέλγω), *mare-milkers, Hippemolgoi*, a Skythian tribe, N 5.

ἱππιο-χαίτην, acc., (χαίτη), *of horse-hair, of horse's mane*, Z 469.

ἱππιο-χάρμην, acc., (χάρμη), *fighter from a chariot*, Ω 257, λ 259.

ἱππο-βότοιο, ῳ, ον, (βόσκω), *horse-nourishing, horse-breeding*, el ithet esp. of Argos, B 287.

Ἱππο-δάμας, αντα, Troja ι warrior, slain by Achilleus, Υ 401.

Ἱππο-δάμεια, (1) daughter of Anchises, N 429.—(2) attendant of Penelope, σ 182.—(3) κλυτός, wife of Peirithoos, B 742.

ἱππό-δαμος, -δάμοιο, ου, ⟨ν, οι, ων, οισι, ους, (δαμᾶν), *horse taming*, epithet of heroes of Trojans, γ 17, 181. (Il.)

Ἱππό-δαμος, slain by Odysseus, Λ 335†.

ἱππο-δάσεια, ης, ας, (δασύς), *with thick horse-hair plume, bushy with horse-hair*, N 714.

ἱππό-δρομος, *course for chariots*, Ψ 330†.

ἱππόθεν, *from the* (wooden) *horse*, θ 515, λ 531.

Ἱππό-θοος, (1) son of Priamos, Ω 251.—(2) Λήθοιο Πελασγοῦ υἱός, P 289.

ἱππο-κέλευθε (κελεύω), *horse-urging, swift-driving*, Patroklos, Π 126. (Il.)

ἱππο-κόμου, ον, οι, ων, (κόμη), *decked with horse-hair*, Π 338.

ἱππο-κορυσταί, άς, (κορύσσω), *chariot-equipping, fighters from chariots*, epithet of heroes; also of Maionians and Paionians, B 1, Ω 677.

Ἱππο-κόων, cousin of Rhesos, K 518†.

Ἱππό-λοχος, (1) son of Antimachos, slain by Agamemnon, Λ 122.—(2) a Lykian, son of Bellerophontes, father of Glaukos, Z 206.

ἱππό-μάχος, *fighting on horse-back* (v. l. ἱππύδαμοι), K 431†.

Ἱππό-μᾰχος, son of Antimachos, slain by Leonteus, M 189†.

Ἱππό-νοος, a Greek warrior, slain by Hektor, Λ 303†.

ἱππο-πόλων (colere), *horse-rearing*, *horse-training*, Θρῃκῶν, N 4 and Ξ 227.

ἵππος, sing., du., (-οῖιν), and pl., comm., but usually fem., (no voc.), equus, equa, *horse, mare*, ἄρσενες, θήλεες, and θήλειαι. In battle and for common use, horses were not ridden but harnessed, hence du. and pl. = freq. *span*, i. e. *war-chariot with horses*, and this even when only the chariot is referred to, Γ 265, 113, Δ 142, Ε 163; opp. infantry, foot, Σ 153; opp. warriors, B 554; ἁλὸς ἵπποι, in simile, δ 708.

ἱπποσύνη, αων, ας, *art of fighting from chariot*, ω 40 and ll. [ῠ]

ἱππότᾰ, ὁ, *chariot fighter, knight;* esp. as epithet of Nestor, Β 336, 628.

Ἱπποτάδης, *son of Hippotes*, Aiolos, κ 36†.

Ἱππoτίων, slain by Meriones, Ξ 514; father of Morys, N 792. [ῑ]

ἵππ-ουρις, ιν, (οὐρά), *with horse-tail plume*, Γ 382.

ἵπτομαι, only 3 sing. ἵψεται, aor. ἵψᾰο, (icere), castigare, *chastise*, spoken of gods and of kings, A 454, B 193.

ἱρεύς, see ἱερεύς. ἱρεύσασθαι, see ἱερεύω.

Ἱρή, town of Agamemnon, in Messene, I 150.

ἵρηξ, κος, ι, ες, ων = accipiter, *hawk*, O 237. [ῑ]

Ἶρις, ιν, ι, epithets: fleet as the wind, Θ 409; swift, Β 786, Ε 353, 790, Θ 399, O 172; *Iris*, in the Iliad, messenger of the gods, with golden wings, Θ 398. She delivers on the battle-field messages to gods and men; to the latter, usually in assumed human form.

ἶριν, ἴρισσιν, (strictly acc. sing. and dat. pl. from preceding), *rainbow*, Λ 27, P 547.

ἱρόν, ά, see ἱερός.

Ἶρος, lit. *messenger*, nickname of Ἀρναῖος; impudent beggar and parasite of suitors, vanquished in boxing-match by Odysseus, σ 1 sqq., 73, 239.

ἴς, ἶνα, ἶνες, ἴνεσι, (Ϝίς), *sinews*, nervi, sing., *muscular strength*, vis; then, in general, *strength, force, power*, e. g. of wind and waves; freq. in periphrasis, with κρατερή or ἱρή, σ 3.

ἰσάζουσα, ipf. iter. mid. ἰσάσκετο, (ἴσος), aequans, *balancing*, M 435; *made herself equal*, Ω 607. [ῐ]

ἴσαν, (1) ibant. — (2) noverant, see ΕΙΔ IV.

Ἴσανδρος, son of Bellerophontes, slain by Ares, Z 197. (Il.)

ἴσασι, noverunt, see ΕΙΔ IV. ἰσάσκετο, see ἰσάζουσα. ἴσθι, scito.

ἴσθμιον, τό, (ἰσθμός), *close-fitting necklace*, σ 300†. (See cuts, Nos. 2, 43, and 44, 65, 100.)

I. ἴσκε, ipf., (in-sece, *say*), *said;* λέγων, *spoke relating*, τ 203, χ 31.

II. ἴσκοντες, ουσα, (ἴσος), assimulare, *imitate, make like*, δ 279; ἐμὲ σοί, *taking* me *for* thee.

Ἴσμαρος, city of Kikones, ι 40.

ἰσό-θεος, *godlike* (in figure); epithet of heroes, Γ 310; in Odyssey, of Telemachos, α 324. [ῑ]

ἰσό-μορον, acc., *having an equal share, equally powerful, equal*, O 209†. [ῑ]

ἰσό-πεδον, acc., τό, *level ground*, N 142†.

ἴσος, ον, οι; η, ης, ῃ, ην, ας; ον, α, (Ϝίσος, cf. ἴίση), *like*, par, in size, number, quantity, exterior, nature = idem or unus, N 704, also with φρονεῖν; aequus, *equal*, ἀτεμβόμενος ἴσης, *cheated of his* (of right belonging to him) *just share;* ἴσον ἐμοὶ φάσθαι, *imagine himself my equal*, A 187. — ἴσα (αἶσα ?), β 203, *reparation;* elsewh. e. g. ἴσον, adv., pariter, *on equal terms with*, ξ 203, with dat., I 616; κατὰ ἴσα = ἐπὶ ἴσα, *equally balanced, undecided;* of battle opp. ἑτεραλκέα.

Ἶσος, illegitimate son of Priamos, slain by Agamemnon, Λ 101†.

ἰσο-φαρίζει, οι, ειν, prs., (φᾶρος from φέρω), τινί, *make one's self equal, vie with, rival*, in any thing, τι, Z 101, I 390. (Il.)

ἰσο-φόροι, *drawing alike, equally strong*, σ 373†. [ῑ]

ἰσόω only ἰσωσαίμην (ἴσος) τοῖσιν ἐν, to them *would I compare myself*, η 212†.

ἴσπω only ἔσπετε = σέσπετε, imp. red. aor., (σεπ-, sec-), *declare*, B 484. (Il.)

ἵστημι, I. trans., collocare, prs.,

(imp. ἵστη, inf. ἱστάμεναι), ipf. also iter. ἵστασκε, fut. στήσειν, 1 aor. ἔστησε, στῆσα, ε, ἔστησαν (ἵστᾶσαν, Μ 56, γ 182 ; elsewh. read ἵστασαν), in general ; *set*, *place*, of things ; *cause to rise*, cloud, fog ; excitare, pugnam, rixam, *rouse*, *begin*, battle, strife, π 292 ; *stop*, mill ; νῆα, *bring to land*, τ 188 ; *weigh off*, τάλαντα, pounds ; pass. aor. ἱστάθη *stood firm*, ρ 463. II. **intr.**, *set one's self*, *stand*, mid. prs., ipf., fut., also act. 2 aor. **ἔστην** = στῆν, *I stood*, στῆμεν, ἔστητε, ἔστησαν, στῆσαν, ἱστᾶν, στάν, and iter. στάσκε, subj. στῶ, στήῃς, ῃ, ομεν, στέωμεν, dissyllable by synizesis, Λ 348 ; inf. στήμεναι, pf. **ἔστηκα,** *I stand*, ας, ε, ασιν, (ἔστητε, Δ 243, 246 ?), and sync. pf. ἔστατον, μεν, τε, ἐστᾶσι, imp. ἔσταθι, τε, part. ἐστεῶτα, ες (in first foot of verse, θ 380, Β 170). ἑστᾶότος, α, ες, ων (in second foot) ; plupf. ἑστήκει, ἕστασαν, of things with and without life, *rise up*, *arise*, Α 535, cf. ὀρθός, dust, battle ; μὴν ἱστάμενος, *coming*, *advancing* month ; *stand firmly*, *still*. III. mid. **στήσασθαι,** *set up for one's self*, or something *of one's own* ; μάχην, pugnam committere, join battle, Σ 533, ι 54.

Ἱστίαια (pronounce Ἱστjαίαν), city in Euboia, Β 537†.

ἱστίη, ἡ, (ἱστία), *hearth*, ξ 159. (Od.) [ῑ]

ἱστίον, ῳ, pl. α, (ἱστός), *sail*, *sails*, Α 481, 433, β 426. (See adjoining cut, from ancient coin bearing the inscription, ΝΙΚΟΜΗΔΙΩΝ . ΔΙΣ . ΝΕΩΚΟΡΩΝ.)

ἱστο-δόκη (δέχομαι), *mast-receiver*, *mast-crutch*, a saw-horse-shaped support on the after-deck to receive the mast when lowered, Α 434†. (Plate IV.)

ἱστο-πέδη (πέδη), *mast-stay*, a thwart or transverse beam with a depression into which the mast fitted, which was by this means, as well as by the ἐπίτο-

νοι, prevented from falling forward, μ 51. (See cut, letter *b*.)

ἱστός, οῦ, ῳ, όν, οἱ, οὕς, (ἵστημι, that which stands), (1) *mast* in middle of ship, held in place by μεσόδμη, ἱστοπέδη, πρότονοι, ἐπίτονοι ; during stay in port the mast was unstepped and laid back upon the ἱστοδόκη (cf. preceding cut, and Nos. 64, 91, 109).—(2) *weaver's beam*, *loom*. The frame of the loom was not placed, as in modern hand-looms, in a horizontal position, but stood upright as appears in the cut, representing an ancient Egyptian

loom. The threads of the warp hung perpendicularly down, and were drawn tight by weights at their lower ends. To set up the beam and so begin the web is (ἱστόν) στήσασθαι. In weaving, the weaver passed from one side to the other before the loom (ἐποίχεσθαι) as he carried the shuttle (κανών), on which was wound the thread of the woof, through the warp, and then drave the woof home with a blow of the κερκίς.—(3) warp, and in general web, woven stuff.

ἴστω, scito, see ΕΙΔ IV.

ἴστορι, α, dat. acc., (οἶδα), one who knows, judge, Σ 501, Ψ 486.

ἰσχἄλέοιο, gen. sing., (ἰσχνός), dry, withered, τ 233†.

ἰσχάνδας, α, mid. ἀσθω, ipf. iter. ἰσχανάασκον, also pres. ἰσχάνει, ipf. ἴσχανε, ἔρην, and ἰσχανόωσι, όων, όωσαν, mid. όωνται, όωντο, (ἴσχω), retinere, detain, o 346; arcere, keep off, P 747; mid. restrain one's self, M 38; and delay, T 234; but with gen. or inf., desire, P 572, Ψ 300.

ἰσχίον, ῳ, α, (ἰξύς), hip-joint, E 306, κοτύλη; then coxa, parts about the hips, flanks, or loins, E 305. [ῐον.]

ἴσχωσι, prs., inf. ἰσχέμεν(αι), and ipf. act. and mid. (red. prs. from ἔχω), tenere, retinere, hold, restrain; τινός, arcere, keep away from, E 90; mid., put restraint upon one's self, stay, χ 367; stop, ω 54; τινάς, desist from.

ἰτέαι (Fιτ., vimen, withe), willows, Φ 350 and κ 510.

ἴτην, ibant ambo.

Ἴτὔλος, son of Aëdon. τ 522†. [ῐ]

Ἰτὔμονεύς, ἦα, son of Hypeirochos, slain by Nestor, Λ 672†. [ῐ]

ἴτυς, υν, (Fιτέη), felloes of wheel, Δ 486. (Il.) [ῐ]

ἴτω, ito, from εἶμι.

Ἴτων, ωνα, town in Thessaly, B 696†. [ῐ]

ἰϋγμῷ, dat., (ἰΰζω), cry of joy, Σ 572†. [ῐ]

ἰΰζουσιν, οντες, (ἰού), scream (with intent to scare away), o 162 and P 66. [ῐ]

Ἰφεύς, έα, a Trojan slain by Patroklos, Π 417†.

Ἰφθίμη, daughter of Ikarios, wife of Eumelos, δ 797†.

ἴφθῑμος, η, α, etc., (τιμή?), strong, mighty; deriv. and signif. still uncertain, A 3.

ἴφῐ (Fῑφι, really old case form from Fίς, ἴς), νἱ, by violence, κταμένοιο; with might, ρ 443.

Ἰφῐ-άνασσα, daughter of Agamemnon, I 145 and 287. [ῐφ.]

Ἰφι-δάμας, αντος, son of Antenor

and of Theano, Λ 21 sqq. (Il.) [-◡ ◡-]

Ἰφι-κλείης, γ, βίης, periphrasis for Ἴφικλος, son of Phylakos, father of Podarkes and Protesilaos, B 705, N 698, Ψ 636, λ 289 sqq.

Ἰφι-μέδεια, wife of Aloeus and mother of Otos and Ephialtes, λ 305. [-◡◡-]

Ἰφί-νοος, son of Dexios, slain by Glaukos, H 14†. [-◡◡]

ἴφια (Fίς) μῆλα. fat sheep, E 556, λ 108. [ῑφι.]

Ἰφῐς εὔζωνος, from Skyros, wife of Patroklos, I 667†.

Ἰφιτίδης, Archeptolemos, Θ 128†.

Ἰφϊτίων, ωνα, Ὀτρυντείδην, slain by Achilleus, Υ 382.

Ἴφῐτος (Fίφιτος), (1) Εὐρυτίδης, an Argonaut, guest-friend of Odysseus, slain by Herakles, φ 14-37.—(2) Ναυβολίδαο, an Argonaut, from Phokis, father of Schedios and Epistrophos, P 306, B 518.—(3) father of Archeptolemos.

ἰχθῠᾷ, pr. and ipf. iter. ἰχθυάασκον, (ἰχθύς), fish, μ 95 and δ 368.

ἰχθυόεντι, τα, (ἰχθύς), abounding in fish, full of monsters of the deep, ι 83, I 4, δ 381.

ἰχθύς and pl. ύες, ύσιν, ύας, ῦς, piscis, fish, only eaten in lack of other food, δ 368.

ἴχνια, pl. with the form ἴχνεσι, (Fίκω), vestigia. steps, β 406; ρ 317, odoratione, scent; but N 71 (see ἴκελος), outlines, similar lines, resemblance.

ἰχώρ, acc. ἰχῶ, (ἰκμάς). fluid that flows in veins of the gods, E 340 and 416. [ῐ]

ἴψ, pl. ἶπες, (Fισπ., vespa?), worm that devours horn and wood, borer, φ 395†.

ἴψαο, ἴψεται, chastise, strike; see ἴπτομαι.

ἰωγῇ (Fάγνυμι) Βορέω ὑπ', under shelter from Boreas, ξ 533†. [ῐ]

ἰωή, ῆς, (ἀυτή), sound (of voice). K 139; tone, note, ρ 261; roaring, whistling (of wind).

ἰωκή, pl. άς, also acc. sing. ἰῶκα, (ἰώκω), attack, E 521; personified, E 740. (Il.) [ῐ]

ἰωχμόν (ἰῶκα), άν', through the battle-tumult, Θ 89 and 158. [ῐ]

Κ υ

κʹ = (ἱ, ϛϛ, (2) καί.

κάββαλε, deiecit, from καταβάλλω.

κὰγ (κατὰ) γόνυ, on the knee, Υ 458†.

Κάβησόθεν, from Kabesos, N 363†.

κάγκᾰνᾰ, arida, dry, Φ 364.

καγχᾰλόωσι, ὁων, ὁωσα, (χάσκω), laugh aloud, exult, Γ 43.

καδ=κατά before δ, Φ 318. καδ-δραθέτην, aor. from καταδαρθάνω, ο 4)4.

καδδῦσαι, aor. part., penetrantes, from καταδύω.

Καδμεῖοι, Kadmeioi, Thebans, Δ 391; = Καδμείωνες, Δ 385.

Κάδμος, original founder of Thebes; his daughter Ino, ε 333†.

Κάειρα, fem. of Κάρ, from Karia, Karian, Δ 142†. [ᾰ]

καήμεναι, inf. aor. pass. from καίω, cremo.

καθ-αιρέω, fut. -αιρήσουσι, aor. -είλομεν, subj. -έλῃσι, part. -ελοῦσα; also in tmesi, ipf. ᾕρεε, εον, aor. ἕλον, γσιν, ἑειν, take down, Ω 268, ι 149; close the eyes of the dead, Λ 453; overpower.

κᾰθαίρειν (καθαρός), ipf. κάθαιρον, aor. ἐκάθηρε, κάθηραν, etc., cleanse, clean; σ 192. adorn; abluere, wash off, away, soil, blood, Ξ 171, ζ 93; τινά αἷμα, Π 667.

κάθ-αλλομένη, aor. κατᾶλτο, rush down, Λ 298†.

καθ-άπαξ, once for all, φ 349†.

[∪ ∪ —]

κᾰθ-άπτεσθαι, prs., ipf. καθάπτετο, (ἅπτω), compellare, address, ἐπέεσσι μαλακοῖσιν; also reprehendere, upbraid, Ο 127.

καθαρῷ, ᾷ, purus, c'ean; ἐν κ., in a clear, open space, Θ 491; θάνατος, honorable.

κατʹ ἕξεαι, subj. -εζώμεσθα, imp. -έζευ, ipf. καθέζετο, -εζέσθην, freq. in tmesi, consido, sit down; πρόχνυ, placing herself upon her knees, I 570.

καθῆκα = καθῆκα, from ἵημι. καθείατο = καθῆντο, from κάθημαι.

καθ-εῖσε, εἷσαν, aor., freq. in tmesi, (ἕζω), bid be seated, Η 57, Ψ 698; set, place, δ 524.

καθέξει, fut. from κατ-έχω.

κᾰθ-εύδετον, du., inf. prs., ipf. κᾰθεῦδε, dormire, sleep, A 611. (Od.)

κᾰθ-εψιόωνται (ἐψιάομαι) σέθεν, te irrident, deride, insult, τ 372†.

κᾰθ-ήμενος, etc., imp. κάθησο, pf., plupf. καθῆστο, pl. καθείατο, (ἥμαι), sedere, sit, A 134 and Λ 76, Ω 403.

καθῆραι, αν, aor. from καθαίρω.

κᾰθ-ίδρυε, considere iussit, ν 257†.

κᾰθ-ίζᾰνον, 3 pl. ipf., considebant, were gathering to the assembly and taking seats there, ε 3†.

κᾰθ-ίζων, prs., ipf. καθῖζε, ον, often in tmesi, I. act. and mid., sedere, sit, ἐπὶ κλισμοῖς, etc.—II. act. prs. ipf. aor. κάθισαν, imp. ισον, part. ἱσσας, place, I 488; considere iubeo, bid be seated, Τ 280, Z 360; convoke, β 69.

κᾰθ-ίημι, only -ίετε, aor. καθῆκα (elsewh. in tmesi), let down, lower; λαυκανίης, pour down through the throat, moisten the throat, Ω 642.

κᾰθ-ίκεο, ετο, (ἵκω), touch, reach, α 342.

κᾰθ-ίστα, imp. prs., aor. imp. στῆσον, inf. στῆσαι, set down; νῆα, bring to land, anchor; ν 274, bring, carry.

καθ-ορῶν, mid. -ορᾶται, ὁρώμενος, look down upon, τι, Ω 291.

κᾰθ-ύπερθεν, desuper, from above, Γ 337; supra, M 153, Σ 353; ultra, besides, Ω 545.

καί, (1) copulative: as well as, O 634, λ 417; et, and, A 7, α 5; distributive = (et—et), both—and, λ 417, A 395; uniting two imperatives (in transition of thought), σ 171; καὶ δέ, and besides, ξ 39; δή, and already, A 161, μ 330; κ. μέν, and yet, A 269; κ. τέ, and besides also, A 521; κ. τόν, at beginning of verse, et hunc quidem, Ψ 748; or even, or also, β 374, instead of τέ, B 49, Z 268, α 159.—(2) also, expressing a natural (logical or actual) harmony between two clauses: ὅς (τε), which also, Υ 165, E 62, λ 111; in protasis and apodosis, Z 476, B 367; esp. freq. introducing apodosis, A 478;

καὶ τότε δή—γάρ τε, A 63, nam et, etenim; instead of rel. form, β 114; κ. λίην, yes to be sure, by all means, A 553; ἔπειτα, and finally; ἠὲ καὶ (οὐκί), or also (not), δ 809; cf. French ou bien, B 300; cf. A 95; νῦν, and now also, joining to a general sentence a special illustration of truth previously announced, A 109, B 239, κ 43; καὶ ἄλλους, φ 293; κ. ἄλλοτε, previously also; κ. ἄλλως, already without this, φ 87; καὶ αὐτοί, α 33 (περ, A 577), of themselves also, sponte.—(3) emphatic, also, even: e. g. καὶ δέ, besides, moreover, N 484; κ. βουλοίμην, Γ 41; δέ τε, Υ 28; μᾶλλον, etiam magis, even more, Θ 470.—(4) concessive. e. g. where force may be given by although, though thou shouldst destroy, P 647; μάλα περ, with part., A 217, P 571.—(5) separated from ἄλλα, which it emphasizes, by δέ or γάρ intervening, ξ 39; κ., also, emphasizing the following word, Γ 184 (as well as to other places); καὶ εἰ=et si and etsi, even if; εἰ καί, etiamsi, if even, although; shortened in η 221; by elision, κ'; by crasis, χἠμεῖς, καὐτός, κἀγώ, κἀκεῖνος.

καιετάεσσαν (κείω), full of caverns, δ 1† (v. l. κητώεσσαν, q. v.).

Καινείδης, Koronos, B 746†.

Καινεύς, king of Lapithai, A 264†.

καίνυμαι, ipf. ἐκαίνυτο, pf. κέκασται, σμίνος, plupf. ἐκέκαστο, superiorem esse, excellere, be superior, excel, τισί, Δ 339, ι 509; ἐπί τινας, Ω 535, cf. ω 509; ἔν τισι, δ 725; μετά τισι, ρ 82; τῶν, Ω 546; ἐπί τινι, excellere re, Υ 35; superare, surpass, τινά τινι, B 530, τ 395; with inf., β 158, γ 282.

καί—περ, always separated, although.

καιρίῳ, ιον, letalis. fatal, Θ 84; ἐν καιρ., in a vital part, Δ 185. (Il.)

καιροσέων, better καιροσσέων for καιρουσσῶν (καιροεσσέων, pronounced with synizesis), gen. pl. fem. from adj. καιρόεις, with many καίροι, i. e. loops or thrums to which the threads of the warp were attached; κ. ὀθονέων, from the fine-woven linen, η 107†.

καίουσι, 3 pl. ind., subj. -ωμεν, inf. -έμεν, imp. part. prs., ipf. καῖε, aor. ἔκηε, κῆε, subj. κήομεν, opt. κήαι, αιεν, etc., mid. κήαντο, ἄμενος, οι, pass. prs., ipf. καίετο, ετο, etc., aor. ἐκάη, inf. καιΐ-μεναι, kindle, burn; mid. for one's self, I 88, 234; pass., ardere, cremari, be lighted, blaze.

κάκ=κατά by apocope and assimilation before κ.

κἀκιζόμενον (κακός), play the coward, Ω 214†.

κακ-κεῖαι and κακ-κῆαι, see κατακαιέμεν.

κακ-κείοντες, see κατα-κείω.

κάκο-είμονας, acc. pl., (Fεῖμα), ill-clad, σ 41†.

κάκο-εργίης, gen. sing., (Fέργον), ill-doing, maleficentia, χ 374†.

κάκο-εργός, (Fέργον), maleficus, vil'ainous, importunate, σ 54†.

Κᾱκο-ΐλιον, acc., evil Ilios, τ 260, 597, ψ 19.

κάκο-μηχάνου, ε, (μηχάνη), contriving evil, malicious, π 418.

κάκο-ξεινώτερος, having sorrier guests, υ 376†.

κακο-ρραφίης, ῃ, ῃσι, (ῥάπτω), maliciousness, evil device, μ 26.

κακός, ή, όν, etc., malus, bad, worthless, wicked, in widest signif., in appearance, position, usefulness, courage, morals, way of thinking; hence ugly, vile, useless, cowardly, low, injurious, fatal; esp. as subst., κακόν, ά, =malum, a, evil, pest; of Skylla, μ 118; adv. κακῶς, male, A 25, β 203; comp. κακώτερος, ον, worse, Τ 321; feebler, Χ 106; malicious person, ζ 275; κακίων, ιον, ιον, sup. κάκιστος, ον, poorer, ξ 56; less honorable, I 601; worse, σ 174; deteriores, β 277; the worst, δ 199.

κάκό-τεχνος (τέχνη), devising evil, wily, Ο 14†.

κάκότητος, gen., τι, τα, (κακότης), scelus, wickedness, cowardice; malum, evil, misery, distress, ρ 318; esp. in war, e. g. Α 382.

κάκο-φράδές, voc., (φράζω, φρήν), bad in counsel, foolish, malevolc, Ψ 483†.

κακόω, imp. κάκου, aor. κακῶσαι, etc., pf. pass. part. κεκακωμένος, οι, (κακός), vexare, τινά, pain, injure, maltreat, υ 99; ζ 137, disfigured, foedatus.

κάκτανε, see κατακτείνω. κακώτερος, see κακός.

κᾰλάμην, acc., (calamus, German halm), reed, T 222; looking upon the poor husk which remains, thou art yet able to recognize what I was, ξ 214.

κᾶλα-ύροπα, (from κάλως and Ϝροπα), shepherd's staff, Ψ 845†.

κᾰλέω, prs. ipf. act. and pass. comm. uncontracted forms : καλέει, etc., yet not always, e. g. inf. καλήμεναι, part. καλεῦντες ; ipf. κάλεον, pass. καλεῦντο, iter. καλέεσκον, καλέσκετο ; fut. καλέει, έων, aor. ἐκάλεσσας, αν, also κάλεσας, κάλεσσαν, καλέσσας, etc. (with σ and σσ), mid. καλέσσατο, etc., perf. pass. κέκλημαι, plupf. κεκλήατο, 3 fut. κεκλήσῃ, (calare), (1) call ; ἀμυδις, together ; with εἰς-, -δε, ἐπὶ οἱ, βουλήν, to the council ; θανατόνδε, Π 693 ; invitare, invite, also mid.—(2) nominare, A 403, pass. (esp. pf. and plupf. and 3 fut.) ; vocari, be called, be, pass for, κεκλημένος εἴη(ν), ζ 244 (B 260) ; καλέσκετο, Ο 338, Ξ 210 ; also καλέω, ξ 147, I call him dearly loved, he is tenderly loved by me.

Κᾰλήσιος, companion of Axylos, slain by Diomedes, Ζ 18†.

Κᾰλητορίδης, Aphareus, Ν 541†.

κᾰλήτορα, acc., (καλέω), calator, crier, Ω 577†.

Κᾰλήτωρ, (1) son of Klytios, cousin of Hektor, slain by Aias, Ο 419.—(2) father of Aphareus.

καλείπειν, καλείψειν, see καταλείπω.

Καλλι-άνασσα and Καλλιάνειρα, Nereids, Σ 46, 44†. [—◡◡ —◡]

Καλλίαρος, town in Lokris, Β 531†. [—◡◡◡]

καλλί-γύναικα, with beautiful women, Hellas, Achaia, Sparta, ν 412.

καλλί-ζωνος, ων, (ζώνη), with beautiful girdles (see cut No. 47), Η 139.

Καλλί-κολώνη, lit. Fair-mount, near Ilios, Υ 151.

καλλι-κόμοιο (κόμη), cf. ἠΰκομος. with beautiful hair, I 449.

καλλι-κρήδεμνοι (κρή-δεμνον), with beautiful fillets or head-bands, ὅ 623†.

κάλλιμος, ον, α, glorious, λ 640. (Od.)

κάλλιον, see καλός.

καλλι-πάρηος, ῳ, ον, (παρειά), beautiful-cheeked, fair-cheeked, A 143.

κάλλιπε, πίειν, see καταλείπων.

καλλι-πλοκάμου, οιο, ῳ, with beautiful locks or braids, cf. ἐϋπλοκαμίδες (πλόκαμος), Ξ 326. (See cut No. 47.)

καλλι-ρέεθρον, beautifully flowing, κ 107. (Od.)

καλλι-ρρόοιο, ῳ, ον, (-σροος, ῥόος), beautifully flowing, B 752, ε 441.

κάλλιστος, see καλός.

καλλί-σφῠρος, ον, ον, with beautiful ankles, (σφυρά), slender-footed, ε 333.

καλλί-τρῐχος, α, ε, ες. ας, (θρίξ). with soft fleece, ι 336 ; with beautiful manes, Θ 348.

κάλλιφ'=κατέλιπε.

καλλι-χόρου (χορός), with beautiful places, with large squares for the choral dance, λ 581†.

κάλλος, εος, εϊ, beauty ; σ 192, means for enhancing beauty [unguent?]

κᾰλός, ή, όν, adv. καλῶς, β 63 ; comp. καλλίονες, ιον, sup. κάλλιστος, ον, ους, αι, pulcher, δέμας, beautiful, of form, in build ; fitting, becoming, τινί, be any one ; εἰπεῖν, ἀγορεύειν, well. Adv. καλά, in the middle of verse, Θ 400, and καλόν with ἀείδειν, A 473.

κάλους, acc. pl. from κάλως, ropes, halyards ; which, passing through a hole at top of mast, and made fast at bottom of same, served to raise and lower the yard. (See cut.)

κάλπῑν, τήν, water jar, η 20†. (See cut, from picture on ancient vase, on next page.)

Κᾰλύδναι νῆσοι, near Kos, Β 677†.

Καλυδών, ῶνος, city on the river Euenos in Aitolia ; ἐραννῆς, αἰπεινῇ, πετρήεσσαν, I 530, Ν 217, Β 640.

κάλυμμα, το, (καλύπτω). veil, Ω 93†. (See cuts Nos. 2, 47, 66, 74.)

κάλῠκας, τάς, (κάλυξ), women's ornaments, Σ 401† ; perhaps cup-shaped ear-rings. (See cut No. 8.)

κᾰλύπτρην, τήν, (καλύπτω), woman's

veil, ε 232. (Cf. adjoining cut, and Nos. 2, 47, 74.)

κᾰλύπτων, part. prs., fut. καλύψω, aor. (ἐ)κάλυψε, also mid., pass. pf. κεκαλυμμένος, plupf. κεκάλυφθ' = ἐκεκάλυπτο, aor. καλυφθείς, (calim, occultus), veil, θ 85; cover, Κ 29, Ψ 693 (mid., veil one's self, Γ 141); τινί, cover up with, Σ 352; πρόσθεν στέρνοιο (οἱ), hold as protection before the breast (before one's self); σάκος ἀμφί τινι, protect one with the shield; pass., wrapped up in, α 443 (ἐντυπάς, closely); hidden, θ 503; fig. τὸν δὲ σκότος ὄσσε, Δ 461, so also κατ' ὀφθαλμῶν νύξ, Ν 580, darkness overshadowed his eyes; τέλος θανάτοιο, end of death, complete death, Ε 553; grief, a cloud of grief enveloped him, Λ 249, ω 315.

Κᾰλυψώ, οῦς, daughter of Atlas, dwelling in Ogygia, where she rescues, and detains for seven years, the shipwrecked Odysseus, η 259; until compelled by command of Zeus to dismiss him, ε 28, η 265; epithets, δολόεσσα, δεινὴ θεός, ἐυπλόκαμος, αὐδήεσσα, ἠυκόμοιο, νύμφη πότνια.

Κάλχας, αντος, son of Thestor, Grecian seer before Troy, Α 69, 86; θεοπρόπος οἰωνιστής, Ν 70. (Il.)

κάμ = κατά by apoc. and assimil. before μ.

κάμαξι, dat. pl., (ἡ κάμαξ), vinepoles, vine-props, Σ 563†. [◡ — ◡]

κᾰμᾰτος, οιο, ῳ, ον, (κάμνω), labor, aerumna, fatigatio, t il, distress, fatigue; ξ 417, fruit of our toil.

κάμβᾰλε = κατέβαλεν, ζ 172.

κάμε, aor. from κάμνω, wrought.

Κάμειρος, town on west coast of Rhodos, Β 656†. [ᾰ]

κᾰμῖνοῖ, τῇ, nom. καμινώ, (κάμινος), baker-woman, σ 27†.

καμ-μίξας, aor. from καταμίγνυμι.

καμ-μονίην, τήν, (κατα-μένω), victory as reward of endurance, Χ 257†.

κάμ-μορον, ε, (κατά-μορος?). ill-starred, hapless, β 351; applied to Odysseus.

κάμνεις, ει, prs., ipf., aor. ἔκαμον κάμε, ετον, subj. κάμω, ῃσι, part. καμόντα, ας, ων; pf. κέκμηκας, κεκμηώς, ῶτι, ῶτα, ότας, mid. fut. καμεῖται, aor. καμόμεσθα, ἐκάμοντο, I. laborare, weary one's self out, become tired, Λ 802, κ 31, Ζ 261 sq., Θ 22, Δ 27; with acc. of part. γυῖα, ὦμον, χεῖρα, μ 280, Π 106; with part., φ 150, Φ 26, Η 5; with neutr. subj., μ 232; ὄσσε, πόδες, Ψ 444; καμόντες, confecti, those who have finished their toil, the dead.—II. elaborare, make ready with care and labor, work, (aor. act.), Δ 187, ψ 189; with τεύχων, work skillfully; aor. mid., ι 130, would have transformed into a well-tilled, habitable island; acquire for one's self, Σ 341.

κάμπτω, only aor. **κάμψειν**, aor. ἐκαμψε, κάμψῃ, flecto, bend; Δ 486, bend into a tire; γόνυ, bend the knee = sit down to rest when weary with running, Η 118; ε 453, let sink upon the ground.

καμπύλον, α, (κάμπτω), bent, curved, Ε 231. [ῠ]

κᾰνᾰχησε, aor. from -έω, (κάναχος), rang, τ 469†. [◡ ◡]

κᾰνᾰχή, ήν, sonitus, strepitus, Τ 365, gnashing; ζ 82, rattle of harness of mule team in motion.

κᾰνᾰχιζε, ipf., (καναχή), creaked, Μ 36; re-echoed, κ 399. [◡ ◡ — ◡]

κάνεον, sing. and pl. κάνεια, έοισι, (κάνη), basket for wheaten bread; dish for meat and sacrificial barley, α 147, ρ 343. [ᾰ] καν-νεύσας, aor. part. from κατα-νεύω.

κανών, ίνεσσι, όνας, masc., (κάνη), (1) shuttle or spool, by which the thread of the woof was drawn through the thread of the warp, Ψ 761.—(2) handle on interior of shield, grasped by the left hand, Θ 193, N 407. (Il.) (See cuts Nos. 12, 17, 85; rudely represented in adjoining cut, after Assyrian relief.)

κάπ = κατά, before π and φ.

Κᾰπᾰνεύς, ῆος, one of the Seven against Thebes, father of Sthenelos, Ε 319; ἀγακλειτοῦ, κυδαλίμοιο.

Κᾰπᾰνηϊάδης and Κᾰπᾰνήϊος υἱός, Sthenelos, Ε 109, 108.

κᾰπέτοιο, ον, from ἡ κάπετος, (σκάπτω), ditch, grave, Σ 564, Ω 797. (Il.)

κάπῃσι, dat. pl., praesepe, manger, δ 40, Θ 434. [ᾰ]

κάπνισσαν, 3 pl. aor. from καπνίζω, lighted fires, B 399†.

καπνός, οῦ, sing., (καπύω), fumus, smoke; μ 202, cloud of spray from violently agitated water.

κάπ - πεσον, εν, aor. from κατα-πίπτω.

κάπριος, ῳ, ον, (κάπρος), with and without σῦς, aper, wild-boar, M 42, P 282. (Il.)

κάπρου, ῳ, ον, ω, οισι, wild-boar, P 21; Τ 197, boar.

Κᾰπυς, νος, son of Assarakos, father of Anchises, Υ 239†.

καπύω, aor. in tmesi, ἀπὸ ἐκάπυσσεν, breathed forth, X 467†.

I. κάρ = κατά, before ρ.

II. κάρος, ἐν—αἴσῃ, (from κείρω?), = a whittling; cf. Lat. flocci; I care for him not a whit, I 378; the derivation of the word is uncertain.

III. κάρ, ἐπί—, headlong, Π 392†; here belong κάρη, ητος, ητι, and καρήατος, -τι, pl. -τα, also gen. κρατός, τί, pl. κράτων, κρασίν, K 152; κράτεσφι, K 156; also κράατος, -τι, acc. pl. -τα, and κράτα, (κορυφή, κόρυμβος, Lat. cer-ebrum, cer-vices), caput, head, as part of body, also pl. θ 92, spoken of one head; of mountain summit, Υ 5; λιμένος, the end reaching farthest into the land, ι 140.—κατὰ κρῆθεν, from head (to foot), utterly, entirely, Il 548, λ 588.

Καρδᾰμύλη, town subject to Agamemnon, in Messene, I 150. [ῠ]

καρδίη, ης, see κραδίη, cor, heart.

Κᾶρες, Karians in S.W. of Asia Minor, βαρβαροφώνων, B 867. (Il.)

κάρη κομόωντες, ας, = capite comati, long - haired, B 11, α 90; of Achaians, who cut their hair only in mourning, or on taking a vow, Ψ 146, 151; while slaves and Asiatics habitually shaved their heads.

κάρηνα, ων, τά, (κάρ III.), capita, cacumina, heads, summits, also battlements, B 117. [ᾰ]

Κάρησος, river rising in Mount Ida, M 20†. [ᾰ]

κάρκαιρε, ipf., quaked, Υ 157†.

καρπᾰλίμοισι, dat. pl., adv. -ίμως, pernices, swift, quick, epithet of feet, Π 342, A 359, β 406.

καρπός, masc., only sing., fructus, fruges, fruit, ἐπὶ καρπῷ (σ 258), by the ball, joint of the hand, wrist.

καρρέζουσα, see κατα-ρέζω.

καρτερό-θῡμον, ε, ων, (κρατερός), strong-hearted, E 277, Ξ 512. (Il.)

καρτερός, see κρατερός.

κάρτιστος, ον, ην, οι, οις, (κάρτος), robustissimus, potentissimus; neutr., μ 120, the greatest valor.

κάρτος, see κράτος.

ἐκαρτύναντο, ipf. mid., (καρτύνω), φάλαγγας, were strengthening their ranks, Λ 215. (Il.) [ῠ]

Κάρυστος, fem., town at southern extremity of Euboia, B 539†. [ᾰ]

καρφᾰλέον, έων, ntr., (κάρφω), aridus, dry; of sound, dull, hollow, N 409. (Il.)

κάρφω, fut. κάρψω, aor. κάρψε, shrivel
up, ν 398 and 430.

καρχᾰλέοι ἐίψῃ, rough with thirst,
i. e. the throat rough and dry, Φ
541†.

καρχᾰρ-όδοντε, ων, sharp-toothed,
sharp-biting, of dogs, K 360. (Il.)

κασί-γνητος, οιο, ον, etc., and
-γνήτη, ην, αι, ῃσι, own brother, sister
(of the same mother), Z 420, Δ 155,
441; also consobrinus, cousin, O
545.

Kάσος, island near Kos, B 676†.

Κασσ-άνδρη, the most beautiful
daughter of Priamos, prophetess, captive of Agamemnon, murdered by
Klytaimnestra, N 366, Ω 699, λ 422.

κασσίτερου, οιο, ῳ, ον, tin, as ornament of weapons and chariots; χεῦμα,
stream or border of tin, to give strength,
Ψ 561.

Kαστἴ-άνειρα, καλή, Αἰσύμνηθεν,
mother of Gorgythion, Θ 305†.

καστορνῦσα, see κατα-στορέννυμι.

Kάστωρ, ορος, (1) son of Zeus and
Leda, brother of Polydeukes and Helena, participated in Kalydonian boar-
hunt and in Argonautic expedition, Γ
237, λ 299 sqq.—(2) son of Hylakos,
ξ 204.

κά σχετε instead of κατ-έσχετε, Λ
702, retinuit.

κατά (and καταί, also κάτα, κατ', in
anastrophe and tmesi, also κάτ', ρ 246;
by assimilation also καβ, καγ, καδ, κακ
[καλ?], καμ, καπ [before π and φάλαρ],
καρ, κάτ-θανε], I. with gen. of place:
from above down, down from, 'Ολύμπου,
οὐρανοῦ, cf. κ 362; down over, ὀφθαλμῶν,
κρῆθεν, desuper, ἄκρης, from crown
(to sole), wholly; ἵππων, down from the
chariot, E 111; ῥινῶν, down into the
nostrils; ι 330, down into the depths of
the cave, χθονός, to the ground (Γ 217),
down under the ground, Ψ 100 ;·γαίης,
upon the ground.—II. with acc., (1)
local: down, ῥῖνας, through the nostrils, cf. σ 97; ὕδωρ, into the water, cf.
Z 136; κέρας, on the horn (horn sheath
for the part of line next the hook); in
region of, upon, on, στῆθος, αὐχένα, στόμα, ἀσπίδα, ὁδόν; in neighborhood of,
στρατόν, usually per castra, passim in castris, through the camp,
everywhere throughout the camp, A 10,
409, 484; with verbs of motion, per,

through, νῆας, λαῶν, ὦλκα; then within,
in the midst of, 'Αχαιίδα, 'Ελλάδα, μόθον, κλόνον, ὑσμίνην, Φ 310; ὕλην,
ἄστυ, δῶμα, βωμόν, upon; θυμόν, in
heart, inwardly; φρένα, in mind; φρ.
καὶ κ. θυμόν, in heart and mind.—(2)
distributive: στίχας, according to ranks;
φῦλα, B 362; σφέας, by themselves;
ἐμ' αὐτόν, ipse solus.—(3) with, according to: secundum, κῦμα, ῥύον, β
429; θυμόν, according to wish, A 136,
cf. I 108; αἶσαν (opp. ὑπὲρ αἶσαν) =
μοῖραν (freq. κατά, II 367), according to
propriety, fitly; κόσμον, in order; οὐ κ.
κ., shamefully, θ 489; after the semblance
of, τ 233; for the purpose of trade, πρῆ-
ξιν, cf. δαῖτα, A 424; ληΐδα, χρέος τινός,
alicuius causa, for the sake of seeing Teiresias.

κατα-βαίνων, prs., ipf., aor. (3 pl.
ἔβησαν and ἔβαν, subj. βείομεν, K 97;
imp. βῆθι, inf. βήμεναι, βῆναι), mid.
-εβήσετο (subj. βήσεται, imp. βήσεο),
descendere, step down, descend, τινός,
from, Ω 329; οὐρανόθεν, ζ 281; εἴς τι,
ἐπί τι, δόμον 'Α. εἴσω, ψ 252; also θάλαμον, β 337; but κλίμακα, descend
the ladder; ἐφόλκαιον, climbing down
along the rudder; only in σ 206, ψ 85,
with pregnant signif., she descended
(the ladder and left) the upper chamber.

κᾰτὰ βάλλων, prs., ipf., aor., (inf.
βαλέειν); always in tmesi exc. ipf. κα-
τέβαλλεν, O 357, and aor. κάββαλε
(better so written than κάμβαλε); de-
iicere, cast down, Ψ 125, μ 252; destruere, destroy, B 414; prosterne-
re; deponere; effundere, δάκρυ;
let fall.

κᾰτα-βείομεν, aor. subj. from -βαί-
νω.

κᾰτα-βλώσκοντα, part. prs., perme-
antem, running about, π 466†.

κᾰτα βρόξειε, opt. aor. from -βρύχω,
devoraret, swallow (down), δ 222†.

κᾰτα-γηράσκουσι, prs., ipf. -εγήρα,
senescunt, grow old, τ 360. (Od.)

κᾰτ-αγίνεον, ipf. from ἀγινέω, (ἄγω),
devehebant, carry down, κ 104†.

κᾰτ-άγνυμι, fut. ἄξω, aor. ῆξε, ἐαξε,
αμεν, subj. ἄξῃς, confringere; N
257, (pluralis maiestatis), shatter.

κᾰτ-άγων, part., εῑν, inf. prs., fut. inf.
-αξέμεν, aor. -ήγαγε, (also tmesis), mid.
ipf. -ήγετο -άγοντο, aor. -ηγαγόμεσθα,

deducere, *lead down*, λ 164; retulit, *bring back*, δ 258; *drive from one's course*, τ 186; mid., appellere, *land*, *bring to land* (νηί, κ 14U), νηῦς, π 322.

κᾰτὰ δάσονται, fut. from δαίω, inter se dividunt = lacerabunt, *tear*, X 354.

κᾰτᾰ δάπτεται, pass. prs., aor. act. ἐδαψαν, ἑάψαι, lacerare, *wound*, π 92.

κᾰτα-δαρθάνω, aor. 1 sing. 3 pl. ἐδρᾰθον, 3 du. καδδρᾰθέτην, subj. δρᾰθῶ, obdormivi, dormio, *sleep*; τοιόνδε, tam placide dormivi, ψ 18. (Od.)

κᾰτᾰ-δέρκεται αὐτούς, *look down upon*, ἀκτίνεσσιν, λ 16†.

κᾰτ-έδευσας, aor., (δεύω), conspersisti, *wet through*, I 490.

κατα-δέω, ipf. ἔδει, aor. (often tmesis) κατ-έδησεν, σαν, subj. δήσῃ, colligare, alligare, *bind fast*; ἐν δεσμῷ, vinculis; κελεύθους, νόστον, *stop*.

κᾰτᾰ-δημο-βορῆσαι, inf. aor., (βιβρώσκω), communiter consumere, *consume in common*, Σ 301†.

κατα-δράθω, subj. aor. from-δαρθάνω, obdormiero, *fall asleep*.

κατα-δύεται, fut. δυσόμεθα, aor. -εδύσετο. (imp. δύσεο), and 2 aor. act. -έδυ (subj. δύω, inf. δῦναι, δύμεναι, part. δύς, δύντι, τα, τες, fem. δῦσα, pl. καδδῦσαι, Τ 25), freq. in tmesi, occidere, *set*, ἠέλιος, φάος ἠελίοιο; intrare, *enter*, δόμον, πύλιν, ὅμιλον, μάχην, μῶλον Ἄρηος; εἰς Ἀ. δόμους, κατά τι, Τ 25; inducere, *put on*, τεύχεα.

κατα ειμένος and -είννυσαν, see κατα-έννυμι.

κατα-είσατο, see κάτ-ειμι.

κᾰτᾰ-έννυμι (Ϝέσνυμι, vestis), aor., contegebant, *cover*, Ψ 135, and pf. pass. -ειμένον, contectum, τ 431.

κᾰτ-αζήνασκε (ἀζαλέος), exsiccabat, *parch, wither up*, λ 587†.

κᾰτᾰ-θάπτειν and aor. inf. κατθάψαι, sepelire, *bury*, Ω 611. (Il.)

κατα-θείομαι, -θείομεν, see κατα-τίθημι.

κᾰτ-έθελξε, aor. from θέλγω, *had charmed*, κ 213†.

κᾰτα-θνήσκων, part. prs., aor. tmesis, 3 pl. θάνον and sync. κάτθἄνε, pf. τεθνήκᾰσι, opt. τεθναίη, inf. τεθνάμεν, part. τεθνηῶτος, ῶτι, ῶτα, ῶτων, ῶτας τεθνηυίης, mori, defungi, *die*; part., mortuus, also joined with νέκυς, νεκροί, λ 37.

κᾰτα-θνητός, ὧν, οἷσι, mortalis, mortal, ἄνδρεσσιν, ἀνθρώπων, Κ 440.

κατα-θρώσκω, only aor. κάδ δ' ἔθορε, desiluit, *spring down*, Δ 79†.

κᾰτᾰ-θύμιος, ον, *floating before the mind*; Κ 383, *think not of*—.

κᾰτὰ χρόα καλὸν ἰάπτῃ, subj. prs., *harm her fair body, destroy her beauty*, β 376. (Od.)

κᾰται-βᾰταί (βαίνω), *that may be descended, passable*, ν 110†.

κᾰτ-ἤκισται, pf. pass., (αἰκίζω), foedata, *disfigured, soiled*, π 290 and τ 9.

κᾰτ-άϊξαντα, τε, ασα, see ἀίσσω; ω 488, *springing down, in haste*.

κᾰτ-αισχύνειν, subj. -ητε, part. οντα, (αἶσχος), foedare, *disgrace*, γένος; δαῖτα, *dishonor*.

κᾰτᾰ-ίσχεται, see κατ-ίσχει.

κᾰταῖ-τυξ (τεύχω), *low leather helmet* or *skull-cap*, Κ 258†. (See cut No. 121.)

κᾰτᾰ-καίριον τέλος, *mortal spot*, Λ 439†.

κᾰτᾰ-καιέμεν, inf., Η 408, καίων, part. ipf. -έκαιον, aor. -ίκηα,-έκηε, subj. κήομεν, inf. κῆαι (κακκῆαι), aor. pass. -εκάη, (also in tmesi), comburere, *burn*; pass., comburi; I 212, *burn out*, deflagraverat.

κατὰ κάλυπτοι, opt. prs., aor. (ἐ)κάλυψεν, etc., (also in tmesi), aor. mid. καλυψάμενος, occulere, *cover up* (by drawing down over the head the veil), κρᾶτα, having veiled his head, θ 92.

κατα-κεῖται, better κῆαι, aor. from καίω.

κᾰτᾰ-κείαται, 3 pl. ind. prs., κεῖσθαι, κείμενος, ipf. -έκειτο, iacent, cubare, *lie*; ἐπὶ πλευράς, on the side; fig. *rest*, Ω 523; Ω 527, positi sunt.

κᾰτᾰ-κείρετε, ipf. -εκείρετε, aor. -έκειραν, consume, δ 686. (Od.)

κᾰτᾰ-κείομεν, subj., imp. κείετε, (κεῖμαι), decumbere, *lie down*, in desiderative signif. only κακκείοντες ἔβαν, cubitum discesserunt, Α 606, α 424.

κατα-κῆαι, κηέμεν, κήομεν, see κατα-καίω.

κᾰτα-κλάω, only ipf. 3 pl. -έκλων, and aor. pass. -εκλάσθη, conculcabant, *tread down*, Υ 227; τινι φίλον ἦτορ, δ 481, fig. my heart *broke*, gave way (from fear, grief); ι 256, δεισάντων, added as explanatory.

κᾰτα-κλίνας, aor. part. from κλίνω, *having laid it down*, κ 165†.

Κᾱτακλῶθες, see Κλῶθες.

κᾰτα-κοιμάομαι, only aor. -εκοιμή-θημεν, imp. -ηθήτω, inf. -ηθῆναι, *sleep*, Λ 731. (Il.)
κᾰτα κοιρανέουσι, see κοιρανέω.

κᾰτ-εκόσμει, ipf., aor. mid. subj. κοσμήσησθε, (κόσμος), *put in order*, χ 440.

κᾰδ κρέμᾰσεν (κρεμάννυμι), θ 67, 105, ἐκ πασσαλόφιν, *hung on* the nail.

κατάκρηθεν, see III. κάρ, funditus, *utterly*.

κατάκρης, see ἄκρη, funditus.

κᾰτα-κρύπτουσι, ων, fut. κρύψειν, aor. part. κρύψας, ασα, occulere, *conceal*, ὑπὸ κόλπῳ, ι 329; αὑτόν, se, δ 247; also η 205, themselves.

κᾰτα-κτείνει, ειν, subj. ῃ, ωσι, prs., fut. κτενεῖ, κτᾰνέουσιν, aor. opt. κτείνειε, inf. κτεῖναι, part. κτείνας, αντα, 2 aor. ἔκτᾰνον, ες, εν (also tmesis, Ζ 416), ομεν, subj. κτάνῃ, and aor. sync. 3 sing. ἔκτα, 1 sing. and 3 pl. ἔκταν, imp. κάκτᾰνε, inf. -κτᾰμεν(αι), part. κτάς; aor. pass. 3 pl. ἔκτᾰθεν, mid. with pass. signif. fut. κτᾰνέεσθε, and aor. κτάμενος, necare, *slay, kill*, α 75, Ε 558, π 106.

κᾰτ-εκύψε, aor. from κύπτω, *bowed himself*, Π 611. (Il.)

καταλαμβάνω (always in tmesi), see λαμβάνω.

κᾰτα-λέγω (see also -λέχω), only fut. -λέξω, and aor. -έλιξα, ας, εν (also tmesis, λ 151), subj. λέξῃς, imp. λεξον, inf. λέξαι, enumerare, *recount*, τ 497; π 235, *narrate* to me, in detail, in order (ἀριθμήσας); *communicate, relate*, δ 256; *tell, disclose*, πᾶσαν ἀλήθειαν, ταῦτα ἀλήθειαν, as truth, in conformity with truth = ἀτρεκέως = οὐ ψεῦδος; εὖ κατὰ μοῖραν = ἐν μοίρῃ, fitly; δάκεο καὶ κ., Τ 186.

κᾰτᾰ-λειβομένοιο, pass., *trickling down*, Σ 109†.

κατα-λείπετε, ειν, ipf. ἔλειπον, ε, ομεν, fut. λείψομεν, ουσι, also (in tmesi): (κάδ) λείπεις, ipf. λεῖπεν, aor. λίπον, ε; λίπω, οιεν; λιπών, ὀντε, οὖσα, οὖσαν, and by assimilation καλλείπειν, fut. λείψω, ειν, aor. λιπον, ες, ε (also λιφ'), inf. ἐειν, relinquere, *leave*, τί, Ζ 221; custodem, ο 89; νέην, as youthful mother, λ 447; ἀγκλίνας, left the door ajar, χ 156; deserere, Φ 414, *forsake, abandon*, εὐχωλήν; *give*

over, as booty, ἕλωρ, with explanatory inf., γ 271, ε 344.

κᾰτα-(λέχω), from stem ΛΕΧ, fut. λέξεται, 1 aor. λέξατο, imp. λέξαι, 2 aor. sync. ἔλεκτο, inf. λέχθαι, part. λέγμενος, (λέχος), *lay one's self down to rest*, ο 394.

κᾰτὰ ἄλεσσαν, aor. from ἀλέω, since *they had ground out* (the wheat), υ 109†.

κατα-λήξονται, obliviscuntur, *forget*, Χ 389†.

κῡτᾱ-λοφᾰδεια (λόφος) φέρων, carrying it *crosswise over his back* (the feet being tied together and held under the chin of the bearer), κ 169†.

κατα-λύσομεν, fut., aor. ἐλῦσε, (λύω), *loose from under* the yoke, *unharness*, δ 28; *destroy*, Β 117.

κᾰδ λωφήσειε, aor. from λωφάω, κακῶν, *recover itself from* the misery, ι 460†.

κατ-έμαρπτε, ipf., aor., (tmesi, ἔμαρψε), subj. μάρψῃ, consequi, *overtake*, Π 598, Ζ 364; corripere, *seize*, ω 390.

κᾰτ-ᾰμήσατο, aor. mid., (ἀμάω), *had heaped upon himself*, Ω 165†.

κᾰτ-ᾰμύξατο, aor. mid., (ἀμύσσω), χεῖρα, *has scratched* her hand, Ε 425†.

κᾰτὰ ἀμφῐκᾰλύψας, aor. part., (καλύπτω), κεφαλῇ ῥάκος, *drawing down from around* my head my ragged garment, ξ 349†.

κᾰτᾰ-νεύων, part., fut. νεύσομαι, aor. ἔνευσα, σας, σε, subj. σω, imp. σον, inf. σαι, part. καινεύσας, adnuere, n d in assent (opp. ἀνα-), τινί τι; also with inf. fut., δ 6; with ὑπέσχεο, ὑπέστην; also κρατί, κεφαλῇ. *permit*.

κᾰτ-άνεται, pass., (ἄνω), consumitur, *use up, waste*, β 58. (Od.)

κατὰ νήσαντο (νέω), ἄσσα οἱ ... λίνῳ, that which *they have spun to* him with the thread, η 197†.

κάτ-αντᾰ, deorsum, *downward*, Ψ 116†.

κατ-άντηστιν, see ἄντηστιν.
κατ-αντικρύ, see ἀντικρύ.

κατὰ πάτησαν, aor. from πατέω, conculcaverunt, *tread under foot, break*, Δ 157†.

κᾰτᾰ-παυμα (παύω), *alleviation*; γόου, *comfort* in their lamentation, Ρ 38†.

κᾰτᾰ-πανέμεν, inf. prs., fut. παύσω, σέμεν, inf. aor. ἔπαυσα, ε, αν, subj. σῃ

and σομεν, finire, placare, put end
to, appease, δ 583; comprimere (co-
ërceri nos vis, β 244); τινά τινος,
hinder from; ironically=slay, Il 618.
  κατὰ ἐπέδησε, aor. from πεδάω, has
fettered, of Ate or Moira, T 94, λ
292.
  κατα-πέσσω, only aor. subj. πέψῃ,
concoquat, digest, repress, A 81†.
  κατὰ πετάσσας, aor. part. from
πετάννυμι, spreading over it, Θ 441†.
  κατα-πέφνων, πέφνῃ, see κατα-
φένω.
  κάτα-πήγνυμι, only aor. ἐπηξεν, αν,
defixit, panxerunt, stick fast, plant,
and sync. aor. mid. ἐπηκτο, fixus
haesit, Λ 378.
  κατα-πίπτω, only aor., in tmesi, Π
469; elsewh. κάππεσον, ε, ἐτην, ον, decidere, procidere, fall down (prae-
ceps, πρηνής), ἐν κονίῃσιν, ἐπὶ γαίῃ,
χαμάζε, ἀλί, cast one's self into the sea;
θυμὸς παραὶ ποσί, courage utterly for-
sook them, Ο 280.
  κατα-(φένω), only red. aor. subj.
πέφνῃ,part. πέφνων, internimere,slay,
P 539.
  κάτ-επλέομεν, ipf., appulimus, put
in, ι 142†.
  κατ-επλήγη, aor. pass. from πλήσσω,
φίλον ἦτορ, was struck in his heart with
fear, Γ 31†.
  κάτα-πρηνεῖ, ἐσσι, from πρηνής,
down turned; with flat of the hand,
χειρί, χερσί, Π 792.
  κατὰ ἐπτηξαν, πτήξας, aor., and
sync. 3 du. πτήτην, crouch down; δεί-
σαντε ὑπ' ὄχεσφιν, under the chariot
for fear, Θ 136.
  κάτα-πτώσσουσι, inf. σσειν, part.
σσοντ(α), τες, timidi sunt; exti-
mescere, yield to fear, E 254. (Il.)
  κάτα-πύθεται, putrescit, become
rotten, ὄμβρῳ, Ψ 328†.
  κάτ-αρῶνται, ipf. ἠρᾶτο (ἀρά), im-
precari, call curses down upon, τινί
πολλά, Ι 454; ἄλγεα, τ 330.
  κάτα-ρῑγηλά, ntr. pl., (ῥῖγος), for-
midolosa, horrible, ξ 226†
  κάτ-ερεξε, ipf., and καρρέζουσα, part.
prs., (ὀρέγω?), stroke, caress, χειρί τέ
μιν κ., δ 610, A 361.
  κάτα-ρρέον, ntr. part., elsewh. tmesis,
ῥέοντες, ipf. ἔρρεε,ῥέε,(σρεω),defluere,
flow down, absol. and with τινός, ἐκ, Δ
149.

  κάτ-άρχεσθαι, only ipf. ἤρχετο χέρ-
νιβά τ' ινλοχύτας τε, began the sacred
hand-washing and the sprinkling of
the barley meal, γ 445†.
  κάτα-σβέννυμι, aor. ἐσβεσε, (tmesis,
Π 293), σαν (tmesis, Ω 791), imp. σβέ-
σατε, extinguere, rogum vino,
quench, Ω 791. (Il.)
  κατα-στύομαι, only aor. -ἐσσῦτο,
(ἐσ̣Fυτο),ῥἐεθρα, streamed down into the
river-bed, Φ 382†.
  κάτ-εσκίαον, ipf. from σκιάω, (σκιά),
obumbrabant, overshadow, μ 436†.
  κατὰ σμῦξαι, aor. inf., (σμύχω),
burn down, 1 653; pass. σμύχοιτο, Χ
411.
  κατα-στορέννυμι, only aor. ἐστόρε-
σαν, στόρεσ(ε), and -εστόρεσαν, part.
κάστορνῦσα, ρ 32, spread out upon; Ω
798, cover over (grave and contents),
λάεσσι.
  κάτ-εστύγε and ἐστύγον, 3 pl. aor.,
(στυγέω), horruit, be horror-struck at,
τί, κ 113.
  κατα-σχεθεῖν, see κατ-ἐχω.
  κατα τεῖνε, aor., drew in (the reins),
Γ 261. (Il.)
  κάτα-τήκω, only aor. -ἐτηξεν, lique-
fecit, melt, τ 206; and pass. τήκομαι
φίλον ἦτορ, acc., my heart is melting
away; τήκεται, liquefit, τ 205.
  κατα-τίθημι, ipf. ἐτίθει, τίθεσαν, fut.
-θήσω, ει, aor. ἐθηκα, εν, αν (also in
tmesi), 2 aor. subj. θείομεν, inf. θεῖναι,
and part. θέντε, mid. 2 aor. 3 pl. -ἐθεν-
το, subj. θείομαι, inf. θέσθαι; sync. 2
aor. act. 1 pl. κάτθεμέν, 3. θεσαν, imp.
θετε, inf. θέμεν, mid. 2 aor. pl. θέμεθα,
θέσθην, θέμενοι, deponere, collocare, place, lay down, τι ἐπὶ γαίῃ, χθονί,
νηΐ, ἀπήνῃ, ῥυμῷ; ὑπ' αἰθούσῃ; ἐν
λεχέεσσι, δήμῳ, ψαμάθῳ, οισιν; ἐπὶ
χθονός, θρόνου; ἐς μυχόν, μέγαρον,
θάλαμον, εἰς 'Ιθάκην; but ἐκ καπνοῦ,
put away out of the smoke; ἐπ' αὐτῷ,
Ψ 381, holding their heads straight toward him; spread out a bed, τ 317;
propose as prize in contest; ἄεθλον,
(ἐπὶ σοί, in thine honor), institute a
contest.—Mid., sibi or suum, am,
etc.. deponere.
  κάτα-τρύχω, indic. and subj. prs.,
exhaurio, exhaust, consume, ο 309.
  καταῦθι, καταυτόθι, see αὖθι and
αὐτόθι.

  κατα-φαγέειν, ωσι, aor. from -εσθίω.

κᾰτα-φέρω, only fut. -οίσεται, με Ἀϊδος εἴσω, will bring me to the grave, X 425†.

κᾰτα-φθίσει, fut., (φθίω), perdet, destroy, ε 341; mid. aor. -εφθῖτο, exhausta erant; φθίσθαι, periisse; φθιμένοιο, οι, οισιν, defuncti.

κᾰτα-φλέξω, fut. from φλέγω, cremabo, consume, πυρί, X 512†.

κᾰτᾰ-φῡλᾰδόν (φῦλον), tributim, in tribes, in clans, B 668†.

κατὰ (δάκρυ) χέοντα, τες, τας, χέουσα, σαν, σαι, (lacrimas), effundens; aor. -έχευα (for έχεFα), ας, εν, αν (both forms freq. in tmesi), subj. χεύῃ, inf. χεῦαι, aor. mid. κέχῠτο and έχυντο, -έχυντο, infundere, offundere, pour down upon, over, τινί τι; effundere, νιφάδας, etc., shower down; πέπλον, let fall; proiicere, cast down, θύσθλα, ἡνία; superinfundere, ἠέρα, etc., τινί; ἐλεγχείην, etc., τινί, conspergere ignominia, cover with ignominy; πλοῦτον, B 670. — Mid. ὀφθαλμῶν or (οἱ) ὀφθαλμοῖσι, oculis (eius) offusa est; φλόξ, diffusa est; ὅπλα, collapsa sunt.

κᾰτα-χθόνιος (χθών), inferior, subterranean, Ζεύς=Aides, I 457†.

κᾰτ-έαξε, αμεν, aor. from -άγνυμι.

κατ-έδει, ipf. from -δέω, colligavit, bind.

κᾰτ-έδουσι, 3 pl., έδων, part. prs., pf. ἐδηδώς, devorare, comedere, eat up, devour, T 31; consumere, οἶκον, rem familiarem, τ 159; ὃν θυμόν, consume, waste one's heart.

κατὰ (συφεοῖσιν) ἐέργνυ, ipf., (Fέργνυμι), shut up (in the hog-sties), κ 238†.

κατ-είβεις, ετον, mid. -ειβόμενον, ipf. -είβετο, elsewh. tmes. κατὰ (δάκρυον) είβεις, ει, οι, ων, ipf. είβε, effundere, shed; mid., defluere, flow apace, trickle down, and fig. effluxit vita, ebb away, ε 152.

κατ' (ὄσσε) ἰδών, aor. part., looking him straight in the eyes, P 167†.

κᾰδ εἰλύσω, fut. from εἰλύω (FειλFω, volvo), involvam, surround, Φ 318†.

κᾰτ-ειμι, εισιν, inf. -ίμεν, part. -ιόντα, -ιοῦσα, αν, ipf. -ήϊεν, aor. κατειίσατο, delata est, had flown; γαίης, (εἶμι), go, or come down, flow down; appellentem, enter harbor, π 472.

κατ-έκταθεν, 3 pl. aor. pass. from -κτείνω.

κᾰτ-εναίρω, only aor. mid. -ενήρατο χαλκῷ, ferro absumpsit, slay, λ 519†.

κᾰτ-εναντίον (ἀντίος) οἱ ἔλθω, ei obviam fiam, go to meet him, Φ 567†.

κᾰτ-ένωπα (ἰδὼν Δαναῶν), in the face of, turned toward the Danaoi, O 320†.

κατ-επ-άλμενος, -ᾶλτο, see κατ-εφάλλομαι.

κατὰ ἐπείγει, urget, oppress, Ψ 623†.

κατ-ερείπω, only pf. -ερήρῐπεν, collapsum est, and aor. -ήριπεν ὑπ' αὐτοῦ, are prostrated under (by) it, E 92.

κατ-ερήτυεν, ον, ipf., retinebat, hold back, τ 545, from tears.

κατ-ερύκω, ει, ετε, subj. ῃ, imp. ε, and κατερύκᾰνε, Ω 218; ipf. -ερυκες, ε, pass. prs. ομαι, εται, retinere, hold back; cohibet, Φ 63; impedire; pass., delays.

κατ-ερύω, aor. -είρυσε, pass. pf. -είρυσται, inf. -ειρύσθαι, deducere (navem), launch, ξ 332. (Od.)

κατ-έρχεαι, εται, pass. ομένης, fut. -ελεύσομαι, aor. -ήλυθον, -ήλθες, ε, ομεν, ον, inf. -ελθέμεν, pass. -ελθόντ(α), go, come down, go; fly down, descend, ι 484.

κατ-εσθίει, ipf. -ήσθιε (also in tmesi), aor. in tmesi, φάγε, ωσι, έειν, devour, spoken of animals and of Polyphemos, except α 8, π 429, γ 315, ο 12.

κατ-έσσυτο, aor. from -σεύομαι.

κατ-ευνάω, aor. opt. -ευνήσαιμι, pass. aor. part. -ευνηθέντα, parallel form indic. 3 pl. -εύνασθεν, Γ 448, sopire, lull to sleep; pass., decumbere, dormire, lie down, sleep.

κατ-εφ-άλλομαι, only aor. -επᾶλτο, part. -επάλμενος, desiluit, shot down, T 351.

κατ-έχει (also in tmesi), ουσι, subj. έχῃ κάτα, pass. -έχων, -εχούσας, ipf. έχεν κάτα, -έχεν, fut. καθέξει, aor. -έσχε, subj. σχῇ, -έσχηται, ipf. -έχετο, -έχοντο, aor. mid. -έσχετο, part. σχομένοις, parallel forms: aor. act. κατέσχεθον, ipf. κάσχεθε, retinere, impedire; cohibere, hold fast, hold back, restrain; τινά γαῖα, αἶα, B 699, hold within its bosom, cut off from light and life; Σ

332, moriar; τί, prevail, bear sway, ι 6; κεφαλήν, bend over; mid.. se contegere, cover one's self; subsistere, remain, γ 284.

κᾰτ-ηπιόωντο, ipf. from ἠπιάω, leniebantur, assuage, E 417†.

κᾰτ-ηρεφές, acc. pl. masc. έας, (ἐρέφω), covered over, vaulte l, overhanging, ε 367.

κατ-ήριπε, aor. from -ερείπω, corruit.

κατη-φείη, ην, (καταί, φάος, = with downcast eyes, shame, Ἡ 498. (Il.)

κατ-ήφησαν, aor., part. σας, (-ηφέω), were confounded, ἐνὶ θυμῷ, π 342.

κατ-ηφέες, pl. from -ής, (-ηφών), disgraced, ω 432†.

κατ-ηφόνες, nom. pl. from ἡ κατηφών (cf. κατηφείη), abstract noun used as concrete, disgraces=bringers of disgrace, Ω 253†.

κάτ-θανε, aor. from -θνήσκω. κατθάψαι, aor. from -θάπτω. κάτθεμεν, 3 pl. ind., -θέμεν, inf. etc., see κατα-τίθημι. κατ-ίμεν = -ιέναι, see -ειμι.

κατ-ίσχει, 3 sing., inf. ἐμεν(αι), mid. pr. -ίσχεαι, εται, pass. κᾰτάϊσχεται, retinere, hold back; tenere, steer; mid., sibi retinere, keep for one's self; pass., possidetur, is occupied, ι 122.

κατ-οίσεται, fut. from -φέρω.

κᾰτ-όπισθε(ν), pone, post, in the rear, behind, with gen.; adv., behind, th reafter, φ 116.

κάτω (κατά), deorsum, down, ψ 91.

κατ-ωθέω, aor. in tmesi, κᾰδ ἔωσε, threw down, Π 410†.

κᾰτ-ωμᾰδίοιο, gen., (ὦμος), hurled from (above and behind) the shoulder, Ψ 431. (See cut No. 33.)

κᾰτ-ωμᾰδόν (ὦμος), from over the shoulder (of whip in lashing the horses), Ψ 500. (Il.)

κᾰτ-ωρῠχέεσσι (ὀρύσσω), dug in, buried in the earth, firmly set, ζ 267. (Od.)

Καύκωνες, tribe in Paphlagonia, Κ 429; in Elis, γ 366.

καυλῷ, όν, dat. acc. masc., (caulis), spear-shaft (part next the point), Π 115; sword-hilt, Π 338.

καύματος, gen. from τὸ καῦμα, (καίω), aestus, in consequence of the burning heat, E 865†.

καυστείρης, gen. from καύστειρα,

(καίω), μάχης, hot, raging combat, Δ 342. (Il.)

Καύστριος, river in Ionia, B 461.

καυτός, ἡ = καὶ αὐτός, ἡ, Ζ 260, ζ 282.

ΚΑΦ, only part. perf. κεκαφηότα, (καπύω), efflantem, exspirantem, with obj. θυμόν, gasping out, E 698.

κέ, κέν, (from pronominal stem κα), similar in use to ἄν, but: (1) enclitic. —(2) esp. common in relative clauses (149 κέν to 3 ἄν).—(3) often repeated in parallel clauses.—(4) used also with ἄν, Ν 127, see also below II. B, c, 3.— I. with indic.: (A) denoting simple subjective supposition, δ 546; also with fut., Δ 176; expectation with fut., Α 175, π 297; repeated action, with aor., σ 263; esp. (B) in apodosis of conditional sentence, with past tense, when the protasis contains a false assumption, e. g., Λ 311, E 898; the protasis may be represented by a participle, λ 418; or may require to be supplied, ξ 62.—II. with subj.: (A) in principal sentence: subj. of expectation, Α 184, Ξ 235; esp. with apodosis conceived of as likely to follow, A 324. —(B) in subordinate clause: (a) relative clause, subj. of wish, τ 403, ι 356; of expectation, κ 539, β 43, Η 171.— (b) hypothetical relative clause (κέν often wanting) dependent upon: (1) principal sentence with verb in imper., θ 548, α 316, Ψ 855 (inf., Ψ 246).— (2) principal sentence with opt., Α 294, τ 577.—(3) principal sentence with fut. indic., φ 280, Ι 397, Ρ 229.—(4) principal sentence with pres. indic., Ξ 416, τ 565, Λ 409.—(5) principal sentence with past indic. in sense of the present (gnomic use), λ 432, Α 218. —(6) subordinate clause with subj., Φ 103.—(c) in clause joined by conjunction to its principal sentence: (1) by final conjunction: ἵνα, only μ 156; ὄφρα, ut, 9 times, σ 183; ὡς, ut, 32 times, Β 385; ὅπως, δ 545.—(2) temporal conjunction (subj. of expectation), ὄφρα, δ 588, Κ 444; ἕως, always with κεν, Γ 291; εἰς ὅ, always with κεν, β 98.—(3) temporal = conditional. ὅτε, ὁπότε, (α) a supposition having reference to future, Α 567, Χ 366, Κ 130; (β) supposition without reference to time, Ζ 225, Ι 501, λ 218, (not

εὖτε), ὄφρα, dum, while, τ 17, Ω 554;
joined with ἄν, Λ 202, ζ 259, ε 361;
εἰς ὅ κεν, Κ 90, I 610.—(4) εἰ, whether,
χ 76, Α 407, δ 322, Υ 436, ξ 118, Π
861, Δ 249; εἰ, if, of future expectation, 111 times, Π 445, ρ 549, Ξ 369,
Ε 763, φ 305, Α 137, Γ' 302, φ 114, Ρ
40, Σ 92 ; of general expectation, Λ
391; ἐπεί, ξ 153, Χ 125, Λ 764, Α 173,
Ρ 658.—III. with optative (A) in principal sentence. (I) concessive, Χ 253,
Ν 486, Ω 619, φ 162. (II) optative denoting future time, (1) simple futurity,
ο 506, σ 166, μ 387, κ 269, Ω 664, Φ 412,
Β 160, Κ 57.—(2) conditioned probability, I 157, φ 77, Δ 171, Ρ 417.—(3)
possible future, always κέν (or ἄν),
Ρ 103, σ 223, 380.—(4) prevented
realization, δ 595, α 236, Γ 410 (joined
with sentence with εἰ, Β 81, Ε 311).—
(5) assumed situation, κέν (or .ἄν),
λ 488, Ο 697, χ 138, ε 73, μ 83.—(6)
mere possibility, Τ 218, Ι 57, μ 102,
ι 131.—(B) in interrogative sentence :
ἤ, ο 300; ἤ ῥα, ο 431, θ 337, σ 357;
πῶς, ο 195, λ 144; τίς, Κ 303 ; ποῖοι
ἤ, φ 197 ; in rhetorical direct question, Τ 90, Ρ 586, 149, Τ 82.—(C) in
dependent sentence : (a) relative sentence, α 253, Γ 235; Ω 732, υ 368, ω
188, Ε 192, 483, Ο 735; with ἄν, Ν
127; (b) hypothetical relative, only
δ 600; (c) in conjunctional sentence,
(1) final, ὡς, ψ 135, ω 532, β 53 ; ὅπως,
Α 344; ἕως, β 78.—(2) comparative,
ὡς, ψ 60.—(3) temporal implying condition, ὅτε, ν 391, I 525.—(4) dubita-
tive, expressing doubt, εἰ, whether, μ
112, ξ 120, Λ 792, Η 387.—(5) optative, expressing desire, εἰ γάρ, υ 236.
—(6) conditional, protasis introduced
by εἰ, if, preceding the principal sentence (this last with κέν), Ε 273, I 141,
363, τ 590, μ 345 ; principal sentence
preceding, protasis (with κέν) following, Τ 322, η 314, Κ 380, Χ 220.

κεάζω, aor. ἐκέασσε κέασσε κέασε, opt.
κεάσαιμι, pf. pass. κεκεασμένα, aor. pass.
ἱκεάσθη, split, ξ 418, υ 161 ; rend, shive'',
ι 132, η 250.

κέαται, το = κεῖνται. ἔκειντο, from
κεῖμαι.

Κεβριόνης, son of Priamos, Θ 318 ;
Hektor's charioteer, slain by Patroklos, Π 738.

κεδάννυμι, only aor. ἐκέδασσε, and

pass. 3 pl. ἐκέασθεν, part. θέντες,
θείσης, parallel form to σκεδάννυμι,
used for metrical convenience, dis-
pergere, dissipare, disperse, scatter;
γεφύρας, bursts the dikes, Ε 88.

κεδνοῖο, ή, ῷ, ήν, αί, άς, (ά), and sup.
-ότατος, οι, (κεκαδμένος), insignis, excellent, ἄλοχος, μήτηρ, τοκῆες, ἀμφίπολος, ἄναξ, ἑταῖροι, κεδνὰ Fιδυῖα, τ
346.

κέδρινον, acc., (κέδρος), of cedar, Ω
192†.

κέδρος, κέδρου, fem., cedar, of the
tree and of the wood, ε 60†.

κειάμενος, κείαντες (κη-), see καίω.

κείαται, το = κεῖνται, ἔκειντο.

κεῖθεν, adv., (κεῖνος), illinc, dein,
thence, then, Ο 234.

κεῖθι, illic, there, Γ 402.

κεῖμαι, κεῖσαι, κεῖαι, κῖται, 3 pl.
κεῖνται, κείαται, κέαται, κέονται, subj.
κῆται, imp. κεῖσο, σθω, inf. κεῖσθαι, part.
κείμενος, ipf. ἐκείμην, το, μεθα, and κείμην, μεθα, κεῖτο, iter. κέσκετο, 3 pl. κεῖντο,
κέιατο, κεῖατο, fut. κείσομαι, εαι, εται,
ονται, cubare, jacere, positum,
collocatum esse, of things having
life, lie, with various modifications, e. g.
sick, dead, β 102 ; feeble, wounded,
despised, old, Σ 435 ; unburied, idle;
μέγας μεγαλωστί, stretched out at his
full vast length ; πολλός τις, like a
giant; of localities, ι 25 ; of things :
lie (objects of value) ; stand (of articles
of household furniture); proposi-
tum est, the prize is offered, Χ 163.
With follg. constructions : ἐπὶ γαίης,
χθονός, γαίῃ, χθονί, ἐννέα πέλεθρα,
spread out over ; ἐν ἀλγεσι, εἰν ἁλί, νεκύων ἀγύρει = ὁμοῦ νεκύεσσι, among
the dead, θεῶν-γούνασι, rest in the
power of the gods, α 267 ; λέκτρῳ, νήσῳ,
νούσῳ, πεδίῳ, πυρί, ψαμάθοισι, χηλῷ,
and with dat. without preposition,
ὀλέθρῳ.

κειμήλιον, α, (κεῖμαι), treasure, heir-
loom ; β 75, landed property.

κεῖνος, η, ο, older form of ἐκεῖνος,
etc.

κεινή, ῇσι, κεῖν' = κεινά = κενά, χ
249, vacuus, inania, empty.

κείρει, 3 sing., imp. ετε, part. οντες,
τας, ipf. ἐκείρετε, ον, fut. inf. κερέειν,
1 aor. (ἐ)κέρσε, part. σαντες, (Ger.
Scheere, Schaar, Eng. shear), shear
off, κόμην ; cut off, lay waste, devour ;

mid. κειρόμενοι, ipf. κείροντο, aor. ἰnf. κείρασθαι, κόμην, cut one's hair (in grief), Ψ 136.

κεῖσε, illo, there; Ψ 461, usque illuc, thus far.

1. κείων, part., splitting. ξ 425†.

2. κείω, inf. κειέμεν, part. κείων (and κέων), οντες, ουσα (fut. forms without tense-sign with desiderative force), desiring to sleep, freq. with verbs of motion, ξ 532.

κεκαδήσει, σύμεθα, see κήδω, trouble.

κεκαδών, οντο, see χάζομαι, cedo, give way.

κεκασμένος, σθαι, see καίνυμαι, excello, surpass. κεκαφηώς, see ΚΑΦ, exspirans.

κέκλετο, aor. from κέλομαι, vocabat.

κεκληγώς, see κλάζω.

κεκλήατο, ήσγ, see καλέω.

κεκλόμενος, see κέλομαι. κέκλυθι, τε, see κλύω, ausculto. κέκμηκας, -ηώς, see κάμνω. κεκοπώς, see κόπτω. κεκορήμεθα, μένοι, ηότε, see κορέννυμι. κεκορυθμένα, see κορύσσω. κεκοτηότι, see κοτέω. κεκράανται, ντο, see κεράννυμι.

κεκρύφαλον, τόν, (κορυφή), net to confine the hair, Χ 469†. (See cut No. 44.)

κεκύθωσι, see κεύθω.

κελάδεινή, ῆς, όν, (κέλαδος), sounding, rushing; esp. freq. as epithet of Artemis, Π 183; as substantive, Φ 511.

κελάδησαν, aor. from κελαδέω, shouted aloud (in applause), Ψ 869†.

κέλάδον, τόν, (Ger. schellen?), tumult of combat, of hunt; in more general signif., confusion, σ 402.

κελάδων, οντα, part., sounding, Φ 16. Κελάδων, stream in Elis, H 133†.

κελαι-νεφέι, εῖ, έα, ές, (νέφος), shrouded in dark clouds, Zeus; as subst., ν 147; αἷμα, dark.

κελαινόν, ή, ῷ, dark, black; of blood, night, skin, wave, storm; of earth, Π 384.

κελάρύζει, prs., ipf. κελάρυζε, run, trickle, Φ 261.

κελεύθου, κέλευθον, οι, ους, fem. and pl. ntr. α, (callis), path, way; ntr. pl. in wider signif. ἀνέμων (λαιψηρά, airy), ἰχθυόεντα, ὑγρά, ἠερόεντα, gloomy ways (of death); masc. also = iter,

journey, κ 539; πρήσσοντε, traversing; τιθέναι, θέσθαι, open a way; γεφυροῦν, make a way over a ditch; Γ 406, θειῶν; κ 86, outgoings of night and day; others, paths (of cattle), i. e. pastures.

κελευτίόων, όωντε, part. from -άω. (κελεύω), animating, Μ 265. (Il.)

κελεύω (no du. and 3 pl.), subj. ῃς, opt. οι, imp. ε, ετε, part. ων, οντος, ipf. ἐκέλευον, ες, ον, and κέλευον, ε, fut. -σω, inf. σέμεναι, aor. ἐκέλευσα, σε, σαν, and κέλευσα, σας, σε, σαν, imp. κέλευσον, part. σας, (κέλλω, pello), drive on, with the lash; iubere, command, τινά, Δ 286, δ 274; τά με θυμός, H 68, η 187, as my heart bids me; τινί, Δ 428; τινί τι, mandare, Ζ 324, π 136; with inf., B 74, δ 233; with acc. and inf., B 11, β 263; with dat. and inf., B 50, β 6; with dat. of indirect object, followed by acc. and inf., Ψ 129, ι 561, λ 44.

κέλητα, τόν, (from κέλλω, celer), κέληθ' ὥς, ἵππον, courser, racer, ε 371†.

κελητίζειν, inf., (κέλης), ἵπποισι, ride a race-horse, Ο 679†; where the feats of a skillful rider are described.

κέλλω, aor. ἐκέλσαμεν, inf. κέλσαι, part. κελσάσγσι, (collis, pello), appellere, bring to shore, beach, νῆα (ἐν ψαμάθοισι); ι 149, having run the ships to land, we, etc.

κέλομαι (κέλλω), εαι (syniz.), εται, εσθε, ονται, opt. οίμην, imp. κελέσθω, εσθε, inf. σθαι, fut. κελήσεται, aor. ἐκέκλετο (after the trochaic cæsura), κέκλετο, part. κεκλόμενος, οι, urge on, τινὰ θυμός, ἷς, coegit; iubere, hortari, command, exhort, with inf., Α 386, γ 317; with acc. and infin., Α 74. γ 425; with dat., Ζ 286, Κ 419, η 335.

κέλσαι, aor. from κέλλω.

κεμάδα, τήν, a two-year-old deer, Κ 361†.

κέν, see κέ.

κενε-αυχέες, voc. pl. from -ής, (αὐχέω), empty, idle boaster, Θ 230†.

κενεάς, vacuas, κενεόν, ntr., νέεσθαι, ἰέναι, incassum, infecta re, in vain, fruitlessly, B 298.

κενεῶνα, τόν, (κενεός), part of body between hips and ribs, waist, small of back, χ 295; acc. of part., E 284; elsewh. with ἐς.

κενά, inania, empty, see κεινός.

κένσαι, aor. from κεντέω.

Κένταυρος, Centaur, Eurytion, φ 295; pl., Centaurs, a wild Thessalian tribe, Α 268.

κένσαι, inf. aor. from κεντέω, goad on, horses, Ψ 337†.

κεντρ-ηνεκέας, acc. pl., (κέντρον, ἔνεικα), stimulatos, goaded on, ἵππους, Ε 752. (Il.)

κέντροιο, ῳ, (κεντέω). stimuli (flagelli), goad, Ψ 387. (Il.)

κέντορες, οἱ, (κέντρον), ἵππων, stimulatores equorum, Kadmeians and Trojans, Δ 391, Ε 102.

κέονται, το, see κεῖμαι.

κεράασθε, see κεράννυμι.

κεράιζέμεν, inf., part. ζων, ipf. κεράιζε, ζέτον, pass. prs. part. κεραιζομένους, ην, (κείρω), destruere, populari, destroy, lay waste, Π 752, Ε 557; trucidare, slay, Β 861.

κέραιε, see κεράννυμι.

κεράμευς, ὁ, figulus, potter, Σ 601†.

κεράμῳ, ων, properly, great earthen jar buried in the earth (see cut), Ι 469; but in Ε 387, χαλκέῳ, serving as dungeon (cf. the pit into which Joseph was thrown by his brethren).

κεράννυμι; κεράω, κεραίω, give the forms prs. part. κερῶντας, imp. κέραιε, 1 aor. κέρασσε, part. κεράσασα, mid. prs. subj. κέρωνται, imp. κεράασθε, ipf. κερῶντο, όωντο, aor. κεράσσατο, σσάμενος, pass. pf. κεκράανται, plupf. κεκράαντο, temperare, mix, prepare by mixing, wine, bath; mid., mix for one's self, have mixed; alloy, mingle with gold, δ 132.

κεράο-ξόος (κέρας. ξέω) τέκτων, worker in horn, horn polisher, Δ 110†.

κεραόν, τόν, (κέρας). horned, Γ 24; κεραοί, are horned from their very birth, δ 85.

κέρας, αος, αι, ᾳ, pl. α, αων, ᾶσι, ἄεσσι, (κάρ, cere-brum, cornu), horn, of cattle, Ρ 521; of wild-goat, Δ 109;

as substance (where the resemblance in sound between κέρας and κραίνω is played upon), τ 566; as forming half of a bow, φ 395; hence = bow, κέραι ἀγλαέ, arcu superbiens; symbol of immobility, τ 211; the sheath of horn encasing the line just above the hook, and preventing it from being bitten off, Ω 81. [κέρᾱ, but shortened before a vowel, Δ 109, τ 211.]

κεραυνός, ῳ̃, ὑν, thunderbolt, lightning, Ο 117.

κεράω. see κεράννυμι.

κερδάλέος, ον, οισιν, ης, (κέρδος), comp. κέρδιον, sup. κέρδιστος, adrantageous, Γ 41, β 74; helpful, Κ 44; cunning, ν 291, Ζ 153.

κερδάλεό-φρον, voc., selfish, Α 149; crafty, Δ 339.

κέρδος, εα, έων, εσι, gain, π 311; good counsel, ψ 140; Ψ 709, κέρδεα ἐπίστασθαι, εἰδέναι, understand cunning arts; νωμᾶν, devise good counsel.

κερδοσύνῃ (κέρδος), per astutiam, cunningly, ξ 31.

κερκίς, ίδα, fem., rod (in later times comb), by a blow from which the threads of the woof were driven home into the warp, and the web made firm and close, ε 62. (See cut No. 63.)

κέρσε, αντες, see κείρω.

κερ-τομέωσι, subj., opt. έοι, part. έων, έοντες, έουσαν, ipf. ἐκερτόμεον, κερτόμεον, (-τομος), taunt, tease, Π 261.

κερτομίας, acc. pl., Υ 202; as subst. κερτομίοισι, οις, (κείρω, τέμνω, ω 240), sharp-cutting, sc. ἐπέεσσι, taunting, derisive words, yet the noun sometimes expressed, e. g. Δ 6.

κέρωνται, όωντο, see κεράννυμι.

κέσκετο, see κεῖμαι.

κεστὸν (κεντέω) ἱμάντα, embroidered girdle, Ξ 214.

ἐκεύθανον, ipf., occultabant, Γ 453†.

κευθμῶν, gen. pl. from ὁ κευθμός, latebra, lairs, Ν 28†.

κευθμῶνας, τούς, (κεύθω), latebras, crannies, ν 367; hog-sties, κ 283.

κεύθεσι, dat. pl. from τὸ κεῦθος, (κευθω), ὑπὸ—γαίης, in the depths of the earth, Χ 482, ω 204.

κεύθει, ετε, subj. ω, ῃ, imp. κεῦθε, ipf. ἔκευθε, κεῦθε, fut. κεύσω, aor. κύθε and subj. κεκύθωσι, pf. κέκευθε, plupf. ἐκεύθει, celare, occultare, hide, cover,

τινά, τί, pass. 'Αϊδὶ κείνθωμαι, s e p e-
l i a r ; also νόος ἔνδοθι, θυμῶ, νόῳ,
νοήμασι, ἐνὶ φρεσίν ; οὐδέ σε κείσω,
n e c t e c e l a b o, nor will I *conceal* it
from thee ; σ 406, no longer can ye
disguise your eating and drinking; it
is easy to see from your actions that,
etc.

κεφαλή, ῆς, ῇ, ήν, αἱ, ἑων, ῆσι, άς ;
ῆφιν, gen. du., (Ger. h a u p t, c a p - u t),
c a p u t, *head*, ἐκ κ.ῆς ἐς πόδας ἄκρους,
II 640 ; κὰκ=κατὰ κ.; also of animals,
I 548, Λ 39, Γ 273, Ψ 381 ; synonymous with *life*, Δ 162 ; in periphrasis,
for a person, Λ 55, Σ 82, Ω 276 ; esp.
in address, Ψ 94 ; common phrase,
κ.ὴν οὐδάσδε πελάσσαι = lay at one's
feet ; custom of kissing head and
hands, φ 224, 225, χ 499 ; thence come
speech and words, Λ 462, Π 77.

Κεφαλλῆνες, collective appellation
of subjects of Odysseus on islands and
mainland, Β 631, ξ 100, υ 187, ω 355,
378, 429.

κεχάνδει, ότα, see χανδάνω. κε-
χαρ-ησεμεν, ήσεται, ηώς, οίατο, οντο,
see χαίρω. κεχαρισμένος, ε, α, στο,
see χαρίξεαι. κεχηότα, see χαίνω. κε-
χωλώ-, see χολόω. κεχρημένος, see
χρα-. κέχυ(ν)ται, το, see χέω.

κέων, see κείω 2. κῆ-αι, άμενος, see
καίω.

κήδεος, Ψ 160†, sepeliendus.

κηδείους (κήδω,) caros, *dear*, Τ
294†.

κηδεμόνες, οἱ, (κήδω), properly, se-
pultores, *mourners, nearer friends*, Ψ
163, 674.

κήδιστος, οι, (κήδω), carissimus,
κ 225.

κῆδος, εα, εσιν, acrumna, *trouble*,
τῶν ἄλλων οὐ- ; θυμοῖ, grief ; luctus,
Ν 464, pl., *sorrows*.

κήδει, 3 sing., subj. ῃ, opt. οι, inf. ειν,
pass. ων, ipf. ἐκηδε, and iter. κήδεσκον,
fut. -ήσοντες, fut. red. κεκαδήσει, φ 153;
mid. κήδεαι, εται, ονται, opt. οιτο, inf.
εσθαι, pass. όμενος, ῳ, ον, οι, η, ipf.
κήδετο, οντο, iter. -έσ.'ετο, fut. κεκα-
δησόμεθα, *injure*, Φ 369, Ε 404 ; θυμόν,
cruciare, *distress*, ι 402, Ω 240. 542 ;
pass. part. prs. mid., *be concerned for*,
person or thing, τινός, *care for*, Η 204,
Α 196, ξ 146.

κῆεν, see καίω.

κήκϊε, ipf., (κίω), *gush forth*, ε 455†.

κηλέω (καίω) πυρί (Ο 744, κηλείῳ),
in blazing fire, Θ 217.

κηληθμῷ, dat., (κηλίω), *in rapture*
(they listened), ν 2. (Od.)

κῆλα, tela, *weapons of the gods ;* even
of snow. Μ 280. (Il.)

κήξ (καϜαξ, κήυξ) εἰνάλίη, *gull*, ο
479†.

κήομεν, subj. from καίω.

κῆπον, ῳ, ους, masc., (c a m p u s ?),
garden, Φ 258, ὃ 737.

Κήρ, ός, ί, α, du. ε, pl. ες, ας, (κείρω,
Ger. s c h e r e, s c h a r f, Eng. s h e a r),
mode of death, (μυρίαι, Μ 326) κῆρες
θανάτοιο, usher into Hades, ξ 207,
Β 302. Immediately upon the birth,
the *Moira* or *Aisa* was determined for
the life, and the *Ker* for the death (cf.
Ι 411, where the choice of a twofold
destiny is offered to Achilleus ; the passage also shows that the Κήρ impels
to destruction, cf. κηρεσσιφορήτους);
when the time of death for the special
favorites of Zeus approaches, he weighs
the fortunes of combatants. e. g. Patroklos and Sarpedon, Achilleus and
Hektor. (See cut, representing Hermes discharging this function.) Freq.

joined with θάνατος. β 283 ; φόνον, δ
273, β 165 ; hence with adj. μελαίνῃ,
αν, Φ 66 ; like θάνατος, Π 687 ; often
=death, Λ 360, 362, Ε 652, Ι 411;
symbol of hate, Α 228.

κῆρ, ός, όθι, ί, ntr., c o r, *heart*, Π 481;
then, in wider signification, as the
seat of understanding, will, and the
varied emotions, and thus correspond-

ing with varied range of meaning to
our ' *heart* ;' hence (ἐν) φρεσίν, ἐνὶ στήθεσσιν, and ἐν θυμῷ, Z 523, which we
may translate *within me* ; (περὶ) κῆρι,
exceedingly in heart, most heartily, ε
36 ; κηρόθι μᾶλλον (at close of verse),
still more in heart, ρ 458 : also used
periphrastically like μένος, βίη, etc.,
B 851, cf. A 395.

κηρέσσι-φορήτους (φορέω), *urged on
by their evil destinies*, i. e. to death, Θ
527†.

Κήρινθος, town on coast of Euboia,
B 538†.

κηρόθι, see κῆρ.

κηρός, οῖο, όν = c e r a, *wax*, μ 175.
(Od.)

κῆρυξ, ῦκος, ι, α ; ε ; ες, ων, εσσι, ας,
herald ; the heralds convoked the popular assembly, kept order at trials,
bore as sign of their office a staff (see
cut, from archaic relief, No. 120), which
they handed over to him who had the
right to speak ; they served also as
messengers of the chiefs and as their
assistants in sacrifice ; epithets, θεῖοι,
Διὸς ἄγγελοι, Διὶ φίλοι. [P 324, pronounce κήρῡκἰ Ἡπυτίδῃ.]

κηρύσσειν, inf., part. -ων, οντος, ες,
ipf. ἐκήρυσσον (κῆρυξ), *proclaim as
herald, summon, order*, πύλεμόνδε, ἀγορήνδε ; P 325, in the office of herald.

κῆται, subj. from κεῖμαι.

Κήτειοι, Mysian tribe, followers of
Eurypylos, λ 521†.

κῆτος, εος, εἴ, εα, εσι, *monster of the
deep*, e. g. sharks and seals, Υ 147, δ
446.

κητώεσσαν (κῆτος) Λακεδαίμονα,
full of ravines, B 581, δ 1.

Κηφῖσίς, ίδος, λίμνη, lake in Boiotia ;
later Κωπαΐς, E 709†, from

Κηφῖσός, river in Phokis, B 522†.

κηώδει, dat. from -ώδης, (καίω, κῆος?),
fragrant with sweet odors, Z 483†.

κηώεντι, α, usually defined *fragrant ;*
and yet this signif. inconsistent with
Γ 382 ; perh. better (κηϜ-, κύτος,
cā̆v-us) *vaulted*, epithet of treasure
chambers, Ω 191.

κίδνᾰται, ipf. ἐκίδνατο, (σκιϹ-. σκεδάννυμι), d i s p e r g i t u r, *is diffused*,
ἠώς, Θ 1.

κἴθάριζε, ipf., φόρμιγγι, *was playing
upon the lyre*, Σ 570†. (See cut, in next
column, representing a Greek woman.)

κίθᾰρις, ιν, fem., *cithara* (hence
g u i t a r), *lyre*, a 153 ; *skill in playing
upon the cithara*, N 731.

κἴθᾰριστύν, τήν, (κιθαρίζω), *art of
playing the cithara*. (See cut.)

κικλήσκεις, ει, ουσ(ι), inf. ειν, part.
οντος, ουσα, ipf. κίκλησκε, ον, pass. pr.
εται, mid. ipf. ετο, (καλέω), *call, summon*, κληδην, nominatim, by name ;
i n v o c a n s, I 569 ; nominant, ἐπί-
κλησιν, cognomine ; mid., *call together to one's self*, ἀμυδις.

Κίκονες, Thrakian tribe, ι 47, B 846.
κίκυς, ἡ, r o b u r, *force*, λ 393†.

Κίλϊκες, tribe of Greater Phrygia,
dwelling under two leaders in Θήβη
ὑποπλακίη and in Lyrnessos, Z 397,
415.

Κίλλα ζαθέη, town in Troas, A 38,
452.

Κιμμέριοι, fabled people dwelling
at entrance of Hades, λ 14†.

κινέω, aor. **κίνησε**, subj. σῃ (and
σει ? B 147, or perh. fut. ?), inf. σαι,
part. σας, pass. aor. κινήθη, 3 pl. ἐκί-
νηθεν, part. ηθέντος, c o m m o v e r e,
disturb, set in motion (wasps, clouds),

push with the foot (ποδί) ; A 47, as he moved himself forward.

κῑνῡμενος, οιο, ων, part., ipf. *κίνυντο*, (κινέω), proficiscor, *set out, march,* κ 556, Δ 281.

Κῑνύρης, ruler of Kypros, Λ 20†.

κῑνυρή, *wailing, whimpering,* P 5†.

Κίρκη, daughter of Helios, sister of Aietes, inhabiting the island Aiaie, the enchantress, κ 230 sqq.

κίρκος, ον, *hawk* or *falcon* which flies in circles, *ἰρηξ* ; Ἀπόλλωνος ἄγγελός, ο 526.

κιρνάς, part., *κίρνη* ipf. from *κίρνημι* ; **ἐκίρνα**, ipf. from κιρνάω, (parallel form to κεράννυμι), m i s c e r e, *mix;* οἶνον, t e m p e r a r e, *mingle,* η 182.

Κισσηίς, daughter of Kisses = Θεανώ, Z 299†.

Κισσῆς, ruler in Thrake ; his grandson Iphidamas, Λ 223†.

κισσύβιον, ῳ, *bowl, basin,* ι 346. (Od.)

κίστη, *box, chest,* ζ 76†.

κιχάνω, ετε, opt. ἄνοι, ipf. (ἐ)κίχαν(ε), *ἐκίχανον*, and mid. **κιχάνομαι**, εται, ὁμένοι, fut. κιχήσομαι, σεαι, σεται, σόμεθα, inf. σεσθαι, aor. κιχήσατο, and parallel forms κίχημι, subj. κιχείω, ῃσι, εἴομεν, opt. εἴη, inf. ἧναι, ἤμεναι, part. εἰς and ἤμενον, ipf. κίχεις, εν, ἤτην, (ἐ)κίχημεν, aor. ἔκιχε, ον, part. ὤν, [the unaugmented forms of two, four, and five syllables stand after caesura in third foot, the augmented forms of three and four syllables almost always at the end of the verse]. — (1) r e p e r i r e, c o n s e q u i, *overtake, find,* τινά, τί, Γ 291, 383, Z 228, Π 342, X 303. — (2) i n v e n i r e, *light upon,* B 188, μ 122, ξ 139 ; with part., A 26, T 289 ; with adj., δ 546.

κίχλαι, t u r d i, *thrushes,* χ 468†.

κίης, subj. prs., opt. κίοι, οίτην, οιτε, part. κιών, όντι, α, ε, ες, ας, οῦσα, ῃ, αι, ipf. ἔκιε, ον, or κί(εν). κίομεν, κίον, (c i e o). *go, go away,* usually of persons ; more rarely of things, animals, ships, etc.. Z 422, ο 149, π 177.

κίων, ονος, ι, α, ες, ας, masc. and fem., c o l u m n a, *pillar,* α 127, esp. *pillar* supporting the rafters. (See plate II. at end of volume, F and G.)

κλαγγή, ῆς, ῇ, (κλάζω), c l a m o r, *any sharp sound, shout* of men, *cry* or *screech* of birds, cranes, *grunting* of swine, etc. ;

κλαγγῇ, Γ 5 = **κλαγγηδόν**, B 463, with a d i n ; A 49, *twang* of bow string.

κλάζοντε, part. du., aor. ἔκλαγξαν, part. κλάγξας, αντος, pf. part. κεκληγώς, ὦτες, ὦτας (MSS. οντες, ας), *make a loud, sharp sound, shriek* ; M 125, *shouting loudly* (in battle); οὖλον, *screaming loudly* all at once ; of birds, Π 429 ; *bellow, clash, rattle, roar.*

κλαίω, εις, ομεν, ετον, subj. ῃ(σι), ωμεν, opt. οισθα, οιμεν, inf. ειν, part. ων, οντα, ε, ες, εσσι, ας, ουσα, ούσης, ipf. ἔκλαιον, κλαῖον, εν, ον, and iter. εσκε, fut. κλαύσομαι, σονται, aor. κλαῦσε, σας, *weep, wail,* lament ; esp. of lament for the dead (either of natural expression of grief, or of the more formal prescribed ceremony), τινά, T 300, π 450 (δ 169–185) ; τί, Ω 85, ψ 351 ; ἀμφί τινα, Σ 339.

κλαυθμοῦ, οῖο, όν, (κλαίω), f l e t u s, *weeping,* esp. in lament for the dead, γόος, ρ 8.

κλαῦσε, aor. from κλαίω.

κλάσε, aor., (κλάω), f r e g i t, ζ 128 ; aor. pass. ἐκλάσθη, f r a c t a e s t, Λ 584.

κληηδόνι, acc. κληηδόνα, (κλέος), f a m a, *tidings,* δ 317 ; elsewh. exclamation of favorable significance, *good omen,* cf. β 35.

κλειτῷ, όν, οί, ῶν, ούς, (κλέος, i n c l i t u s), *glorious, famous,* esp. of ἐπικούρων, Γ 451, and ἑκατόμβην, A 447.

Κλεῖτος, (1) son of Mantios, ο 249. —(2) Πεισήνορος υἱόν, companion of Polydamas, slain by Teukros, O 445.

κλείω, (1) see κλέω.—(2) see κληίω.

Κλεόβουλος, a Trojan, slain by Aias, son of Oileus, Π 330†.

Κλεοπάτρη, wife of Meleagros = Ἀλκυόνη, I 556†.

κλέος, pl. α, (κλύω, c l u - e n t e s, Gothic, h l i u m a [sense of hearing], Ger. l a u t [sound]), q u a e f a n d o a u d i u n t u r : (1) f a m a, *rumor, tidings* (σόν, ἐμόν, of thee, of me).—(2) g l o r i a, κλέος (σοί) πρὸς Τρώων εἶναι, l a u d i tibi sunto inter Troianos, but they shall be an *honor* to thee before the Trojans, X 514; pl. ἀνδρῶν, l a u d e s, *glorious deeds.*

κλέπτῃ, τῷ, (κλέπτω), *thief,* Γ 11†.

κλεπτοσύνῃ, τῇ, (κλέπτης), *knavery, trickery,* τ 396†.

κλέπτῃ, subj., κλέπτε, imp. prs., aor. ἔκλεψε, inf. κλέψαι, (καλύπτω, c a l - i m, oc-cul-o, clepo), furari, *steal*; νόον, fallere, deceive; νόῳ, cunningly get advantage of, A 132.

κλέομαι, ipf. ἐκλέ(ο), pass. of **κλείουσιν**, subj. κλείω, (κλέϝ-ος), famā celebrare, *make famous*, α 338, ν 299.

Κλεωναί, άς, town in Argolis, B 570†.

κλήδην (καλέω), nominatim, *by name*, I 11†.

κληηδόνα, see κληηδόνι.

κλήθρη, alnus, *alder*, ε 64 and 239.

κληῖς, ῖδος, ι, α, ες, εσσιν, ῖσιν, (κλαϝ-, clav-is), (1) obex, repagula, *bolt, bar* (see cuts Nos. 32 and 38, both from Egyptian originals); cut No. 60, in four compartments, shows above the open, below the closed door: on the left as seen from within; on the right from without; c, g, f, mark the place of the key-hole, through which the thong. ἱμάς, α 442, ran, and the key was passed by which the bolt was first lifted (as is seen at g), ἀνέκοψεν, and then pushed back (ἀπῶσαν). The adjoining cut, from a Greek sepulchral

monument, as well as No. 32, presupposes double bolts, and above on the right we see the key as it is applied, and below on the other half of the door the loosened thong; these bolts of double doors are also called ἐπιβλῆς, ὀχῆες; κρυπτῇ, with hidden, concealed bolt.—(2) clavis, *key*, better described as *hook*, M 456. (See cut

No. 60, f, g.)—(3) iugulum, *collar-bone*. — (4) curved *tongue* of buckle, σ 294. (See cut No. 104.)—(5) *thole-pins, rowlocks*, ἐπὶ κληῖσι, to which the oars were made fast by a thong, and round which they played, see cuts Nos. 126 and 35; for later, different arrangement, see cuts Nos. 41, 94, 64, and the Assyrian war-ship, cut No. 40. ἐπὶ κληῖσι, translate, *at the oars*.

κληῖσταί (κληίω), *that may be closed*, β 344†.

κληῖω, aor. (ἐ)κλήϊσε, inf. ῖσαι, (κληϊς), claudere, shut, ὀχῆας, *drew forward* the bolts closing the door, by means of the thong. (See cut No. 60.)

κλῆρος, ον, ῳ, ους, (κλάω?), sors, (1) *lot*, a stone, or potsherd or broken (κλάω) twig, on which each man scratched his mark, H 175; the lots were then shaken in a helmet, and he whose lot first sprang forth was thereby selected for the matter in hand. —(2) *paternal estate*, patrimonium, ξ 64.

κλητοί, ούς, (καλέω), electos, I 165; invitati, ρ 386.

κλίμακα, τήν, (κλίνω), scalas, *stairs, ladder*, κ 558. (Od.)

κλιντῆρι, τῷ, (κλίνω), lectulo, *couch, sofa*, cf. adjacent cut, No. 73.

κλίνω, subj. **κλίνῃσι**, inf. κλῖναι, part. -ων, aor. ἐκλῖνε, αν, (κλῖναν). part. -ας, ασα, αντες, (clinare). *make to slope* or *incline*, one thing against another; τί τινι, πρὸς ἐνώπια, drew aside the chariots and *leaned them up* against the shining walls of the vestibule; ὄσσε πάλιν, oculos avertere, *turn away* the eyes; μάχην, inclinare pugnam, *turn the tide of* battle; τινάς, fugare. *put to flight*; pass. aor. (ἐ)κλίνθη, ἐκλίθη, -ῆναι, κλινθήτην, -ῆναι, *bend* one's self, crouch down, K 350; ἑτέρωσ', sank on one side; lie down; pf. κεκλίαται, κεκλιμένος, ον, οι, ων, η, plupf. κέκλῑτο, τινί, ad aliquid applicatus, innixus rei, rest upon, lean upon, Ι' 135; iacēre, lie, χθονί, humi; situs, situated, ἁλί, ad mare, near the sea; λίμνῃ, accola lacus, hard by; mid., se applicare, support one's self upon, τινί.

κλῑσίης, ῃ, ην, αι, ῶν, ῃσι, ῃς, ας, (κλίνω), earth hut of shepherds, shed or lodge, wigwam of warriors, cf. Ω 450; couch or easy chair. (See cut No. 79.) κλῑσίηθεν, from the hut; κλῑσίηνδε, to the hut; κλῑσίῃφι, in the hut.

κλῑσιον, τό, buildings adjoining master's house, (cf. in signif., Eng. Lean-to). for servants, strangers, etc., ω 208†.

κλισμῷ, όν, οῖσι, οὐς, (κλίνω), easy-chair, reclining chair, α 145. (Cf. adjoining cut, or cut No. 113.)

κλιτύν, acc. pl. ῦς, (κλίνω), clivus, slope, hill-side, ε 470.

κλονέει, ουσι, part. έων, έοντα, τε, τας, fugare, put to flight (τινά, Il.). absol., Λ 496; Ο 7, drive before one, proturbare; pass. κλονέονται, εσθαι, ipf. έοντο, conturbari, rush wildly

about, be driven in confusion; ὁμίλῳ, in the fray; ὑπό τινι, Φ 527.

Κλονίος, chief of the Boiotians, B 495; slain by Agenor, O 340.

κλόνον, τόν, turbam, tumult, Π 729; ἐγχειάων, press of spears.

κλοπίων, gen. pl. from κλόπιος, (κλοπή), fallacium, deceitful, ν 295†.

κλοτοπεύειν, make fine speeches? Τ 149†. (Of doubtful deriv. and signif.)

κλύδων, ὁ, (κλύζω), billow, surge, μ 421†.

κλύζεσκον, ipf. iter., (κλύζω), were plashing, Ψ 61; ἐκλύσθη δὲ θάλασσα, was dashed high, rose aloft in foam.

κλῦθι, imp. from κλύω, hear.

Κλυμένη, (1) a Nereid, Σ 47.—(2) an attendant of Helena, Γ 144; daughter of Minyas (Iphis), mother of Iphiklos, λ 326.

Κλύμενος, father of Eurydike, mortally wounded at Thebes, γ 452. [ῠ]

Κλῡται-μνήστρη, daughter of Tyndareos, sister of Helena, wife of Agamemnon; her paramour Aigisthos having slain at her desire her husband, she herself was slain with Aigisthos by her own son Orestes, Α 113, γ 266, 310. λ 439. (See cut No. 36.)

Κλυτίδης, son of Klytios.—(1) Δόλοψ.—(2) Πείραιος.

Κλύτιος, (1) son of Laomedon, brother of Priamos, father of Kaletor, O 419, 427, Γ 147, Υ 238.—(2) father of Peiraios in Ithaka, π 327.—(3) father of Dolops.

κλῡτό-εργον (Ϝέργον), maker of famous works, artist, θ 345†.

Κλῡτο-μήδης, son of Enops, beaten in boxing-match by Nestor, Ψ 634†.

Κλῡτό-νηος, son of Alkinoos, θ 119, 123.

κλῡτο-πώλῳ, with noble steeds, always epithet of Aides, Ε 654 sqq. (Il.) Probably in reference to rape of Persephoneie.

κλῡτός, οῦ, όν, οί; also comm. gender, (κλύω, in-clu-tus), illustrious, glorious; 'Εννοσίγαιος, ε 423; also of other gods and men, α 300; of places, Ω 437; of animals, ι 308; of things, ὄνομα, τ 183, ι 364.

κλῡτο-τέχνης, famous for his art, renowned artist, Α 571.

κλῡτό-τοξος, ῳ, ον, (τόξον), with fa-

nous bow, renowned archer, Δ 101, ρ 494.

κλύω, aor. **ἔκλυον,** ες, ε, ον, also **κλύον,** imp. **κλῦθι, κλῦτε,** and aor. sync. **κέκλυθι,** τε, (cluere, in-clutus), (1) *hear,* ἔπος, ἀγγελίην, δοῦπον, αὐδήν, also with gen. ὁπός, **vocem;** with part., δ 505, τινὸς αὐδήσαντος; Γ 87, *hear from* me, the proposition of Alexander; also ἐκ τινος, **ex aliquo.**—(2) **exaudire,** *give ear to, hearken,* τινός, A 43, 218, β 262, γ 385; also τινὸς αὐδῆς, μύθων, τινὶ ἀρῆς; less common with dat., τινί, Π 516.—(3) **obedire,** *hear and comply, obey,* τοῦ μάλα μὲν κλύον, ο 220.

Κλῶθες, lit. *the Spinsters;* as goddesses of fate, η 197†.

κλωμακόεσσαν (κλῶμαξ, grumus), *on rock terraces, rocky,* B 729†.

κνέφας, ἄος, ας, (δνόφος), **crepusculum,** *twilight, dusk,* σ 370.

κνῆ, ipf. from κνάω, *she grated* (ἐπὶ thereon), Λ 639†.

κνήμη, ην, αι, άων, ῃσιν, **crus,** part of leg between the knee and ankle, *shin,* Δ 519.

κνημίς, ἴδας, (κνήμη), **ocrea,** *greaves,* metal plates, lined with some soft material, bent around the shin-bone under the knee, and fastened by clasps at the ankle (see cut No. 39), only in Iliad; the word in the Odyssey, ω 229, signifies *leather leggins.*

κνημοῖσι, ούς, masc., **saltus,** *mountain valleys,* B 821.

κνῆστι, dat. from κνῆστις, (κνῆν), *knife for shaving* or *grating,* Λ 640†.

κνίση, only sing., (κνίϑα, nidor?), *fat,* esp. the *fat caul* or *diaphragm,* in which the thighs of the victim were wrapped, laid upon the fire and burned, together with the pieces of flesh piled upon them (A 460); hence the word also signifies the *steam of the fat* or *sacrifice,* A 66; **κνῖσήεν,** *full of the steam of burnt sacrifice,* κ 10†. [v. l. κνίσση.]

κνυζηθμῷ (κνύζω), *with whimper, whimpering,* π 163†.

κνυζώσω, fut., and aor. κνύζωσεν, ν 401, 433, *make lustreless.*

κνώδαλον, fera, *monster,* ρ 317†.

Κνωσός, μεγάλη πόλις, εὐρείῃ, in Kreta, B 646, Σ 591, τ 178.

κνώσσουσα, part., *deeply s'umbering,* consopita, δ 809†.

κοίλοιο, ον, η, ης, ῳ, ην, only χ 385, κοῖλον, (κόFιλος, cav-us), *hollow;* λιμήν, *deep-embosomed, extending far into the land,* κ 92.

κοιμάω, aor. **(ἐ)κοίμησε,** σατε, imp. σον, part. σας, ασα, (κεῖμαι), *lull, hush to sleep,* τινά; *litter,* δ 336; **consopire,** *put to sleep,* also figuratively; mid. pr. κοιμᾶται, ipf. κοιμᾶτο, ῶντο, aor. (ἐ)κοιμήσατο, σαντα, subj. σωνται, imp. σασθε, and aor. pass. (ἐ)κοιμήθημεν, opt. θείη, inf. θῆναι, part. θέντι, ε, ες, *lay one's self down to sleep,* past tenses, *sleep; sleep the sleep of death,* Λ 241.

κοιράνέουσι, part. έων, έοντα, (κοίρανος), *be lord* or *master, rule,* ἀνά, κατά, διά τινας ; dominari, *play the lord,* ν 377.

κοίρανος, ε, οι, (κῦρος), *ruler;* also with λαῶν, *ruler of the people,* H 234.

Κοίρᾰνος, (1) a Lykian slain by Odysseus, E 677.—(2) from Lyktos in Kreta, charioteer of Meriones, P 611, 614, slain by Hektor.

κοίτη, τῇ, (κεῖμαι), *bed,* τ 341†.

κοῖτος, οιο, ου, ον, masc., *bed,* ξ 455; *night's rest, sleep,* η 138.

κολεόν, οἷο, ῳ, and κουλεόν, ῳ, ntr., (metal) *sword-sheath,* A 194, 220.

κολλήεντα, ntr. pl., (κολλάω), ξυστὰ ναύμαχα, ship-spears, *united together with rings,* O 389†.

κολλητόν, οῖσι, ῇσι, άς, (κολλάω), *firmly bound together, compacted* or *shod with bands,* O 678, ψ 194.

κόλλοπι, dat. from κόλλοψ, *peg* on the lyre, round which the string was made fast, φ 407†.

κολοιῶν, ούς, graculorum, *jackdaws,* II 583. (Il.)

κόλον, ntr., *docked, pointless,* Π 117†.

κολοσυρτόν, τόν, *noisy rabble,* M 147 and N 472.

κολούει, imp. ετε, (κόλος), mutilat, *leaves unfulfilled,* Υ 370; λ 340, *cut short. curtail.*

κόλπῳ, ον, οι, ους, (καλύπτω), *fold* or *belly* of garment round neck and breast, 1 570; *bosom,* Z 136, 400; *bosom of the sea,* Σ 140.

ἐκολώα, ipf. from κολωάω, (κολωός), *screamed, bawled,* B 212†.

κολώνη (κέλλω), collis, *hill,* B 811. (Il.)

κολωόν (ᾠὸν?) ἐλαύνετε, *continue noisy wrangling,* A 575†.

κομόωντε, τες, part. from κομάω, (κόμη), ὄπιθεν, with hair long at back of head, shorn in front, B 542 ; κάρη, long - haired ; ἐθείρῃσι, with long manes.

κομέω, κομέουσι, imp. εἴτων, inf. ἔειν, ipf. ἐκόμει (and iter. ἔεσκε), εἴτην, take care of, tend (by giving bath, food, bed, clothing), τινά, λ 250 ; also of animals, ρ 310, 319.

κόμη, ης, ην, αι, ας, (coma), hair of head ; pl. ζ 231, thick flowing locks ; also foliage, ψ 195.

κομιδή, ῆς, ήν, cultus corporis, (see κομέω), care, attendance, bestowed on men, horses, also on garden, ω 245, 247.

κομίζω, ει, subj. ῃ, imp. κόμιζε, inf. ειν, έμεν, ipf. κόμιζε, fut. κομιῶ, aor. ἐκόμισσα, (ἐ)κόμισε, αν, subj. ίσσῃ, imp. ισσον, (κομέω), (1) wait upon, attend, care for, Z 490, τινά, τί ; esp. receive as guest, entertain, κ 73, ρ 113, cf. 111 ; τινά τινι, nutrire, υ 69 ; pass. ὀμένος, θ 451.—(2) gather up, ψ 355 ; carry away, Γ 378 ; bear off, Ξ 456, B 875 ; bring, Ψ 699 ; mid. aor. (ἐ)κομίσσατο, ἴσαντο, opt. ἴσαιο, receive hospitably, entertain ; X 286, carry off in one's flesh.

κομπέω, ipf. ἐκόμπει, clashed, rattled, M 151†.

κόμπος, ὁ, (κύναβος), stamping of feet, θ 380 ; grinding, gnashing of tusks of boar.

κονάβησε, σαν, aor., ipf. κονάβιζε, (κόναβος), resound (of echo) ; rattle, ring, O 648, Φ 593, N 498. (Il. and ρ 542.)

κόναβος, din, crash, κ 122†.

κονίη, sing., and ῃσι, pulvis, dust ; λ 600, rose from his head ; with ὀμί-χλη, N 336 ; στροφάλιγγι, Π 775, ω 39 ; sand, Ψ 502, 506 ; cineres, ashes, η 153. [ῑ when in final foot of verse.]

κόνις, ιος, ῑ, fem., pulvis, dust, N 335 ; ashes, Σ 23, λ 191.

κονίσσαλος, ω, (σΓαλ), dust-cloud, dust-whirl, Γ 13. (Il.)

κονίοντες, part., fut. κονίσουσι, aor. ἐκόνισε, (κονίῳ), make dust ; πεδίοιο, raise a dust-cloud, speeding over the plain, N 820 ; making dusty, Φ 407 ; pass. plupf. κεκόνῑτο, and pf. κεκονιμέ-νοι, pulvere obducti, covered with dust.

κοντόν, τόν, (κεντέω), pole, ι 487†.

Κοπρεύς, father of Periphetes, O 639†.

κοπρήσοντες, fut. part., (κοπρέω), stercorandi causa, for manure, ρ 299†.

κύπρος, ὁ, only sing., fimus, stercus, lutum, dung, Ω 164 ; farm-yard, cattle-stall, Σ 575.

κόπτων, οντες, part, ipf. κόπτε, ον, aor. κύψε, ας ; 2 pf. κεκοπώς, aor. mid. κύψατο, beat, smite ; παρήϊον, on the cheek ; ποτὶ γαίῃ, strike to earth ; bite, sting, M 204 ; decidere, detrunca-re, χ 477 ; forge, δεσμούς ; mid., X 33, smite one's own head.

Κόρακος πέτρῃ, rocky mountain in Ithaka, ν 408†.

κορέννυμι, fut. κορέεις, έει, aor. opt. κορέσειε, satiare, sate, satisfy, τινά τινι, Θ 379 ; mid. (ἐ)κορέσσατο, σάμεθα, subj. σωνται, opt. σαίατο, inf. σασθαι, part. σάμενος, and pass. pf. κεκορήμεθα, ἦσθε, ἡμένοι, act. part. κεκορηότε, aor. also pass. ἐκορέσθην, satiari, sate one's self with, τινός ; (κατὰ) θυμόν, in heart ; also metaph. be tired of, τινός, or with part. τάμνων, κλαίουσα, υ 59.

κορέω, aor. imp. κορήσατε, sweep out, υ 149†.

κόρη, false reading, read κούρη.

κορθύεται (κόρυς, κάρ, III.), raises itself aloft, I 7†.

Κόρινθος, the city Korinth, the wealthy, on isthmus of same name, Isthmos, B 570 ; Κορινθόθι, at Korinth, N 664 ; ancient name, Ἐφύρη.

κορμόν, τόν, (κείρω), the trunk of the tree I hewed round about (beginning with the root and progressing toward the smaller end), ψ 196†.

κόρος, ὁ, satietas, taedium ; τινός, surfeit, N 636, δ 103.

κόρσην, τήν, temple, Δ 502. (Il.)

κορύθάϊκι, dat., (κόρυθα ἀΐσσοντι), helmet shaking, with waving plume, X 132†.

κορύθ-αίολος (κόρυθα αἰόλην ἔχων), with glancing helm, esp. epithet of Hek-tor and of Ares, B 816, Γ 83. (Il.)

κόρυμβα (κορυφή, κάρη) ἄκρα, the heads or ends, in which the stern of vessel terminated, cf. ἄφλαστα, I 241†. (See cut No. 21.)

κορύνη, ῃ, (κόρυς), battle mace (of

iron). Hence comes **κορὑνήτης**, ην, club-brandisher, H 141, 9.

κόρυς, ὑθος, θι, θα, and ὑν; θες, θων, θισσι, ας, fem., (κάρη, κάρ), helmet, with adjs. βριαρήν, δαιδαλέην, ἱπποδασείης, ἱπποκόμου, λαμπομένης, λαμπρῆς, παναίθῃσι, τετραφάλῳ, φαεινῇ, χαλκήρεος, χαλκοπαρῄου, N 131, 188. (See these adjs., and cuts under them.)

κορύσσων, part., ipf. ἐκόρυσσε, (κόρυς), equip, excitare, augere; pass. and mid. κορύσσεαι, σσεται, σσύμενος, ον, ipf. κορύσσειτο, σσέσθην, aor. κορυσσάμενος, and pf. part. κεκορυθμένος, ον, οι, α, equipped; (χαλκῷ), shod with; arm one's self, τεύχεσι, χαλκῷ; raise the head, Δ 442, cf. 443, 424, cf. κορθύεται.

κορυστήν, du. τά, lit. helmed, hence armed, ready for ba'tle, Δ 457, N 201. (Il.)

κορὑφῆς, ῇ, ἤν, αί, ῇσι, ἁς, (κόρυμβος, κόρυς), vertex, crest; cacumen, summit, dat. without prep., E 554. (Il. and ι 121.)

κορύφοῦται, from -όω, (κορυφή), rises with arching crest, Δ 426†.

Κορώνεια, city in Boiotia, south of lake Kopais, B 503†.

κορώνη, ης, ῃ, αι, ῃσιν, (corona, cornu, cur-vus), any thing crooked or curved, (1) the ring on the door, α 441. (See cut No. 72, and κληίς.)— (2) the curved end of the bow over which the loop of the bow-string must be brought. (See cut No. 37, under ἐνταινύουσιν.)—(3) εἰνάλιαι, τανύγλωσσοι, sea-crows, cormorants. ε 66.

κορωνίσι, dat. pl. fem., (κορώνη), bent into shape of a horn, curved (always in 4th foot of verse), often, τ 182. (See cuts Nos. 21, 41, 94, 95, 109.)

Κόρωνος, Καινείδης, father of Leonteus, king of the Lapithai, B 746†.

κοσμέω, ipf. ἐκόσμει, εον, aor. ἐκόσμησε, inf. ῆσαι, pass. aor. 3 pl. κόσμηθεν, part. -θέντες, (κόσμος), arrange, order, equip troops, get ready chariot; δόρπον, prepare evening meal, η 13; mid. κοσμησάμενος πολήτας, marshaling his own countrymen, B 806.

κοσμηταί (κοσμέω), well laid out, η 127†.

κοσμήτορι, ε, usually λαῶν, marshaler of the people, usually of Atrei-

dai and Dioskouroi; only in σ 152, Amphinomos. (Il.)

κόσμος, ῳ, ον, arrangement, order; constructio, building, ἵππου, θ 492; decus, ornamenta, ornaments, trappings, of women and horses; κόσμῳ, in order, in rank and file; λίην, εὖ κατὰ κόσμον, duly, becomingly, θ 489; οὐ κ. κ., indecōre, shamefully, ν 181.

κοτέουσι, part. ἔων, ἔοντος, τε, ἔουσ(α), pf. part. κεκοτηότι, τ 71; mid. ipf. κοτίοντο, aor. κοτέσσατο, subj. ἔσσεται, part. ἐσσάμενος, η, (κότος), succensere, be angry with, τινί (on account of something, τινός, Δ 168); also οὔνεκα, quod.

κοτήεις, wrathful, E 191†.

κότον, τόν, grudge, rancor, wrath, with dat. of person against whom feeling is felt, τινί; but Π 449, in whom thou wilt excite dire wrath.

κοτύλην, τήν, properly a little cup; E 306, hip-joint.

κοτὑληδονόφιν, from κοτυληδών, (κοτύλη), πρός—, on the suckers at the end of the tentaculae of the polypus pebbles stick fast, ε 433†.

κοτὑλ-ήρῠτον (ἀρύω), that may be caught in cups, streaming, Ψ 34†.

κουλεόν, see κολεόν.

κούρη, sing. and pl., (gen. ἁων, dat. ῃσι), fem. from κοῦρος, young girl or daughter, cf. French fille; τινός, Χρυσηίδος, A 111, for the daughter of Chryses; (Διός) γλαυκῶπις=Athene; also applied to youthful wives, A 98, Z 247.

κούρητες, ων, εσσι, (κοῦρος), Ἀχαιῶν, Παναχαιῶν, T 248, 193, youthful chiefs, princes, princes' sons.

Κουρῆτες, tribe in Aitolia, afterward expelled by Aitolians; their siege of Kalydon, I 529–599.

κουρίδιον, οιο, ῳ, ον, ης, ῃ, ην, ας, (κουρίξ [Curtius], κοῦρος, κούρη ?), bridal, wedded; nobilis, noble, Λ 243 (cf. 242, μνηστῆς), ο 22, in which latter case neither κουριδίοιο nor φίλοιο is subst. The signification of the word is not certainly known; others translate youthful, princely, A 114.

κουρίζων, part., (κοῦρος), young, lusty, χ 185†.

κουρίξ (κουρά), adv., ἔρυσαν, by the hair, χ 188†.

κοῦρος, ῳ, ον, ω, οι, ων, οισιν, ους, properly iuvenis, youth, boy, Ζ 59; son, τ 523 (yet Ν 95); cf. κουρότεροισι, Δ 316, φ 310, iunioribus, fresh with youth, lusty, θηρητῆρες; hence, able to bear arms, valiant, noble, β 96 ; used often (cf. Lat. equites) to denote persons of given rank, and may be translated noble, Α 473; κοῦροι Ἀχαιῶν, etc.

κουρο-τρόφος (τρέφω) ἀγαθή, bona nutrix iuvenum robustorum, ι 27†.

κοῦφα, ntr. pl., as adv., quickly, Ν 158†; κουφότερον, with lighter heart, θ 201†.

Κόων, son of Antenor, slain by Agamemnon, Λ 248-260, Τ 53.

Κόωνδ', see Κῶς.

κράατα, τι, τος, see III. κάρ.

κράδαινόμενον, η, (κραδαίνω), vibratum, quivering, Ν 504. (Il.)

κραδάων, part. from κραδάω, vibrans. brandishing, Η 213, τ 438.

κράδίη, ης, ῃ, ην, and at beginning of verse καρδίη, (κραδάω), cor, heart; then as centre of circulation, anima, life; also animus, courage, Α 225, Μ 247; heart as seat of emotion, desire, Ι 646, with θυμός, Κ 220, Β 171, δ 548, etc., of thought, reason, Φ 441; thoughts were set, δ 260.

κραίνουσι, ipf. ἐκραίαινε, aor. imp. κρῆνον, κρήηνον, ἤνατ(ε), inf. κρῆναι, κρηῆναι, fut. mid. (as pass.) κρανέεσθαι, (creare), perficere, ε 170, accomplish, fulfill, bring to pass; Ι 626, the object of our mission does not appear to me likely to be brought to pass in this way; only θ 391, bear sway.

κραιπνόν, οἶσι, αἱ, ά, as adv. = ὥς, comp. -ότερος, rapidus, from wind and storm; elsewh. quick; Ψ 590, hasty, hot.

Κράνάη, an island, Γ 445†.

κράνἄῆς, ἥν, rocky, Ithaka, α 247. (Od.)

κρανέεσθαι, fut., see κραίνουσι.

κράνειαν, acc., gen. είης, cornus, cornel-tree. its wood esp. hard, κ 242.

κρανίῳ (κράνον), cranio, upper part of the skull, Ο 84†.

Κράπἄθος, ή, Β 676, island near Rhodos; later Κάρπαθος.

κράτα, τί, see III. κάρ.

κράται-γύᾶλοι (γύαλον), with strong

breast-plates, Τ 361†. (See cut No. 59.)

κράταιΐς (κράτος), with its weight, with overmastering force, pondus, λ 597†.

Κράταιΐν, μητέρα τῆς Σκύλλης, μ 124†.

κράταιός, οῦ, ώ, ή, potens, mighty; θηρός=λέοντος, Λ 119.

κράται-πεδον (κραταιός) οὖδας, hard-surfaced earth, pavimentum, ψ 46†.

κράτερός, οἶο, οῦ, ᾧ, όν, ώ, οῖσι; ή, ἧς, ᾗ, ᾗφι (βίηφιν, thrice at end of verse), ἥν, αἱ, ἧσι, άς; όν, (κράτος), and parallel form καρτερός, όν, οί, (κάρτος), strong, mighty, of persons, things, passions, etc.; adv. κρατερῶς, strongly, mightily, Θ 29 ; hold firm thy ground, Π 501.

κράτερό-φρονος, gen., acc. α, (ε), (φρήν), stout-hearted, dauntless, animosus; of heroes and warriors, of lion, θήρ, Κ 184.

κρατερ-ώνυχες, ας, (ὄνυξ), strong-hoofed, strong-clawed, of horses, mules, and κ 218, of wolves and lions.

κράτεσφι, see III. κάρ.

κράτευταί, gen. pl., (κρατός), explained by Aristarchus as stones, head-stones, on which the spits were rested in roasting meat; cf. our fire-dogs, and-irons, possibly in shape like the horns on the altar in cut No. 102, Ι 214†.

κρατέεις, ει, ουσι, inf. έειν, part. έων, (κράτος), be mighty, rule over, Α 288; κρατέων, with might; over any one, τινῶν ; τισίν, bear sway among, λ 485.

κράτος, εἵ, and κάρτος, εἵ, robur, potentia, imperium, might, power, mastery, α 359; victoria, φ 280; φέρεσθαι, reportare, carry off victory.

κρατός, see III. κάρ.

κράτύς = κρατερός, ἀργειφόντης, Π 181, ε 49, mighty.

κρέας, pl. κρέ(α)' (κρέατ(α)', γ 33, ι 162), gen. κρεῶν, κρειῶν, dat. κρέασιν, (cruor), caro. flesh, pl. pieces of flesh, dressed meat. [κρεα, synizesis, ι 347.]

κρεῖον (κρέας), meat-tray, dresser, Ι 206†.

κρείσσων, οντες, οσιν, ον, (κράτ-ϳων), superior, mightier, stronger; ζ 182, nobler and better; βίῃ, superior in strength; with inf. φ 345.

Κρειοντιάδης, son of Κρείων, Lykomedes, Τ 240†.

κρείων, οντα, ὑντων, (ουσα, X 48), properly part., *ruling, ruler; εὐρὺ κρ.,* ruling far and wide, title esp. of Agamemnon, with reference to his position as generalissimo of Greek forces; also of Enosichthon, Zeus; also in one case of servant of Menelaos, δ 22.

Κρείων, (1) king of Thebes, father of Megara, λ 269.—(2) father of Lykomedes, I 84.

κρέμαμαι, see following.

κρέμαννυμι, fut. **κρεμόω**, aor. *κρέμᾶσε, ἄσαντες,* s u s p e n d e r e, *hang, hang up; mid. ipf. ἐκρέμω,* p e n d e b a s, thou didst hang, O 18.

κρέων, gen. pl. from κρέας.

κρήγυον, τὸ—εἶπας, A 106†, s a l u t i f e r u m, *good, useful, helpful.*

κρήδεμνον, ῳ, α, (κάρη, δέω), *headband;* in woman's attire, *a short veil,* as in adjacent cut, α 334; of cities, *battlements,* ν 388; of wine jar, *lid,* γ 392, (See cut No. 68.)

κρηῆναι, aor. from κραίνουσι. **κρῆθεν,** see III. κάρ, f u n d i t u s, *utterly.*

Κρηθεύς, Αἰολίδης, husband of Τυρώ, λ 237, 258.

Κρήθων, son of Diokles, slain by Aineias, E 542, 549.

κρημνοῦ, οἶο, όν, οί, ούς, (κρέμαμαι), *overhanging river bank,* esp. the *gullied banks* of the Skamandros, Φ 26, 175.

κρηναῖαι (κρήνη) *νύμφαι, fountain nymphs,* ρ 240†.

κρήνη, ης, ῃ, ην (δε), αι, εων, (κάρηνα, cf. c a p u t), *fountain, spring, well,* I 14, ι 141. (Cf. cut No. 65.)

Κρῆτες, B 645, Γ 230, *inhabitants of island* Κρήτη; described, τ 172, 175, ἑκατόμπολιν, εὐρείης; also pl. Κρητάων, as divided and speaking different languages, π 62; Κρήτηνδε, τ 186; Κρήτηθεν, Γ 233.

κρητῆρος, ι, α, ες, σι, ας, masc., (κεράννυμι), *mixing-vessel* in which wine and water, in ratio of ⅔ and ⅓, were mingled: μίσγεσθαι; στήσασθαι, place the mixing-bowl at hand, usually near the hearth, and often on a tripod (esp. when several κρητῆρες were used at the feast); the contents were afterward poured into the drinking-cups

by means of the πρόχοος, γ 339; Z 527, set up in our palace a mixing-bowl in commemoration of freedom, in honor of the gods. Cut No. 7 shows (1) the ἀμφιφορεύς, from which the wine was poured into the upper smaller mixing bowl, on which the πρόχοος stands; the second mixing bowl served to contain the water, and then the contents of both bowls may be imagined as mixed in the largest mixing-bowl, which stands upon the tripod, and from which, by means of the πρόχοος, the diluted wine was distributed into the δέπαα. (Cf. cut No. 29.)

κρῖ, τό, nom. and acc., (κριθή), λευκόν, *barley,* Τ 496; also as food for horses, E 196, δ 41.

κριθαί, ῶν, έων, άς, (κρῖ, c e r - e s ?), *barley, barleycorn,* Λ 69.

κρίκε, aor. from κρίζω, *creaked,* of the yoke under a strain, Π 470†.

κρίκον, τόν, (κίρκος, c i r c u s), *yoke-ring,* Ω 272†. (See adjoining cut, from the antique; still clearer cuts Nos. 45, 49.)

κρίνῃ, ωσι, subj., οιμι opt., **κρῖνε** imp., ων, οντες part. prs., aor. ἔκρινε, ιναν, subj. ίνωσι, part. ινας, c e r n e r e, *sieve, select;* c l i g e r e, λοχόνδε, for the ambuscade; pass. pf. part. κεκριμένοι, ους, η, c l e c t i, *chosen,* selected (Ξ 19, -ον, c e r t u m), and κρινθέντες, ες; d e c e r n e r e, *decide,* νεῖκος, the dispute; σκολιὰς θέμιστας, proleptically, *pervert* justice, mid. κρίνονται, subj. ώμεθα, aor. ἐκρίνατο, subj. ηται, ωνται, imp. άσθων, inf. ασθαι, part. άμενος, s i b i c l i g e r e, *choose for one's self;* also, *measure one's self* in battle, ἄρηι, a c i e, B 385; π 269, when our courage and that of the suitors is measured in my

palace, cf. ω 507; ὀνείρους, *expound,
interpret.*

κριόν, ί, masc., (κέρας), a r i e t e m,
ram, ι 447, 461.

Κρῖσα, town in Phokis; ζαθέην, Β
520, near and southwest of Delphi.

κριτός, οἱ, (κρίνω), e l e c t u s, *chosen*,
Η 434 and θ 258.

κροαίνων, part., (κρούω), *galloping*,
Ζ 507, Ο 264.

Κροῖσμος, a Trojan, slain by Meges,
Ο 523†.

κροκό-πεπλος (πέπλος), *with saffron-
colored mantle;* epithet of Eos, Θ 1. (Il.)

κρόκον, τόν, *crocus, saffron*, Ξ 348†.

Κροκύλεια, τά, island or village belonging to Ithaka, Β 633†.

κρόμῦον, οιο, c e p a, *onion*, Λ 630, τ
233.

Κρονίδης, ου, αο, ῃ, ην, η, *son of
Kronos*, standing alone or with Zeus,
Α 552, α 45, =**Κρονίων**, ἱωνος (ἱονος,
Ξ 247, λ 620). (See following.)

Κρόνος, οιο, ου, ον, (κραίνω), father
of Zeus, Poseidaon, Aides, of Hera,
Demeter, and Hestia; overthrown with
the Titans, Θ 415, 479, 383, Ε 721.

κροσσάων, ας, fem., (κόρση?), perh.
walls of the towers, between foundations
and battlements, Μ 258, 444.

κροτάλιζον, ipf., (κρόταλον), ὄχεα,
made rattle (as they drew), *drew the
rattling* chariots, Λ 160†.

κρόταφον, οιο, οισι, οις, masc., t e m-
p o r a, *temples;* sing., Δ 502, Υ 397.

κροτέοντες (κρότος) ὄχεα, *drawing
the rattling* chariots, Ο 453†.

Κρουνοί, "Springs," name of locality in Elis, [ο 295]†.

κρουνώ, du., ὦν, ούς, pl., *sources*, Δ
454; of Skamandros, Χ 147, 208.

κρύβδᾱ, Σ 168†. =**κρύβδην**, λ 455
(Od.), c l a m, *secretly*.

κρύεροῖο (κούος, c r u-o r, Eng. g o r e),
r i g i d u s, *chilling, dread*, Ν 48, δ 103.

κρυόεντος, εσσα, (κρύος), h o r r e n d i,
chilling, horrible, Ι 2. (Il.)

κρύπτᾰδίης, α, (κρύπτω), c l a n d e-
s t i n a, *secret;* Α 542, c l a n d e s t i n i s
c a p t i s c o n s i l i i s d e c e r n e r e.

κρυπτῇ κληΐδι, with a *secret* bolt, Ξ
168†.

κρύπτων, part., ipf. iter. κρύπτασκε,
fut. κρύψω, aor. ἔκρυψαν, κρύψειν, subj.
ψω, inf. ψαι, part. ψαντες, perf. pass.
part. κεκρυμμένον, α, aor. κρύφθη, c e-

l a r e, *hide, conceal*, τί τινι (with desire
for protection); pass. s e c e l a r e, ὑπό
τινι, s u b r e, *hide one's self* under any
thing; τινά, aor., from some one; *keep
secret*, ἔπος τινί, λ 443.

κρύσταλλος, ῳ, masc., (κρύος), g l a-
c i e s, *ice, clear ice*, ξ 477 and Χ 152.

κρύφηδόν (κρύφα), c l a m, *secretly*,
ξ 330 and τ 299.

Κρῶμνα, locality in Paphlagonia, Β
855†.

κτάμεν(αι), ος, see κτείνω.

κτᾶσθαι, aor. ἐκτήσω, (ἐ)κτήσατο, pf.
ἐκτῆσθαι, s i b i c o m p a r a r e, *acquire
for one's self*, property, servants, wife;
τινί τι, a l i c u i a l i q u i d, v 265; pf.
p o s s i d ê r e, *possess*, Ι 402.

κτεάτεσσιν (τὸ κτέαρ, κτάομαι), b o-
n i s, *property, possessions*, Ε 154, α
218.

κτεάτισσα, εν, part. ας, aor. from
-ίζω, (κτέαρ), s i b i c o m p a r a r e, *acquire for one's self;* δουρί, cf. δουρικτήτη, f e r r o = b e l l o, Π 57. [ᾰ]

Κτέᾱτος, son of Aktor and of Molione, Β 621.

κτείνεις, ει, ουσι, subj. ω, inf. ειν,
part. ων, οντ(α), ες, ipf. ἔκτεινε, ον,
κτεῖνε, ον, iter. κτείνεσκε, fut. κτενέω,
έει (εῖ), έειν and κτανέω, έοντα, aor.
(ἔ)κτεινε, opt. αιμι, inf. ναι, part. νας,
(ἔ)κτεινε, aor. 2 aor. ἔκτᾰνον, ες, ε, κτά-
νον, ε, and 3 sing. ἔκτα, αμεν, αν, subj.
κτέωμεν, χ 216, inf. κτάμεν(αι); pass.
prs. κτεινώμεθα, εσθαι, ὀμενος, ῳ, ων,
ους, ipf. κτείνοντο, 3 pl. aor. ἔκταθεν,
and aor. 2 κτάσθαι, ἀμενος, οιο, ῳ, ον,
ων, οισι, ης, with aoristic signif. only
in Ν 262, Ο 554, Σ 337, i n t e r i m e r e,
kill, slay; pass. Ε 465, 'Αχαιοῖς = ὑπ'
'Αχαιῶν.

κτέρας (κτᾶσθαι), *possession*, Κ 216
and Ω 235; pl. **κτέρεα**, έων, always
with κτερεΐζειν, bestow one's possessions upon one=j u s t a f a c e r e, *bury*
with due honors.

κτερίζω, fut. **κτεριῶ**, ιοῦσι, aor. opt.
ίσειε, αίμι, and prs. imp. **κτερεΐζε**, inf.
έμεν, aor. -είξω, είξαι, (κτέρας), *bury*,
e f f e r r e; ἀέθλοις, with funeral games;
κτέρεα κτ., j u s t a f a c e r e, bury with
solemn pomp, α 291.

κτῆμαθ' = κτήματα, dat. ασιν, (κτᾶσθαι), *possession, property*, esp. the *treas-
ures* carried off at the same time with
Helen, Η 350, Ι 382.

Κτήσιος Ὀρμενίδης, father of Eumaios, ο 414†.

Κτήσιππος, from Same, son of Polytherses, a suitor, υ 288, χ 279; slain by Philoitios, χ 285.

κτήσιος, σιν, fem., (κτᾶσθαι), property, Ο 663.

κτητοί (κτᾶσθαι), that may be acquired, Ι 407†.

κτῐδέην (ἰκτίς), κυνέην, helmet of weasel-skin, Κ 335 and 458.

κτίζω, aor. **κτίσσε**, ἔκτῐσαν, incolere, settle in a count y, with acc., Υ 216.

κτίλος, ον, aries, ram, Γ 196 and Ν 492. [ῐ]

Κτῐμένη, daughter of Laertes, sister of Odysseus, settled in marriage in Same, ο 363.

κτῠπέει, έων, ἐουσαι, aor. ἔκτῠπε, κτῠπε, crash, of falling trees, thunder, of Zeus; μέγα, loud; σμερδαλέα, terribly, Η 479, Θ 170.

κτῠπος, ου, ον, sonitus, any loud noise, stamping of feet, blow of horse's hoof, foot-tread, tumult of battle, thunder, Κ 532, φ 237.

κύᾰμοι, beans, Ν 589†.

κυᾰνεος, ον, οι, η, ην, αι, ρσιν, (κύανος), of steel, only Σ 564; elsewh. always steel-blue or dark-colored, Ω 94.

κυᾰνό-πεζαν, with dark feet, Λ 629†.

κυᾰνο-πρωρείους (πρῴρα), νέας, γ 299; elsewh. **πρῴροιο**; always at end of verse, always with νεός, dark-bowed, dark-prowed, Ο 693, ι 482.

κυᾰνοιο, gen., (blue) steel, Λ 24, 35, and η 87.

κυᾰνο-χαῖτο = -χαίτης, dat. γ, (χαίτη), dark-haired; also subst., the dark-haired one, Ν 563; dark-maned, Υ 224.

κυᾰν-ώπιδος (ὤψ), dark-eyed, μ 60†.

κυβερνῆσαι, aor. inf., (κυβερνάω, guberno), steer, γ 283†.

κυβερνήτης, εω, ην, voc. κυβερνῆτα, μ 217; αι, = -ητήρες, θ 557; gubernator, pilot, helmsman, Τ 43, Ψ 316. (Od.)

κυβιστᾷ, 3 sing., ipf. 3 pl. κυβίστων, (κύβη), se praecipitat, turn a somersault, tumble; Φ 354, were leaping about.

κυβιστητῆρε, ες, (κυβιστᾶν), divers, Π 750; elsewh. tumblers.

κυδαίνων, ipf. κύδαινε, ον, aor. κύδηνε, inf. ῆναι, (κύδος), glorify, honor,

Ο 612; ennoble, π 212; θυμόν, rejoice the heart.

κυδαλίμοιο, ον, ω, οισι, (κῦδος), noble in exterior, glorious, epithet of heroes; κῆρ, periphrastically, noble heart.

κυδάνει, ipf. ἐκύδανον, (κῦδος), exalt, Ξ 73; superiores erant, Υ 42.

κυδῐ-ανείρῃ, ἄν, (κυδιᾶν), man-ennobling, bringing renown, ἀγορῇ, μάχῃ, Λ 490, Ζ 124.

κυδιόων, τες, (κυδιάω, κῦδος), triumphing, proud, Φ 519. (Il.)

κυδιστε, ην, (κῦδος), most glorious, exalted, Α 122.

κυδοίμεον, 3 pl. ipf., fut. ήσων, (κυδοιμός), saeviebant, grassabantur, spread confusion, Λ 324; Ο 136, ἡμᾶς, to vent his rage against us.

κυδοιμός, οῦ, όν, din or mêlée of battle; uproar, also personified, Σ 535, Ε 593.

κῦδος, εῖ, ntr., might, majesty, glory, γ 57, 79, Ἀχαιῶν, pride of the Achaioi.

κυδρή, ήν, (κῦδος), glorious, illustrious, λ 580.

Κύδωνες, tribe in northwest of Kreta, γ 292, ρ 176.

κυέουσαν, part., ipf. ἐκύει, with acc., bear in the womb, Τ 117; Ψ 266, be with mule foal.

κύθε, aor. from κεύθει, occuluit, has hid.

Κυθέρεια, epithet of Aphrodite, θ 288; from island **Κύθηρα**, τά, southwest of promontory Maleia, where the worship of the goddess had been introduced by an early Phoinikian colony, ι 81, Ο 432; **Κυθηρόθεν**, from Kythera; adj. **Κυθηρίῳ**, ον, Κ 268, Ο 431.

κυκόωντι, dat. part., ipf. ἐκύκα, aor. κύκησε, pass. prs. part. κυκώμενος, ον, η, aor. du. κυκηθήτην, ήθησαν, immiscere, stir up and mix with, pass., confundi, perturbari, be struck with fear, or panic, Υ 489; be in commotion, foam up, of the sea.

κυκεώ, = ειῶ, τόν, (from κυκεών, κυκᾶν), mixed drink, compounded of barley meal, grated goats' cheese, and (Pramnian) wine, Λ 624; Kirke adds also honey, κ 290, 234.

κυκλήσομεν, fut., (κυκλέω, κύκλος), wheel away, carry forth, of corpses, Η 332†.

κύκλου, ῳ, ον, οι, and α, circle, ring; δόλιον, circle with which hunters enclose game ; ἱερῷ, s a n c t o, solemn circle. as tribunal ; κύκλῳ, *round about ;* the *rings* on the outside of shield, or the *layers* which, lying one above another and gradually diminishing in size toward the ὀμφαλός, made up the shield, Λ 33, Υ 280 ; *wheel*, Ψ 340, pl. τὰ κύκλα.

κυκλόσε, *in a circle,* Δ 212 and P 392.

κυκλο-τερές (τείρω), *circular,* ρ 209 ; Δ 124, stretch, draw into a circle.

Κύκλ-ωπες, wild race of giants, α 71, ζ 5. ι 166 sqq., related to Gigantes and Phaiakians, without towns, fear of gods, or social ties, ι 166 ; chief representative, ὁ **Κύκλωψ,** Polyphemos, the lawless monster, ι 428 ; one-eyed cannibal, κ 200 ; overreached by Odysseus, ι 366, 408.

κύκνων, τῶν, c y g n o r u m, *swans,* B 460 and O 692.

κυλίνδει, pass. ων, ον, pass. prs. εται, εσθαι, ὁμενος, η, ην, α, ipf. (ἐ)κυλίνδετο, v o l v e r e a l i q u i d, *roll,* πῆμά τινι, m o l i r i, metaph., roll calamity against ; pass., v o l v i, *be rolled,* also *throw one's self prostrate, wallow,* in agony, Θ 86 ; in grief, κατὰ κόπρον, in the dirt (of the street, etc.) ; νῶιν πῆμα, evil is rolling upon us.

Κυλλήνη, mountain chain in northern Arkadia, B 603 ; birthplace of Hermes, who is hence called, ω 1, **Κυλλήνιος ;** yet the word in O 518 designates an inhabitant of the town Κυλλήνη, in Elis.

κυλλο-ποδίων, voc. -πόδιον, (κυλλός, πούς). *crook-footed,* epithet of Hephaistos, Φ 331. (Il.)

κῦμα, τος, τι, τα, σι, ntr., (κύω), u n d a, also f l u c t u s, *wave, billow,* B 209, K 574 ; B 396, ν 99, v e n t i s a g i t a t a, keep off the waves raised by the wind ; κατὰ κ., with the current.

κυμαίνοντα, part., (κῦμα), πόντον, f l u c t u a n t e m, *billowy,* Ξ 229. (Od.)

κύμβαχος, ον, (κύμβη), adj., *on the head,* E 586 ; subst.. *crown* or *top of helmet,* in which the plume is fixed, O 536. (See cut No. 20, *b.*)

κύμινδιν, τήν, Ξ 291 : ancient name of bird usually called χαλκίς, *nighthawk.*

Κῦμο-δόκη and **Κῦμο-ζόη,** Nereids, Σ 39, 41†.

κυνά-μυια, *dog-fly,* abusive epithet applied by Ares to Athena, Φ 394.

κυνέη, ης, η, ην, (κύων), *soldier's cap,* of leather or weasel's skin, also of metal stiffened or adorned with metal, χαλκήρης (see cut, p. 58), also fitted with metal plates to protect the checks, χαλκοπάρηος ; with horse-hair plume, ἵππουρις, ἱπποδάσεια, cf. cuts Nos. 11, 85. Sometimes entirely of bronze = *helmet.* κυνέη αἰγείη is a goat-skin cap, like that of the oarsmen in cut No. 41. Ἄϊδος, cap of Hades, rendering invisible, E 845.

κύνεος (κύων), i m p u d e n s, *shameless,* I 373†.

κυνέω, ipf. **κύνει,** εον, aor. **κύσα,** (ἐ)κύσε, (ἐ)κύσσε(ν), opt. κύσειε, inf. σσαι, o s c u l a r i, *kiss,* υἱόν, πάντα, masc., π 21 ; γούνατα, χεῖρας, κεφαλήν τε καὶ ὤμους, μιν κεφαλήν τε καὶ ἄμφω φάεα καλὰ χεῖράς τ' ἀμφοτέρας, π 15, cf. ρ 39 ; κεφαλὰς καὶ χεῖρας, φ 225 ; ἄρουραν, one's native soil.

κυν-ηγέται (ἄγω), v e n a t o r e s, *hunters,* ι 120†.

κυνο-ραιστέων (synizesis), gen. pl. from -στής, (ῥαίω), *fleas,* ρ 300†.

Κῦνος, harbor-town of Lokris, B 531†.

κύντερον, τατον, (κύων), i m p u d e n - t i u s, -i s s i m u m, *shameless, horrible ;* K 503, what *daring exploit* he should perform.

κύν-ῶπα, voc. masc. from A 159 ; -ῶπις, ιδος, fem., *impudent ;* i m p u - d e n s, *shameless,* Γ 180.

Κῦπαρισσήεις, town in Elis, B 593†.

κῦπαρισσίνῳ (κυπάρισσος), *of cypress wood,* ρ 340†.

κῦπάρισσον, ἡ, *cypress,* evergreen, ε 64†.

κύπειρον, τό, *fragrant marsh-grass,* food for horses, perh. galingal, ὁ 603.

κύπελλον, α, οις, (c u p a, Eng. c u p), *goblet,* usually of gold, general word for *drinking-cup.* Ω 305, cf. 285, I 670.

Κύπρις, ιν, and ἰδα, Aphrodite, E 330 ; as goddess of island **Κύπρος,** whither her worship was brought by Phoinikians, θ 83 ; Κύπρονδε, A 21.

κύπτω, aor. opt. κύψει', part. ψας, αντι, *bow down,* λ 585. (Il.)

κύρμα, τό, (κυρέω), *what one lights upon, booty, prey,* P 272 ; usually with ἕλωρ, E 488.

κύρσας, aor. from κύρω.

κυρτόν, ώ, ά, (cur-vus), *rounded, arched, round*, B 218. (Il.)

κυρτωθέν, part. aor. pass. from κυρτόω, curvatum, *arched*, λ 244†.

κύρω, ipf. **κῦρε**, *collide with*, ἅρματι; aor. part. **κύρσας** ἐπὶ σώματι, *having lighted upon* a lifeless body; αἰὲν ἐπ' αὐχένι κῦρε, *was constantly aiming at* the neck, Ψ 821; mid., Ω 530, κύρεται κακῷ, *encounters, falls in with*.

κύστιν, τήν, *bladder*, E 67. (Il.)

Κύτωρος, town in Paphlagonia, B 853.

κῦφός (κύπτω), *bowed, bent*, β 16†.

Κῦφος, town in Perrhæbia in Thessaly, B 748†.

κύω, see κυέω and κυνέω.

κύων, κυνός, κύνα, κύον, κύνες, ὦν, σί(ν) and κύνεσσι(ν), νας, masc., six times fem., canis, *dog, bitch*; θηρευταί, τραπεζῆες; Ἀΐδαο = Kerberos, Θ 368, λ 623; *sea-dog*, perhaps *seal*, μ 96; dog of Orion, Χ 29 = Seirios; as symbol of shamelessness, applied to women=feminae impudicae, then with general sense, impudens, *impudent*; dastardly dogs, N 623; with λυσσητήρ, rabida, *raging hound*, Θ 299.

κῶας, εα, εσιν. *fleece*, serving for seat or bedding, π 47, Ι 661, γ 38.

κώδειαν, *poppy-head*, Ξ 499†.

κωκῡτός, ό, (κωκύω), (1) *howling, wailing*, Χ 409 and 447.—(2) as proper name, a river of the lower world, flowing out of the Styx, κ 514.

κωκύω, 3 sg. prs. **κωκύει**, ipf. ἐκώκυε, ον, aor. ἐκώκυσεν, κώκυσ', part. κωκύσασα, -άνων, (1) *shriek, wail*, always of women, ε 37, β 361.—(2) trans., *lament*, τινά, ω 295.

κώληπα, τήν, (κῶλον?), poplitem, *bend or hollow of the knee*, Ψ 726†.

κῶμα, τό, (κοιμάω), sopor, *deep sleep*, σ 201.

Κῶπαι, town on lake Kopaïs in Boiotia, B 502†.

κώπη, ῃ, ην, ῃσι(ν), ῃς, ας, (capio, Eng. haft), *sword-hilt*, Α 219; *butt or handle of oar* (same word used to-day in Greece for oar), ι 489; incumbere remis, lay one's self to the oar, μ 214; *handle of key*, φ 7. (See cut No. 72.)

κωπήεντι, τα, (κώπη), *hilted*, Π 332, Ο 713.

κωρύκῳ, τῷ, perae, *leather sack or wallet*, ε 267. (Od.) [ῠ]

Κῶς, acc. Κόωνδε, *to Kos*. Ο 28, island in Ikarian sea, opposite the coast of Karia.

κωφῷ, όν, ήν, (κόπτω), (1) *blunted*, Λ 390.—(2) *noiseless, silent* (before it breaks), Ξ 16.—(3) γαῖαν, *dull, senseless, lifeless*, Ω 54.

Λ.

λᾶας, ᾶος, ᾶϊ, ᾶαν, du. ᾶε, pl. άων, άεσσι, saxum, *stone*, Γ 12, Μ 445, λ 594, ν 163, ξ 10; *hewn stone*, κ 211.

Λᾶας, αν, town in Lakonike, B 585†.

λαβρ-ἀγόρην, τόν, (λάβρος), *reckless talker*, Ψ 479†.

λαβρεύεαι, 2 sing. prs., (λάβρος), *talkest rashly*, Ψ 474 and 478.

λάβρος, ον, and sup. -ότατον, rapidus, *swift*, o 293.

λαγχάνω, ipf. ἐλάγχανον, λάγχανον, aor. ἔλαχον, λάχ(εν), ομεν, ον, subj. λάχῃσιν, ῃ, inf. εῖν, part. ών, όντα, sortiri, *obtain by lot*, τί, Ι 367, Ο 190; ληΐδος αἶσαν, praedae portionem, share of spoil; Κῆρ λάχε γεινόμενον, *had me allotted to her* at birth, i. e. *obtained power over me* from my birth; pf. λελόγχᾱσι, adepti sunt, *have obtained*, τιμὴν δώρων, κτερέων; red. aor. subj. λελάχητε, ωσι, θανόντα πυρός, mortuo ignem impertire, put in possession of fire = *solemnly burn*, Η 80; *choose by lot*; ι 160. *fall by lot*.

λαγωόν, ούς, masc., leporem, es, *hare*, Κ 361, ρ 295.

Λαέρκης, (1) son of Aimon, father

of Alkimedon, Myrmidon, Π 197.—(2) χρυσοχόος in Pylos, γ 425.

Λαέρτης, son of Akreisios, father of Odysseus, king in Ithaka, α 430, ω 206, 270, δ 111, χ 185, δ 555.

Λαερτϊάδης, son of Laertes, Odysseus, Β 173, ε 203, ι 19, Γ 200.

λαζοίατο, 3 pl. opt. prs., ipf. λάζετο (ἐλάζετο, Ε 840), take into the hands (χερσί), μάστιγα ; ἀγκάς, amplecti, embrace ; γαῖαν ὀδάξ, bite the dust, fall in combat ; μῦθον πάλιν, caught back again the words (of joy which were on his lips), ν 254.

λᾱθῐ-κηδέα, acc. masc., (λαθεῖν κῆδος), banishing care, Χ 83†.

λάθρη (λαθεῖν), clam, secretly, unbeknown; also with gen., τινός, aliquo; sensim, imperceptibly, Τ 165.

λάϊγγες, ᾰς, (λᾶας), pebbles, ε 433 and ζ 95. [ᾰ]

λαίλαψ, λαίλᾰπι, α, fem., thundershower, hurricane; also fig. with ἴσος, Μ 375, Υ 51.

λαιμόν, τόν, guttur, throat, gu'let, Ν 388, Σ 34, χ 15. (Il.)

λάϊνεος and **λάινος, ον, οι,** (λᾶας), saxeus, of stone, stony ; Μ 177, τεῖχος, yet the passage is of doubtful authenticity.

λαισήϊα, τά. (λάσιος ?), πτερόεντα, fluttering shield or target, Ε 453 and Μ 426, so called on account of the fluttering apron of untanned leather, λάσιος, hanging from the shield. (See adjoining cut, and esp. No. 85.)

Λαιστρυγών, όνος, όνες, fabled tribe of savage giants, κ 106, 119, 199. Hence adj., **Λαιστρυγονίη,** κ 82, ψ 318.

λαῖτμα, τό, (λαιμός ?), depth or gulf of the sea, used alone or with θαλάσσης, ἁλός, Τ 267. (Od.)

λαῖφος, ε(α), ntr., shabby, tattered garment, ν 399 and υ 206.

λαιψηρόν, οἷς, ά, (λαῖλαψ), rapidus, nimble, swift, λαιψηρὰ ἐνώμα, plied nimbly, Ο 269.

λάκε, aor. from λάσκω.

Λᾰκεδαίμων, ονος, fem.,. district whose capital was Sparta, δῖαν, γ 326; ἐρατεινῆς, Γ 239 ; εὐρύχορον, ν 414; κοίλην κητώεσσαν, δ 1.

λακτίζων, part., (λάξ), kicking with the heel, struggling convulsively, of the mortally wounded, σ 99 and χ 88.

λαμβάνω, only 2 aor. **ἔλαβε,** also other augmented forms ἐλλαβ(ε), etc., (1) prehendere, take hold of, τί (ἐν) χείρεσσι ; τι ὰ ποδός, grasp by the foot, etc. ; ἀγκάς, amplecti, embrace ; τινός, also mid. ἐλλάβετ(ο), comprehendit, seize, and λελαβέσθαι, scil. αὐτοῦ, δ 388.—(2) of mental states, subjects such as χόλος, incessit, take possession of, seize, τινά (also with acc. of part., γυῖα).—(3) accipere, receive.—(4) capere, take captive, carry off as booty ; η 255, domi recipiens.

Λάμος, king of Laistrygones, κ 81†.

λαμπετόωντι, part. pr., (-άω, λάμπω), blazing, Α 104.

Λαμπετίδης, son of Lampos, Dolops, Ο 526†.

Λαμπετίη, a nymph, daughter of Ἥλιος, μ 132, 375.

Λάμπος, (1) son of Laomedon, father of Trojan Dolops, Γ 147, Ο 526. —(2) horse of Eos, ψ 246 ; of Hektor, Θ 185.

λαμπρός, όν, οἷσι, ἧσιν, sup. ότατος, bright, shining, τ 234. (Il.) λαμπρὸν παμφαίνῃσι, splendide luceat, Ε 6.

λαμπτήρων, gen. pl., ἧρσι, ἧρας, λάμπω), fire pans or basins, σ 307, τ 63 ; for holding blazing pine splinters, used to illuminate rooms. (See cuts on next page, after bronze originals from Pompeii.)

λάμπω, only prs. and ipf. (ἐ)**λάμπ(ε)** and λάμφ', act. and mid.. splendere, shine, gleam, be radiant ; subject a person, (χαλκῷ, πυρί, τεύχεσι), or thing, ꝛ. g. metal, torches, weapons, ὀφθαλμώ, ὄσσε, also πεδ. χαλκῷ, Υ 156.

λανθάνω, ipf. (ὲ)λάνθανε, ον, parallel form λήθω, chief forms: ipf. ἔληθον. λῆὲ(ε), etc., iter. λήθεσκε, fut. λήσεις, aor. (ἔ)λαθ(ε), λάθον, 3 du. λαθέτην, mid. ipf. λανθἄνόμην, prs. λήθεαι, ipf. λήθετο, aor. λάθιτ(ο), opt. 3 pl. λαθοίατο, and aor. red. λελάθοντο, λελαθέσθω, pf. λέλασται, σμεθα, σμένος, ον, (1) l a t e r e, *escape notice of*, τινά, Α 561, Ν 272; with part., Ν 560, 721, π 156, θ 93, Ρ 89; also with ὅτι (ὅτε, Ρ 626), and ἔπως; λαθών (τινα), c l a m, *unperceived by*, Ι 477, Λ 251, ρ 305.—(2) λελάθῃ τινά τινος, Ο 60, *make forget*.—(3) mid. τινός. o b l i v i s c i. *forget*, Δ 127, γ 224.

λάξ, (c a l x), *with the heel*, joined with ποδί, Κ 158 and ο 45.

Λᾱΐ-γονος, (1) son of Trojan Onetor, slain by Meriones, Ἡ 604.—(2) son of Trojan Bias, slain by Achilleus, Υ 460.

Λᾱο-δάμας, ντος, ντα, voc. δάμα, (1) son of Antenor, a Trojan, slain by Aias, Ο 516.—(2) son of Alkinoos, boxer, θ 119, 132, η 170, θ 117, 141.

Λᾱο-δάμεια, daughter of Bellerophontes, mother of Sarpedon, Ζ 198.

Λᾱο-δίκη, (1) daughter of Agamemnon, Ι 145, 287.—(2) daughter of Priamos, wife of Helikaon, Γ 124, Ζ 252.

Λᾱό-δοκος, (1) Antenor's son, Δ 87. —(2) comrade of Antilochos, Ρ 699.

Λᾱο-θόη, daughter of Altes, mother of Lykaon, Φ 85, Χ 48.

Λᾱο-μεδοντιάδης, (1) Priamos, Γ 250.—(2) Lampos, Ο 527.

Λᾱο-μέδων, son of Ilos, father of Priamos, Υ 237, Ζ 23, Ε 269, 640; his faithlessness, Φ 443; his daughter was wooed by Herakles, to whom she was promised by Laomedon on condition that Herakles freed her from the sea-monster which Poseidon had sent to ravage Troas. Herakles performed his part of the agreement, and when Laomedon refused Hesione, Herakles slew him, Ε 638 sqq.

λᾱός, etc. (no du.), masc., (κλαϝός? c l u e n t e s?), *people*, m u l t i t u d o, Δ 199, Ε 573; usually pl., *soldiers, vassals*, γ 214, e x e r c i t u s, *army*, opp. fleet or troops fighting from chariots.

λᾱο-σσόος, ον, (σεύω), *driving the people on* (to combat), *rousing the people*, epithet of Ares, Eris, Athene (Apollon, Amphiaraos), Ν 128, χ 210.

λᾱο-φόρον ὑδόν, *public way*, Ο 682†.

λᾱπάρης, gen., ην, fem., *the soft part of the body* between the hips and the ribs, *flank, loins*, Γ 359. (Il.)

Λᾱπίθαι, *Lapithai*, a tribe inhabiting Mount Olympos in Thessaly, Μ 128, 181, φ 297.

λάπτω, only fut. part. **λάψοντες**, *lap up* with the tongue, Ἡ 161†.

Λάρῑσα, ης, town in Asia Minor near Kyme, Β 841, Ρ 301.

λάρνᾰκα, την, *chest*, Σ 413; *vase*, Ω 795.

λάρῳ, τῷ, l a r o, *cormorant*, ε 51†.

λᾱρόν, sup. -ώτατος, *dainty, choice*, Ρ 572, β 350.

λάσιος, ον, οισι, ην, (ὲασύς?), v i l l o s u s, *shaggy, woolly*, ι 433; epithet of στῆθος, also of κῆρ, as sign of strength and courage, Α 189.

λάσκω, only aor. **λάκε**, *crashed*,

cracked, bones, brass ; pf. λελᾱκώς, λελᾱκυῖα, *bellowing,* μ 85 ; *shrieking,* X 141.

λαυκᾰνῐης, της, g u t t u r i s, X 325, there appeared an unprotected spot *on the throat.* (Il.)

λαύρην, τήν, and (στόμα) λαύρης, *side passage,* pathway between the house of Odysseus and the outer wall (of the court), χ 128, 137. (See plate III., *i. n.*)

λᾰφύσσει, ετον, 3 du. Σ 583, glut i r e, *gulp down,* Λ 176. (Il.)

λάχε, aor. from λαγχάνω.

λάχεια, *with good soil for digging, fruitful,* ι 116 and κ 509.

λάχνη, y, *woolly hair, down,* K 134 ; *sparse hair,* B 219 ; λ 320, *sparse beard.*

λαχνήεντι, α, ας, (λάχνη), *hairy, shaggy,* I 548. (Il.)

λάχνῳ, τῷ, l a n a, *wool,* ι 445†.

λάω, pres. part. **λάων,** aor. λᾰε, *burying his teeth in,* τ 229.

λέβης, nom. sing., gen. pl. -ήτων, *caldron* for warming water, or for boiling food over fire, Φ 362 ; *wash-basin,* held under the hands or feet while water was poured from a pitcher over them (see cut), τ 386 ; ἀνθεμόεντα, adorned on the exterior with designs in imitation of palm leaves or flowers.

λέγωμεν, λέγε, ειν, ων, οντες, ipf. (ἐ)λέγ(ε), λέγομεν, aor. ἔλεξεν, mid. prs. λεγόμεθα, εσθε, εσθαι, ipf. λέγοντο, aor. λέξατο, αιτο, ασθαι, 2 aor. ἐλέγμην, λέκτο, pass. 1 aor. ἐλέχθην, l e g e- r e, c o l l i g e r e, *pick up, gather,* ὀστέα, αἱμασιάς ; n u m e r a r e in, *count among,* ἐν, μετὰ τοῖσι ; e n u m e r a r e, *reckon up, narrate* (only Od. and B 222), τί, ξ 197, τ 203 ; τί τινι, ε 5, λ 374 ; mid.; s i b i c o l l i g e r e, sibi e l i g e r e, s e a d n u- m e r a r e, *collect for one's self, select for one's self, add one's self to ;* n a r r a r e,

relute, N 292, γ 240 ; B 435, μηκέτι δὴ νῦν ταῦτα λεγώμεθα, let us now speak no longer of these things (but act); N 275, what need to relate these things? (See also ΛΕΧ.)

λειαίνω, fut. **λειανέω,** aor. 3 pl. λείηναν, part. ας, (λεῖος, l ē v i s), *smooth,* Δ 111 ; *level off,* θ 260.

λείβειν, ων, ipf. λεῖβε, ον, aor. λεῖ- ψαι, part. ψαντε, (l i b a r e), e f f u n d e- r e, *shed,* δάκρυα ; l i b a r e, *pour a liba- tion,* Ω 285 ; οἶνον, also with τινί, *per- form a drink-offering.* (See adjoining cut ; cf. also Nos. 24 and 102.)

λειμών, ῶνος, ι, α, ες, ας, (λείβω), *meadow,* ζ 292 ; λειμωνόθεν, *from the meadow,* Ω 451.

λεῖος, ψ, η, ην, α, (l ē v i s), *smooth, even, level ;* πετράων, ε 443, *free from* rocks ; λεῖα δ' ἐποίησεν, *made even.*

λείπω, prs. ipf. also λείπ(ε), fut. λείψω, aor. ἔλιπον, also λίπον, ες, ε, ἔτην, ομεν, λίπ' = ἔλιπ', and λιπέ, imp., pf. λέλοιπεν ; mid. prs., ipf. λείπετ(ο), aor. λιπόμην, r e l i c t u s s u m ; pass. pf. λέλειπται, inf. -εῖφθαι, part. -μμένος, ον, οι, plupf. λελείμμην, -ειπτο, 2 fut. λε- λείψεται, **aor. 3 pl. λίπεν,** l i n q u o, r e-

linqucre, *leave, forsake;*
ξ 213, me deficiunt, *are
wanting; fuil,* ἰοὶ ἄνακτα.—
Pass. and aor. mid., relin-
qui, remanere, *be left,
remain;* ὄπισθεν, vivum, M
14, *survive;* τινός, *to be left
behind one* (with acc. of distance? δουρὸς ἐρωήν); Π
507, postquam currus
orbati sunt domino-
rum, after the chariots *had
been forsaken* (λίπεν [v. l.
λίπον]) by their masters.

λειριόεντα, όεσσαν, (λεί-
ριον), *lily-white;* ὄπα, *tender, delicate,* Γ 152. (Il.)

Λειώδης, son of Oinops,
θυοσκόος of the suitors; he
shares their fate, φ 144, χ 310.

Λειώκριτος, (1) son of Arisbas,
slain by Aineias, P 344.—(2) son of
Euenor, suitor, β 242; slain by Telemachos, χ 294.

λείουσι, see λέων. λέκτο, see λέγω,
and ΛΕΧ.

Λεκτόν, promontory on the Trojan
coast, opposite Lesbos, Ξ 284.

λέκτρον, οιο, ῳ, οισι, (λέχω), lectus,
bed; freq. pl., παλαιοῦ θεσμόν, to the
site of the ancient bed; λέκτρονδε
(with δεῦρο, hither), *to bed!* θ 292.

λελαβέσθαι, -βῆσι, see λαμβάνω.
λελάθῃ, οντο, see λανθάνω.

λελακυῖα, see λάσκω. λελασμένος,
ον, see λανθάνω.

λελάχητε, ωσι, see λαγχάνω.

Λέλεγες, piratical tribe on south and
west coast of Asia Minor, Κ 429, Φ 86.

λεληκώς, *shrieking,* see λάσκω.

λελιημένος, οι, pf., (λίην, λῆν), rapidus, *hastily,* with ὄφρα, Δ 465, E 690.
(Il.)

λέλογχε, ασι, see λαγχάνω. λέξεο,
λίξο, see ΛΕΧ.

Λεοντεύς, son of Koronos, one of
the Lapithai, suitor of Helena, B 745,
Ψ 841.

λέπαδνα, τά, *breast collar,* strap
passing around the breast of the horses
and made fast to the yoke, E 730. (See
above cut. g; also cut No. 49, f.)

λεπταλέη (λεπτός), tenera, *delicate,*
Σ 571†.

λεπτῷ, όν, οἱ, ἡ, ῇ, ἁς, ά, (λέπω), sup.
-ότατος, η, *peeled, husked,* Υ 497; te-

nuis, tener; exiguus, *thin, fine,
delicate, narrow.*

λέπω, aor. ἔλεψεν; ἕ = φύλλα, *has
stripped off* from it the leaves, A 236†.

Λέσβος, island on the coast of Asia
Minor, opposite the gulf of Adramyt-
tium, γ 169, Ω 544. Λεσβόθεν, *from
L.,* I 664. Λεσβίδας γυναῖκας, 1 129,
271.

λέσχην, τήν, (λέγω, collect), *place
of meeting, country tavern,* σ 329†.

λευγαλέοιο, ῳ, οι, οισ(ι), η, ῃσι, (λοιγός, λυγρός, lugubris), miser, inho-
nestus, funestus, *wretched, shameful, ruinous,* πόλεμος, ἔπεα; I 119,
ruinous obstinacy; adv., λευγαλέως,
foede, *disgracefully,* N 723.

λεύκαινον, 3 pl. ipf., (λευκός), *made
white with foam,* μ 172†.

Λευκάς, άδος, Leukas, lit. "White-
rock" (cf. Ger. Weissenfels), at entrance of lower world, on border of
Okeanos, ω 11†.

λευκ-ασπίδα, acc., and -ασπις, *with
white shield, white-shielded,* X 294†.

Λευκοθέη = Ἰνώ, daughter of Kadmos ; saves Odysseus from drowning
by throwing him her veil, ε 334, 461.

λευκοῖο, ῷ, όν, οἱ, ούς, ἡ, ἡν, ἐν, ά,
comp. -ότερος. στέρην, (lux, λεύσσω,
γλαυκός), *bright, shining, gleaming,* lu-
cens, splendens, nitens; candi-
dus, *white,* K 437.

Λεῦκος, companion of Odysseus,
Δ 491†.

λευκ-ώλενος, ῳ, ον, οι, (ὠλένη), *with
white elbows, white armed,* epithet of

Hera, and of women in general, A 55, 572.

λευρῷ (λεῖος), p l a n ò, *level, η* 123†.

λεύσσω, prs., ipf., λεῦσσ(ε), (λευκύς), c e r n e r e, *see clearly; ἐπὶ τόσσον,* so far; *τινά,* c o n s p i c e r e, *behold,* Υ 346, θ 200.

λεχε-ποίην (λέχος, ποίη`), making his bed in the grass,* of river Ασōpos, Δ 383 ; of towns, *meadowy, grassy,* B 697.

λέχος, ει, ε(α), ἑων, ἑεσσ(ιν) ἐσσι, (λέχω), *bedstead,* ψ 189; *bed-clothing,* στορέσαι, *make the bed,* I 621, Ω 648, pl.; πυκινόν, *firmly built, η* 340, ψ 179; *the entire bed, including couch and bedding,* A 609, Γ 447 ; πορσύνειν, *prepare and share,* γ 403, Γ 411 ; τρητά, *smoothly polished* ; δινωτά, *smoothly turned* (posts and bars) ; pl., *the whole bed, composed of all its parts,* ε 1, δ 730, Ω 743; *bier, funeral couch,* ω 44, Ψ 165, Ω 720.

ΛΕΧ, (1) act.: aor. **ἔλεξα,** imp. λέξον, *put to rest,* Ω 635 ; fig., Ξ 252.—(2) mid.: fut. and 1 aor. and syncop. 2 aor. imp. λέξο, λέξεο, *lay one's self to rest,* θ 519, I 67, Ξ 350, δ 413, ρ 102 ; *lie at ease,* B 435.

λέων, οντος, etc., (exc. οιν), dat. pl. λείουσι (λέουσι, X 262), leo, *lion,* bold in the midst of pursuit, Γ 23 ; *attacks flocks or herds,* Ε 140; λέοντα γυναικξίν (instead of λέαιναν), *destruction to women, as goddess of sudden death.*

λήγεις, imp. λῆγ', inf. -έμεναι, ipf. ἔληγε, λῆγ(ε), fut. λήξω, ειν, aor. 3 pl. λῆξαν, opt. αιμι, ειεν, *leave off, cease,* τινός, Ζ 107 ; or with part., Φ 224 ; ἐν σοί (with thee), I 97 ; *abate,* μίνος, *martial fury;* χεῖρας φόνοιο, *stay my hands from slaughter,* χ 63.

Λήδη, wife of Tyndareos, mother of Kastor and Polydeukes, and of Klytaimnestra, λ 298, 300.

ληθάνει, ἐκ . . . πάντων, *does not allow me to think on* all, η 221†.

λήθη (λήθω), o b l i v i o, *forgetfulness,* B 33†.

Λῆθος, son of Teutamos, father of Hippothoos, B 843, P 288.

λήθω, see λανθάνω.

ληϊάδᾰς (ληΐς) γυναῖκας, c a p t i v a s f e m i n a s, *female captives,* Υ 193†.

ληϊ-βοτείρης (λήϊον, βόσκω) συός, *crop-destroying,* sow, σ 29†.

ληΐζομαι, fut. λη ΐσσομαι, aor. ληΐσ-σατο, *carry off as booty,* τινά, α 398, Σ 28 ; πολλά, ψ 357.

λήϊον, ίου, *crop* (uncut), s e g e t e s, B 147.

ληΐδος, τῆς, acc. ἴδα, (λάϜω), p r a e-d a, *prey, booty,* consisting of men, beasts, or treasure, Λ 677, κ 41. [ῑ]

ληϊστῆρες (ο 426, ληΐστορες), -ρσι, (ληΐζομαι), p r a e d a t o r e s, *pirates,* γ 73. (Od.)

ληϊστοί, ή, (ληΐζομαι), *may be plundered* (i. e. taken by plunder), I 406, 408.

ληϊτῐδι, τῇ, (ληΐς), *the dispenser of booty* (Athena), Κ 460†.

Λήϊτος, son of Alektryon, chief of the Boiotians, B 494, N 91, P 601, Z 35.

ληκύθῳ, τῇ, *oil-flask, oil-bottle,* ζ 79 and 215.

Λῆμνος, *Lemnos,* an island west of Troas, with (probably in the time of Homer) a city of the same name, Ξ 230, 281 ; ἠγαθέη, sacred to Hephaistos (also to the Kabeiroi), on account of its volcano, Moschylos ; now called Stalimene [(ἐ)ς τῆ(ν) Λήμνον].

λήσω, σομαι, see λανθάνω.

Λητώ, οῦς, οῖ, voc. οῖ, *Leto, Latona,* mother of Apollon and of Artemis by Zeus, λ 580, A 9, ἐρικυδέος, ἠΰκομος, καλλιπαρῄου.

λιαζόμενον, ipf. λιά έτο, aor. λιάσθης, η, εν, εἰς, e f f u g e r , *retire, withdraw* (from), κῦμα, ὕπα ὑα, τινός, or with prep.; *sink down,* Υ 418; προτὶ γαίῃ, πρηνής; *droop,* πτερά.

λιᾰρῷ, όν, t e p i d u s, *warm, lukewarm,* A 477 ; *sweet, gentle,* Ξ 164.

Λιβύη, *Libya,* west of Aigyptos, δ 85, ξ 295.

λῐγᾰ, adv., (λιγύς), *shrilly, piercingly,* θ 527, κ 254.

λιγαίνω, ipf. 3 pl. ἐλίγαινον, (λιγύς), *cry with loud voice,* Λ 685†.

λίγδην (λοκίς, l a c e r o), *scraping, grazing;* βάλλειν, χ 278†.

λιγέως, adv. from λιγύς.

λίγξε, aor., (λίγγω? λίζω), *twanged,* Δ 125†.

λῐγυ - πνείοντας (λιγύς), *whistling* (gusts), δ 567†.

λῐγὔρῇ, ήν, ῇσι, (λιγύς), *shrill-voiced,* Ξ 290 ; ἀοιδή, *loud-sounding, shrill* (the word orig. began with two consonants).

λιγύς, ύν, ύ, έων ; εῖα, εῖῃ, εῖαν, adv. λϊγέως (orig. beginning with two consonants), *penetrating, clear, piercing, shrill, whistling, loud*, φόρμιγγι, ἀγορητής.

λϊγυ-φθόγγοισιν (φθόγγος), *loud-, clear-voiced*, B 50, β 6.

λῐγῠ-φώνῳ (φωνή), *harsh-screaming*, T 350†.

λίζω, see λίγξε.

λίην, (λῆν, desire), *gladly, fully, exceedingly;* with negative, *very much, altogether;* καί λ., and *certainly,* and *by all means*, A 553. [ῑ, but ten times ῐ.]

λϊθᾰκι, dat. sing., (λίθος), *stony, hard*, ε 415†.

λϊθάδεσσι, ταῖς, (λίθος), *stone*, ξ 36. (Od.)

λιθέῳ, εοι, (λίθος), saxeus, *of stone*, ν 107.

λῐθος, οιο, ου, ῳ, ον, οι, οισ(ι), ους, masc. and fem. (twice), *rock*, γ 296 ; ν 156, *stone*, in field, or for building ; *stone seats*, θ 6; symbol of firmness and harshness; λίθον ἔθηκεν=ποίησε.

λικμώντων, gen. pl. of part., (λικμάω, λικμός), *winnow*, E 500†.

λικμητῆρος, τοῦ, (λικμάω), *winnower*, who threw the grain with winnowing shovel against the wind, thus separating it from the chaff, N 590†.

λικρῐφίς, adv., (λέχριος, obliquus), *sideways, to one side*, Ξ 463.

Ἀϊκύμνιος, brother of Alkmene, slain by Tlepolemos, B 663†.

Ἀϊλαια, town in Phokis, at the source of the Kephisos, B 523†.

λιλαίομαι, prs., ipf. λιλαίετο, (λιλάvjoμαι), cupere, gestire, desiderare, *desire*, with inf., or with gen. τινός, e. g. ὁδοῖο, ν 31; also of inanimate objects, missiles, χρόος ἆσαι, etc., φόωσδε (sc. ἐλθεῖν), λ 223.

λῐμήν, ένος, ένι, ένα, ες, έ(νεσ)σι, ας, (λίμνη), portus, *harbor*, pl. also in signif. of *inlets, bays*, Ψ 745, ν 96, δ 846.

λίμνη, ης, ῃ, ην, (λείβω), lacus, stagnum, palus, *lake, swamp, marsh*, Φ 317 ; γ 1, *sea*.

Λιμν-ώρεια, lit. "she who guards a harbor," a Nereid, Σ 41†.

λῑμός, ῳ̑, όν, fames, *hunger, famine*, T 166, ε 166.

Λίνδος, town in Rhodos, B 656†.

λῖνο-θώρηξ (λίνον), *wearing a linen cuirass*, B 529. (As represented in adjoining cut; cf. also No. 12.)

λῖνον, οιο, ου, ῳ, (λῖτα, linum), *flax, yarn, fishing-line, thread*, esp. the *thread of human destiny*, spun to each one at birth by Αἶσα and Κλῶθες, Υ 128, Ω 210, η 198 (see cut under ἠλακάτη) ; *fisher's net*, E 487 ; *linen cloth, linen*, fleecy (as bed covering), I 661.

λῖνον, *lay of Linos*, lament over the death of the youth Linos (perh. personification of spring), Σ 570†.

λῐπᾰ (ἀλείφω, liquor), old oblique case of a subst., or acc. ntr. of adj., as adv.=*shining with fat, unctuously*, γ 466.

λῐπᾰρο-κρήδεμνος (κρήδεμνον), *with shining head-band*, Σ 382†.

λῐπᾰρο-πλοκάμοιο (πλόκαμος), *with shining braids*, T 126†.

λῐπᾰρῳ̑, όν, οῖσι, ούς, ήν, άς, ά, (λίπα, Ger. kleben), nitens, nitidus, *anointed, shining* (beautiful, white); *wealthy, comfortable*, λ 136 ; so also adv. λιπαρῶς, δ 210.

λῐπόω (λῐπα), nitere, v. l., τ 72†.

I. λίς, ῑν, (λῖς, λέων), *lion*, Λ 239, 480.

II. λῖς, adj., (λισσός), πέτρη, *smooth rock*, μ 64, 79.

III. λίς, λῑτί, λῖτα, dat. acc., (λίνον), *linen;* cover of seat, κ 353 ; of chariot when not in use, Θ 441; of dead, Σ 352; of cinerary urn, Ψ 254.

λίσσομ(αι) from γλίτjομαι, pres.,

ipf. (ἐ)(λ)λίσσετο, etc., iter. λισσέσκετο, 1 aor. ἐλλισάμην, subj. λίσῃ, imp. λίσαι, 2 aor. ἐλιτόμην, opt. οἴμην, inf. λιτέσθαι, precari, *beseech, pray*, τινὰ εὐχῇσι εὐχωλῇσι λιτῇσί τε, Ζηνός, by Zeus, πρός, ὑπέρ τινος, for the sake of, by, γούνων (λαβών, ἁψάμενος), etc., β 68, Ι 451, κ 481; various constructions: with inf., with acc. and inf., with ὅπως, θάνατόν οἱ, sibi necem; ταῦτα ὑμέας, haec vos precor.

λισσή (λεῖος) πέτρη, lēve saxum, *smooth* rock, γ 293. (Od.)

λιστρεύοντα, part., *dig about*, ω 227†. (See follg.)

λίστροισι, dat. pl. ntr., *scraper* or *hoe* for cleaning the floor of large hall of house, χ 455†.

λῖτα, see III. λίς.

λῖτάνευε = ἐλλιτάνευε, ipf., fut. -εύσομεν, aor. ἐλλιτάνευσα, (λιταί), implorabat, *beseech; πολλά*, impense, earnestly, X 414; γούνων (ἁψάμενοι), by one's knees (grasping the knees), Ω 357.

λῖταί, ῇσι, (λίσσομαι), preces, *prayers*, with ἐλλισάμην, λ 34; personified, Ι 502–4, daughters of Zeus, *penitential prayers* following after their sister ἄτη (the blindness, the delusion which has caused the fault), moving limpingly and with eyes fixed on the ground.

λιτί, see III. λίς.

λό' = λόε, see λούω.

λοβοῖσιν, masc., auriculis, *lobes of the ears*, Ξ 182†.

λόγος, οισ(ιν), (λέγω), *story, tale; words, talk, language*, Ο 393.

λόε, εσσαι, etc., see λούω.

λοετρά, ῶν, τά, (λούω), lavacrum, *baths*, Ὠκεανοῖο, in Oceano, ε 275.

λοετρο-χόῳ, ον, (χέω), adj., *pouring or containing water for the bath*; τρίποδα, tripod with the water-kettle, Σ 346, θ 435; but υ 297, subst. *bath-maid*.

λοέω, see λούω.

λοιβῆς, ῇ, ήν, (λείβω), *libation*, Δ 49, Ω 70.

λοίγι(α) (λοιγός), perniciosa, *pestilent, deadly*, φ 533; *ending fatally* (ἔργα), A 518.

λοιγός, όν, masc., (lugēre), pernicies, interitus, *death, ruin*, by sickness or war; νεῶν, iacturam, *destruction*, Π 80.

λοιμός, οἶο, (λείβω?), lues, *pestilence*, A 61 and 97.

λοῖσθος (λοιπός), postremus, *last*, Ψ 536†. Hence λοισθήϊον, ultimum praemium, prize *for the hindmost*, Ψ 785 = λοισθήϊ(α), Ψ 751.

Λοκροί, *Lokroi*, a tribe occupying one of the divisions of Hellas, and dwelling on the Euripos, on both sides of Mount Knemis, B 527, 535, N 686.

λοπόν, τόν, (λέπω), τ 233†, *peel* (tunica), of an onion.

λούω, the forms may be classed under two stems, λοϜ- and λοε.—I. λοϜω (lavo), ipf. λό-(ϝ)ε, λοῦον, aor. λοῦσ(εν), αν, subj. λούσῃ, inf. λοῦσαι (λοῦσαι), imp. λόεσον, λούσατε, part. λοέσσασα, mid. prs. λούεσθαι λοῦσθαι, aor. λούσαντο, σαιτο, ασθε, ασθαι, pass. pf. λελουμένος.—II. ipf. λόεον, aor. λοέεσσαι, σσας, mid. fut. λοέσσομαι, aor. λοέσσατο, σσάμενος, η, (parallel form λοϜέσω), lavare, *bathe, wash*, mid., *have one's self washed*, in waters of river, Z 508; Ὠκεανοῖο, washed by Okeanos.

λοφίην, τήν, (λόφος), *comb*, or *bristly ridge* of boar's back, τ 446†.

λόφος, ον, ων, masc., (globus), (1) *crest* or *plume of helmet*, usually of horse-hair, E 743. (See adjoining cuts, and Nos. 3, 11, 12, 17, 18, 20, 36, 79, 122, 128.)—(2) cervices, *back of neck* of animals, Ψ 508; and of men, K 573. —(3) collis, *hill, ridge*, λ 596.

λοχάω, prs. λοχόωσι, ῶσι, όωντες, aor. λοχῆσαι, ήσας, mid. fut. -ήσομαι, aor. ησάμενος, (λόχος), insidiari, *lie in wait*, ν 268, χ 53; τινά, *waylay*, ν 425; so also mid., δ 670.

λόχμη, τῇ, (λόχος), *thicket, lair of wild beast*, τ 439†.

λόχος, ον, ῳ, ον, οι, (λέχω), *place for lying in wait*, (1) *the lying in wait, ambush*, Λ 379; λ 525, πυκινόν, crowded and κοῖλος, hollow, of wooden horse before Troy.—(2) *the men who lie in* wait, Θ 522; πυκινόν, numerous; εἶσε, Z 189, laid an ambush. λοχόνδε, into the ambush, A 227; λόχῳ, for the ambush, Σ 513.—(3) δ 395, way to capture. —(4) band, troop, υ 49.

λύγοισι, ους, fem., (properly vitex agnus castus), Abraham's balm, willow twig, osier, ι 427; μόσχοισι, Λ 105, with tender willows.

λυγρός, ῷ, όν, ῶν, οἷς; ἧς, ῇ, ἥν; ά, (lugeo, λευγαλέος), miserabilis, miserandus, funestus, wretched, pitiable, ruinous, Ω 531, P 642, σ 134; perniciosus, δ 230, λ 432; ignavus, worthless, N 119, 237, σ 107; vilis, contemptible, π 457; adv. λυγρῶς, foede, E 763.

λύθεν = ἐλύθησαν, from λύω.

λύθρῳ, τῷ, (lues), cruore, gore, with and without αἵματι; πεπαλαγμένος, defiled, Z 268, cf. Λ 169, χ 402.

λῠκᾰ-βαντος, τοῦ, (lux, βαίνω), year, ξ 161 and τ 306.

Λύκαστος, ή, a town in southern part of Kreta, B 647†.

Λυκάων, (1) father of Pandaros, E 197, 95.—(2) son of Priamos and of Laothoe, Γ 333; slain by Achilleus, Φ 114 sqq.

λυκέην, τήν, (λύκος), wo'f-skin, K 459†.

λῠκη-γενεῖ (lux), light-born, epithet of Apollo as sun-god, Δ 101, 119.

Λῠκίη, (1) division of Asia Minor, B 877; Λυκίηνδε, to Lykia, Z 168; Λυκίηθεν, from Lykia, E 105; the inhabitants, Λύκιοι, led by Glaukos, H 13, and by Sarpedon, E 647, Ξ 426, Π 490.—(2) district on river Aisēpos; its chief town Ζέλεια, B 824, E 173.

Λῠκο-μήδης, son of Kreon in Boiotia, P 346, T 240.

Λῠκό-οργος, (1) son of Dryas, banishes from his land the worship of Dionȳsos (Bacchus), Z 134.—(2) an Arkadian, slays Areithoos, H 142–148.

λύκοιο, οι, ων, ους, (Γλύκος), lupus, wolf, K 334; symbol of blood-thirstiness, Δ 471, Λ 72.

Λῠκο-φόντης, a Trojan, slain by Teukros, Θ 275.

Λῠκό-φρων, son of Mastor, from Kythera, companion of Aias, O 430.

Λύκτος, city in Kreta, east of Knosos, B 647, P 611.

Λύκων, a Trojan, slain by Peneleos, Π 335, 337.

λύμᾱτ(α), τά, (lues, lu-strum), filth, dirt, A 314, Ξ 171.

λυπρή (λύπη), tristis, poor, ν 243†.

Λυρνησ(σ)ός, town in Mysia, under sway of Thebe ὑποπλακίη, B 690, T 60, Υ 92, 191.

Λῠσ-ανδρος, a Trojan, slain by Aias, Λ 491†.

λῡσι-μελής (μέλος, member; false derivation, υ 56 sq.), relaxing the limbs, ψ 343.

λύσιος, ιν, (λύω), ransoming, Ω 655; θανάτου, rescue from death, ι 421.

λύσσα, αν, fem., (λύκος), rabies, martial rage, I 239, Φ 542.

λυσσητῆρα, τόν, (λύσσα), one who rages, with κύνα of Hektor, Θ 299†.

λυσσώδης (λύσσα), raging, of Hektor, N 53†.

λύχνον, τόν, (λευκός, lux), light, lamp, τ 34†.

λύω, prs., ipf. (also λύε, ομεν, ον), fut., aor. [also λῦσεν, σαν, σασ(α)], pass. pf. λέλυται, υνται, opt. ῦτο, plupf. υντο; aor. λύθη, 3 pl. λύθεν, also aor. mid. λύτο, λύντο, solvere, (1) loose, open, release, let go; τινά τινι, set free (ἀποίνων, for ransom).—(2) dismiss, assemblies; componere lites, adjust disagreements.—(3) τινός or τινί γυῖα, μένος, ψυχήν, interimere, kill; also of animals, with the weapon as subject, e. g. πέλεκυς, γ 450.—(4) unnerve, weaken, γυῖα, γούνατα (also as effect of amazement, σ 212), βίην; of sleep, λύθεν δέ οἱ ἅψεα πάντα, all her limbs lost their strength.—(5) delere, break down, destroy, κάρηνα, κρήδεμνα, towers, battlements; μελεδήματα θυμοῦ, dissipate cares, anxiety. — Mid. prs. λυώμεθα ἵππους, let us put out our horses; ipf. λυόμην, οντο, fut. λύσομαι, μενος, aor. ἐλύσαο, ατο, σασθ(αι), 2 aor. λύμην, λύτο, λύντο, se, sibi, or sua solvere, release, set free (for one's self or one's own), freq., redimere, ransom, A 13. [ῠ before σ, elsewh. in arsi; except thrice ŭ.]

λωβάομαι, aor. λωβήσασθε, opt. λωβήσαιο, maltreat; τινά λώβην, ignominia afficere, do despite, N 623.

λωβεύω, εις, (λώβη), mock, ψ 15 and 26.

λώβη, ης, ην, (labes), ignominia, outrage, insult; τῖσαι, ἀποδοῦναι, pay, atone for; τίσασθαι, exact retribution for; Σ 180, shame upon thee, if—; Γ 42, ignominiosus, cowardly wretch.

λωβητῆρα (λώβη) ἐπεσβόλον, foul slanderer, B 275; λωβητῆρες ἐλεγχέες, vile scoundrels.

λωβητόν (λωβάομαι) τιθέναι τινά, make contemptible, Ω 531†.

λώϊον=λώϊτερον, melius, satius, better, preferable; ρ 417, largius, more freely.

λώπην (λέπω), mantle, ν 224†.

λωτοῦντα, part. from λωτόω, Lotos-producing, clovery fields, M 283†.

λωτός, οῖο, όν, masc., (1) Lotos, a kind of clover, food of horses (trifolium melilotus or lotus corniculatus, Linn.), δ 603, Ξ 348. — (2) Lotus—tree and fruit; the latter of the size of olives, and in taste resembling dates, still prized in Tunis and Tripoli, under the name of Jujube, ι 91 sqq.

Λωτο-φάγοι (see λωτός 2), Lotos-eaters on coast of Libya, ι 84 sqq.

λωφάω, fut. λωφήσει, will retire, Φ 292†.

M.

μ' usually = με; less often = μοι, Z 165, κ 19.

μά, from μάν, in oath; vero, with acc. of the divinity, or of the witness invoked (sc. ὄμνυμι): preceded by ναί =nae, it has an affirmative; by οὐ, a negative force.

Μάγνητες, a Thessalian tribe, sprung from Aiolos, B 756.

μαζοῖο, ῷ, όν, masc., papilla, nipple, teat, then mamilla, mamma, esp. the mother's breast; λαθικηδέα, banishing cares; ἐπέχειν, offer; ἀνέσχεν, obsecrandi causa.

μαῖα, voc., good mother, φίλη, used esp. in addressing the nurse, υ 129, ψ 11.

Μαιάδος υἱός, Hermes; Maia is the daughter of Atlas, ξ 435†.

Μαίανδρος, the river with many windings which flows into the sea at Miletos, B 869†.

Μαιμαλίδης, son of Maimalos, Peisandros, Π 194†.

μαιμάω, only pres. μαιμώωσι, ῶσι, ώων, ώωσα, etc., aor. μαίμησε, eagerly desire, N 75, 78, itch or quiver with desire.

μαινάδι, τῇ, (μαίνομαι), mad woman, X 460†.

μαίνεαι, etc., prs. and ipf. 3 sing. μαίνετο, (μαν, mens), furere, rage, be furious, of combatants, also of hand

and weapons; with anger, of Polyphemos, ι 350; of fire on mountains; madly raving (under Bacchic frenzy), Z 132; of madness from wine, σ 406.

μαίεσθαι, fut. μάσσεται, (μα-, μίμαα), seek, ξ 356; perscrutari, explore, ν 367; find a wife for any one, I 394, [μάσσεται, v. l. γαμέσσεται].

Μαῖρα (μαρμαίρω), lit. "shining" or "sparkling," (1) a Nereid, Σ 48†.—(2) attendant of Artemis, mother of Lokros, λ 326†.

Μαίων, son of Haimon in Thebai, Δ 394, 398.

μάκαρ, αρος, αρες, άρων, άρεσσι, sup. μακάρτατος, (macte), beatus, (1) blessed, of gods, opp. δειλοὶ ὀιζυροὶ βροτοί.—(2) of men, happy, fortunate, λ 483.—(3) wealthy, α 217.

Μάκαρ, ος, son of Aiolos, ruling in Lesbos, Ω 544†.

μάκαρίζοι, opt. prs., (μάκαρ), pronounce happy, τινά, ο 538. (Od.)

μικεδνής, gen. fem., (μακρός), tall, η 106†.

μάκελλαν, τήν, broad, heavy hoe, mattock, Φ 259†.

μακρός, ῷ, όν, οἱ, οἶσι; ἡ, ήν, αἱ, ᾶσ(ι), άς; όν, ά, comp. μακρότερον, ην, also μάσσον, sup. μακρότατ(α), τη, cf. μήκιστον, long, (1) of space, κύματα; high and deep, esp. μακρόν, ά; as adv., far, -ον ἀύσας, always at close

of verse (exc. Γ 81); αὐτιῖν, Θ 160, ζ
117; βιβάς.—(2) of time, diutinus,
long.

μᾱκών, see μηκάομαι.

μάλᾰ, adv., (μαλερός ?), sup. μάλιστα, (before or after the modified word),
eagerly, ἐσθίειν; gladly, ἔκλυον; with
adjs., very, quite; πάντες, quite all, all
together; with demonstratives, fully,
utterly, τοῖον; μάλα κνέφας, utter darkness; with advs., e. g. εὖ, πάγχυ,
strengthens their meaning, quite, utterly, ρ 217; αὐτίκα, on the very moment; with verbs = valde; καί (or
οὐδ') εἰ μάλα, quantumvis; μάλα
περ with part.=quamvis; also with
καί περ, A 217.—(2) strengthening an
assertion: certainly, verily, Γ 204; no
doubt, ι 135; comp. μᾶλλον, only the
more, so much the more, with κηρόθι, at
heart, ε 284; with πολύ, ἔτι, καί, η 213;
sup. μάλιστα, maxime, with gen.
part., with ἐκ; far, by far, with other
superlatives, B 57, Ω 334. [μᾱλᾰ, by
arsis often ‿ ‑.]

μᾰλᾰκός, οῦ, ῷ, όν, οἱ, οἷσι; ἧς, ῇ,
ήν, comp. -ώτερος (Ger. schmalz?
mollis), soft, mild, gentle, tender, B 42,
γ 38; spongy meadow, Σ 541; mitis,
dulcis, K 2, σ 201, Z 337; X 373,
easier to handle; adv. -ῶς, placide,
softly, γ 350.

Μάλεια, αν, ῶν, άων, southern
promontory of the Peloponnesos, ι 80,
τ 187, γ 287.

μᾰλεροῦ, ῷ, devouring; of fire, I 242.
(Il.)

μαλθᾰκός (mollis), effeminate, cowardly, P 588†.

μάλιστα, μᾶλλον, see μάλα.

μάν (=μήν), profecto, verily, truly,
in sooth, Θ 373, Π 14; come! E 765;
ἦ, B 370; δή, P 538; οὐ, Δ 512; αὖτε,
by no means in his turn, N 414; μή,
Θ 512; θην, but yet by no means, ε
211, v. l. μέν. [—]

μανθάνω, aor. μάθον, ἔμμαθες, εν,
novi, know, ἔμμεναι ἐσθλός, Z 444.

μαντεύομαι, prs., ipf. μαντεύετο, fut.
μαντεύσομαι, (μάντις), vaticinor, divine, prophesy, τινί τι, κακά, ἀτρεκέως, ρ
154.

μαντήϊα, τά, (μαντεύομαι), vaticinia, predictions, oracles, μ 272†.

Μαντῑνέη, a city in Arkadia, B
607†.

Μάντιος, son of Melampus, brother
of Antiphates, father of Polypheides
and of Kleitos, o 242, 249.

μάντις, ιος, (μάντηος in arsi, κ 493),
ι, ιν, ιες, (μαίνομαι), prophet, seer, ex-
pounder of omens, which were drawn
from flight of birds, from dreams, and
from sacrifices, e. g. Teiresias, Kalchas,
Melampus, Theoklymenos, Ω 221, A
62.

μαντοσύνη, ην, ας, (μάντις), gift of
divination, A 72; vaticinia.

μάομαι, see μαίομαι.

Μᾰρᾰθών (μάραθον, "fennel"), village in Attika, η 80†.

ἐμᾰραίνετο, ipf., aor. ἐμαράνθη, sensim extinguebatur, died gradually
away, Ψ 228. (Il.)

μαργαίνειν (μάργος), furere, rage;
madly attack, ἐπὶ θεοῖσιν, E 882†.

μάργε, voc., and ῃ, ην, vesanus,
furious, madman! σ 2. (Od.)

Μᾰρις, son of Amisodaros, slain by
Thrasymedes, Π 319.

μαρμαίροντες, ας, α, (μαῖρα), sparkling, coruscantes, of weapons, eyes;
of Trojans, χαλκῷ, resplendent with armor, N 801.

μαρμᾰρέην (μαῖρα), flashing, sparkling, of shield, shield-rim, sea, P 594.

μαρμάρῳ, ον, adj. and subst., [sc.
πέτρος or πέτρη], (μαῖρα), stone of
crystalline structure, which sparkles
in the light, block of stone, M 380, ι
499.

μαρμᾰρυγάς, τάς, (μαρμαρύσσω),
ποδῶν, quick twinkling of dancers' feet,
Θ 265†.

μάρνᾰται, prs., (opt. -οίμεθα), ipf.
(ἐ)μάρναο, ατο, άμεθα, elsewh. unaugmented, aor. ἐμαρνάσθην, pugnare,
fight, (ἐπί) τινί, against some one, ἔγχει;
περὶ ἔριδος, out of rivalry; as boxer,
σ 31; with words, wrangle, A 257.

Μάρπησσα, daughter of Euenos,
wife of Idas, who recovered her after
she had been carried off by Apollo,
mother of Kleopatra, I 557 sqq.

μάρπτω, subj. μάρπτῃσι, ipf. ἔμαρ-
πτε, μάρπτε, fut. μάρψει, aor. subj. μάρψῃ, inf. -αι, part. -ψας, comprehendo,
seize, κ 116; ἀγκάς, complecti, embrace; consequi, overtake, X 201;
attingere, touch, Ξ 228; Θ 405, in-
flixerit, inflict upon; ὕπνος, oppres-
sit, lay hold of, υ 56.

μαρτῠρίησι, ταῖς, (μάρτυρος), testimonio, on testimony of, λ 325†.

μάρτῠρος, οι, testis, witness, π 423, Α 338.

Μάρων, son of Euanthes, priest of Apollo in Ismaros, ι 197†.

Μάσης, ητος, town in Argolis, near Hermione, Β 562†.

μάσσεται, fut. from μαίομαι, quaeret, seek.

μᾶσσον, see μακρός.

μάσταξ, μάστᾰκ(α), τήν, (μαστάζω, mandere), mouth, δ 287, ψ 76; mouthful, food, Ι 324.

μαστίζω, aor. μάστιξεν, (μάστιξ), was lashing, ἵππους; ἐλάαν.

μάστιξ, μάστῑγι, α, ας, fem., flagellum, whip, scourge, ζ 316; Διός, Μ 37; Ν 812, chastisement.

μάστις, μάστῑ, ιν, fem., flagellum, whip, Ψ 500, ο 182.

μάστῑε, imp., whip, Ρ 622; mid. prs. μαστίεται πλευράς, lashes his sides, Υ 171.

Μαστορίδης, son of Mastor, (1) Halitherses in Ithaka, β 158, ω 452. —(2) Lykophron, Ο 438, 430.

ματάω, οὐκ ἐμάτησεν, (μάτην), be idle, delay, linger, Π 474; nec cessavit, Ψ 510; μὴ ματήσετον, ne cessaveritis.

μᾰτεύσομεν, fut. quaeremus, seek, Ξ 110†.

μᾰτίη, τῇ, (μάτην), irrito labore, useless labor, κ 79†.

μαχαίρη, αν, ας, fem., broad, short sacrificial knife, Γ 271, Λ 844. (See following cut, and No. 115.)

Μαχάων, voc. ᾶον, son of Asklepios, ruler in Trikka and Ithome in

Thessaly, excelling in art of healing, Λ 512, 613, Δ 200, Β 732; wounded by Hektor, Λ 506, 598, 651.

μαχειόμενος, εούμενον, see μάχομαι.

μάχη, η, ῃ, ην, αι, ας, pugna, battle, combat, fight; μάχῃ (ἐνὶ), in pugna, δ 497; στήσασθαι, set the battle in array, form one's line for battle, a ciem instruere, ι 54; committere, join battle, fight a battle, μάχεσθαι, τίθεσθαι; ἐγείρειν, excitare, rouse the fight, Ν 778 = ὀρνύμεν ὀτρύνειν; also used of single combat, Η 263 and Λ 255; field of battle, Ε 355.

μᾰχήμων (μάχη), warlike, Μ 247†.

μᾰχητής, ῆν, αἱ, άς, (μάχομαι), pugnator, warrior, Ε 801.

μᾰχητόν (μάχομαι), that may be vanquished, μ 119†.

μαχλοσύνην (μάχλος), lust, Ω 30†.

μάχομαι, μάχονται, ὁμεσθ(α), etc., ipf. ἐμάχοντο, μαχόμην, οντο, etc., parallel forms μαχέομαι, prs., opt. μαχίοιτο, εοίατο, Α 344; μαχειόμενος, ρ 471; εούμενον, οι, ipf. iter. μαχέσκετο, Η 140; fut. alternates between μαχήσομαι and μαχέσσομαι, etc., μαχεῖται, έονται; also aor. μαχήσασθαι and ἐσασθαι, ἐσσάμεθ(α), αἱμην, άμενον, pugnare, fight, of armies and of single persons, ἀντία, ἐναντίον τινός, (ἐν)αντίβιον, or (ἐπί) τινί; μάχην, Σ 533; for any thing, περί τινος (τινί, ἀμφί τινι), εἵνεκα; also of combat between beasts, and in general signif. e. g. of single combat and of quarrel with words, Α 8, Β 377; contradicere, Ι 32.

μάψ (ἐμμαπέως), raptim, temere, hastily, rashly, ὁμόσαι, ἀτὰρ οὐ κατὰ κόσμον; recklessly, wantonly, Ε 759, γ 138; cf. Β 120, Ν 627, Β 214; incassum, in vain, Β 120; likewise μαψιδίως, Ε 374, β 58.

Μεγάδης, son of Megas, Perimos, Π 695†.

μεγᾰ-θῡμος, ου, ον, ε, οι, ων, (θυμός), high-hearted, animosus, Β 53; usually of nations; of a bull, Π 488.

μεγαίρω, aor. μέγηρε, subj. μεγήρῃς, part. -ας, (μέγας), invidēre, grudge, τινί τι, Ψ 865; βιότοιο, grudging him the life of his enemy, Ν 563; object, with inf.; οὔτι μεγ., nihil moror.

μεγᾰ-κήτεος, εῖ, εα, (κῆτος), with great hollows; νηῦς, wide-bellied; πόντος, wide-yawning, γ 158.

μεγαλ-ήτορος, ι, α, ες, ας, (ἦτορ), ferox, *great-hearted, haughty*, N 302, τ 176.

μεγαλίζομαι, imp. εο, (μέγας), superbio, *exalt one's self*, θυμῷ, K 69.

μεγάλως, adv. from μέγας.

μεγαλωστί, from μεγάλως, μέγας μ., *stretched over a vast space*, Σ 26, ω 40.

Μεγα-πένθης, son of Menelaos by a slave, ο 100, 103, δ 11.

Μεγάρη, daughter of Kreon in Thebai, wife of Herakles, λ 269†.

μέγαρον, οιο, ον, etc., *hall, large room*; μεγαρόνδε, *to the hall, into the hall.*— (1) *men's dining-hall, chief room of house*, the roof supported by columns, the light entering through the doors, the opening for the smoke overhead, and the loop-holes (ὀπαῖα) just under the roof. The cut, combined from different ancient representations, is de-

μέγας, αν, α (μέγ'), μεγάλου, ψ, ω, οι, ων, οισι, ους; η, ης, ῃ, ην, ῃσι, ας; α; comp. μείζων, ονι, ονα, ονες; ον; sup. μέγιστος, ον, ε, ους, αι, ον, α, magnus, *great*, in various senses, e. g. also altus, longus, latus, amplus; ἔργον, facinus, *monstrous* deed; nimius, εἰπεῖν, *speak too big, too boldly*, provoking divine wrath; so also ntr. μέγα, with comp., multo, B 239; with super., longe, B 82; with positive, valde, B 480, Π 46; with verbs of mental condition or action, A 517, 256, B 27, Π 822, I 537, Π 237; also μεγάλ(α), *mightily, strongly, aloud*, A 450; with advs., valde; adv. μεγάλως, valde, *exceedingly*, π 432.

μέγεθος, τό, (μέγας), magnitudo (corporis), *bodily size*, B 58, ε 217.

Μέγης, ητος, acc. ην, son of Phyleus, Odysseus's sister's son, chief of the inhabitants of Dulichion and of

signed to show the back part of the μέγαρον in the house of Odysseus, cf. plate III. for ground-plan.—(2) *women's apartment*, behind the one just described, see plate III. G, also in pl., τ 16. — (3) *housekeeper's apartment in upper story* (ὑπερῷον), β 94.—(4) *sleeping-apartment*, λ 374. — (5) in wider signif. cf. aedes, in pl., *house*, A 396.

the Echinades, E 69, N 692, O 520, 535, B 627, T 239.

μέγιστος, superl. from μέγας.

μεδέων, part., *bearing sway*; Ἰδηθεν, from Ida (as his seat), of Zeus, Γ 276.

Μεδεών, ῶνος, town in Boiotia, B 501†.

μέδομαι, μέδεσθαι, prs., ipf., fut. μεδήσομαι, (μεδέων), *be mindful of, pro-*

vide for, τινός, E 718, γ 334; κακά
τινι, mala moliri, devise mischief.

μέδων, οντες, (μέδομαι), lord, ἁλός, α
72; pl., counselors, B 79.

Μέδων, οντος, (1) son of Oileus,
step-brother of Aias, from Phylake,
chief of warriors from Methone in
Phthia, N 693, 695 sq., B 727; slain
by Aineias, O 332.—(2) a Lykian, P
216.—(3) herald in Ithaka, δ 677, ρ
172, χ 357, 361, ω 439.

μεθ-αιρέω, only aor. iter. μεθέλεσκε,
reached after and caught, excipiebat,
θ 376†.

μεθ-άλλομαι, aor. part. μετάλμενος,
springing upon, after, E 336, Ψ 345. (Il.)

μεθείω, subj. aor. from μεθ-ίημι.

μεθ-έλεσκε, aor. iter. from μεθ-αιρέω.

μεθέμεν, aor. inf. from μεθίημι.

μεθ-έπεις, ipf. μέθεπε, aor. part.
μιτασπών, (ἕπω), persequi, petere,
follow after, follow closely, τινά, τί;
pervenire, arrive; ἵππους Τυδείδην,
turned the steeds after Tydeides; mid.
aor. μετασπόμενος, consecutus; ipf.
μετά-είπετο, subsequebatur, Σ 234.

μεθ-ήμενος, part., (ἥμαι), μνηστῆρσι,
sitting among the suitors, α 118†.

μεθ-ημοσύνῃ, ῃσι, (μεθήμων), negli-
gentia, remissness, N 108 and 121.

μεθ-ήμων, ονα, (ἵημι), negligens,
careless, remiss, B 241, ζ 25.

μεθ-ίημι, (εις, ίει, δ 372, prs. and ipf.
(others write ίης, ίῃ, and pres. ιείς, ιεί),
prs. inf. ιέμεν(αι), subj. μεθιῇσι (sometimes written ίῃσι), ipf. 3 pl. μεθίεν,
fut. μεθήσω, etc., inf. ησέμεν(αι), aor.
μεθέηκα, ε(ν), and μεθῆκεν, subj. μεθείω,
ῃῃ (or είῃ, distinguish from opt. είῃ, ε
471), inf. έμεν, (ἵημι) (1) properly,
send after, ίόν; immittere, τὶ ἐς πο-
ταμόν.—(2) dimittere, let go, τινά,
also ῥῖγός με; give up, χόλον τινά,
about any one, τινί, as a favor to some
one, A 283; also νίκην, concedere,
give up to, surrender; τοῦτον ἐρύσαι,
hunc trahendum.—(3) with part.
cease, Ω 48; τινός, χόλοιο Τηλεμάχῳ,
desist from, cease from anger at wish
of Telemachos; neglect, σεῖο τειρομέ-
νοιο, te saucium.—(4) cessare, re-
lax, also with inf., N 234.

μεθ-ίστημι, fut. μεταστήσω, substi-
tute, i. e. exchange, ἃ 612; mid. ipf. μεθ-
ίστατο ἑτάροισι, retired among his com-
rades, E 514.

μεθ-ομίλεον, ipf., (ὁμιλέω), τοῖσιη
had dealings with them, A 269†.

μεθ-ορμηθείς, aor. part., (ὁρμάομαι),
persecutus, make a dash after, Υ 192,
ε 325.

μέθυ, τό, (Eng. mead), wine, ι 9, η 179.

μεθύοντι, ύουσαν, (μέθυ), drunken,
σ 240; ἀλοιφῇ, soaked with fat.

μειδάω, aor. μείδησεν, ἦσαι, ήσας,
ασα, A 596, and μειδιάω, part. μειδιόων,
όωσα, (σμιδ-, mirus, smile), subri-
dere, smile, Ψ 786.

μείζων, ον, see μέγας.

μείλανι=μέλανι, nigro, Ω 79†.

μείλια, τά, (μέλι), soothing gifts, gifts
as means of reconciliation, I 147 and 289.

μειλίγματα, τά, μειλίσσω, that which
appeases hunger, sedamina appetitus, i. e. dainty bits, κ 217†.

μείλινον, see μέλινος.

μειλισσέμεν, prs. inf.; mid. prs. imp.
-ίσσεο, (μείλιχος), placare (mor-
tuos); πυρός, cf. construction with
λαγχάνειν, appease the dead with fire,
i. e. with funeral rites, H 410; mid.,
extenuate, γ 96.

μειλίχιον, ίοισ(ιν), ίῃ, and ‾μείλιχος,
(μείλια), placidus, comis, mitis,
gentle, mild; μῦθος, μειλιχίοις, sc. ἔπεσι;
θ 172, gentle, winning modesty.

μείρεο, see μείρω.

μείς, ὁ, Τ 117; also μηνός, ί, μῆνα,
ες, ας, ῶν, (metior) mensis, month,
φθίνοντος, the waning month, i. e. as
this month draws to a close, ξ 162.

μείων, see μικρός.

μελαγ-χροιής (χροιά, χρώς), bronzed,
swarthy, π 175†.

μέλαθρον, ου, ῳ, ὄφιν, τό, (κμέλα-
θρον, camera), vaulting of roof, rafters,
roof; τ 544, on the ridge-pole aloft
(near the smoke-hole); χ 239, she,
flying up to the roof of the sooty hall,
sat there just like a swallow to look
upon (i. e. on one of the cross-beams
under the rafters; see cut under μέγαρον).

μελαίνετ(ο), ipf., (μέλας), she colored
herself dark on her fair skin, her fair
skin was stained by the dark blood;
also of fresh upturned earth, E 354
and Σ 548.

Μελάμ-πους, ποδος, son of Amy-
thaon, famous seer in Pylos. Wishing

to fetch from Phylake in Thessaly the famous cattle of Iphiklos, and thus gain the beautiful Pero for his brother Bias, he was taken captive by herdsmen of Iphiklos, as he had predicted, and held prisoner for one year, when, in consequence of good counsel given by him, he was set free by Iphiklos, gained what he sought, and settled in Argos, λ 287 sqq., ο 225 sqq.

μελάν-δετα (δέω), mounted in black, i. e. with dark hilt or scabbard, Ο 713†.

Μελᾰνεύς, father of Amphimedon in Ithaka, ω 103.

Μελανθεύς = Μελάνθιος, son of Dolios, insolent goat-herd on estate of Odysseus, ρ 212, υ 173, φ 181, χ 135 sqq., 182 ; brother of the shameless maid-servant Μελανθώ, σ 321, τ 65.

Μελάνθιος, a Trojan, slain by Eurypylos, Ζ 36.

Μελάνιππος, (1) an Achaian chief, Τ 240.—(2) a Trojan, son of Hiketaon, slain by Antiochos, Ο 547–582.—(3) a Trojan, slain by Teukros, Θ 276.—(4) a Trojan, slain by Patroklos, Π 695.

μελᾰνό-χροος, 2 declension, τ 246, pl. -χροες, 3 declension, (χρώς), black, Ν 589.

μελάν-ῠδρος (ὕδωρ), with dark water, Ι 14, υ 158, only at close of verse.

μελάνει, prs., darkens, (μέλας), spoken of the water of the sea, under its white surface-foam (v. l. μελανεῖ), Η 64†.

μέλας, αινα, αν, etc., pl. μέλανες, αιναι, ανα, dat. sing. μείλανι, Ω 79 ; dat. pl. masc. and ntr. wanting; comp. μελάντερον, dark, in different degrees up to black (opp. λευκός) ; of sea in commotion, when surface is ruffled by ripples, so that it does not reflect light, but appears dark, δ 359 ; dark (painted) ships, θ 34 ; land, spring (on account of depth) ; pitch-dark, Δ 277 ; μέλαν, as ntr. subst. the dark, i. e. bark of oak, δρυός. Metaph. dark, gloomy, of death, etc., θανάτου νέφος, κήρ, ὀδύναι.

Μέλας, son of Portheus, Ξ 117†.

μελδόμενος, part., (σμίλδω, Eng. melt), filled with melting fat, liquefaciens, Φ 363†.

Μελέ-αγρος, (ᾧ μέλει ἄγρα), son of Oineus and Althaia, husband of Kleo-

patra, slayer of Kalydonian boar. A quarrel arose between the Kuretes, of Pleuron, and the Aitolians, for the head and skin of the boar ; the Aitolians had the upper hand until Meleager, on account of the curses of his mother, withdrew from the struggle; but he was afterward induced by his wife to enter the conflict again, and he drove the Kuretes vanquished into Akarnania, Ι 543 sqq., Β 642.

μελεδήματα, τά, (μέλω), care, anxiety, θυμοῦ, of the soul ; πατρός, anxiety for his father kept him awake, ο 8.

μελεδών (μέλω), μελεδῶνες ὀξεῖαι, sharp cares, τ 517†.

μέλει, see μέλω.

μελεϊστί, adv., (μέλος), limb from limb, Ω 409, ι 291, σ 339.

μέλεος, η, ον, irritus; Ψ 795, unrewarded ; ntr., in cassum, in vain.

μέλι, τος, τι, τό, mel, honey, as food, ν 69; also as draught, mixed with wine; honey and fat were burned upon the funeral pyre, Ψ 170, ω 68 ; mixed with milk as libation to shades of dead, μελίκρητον. Metaph. of speech of well-disposed, Α 249, Σ 109. Cf. μελίγηρυν.

Μελί-βοια, town in Thessalian Magnesia, Β 717†.

μελί-γηρυν, sweet-voiced, μ 187†.

μελίη, ης, ῃ, ην, ῃσι, fraxinus, ash, Ν 178, Π 767 ; shaft of lance, lance, freq. with Πηλιάδα, from mount Πήλιον ; presented by the Centaur Cheiron to Πηλεύς, Π 143 ; εὔχαλκον, well shod with brass ; χαλκογλώχινος, brazen-pointed.

μελί-ηδής, έος, έα, (ἡδύς), honey sweet, Σ 545, Κ 569, ι 94 ; fig. ὕπνος, sweet, νόστον, θυμόν, life.

μελι-κρήτῳ, τῷ, (κεράννυμι), honey drink, potion compounded of milk and honey as a libation to spirits of the lower world, κ 519, λ 27.

μέλινος, ρ 339, and μείλινον, α, (μελίη), fraxineus, beechen, ashen, Ε 655. (Il.)

μέλισσαι, άων, fem., (μέλι), bees, Μ 167.

Μελίτη, a Nereid, Σ 42†.

μελί-φρων, ονος, ονα, (φρήν), having mind, substance, essence like honey ; honey sweet=μελιηδής, dulcis.

μέλλω, εις, ει, ετι, ουσι, opt. οι, οιμεν, ipf. ἔμελλον, ες, (ε)ν, ετε, ον, and μέλλε, μέλλον, (1) is sum qui, be able, can, with inf. prs., Ξ 125, α 232, δ 200; with inf. aor., δ 377, χ 322; with πού, denoting probability or suspicion, may well, must, οὕτω που Διί μέλλει φίλον εἶναι, thus, methinks, must it please Zeus.—(2) like -urus sum, (a) be on the point of, α 232, ζ 135, with inf. fut. (prs. aor.); (b) it is one's fate, destiny, I have to, Λ 700, Π 46; often negatived, with inf. prs. aor.; must, Ω 46, ι 477.

μέλεα, έων, εσσι, ntr., membra, limbs, σ 70, Ρ 211; corpus, body, Η 131, Ν 672, ο 354.

μέληθρα, τά, (μέλπω), sport, κυνῶν, Ν 233; κυσίν, Ρ 255. (Il.)

μέλποντες, part., extol in song, Α 474; mid. ἐμέλπετο (φορμίζων), was playing (on the lyre), δ 17, ν 27; μελπομένῃσιν ἐν χορῷ, celebrate a choral dance; μέλπεσθαι Ἀρηϊ, fig., dance a measure in honor of Ares in close combat = fight on foot, Η 241.

μέλω, ι 20, elsewh. 3 prs. μέλει, ουσι; imp. ἔτω, όντων; inf. ἔμεν, ειν; part. ουσα, ipf. ἔμελε, μέλε, fut. -ήσει, ήσουσι, ησέμεν, pf. μέμηλε(ν), subj. ῃ, part. ὥς, plupf. μεμήλει, curae esse, it is a care, to me, μοί τι; may often be translated personally, care for, attend to, engage in, ἔργα; Κ 92, angit, distresses, Ω 152, φρεσί, in thy soul; with inf., π 465; part., ε 6; ι 20, be an object of interest; μεμηλώς τινος, studiosus rei; mid. in similar signif. with act. prs. μελέσθω, angat; fut. μελήσεται, pf. μέμβλεται, plupf. μέμβλετο, χ 12.

μέμαα, du. μέμᾰτον, pl. ᾰμεν, ᾰτ(ε), άασι, imp. ᾰτω, part. ᾰώς, ῶτος, τι, τα, τε, τες, σιν, τας, (μεμᾰότες, ότε, Β 818), μεμᾰυῖα, αν, αι, plupf. μέμᾰσαν, (μαίομαι), charge, press forward, ἐπί τινι (yet not so, Φ 174), ἐγχείῃσι; gestire, moliri, plan, λ 315; with inf., appetens sum, desirous, τινός; part., cupidus, rapidus, eager, quick.

μεμᾰκυῖαι, see μηκάομαι.

μέμβλωκε, see βλώσκω.

μέμβλεται, το, see μέλω.

μεμηκώς, see μηκάομαι.

μέμηλε, ει, ῃ, see μέλω.

μεμνώμεθα, έῳτο, see μιμνήσκω.

Μέμνων, ονος, son of Tithonos and of Eos, came to the aid of Priamos

after the death of Hektor, and slew Antilochos, λ 522, cf. δ 188.

μέμονας, εν, pf., (mens), have in mind, purpose, with inf. prs. fut. or aor., ἴσα θεοῖσι (cf. φρονέειν ἴσα), thinks to make himself equal with the gods, Φ 315; διχθά, yearns with a twofold wish, hesitates.

μέμυκε, see μυκάομαι.

μέν (from μήν, μὲν, Η 77, 389, Λ 442, Χ 482), I. in affirmation : profecto, in truth, Α 216; μὲν δή, with imp., now then, Α 514; νῦν, now certainly; εἰ, if then in fact; ἤ, (1) in oath, in very truth, ξ 160; (2) in assertion : truly, yet, κ 65, λ 447; (3) in antithesis, Ω 416.—καὶ μέν, (a) and yet, Α 269; (b) but even, ν 45; (c) and truly, κ 13, τ 244; οὐ μέν, non profecto, not indeed, Β 203, Ρ 19, ρ 381 (see also II.); οὐ μὲν γάρ=ἐπεὶ οὐ μέν, α 78, 173; οὐ μέν τοι, ψ 266; οὐδὲ μέν, κ 447; οὐδὲ μὲν οὐδέ, Β 703; neque vero ne hi quidem, nor by any means; ἀτὰρ μέν, but in truth, β 122; μὲν=δέ, Γ 308; after pronouns, in recapitulation, Α 234; in repetition, Α 267.—II. in first of two corresponding clauses, (1) without δέ, quidem, indeed, Α 211; also οὐ μὲν δή, but still not, ε 341; οὐ μέν τοι, yet by no means, σ 233; μὲν οὐδέ, (a) =ἀλλ' οὐ μὰν οὐδέ, nec vero ne—quidem, but not even, κ 551.—(b) but yet not, Τ 295; verily in no respect, δ 807; οὐδὲ μέν, but also not, Α 154; nor indeed, Ψ 311; after negative, οὐ, θ 553, γ 27.—(2) with following δέ, et—et, quidem—sed, cum—tum, both—and, as well—as, although—yet, Α 53 sq., α 22 sqq., Γ 51, α 24, γ 153.—(3) instead of δέ, ἀλλά may follow, Α 24; ἀτάρ, Α 166; αὖ, Λ 109; αὐτάρ, Α 127; αὖτε, Γ 240.—(4) other combinations: μὲν οὖν, so then, δ 780; μὲν που, methinks indeed, Γ 308; μέν τοι (but β 294, δ 836, τοι=tibi): (a) in assertion, yet really, δ 157, π 267.—(b) introductory, before αὐτάρ, δ 411; before δέ, β 294.—(c) adversative, σ 233, Θ 294.

μενεαίνω, εις, ει, ομεν, ετε, ων, ipf. μενεαίνομεν, aor. μενεήναμεν, (μέμονα, mens, μῆνις), eagerly desire, with inf. aor. prs. (fut.), Ν 628, Δ 126; irasci, be angry, Τ 68, Ω 22, α 20, succensere alicui, τινί; but ἔριδι, contend in angry strife; Π 491, transfixus indignabatur.

μενε-δήιος, *withstanding the enemy, brave*, M 247 and N 228.

Μενέ-λāος, son of Atreus, brother of Agamemnon, his wife Helene seduced by Alexandros, Γ 27; slays Skamandrios, Pylaimenes, Peisandros, Dolops, Thoas, Euphorbus, Podes; ἀρήιος, ἀρηίφιλος, διοτρεφές, δουρικλειτός, κυδαλίμοιο, ξανθός; his return home, occupying eight years, δ 82 sqq.

μενε-πτόλεμος, οι, *persistent in battle, steadfast*, γ 442. (Il.)

Μενεσθεύς, son of Peteos, B 552, M 331; leader of the Athenians, N 195; πλήξιππον, Δ 327.

Μενέσθης, a Greek, slain by Hektor, E 609†.

Μενέσθιος, (1) son of Areithoos, slain by Paris, H 9.—(2) a Myrmidon, son of Spercheios, Π 173.

μενε-χάρμης, ην, αι, and **-χαρμος**, Ξ 376, (χάρμη), *stanch in battle, steadfast.*

μενο-εικέ(α), masc., ntr., ές, (εἴκω), *suiting the heart, satisfying*, largus, Τ 144, ζ 76.

μενοινώω (instead of άω), ᾱς, ᾱ̃=άᾳ, ῶν, prs., ipf. μενοίνα, εον, aor. -ησεν, subj. ἡσῃ=ἡγσι, Ο 82; ἡσωσι, (μένος, μενεαίνω), cupio, peto, *desire, seek*, δ 480, ο 111, ρ 355; τινὶ κακά, moliri, *devise*, λ 532; *ponder*, Μ 59; πολλά, Ο 82.

Μενοιτιάδης, αο and εω, *son of Menoitios*, Patroklos, Π 554, Σ 93, Ι 211.

Μενοίτιος, son of Aktor, Λ 785; in Opus, Σ 326; father of Patroklos, Λ 605, Τ 24.

μένος, εος, εἰ, ος, εα, έων Θ 361, εα, ntr., (MEN, MA, mens, μῆνις), *vehement impulse*, ω 319, Τ 202, Ρ 503; *force, might*, Η 210; ἐν γούνεσσι, Ρ 451; freq. with χεῖρες, Ζ 502, Υ 372, λ 502; κρατερόν, Η 38, Κ 479, Ν 60; coupled with ἀλκή (power of defense), Ι 706, Ζ 265, χ 226; πυρός, Ζ 182, λ 220; ἀνέμων, Ε 524; *vital force, life*, Ρ 298, 29, Ζ 27; joined with ψυχή, Ε 296, Γ 294; θυμός, Θ 358; often in periphrasis, e. g. μ. Ἀτρείδαο=Ἀτρείδης, etc., Λ 268, Ψ 837, η 178, θ 423; ιερόν, η 167, ν 20; μένε' ἀνδρῶν, Δ 447, Θ 61, δ 363; *resolve*, with θυμός, Ε 470, Χ 346; *courage, valor*, Φ 151, Κ 366, Π 529; πολύθαρσες, Ρ 156;

with θάρσος, Ε 2; Β 536, Γ 8; *wrath*, Θ 361, Α 207; *fury*, cf. ἔριδος, Α 103; δάμασσε, λ 562; mens, *temper*, τ 493, Ε 892; in general signif. determined by context, ἐν φρεσί, Φ 145, Α 103; ἐν θυμῷ, Ρ 451, Ψ 468, Χ 312.

Μέντης, (1) chief of Kikones, Ρ 73.
—(2) son of Anchialos, α 180, chief of Taphians, α 105, guest friend of Odysseus, under whose form Athena visits Telemachos.

μέντοι, see μέν, ad fin., II., 4.

Μέντωρ, ορος, son of Alkimos, friend of Odysseus, in whose form Athena conducts Telemachos to Pylos, and seconds Odysseus against the suitors, β 225, 243, γ 22, 340, χ 206, 208, ω 446.

μένω, prs., ipf. ἔμεν(ε), ον, iter. μένεσκον, fut. μενέω, εις, ουσι, ειν, ων, aor. ἔμεινα, ας, ε, αμεν, αν, and μειν(ε), αμεν, ατ', αν; ῃ; ειας, (mens, maneo), (1) maneo, *remain, wait*, with inf., Ο 599; εἰσόκε, Ι 45; *hold one's ground in battle*, Π 659.—(2) τί, expecto, *await*, Ο 709; τινά, ο 346; *withstand*, Ζ 126; *await*, Α 535, Φ 609; *wait for*, τινά, Υ 480, Φ 571, ἡῶ, Λ 723; *sustain, resist*, Ο 406, Χ 93, Μ 169, Ι 355, there *he dared* once *to encounter* me alone.

Μένων, a Trojan, slain by Leonteus, Μ 193†.

Μερμερίδης, *son of Mermeros*, Ilos, α 259†.

μέρμερ(α), τά, (smar, maere, merke), *remarkable, signal* (ἔργα, πολέμοιο); in bad sense, *infamous, horrible*, Κ 48 (Κ 524, Θ 453). (Il.)

Μέρμερος, slain by Antilochos, Ξ 513†.

μερμηρίζω, εις, ει, ων, ipf. μερμήριζε, ον, aor. μερμήριξα, ε(ν), subj. ω, inf. -αι, (smar, schmerz ?), (1) deliberare, *ponder, reflect*, ἐνὶ (μετὰ) φρεσί, κατὰ φρένα (θυμόν), Α 189; with ἤ—ἤ, utrum—an, ὡς, ὅπως, inf. ω 235.—(2) meditari, *imagine*, τινὰ ἀμύντορα, π 256, 261.

μέρμιθα, τῇ, *cord*, κ 23†.

μέροπες, ων, εσσι, (mors), *mortals, mortal*, ἄνθρωποι, ων, also βροτοῖσιν, Β 285.

Μέροψ, seer and ruler in Perkote on Hellespont, father of Adrastos and Amphios, Β 831, Λ 329.

(μέρω, μέρομαι, μείρομαι), ipf. μείρεο, pf. 3 sing. ἔμμορε, plupf. pass. εἴ-
μαρτο (for σέσμαρτο), cause to be divided,
receive as portion, (a) with acc., I 616.
—(b) with gen., τιμῆς, A 278, O 189, ε
335.—(c) plupf. pass., it was decreed by
fate, with acc. and inf., Φ 281, ε 312,
ω 34.

μεσαι-πόλιος (μέσαι, locative from
μέσος), half-gray, grizzled, N 361†.

Μεσαύλιος, servant of Eumaios, ξ
449, 455.

μεσηγύ(s), see μεσσηγύ.

μεσήεις (μέσος), mediocris, mid-
dling, M 269†.

μεσό - δμης, τῆς, (δέμω), (1) prop.
what is constructed in the middle, represented in the cut (see a) as a metal shoe

in which the foot of the mast was firmly fastened, so that it (the mast) could
be turned backward on the pivot (c) to
a horizontal position, until it rested upon
the ἱστοδόκη, β 424. See also plate IV.,
where the μεσόδμη is somewhat differently represented as a three-sided
trough, or mast-box. — (2) pl., small
spaces or niches opening into the μέγαρον, and enclosed on three sides, behind
by outside wall, on either side by the
low walls which served as foundations
of the columns, τ 37. (See table III.,
r, and cut No. 90.)

μέσον, etc., see μέσσος.

μεσσᾶτω, (μέσσος), ἐν, in the middle,
Θ 223 and Λ 6.

μεσσ-αύλοιο, ον, (αὐλή), court, farm-
yard, P 112; cattle-yard, Λ 548, βοῶν;
of Polyphemos, κ 435.

Μέσση, harbor town near Tainaron
in Lakonike, B 582†.

μεσσηγύ(s) and μεσηγύ(ς), in the
middle, Λ 573, Ψ 521; meantime, η 195;
elsewhere with gen., between, betwixt, χ
341. [ῡς, ὔ.]

Μεσσηίς, spring in Thessalian Hellas, Z 457†.

Μεσσήνη, district about Pherai, in
what was afterward Messenia, φ 15;
the inhabitants, Μεσσήνιοι, φ 18.

μεσσο-παγές (πήγνυμι), fixed up to
the middle; ἔθηκεν ἔγχος, drove the
spear half its length firm into the bank,
Φ 172; v. l. μεσσοπαλές, vibrating
through half its length, quivering.

μέσσος, nom. and gen. pl. wanting,
dat. pl. οισ(ιν); η, gen. sing., nom. and
gen. pl. wanting, dat. pl. ῃσ(ιν); ον, α,
with parallel form μέσῳ, ον, οισι,
(μεδϳος, medius), medius, ntr., freq.
as subst., middle; (ἐν)μέσσῳ, ἐς (κατὰ)
μέσον, δικάζειν, judge impartially, Ψ
574; ἐς μ. θεῖναι, in medio propo-
nere, offer as prize; μέσον ὑπέρ, half-
way over; μέσον αἰόλοι, pliant in the
middle.

μέσφ(α) (μέσοφα), ἠοῦς, till dawn,
Θ 508†.

μετά, amid, among, B 446, Σ 515;
after, Ψ 133; postea, afterward, ο
400.—Prep., (1) with dat., amid, also
of things; among, μ. νηυσίν, N 668;
also between, of two things, or such as
exist in pairs, γέννσσι, ποσσί (πίσy μ.
π. γυναικός = nascatur), φρεσί, in
thought, properly intra praecordia,
Δ 245; πνοιῇς, στροφάλιγγι, as it were
with the breath of the wind, of the
whirlwind; πύματον μετὰ οἷς ἐτ., ultimum e sociis suis. — (2) with
gen., along with, μάχεσθαι μετά τινος,
in league with any one.—(3) with acc.,
inter, amid, infrequent, B 143; usually to denote direction toward, often
with plural subst., Γ 264, H 35, K 205,
P 458, 460, joined with ἐς, Δ 70, A
423, μ 247, cf. E 804; coupled with
ἐπί, Π 534; also after, of individuals,
K 73, ζ 115; in hostile sense, ὁρμᾶσθαι; of space, A 423; and of time,
post; in order of worth, rank, secundum = next after; so also where a

superlative is implied, e. g. ἀριστῆες, μετέπρεπε, Π 195; θ 583, the dearest according to blood and race; finally, with verbs of motion and of intention, after, in pursuit of, πλεῖν μετὰ χαλκόν, οἴχονται μετὰ δεῖπνον; denoting conformity with, secundum, μ. ὄγμον, along the furrow. In anastrophe μέτα = μέτεστι, so μέτα, φ 93, coupled with ἐν.

μετα-βαίνω, aor. imp. -βηθι, pass over (in narration, καὶ ἄεισον), θ 492; μετὰ δ' ἄστρα βεβήκει, μ 312, had passed over (the meridian) = were declining toward the horizon, μ 312.

μετὰ νῶτα βαλών, aor., terga vertens, turn one's back, θ 94†.

μετ-εβούλευσαν, aor. from -βουλεύω, ἄλλως, have changed their purpose, ἀμφ' (de) Ὀδυσῆι, ε 286†.

μετ' ἄγγελος, Ο 144 and Ψ 199, is not a single word, but μετά belongs in one case to θεοῖσι, and in the other to ἀνέμοισι.

μετα-δαίνυται, prs., fut. δαίσομαι, σεται (δαίνυμαι, δαῖς), have a share in the feast, Ψ 207, with gen. partitive, elsewh. ἡμῖν, nobiscum.

μετα-δήμιοι, ον, (δῆμος), among the people, in the community, ν 46; at home, θ 293.

μετα-δόρπιος (δόρπος), adj., inter caenam, during supper, δ 194† (cf. 213, 218).

μετα-δρομάδην (δρόμος), running after, Ε 80†.

μετα-ἵζειν (ἵζω), sit among them, π 362†.

μετ-αΐσσων, prs. part., -αΐξας, aor. part., rushing after, Φ 564.

μετ-εκίαθε, ον, ipf., (κιάθω), subsequi, follow after; τινά, persequi, Σ 581; tr insire, pass over to; πεδίον, permeare.

μετα-κλαύσεσθαι, fut., (κλαίω), postea fleturum esse, shall hereafter lament, Λ 764†.

μετα - κλινθέντος, aor. pass. part., (κλίνω), if the tide of battle should shift about, Λ 509†.

μετα-λλήξειε, αντι, aor. from λήγω (σλ- ?), χόλοιο, cease from, Ι 157. (Il.)

μετ-αλλῶ, ᾷς, ᾷ, ῶσιν, imp. άλλα, aor. ἀλλησαν, ἦσαι, (Ameis derives from μετά and λάω, look after); sciscitari, search after, Ε 516, ο 362; inquire

about, τινά, Κ 125, Ν 780; τί, π 465, ξ 128; percontari, question, τινά, Α 553, τ 6; also τινά τι, or ἀμφί τινι, ρ 554; coupled with verbs of similar meaning, Α 550, γ 69, ψ 99, η 243.

μετάλμενος, aor. part. from μεθάλλομαι.

μετὰ-μάζιον, ntr., (μαζός), στῆθος, on the breast, between the nipples, in the middle of the breast, Ε 19†.

μετ-έμισγον, ipf., fut. -μίξομεν, (μίσγω), placed (pine splinters) in the midst, σ 310; χ 221, we will merge thy possessions with those of Odysseus (for subsequent division among us).

μεταμώνια (for -ανεμώνια?), ntr., vana, irrita, vain, fruitless; θεῖεν, reddant, Δ 363; v. l. μεταμώλια.

μετὰ-νάστην, τόν, (ναίω), new-comer, interloper, inquilinum, Ι 648. (Il.)

μετ-ενίσσετο, ipf., (νίσσομαι), βουλυτόνδε, passed over (the meridian) toward (his place of unyoking) setting, Π 779.

μετ-αξὖ, between, Α 156†.

μετὰ-παυόμενοι (παύω), resting between whiles, Ρ 373†.

μετα-παυσωλή (παύω), intermissio, rest, pause, πολέμοιο, Τ 201†.

μετα-πρεπέ(α) τόν, (πρέπω), conspicuous among, ἀθανάτοισιν, eximiam inter immortalium (domos), Σ 370†.

μετα-πρέπω, ει, (tmesis, θ 172), ipf. -έπρεπον, ε(ν) (tmesis, σ 2), ον, (πρέπω), be prominent among, excellere, among, τισί, on account of, dat. Π 596, inf. Π 194.

μετα-σεύομαι, ipf. -εσσεύοντο, aor. ἔσσυτο, (σεύω, σFυ-), hurry after, Φ 423; τινά, Ψ 389.

μετα-σπών, μετα-σπόμενος, see μεθέπω.

μέτασσαι, αἱ, (μετά), yearlings, properly those born in the middle one, of the three bearings in the year, summer lambs, ι 221†, see δ 86.

μετασσεύομαι, see μετα-σεύομαι.

μετ-έστενον, ipf., (στένω), postmodo deploravi, lament afterward, δ 261†.

μετα-στοιχί (στοῖχος), secundum lineam, in a line, in a row, side by side, Ψ 358 and 757.

μετα-στρέφω, fut. -στρέψεις, aor.

subj. στρέψῃ, ωσι, opt. ειε, convertere, K 107, *turn away* his heart *from* anger; O 52, *change* his purpose in conformity to thy and my will; *change* one's ways, O 203; β 67, *reverse* (your fortunes), sending misfortune instead of prosperity; pass. aor. μεταστρεφθείς, έντι, τα, τε, qui corpus convertit, *having turned themselves about*, P 732.

μετ-έθηκεν (τίθημι), κε—, *would not have caused* such a din *among* us, σ 402†.

μετα-τρέπομ(αι), ῃ, εται, τινός, properly, *turn one's self about* at=*regard, consider*, always with neg., A 160; exc. μετὰ δ' ἐτράπετο, aor., se convertit, *turned himself about*, A 199.

μετα-τροπαλίζεο, ipf., (τροπαλίζω), (non) revertebaris ad me, *turn about*, i. e. thou didst flee *without looking behind thee*, Υ 190†.

μετ-αυδάω, only ipf. ηύδων, α, (αὐδή), *spake among*, ἔπεα, Θ 496, α 31, B 109.

μετά-φημι, aor. **μετ-έφη** and **μετέειπον**, ἐειπ(εν) and ἐειφ', τοῖσι, *among* (them) he (she) *spoke*, B 411 ; B 795, allocuta est, not a genuine verse: tmesis, μετὰ ἔειπ., Γ 303, κ 561.

μετα-φραζόμεσθα, prs. 1 pl., (φράζομαι), postea considerabimus, *will afterward consider*, A 140†.

μετά-φρενον, ου, φ, and pl. α, of single person, M 428, (φρένες), properly, *behind the diaphragm, the back*.

μετα-φωνέω, ipf. -εφώνεον, ε(ν), (φωνή), τοῖσι, *made my voice heard among them*, κ 67, sc. τοῖσι.

μετ-έᾱσι, from I. μέτ-ειμι.
μετ-έειπ., see μετά-φημι.

I. **μέτ-ειμι** (μέτα = μέτεστι, φ 93), 3 pl. **ἔᾱσι**, ἔμμεναι = εἶναι, ἰών (tmesis, λ 78), subj. ἔω = εἴω, ἐῃ, fut. ἔσσομαι (tmesis, ἔσσεται, I 131), versari inter, *be among*, τισίν; only B 386, intercedet, *intervene*.

II. **μέτ-ειμι**, εισιν, ipf. tmesis, ῄει, aor. mid. εἰσάμενος, (ἰέναι), *go after*, sequor; N 298, *march forth; go* or *ride among*, N 90, P 285.

μετ-εῖπον, etc., see μετά-φημι.
μετ-εισάμενος, see II. μέτ-ειμι.
μετ-είω, ἔμμεναι, see I. μέτ-ειμι.
μετ-έπειτα, *afterward*, Ξ 310, κ 519.
μετ-έρχομαι, εται, όμενος, fut. ελεύ-

σομαι, aor. ἐλθοί, imp. ἐλθε, part. ἐλθών, *come upon*, α 229; τισίν, *come among*, α 134; ingruere, irruere, *attack*, λέων ἀγέληφι, μετ' ἐλάφους; στίχας, obire ordines, *pass through to marshal* the ranks, E 461; τινά, *seek for*, pursue; πατρὸς κλέος, *I go to seek* tidings of my father; ἔργα, *attend to* the farm; γάμοιο, curare.

μετ-έσσυτο, see μετα-σσεύομαι.
μετέω, see I. μέτ-ειμι.
μετ-ήορα, ntr., (ἀείρω), Θ 26, γένοιτο, would *be raised aloft*, would float in the air; into the air, Ψ 369.

μετ-οιχόμενος, η, ipf. ᾠχετο, ἀνὰ ἄστυ, permeare urbem; K 111, *go to seek*; persequi; comitari.

μετ-οκλάζει, *keeps changing his position* (from one knee to the other), N 281†.

μετ' ὄπασσα, (ὀπάζω), *gave* (to accompany them) *at the same time* a leader, κ 204†.

μετ-όπισθ(εν), *behind, in the rear* (toward the west), ν 241; λελειμμένοι, *left behind*; with gen., pone, *behind*, ι 539.

μετ-οχλίσσειε, aor. opt., (ὀχλίζω), *push back, away* (strictly with a lever), Ω 567.

μετρήσαντες, aor. part., (μετρέω), emensi, *having passed over*, γ 179†.

μέτρον, (α), ntr., *measure, measuring-rod*, M 422; *jar and its contents*, measure, H 471, of wine, of flour; measures of the way = length of the journey, δ 389; *full measure, prime*, ἥβης; ὅρμου, proper mooring-place.

μετ-ώπιον, adj., acc. sing. masc. (μέτ-ωπον), *on the forehead*, Λ 95 and Π 739.

μέτ-ωπον, φ, α, ntr., (ὤψ), frons, *forehead*, also *front of helmet*, Π 70.

μεῦ = (ἐ)μοῦ, see ἐγώ.

μέχρι(ς), with gen., tenus, *as far as*, θαλάσσης, N 143, and τέο μ., *how long?* Ω 128.

μή, negative prohibitory particle, ne: I. where the subject desires to avert something, (1) prohibition, with imp. pres., Π 22, Γ 414; aor., Δ 410, ω 248; subj. aor., E 684 (in threat, A 26; as mild assertion, ε 467); μή τι, do not in any way, true reading in α 315.—(2) exhortation, M 216, μὴ ἴομεν (subj.).—(3) wish, with opt., Γ

160; with ὄφελες, I 698; with inf.,
B 413; in imprecation, B 259.—(4)
solemn promise, fut. indic., K 330;
inf., ε 187; protest, indic., O 41; inf.,
T 261, Ψ 585.—(5) purpose, A 522,
α 133.—(6) fear lest, o 12, A 555; with
indic. aor., ε 300; in independent
clause, A 587; dependent upon other
verbs, A 555, K 98, Π 446; in indirect
question, K 101.—(7) threat, Ξ 46.—
II. where the subject intends to deny
the truth of its assertion : (1) in conditional clauses, nisi, unless, Γ 374 (invariable, except where an idea not the
sentence is denied, cf. si non, Γ 289).
—(2) in concessive sentence invariable,
εἰ καί and καὶ εἰ, etc.—(3) in relative
sentence implying a condition, δ 165 ;
after indefinite general antecedent, B
302.—(4) in temporal clauses implying
condition, π 197, N 319.—(5) always
with infin.—(6) in interrogations expecting negative answer, num; always
ἢ μή, pray can it be? you don't mean?
ζ 200, ι 405, 406. With other particles : μὴ οὐ, ne non, lest not, A 28,
566; μὴ δή, think not, I pray you, A
131 ; μὴ μάν, Θ 512, see μάν. (For
place in sentence, see οὐ.)

μηδέ, (1) but not, Γ 160.—(2) neque, and not, nor, ne—quidem, μηδέ
τι, nor by any means (in first, second,
and fifth foot), Δ 184, Υ 121, γ 96.
Also doubled, yet not correlative like
μήτε — μήτε, but continuative, c. g.
nor—, also not, Δ 303.

μηδέν, nihil, nothing, Σ 500†.

Μηδεσι-κάστη, illegitimate daughter of Priamos, wife of Imbrios, N
173†.

μήδεαι, εται, οίμην, εο, ipf. μήδετ(ο),
δονθ' = δοντο, fut. μήσεται, aor. (ἐ)μή-
σατ(ο), (μέδων, meditor), B 360, take
counsel for one's self; devise, τινί τι, Ξ
253; κακά τινι, H 478; ὄλεθρόν τινι,
ξ 300, κ 115; λυγρὸν νόστον, γ 132;
τινά τι, prepare for, Ψ 24, X 395, ω
426; νόστον, parare, γ 160.

I. μήδεα, τά, (μέδων, meditor),
plans, counsels ; πυκνά, shrewd; εἰδώς,
fertile in plans; πεπνυμένα, prudent;
ἄφθιτα, enduring ; φίλα, friendly ; εὖ
φρεσὶν οἶδεν, knows well in her
thought, λ 445.

II. μήδεα (μαδᾶν, madere), privy
parts, ζ 129, σ 87. (Od.)

Μηθώνη, home of Philoktetes, B
716.

μηκάομαι, only pf. μεμηκώς, μεμά-
κυῖαι, whence ipf. (ἐ)μέμηκον, ι 439 ;
and aor. part. μάκών, shrieking, screaming, always of wounded animals, exc.
σ 98; pf., of hard-pressed game, K
362 ; elsewh. balare, bleat.

μηκάδες, ας, fem., (μηκάομαι), bleating (she-goats), ι 124.

μη-κ-έτ(ι), non iam, no longer, B
259, 435, γ 240.

Μηκιστεύς, ῆος, έος, (1) son of Ta-
laos, brother of Adrastos, father of
Euryalos, B 566, Ψ 678.—(2) son of
Echios, companion of Antilochos, slain
by Polydamas, acc. -ῆ, O 339, Θ 333,
N 422.

Μηκιστηϊάδης = Euryalos, Z 28.

μήκιστον, ους, longissimum, os,
tallest, H 155 ; μήκιστα, finally, ε 299.

μῆκος, τό, (μᾱκρός), lofty stature,
ν 71; elsewh. longitudine, length.

μήκων, ὁ, poppy stalk, Θ 306†.

μηλέαι, ας, pl. fem., (μῆλον), apple-
trees; in synizesis, ω 340. (Od.)

μηλο-βοτῆρας, τούς, shepherds, Σ
529†.

I. μῆλον, ῳ, ων, τό, malum, apple,
η 120, I 542.

II. μῆλον, ntr., μ 301, ξ 105, small-
cattle, domestic animals ; τί, a single
head; esp. in pl., herds of sheep and
goats; ἔνορχα, ἄρσενα, he-goats, rams.

μήλοπα, τόν, shining white, η 104†.

μήν (μάν), profecto, verily, in truth
(never alone) ; ἤ—, B 291; οὐ—, Ω
52 ; ἄγε—, on then, A 302 ; καὶ μήν,
and verily, Ψ 410, π 440; also in truth,
T 45, λ 582.

μήν, νός, see μείς.

μήνη, ης, (μήν, mensis), moon, Ψ
455 and T 374.

μηνιθμόν, τόν, (μηνίω), wrath, Π 62
(only Π).

μήνιμα, τό, (μηνίω), θεῶν, cause of
divine wrath, curse, X 358.

μῆνις, ιος, ιν, fem., (μαίνομαι), ira,
wrath, rancor, A 1.

μηνίει, prs., imp. μήνϊ(ε), ipf. (ἐ)μή-
νϊ(εν), aor. μηνίσας, (μῆνις), irasci,
succensere, be wroth with, A 422,
M 10, ρ 14.

Μήονες, inhabitants of, Μηονίς,
woman from, Μηονίη, i. e. Lydia, Δ
142, Γ 401, B 864.

μή-ποτε, (1) nunquam, *never,* I 133.—(2) ne unquam, *lest ever,* X 106.

μή που, ne forte, *lest in any way,* Ξ 130, δ 775, τίς, with subj. in threat.

μή πω, with imp., ne (non) iam, *not yet, that not yet,* χ 431, ψ 59, P 422, Σ 134 ; with opt., ν 123.

μή πως, with subj. or opt. : *that in no way, lest somehow,* ι 102 ; expressing purpose or fear, with subj., P 95 ; in indirect question, *whether not,* K 101.

μῆρα, see μηρία.

μηρίνθοιο, ῳ, ον, fem., (μηρύω), cord, Ψ 854 (only Ψ).

μηρί(α) and μῆρ(α), τά, (μηρύς), *pieces of the flesh of the thighs,* which, together with other pieces, were wrapped in a double layer of fat (πίονα ὠμοθέτησαν), placed upon the altar (ἐπιθεῖναι), and burned, A 40, γ 456.

Μηριόνης, son of Molos, N 249; K 270, from Kreta; θεράπων, of Idomeneus, N 246; ἀτάλαντος Ἐνυαλίῳ, H 166 ; Ἄρηι, N 528 ; exploits, N 566, 650, Ξ 514, Π 342, 603.

μηρός, οῦ, όν, ῷ, οί, ούς, masc., fe-mur, ham, *upper fleshy part of the thigh;* "to smite one's thighs" as sign of surprise or excitement, M 162; ἐξέταμνον μηρία, they cut out (from the thighs of the victims, sc. μηρῶν) the thigh-pieces, γ 456, q. v.

μηρύσαντο, aor. mid. from μηρύω, *drew up, furled by brailing up,* μ 170†. The process was what it is to-day. (See cut No. 5, Egyptian representation of a Phoenician ship.)

μήστωρα, ε, ες, ας, masc., (μήδομαι), properly, *deviser, preparer; auctor,* μ. φόβοιο, *author* of flight, but E 272, *well understanding* pursuit and flight; μ. αὐτῆς, *raisers of* battle cry, cf. βοὴν ἀγαθός, elsewh. *counselor.*

Μήστωρ, son of Priamos, Ω 257†.

μήτε — μήτε, nec — nec, neve — neve, *neither—nor;* followed by simple τέ, N 230 ; μητέ τι, with imp., and do not, K 249, ξ 387.

μήτηρ, έρος, έρι, έρα, (ῥ' ἐμήν and ἰνί, ψ 113), voc. μῆτερ, acc. pl. έρας ; also μητρός, ρί, mater, *mother,* of men, Δ 130, α 215 ; of animals, κ 414 ; freq. with epithets, πότνια, αἰδοίη, κεδνή ; with μήλων = *producing, abounding in*

sheep, Λ 222 ; — θηρῶν, in wild-beasts, Θ 47.

μήτῑ, see μῆτις. μήτῑ, see μῆτις.

μητιάω, 3 pl. μητιόωσι, part. όωντι, ες, όωσι, όωσα, mid. prs. άασθε, ipf. μητιόωντο, (μῆτις), *deliberate,* H 45 ; *conclude, βουλάς ; devise, τί, κακά, νόστον τινί ; Σ 312, κακά, mal e sua-denti ; mid., *debate with one's self, consider.*

μητίετα (μητίομαι), only of Ζεύς and Ζεῦ at close of verse, *all-wise, counselor,* A 175, 508.

μητιόεντα (μῆτις) φάρμακα, *helpful* herbs, δ 227†.

μητίομαι, fut. ἴσομαι, aor. ισαίμην, ίσασθαι, (μητίομαι, μῆτις), *devise, τινί τι, τινά τι ; cf. μήδομαι, perpetrate against* one.

μητιόωσα, όωσι, see μητιάω.

μῆτις, ῐς, ῑ, ῑν, fem., (metior), con-silium, (1) *shrewdness, wisdom, μῆτιν ἀτάλαντος,* equal in *insight* to the gods.
—(2) *proposal, plan,* P 634 ; ὑφαίνειν, *think out,* H 324, δ 678.

μῆτίς, μήτῑ, nullum, X 120, ν 46 ; usually separated, μή τι, e. g. with imp., *by no means ;* also with subj. and inf. In most cases the force of the two words μή and τις, which are usually separated by a word, may be separately given, X 358, ν 229, Δ 234.

μητρο-πάτωρ, *one's mother's father,* Λ 224†.

μητρυιή, ῆς, noverca, *step-mother,* N 697. (Il.)

μητρώιον δῶμα, materna domus, *maternal home,* τ 410†.

μήτρως, acc. ωα, avunculus, *ma-ternal uncle,* Π 717. (Il.)

μηχανόωντας, part. pr. (for άοντας), mid. prs. -όωνται, opt. όωτο, ipf. μη-χανάασθε, όωντο, (μηχανή), *set at work, perpetrate,* σ 143 ; mid. in similar signif., also *devise,* π 134, τινί κακά.

μῆχος, τό, *help, remedy,* B 342.

Μήων, see Μήονες. μία, see εἷς.

μιαίνω, aor. subj. μιήνῃ, pass. pr. μιαίνεσθαι, ipf. μιαίνετο, aor. 3 pl. ἐμί-ανθεν and ἄνθησαν, *dye, stain,* Δ 141 ; pass., inquinari, *be soiled* (with blood and dust).

μΐαι-φόνος, ε, cruore inquina-tus, *blood-stained,* Ares, E 31. (Il.)

μΐᾰρός (μιαίνω), cruore inqui-natus, *stained,* Ω 420†.

μΐγαζομένους, part. prs., (μίγνυμι), φιλότητι, united in love, θ 271†.

μίγδᾰ, adv., (μίγνυμι), promiscuously, θευῖσι, Θ 437 ; together, ω 77.

μίγνυμι, aor. inf. μῖξαι, pass. pf. μεμιγμένον, οι, η, α, plupf. ἐμέμικτο, aor. (ἐ)μίχθη, 3 pl. ἔμιχθεν, inf. θήμεναι, part. θείς, aor. 2 ἐμίγην, ης, η, μίγη, ἧσαν=μίγεν, subj. ἧς, ἔωσι, opt. εἴην, ης, η, μιγεῖεν, inf. ἥμεναι and ἦναι, part. ἔντα, εἶσα, fut. μιγήσεσθαι, mid. fut. μίξεσθαι, aor. ἔμικτο, μίκτο ; moreover, pass. μίσγεαι, εται, ηται, ἔμεναι and εσθ(αι), ἐμένων, ipf. μίσγετο, ὀμεθ(α), οντο, and iter. μισγέσκετο, ἐμισγέσκοντο, miscere, mix, οἶνον καὶ ὕδωρ; also wine with wine, Γ 270 ; ἅλεσσι, with salt ; γλῶσσα, mixed language ; pass., come in contact, with dat., ἔγκασι, κονίῃ ; have relations with, ξεινίῃ, hold intercourse in guest friendship, with dat., also ἔν τισι, ἔς τινας ; also, come into hostile relations with, τινί, παλάμῃσί τινος, ἐν δαΐ ; be united in sexual intercourse, esp. (παρά) τινί, with one ; φιλότητι καὶ εὐνῇ, also ἐν φιλότητι or εὐνῇ, or ἐν ἀγκοίνῃσί τινος ; Ο 33, ἣν ἐμίγης, whose embraces thou hast enjoyed.

Μίδεια, town in Boiotia on Lake Kopais, Β 507†.

μικρός, parvus, small, little ; δέμας, in bodily stature, E 801 ; comp. μείων, minor ; κεφαλῇ, less in stature, or shorter by a head, Γ 193.

μίκτο, μῖκτο, see μίγνυμι.

Μίλητος, (1) Ionian city in Karia, B 868.—(2) city in Kreta, mother-city of foregoing, B 647.

μιλτο-πάρῃοι (μίλτος, " vermilion," παρειή), red-cheeked, painted red on sides or bows, B 637, ι 125.

Μίμας, ντος, promontory in Asia Minor opposite Chios, γ 172†.

μιμνάζειν, inf. prs., (μίμνω), permanere, remain, B 392 and K 549.

μιμνήσκ(ε), imp. prs., fut. μνήσει, aor. ἐμνήσας, ῃσῃ, ἥσασα, (μένω, mens), commonefacere, remind, τινά τινος ; mid. prs., fut. μνήσομαι, etc., aor. ἐμνήσατο, μνήσαντο, opt. -σαίατο=σαίαθ᾽, imp. μνῆσαι, ασθαι, etc., iter. μνησάσκετο ; moreover from μνάομαι, prs. μνωομένω, ῳ, ipf. μνώοντ(ο), (1) bethink one's self of, provide for, with gen., περί, η 192 ; φύγαδε, think on flight.— (2) memorare, mention, μνησθῆναι

τινος, δ 118.—(3) pf. μέμνημαι, (σ)αι and ῃ, ητ(αι), etc., subj. ὤμεθα, opt. ῄμην, ἔῳτο, plupf. μεμνήμην, ηντο, 3 fut. μεμνήσομαι, ἥσεσθαι, meminisse, remember, τινός and τινά, τί ; σ 267, curare, care for.

μίμνω, only prs. (part. μιμνόντεσσι, etc.) and ipf., also unaugmented μίμνομεν, ον, (μι-μένω), manere, permanere, withstand, enemy, rain, wind; exspectare, await, ῃσι, π 367.

μῖν, Κ 347 μῖν, enclit., (for ιμιμ, old Lat. emem), eum, eam, id, ζ 48, Γ 232 ; never reflexive, δ 244 ; never for pl., ρ 268, κ 212.

Μινύειῳ (ῃῳ), εῖον, Minyeian, from ancient stem of Minyai in Orchomenos, λ 284 and B 511.

Μινυήϊος, river in Elis, Λ 722.

μινύθει, ουσι, subj. ῃ, ipf. iter. εσκον, (μίνυνθα), minuo, lessen, diminish, Ο 492, ξ 17 ; minui, δ 467 ; μ 46, the skin round (the bones) is wasting.

μίνυνθα (minus), paullulum, a little while ; περ οὔτι μάλα δήν, nor was it long=was quickly over, χ 473.

μινυνθάδιος, ῳ, ον, οι, comp. -διώτερον, Χ 54 (μίνυνθα), brief (of pain, life), Ο 612.

μινύριζε, imp. prs., ipf. 3 pl. μίνύριζον, (μινυρός), whimper, whine, moan, Ε 889 and δ 719.

Μίνως, ωος, ωα, and ω, son of Zeus and of Europa ; ruler in Knosos in Kreta, Ν 450 ; father of Deukalion and of Ariadne, λ 322 ; rules over his subjects in lower world, λ 568 sqq.

μισγ-άγκειαν, τήν, (ἄγκος), meeting of mountain glens, basin, Δ 453†.

μίσγω, see μίγνυμι.

μίσησε, aor. from μισέω, Ρ 272†, suffered not that he should—.

μισθός, οῦ, οῖο, ῷ, όν, ούς, (Ger. Miethe), wages, κ 84, σ 358.

μιστύλλε(ν), ον, ipf. from μιστύλλω, (mutilus), cut up into bits, preparatory to roasting flesh on the spit, Α 465.

μίτον, τόν ; παρὲκ —, forth from the upright threads of the warp, Ψ 762†. (See cuts Nos. 63, 129.)

μίτρη, ης, ην, fem., band or girdle round the waist and abdomen, below the στατὸς θώρηξ, the exterior of metal plates, the interior lined with wool (see cut No. 36), shorter than the ζῶμα, which it covered, while over both and the θώρηξ passed the ζωστήρ. (See cuts Nos. 3, 78.)

μιχθείς, see μίγνυμι.

μνάομαι, μνάᾳ, ἀασθαι and ᾶται, ὦνται, ἀσθω, ἄσθαι, ὤμενος, ipf. μνώμεθ(α), ὤοντο, iter. μνάσκετ(ο), (Ger. minne), woo, γυναῖκα, ἀκοιτιν, δάμαρτα, ω 125; used also absolutely: μνωομένω, etc.; see μιμνήσκω.

μνῆμ(α), τό, (μέμνημαι), memorial, χειρῶν, from Helen's hands (of her handiwork), ο 126.

μνημοσύνη (μνήμων) πυρὸς γενέσθω, let there be remembrance of, let us be mindful of fire, equivalent to a pass. of μέμνημαι, Θ 181†.

μνήμων (μνῆμα), memor, φ 95, and φόρτου, bent on freight.

μνῆσαι, μνησάσκετο, see μιμνήσκω.

Μνῆσος, a Paionian, slain by Achilleus, Φ 210†.

μνηστεύειν, prs., aor. part. -εύσαντες, (μνηστή), woo, δ 684 and σ 277.

μνηστῆρες, ἡρων, ῆρσι and ἡρεσσι(ν), ᾶς, (μνηστή), suitors, proci, esp. of Penelope, in number 108, with ten servants, π 247.

μνῆστις, ἡ, (μιμνήσκω), remembrance, δόρπου, ν 280†.

μνηστός, only fem. **μνηστή**, ῇ, ήν, (μνάομαι), wooed and won, wedded, ἄλοχος; opp. παλλακίς, δουρικτήτη, etc., Ζ 246, α 36.

μνηστύος, ύν, gen. and acc. from μνηστύς, (μνάομαι), wooing, courting, β 199. (Od.)

μνωόμενος, μνώμενος, ὤοντο, see μνάομαι.

μογέοντες, part., aor. (ἐ)μόγησα, ας, αν, ἐμόγησε(ν), subj. μογήσῃ, part. σας, (μόγις), laborare, toil, labor; part. = aegre, hardly, Λ 636; fessum esse, worn, with dat. instrum., ε 224, also with gen.; and ἐξ ἔργων, tired with work in the fields; perpeti, suffer, undergo, πολλά, εἵνεκά τινος and ἐπί τινι, for the sake of.

μόγις, aegre, vix, scarcely [ῐ, Χ 412], Ι 355.

μόγῳ, τῷ, prae labore, through my toil, Δ 27†.

μογοσ-τόκος, οι, (τίκτω), exciting pains (of labor), Eileithyia, Π 187. (Il.)

μόθον, ον, masc., (σμυθ.), din of battle, Η 117; ἵππων, of war-chariots.

μοῖρ(α), ῃ, αν, αι, ἀων, ας, (μέρο-

μαι), pars, then portio, part, portion, in booty, the feast; οὐδ' αἰδοῦς μ. ἔχουσιν, expertes sunt pudoris; then generally share, to every thing its share, τ 592; proper share, κατὰ μοῖραν, suitably; ἐν μοίρῃ, merito; opp. παρὰ (ὑπέρ, Υ 336) μοῖραν; finally, fatum, sors, the lot in life assigned to every one at birth, θανάτου; μοῖρά ἐστιν = εἵμαρται, it is fated, ordered by destiny, with inf.; opp. ἀμμορίη, in sense of good fortune; doom, Ζ 488; last of all, Fatum, Destiny as the blind controlling power, recognized even by the gods; plur. only Ω 49.

μοιρη-γενές, voc., favored by Μοῖρα at one's birth, child of destiny, Γ 182†.

μοιχ-άγρι(α), τά, (μοιχός, ἄγρα), μ. ὀφέλλει, owes the fine imposed upon one taken in adultery, θ 332†.

μολεῖν, see βλώσκω.

μόλιβος, ἡ, plumbum, lead, Λ 237†.

Μόλων, ονα, (1) companion of Thymbraios, slain by Odysseus, Λ 322. —(2) Μολίονε = Ἀκτορίωνε, Eurytos and Κteatos, Λ 709, 750.

μολοβρός, όν, ("filthy pig," so Curtius), glutton, as insulting epithet, ρ 219 and σ 26.

Μόλος, father of Meriones, Κ 269, Ν 249.

μολοῦσα, μολών, see βλώσκω.

μολπή, ῆς, ῇ, (μέλπω), lusus, play, sport, with music and dance, ζ 101, Α 472; music (vocal and instrumental); dance, Σ 572.

μολυβδαίνῃ, τῇ, (μόλυβδος), piece of lead attached to fishing-line as sinker, Ω 80†.

μονόω, only **μονωθείς**, έντα, part. aor. pass., and **μούνωσε**, aor. act., propagate the race single, so that there is in each case but a single heir, π 117; pass., left alone.

μόριμον (μόρος), decreed by fate, with inf., Υ 302†.

μορμύρων, οντα, part., (μύρω), roaring by, ἀφρῷ, with foam, Σ 403. (Il.)

μορόεντα (μόρον), mulberry-colored = dark-colored, so the old commentators; modern criticism has proposed other explanations, e. g. shining, from ΜΑΡ, yet nothing so far conclusive, σ 298.

μόρος, ον, masc., (1) from μείρομαι: due (cf. μοῖρα, αἶσα), ὑπὲρ μόρον, Φ

517, a 34; fatum, destiny, doom [Λ 409], π 421, υ 241, Τ 421.—(2) abstract noun corresponding to βροτός, mors, death, Σ 465, Χ 280, Ω 85.

μόρσιμος, ον, ntr., (μόρος), ἐστιν (ἤεν), is (was) ordered by fate, with inf., Τ 417, Ε 674; also of persons, destined to death, Χ 13, to marriage, π 392; ἦμαρ, day of death, Ο 613.

Μόρυς, υος, son of Hippotion, Ν 792; a Mysian, slain by Meriones, Ξ 514.

μορύσσω, pf. pass. part. **μεμορυγμένα** or **-χμένα**, foedata, stained, ν 435†.

μορφή, ἤν, venustas, grace, of speech; fills his words with grace, θ 170. (Od.)

μόρφνον, swamp-eagle, (μορφνός), or (cf. ὄρφνη) dark-colored (?), Ω 316†.

μόσχοισι, recentibus, fresh, tender, see λύγοισι, Λ 105†.

Μούλιος, (1) an Epeian, slain by Nestor, Λ 739.—(2) a Trojan, slain by Patroklos, Π 696.—(3) a Trojan, slain by Achilleus, Υ 472.—(4) a native of Dulichion, herald of Amphinomos, σ 423.

μουνάξ, adv., (μοῦνος), singly, θ 371.

μοῦνος, ου, ῳ, ον, οι, η, (μόνος), solus, alone, Λ 467; unicus, single, β 365; desolate, forsaken, desertus, κ 157.

Μοῦσ(α), αι, άων, (mens, monere), Muse, Muses, daughters of Zeus, θ 488, Β 598, and of Mnemosyne, dwell in Olympos, Β 484, in number, nine, ω 60; sing before the gods, Α 604; λίγεια, ω 62; and inspire the bard, Α 1, α 1, Β 484.

μοχθήσειν, fut. from μοχθέω, (μόχθος), laboraturum, will be worn; κήδεσι, curis, Κ 106†.

μοχθίζοντα, part. from μοχθίζω, (μόχθος), suffering, e vulnere, Β 723†.

μοχλέω, ipf. **ἐμόχλεον**, (μοχλός), heave up (with levers), Μ 259†.

μοχλός, ῳ, όν, οἶσι, (moles), lever, han l-spike, not roller, ε 261; (in ι) stake.

Μύγδων, ονος, king of Phrygia, Γ 186†.

μυδαλέας, acc. pl. fem., (madeo), madidas, dripping (with blood), Λ 54†.

Μύδων, ωνος, (1) son of Atymnios, charioteer of Pylaimenes, slain by Antilochos, Ε 580.—(2) a Paionian, slain by Achilleus, Φ 209.

μυελόεντα, ntr., (μυελός), medullosa, full of marrow, ι 293†.

μυελός, όν, masc., medulla, marrow, Υ 482; ἀνδρῶν, β 290, spoken of strengthening food.

μυθέομαι, pr., and ipf. ἐμυθεόμην (elsewh. unaugmented), iter. μυθέσκοντο, in ore habebant, used to call, Σ 289; fut. ἤσομαι, σεαι, aor. ἤσατο, etc., (μῦθος), say, speak, Η 76, Χ 184, α 124, λ 345; κειρομίας, utter taunts; with acc. with inf., Φ 462; report, Α 74, λ 328, β 202; with οἷος, describe, τ 245; relate, μ 155; also memorare, speak of, λ 517; interpretari, Α 74; communicate, ν 191.

μῦθο-λογεύειν, narrare, re'ate, τινί τι, μ 450.

μῦθος, οιο, ον, etc., dat. pl. οισ(ιν), masc., speech, opp. ἔργον, Ι 443; oratio, narratio, δ 597; sermo, conversation, δ 214; iussum, request, wish, o 196; consilium, counsels, Α 545; in general signif. = res, matter, its circumstances, its occasion; φ 71, demeanor, conduct.

μυίης, μυῖαν, αι, άων, ας, musca, house-fly, carrion-fly, horse-fly, the last as symbol of audacity, Ρ 570.

Μυκάλη, promontory in Asia Minor, opp. Samos, Β 869†.

Μυκάλησσός, town in Boiotia, Β 498†.

μυκάομαι, part. **μυκώμεναι**, aor. 3 sing. μύκε, 3 pl. μύκον, pf. μεμυκώς, plupf. ἐμεμύκει, (1) mugio, bellow, of cattle; of Skamandros in comparison, Φ 237.—(2) crepare, creak, grate, of city gates; resound, Υ 260.

μυκηθμοῦ, ῳ̃, masc., mugitus, lowing, bellowing, Σ 575 and μ 265.

Μυκήνη, daughter of Inachos, β 120; eponymous heroine of city **Μυκήνη** (-ηθεν, from M.), and ἦναι, Mykene or Mykenai, residence of Agamemnon; the inhabitants **Μυκηναῖοι**.

μύκον, aor. from μυκάομαι.

μυλάκεσσι, τοῖς, with millstones, then generally, mighty stones, cf. saxis, M 161†.

μύλης, ην, αι, mola, (hand) mill, ν 106. (Od.) Without doubt, not very different, except that they were of ruder make, from the Roman handmills found in Switzerland, and represented in the cut on next page.

μὔλη-φάτου (φένω), *cracked* or *ground in a mill*, β 355†.

μὔλο-ειδέϊ (μύλη), *like a millstone*, Η 270†.

μύνῃσι, ταῖς, (munio), *through excuses*, φ 111†.

Μύνης, ητος, son of Euenos, slain by Achilleus, Β 692 and Τ 296.

μὔρίκης, ην, ἵκαι Φ 350, ῥσιν, *tamarisk, marsh-shrub* (tamarix gallica Linn.), Κ 466. Hence μὔρῑκίνῳ ὄζῳ, *tamarisk-shoot*, Ζ 39†.

Μὔρίνη, an Amazon, whose funeral mound was called "Thorn-hill," Βατίεια, Β 814†.

μὔρίον, ίοι, ίαι, ίον, ί(α), innumerus, immensus, *countless*, θ 110, Β 468; μυρίον, with gen., immensum, *a vast quantity*, Φ 320.

Μυρμῐδόνες, εσσι, a Thrakian tribe in Phthiotis, followers of Achilleus, Π 269, Β 684, Α 180, λ 495; their chief centres, Phthia and Hellas.

μὔρονται, prs., part. and freq. ipf. 3 pl. μύρονθ', (mare), *flow, dissolve in tears, lament*, Τ 340; ἀμφί τινα, Τ 6.

Μύρσῐνος, village in Elis, later τὸ Μυρσύντιον, Β 616†.

Μυσοί, (1) a tribe on the Danube, Ν 5.—(2) kindred with foregoing, *Mysians* in Asia Minor, occupying territory from River Aisepos to Mount Olympos, Β 858, Κ 430, Ξ 512, Ω 278.

μυχμῷ, τῷ, (μύζω), fremitus, *moaning*, ω 416†.

μὔχοίτατος, φ 146, postremus, *farthest away from* (the rest); more common μὔχός, ῷ, όν, (όνδε, χ 270), ούς, *rear portion, inner part*, of hall, house, cave, harbors, Φ 23; hence μυχῷ, *in the farthest, innermost corner of*, penitus, κλισίης, Ἀργεος, σπείους.

μύω, aor. 3 pl. μὔσαν, *have closed*, Ω 637†.

μυῶν, nom. sing., gen. pl. ὠνων, masc., (μῦς, mus-culus), *mass of muscle, muscles*, Π 315, 324.

μῶλος, ον, masc., *tumult of battle*, Ρ 397; freq. with Ἄρηος, *moil of war*, Η 147.

μῶλυ, τό, *moly*, a magic herb, given by Hermes to Odysseus, to shield him against the spells of Circe, κ 305†. Identified by the ancients as a kind of *garlic* (allium nigrum Guan.).

μωμένη, subj. prs. from -εύω, ζ 274†, and μωμήσονται, fut. from -έομαι, Γ 412†, vituperet, -abunt, *blame, reproach* (μῶμος).

μῶμον, τόν, μ. ἀνάψαι, set a *brand of shame* upon us, β 86†.

μώνυχες, ας, explained by ancient commentators as μον-όνυχες, *single-, uncloven-hoofed*, solidis ungulis, Ε 236, opp. cattle and sheep; a derivation from μέμαα, *eager-, quick-footed*, has been proposed by modern scholars.

N.

νῦ ἐφελκυστικόν, affixed to follg. forms: pl. σι; εἴκοσι; suff. φι and νόσφι; the particle κε; and to forms of the verb ending in ε and ι of 3d person.

ναί (νή, nae, ne), *verily*, Α 286; also with μά, q. v.

ναιετάω, part. άων, όωσα, (α 404, Β 648), άοντα, prs. and ipf., iter. ναιετάασκον, (ναίω), habitare, versari,

inhabit, exist, Λακεδαίμονι, Γ 387; of
localities, are situated, inhabited, sita
est, dwells, where the island is conceived as a thing endowed with life =
exists, a 404; also transitive, B 539;
part. εὖ ναιετάων, etc., habitable.

ναίω, prs., (inf. ναιέμεν), and ipf.
(iter. ναίεσκε, ον), mid. ἐὖ ναιόμενον, η,
etc., inhabited, peopled, of cities, (ναοͅω),
(1) dwell, κατά, περί, πρός τι; ἐν,
παρά τινι; αἰθέρι, locat. enthroned in
the aether; νῆσοι, lie, B 626; trans.,
inhabit, οἰκία, Η 221, ν 288.—(2) 1 aor.
νάσσα οἱ πόλιν, δ 174, would have assigned him a town to dwell in; also 1
aor. pass. 3 sing. νάσθη Ἀργεῖ, sedes
posuit, settled in—, Ξ 119.

νάκην, τήν, αἰγός, hairy skin, ξ
530†.

νάπαι, αἱ, (γναμπτός), forest glens
or dells, Θ 558 and Π 300.

νάρκησε, aor. from ναρκάω, was
palsied, Θ 328†.

νάσθη, νάσσα, see ναίω.

νάσσω, aor. **ἔναξε**, stamped down,
γαῖαν, φ 122†.

Νάστης, son of Nomion, leader of
Karians, slain by Achilleus, B 867 sqq.

Ναυβολίδης, son of Naubolos, (1)
Iphitos, B 518.—(2) a Phaiakian, θ
116.

ναύ-λοχον, οἱ, (λεχ, λέκτο), ship-
sheltering, of harbors, δ 846 and κ 141.

ναύ-μάχα, pl. ntr., navalia, for
naval combat, of ship-pikes, O 389†.

ναῦς, see νηῦς.

Ναυσί-θοος, son of Poseidon, father
of Alkinoos, colonizes the Phaiakians
in Scheria, η 56 sqq.

Ναυσι-κάα, daughter of Alkinoos,
ζ 17 sqq., η 12, θ 457, 464.

ναυσι-κλειτοῖο, navibus clari, renowned for ships, intrepid seaman, ζ
22†, = **ναυσι-κλῦτοί**, epithet of Phaiakians and Phoenikians, ο 415.

ναῦται, άων, έων, φσι(ν), masc.,
nautae, sailors, Δ 76, θ 162.

Ναυτεύς, a Phaiakian, θ 112†.

ναυτιλίῃ, τῇ, navigatione, sea-
manship, θ 253†.

ναυτίλλεται, subj. εσθαι, inf., (ναυ-
τιλίη), navigat, sail, δ 672 and ξ 246.

ναῦφι(ν), see νηῦς.

νάει, ουσι, ipf. (νᾶον, v. l. and better),
ναῖον, flow; ὀρῷ, ran over with whey,
ι 222.

Νέαιρα (possibly personification of
new moon), name of nymph, mother
by Helios of Lampetie and Phaethusa,
μ 133†.

νεαροί (νέος), teněri, youthful, B
289†.

νεάτη, αι, elsewh. **νείατος**, ον, α,
(νέος), properly novissimus, always
local, extremus, last, B 824; infi-
mum, lowest; νείατος ἄλλων, imum e
ceteris.

νεβρῷ, όν, οἱ, ούς, masc., (νέος),
fawn, Θ 248; ἐλάφοιο, X 189; symbol
of timorousness, Δ 243.

νέες, εσσι, see νηῦς.

νέηαι, see νέομαι.

νεη-γενέας, τούς, (-γενής), new-born,
δ 336 and ρ 127.

νε-ήκεσι (ἀκή), freshly whetted, N 391
and Π 484.

νε-ήλύδες (ἤλυθον), newly come, K
434 and 558.

νεηνίῃ, ίαι, adolescenti, youth;
masc. ἀνδρί, ξ 524; fem. νεήνιδι, ισι,
maiden, η 20, Σ 418.

νείαι, see νέομαι.

νειαίρῃ, αιραν, (see νεάτη, from
νέος), inferior, lower; γαστήρ, lower
part of belly, abdomen, E 539. (Il.)

νείατος, see νεάτη.

νεικείω, subj. είῃσι, είῃ, inf. ειν, part.
ων, ipf. 3 pl. νείκειον, and iter. νεικεί-
εσκε, ον, other forms from νεικέω, 3 pl.
νεικεῦσι(ν), imp. νείκεε, ει, inf. εῖν, ipf.
νείκεε, (ἐ)νείκεον, iter. νεικέ'σκε· fut.
νεικέσω, aor. ἐνείκεσας, (ἐ)νείκεισ',
(νεῖκος), (1) quarrel, τινὶ εἵνεκά τινος,
ἔριδας καὶ νείκεα ἀλλήλοις, contend with
railing and strife, Υ 252.—(2) upbraid,
reprove, opp. αἰνεῖν, K 249, Ω 29; freq.
with ἐπέεσσιν and with adj., Γ 38, ρ
374; μάλα, angrily; ἄντην, face to
face, outright, ρ 239.

νεῖκος, εος, ει, εα, ntr., (νίκη?), heat
of combat, M 348; πολέμοιο, N 271;
in general, strife, Γ 87; of Trojan war,
ἔριδος νεῖκος, P 384; φυλόπιδος, Υ
140; iurgia, dissensions, Ξ 205; with
ἔρις, ν 267; quarrel, Ψ 483; dispute,
θ 75, Δ 37; lites, strife at law, μ 440;
reproof, 1 448; taunt, H 95.

νεῖμα = ἔνειμα, aor. from νέμω.

νειόθεν (νέος), from below, ἐκ κραδίης,
from the depths of his heart, K 10†,
and **νειόθι** λίμνης, far below in the
depths of the sea, Φ 317†.

νειοῦ, ῷ, όν, fem., (νέος), *new land, fallow land*, land newly ploughed after having lain fallow ; thrice ploughed, after such rest, in Σ 541, ε 127.

νεῖται, from νέομαι. νειφέμεν, v. l. for νιφέμεν.

νεκάδεσσιν, ταῖς, (νεκρός), *heaps of slain*, E 886†.

νεκρός, οἷο, οῦ, οἷσ(ιν), etc., (necare), mortuus, *dead*, τεθνηῶτα, μ 10 ; *corpse*, Ψ 197, Δ 467 ; also with (κατα) τεθνηῶτες, Z 71, Σ 540.

νέκτᾰρ, αρος, (νη-κτείνω), *nectar*, reddish, fragrant drink of the gods, Δ 3 ; preserves from decay, Τ 38 ; ἀπόρρωξ, lit. "fragment," sample of nectar, i. e. wine of the choicest sort, ι 359.

νεκτᾰρέου, ῳ, (νέκταρ), Γ 385, Σ 25, *fragrant, perfumed with nectar*.

νέκῦς, υος, υι, ῦν, ύες, ύων, ύεσσι(ν), ύσιν, ύας, ῦς, (necare), = νεκρός, mortuus, *dead*, as subst., Ψ 160, 168, 190, N 509 ; κατατεθνηῶτες, Η 409, λ 37, κ 530 ; *corpse*, Ω 108.

νεμέθοντο, ipf., pascebantur, *were feeding*, Λ 635†.

νεμεσῶ, subj. ῆσι, imp. α, ᾶτον, aor. νεμέσησαν, subj. σήσῃ, fut. mid. σήσεαι, σήσετ(αι), verbal adj. σητός, also νεμεσσῶμαι, σσᾶται, ipf. ἐνεμέσσα, aor. mid. σσήσαιτο, aor. pass. νεμεσσήθη, θητε, θεν, Β 223 ; θωμεν, θείς, θεῖσα, verbal adj. σσητόν, (νέμεσις), *take it ill, be vexed with*, τινί (τι), ζ 286, Ψ 494 ; indignari, *be angry with*, with part. φ 169, with οὕνεκα ; mid., indignari (esp. aor. pass.), *become angry*, τί, τινί ; with relative, α 158, or infin. clause, irasci ; verbal adj., *causing indignation, reprehensible*, iniquum; only Λ 649, magni faciendus, reverendus, *to be dreaded*.

νεμεσίζομ(αι), only sing. prs. (imp. -ζέσθω), and ipf. νεμεσίζετο, (νέμεσις), magni facere, revereri, *dread, fear*, θεούς ; *be wroth with for*, τινί τι, Ε 757 ; followed by acc. and inf., Β 296 ; *be ashamed*, Ρ 254, β 138.

νέμεσις, ἐσσί Ζ 335, ιν, fem., ignominia, *disgrace*, N 122, Z 351 ; (ἐξ) ἀνθρώπων, *censure of men* ; οὐ νέμεσις, non vituperandum, *'tis no cause for anger*.

νεμεσσάω, σσητόν, see νεμεσῶ, νεμέσσ(ε)ι, see νέμεσις.

νέμει, τῷ, ntr., (νέμεσθαι), *wood-pasture, glade*, Λ 480.

νέμει, prs., ipf. νέμε, ἔνεμον, aor. ἔνειμε, νεῖμεν, αν, imp. νεῖμον, (1) distribuere, *dispense*, τινί τι, ζ 188.— (2) pascere, *drive to pasture*, ι 233 ; pass. νέμοιτο, consumeretur, *was consumed*, only Β 780 ; mid. (1) pasci, *feed, browse, graze*, νέμεαι, ονται, εσθαι, Ε 777, υ 164 ; (2) frui, *feed one's self upon, possess*, νέμεται, ὁμεσθ(α), subj. ηαι, opt. οιτο, Z 195, Ψ 177.—(3) incolere, *inhabit*, νέμονται, ἐνέμοντο, Υ 8, Β 496, 751.

νένιπται, see νίζω.

νεο-αρδέ(α), acc. (ἄρδω), *freshly watered*, Φ 346†.

νεο-γῐλῆς, *new-born*, σκύλακος, μ 86†.

νεό-δαρτον (δείρω), *newly flayed*, χ 363†.

νεο-θηλέα, acc. (θάλλω), *fresh-sprouting*, Ξ 347†.

νεοίη (νέος), adolescentia, *youth, youthful thoughtlessness*, Ψ 604†.

νέομαι and νεῦμαι, νεῖαι, νεῖται, νίονται, subj. νέηαι, ηται, ὠμεθ(α), opt. νεοίμην, μεθα, οίατο, imp. νεέσθω, σθων, inf. νεόμην, νέοντο, (νεσσομαι, νισσομαι), often with fut. signif., (1) redire, *return*, οἰκόνδε, λ 176, ο 72, σ 241, ω 460, Μ 32, κὰρ ρόον.—(2) ire, *go*, Υ 6, Ξ 335, δ 8, ξ 261; venire, *come*, χ 484; ὑπὸ ζόφον, Ψ 51.—(3) abire, *go away*, φ 374.

νέον, see νέος.

νεο-πενθέα (πένθος), *fresh-mourning*, θυμόν, λ 39†.

νεό-πλῠτα (πλύνω), *newly washed*, ζ 64†.

νεο-πρίστου (πρίω), *fresh-sawn*, θ 404†.

Νεο-πτόλεμος, son of Achilleus, educated in Skyros, Τ 327; conducts the Myrmidons home from Troja, weds Hermione, daughter of Menelaos, γ 189, δ 5; slays Eurypylos, λ 520.

νέος, οιο, ον, etc., no dat. pl., νέην, αι, νέον, α ; comp. νεώτερος, ου, ῳ, ον, ω, οι ; sup. νεώτατος, η, (novus, new), novus, recens, *new, fresh*, opp. παλαιοί, δ 720, θ 58 ; adolescens, *young* (ἑταῖροι), Α 463 ; also substantively, τ 433, Ι 36, θ 202 ; νέον, nuper, *just now, lately*, π 181, 199.

νεός, see νηῦς.

νεο-σμήκτων (σμάω), *freshly polished*, N 342†.

νεοσσοί, οἷσι, (νέος), pulli, *young* (birds), B 311, I 323.

νεό-στροφον (στρέφω), *newly twisted*, νευρήν, O 469†.

νεο-τεύκτου (τεύχω), *newly wrought*, κασσιτέροιο, Φ 592†.

νεο-τευχέες, pl. from -τευχής, (τεύχω), new'y made, E 194†.

νεότητος, τῃς, (νέος), adolescentia, *youth*, Ξ 86, Ψ 445.

νε-ουτάτου, ον, (οὐτάω), *lately wounded*, Σ 536, N 539.

νί-ποδες (νέω), *web-footed*, lit. "swimfooted;" or better, with Curtius, *offspring*. cf. Lat. nepos, δ 404†.

νέρθε(ν), adv., (ἔνερος), *below*, H 212, Λ 535 ; with gen., *under*, γῆς, λ 302.

Νεστόρεος, adj. from Νέστωρ, Θ 192, 113, B 54.

Νεστορίδης, *son of Nestor*, (1) Antilochos, O 589.—(2) Peisistratos, δ 71, o 6, 44, 202 ; pl. Antilochos and Thrasymedes, Π 317.

Νέστωρ, ορος, son of Neleus and Chloris, king in Pylos, Γερήνιος ἱππότα, B 336 ; ὁ γέρων, Λ 637 ; t1 i sec l i s e n e x, survivor of three generations of men, A 247 sqq. ; λιγὺς Πυλίων ἀγορητής, A 248, Δ 293 ; his youthful exploits, Δ 319, Λ 669 sqq., A 262 sqq., Ψ 630 sqq. ; after the Trojan war, again in Pylos, γ 17, cf. 412 sqq.

νεύμαι = νέομαι.

νευρή, ῆς, ῆσι(ν), ῇ, ήν, fem., (σνευρή, Schnur), *bow-string*, Δ 118, Θ 300.

νεῦρον, α, ntr., (νερϜον, nervus), *sinew, tendon, of body*, Π 316 ; *bowstring*, Δ 122 ; *cord*, with which the arrow-head was bound to the shaft, Δ 151.

νευστάζων, part. prs., (νεύω), *nodding*, Υ 162 ; κεφαλῇ, *letting the head droop* ; ὀφρύσι, *giving a sign by nodding* with the eyebrows, innuens, μ 194.

νεύοιεν, οντα, όντων, ipf. ἔνευε and νεῦον, aor. νεῦσ(εν), from νεύω, nuo, *nod;* capite, π 283, I 223, N 133 ; annuit, promisit, *assent or promise by a nod*, Θ 246 ; but κεφαλάς, demittere, *let* their heads *hang down* ; often also of helmet, of plume, *nod*, Γ 337, χ 124.

νεφέλη, ῃ, ην, αι, άων, ῃσι(ν), ας, fem., (κνεφ., nebula), nubes, *cloud;*

ἄχεος, grief's *dark cloud* enshrouded him, P 591.

νεφελ-ηγερέτα, nom., (ἀγείρω), Ζεύς, Zeus, *the cloud-compeller, cloud-gatherer,* A 511, a 63.

νέφος, εῖ, εα, έων, (έ)εσσι(ν), ntr., (κνέφας, δνοφερός, nebula), nubes, *cloud*, Δ 275 ; θυόεν, fragrant, O 153 ; ἀχλύος, dark mist ; θανάτου μέλαν ν., *death's gloomy cloud*, Π 350, δ 180 ; the gods have at control red, blue, black, and golden clouds. *Thick cloud, company*, Ψ 133, P 755.

I. νέων, ipf. ἔννεον, (σνεϜω), *n a r e, swim*, Φ 11, ε 344.

II. νέω, aor. mid. νήσαντο, (n e r e), *have spun* to him with the thread, η 198†.

νη-, *negative prefix*, as in Lat. neuter, nemo, noenum (nenum), nullus.

νῆα, νηάδε, see νηῦς.

νη-γάτεον, ῳ, (νέον, γέγαα), *newmade*, B 43 and Ξ 185.

νήγρετος, ον, (νη, ἐγείρω), *without waking*, εὕδειν, ὕπνος, *deep*, ν 80.

νηδύίοισι, τοῖς, ntr., (νηδύς), intestinis. *bowels*, P 524†.

νή-δυμος, ον, ὕπνος, *fast, deep sleep*, B 2, ν 79 ; derivation doubtful, possibly from δύη, "pain," i. e. *painless, refreshing without pain ; yet* see Curtius.

νήδυος, νηδύν, fem., *belly, stomach*, N 290, ι 296 ; *womb*, Ω 496.

νῆες, νήεσσι, see νηῦς.

νηέω, ipf. νήει, νήεον, aor. νήησαν, ῆσαι, ήσας, (νέω), *heap or pile up*, Ψ 139 ; upon wagon or car, ἐπ᾿ ἀπήνης ; *fill with cargo*, I 358, and mid. νηησάσθω, σασθαι νῆα, fill one's ship with cargo.

Νηιάς, αδες, κοῦραι Διός, ν 104, 356, *Naiads*, pl. from Νηΐς, Υ 384, Z 22.

Νήιον, *spur of Mount Neriton in Ithaka*, α 186†.

νήϊον (νηῦς), with and without δόρυ, *ship-timber*, Γ 62, ι 384.

νηΐς, see Νηιάς.

νῆϊς, ϊδα, (νη-ίδμεναι), ignarus, *unpracticed in*, ἀέθλων, θ 179 ; absol., *inexperienced*, H 198.

νη-κερδέα, δές, (κέρδος), *useless*, P 469, ξ 509.

νηκούστησε, aor. from νηκουστέω, (νη-ἀκουστός), οὐδ᾿ — θεᾶς, *nor did he disob y* the goddess, Υ 14.

νηλεής 219 νίζειν

νηλεής, sync. νηλής, νηλεῖ, ἑα; εἴς, (νη-έλεος), pitiless, ruthless, often relentless, fig. of θυμός, ἦτορ, δεσμῷ, χαλκῷ, ἦμαρ, day of death, ὕπνῳ, irresistible, μ 372.

Νηλείδης, Nestor, Ψ 652 = Νηληϊάδης.

νηλείτιδες, fem. from νη-ἀλείτης, guiltless, innocent, π 317; v. l. νηλίτεῖς.

Νηλεύς, ῆος, son of Poseidon and of Tyro, husband of Chloris, λ 254, 281; father of Pero, o 233, and of Nestor; driven by his brother Pelias from Iolkos in Thessaly, he wanders to Messenia and founds Pylos, γ 4; in war with Herakles, all his twelve children were slain except Nestor, Λ 692; who is called Νηλιάδης, Θ 100, Ο 378, Λ 618; Νηλήιος, Neleian, Ψ 514, Λ 597, Β 20.

νηλής, see word before Νηλείδης.

νηλιτεῖς, see νηλείτιδες.

νῆμα, νήματος, τα, ntr., (II. νέω), that which is spun, yarn, β 98. (Od.)

νημερτής, έ(α), ές, adv. έως, (ἁμαρτάνω), unerring, infallible, verax; νόος, candidus; ntr. with εἰπεῖν, etc., verum (a) dicere, speak the truth, γ 101.

Νημερτής, ή, a Nereid, Σ 46†.

νηνεμίη, ης, fem. from νήνεμος, Θ 556, (νη-ἄνεμος), windless, breeze!ess; also as subst., calm, Ε 523, ε 392.

νηός, ῷ, όν, ούς, masc., (ναίω), dwelling of a god, temple, Α 39, ζ 10; for an idea of the interior of the cella, cf. cut under βωμός, with statue of Aphrodite and altar.

νηός, gen. from νηῦς.

νη-πενθές (πένθος), soothing sorrow, epith. of Egyptian magic drug which lulled sorrow for a day (Opium?), δ 221†.

νηπιάας, see νηπιέη.

νηπιάχεύων (νηπίαχος), playing childishly, Χ 502†.

νηπίαχον, οι, οις, (νήπιος), childish, Β 338.

νηπιέη, έγσι(ν), άας, (νήπιος), infancy, Ι 491; childish follies, α 297.

νήπιος, ον, ε, οι; η; α, (νη-πυ, im-pu-bes, puer?), young; offspring, Ρ 134; common phrase, ν. τέκνα, also of animals; foolish, blind, Β 873; with αὔτως, so young! Ζ 400; infantile, feeble, βίη.

νή-ποινοι(ποινή), inulti, unavenged, α 380, β 145; νήποινον, impune, with impunity, α 160.

νη-πύτιον, ι(ε), ιοι, ίοισιν, children, Υ 244; foolish, Υ 211.

Νηρηΐδες, Nereids, Σ 38, 49, 52, the daughters of Nereus, the old man of the sea, who is never mentioned in Homer by name, but only as ἅλιος γέρων, Α 538.

Νήρικον, orig. a promontory on the coast of Akarnania; later, by cutting through an isthmus, the island of Leukas; subjugated by Laertes, ω 377†.

Νήριτον, mountain in northern part of Ithaka, ν 351, Β 632, ι 22.

Νήριτος, an Ithakan, ρ 207†.

νήριτος, see εἴκοσιι-ήριτ'.

Νησαίη, a Nereid, Σ 40†.

νῆσος, ου, ῳ, ον, οι, ων, οισι(ν), ους, fem., (νέω, nare), island, α 85, Β 108.

νήστιες, ίας, (νη-ἔδω), not eating, fasting, σ 370. (Od.)

νητός, adj., (νέω, νηέω), piled up, β 338†.

νηῦς, νηός, ί (dat. of accompaniment, λ 161), α, ές, ῶν, εσσι, and νηυσί, ας, and νηάδε; also τὴν νέα, pl. νέες, ῶν, εσσιν, and ναῦφιν, νέας (νέω, nare), navis, ship; its parts, as named in Homer (see cut under ἔδαφος), are as follows: of the hull, τρόπις, πρώρη, πρύμνη, ἐπηγκενίδεσσι, πηδάλιον, οἴϊα, ἱστός, ἱστοπέδη, ἱστοδόκη, ζυγά, κληΐδες, κώπη, ἐρετμά, τροπός; of the rigging, ἱστία, πείσματα, πόδες, ἐπι- and πρότυνος, πρυμνήσια; see these words separately. When the word stands alone, ship of war is commonly implied; ν. φορτίδος, ship of burden, ε 250, ι 323; pl. νῆες, freq. signifies in Iliad camp, including νῆες and κλισίαι, Β 688. (See also plate IV., at end of volume.)

νηχέμεναι, inf. prs., ipf. νῆχε, ον, and νηχόμενος, οι, οισι, fut. νήξομ(αι), (σνήχω), natare, swim, ε 375. (Od.)

νίζειν, imp. νιζ(ε), ipf. νίζε, ον, and mid. νίζετο, fut. νίψω, ει, aor. νίψ(εν), imp. νίψον, mid. aor. νίψατο, ασθαι, ἀμένος, οι, (νίγjω, νιβ), lavare, wash, τινὰ πόδας, the hands and feet for some one, τὶ ἀπό τινος, abluere, wash off; mid. wash one's self; χεῖρας, wash one's hands; with dat. of place (locative), Π 229; ἁλός, with water from the sea; χρόα ἄλμην, washed off from his body the salt sea-spray, ζ 224; pass. νένιπται αἷμα, the blood is washed off.

νικᾷς, ᾷ, etc., prs., ipf. (ἐ)νίκα, (ἐ)νίκων, iter. νικάσκομεν, fut. νικήσει, ουσι, ἔμεν, aor. ἐνίκησα, ας, ε, and νίκησα, etc., pass. aor. νικηθείς, θέντι, (νίκη), vincere, conquer, with dat. of manner; surpass, excel, with dat. of means; vanquish, be superior to, τινά τινί, e. g. ἀγορῇ, κάλλεϊ, μάχῃ, πόδεσσι, πύξ; phrases: Ψ 604, youth got the better of judgment; λ 545, gain a victory; σ 319, shall not outwatch me.

νίκη, only in sing., victory, in battle and before the tribunal, λ 544; νίκης πείρατα, Η 102, cords of victory.

Νιόβη, daughter of Tantalos, wife of Amphion, king of Thebes. She exultingly compared her twelve children with the two (Apollo and Artemis) of Leto, and was punished by the death of all her children: the six sons by the arrows of Apollo; the daughters by the arrows of Artemis, while she herself, in grief at their death, was changed to stone. The legend arose from a natural rock-figure in Mount Sipylos, which resembles a woman in sitting posture, Ω 602, 606.

νίπτω, see νίζω.

Νιρεύς, ῆος, son of Charopos and Aglaia of Syme, the most beautiful of the Greeks next to Achilleus, Β 671 sqq.

Νῖσα, village on Mount Helikon in Boiotia, Β 508†.

Νῖσος, son of Aretos, father of Amphinomos of Dulichion, π 395, σ 127, 413.

νίσομαι, νίσσεται, ὁμεθα, ὁμενον, ipf. νίσσοντο, (νέσσομαι), ire, go, πόλεμόνδε, into the combat; ἀβιρε, Μ 119; redire, οἴκαδε.

Νίσυρος, small island, one of the Sporades, Β 676†.

νιφάς, άδες, άδεσσι, fem., (σνιφ., nives, snow), snow, Ο 170; flakes, χιόνος, Μ 278. (Il.)

νιφετός, όν, (νιφάς), snow-storm, snows, nives, Κ 7 and δ 566.

νιφόεντος, τι, τα, (νιφάς), nivosi, snow-clad, snow-capped, Ν 754, τ 338, Kreta, Olympos, Tmolos, Thrakian mountains.

νιφέμεν, inf., (νιφάς), ningere, snow, Μ 280†. (v. l. νείφεμεν.)

νίψ, νιψάμενος, etc., see νίζω.

νοέω, εις, imp. νόει, part. νοέοντι, ούσῃ, ipf. νόει, fut. νοήσω, εις, ει, aor. ἐνόησα, σας, σ(εν), and νόησα, εν, subj. σῃ, imp. νόησον, inf. νοῆσαι, part. σας. mid. aor. νοήσατο, (γι-γνώ-σκω?), (1) sentire, perceive, observe, become aware of, Χ 136, Ο 453, Γ 396, π 5; freq. with part., υ 367 and Β 391, Γ 21, 30, Δ 200, Χ 463, δ 653; ὀξὺ ν., sharply or quickly see, discern, Γ 374; (ἐν) ὀφθαλμοῖς (Ω 294), Ο 422; coupled with θυμῷ and οἶδα, σ 228; φρεσίν, α 322; see with mind, discern, Α 343; ἐπεφράσατο, θ 94; ἀθρεῖν, τ 478.—(2) think, Κ 247; ἀλλα, of something else, Ψ 140, 193, β 393; πεπνυμένα πάντα, think always prudent thoughts, σ 230; ἐναίσιμον, η 299.—(3) imagine, devise, ρ 576; μῦθον, Η 358; νόον, Ι 104; τεχνήσομαι ἠδὲ ν., Ψ 415.—(4) ponder, reflect (ἐν and μετά, γ 26, Υ 310), φρεσί, Ο 81; μετὰ φρ. καὶ κατὰ θυμόν, Υ 264; with ὅππως, ο 170, Κ 224; νοέων, π 136, ρ 193; prudent, discreet, Α 577, Ψ 305.—(5) be minded, intend, φρεσί, with inf., Χ 235, Ω 560; τί, Α 543.—(6) think of, remember to, with inf., Ε 665, cf. ι 442; οὐ ν., with inf. (mid. only Κ 501), Ι 537, λ 62, with subst. clause, Υ 264, Χ 445, nor did she think.

νόημα, ατος, τι, τα, σι, (νοέω), that which is thought, thought, β 363; idea, Η 456; abstract, η 36; plan, Ρ 409; wish, Κ 104, Σ 328; schemes, β 121; reason, υ 346, Τ 218; disposition, character, ζ 183, Ω 40, η 292, σ 215; sense, heart, υ 82.

νοήμονες (νοεῖν), discreet, β 282, ν 209. (Od.)

Νοήμων, ονος, (1) a Lykian, slain by Odysseus, Ε 678.—(2) son of Phronios in Ithaka, δ 630, β 386.—(3) a Pylian, Ψ 612.

νόθος, ον, ην, (ἄνθος, ἐνήνοθε), illegitimate son, or, Ν 173, daughter.

νομεύς, ῆες, ῆας, masc., (νέμω), pastor, shepherd, Ο 632; ἄνδρες, Ρ 65.

νομεύων, part., ipf. ἐνόμευε, (νομεύς), pascere, pasture, ι 217, 336. (Od.)

Νομίων, father of Nastes and Amphimachos of Karia, Β 871†.

νομός, οῖ, ῷ, όν, (νέμομαι), pascua, pasture, Ε 587; ἐπέων, fig. wide is the field of words, on this side, and on that, i. e. varied is their range of meaning, Υ 249 ; ὕλης, woodland pasture.

νόος, οιο, ου, ῳ, ον, (γιγνώσκω), (1) *consciousness*, κ 240, 494 ; *power of thought, understanding, prudence*, μετὰ φρεσί, Σ 419 ; ἐν στήθεσι, ν 366 ; νόῳ, *cunningly*, Α 132 ; *wisely*, ζ 320 ; Ο 643, πέπνυσαι ; νόῳ, Ω 377 ; with βουλή, μ 211, π 374, δ 267.—(2) *thought, thoughts*, Ο 80, τ 479.—(3) *desire* or *aim;* here follow a variety of shades of meaning, all covered by the single English word *mind*, e. g. ὀρνυται, α 347 ; μενοινᾷ, β 92, Χ 382, β 124 ; with θυμός, *thought* and *wish*, Δ 309 ; *disposition*, σ 136, Π 35, γ 147, ζ 121, ν 229, α 3 ; *thought*, Ι 104 ; *design, counsel*, Διός, Ο 242, Π 103, Ρ 176, ξ 490, Ο 699, 52, δ 493, ε 23 ; *interior of one's soul, heart*, κεῦθε νόῳ, Α 363, ω 474 ; ἴσχανε, τ 42. Cf. Γ 63, θ 78 ; *thought* (intention, plan), Ψ 149, δ 256, χ 215 ; νόος καὶ μῆτις, *reason* and reflection, Κ 226, Ψ 590, τ 326.

νόσος, see νοῦσος.

νοστέω, only fut. **νοστήσω**, inf. σέμεν and σειν, and aor. νοστήσῃ, etc., (νόστος), r e d i r e, *return*, in various signif., but esp. φίλην ἐς πατρίδα γαῖαν, οἴκαδε, ὄνδε δόμονδε, ἐκ —, out of dangers, Τροίης, πυρός, Κ 247 ; πολέμοιο ; κεῖσέ με νοστήσαντα, while I tarried there on my return home.

νόστιμος (νόστος), r e d i t u r u s, *destined to return*, ν 333, δ 806 ; νόστιμον ἧμαρ, day of one's return.

νόστος, οιο, ου, ῳ, ον, masc., (νέομαι), r e d i t u s, *return home;* Ἀχαιΐδος, to Achaia; ν 379, *his delayed return;* ε 344, νόστου, *return*, namely to the land of the Phaiakians.

νόσφ(ιν), (1) s e o r s u m, *apart, away;* ἀπό, from. — (2) *aloof from, except*, with gen. = s i n e, θεῶν, Ἀχαιῶν; Β 346, form their plans *at variance with* those of the Achaians.

νοσφίζεαι, οἴμεθα, prs., aor. νοσφίσατο, (σ)σαμένη, ην, aor. pass. νοσφισθείς, (νόσφι), d i s c e d e r e, *depart from, τινός ; τινά* (Od.), d e r e l i n q u e r e, *abandon;* n e g l e g e r e, *disregard*, Ω 222.

νοτίῃσι, ταῖς, (νότιος), i m b r i b u s, *rains, showers*, Θ 307†.

νότιος, ῳ, (νότος), h u m i d u s, ntr., *harbor water, roadstead*, δ 785.

Νότος, οιο, ου, (Ger. n e t z e n, n a s s), *south wind*, bringing rain, Β 145, γ 295; ἀργεστᾶο, Λ 306, Φ 334.

νοῦς, see νόος.

νοῦσος, ῳ, ον, fem., m o r b u s, p e s t i l e n t i a, *sickness, disease*, Α 10.

νῦ(ν), enclitic, *now; νύ περ, of course*, just *now;* Γ 164, *doubtless, methinks;* οὔ νυ, *surely* not ; τί νυ, q u i d t a n d e m, why *pray!*

νυκτερίς, ίδες, fem., (νύξ), v e s p e r t i l i o, *bat*, μ 433 and ω 6.

νύμφη, ης, ῃ, ην, ᾰ, αι, ἀων, ῃς, ᾱς, (n u b o), *bride*, Σ 492 ; also of married woman still comparatively young, Γ 130.

Νύμφη, *goddess of subordinate rank, Nymph*, e. g. Kalypso, ε 153 ; Kirke, κ 543 ; Naiads, ν 107 ; mountainnymphs, Ζ 420, ζ 123 ; offerings made to them, ρ 211, μ 318 ; Phaethusa and Lampetie, μ 132 ; κοῦραι Διός, ζ 105.

νυμφίου, ίον, masc., (νύμφη), *newly married*, η 65 and Ψ 223.

νῦν (n u n c), *now*, of present time, more or less protracted ; *νῦν δή*, n u n c i a m, n u n c t a n d e m, *now at this moment, just now*, Β 435 ; νῦν αὖ, but *now*, ν 149 ; ν. αὖτε, now on the contrary, now once more, Α 237, Ε 117 ; used with preterit tenses, where an unexpected result discloses a truth at variance with one's previous supposition, νῦν δέ, n u n c a u t e m, but *now*, Α 417.

νύξ, νυκτός, τί, τ(α) and νύχθ᾽, νύκτες, ῶν, ᾰς = n o x, *night*, acc. with φυλάσσειν, ἰαύειν, watch, sleep *the livelong night ; νύκτας τε καὶ ἧμαρ*, n o c t u d i u q u e ; διὰ νύκτα, of space and time, Β 57 ; ἀνὰ νύκτα, νυκτός, ἐπὶ νυκτί, n o c t u ; *by night*, ο 34 ; also fig. *the night of death*, Ε 310. As goddess, *Night*, Ξ 259.

νυόν, οί, ούς, fem., (σνυσον, n u r u m, S c h n u r), n u r u s, *sister-in-law*, Γ 49.

Νυσήιον, τό, *region about Nysa*, where Dionysos grew up, Ζ 133†.

νύσσα, ης, ῃ, fem., m e t a, *turning post*, or *pillar*, round which the chariots turned, and returned to the starting-point, Ψ 332 ; elsewh. *starting-point* or *line*.

νύσσων, οντες, pass. ὀμένων, aor. νύξ(εν), ᾰς, *prick, pierce*, Η 704 ; esp.

with weapons, M 395; τινά τι, Υ 487, Λ 563.

νῶ, see νῶι.

νωθής (νη- ὄθεσθαι?), iners, *lazy*, Λ 559†.

νῶι, nom., (νῶι(ν) gen. dat., νῶι, νώ acc. du., (nos), *we* (two); Π 99, νῶιν, dat.

νωΐτερον, ην, *of us both*, O 39 and μ 185.

νωλεμές (νη-ορεμές, ἠρέμα), *without pause*, Ξ 58; freq. with αἰεί at the close of verse, χ 228; adv. νωλεμέως, *unceasingly*; *firmly*, Δ 428.

νωμάω, νωμᾷς, ᾷ, ῶν, prs., ipf. ἐνώμων, ας, α, νῶμα, aor. νώμησεν, σαν, σαι, (νέμω), distribuere, dispen-

sare, *deal out, distribute*, food and drink, A 471; *ply*, πόδας καὶ γούνατα; huc illuc versare, *handle, wield* (weapons); *hold, control*, πόδα, the sheet; οἰήια, the rudder; esp. νόον, ν 255, *revolve*; κέρδεα, shrewd plans.

νώνυμος, ον, νωνύμνους, (νη-ὄνομα), inglorius, *nameless*, α 222, M 70.

νώροπι, α, (nero, ἀνήρ), only of χαλκός, *manly*, as man's defense, B 578, H 206, ω 467.

νῶτον, ον, ῳ, α, οισι(ν), (nates) tergum, *back*, also pl., cf. terga; *back pieces*, as best portions of meat at feast, H 321; θαλάσσης, B 159.

νωχελίη, τῇ, (νη-ώκύς), inertiae, tarditati, *sloth*, T 411†.

Ξ.

ξαίνειν (ξέω), *comb* or *card* wool, χ 423†.

ξανθός, ῷ, όν, ή, ῆς, ήν, άς, ά, (1) flavus, *blond, fair*; κάρη, fair countenanced, ο 133; κόμης, A 197; τρίχες, ν 399; of mortals and of Demeter.—(2) *sorrel*, of horses, Λ 680.

Ξάνθος, (1) son of Phainops, a Trojan, E 152, slain by Diomedes.—(2) *Sorrel*, name of one of the horses of Achilleus, Π 149; of Hektor, Θ 185. —(3) (a) river in Lykia, flowing from Mount Tauros into the Mediterranean, B 877; (b) another name for the Trojan Skamandros, Φ 15, Ξ 434, Z 4. Personified as god of this stream, Υ 40, 74, Φ 146.

ξεινῆιον, α, (ξεῖνος), *gift given by host to his guest on his departure*, K 269; *between host and guest*, Z 218; hospitium, *entertainment*, Σ 408; ironically: *hospitable return*, ι 370; *recompense*, χ 290; as adj. joined with δῶρα, ω 273.

ξεινίζειν (ξεῖνος), hospitio excipere, *receive as guest*, γ 355; fut. ξεινίσσομεν, aor. (ἐ)ξείνισσα, ε, and ξεινίσαι, σας, *entertain*.

ξείνιος, ον, ον, and ξένιον, hospitalis, Zeus, *protector of guests* (strangers), N 625, ι 271; τράπεζα, *hospitable*

table, ξ 158; as subst. (sc. δῶρον, α), *gift bestowed upon the guest*, ξεινιον, ια, ξεινίων, ν 296, ξ 404, ο 514; παραθεῖναι, δοῦναι.

ξεινο-δόκος, ου, ῳ, ον, οι, (δέκομαι), *hospitable*, ἀνήρ, ο 55; *host*, σ 64.

ξεῖνος, οιο, ου, ῳ, ον, οι, ων, οισ(ιν), ους, *strange*, ἄνθρωποι, πάτερ; elsewh. as subst., hospes, *stranger, guest*, under the protection of Ζεὺς ξείνιος; *guest-friend*, which relation existed from the time when ξεινήια, as pignora, were exchanged; hence hereditary, πατρώιος, Z 215.

ξεινοσύνης, τῆς, *hospitality*, φ 35.

ξενίη, τῇ, hospitio, *entertainment*, ω 286; μίξεσθαι, hospitio mutuo usuros, enjoy each the hospitality of the other, ω 314.

ξένιος, see ξείνιος.

ξερόν, τό, *dry land*, ε 402†.

ξέσσε, aor. from ξέω.

ξεστοῦ, οἷο, ῶν, οἷσι, όν, (ξέω), *hewn, polished*, of cut stone, αἴθουσαι; *polished*, τ 566.

ξέω, ipf. ἔξεον, aor. ξέσσε(ν), *smooth, hew, po'ish*, ψ 199, ε 245. (Od.)

ξηραίνω, only aor. pass. ἐξηράνθη, *was dried up*, Φ 345.

ξίφος, εος, εῖ, ει, ἐεσσ(ι), (ξύω), *sword*,

Δ 530, λ 97; a *two-edged sword*, united by bands of dark metal (μελάνδετον) to the hilt (κώπῃ, ἀργυροήλῳ), worn in a sheath (κουλεός); sword and sheath were suspended by a strap (τελαμών) passing over the shoulder. (See adjacent cut.) [ῐ]

ξύλον, α, Ψ 327, truncus, *trunk of a tree;* pl. ligna, *wood.*

ξυλόχοιο, ῳ, ον, *thicket, jungle,* Λ 415, δ 335.

ξυμ-, form used in compounds of βάλλω, πᾶς, and ξυν-, in composition with ἀγείρω, ἄγνυμι, ἄγω, δέω, ἐλαύνω, ἔσεσθαι, ἔχω, ἰέναι, ἱέναι,—ξύνεσις and ξυνοχή, see under συμ-, συν-.

ξυν-εείκοσι, *twenty together,* ξ 98†.

ξυν-έηκε, ἑηχ΄, ες, see συν-ίημι.

ξυνήϊα (ξυνός), communia, *common property,* Α 124, Ψ 809.

ξυνίει, ιον, see συν-ίημι.

ξυνιόντος, ξύνισαν, see σύν-ειμι.

ξυνός, ή, όν = κοινός, communis, *common,* Ο 193 ; Ἐννάλιος, *even-handed, changing.*

ξυροῦ, ntr., (ξύω), ἐπὶ — ἀκμῆς, is poised upon a *razor's* edge, hangs by a hair, in ipso discrimine, Κ 173†.

ξυστόν, ῷ, οἶσι, (ξύω), hastile, (*polished*) *shaft* of a spear; ναύμαχον, ship-*pike.*

ξύω, ipf. ξῦον, aor. ἔξῦσε, (ξέω), *scrape,* χ 456; *make smooth,* Ξ 179.

O.

ὁ-, protheticum (= ἁ copulat.), see ὄτριχας, ὅπατρος, οἰετέας.

ὁ, ἡ, τό, (Goth. sa, sô, thata); peculiar forms : τοῖο, τοῦιν, τοί, τοῖσι, ταί, τάων, τῇς(ι), I. demonstr., (a) simply pointing out, (1) substantively, Α 9, 12, 29, 43, 55, 57, 58, Ο 539; τοῖσι μετέφη, spoke among *them;* ἐκ τοῦ, exinde, since then, ever since; ὁ δέ,

emphatic, accompanying not change of subj., but fresh act of same subject, nearly = αὐτός δε, Α 191; anticipatively, *it* indeed (the spear) no one thought of, to draw out = no one thought of drawing it out, Ε 665, Ο 599, Ρ 406; repeated in simile, Β 459. —(2) before an appositional subst. nearly = hic ille, indicating something as present, before one, known, etc., A 20, these things, as ransom, ν 215, Α 33, ὁ γέρων, he, the old man, Λ 637, Α 11, ρ 10, Α 207, 167; Λ 69, the handfuls (as every one knows) fall; denoting opposition, Δ 399, λ 4, Κ 498, ι 375; with second of two substantives, χ 104, ν 310; with the first of several appositives, Λ 660; in arsis of first foot for emphasis, θ 388, τ 483, α 351; in classification with μέν—δέ, ξ 435, Ε 145, μ 73; in antithesis often only in second member, Β 217, Ν 616.—(b) referring back to what has already been mentioned, μ 201, Α 33, γ 306; ὁ δε, after hypothetical relative sentence, λ 148; emphasizing the subject, Δ 491; with partitive division of numbers, Ε 272.—(c) calling attention to something which follows, before relative clause, Κ 322, ψ 28, φ 42; after substantive, especially in arsis of first foot, Δ 41, Ε 320, Ι 631, κ 74.—II. individualizing, fulfilling the proper function of the article, (a) rendering adj. substantive, ρ 218, Π 53, ξ 12, Α 576, Ψ 702, 325, 663, Φ 262, Θ 430, Ψ 572; here belong also, Λ 613, τὸ πρίν, τὸ πάρος, τὰ πρῶτα; never, in this use. before inf., which is to be construed as appositive of τό, e. g. harmful is this, to watch (cf. ·ν 52, α 370); (b) preceding the attribute, e. g. ὁ καλὸς παῖς, Κ 536, Ξ 376, Δ 42, λ 515, Ξ 503, Ο 37, Κ 408, Ξ 274; inversion of usual position of attribute, owing often to requirements of metre, e. g. ὁ παῖς καλός, Φ 317, Α 340, λ 492; (c) preceding the appositive (but only once expressed), λ 298, Λ 288, Ξ 213; with pron., η 223, Θ 211 (rarely after demonstr., σ 114, τ 372, β 351); with gen. of poss. pron. only Ι 342; with πᾶς, ν 262, ω 79, etc.; ὁ αὐτός, rarely, η 55, 326, cf. θ 107; (d) expressing possession or propriety, own, proper, Λ 142, λ 492, θ 195, Λ 763, ο 218, λ 339.

ὅ, ἥ, τό, esp. freq. forms beginning with τ, pr. relat., α 300, β 262; οἵ τοι, ζ 153; ταί τε, μ 63; ὅτε, quicunque, whoever, μ 40; since he, Α 412; ὅ τις, α 47, ρ 53; τῇ περ, in which very way, θ 510; τὸ μέν, Α 234.

ὀδρων, ὤρεσσιν, fem., (οσαρ-, cf. ὅρμος, sermo), uxorum, ibus, wives, Ι 327, Ε 486.

ὀαρίζετον, ζέμεναι, ipf. ὀάριζε, (ὅαρ, sermo). chat, τινί; converse familiarly, Ζ 516, Χ 127 sq.

ὀαριστής, ὁ. (ὀαρίζω), bosom friend, τ 179†.

ὀαριστύς, ύν, fem., (ὀαρίζω), familiar converse, πάρφασις, fond discourse, beguiling the mind, etc., Ξ 216; iron. intercourse, combat, πολέμου, προμάχων.

ὀβελοῖσ(ι), οὑς, masc., veru, spit, Α 465. (See cuts under πεμπώβολα.)

ὀβρῑμο-εργός, όν, (Ϝέργον), immania exsequens, worker of monstrous deeds, impious, Ε 403 and Χ 418.

ὀβρῑμο-πάτρη, ης, daughter of the mighty father, Ε 747, γ 135.

ὄβρῑμος, ον (ε), incorrectly written ὄμβρ. Γ 357, (βρίθω), mighty, of Ares, Ο 112, Ν 444; of heroes, Θ 473, Τ 408; of things, ponderous, heavy, Γ 357, Δ 453, ἄχθος, ι 233; θυρεόν, ι 241.

ὀγδοάτῳ, την, γ 306, Τ 246, and ὄγδοος, ον, octavus, eighth; ὀγδώκοντα, octoginta, eighty, Β 568.

ὅγε, ἥγε, τόγε, (see γε), freq. with slight force which can not be given in translation, Α 65, 93, 68, 97.—(1) as outward sign, indicating an antithesis, Ρ 122; αὐτάρ, Λ 226, Μ 40, Ψ 35.—(2) in second member of antithesis, (a) referring to what has gone before, Μ 239, δ 789, Α 190; in first member of antithesis, recapitulating, β 132, γ 90, δ 821; δ' ὅγε, Α 226, Ρ 130; special cases: Ν 8, 395, Ο 392, 479, 710; after ἄρα, Η 169, Ι 511, χ 329, 379; after recapitulating pron. or adv., Ν 88, 94, 538; ὥς, Λ 136, Μ 171; idem, Λ 478, Π 455; (b) pointing forward, κ 91; in simple anticipation, Α 120, ζ 182, ξ 119, in opposition to what has gone before, τ 283, π 470.

ὄγκιον, τό, (ὄγκος), iron-basket, basket or chest for containing iron, φ 61†.

ὄγκοι, ους, masc., (uncus), barbs of arrow, Δ 151. (Il.)

ὄγμον, ον, ους, masc., (ἄγω), lira, furrow; Σ 552, 557, swath made by mower or reaper.

Ὀγχηστός, town on Lake Kopais in Boiotia, with grove of Poseidon, Β 506.

ὄγχνη, ῃ, ην, αι, ας, fem., pirus, pear-tree; but also pirum, pear, η 120. (Od.)

ὀδαίων, ntr. pl. gen., (ὀδύς), freight, cargo, θ 163 and ο 445.

ὀδάξ, adv., (δάκνω), with the teeth, λάζεσθαι, ἕλον γαῖαν, οὖδας, bite the ground, of slain in combat, Χ 17; ἐν χείλεσι φύντο, bit their lips in wrath.

ὅδε, ἥδε, τόδε, dat. pl. τοῖσδε and τοίσδεσ(σ)ι, pron. dem., hic, this, points out what lies before one, Γ 192, θ 403; yet not yet named or known, Γ 166, 226; cf. οὗτος, Γ 178, 200, 229, Τ 8.—(1) referring to the speaker, π 205, α 76, Τ 140; and to what falls within his familiar horizon, e. g. house, α 232; city, η 26; land, ο 484, people, cf. French céans, English, these here, β 317, τ 372, ο 388, 429, in widest, most general sense, χ 154, Ζ 326, Θ 237, Α 257, Ξ 3, ρ 158, θ 197, Β 324, ω 444.—(2) referring to that which is present in widest sense, υ 116, Θ 541, Φ 155, Ω 765 (usually following its subst.); yet ἥδε ὁδός, τόδε κακόν, μ 216; that in which the speaker feels a lively interest, γ 56, δ 94, β 280, Α 127, 134; emphatically of that which is absent, α 185; τόδε (δεῦρο), here, ἱκάνω, ρ 444; explanatory, τῷδ' ἐπὶ θυμῷ.—(3) pointing out what is to follow, δ 486, Κ 111; esp. τόδε, referring to: inf., Ο 509, α 376; indirect question, Η 393; substantive clause introduced by that, υ 333, χ 350, Α 41; hypothetical sentence, Ο 208; μή, π 291; ὡς, ρ 242; relative clause, θ 564, σ 221, Α 110, Β 274; freq. where there is an asyndeton, β 93, ρ 274, Β 301, Ο 36; γάρ, β 162, Π 238.—(4) special phrases: ἥδε δέ μοι κατὰ θυμὸν ἀρίστη φαίνετο βουλή, ι 318, 424, Β 5, Κ 17; εὖ γὰρ ἐγὼ τόδε οἶδα, with asyndeton, ο 211; ἀλλ' ἄγε μοι τόδε εἰπέ, with following question, α 169, Κ 384, α 206, Ω 380.

ὀδεύειν, inf., (ὁδός), ire, go, ἐπὶ νῆας, Λ 569†.

Ὀδίος, (1) leader of the Halizones, slain by Agamemnon, Β 856, Ε 39.—(2) herald of the Greeks, Ι 170.

ὁδ-ίτης, αι, άων, masc., (ὁδός, εἶμι), wayfarer, λ 127, also ἄνθρωπος, wending his way, Π 263, ν 123.

ὀδμή, ἥν, fem., odor, smell, fragrance, Ξ 415, ι 210.

ὁδοί-πορος, masc., (περᾶν), wayfarer, (fellow) traveler, Ω 375†, hence ὁδοι-πόριον, ntr., reward for the journey (feast), ο 506†.

ὁδός, οἶο, οὗ, ᾧ, όν, ούς, fem., (1) way,

journey, Lat. iter, Α 151, as envoy; expeditio, γ 288, ξ 235; also by sea, β 273; ἦρχε δ' ὁδοῖο, she began the way, took the lead; πρήσσειν ὁδοῖο, accomplish the way, leave it behind.—(2) path, road, via, δ 389, cf. π 138; ἱππηλασίη, carriage-road; λαοφόρον, highway; πρὸ ὁδοῦ ἐγένοντο, progressed on their way.

ὀδούς, ὀδόντι, α, τες, ων, οῦσι, όντας, masc., dens, tooth, τ 450; λευκῷ, τ 393.

ὀδύνη, ῃ, αι, άων, ῃσι, ας, (δύη?), dolor, pain, Λ 398, Ε 417; animi= sorrow, α 242, β 79; Ο 25, Ἡρακλῆος, grief for Herakles.

ὀδυνή-φατον, α, (φένω), pain-assuaging, Ε 401. (Il.)

ὀδύρομαι, εαι, εται, εο, and part., ipf. ὀδύρετο, οντο, (ὀδύνη?), lamentari, grieve, mourn, Χ 79, α 55, θ 577, στοναχῇ τε γόῳ τε; τινός, for any one, Ψ 224, ξ 40; τινί, conqueri apud, lament before, δ 740; Β 290, lamenting to each other, they desire to return home; mourn for, deplore, commiserari, Τ 345, δ 100, ν 379.

Ὀδυσ(σ)ήιος, σ 353, adj. from Ὀδυσ-(σ)εύς, (σ)ῆος, σέος, σεῦς; σῆι, σεῖ; σσῆα, σσέα, σῆ, Odysseus, son of Laertes and Ktimene, king of Kephallenes, inhabiting Ithaka, Same, Zakynthos, Aigilops, Krokyleia, and a strip of opposite mainland, husband of Penelope, father of Telemachos; for Homeric explication of his name, see τ 407; the shrewd, much-tried hero of the Odyssey, πολύτροπος, πολύμητις, always able to evade danger by stratagem, and esp. conspicuous for his self-control.

ὀδύσσομαι, aor. ὠδύσαο, ατ(ο), aor. ὀδύσαντο, part. σσάμενος, οιο, pf. ὀδώδυσται, irasci, odisse, be angry with, hate, τινί; pf. pass.; ε 423, mihi iratus sit.

ὀδώδει, see ὄζω; ὀδώδυσται, see ὀδύσσομαι; δεκσι ᾆς ὗις.

ὄζος, ῳ, ον, οι, οισιν, ους, shoot, twig, Ζ 39, Κ 467, Π 768; Ἄρηος, scion of Ares, epithet of daring heroes, Β 540, 745.

ὄζω, only plupf. ὀδώδει, give out a smell, transl. was exhaled; fragrabat, ε 60 and ι 210.

ὅθεν (ὅς), unde, whence, Β 307, Δ 58,

η 131; also with personal antecedent, γ 319.

ὄθ(ϊ) (ὅς), ubi, *where*, B 572, 722; also further defined by follg. preposition, λ 191, ξ 533; — τε, introductory to a general description, *where also*, a 50, μ 3; — περ, ξ 532, even where; καί —, only ι 50. [ὅθῖ, Δ 516.]

ὄθομαι, εται, ipf. ὄθετ(ο), (ὄθνος, odium), always with negation, non respicio, *heed*, A 181; τινός, *trouble one's self about*, usually with inf., with part., E 403.

ὀθονέων, ησιν, ας, fem., *fine linen*, Γ 141, Σ 595, of women's garments; *a web*, or *piece of fine linen*, η 107.

Ὀθρυονεύς, ῆος, Trojan ally from Kabesos, N 363, 370, 374, 772.

οἷ, sibi, ei, see οὖ.

οἵα, see οἷος.

οἴγνυμι, aor. ὤξε, and ὦιξε, αν, ὀίξασα, pass. ipf. ὠίγνυντο, aperire, *open*, θύρας, πύλας ; but γ 392, οἶνον, *broach* the wine.

οἶδα, ας, ε, see ΕΙΔ, IV.

οἰδάνει (οἰδέω), *swells*, (enrages), I 554, νύον; pass. οἰδάνεται κραδίη χόλῳ, swells with wrath, I 646.

οἰδέω, ipf. ᾤδεε, *had* all his body *swollen*, χρόα, ε 455†.

Οἰδιπόδης, **Οἰδιπόδᾱο**, *Oidipus*, λ 271, Ψ 679, son of Laios and Epikaste, father of Eteokles, Polyneikes, and Antigone.

οἴδματι, τῷ, ntr., (οἰδέω), *swell of the sea*, *billow*, Φ 234 and Ψ 230.

οἰετέας, acc. pl., (οἰέτης, ὁ-Fέτης), *of equal age*, B 765†.

ὀιζῡρός, οῦ, οῖο, όν, οἶσι, αί, comp. -ώτερον, P 446; sup. -ώτατον, ε 105; (ὀιζύς), miser, *wretched*, A 417, γ 95.

ὀιζύς, ύος, ύι η 270, υν, fem., (οἴ, vae), miseria, aerumna, *woe*, *suffering*, *misery*, Ζ 285, Ξ 480, O 365, δ 35.

ὀίζῡε, imp., ipf. ὀιζύομεν, aor. part. ὀιζύσας, (ὀιζύς), *endure hardship, lament, suffer*, περί τινα, circa; ἀμφί τινι, propter; κακά, perpeti, Ξ 89.

οἰήιον, α, ntr., (οἴσω, Fοιήιον), *tiller*, then in wider signif. *rudder*, ι 483; usually pl. because the Homeric ships had two rudders, μ 218. (Cf. following cuts and No. 64.)

οἰήκεσσι, dat. pl., (οἴσω), *rings in the*

yoke through which the reins passed, Ω 269†. (Cf. cuts Nos. 49 *h*, 10, 84 *f*.

οἴκᾱδε (old acc. form with δε), domum, *homeward*, *home*, hence freq. = *to one's house, tent*; with verbs of motion, A 19, 170, B 154, 236, Γ 72, Δ 103, H 79, I 418, β 176, δ 701, ε 108, η 326, κ 484, λ 132, ν 169, ο 431.

οἰκεύς, οἰκῆι, pl. οἰκῆες, ων, ας, (οἶκος), *inmates of house*, Ζ 366; *servants*, E 413.

οἰκέομεν (οἶκος), habitamus, *inhabit, dwell*, ζ 204; ipf. ᾤκει, ι 200; ᾤκεον, Υ 218; pass. οἰκέοιτο, Δ 18, *be inhabited*; aor. ᾤκηθεν, *settled*.

οἰκί(α), τά, (οἶκος), domicilium, *abode*; ναίων, habitans, dwelling, Ζ 15, H 221; Ἑλλάδι, Π 595; nidus, *nest*, M 168, Π 261, M 221; dwelling of Aïdes, Υ 64.

Ὀικλείης, ο 244, son of Antiphates, father of Amphiaraos.

οἰκόθεν (οἶκος), *from home*, A 632; de suo (de re familiari), H 364.

οἴκοθῐ (οἶκος), domi, at home, Θ 513,
φ 398; of like signif. οἴκοι (locative
from οἶκος), Α 113, θ 324.

οἴκόνδε (οἶκος), domum, home;
ἄγεσθαι, the bride, ζ 159; to women's
apartment, α 360, φ 354; homeward, Β
158.

οἶκος, οιο, ου, ῳ, ον, οι, ων, ους,
masc., (Ϝοῖκος, vicus), house, domus
and domicilium, Ο 498; roof, abode,
ι 478, ω 208; tent, Ω 471; room, υ
105; hall, τ 598; household, β 45, η
68,o 375; res familiaris, substance,
β 48,ρ 455, τ 161,β 238.

οἰκτείρων, aor. ὤκτειρε, (οἶκτος), misereri, pity, Ψ 548, Ω 516.
οἴκτιστος, see οἰκτρός.

οἶκτος, masc., (οἵ), ἔλε (τινάς), misericordia tetigit (eos), pity, β 81,
ω 438.

οἰκτρός, comp. -ότερ(α), sup. -οτάτην
and οἴκτιστῳ, ον, (οἶκτος), miserabilis, pitiable, Λ 242, λ 381, 421, Χ 76,
μ 258; οἰκτρ(ὰ) ὀλοφύρεσθαι, miserа-
biliter lamentari, κ 409; οἴκτιστα
θάνοιεν, miserrime morerentur,
χ 472.

οἰκ-ωφελίη (οἶκος, ὀφέλλω), bettering
one's estate, thrift, ξ 223†.

Ὀϊλεύς, ῆος, (1) king in Lokris,
father of the lesser Aias and of Medon, Ν 697, Ο 333, Β 727, see Αἴας.—
(2) charioteer of Bienor, slain by Agamemnon,Λ 93. Hence Ὀϊλιάδης, Aias,
Μ 365, Ν 712, Ξ 446, Π 330, Ψ 759.

οἶμα, ματ(α), ntr., (οἴσω), impetus,
spring, swoop, Π 752, Φ 252.

οἰμάω, aor. οἴμησε(ν), irruit, dart
upon, Χ 308, ω 538; μετὰ πέλειαν, in
columbam, swoop after a dove, Χ
140.

οἴμης, pl. ας, (εἶμι), song, lay, θ 481,
χ 347; θ 74, cuius cantici
gloria.

οἶμοι, pl. masc., (εἶμι), stripes, bands,
Λ 24†.

οἰμωγή, ῆς, ῇ, fem., (οἰμώζω), lamentatio, cry of grief, Χ 409; διδηε,
resounds, υ 353.

οἰμώζω, aor. ᾤμωξε, opt. οἰμώξειε,
part. οἰμώξας, (οἴμοι, vae mihi), lamentari, aloud, with loud voice
(μέγα), wail, lament; σμερδαλέον, bitterly; ἐλεεινά, pitiably, Μ 162, Κ 522,
Χ 33, Ψ 12, ι 506.

Οἰνείδης, son of Oineus, Tydeus,

E 81 ?, Κ 497; Οἰνεύς, ῆος, son of
Portheus, king of Kalydon in Aitolia,
husband of Althaia, father of Tydeus
and of Meleagros, guest friend of Bellerophontes; Artemis, in anger, sends
upon his territory the Kalydonian
boar, Β 641, Ζ 216, Ι 535, Ξ 117.

οἰνίζεσθε, imp. prs., ipf. οἰνίζοντο,
(οἶνος), supply one's self with wine, Θ
506, Η 472, Θ 546.

οἰνο-βαρείων, part.,(βαρύς), heavy or
drunk with wine, ι 374, κ 555, φ 304.

οἰνο-βαρές, voc.; (βαρύς), = foregoing, Α 225†.

Οἰνόμαος, (1) an Aitolian, slain by
Hektor, Ε 706.—(2) a Trojan, Μ 140,
Ν 506.

οἰνο-πέδοιο (πέδον), adj., with soil
fit to produce wine, wine-producing;
ἀλωῆς, wine-yielding soil, earth, α 193
subst., vineyard, ι 579.

Οἰνοπίδης, son of Oinops, Helenos,
Ε 707†.

οἰνο-πληθής (πλῆθος), abounding in
wine, o 406†.

οἰνο-ποτάζει, ζων, (ποτόν), quaff
wine, ζ 309, Υ 84.

οἰνο-ποτῆρας, τούς, (ποτόν), wine-
drinkers, θ 456†.

οἶνος, οιο, ου, ῳ, ον, (Ϝοῖνος, vi-
num), wine, always mixed with water
before drinking (see κρητήρ, ἀμφιφορεύς, ἀσκός, πίθος, πρόχοος, νέμειν);
αἴθοπα, sparkling, Α 462; see ἐρυθρόν,
μελιηδέα, μελίφρονα, ἡδύν, ἡδυπότοιο,
εὐήνορα; γερούσιον, reserved in honor
of the elders; places famed for quality
of wine: Epidauros, Phrygia, Peda-
sos, Arne, Histiaia, Lemnos, Thrake,
Pramne, land of the Kikones.

οἰνο-χοέω, ipf. οἰνο-χόει (see Α 598,
o 141), ἐῳνοχόει, part. οἰνοχοεῦντες?
γ 472; aor. -χοῆσαι (-χοή), and οἰνο-
χοεύει, ειν, ων, (χοεύς). pour out wine,
τινί (in φ 142, sc. οἰνοχόος); nectar,
Δ 3.

οἰνοχόος, οιο, ον, masc., (χέω), wine-
pourer, cup-bearer, Β 128, ι 10.

οἶνοψ, οἶνοπος, ι, α, ε, (οἶνος ?), glancing, gleaming, epithet of the sea and of
cattle, dark red, ε 132.

Οἶνοψ, an Ithakan, father of Leio-
des, φ 144†.

οἰνόω, only aor. pass. part. οἰνωθέν-
τες, vino ebrii, drunken with wine,
π 292 and τ 11.

δίξασα, see οἴγνυμι.

οἶο = οὖ, gen. from οὕ, s u n s.

οἰόθεν (οἶος) οἶος, *all alone*, H 39. (Il.)

οἴομαι, see ὄίω.

οἰο-πόλῳ, οισιν, (πέλομαι), d e s e r-
t u s, *lonely*, N 473, λ 574.

οἶος, ου, ῳ, ον, ω, οι, οισι(ν), ους, η,
ης, ην, αι, ῃς, s o l u s, *alone; οὐκ οἴη.
ἅμα τῆγε*, etc., Γ 143 ; with εἶς, μία,
δύ(ο); with νόσφι, ἄνευθέ τινος, ἐν,
μετά τισι ; καὶ οἶος, e t i a m, *even alone,
unassisted*, Ω 456 ; u n i c u s e x i m i u s,
alone of its kind, best, Ω 499 ; with ἀπό,
isolated, ι 192 ; οἶον, sc. με, met me *in
single combat*, I 355.

οἶος, οἴη, οἶον, rel. pron. like ὅς,
orig. demonstrative like t a l i s, B 320,
that *such a thing* had happened ; apparently often = ὅτι τοῖος, *because
such*, δ 611, ε 183, 303, ξ 392, π 93,
Ζ 166 ; cf. ρ 160 and ω 512 ; then rel.
q u a l i s, *as; οἶον ὅτε, as* when, ν 388 ;
εῖος, with inf., ξ 491 ; οἷός τε, τ 160,
*such as to, able to, capable of; οἶον, οἷα
(τε), as* (often), ι 128 ; οἶον δή, causal,
since now, σ 221. [ὅῐος, N 275, Σ 105,
η 312, ν 89.]

οἱός and *ὅιος*, see οἶς.

οἰο-χίτων(α), τόν, *with tunic only,
lightly clad*, ξ 489†.

οἰόω, aor. pass. **οἰώθη**, *leave alone,
abandon*, d e r e l i c t a e s t (a d i i s), Z
1 ; d e s e r t u s e s t a s u i s, Λ 401.

ὄις, ὄιος and *ὀΐος, ὄιν*, pl. ὄιες (ὄιες
ι 425, ὄιεσι), ὄίων, ὀίεσσι and ὄεσσι, ὄις,
o v i s, *sheep*, masc. and fem., with ἀρνειός, ἄρσην or θήλεια.

ὄίσατο, see ὄίω. **οἴσετε, σέμεν(αι)**,
see φέρω. **οἶσθα**, see ΕΙΔ, IV.

ὀισθείς, see ὄίω.

ὀιστεύοντα, aor. imp. ὀίστευσον,
part. σας, (ὀιστός), *shoot arrows*, τόξῳ,
μ 84 ; τινός, at any one. The following cuts, from Assyrian reliefs, give a
good idea of the way in which the
arrow was held in the fingers and
placed upon the bow ; see also cut
under πῶμα.

ὀιστός, οῦ, ῷ, όν, οἱ, ῶν, ούς, (ὀιστύς,
φέρω, q u i f e r t u r), s a g i t t a, *arrow*,
of wood or reed, with barbed metal
point, the lower end feathered and
notched (γλυφίδες), or with projections, enabling the fingers to clasp
firmly the arrow to draw it back ;
poisoned arrows are mentioned only
α 261, Δ 213 ; πικρός, pointed, Ψ 867.

οἶστρος, ὁ, *gadfly*, χ 300†.

οἰσύῃσι (οἰσύα, v i t e x), ῥίπεσσι,
willow (withes), ε 256†.

οἶτον, τόν, (οἴσω, f o r s ?), f o r t u n a,
fate, always in bad sense, I 563 ;
usually joined with κακόν, m i s e r ā
f o r t u n ā p e r i r e, *perish by a wretched fate*, Γ 417, Θ 34, α 350.

Οἴτυλος, town on coast of Lakonike,
B 585†.

Οἰχαλίη, town on river Peneios,
home of Eurytos, B 730 ; **Οἰχαλίηθεν**,
from Oichalia, B 596 ; **Οἰχαλιεύς**, Eurytos, B 596, θ 224.

οἰχνέω, 3 pl. **οἰχνεῦσιν**, ipf. iter.
οἴχνεσκον, ε, (οἴχομαι), m e a r e, *go,
come*, E 790, γ 322.

οἴχεται, etc., prs., ῷχετο, etc. ipf.
(properly perf. with present signif.
from Ϝικ-, Ger. w e i c h e), (1) *skip away,
escape*, N 672, E 472, X 213, ι 47, α
242 ; part. οἴχομενος = a b s e n s, α 281; *begone, be away*, also p r o f e c t u s s u m,
set out for, A 366 ; c. t e r m. in q u o,
δ 821 ; c. t e r m. in q u e m, ἐς, ἐπί,
μετά, κατά, (πάντη), παρά, πρός, with
acc., κεῖσε, Πύλονδε ; a b i r e, *depart*, κ
571, E 511 ; f e r r i, *fly, speed, haste,
run*, A 53 ; κατὰ γαίης, χθονός, *under
the earth*, μετὰ ζουρὸς ἐρωήν ; ὁδόν,
p r o f e c t u s, *since thou hast set out* (on
thy long and weary journey), δ 393.

ὄίω (~ ~ | – E 894), *οΐω*, mid. ὄίομαι,
εαι, ται, etc., opt. ὄιοιτο, ipf. ὠίετο, aor.
ὀίσατο, pass. ὠίσθην, θη, ὀισθείς (ὀϜίω,
o p i n o r ?), s u s p i c o r, *suspect*, τί, τάδε,
γόον (θυμός) ; often parenthetical, like
Lat. o p i n o r, π 309 ; *think, intend,
mean*, A 170, 296. Construed with, (1)

acc. and inf., A 59, 170, 204, 289, 427, 558, Ω 727, γ 27, χ 215, A 78, T 334, α 173, χ 210; subject to be supplied from context, α 201, 323, ζ 173, ο 173, 278, π 372, M 66, 217, O 292, Υ 195, κ 193.—(2) with inf. where subj. remains unchanged, A 296, Z 341, Φ 92, θ 180, τ 215, Δ 12, O 728, τ 581, φ 91. —(3) acc., χ 159, β 351, χ 165; with attraction, γ 255, υ 224.—(4) ὅίσατο κατὰ θυμὸν μή ... ἀμφράσσαιτο, ne ... agnosceret, there rose in his mind the apprehension lest, etc., τ 390.—(5) impers., τ 312, ἀλλά μοι ὧδ' ἀνὰ θυμὸν ὀίεται ὡς ἔσεταί περ.

οἰωνιστής, ῆν, masc., (οἰωνός), understanding the flight of birds, N 70; elsewhere as subst.

οἰωνο-πόλων, gen. pl., (πολέω), augurum, occupied with flight of birds, seers, A 69 and Z 76.

οἰωνός, ῷ, όν, οἱ, ῶν, οἶσι(ν), οὕς, (avis), bird of prey, γ 271; coupled with κύνες, γ 259; bird of omen, δεξιός, seen in the east, auspicious quarter, ο 531; omen, the one best omen is, etc., M 243.

ὀκνείω, prs., ipf. ᾤκνεον, (ὄκνος), with inf., dubitare, shrink, E 255 and Υ 155.

ὄκνος, ῳ, masc., (cunctari), inertia, sluggishness, E 817. (Il.)

ὀκριόωντο, ipf., (ὀκριάω, from ὀκριόεις), — πανθυμαδόν, exasperabantur, were hot with furious passion, σ 33†.

ὀκρίόεντι, τα (θ'), (ἄκρος), having sharp corners or points, jagged, rugged, θ 327, Π 735, ι 499.

ὀκρυόεντος, οἴσσης, (κρύος), horrendi, ae, chilling, horrible, I 64 and Z 344.

ὀκτά-κνημα, adj. ntr. pl., (κνήμη), eight-spoked, E 723†, of wheels, as in adjoining cut, from a painting on a

Panathenaic amphora found at Volsci.

ὀκτώ, octo, eight, B 313, χ 110; ὀκτω-καιδεκάτῃ, duodevicesima die, ε 279, η 268, ω 65.

ὀλβιό-δαιμον, voc., (ὄλβιος), blessed by the deity, Γ 182.

ὄλβιος, ον, ον, ε, οι, (ὄλβος), beatus, blessed, λ 450, ρ 354; rich, σ 138; pl. ὄλβια, blessings (in their lives), η 148; ποιήσειαν, may they bless! ν 42.

ὄλβος, ῳ, ον, masc., wealth; γ 208, good fortune.

ὀλέεσθαι, ὀλέεσκε, see ὄλλυμι.

ὀλέθριον, (ὄλεθρος) ἦμαρ, day of destruction, T 294 and 409.

ὄλεθρος, ον, ῳ, ον, (ὄλλυμι), pernicies; αἰπύς, sheer, utter ruin; ψυχῆς, vitae discrimen, most perilous spot to life, X 325; πείρατα ὀλέθρου, destruction's net; Ω 735, a wretched fate.

ὀλεῖται, see ὄλλυμι.

ὀλέκουσι, prs. with part., ipf. ὄλεκον, iter. ὀλέκεσκεν, pass. prs. ὀλέκονται, ipf. ὀλέκοντο, (ὄλλυμι), perdere, pessumdare, destroy, θ 279, χ 305, Π 17, A 10.

ὀλέσαι, ας, σσαι, σσας, ὀλέσθαι, see ὄλλυμι.

ὀλετῆρα, τόν, (ὄλλυμι), destroyer, Σ 114†.

ὀλίγη-πελέων, ἔουσα, swooning, O 245; infirma, τ 356.

ὀλιγη-πελίης, τῆς, (πέλομαι), weakness, faintness, ε 468†.

ὀλίγιστος, see ὀλίγος.

ὀλίγο-δρανέων, part., (δρᾶν), able to do but little, feeble, O 246. (Il.)

ὀλίγος, ον, ῳ, ον, οισι, η, ης, ᾳ, ην, ον, sup. ὀλίγιστος, T 223, paullus, brevis, exiguus, little, small; πῖδαξ, feeble flowing; ὀπί, feeble; ntr. ὀλίγον, paullum, a little, P 538, θ 547; with comp., paullo, by little, T 217; ὀλίγου, paene, almost, ξ 37; super., T 223, scanty shall be the reaping.

Ὀλιζών, town in Magnesia in Thessaly, B 717†.

ὀλισθάνω, aor. ὄλισθε, (for ὀγλισθάνω, Ger. glitschen), slipped and fell, Ψ 774; with ἐκ, Υ 470, fell from him.

ὄλλυμι, part. ὀλλύς, ύντων, τας, ὀλλῦσαι, fut. ὀλέσω, σσεις, σσι, aor. ὤλεσα, ας, (εν), σσαν and ὄλεσσε(ν), σσαν, subj. σσῃς, ῃ, σωσιν, opt. σειε imp. σσον, inf. σσαι, part. σσας, σαντ(α), τες, σασα, perdere, pessum dare, delere, interimere, *destroy, kill,* amittere, *lose,* θυμόν, μένος, Λ 83, Θ 449 ; pass. mid. prs. ὀλλύμενοι, ων, ους, άων, ipf. ὄλλυντ(o), fut. ὀλεῖται, ὀλέεσθε, σθαι, aor. ὀλόμην, ὄλεθ' = τ(o), οντο and ὤλεο, ὤλετο, subj. ὄλωμαι, ὄληαι, ται, ωνται, opt. οισθε, inf. ἔσθαι, see οὐλόμενος, perire, *perish,* ὑπό τινι; with acc. of manner of death, etc., μόρον, οἶτον, ὀλέθρῳ ; with dat. of means, δόλῳ ; also pf. ὄλωλας, εν, ῃ, and plupf. ὀλώλει, periit, etc., Ω 729, Κ 187.

ὅλμον, τόν, (Folμ., volvo), *smooth round stone, quoit,* Λ 147†.

ὀλοιή, ῇσι, dat. pl., (ὀλοός), perniciosa, *destructive, deadly,* Χ 5, Α 342.

ὀλολυγῇ, τῇ, (ὀλολύζω, ululare), *with a loud cry,* Ζ 301†.

ὀλολίζω, aor. ὀλόλυξε, αν, αι, always of female voices, ululare, *lament aloud,* δ 767 ; eiulare, *rejoice aloud,* χ 408, 411.

ὀλόμην, see ὄλλυμι.

ὀλοοί-τροχος, masc., (FoλFοι-, volvo-), *rolling stone, round rock,* Ν 137†.

ὀλοός, οἶο, ῷ, όν, οἷς ; ή, ἧς, ήν, ῇς, άς ; ά, comp. ώτερος, sup. ώτατος, τε, (ὄλλυμι), perniciosus, *destroying,* of gods, Μοῖρα, Κήρ ; of men and things, Γ 133, Ω 39, Χ 5, Π 849 ; κῆρ, saevum ; but κῆρ' = Κῆρα, saevam.

'Ολοοσσών, όνος, town on river Eurotas in Thessaly, situated on white cliffs, Β 739†.

ὀλοό-φρων, ονος, (φρήν), *baleful, savage, stern,* saevus, Β 723, α 52.

ὀλοφυδνόν (ὀλοφύρομαι?), *pitiful, loleful,* miserabile, ἔπος, Ε 683, τ 362.

ὀλοφύρομαι, εαι, etc., prs. aor. ὀλοφύραο, ατο, lamentari, miserari, *wail, lament, pity,* πολλά, much, οἰκτρ(ά), piteously, αἰνά, dreadfully, pitiably, ν 321, τ 543 ; freq. with προσηύδα, Λ 815, λ 472, κ 265, cf. Ο 114; with inf., χ 232 (cf. ὀκνεῖν), *bewail* that thou must be brave before the suitors; τινός (Il.), misereri, *feel pity,* Π 17, Χ 170; τινά, miserari, *show pity,* Ω 328, κ 157, τ 522.

ὀλο-φώϊα (φάος, salus?), perniciosa, *destructive,* εἰήνεα ; subst., *wiles,* δ 410.

'Ολυμπιάδες, Β 491†, Muses, cf.

'Ολύμπιος, οι, α, Α 583, 399, 18, *Olympian,* inhabiting Οὔλυμπος or 'Ολυμπος, *Olympus,* the mighty mountain, dwelling of gods, on left bank of river Peneios in Thessaly, penetrating with its snow-capped peaks into the upper αἰθήρ ; ἀγάννιφος, αἰγλήεντος, αἰπύν, θεῶν ἕδος, μακρός, πολυπτύχου.

ὀλύρας, τάς, (ἀλέω ?), a kind of grain not unlike *barley,* Ε 196 and Θ 564.

ὄλωλε, see ὄλλυμι.

ὀμάδησαν, aor. from ὁμαδέω, (ὄμαδος), *made a din,* α 365. (Od.)

ὄμᾰδος, ῳ, ον, masc., (ὁμός), *noise, din,* strictly of many voices, also of battle-cry, κ 556. (Il.) [σομάδῳ, Ρ 380 ?]

ὁμᾰλὸν ποίησαν, levigabant, *made smooth,* ι 327†.

ὀμ-αρτέων, part. prs., aor. ἤσειεν, ἤσ·νθ' = ἤσαντε, τες, (ὁμοῦ, ἄρτιος), *meet, keep pace with,* ν 87 ; comitari, *attend,* Ω 438 ; *encounter,* Μ 400.

ὁμαρτῇ, see ἁμαρτῇ.

ὄμβριμος, -πάτρη, false reading for ὄβριμος, ὀβριμοπάτρη.

ὄμβρος, ῳ, ον, masc., (imber, μύρεσθαι ?), imber, *rain,* also of heavy *snow-fall,* Μ 286.

ὀμεῖται, fut. from ὄμνυμι.

ὀμ-ηγερέες, έεσσι, (ὁμοῦ, ἀγείρω), *assembled together,* Ο 84.

ὀμ-ηγυρίσασθαι, aor. from -ηγυρίζομαι, (ἄγυρις), congregare, *convoke,* π 376†.

ὀμήγυριν, τήν, concionem, *assembly,* Υ 142†.

ὀμ-ηλικίη, ης, ῃ, ην, (ὁμοῦ, ἧλιξ), *sameness of age,* Υ 465 ; aequales, (collective), *those of like age,* Γ 175, Ν 485; also aequalis, *companion,* ζ 23, χ 209.

ὀμ-ήλικα, ες, ας, (ὁμοῦ, ἧλιξ), aequalis, τινός, *of like age with,* τ 358.

ὀμ-ηρέω, aor. ὡμήρησε, (ἀραρεῖν?), μοι, *met me,* π 468†.

ὁμιλᾰδόν, adv., (ὅμιλος), catervatim, *in crowds,* Μ 3. (Il.)

ὁμῖλεῖν, prs., ipf. ὁμίλει, έομεν, εον, aor. ὡμίλησα, ἤσωσι, ἤσειεν, ἤσαντες, (ὅμιλος), *introduce one's self among, associate with* (ἐνί, μετά, παρά), τισιν, π 271 ; versari inter, cum, σ 167; manus conserere, *meet in battle,* Ν 779 (μετά), τισίν ; *throng about,* περί τινα, Π 641, ω 19.

δμῖλος, ου, ῳ, ον, masc., (ὁμοῦ, εἰλέω), crowd, throng, ἵππων τε καὶ ἀνδρῶν, etc.; tumult of battle, ὁμίλῳ, Φ 606; army, host, K 231 (in camp or otherwise), λ 514; then acervus, ‚coetus, mass, company, o 328, π 29.

ἐμίχλη, ην, (μιχ), nebula, cloud, A 359, Γ 10; κονίης, dust-cloud. (Il.)

ὄμμα, τ(α), σι, ntr., (ὤμμαι, perf. from ὁράω), oc-ulus, eye, A 225, Λ 614; Θ 349, better οἶματ.

ὄμνῡθι, from ὄμνυμι; also from ὀμνύω, ὀμνΰέτω, imp. prs., and ipf. ὤμνυε; fut. ὀμοῦμαι, εῖται, aor. ὤμοσα, ε, σαμεν, elsewh. ὀμ-, also with σσ, iurare, swear; alicui, τινί (πρός τινα), ὅρκον; affirm by oath, swear, iure iurando affirmare, τί; or with inf. as object, ἤ μέν, A 76, μή, I 132, Ψ 585, β 373; acc. with inf. μή-ποτ', T 127, cf. ξ 332; with inf. fut. aor. and perf. according to the sense; swear by a thing, τινά, O 40.

ὁμο-γάστριος, ον, (γαστήρ), ger-manus, brother by the same mother, own brother, Φ 95; κασίγνητος, Ω 47.

ὁμόθεν, ἐξ-, = ἐξ ὁμοῦ, from the same (root or spot), ε 477†.

ὁμοῖος, ον, οι, η, ης, ῳ, ην, αι, ας, (ἅμα), similis, Ger. samt, Eng. same), idem, same, π 182; with οὗ, A 278; M 270, similis, like, similar, τινί, in something, τί or ἐν πολέμῳ, or θείειν, also with other infs.; in abbreviated comparisons, β 121, P 51; Ψ 632, equal, distinguish from follg.

ὁμοιῖου and ὁμοῖἰον, making like, breaking down distinctions, shared by all alike, ω 543.

ὁμοιόω, only aor. pass. ὁμοιωθήμεναι ἄντην, A 187, match himself face to face; μῆτιν, in shrewdness, γ 120.

ὁμόκλᾱ, ipf. from ὁμοκλάω = -κλέω, ipf. ὁμοκλέομεν, εον, aor. ὁμοκλήσειε, etc., and iter. κλήσασκε,(καλεῖν, κελεύω), call out to, exclaim, Σ 156; Υ 448, E 439, δεινά; Ω 248, iubere, com-mand, τ 155; with inf., ω 173; acc. with inf., Η 714.

ὁμο-κλῆ, ήν, αί, fem., (ὁμοκλᾶν), loud call, M 413; commands, ρ 189.

ὁμο-κλητῆρος, τοῦ,(ὁμοκλή), one who calls out aloud; ἀκούσας, hearing the call, cry, M 273 and Ψ 452.

ὁμόργνυμι, ipf. ὀμόργνυ, mid. ὠμόρ-

γνυντο, aor. ὀμορξάμενος, ον, ην,(mer-gere), wipe off; δάκρυα, his tears; παρειάων, de genis, from his cheeks, Σ 124.

ὁμός, οῦ, όν, ή, ῷ, ήν, (ἅμα, simul, similis, Ger. sam, samt, Eng. same), idem, same, Δ 437, κ 41; communis, common, N 333.

ὁμόσας, etc., see ὄμνυμι, iurare.

ὁμόσε (ὁμός), eodem, together, M 24 and N 337.

ὁμο-στιχάει (στείχω) βόεσσιν, una cum bobus incedit, keeps pace with, O 635†.

ὁμό-τῑμον, masc.,(τιμή), equally hon-ored, entitled to equal honor, O 186†.

ὁμοῦ (ὁμός), together, Δ 122, λ 573; simul, alike, at once, A 61, Λ 245, μ 67; una cum, νεφέεσσιν.

ὁμο-φρονέοις, ἐοντε, du. part., (φρο-νέω), be of one mind, ι 456; νοήμασι, in unity of purposes, ζ 183.

ὁμο-φροσύνην, ῃσι, fem., (ὁμόφρων), concordia, ζ 181; familiaritas, intimacy, o 198.

ὁμό-φρονα (φρήν) θυμόν, having like desire, harmonious, X 263†.

ὁμωθῆναι, aor. pass. from ὁμόω — φιλότητι, to be united in love, Ξ 209†.

ὀμφαλόεν, Ω 269, with a knob or cap (see cut No. 5); ὀμφαλοέσσης, αν, αι, ας, (ὀμφαλός), ornamented with studs, τ 32, or with a single great boss, with corresponding deep concavity in in-terior (see cuts Nos. 17, 121). (Il.)

ὀμφαλός, οῦ, όν, οί, (1) umbilicus, navel, Δ 525, Φ 180.—(2) boss or pro-jection on centre of shield, terminating in a button or in a point; pl., studs upon shield serving as ornament, Λ 34. —(3) a knob or pin on the centre of the yoke (see cut No. 49, a), also among the Assyrians (see cut No. 55), while the Egyptians ornamented each end of the yoke with a ball of brass (see cut on next page), Ω 273.—(4) in wider signif., middle point, centre, θα-λάσσης, a 50. (Il.)

ὀμφᾰκες, αἱ, (ἀν-, φαγεῖν?), unripe grapes, η 125†.

ὀμφή, ῆς, ῇ, fem.,(Ϝέπος, vox), voice, θειῶν, Υ 129; θεοῦ, γ 215; also of dream, B 41 (see πανομφαῖος); always of divine prophetic voices.

ὀμ-ώνὕμοι, pl., (ὄνομα), cognomi-nes, having the same name, P 720†.

ὁμῶς (ὁμός), (1) *together*, πάντες, δ
775.—(2) *alike, at once, also*, P 644, κ
28, ν 405; with dat. = pariter ac,
equally as, just as, E 535.

ὅμως (ὁμῶς), tamen, *yet*, M 393†.

ὄναρ, τό, somnium, *dream, vision*,
K 496; opp. ὕπαρ, *reality*, τ 547, υ
90.

ὄνειαρ, ὀνείἄθ' = ὀνείατα, ntr., (ὀνίνημι), *protector, defense*, X 433; *relief,
refreshment*, δ 444; pl., *rich presents*,
Ω 367; elsewh. *food, victuals*.

ὀνείδειον, οισ(ιν), (ὄνειδος), *reproach-
ful*, μῦθον, ἐπέεσσιν, Φ 393; without
ἐπ., *reproaches*, X 497.

ὀνειδίζων, aor. 2 sing. ὀνείδισας, imp.
-ισον, (ὄνειδος), *reproach*, ἔπεσιν; τινί
τι, I 34, or ὅτι, B 255, *censure*; expro-
brare, *cast in one's teeth*, σ 380.

ὄνειδος, εα, εσι, ntr., (Goth. naiteins,
neith, Ger. Neid), probrum, *reproach*, pl. κατ' χεῦαν μητέρι, χ 463,
have covered (overwhelmed) *my mother with reproach*; Π 498, *matter of reproach, disgrace*.

ὀνείρατα, see ὄνειρος.

ὀνειρείῃσι, fem. adj., (ὄνειρος), ἐν —
πύλῃσι, *at the portals of dreams*, δ
809.

ὀνειρο-πόλοιο, ον = (ὀνειροπολούμε-
νος), A 63, *interpreter of dreams.*

ὄνειρος, ὁ, (τὸ ὄνειρον, δ '41), φ, οι,
ε, οι, ων, ους, and τὰ ὀνείρατ(α), υ 87,
(ὄναρ), somnium, *dream*, B 6, 8, 16;
in simile, of disembodied spirits, λ 207,
222; *represented as a people located*

on the way to Aides, ω 12; *they come
to mortals through two gates*, τ 562
sqq., cf. δ 809.

ὀνήμενος, ὄνησα, see ὀνίνημι.

ὀνήσιος, τῆς, (ὄνησις, ὀνίνημι), ἀν-
τιάσειεν, *would that he might have such
a portion of prosperity*, i. e. *none whatever*, φ 402†.

Ὀνητορίδης, γ 282, Phrontis.

Ὀνήτωρ, priest of Idaean Zeus; his
son Laogonos, Π 604.

ὄνθος, ου, ον, masc., fimus, *dung*,
Ψ 775. [Ψ]

ὀνίνησι, fut. ἥσει, ειν, aor. ὤνησας,
εν, αν, and ὄνησα; mid. fut. ὀνήσεαι,
εται, ὁμεθ(α), 2 aor. imp. ὄνησο, part.
ὀνήμενος, (cf. ὦνος), iuvare, *help, aid,
cheer*, Θ 467; τινά, A 395, 503, ξ 67;
by what means, τινί, A 503; μέγα,
multum, Ω 45, τοῦτο, in this; mid.
iuvari, ὃν θυμόν, *have profit* in his
own soul, H 173; frui, *enjoy*, τινός,
Π 31, τ 68; part. ὀνήμενος, sc. ἔστω,
may he be blessed, β 33.

ὄνομ(α) and οὔνομα, οὔνοματ(α), ntr.,
(ὄ-γνομα, nomen), *name*; καί τ' οὔνομα, vel nomen, Γ 235; = memoria, δ 710, ω 93; μοί ἐστιν, with nom.,
τ 183, 247, σ 5, ι 366 (η 54, τ 409, with
ἐπώνυμον); τίθεσθαι, indere, *give a
name to* —; ὅ, ττι σε κάλεον, θ 550;
fama, glōria, ν 248.

ὀνομάζοι, ε, ειν, ων, ipf. ὀνόμαζες,
ον, aor. ὠνόμασας, (ὄνομα), *name, mention*, I 515; *address by name*, ἐξονομα-
κλήδην, X 415: πατρόθεν ἐκ γενεῆς,

according to his descent on the father's side, K 68.

ὄνοσαι, ονται, οιτο, fut. ὀνόσσεται, σθαι, aor. ὠνοσάμην, ὀνόσασθ(ε) Ω 241, ὀνόσαντ(ο), οσσάμενος, and 2 aor. ὤνατο P 25, vitupero, censure, scorn, (exc. P 173, φ 427), always in rhetorical question or with negation, Δ 539, P 39J ; κακότητος, ε 379, fore ut te poeniteat miseriae, that thou wilt disparage, esteem lightly.

ὀνομαίνω, only aor. ὀνόμηνας, εν, ω, ῃς, (ὄνομα), declare, λ 251 ; recount, uame, B 488, δ 240 ; name as witnesses, Ξ 278 ; call by name, K 522 ; name as, constitute, Ψ 90.

ὀνομακλήδην, see ἐξονομ.

ὀνομά-κλῦτος (κλύω), of famous name, renowned, X 51†.

ὀνομαστήν (ὀνομάζω), οὐκ —, not to be uttered (because ill-omened Ilios, malum omen), τ 260. (Od.)

ὄνος, masc., asinus, ass, Λ 558†.

ὀνύσασθε, -αιτ, ὀνοσσάμενος, see ὄνοσαι.

ὀνοστά, verbal adj. from ὄνομαι, οὐκέτ —, non vituperanda, no contemptible, I 164†.

ὄνυξ, ὀνύχεσσι, masc., unguibus, claws, talons of eagle, M 202.

ὀξῦ-βελής (βέλος), sharp-pointed, Δ 126†.

ὀξύόεντι, τα, (ὀξύ), piercing, δόρυ, Ξ 443 ; ἔγχεα, τ 33, 306. (Il.)

ὀξύς, ἐι, ύν, ἐες, ἐσι(ν) ; εἱ(α) O 313, εἱῃ, εἱ(αι) Λ 272, ῳς, ας ; εἱα, ἑα, sup. ὀξύτατον, (acer, acus), sharp (penetrating), pointed, of weapons and utensils, P 520 ; cliffs, ε 411 ; keen, φάσγανον, ἄορ; of light, P 372, and sound, clear, shrill, piercing, especially ntr. sing. and ntr. pl. ; with verbs of perceiving and of calling, sharply, keenly, quickly, Γ 374 ; and of pains, Λ 268 ; of grief, etc., bitter, τ 517 ; the wildly charging Ares, Λ 836.

ὅο and ὅου for οὗ, see ὅς, ἥ, ὅ.

ὀπάζω, prs., ipf. ὅπαζεν, ὥπαζε, ζον, fut. ὀπάσσω, ομεν, aor. ὥπασα, ε, αν, and ὅπασσα, ε(ν), opt. σαιμι, σειαν, imp. σσον, inf. σσαι, part. σσας, fut. mid. ὀπάσσομαι, aor. σσατο, σπάμενος, (ἔπω, sequor), make to follow, τινί τινα (ἄμα, Σ 452, ο 310), as escort, also μετ' ἀμφοτέροισι; also of things, θ 430, κῦδός τινι, ἔργοις; of dowry of

bride, X 51 ; bestow, confer, θ 498 ; often with inanimate subj., γῆρας, follow hard upon, beset, Δ 321 ; mid., take to one's self as escort, T 238 ; κ 59, take with one.

ὄπαια, ntr. pl., (ὀπή), ἀν' ὀπαῖα, through the loop-holes, i. e. between the rafters, under the caves. These open spaces were afterward filled up, and a specific name, μετόπαι, given to them. This seems the simplest interpretation of α 320†, for that swallows and other birds often flew through these apertures, and into the apertures, can not be doubted. (See cut No. 90.)

ὁ-πάτρος, ον, (πατήρ), eiusdem patris, of the same father, Λ 257 and M 371.

ὀπάων, ονα, masc., (ἔπω), comes, armor-bearer, esquire, K 58. (Il.)

ὅ πῃ, see ὅς πῃ.

ὅπ(π)ῃ, adv., quâ, (1) where, κ 190 sq.; whither(soever), M 48.—(2) as, θ 45.

ὀπηδεῖ, prs., ipf. ὀπήδει, (ὀπηδός, ὀπάζεσθαι), (ἅμα, η 165, ι 271) τινί, comitari, attend, follow, ἀρετῇ, etc., θ 237, P 251, ἐκ Διός, by a Jove ; μοί, E 216, I carry it with me in vain.

ὀπίζομαι, εο, prs., ipf. ὠπίζετ(ο), (ὄπις), revereri, reverence, τί, Σ 216, Od. always joined with Διός, θεῶν μῆνιν ; τινά, only X 332.

ὀπιθε(ν), see ὄπισθεν.

ὀπιπεύεις, and part. aor. εὔσας, (ὄπις), Δ 371, circumspicere, gaze at, τί ; stare at, γυναῖκας.

ὄπις, ιδος, ιδα, and ιν, fem., (ὄπωπα), eye, θεῶν, in sense of avenging eye, ultio, ξ 88 ; elsewh. divine punishment, only ξ 82 without θεῶν, Π 388. (Od.)

ὀπι(σ)θε(ν), adv., (ἀπό?), τὰ ὄπ., a tergo; στῆ, accessit, approached from behind, Λ 197 ; behind, ρ 201, οἱ ὄ., relicti ; (from) behind, Σ 548, Φ 256 ; postea, afterward, χ 55 ; in posterum, hereafter, Δ 362 ; = prep. with gen., N 536.

ὀπί(σ)σω (ἀπό?), backward, M 272, Γ 218 ; behind him, X 137 ; postmodo, hereafter, Γ 160, 411 ; πρόσω καὶ ὀπ., before and behind, forward and backward, describing foresight, Α 343, Γ 109 ; λείπειν, leave behind.

Ὀπίτης, a Greek, slain by Hektor, Λ 301†.

ὥπλέον, ipf., (ὅπλον), were getting ready, ζ 73†.

ὁπλέων, gen. pl. from ὁπλή, ungularum, hoofs, Λ 536 and Υ 501.

ὁπλίζω, aor. ὥπλισσε, imp. ὅπλισσον, inf. ἴσαι, pass. and mid. prs. ὁπλίζονται, ὡμέθα, ipf. ὁπλίζετο, ὑντο, aor. ὥπλίσαθ' = ὁπλίσσατο, ἁμεσθ(α), subj. ὁμεσθα, aor. pass. 3 pl. ὑπλισθεν, make ready, chariot, prepare, food, Ω· 190; get ship ready for sailing; mid. pass., make one's self ready, ψ 143, Η 417; equip, arm one's self, Θ 55; mid. sibi parare (cenam), π 453 = ὅπλεσθαι, Τ 172, Ψ 159; equos suos adiungere, harness one's horses, Ψ 301.

ὅπλον, ῳ, ων, οισιν, (α), utensil, implement, (1) tools, Σ 409, γ 433.—(2) rope, cable, rudens, φ 390, ξ 346; pl. cordage, rigging, β 390.—(3) armatura, weapons, armor, Κ 254, Σ 614.

ὁπλότερος, οι, ων, ἀων, comp.; sup. -οτάτη, ην, (ὅπλον), stronger, fresher, younger; γενεῇ, γινεῆφιν, in age, Β 707, Ι 58; cf. Δ 325, γ 465.

'Οπόεις, όεντος, masc., city in Lokris, home of Menoitios, Ψ 85, Σ 326, Β 531.

ὁπός, masc., (sucus), coagulum, sap of wild fig-tree, used, like rennet, to curdle milk, Ε 902†.

ὁπός, τῆς, see ὄψ.

ὁππόθεν (ὁκϝό-), interrogative adv., unde, whence, α 406, ξ 47. (Od.)

ὅππoθ(ι), rel. adv., ubi, where, Ι 577, γ 89.

ὁποῖος, ρ 421, τ 77, and ὁπποῖον, οἵης, οἷ(α), (ὁκϝοῖος), qualis, of what sort, (1) interrogative, α 171; ὁπποῖ' ἄσσα, about what sort of garments, τ 218.—(2) rel., ρ 421, Υ 250.

ὅπου, ubi, where, γ 16. (Od.)
ὑππόσ-, see follg.

ὁπόσσον, ὁπ(π)ό(σ)σ(α), ntr., how many, ξ 47; ὁπόσᾶ, quantum, Ω 7; quatenus, Ψ 238; ἐπέλθω, quantum ϝermeavero, however far I may seek, ξ 139.

ὁπ(π)ν̣τε, adv., (ὁκϝότε), quando, when, with indic. after principal tenses, δ 633, υ 386; with opt. after historical tenses, Ι 191.—Conjunction = quom, I. temporal with ind., when, σ 409, Γ 173; fut. κέν [π 282].—II. conditional, when that is spoken of which has not yet taken place, (a) with subj., (1) if,

in case that, where something is anticipated before the action of the principal verb follows, Α 163, Φ 112.—(2) in general propositions, Ο 210, Π 53, Ρ 98, δ 651, ρ 470; esp. in similes, Ο 382, ρ 128.—(3) designating repeated action in present, (b) with opt., (1) in cases of indefinite frequency in past, Τ 317, the verb in the principal sentence is ipf. or aor. (iter.), Γ 233, Ο 284, Σ 544, ξ 217.—(2) through assimilation with mode of principal verb, Υ 148, σ 148; (c) with subj. with κέν, in principal sentence: imp., κ 293 (ζ 303, ἄν); fut., Χ 366, Ι 703, Ξ 505, β 358, ν 394, χ 216 (ἄν, α 40, Π 62, Υ 317); prs. indic., γ 238, υ 83 (ἄν, λ 17); subj., θ 445, with ἄν.

ὁππότερος, ῳ, οι, οισι, η, αι, uter, which (of two), Γ 71, μ 57; ὁππιτέρωθεν, ex utra parte, Ξ 59†.

ὁπτἄλέα, έων, (ὀπτός), assata, roasted, Δ 345, μ 396.

ὁπτάω, only 3 pl. ipf. ὅπτων = ὥπτων, aor. ὥπτησε, σαν, ὅπτησαν, ἦσαι, ἤσας, σαντες, pass. aor. ὁπτηθῆναι, (ὀπτός), assarc, roast (on the spit), γ 33, Α 466; κρεῶν, partitive gen., ο 98.

ὁπτῆρας, τούς, (ὄπωπα), speculatores, scouts, spies, ξ 261 and ρ 430.

ὀπτόν, ά, (ποπ-, popina, πεπ, coctum), roasted, broiled, π 443. (Od.)

ὀ-πυίοι, ἐμειν(αι), οντες, ipf. ὥπυιε, ὅπυιε, (pubes), uxd, take to wife, uxorem ducere, Ν 429, Π 178; ὀπυίοντες, married; ὀπυιομένη, nupta.

ὄπωπα, see ὁράω.

ὀπωπῆς, τῆς, (ὄπωπα), visus, sight (vision), ι 512; adspectus, ὅπως ἤντησας, as thou hast met the view, as thine eyes have seen, γ 97.

ὀπώρη, ης, ῃ, ην, (ὀπτός, ὥρη), time of ripening, extending from the rising of Seirios (end of July) to the setting of the Pleiades, and corresponding nearly to our dog-days; τεθαλυῖα, luxuriant, exuberant fruit-time, λ 192.

ὀπωρινός, ῷ, (ὀπώρη), belonging to ὀπώρη, midsummer; ἀστήρ, Seirios, Ε 5.

ὅπ(π)ως, adv., (ὅκϝως), ut, I. interrogative, in indirect question, quomodo, how, Κ 545, Β 252; with fut. indic., often involving an intention, Ρ 635, Δ 14, α 57; with subj., ξ 329, and κέν, δ 545, Ι 681, α 296; it passes into final ut, in order that, γ 19, α 77, ν

365, ξ 181 ; joined with opt. after historical tenses, Ξ 160, ν 319, ζ 319. The transition from the use of ὅπως as indirect interrogative to that of a final conjunction can not be traced.— II. relative, as, corresponding to ὥς, ο 111 ; τοῖον, π 208, δ 109, as he is now so long away ; conditional, with subj., ζ 189, with κεν, Υ 243 ; temporal, with preterit tense, Ε 27, Λ 459, γ 373, yet in all these passages there exists a v. l. ἐπεί.

ὁράω, ὁρόω, ὦ, άας, ᾶς, ᾷ, ὦμεν ; ὄψτε ; ὅρα ; ἂν ; ὁων, ὁωντες, ὁωσα, ὦν, ὦντες, ὦσα ; mid. ὁρῶμαι, ἆται ; ὅρηαι, ηται ; ᾦτο, άασθαι, ᾶσθαι, ὠμενος, οι ; ipf. ὁρᾶτο, ὦντο ; pf. ὄπωπα, ας, plupf. ὀπώπει, aor. εἶδον and -όμην, see ΕΙΔ, V. ; fut. mid. ὄψεαι, ει, εται, εσθ(αι), ὁμενος, η, αι ; but ὄψεσθ(ε) (Ω 704, θ 313) is aor. imp., (Fop., vereor, Ger. gewar, Eng. wary), videre, be aware of, behold, τινά, τί (ἐν, before, θ 459) ὀφθαλμοῖσιν ; mid. (e. g. δ 47, Χ 166), look on with interest, gaze ; φάος ἠελίοιο=ζῆν ; also intelligere, notice, ρ 545 ; look at, over, down upon, εἰς, ἐπί, κατά τινα, τι ; κατ' ὅσσε, into the eyes, Ρ 167 ; also with follg. ὅτι, Η 448 ; οἷος, Φ 108 ; part., Ι 360.

ὄργυι(α), αν, fem., (ὀρέγω), fathom, distance spanned by the outstretched arms, Ψ 327. (Od.)

ὀρεγνύς, part., parallel form to ὀρέγων, οντας, fut. ὀρέξω, ομεν, ειν, aor. ὤρεξε, ὀρέξῃς, ῃ, ειαν, αι, ας ; mid. ὀρίγεσθαι, pf. 3 pl. ὀρωρέχαται, Π 834 ; plupf. ὀρωρέχατο, Λ 26 ; aor. ὠρέξατ(ο) and ὀρέξατ(ο), ἀσθω, ασθαι, ἀμενος, η, (por·rigo, reach), (1) stretch out, the hands toward heaven, or toward some person.—(2) extend to, and give, mid., stretch themselves (with the neck), Λ 26 ; grasp after any thing, with the hand ; stretch themselves, go at full speed, of horses ; stride, Ν 20 ; ἐγχει, lunge out, with the spear ; τινός, at any thing ; aim at or hit, δουρί ; with ἔφθη. φθῆσι, and part., hit first, any one τινά, something τι ; Ω 506, reach out the hands to the mouth (chin) of the murderer of my son ; a general expression for the act of supplication, described in word γουνοῦσθαι, and not entirely consistent with Ω 478. Hence ὀρεκτῆ-

σιν, porrectis (hastis), by thrusting with their spears, Β 543.

ὀρέοντο, ipf., parallel form to ὄρνυμι, coorti sunt, rushed forth, Β 398 and Ψ 212.

'Ορέσ-βιος, a Boiotian from Hyle, slain by Hektor, Ε 707†.

ὀρεσί-τροφος, mountain-bred, Μ 299, ζ 130.

ὀρεσ-κώοισι, ους, (κεῖμαι), having mountain-lairs, Α 268 and ι 155.

ὀρέστερος, ροι, (ὄρος, cf. ἀγρότερος), of the mountains, mountain-dragon, Χ 93 ; wolves, κ 212.

'Ορέστης, (1) a Trojan, slain by Leonteus, Μ 139, 193.—(2) a Greek, slain by Hektor, Ε 705.—(3) son of Agamemnon, returns to Mykenai in the eighth year of the reign of Aigisthos, γ 306, whom, with his own mother, Klytaimnestra, he slays (see cut under ἔδρη, from painting on ancient Greek vase), and assumes his hereditary throne, λ 461, α 30, 40, 298, δ 546, Ι 142, 284.

ὀρεστιάδες (ὄρος) νύμφαι, mountain-nymphs, Ζ 420†.

ὄρεσφι, see ὄρος.

ὀρέχθεον, ipf., (ῥοχθέω), rattled in the throat, bellowed in last agonies, Ψ 30†.

ὄρθαι, see ὄρνυμι.

'Ορθαῖος, a Trojan, Ν 791†.

"Ορθη, town in Thessaly, Β 739†.

ὀρθι(α), ntr. pl., (ὀρθός), with high, shrill voice, Λ 11†.

ὀρθο-κραιράων, gen. pl. fem., (κέραα), (1) βοῶν, with straight, upright horns, opp. the horns of sheep and goats, μ 348, Θ 231.—(2) νεῶν, Σ 3, Τ 344, also applied to ships, with reference to pointed bow and stern, yet possibly from κεραία, with straight or extended yards, antennis porrectis instructarum.

ὀρθός, όν, (ά), ὦν, (arduus), erectus, upright, usually with στῆ ; ἀναΐξας, starting up from his seat.

ὀρθόω (ὀρθός), aor. ὤρθωσε, raise up, Η 272 ; ὀρθωθείς, raised up, upright ; Κ 21, rising up.

ὁρίνω, ει, ετον, ων, ipf. ὄρινε(ν), aor. ὤρινας, ε(ν), ὤρινα, ὄρινα, ε, ι, ῃς, ῃ, αις, pass. pr. ὀρίνονται, ὀρινομένῳ, ων, οι, ους, η, ipf. ὠρίνετο, aor. ὠρίνθη, ὀρίνθη, είη, ἐντες, (ὄρνυμι), stir, raise ; γόον, Ω 760, aroused ; shock, Δ 208 ; dispersed, affrighted, χ 23; θυμόν, stir the heart with anger, θ 178, and other passions, Β 142, Γ 395, Δ 208, Λ 804, ρ 47, 150, 216, φ 87; fear, σ 75, χ 23; move to pity, touch, Λ 792, Ο 403, ξ 361, ο 486; κῆρ, ἦτορ, Π 509; pass. also grassari, rage wildly through, χ 360; conturbari, troubled, confused, Β 294, Ο 7, Π 377.

ὅρκιον, Δ 158; ὅρκι(α), pl., (ὅρκος), pledge, pignora foederis, (1) oath, Δ 158, τ 302.—(2) victims for sacrifice, Γ 245, 269; ταμεῖν, slaughter, hence foedus ferire, conclude a treaty, Β 124; πιστά, worthy of confidence, because under the protection esp. of Zeus, Γ 105, 107; Δ 155, as death for thee, fatal to thee; cf. also φυλάσσω, τελέω, δηλέομαι, συγχέω, ψεύδομαι, κατὰ πάτησαν.

ὅρκος, ον, ῳ, ον, ους, masc., (ἕρκος), (1) object by which one swears, the power called upon as witness and avenger in taking an oath, Β 755, Ο 38.—(2) oath, ἑλέσθαι τινός or τινί, take an oath from one, Χ 119, δ 746; καρτερόν, μέγαν, by the three realms, of the universe, of the gods, Τ 108; also in general, μέγας, mighty; θεῶν, oath by the gods, cf. Υ 313; γερούσιον, oath of the princes binding the entire people, Χ 119; ὅρκῳ πιστωθῆναι, bind yourselves by oath, ο 436.

ὁρμαθοῦ, τοῦ, (ὅρμος), chain, of bats hanging together, ω 8†.

ὁρμαίνων, ουσ(α), etc., part. prs., ipf. ὥρμαινε, aor. ὥρμηνε, αν, (ὁρμάω), animo volvere, turn over in the mind, Ξ 20; debate, ponder, χαλεπὰ ἀλλήλοις; (ἐνὶ) φρεσίν, κατὰ φρένα (καὶ κατὰ θυμόν), ἀνὰ θυμόν; also with ὅπως, or a double question.

ὁρμάω, only aor. ὡρμήσαμεν, σαν; ὁρμήσῃ, σειε, (ὁρμή), excitare, set in motion, τινὰ ἐς πόλεμον, πόλεμον; pass. ὁρμηθεὶς θεοῦ, a numine divi, inspired by the gods; surgere, with στῆναι ἐναντίβιον, ad resistendum, make an effort to resist; τινός, contra aliquem; mid. ipf. ὡρμᾶτ(ο), ῶντ(ο), aor. ὡρμήσατ(ο), ἤσωνται, and pass. ὡρμήθη, ήτην, ησαν, and ὁρμηθήτην, ῆναι, θείς, θέντος· ι, α, ε, ες, surgere, ruere, set out, rush on, with inf., Κ 359; ἐκ-, currere; μετά τινα, cursu persequi, pursue; ἦτόρ οἱ, animus

eius gestiebat, his heart desired; irruere, charge upon, τινός (ἐπί τινι) ἔγχεϊ, etc.; σὺν τεύχεσι, rise up in armor.

Ὀρμενίδης, αο, son of Ormenos, Amyntor, Ι 448; Ktesios, ο 414.

Ὀρμένιον, τό, town in Magnesia, Β 734†.

Ὄρμενος, (1) a Trojan, slain by Teukros, Θ 274.—(2) a Trojan, slain by Polypoites, Μ 187.—(3) and (4) see Ὀρμενίδης.

ὄρμενον, see ὄρνυμι.

ὁρμή, ῆς, ῇ, ήν, (ruo, ῥέω), impetus, ἐς ὁ. ἔγχεος ἐλθεῖν, come within the cast of a spear; Δ 466, curtus eius erat impetus, short was his effort; ε 416, irritus mihi erit, vain was my effort; β 403, profectionem, departure.

ὁρμήματα, τά, (ὁρμᾶσθαι), longings and sorrows of Helene, Β 356; others construe as obj. gen., struggles and sorrows for Helene, i. e. for her recovery.

ὁρμίζω, only aor. ὡρμίσαμεν, σαν, subj. ὁρμίσσομεν, (ὅρματα), make fast, moor, by means of stones cast from the ship, ἐπ' εὐνάων, Ξ 77, δ 785.

1. ὅρμον, ον, (ὁρμή?), landing, the running of the flat-bottomed ship upon the shore, Α 435; μέτρον, anchorage, ν 101.

2. ὅρμον, ους, masc., (σειρά, series), necklace, ο 460, Σ 401. (See adjoining cut, also Nos. 43, 44.)

Ὀρνειαί, town in Argolis, Β 571†.

ὄρνεον, τό, (ὄρνις), aviculam, bird, N 64†.

ὄρνῑς, ῑθος, ι, ες, ων, εσσι(ν) and ὑρνῑσι, avis, ales, bird, in widest signif. small and large, also of birds of prey (freq. with name of the species added, λάρῳ, αἰγυπιοῖσιν), hence also birds of omen, K 277, ω 311, β 155; omen praesagium, evil omen, Ω 219.

ὄρνυμι, imp. ὄρνῠθι, τε, inf. ὔμεν(αι), ipf. ὤρνῠε, ον, fut. ὄρσομεν, ὄρσουσα, aor. ὦρσε, σαν, ὄρσῃ, ωμεν, (and ομεν), ητε, ὄρσας, ὄρσασ(α), aor. iter. ὄρσασκε, 2 aor. ὦρορε(ν), subj. ὀρώρῃ, (orior, ruo), rouse, ἐξ εὐνῆς, also, awake, K 518; excitare, impellere, excite, impel, Δ 439; τινὰ (ἐπί) τινι or ἀντία τινός, instigare; of mental states and emotions, arouse, Ψ 14; υ 346, excite. Distinguish pf. ὄρωρε, ῃ, plupf. ὀρώρει (Ψ 112, ἐπὶ, ad eos surrexerat, arose as their chief), ὠρώρει and mid. ὄρνῡτ(αι), ὄρνυσθ(ε), μένοιο, etc., ipf. ὤρνυθ' = ὤρνυτ(ο), ὄρνυτο, υντο, pf. ὀρώρεται, ηται, fut. ὀρεῖται, aor. ὦρετο, ὦρτ(ο), ὄροντο, ὄρηται, ὄροιτο, ὄρσ(ο) and ὄρσεο, σευ, inf. ὄρθαι, part. ὄρμενον, α, orior, rise, arise, of wind, dust, Λ 151; battle, tumult K 523, fire; often like ordior, with inf. η 14, begin; of persons, from the seat or the bed, or (for battle) against some one, χαλκῷ; ruere, πρόσω, flying onward; φίλα γούνατα, have strength; spring up, H 162, χ 364.

ὀροθύνει, prs., aor. ὀρόθυνε, imp. νον, (ὄρνυμι), excitare, urge on; Φ 312, cause all the river-beds to swell.

ὄρονται, το, (Ϝορ-, ὁράω, Goth. waren, Eng. be-ware), ἐπὶ δ' —, keep ward over them, γ 471. (Od.)

ὄρος, εος, εἴ, εα, έων, εσ(σ)ι, for gen. and dat. usually εσφι, and οὔρεος, εἴ, εα, εσι(ν), mons, mountain; Νήριτον, ι 21; Παρνησοῦ, τ 431, etc.

ὀρῷ, όν, masc.,(ῥέω), serum lactis, whey, the watery portion of curdled milk, ι 222 and ρ 225.

ὄρουσ(εν), σαν, aor. from ὀρούω, part. σας. (ὄρνυμι), ruit, irruit, rush forth, dart forward, of persons and things, of missiles, Λ 359, N 505.

ὀροφῆς, τῆς, (ἐρέφω), tecti, roof or ceiling, χ 298†.

ὄροφον, τόν, (ἐρέφω), reeds used for thatching houses, Ω 451†.

ὁρόω, see ὁράω.

ὅρπηκας, τούς, surculos, saplings, shoots, Φ 38†.

ὄρσ', ὄρσεο, ὄρσευ, ὄρσας, ὄρσασκε, see ὄρνυμι.

Ὀρσίλοχος, (1) son of Alpheios, E 547 = Ὀρτίλοχος, father of Diokles, γ 489, ο 187, cf. φ 16.—(2) son of Diokles from Pherai, grandson of foregoing, E 549.—(3) a Trojan, slain by Teukros, Θ 274.—(4) fabled son of Idomeneus, ν 260.

ὀρσο-θύρη, ην, fem., (ὄρρος), back door, in the side wall of the men's hall (μέγαρον) of house of Odysseus, leading into the passage (λαύρη), χ 126, 132, 333. (See cut No. 90, and plate III., b, at end of vol.)

Ὀρτίλοχος, v. l. for Ὀρσίλοχος.

Ὀρτυγίη (ὄρτυξ), a fabled land, ο 404, ε 123.

ὀρυκτή, ῇ, ἥν, (ὀρύσσω), fossa, dug, adj. joined with τάφρος, M 72. (Il.)

ὀρυμαγδός, only sing., (rugire), any loud inarticulate noise, crash, roar, rattling; esp. the din of battle, P 424, B 810, K 185.

ὀρύσσω, aor. ὄρυξα, αν, subj. ομεν, inf. αι, part. ας, fodere, dig, κ 517; but κ 305, effodere, dig up.

ὀρφανικόν, οί, (ὀρφανός), orphaned, fatherless; ἦμαρ, X 490, the day that makes one an orphan, orphanhood.

ὀρφαναί, orbae, orphan daughters, υ 68†.

ὀρφναίην, acc., (ὄρφνη, ἔρεβος), tenebricosam, murky, νύκτα, ι 143. (Il.)

ὄρχαμος, ον, ε, (ἄρχομαι), the first of a row, leader, chief, ἀνδρῶν, acc.; of Eumaios (at close of verse), ξ 22, 121, ο 351, 389, π 36, ρ 184; of Peisistratos, γ 454, 482; Philoitios, υ 185, 254; Asios, B 837, M 110; Polites, κ 224; Achilleus, Z 99; Peisistratos, γ 400; voc. with λαῶν, of Menelaos (seven times); Agamemnon, Ξ 102; Patroklos, as dead, T 289; Achilleus, Φ 221; Odysseus, κ 538.

ὄρχατος, ου, ον, οι, masc., (ὄρχος), trees planted in rows, orchard, η 112; φυτῶν, Ξ 123.

ὀρχέομαι, ipf. ὠρχείσθην, ὠρχεῦντ(ο), aor. inf. ὀρχήσασθαι, (ὄρχος), dance, properly in a ring or row, Σ 594, θ 371.

ὀρχηθμοῖο, τοῦ, *choral dance*, θ 263,
N 637.

ὀρχηστήν, ὀρχησταί = ὀρχηστῆρες,
Σ 494†, *dancers*, Π 617. (Il.)

ὀρχηστύς, ύϊ, ύν, fem., saltatio,
d:nce, α 152, 421.

'Ορχομενός, (1) Μινυηίῳ, λ 284;
Μινύειον, B 511; very ancient city on
Lake Kopais, in Boiotia, seat of the
treasure-house of Minyas.—(2) city in
Arkadia, B 605.

ὅρχον, ους, masc., *row of vines*, η
127 and ω 341.

ὄρωρε, ει, ηται, see ὄρνυμι.

ὀρωρέχαται, το, see ὀρέγω.

I. ὅς, ἥ, ὅ, ὅου (ὅο? B 325, α 70),
ἕης, also οὔ, ἧς, etc., dat. pl. ᾗσ(ιν) E
54; orig. demonstr.; then correlative
as in Z 59, μηδ᾽ ὅν τινα—μηδ᾽ ὅς; then
apparently also interrogative.

(I.) demonstr. pr., *this, that; he, she,
it, ἥ*, only ω 286, B 872, δ 367, o 254,
ρ 221, 425, ν 289, 291, Z 132, 316,
399, H 356, Φ 198, X 201; doubled,
like h i—illi, Φ 353 sq.; in first member of correlative period, τά, A 125, δ
349; ὅ, Σ 460.

(II.) relat. pron., *who, which*.—(A) position in sentence: after monosyllabic
preps., but before those of more than
one syllable; before, or following at
an interval, a gen. part., ε 448. The
relative sentence is sometimes thrown
in parenthetically, χ 51; often precedes demonstrative, δ 349; specifying clauses in this case added by a
dem. pron., the place of which, in
apod. of conditional clauses, is sometimes supplied by δέ; two or more
relative sentences succeed each other,
either without connective, ψ 229, or
the second relative falls away, β 54,
δ 737, ξ 86; or may be replaced by
a dem. or pers. pron., A 95.—(B) Construction (a) with respect to antecedent, (1) ad sensum, genere, K
278; numerus plur. after collec-
tives, ι 96, 332; vice versâ = οἷα, μ
97, Z 228.—(2) the antecedent must
sometimes be supplied, σ 286; τῶν,
δ 177.—(3) antecedent assimilates to
itself the case of the relative, Ψ 649,
ω 30; more often the reverse, K 416.
—(4) antecedent drawn into the rel.
clause (attraction), B 38.—(b) as regards mode, (1) with ind. of existing

circumstances, A 37; so especially in
descriptions, also with κέ.—(2) with
subj. of possibility (the realization of
which is expected), esp. in general
statements or in comparisons, δ 165.
—(3) with opt., of desire, H 342; after
principal verb in the preterit tense,
to denote an action repeated indefi-
nitely often, ι 94; with κέ, as in principal sentences, A 64.—(C) relative
clauses may be classified, (a) simply
descriptive or explanatory, H 349, I
110, K 323.—(b) hypothetical, ο 72.
—(c) final, δ 389, mittit qui dicat,
ὅς (κεν) ἐρεῖ, (κεν) εἴπῃ, κεν εἴποι; so
also after principal verb in preterit
tense, also ὃς εἴπεν.—(d) causal, B
239, 275, σ 222.—(e) apparently interrogative (in indirect question), δ
740, ρ 363, B 365, Φ 609.—(D) joined
with particles, ὃς δή, *who plainly*; ὃς
καί, *who also, who too*; ὃς ῥά (τε, B
522); τῇ γάρ, Z 393.

II. ὅς, ἥ, ὅν (properly σϜος, Lat.
svos, suus, then Ϝός, Ϝοῖο, etc.; Ϝ
afterward replaced in all forms by
rough breathing), also the form ἥφι,
one's own, α 402, ι 28 [ν 320]; tuus,
T 174; eius, [δ 192]; usually reflexive, suus, e. g. α 269; ὄνδε δόμονδε,
to his own house; freq. with pron., τό,
τά, etc., Φ 305, M 280, ξ 153, Σ 451, ι
250. It often precedes its noun, π 411,
σ 8 (precedes the preposition, Z 500);
and often follows it, E 71, Ω 36, γ 39
(follows preposition, ο 251). The noun
to which it refers is often not the subject, though in the same sentence, Π
753, α 218, ι 369, λ 282, Ψ 153, ω 365;
sometimes in another sentence, K 256,
δ 618, 643.

ὀσίη, οὐχ —, non fas (est), it is
against *divine* law to—; with inf., π
423. (Od.)

ὅσος, οι, η, ην, αι, ὅσον, α, and ὅσσος,
οι, οισιν, ους, η, ῃ, ας, ον, (α), quan-
tus, pl. quot. Quantitative adj. with
varying meaning according to its antecedent, e. g. *as much as, how much,
as great as, how great; as far as, how
far;* its proper antecedent is τόσος,
after which it is translated *as*; with τίς
or τί = quidam, fere, hence ὅσσον
τε = fere; agrees in gender with the
noun to which it refers, B 845; ὅσον
ἔπι, *as far as*, B 616; elsewh. ὅσσον

τ’ ἔπι, Ψ 251, ν 114 = per quantum spatium; ἐπί θ’ ὅσσον, P 368 ; ὅσσοι νῦν βροτοί, θ 222; ntr. ὅσ(σ)ον, (1) as far as (a certain distance), I 354.—(2) quantopere, by as much as, by how much, before comparatives and superlatives, A 186, 516.

ὅς περ, B 318 ; ὅ περ, H 114 ; ἥ περ, Ψ 79, etc. ; τοί περ, τῶν περ = pr. rel. with πέρ (q. v.), (1) the very one who (which), B 318.—(2) which however, B 286.

ὄσσα, ῃ, αν, (Fόκja, vox), fama divinitus excita, rumor, α 282; ἐκ Διός, personified as messenger of Zeus, Fama, B 93, ω 413. Ὄσσα, mountain in Thessaly, λ 315.

ὄσσα, see ὅσος.

ὀσσάκι, quoties, as often as, Φ 265 ; relative to τοσσάκι, λ 585.

ὀσσάτιον, masc., quantum, how great, E 758†.

ὄσσε, τώ, (ὄκjέ, oculi), eyes; its adj. often pl., N 435; its verb occurs in all three nos., M 466, O 608, N 617.

ὀσσόμενος, ον, η, part. prs., ipf. ὄσσετο, οντο, (ὄσσε), see forebode, κ 374, Σ 224 ; give to forebode, threaten, β 152, Ξ 17 ; ἐνὶ φρεσί, α 115 ; υ 81, see in spirit, picture to one's se'f.

ὄσσος, see ὅσος.

ὅς τε, ἥ τε, τό τε, (masc. also ὅτε, quicunque, μ 40, ξ 221, Π 54, O 468); τάς τε, Λ 554 ; τά τε, B 262, E 52, ε 438 = οἶα, ν 60 ; differing from ὅς only in binding more closely together, and emphasizing the mutual relation between the chief and dependent clause, that which, Δ 361, E 332, I 117, O 130, δ 207, η 312, ξ 466; then, without general sense, like quippe qui, (ἅτε), which in fact, either causal, or of what is permanent or usual, ν 60: e. g. custom, Λ 779; manner, γ 73, X 127 ; occupation, Λ 238 ; ὅς ῥά τε, who, in fact.

ὀστέον, ου, ῳ, ον (α), ὄφιν, for gen. and dat. pl., (ossa), bone, Λ 97, M 384; λευκά, the bleached bones of the dead, λ 221, Ψ 83.

ὅστις, ἥτις, ὅτι, οὕτινος, ἧστινος, ὕντινα, οἵτινες, αἵτινες, οὕστινας, ἅστινας; also from ὅτις, ὅττ(ι), ὅττεο = ὅτ(τ)ευ, ὀτέῳ, pronounce ὅτjῳ, M 428 ; ὅτινα, ὅτεων, ὀτέοισι, ὕτινα, and ἅσσα (q. v.), quicunque, whosoever, which-

soever, also distributive before (ι 96) or after pl., γ 355; also indirectly interrogative, Γ 167; οὐκ οἶδ’ ὅστις, mihi ignotus.

ὅτ’, (1) = ὅτε. — (2) = ὅ τε, i. e. ὅτ: τε.—(3) doubtful whether ε or ι is elided, the meaning is because, A 244.

ὅταν, better ὅτ’ ἄν, see ὅτε.

ὅ τε, see ὅς τε.

ὅτε, (see ὅ), quom.—I. temporal, correlative with τότε, ἐνθα, ἔπειτα.—(A) with indic., (1) pres., when, where, since, B 743 ; -δή, β 314 ; ὅτε τε, when usually, B 471; with fut. and κέν, Υ 335.—(2) with preterit tenses, when, how, memini cum, A 396, Φ 396, P 627 ; with pf., Φ 156; plupf., E 392 ; ὅτε τε, with aor., E 803 ; ipf., η 324 ; ὅτε δή ῥα, Γ 221; with aor., ὡς ὅτε, as, then, when, Γ 33, Δ 319.—(3) iterative, ὅτε περ, E 802 ; introducing a simile, ὡς δ’ ὅτε, with aor., Γ 33 ; with fut., A 518. —(B) with subj., when, (1) of possibility with expected realization, Φ 323, ψ 258, π 267 ; with ἄν, Z 448, Δ 164, Θ 373, H 459, Θ 406, (πρίν—πρίν γ’ ὅτ’ ἄν, δ 478); with κέν, Z 225, I 138, ν 180, ο 446, A 567, θ 243, Υ 130; εἰς ὅτε κεν, against the time when, β 99.—(2) iterative (a) in general, κ 486, Δ 263, η 72, π 72, φ 132, τ 567, Ω 417; after past tense, Ξ 522 ; with κέν, K 130, I 501; ἄν, Δ 53, ν 100, B 397, λ 17 ; (b) in maxims or conventional phrases, ι 6, σ 134, O 207, ξ 59 ; κέν, λ 218, Υ 168 ; (c) in similes, B 782, P 756, csp. ὡς δ’ ὅτε preceding the principal sentence (with τοῖοι, Δ 141; elsewh. follg. with ὥς), B 147, X 189, ε 328, ψ 158 ; follg. the principal sentence, A 325, Δ 130; ὡς δ’ ὅτ’ ἄν—ὥς, κ 217, K 5, Ω 480, ε 394, ψ 233 ; ὡς ὅτε, without verb, tanquam, just like, λ 368 ; ἕως ὅτε, only ρ 358.—(C) with opt., when, (1) conditional, N 319, μ 114, Σ 465, ν 390, π 197, Ξ 248, ψ 185, N 319, ε 189.—(2) iterative, the principal sentence being iterative (a) in sense, A 610, K 78, Σ 566, P 733, θ 220, λ 510, 513, ι 208, Γ 233, ξ 220 ; with κέν, I 525 ; (b) in form, its verb being iterative, θ 87, Γ 217.—II. causal, quom, quando, whereas, since, A 244.

ὀτὲ μέν before ἄλλοτε or ὀτὲ δέ, Υ 49, Λ 566 = modo—modo, now—now.

ὀτέοισι, ὕτευ, ὀτέῳ, see ὅστις.

ὅτί, ὅττί (ntr. from ὅτις, never suffers elision), (1) as adv.=quam, with superlatives, Δ 193. — (2) as conj.= quod, that, ὅττι ῥα, φ 415; and because, B 255, ξ 52, 441.

ὅ, τι, ὅ, ττι, see ὅστις.

ὅτινα, ὅτινας, ὅτις, see ὅστις.

ὀτραλέως, adv., (ὀτρηρός), nimbly, quickly, Γ 260, τ 100.

'Οτρεύς, ῆος, son of Dymas, king in Phrygia, Γ 186†.

ὀτρηρός, ώ, οἱ, ούς, ή, (ὀτρύνω, τρέω), nimble, busy, ready, A 321, δ 23; adv. -ῶς, δ 735.

ὅ-τριχας, acc. pl., (θρίξ), with like hair, like-colored, B 765†.

'Οτρυντείδης, Iphition, Υ 383, 389, son of 'Οτρυντεύς, king of Hyde, Υ 384.

ὀτρυντύς, ύν, fem., (ὀτρύνω), encouragement, T 234, 235.

ὀτρύνω, εις, ει, έμεν, etc., ipf. ὤτρυνον, ὄτρυνον, ε(ν), iter. ὀτρύνεσκον, fut. ὀτρυνέω, έει, έων, etc., aor. ὤτρῡνα, (εν), ὀτρύνῃσι(ν), ῡναι, also unaugmented, impellere, urge on, τινὰ εἴς (ἐπί, προτί) τι, εἴσω, -δέ; also with inf., ξ 374, O 402; rarely ἵππους, κύνας, τί, hasten, maturare, ὁδόν τινι, speed one's departure; ἑταίρους, send forth; mid. ὀτρύνεσθε, ωμεθ(α), ipf. ὠτρύνοντο, etc., make haste, κ 425.

ὅττι, see ὅτί. ὅ,ττι, see ὅστις.

οὐ, οὐκί, οὐχί, before vowels οὐκ, before rough breathing οὐχ, particle of objective or absolute negation, the thing is declared not to be so, while μή (subjective negation) declares that one thinks it is not so, not, no; position, usually, at end of verse, often doubled, e. g., γ 28, θ 280, κ 551, θ 32, A 86, Θ 482.—(1) in independent assertion, also subjective (opt. with κέ, A 271; fut. subj., A 262; subj. and κέ, H 197; with reference to what is past, ω 61; hypothetical, E 22).—(2) in dependent assertion after ὡς, ὅτι, ὀθούνεκα (not in protestation), δ 377; with inf., P 176; after verbs of thinking; in relative sentence, A 234, B 36.—(3) in causal sentence after ἐπεί, A 119; ὅτι, A 244; οὕνεκα, A 111, and conclusion. —(4) where subst. or word used substantively replaces subordinate clause, β 50.—(5) joined closely to a verb, changing its meaning into its converse,

esp. with φάναι, ἐῶ, ἐθέλω, τελέω, χραίσμῃ, cf. also Δ 57, ν 143, ω 251, β 274, Γ 289; οὔτι, not a whit, by no means, δ 292; οὐ πάμπαν, οὐ πάγχυ, nequaquam, in no wise.—(6) in questions expecting affirmative answer, K 165, η 239; also in question containing a summons, η 22; cf. E 32 and ἠὲ καὶ οὐκί.—(7) οὐ μά, see μά; οὐχ ὥς, φ 427; οὐ μὰν οὐδέ, Δ 512.

οὗ, οἷ, ἕ, (orig. form σϜοῦ, etc., traces of Ϝ at hand in many forms, sui), as reflexive always retains its accent; as simple pron. of 3 pers. enclitic; gen. ἕο, εἷο, εὗ, ἕθεν, eius, and more freq. sui (εὗ, only Υ 464, sui; elsewh. eius, and enclitic); dat. οἷ, ei (ἑοῖ, without Ϝ, before αὐτῷ, sibi, N 495); and sibi; acc. ἕ, and (not enclitic, without Ϝ) ἕε, se; not eum, eam, eos, but B 196 = eum, A 236 = id. ἕ αὐτόν, ἥν, se ipsum, am, himself, herself.

οὔασι, ατα, see οὖς.

οὖδας, εος, εἴ, ει, (ὁδός, οὐδός), solum, surface of the earth; ἄσπετον, immensum; οὐδάσδε, and freq. οὔδει, to the ground, on the earth, κ 440; ὀδὰξ ἕλον οὖδας, they bit the dust, see ὀδάξ; also pavimentum, pavement; κραταίπεδον, hard-surfaced, ψ 46.

οὐδέ (οὐ δέ), neque, (1) and not, τὸ (τὰ) ἤδη (οἷδεν) ὅ (ὅττι), B 38; ι 408, with double meaning nor, and not; introduces an apodosis, E 789; causal (subordinative), B 873, δ 493, 729; οὐδὲ γὰρ οὐδέ, for by no means, E 22; οὐδέ τε, (a) continuative, in a negative sentence, nor, P 42; (b) in an affirmative sentence, and not, nor, β 182, A 406; — τι, nor at all (separated by intervening words, N 521, P 401, X 279), very freq. before οἶδα, χρή, χρεώ, with acc., δ 492; and with other verbs, A 468, Ξ 66; πολύς, λίην, πρίν, T 169; πάμπαν, by no means, ω 245.—(2) yet not, and also not, Γ 215, ν 243; οὐδὲ μέν, nec vero, A 154; non profecto, B 203; non enim, ο 246; — μὲν οὐδέ, but also not, B 703, cf. ψ 27.—(3) ne — quidem, not even, ἡβαιόν, ne paullulum quidem, strengthens preceding negation, N 106; — περ, λ 452, elsewh. always separated; — εἰ, not even if, γ 115; — ὥς, ne sic quidem, not even thus, φ 427.—(4) — οὐδέ (not even), nor yet, A 332, β 369, δ 492.—(5) but not, after μέν, better separated, οὐ δέ, E 138; and yet not, nor yet, A 124, Ι' 215; οὐδέ —δέ, but not, —but, Γ 348.

οὐδενί, τὸ ὂν μένος, in his courage, οὐδενὶ εἴκων, yielding to no one; elsewh. ntr. οὐδέν, nihil, nequaquam, nothing, by no means, in no respect, A 244, X 332, Ω 370, δ 195.

οὐδενόσ-ωρα (ὥρα), worth no notice, contemnenda, Θ 178†.

οὐδέ πη, neque usquam, nor anywhere, μ 433 = οὐδέ ποθι, ν 114; οὐδέ ποτε, neque unquam, nor ever, never, E 789, β 26; οὐδέ πω, — τί πω, nondum, not yet, A 108; neque ulla ratione, nor in any way.

οὐδετέρωσε, in neutram partem, Ξ 18†.

οὐδός, οἷο, οὔ, όν, masc., (ὁδός), limen, δ 680, threshold of women's apartment; λάϊνος, lapideum, but ν 258, χ 127 = κρηπίδωμα, fundamentum, stone foundation walls.

οὐδός, ῷ, όν, fem., (ὁδός), way, ρ 196; γήραος, the path of old age; ἱκέσθαι, arrive at, tread upon the path of old age, commonly interpreted as threshold (see foregoing), which does not suit all passages.

οὖθαρ, ατα, ntr., uber, udder, metaphorically, fertile, fat land, I 141.

οὔκ, see οὐ.

Οὐκ-αλέγων, οντα, Trojan counsellor, Γ 148†.

οὐκ-έτι, non iam, non amplius, no longer, H 357; — πάμπαν, or — πάγχυ, no more at all.

οὐκ-ί = οὐκ, at close of verse, δ 80.

οὐλάς, τάς, (ὅλος?), barley-corns, roasted, mixed with salt, and sprinkled between the horns of victim, mola salsa, γ 441†.

οὐλἄμόν, τόν, (2. οὖλος, εἰλέω), ἀνδρῶν, throng, crowd (of men), Δ 251. (Il.)

οὖλε (1. οὖλος), imp. pres., salve, — καὶ μάλα χαῖρε, hail and a hearty welcome to thee, ω 402†.

οὐλῆς, ήν, fem., (ἕλκος, vulnus?), scar, cicatrix, τ 391, φ 219. (Od.)

οὔλιος (ὀλοός, οὖλος), perniciosus, baleful, deadly, Λ 62†.

οὐλο-κάρηνος (2. οὖλος), with thick, curly hair, τ 246†.

οὐλόμενον, (ε), η, ης, ῃ, ην, ων, prs. part. from οὔλομαι = ὄλλυμι, accursed, δ 92.

1. οὖλῳ, ον, (σολϜος, salvus, sollus), solidus, whole, ρ 343 and ω 118.

2. οὖλος, ων; η, ην, ας; ον, (ϜολϜρος, vellus, Ger. wolle, Eng. wool), woollen, Π 224, ταπήτων and χλαῖναν, ας, τ 225, Ω 646, δ 50, ρ 89; bushy, thick, crisp, κόμας, ζ 231, ψ 158; ntr., confusedly, incessantly, P 756.

3. οὖλος, ον, ε, (ὀλϜός, ὀλοός), perniciosus, destructive, murderous, Ares, E 461; Achilleus, Φ 536, E 717; of dream, baneful, B 6, 8.

οὐλο-χύτας, τάς, (οὐλάς, χέω), sprinkled-barley, poured or scattered from baskets, δ 761, between the horns of the victim, A 458, as initiatory sacrificial rite; κατάρχεσθαι, = begin the solemn rites.

Οὔλυμπος, see Ὄλυμπος.

οὐμός = ὁ ἐμός, θ 360†.

οὖν, particle, never standing alone, igitur, then, therefore, (1) resumptive, Γ 340, N 1; ἐπεὶ οὖν, ξ 467.—(2) continuing or further developing a thought, α 414, hence; μὲν οὖν, δ 780.—(3) carrying the thoughts backward, ἐπεὶ οὖν, since once for all; ὡς οὖν, so when, when then, A 57 and Γ 4, O 363, ρ 226. —(4) used in appending an attendant circumstance in harmony with what precedes, neither certainly nor; neither, nor yet; according as it occurs in the first or second of correlative clauses: μήτ' οὖν—μήτε, ρ 401; οὔτ' οὖν—οὔτε, α 414; οὐδέ τις οὖν, ξ 254; γὰρ οὖν, for certainly, B 350; εἴ γ' οὖν, if in any case, E 258.

οὔνεκα = οὗ ἕνεκα, (1) quamobrem, therefore, corresponding to τούνεκα, Ι' 403.—(2) quod, quia, because, A 11, δ 569.—(3) that, ε 216.

οὔνεσθε, see ὄνομαι.

οὔνομα, see ὄνομα.

οὔ περ, not at all, Ξ 416. οὔ πη, (1) nequaquam, in no way, ε 410.—(2) = οὔ ποθ(ι), A 278, N 309, nusquam, nowhere. οὔ ποτε, nunquam, Z 124. οὔ πω, (1) nondum, not yet, A 224, β 118.—(2) = οὔ πως, in no wise, Γ 306. οὔ πώ ποτ(ε), φ 123, μ 98, never yet at any time. οὔ πως, nulla ratione, nequaquam, nohow, on no *terms*; ἐστι, with inf., ε 103, ι 411; absolutely, χ 136.

οὔρα, see οὖρον.

οὐραῖαι, fem. pl., (οὐρά), τρίχες, hairs *of the tail,* Ψ 520†.

Οὐρᾶνίωνες, ων, (οὐρανός), caelites, *heavenly, celestial,* Ω 547; θεοί, A 570, ι 15; also as subst., E 373, 898.

οὐρᾶνόθεν (οὐρανός), caelitus, *from heaven,* also with ἐξ —, Θ 19; ἀπό —, Φ 199. **οὐρᾶνόθι** πρό, *before,* i. e. not yet having passed through and beyond the vault of *the heavens, under the sky,* Γ 3†.

οὐρᾶνο-μήκης (μῆκος), *high as heaven,* ε 239†.

οὐρᾶνός, οῦ, ῷ, όν, masc., *heaven,* (1) conceived of as fortress of brass or iron; above the αἰθήρ, B 458; hence οὐρανὸν ἵκει, makes its way up to heaven, ι 20, ο 329.—(2) as home of gods; ἔχουσιν, inhabit; Olympus towers aloft and its summit penetrates into heaven, A 497; invoked as witness to oath, εὐρύς, Ο 36, ε 184.

οὔρεα, see ὄρος, mons, *mountain.*

οὐρεύς, only pl. **οὐρῆες,** εῦσι, ῆας, mulus, *mule,* Α 50; but in interpolated verse, Κ 84 = οὔρους, *guard, sentry.*

οὐρή, dat. οὐρῇ, pl. -ῇσιν, cauda, *tail,* of wild beasts, Η 215; of the hound Argos, ρ 302.

οὐρίαχος, ον, (οὐρά), ἔγχεος, *the thicker, butt end* of spear, Ν 443, Π 612. (Il.) (See cut under ἀμφϊ-γύοισιν.)

1. **οὖρον,** α, (ὄρνυμι), ἡμιόνοιιν, ων, mules' *range,* θ 124, Κ 351, as much as a pair of mules can plough, for which the later word was πλέθρον, i. e. πέλεθρον,point at which the team, having finished the furrow, turns, *furrow's length;* δίσκου, Ψ 431, *discus-throw;* as measure of distance, θ 124.

2. **οὖρος,** ον, οι, masc., (aura), *fair wind,* ε 268; proleptically ἴκμενον, following, favoring, β 420.

3. **οὖρον,** τόν, pl. οισι, (ὄρος), *landmark, boundary,* Φ 405, Μ 421.

4. **οὖρος,** ον, masc., (Φόρος, ὁρᾶν), *guardian,* ο 89; Ἀχαιῶν, *bulwark* of the Achaians, γ 411.

5. **οὖρος,** εος, dat. pl. οὔρεσι, see ὄρος, mons.

6. **οὖρός. οὐρούς,** τούς, (ὀρύσσω), *ditches* or *channels,* serving as ways for

the ships, leading from the camp down to the sea, Β 153†.

οὖς, acc. sing., ὡσίν, dat. pl., and **οὔατος,** τ(α), ασι, auris; ἀπ' οὔατος, far from the *ear,* = unheard, Σ 272; from resemblance to an ear, *handles,* Λ 633.

οὐτάζων, prs. part., ipf. οὔταζον, pass. -ζοντο, aor. οὔτασε(ν), ῃ, αι, pf. pass. οὔτασται, μένος; also from οὐτάω, aor. **οὔτησε,** iter. οὐτήσασκε, aor. pass. οὐτηθείς; from οὔτημι, imp. οὔτᾱε, aor. 3 sing. οὖτα, iter. οὔτασκε, inf. οὐτάμεν(αι), and pf. pass. οὐτάμένην, οι, icere, *hit, wound* by cut or thrust, αὐτοσχεδίην and αὐτοσχεδόν, τινά, also with acc. of part hit; with double acc., Δ 467, Ν 438, χ 294; with κατά, Λ 338, Ξ 446; ἕλκος, vulnus infligere.

οὔτε, neque, *neither, nor;* usually corresponding to οὔτε or οὐ; also to οὐδέ, or to τέ, καί, δέ; οὔτε τι, δ 264, Α 108.

οὐτήσασκε, see οὐτάζων.

οὔτι, see οὔτις.

οὐτϊδᾶνός, οἷο, οἷσιν, *worthless,* Α 231.

οὔτϊς, τινι, τιν(α), τινες, τι, parts often written separately, nullus, *no one,* **οὔτι,** as adv., nequaquam, *not at all, by no means,* with verbs, β 411, Β 338, β 235, Α 241; — γε, Η 142, Ι 108, Ψ 515; with adjs., Θ 81, Α 153; with advs., Α 416; οὔ μέ τι, Υ 361.

Οὔτις, τιν, fabled name, *No-man,* ι 366, 369.

οὔτοι, *certainly not,* α 203, ι 27, 211.

οὗτος, αὕτη, τοῦτο, hic, *this,* referring to what is in the mind, or to what is mentioned or known, Γ 178, 200, 229, Τ 8; in reference to second person, Κ 82; in contrast to ἐγώ, γ 359, σ 57, Θ 141; used antithetically, ν 230, Ζ 352, χ 254, 70, 78; καί μοι τοῦτ' ἀγόρευσον, α 174, δ 645, ν 232; used correlatively, Γ 177; referring back to something already mentioned, π 373, Α 126,β 256; freq. with γέ : where apparently referring to what follows, κ 431, α 267, ε 23, ν 314, η 299, φ 200, to be, however, explained as epexegetical (offering additional explanation), or οὗτος refers to what is known or has preceded; it is never used like ὅδε in wider signif., nor in reference to time.

οὖτως, before consonants οὖτω, (οὖτος), sic, thus, so, in reference to what is present in sight or thought, ε 377, Φ 184; with verb in 2 pers., κ 378, Δ 243, K 37, E 249; in 3 pers., Γ 42, 169, E 717; referring back (1) to a single thought, γ 358, φ 257, A 131, H 198, T 155 (closing a sentence, δ 485, ε 146, λ 348).—(2) to a hypothetical sentence, β 334, τ 128, K 129.—(3) — δή, sic igitur, thus then, B 158, ε 204, θ 167, so true is it that; interrogative, Ξ 88, O 201, 553; — θην, N 620; referring apparently to what follows, N 225, Ξ 69, Ω 373, δ 148, θ 465; tantopere, B 120; — ὡς, ξ 440, ο 341 cf. ita—ut, σ 236; so certainly as, N 825.

οὐχ, before rough breathing, see οὐ.

οὐχί, non, no, not, O 716, π 279.

ὄφειλον, ipf. indic. pl., and pass. ipf. ὀφείλετο, owe, with χρεῖος, a debt, Λ 688, 686, 698.

'Οφελέστης, αο, (1) a Trojan, slain by Teukros, Θ 274.—(2) a Paionian, slain by Achilleus, Φ 210.

1. ὀφέλλω (ὀφείλω), ὀφέλλεις, ει, ετε, ipf. ὄφελλον, ὤφελλον, ες, ε, aor. ὄφελον, ες, (εν), and ὤφελε, ετ(ε), pass. prs. ὀφέλλεται, debere, owe, χρεῖος, a debt; in aor., debebam, of impossible wish, ought to have, etc., freq. with αἴθε, εἴθε, ὥς, also with μή, utinam, would that, Λ 380, Φ 279, Ω 764, β 184, I 698, P 686.

2. ὀφέλλεις, ει, ωσι, ειεν, ειν, ουσα, ipf. ὤφελλον, ες, (ε), ὀφέλλε(ν), pass. ὀφέλλετο, augere, increase, augment, Γ 62, Υ 242, π 174; B 420, laborem auxit ingentem, prolepsis, increase so as to be dreadful; Ψ 524, stand in stead; μῦθον, multiply words.

ὄφελος, τό, commodum, advantage; with εἶναι, γενέσθαι, prodesse, profit, N 236, X 513.

'Οφέλτιος, (1) a Greek, slain by Hektor, Λ 302.—(2) a Trojan, slain by Euryalos, Z 20.

ὀφθαλμός, οἴο, οῦ, ῷ, όν; ὤ, οἴιν; οἱ, ὦν, οἶσ(ιν), οὕς, (ὄπωπα), oculus, eye, A 587; βολαί, δ 150, glances; ἐς ὀφθαλμούς, in conspectum, before one's eyes; cf. ἐν ὀφθαλμοῖσιν, θ 459; cf. also δ 47.

ὄφιν, masc., [ō], anguem, snake, M 208†.

ὄφρα, I. temporal: (1) aliquamdiu, sometime, O 547.—(2) dum, as long as, while, (a) with indic. of actuality, B 769.—(b) with subj. of probability, (a) so long, as long as, Ψ 47, Λ 477, σ 132; κεν, θ 147, Ω 553; ἄν, X 388; κέν and ἄν—τόφρα, β 124, ε 361, ζ 259, Λ 202; (b) until, with κέν, τ 17; with ἄν, Σ 409, P 186.—II. final: in order that (freq. of the intention of destiny, B 359); ὄφρα τάχιστα, Δ 269; ὄφρ' εἴπω, φ 276; εὖ εἰδῇς, A 185, (a) with indic. fut., δ 163, ρ 6.—(b) with subj. 140 times (κέν 9, ἄν 7 times), the verb of principal sentence being (a) imp. or imp. inf., θ 27, χ 391, P 685 (κέν, σ 182, Ω 636; ἄν, ρ 10), I 370, X 343 (κέν, κ 298); (β) subj., Ψ 83, ψ 255 (κέν, B 440); (γ) opt., Ω 75, ο 431; (δ) indic. fut., Z 365, Π 423 (κέν, τ 45, γ 359); pres., π 195, 31, M 281 (μή, A 579; ἄν, σ 363); pret., π 234, γ 15, Δ 486 (ἄν, κ 65, O 23).—(c) with opt., H 340, 349; assimilated through influence of principal verb, υ 80.—III. special cases, referrible to I. or II. with subj., Z 258 (ἄν, Υ 24; κέν, Ω 431).

ὀφρυόεσσα, from ὀφρύς, cf. supercilium, on the brow or edge of a steep rock, beetling, high-throned, X 411†.

ὀφρύς, ὀφρύος, ὑσι, ὑας = ὑς, fem., brow, I 620; Υ 151, brow of a hill.

ὄχ(ἄ) (cf. ἔξοχα), always before ἄριστος, α, etc., eminenter, by far, A 69, ω 429, γ 129.

ὄχεσφι, see ὄχος.

ὀχετ-ηγός (ὀχετός, ἄγω), laying out a ditch, Φ 257†.

ὀχεύς, ἦα, ἦες, ας, masc., (ἔχω), holder, (1) chin-strap of helmet, Γ 372.—(2) clasps on belt, Δ 132.—(3) bolt (as in cut No. 32), M 121.

ὀχέειν, ἐονται, pass. ἔεσθαι, ipf. 3 sing. ὀχεῖτο, ipf. iter. ὀχέεσκον, fut. mid. ὀχήσονται, aor. ὀχήσατο, vehere, bear; play, νηπιάας; elsewh. endure; pass. and mid., vehi, be borne, drive, sail, P 77, ε 54.

'Οχήσιος, an Aitolian, father of Periphas, E 843†.

ὀχθέω, ὤχθησαν, ἐχθήσας, (ἄχθος), aegre ferre, indignari, bear with indignation, take ill, A 570; μέγ', in great wrath he spake, δ 30, ψ 182.

ὄχθης, gen., ῃ, ην, ας, ῃσιν, ας, fem., (ἔχω), ripa, litus, *bank, shore*, Φ 17, 171, 172, ι 132.

ὀχλεῦνται = ἐονται, from ὀχλέω, (ὀχλύς), *are swept away*, Φ 261†.

ὀχλίσσειαν, 3 pl. opt. aor. from ὀχλίζω, (ὀχλός), *would heave from its place, raise*, M 448, ι 242.

1. **ὄχος, ὄχεα**, ἔων, ἔεσσι, εσφι, εα, ntr. pl., (Fεχ, veho), *chariots*, Λ 160, Δ 297.

2. **ὄχος, ὄχοι**, pl., (ἔχω), νηῶν, *shelters for ships*, ε 404†.

ὄψ, ὀπός, ἡ, ὄπ(α), usually with F, Fοπός, Fόπα but ὀπί, fem., (Fεπ-, vocis), vox, (1) *voice; ὀλίγῃ*, with faint, feeble voice; also of insects and animals, Γ 152, Δ 435.—(2) *speech, words*, H 53.

ὀψέ (ὄπισθε), postea, *afterward*, P 466, Δ 161; sc ο, *late*, I 247, ε 272, Φ 232.

ὀψείοντες, desiderative part. from 'ψομαι, *desiring to see*, with gen., Ξ 3ι†.

ὀψί-γονος, ων, (ὀψέ, γόνος), *late-born, posterity*, posteri, postumus, Π 31, Γ 353.

ὀψίμον (ὀψέ), *late* (coming), B 325†.

ὄψις, ὄψει, fem., (ὄψομαι), *power of sight; ἰδεῖν*, see with one's eyes, Υ 205, ψ 94; conspectus, species, *appearance, exterior*, Z 468, Ω 632.

ὀψί-τέλεστον (τελέω), *late of fulfillment*, B 325†.

ὀψόμενος, etc., see ὁράω.

ὄψον, ου, ntr., (ἔψω), *that which is cooked and eaten with bread; onion*, Λ 630, ποτῷ, as relish with wine; γ 480, *flesh*.

Π.

πάγεν = πάγησαν, πάγη, see πήγνυμι.

πάγοι, masc., (πήγνυμι), scopuli, *cliffs*, ε 405 and 411.

πάγ-χαλκος, and -χάλκεος, ον, (χαλκός), *all of bronze*, θ 403; fig., a man with sinews of brass, Υ 102.

παγ-χρύσεοι (χρυσός), *all of gold*, B 448†.

πάγχῦ (χέFω, instead of παγχύδην, cf. ῥύδην, lit. "pouring out, heaping up every thing"?), prorsus, *altogether, wholly, absolutely*, ρ 217.

πάθε, ἔειν, ῃσθα, see πάσχω.

παιδνός (παῖς), puer, *lad, mere child*, φ 21 and ω 338.

παιδο-φόνοιο (φόνος), *murderer of one's children*, Ω 506†.

παίζουσι, part. όντων, ούσας, aor. imp. παίσατε, (παῖς), ludere, *play*, also of dance, θ 251; σφαίρῃ, game at ball, ζ 100.

Παιήων, ονος, *physician of the gods*, E 401, 899; from him the Egyptian physicians traced their descent, δ 232.

παιήονα, *song of triumph* or *thanksgiving* (addressed to Apollon), A 473, X 391.

Παίων, ονες, *tribe in Makedonia and Thrake*, on river Axios, allies of Trojans, Π 291; ἀγκυλότοξοι, K 428; δολιχεγχέας, Φ 155; ἱπποκορυστάς, Π 287.

Παιονίδης, Agastrophos, son of Παίων, Λ 339, 368.

Παιονίη, *fertile territory of the* Παίονες, P 350, Φ 154.

παιπαλόεντος, ἔσσης, ῃ, αν, (πάλλω?), *rugged, rough*, N 17, 33, P 743, κ 97. (A word of uncertain meaning.)

παῖς, in thesis of first foot, παῖς π 337, δύς, δί, (α), πάϊ; (ε); ες, ων, σι and δεσσι(ν), (πάF-ις, pover=puer), *child*, σ 216, δ 688; *maiden*, δ 13; *daughter*, η 313, α 278; *son*, Δ 512, I 37; *young*, Φ 282; with νέος, δ 665.

Παισός, *town on the* Propontis, E 612, see Ἀπαισός.

παιφάσσουσα, intensive form from stem of φά-ος, exsplendescens, *dazzling*, B 450†.

πάλαι (πάρος), olim, *long ago*, opp. νέον, I 527, νῦν, I 105; iamdiu, pridem, *long, all along*, ρ 366, υ 293, ψ 29.

πάλαι-γενεῖ, ἐς, dat. and voc. sing., (γένος), grandaevus, *full of years*, Γ 386, χ 395.

παλαιός, οῦ, ῷ, οἱ, ἡ, αἱ, ὦν, ἁ, (πάλαι), senex, *old, aged, ancient*, Ξ 108, α 395 ; φωτί, Ξ 136; vetustus, β 293, 340; comp. παλαιοτέρους, seniores, Ψ 788.

πᾶλαισμοσύνη, ης, (παλαίω), luctatio, *wrestling-match*, Ψ 701, θ 126.

πᾶλαισταί, masc., (παλαίω), luctatores, *wrestlers*, θ 246†.

πᾶλαι-φᾶτον, α, (φημί), pridem edita, *uttered long ago; θέσφατα*, v aticinia; δρυός, *famed in fable, mythical*, τ 163.

πᾶλαίω, ipf. ἐπάλαιον, fut. παλαίσεις, aor. ἐπάλαισεν, (πάλη), luctari, *wrestle*, Ψ 621, δ 343.

πᾶλάμη, ἄων, γσ(ιν), ῃφιν, palma, *palm of the hand*, Γ 338, β 10; *hand, fist*, Γ 128, Θ 111.
1. πᾶλάσσω, fut. πᾶλάξέμεν, pass. ipf. (ἐ)παλάσσετο, pf. πεπαλαγμένον, αι, plupf. πεπάλακτο, (πάλλω), conspergere, inquinare, *besprinkle, stain, defile*, ν 395, Λ 169; χεῖρας, Λ 98.
2. πᾶλάσσω, mid. pf. πεπάλασθε, άσθαι, (πάλλω), — κλήρῳ, of men, *select among themselves by lot*, which was shaken in helmet, Η 171 and ι 331.

πᾶλη, ἡ, (πάλλω), luctatio, *wrestling*, Ψ 635 and θ 206.

πᾶλίλ-λογα (πάλιν, λέγω), rursus colligenda, recollecta, Α 126†.

πᾶλιμ-πετές, ntr., as adv., (πέτομαι), strictly retro volando, recidendo, = retrorsum, *back, back again*, Π 395, ε 27.

πᾶλιμ-πλάζω, only pass. aor. part. -πλαγχθέντα, ας, strictly retro repulsum, *repulsed, ν 5 ; driven back* (in disgrace), = male mulcatos, Α 59.

πᾶλῖν (πάρος), retro, *back, back, again*, Α 59 ; ποίησε, *transform*; also with gen., *back from*, τρέπειν, Υ 439 ; with αὖτις, *back again*; ὀπίσσω, with strengthening force; λάζετο, retractavit, *take back, unsay*; ἐρέει, Ι 56, contradicet, *gainsay*.

πᾶλιν-άγρετον (ἄγρα), recipiendum, *revocable*, Α 526†.

πᾶλιν ὁρμένω, du. part. aor. mid. from ὄρνυμι, retro ruentes, *rushing back*, Λ 326†.

πᾶλίν-ορσος (ὄρνυμι), resiliens, *springing back*, Γ 33†.

πᾶλίν-τῖτα (τίνω), ntr., retributa, — ἔργα = *vengeance*, α 379 and β 144.

πᾶλίν-τονον, α, (τείνω), *bent back*, having impulse to bend backward, *elastic, quivering*, Θ 266, φ 11.

πᾶλι-ρ-ρόθιον (ῥόθος), *foaming back, refluent*, ε 430 and ι 485.

πᾶλί-(ι)ωξις, ιν, (ἰωξις, διώκω), *pursuit back again, rally*, Μ 71.

πᾶλλᾶκίς, ίδος, ίδι, fem., concubine, Ι 449, ξ 203.

Παλλάς, άδος, epithet of Athena, according to the explanation of the ancients, from πάλλω, as brandishing the Aigis and the spear, Κ 275, δ 828, Α 200, 400, Ε 1, α 125, Ε 510.

πάλλειν, ων, prs., ipf. πάλλον, ε(ν), ομεν, and mid. prs. πάλλεται, ὑμενος, η, ων; act. aor. πῆλε, πῆλαι, mid. 2 aor. πάλτο, *swing, brandish*, χερσίν; *shake*, κλήρους ; mid., *cast lot for one's self* or (of several) *among each other*; iaculari, *hurl weapons* ; Ο 645, ἐν ἄντυγι, hit himself on the shield-rim = stumbled over the shield ; Χ 461, quivering at heart, with palpitating heart ; Χ 452, my heart leaps up to my mouth.

Πάλμυς, υος, a Trojan chief, Ν 792.

πάλτο = ἔπαλτο, from πάλλω.

πᾶλύνειν, ipf. ἐπάλυνε, πάλυνε, ον, aor. part. παλύνας, (πάλλω, pul-vis), *strew* or *sprinkle upon*, barley meal upon meat (Σ 560, for repast), ἀλφίτου ἀκτῇ ; inspergere, ἄλφιτα.

παμ-μέλαν(α), μέλανας, *entirely, jet black*, κ 525. (Od.)

Πάμμων, son of Priamos, Ω 250†.

πάμ-πᾶν, prorsus, *altogether*, joined with verb, Τ 334 ; with adj., γ 348 ; usually with neg. οὔ, οὔτι, οὐκέτι, οὐδὲ = *not at all, by no means* ; μή —, *let no man whatever*, σ 141.

παμ-ποικίλοι, pl., *all variegated, embroidered all over*, πέπλοι, Ζ 289 and ο 105.

πάμ-πρωτος, *very first*, Η 324, Ι 93 ; -πρῶτον, δ 780 (Od.), and -πρωτα, Δ 97, Ρ 568, *first of all*.

παμφαίνῃσι, subj., and -ων, ονθ' = οντα, οντας, αἶνον, part. prs., ipf. 3 pl. πάμφαινον, (redup. from φαίνω), *gleam, shine*, with dat., in or with, Ζ 513,

Ξ 11; στήθεσι, with white-shining, i. e. naked breasts.

παμφανόωντος, α, όωσα, όωσαν, (as if from -φανάω, φανός), bright-shining, beaming, glistening, E 619, δ 42, B 458.

πᾰν-άγρου, gen., (ἄγρα), all-catching, of fisher's net, E 487†.

πᾰν-αίθησι, dat. pl., (αἴθω), all glowing, burnished, Ξ 372†.

πᾰν-αίολος, ον, (αἴολος), all gleaming, glancing, Δ 186, K 77.

πᾰν-ᾰπάλῳ, dat., (ἀπαλός), very tender, youthful, ν 223†.

πᾰν-άποτμος (πότμος), all hapless, Ω 255 and 493.

πᾰν-άργυρον, all of silver, ι 203 and ω 275.

πᾰν-ᾰφ-ήλῐκα (ἧλιξ) τιθέναι, deprived of all playmates, X 490†.

Πᾰν-αχαιοί, ῶν, collective Achaians, host of the Achaians, B 404, α 239, etc.

πᾰν-ᾰ-ώριον (ἀ-, ὥρη), all-immature, having left home I 440, as νήπιος, Ω 540†.

πᾰν-δᾰμάτωρ (δαμᾶν), all-subduing, Ω 5 and ι 373.

Πανδᾰρεος, ου, friend of Tantalos; his daughter Aëdon, τ 518; the latter carried off by the Harpies, υ 66.

Πάνδᾰρος, son of Lykaon, leader of Lykians, faithless archer, Δ 88, E 168, 171, 795, B 827; slain by Diomedes, E 294.

πᾰν-δήμιος (δῆμος), belonging to all the people, public, σ 1†.

Πανδίων, a Greek, M 372†.

Πάνδοκος, ον, a Trojan, wounded by Aias, Λ 490†.

Πᾰν-έλληνες, united Greeks, i. e. inhabitants of Hellas or northern Greece, B 530†.

πᾰν-ῆμαρ, adv., all day long, ν 31†.

πᾰν-ημέριος, ον, οι, οις, ίης, ίῳ, (ἦμαρ), all day long, i. e. (1) from morn to eve, δ 356, λ 11.—(2) what remains of a day, A 472, cf. A 592.

Πανθοΐδης, son of Panthoos, (1) Euphorbos, P 70. — (2) Polydamas, Ξ 454.

Πάν-θοος, ου, ῳ, son of Othrys, father of Euphorbos and Polydamas, priest of Apollon, at Delphi, then at Troja, a counsellor, Γ 146, P 9, 23, 40, 59, O 522.

πᾰν-θῡμαδόν, adv., in full wrath, σ 33†.

παν-νύχιος, ον, οι, η, and -νύχος, ον, οι, (νύξ), the whole night long, the rest of the night, β 434. ·

πᾰν-ομφαίῳ, dat., (ὀμφή), author of all omens, all-disclosing, ὀμφαί, Θ 250†.

Πάν-οπεύς, (1) father of Epeios, Ψ 665.—(2) city in Phokis on the Kephisos, B 520, P 307, λ 581.

Πάν-όπη, a Nereid, Σ 45†.

πᾰν-ορμοι, offering moorage at all points, convenient for landing, ν 195†.

πᾰν-όψιος (ὄψις), in every body's eyes, openly, palam, Φ 397†.

παν-συδίη (σεύω ; v. l. πασσυδίῃ), summo impetu, with all haste, Λ 709.

πάντη, also -ῃ, (πᾶς), on all sides, in all directions, μ 233, P 354.

πάντοθεν (πᾶς), from every quarter, Π 110.

παντοίου, οι, ων, οισ(ι), ους ; η, ης, ην, αι, ῃς, ας, (πᾶς), varius, of every kind, manifold, B 397 ; in various guise, ρ 486.

πάντοσε (πᾶς), in first or fifth foot, on every side, E 508 ; in other feet, πάντοσ ; (πάντοσ ἐίσην, round, Γ 347).

πάντως, adv., omnino, by all means ; with οὐ, by no means, τ 91, Θ 450.

πᾰν-ὑπερτάτη, extrema, farthest off, last, ι 25†.

πᾰν-ύστατος, the very last, ι 452, Ψ 547.

παππάζουσι (πάππας) τινά, say papa, call one father, E 408†.

πάππᾰ, voc., papa, father, ζ 57†.

παππαίνετον, indic. 3 du., part. -ων, οντι, ες, ι, aor. πάπτηνε, part. -ας, αντα, ασ(α), look narrowly, cautiously about one, ἀμφὶ ἕ ; at, or over ἀνά, κατά τι, κατὰ δόμον ; look in quest of, desiderare, τινά, Δ 200 ; δεινόν, torva tueri, glare fiercely.

πάρ, (1) = παρά, q. v., in anastrophe, ὄχθας πάρ Λ 499.—(2) = πάρεστι, I 43; = πάρεισι, A 174 ; γ 325, praesto sunt, are at hand.

πᾰρά, ᾱ κ 242 ; an old case-form (cf. πάρος) appears as locative **πᾰραί**, B 711: with gen., O 175 ; acc., B 711, Γ 359 ; dat., O 280 ; apoc. πάρ, orig. as adv., alongside, by, near, A 611, usually preposition.—I. with gen., from beside, from, τινός, from some one ; ναῦφι, from the ships ; esp. with verbs of receiving to denote the source, πὰρ Ζηνός.—II. with dat., beside, with, by, Α 329; ὄχεσφιν, Ε 28; ναῦφιν, Π 281; usually with verbs implying rest, but also as locative with verbs of placing, ο 488 (θεῖναι, εἷσε, etc.), πεσεῖν, κυλινδέσθαι; penes, λ 175.—III. with acc., (1) to (a place), beside, unto, along by, esp. with verbs of motion, yet also with verbs with which, in English, no idea of motion is associated, φ 64, Ζ 34.— (2) secundum, close to, by, Β 522, Α 34, Μ 352.—(3) praeter, beyond, Λ 167; in excess of, δύναμιν; μοῖραν, contrary to right.—IV. by anastrophe, πάρα, Σ 400, Ω 429; παρ' (for greater clearness, πάρ', Σ 191) and πάρ, q. v.; also = πάρεστι, π 45, Ε 608; Τ 148, penes te est, it rests with thee; or = πάρεισι, δ 559.—V. in composition, the word appears in the significations already mentioned, but notice with βάλλω, τίθημι, the meaning before, Ε 369, Ι 90; and the idea of beguiling or cunningly diverting which may sometimes be expressed by amiss, aside, Α 555, π 287.

παρα-βαίνω, παρ ... βαινέτω, let him mount by (thy) side (on the chariot), Λ 512; pf. part. παρβεβαώς, ὦτε, standing by one (τινί) upon the chariot, Λ 522. (II.)

πᾰρὰ βάλλετε, imp. prs., and aor. (ἐ)βάλεν, ἔβαλον, throw down (fodder) before, Θ 504, Ε 369, δ 41; mid. βαλλόμενος, staking, Ι 322.

πᾰρ-έβασκε, was standing by his side as combatant, Λ 104†.

πᾰρα-βλήδην, adv., (βάλλω), covertly, maliciously, Δ 6†.

παρα-βλώσκω, pf. **παρμέμβλωκε**, go with help to the side of, Δ 11 and Ω 73.

πᾰρα - βλῶπες (βλέπω), looking askance (from shame, with acc. of respect), Ι 503†.

πᾰρ - εγίγνετο, intererat, was present at; δαιτί, cenae, ρ 173†.

παρα-δαρθάνω, only 2 aor. ἐδρᾰθεν, slept beside me (υ 88), and δρᾰθέειν φιλότητι, share the pleasures of love with—, Ξ 163.

παρα-δέχομαι, aor.-**εδέξατο**, perceperat, receive at hands of—, Ζ 178†.

παραδραθέειν, see παραδαρθάνω.

παραδραμέτην, see παρατρέχω.

πᾰρα-δράω, only **δρώωσι**, τινί, perform in the service of, ο 324†.

πᾰρᾱ-δύμεναι, aor. inf., (δύω), steal past, Ψ 416†.

πᾰρ-αείδειν, σοί, sing before, χ 348†.

πᾰρ-αείρω, aor. pass. -**ηέρθη**, hung down, Π 341†.

παραι-βᾰται (βαίνω), warriors, who stand beside the charioteer, and fight, Ψ 132†.

παραιπεπίθῃσι, πιθών, see παραπείθω.

πᾰρ-αίσια (αἶσα), adverse, Δ 381†.

πᾰρ-ᾱΐσσοντος, part. prs., aor. ἠΐξεν, αν, (ἀίσσω), charge by; τινά, Λ 615.

παραιφάμενος, see παράφημι.

παραί-φᾰσις (φημί), persuasion, encouragement, Λ 793 and Ο 404.

παρακάββᾰλε, see follg.

πᾰρᾰ-κατα-βάλλω, aor. **κάβ-βᾰλεν**, ον, lay about, Ψ 127 and 683.

παρα-κατα-λέχω, aor. mid. **ἔλεκτο**, (λέχος), τῇ, he had laid himself down by her, Ι 565†.

πᾰρά-κεῖται, ipf. ἔκειτο, iter. ἐκίσκετο, freq. in tmesis, κ 9, ν 424, Κ 75, 77; lay near him (οἱ), φ 416; before him stood, Ω 476; licet, χ 65.

παρὰ κίων, passing by, Π 263†.

πᾰρα-κλῐδόν, adv., (κλίνω), evasively, δ 348 and ρ 139.

πᾰρα-κλίνας, aor. part., (κλίνω), inclining to one side, υ 301; turning aside, Ψ 424.

πᾰρα-κοίτης, ας, acc. pl., (κοίτη), bed-fellow, husband, maritus, Ζ 430 and Θ 156.

πᾰρά-κοιτις, ῑ, ιν, (κοίτη), wife, uxor, Γ 53, Φ 479.

πᾰρα-κρεμάσας, aor. part., (κρεμάννυμι), letting hang down, Ν 597†.

πᾰρ-ελέξᾰτο, aor., subj. λέξομαι, (λέχος), sleep by the side of; τινι φιλότητι, have intercourse with, Ξ 237, λ 242.

πᾰρ-ᾰμειψάμενος, aor. part., (ἀμείβω), driving past, τινά, ζ 310†.

πᾰρᾰ μένῃ, subj., -μένετε, μενόντων, imp., μενέμεν, inf. prs., ipf. μένον, aor. μεῖνα, -έμεινεν, (μένω), and **μίμνων**, ipf. -έμιμνεν, remain with, τινι, γ 115, Λ 402, Ο 400; tarry, hold out, π 74, β 297.

πᾰρᾰ-μῦθησαίμην, opt., σασθαι, inf. aor., (μυθέομαι, μῦθος), encourage, exhort, with inf., Ι 684, Ο 45.

παρα-νηέω, see παρ-ενήνεον.

πᾰρᾰ-νήξομαι, fut., (νήχω), swim along near (the shore), ε 417†.

παρ-αντᾰ (ἄντα), sideways, Ψ 116†.

παρ-απαφίσκω, aor. ἤπᾰφε, cajo'e, Ξ 360; with inf. in tmesis, ξ 488.

πᾰραι-πειθω, aor. ἔπεισεν, 2 aor. red. subj. πεπίθῃσι, part. πεπιθοῦσα, παρ-πιπῐθών, ὄντες, win over, wheedle, Η 120; with inf., χ 213.

πᾰρᾰ-πέμπω, aor. ἔπεμψε, guided past, μ 72†.

πᾰρα-πλάζω, aor. ἔπλαγξε, drive away from, τινός, ι 81, τ 187; confuse, perplex, ν 346; part. aor. -επλάγχθη, went aside, Ο 464.

πᾰρα-πλῆγας, acc. pl. from -πλήξ, (πλάζω), beaten on the side by waves, i. e. shelving, sloping, ε 418.

πᾰρα-πλώω, 3 sing. aor. -έπλω, (πλέω), praetervecta est, sailed by, μ 69†.

πᾰρα-πνεύσῃ, subj. aor. from πνέω, blow out by the side, escape, κ 24†.

πᾰρα-ρρητοί, οἶσι, (ῥητοί, verbum),(1) to be influenced by words, ἐπέεσσι, placable, Ι 526.—(2) ntr., persuasion, Ν 726.

πᾰρα-στᾰδόν, adv., (παρίστημι), ϛoing up to, Ο 22. (Od.)

πᾰρα-σφάλλω, aor. ἔσφηλεν, caused to glance away, Θ 311†.

παρα-σχέμεν, aor. inf. from παρέχω.

παρὰ ἐτᾰνυσσεν, aor. from τανύω, (τείνω), spread out before, α 138. (Od.)

πᾰρᾰ-τεκταίνομαι, aor. opt. τεκτήναιο, αιτο, (τέκτων), transform, alter, Ξ 54, with ἄλλως; ἔπος, fashion the matter differently than the truth, invent a new story, ξ 131.

παρα-ρίθημι, 3 sing. παρτιθεῖ α 192, ipf. παρ(ὰ) τίθει, ἐτίθει πάρα ε 196, fut. παραθήσομεν, aor. παρέθηκ' = παρέθηκε(ν), πὰρ ἔθηκεν, θῆκεν, παρ' ἔθηκαν ε 199, aor. 2 πάρθεσαν, πὰρ and παρὰ θέσαν, πὰρ ἔθεσαν, subj. -θείω, opt. -θεῖεν, imp. -θες, mid. aor. -θέτο, opt. παραθείμην, -θεῖτο, part. παρθέμενοι, place or spread before one, food or drink, δ 57, α 192; bestow, give, ε 91; mid., set before one's self, have set before one; κεφαλάς, ψυχάς, stake one's life, β 237.

πᾰρα-τρέπω, aor. τρέψας, turning sideways; ἔχε, he held or guided, Ψ 398; παραὶ δέ οἱ ἐτράπετ', his spear

was turned to one side, i. c. the stroke was baffled.

πᾰρα-τρέχω, aor. ἔδρᾰμον, εν, ἔτην, run by, Κ 350; outrun, overtake, Ψ 636.

πᾰρ-έτρεσσαν, aor. from τρέω, sprang to one side, shied, Ε 295†.

πᾰρα-τροπέων, part. pres., (τροπή), misleading, δ 465†.

πᾰρα-τρωπῶσι, from -τρωπάω, (τρέπω), change purpose, = placant, Ι 500†.

πᾰρ-ετύγχανε, ipf. from τυγχάνω, chanced to be at hand, Λ 74†.

πᾰρ-αύδα, imp., ὤν part. pres., aor. αυδήσας, (αὐδάω, αὐδή), address with intent to persuade, μύθοις; ταῦτα, persuade; θάνατόν τινι, extenuate, make light of, λ 488. (Od.)

πᾰρ-αυτόθι, eo ipso loco, in that very place, Μ 302†.

πᾰρά-φημι, suadeo, advise, Α 577; aor. mid. παρφάσθαι, φάμενος, ἐπέεσσιν, delude, mislead; παραιφάμενος, Ω 771, appeasing.

πᾰρα-φθάνω, aor. opt. φθαίῃσι, part. φθάς, aor. mid. φθάμενος, overtake, pass by, Κ 346, Χ 197, Ψ 515.

παρ-βεβαώς, see παραβαίνω.

παρδᾰλέη, ην, leopard-skin, Γ 17 and Κ 29.

πάρδᾰλις, see πόρδαλις.

πᾰρ-έζω, aor. εἷσαν, iuxta sistebant or collocabant, place or make sit near, γ 416; mid. pres. παρέζεο, imp. part. εζόμενος, ipf. ἕζετο, tmesis, ξ 448; adsidebat, iuxta considebat, sit or take one's place near, Α 407, δ 738.

πᾰρειαί, άων, ῶν, άς, (οs, oris), genae, cheeks, Λ 393, υ 353; of eagles, β 153.

παρείθη, aor. pass. from παρ-ίημι.

1. πᾰρ-ειμι, εστι, εστε, εασιν, opt. εἴη, inf. ἔμμεναι and εἶναι, part. ἐών, etc., ipf. 2 ἦσθα, 3 ἔην, παρῆεν, παρῆν, 3 pl. εσαν, fut. ἔσσομαι, ἔσσεται, ἔσται, (εἰμί), be present, at hand, ready, τινί, versari cum, adesse; praesto esse, ρ 457; τινί, belong to, ξ 80; δύναμις, be at command, ψ 128; παρεόντων, of her store.

2. πᾰρ-ειμι, ιών, praeteriens, passing by, δ 527; accedens, drawing near, ρ 233, tmesis, Λ 558; ἴσαν, ἤισαν, ω 11, 13, praeterire.

πᾰρ-εῖπον, subj. εἴπῃ, part. ειπών, οὖσ(α), hortari, persuadere, persuade, win over, Α 555, Ζ 337.

παρ-έκ, before vowels **πᾰρ-έξ**, I. adv., *along past*, ε 439; *close by*, Λ 486; *away from* the point, *evasively*, εἰπεῖν, ἀγορεύειν; *except this*, ξ 168. — II. prep., (1) with gen., extra, *outside of*.—(2) with acc., praetereundo, ultra, *beyond, away from*, νόον, contrary to prudence, ἄγρσιν, by beguiling speeches, Κ 391; *along beyond*, μ 276; Ἀχιλῆα, inscio Achille, *without the knowledge of* Achilleus, Ω 434.

παρεκέσκετο, ipf. iter. from *παρά-κειμαι*.

πᾰρ-εκ-προ-φῠ́γῃσιν, subj. aor. (φεύγω), effugiat, *elude the grasp*, Ψ 314†.

πᾰρ-ελαύνω, fut. **-ελάσσεις**, aor. ἐλασσ(ε) = ἤλασε, ἤλασαν, praetervehi, *drive* or *pass by*; curru, Ψ 382; nave, μ 197; τινά, aliquem.

πᾰρ-έλκετε, imp. pres., *put off*, φ 111; mid. ἕλκετο, *draw aside to one's self, get hold of*, σ 282.

παρέμμεναι, see 1. πάρειμι.

πᾰρ-ενήνεεν, ον, intensive ipf., (νηέω, νέω), *heap up*, α 147 and π 51.

παρέξ, see παρέκ.

πᾰρ-εξ-ελθᾶν, inf. pres., (ἐλαύνω), praetervehi, *drive* or *be borne past*; aor. tmesis, ἐλασσαν, with acc., Ω 349; subj. -ελάσγσθα, Ψ 344.

πᾰρ-εξ-έρχομαι, aor. **ἐλθεῖν**, part. ἐλθοῦσα, *slip by*, κ 573, Κ 344; elsewh. eludere, *deceive*.

παρέπλω, see παρα-πλώω.

πᾰρ-έρχεται, ερχομένην, fut. ἐλεύσεαι, aor. ἦλθεν, subj. ἔλθῃ, opt. ἔλθοι, inf. ἐλθέμεν, *pass by*; τινά, *outstrip*, θ 230; *surpass*, ν 291; *evade*, Α 132.

πάρεσαν, see 1. πάρειμι.

πᾰρ-ευνάζεσθε, ipf., (εὐνάζομαι, εὐνή), *lie beside*, χ 37†.

πᾰρ-έχει, ουσιν, subj. ἔχωσι, opt. ἔχοιμι, part. ἔχουσαι, ipf. εἶχον, 3 pl. ἔχον, fut. ἕξω, ει, aor. subj. σχῃ, inf. σχέμεν, σχεῖν, tmesis Ψ 50, praebere, *hold ready*, Σ 556; *supply*, food and the like, σ 133, 360; *furnish, provide*, τ 113, Ψ 835; with inf., δ 89. [πάρσεχῃ, in arsi, τ 113.]

παρηέρθη, see παρ-αείρω.

πᾰρ-ήϊον, α, ntr., (παρειά), *cheek, jaw*, χ 404, Ψ 690; *cheek-piece* of a bridle, Δ 142.

παρήλασε, see παρ-ελαύνω.

πᾰρ-ήμενος, ον, ω, οι, part. from ἧμαι, — τινί, adsidere, *sit down at*

or *near*, δαιτί; also versari apud, circa, *dwell with* or *among*, ν 407; of nearness that annoys, Ι 311.

πᾰρ-ηορίῃσι, ας, pl. fem., (παρήορος), *head-gear, bridle and reins* of third or running horse, Θ 87, Π 152, represented in plate I. as hanging from the ζυγόν.

πᾰρ-ήορος, ον, masc., (ἀείρω), *floating* or *hanging beside*, (1) *flighty, foolish*, Ψ 603.—(2) a horse *harnessed by the side of the* pair, ready to take the place of either of them in case of need, tolutim iuxta currens, Π 471, 474. Plate I. represents the παρήορος in the background as he is led to his place. See also the adjacent cut, the first horse.—(3) *stretched out, sprawling*, Η 156.

πᾰρ-ήπαφε, see παρ-απαφίσκω.

πὰρ θείω, θέμενοι, see παρα-τίθημι.

παρθενικῇ, αί, (παρθένος), *maidenly, youthful* (νεῆνις, *maiden*, η 20); *maiden*, λ 39.

παρθένιος, *son of an unmarried girl*, Π 180; παρθενίην ζώνην, *virgin's* girdle.

Παρθένιος, river in Paphlagonia, Β 854†.

παρθεν-οπῖπα, voc. from -οπίπης, (ὀπιπεύω), *one who stares at maidens, seducer*, Λ 385†.

παρθένος, οι, fem., virgo, Χ 127, Σ 593, ζ 33; *young wife*, Β 514.

πάρθεσαν, aor. from παρατίθημι.

παρ-ιαύων, part. and ipf. 3 pl. ἴαυον, iuxta cubans, *sleeping by* or *with*, Ι 336, 470, ξ 21.

πᾰρ-ίζεν, ipf., (ἵζω), τινί, adsidebat, *sat down by*, δ 311†.

πᾰρ-είθη, aor. pass. from ἵημι, dependebat, *hung down*, Ψ 868†.

παρὰ ἰθύνετε, subj. pres., *would be able to steer by*, μ 82†.

Πάρις, Γ 437, Ζ 280, 503, 512, son of Priamos, seducer of Helene; see Ἀλέξανδρος.

πᾰρ-ίστημι, inf. -ιστάμεναι, aor.
έστης and έστης, η, subj. παρστήετον,
opt. παρασταίης, παρσταίη, pl. παρα-
σταῖεν, imp. πάρ-στητε, part. παρα-
στάς, παρστάς, ᾶσα, pf. παρέστηκεν,
inf. παρεστάμεναι, plupf. 3 pl. παρέ-
στᾰσαν, mid. pres. παρίσταμαι, σαι,
ται, σο, μενος, οι, η, ipf. ίστατο, mid.
accedere, approach, τινί, ad aliquem, B 244, E 570; opitulari, bring
aid, K 290, ν 301; act. aor. pf. plupf.
adstare, stand by or near, σ 344, α
335; plupf. aderant, H 467; aor.
accessi, draw near, Γ 405, E 116;
hostiliter, with hostile intent, X
371, ι 52, with friendly intent, O 442;
part. drawing near, ψ 87, Λ 261.

πᾰρ-ίσχομεν (ίσχω), offer, I 638;
inf. παρισχέμεν, hold in readiness, Δ
229.

παρ-κατ-έλεκτο, see παρα-κατα-λέχω.

παρ-μέμβλωκε, pf. from -βλώσκω.

παρμένω, see παρα-μένω.

Παρνησός, οῦ, όνδε, Parnassus, a
double-peaked mountain range in
Phokis; in a ravine on its southern
side lay Delphi, τ 394, φ 220, ω 332.

πάροιθ(εν), (loc. παροι, cf. παραί
from πάρος), in front, Υ 437; antea,
heretofore, Ψ 20, also τὸ π.; with gen.,
coram, pro, in presence of, before, A
360, O 154.

πᾰροίτεροι, αι, (πάρος), anteriores, (those) in front, Ψ 459, 480.

πᾰρ-οίχομαι, ipf. ᾤχετο, pf. ᾤχηκε,
praeteriit, K 252, v. l. οίχωκε, two
thirds of the night have passed by.

πάρος (παρά), τὸ π. 28 times, N 228,
θ 31; also with πρ. γέ (μέν), ὡς τὸ π.
περ 11 times; relative with τὸ π. περ
12 times, M 346, antea, otherwise,
formerly, with pres., A 553, ε 88, η
201; neg. with follg. πρίν γε, E 218;
with inf. = priusquam, before, α 21;
π. σχέμεν, hold onward, drive forward,
the gen. depends upon πρότερος, Θ
254.

παρ-πεπιθών, aor. from παρα-πείθω.

Παρρᾰσίη, ης, town in Arkadia, B
608†.

παρ-σταίην, στάς, στήετον, see παρίστημι.

παρ-τιθεῖ, see παρα-τίθημι.

παρ-φάμενος, φάσθαι, see παράφημι.

πάρ-φᾰσις (φημί), persuasion, allure-
ment, Ξ 217†.

παρ-φύγέειν, aor. inf., (φεύγω), slip
by, flee past, μ 99†.

πᾰρ-ᾤχηκα, pf. from παρ-οίχομαι.

πᾶς, πᾶσα, πᾶν, (παντ-ς, ja, orig.
from παϜαντ), declined throughout as
in Attic dialect, yet dat. pl. πᾶσι and
πάντεσσι, gen. pl. fem. πασέων, πασά-
ων, sing. omnis, omnes, all; ἅμα
π., together; π. ὁμῶς, alike; μάλα π.,
entirely; ἐν π., quite; with numbers,
in all, ε 244, θ 258, ξ 103; with superlatives, none but, the very, π 251.—
(2) totus, whole, B 809; ἀληθείην, the
entire truth; ρ 549, νημερτέα.—(3) pl.,
all sorts or kinds, A 5, 15, E 52, 60, δ
279, ε 196, δ 417; all over, πάντα, τ
475.—(4) πάντα, ntr. pl. adv., B 643,
in all respects, in Iliad almost always
in comparisons; in Odyssey only so
in ω 446; with adj. only, θ 214, ν 209;
all over, π 21, ρ 480.

Πᾱσῐ-θέη, one of the Graces, Ξ
276.

πᾶσι μέλουσα (μέλει), object of interest to all, famous, μ 70†.

πασσᾰλόφιν = πασσάλου, dat. φ,
nom. πάσσᾰλος, (πήγνυμι), nail or pin
in wall; κὰδ δ᾽ ἐκ π. κρέμασεν, he hung
it upon the peg, suspendit ex clavo,
θ 67.

πάσσασθαι, see πατέομαι.

πάσσειν, ων, ipf. ἔπασσε(ν), πάσσε,
with ἐπί, strew or sprinkle upon, E 401,
900; also with gen. part., I 214.

πάσσονα = παχίονα, from παχύς.

πασσυδίη, see πανσυδίη.

πάσχω, etc., pres., ipf. ἔπασχον, ipf.
mid. πασχόμην, fut. πείσομαι, εται,
εσθαι, aor. ἐπάθον, ες and πάθον, ες,
εν, etc., inf. ἔειν, pf. πέπονθα, ας, 2 pl.
πέποσθε (πέπᾱσθε?), Γ 99, κ 465, ψ
53; part. πεπᾱθυΐη, plupf. ἐπεπόνθει,
(πάθος), pati, suffer ill; τ 464, with
respect to the scar, how he had come
by it; ἔκ τινος, suffer at hands of; μή
τι πάθω, ῳς, lest something should befall me (thee), = lest I should die, of.
δ 820; τί παθών, with finite verb, by
what mischance, ω 106; κακῶς, while
I am maltreated, π 275.

πᾰτάγος, ῳ, dashing of waves, chattering of teeth, crash of falling trees,
roar of combat, N 283. (Il.)

πᾰτάσσει, ipf. ε(ν), (πάταγος), beat,
θυμός; κραδίη, H 216. (Il.)

πατέομαι, aor. (ἐ)πᾱσάμην, (ἐ)πασ-

σάμεθ(α), ἐπάσαντο, πάσσασθαι, σσάμενος, ω, plupf. πεπάσμην, (pa-sci, pa-
bulum), comedo, *eat*, σπλάγχνα,
ἀκτήν; elsewh. τινός, frui, *partake of*,
enjoy, δ 61.

πατέω, see κατὰ πάτησαν, conculcaverunt, *tread under foot*.

πἄτήρ, ἑρος, ἑρι, ἑρ(α), ἑρ (ε lengthened, θ 408, σ 122, υ 199), ἑρων, ἑρας,
and sync. πᾶτρός, Z 479; ἱ, ὦν (πατρό-
θιν, on the father's side, K 68†), pater,
father, ἀνδρῶν τε θεῶν τε, freq. title of
Zeus; in invocation, Ζεῦ πάτερ(Diespiter); pl., maiores, *ancestors*, Δ
405.

πᾶτος, ον, ον, masc., *path*, *trodden
way*, Υ 137; ἀνθρώπων, Z 202 = intercourse with men, as if it were πατῶν
πάτον θηρῶν.

πάτρη, ης, γ, fem., (πατήρ), patria, *native country, fatherland*; N 354,
home.

πατρίς, ίδος, ίδι, ίδ(α), fem., (πατήρ),
native, *of one's fathers*, B 140, α 407;
patria, ψ 315, ω 266.

πατρο-κἄσιγνήτοιο, ψ, ον, *father's
brother*, patrui, Φ 469. (Od.)

Πάτροκλος, οιο, ου, ψ, ον, (ε), and
κλῆος, ῆ(α), (before ἵππιν), εις, son of
Menoitios, Π 760, from Opus, elder
comrade of Achilleus, fled as a youth
to Peleus, on account of involuntary
homicide, Λ 765 sqq. When the Trojans had burst into the camp of the
Greeks, he put on Achilleus's armor,
and drove them back, but was slain by
the united efforts of Apollon, Euphorbos and Hektor, Π; funeral games in
his honor, Ψ.

πατρο-φονῆα, τόν, (φονεύς), parri-
cide, α 299. (Od.)

πατρο-φόνος, masc., (φόνος), parri-
cide, I 461†.

πατρώϊος, ιον, ιοι, ια, (πατήρ), pa-
ternus, *from one's father, hereditary*;
patrius, paternal, Υ 391, Φ 44; hereditary, β 286; ntr. pl. as subst., patri-
mony, π 388, χ 61.

παῦρος, οι, οισι, ους, α, and comp.
παυρότερον, οι, οισι(ν), ους, parvus,
exiguus, *little, feeble*, B 675; pauci,
few, I 545, ᴥ 56.

παυσωλή, fem., (παύω), *rest*, B 386†.

παύω, prs., inf. ειν and ἐμεναι, ipf.
iter. παύεσκον, fut. παύσομεν, aor.
ἐπαυσας, ε, elsewh. unaugmented, I.

check, *restrain*, ε 451; κ 2? *calm*, τι, Τ
67, A 282; τινά τινος, arc..re a, *keep
back from*, Ο 15, Φ 137; privare re,
deprive of, B 595; exsolvere re,
make leave off, δ 659, 801; also with
inf., Λ 442; with part., Λ 506.—II.
mid. prs. παύομαι, ipf. iter. παυέσκετο,
fut. παύσεσθ(αι), aor. ἐπαύσατο, σάμεθα, elsewh. unaugmented, 1 pl. subj.
ὤμεσθα, pf. πέπαυμαι, ται, μίνοι, *cease*,
take rest from, leave off, Θ 295, υ 110,
Ψ 228, μ 168; τινός, τ 268, Λ 467,
Σ 241; with part., X 502; exsolvi
re, θ 540.

Παφλἄγών, όνος, ες, inhabitant of
the district of Asia Minor lying south
of the Pontos Euxeinos, and bounded
by the rivers Halys and Parthenios,
and by Phrygia, B 851, E 577, N 656,
661.

παφλάζοντα, part.,(πομφόλυξ),*foaming*, N 798†.

Πάφος, fem., city in Kypros, θ
363†.

πάχετος, ον, (παχύς), *thick*, ψ 191,
θ 187.

πάχιστος, sup. from παχύς.

πάχνη, fem., (πήγνυμι), pruina,
hoar frost, ξ 476†.

παχνοῦται, pass. prs., (παχνόω),
congelatur, horret, *is chilled with
dread*, P 112†.

πάχος, ntr., (παχύς), *thickness*, ι
324†.

πἄχύς, ἑος, ύν, ύ, είη, comp. πάσσονα, sup. πάχιστος, (pinguis), *thick*,
in various senses, e. g. *clotted, stout,
mighty*, of blood, body, and members,
μηροῦ, Π 473; neck, ι 372; hand, fist,
E 309, ζ 128; stone, staff, M 446, Σ 416.

πεδάω, πεδάφ, ipf. iter. πεδάασκον,
aor. ἐπέδησ(εν), πέδησε, ῆσαι, (πέδη),
fetter, ψ 17; *bind fast*, ν 168; *delay*,
Ψ 585, δ 380; ἀπό, arcere, ω 353;
Μοῖρα, *entangle in fetters*, Δ 517; with
inf., X 5, γ 269, constrained her to
yield.

πέδας, τάς, (πούς), compedes,
fetters, N 36†.

πέδιλα, πέδιλ' ν 225, (πούς), *sandals*,
for men or women, B 44, Ξ 186; of
ox-hide, ξ 23; the gods wear golden
sandals, which bear them over land
and sea, Ω 340.

πεδίον, οιο, ου, ψ, ον, ια, (πέδον),
plain, campus; πεδίονδ(ε), *toward*

the plain, earthward, Ψ 189, Θ 21; πεδίοιο, on or over or through the plain, διώκειν, φέβεσθαι, θέειν, ἔρχεσθαι, Ε 222, Κ 344.

πεδόθεν, from the ground, from the beginning, from childhood, a pueritia, ν 295†.

πέδονδε (πέδον), to the ground, to the plain, earthward, Ν 796, λ 598.

πέζῃ, τῇ, (πέζα, from πεδja, πούς), metal ring at end of pole (see cut No. 45), Ω 272†.

πεζός, όν, οἱ, ούς, masc., (πέζα), pedester, Λ 341; on foot, pedibus, Ε 204; on land, Ι 329.

πείθω, etc., ipf. ἔπειθον, (εν), elsewh. unaugmented, fut. πείσεις, σει, σειν, σέμεν, aor. πείσῃ, σειε, red. aor. πεπίθοιμεν, οιεν, εῖν, οὖσα, (fides), persuade, win over, talk over, τινά, Α 132; τινὸς φρένας, τινὶ φρένας, θυμόν; mollify, Α 100.—pf. πέποιθα, ε, ασι, ὡς, ὅτες, όρας, subj. πεποίθω, ῃς, ομεν, plupf. πεποίθεα, 1 pl. ἐπέπιθμεν, confidere, trust in, τινί, with inf., Ξ 55.—mid. πείθομαι, πείθεθ' = θεται, etc., 3 pl. opt. πειθοίατο, ipf. ἐπείθετο, πείθοντο, fut. πείσομ(αι), πείσεαι, εται, ονται, εσθαι; 2 aor. ἐπίθοντο, elsewh. unaugmented πιθόμην, etc., opt. πεπίθοιθ = θοιρο, obedire, obey, τινί, μύθῳ; δαιτί, obey (the call to) the feast; πάντα, in all things; τί, partially; ἅ τιν' οὐ πείσεσθαι ὀίω, quae multos non secuturos opinor; credere, confide in, τεράεσσι, τινί, ν 45.

πείκετε, see 3. πέκω.

πεινάων, οντα, οντε, inf. ἡμεναι, (πείνη), esurio, suffer hunger, hunger after, τινός, ν 137.

πείνη, fem., (πενία, penuria), hunger, fumine, ο 407†.

πειράζειν, ων, prs., (πειρᾶν), tentare, make trial of, test; τινός, π 319.

Πειραΐδης, αο, son of Peiraios, Ptolemaios, Δ 228†.

Πείραιος, comrade of Telemachos, son of Klytios, ο 544, ρ 55.

1. πειραίνω, only aor. part. πειρήναντες, (see πεῖραρ), bind to, χ 175 and 192.

2. πειραίνω, only pf. pass. 3 sing. πεπείρανται (2. πεῖραρ), is accomplished, μ 37†.

1. πεῖραρ, ατα, cord, rope, μ 51, also fig. laquei, ὀλέθρου, exitii, snares or

cords of destruction, cf. Psalm xviii. 6, 2 Sam. xxii. 6; ὀιζύος, miseriae, net of woes, ε 289; πολέμοιο, νίκης, cords of war, of victory, Ν 358.

2. πεῖραρ, ατα, ασι, αθ' = ατα, (πέραν), finis, fines, end, of earth, Okeanos, sea, ψ 248; ἑλέσθαι, obtain a decision, Σ 501; chief points in each matter, Ψ 350; γ 433, that which brings to completion or end, implement, tool.

πειρᾶν, imp. -άτω, (πείρα, experior), tentare, test, τινύς; also adoriri, attack; conari, attempt, with inf., Θ 8; ὅπως, δ 545.—mid. πειρᾶται, ipf. ἐπειρᾶτο, ῶντ(ο), fut. πειρήσομ(αι), etc., aor. ἐπειρήσαντ(ο) = ανθ', elsewh. unaugmented, pf. πεπείρημαι, aor. pass. πειρήθη, etc., conari, with inf., also with μή, εἰ; experiri, tentare, make trial of, put to proof, τινός, Β 193, ν 336, Κ 444, Β 73; τί, as to something, θ 23; with εἰ, Ν 806; decertare cum, contend with (ἀντίβιον, adversus, περί, de); of things, τινός; σθένεος, test one's strength, cf. Ψ 432; also τί, make trial of something; explorare, τινί, dat. of instr.; μύθοισιν, try one's self, find out one's skill, in words.

πειρητίζων, ipf. πειρήτιζε(ν), ον, (πειράω), tentare, try, test, τόξον; τινός, make trial of, sound, ο 304; decertare cum, contend with; στίχας, adoriri ordines, attack the lines, Μ 47.

Πειρί-θοος, son of Zeus and of Dia, wife of Ixion, king of the Lapithai in Thessaly, friend of Theseus, husband of Hippodameia; the quarrel with the Centaurs arose out of the wedding banquet, Μ 129, 182, φ 298, Ξ 318, Α 263.

πείρινθα, τήν, (πείρατα), wagon box or body, perh. of wicker-work, ο 131.

Πείροος, εω, son of Imbrasos, chief of the Thrakians, Δ 520; slain by Thoas, Δ 525.

πείρων, οντες, ipf. ἔπειρε(ν), ον, πεῖρε(ν), aor. ἐπείρων, πείραν, pf. pass., part. πεπαρμένος, η, ον, (πειρᾶν), transfodere, pierce through, Υ 479; peregit, transfix, Π 405; pierce with spits, spit, γ 33, κ 124; also pass., Φ 577; stuck full of, studded, ἥλοισι; pierced with pains, Ε 399; pervehi, fig.

cleave the waves, one's way, etc., β 434, Ω 8, θ 183.

πείσῃ, τῷ, (πείθομαι), ἰν—μένε, remained *in obedience, subjection*, υ 23†.

Πείσ-ανδρος, (1) son of Antimachos, slain by Agamemnon, Λ 122, 143.—(2) a Trojan, slain by Menelaos, N 601–619.—(3) son of Maimalos, chief of Myrmidons, Π 193.—(4) son of Polyktor, suitor of Penelope, σ 299; slain by Philoitios, χ 268.

Πεισ-ηνορίδης, *son of Peisenor*, Ops, α 429, β 347, υ 148.

Πεισ-ήνωρ, (1) father of Kleitos, O 445.—(2) father of Ops.—(3) herald in Ithaka, β 38.

Πεισί-στρατος, Nestor's youngest son, Telemachos's companion to Sparta and to Pherai, γ 36, δ 155, o 46, 48, 131, 166.

πεῖσμα, ἄτος, ατ(α), ntr., *stern-cable*, used to make the ship fast to land, ζ 269, κ 96, ν 77; *cord plaited of willow withes*, κ 167. (Od.)

πείσομαι, see πάσχω, and πείθω.

(πέκω) **πείκετε**, imp. prs., (pecto), *comb* or *card* (wool), σ 316; aor. mid. πεξαμένη χαίτας, combing her hair, Ξ 176.

πέλἄγος, ει, εσσι(ν), ntr., (πλάζω), *wave, tide; ε 335, high* or *open sea*.

Πελάγων, (1) chief of the Pylians, Δ 295.—(2) attendant of Sarpedon, E 695.

πελάζειν (πέλας), aor. ἐπέλασσα, ε(ν), αν, and πέλασ(σ)ε(ν), σαν, subj. πελάσῃς, (σ)σῃ, σσομεν, imp. σσετον, inf. πελά(σ)σαι, (1) *bring near, make to approach*, adigere, τινά (τί) τινι, local dat. χθονί, οὔδει, to the earth; ἱστοδόκῃ, into the mast-crotch; ὀδύνῃσι, *bring into*, so also (Od.) εἴς τι, ἐν τινι, κ 404, οὐδάσδε; mid. only 3 pl. opt. aor. νηυσὶ πελάσαιάτο, P 341.— (2) appropinquare, *approach, draw near*, νήεσσι. — Pass. pf. πεπλημένος, aor. πελάσθη, and 3 pl. πέλασθεν, also sync. aor. ind. πλῆτο, pl. πλῆντο, ἔπληντο, appropinquare, Δ 449, μ 108; οὔδει, χθονί, sink to earth.

πέλας, iuxta, *hard by*, κ 516; with gen. only o 257. (Od.)

Πελασγικός, όν, epithet of Zeus in Dodona, Π 233; in Argos, q. v.

Πελασγός, οί, original population of Greece, first in region about Do-

dona; then in Thessaly, B 840, Boiotia, Attika, also in Peloponnesos, P 288; Homer mentions other Pelasgians from Kyme, on side of Trojans, K 429; and still others in Kreta, r 177.

πέλεθρα, τά, (πέλομαι?), *plethron*, a square each of whose sides is 100 feet, i. e., as measure of surface, about ¼ acre, Φ 407, λ 577; see οὖρον.

πέλεια, αν, αι, and πελειάδες, άσιν, fem., (πέλειος), *wild pigeon*, Φ 493, Λ 634.

πελεκκάω, aor. **πελέκκησεν**, *hew, shape with axe*, ε 244†, from

πέλεκκῳ, ntr. dat., (πέλεκυς), *axe-helve*, N 612.

πέλεκυς, υν, εις, εων, εσσι, εας, *axe* or *hatchet* for felling trees, Ψ 114, P 520; double-edged, ε 234, see ἡμιπέλεκκα; serves also, in case of need, as weapon, O 711; symbol of firmness and resolution, Γ 60; *sacrificial axe*, γ 449; r 573, *wedge-shaped blocks of iron*, resembling axes, which were placed in line, and then the attempt was made to shoot an arrow through all the helve-holes.

πελεμιξέμεν, aor. πελέμιξεν, ίξαι, (πέλω), *brandish, shake*, Π 766; φ 125, *make quiver*.—Pass. ipf. πελεμίζετ(ο), aor. πελεμίχθη, concuti, *quake*, Θ 443; repulsus est, *drive back*, Δ 535.

πελέσκετο, πέλευ, see πέλω.

Πελίης, αο, *Pelias*, son of Poseidon and Tyro, λ 254; king of Iaolkos, exiled his brother Neleus, and forced Jason, the son of his other brother Aison, into the Argonautic expedition; father of Alkestis, B 715.

πέλλας, τάς, *milk bowls* or *pails*, Π 642†.

Πελλήνη, fem., town in Achaia, B 574†.

Πέλοψ, οπος, *Pelops*, son of Tantalos, father of Atreus and of Thyestes, gained with his wife Hippodameie, the daughter of Oinomaos, the throne of Elis, B 104 sqq.

πέλει, ipf. πέλε(ν), aor. ἔπλε; mid. **πέλεται**, ονται; ηται, ὠμεθ(α), ωνται; οιτο; ευ, ipf. πέλοντο, iter. πελέσκετο, aor. ἔπλευ = εο, ἔπλεθ' = ἔπλετ(ο), (πάλλω), verti, *be hurled*, Λ 392; *be in motion*, ἐπί τινι, ν 60; versari circa, *be busy about;* then, in general, versari, locum habere, δ 45, usu-

ally in mid.; πέλε, project, E 729;
cf. πέλονται, N 632; esse, esp. with
adj., e. g. τοὶ φίλον ἔπλετο (factum
est) θυμῷ, H 31; πέλει, rises (to
heaven), Γ 3.

πέλωρ, ntr., monster; the Kyklops,
ι 428; Skylla, μ 87; Hephaistos, Σ
410; also πέλωρον, ου, α, B 321, κ 168,
219, λ 634.

πελώριος, ον, α, (πέλωρ), immanis,
ingens, monstrous, huge, Γ 229, γ 290,
ι 187, 190, Λ 820, Θ 424, K 439, Σ 83
= πέλωρον, ι 257, ο 161, M 202.

πεμπάζομαι, aor. subj. 3 sing.
πεμπάσσεται, (πέντε), he reckons up
for himself (on his five fingers), δ
412†.

πεμπταῖοι, pl., (πέντε), on the fifth
day, ξ 257†.

πέμπτος, ῳ, ον, ης, quintus, fifth,
ι 335, Π 197.

πέμπω, etc., prs., ipf. ἔπεμπε, ον, and
πίμπ(ε), ον, fut. πέμψω, ἐμεναι = ειν,
aor. ἔπεμψ(εν), αν, and πέμψεν, αν, etc.,
mitto, send, (ἐπί) τινι, εἰς, ἐπί, προτί
τινα; also with -δε, ζε; with inf., Π
454, ν 206.—(2) dimitto, dismiss,
send home, ψ 315.—(3) comitari,
escort, τ 461, θ 556.

πεμπ-ώβολα, ntr. pl., (ὀβολός), five-
tined forks, on which the flesh or
inwards were spitted preparatory to
roasting, A 463. (Cf. adjoining cut
combined from several ancient representations.)

πενθερός, ῷ, masc., socer, father-in-
law, θ 582 and Z 170.

πενθήμεναι, inf., 3 du. indic. πενθεί-
ετον, aor. inf. πενθῆσαι, (πένθος), desiderare, lugere, lament, mourn for,
σ 174; esp. for the dead, Ψ 283, γα-
στέρι, by fasting, T 225.

πένθος, εος, ntr., (πενία), desiderium, luctus, longing, grief, Σ 73,
Δ 197; τινός, for any one, Λ 249;
ἀέξειν, cherish grief.

πενίη, τῇ, (πένεσθαι), penuriae,
poverty; εἴκων, cedens, ξ 157†.

πενιχροῦ, τοῦ, egeni, needy, γ 348†.

πενώμεθα, subj. prs., inf. πένεσθαι,
ipf. (ἐ)πένοντο, be busily engaged (about),
περί τι, prepare; esp. feast, meal, ξ
251.

πεντά-ετές, ntr., (ϝέτος), five years
long, γ 115†.

πεντά-έτηρον (ϝέτος), five years old,
B 403, ξ 419.

πεντάχά (πέντε), in five divisions,
M 87†.

πέντε, quinque, K 317, γ 299.
πεντήκοντ(α), quinquaginta, Z 244,
B 509. πεντηκοντό-γυιον, of fifty
acres, I 579†. πεντηκόσιοι, five hundred, γ 7†.

πεπαθυῖα, see πάσχω.
πεπείρανται, pf. pass. from πειραίνω.
πεπαλαγμένος, πεπάλακτο, see πα-
λάσσω.

πεπαρμένος, see πείρω.
πεπάσμην, see πατέομαι.
πεπερημένος, see περάω.
πέπηγε, see πήγνυμι.

πεπιθεῖν, πέπιθμεν, πεπι-
θήσω, see πείθω.

πέπληγον, πεπληγώς, see
πλήσσω.

πεπλημένος, see πελάζω.

πέπλος, οιο, ον, οι, οισι, ους,
masc., cover for chariot, E 194;
chairs, η 96; funeral urns, Ω
796; esp. woman's over-garment
or robe, E 315, Z 90, σ 292.
(Cf. cut No. 2, and the cut
on next page.)

πεπνυμένος, etc., see πνέω.
πέποιθα, see πείθω.
πέπονθα, πέποσθε, see πά-
σχω.

πεποτήαται, see ποτάομαι.
πεπρωμένον, πέπρωται, see
(ἐ)πορον.

πεπταμένας, πέπταται, πέπτανται,
see πετάννυμι.

πεπτεότ(α), see πί-
πτω.

πεπτηώς, ῶτα, see
πτήσσω.

πεπύθοιτο, πέπυ-
σμαι, see πυνθάνομαι.

πέπον, voc., plur.
ονες, from nom. πέ-
πων, (πέσσω), proper-
ly, cooked, ripe, mel-
low, then as term of
endearment, dear, pet,
Z 55, P 120, ι 447; in
bad sense, coward, weakling, B 235, N
120.

πέρ (περί), post-positive and enclitic,
perquam, (1) to emphasize assertion,
very, A 416, Γ 201, H 204; very first
time, Ξ 295; by all means, at all events,
at least, A 211, B 236, ρ 13, Θ 242, υ
7, 181, I 301, A 353; even, γ 236.—(2)
concessive after part. (cf. καίπερ), although, A 241, 588, Z 85 (also preceding part., A 131, 217, 546, 587); with
ἔμπης, o 361; with καί, A 577; καίπερ, although, Θ 125, I 247, ε 73.—(3)
with conditional particles, if besides, A
81, H 117; if that is to say, α 188;
also with κέ, e. g. αἴ κέ περ, H 387.—
(4) with temporal conjunctions, ὅτε
περ, E 802, K 7; πρίν, O 588.—(5)
after relatives (sometimes separated
from the relative) calling attention to
what is known, or familiar, may often
be rendered by just, ν 284; or by yet,
for that matter, B 286, β 156, ν 249;
coinciding in meaning with (1), Ψ 79.

πέραν, see περάω 1. 2.

Περαιβοί, Pelasgian tribe about
Dodona and on the river Titaresios,
B 749†.

περαιόω, only aor. pass. περαιωθέν-
τες, (πέραν), transvecti, (get the
start in) crossing over, ω 437†.

περάτῃ, τῇ, (πέραν), in extrema
parte, at the farthest or opposite
border; opp. east = in the west, ψ
243†.

1. περάω, 3 pl. περόωσι, inf. περάᾶν,
part. περῶντα, ipf. 3 pl. πέραον, iter.
περάασκε, fut. περήσω, ησάμεναι = ήσειν,
aor. ἐπέρησε, πέρησε, σαμεν, (πέραν),
pass through, penetrate, traverse, τί, διά
τινος, permeare, pervehi, trai-
cere; also διά τινος, ἐπὶ πόντον, ἐφ᾽
ὑγρήν, δ 709.

2. περάω, inf. περάαν, aor. ἐπέρασσα,
ας, εν, αν, and πέρασαν, άσητε, άσειε,
pf. pass. part. πεπερημένος, (πέραν,
πράσσω, πιπράσκω), vendere, export
for sale, sell, (ἐς), Λῆμνον, Φ 40; πρὸς
δώματα, κατ᾽ ἀλλοθρόους ἀνθρώπους,
o 453.

Πέργαμος, fem., citadel of Ilios, Δ
508, E 446, Z 512, H 21.

Περγασίδης, son of Pergasos, Δηι-
κόων, E 535†.

πέρην (πέραν), adv., ultra, beyond,
with gen., B 626; opposite, with gen.,
B 535.

περησέμεναι, see περάω 1.

πέρθω, πέρθοντε part. pres., fut. πέρ-
σειν, aor. ἔπερσεν, πέρσα, σε(ν), σειαν,
σας, σαντες, and 2 aor. ἔπράθον (ἐπρά-
θομεν, A 125), (perdo), delere, sack,
destroy, Σ 342, nearly always of cities;
pass. pres. περθομένη, ipf. πέρθετο, M
15; fut. πέρσεται, Ω 729; 2 aor. sync.
πέρθαι, Π 708, deleri, vastari, be
laid waste.

πέρι, properly locative of orig. comparative form para, with signif. in
higher degree or measure, I. as adv.,
(1) more, magis, hence often with
gen. comp., see below; then valde,
very, exceedingly, Σ 549, Π 186; often
with verbs, e. g. μ 279, θ 63, δοῦναι;
often also like valde, when standing
with the locative forms κῆρι, φρεσί,
θυμῷ, really belonging to the verb or
adjective (ἄσπετον, Π 157, γ 112, 95).
—(2) round about, circa, Γ 384; esp.
freq. with locatives (αὐλῇ, in the court,
κ 10; καπνῷ, in the smoke, A 317;
χειῇ, in the hole, X 95), in which cases
it belongs to the verb. The transition
to follg. use often can not be traced:
II. as prep., περί (by anastrophe
πέρι), (1) with gen., (a) super, over,
σπείους, over the cave; τρόπιος, a-strad-
dle of the keel; (b) the meaning passes
from the original signif. round about,
circa, to that of about, for, in behalf
of, de, pro, esp. with verbs of fighting, defending, striving, Π 1; (c) with
verbs of saying, inquiring, etc., = de,
concerning, α 135, ρ 563; (d) special
phrases, H 301, πέρι may be construed
with θυμοβόρος as adverbial, very destructive, and ἔριδος as causal genitive,
out of strife; the explanation of the
genitive in phrases like (e) πέρι ἐμμε-

ναι, adjectives like καρτερός, πέρι, m re, *in higher measure, better,* is to regard them as genitive after com-'parative, Δ 257, δ 190, α 66, P 279; also dative of respect in which, θ 102, Ψ 318.—(2) with dative (a) locative, freq. περί as adverb really belongs to the verb, χροΐ, *on* the body ; στήθεσσι, *on* the breast; yet with verbs of fighting it is to be translated *for, in behalf of*, cf. de, pro, P 133 ; also circa, B 389 and λ 424, dying *around* the sword, i. e. pierced by the sword still remaining in wound; (b) of advantage, be anxious *about, for,* one, K 240.—(3) with acc., (a) *round about,* δ 368, Z 256, Ω 16, Λ 609, Α 448 ; (b) *along,* M 177 ; *close by, round about,* Γ 408, B 757, γ 107, κ 410 ; πονεῖν περί τι, of object for which one is interested, circa, *about, respecting;* Φ 11, *about, in* the eddies.

πέρι stands for περίεστι, K 244, μ 279.

περί-άγνῦται (Ϝάγνυμι), *breaks around, spreads around* (voice of Hector), Π 78†; in tmesi, Λ 559, are *broken over.*

περί ἄγωσιν, subj., (ἄγω), μίν, circa eum ducant, *draw about* him, δ 792†.

περί βαίνε, ipf., aor. περίβη, ησαν, ῆναι, βάντα, pf. βεβαῶτα, ὦσα, plupf. βεβήκει, βέβασαν, (περί) τινί, *go about, surround* (to protect), defendere, τινός.

περί-βάλλει, ετον, ipf. βάλλε, περίβαλλε, aor. βαλόντε(ς), *throw about* or *around,* a rope around, θόλοιο ; *throw* arms *around, flap* wings around, Λ 454; superare, *excel,* Ψ 276, o 17.—Mid. βαλλομένους, ipf. βάλλετο, aor. βάλόμην, βάλετ(ο), *throw over one's self, put on,* φᾶρος, B 43; ζώνην ἰξυῖ, κ 544.

Περί-βοια, (1) daughter of Akessamenos, mother of Pelegon, Φ 142.— (2) daughter of Eurymedon, mother of Nausithoos by Poseidon, η 57.

περί-γίγνεται, ὁμεθ(α), εσθαι, superat, *surpass,* τινός, θ 102, Ψ 318.

περι-γλάγεας (γλάγος, lac), *filled with milk,* Π 642†.

περι-γνάμπτοντα (γνάμπτω, νάπος), Μάλειαν, *doubling* Malea, ι 80†.

περί-δείδια, pf., aor. περί-δεισαν, σασ(α), σαντες, (δειδ-, δϳι, hence vowel

long by position, where others read -ὀδεισαν), timere alicui, *fear for,* τινί ; νέκυος, P 240 ; ne, lest, μή, P 242. (II.)

περί-δέξιος, ambidexter, *very skillful, expert,* ᴅ 163†.

περί-δίδωμι, περί-δώσομαι, ὠμεθον, subj. aor. mid., (δίδωμι), *stake upon,* with gen. of thing risked, Ψ 485, ψ 78 ; πέρι δῶκε, *gave in high degree, abundantly,* α 66, η 110.

περί-δῑνηθήτην, 3 du. aor. pass., (δινέω), ran *round and round,* πόλιν, X 165†.

περί γὰρ δϊε, aor., (δϳι, δίω), valde timuit (ei) ne, *greatly feared* lest, E 566, P 666.

περί-δράμον, see περι-τρέχω.

περί-δρομος, οι, (δρόμος), *running round, round, circular,* E 726, B 812; ξ 7, *detached, alone.*

περι-δρύφθη (δρύπτω), aor. pass., *he had the skin all torn off* from his elbows, Ψ 395†.

περὶ ἔδῡνεν, Π 133 ; aor. δύσετο, χ 113, induit, *put on;* but aor. περίδῦσε, *stripped off,* Λ 100.

περι-δώσομαι, δώμεθον, see περιδίδωμι.

πέρι τ᾽ εἰμί, περίειμι, εσσι, εστι, εστε, inf. ἔμμεναι, τινός, superior sum, *be superior, excel,* τι, in respect to, in ; τόσσον, tanto, θ 27; also with dat. whereby, v. l. βουλῇ, Α 258.

περι-έρχομαι, aor. **ἤλυθεν** and ἦλθε(ν), *come around, encompass,* τινά ; of a sound, ρ 261 ; οἰνός τινα φρένας, *stole around* his senses, ι 362.

περι-έχω, aor. mid. **σχόμεθα,** imp. σχεο, tueri, *protect,* ι 199; τινός, Α 393.

Περι-ήρης, εος, father of Boros, Π 177†.

περί-ήχησεν, aor. from ἠχέω, *rang all over,* H 267†.

περι-ίδμεναι, see περί-οιδα.

περί-ίστημι, put on, **ἔστη,** -στησαν, 3 pl. subj. -στείωσι, mid. ipf. -ίστατο, pass. aor. -στάθη, *station one's self about,* circumsistere, B 410; cingere, P 95; pass., λ 243, *rose and stood around.*

περι-καλλής, έος, έϊ, έ(α), έας, ές, (κάλλος), pervenustus, *very beautiful.*

περί-καλύπτει, ipf. κάλυπτε, aor.

ἰκάλυψα, ε, τινί τι, cover all over with; κῶμα, wrap in the cloak of sleep, Ξ 359, Κ 201, σ 201.

περί-κειται, μενον, ipf. -κειτο, τινί, lie around, as a veil or covering, φ 54; amplecti, Τ 4; Ι 321, naught remains to me, I have won nothing.

περι-κήδετο, ipf., (κήδομαι), τινός, care for; οἱ βιότου, curabat eius rem familiarem, take care of his possessions.

περί-κηλα, ntr. pl., (κῆλον), per-arida, well-seasoned, ε 240 and σ 309.

Περι-κλύμενος, son of Neleus and of Pero, λ 286†.

περι-κλυτός, οῦ, όν, ά, (κλύω), prae-clarus, famous, renowned, of gods, Α 607, θ 287; of men, α 325, Σ 326; of things, δῶρα, Ι 121; ἔργα, Ζ 324, ἄστυ, δ 9.

περι-κτεινώμεθα, pres. subj., ipf. κτείνοντο, circa interimi, be killed round about, Δ 538 and Μ 245.

περι-κτίόνων, εσσι, ας, nom. -κτίων, (κτίω), dwellers around, neighbors, vici-nus, Ρ 220, Τ 104, β 65.

περι-κτίται, οἱ, (κτίω), dwellers about, vicini, λ 288†.

περὶ ἔλεψε (aor. from λέπω), φύλλα, has peeled off from it round about the leaves, Α 236†.

περί-μαιμώωσα, part. from μαιμάω, feeling or groping about for, with acc., μ 95†.

πέρι μάρναο, imp. pres., (μάρναμαι), ἐμεῦ, fight for me, Π 497†.

περί-μετρον (μέτρον), beyond meas-ure, very large, β 95. (Od.)

Περι-μήδης, (1) companion of Odys-seus, λ 23, μ 195.—(2) father of Sche-dios, Ο 515.

περι-μήκετον, acc., (μῆκος), very lofty, Ξ 287, ζ 103.

περί-μήκεος, ει, εες, -μηκες, εα, (μῆ-κος), permagnus, very long or high, ι 487, Ν 63.

περί-μηχανόωνται, pres., ipf. όωντο, (μηχανή), cunning'y devise; τινί, against any one, ξ 340 and η 200.

Πέρϊμος, a Trojan, son of Meges; slain by Patroklos, Π 695†.

περί-ναιετάουσιν, pres., (ναίω), are inhabited, i. e. lie round about, ὃ 177; dwell about, β 66.

περί-ναιέται, οἱ, neighbors, Ω 488†.

περι-ξέστῃ (ξέω), polished on every side, μ 79†.

περὶ οἶδ' = περί-οιδε, better πέρι οἶδε, inf. ἴδμεναι, plupf. ᾔδη, (οἶδα), with inf., know better, understand something (τί) better than others (ἄλλων) ; τ 285, be master of.

περι-πέλομαι, aor. part. περι-πλομέ-νου, ων, ους, aor. (πέλομαι), Σ 220 (ex, ὑπό), hostibus versantibus circa urbem, in conséquence of the enemies having surrounded the city; elsewh. ἐνιαυτοῦ, ὦν, as the years revolved, in the course of the years.

περί-πευκές, ntr., (πευκ-, πικ-, pique), very sharp, Λ 845†.

περι-πλέχθη, θείς, aor. part. from πλέκω, amplexus, embrace, τινί, ξ 313 and ψ 33.

περι-πληθής (πλῆθος), very full (of people), populous, ο 405†.

περι-πλομένων, see περι-πέλομαι.

περι-πρό, around and before (him), Λ 180 and ΙΙ 699.

περι-προ-χυθείς, part. aor. pass. from χέω, pouring in a flood over, Ξ 316†.

περί-ρρεε (for σρεϜε, ipf. from ῥέω), streamed around, with acc., ι 388†.

περι-ρρηδής (ῥέω, cf. Liv. 2, 20, 3, "moribundus ad terram de-fluxit;" or perh. better from Ϝρα-ὃινός), τραπέζῃ, falling down across the table, χ 84†.

περι-ρρύτος (for σρυτος, ῥέω), sea-girt, τ 173†.

περι-σθενέων, part., (σθένος), exult-ing in his might, χ 368†.

περι-σκέπτω (σκέπω), covered, shut in on all sides ; others translate, con-spicuous from every side, α 426. (Od.)

περι-σσαίνοντες, and mid. ipf. -σσαί-νοντο, (σϜαίω, schwänzeln), wag with the tail (οὐρῇσι) about one (τινά), fawn upon, κ 215. (Od.)

περι-σσείοντο, ipf. pass., (σείω, σϜι, schwingen), were tossed about, floated in the air, Τ 382 and Χ 315.

περι-σταδόν, adv., (ἵσταμαι), draw-ing near from every side, Ν 551†.

περι-στάθη, see περι-ίστημι.

περι-στείχω, 2 sing. aor. -στειξας, circumibas, didst walk about, δ 277†.

περι-στέλλω, aor. pass. στείλασα, wrapping up (in funeral clothes), ω 293†.

περι-στενάχίζεται, ipf. -το, re-echoes

on every side, αὐλῇ, (even) in the court, κ 10; ποσσίν, with the tread of feet.

περι-στένεται (στένω), is too small, i. e. stuffed full, II 163†.

περι-στέφει, 3 sing., surrounds on all sides, complet, ε 303; but θ 175, his grace is not embellished on every side by (seemly) words.

περί-στησαν, see περι-ίστημι.

περι-στρέφω, aor. part. **στρέψας**, whirling around, T 131, θ 189; pass. στρέφεται (better τρέφεται, curdles, thickens), whirls around, E 903.

περί-σχεο, see περι-έχω.

περι-ταμνόμενον, ους, (τέμνω) cutting off for one's self, intercepting, i. e. driving away, λ 402. (Od.)

περι-τελλομένου, ων, ους, (τέλλω), ἔτεος, ἐνιαυτῶν, in the revolution of the year, the years; revolving, Θ 404, B 551.

περι-τίθημι, aor. ἔθηκαν, θῆκαν, opt. 3 pl. θεῖεν, place round about, splinters in the fire-pan, σ 308; δύναμίν τινι, bestow, γ 205; mid. aor, θήκατο χροΐ, put on one's body, θέτο κρατί, θέτ' ὤμῳ.

περὶ τρέπω, aor. ἔτράπον, went round, κ 469†.

περι-τρέφω, ipf. **τρέφεται**, thickens, i. e. curdles, E 903; ipf. τρέφετο, ice was forming (thickening) on the shield, ξ 477.

περὶ τρέχω, aor. ἔδραμε, -δραμον, it rolled about in every direction, Ξ 413; ran up with help (from every side), X 369.

περι-τρέω, aor. **τρέσαν**, fled on every side in fear, Λ 676†.

περι-τρομέοντο, ipf. (τρομέω), his flesh quivered with fear, μέλεσσιν, on his limbs, σ 77†.

περι-τροπέων, έοντες, part. pres., (τρέπω), revolving, B 295; turning (ourselves) often about, ι 465.

περί-τροχον, ntr., round, Ψ 455†.

περι-φαινομένοιο, ῳ, visible from every side, N 179; subst., conspicuous place, ε 476.

Περί-φᾶς, αντος, (1) son of Ochesios, an Aitolian, slain by Ares, E 842, 847.—(2) son of Epytos, Trojan herald, P 323.

Περί-φήτης, (1) a Mysian, slain by Teukros, Ξ 515.—(2) son of Kopreus, from Mykenai, slain by Hektor, O 638.

περι-φράδέως, adv., carefully, A 466, ξ 431.

περι-φραζώμεθα, subj., (φράζω), νόστον, let us consider the return, α 76†.

περί-φρων, ονι, masc. and fem., (φρήν), very thoughtful, sagacious, E 412, α 329.

περι-φῦναι, φύς, φῦσ(α), amplecti, embrace, τ 416; τινά, π 21. (Od.)

περι-χέω, aor. ἔχευεν, χεῦεν, χέυεν, subj. χεύῃ, part. χεύας, — τινί τι, pour or shed over, E 776; χρυσόν τινι, gild, γ 426; mid. χεύεται for ηται, subj. aor. ἀργύρῳ, silvers; plupf. κέχυτο, was shed over, B 19.

περι-χώσατο (χώομαι), was very wroth; τινός, on account of—, I 449, Ξ 266.

περι-ωπῇ, ῆν, (ὄπωπα), look-out place, Ξ 8, Ψ 451, κ 146.

περι-ώσιον, ntr. adv., (ὅσιος), beyond measure, Δ 359, π 203.

περκνός, with acc., dappled, Ω 316†.

Περκώσιος, inhabitant of Περκώτη, a town in Troas, Λ 228, O 548, B 835.

πέρνημι, part. **περνάς**, ipf. iter. πέρνασχ' = πέρνασκε, pass. prs. περνάμενα, (πέραν), vendere, sell, Σ 292, X 45. (Il.)

περονάω, aor. **περόνησε**, (περάαν), transfixit, pierce, H 145; mid. ipf. περονᾶτο, aor. ἤσατο, fastened, made fast about her, K 133.

περόνη, ῃ, ην, fem., (πείρω), clasp, brooch, buckle, E 425, σ 293; of modern form, as the cut from ancient original shows.

περόωσι, 3 pl. for περάουσι, from περάω.

πέρσα = ἔπερσα, aor. from πέρθω.

Περσεύς, (1) son of Danae, Ξ 320. —(2) son of Nestor, γ 414, 444.

Περσε-φόνεια, ης, ῃ, daughter of Zeus, λ 217, and of Demeter, wife of Aides, κ 494, 509, λ 213; ἐπαινή, I 457.

Πέρση, daughter of Okeanos, wife of Helios, mother of Aietes and of Kirke, κ 139†.

Περσηϊάδης, descendant of Perseus, Sthenelos, T 116†.

πεσέειν, ἐεσθαι, see πίπτω.

πεσσοῖσιν, dat. pl. masc., at draughts

or *checkers, a* 107†. (Similar Egyptian game illustrated in the following cut.)

πίσσω, only prs., (coquo), *ripens,* η 119; χύλον, κήδεα, *conceal, brood over;* γέρα, *digest = enjoy,* B 237; Θ 513, *carry off* the missile in one, and *nurse* the wound.

πεσών, see πίπτω.

πετάλοισι, dat. pl. ntr., f o l i i s, *leaves,* B 312, τ 520.

πετάννυμι (see πιτνάω, -ημι), aor. **πέτᾰσ(ε),** αν, opt. άσειε, part. άσ(σ)ας, (patere), pandere, *spread out,* ζ 94, ε 269; χεῖρε, the arms, ι 417; to swim, ε 374; elsewh. as suppliant, Ξ 495; θυμόν, *open* the heart; pass. πέπταται, ανται, αρο, expanditur; πεπταμέ-νας, patentes; aor. 3 pl. πετάσθη-σαν, φ 50; part. θεῖσαι.

πετεηνά, ηνῶν, οῖς, (πέτομαι), *winge l,* B 459; *birds, flying things,* O 238, P 675; *fledged,* π 218.

Πετεών, ῶνος, fem., village in Boiotia, B 500†.

Πετεώς, ῶο, son of Orneus, father of Menestheus, Δ 338, M 355.

πέτομαι, πέτεται, ονται, εσθαι, ipf. **πίτετ(ο),** ἐσθην, οντο, ἐπέτοντο, aor. ἐπτᾰτ(ο), subj. πτῆται, part. πτᾰμένη, volare, *fly* (strictly and fig., c u r r e r e, *run,* ποτὶ πτόλιος, X 198); of steeds, οὐκ ἄκοντε πετέσθην, E 366, Θ 45; with ἐκ, *fall from, escape from,* μ 203.

πετραίην, acc. fem., (πέτρη), *inhabit-ing a rock,* μ 231†.

πέτρη, ης, ῃ, ην, αι, άων, ῃσ(ιν), ας, saxum, *rock,* N 137, ι 243; symbol of firmness, O 618; of hard-hearted-ness, Π 35; *cliff, reef,* γ 293, κ 4; *rocky mountain,* ν 196, δ 501; *cave,* B 88; X 126, *stone seat.*

πετρήεσσα, ῃ, αν, (πέτρη), saxo-sus, *rocky,* B 496, δ 844.

πέτρῳ, ον, masc., saxum, *piece of rock, stone,* H 270.

πεύθομαι, see πυνθάνομαι.

πευκᾰλίμῃσι(ν), *prudent, sagacious;* φρεσίν, Ξ 165. (Il.)

πευκεδᾰνοῖο, *destructive,* K 8†.

πεύκης, ας, fem., pinus, *pine, fir,* Λ 494. (Il.)

πεύσομαι, see πυνθάνομαι.

πέφανται, see (1) φαίνω.—(2) φένω.

πεφάσθαι, see φένω.

πεφασμένος, see φαίνω.

πεφήσεται, fut. pf., (1) from φαίνω. —(2) from φένω.

πεφιδέσθαι, δήσομαι, see φείδομαι.

πέφνον, see φένω.

πέφρᾰδον, δέειν, see φράζω.

πέφρικε, see φρίσσω.

πεφύασι, see φύω.

πεφυγμένον, πεφυζότες, see φεύγω.

πεφῠλαγμένον, see φυλάσσω.

πεφυυῖα, see φύω.

πεφυρμένη, ον, see φύρω.

πῆ; (v. l. πῇ), qua? (1) *whither?* E 472, Θ 94.—(2) *how?* N 307.

πή (v. l. πῇ), enclitic, aliquâ, (1) *anywhere,* χ 25; *somewhere,* Γ 400.— (2) *in any way,* Σ 267, Ω 373.

πηγεσι - μάλλῳ (πήγνυμι), *thick-fleeced,* Γ 197†.

πηγαί, ἑων, ῇς, άς, fontes, *sources,* Φ 312, ζ 124.

πήγνυμι, fut. **πήξεις,** aor. ἐπηξε = πῆξε, αμεν, ῃ, αι, ας, αντ(α), (pango, pax), *fix, plant firmly* in any thing, ἐν, with local dat. χ 83, ἐπὶ τύμβῳ, λ 87; without prep., λ 129; *impale,* ἀνὰ σκολόπεσσιν, Σ 177; pass. prs. πήγνυ-ται, ipf. πήγνῠτο, aor. 3 pl. πῆχθεν, and 2 aor. (ἐ)πάγη, ῃ pl. πάγεν, 2 pf. πί-πηγε, plupf. ἐπεπήγει, haerere, *stick fast,* pf. *remain fast,* ἐν καιρίῳ, in a mortal part, Δ 185, Γ 135, N 442, Θ 298; X 453, rigescunt, *stiffen.* In ε 163, πῆξει may be construed as imp. 1 aor. mid. or inf. 1 aor. act. used im-peratively.

πηγῷ, ούς, (πήγνυμι), *firm, stout, tough,* I 124; κύματι, *mighty* wave, ε 388.

πηγῠλίς (πάγος), *frosty, ice-cold,* ξ 476†.

Πήδαιον, place in Troja, N 172†.

Πήδαιος, son of Antenor and of Theano, slain by Meges, E 69†.

πηδάλιον, ῳ, (α), (πηδόν), *rudder,* γ 281, ε 255. Strictly the word seems to denote the *handle* or *bar* connecting the two rudders (for two were used even in historical times), and serving to move them. See cuts Nos. 94, 95;

cf. Nos. 21, 40, 41, 48, 64, and adjoining cuts representing rudder of an Egyptian ship; in the first cut both rudders are portrayed, regardless of perspective, as on the same side of the vessel.

Πήδασος, (1) town of the Leleges in Troas, on the Satnioeis, destroyed by Achilleus, Z 35, Υ 92, Φ 87.—(2) subject town of Agamemnon, I 152, 294.—(3) son of Abarbaree, slain by Εuryalos, Z 21.—(4) steed of Achilleus, Π 152, 467.

πηδάω, ipf. **ἐπήδα,** aor. **πηδῆσαι,** salire, *leap, ὑψόσε,* in the air, Φ 302; *speed, escape,* Ξ 455. (Il.)

πηδῷ, τῷ, ntr., *with the oar-blade,* used collectively, η 328. (Od.)

πηκτόν, ntr., (πήγνυμι), *well joined together, firm,* Κ 353, ν 32.

πῆλαι, λε, see πάλλω.

Πηλεγών, son of Axios, father of Asteropaios, Φ 141, 152, 159.

Πηλεΐδης, αο, εω, and **Πηληϊάδης,** αο, εω [synizesis, also in Πηληΐδεω, Α 1, Ο 64, θ 75], and **Πηλείων, ωνος, ι, α,** *son of Peleus,* Achilleus, A 223, Ο 74, Χ 58, Ψ 41, Λ 322, Ω 431, Υ 80, Λ 197, ω 18, Ψ 249, Υ 27, 88. **Πηλειωνάδε,** *to Peleus's son,* Ω 338†.

Πηλεύς, ῆος, (έος, when joined with *υἱός, όν), Peleus,* son of Aiakos, fugitive from Aigina to the Myrmidon Eurytion in Phthia, whose daughter Antigone he marries, but afterward the Nereid Thetis: his daughter by the former Polydora, Π 175 sqq.; his son by the latter Achilleus, I 147, 252, 289, Σ 87, Ω 61, Φ 188; hence **Πηλήϊος,** adj., Σ 60.

Πηληϊάδης, see Πηλεΐδης.

πήληξ, ηκι, α, fem., galea, *helmet,* Π 105, Ο 608, α 256. (Il.)

Πηλιάς, άδα, μελίη, ην, *Pelian* spear (from Mount Pelion), gift of Centaur Cheiron to Peleus, Υ 277, Π 143. (Il.)

Πήλιον, mountain in Thessaly, Β 757, Π 144, λ 316.

πῆμ(α), ατος, άτ(α), ntr., (πά-θος), malum, *suffering, woe, harm,* Ω 547, ε 179; κακοῖο, perpessio mali, *endurance* of calamity; δύης, doloris, *depths* of wretchedness; of persons, and pestis, *bane, nuisance,* ρ 446.

πημαίνει, fut. πημανέειν, aor. 3 pl. opt. -ήνειαν, (πῆμα), *injure, distress,* Ο 42; ὑπὲρ ὅρκια, *work mischief* by violating the oaths; aor. pass. πημάνθη, ανθῆναι, laedi, *τί, to suffer* any *hurt* or *harm,* θ 563.

Πηνειός, river in Thessaly, flowing through the vale of Tempe into the Thermaic gulf, Β 752, 757.

Πηνέλεως, εω, leader of Boiotians, Β 494, Ξ 496, 487, 489, Π 340, Ρ 597.

Πηνελόπεια, ης, *Penelope,* the heroine of the Odyssey, κούρη Ἰκαρίοιο, α 329; Ὀδυσσῆος παράκοιτις, φ 158; μήτηρ Τηλεμάχοιο, φ 311; ἐχέφρων, δ 111; περίφρων, δ 787, ε 216.

πηνίον, τό, (pannus, fano). *thread of the woof* passed from one side to the other in and out through the upright threads of the warp, before which the weaver stood, Ψ 762†.

πηός, ούς, affinis, *brother-in-law,* Γ 163, θ 581.

Πηρείη, ἡ, region in Thessaly = Πιερίη? Β 766†.

πήρης, gen., ην, fem., (pera), knapsack, beggar's wallet, ρ 357, 411. (Od.)

πηρόν, acc., caecum, blind, Β 599†.

Πηρώ, οὖς, daughter of Neleus and of Chloris, wife of Bias, λ 287†.

πήχει, dat., acc. υν, du. εε, (1) elbow, lower arm, Φ 166; brachium, Ε 314, ρ 38.—(2) the centre-piece, which joined the arms of the ancient bow; in shooting, this piece was grasped by the left hand, and the arrow passed between the finger of the hand and the centre-piece of the bow (see cuts Nos. 112, Herakles; 133, Paris; 67, 96, 97, Assyrians), Λ 375, φ 419.

πῖαρ, ntr., (πιϜαρ), fat, of cattle, Λ 550; rich, fat soil under the surface of ground, ι 135.

πίδᾰκος, ῆς, fontis, spring, Π 825†.

πιδηέσσης, rich in springs, Λ 183†.

Πιδύτης, ην, a Trojan from Perkote, slain by Odysseus, Ζ 30†.

πίε, έειν, aor. from πίνω.

πιέζειν, ipf. ἐπίεζε, πιέζον, pass. aor. πιεσθείς,(premo), comprimo, squeeze, press, μ 174, Π 510; ἐν δεσμοῖς, vinculis constringere, load with fetters.

πίειρα, irreg. fem. from πίων.

Πιερίη, region about Olympos in Makedonia, Ξ 226, ε 50; see Πηρείη.

πιθέσθαι, see πείθω.

πιθέω, apparent coll. form of πείθω, 2 fut. πεπιθήσω, persuadebo, persuade, with inf., X 223; πιθήσεις, obedies, obey, φ 369; aor. part. πιθήσας, with dat., fretus, confisus, relying on.

πίθοι, ων, great earthen jars for wine and oil, ψ 305, β 340, half buried in earth, as in cut No. 68.

πικρόγαμοι, nom. pl., πάντες κ' ὠκύμοροί τε γενοίατο—τε, for all would be a speedy death and a bitter marriage, α 266, δ 346, ρ 137.

πικρός, όν, (fem., δ 406); ἥν, ἅς, όν, ά, sharp-pointed, of arrows, missiles, Δ 118; also of taste, Λ 846; and of smell, pungent, δ 406; bitter, Λ 271; hateful, ρ 448.

πίλνᾰται, ipf. πιλνᾶτο, (πέλομαι), versatur, move about, frequent, Τ 93; vertebantur, were rolling along, χθονί, on the ground, Ψ 368.

πῖλος, masc., pilus, felt, Κ 265.

πίμπλανεται, (πίμπλημι, plenus), impletur, is filled with, μένεος, Ι 679†.

πίμπλημι, 3 pl. πιμπλᾶσι, aor. 1 πλῆσε, σαν, opt. σειαν, part. σασα, impleo, fill, τί, Ξ 35, Φ 23; τί τινος, Ρ 573; not with dat. (Π 373 is dat. of accompanying circumstance, amid); mid. ipf. πίμπλαντο, 1 aor. opt. 3 pl. πλησαίατο, σάμινος, οι, like act., ξ 112; usually with reflexive reference to subject (sibi, suum), ξ 87; θυμόν, satisfy themselves, τ 198; pass. aor. ἐπλήσθη, 3 pl. πλῆσθεν, also 2 aor. mid. πλῆθ' = πλῆτο, pl. πλῆντο, impleri, be filled with, μένεος, irâ, δ 662, υ 349; δακρυόφι, δ 705; φρένας, his breast was filled, Ρ 499. (X 402, πίτναντο.)

πίνᾰκι πυκτῷ, writing-tablet, folding tablet, Ζ 169; elsewh. πίνακας κρειῶν, wooden plates or trenchers with meat, α 141; νεῶν, μ 67, ship's timbers.

ἐπινύσσω, ipf. from πινύσσω, (πινυτός), sharpen the wits, Ξ 249†.

πινυτή, ήν, prudence, understanding, Η 289, prop. fem. from πινυτός, οὖς, ἡ, ῇ, (πινύσσω, πνέω), prudens, discreet, α 229. (Od.)

πίνων, prs., inf. ἐμέναι, ipf. iter. πίνεσκεν, fut. part. πιόμενος, aor. ἔπιον, πίε, πίον, subj. πίω, πίησθα, πιῃ, opt. πίοιμι, πίοι(εν); πιέμεν, πιεῖν, πιών, bibere, drink; οἶνον, ὕδωρ, αἷμα, γάλα, ὀρόν, φάρμακα, Δ 262, portionem, each his portion; also with gen. part., λ 96 (Od.); drain, quaff, κρητῆρας, κύπελλα; also with dat. of place, like the French boire dans une tasse, drink out of a cup, ξ 112. [ῑ in aor., but in arsis also πιέμεν.]

πίομαι, see πίνω.

πιότατον, sup. from πίων.

πίπτει, ουσι, ωσι, ων, όντων, ipf. ἔπιπτε, ον, πίπτε(ν), ον, fut. 3 pl. πεσέονται, σέεσθαι, aor. 2 ἔπεσ(εν), ον, πέσε(ν), ἔτην, ον; χ(σι-ν), ἧτον, ωμεν, ωσι; οι, ουσι; ἕειν; ὧν, ὄντος, ὄντ(α), οὖσ(α), όντες, pf. part. πεπτεῶτα, ας [pronounced with synizesis], (ΠΕΤ), cadere, per aëra ferri, fall, be borne through the air, Μ 278; with locative, χαμαί, πεδίῳ (with ἐν, Ν 205; ἐπί, β 398; ὑπό, Π 378; μετά, Τ 110; ἔραζε, χαμάδις, ἄλλυδις); fall over, crash, Ψ 120, μ 410; fall in battle, Τ

227, A 243; at the hands of, ὑπό τινος (τινι), Λ 158; petere aliquid, *fall upon, attack*, with ἐν, N 742; *subside*, of wind, τ 202; ἐκ, fall out of, forfeit, θυμοῦ, ex favore.

πίσεα, ntr. pl., (πίνω), *meadows*, Υ 9, ζ 124.

πίσσα, fem., (πικρός), pix, *pitch*, Δ 277.

πιστός, όν, ά, sup., πιστότατος, fidus, *trusty*, with inf., Π 147; πιστά γυναικί, mulieribus confidendum; freq. ὅρκια, foedus fidum. πιστόω, aor. mid. ἐπιστώσαντ(ο) = πιστώσαντο, aor. pass. 2 du. subj. ωθῆτον, inf. ωθῆναι, part. ωθείς, (πιστός), pass. confidere, *trust*, φ 218; bind one's self, fidem facere, ὅρκῳ, by oath; mid. *mutually bind each other*, Z 233.

πίσυνος, οι, (πείθω), confisus, fretus, *relying upon*, τινί, E 205, Λ 9.

πίσυρες, ας, (Aeolic for τέσσαρες), quatuor, ε 70, O 680.

Πιτθεύς, ῆος, king in Troizen, father of Aithra, Γ 144†.

πιτνάς, pres. part., ipf. πίτνα, pandere, *extending*; ipf. mid. πίτναντο, *floated, fluttered*, X 402.

Πίτεια, town in Mysia, B 829†.

πίτυς, υσσιν, dat. pl. fem., pinus, *pine* or *fir*, N 390, ι 186.

πίφαυσκέμεν, ων, ipf. πίφαυσκε, ον, mid. πιφαύσκομαι, εαι, εται, imp. εο, part. ὅμενος, (πι-φαF-σκω, φάος), *let gleam, display*, φλόγα; M 280, *letting loose* his missiles, hence *manifest, make known*, ἔπος πάντεσσι, τί τινι. [in arsis ῑ, K 478.]

πίων, **πίονος**, ι, α, ες, fem. **πίειρα**, ῃ, αν, ας, sup. πιότατον, (opίmus?), *fat*, (1) of animals, plump, *fat*, μηρία, νῶτα, δημός; cellular tissue, paunch.— (2) of fields and soil in general, *fertile*, Ι 577.—(3) of localities and cities, *wealthy*, opulentus, E 512.

πλαγκταί, ἀς πέτρας, *clashing* rocks, against which every thing is dashed to pieces, myth suggested by natural phenomena in strait of Messina or the Lipari Isles, μ 61, ψ 327.

πλαγκτέ, voc., (πλάζω), either *mad*, (sc. φρένας), or, better, *vagabond*, φ 363†.

πλαγκτοσύνης, τῆς, (πλαγκτύς), *roving, roaming*, o 343†.

πλάγχθη, see πλάζω.

1. **πλάζω**, ipf. **πλάξ(ε)**, (πέλαγος, plash), *bespattered*, Φ 269.

2. **πλάζω**, **πλάζουσι**, ων, ipf. πλάζε, aor. πλάγξ(ε), (πλήσσω), *drive away* (from object of one's aim), freq. with ἀπό, with inf. of result, ω 307; μέγα, greatly hinder, B 132; *confuse*, β 396; *turning its course, deflecting*, P 751; pass. mid. πλάζομαι, ετ(αι), εσθαι, ὅμενος, ου, οι, ipf. πλάζετ(ο), fut. πλάγξομαι, aor. πλάγχθη, θείς, θέντα, ες, oberrare, vagari, *rove, wander*, ν 204; κατά, with acc., ο 312, π 151; ἐπὶ δῆμον, ξ 43, γ 252; *be cast about*, κύματι, on the wave (collective), ε 389; *be cast away*, α 2; ἀπό, from, aberrare, ζ 278; *dash back*, Λ 351.

Πλάκος, ἡ, mountain above Thebe, in Mysia, Z 396, 425, X 479.

πλανάω, mid. **πλανόωνται**, vagantur, *rove*, Ψ 321†.

Πλάταια, town in Boiotia, B 504†.

πλατάνιστῳ, fem., *plane-tree*, not unlike our maple, B 307.

πλατύς, **πλατέος**, εῖ, έ(α), *broad*, Η 86, N 588; αἰπόλια αἰγῶν, *wide-roaming* herds of goats.

πλέες, ας, see πλείων.

πλεῖος, ου, οι; η, αι; ον, πλέον, πλείοις, comp. πλειοτέρῳ, plenus, *full*, K 579, Θ 162; with gen., δ 319, ο 446.

πλεῖστον, οι, ους, η, ην, αι, ον, α, (πολύς), plurimum, ι, *most*, O 616; ntr. as adv., maxime, *especially*, Δ 138, Τ 287.

πλείων, **πλέων**, πλέονες (πλέες), όνων, όνεσσι (πλείοσι), πλέονας (πλείονς, πλέας), ntr. πλέον, πλείον(α), comp. from πολύς, plus, plures, maior, *more, greater*, with ὁ, τό, etc., β 277, K 506, Λ 165, *greater part*. [σ 247, synizesis = πλεῦνες.]

πλεκτοῖς, ήν, verbal adj., (πλέκω), *braided, twisted*, χ 175, Σ 568.

πλέκω, aor. **ἔπλεξε**, p'ait, *twist*, Ξ 176; aor. mid. πλεξάμενος, κ 168.

πλευραί, ῶν, ἀς, ribs, Λ 437; *sides* or *flank*, latera, ρ 232, Υ 170 = **πλευρά**, acc. pl. ntr., *on the side*, Δ 468†.

Πλευρών, ῶνος, town in Aitolia, B 639, N 217, Ξ 116; inhabitant, Πλευρώνιος, Ψ 635.

πλείω, **πλεῖθ'** = πλεῖτε, πλείειν, πλέων, ουσα, σας, πλείοντες, ipf. ἔπλεον, εεν, ἐόμεν, εον and πλέεν, ἴομεν, πλέον, fut. πλεύσεσθε, (πλέϜω), navigo, sail; ὑγρὰ κέλευθα, sail the watery ways, γ 71. [πλέων, synizesis, a 183.]

πλέων, έον, see πλείων.

πληγή, πληγῆς, ῇ, έων, ῇσι(ν), fem., (πλήσσω), blow, v e r b e r a, stroke, from stick, whip, or thong, O 17, δ 244; Διός, Ξ 414, stroke of lightning.

πλῆθ' = πλῆτο, see πίμπλημι.

πλῆθε, see πλήθω.

πλῆθος, dat. πλήθεϊ, ει [P 330, Ψ 639], and πληθύς, ύος, ύϊ, ύν, (πλήθω), multitudo, esp. opp. chiefs, B 143, 278 (with pl. verb), 488, I 641.

πλήθω, πλήθει, ουσι, ωσι, ipf. πλῆθε, be or become full, with gen., of rivers, swell, Π 389; part. πλήθων, οντι, ουσαν, ούσας, plenus, full, ι 8; swollen, E 87, Λ 492; σελήνην, lunam plenam.

πληϊάδες, Pleiades (seven stars in the constellation Taurus), from πλέω, as the opening and close of navigation was marked by their rising and setting; the popular etymology made them doves (πελειάδες), flying before the hunter Orion, ε 272, μ 62. The Romans called the constellation V e r giliae, from vergo, to turn.

πληκτίζεσθαι (πλήσσω), depugnare, contend with, Φ 499.

πλήμνη, αι, fem., (πλήθω), hub or nave of a wheel, E 726, Ψ 339.

πλη-μυρίς, fem., (πλήμμυρις?), rise of the sea, flood (tide), ι 486†.

πλήν (πλέον), with gen., except, θ 207†.

πλῆντο, (1) from πίμπλημι, implebantur.—(2) from πελάζω.

πλῆξα, ε, see πλήσσω.

πληξ-ίππῳ, ον, (πλήσσω), striking or driving horses, B 104.

πλησίον, du. ίω, pl. ίοι, ίαι, (πέλας), propinquus, vicinus, near, ἄλλον, neighbor, θ 328; elsewh. adj., with gen. or dat.; ntr. as adv., prope, hard by, μ 102.

πλησ-ιστίον (πλήθω, ἱστίον), filling the sail, λ 7 and μ 149.

πλήσσω, aor. πλῆξα, ε, etc., 2 aor. (ἐ)πέπληγον, inf. πεπληγέμεν, pf. πεπληγώς, υῖα, (πλαγ-, plango), strike, with hand, foot, staff, whip, missile, weapon, Π 791, σ 57, υ 17, χ 20; smite, μ 412; pass. πληγείς, Θ 12, Ψ 694, O

117; κληΐδι, thrust open by, φ 50; θ 264, χορόν, trod a measure; hit and wound, K 489, Π 332; with double acc. (on), κ 161, Λ 240; mid. 2 aor. πεπλήγετο, οντο, reflex. se or sua, Π 125, having smote his thighs.

πλῆτο, (1) from πίμπλημι, implebatur.—(2) from πελάζω.

πλίσσοντο, ipf., strode out, ζ 318†.

πλοκάμους, masc., (πλέκω), locks, braids, Ξ 176†.

πλόον, masc., (πλέω), navigationem, voyage, γ 169†.

πλοῦτος, οιο, ῳ, ον, (πλήθω), divitiae, wealth, A 171, Π 596, ξ 206.

πλοχμοί = πλόκαμοι, locks, P 52†.

πλυνοί, masc., wash-troughs or basins in the earth, lined with stone, ζ 40.

πλύνω, πλυνούσῃ, ipf. iter. 3 pl. πλύνεσκον, fut. έουσα, αι, aor. 3 pl. πλῦναν, part. ασα, (fluo), wash, clean, ζ 31, 59, 93.

πλωτῇ, dat. sing., (πλωτός), floating, κ 3†.

πλώουσι, οιεν, ειν, ipf. πλῶον, (πλόϜω from πλέω), swim, float, ε 240, Φ 302.

πνεύμονι, dat. masc., lung, Δ 528. (Il.)

πνέει, and πνείει, οντε, ες, ας, ουσα, αν, (πνέϜω), spirare, breathe, live, P 447, σ 131; smell, δ 446; blowing, η 119; breathing courage, μένος, χ 203; μένεα, with souls inspired with courage; mid. pf. πέπνυσαι, inf. ὔσθαι, plupf. πέπνυσο, have discretion, κ 495; be prudent, Ω 377; part. pf. πεπνυμένος, etc., prudens, discreet, Γ 203, α 213, δ 206, θ 388, γ 52, β 38.

πνοιῇ, ῆς, ῇ, ήν, αί, ῇσ(ιν), άς, fem., (πνέω), spiramen, breath, Υ 439; panting, Ψ 380; hot breath, blast, Φ 355; elsewh. of wind, ζ 20, κ 507.

Ποδᾰ-λείριος, son of Asklepios, brother of Machaon, B 732, Λ 833.

ποδά-νιπτρα, ntr., (νίπτω), water for washing the feet, τ 343 and 504.

Ποδ-άργη, a Harpy (storm-wind), mother of Achilleus's horses, Π 150, Υ 400.

Πόδ-αργος, horse of Hektor, Θ 185; of Menelaos, Ψ 295.

ποδ-άρκης (ἀρκέω), swift-footed, A 121. (Il.)

Ποδ-άρκης, son of Iphiklos, brother

of Protesilaos, chief of the contingent from Phylake and Pyrasos, B 704, N 693.

ποδ-ηνεκέ(α), ές, (ἠνεκής, stem ἐνεκ, see φέρω), *extending to the feet*, K 24, O 646.

ποδ-ήνεμος (ἄνεμος), *swift as the wind*, B 786, of Iris. (Il.)

Ποδῆς, οὖς, ἦν, son of Eetion, slain by Menelaos, P 575, 590.

ποδ-ωκείῃσι, dat. pl. fem., (ὠκύς), *swiftness of foot*, B 792†.

ποδ-ώκης, εος, εἴ, εα, εες, εσι, εας, (ὠκύς), *fleet-footed*, K 316, B 860, Ψ 249, 262, λ 471, 538,

ποθέεσκε, see ποθέω.

πόθεν, interr. adv., *whence?* unde? γ 71, ο 423; also like Lat. cujas, with gen., π. ἀνδρῶν, unde gentium, from what quarter of the world? Φ 150, α 170.

ποθέν, indefin. adv., alicunde, *from some quarter*, ω 149; freq. with εἰ.

ποθέω, έεις, ποθήμεναι, inf. prs., ipf. πόθει, εον, aor. πόθεσαν, ἴσαι, desidero, *desire, long for*, β 375; τινά, Α 492, λ 196.

ποθή, ῇ, ἦν, (ποθέω), desiderium, *longing for*, τινός, Α 240, θ 414; σή, tui; also = inopia, *lack*, κ 505, β 126.

πόθι, interr. adv., ubi? *where?* α 170, ω 298. (Od.)

ποθί, indefin. adv., alicubi, *anywhere*, υ 114; aliqua, *somehow*, Τ 273, α 348; esp. αἴ κέ ποθι, *if in any case, if at all*, to see whether, α 379, β 144, μ 215, χ 252, ρ 51, 60, δ 34.

πόθος, ῳ, masc., (ποθέω), desiderium, *yearning (after)*, σός, tui, P 439.

Ποιάντιος υἱός, son *of Poias*, Philoktetes, γ 190†.

ποιέω, prs., ipf. ἐποίει, ποίει, ποίεον, fut. ποιησέμεν, aor. ἐποίησεν, σαν, ποίησε, σαν, σαι, etc., *make*, act., (1) *create*, εἴδωλον, φάος τινί ; *build, make*, σάκος ταύρων, shield of bulls' hides ; ἀθύρματα, make sport, play ; with acc. and inf., ψ 258, efficere ; pass. pf. πεποίηται εὐνή, η 342; σοὶ ἄριστα, optima tibi facta sunt per domum?—(2) with double acc., *cause to become, make so and so*, τινά τι (second acc. either subst. or adject.), ἄκοιτιν θνητῷ, give in marriage to a mortal; ἄιστον, cause to be forgotten; ὄλβια,

bless; ἐνὶ φρεσί, put in one's thoughts. —mid. ποιεῖται, ipf. ποιεύμην, fut. ποιήσεται, aor. ποιήσατ(ο), σαντο, σασθαι, sibi facere, comparare, *make for one's self, procure*; τινά ἄλοχον, uxorem ducere; ἀκοίτην, nubere; υἱόν, adoptare; ῥήτρην, bind one's self by an agreement.

ποίη, ης, ῃ, ην, (ποΓίη), gramen, *grass*, σ 370, Ξ 347.

ποιήεντος, gen., ποιήενθ' = ποιήεντα, ποιήισσαν, (ποΓιηΓεις, ποίη), graminosus, *grassy*, B 503, δ 337.

ποιητοῖο, οἶσι(ν), ἦν, ῇσι, άς, (ποιέω), *with* and *without* εὖ, (well) *made*, K 262; πύκα, firmly *built*, α 333.

ποικίλλε, ipf. from ποικίλλω, (ποικίλος), *skillfully work* or *make*, Σ 590†.

ποικίλμασιν, τοῖς, ntr., (ποικίλλω), *rich work, broidery*, Z 294 and ο 107; cf. the embroideress in cut.

ποικιλό-μήτην, voc. μῆτα, (μῆτις), prop. *with changing, versatile mind*, versatili ingenio, *rich in invention*, χ 115.

ποικίλον, ῃ, ον, (α), (pic-tus), *parti-colored, spotted, mottled*, of skin of animals ; *embroidered in various colors*, E 735, σ 293, X 441 ; *skillfully wrought*, of objects in metal or wood, Δ 226, K 501.

ποιμαίνων, οντ(α), (ποιμήν), part. prs., ipf. iter. ποιμαίνεσκεν, pascere, *tend as shepherd* (ἐπ᾽ ὕεσσι, Z 25), μῆλα, ι 188; pass. ipf. ποιμαίνοντο, pascebantur, *were tended*, Λ 245.

ποιμήν, ένος, ένι, ένα, ένες. ἐσιν, (πῶυ), pastor, herdsman, of sheep or oxen; λαῶν, shepherd (defense) of the people, epithet of chiefs, B 243.

ποίμνῃσιν, dat. pl. from ἡ ποίμνη, (ποιμήν), gregibus (tenetur), (is occupied by) *flocks*, ι 122†.

ποιμνήϊον σταθμόν, (ποίμνη), cattle-stall, sheep-fold, B 470†.

ποινή, ῆς, ήν, (ποϜινή), poena, purus), purification, expiation, quit-money for bloodshed, penalty, τινός, for a person, i. e. murder of a person, I 633; for a thing, satisfaction, price, Γ 290, E 266, P 207; ἄτιτοι, unpaid; ἀπετίνυτο, exacted satisfaction for himself from many, Π 398.

ποῖον, οι, οίη, ῳ, interr. adj. pron., qualis? of what sort? εἶτ' ἀμυνέμεν, what sort are ye to defend? how would ye be disposed to defend? φ 195; ποῖόν σε ἔπος φύγεν ἕρκος ὀδόντων, in questions expressive of indignation or surprise, α 64, φ 168.

ποιπνύοντα, ύουσαι, ipf. (ἰ)ποίπνῦον, aor. part. ποιπνύσαντι, (red. from πνέω), prop. puff, pant, bestir one's self, Ξ 155; make haste, υ 149; esp. of attendants, servants, Σ 421, A 600.

πόκον, τόν, (πέκω), shorn wool, fleece, vellus, M 451†.

πολέες = πολλοί.

πολεμήϊα, ntr., (πόλεμος), ἔργα, toil of battle, B 338 (οἶδε, understands); with δοῦναι, bestow renown in battle, glory; τεύχεα, warlike equipment.

πολεμίζω, prs. and ipf. πολέμιζε, ον, and πτολεμίζω, ειν, ων, fut. ἰξομεν and πολεμίξομεν, (πόλεμος), pugnarc, fight, πόλεμον, pugnam; τινί, contra aliquem = ἄντα τινός, ἐναντίβιον, opp. μετά τισιν, jointly with; impugnare, to fight with, Σ 258.

πολεμιστής, ήν, ά, αί, and πτολεμιστῇ, (πολεμίζω), bellator, warrior, K 549.

πόλεμος, οιο, ου, ῳ, ον, οι, ων, ους, and πτόλεμος, οιο, ου, ῳ, ον, ους, (πελεμίζω), tumult of combat, fight, A 492, Δ 15; esp. freq. plur., ξ 225, χ 152; also in periphrasis, ἔρις, νείκος, φύλοπις πολέμοιο, discord, fury, din of the combat. π(τ)όλεμόνδε, into the combat, Θ 400.

πολεύειν (πέλεσθαι), versari, live in, χ 223†.

πολέων = πολλῶν.

πόληας, ες = πύληις.

πυλίζω, aor. πολίσσαμεν, and plupf. pass. πεπόλιστο, condere, build, H 453 and Υ 217.

πολιήτας, τούς = πολίτας, cives, citizens, B 806†.

πόλινδ(ε), in urbem, to the city, E 224, N 820, α 189.

πολΐο-κροτάφους, τούς, with hoary temples (κρόταφος), gray with age, Θ 518†.

πολιοῖο, ον, οί, ῆς, ήν, άς, (πελλός, pullus), canus, hoary, of hair (capilli, pili); of iron, sea, ἁλός, with hoary foam, A 350.

πόλῑς, ιος [and ιος, B 811, Φ 567], ει, ιν, ιις, ίων, ίεσσι, ιας [pronounce ἴς, ἴας? θ 560], εις; πτόλιος, Δ 514, etc.; ιν, B 130, etc.; also πόληος, ηϊ, Γ 50; ηες, ηας, urbs, civitas, city, with name as appos., e. g. Τροίην, λ 510; or as limiting gen., B 133; opp. ζ 178, ἄστυ, fortified dwelling-place, πόλις, inhabited city; P 144, community and city; ἄκρη, acropolis, citadel, upper town.

πολῖται, ας, masc., (πύλις), cives, citizens, η 131, O 558.

Πολίτης, αο, (1) son of Priamos, B 791, N 533, O 339, Ω 250.—(2) companion of Odysseus, κ 224.

πολλάκι(ς), adv. from πολλός, saepe, many times, Γ 232, N 666, τ 76.

πολλός, όν, see πολύς, ύ.

Πολύ-αιμον'ίδης, αο, son of Polyaimon, Αιποραον, Θ 276†.

πολύ-αιν(ε), voc., (αἶνος), much-praised, 'Οδυσεῦ, I 673, Α 430.

πολύ-άϊξ, άϊκος, (ἀΐσσω), impetuous; κάματος, weariness caused by impetuousness in fight, E 811; elsewh. πολέμοιο, furious combat, Α 165.

πολύ-ανθος (ἄνθος), much-, luxuriantly blooming, ξ 353†.

πολύ-άρητος (ἀράομαι), much-, warmly desired, ζ 280 and τ 404.

πολύ-αρνι, τῷ, (-Ϝαρνι, lamb), rich in lambs, possessor of many flocks, B 106†.

πολύ-βενθέος, gen., (βένθος), very deep, A 432; elsewh. of sea. (Od.)

Πόλύ-βος, (1) son of Antenor, Λ 59.—(2) an Egyptian, δ 126.—(3) an Ithakan, father of Eurymachos, ο 519. —(4) a Phaiakian, θ 373.—(5) a suitor in Ithaka, χ 243, 284.

πουλύ-βοτείρη, αν, (βόσκω), much-or all-nourishing, alma, only of the earth, χθονί, α, Ζ 213, A 619, exc. Λ 770, 'Αχαιΐδα.

πολύ-βουλος (βουλή) 'Αθήνη, deep in counsel, exceeding wise, E 260, π 282.

πολὔ-βοῦται (βούς), rich in cattle,
I 154 and 296.

πολὔ-γηθέες (γηθέω) Ὧραι, ever gay
(conceived as never ceasing from the
choral dance), Φ 450†.

πολὔ-δαίδᾰλος, ου, ψ, ον, οι, per-
quam artificiosus, highly, cunningly wrought, of objects in metal and
wood; of men, solertes, only Ψ 743,
skilful.

πολὔ-δακρυς, υ, and -δακρῦον, P
192, epithet of μάχη, ὑσμίνη, ἄρηα, occasioning many tears, doleful, deplorable,
Γ 132.

πολὔ-δάκρῦτος, οιο, much-lamented,
Ω 620; tearful, γόοιο.

Πολύ-δαμνα, wife of the Egyptian
Θῶν, δ 228†.

πολὔ-δειράδος, gen. from -δειράς,
(δειρή), many-ridged, Οὐλύμποιο, A 499.
(Il.)

πολὔ-δένδρεον, masc., (δένδρον),
thickly planted with trees, δ 737, ψ 139,
359.

πολὔ-δέσμου, gen., (δεσμός), firmly
(=in many places) bound together,
epithet of Odysseus's raft, ε 33 and
338.

Πολὔ-δεύκης, acc. εα, Pollux, son of
Zeus and of Leda, brother of Kastor,
Γ 237, λ 300. (decus.)

πολὔ-δίψιον, ntr., (δίψα), thirsty, dry,
of Argos in valley of Inachos, Δ 171†.

Πολὔ-δώρη, daughter of Peleus,
wife of Spercheios, mother of Menestheus, Π 175†.

πολὔ-δωρος (δῶρον), richly dowered,
Z 394.

Πολὔ-δωρος, (1) youngest son of
Priamos by Laothoe, Υ 419, Φ 91,
X 46; slain by Achilleus, Υ 407.—(2)
a Greek, Ψ 637.

Πολὔ-ειδος, v. l. for Πολύ-ιδος.

πολὔ-ζύγῳ (ζυγόν), with many rowers'
benches = great, B 293†.

πολὔ-ηγερέες (ἀγείρω), numerously
assembled, reading of Aristarchos in
Λ 564†.

πολὔ-ηράτου, ῳ, ον, (ἔραμαι), greatly
loved or desired, desideratus; ἥβη,
lovely youthful bloom; Θήβη, λ 275.

πολὔ-ηχεῖ, έα, many-toned, of nightingale, τ 521; echoing, resounding, Δ
422.

πολὔ-θαρσές, bold, intrepid, audax,
P 156.

Πολὔ-θερσείδης, αο, son of Polytherses, Ktesippos, χ 287†.

Πολὔ-ϊδος (Fιδος), (1) son of Eurydamas, slain by Diomedes, E 148.—
(2) seer in Korinthos, father of Euche-
nor, N 663, 666.

πολὔ-ιδρείησι(ν) (ἴδρις), consilio,
much knowledge, shrewdness, β 346 and
ψ 77.

πολὔ-ιδρις, ιν, very shrewd, subtle,
versutus, ο 459 and ψ 82.

πολὔ-ίππου, rich in horses, N 171†.

πολη-καγκέα (κάγκανος), very dry,
parching, Λ 642†.

πολὔ-καρπος, ου, (καρπύς), frugi-
fer, fructuosus, fruitful, η 122 and
ω 221.

Πολὔ-κάστη, youngest daughter of
Nestor, γ 464†.

πολὔ-κερδείησι (κέρδος), astutiâ,
great craft, ω 167†.

πολὔ-κερδέα, acc. masc., (κέρδος),
astutum, cunning, ν 255†.

πολὔ-κεστος (κεντέω), rich'y embroidered, Γ 371†.

πολὔ-κηδέ(α), acc., (κῆδος), aerum-
nosum, woful, wretched, ι 37 and ψ
351.

πολὔ-κληῗδι, ῖσι, (κληΐς), with many
thole-pins, many-oared, B 74, H 88.

πολὔ-κλήρων, gen. pl., (κλῆρος),
locupletium, wea'thy, ξ 211†.

πολὔ-κλητοι (καλέω), called together
in large numbers = from many a land,
Δ 438 and K 420.

πολὔ-κλύστῳ (κλύζω), loudly surg-
ing, δ 354. (Od.)

πολὔ-κμητος, ου, ον, (κάμνω),
wrought with much labor, well-wrought,
of iron, Z 48; θάλαμος, δ 718, firmly
built.

πολὔ-κνημον (κνήμη), with many
glens or ravines, B 497†.

πολὔ-κοιρανίη, fem., (κοίρανος), rule
of many, mob-rule, B 204†.

πολὔ-κτήμων (κτῆμα), with much
possessions, E 613†.

Πολὔ-κτορίδης, αο, son of Polyktor,
Peisandros, σ 299†.

Πολύ-κτωρ, ορος, (1) fabled name,
Ω 397.—(2) ancient hero in Ithaka,
ρ 207.—(3) father of Peisandros.

πολὔ-λήϊος (λήϊον), rich in harvests,
E 613†.

πολύ-λλιστον (λίσσομαι), object of
many (fervent) prayers, ε 445†.

Πολῠ-μήλη, daughter of Phylas, mother of Eudoros, Η 180†.

πολῠ-μήλου, gen., acc. ον, (μῆλα), rich in sheep, rich in flocks, Β 605, 705. (Il.)

Πολῠ́-μηλος, son of Argeas, a Lykian, slain by Patroklos, Η 417†.

πολῠ́-μητις, ιος, (μῆτις), rich in devices, crafty, shrewd, freq. epithet of Odysseus, Α 311; of Hephaistos, Φ 355.

πολῠ-μηχᾰνίην (μηχανή), manifold cunning, ψ 321†.

πολῠ-μήχᾰνος, (ε), (μηχανή), fertile in devices, full of expedients, ever ready, epithet of Odysseus, α 205, Β 173.

πολυ-μνήστη, ην, (μνάομαι), much-wooed, eagerly sought, δ 770. (Od.)

πολῠ́-μῡθος, ον, of many words, fluent, Γ 214 and β 200.

Πολῠ́-νείκης, son of Oidipus, brother of Eteokles, mover of the expedition of the Epigoni (descendants) against Thebes, Δ 377†.

Πολῠ́-νηος, father of Amphialos, a Phaiakian, θ 114†.

Πολῠ́-ξεινος, son of Agasthenes, chief of Epeioi, Β 623†.

πολῠ-παίπαλοι (παιπάλη), very artful, cunning, ο 4:9†.

πολῠ-πάμονος, gen., (πέπαμαι), opulenti, exceeding wealthy, Δ 433†.

πολῠ-πενθέος, gen., έα, ές, (πένθος), deeply mournful, ψ 15, Ι 563.

Πολῠ-πημονίδης, fabled name ('Αφείδας, "Spendthrift"), son of the Great Possessor, ω 305†.

πολῠ-πῑ́δᾰκος, α, gen., also -πῑδᾰκου, (πῑδαξ), rich in springs, Υ 59, Ξ 157. (Il.)

πολυ-πικρα, as adv., (πικρός), very bitterly, π 255†.

πολυ-πλάγκτοιο, ῳ, οισι, ους, (πλάζω), baffling, driving far from one's course, Λ 308; elsewh. far-roving, much-wandering.

Πολῠ-ποίτης, αο, son of Peirithoos, one of the Lapithai, Β 740, Ζ 29, Μ 129, 182, Ψ 836, 844.

πολυ-πτύχου, gen., (πτύσσω), with many folds, many-furrowed, Θ 411. (Il.)

πολῠ-πῡρος, ον, ῳ, ον, (πῡρός), abounding in wheat, ο 406, Λ 756.

πολύ-ρρηνος, λ 257, and pl. -ρρηνες, (Ϝρην, Ϝάρνα), rich in sheep, Ι 154 and 296.

πολῠ́ς, πολλή, πολῠ́, besides the regular Attic forms (excluding πολλοῦ, which does not occur), are found in Homer also πολῠ́ς, Ν 705, πουλύς, ύν, ύ ; πολέος [pronounce πολjος, v 25], pl. πολέες, εῖς, Λ 708 ; πολέων [dissyll., Π 655], άων, έων, dat. πολέσι, έεσσ(ι), έσσ(ι), Ρ 236, acc. πολέας, Ν 734 ; πουλύν, fem., Κ 27 ; also πολλός ; ntr. πολλόν ; comp. πλείων, ονες, οσιν, ους, ον(α), πλέων, πλέον, πλέονες, όνων, όνεσσι(ν), ονας, sup. πλεῖστον, οι, ους, η, ην, αι, α (plus, Ger. viel, voll), multus, of number, many ; of size, strength, much ; of time, long, amplus, wide, broad, of space ; πολλοί, vulgus, plerique, the multitude, the larger part ; also with gen., τὰ πολλά, pleraque, the most ; τόσσον πολλόν, so far into the conflict, Υ 178 ; often coupled with other adjs., with καί, τέ—καί, τέ—τέ, β 188, Ζ 452, ο 159, Β 213 ; ntr. πολῠ́, with comp., increasing comparative force = multo, far, by far, much, β 180, Α 169, Λ 162, Ξ 467 ; in like manner with sup., longe, Α 581, Δ 51, Η 162, Ξ 442 ; with βούλομαι, malo, prefer, Α 112 ; with φθάνω, Ν 815, and other words of distance where a comparative idea is involved ; so likewise πολῠ́ν, Ζ 479, Ψ 587, Α 91, Ζ 39 ; ἐπιδευέες, ω 171 ; with verbs, Ε 636, Τ 218, Ψ 742, Τ 113 ; πολλά, multa, multum, much, ο 401 ; saepe, often, Ρ 430, ι 128 ; valde, exceedingly, Ζ 458, Θ 22 ; impense, intently, earnestly, Δ 229, Ε 358 ; fervently, ardently, Α 35, γ 267, δ 433.

πολῠ-σκάρθμοιο (σκαίρω), much-, far-springing, agile, fleet, epithet of the Amazon Myrine, Β 814†.

πολῠ-σπερέων, έας, (σπείρω), wide-spread, spread over the earth, λ 365.

πολῠ-στᾰφῠλον, rich in grapes, Β 507 and 537.

πολύ-στονος, α, (στόνος), much-sighing, mournful, miser, τ 118 ; causing many sighs, grievous, Ο 451.

πολύτλας = πολυ-τλήμων, (τλῆναι), much-enduring, steadfast, esp. epithet of Odysseus, Θ 97, ε 171, Η 152, σ 319.

πολύ-τλητοι (τλῆναι), aerumnosi, having borne much, wretched, λ 38†.

πολυ-τρήρωνα, abounding in doves, Β 502 and 582.

πολυ-τρήτοισι (τρητός), *pierced with many holes, porous*, a 111. (Od.)

πολύ-τροπος, ον, (τρέπω), *versatile, versutus*, a 1 and κ 330.

πολυ-φαρμάκου, οἱ, *skilled in drugs*, Π 28, κ 276.

Πολυ-φείδης, εος, *son of Mantios, grandson of Melampus*, ο 249 and 252.

πολύ-φημος, ον, (φήμη), *abounding in songs*, χ 376 ; *many-voiced, buzzing*, β 150.

Πολύ-φημος, (1) *son of Poseidon, Kyklops*, α 70, ι 371 sqq.—(2) *one of the Lapithai*, A 264.

πολυ-φλοίσβοιο, gen., (φλοῖσβος), θαλάσσης, (close of verse), *loud-roaring*, A 34, ν 85.

Πολύ-φήτης, αο, *chief of the Trojan allies from Askania*, N 791†.

Πολύ-φόντης, *son of Autophonos, slain before Thebes by Tydeus*, Δ 395†.

πολύ-φόρβου, ἦν, (φορβή), *bountiful*, alma, I 568, Ξ 200. (Il.)

πολύ-φρονος, α, (φρένες), *very sagacious*, prudens, Σ 108, θ 297.

πολύ-χαλκος, ου, ον, *abounding in bronze; οὐρανός, wrought of bronze, all-brazen*, E 504, γ 2.

πολύ-χρῡσος, οιο, ον, *rich in gold*, Σ 289, γ 305.

πολύ-ωπῷ (ὀπή) *many-meshed*, χ 386†.

πομπεύς, only pl., πομπῆες, ας, (πομπός), comites, *conductors, escort*, γ 325, ν 71. (Od.)

πόμπευον, ipf. from πομπεύω, (πομπεύς), comitata sum, *conduct*, ν 422†.

πομπή, ῆς, ῇ, ἦν, (πέμπω), *escort*, η 193, Z 171 ; *sending away, dismissal*, ν 41, ε 233.

πομπός, όν, οἱ, οἶσιν, (πέμπω), comes, *escort*, N 416 ; also fem., δ 826.

πονέομαι, subj. πονεώμεθα, opt. ἑοιτο, inf. ἑεσθαι, part. εὑμενος, ον, ipf. (ἐ)πονεῖτο, πονέοντο, fut. ἡσομαι, aor. πονήσατ(ο), σάμενος, οι, plupf. πεπόνητο, (πόνος), *be busy about, τί, περί τι*, Ω 444 ; *toil in the fight*, Δ 374 ; *generally, work upon*, with dat. of instrument ; elaborare, *make with care*, Σ 380, ι 310.

πόνος, οιο, ου, ον, ων, οισ(ι), (πένο-

μαι), labor, esp. *toil of battle*, Z 77 ; aerumna, *distress, grief*, B 291, that is indeed a grief, to return unsatisfied.

Ποντεύς, *a Phaiakian*, θ 113†.

ποντόθεν, e mari, *from the sea*, Ξ 395†. πόντονδε, in mare, *into the sea*, ι 495 and κ 48.

Ποντό-νοος, *herald of Alkinoos*, η 182, θ 65, ν 50, 53.

ποντο-πορούσης (πορέω), and πο-ρευέμεναι, εὐων, *traversing the high sea*, λ 11, ε 277 sq.

ποντο-πόρος, οιο, οισι(ν), *sailing through the sea*, H 72, μ 69.

πόντος, οιο, ου, ῳ, ον, (pons), *high sea*, ι 285, A 350, B 145 ; *deep*, δ 508; with adj. specifying the name, Θρηίκιος, Ἰκάριος.

ὦ πόποι (παπαί), interj. of astonishment, displeasure, wrath, grief, only B 272, of pleasurable surprise ; usually at beginning of verse followed by ἤ μάλα δή (ῥα), etc., ν 383, 209, A 254.

πόρδαλις, ιος, ίων, also πάρδαλις, *panther, leopard*, δ 457, N 103.

Πορθεύς, εῖ, *father of Oineus*, Ξ 115†.

πορθέω, ipf. (ἐ)πόρθεον, (πέρθω), devastare, *lay waste*, ξ 264.

πορθμῆες, pl. from -εύς, (πόρος), *ferry-men*, υ 187†.

πορθμῷ, τῷ, (πόρος), *strait, sound*, δ 671 and ο 29.

πόριες, see πόρτιος.

πόρκης, masc., (πλέκω?), *iron ring*, passing round the spear at meeting of head and shaft, Z 320 and Θ 495. (See cut No. 4.)

πόρον, acc., pl. οἱ, οἱς, ους, masc., (πείρω), vadum, *ford*, B 592, Ξ 433 ; pl. *path*, μ 259.

(ἔ)πορον, (ἐ)πορ(εν), aor. πόρῃσι, πόρῃ, πόρωμεν, ωσι, πόροι, όντες, (portio, impertio), comparare, *procure*, Ω 30; bestow, Λ 353, T 21 ; *provide*, υ 71; *present*, Z 218, Π 185 ; *commit to*, Z 168 ; *give*, κ 394 ; *grant*, σ 202 ; with inf., I 513 ; in general, *be the cause of*, τ 512 ; pass. perf. πέπρωται, *it is decreed by fate*, with acc. and inf., Σ 329 ; τινί τι, Γ 309 ; πεπρωμένον, praebitum, debitum, *destined*, αἴσῃ, Π 441, O 209.

πόρπας, τάς, nom. ἡ πόρπη, (πείρω), *buckle, brooch*, Σ 401†. (See cut No. 104.)

πορσᾰνέουσα, ipf. πόρσῡνε, from πορσαίνω, σύνω, (πορεῖν), prop. make ready; λέχος καὶ εὐνήν, share bed and couch, γ 403, Γ 411.

πόρτᾰκῐ, τῇ, (πόρτις), vitulo, calf, P 4†.

πόρτιος, E 162, and πόρτιες, κ 410, fem., iuvencae, heifer.

πορφύρεος, ῳ, ον, οισ(ιν), ῃ, ην, ον, (α), (purpura), purple, spoken of non-transparent substance with a reddish gleam, yet without distinct notion of color; of waves, dark-gleaming, β 428; of sea near the shore, Π 391; θάνατος, of death in battle, E 83.

πορφύρῃ, subj. pres., ipf. πόρφυρε, (φύρω), boil up, of waves, Ξ 16; elsewh. of mental disquiet, be troubled, δ 427.

πόσε; quo? whither? Π 422.

Ποσειδάων, Poseidon, Neptunus, son of Kronos, brother of Zeus and Aides, husband of Amphitrite, lord of the sea, O 190; dwells in Αἰγαί, also in Olympos; sends storm or favoring wind; enemy of Trojans because of faithlessness of Laomedon, Φ 443 sqq.; of Odysseus, because of Polyphemos, α 20; sets in turmoil the sea with his trident, and causes earthquakes, ἐνοσίχθων, ἐννοσίγαιος; γαιήοχος, earth-upholder, θ 322; κυανοχαῖτα, dark-haired, with hair the color of the sea; to him, as to the gods of the lower world, were sacrificed black bulls, γ 6; also boars and rams, λ 131.

Ποσῐδήϊον, place sacred to Poseidon, ζ 266; ἄλσος, grove, B 506.

1. πόσις, ιος, ιν, fem., (ποτός), potio, drink, A 469, κ 176.

2. πόσις, ιος, εἴ, ει, ιν, ιας, masc., (δεσπότης, potens), husband, spouse, H 411, δ 137.

ποσσ-ῆμαρ, quot dies? how many days? Ω 657†.

πόσσον, acc., quotum, how many a year ago? ω 288†.

ποταμόν-δε, in flumen, into, to the river, Φ 13, κ 159.

ποταμός, οῖο, οῦ, ῷ, όν, ώ, οί, ῶν, ούς, (δι-πετέος), flumen, river, ε 453; freq. personif. as river-god, E 544, Ξ 245.

ποτάομαι, ποτῶνται, B 462; but ποτέονται, ω 7; pf. πεπότηται, πεποτήαται, (πέτομαι), volare, fly, flutter; of souls of departed, λ 222.

πότε, quando? when? T 227.

ποτέ, enclitic, aliquando. once, Ξ 45; quondam, B 547, Z 99; olim, hereafter, Δ 182.

ποτέομαι, sec ποτάομαι.

ποτέροισι, utris, to which (party), E 85†.

ποτῇ, (πέτομα), in flight, ε 337†.

ποτῆς, ποτῆτος, τα, fem., (πότος), potionis, drink, δ 788, T 306.

ποτητά, τά, (ποτάομαι), volucres, birds, μ 62†.

ποτί and ποτι-, see πρός, προσ-.

ποτῐ-δέγμενος, etc., part., (δέχομαι), expectans, awaiting, τινά, τί, εἰ, ψ 91; ὁππότ' ἄν, H 415.

ποτι-δόρπιον, for (his) supper, ι 234 and 249.

ποτι-κέκλιται, perf. from -κλίνω.

ποτι-νίσσεται, go in at, enter (through the gates, spoken of precious possessions), I 381†.

ποτι-πεπτηυῖαι, pf. part. (-πτήσσω), λιμένος, sinking down toward the harbor, ν 98†.

ποτι-πτυσσοίμεθα, see προσ-πτύσσομαι.

ποτι-τερπέτω (τέρπω), oblectato, let him care for, O 401†.

ποτι-φωνήεις (φωνή), capable of addressing, endued with speech, ι 456†.

πότμος, ον, masc., (πίπτω), the lot which falls from the helmet, sors; ill fate, ἐφιέναι τινί, (θάνατον καὶ) π. ἐπισπεῖν, meet death, fulfill one's fate, B 359.

πότνῐ(α), πότνᾰ, (πόσις), mistress, queen, θηρῶν; august, θεά; revered, bearing sway, μήτηρ.

ποτόν, οῖο, ῷ, όν, ntr., (πίνω), potio, drink, A 470, α 148.

πού, ubi? where? E 171; quo? whither? N 219. πού, enclitic, aliquando, somewhere, λ 458; methinks, doubtless, perhaps, A 178, B 116, 136, I 23, θ 491, λ 449.

πουλύ - βοτείρῃ, αν, Γ 89, 265, almae, bountiful, = πολυβ.

Πουλύ-δάμᾱς, αντος, son of Panthoos, a Trojan, Ξ 449, 453, O 339, 518, 521, Π 535; πεπνυμένος, Σ 249.

πουλύ-ποδος, τοῦ, polypus (cuttlefish), ε 432†.

πουλύς, θ 109 = πολύς.

πούς, ποδός, ί, α, οἷιν τ 444, ες, ῶν, ποσ(σ)ί(ν), πόδεσσι(ν), ας, pes, foot, of

men, animals, also of birds, *talons*, u n-
gulae ; coupled with χεῖρες, χ 477 ;
λάξ ποδί, push with the foot, kick ; ἐς
πύδας ἐκ κεφαλῆς, or ἐκ κ. ἐς π., from
head to foot, Σ 353 ; in foot race, swiftness of foot, N 325 ; r a d i c e s m o n t i s,
foundations, Υ 59 ; rope fastened to
lower corners of sail to control it,
sheet (see plate IV.), ε 260.

Πράκτιος, river in Troas, north of
Abydos, B 835†.

Πραμνεῖος οἶνος, *Pramneian* wine,
of dark color and fiery taste, κ 235.

πρᾰπῐ́δων, δεσσι(ν) = φρένες, (1)
praecordia, *diaphragm, midriff,* Λ
579. — (2) fig. *heart,* X 43 ; *mind.
thoughts,* Σ 380, η 92.

πρασιή, αί, *garden-bed,* ω 247 and η
127.

πρέπω, *be conspicuous,* ipf. ἔπρεπε,
διὰ πάντων, M 104†.

πρέσβᾰ, fem., (πρέσβυς), prop. *old,*
then *august, honored,* E 721.

πρεσβήιον, (πρέσβυς), *gift of honor,*
Θ 289†.

πρεσβῠ-γενής, *first-born,* Λ 249†.

πρεσβύτερος, οισιν, comp., -ύτατος,
ον, η, ην, sup. from πρεσβύς, s e n i o r,
elder, O 204 ; n a t u (γενεῇ) m a x i m u s,
oldest, Z 24.

πρήθω, aor. (ἔ)πρῆσε, σαι, *b'ow, let
stream forth,* Π 350 (with ἐν, A 481);
scatter, shower upon, πυρί, fire, Θ 217 ;
also πυρός, B 415, 1 242.

πρηκτῆρα, τόν, (πράσσω) ἔργων,
doer, I 443 ; pl. ῆρες, *traders,* θ 162.

πρηνής, έα, έες, εῖς, ές, (πρό), p r o -
n u s, *forward, on the face* (opp. ὕπτιος,
Ω 11); *head foremost,* praeceps, Z
43, Π 310.

πρῆξις, ῑν, fem., (περάω), *accompiish-
ment, result; οὔτις τινὶ γίγνεται, πέλετο,
no good comes of ; enterprise,* γ 82.

πρήσσει, etc., prs., ipf. iter. πρήσ-
σεσκον θ 259, fut. πρήξεις, ει, aor.
ἔπρηξας, πρῆξαι, αντα, always after
caesura in fourth foot, (πέραν), *accomplish, complete, pass over,* κέλευθον, Ψ
501 ; ὁδοῖο, gen. part., Ω 264, γ 476,
ο 47, 219 ; fut. and aor., *further, help,*
ἔργον, οὔτι.

πρῐ́ατο, 3 sing. aor., (περάν), e m e -
b a t, κτεάτεσσιν, *buy* with treasure, α
430. (Od.)

Πρῑαμίδης, αο, εω, *son of Priamos,*
B 817, Υ 77. (Il.)

Πρῐ́αμος, son of Laomedon, Υ 237,
king of Troja ; husband of Hekabe,
who bore him 19 out of his 50 sons ;
already aged at the time of the Trojan
war, γέρων, N 368, Ω 217, 777 ; descendant of Dardanos, Γ 303. His
children : Hektor, Γ 314 ; Helenos, H
44 ; Echemmon, Chromios, E 160;
Lykaon, Φ 35 ; Paris, Z 512 ; Polites,
B 791 ; Gorgythion, Θ 303 ; Demo-
koon, Δ 499 ; Deiphobos, M 95 ; Isos,
Antiphos, Λ 102 ; Kassandra, N 365,
λ 421 ; Laodike, Γ 124.

πρίν (comp. from πρό), A. adverb:
p r i u s, *before,* B 112 ; τὸ πρίν γε, E
54 ; with indic., M 437 ; fut. or subj.,
p o t i u s, *sooner, first,* A 29, Σ 283, ν
427, Ω 55]; with opt. and κε, γ 117;
πρίν γ᾽ ἤ, E 288, X 266 ; also οὐ πρίν
(γε), or οὐ πάρος, or οὐ πρόσθεν with
follg. πρίν γε (or ἀλλ᾽ ὁπότ᾽ ἂν δή,
Π 62, Φ 340), E 218, E 288.—B. conjunction, *before.* I. with inf. without
temporal or modal limitation, to char-
acterize the subordinate action as un-
real or impossible (if the subordinate
clause has a subject, it stands in acc.,
Z 81); tense of inf. usually aor. after
affirmative (N 172), and negative principal sentence, A 98, T 423, Φ 225,
X 266, ψ 138, δ 747; also after opt.
or potential sentence, Z 465, Δ 115,
Ω 245, δ 668, χ 64, κ 384; cf. also E
218, 287, M 171, β 127, δ 254.—II.
followed by subj. or opt., the principal
sentence, as before, being negative :
(1) after principal tenses, πρίν with
subj. represents subordinate action at
once as fut. and as the condition of
principal action, Σ 135, κ 175 ; πρίν
γ᾽ ὁπότ᾽ ἂν, β 374, δ 477; also after
inf. used imperatively, Ω 781 ; even
after historical tense, Σ 190.—(2) after
historical tenses, πρίν with opt. represents subordinate action as future,
viewed from past standpoint of principal verb, Φ 580; πρίν γ᾽ ὅτε, I 489;
transition in same sentence from II.
1 to I., β 374. [πρίν (orig. προιν for
προιον), yet not infrequently also πρῖν,
δ 32, 212, B 344, 354, 413, etc.]

πριστοῦ, adj., (πρίω), ἐλέφαντος,
sawn ivory, σ 196 and τ 564.

πρό, pro, I. adv., *before, forth,* οὐ-
ρανόθι, Ἰλιόθι, *in and under* (before)
the sky, *around and before* Troja ; also

temporal, ἠῶθι, *in the morning early*,
Λ 50: πρὸ φόωσδε, Π 188, *forward into
the light.*—II. prep. with gen., (1) of
space, προ, ante, coram, *in front of,
in presence of,* τ 435, Ω 734; πρὸ ὁδοῦ,
forward in the way, *onward.*—(2) temporal, ante, before, ο 524.—(3) *in behalf of, for,* μάχεσθαι, ὀλέσθαι; πρὸ ὃ
τοῦ for ὁ πρὸ τοῦ, unus pro altero,
one for the other, Κ 224; πρὸ φόβοιο,
for (because of) fear.

προ-άλεῖ, dat. sing., (ἅλλομαι?), *descending*, Φ 262†.

προ-βαίνω, pf. **-βέβηκας**, ε, plupf.
βεβήκει, and part. pres. -βιβάς, Ν 18;
and, as if from βιβάω, βιβῶντος, Π 609;
βιβῶντι Ν 807, βιβῶντα Γ 22, procedere, *advance;* τινός, antecedere,
surpass; τινί, aliqua re, Π 54.

προ-βάλλω, only aor. **-βάλόντες,**
iter. βάλεσκε, projicere, *cast before,*
ε 331; ἔριδα, injicere, inire, *begin;*
mid. aor. -βάλοντο, *cast down before
them,* Α 458; Ψ 255, fundamenta
iecerunt; opt. -βαλοίμην (mente
te longe), antecellam, *excel.*

πρό-βᾰσίν, τήν, bona moventia,
live stock, cattle, β 75†.

πρό-βατ(α), τά, (προβαίνω), pecora, *droves* or *flocks,* Ξ 124 and Ψ 550.

προ-βέβουλα, pf., (βούλομαι), praefero, *prefer before,* Α 113†.

προ-βιβάς, -βιβῶν, see προ-βαίνω.

προ-βλής, dat. βλῆτι, pl. βλῆτες, ας,
(προβάλλω), *projecting,* Μ 259.

προ-βλώσκειν, ἔμεν, aor. -μολον,
imp. μολ(ε), part. μολών, οὖσα, prodire, *go* or *come forward, forth,* τ 25,
ο 468, Σ 382, Φ 37.

προ-βοάω, part. **βοῶντε,** (βοή), *shouting loudly* (above the rest), Μ 277†.

προ-βόλῳ, τῷ, masc., (βάλλω), *jutting rock,* μ 251†.

προ-γενέστερος, οι, (γένος), senior,
Β 555.

προ-γίγνομαι, aor. **γένοντο,** progressi sunt, Σ 525; in tmesis, ὁδοῦ,
Δ 382, *advanced* on their way.

πρό-γονοι, masc., (γόνος), *earlier
born,* or *spring lambs, larger lambs,* ι
221†.

προ-δᾰείς, part. aor., (ἰδάην), ante
sentiens, *know beforehand,* δ 396†.

προ-δοκῆσιν, dat. pl., fem., (δέχομαι), ἐν, *in ambush, lurking-place,* Δ
107†.

προ-δόμῳ, τῷ, masc., (δόμος), *vestibule, portico,* with pillars before the
house (see plate III., *D D,* at end of
volume), Ι 473, δ 302, cf. θ 57.

προ-έεργε, ipf., *hinder* (by standing
before), with inf., Λ 569†.

προ-έηκα, ε, see προ-ίημι.

προ-εῖδον, subj. **ἴδωσι,** part. ἰδών,
ὄντες, praevidere, *look forward, catch
sight of,* ε 393, prospiciens; ἰδώνται, ν 155, prospicient.

πρό-ειμι, **πρὸ ἐόντα,** praeterita,
Α 70.

πρὸ εἴπομεν, praediximus, α
37†.

προ-έμεν, aor. inf. from προ-ίημι.

προ-ερέσσαμεν, σσαν, aor. from
-ερέσσω (ἐρετμός), appellere, *drive
forward with oars,* Α 435, ι 73, ν 279,
ο 497.

προ-έρυσσεν, aor., (ἐρύω), *had drawn
forward,* Α 308.

πρό-ες, imp. aor. from -ίημι.

προ-έχω, προύχοντο, part. οντι, α,
ουσιν, ούσῃ, σας, ipf. προέχ(ε), *jut forward,* μ 11, ω 82; *lofty,* τ 544; mid.
ipf. προύχοντο, *had before them,* γ 8;
πρὸ ἔχοντο, *were holding before them,* Ρ
355.

προ-ήκεα, ntr. pl., (ήκης, ἀκή),
praeacuta, *pointed at the end, with
sharp blades,* μ 205†.

προ-θελύμνῳ, ους, α, (θέλυμνον),
along with the root ; Ν 130, *overlapping,*
of layers of ox-hide forming a shield.

προ-θέουσι, see προ-τίθημι.

προ-θέησι, subj., ipf. iter. θέεσκε,
praecurrere, *outstrip,* Κ 362, λ 515.

Προ-θο-ήνωρ, ορος, son of Areilykos,
chief of Boiotians, Β 495, Ξ 450, 471.

Πρό-θοος, son of Tenthredon, leader of Magnesians, Β 756, 758.

προ-θορών, see προ-θρώσκω.

Προ-θόων, ωνα, a Trojan, slain by
Teukros, Ξ 515†.

προ-θρώσκω, aor. θορών, prosiliens, *springing forward,* Ξ 363. (Il.)

προ-θῦμίῃσι, ταῖς, *zeal, courage,* Β
588†.

πρό-θῦρον, ον, οιο, οισ(ιν), *pillared
porch at entrance of court* (see plate
III., *A*); *gateway,* α 103, γ 493; *porch
before the house-door* (see plate III.,
t), *doorway,* θ 304, σ 10.

προ-ϊαλλε(ν), ipf., (ἰάλλω), *sent forth,*
Θ 365.

προ-ιάπτω, fut. ίάψει, ειν, aor. ίαψεν, *send (forth)*, usually of what is untimely, premature, A 3.

προ-ίημι, ίησι, 3 pl. ιεῖσι, imp. ίει, ipf. ίειν, ίεις, ίει, aor. ἦκε,= ἦκε, ἑηκα, ε(ν), 3 pl. εσαν, imp. ες, ἑτω, inf. ἑμεν, emittere, *send forth*, τινά, with inf. of purpose, κ 25; θεῷ, in submission to the god; also of missiles, *shoot, dart, sling;* ὕδωρ, *pour forth; ἔπος, let drop; κῦδος, bestow upon; let slip,* ε 316; τ 468, *let go,* so that it fell.

προ-ίκτης, γ, masc., (ἰκέτης), mendicus, *beggar,* ρ 352. (Od.)

προίξ, προικός, (procus, precor), *gift, pres nt,* ρ 413; but ν 15, that a single person should win for himself gratitude for a gift.

προ-ίστημι, aor. **στήσας,** in *having* put thee *forward before* the Achaians to fight, Δ 156†.

Προῖτος, king of Argives, Z 157, 177 ; husband of Anteia, Z 160.

προ-κἄθ-ιζόντων, gen. pl. part., (ίζω), *alighting after having flown forward,* B 463†.

προ-κἄλέσσατο, aor., subj. ἑσσεται, imp. εσσαι, (καλέω), evocare, *challenge,* H 39 ; to combat, χάρμῃ ; μαχέσασθαι, H 218.

προ-κἄλίζεο, imp., ipf. καλίζετο, (καλέω), evocare, *challenge,* Γ 19 ; χερσί, to boxing contest, σ 20 ; with inf., Δ 389, θ 228.

προ-κείμενα, part., *lying before* (them), α 149.

πρό-κλύτα, (κλύω), ante audita =celebrata, ἔπεα, *ancient* legends, Υ 204†.

Πρόκρις, ιδος, daughter of Erechtheus, king of Athens, λ 321†.

προ-κρόσσας, fem. pl., (κρόσσαι), *in rows, in tiers,* Ξ 35†.

προ-κυλίνδεται, pass., (κυλίνδω), provolvitur, *roll forward,* Ξ 18†.

προ-λέγω, pf. pass. part., **λελεγμένοι,** delecti, *chosen, élite,* N 689†.

προ-λείπω, aor. λιπεῖν, ὤν, ὄντες, pf. λέλοιπεν, deserere, *leave behind,* γ 314; deficere, *forsake,* β 279.

προ-μάχιζε, imp. pres. and ipf., (μαχίζω), pugnare, τινί, *fight in the front rank before others,* Υ 376 and Γ 16 = **προμάχεσθαί** τινος, Λ 217 and P 358.

πρό-μάχος, οιο, ον, οι, ωι, οισ(ιν),

ους, (προ-μάχομαι), propugnator, *champion, foremost fighter,* σ 379, ω 526. (Il.)

Πρό-μαχος, son of Alegenor, Boiotian chief, Ξ 476, 482, 503.

προ-μῖγῆναι, aor. inf. pass., (μίγνυμι), *have intercourse with before,* τινί, Ι 452†.

προ-μνηστῖνοι, αι, (πρυμνή ?), *one after another, successively,* φ 230 and λ 233.

προ-μολών, see προ-βλώσκω.

πρόμος, ον, (sup. from πρό, cf. primus), *foremost fighter,* H 75.

προ-νόησαν, ἦσαι, (νοέω), praesenserunt, *suspect,* Σ 526; ante excogitare, *devise beforehand,* ε 364.

Πρό-νοος, a Trojan, slain by Patroklos, Π 399†.

πρόξ, acc. pl. **πρόκας,** capreas, *roe, fawn,* ρ 295†.

προ-πάροιθε(ν), adv., pro, ante, porro, coram, *forward, formerly,* K 476, O 260; usually prep. with gen. (prepos. and postpos.), ante, *before,* O 66, Γ 22 ; ἠιόνος, *along the shore.*

προ-πάσας, πᾶν, totas, *all* (day) *long, all* (the ships) *together,* ι 161.

προ-πέμπω, aor. **ἔπεμψε** and **προύπεμψα,** ε, *send forth,* A 442, ρ 54.

προ-πέφανται, see -φαίνω.

προ-πεσόντες, aor. part., (πίπτω), incumbentes, *bending forward,* ι 490 and μ 194.

προ-ποδίζων, (πούς), *striding forward,* N 158 and 806.

προ-πρηνέα, ές, (pronus), *leaning forward,* Γ 218; *bent,* χ 98 (v.l. πρηνέι).

προ-προ-κυλινδόμενος, *wandering from place to place,* ρ 525 ; Διός, ad pedes Jovis provolutus, *rolling as suppliant before,* X 221.

προ-ρέει, ρέων, etc., pres., profluere, M 19, ε 444.

πρό-ρριζος, οι, (Ϝριἔja, ρίζα), radicitus, *with the roots,* Λ 157 and Ξ 415.

πρός, orig. **πρότι,** then προτί, to avoid the lengthening of a preceding vowel by position (exc. ω 347), **ποτί,** (πρό), I. adv., insuper, *moreover, in addition,* δέ, E 307, K 108.—II. prep. (a) with gen., *of point from which,* θ 29 (*toward,* K 428, X 198, ν 110, φ 347) ; origin, *from,* A 160, 239 Διός, which come from Zeus ; *in the eyes of, before*, A 339, X 514. II 85, λ 302, σ 162 ; *in subjection to, ἄλλης*, Z 456 ; in oaths and entreaties, *by, before*, ν 324, Τ 188; (b) with dat., practer, *besides*, κ 68; locat., *on*, ε 434, λ 423 ; *to, upon*, with βάλλειν, η 279 ; ῥαίειν, τρέπεσθαι, Ξ 403 ; (c) with acc. (1) local: *to, toward*, Μ 332 ; with verbs of going, moving, 1 147 ; smiting, Δ 108, *upon ;* of looking, talking, *at, with* (ξ 331, swear to), Γ 155, Λ 643, 403 ; of changing, *with*, Z 235 ; *against*, with verbs of fighting, P 98, 104.—(2) temporal: toward, sub vesperam, ρ 191.

προσ-άγω, aor. **ἤγαγε**, advehere, τινί, *bring upon* (us), ρ 446†.

προσ-ᾱῖξας, aor. part. from ἀίσσω, advolans, adortus, *hurry up to*, χ 337, 342, 365.

προσ-ἀλειφεν, ipf. from ἀλείφω, illinebat, *anoint*, τινί, κ 392†.

προσ-αμύνει, *ομεν*, pres., aor. inf. ῡναι, ward off (sc. αὐτόν), Ε 139 ; τινί, *help, aid*, Β 238, Π 509.

προτι-άπτω (aptus), *attach to, accord*, Ω 110†.

προσ-άρηρότα, ntr. pl. pf. part., (ἀραρίσκω), *closely fitted*, Ε 725†.

προσ-αυδάω, imp. αὐδάτω, ipf. ηὔδων, α, αὐδήτην, ων. κ 418, ν 253, (αὐδή), alloqui, *address*, Μ 353, ψ 208, ω 320 ; τινά, Δ 192, X 7, δ 680 ; ἐπίεσσι, ο 440 ; μειλιχίοις, P 431 ; ἔπεα πτερόεντα, Ε 871, Δ 92, β 362 ; with part., Φ 367, χ 435 ; φωνήσας, Α 201, α 122 ; with part. as subj., P 33, ξ 79, O 114, Z 163, Ε 30, φ 192.

προσ-βαίνω, aor. **ἔβη**, ἐβην, βάς, aor. mid. ἐβήσετο, adire, pervenire ad, assequi, *go to, arrive at*, τινά, τί, Β 48, Ψ 117.

προσ-βάλλω, **ἔβαλλε**, ipf., aor. βαλών, όν, in tmesi, proiicere, *dash against*, πέτρῃσι, ι 284; ἀρούρας, (sc. ἀκτῖσιν), collustrabat, *strike with rays, illumine*, Η 421 ; προτι-βάλλεαι, mid., increpas, *reprove*, Ε 879.

προσ-εδέρκετο, ipf. from ποτι-δέρκεται, adspicit, *look at*, υ 385, Π 10.

ποτι-δέγμενος, etc., part. pres., (δέχομαι), exspectans, *await*, τινά, τί, εἰ, ψ 91, ὁππότ᾽ ἄν, Η 415.

πρόσ-ειμι, part. ἰόντι, α. accedenti, em, *approach*, Ε 682. (Il.)

προσ-έειπε, ον, opt. προτι-είποι, (εἶπον), alloqui, *address*, Ω 361, ω 350 ; τὸν δ᾽ αὖτε, Α 206, α 178 ; elsewh. τινά, Α 441, δ 542 ; with part., Α 105, Γ 386, ζ 56, ρ 405 ; μύθοισι, Γ 437, τ 252, δ 484 ; πρός τινα μῦθον, *address a speech to*, δ 803.

προσ-ερεύγεται, πέτρην, *breaks foaming against* the rock, O 621†.

πρόσθε(ν), adv., (πρό), *in front* (of him), ε 452 ; ἔχειν, *hold before*, P 7 ; Υ 163, στέρνοιο ; precede, *ἰέναι* τινί; βάλλειν, in citare, drive, urge; Ψ 639, *outstripping me by their superiority in number* ; antea, *heretofore, formerly*, Ν 440 ; before, Ν 66, Ω 698 ; *οἱ π., the men of old, forefathers*. As prep. with gen. (prepos. and postpos.), ante, *before*, Ι 473, Μ 445 ; τινὸς ἵστασθαι, *come before one for his protection*, hence = ὑπέρ, Φ 587, θ 524 ; local and temporal, Β 359 ; Ν 66, τοῖιν is gen. part.

προσ-έκειτο, ipf., *were attached*, Σ 379†.

προσ-κηδέος, gen. from -κηδής, (κῆδος), diligentis, *loving, affectionate*, φ 35†.

προσ-έκλῑνε, ipf., pf. pass. ποτι-κέκλῖται, acclinare, *lean upon*, with dat., φ 138 ; apposita est ei, *place near*, ζ 308.

προσ-έλεκτο (λεχ-), accubuit iuxta, *reclined beside* (me), μ 34†.

προσ-πελάσᾱς, aor. part. from πελάζω, appellere, *drive upon*, νῆα ἄκρῃ, ι 285†.

προσ-επιλνᾶτο, ipf., (πίλναμαι, πέλομαι), appropinquavit, *draw near*, ν 95†.

προσ-πλάζον, part. pres., ipf. -έπλαζε, (πέλαγος, Ger. plätschern, Eng. plash), γενείῳ, *dash against*, λ 583 and Μ 285.

προσ-πτύσσομαι, opt. ποτι-πτυσσοίμεθα, fut. προσ-πτύξεται, aor. -πτύξα-το, subj. -πτύξομαι, *fold to one's self*, embrace, τινά, ι amplecti, λ 451 ; receive warmly, θ 478 ; *welcome, greet*, γ 22 ; μύθῳ, adire precibus, *entreat*.

πρόσσοθεν, *before* him, Ψ 533†.

πρόσσω, see πρόσω.

προσ-στείχω, aor. **ἔστιχε**, *strode toward*, υ 73†.

προσ-τίθημι, aor. **ἔθηκεν**, apposuerat, *place upon* (the entrance), ι 305†.

πρόσ-φασθαι, see πρόσ-φημι.

πρόσ-φᾱτος, Ω 757, *that may be addressed*, appearing about to speak, so unchanged = *with countenance undistorted and undisfigured*, cf. ποτιφωνήεις.

πρόσ-φημι, aor. ἔφην, ης, η, and pres. φάσθαι, alloqui, *speak to, address*, Κ 369, ο 9; ἔπος, ψ 106; τινά, Η 405, Ν 46, ν 49; ἀπαμειβόμενος, Α 560, α 63, Α 84, 130, ε 214, ω 406; with other parts., Α 148, 517, 364, Θ 38, Ι 196, ι 446, Ε 427.

προσ-φῦέ(α), with dat., (φύομαι), *grown upon*, i. e. *fastened to*, τ 58†. (See cut No. 113.)

προσ-φύς, φῦσα, aor. part., (φύομαι), *clinging*, μ 433 and Ω 213.

προσ-φωνέω, ipf. ἐφώνεε, εον, (φωνή), alloqui, *address, accost*, ε 159; τινά, Γ 389, Λ 346, 464, χ 355, ο 194; with part., Γ 413, σ 25, Θ 292, Γ 389; χ 69, μετεφώνεε is the better reading.

πρό(σ)σω, (porro), *forward*, Π 265; in posterum, *in the future*, Α 343.

πρόσ-ωπον, α and ἄτα, dat. ἄσι, ntr., (ὅπωπα), *countenance*, Σ 24, Π 414.

προ-τᾰμών, aor. part., (τάμνω), *cutting up*, Ι 489; *cutting before one*, forward, from root toward the top, ψ 196; mid. aor. opt. -τᾰμοίμην, *cut straight before me, draw straight before me*, σ 375.

πρότερος, οιο, ῳ, ον, ω, οι, ων, οισι, ους, η, ῃ, ην, ῃς, (comp. from πρό), prior, *former*, Γ 140; also, instead of prius, Τ 183, β 31, Δ 67; senior, γενεῇ, *elder*, Ο 166; maiores, *men of former time*, Δ 308; πόδες, anteriores, *forefeet*, τ 228.

προτέρω, *forward, further*, Γ 400, Κ 469, ε 417.

προ-τεύχω, pf. pass. inf. τετύχθαι, facta esse, *have happened, be past*, Π 60. (Il.)

προτί, see πρός; προτι-, see προσ-.

Προτιάων, ονος, father of Astynoos, in Ilios, Ο 455†.

προτι-ειλεῖν (Fελ-), *press forward*, ποτὶ νῆας, Κ 347†.

προ-τίθημι, 3 pl. ipf. -τίθεν, aor. προύθηκεν, *place before*, tables, α 112; cast before dogs, Ω 409; προ-θέουσι in Α 291 irregular inflection (cf. δίδη, διδώσομεν, φορῆναι) for τιθέασι, *place before, give into hands of, permit.*

προτι-μῡθήσασθαι, alloqui, λ 143†.

προτι-όσσομαι, imp. εο, ipf. ὄσσετ(ο), (ὄσσε), adspicere, *look upon*, η 31, ψ 365; then, with eyes of the mind, *forebode*, Χ 356 = recognize thee for what I had foreboded.

πρό-τμησιν, τήν, (τέμνω), *parts about the navel*, Λ 424†.

προ-τόνοισιν, ους, pl. masc., (τείνω), *fore-stay*, rope extending from the mast to the inner portion of stem, Α 434, β 425. (See cut under the word Σειρήν.)

προ-τρέπω, 3 pl. ipf. mid. τρέποντο, 2 aor. subj. τράπηται, opt. τραποίμην, inf. ἔσθαι, se convertere ad, *turn in flight to, give one's self to*, ἐπί τι, ἐπί τινος, ἄχεϊ, Ζ 336.

προ-τροπάδην, adv., (τρέπω), *in headlong flight*, Π 304†.

προ-τύπτω, aor. προύτυψε, αν, *charge forward*, ω 319, a prickling, smarting sensation *forced itself forward through his nostrils* (preceding the tears which he could hardly restrain).

προύθηκε, see προ-τίθημι.

προύπεμψε, see προ-πέμπω.

προύχοντα, το, προυχούσῃ, etc., see προέχω.

προ-φαίνω, ipf. προύφαινε, ον, *shine forth from*, ι 145; *revealed*, μ 394; mid. ipf. προύφαίνετο, pf. προπέφανται, *be visible*, ν 169, Ξ 332; aor. pass. προφανέντα, τε, εἶσα, *appearing*, Θ 378, Ρ 487, with εἰς, ἐν, ἀνά with acc.

πρό-φᾰσιν, τήν, *pretense, ostensibly*, Τ 262 and 302.

προ-φερέστερος, ον, οι, αι, and sup. -φερέστατος, (προφερής), *preferred*, τινός, above some one; τινί, *superior in*, φ 134; with inf., better in drawing, Κ 352.

προ-φέρω, φέρῃσι, ωμεν, οις, ε, ων, ουσα, αι, *bear forth, away*, ν 64; *proffer*, Ι 323, Ρ 121; τινὶ ἔριδα, *rivalling one another*, ζ 92; ὀνείδεα, convitiari, *revile*; μένος, *display* courage; mid. pres. -φέρηται ἔριδα, *challenge*, Θ 210, *begin combat*, Γ 7.

προ-φεύγω, aor. subj. φύγῃ, opt. φύγοισθα, inf. φυγεῖν, part. -ών, ὄντα, effugere, *flee away*, Λ 340; with acc., λ 107.

πρό-φρασσ(α) (... φρᾰδέος, φρήν), propensus; *seriously*, κ 386; *cheerfully*, Φ 500.

πρό-φρων, ονι, ονες, adv. -φρονέως, (φρήν), joined with verb, cf. lubens, or lubenti animo, *gladly*, Ξ 357, E 810; *with good cheer*, ξ 54; *zealous, friendly*, π 257; *kind'y*, β 230.

προ-χέει, ειν, profundit, *pour forth*; pass. -χέοντο, ipf., effusi sunt, Φ 6. (Il.)

πρό-χνυ, adv., (γόνυ), *on her knees*, I 570; ἀπολέσθαι, be brought low and perish, perish *utterly*, Φ 460.

προ-χοῆσ(ιν), άς, fem., (χέω), *mouth, stream*, υ 65, P 263.

πρό-χοος, ῳ, ον, fem., vessel for drawing off wine, *pitcher, vase*, σ 397 (for the form see cuts Nos. 29, 76); used also to pour water over the hands or feet into a kettle below in washing (see cut No. 82).

πρῦλέες, έων, έεσσ(ι), (proelium?), *foot-soldiers*, Λ 49, M 77, O 517, E 744, hyperbolically, fitted to, sufficient to protect the combatants of a hundred cities.

Πρυμνεύς, έως, a Phaiakian, θ 112†.

πρύμνη, ης, puppis, *stern*, A 409, Σ 76, 447. πρύμνηθεν, (seize) *by the stern-post*, O 716†.

πρυμνήσι(α), τά, (sc. πείσματα), *stern*-(cables), by which the ship was made fast to the shore (κατέδησαν, ἀνάψαι), hence ἔλυσαν πρυμνήσια = naves solverunt, β 418.

πρυμνός, οῖο, όν, οῖσι, ῆς, ῇ, ήν, όν, extremus, *extreme end*, either *upper, lower*, or *hinder* part, Π 314, *thigh*; Π 124, 286, *stern*, cf. M 446, *below*; E 292, *root of the tongue*; M 149, *wood at the root*; E 339, ntr. θέναρος, *end of the palm*, just below the fingers; -όтатоν, sup.,ρ 463 = summum, where it joins the back.

πρυμν-ωρείη, τῇ, (ὄρος), *foct oj' a mountain*, Ξ 307†.

Πρύτᾰνις, ιος, a Lykian, slain by Odysseus, E 678†.

πρώην, adv., (πρό), nuper, *lately*, E 832. (Il.)

πρωθ-ήβαι, ας, masc., and fem. ην, (ἥβη), pubes, *in the bloom of youth*, θ 518, α 431.

πρῶι, adv., (πρό), mane, *in the morning*, θ 530; v. l. ω 28, praematurc, *untimely*.

πρωΐ̈ʼ = πρωιζά, (πρῶι), *day before yesterday*, B 303†.

πρώιον, mane, *early in the morning*, O 470†.

πρών, P 747; πρώονες, ας, masc., (πρό). *foreland, headland*, M 282. (Il.)

Πρωρεύς, a Phaiakian, θ 113†.

πρώρη, adj., (πρό), νηῦς, prora, *prow*, μ 230†.

Πρωτεσί-λαος, son of Iphiklos, leader of Thessalians; the first to tread on Trojan soil, and the first to fall, B 698, 706, O 705, N 681, Π 286.

Πρωτεύς, father of Eidothea, servant of Poseidon, whose seals he herds in the sea near Egypt, the wise old man of the sea, δ 365, 385.

πρώτιστος, ῳ, sup. from πρῶτος, (with πολύ, longe), primus, *first*, ntr. πρώτιστον (before vowel in third foot) (Od.) and πρώτισθʼ, λ 168 = πρώτιστα (before consonants in third foot), primum, *first of all, chiefest of all*, Ξ 295, γ 57, 419, ι 224.

πρωτο-γόνων, *firstling*; ἀρνῶν, Δ 102. (Il.)

πρωτο-πάγέα, acc. sing. masc., εἷς, pl., (πέπηγα), *new-made*, E 194 and Ω 267.

πρωτο-πλόον (πλόος), adj., *going to sea for the first time*, θ 35†.

πρῶτος, ῳ, ον, ω, οι, οισι(ν), ους, η, ης, ῃ, ην, αι, ας, (sup. from πρό), primus, *first*, in position, οἱ π., propugnatores, θύραι = πρόθυρα; in time and rank (ἆθλα, Ψ 275); ntr. πρῶτον, so also πρῶτα (which only occurs before consonants in first, fifth, and esp. in third foot, after ἐπειδή, ὡς, A 276), primum, *first of all, as soon as*; τὸ πρῶτον before vowels, before the feminine caesura, after ὡς, Δ 267; ἐπειδή, δ 13; τὰ πρῶτα in third and fourth foot only before consonants; after ὡς, θ 268, cf. A 6, Z 489, M 420, θ 553; after relative conjunctions, ubi primum, *as soon as*. (In ω 28, πρῶι, praemature, is the better reading.)

πρωτο-τόκος (τίκτω), *about to bear for the first time*, of heifer, P 5†.

Πρωτώ, οῦς, a Nereid, Σ 43†.

πρώονες, see πρών.

πταίρω, aor. ἔπταρεν, μέγ —, *sneezed a'oud*, ρ 541†.

πτάμενος, πτάτο, see πέτομαι.

πτελέην, αι, ας, ein, Z 419. (Il.)

Πτελέος, (1) harbor-town in Thessalv, B 697.—(2) colony of Thessalian Ptcleos in Elis, B 594.

πτέρνης, τῆς, *heel*, X 397†.

πτερόεντες, τ(α), (πτερόν), *winged, flying*, of arrows, as feathered at the lower end, Υ 68, Δ 117.—(2) of shields, λαισήια, because of the fluttering apron attached to them, E 453 (see cuts Nos. 79 and 85).—(3) ἔπεα, A 201.

πτερόν, ά, ntr., (πέτομαι), *feather, wing* (torn, o 527), πυκνὰ βάλλειν, ply rapidly; symbol of lightness, Τ 386, and swiftness, η 36; compared with oars, λ 125.

πτέρυξ, πτέρῠγος, εσσι(ν), (πτερόν), *pinion, wing*, B 316.

πτήσσω, aor. **πτῆξε**, *make bend with fear, terrify*, Ξ 40, interpolated verse; pf. part. πεπτηώς, ῶτες, *cowering, crouching* in fear, ξ 354, χ 362.

πτοιέω, only 3 pl. aor. pass. **ἐπτοίη- θεν**, pavebant, *be dismayed*, χ 298†.

Πτολεμαῖος, son of Peiraios, father of Eurymedon, Δ 228†.

πτολεμίζω, ιστής, μος, etc., see πολεμίζω, etc.

πτολίεθρον, α, (πόλις), *city*, always with follg. gen. of proper name, Ἰλίου; Τρώων, A 163, a city of the Trojans, =any whatever, not Ilios.

πτολί-πορθος, ῳ, ον, and **-πόρθιον** (ι 504, 530), masc. and fem., (πέρθω), *destroyer, sacker of cities*, B 728, E 333, σ 356, ω 116 of Odysseus. (Il.)

πτόλις, see πόλις.

πτόρθον, τόν, surculum, *sapling*, ζ 128†.

πτύγμ(α), τό, *fold*, E 315†.

πτυκτῷ, dat., (πτύσσω), *folded*, Z 169†.

πτύξ, πτυχί, ές, ας, fem., (πτύσσω), (1) *layer of shield*, Σ 481; usually the outermost, smallest layer, e. g. in shield of Achilleus (see cut No. 135).—(2) *ravine, mountain valley*, Λ 77.

πτυόφιν=gen. sing. from τὸ πτύον, (πτύω), *winnowing shovel* or *fan*, used to throw up grain and chaff against the wind, N 588†.

πτύσσω, aor. part. **πτύξασα**, *having folded together*, α 439, ζ 111; pass. ipf. ἐπτύσσοντο, *were bent*, N 134, doubtful reading.

πτύοντα, part. pres., (πτύω, spuo), *spitting forth*, Ψ 697†.

πτώξ, ῶκα, masc., (πτώσσω), timi-

dus, *timid*, X 310; as subst. *hare*, P 676.

πτωσκάζεμεν, inf., (πτώξ), *crouch in fear*, Δ 372†.

πτώσσεις, ουσι, etc., pres., ipf. πτώσσον Φ 26, (πτήσσω, πτώξ), *cower, hide*, Δ 371; ὑπό τινι, before, H 129, pavere; *go cringing, begging about*, κατὰ δῆμον; νίφεα, *forsake in fear* the clouds, sky.

πτωχεύω, ῃ, ειν, ipf. iter. πτωχεύεσκ(ε), fut. εὔσων, (πτωχός), mendicari; trans. *gain by begging*, ρ 11, 17.

πτωχός, ῷ, όν, οἱ, ῶν, οὐς, (πτώσσω), mendicus, *beggar-(man)*, ἀνήρ, φ 327, ξ 400. (Od.)

Πυγμαῖοι, fabled race of dwarfs, manikins, thumbkins, lit. "fist-lings," (πυγμή), Γ 6†.

πυγ-μάχης, τῆς, (πυγμή), *boxing*, Ψ 653 and 665; from

πυγ-μάχοι, masc., (πυγμή, pug-nus). pugiles, *boxers*, θ 246†. (Cf. cut.)

πυγμῇ, τῇ, (pug-nus, Eng. fight), in the boxing-match, Ψ 669†.

πῠγούσιον, accus. masc., (πυγών), *a cubit long*; ἔνθα καὶ ἔνθα, in length and breadth, κ 517 and λ 25.

πύελον, τήν, *feeding-trough*, τ 553†.

πυθέσθαι, aor. inf. from πυνθάνομαι.

πυθμένι, α, ες, masc., (fundus, bottom), *bottom of a vase*, Λ 635; of trees, *trunk, butt-end*, ν 122, 372.

πύθω, fut. **πύσει**, Δ 174, putrefacict, *cause to rot*; pass. πύθεται, ομένων, putrescere, *rot*, Λ 395, μ 46.

Πῡθώ, οῦς, οῖ, ώ, and **Πῡθῶνα** B 519, Pytho, oldest name of oracle of Apollo on Parnassos, θ 80, Ι 405, B 519; Πυθῶδε, to Pytho, λ 581.

πῠκά, *thickly, strongly*, crebro, I 588; φρονεῖν, τρέφειν, *wisely, carefully*, E 70.

πῠκάζοιεν, opt., ειν, inf. pres., aor. πύκασι(ν), αι, ας, ἀσᾶσα, pf. pass. part. πεπῠκασμένος, α, (πύκα), *cover closely*, κάρη; *wrap up, cover*, with dat., ἅρματα, *chariots overlaid with gold*; ῥάκεσιν ὤμους, his shoulders *wrapped in* rags; τινὰ φρένας, grief *overshadowed*, *encompassed* his soul; λ 320, before their chins were thickly covered with down.

πὔκΐ-μήδεος, gen., (μῆδος), prudentis, *deep-counselled*, α 438†.

πὔκϊνός, οὔ, όν, (ά), and πυκνόν, οἱ, ήν, αἱ, ᾗς· ᾀς, όν, (ά), and πυκνόν, οἱ, οἶσιν, οὕς, ή, ήν, αἱ, ᾗσι, ά, (πύκα), prop. spissus, frequens, *firm, close, compact;* πτερά, flap *rapidly* (in closely succeeding motions) the wings, β 151; *close-packed, crowded,* χηλός, λόχος; *firmly put together,* λέχος ψ 117, but in I 621 the adj. is rather to be understood as applying to the several bed-coverings, *closely spread;* *thick-foliaged,* ὄζος, δρυμός, θάμνος, ὕλη; *mighty, sore,* delusion, Ω 480; grief, Π 599; prudens, *wise, sagacious,* B 55, Σ 216, Ξ 294, Ω 282; adv. πυκινόν, ά, πυκνόν, ά, and πὔκϊνῶς, *close, fast,* then frequenter, *often, deeply,* τ 95, T 312; prudenter, *wisely,* Φ 293, α 279.

Πῡλαι-μένης, εος, king of Paphlagonians, ally of Trojans, B 851; slain by Menelaos, E 576, yet appears again N 658; his son, Harpalion, N 643.

Πῡλαῖος, son of Lethos, chief of Pelasgians, B 842†.

πὔλ-άρτᾱο, τοῦ, (-άρτης), *door-closer, gate-fastener,* epithet of Aides, Θ 367, λ 277.

Πυλ-άρτης, a Trojan, (1) wounded by Aias, Λ 491.—(2) by Patroklos, Π 696.

πὔλᾰ-ωρούς, τούς, (Ϝορᾶν), *gate-keepers,* Φ 530. (Il.)

πὔλαι, άων, ῳσ(ι), ας, fem., (πέλομαι?), *gate* (always pl. as in two wings), B 809; of cities, camp, heaven, dreams, τ 562; of the sun, ω 12; 'Αΐδᾱο, of death, I 312.

Πυλη-γενής, see Πυλοι-γενής.

Πυλήνη, town in Aitolia, B 639†.

Πέλίοι, H 134, Ψ 633, Λ 753, ο 216, *inhabitants of* Πύλος.

Πυλοι-γενής, *born in Pylos,* Nesto., B 54; horses, Ψ 303.

Πὔλόνδε, to *Pylos,* Λ 760, β 317, γ 182, and freq.

Πὔλόθεν, π 323, *from Pylos*†.

Πὔλος, *Pylos,* a city in Triphylia, south of Alpheios, Λ 671 sq. In the Odyssey a city in the Messenian Elis, opposite the south end of Sphakteria,

γ 4, ἠγαθέῃ, ἱερῆς; joined with ἠμαθόεντος, τι, the word seems to designate not the city only, but the entire realm of Pylos.

πύλος, ἐν πύλῳ, E 397†, *in the gateway,* sc. Πυλάρταο, words from some ancient myth describing the combat of Hades and Herakles: the myth having been forgotten, later commentators wrote ἐν Πύλῳ, and thus gave to the combat an earthly arena.

Πύλων, ωνος, a Trojan, slain by Polypoites, M 187†.

πῡμάτῳ, ον, η, ης, ην, ας, ον, α, extremus, ultimus, *last,* η 138, Λ 759, Ψ 373, ι 369; N 616, *root of* the nose; ntr. used adverbially, X 203, δ 685.

πυνθάνομαι, ipf. πυνθανόμην, and πεύθομαι, οἶαθ' = οἶατο 3 pl. opt., εσθαι, ἐσθω, ὁμενος, ipf. (ἐ)πεύθετ(ο), ὁμεθ(α), fut. πεύσομαι, σεαι, σεται, σόμενος, ον, aor. ἐπύθοντο, and 1 sing. πυθόμην, 3 du. ἐσθην, ηαι, ηται, ησθε, οἴμην, οιτο, οἶατο, and aor. red. πεπυθοίατ(ο), pf. πέπυσμαι, σσαι, σται, ὑσθαι, plupf. (ἐ)πέπυστο, 3 du. πεπύσθην, comperio, exploro, *learn by inquiry,* β 215, *from* some one, τινός, P 408; usually = audio, *ascertain at first hand,* τί, κ 147, π 412, Ο 379; comperio, *hear tell of,* τινός, de, ν 256, ξ 321, but Z 465, βοῆς = audire; τί τινος, P 408, from some one, also ἐκ τινος; the fact heard freq. expressed by τινά, with part. or adj., Z 50, Λ 135, cf. E 702; τινός, with part., Λ 257, these things from you wrangling, T 322.

πύξ, possibly for πυξί, adv., (pugnus, πυγμή), *at boxing,* Γ 237, θ 103.

πύξῐνον, ntr., (πύξος), *of box-wood,* Ω 269†.

πῦρ, πυρός, ί, ά, (Ger. Feuer), ignis, *fire,* also in fire-pans for illumination; as symbols of danger, K 246; pl. *watch-fires;* πυρὸς θερέω, warm myself *at the fire,* ρ 23.

πῦρ-άγρην, τήν, (άγρέω). *fire-tongs,* γ 434 and Σ 477.

Πῦρ-αίχμης, chief of the Paionians, ally of Trojans, B 848; slain by Patroklos, II 287.

πυρακτέω, ipf. ἐπὔράκτεον, *I brought to a glow,* ι 328†.

Πόρᾰσος, (1) a Trojan, wounded by

Aias, Λ 491.—(2) town in Thessaly, B 695.

πυργηδόν, adv., (πύργος), like a tower, *in solid masses*, M 43. (Il.)

πύργος, ου, ψ, ον, οι, ων, οις, ους, masc., *tower, turreted wall*, ζ 262; *bulwark*, "strong tower," of Aias, λ 556; *compact body, column*, Δ 334.

πύργωσαν, 3 pl. aor., (πυργόω), *surround with towers. fortify*, λ 264†.

πῦρετόν, τόν, febrim, *fever*, X 31†.

πῦρή, ῆς, ῇ, ήν, αἱ, rogus, *funeral-pyre*; ἀλεγεινῆς, grievous, for the friends of the deceased, Ψ 110–177, 192–258, Ω 786–799. (Cf. cut.)

πῦρη-φόρον, see πυρο-φόρος.

πῦρι-ήκεα, acc., (ἀκή, -ήκης), *with blazing point*, ι 387†.

πῦρί-καυστος, 2, (καίω), praeustus, *charred*, N 564†.

Πῦρις, ιν, ο Lykian, slain by Patroklos, Π 416†.

Πῦρι-φλεγέθων, river in lower world, κ 513†.

πυρ-καϊή, ῆς, ήν, (καίω), *place where fire is kindled. funeral-pyre*, bustum, Ψ 158, 228, Ω 791; also H 428, 431, πυρκαϊῇ, they piled the corpses on the funeral-pyre. (Il.)

πύρνον, α, ntr., (πυρός), *wheaten loaf*, ο 311. (Od.)

πῦρόν, acc. sing.; pl. πυροί, ῶν, ούς, *wheat* (grains) used unground, as food for animals rather than for men; *yet*, υ 109.

πῦρο-φόροιο, οι, and πυρη-φόρον, *wheat-bearing*, M 314, γ 495.

πυρ-πολέοντας, part., (colere), *tending fires*, κ 30†.

πυρσοί, masc., (πῦρ), *torches, signal-lights*, Σ 211†.

πώ, encl. adv., *yet*, οὔ πω, nondum, *not yet*, also nequaquam, *in no wise*; οὐ πώ ποτε, nunquam, *never*, of past.

πωλέομαι, **πωλέ(εαι)**, εἶται, εὔμενος, ipf. πωλεύμην, εἶτ(ο), iter. πωλέσκετο, fut. πωλήσεαι, (πέλομαι), versari, frequentare, *frequent, consort with*, εἰς, ἐπί, μετά τινας, δεῦρο, ι 189, δ 384, β 55, A 490, χ 352, E 350.

πῶλοι, οισιν, ους, comm., (pullus), *foal*, Λ 680, Υ 222, ψ 246.

πῶμ(α), dat. pl. ασιν, ntr., *cover*, of chest, Π 221; of vase, β 353; also of quiver, Δ 116. (See Herakles in cut.)

πώ-ποτε, unquam, *ever yet*, always after οὐ, referring to the past, μ 98.

πῶς, quomodo? *how?* in exclamatory question, κ 337; with γάρ, *how then? κ* 337, A 123; with γὰρ δή, δέ, δή, quomodo tandem, *how pray?* νῦν, σ 223; with τ' ἄρα, igitur, therefore.

πώς, enclit., *somehow; αἴ κέν πως*, A 66, si qua, *if perhaps; οὐ μέν πως*, nequaquam, *by no means*, Δ 158.

πωτάομαι, ipf. **πωτῶντο**, (πέτομαι), ferebantur, *flew*, M 287†.

πῶν, εα, εσι, (pa-scor, Germ. Vieh), *flock, ὀίων, μήλων*, Γ 198, ω 112.

P.

P. Many words beginning with ρ began orig. with two consonants, esp. Ϝρ and σρ; what this initial consonant orig. was can not always be determined.

ῥά, ῥ', see ἄρα.

ῥάβδον, ῳ, οισι, masc., (ῥέπω?), *rod, staff,* esp. *magic wand* of Hermes, Ω 343; Kirke, κ 238; Athena, ν 429; *fishing-rod,* μ 251; *pins,* M 297.

ῥαδάλόν, v. l. = ῥοδανόν, Σ 576.

Ῥαδά-μανθυς, νος, son of Zeus, brother of Minos, Ξ 322, η 323; *ruler* in Elysion, δ 564.

ῥαδινήν, (Ϝραδ-), *slender, pliable,* Ψ 583†.

ῥάθάμιγγες, fem., guttae, *drops,* esp. of blood (mingled with dust), Λ 536; κονίης, *particles* of dust, Ψ 502. (Il.)

ῥαίνω (from ῥαδιηω), ipf. pass. **ῥαίνοντο,** aor. act. imp. ῥάσσατε, pass. pf. ἐρραδάται, plupf. ἐρράδατο, conspergere, *besprinkle,* τί τινι, Λ 282, υ 150, Μ 431.

ῥαιστῆρα, acc. masc. and fem., malleum, *hammer,* Σ 477†.

ῥαίω, subj. **ῥαίησι,** ipf. ἔρραιε, fut. ῥαισέμεναι, aor. ῥαίσῃ, αι, *shatter, νῆα;* τινά, *wreck,* ζ 326, ε 221; pass. pres. ῥαίοιτο, ομένου, aor. ἐρραίσθη, *be dashed,* ι 459, πρὸς οὐδέι, on the ground; *shiver,* Π 339.

Ϝράκος, εα, έων, εσιν, έεσσι, ntr., (λάκος, modern Greek βρακίον?), *ragged garment, tatters,* ζ 178. (Od.)

ῥαπτόν, άς, sartum, *patched,* ω 228 and 229, from

ῥάπτειν, ipf. 1 pl. ῥάπτομεν, aor. ῥάψε, ψαι, sarcio, *rivet together,* M 296; κακά, etc., τινί, *devise,* γ 118, π 379.

ῥάσσατε, imp. aor. from ῥαίνω, conspergite, *sprinkle.*

ῥάφαί, αι, *seams,* χ 186†.

ῥάχιν, fem., *chine,* piece cut lengthwise along the spine, I 208†.

ϜΡέα, monosyll. Ο 187, Ῥείης Ξ 203, (εὐρείης, the broad earth?), *Rhea,* daughter of Uranos, daughter and sister of Kronos, mother of Zeus, Poseidon, Aides; of Hestia, Demeter, Hera.

ῥέα, monosyll., facile, *easily,* only Il., μάλα, Υ 101. **ῥεῖα,** facile, *easily,* with verbs of moving, E 304; ζώοντες, *lightly* living, i. e. without care or pain, ε 122.

ῥέεθρα, τά, (ῥέω), undae, *stream, current,* also *bed,* B 461, ζ 317.

ῥέζω, pres. and ipf., ipf. iter. ῥέζεσκον, fut. ῥέξω, ει, ομεν, ειν, aor. ἔρρεξε, ἔρεξα, etc., ῥέξ(ε) I 535, pass. aor. part. ῥεχθέν, ἐντος, (Ϝρεγjω, from Ϝεργjω, Ger. wirken, Eng. work), *handle, deal with,* εὖ κακῶς τινα; *attempt, avail,* Τ 90; *bring to pass,* θ 148; ἔργον, usually in bad signif., χ 315; I 647, *treat with contumely;* ἱερά, θαλύσια, ἑκατόμβην, *perform, offer,* sacra facere, and generally sacrificare, γ 5, l 535.

ῥεθέων, gen. pl. ntr., (ὄρνυμι), *limbs,* Π 856, Χ 68.

ῥεῖα, see ῥέα. **Ῥείη,** see ϜΡέα.

Ῥείθρον, harbor in Ithaka, α 186†.

Ϝρέπω, ipf. **Ϝρέπε,** *sank* (in the scale), αἴσιμον ἦμαρ, fatalis dies, *destiny,* Θ 72, Χ 212.

ῥερυπωμένα, see ῥυπάω.

ῥεχθέν, ἐντα, see ῥέζω.

ῥέων, etc., (from σρεϜω), pres., ipf. ἔρρεε, ει, εον, and ῥέε, ον, aor. ῥύη γ 455, fluere, *flow,* ὕδατι, αἵματι, *trickle;* fig., A 249; *drop off,* κ 393.

Ϝρηγμῖνος, ῖνι, ῖνα, masc., (ῥήγνυμι), *surf, breakers,* Υ 229, not on the shore alone.

ῥήγνυμι, ῥηγνῦσι, ipf. iter. ῥήγνυσκε, fut. ῥήξω, ειν, aor. (ἐρ)ρῆξ(εν), etc., (frango), *break, shatter;* πύλας, *burst through;* also of hostile ranks, φάλαγγας, στίχας; pass. pres. ipf. ῥήγνῦτο, υντο, mid. aor. ἐρρήξαντο, ῥήξασθαι, ἁμένος, etc., subj. ῥηξόμεθα, *break,* intrans. κῦμα, Σ 67; *unchain, let loose,* Υ 55; *burst, scatter,* M 440.

Ϝρῆγος, εϊ, εα, εσσι, (ῥάκος, Ger. Laken), *covering, blanket,* χ 349; *woolen rug,* ζ 38, ν 73; *cushion and cover, mattress and blanket* for chair and bed,

I 661, η 336. (Cf. the Assyrian and Greek θρόνος with θρῆνυς attached.)

Ϝρηθέντι σ 414, υ 322, part. aor. pass. from ἐρῶ, (εἰπεῖν), over a just word *clearly spoken.*

ῥηΐδῐη, ιον, ι(α) Υ 265, adv. ἰδίως, Ε 808, φ 92, comp. ῥηΐτεροι, sup. ῥηΐτᾰτ(α), ῥηΐστη, facilis, *easy,* δ 565, φ

75; τινί, also with inf., Σ 258, Ω 243; Μ 54, facilis transitu, easy to pass.

Ϝρηκτός, verbal adj. from Ϝρήγνυμι, *that can be broken, vulnerable,* Ν 323†.

'Ρήνη, concubine of Oïleus, mother of Medon, Β 728†.

ῥηξ-ηνορίην, τήν, *might to break through hostile ranks, impetuosity,* ξ 217†, from

ῥηξ-ήνωρ, ήνορος, ι, α, *bursting hostile ranks, irresistible,* epith. of Achilleus, Η 228, δ 5.

'Ρηξ-ήνωρ, ορος, son of Nausithoos, brother of Alkinoos, η 63 and 146.

ῥῆσις, gen. ῥήσιος, fem., (ἐρεῖν), sermo, *speech,* φ 291†.

'Ρῆσος, son of Eïoneus, Κ 435, king of the Thrakians, slain by Odysseus and Diomedes, Κ 474, 519.

ῥήσσοντες, part. pres., (ῥήγνυμι?), *treading, stamping,* Σ 571†.

Ϝρητῆρ(α), τόν, (ἐρεῖν), oratorem, *speaker,* Ι 443†.

Ϝρητῷ (ἐρεῖν), conducta, *stipulated,* Φ 445†.

Ϝρήτρην, τήν, (ἐρεῖν), *stipulation, bargain,* ξ 393†.

Ϝρῑγεδᾰνή (ῥιγέω), *hateful, horrible,* Τ 325†.

ῥιγέω, fut. ῥιγήσειν, aor. ἐρρίγησε, σαν, and ῥίγησ(ε), pf. ἔρρῑγα, (ε), subj. ἐρρίγησι, plupf. ἐρρίγει, (ῥῖγος, frigus), horrere, *shudder at, start* (with fright) *from,* comm. absol. Δ 148, Ο 34, ε 116; ἰδών, Δ 279, Μ 331, 208, Π 119; pf. like pres. with inf., Γ 353; with μή, ψ 216, pertimui, ne—.

Ϝρῑγιον, comp., (ῥῖγος), frigidius, *colder,* ρ 191; magis horrendum, peius, *harsher, worse,* Α 325, υ 220; sup. ῥίγιστα, pessima, Ε 873.

'Ρίγμος, son of Peiroos, from Thrake, ally of Trojans, Υ 485†.

ῥῖγος, τό, frigus, *cold,* ε 472†.

ῥιγόω, fut. ῥῑγωσέμεν, frigēre, *be cold,* ξ 481†.

ῥίζης, gen., ῃ, αν, αι, ῶν, ῃσι(ν), (Ϝριδ̑ι̯α, radix, root, cf. thorough-wort), ψ 196, roots of the eye, ι 390.

ῥιζόω, aor. ἐρρίζωσε, *plant, fix firmly,* ν 163; pf. pass. ἐρρίζωται, *is planted out,* η 122.

ῥίμφᾰ, *swiftly,* Ζ 511, θ 193.

ῥίν, see ῥίς.

Ϝρῑνόν, οῦ, ntr., corium, *hide,* Κ

155; in ε 281, *shield*, according to the ancient commentators = *cloud*, v. l. ἐρῖνον interpreted as = ἐρινεός, which suits some passages equally well, but not all.

Ϝρῑνός, οῦ, ῷ, όν, οί, οῖς, ούς, fem., cutis, corium, *hide, skin*, of animals, K 262, Υ 276 ; of men, E 308; usually, with and without βοῶν, *ox-hide*, i. e. *ox-hide shield*, N 406, Δ 447; Π 636, the thud of bronze, of leather, and of ox-hide shields.

ῥῑνο-τόρος, (τορέω), *shield-piercing*, Φ 392†.

ῥίον, ntr., *peak, crag*, of Olympos, Θ 25 ; γ 295, *headland*.

ῥῑπή, ῆς, ῇ, fem., (ῥίπτω), impetus, *impulse, weight, flight, rush*, θ 192, Θ 355, Φ 12.

'Ρίπη, town in Arkadia, B 606†.

Ϝριπτάζων, part., (ῥίπτω), *hurl about*, Ξ 257†.

Ϝρίπτω, ipf. iter. **ῥίπτασκον**, fut. ῥίψω, ει, aor. ἔρριψε(ν), and ῥῖψ(ε), (Ϝριπ-, Ger. werfe), *hurl, throw*, τὶ μετά τινα, *toss into the hands of*, Γ 378.

ῥῖπεσσι, fem., (scirpus), οἰσυΐνῃσι, *with willow withes*, viminibus, ε 256†.

Ϝρίς, ῥῑνός, ῥῖνες, ῶν, ας, nasus, *nose*, N 616, δ 445 ; pl., nares, *nostrils*, Ξ 467, ε 456, Τ 39, per nares instillavit.

ῥοδἄνόν, *waving, swaying*, Σ 576†.

'Ρόδιος, see 'Ρόδος.

'Ροδίος, river in Troas, rising in Mount Ida, M 20†.

Ϝροδο-δάκτῠλος, *rosy-fingered*, 'Ηώς, epithet originating in an appearance of the eastern sky before sunrise peculiar to southern latitudes, β 1.

Ϝροδόεντι, dat., (Ϝρόδον, rosa), *fragrant with roses*, Ψ 186†.

'Ρόδος, fem., *Rhodes*, famous island southwest of Asia Minor, B 654 sq., 667 ; the inhabitants, 'Ρόδιοι, B 654.

ῥοάων, ῆσ(ι), άς, (ῥέω), fluctus, *stream*, B 869, ζ 216, ω 11.

ῥόθιον (ῥόθος), *gurgling, plashing, roaring*, ε 412†.

ῥοιαί, nom. pl., *pomegranate* (of tree and fruit), η 115 and λ 589.

ῥοιβδήσειεν, opt. aor. from ῥοιβδέω, (ῥοῖζος), *suck in*, μ 106†.

ῥοίζησεν, aor. from ῥοιζέω, *whistled*, K 502†.

ῥοίζῳ, ον, fem., *whistling, whizzing, whirr*, II 361; of shepherd's call, ι 315.

ῥόος, όοιο, όον, masc., (σρόος, ῥέω), *stream, flow* of water, Σ 402, M 25 ; κὰρ ῥ., *along in the current*, ε 327.

Ϝρόπαλον, ῳ, (α), οισι, ntr., (ῥέπω), *club, cudgel*, fustis, Λ 559, ι 319, λ 575.

ῥοχθεῖ, prs., ipf. ῥόχθει, *roar*, μ 60 and ε 402.

ῥύατο, see ῥύομαι.

ῥῦδόν, adv., (ῥέω), ἀφνειοῖο, *with floods of gold*, enormously rich, ο 426†.

ῥύη, aor. from ῥέω.

ῥῦμός, οῦ, ῷ, (ἐρύω), temo, *pole*, Z 40, K 505. (Cf. cut No. 45 for method of attachment of pole to chariot-box ; cf. also Nos. 49, 99.)

ῥύομαι (ἐρύεσθαι), **ῥύεται**, etc. prs., (inf. also ῥῦσθαι), aor. with σσ, σ, and ῥύατο, ipf. iter. ῥύσκεν Ω 730, (servo), tueor, *protect*, (1) *save, rescue*, ὑπέκ, ὑπό τινος, out of, from, P 645, 224.— (2) *hide*, M 8, ζ 129. [ῡ only in aor., also ῥύατο, but ῥῡσάμην, O 29.]

ῥῡπάω, ῥῠπόω, όωντα, ntr. pl., sordēre, *be filthy*, ψ 115 ; pf. pass. ῥερυπωμένα, ζ 59 (from ῥυπόω, transitive).

ῥύπα, τά, sordes. *filth*, ζ 93†.

ῥῦσατ(ο) (ἐρύκω), aor., retinebat, *detain*, ψ 244† ; see also ἐρύομαι and ἐρύω.

ῥύσαι, see ῥύομαι.

ῥύσι(α), τά, (ῥύω), ἐλαύνεσθαι, *booty dragged away*, of cattle, Λ 674†.

ῥῡσί-πτολι, Z 305, v. l. for ἐρυσί-πτολι.

ῥύσκεν, see ῥύομαι.

ῥῦσαί (ἐρύω, with furrows *drawn* over the face, sulcosae), rugosae, *wrinkled*, I 503†.

ῥῦσί-πτολι, *protectress of the city*, Z 305.

ῥυστάζοντας, acc. pl. part. prs., ῥυστάζεσκεν, (ἐρύω), *drag about*, Ω 755; *maltreat*, π 109.

ῥυστακτύος, τῆς, (ῥυστάζω), *misusage, ill-treatment*, σ 224†.

I. ῥῦτῆρα, masc., (ἐρύω), *one who draws a bow*, φ 173, σ 262.

II. ῥῦτῆρα, τόν, (Fερ-, Eng.warden), custodem, *guard*, ρ 187 and 223.

III. ῥῦτῆρσι, τοῖς, (ἐρύω), Π 475, they ran in between the reins, *in taut reins*, which by the fall of the παρήορος had been drawn to one side and entangled. The word is sometimes translated *traces*, but there is no mention of the use of traces in Homer. (Cf. plate I., at end of volume.)

Ῥύτιον, town in Kreta, B 648†.

ῥῦτοῖσι (ἐρύω), *dragged to the spot*, i. e., too large to carry, ζ 267 and ξ 10.

ῥωγαλέον, ἐην, ἑᾱ ξ 343, *pierced*, *torn*, *ragged*, B 417.

Fρῶγας (ῥήγνυμι), *clefts*, i. e. *loopholes* or *windows*, in the rear wall of the μέγαρον, to lighten the stairway behind them, χ 143. (See cut No. 90.)

ῥώομαι, ipf. (ἐρ)ρώοντο, aor. ἐρρώσαντο, (ruere), *were in rapid motion*, γούνατα, κνῆμαι; χαῖται, *fluttered*; *rushed forward*, Λ 50; *moved in armor*, *marched in pomp around*, ω 69; *danced*, Ω 616; Σ 417, *were running hard by* (of automatons).

ῥωπήϊα, ntr., (ῥώψ), fruticeta, *undergrowth*, Φ 559, ξ 473.

ῥωχμός, masc., (ῥώξ), *place gullied out, hollow*, Ψ 420†.

ῥώψ, acc. pl. ῥῶπας, fem., (ῥέπω), sarmenta, *twigs, brushwood*, κ 166, π 47.

Σ.

σ' = (1) σέ, X 351.—(2) σοί, A 170, Φ 122, cf. κ 19, δῶκε δὲ μ'.—(3) σά, α 356.

Σαγγάριος, οιο, river flowing through Bithynia and Phrygia, and into Pontos Euxeinos, Γ 187, Π 719.

σαίνω (from σFανjω, Ger. schwänzeln), σαίνωσ(ι), οντας, ipf. σαῖνον, *fawn upon*, with wagging of tail, π 6.

σακέσ-πάλος (πάλλω), *shield-swinging*, E 126†.

σάκος, εος, εΐ, εα, εσ(σ)ι(ν), ntr., *the great shield*, H 219, 222. (See cuts Nos. 9, 17, 18.)

Σᾰλᾰμίς, island near Athens, B 557, H 199, home of Aias, the son of Telamon.

Σαλμωνεύς, ῆος, son of Aiolos, father of Tyro, λ 236†.

σάλπιγξ, ἡ, *trumpet*, Σ 219†.

σαλπίζω, aor. σάλπιγξεν, *resounded, quaked*, Φ 388†.

Σάμη, island near Ithaka, ι 24, π 249, Kephallenia, or a part of it.

Σάμος, = (1) Σάμη, B 634. — (2)

Θρηικίη, *Samothrake*, island off the coast of Thrake, N 12.

σᾰνίς, ἴδος, ίδες, ίδων, ίδεσσιν, ίδας, fem., *boards, planks*, esp. the *wings of folding doors*, fores, I 583, Σ 275; *scaffolding*, stage, φ 51.

σάος, comp. σᾰώτερος, *more safely*.

σᾰο-φροσύνης, τῆς, dat. pl. γσι, *sound sense, discretion*, ψ 30; ψ 13, bring into the *ways of reason*.

σᾰό-φρων, ονα, *discreet*, δ 158 and Φ 462.

σαόω, imp. σάω, v. l. σῶ ν 230 (full form σάοε), and 3 sing. ipf. σάον, σάω, σάοε, fut. σαώσω, aor. ἐσάωσα and σάωσε, etc., fut. mid. σαώσεαι; pass. aor. 3 pl. ἐσάωθεν, also σώοντες, ipf. iter. σώεσκον and (from σοάω) subj. σόως, σόω, also v. l. σόγς, γ, I 681, 424, and finally σώζων ε 490, (σάος, salus), servare, conservare, *save, preserve*, I 78, ν 230, O 290, χ 372; ἔνθεν, inde nequaquam servaberis, thence in no way shalt thou *deliver thyself*, φ 309.

σαπήη, see σήπω.

σαρδάνιον (σαίρω?), grim, sarcastic, υ 302†.

σαρκός, τῆς, sing. only τ 450; pl. σάρκες, εσσι, ας, flesh, Θ 380, ι 293, λ 219.

Σαρπηδών, όνος, etc., also οντος, οντι, voc. Σαρπῆδον, son of Zeus, chief of Lykians, ally of Trojans, Ψ 800, Β 876, Ε 658, Μ 392, Π 464, Ε 633; slain by Patroklos, Π 480 sqq.; his burial, Π 667.

Σατνιόεις, εντος, forest stream in Mysia, Ζ 34, Ξ 445, Φ 87.

Σάτνιος, son of Enops, wounded by Aias, Ξ 443†.

σαυρωτῆρος, τοῦ, (σαῦρος), a spike at butt-end of spear, by which it was driven into the ground, Κ 153†. (See cut No. 4.)

σάφά, adv., (σάφής), clearly, plainly, εἶπον, ἴδμεν, ρ 106, Β 192.

σάω, σαῶσαι, etc., see σαόω.

σαώτερος, see σάος.

σβέννυμι, aor. ἔσβεσε, σβέσαν, σβέσατ(ε), σβέσ(σ)αι, extinguere, sedare, quench, calm, Ι 678; 2 aor. ἔσβη, extinctus est, go out, Ι 471; cessavit, cease, γ 182.

-σε, = -δε, suffix denoting motion toward; κυκλό-, ὑψό-, πάντο-, ὀμό-, πό-, κεῖ-σε.

σεβάσσατο τόγε θυμῷ, aor. from σεβάζω, (σέβας), veritus hoc est in animo, feared, Ζ 167 and 417.

σέβας, τό, reverentia, astonishment, awe, Σ 178; μ' ἔχει, miror.

σέβεσθε, imp. prs., (σέβομαι), are ye ashamed? Δ 242†.

σέθεν = σοῦ, see σύ.

σεῖ(ο) or σεῦ = σοῦ, see σύ.

σειρήν, τήν, pl. άς, fem., (εἴρω, sero), cord, Θ 19, Ψ 115, χ 175.

Σειρήνοιιν, ἧνες, (σύριγξ, susurrus?), Syrens, sweetly singing enchantresses, whose allurements Odysseus found means to resist, μ 39, 42, 44, 52, 158, 167, 198, ψ 326. The cut, from an ancient gem, represents them as bird-footed, an addition of later fable; for Homer, they are beautiful maidens.

σείων (σϜειω, Ger. schwinge), οντε, ipf. σεῖον, aor. σεῖσ(ε), ασα, vibrare, brandish, spear, ægis, Ο 321; concutere (pulsare) fores, shaking (beat-

ing) the doors, Ι 583; iugum, shake the yoke, γ 486; pass. mid. prs. σειόμενον, (α), ipf. σείετο, (ἐ)σσείοντ(ο), aor. σείσατο, concuti, be shaken, Υ 59; vibrata, Ν 558; commovit corpus, moved herself, Θ 199.

Σέλαγος, ου, father of Amphios from Paisos, Ε 612†.

σέλας, αι, τό, (σϜελ-, σείριος), brightness, gleam of fire, Θ 509; fire, Ρ 739; flash of lightning, Θ 76; incendii, blaze of the burning ships, Ο 600; of angry look, Τ 17; wondrous radiance, Τ 379, Σ 214.

σελήνη, ης, ῃ, ην, fem., (σέλας), luna, moon, πλήθουσαν, plenam, Σ 484; symbol of splendor, δ 45.

Σεληπιάδης, αο, Euenos, son of Selepios, Β 693†.

σέλινον, ου, (celery), ntr., apium, parsley, Β 776 and ε 72.

Σελλήεις, εντος, masc., river, (1) in Elis near Ephyra, Β 659, Ο 531.—(2) in Troas near Arisbe, Β 839, Μ 97.

Σελλοί, priests of Zeus at Dodona, Π 234†.

Σεμέλη, daughter of Kadmos, mother by Zeus of Dionysos, Ξ 323 and 325.

σέο = σεῦ = σοῦ, see σύ.

ΣΕΡ (σϜερ, serere, hence σειρά, ὅρμος), pass. perf. ἐερμένον (αι) σ 295, plupf. ἔερτο ο 460, was strung with (beads of amber and gold); Ε 89, firmly compacted.

σεῦα, aor. from σεύω.

σεύω, aor. ἔσσευα, ε, σεῦα, ε(ν), αν, ῃ, ας, pass. pf. ἐσσύμαι, part. ἐσσύμενος, οι, etc. = citus, quick, with gen., cupidus, *desirous;* mid. prs. σεύονται, ipf. ἐσσεύετο, οι το, aor. σεύατ(ο), ἐσσεύαντο, σεύωνται, αιτο, ασθαι, ἅμενος, 2 aor. sync. ἐσσύμην, ὕο, ὗτ(ο), *set in violent motion, chase, drive,* Z 132; drive away, ζ 89, ξ 35; *hurl, throw,* Λ 147, Ξ 413; *set on,* Λ 293; E 208, *I have really by my shot caused* the red blood *to flow* from both; mid. freq. = act., yet also = pass., festinare, *hasten,* τ 448, Z 518; appetere, *strive for,* δ 416, N 630; *start up* (Il.), O 271; *chase,* Γ 26, Λ 415; evolare, *fly away,* Ξ 519.

σήκασθεν, 3 pl. aor. pass. from σηκάζω, (σηκός), inclusi fuissent, *pen up,* Θ 131†.

σηκο-κόρον, masc., (σηκός, κορέω), *cleaner of cattle-pens* or *sheep-folds,* ρ 224†.

σηκῷ, οἱ, ῶν, ούς, masc., (sepes), *pen, fold,* ι 219, 319, Σ 589.

σῆμα, ἅτι, ατ(α), also σήμαθ᾽ before ἄ, ntr., *sign, mark* (by which any thing is identified), ψ 188; of recognition for us two, Ψ 326, τ 250; *mark on a lot,* H 189; on a horse, *spot, star,* Ψ 455; *a sign from heaven,* thunder, lightning, φ 413, N 244; prodigium, X 30; *funeral mound,* B 814, H 86; *mark to show the length of a throw,* θ 195; baleful *characters,* not alphabetic writing, but pictorial, Z 168.

σημαίνει, ουσιν, (ε), έτω, ειν, ων, ipf. σήμαινε, fut. σημανέω, aor. σήμηνε, (σῆμα), *point out,* τέρματα, Ψ 358; *bear sway, command,* A 289; ducere, τινί, K 58, P 250; τινός, Ξ 85; ἐπί τινι, over some one, χ 427; mid. aor. ἐσημήναντο κλῆρον, suam sortem insignire, *mark,* H 175.

σημάντορος, ι, ες, ας, nom. ὁ σημάντωρ, (σημαίνω). commander, *leader,* Δ 431; *driver,* Θ 127; βοῶν, pastor.

σήμερον (τῇ ἡμίρᾳ, ho-die), hodie, *to-day.* Λ 431.

σήπεται, pf. σέσηπε, aor. pass. subj. 3 sing. σαπήῃ, putrescere, *rot,* B 135, T 27. (Il.)

Σήσαμος, town in Paphlagonia, B 853†.

Σηστός, Thrakian city on the Hellespont, opposite Abydos, B 836†.

σθεναρή (σθένος), valida, *strong,* I 505†.

Σθενέ-λαος, son of Ithaimenes, slain by Patroklos, Π 586†.

Σθένελος, (1) son of Kapaneus, Nestor's attendant, Θ 114; combatant before Thebes and Ilios, E 111, 108, 241, 835, B 564, Δ 367, Θ 114, I 48, Ψ 511.—(2) son of Perseus and of Andromeda, father of Eurystheus, T 116, 123.

σθένος, εος, εϊ, ει, (στα-), robur, vis, *strength,* fluminis, Oceani; *valor,* P 212, 499; in periphrasis, Ἰδομενῆος, Ὠρίωνος, Ἠετίωνος = the mighty Idomeneus, etc.; Σ 274, in concione = consultando vim assequemur, seek strength in the council, i. e. in counsel.

σίαλοιο, ον, οισιν, ους, etc., with and without συός, *fat hog,* I 208, β 300.

σιγαλόεντι, τα, nitido, a, *shining, glittering,* of garments, X 154; reins, E 226; rugs, ζ 38; ὑπερῴϊα, π 449.

σίγα (σῖγ-, Ger. schweige), hush! imp., Ξ 90, τ 42.

σιγῇ, dat. from ἡ σιγή, silentio, *silently,* Γ 134, H 195, ο 391.

σίδήρεος, ψ, ον, α, η, and σιδήρειος, ον, η, ῳ, αι, (σίδηρος), ferreus, literally ὀρυμαγδός, "iron din of war," crash *of iron weapons;* fig. *hard* or *firm as iron,* inflexus, X 357; intrepidus, Ω 205; indefessus, μ 280.

σίδηρος, ον, ῳ, ον, masc., ferrum, *iron;* αἴθωνι, reddish, others glittering; πολιόν, ἰόεντα, violet blue = dark or steel blue; symbol of firmness, inexorableness, τ 494; πολύκμητος, *well-wrought, wrought with much labor,* of iron tools or weapons.

Σιδών, ῶνος, Phoenician city, ο 425; *inhabitants of Sidon,* Σιδόνες, Ψ 743; πολυδαίδαλοι, sollertes, skillful, and Σιδόνιοι, δ 84, 618, ο 118, Z 290; their country, Σιδονίην, ν 285; Σιδονίηθεν, Z 291†, *from Sidonia.*

σίζ(ε), ipf. from σίζω, hissed, ι 394.

Σικανίη, Sikania, earlier form for *Sikelia,* (Sicily), ω 307; inhabitants, Σικελοί, ή, ν 383, ω 366, 389, 211.

Σικυών, ῶνος, comm., *Sikyon,* a city on south shore of gulf of Corinth, subject to Agamemnon, B 572, Ψ 299.

Σιμόεις, (1) small river rising in Mount Ida, and flowing across the Trojan plain into the Skamandros, E 774, 777, M 22, Δ 475, Z 4, Υ 52.

(See plate V., at end of volume.)—(2) personified, *Simoeis*, the god of the river just described, Φ 307.

Σῑμοείσιος, son of Trojan Anthemion, slain by Aias, Δ 474, 477, 488.

σίνεται, ῆαι, οιτο, ipf. iter. σινέσκοντο, ra p e r e, *seize, despoil*, τί τινι, ζ 6 (n o c e t, *harms*, in ungenuine verse, Ω 45).

σίντης, ην, αι, (σίνεται), r a p a x, *ravenous*, Λ 481, Υ 165. (Il.)

Σίντιες (lit. "plunderers"), inhabitants of Lemnos, ἀγριοφώνους; θ 294, A 594.

Σίπυλος, branch of the Tmolos mountain range, near Magnesia, on the borders of Lydia, Ω 615†.

Σῐσῡφος (σοφός), son of Aiolos, father of Glaukos, founder of Ephyra (ancient name for Acropolis of Corinth), Ζ 153 sq.; κρατέρ' ἄλγεα πάσχων, in the lower world, λ 593.

σιτέσκοντο, ipf. iter. from σιτέω, (σῖτος), c e n a b a n t, *used to eat*, ω 209†.

σῖτος, οιο, ου, ῳ, ου, masc., f r u m e n t u m, *grain*, esp. *wheat; wheaten bread*, ι 9, α 139 ; c i b u s, *food*, Ω 602, Τ 306.

σῖτο·φάγῳ, *eating grain* or *bread*, ι 191†.

σιφλώσειεν, opt., (σιφλόω), m a l e p e s s u m d e t, *deform, ruin*, Ξ 142†.

σιωπᾶν, inf. pres., aor. opt. 3 pl. ἡσειαν, inf. ῆσαι, s i l e r e, *keep silence*, ρ 513 and Ψ 568.

σιωπῇ, dat. fem., t a c i t e, *silently*, Ι 190, ν 309 ; c l a m, *secretly*, Ξ 310 ; ἀκὴν ἐγένοντο σ., *were* (became) hushed in silence.

σκάζων, οντε, and mid. σκάζεσθαι, c l a u d i c a r e, *limp*, Τ 47, Λ 811. (Il.)

Σκαιαὶ (πύλαι), the only one of the gates of Troy mentioned by name by Homer ; it appears to have faced the Greek camp, and to have afforded a view over the Trojan plain, Γ 145, 149, 263, Ζ 237, 307, 393, Ι 354, Λ 170, Π 712, Σ 453, Χ 6, 360.

σκαιόν, ή, ῶν, s c a e v u s, s i n i s t r a, *left* (hand), Α 501 ; *western*, γ 295.

σκαίρουσι, οντες, s a l i u n t, *skip*, κ 412 ; t r i p u d i a n t e s, *beat the ground with feet in dance*, Σ 572.

(σκαλμοί, that *part of the gunwale* just under the thole-pin on which the

oar rests as it plays. See cut No. 35, *e*.)

Σκάμανδρος, (1) πεδίον, *plain of the Skamandros*, also λειμών, Β 465, 467.—(2) real name of Astyanax, Ζ 402.—(3) son of Strophios, a Trojan, slain by Menelaos, Ε 49.

Σκάμανδρος, the *Scamander* (called by gods Ξάνθος [yellow], now the Mendere Su,= "Scamander water"), river rising on Mount Ida, Μ 21.

Σκάνδεια, harbor of Kythera, Κ 268†.

Σκάρφη, locality in Lokris, near Thermopylai, Β 532†.

σκάφίδες, fem., *bowls*, ι 223†.

σκεδάννυμι, aor. (ἐ)σκέδασ(εν), imp. σκέδασον, (s c i n d o), *scatter, disperse*, Υ 341 ; *shed*, Η 330.

σκέδάσιν, τήν, (σκεδάννυμι), d i s p e r s i o, *scattering*; θεῖναι, scatter, α 116 and ν 225.

σκέλλω, aor. opt. σκήλειε, e x s i c c a r e t, *parch*, Ψ 191†.

σκέλος, τό, πρυμνόν σκίλος, upper part of *thigh*, Π 314†.

σκέπαρνον, ntr., *adze*, ε 237 and ι 391.

σκέπας, ntr., (σκέπω), *cover, shelter*, against the wind, ἀνέμοιο, ζ 210. (Od.)

σκεπάω, σκεπόωσι, *ward off*, κῦμα (ἀνέμων, raised by the winds), ν 99†.

σκέπτεο, imp. pres., ipf. σκέπτετ(ο), aor. σκεψάμενος, (specio, Ger. spähe, Eng. s p y), *look about* (after), μετά τινα ; αἰ κεν, to see whether, with subj., Ρ 652 ; c a v e b a t, Π 361.

σκηπάνιῳ, ntr., (σκῆπτρον), *staff*, sceptre, Ν 59 and Ω 245.

σκήπτρον-οὖχος, οι, ων, (σκῆπτρον), *bearing a staff* or *sceptre*, sceptred, δ 64.

σκῆπτρον, ου, ῳ, ου, α, (s c a p u s, Ger. S c h a f t, Eng. s h a f t), *staff*, of wanderer and beggar ; *sceptre* of kings, priests, heralds, judges. (Cf. cut on next page representing Agamemnon.) He who rose to address the assembly received the sceptre on rising from the herald ; symbol of royal power and dignity, Β 46 ; see also β 37, λ 91.

σκηπτόμενος, ον, i n n i x u s, τινί, *leaning on one's staff*; ironically, Ξ 457 = h a s t a t r a n s f i x u m.

σκηρίπτεσθ(αι), ὅμενος, i n n i t i, *lean upon*, ρ 196; c o n t r a n i t e n s, *push against*, λ 595.

σκιάσῃ, subj. aor., (σκιά), obumbret, overshadow, Φ 232†.

σκιάω, ipf. σκιόωντο, obumbrabantur, were darkened, β 388; A 157, σκιόωντα, according to Aristarchos, shadow-casting, v. l. σκιοέντα.

σκίδνᾰται, ασθ(ε), ασθαι, ipf. σκίδναθ' = σκίδνατο, pl. ἐσκίδναντ(ο), disperse, ἐπί, κατά, πρός τι; with inf., Ω 2; ὑψόσι, dash on high; diffuse its waters, η 130.

σκίερῷ, όν, (σκιά), opacus, shady, Λ 480 and υ 278.

σκῐῇ, αἱ, umbra, shadow, λ 207; of the departed, shade, ghost, κ 495.

σκιόεντr, opaca, affording shade, shadowy, E 525, α 365. The danger of protracted exposure to the intense rays of a southern sun gives such words as shade and shadowy much more meaning to an inhabitant of Greece or Ionia than they have to us. σκιόωντα, see σκιάω.

σκιρτάω, opt. σκιρτῷεν, (σκαίρω), bound along, Υ 226 and 228.

σκολιάς, 3, crooked = perverted, unjust, (opp. ἰθύντατα), Π 387†.

σκόλοπες, εσσι(ν), ας, masc., stake for impaling, Σ 177; palisades, O 344.

σκοπέλου, ῳ, ον, οι, οισιν, masc., scopulus, cliff, B 396, μ 73.

σκοπιάζέμεν, ων, ipf. ἐσκοπίαζον, (σκοπιή), speculari, watch, K 40, search out.

σκοπιῆς, ῇ, ήν, αἱ, άς, (σκοπός), specula, look-out place, on a rock or mountain, X 145; ἔχειν, speculari, θ 302.

σκοπός, οῦ, όν, οἱ, masc., (σκέπτομαι), speculator, watcher, look-out; χ 156, their (the suitors') look-out was better, = they kept a sharper watch; overseer, person in charge, Ψ 359, χ 396; mark, target, χ 6; ἀπὸ σκοποῦ, away from the mark, contrary to our idea.

σκότιον, clandestinum, in secret, Z 24†.

σκοτο-μήνιος, fem., (σκότος, μήν), illumis, darkness from absence of the moon, darkness, ξ 457†.

σκότος, ον, masc., (σκύτος?), tenebrae, darkness, gloom, τ 389; esp. (ll.) the darkness of death, μὶν (ὄσσε, as to the eyes), κάλυψε, Δ 461; εἷλε, E 47.

σκυδμαινέμεν (σκύζομαι), be wroth, τινί, Ω 592†.

σκύζεν, imp., εσθαι, ομένῳ, η, ης, (σκυδρός), be angry, wroth, τινί, ψ 209.

σκύλάκος, εσσι, ας, fem., whelp, puppy, ι 289. (Od.)

Σκύλλα, and η, ην, daughter of Κραταιίς, Scylla, a monster dwelling in a cave opposite Charybdis, μ 85, 235, 108, 125, 223, ψ 328.

σκύμνους, masc., (lion's) whelps, Σ 319†.

Σκῦρος, island northwest of Chios, λ 509, T 326. Σκυρόθεν, T 332, from S., town of same name on the island, I 668.

σκῦτος, ntr., (cutis), corium, hide, ξ 34†.

σκῦτο-τόμος, leather-worker, H 221†.

σκύφον, masc., (drinking) cup, ξ 112†.

σκώληξ, masc., earth-worm, N 654†.

σκῶλος, masc., palus, pointed stake, N 564†.

Σκῶλος, locality in Boiotia, B 497†.

σκῶπες, masc., horned owl, ε 66†.

σμάραγεῖ, aor. subj. ήσῃ, roar, thunder, B 210, Φ 199; re-echo, B 463.

σμερδαλέος, ῳ, ον, ω, ων, η, ην, ἐ(α), fearful, terrible (to look upon), λ 609, μ 91; ntr. as adv., έον (ἐα only before F and κτυπέων), of a cry or sound, χ 81; of look, X 95.

σμερδνή, terrible, E 742; όν as adv. with βοάν.

σμήχω, ipf. ἔσμηχε, detersit, wipe off, cleanse, ζ 226†.

σμικρῇσι, parvis, small, P 757†.

Σμινθεῦ, voc., epith. of Apollo, Λ 39, explained by ancient commentators as meaning the destroyer of field-mice (σμίνθοι). (The following cut, repre-

senting a mouse at work, is reproduced from the tetradrachm of Metapontion.)

σμύχοιτο, see κατὰ σμῦξαι.

σμῶδιξ, διγγες, fem., vibex, wale, B 267 and Ψ 716.

σόη, see σαόω.

σοῖο, see σός.

σόλον, τόν, rudely formed *mass of iron,* Ψ 826, 839, 844, the adj. αὐτοχόωνον (self-fused) suggests that a meteoric stone may have been meant.

Σόλυμοι, a Lykian tribe, Z 184, 204, ε 283.

σόος, ον, οι, οις, η, salvus, integer, *safe, sound* (acc. σῶν, P 367), A 117, O 497, Ω 382; χ 28, nom. σῶς, certus, *certain.*

σορός, masc., *funeral urn,* Ψ 91†.

σός, ή, όν, etc., (σύ), tuus ; joined with πόθος, ποθῇ, desiderium = tui, *for thee ;* ntr. used substantively = cum patrimonio versans, *with thy possessions,* β 369.

Σούνιον, ntr., southernmost promontory of Attika, γ 278†.

σοφίης, τῆς, (σοφός, sapiens), *skill, accomplishment,* O 412†.

σόφς, φ, see σαόω.

Σπάρτη, fem., capital of Lakonike, residence of Menelaos and Helena, visited by Telemachos ; εὐρείη, λ 460; καλλιγύναικα, ν 412; B 582, Δ 52, α 93, β 214, 359. Σπάρτηθεν *from Sparta,* β 327, δ 10. Σπάρτηνδε, *to Sparta,* α 285.

σπάρτα, τά, (σπεῖρα), *ropes,* B 135†.

σπάω, aor. **ἔσπασεν,** σπάσεν, mid. aor. (ἐ)σπάσατ(ο), σπασάμην, imp. σπάσασθε, σσάμενος, pass. aor. part. σπασθέντος, *draw forth,* Λ 458; with ἐκ, E 859; mid. suum aliquid extrahere, one's hand, one's sword, etc.; κ 166, *I pulled up for myself.*

σπεῖο, imp. aor. from ἕπομαι.

σπεῖος = σπίος, specus, *cave.*

σπεῖρον, ου, α, ων, ntr., (σπείρω), *cover, garment, shroud,* β 102 ; *sail,* ε 318, ζ 269.

σπεῖσαι, σασκε, see σπένδω.

Σπειώ, a Nereid, Σ 40†.

σπένδῃσθα, subj. pres. 2 sing., ῃ, ων, οντ(α), ες, ας, ipf. iter. σπένδεσκε, ον, aor. 3 pl. σπεῖσαν, subj. σῃς, σομεν, inf. σαι, pass. σας, σαντες, aor. iter. σπείσασκε, *make a libation,* i. e. to pour out unmixed wine upon the ground, or on the altar (μ 363), in honor of the divinity, before drinking, οἶνον, τινί; yet also ὕδατι, with water, μ 363, in case of need ; δέπαι, from the goblet.

σπέος, σπείους ε 68, σπῆϊ Σ 402, σπέος, σπεῖος ε 194, σπέσσι α 15, σπήεσσι, *cave, cavern, grotto.*

σπέρμα, ntr., (σπείρω), *seed, germ ;* πυρός, *spark,* ε 490†.

Σπερχειός, river in Thessaly ; as river-god the father of Menestheus, Π 174, 176, Ψ 144.

σπέρχωσιν, subj. pres., mid. opt. pres. σπερχοίατ(ο), and ὅμενος, οιο, ους, ῃ, *move rapidly, hasten ;* ἐρετμοῖς, *row rapidly,* ν 22 ; part. = adv. *hastily, rapidly.*

σπέσθαι, inf. aor. from ἕπομαι.

σπεύδουσιν, imp. ετον, ειν = ἔμεν, ων, ὄντεσσι, ουσ(α), etc., aor. 3 sing. σπεῦσε, subj. σομεν, imp. σατε, mid. fut. σπεύσομαι, *hasten,* Σ 373, εἰς τι, τινα, with part., = *quickly,* ι 250 ; περί τινος, *struggle for,* P 121 ; *hurry forward,* τί, γάμον, τ 137.

σπῆϊ, σπήεσσι, see σπέος.

σπιδέος, *broad,* Λ 754†. (v. l. ἀσπιδέος.)

σπιλάδες, εσσι(ν), fem., scopuli, *reefs,* ε 401, 405. (Od.)

σπινθῆρες, masc., scintillae, *sparks,* Δ 77†.

σπλάγχν(α), ων, ntr., viscera, *inward parts, entrails,* esp. *heart, liver, and lungs ;* these were roasted and eaten while the other parts of the victim were burning on the altar, and served as relish to the sacrificial banquet which followed ; the practice described A 464, γ 9.

σπόγγῳ, οισι, masc., (σΓόμ-γος, fungus, sponge), *sponge,* as means of cleansing the hands, Σ 414 ; tables and seats, α 111.

σποδιῇ, τῇ, *ash-heap*, ε 488†.
σποδοῦ, fem., *ashes*, ι 375†.

σπονδαί, αἱ, (σπένδω), libationes, *drink - offering, libation*, a portion of pure wine poured out before drinking in honor of the gods; *treaty ratified by libations of unmixed wine*, B 341, and Δ 159.

σπουδῆς, ῇ, fem., (studium?), *labor, effort*, φ 409; ἀπὸ σπ., ex animi sententia, *in earnest*; σπουδῇ, *eagerly, quickly*, ν 279, ο 209; *with difficulty, scarcely*, γ 297.

σταδίῃ, ἐν, (ὑσμίνῃ), *in close combat*, N 314, H 241.

στάζω, aor. στάξ(ε), imp. στάξον, instillare, *drop, let fall*, T 39, 348.

στάθμη, ην, fem., (στῆσαι), *chalk line*; ἐπὶ — ἰθύνειν, straighten or make true to the line, ε 245; phrase used of hewing timber, setting up things in a row, digging a ditch, τάφρον, φ 121.

σταθμοῖο, ῷ, όν, οἶιν, οἱ, ὧν, οἷσι(ν), ούς, (σταθῆναι), (1) stabulum, *stall*, shelter for men and beasts, used in general for sh-pherd's quarters, T 377, ρ 20; *sheep-pen*, B 470; σταθμόνδε, *to the stall, homeward.*—(2) postis, *post*, Ξ 167, α 333, η 89.—(3) *weight in balance*, M 434.

στάμεν(αι), inf. aor. = στῆναι, see ἵστημι.

σταμίνεσσιν, ταῖς, *braces* serving to enable the ribs to resist the inward pressure of the water (see cut No. 15, b), ε 252†. (Yet see also plate IV., where σταμίνες are taken as synonymous with ribs.)

στάν, 3 pl. 2 aor. from ἵστημι.
στάξ', aor. from στάζω.
στάς, part. 2 aor. from ἵστημι.
στἄτός (ἵστημι), ἵππος, *stalled* horse, Z 506, O 263.

σταυρούς, οἶσιν, (ἱστάναι), *stake, pale*, Ω 453 and ξ 11.

σταφυλῇ, ῇ, αἱ, ῇσι, fem., (ἀ-σταφίς), uva, *bunch of grapes*, η 121.

σταφύλῃ, τῇ, *plummet*; ἶσαι, matched to a hair in height, B 765†.

στάχύεσσιν, nom. ὁ στάχυς, aristis, *ears of grain*, Ψ 598†.

στέαρ, στέατος [dissyll.], ntr., (στῆναι), *hardened fat, tallow*, φ 178 and 183.

στείβοντες, ipf. στεῖβον, (στειμφ-, Ger. stampfen, -tapfen), *tread, wash*

clothes *by stamping* on them, ζ 92; *trample upon*, Λ 534.

στεῖλα(ν), aor. from στέλλω.

στειλειῆς, τῆς, (στέλλω), *hole in axe*, for helve, φ 422†.

στειλειόν, ntr., (στέλλω, Ger. Stiel), *axe-helve*, ε 236†.

στεῖνος, εἴ, ει, ntr., (στενός), angustiae, *confined space*, M 66; ὁδοῦ κοίλης, *narrow entrance*, Ψ 419.

στείνοιτο, ὄμενος, ipf. στείνοντο, (στεῖνος), *be crowded*, Ξ 34; ι 219, *be packed full*, with gen.; *dammed, weighed down*, Φ 220, ι 445; *be too narrow*, σ 386.

στεινωπός, ῷ, όν, adj., (στεῖνος), *narrow*; ὁδός, fauces, *narrow pass*, H 143; (πόντου) fretum, *strait*, μ 234.

στείομεν, subj. 2 aor. = στείωμεν, see ἵστημι.

στεῖραν, adj. fem., (στερεός), sterilem, *unfruitful, barren*, κ 522. (Od.)

στείρῃ, fem., (στῆναι), *fore part of keel, stem, cut-water*, A 482, β 428. (See cut No. 34, e.)

στείχῃσι, ειν, ων, οντα, ες, ipf. ἔστειχε, στεῖχεν, aor. ἔστιχον, (στίχος, στίχες), *go forward, advance*, ι 444, with θύραζε, also with acc. with ποτι, ἐς, ἀνά, *go, march*, B 833; also standing alone, I 86; of the sun, *climb*, λ 17.

στέλλω, στέλλοιμι, οντα, ας, prs., fut. στελέω, aor. στεῖλα, αν, (Ger. stellen), *put in order, arrange*, Δ 294; *make ready*, β 287; *send*; ἱστία, *take in sail*; mid. στείλασθε, *make yourselves ready*, Ψ 285; ἱστία, *take in their sails*, letting them down from the yards and getting them into the hold, A 433.

στέμμα, ματ(α), ntr., (στέφω), infula vittae, *chaplet* or *fillet of priest*, which Chryses (A 14) takes off, because he comes as suppliant; the cut on the next page shows the band in two positions—as extended at full length, and as wrapped around the head : in the second representation the ends should hang down by the sides of the head below the ears, A 28.

στενάχεσχ' = στενάχεσκε, see στενάχω.

στεναχίζω, ων, mid. ipf. στεναχίζετο, *wail, sigh*, ι 13, T 304; *groan*, B 95.

στενάχω, ουσι, ων, etc., ipf. iter.

στενάχεσκε Τ 132, mid. ipf. στενάχοντο, (στένω), wail, Π 489; groan,
Φ 417; puff, pant, Π 393; roar, Π 391;
τινά, τί, bewail, ι 467, Τ 301; with
βαρέα, Θ 334; πυκνὰ μάλα, Σ 318;
ἀδινά, Ω 123; μεγάλα, δ 516; mid. =
act.

Στέντωρ, ορος, a Greek whose voice
was as loud as the united cry of fifty
men, Ε 785†.

στένω, **στένει** Υ 169, ipf. ἐστενέ(ν),
groan, sigh; κῆρ, in heart, Κ 16; rage,
heave, Ψ 230.

στερεοῖς, ή, ῷσι, comp. -εωτέρη,
(Ger. starr), hard, λίθος, ἐπίεσσι, κρα-
δίη; stiff, βοέη; adv. **στερεῶς**, firmly,
Κ 263, ξ 346; obstinately refuse, Ψ 42.

στερέω, aor. inf. στερέσαι, deprive,
τινός, ν 262†.

στέρνον, οιο, ων, οισι(ν), ntr., (στόρ-
νυμι, Ger. Stirn), breast, Β 479, Λ
842, Ψ 365, 508.·

στεροπή, ῆς, ήν, fem., (ἀστράπτω),
thunderbolt, lightning, Λ 66, 184; gleam,
radiance, Τ 363, δ 72.

στεροπ-ηγερέτᾰ (ἐγείρω) Ζεύς, he
who wakes the lightning, thunderer, Π
298†. (Equally admissible is the derivation from ἀγείρω, he who gathers the
lightning.)

στεῦται, ipf. στεῦτο, (στῆναι), denotes the expression of a wish by a
movement or gesture, and is always
followed by inf. (always fut. exc.
ρ 525), have the appearance, make as·
if, with part., λ 584, stand as if thirsty;
pretend, ρ 525, to have heard; also
engage, threaten, promise.

στεφάνη, ης, ην, ας, fem., (στέφανος),
that which surrounds or encompasses,
(1) head-band or fillet, as woman's ornament, Σ 597. (See cuts Nos. 17, 43,
44.)—(2) brim of helmet projecting over
the forehead, visor, Λ 96; the helmet itself, Κ 30, Η 12. (See cuts Nos. 12,

85, 87, 88, 93, 122.)—(3) edge of a
cliff, Ν 138.

στέφᾰνος, masc., (στέφω), crown,
ring, Ν 736†.

στεφανόω, pass. pf. ἐστεφάνωται,
plupf. -το, (στέφανος), place all around;
πόντος, encompasses; Γοργώ, the Gorgon's head was placed upon it around
=at the centre; νέφος, cingebat;
τά τ' οὐρανός, by which the heaven is
encircled; Ε 739, fig. around which
panic fear was spreading itself on every
side.

στέφει (στεμφ-, stipare, Ger. stop-
fen), grants in abundance grace, μορφήν,
θ 170; ἀμφὶ στέφει, Σ 205, circumde-
dit.

στέωμεν, στῆ, στήῃ, aor. subj. from
ἵσταμαι.

στῆθος, εος, εϊ, εα, εων, εσσι(ν), for
gen. also εσφι, ntr., (στῆναι), breast,
sing. and pl. for both sexes, of men
and beasts, Β 218, Σ 51; since κῆρ, Ξ
140, κραδίη, Κ 95, ἦτορ, Α 189, are
situated in the breast, it is made also
the seat of θυμός, Ι 256, and in general of feelings, passions, and of reason,
Α 93, Δ 208, Ε 125, Ν 732, Ξ 316,
Υ 20; so also of voice, Δ 430; of
breath, Ι 610.

στήλη, ην, ας, fem., (στέλλω), co-
lumna, pillar, Ν 437; esp. grave-
stone, Π 457 (cf. cut), Μ 259.

στήμεναι, inf. aor. from ἵσταμαι.

στηρίζω, aor. (ἐ)στήριξε, ξαι, mid.
ασθαι, plupf. ἐστήρικτο, (στερεός), Ger.
starr), fix firmly, Λ 28; support one's
self, stand upon, μ 434, Φ 242, ποσίν,
πούεσσιν; κακὸν κακῷ, was piled upon,
Π 111; οὐρανῷ κάρη, rests her head
in the heaven, Δ 443.

στῐβᾰρόν, ῷ, οί, οῖς, ῆς, ῇσι(ν), comp.
-ώτερον, adv. -ῶς, (στείβω), close-pressed,

trodden firm, firm, compact, strong, of bodily members and weapons, E 400, 746, M 454.

στίβη, fem., (στείβω), *rime, hoar-frost*, ε 467 and ρ 25.

στίλβων, οντας, part., (allied to στεροπή), *glittering, gleaming*, τινί, with oil, Σ 596, also with beauty, grace.

στιλπναί (στίλβω), *sparkling* (dew-drops), Ξ 351†.

στίχός, ες, ας, fem., (στιχ-, στοῖχος), *row, rank*, or *file* of warriors; ἐπὶ στίχας, proleptically, *to the ranks* (so that they formed ranks), B 687, Γ 113; κατὰ στ., *by ranks*, Γ 326.

στιχάομαι, ipf. **ἐστιχόωντο**, (στίχες), *advance in rows*, in battle array, agmine incedere or vehi, B 92, Ξ16, Γ 266.

Στίχιος, Athenian leader, slain by Hektor, N 195, O 329, 331.

στόμ(α), ατος, ατι, ατ(α), ων, *mouth*, *throat*, of man and beast, B 489; διὰ στ. ἄγοντο = *utter*; ἀνὰ στ. ἔχων, *have in one's mouth*; ἐπὶ στ., prae-ceps; *mouth* of rivers, harbors, ε 441; στόμα ἠιόνος, *inlet* of the shore; O 389, *at the point*.

στομάχοιο, ον, ους, masc., (στόμα), *gullet, throat*, Γ 292. (Il.)

στοναχέω, aor. inf. **στοναχῆσαι**, *wail*, Σ 124†.

στοναχή, ῆς, ῇ, ῆσι, άς, *sighs, groans*, B 356, ε 83.

στοναχίζω, see στεναχίζω.

στονόεντα, ες, εσσα, αν, (στόνος), *plenum suspiriórum, mournful*, ι 12; ἀοιδή, of *funeral dirge*, Ω 721; elsewh. *causing sighs and groans, griev-ous*, Θ 159.

στόνος, ον, masc., (στένω), *sighing, groaning*, Φ 20, ψ 40, χ 308.

στορέννυμι, aor. **ἐστόρεσεν**, σαν, στόρεσ(ε), σαν, σον, σαι, σας, pass. plupf. ἔστρωτο, (sternere), *spread out*, bed, couch, carpet, I 621, Φ 171; *scatter*, I 213; *calm*, γ 158.

Στρατίη, town in Arkadia, B 606†.

Στρατίος, son of Nestor, γ 413 and 439.

στρατός, όφιν, οῦ, ῷ, όν, οί, masc., (στρώννυμι).—(1) In Iliad *the encamped army* of the Greeks, consisting of 1186 ships; streets throughout this camp, K 66; the tents or huts stood parallel with the ships, and opposite the inter-vals between them, O 653 sq. At first the camp was surrounded by no wall, Achilleus's presence rendering such defense needless; but after his with-drawal, by advice of Nestor, H 436–441, a massive wall with towers and gates, M 118–123, was built. (Il.) — (2) *the host, the army* of the Greeks or Trojans, β 30.

στρατόομαι, ipf. **ἐστρατόωντο**, (στρα-τός), *be encamped*, Γ 187, Δ 378, πρὸς τείχεα, *assault*.

στρεπτοῖο, οί, οῖσι, ἡ, αἱ, (στρέφω), (1) *twisted and braided*; χιτών, *ringed* coat of mail (cf. cut No. 36), E 113. — (2) exorabilis, *that may be turned, placable*, φρένες, θεοί; γλῶσσα, *voluble*, Υ 248.

στρεύγεσθαι (στράγγω, Eng. s t r u g-g l e), *grow weary, exhausted*, O 512, μ 351.

στρεφε-δίνηθεν, aor. pass. 3 pl., (στρέφω, δινέω), vertigine rotati sunt, lit. his eyes *whirled round and round* = every thing was in a whirl before his eyes, Π 792†.

στρέφω, στρέφει, ipf. ἔστρεφον, ε, aor. στρέψ(ε), αν, αι, ας, αντα, ες, aor. iter. στρέψασκον, (τρέπω?), *turn*, also with chariot (ἵππους), in combat and in race, Ψ 323; or with plough, Σ 544, 546; ὅιν εἰς ἔρεβος, *turn* the sheep toward the land of shadow. — Pass. pres. στρέφεται, ὄμεσθα, subj. εται M 42, ipf. ἐστρέφετ(ο), fut. στρέψεσθ(αι), aor. στρεφθείς, έντος, τι, τε, εἶσ(α), *turn one's self, turn*; ἔνθα καὶ ἔνθα, huc illuc; νωλεμίως, *twisting myself tight-ly into*, i. e. *twisting his wool tightly around me*, ι 435.

στρέψασκον, see στρέφω.

στρόμβον, τόν, (στρέφω), *top*, Ξ 413†.

στρουθοῖο, masc., *sparrow*, B 311. (Il.)

στροφάλιγγι, τῇ, (στρέφω), vor-tici, *eddy, whirl*, Π 775†.

στροφάλίζετε, imp., (στροφάλιγξ) *twirl, ply*, σ 315†.

Στρόφιος, father of Skamandros, E 49†.

στρόφος, ὁ, (στρέφω), *cord, rope*, ἀορτήρ, as support, ν 438. (Od.)

στρώννυμι, see στορέννυμι.

στρωφάω, στρωφῶσιν, ῶσ(α) (στρέ-φω), *turn constantly* (thread, yarn), ἠλά-κατα; mid. ᾶσθ(αι), ipf. στρωφᾶτ(ο), *tarry, dwell*, I 463 ; N 557, *engage in combat against*.

στῦγερός, οῖο, οῦ, ῷ, όν, οί, ή, ῆς, ῷ, ήν, άς, adv. -ῶς, (ἔστυγον), *hated, hateful*, Ψ 79 ; λ 201, *wretched*.

στῦγέει, έουσι, έῃ, and ἔησιν, aor. ἔστυγον, and 1 aor. opt. στύξαιμι : this last form. *make hateful* ; the other forms, *hate, shudder at, be disgusted with*, Θ 370, ν 400.

Στύμφηλος, fem., town in Arkadia, B 608†.

Στύξ, Στῦγός, *Styx*, lit. "Hateful," river in the lower world, by which the gods swore their most sacred oaths ; its branches, Titaresios and Kokytos, B 755, κ 514, Θ 369, Ξ 271, Ο 37.

Στύρα, τά, town in Euboia, B 539†.

στῦφελίζετε, ειν, aor. (ἐ)στυφέλιξε(ν), ῃ, αι, part. pres. -ομένους, (στύφω), *smite*, E 437, H 261 ; *scatter*, Λ 305 ; *thrust out of*, ἐκ(τός), Α 581 ; *maltreat*, σ 416, π 108.

σῦ (for τύ, τϝέ), also τύνη, gen. τεοῖο Θ 37, σεῖ(ο), σέο encl., σεῦ Z 454, σέθεν, dat. τοι encl., τοί γε, σοί, τεΐν Λ 201, δ 619, acc. σέ, encl. and orthotone, (du. σφω(ι), and pl. ὑμεῖς, q. v.), pers. pron. of second person, t u, *thou*, often strengthened by γέ or πέρ ; also orthotoned when joined with cases of αὐτός.

σῦ-βόσϊα, ntr., also written -βόσεια, (βόσις), συῶν, *herds of swine*, Λ 679, ξ 101.

σῦ-βώτης, εω, ῃ, ην, βῶτα, masc., (βόσκω), *swine-herd*, δ 640 ; δῖος, *excellent, illustrious*. (Od.)

σῦ-γε, tu quidem.

συγ-κάλέσας, aor. part., c o n v o - c a n s, *summoning*, B 55 and K 302.

συγ-καλύπτω, see σὺν κάλυψε.

συγ-κλονέω, ipf. **συν-εκλόνεον**, p e r - t u r b a b a n t, *confound*, N 722†.

συγ-κύρσειαν, aor. opt. from κυρέω, c o n c u r r e r e n t, *strike together*, Ψ 435†.

συγ-χέω, imp. χει, ipf. -χει, aor. ἔχευε, αν, inf. χεῦαι (for χεϝ-αι), part. χέας, mid. 3 sing. aor. sync. -χῦτο, c o n f u n d e r e, *confound, confuse*, θυμόν, νόον ; π 471, σύγχῦτο, *were entangled ; ὅρκια*, f o e d u s l a c d e r e, *violate*, Δ 269 ; κάματον, ἰούς, *make of no effect ; ἄνδρα, break down*, θ 139.

σῦκέη (συκῆ, ω 246), ἕαι, ἕας, all forms pronounced with synizesis, *fig-tree*, η 116. (Od.)

σῦκον, σύκῳ, ntr., *fig*, η 121†.

σῦλάω (for σκυλάω, s p o l i o), ipf. (ἐ)σῦλᾱ, συλήτην, fut. συλήσετε, σειν, σων, aor. σύλησω, σωσι, σειε, σας, *strip off*. E 164, τεύχεα (ἀπό) τινος, Λ 110, and τινά ; also τινά τι, N 201 ; d e - m e r e, πῶμα, *take the lid off the quiver*, Δ 116 ; p r o m e r e (ἐκ γωρυτοῦ), *take out* (of its case), Δ 105.

σῦλεύειν, ipf. ἐσύλευον, (σκῦλα), s p o l i a r e, *spoil*, τινά, E 48 ; *take away* any thing from him (Achilleus), Ω 436.

συλ-λέγω, aor. -λέξας, c o l l i g e r e, *collect, gather* ; mid. fut. -λέξομαι and aor. λέξατο, s i b i or s u a c o l l i g e r e, Σ 413, β 292.

συμ (more freq. ξυμ), -βάλλω, **βάλλετον** (ξυμ), σὺν ἔβᾰλον and σύμβᾰλον, imp. ετ(ε), aor. sync. 3 du. ξυμβλήτην, inf. -βλήμεναι, mid. fut. συμβλή(σ)εαι Υ 335, aor. σὺν ἐβάλοντο, aor. sync. ξύμβλητο, ηντο, subj. ηται η 204, part. ἡμενος, m i s c e r e a q u a s, c o m - m i t t e r e a r m a, p u g n a m, *throw, bring*, or *put together* ; of rivers, *unite their waters* ; of weapons, *bring in contact ; τινάς*, of men, *bring against each other in battle*, Υ 55, Γ 70 ; τινί (with hostile intent, Π 565, Φ 578), *meet*, as also mid. ; usually *meet*, also *encounter*, c o n c u r r e r e, μάχεσθαι, M 377.

Σύμη, fem., island off the coast of Karia, north of Rhodos ; Σύμηθεν, *from Syme*, B 671†.

συμ (ξυμ) **-μάρψας**, aor., (μάρπτω), *seizing at the same time*, ι 289 ; but K 467, *break off*.

συμ (ξυμ) **-μητιάασθαι**, c o n s u l e r e, *take counsel*, K 197†.

συμ-μίσγεται, aor. 3 pl. σὺν ἔμιχθεν, *flow into*, B 753 ; *mingle*, Ψ 687.

συμ-μύω, pf. σὺν μέμῦκε, *have closed*, Ω 420†.

σύμ (ξύμ) **-παντες**, ων, ασι, ας and α, c u n c t i, a, *all (together)*, B 567, η 214.

συμ-πήγνυμι, aor. συνέπηξεν, *curdled*, E 902†.

συμ-πίπτω, aor. σὺν ἔπεσε, ον, c o n - c u r r i t, *rush together, meet*, ε 295, Η 256.

συμ-πλάτάγησεν (πλάταγος) χερσίν, *smote his hands together*, Ψ 102†.

συμ-φερτή, Ν 237†, where ἀρετή is to be repeated in the predicate, the united bravery even of weak men is (real) bravery.

συμ-φέρω, ipf. mid. -φερόμεσθα, fut. -οισύμεθα, meet in battle, μάχῃ, Λ 736 ; πτόλεμόνδε, Θ 400.

συμ-φράδμονες, pl., (φράζω), joint counsellors, Β 372†.

συμ - φράζομαι, φράσσομαι, aor. φράσσατο, secum (θυμῷ) meditari, take counsel with one's self, ὅπως, ο 202 ; τινί (βουλάς), cum aliquo consilia inire, concert plans with, Α 537 ; have neither word nor deed in common with, I 374.

σύν, from ξύν, which is used when it is desired to lengthen a preceding vowel by position, (κοινός, cum), as also freely in compounds, with, along with, together, Κ 224, κ 42 ; σὺν τινι, cum aliquo; unā cum, along with, Ρ 57 ; by the aid of, σὺν Ἀθήνῃ ; of things, with, Ε 220, ἔντεσι, also with νηί ; often with weapons, instrumental, ἔντεσι, τεύχεσι ; with ἀπέτισαν, Δ 161, gravi poena, with a great price; denoting accompaniment, along with, αὐτῇ σὺν πήληκι, Ξ 498, cf. I 194. Σὺν freq. follows its case, ι 332, ν 303.

συν (ξυν) -αγείρων, aor. ξυνάγειρα, gather together, assemble, pass. -αγειρόμενοι, and 2 aor. mid. sync. αγρόμενοι, assembled ; aor. mid.-αγείρατ(ο), collect for one's self, ξ 323.

συν (ξυν) -άγνυμι, aor. ἐ(F)αξε, αν, αι, tmesis, confringere, dash to pieces, νῆας, ἄρματα, Ψ 467 ; Λ 114, crush with his teeth.

σὺν (ξυν) -άγω, subj. ξυνάγωμεν, ουσα, οντες, σὺν ἄγοιμι, ipf. ξύναγον, ε, lead together, νηόν, ad templum convocare; ὅρκια, bring together the animals for sacrifice, Γ 269 ; collect, φόρτον ; on the other hand, ἄρηα, ἔριδα ἄρηος, etc., join battle, stir up battle, Ε 861, Π 764.

συν-αείρω, aor. ἤειραν, joined in raising him, Ω 590 ; on the other hand, ipf. ἤειρεν Κ 499, aor. subj. ἀείρεται Ο 680, are from ΣΡΕΡ (εἴρω, σειρά), couple together.

σὺν - αίνυτο, ipf., gathered up, Φ 502†.

σὺν-αιρέω, aor. ελεν, Π 740, tore away ; - ελών, υ 95, laying hold of at once.

συν-αντάω, ipf. du. αντήτην, mid. aor. subj. αντήσωνται, τινί, meet, Ρ 134 and π 333.

σῠν-αντόμενος, ipf. ἤντετο, 3 du. αντέσθην, meet, τινί ; Φ 34, encounter.

συν-αράσσω, fut. ἀράξω, aor. ἀραξ(εν), pass. ἀράχθη, always in tmesis, dash to pieces, Ψ 673, ε 426.

συν (ξυν) -δέω, ipf. 3 pl. δέον, aor. -έδησα, ξυνέδησε, δῆσαι, bind together, -έδησα fast, Α 399, χ 189 ; σφενδόνῃ, bind up with a bandage, Ν 599.

συν-έδραμον, see συν-τρέχω.

συν-είργω, ipf. -ἐεργον, (for FίFεργον), aor. ἐέργαθον, bind together ; ξ 72, cinxit ; Ξ 36, shut in.

(συν =) ξυν-εείκοσι, twenty (men) together, ξ 98†.

1. σύν-ειμι, fut. ἔσεσθαι, be together ; ὀιζυῖ, be together with, participate in, η 270†.

2. σῠν-, ξῠν-ειμι, ιόντες, ων, ας, ipf. ξύνισαν, du. συνίτην, come or go together, esp. in hostile signif. encounter, περὶ ἔριδος ; ἔριδι, in a spirit of strife.

σὺν (ξυν) -ελαύνεις, έμεν, aor. ἤλ‿ησ(ε), ελάσσαμεν, subj. ελάσσομεν, inf. σεαι, cogere, drive together, booty ; ὀδόντας, gnash (together), σ 98 ; τινὰς ἔριδι, bring together in combat ; only Χ 129, intrans. engage in battle.

σύν-ελον, see συν-αιρέω.

σῠν-εοχμῷ, masc., (vehi), junction, Ξ 465†.

σὺν ἐρείσαι, aor. from ἐρείδω, close, λ 426†.

σῠν-έριθος, comm., fellow-worker, ζ 32†.

(συν) ξῠν-εσις, fem., (ἵημι), conflux, κ 515†.

σῠν-εχές (-σεχές, ἔχω), also with αἰεί, perpetuo, continuously, ι 74.

συν (ξυν) -έχω, ἔχουσι, οντες, ουσαν, (tmesis), ipf. εχον, hold together, meet, Δ 133, Υ 415 ; pf. οχωκότε, bent together over, Β 218.

σῠν-ημοσῠνας, τάς, (συνίεμαι), compacts, Χ 261†.

συν -ήορος (ασFερ-, σειρά, εἴρω), δαιτί, linked with, accompaniment to the feast, θ 99†.

συν-θεσίαι, ἀων, fem., (συντίθημι), conditiones, treaty, Β 339 ; but Ε 319, instructions.

συν - θεύσεται, fut., (θέω), go well, υ 245†.

συν (ξυν) -ίημι, imp. prs. ξυνίει, 3 pl. ipf. ιον = ιεν, aor. ίηκεν, 2 aor. imp. ξύνες, mid. 2 aor. ξύνετο, subj. συν-ώμεθα, covenant, agree, N 381; committere, ἔριδι μάχεσθαι, bring together in thirst for combat, to fight, A 8; perceive, hear, attend, ὄπα, ἔπος; also τινός, some one, B 63; something, A 273; with part., δ 76; mid. in the same sense, δ 76.

συν - ίστημι, pf. - εσταότος, having arisen, Ξ 96†.

συν-οισόμεθα, see συμ-φέρω.

σὺν ὀρίνῃς, subj., commoveas, move, Ω 467; ὀρινόμεναι, set in motion, Δ 332.

(συν) ξυν-οχῇσιν, ταῖς, (ἔχω), coniunctio, ὁδοῦ, meeting of out- and home-stretch, Ψ 330†.

συν-ταράσσω, aor. ἐτάραξε, subj. ταράξῃ, confuse, throw into disorder, Θ 86; interrupt, spoil, A 579.

σὺν - τίθημι, aor. θέτο, imp. θεο, θεσθ(ε), (θυμῷ), sentire, perceive, hear, τί, τ 268, υ 92; take heed to, o 318.

σύν-τρεις, ternos, by threes, ι 429†.

συν-τρέχω, aor. ἐδράμον, concurrerunt, rushed together, Π 337 and 335.

συν-ώμεθα, see συν-ίημι.

σύριγξ, σύριγγος, ων, ξι, fem., pipe or tube, hence (1) spear-case, T 387.— (2) shepherd's pipe, K 13.

Σῦρίη, fem., mythical island, beyond Ortygia, far in the West, ο 403†.

συ-ρρήγνυμι (Ϝρήγνυμι), pf. pass. συν-έρρηκται, is broken, θ 137†.

σῦς, σὐός, ἱ, σῦν, σύες, ῶν, σί(ν), εσσι(ν), ας, comm., sus, swine, hog, boar or sow; κάπριος, wild boar, Λ 293, M 146, E 783, δ 457, κ 239.

σῦτο = ἔσσυτο, see σεύω.

συφειοῦ κ 389, συφεόνδε, εοῖσιν, εούς, masc., hog-pen, sty. (Od.)

σὐ-φορβός, όν, ἑ, ῶν, masc., (φέρβω), swine-herd; παῖδα, Φ 282. (Od.)

σφ' = σφέ and σφί, see σφεῖς.

σφάζουσι, ειν, ipf. ἔσφαζον, aor. ἔσφαξαν, σφάξ(ε), pass. prs. σφαζόμενοι, ων, pf. ἐσφαγμένα, iugulum aperire, only of victims for sacrifice, γ 454, cut or slit the throat, so as to catch the blood (also of beast already dead, γ 449), see cut under ἀμνίον, and A 459.

σφαίρῃ, σφαῖραν, fem., ball, ζ 100. (Od.) σφαιρηδόν, adv., like a ball, N 204.

σφάλλω (fallo), aor. σφῆλε, overthrow, make totter, ρ 464; σφῆλαι, Ψ 719.

σφάρἄγεῦντο, 3 pl. ipf. from σφαραγέομαι, (σφάραγος), hissed, ι 390; were full to bursting, ι 440.

σφάς, σφέ, see σφεῖς.

σφεδᾰνόν, adv., (σφαδάζω), eager'y, impatiently, Λ 165. (Il.)

σφεῖς (σϜε-, 8vo-), used as du. arc, dat. σφ(ίν), acc. σφέας, σφ(έ), see also σφωέ; much more common arc the pl. forms; gen. (ἀπὸ σφείων) σφέων orthotone and encl., σφῶν before αὐτῶν; dat. σφίσι(ν) orthotone and encl., σφ(ιν) encl.; acc. σφέας orthotone and encl., but not σφείας, v. ι 213 [pronounced as monosyll., B 96 and elsewh.]; σφᾶς encl., E 567; also σφ(έ), pron. of 3d pers., (a) reflexive, sui, sibi, se, ἀπὸ σφείων, μετὰ σφίσιν, A 368; κατὰ σφέας, B 366, and joined with αὐτῶν, οὕς; (b) direct, eorum, eis, etc., esp. common dat. σφί; of things, ι 70, κ 355.

σφέλἄς, α, ntr., footstool, short, thick block of wood placed before the seats of the men at banquet, σ 394 and ρ 231.

σφενδόνη, τῇ, (funda), s'ing, as in the cut in the hands of Assyrian; serves also as bandage for wound, N 600†.

σφετέρου, ψ, ον, γσι, άων, (α), 3d

ρoss. pron. of 3d pers. pl., *their,* s u i ; cf. α 7 ; ad sua, α 274.

σφηκόω, plupf. pass. **ἐσφήκωντο,** (σφήξ), *were bound together,* P 52†.

Σφῆλος, οιο, son of Bukolos, father of Iasos, O 338†.

σφῆλε = ἐσφηλε, see σφάλλω.

σφῆξ, σφῆκες, εσσιν, v e s p a e, *wasps;* also *hornets,* M 167 and Π 259.

σφι, σφιν, see **σφεῖς.**

σφοδρῶς, adv., (σφεδανόν), *earnestly, eagerly,* μ 124†.

σφονδυλίων, τῶν, masc., *vertebra of spine,* pl. *backbone,* Υ 483†.

σφός (σϝος, s v o s), s u u s, *their,* **σφοῦ,** σφούς, σφῆς, σφῷ, σφῇσι, σφάς, β 237 ; σφῷ, σφοῖς, Σ 231, always referring to a pl. subst.

σφύραν, τήν, *hammer,* γ 434†.

σφῦρόν, ά, ntr., *ankle,* Δ 518, Z 117.

σφω(έ), ὥϊν, pron. of 3d pers. du., *they two, both of them,* A 8. (See also σφίν, σφέας, σφέ, under σφεῖς.)

σφῶϊ and **σφω,** A 257, 574 ; gen. σφῶϊν, σφῶν, δ 62 ; pron. of 2d pers. du., *ye, you two.*

σφωΐτερον, poss. pron. of 2d pers. du., *of you both,* A 216†.

σχεδίης, η, ην, (σχέδος, Ger. S c h e i t), *float, raft,* raft of Odysseus described, ε 234 sqq., the parts of which it is attempted to represent in the cut under ἁρμονιάων : *a,* the beams forming the ἔδαφος, *h ; b,* σταμίνες ; *c,* γόμφοι ; *d,* ἁρμονίαι ; *e,* ἐπηγκενίδες ; *f,* ἴκρια ; *g,* ἱστός.

σχεδίην, adv., (ἔχω), *in hand-to-hand fight,* E 830†.

Σχεδίος, (1) son of Iphitos, chief of Phokians, B 517, P 306.—(2) son of Perimedes, a Phokian, slain by Hektor, O 515.

σχεδόθεν (ἔχω), *from close at hand,* then *near at hand, near* (τινός, τ 447), β 267, Π 807 ; position in verse always

the same, after caesura of third foot, ν 221.

σχεδόν, adv., (ἔχω), *near, hard by ;* πηός, near kinsman, κ 441 ; with dat., τινί ; with verbs also with gen., τινός ; never with prep. ; εἶναι, be at hand, N 268 ; M 53, the ditch, i. e. its farther bank, was not near.

σχεθέειν, see ἔχω, aor. ἔσχεθον.

σχεῖν, σχέμεν, σχέο, see ἔχω.

Σχερίη, fem., *Scheria,* the land of Phaiakes, which the ancients located in Kerkyra, whereas it really existed only in the poet's fancy, ε 34, ζ 8–263.

σχέτλιος, ε, οι, η [pronounce σχετλῖη or σχέτ-λίη, Γ 414], αι, (α), (ἔχω), strictly, *holding out, enduring,* then *merciless, unflinching, dreadful,* both in extravagant, Κ 164, and in seriously meant sense ; always in the latter sense where reference is made to presumption or crime ; ἔργα, *impious ;* ὕπνος, κ 69, *wicked.*

σχέτο, aor. mid. from ἔχω.

σχίζης, η, ησ(ιν), fem., (σκιδ-, s c i d i), *split wood, log,* A 462 ; δρυός, with the oaken billet, ξ 425.

σχοίατ(ο), opt. aor. from ἔχομαι.

σχοίνῳ, τῷ, masc. coll., *rushes,* ε 463†.

Σχοῖνος, town on river of the same name in Boiotia, B 497†.

σχόμενος, part. aor. mid. from ἔχω.

σώεσκον, σώζων, see σαόω.

σῶκος, masc., (σώζων), *saviour,* Υ 72†.

Σῶκος, son of Hippassos, a Trojan, Λ 427, 428, 440, 450, 456 ; slain by Odysseus, Λ 447.

σῶμα, τος, τι, τ(α), ntr., *corpse, carcass,* H 79, λ 53.

σῶς (σόος, τ 300), acc. σόον, σῶν A 117, Θ 246 (from σάος, see σαόω, s a-l u s), *safe, unharmed,* X 332 ; *certain,* ε 305.

Τ.

τ', (1) = τε.—(2) = τοί, σοί, a 60, 347.—(3) = τοι after μέν, sce μέν, II. 4.

τᾰγοί, pl. masc., (τάσσω), *arrangers, leaders* (v. l.), Ψ 160†.

τᾰθείς, τάθη, aor. pass. from τείνω.

τᾰλᾰ-εργοῦ, όν, οἱ, (Ϝέργον), *enduring labor, patient, drudging,* mules, δ 636, Ψ 666.

Τᾰλαι-μένης, chief of Maiones, B 865†.

Τᾰλᾰϊονίδης, αο, *son of Talaos,* Mekisteus, B 566, Ψ 678.

τάλαντον, τα, ntr., (τλῆναι, tollo), (1) *scales, balance,* Μ 433, χρύσεια, Διός, ἱρά, in which Zeus balances the fates of men. (See cut No. 69, where Hermes occupies the place of Zeus.)—(2) a definite weight, perhaps about a *pound,* χρυσοῖο, I 122, and elsewh.

τᾰλᾰ-πείριος, ον, οι, (τλῆναι, πεῖρα), *enduring trials, much tried,* η 24, ρ 84. (Od.)

τᾰλᾰ-πενθέα, acc. (πένθος), *bearing griefs, patient in suffering,* ε 222†.

τάλᾰρον, οισι, masc., (τάλαντον), *basket,* of silver for wool, δ 125; of wicker-work for fruit, etc., Σ 568.

τάλᾰς, only voc. **τάλᾰν,** (ταλάσσῃ), *foo'hardy, wretch,* σ 327 und τ 68.

τᾰλᾰσί-φρονος, α, *stout-hearted,* Δ 421, esp. of Odysseus.

ταλάσσῃς, ῃ, see τλῆναι.

τᾰλα-ύρῖνον, masc. and ntr. from -Ϝρῖνον, (Ϝρινός), *shield-bearing* (suspended by τελαμών, cut No. 121), in general, *brave, intrepid, valiant,* joined with Ἄρηα; —πολεμιστήν, Ε 289; ntr. as adv., *bravely,* Η 239. (Il.)

τᾰλᾰ-φρονα = ταλασί-φρονα, *stout-hearted,* Ν 300†.

Ταλθΰ-βιος, herald of Agamemnon, Η 276, Α 320, Γ 118, Δ 192, Τ 196, 250, 267, Ψ 897, represented in the following cut from very ancient Greek relief.

τάλλα, τάλλα, see ἄλλος.

τάμε, ταμέειν, sce τάμνω.

τᾰμεσί-χροα, ας, (τάμνω, χρώς), *cut-*

ting the skin, sharp-cutting, χαλκόν, ἐγχείας, Ν 340. (Il.)

τᾰμίη, ης, ην, αι, fem., (τάμνω), *housekeeper, stewardess,* γ 392; with and without γυνή, Ζ 390; ἀμφίπολος, π 152.

τᾰμίης, masc., (τάμνω), *steward, dispenser,* Τ 44; τ. πολέμοιο, of Zeus, as controller of the combat, Δ 84; ἀνέμων, of Aiolos, κ 21.

τάμνω, τάμνῃ, ετε, ων, ipf. ἔταμνον, (ἐ)τάμνε, parallel form **τέμνειν** and **τέμει** (also written τεμεῖ), aor. τάμε, ον, ησιν, ωμεν, ητε, οι, ἕειν, ών, ταμόνθ' = όντα, όντες, secare, *cut;* of flesh, *cut up, cut in pieces,* μελεϊστί, *furrow,* with the plough, Ν 707; also of ships, *cut through the waves;* χρόα, *wound, maim;* ὅρκια, *conclude a treaty with sacrifice,* foedus icere, Β 124, Γ 105; Δ 155, I *made a truce* which was death to thee; *slaughter; cut off,* τρίχας; *cut out,* the tongues of victims, an arrow from a wound; *fell trees; lop off* saplings from the wild fig-tree. ἐρινεὸν ὀρπηκας ; *hew* beams; *mark off* an enclosure, τέμενος ; mid. pass.

ταμνομίνη, ους, ipf. τάμνετο, οντ(ο), mid. aor. ταμίσθαι, pf. pass. τετμημίνον, ρ 195, *ready cut*; mid. contains reflexive idea, sibi, Σ 528, I 580.

τᾰνᾰ-ήκεϊ, dat., (ταναός, ἀκή), *with long edge* or *point*, of spear and sword, H 77, δ 257.

τᾰνᾰοϊο, for ταναϝοϊο, (tenuis), *long*, Π 589†.

τᾰναύ-ποδα (τανἄϝΰς), *long-*, i. e. *slender-legged*, ι 464†.

τᾰν-ηλεγέος (ταναός, ἄλγος), *containing long - enduring grief, deeply painful, long - lamented*, always with θανάτοιο, Θ 70, β 100, λ 171.

Τάνταλος, son of Zeus, king in Sipylos, father of Pelops, grandfather of Atreus ; revealed the secrets of the gods, and was punished therefor in Hades, λ 582 sqq.

τᾰνΰ—, stem of τᾰνΰς, (tenuis), *thin, stretched out*, freq. in compounds, c. g. Γ 228.

τᾰνΰ - γλωσσοι (γλῶσσα), *slender-, long-tongued*, ε 66†.

τᾰνυ-γλώχῖνας (γλωχίν), *with slender, sharp point*, Θ 297†.

τᾰνΰ-ήκεας, -ηκες, -ήκεσιν, (ἀκή), *with thin, fine edge* or *point ; keen, ἄορ; tapering*, Π 768.

τᾰνΰ-πεπλος, φ, ε, *in finely woven garment, richly clad ;* others translate, *with long flowing garment*, Γ 228, δ 305.

τᾰνΰ-πτέρΰγι, γεσσι, (πτέρυξ), *with wide-extending wings*, Μ 237 and Τ 350.

τᾰνΰσί-πτεροι (τανύω, πτερόν), *broad-winged*, ε 65 and χ 468.

τᾰνυστΰος, τῆς, (τανύω), *stretching* or *stringing the bow*, φ 112† (illustrated in cut No. 37).

τάνυται, see τανύω.

τᾰνΰ-φλοιον, *with thin*, i. e. *smooth and tender bark*, Π 767†.

τᾰνΰ-φυλλος, ον, *with long, slender leaves*, ν 102. (Od.)

τάνυμι, pass. τᾰνΰται, extenditur, *is stretched out*, Ρ 393†.

τᾰνΰω, ουσι, ειν, ων, fut. τανΰουσι, φ 174, aor. (ἐ)τάνυ(σ)σε(ν), τάνυσσαν, (σ)ση, σειε, σσαι, σσας, pass. pf. τετάνυσται, plupf. τετάνυστο, aor. 3 pl. τάνυσθεν, σθείς, (ταν, τείνω), tendere, *stretch, strain, stretch out, put in place*,

or *arrange* any thing long or broad, e. g. spears, tables, etc.; *string* a bow; *draw* the shuttle *from one side* of the warp *to the other*, κανόνα; ἵππους, *put upon their pace, drove at full speed;* of Zeus and other gods, when the comparison is with a net or noose, *extend, spreau over, involve in*, yet the meaning *strain, tighten, make more intense* seems also to suit these passages, ἔριδα πολέμοιο, μάχην, πόνον, ἔριδος καὶ πολέμου πεῖραρ ἐπ᾿ ἀμφοτέροις, Ν 359; pass., *be stretched out, extended ;* π 175, the cheeks *became full again;* mid. ipf. τανΰοντο, aor. τανυσσάμενος, and corresponding in formation and meaning, aor. pass., Π 475, *ran at full stretch ; having strung his* bow, Γ 112; ι 298, *stretch one's self out.*

τάπης, ητα, ήτων, ησι, ητας, masc., *carpet, rug*, used as cover for seat and bed, κ 12, I 200. (See cuts Nos. 73, 112.)

ταπρῶτα, see πρῶτος.

τάρ from τέ and ἄρα, Α 8.

τᾰράσσω (τραχΰς), aor. ἐτάραξε, ταράξη, pf. τετρηχυῖα, plupf. τετρήχει, *stir up, trouble ;* pf., *be in confusion*, Β 95, Η 346.

ταρβέω, ταρβεῖς, εῖ, imp. ει, ipf. τάρβει, aor. τάρβησεν, σαν, σειεν, σας, σαντε, (τάρβος), *be terrified, fear, θυμῷ,* aor. τινά and τί (Il.), *dread*, Α 331, Ζ 469.

τάρβος, ntr., (tor-vus), terror, *dread*, Ω 152 and 181.

ταρβοσΰνη, τῇ, terrore, σ 342†.

Τάρνη, Lydian city on Mount Tmolos, later Sardes, Ε 44†.

ταρπήμεναι, ἦναι, see τέρπω.

ταρσόν, σοί, masc., (τερσαίνω, torreo), *crate* (properly a surface for drying any thing upon), ι 219; *flat of the foot*, Λ 377, 388.

Τάρταρος, masc., *Tartaros*, dungeon, place of confinement of, the lower world, situated as far below the earth as the heaven above it ; here the Titans were shut up, Θ 13, 481.

ταρφέες, έσιν, έας, ειαί, άς, ἑ(α), (τρέφω), *thick, close together, frequent;* ntr. as adv., *often, thickly*, Μ 47.

Τάρφη, town in Lokris, Β 533†.

τάρφεσιν, nom. τὸ τάρφος, (τρέφω), *thicket*, Ε 555 and Ο 606.

ταρχΰσουσι, fut., aor. subj. σωσι,

(τέρσαίνω, torreo?), orig. perh. dry, burn, then solemnly bury, στήλῃ, Π 456. (Il.)

ταυρείη, ην, (ταῦρος), of ox-hide, Κ 258. (Il.)

ταῦρος, οιο, ου, ον, ων, οισι, ους, taurus, bull, with and without βοῦς, Λ 728, Ρ 389.

τάφήϊον, ntr. adj., (τάφος), φᾶρος, winding-sheet, shroud, β 99. (Od.)

Τάφιοι, inhabitants of the island Τάφος, α 417; this Taphos has been identified with the island Meganisi between Leukas and Akarnania; the Taphians were notorious among the neighboring islands and on the opposite mainland for piracy, α 105,181, 419, ξ 452, ο 427, π 426.

1. τάφος, τό, (τέθηπα), astonishment, φ 122. (Od.)

2. τάφος, ου, ῳ, ον, masc., (θάπτω), exsequiae, burial; τελέσαι, perform the rights of burial, Ω 660; funeral banquet, δαινύναι, γ 309.

τάφρος, οιο, ου, ῳ, ον, fem., (θάπτω), fossa, ditch, trench, φ 120; esp. for fortification, e. g. round the encampment of Grecian ships, Θ 179.

τάφών, aor. part., pf. τέθηπα, εν, ώς, ότες, ότας, plupf. ἐτεθήπεα, be astonished, amazed, τινά and κεῖνο, ζ 166, 168.

τάχ(ᾰ), adv. from ταχύς, quick'y, soon, Α 205, α 251.

τᾰχέως, quickly, Ψ 365†.

τάχισθ' = τάχιστ(α), etc., see ταχύς.

τάχος, ει, ntr., (ταχύς), speed, Ψ 406. (Il.)

τᾰχύ-πωλος, ων, (πῶλος), with swift horses, epithet of Δαναοί and Μυρμιδόνες, Ψ 6.

τᾰχύς, ύν, ύ, έες, έεσσι, έας, -εῖα, είης, -έ(α), comp. θάσσων, ονα, θᾶσσον, sup. τάχιστ(α) τάχισθ' θ 561, quick, swift, fleet; πόδας, pedibus, Σ 2; of messengers, arrows, warriors, πόδες; with inf. θείειν, Π 186; οἰωνοί, ξ 133; κύνες, Γ 26; ἐλάφοιο, αἰχμή; comp. ntr. cf. ocius, Β 440; η 152, nearly equals ὅτι τάχιστα, quam celerrime, as quickly as possible.

τᾰχῠτῆτος, τα, fem., swiftness, speed, Ψ 740 and ρ 315.

τέ (τίς, τέο, quis, que), enclitic, usually postpositive, corresponding in meaning and use to que, exc. Β 136,

Γ 33; I. connects things which by nature belong together, (1) -que, whether single words, Α 5, 38, Ζ 476; or sentences, Α 38, 192, 467.—(2) is often repeated, cf. et—et, Α 167, 13, 157; may connect principal and subordinate sentence, Α 81, Γ 12, Κ 225, Ψ 845; Α 218, only expressed in principal sentence; τέ—δέ, Η 418, Γ 366. —(3) τέ—καί (π 249, Α 417; in caesura, Γ 227), without marked emphasis of second clause; τέ, often repeated (γ 418, Ζ 239, Α 264), or καί (ν 365), or (Ζ 283, Α 465) first one, then the other; τε ἠδέ, Α 400; τε ἰδέ, δ 604.—II. affixed to prons. and to particles, it still serves as a connective, but can rarely be translated into English (cf. quisque, undique), (1) it may be affixed to all relatives except ὅστις, Α 86, 238, 279.—(2) to subordinate conjunctions, e. g. ὡς, ὅτε, εἴ περ, ἐπεί, Γ 33, Β 522.—(3) to co-ordinate conjunctions, e. g. καί τε, Α 521; μέν τε—δέ τε, Β 90 (ἀλλά τε, οὐδέ, δέ τ' οὐ, in second member, or δέ, δ' αὖτε, αὐτάρ), or when μέν in the first member is wanting, we find in the second member δέ τε, ἀλλά τε (after εἴπερ, Τ 164), ἀτάρ τε, Δ 484 (after ἤ ῥά τε); also οὐδέ τε, (a) nor also, (b) but not; ἤ τε, aut, either; doubled, whether—or, Λ 410, Ρ 42, and simple, quam, than, π 216; γάρ τε, namque.—(4) τ' ἄρα, with interrogative, Α 8, cf. Β 522. — (5) τίς τε, any body, δ 585. —(6) ἤ τε, Ε 201, Λ 362, Κ 450, μ 138; in οὔ νύ τ', τοι is to be understood.

Τεγέη, city in Arkadia, Β 607†.

τέγεοι, pl., (τέγος), roofed over, Ζ 248†.

τέγεος, τοῦ, tecti, κ 559, roof; apartment, hall, chamber, α 333. (Od.)

τεΐο = σοῦ from σύ.

τεθαλυῖα, τέθηλε, see θάλλω.

τέθηπα, ότες, see ταφών.

τέθναθι, άμεν(αι), ᾶσι, εώς, εΐώς, ηώς, see θνήσκω.

τεΐν = σοί, tibi.

τείνω, subj. τείνῃ, aor. ἔτεινε, τεῖναν, εἰς, ας, pass. pf. τέτᾰται, plupf. τέτᾰτο, 3 du. τετάσθην, 3 pl. τέταντο, aor. τάθη, θείς, tendo, stretch, τόξον; ἡνία ἐξ ἄντυγος (see cut No. 10), bind firmly on the chariot rim; ὀχεύς, chin-strap *was drawn tight*; ἐνὶ δεσμῷ, *bind* in chains ; φάσγανον, d e p e n d c b a t, *hung*; λαίλαπα, *spread* a tempest ; πολέμου τέλος ἴσον, *strain* the even tug of war, cf. μάχη ἐπὶ ἴσα ; ἐπί τινι μάχη τέταται (cf. πεῖραρ), the combat *spreads itself* around; δρύμος ἵπποισι, the horses *ran at full speed, at full stretch ;* ταθείς, *stretched out, prostrate,* p o r r e c t u s.

τεῖος, see τέως.

Τειρεσίης, ᾱο, Boiotian seer, dead before the Trojan war; his temple and oracle in Orchomenos, κ 537, λ 50, 89, 479, ψ 251, κ 524, λ 32, 139, 151, μ 267, ψ 323. He alone of all the shades retains his consciousness, but, like them, needs the draught of blood in order to converse with Odysseus.

τείρεα, τά, s i d e r a, (τέρας, ἀστήρ), *constellations,* Σ 485.

τείρω, prs. ipf., (ἔτειρε, ετο, also unaugmented), act. and pass., t e r e r e, *wear away, fatigue,* P 745, E 153 ; *distress, afflict,* N 251, Z 255, δ 369 ; *torment,* O 61, Π 510 ; pass., *be hard pressed,* Z 387.

τειχεσι-πλῆτα (-p e l l e r e), voc., *stormer of walls, cities,* E 31 and 455.

τειχίζω, ἐτειχίσσαντο, aor. mid., *built themselves,* Η 449†.

τειχιόεσσαν (τεῖχος), *well-walled,* B 559, 646.

τειχίον, ntr. dimin. from τεῖχος, *wall of private building,* π 165 and 343.

τεῖχος, εος, εϊ, ει, εα, εσσιν, (Ger. D e i c h), *wall round a city,* Δ 308, P 558 ; *fortification, rampart* (draw a line of wall, ἐλαύνειν), M 4, ποιήσαντο ; Η 436, ἔδειμαν.

τείως, see τέως.

τέκε, τεκέειν, see τίκτω.

τεκμαίρομ(αι), εται, aor. τεκμήρατο, αντο, (τέκμωρ), *decree, appoint,* Z 349 ; τινί τι, η 317 ; *intend, predict,* ὄλεθρον, κακά, Η 70.

τέκμωρ, τό, *goal, end;* Ἰλίου, *overthrow ;* Α 526, *pledge.*

τέκνον, voc. φίλε τέκνον, X 84, α, ων, voc. φίλα τέκνα, K 192, (τίκτω), *child,* Σ 73 ; in fond, conciliatory address, K 192 ; *young,* B 311, Λ 113.

τέκον, see τίκτω.

τέκος, εος, εϊ, έων, (τίκ(ε)εσσιν, ntr., (τίκτω), *child,* Φ 229, E 71 ; as term of

endearment, Ι 162, Θ 39, ψ 5, ζ 68 ; *young,* Θ 248.

τεκταίνομαι, aor. **τεκτήνατο,** αιτο, (τίκτω), μῆτιν, *devise,* K 19 ; *contrive, build,* E 62.

Τεκτονίδης, ᾱο, *son of Tekton* (shipbuilder), Polynaos, θ 114†.

τεκτοσύνάων, fem. pl., (τέκτων), *carpenter's art,* ε 250†.

τέκτων, ονος, ονα, ες, masc., (τίκτω, τεύχειν), *maker, builder, carpenter,* δούρων, νηῶν, Z 315 ; κεραοξόος, *worker* in horn ; ἄνδρες, N 390.

Τέκτων, ονος, father of Phereklos, E 59†.

τελᾰμών, ῶνος, ι, α, ε, ων, masc., (ταλ-, t u l-), (1) *any belt* or *strap for bearing* or *supporting,* e. g. strap for sword (see cut No. 93), for dagger (No. 115), for shield (see cut), Ξ 404 ;

often cunningly wrought, λ 610.—(2) *thong* bound about or piercing the ankles, to drag dead body away, P 290 ; cf. cut No. 18, where the ankles of the slain Achilleus are already pierced for the thong.

Τελᾰμών, ῶνος, son of Aiakos, brother of Peleus, king in Salamis, father of Aias and Teukros, Θ 283, N 177, P 284, 293, λ 553.

Τελαμωνιάδης, αο, *son of Telamon,* Aias the greater, N 709.

Τελαμώνιος, son of Telamon, (1) Aias, ὁ μέγας, υἱόν, Λ 591.—(2) Teukros, N 170, O 462.

τελέθει, ουσι, οντες, (τέλλω), *is already here,* νύξ, Η 282 ; generally = *to be,* η 52, Ι 441.

τελείων, gen. pl., (τέλος), *perfect, unblemished,* of victims, A 66 ; sup. τελειότατον, *most perfect,* πετεηνῶν, a l i t u m, Θ 247 = a q u i l a m (J o v i s a l i t e m).

τελείει, ipf. ἐτέλειον, and prs. pass.
εἴεται, (τελέω), bring to pass, fulfill,
I 456, O 593, ξ 160, τ 305, 561; execute, ζ 234, ψ 161.
τελεσ-φόρον εἰς ἐνιαυτόν, bringing to
perfection or maturity, full (year), T 32.
(Od.)
τελευτᾷ, fut. ήσω, εις, ει ο 524,
ουσι, ειν, aor. τελεύτησεν, σαν, σω, σης,
σαι, σας, aor. pass. τελευτηθῆναι, and
fut. mid. ήσεσθαι in pass. signif.,
(τελέω), bring to pass, fulfill, νοήματα,
Σ 328; ἐέλδωρ, φ 200; in general,
λ 80, γ 62; carry out, β 275; ἔργα,
ὅρκον, complete, Ξ 280; κακὸν ἡμάρ
τινι, bring misfortune upon.
τελευτή, ήν, (τελέω), end, accomplishment, α 249; object, I 625, κρανέεσθαι,
to be secured.
τελέω, έει, έωμεν, έοιεν, έοντες, ipf.
τέλεον, fut. έω, έει, έουσι, aor. ἐτέλεσσα,
ας, ε, αν, and τέλεσ(ε), σσαν, fut. (σ)σω,
σσης, (σ)σῃ, σωσι, σαιμι, σειας, σει(εν),
σαιμεν, σον, (σ)σαι; pass. prs. εἶται, ipf.
ἐτελείετο, pf. τετέλεσται, σμίνος, ον, α,
plupf. τετέλεστο, aor. (ἐ)τελέσθη, fut.
εἶται, εἶσθαι, and ἐεσθαι, (τέλος), bring
to goal, (1) complete, τί, with part.,
quite, altogether, M 222, ε 409.—(2)
fulfill, accomplish, ἔπος, μῦθον, T 107;
τάδε δὴ νῦν πάντα τελεῖται, β 176;
τὸ (δὲ) καὶ τετελεσμένον, fulfilled,
ἔσται, π 440, in other phrases τετελεσμένον means practicable.—(3) θέμιστας, pay tribute, I 156.
τελήεσσας, τάς, (τέλος), rich in fulfillment, effective, δ 352.
τέλος, τέλοσδε, τελέεσσι(ν), ntr.,
(τέρμα, Ger. Ziel), end, sum, B 122, (1)
sum and substance, μύθον; Π 630, πολέμοιο, victory in battle; ἐπέων, in
words, ι 5, ρ 476.—(2) accomplishment,
reality, γάμοιο, ἀρῆσιν; θανάτοιο, periphrasis for death, E 553.—(3) completion, Σ 378; μύθων, conclusion of the
matter.—(4) manipulus, division of
the army, company (Il.), Λ 730.
τέλσον, ntr., (τέλος), marks off the
limit of the corn-field, ἀρούρης, N 707.
τέμενος, ἔνεα, ntr., (τέμνω), land
marked off and set apart as property
of king, λ 185; as sacred to a god, θ
363.
Τεμέση, fem., town famous for its
copper mines (in Kypros?), α 184†.
τέμνω, τέμει, τεμεῖ, see τάμνω.

Τένεδος, small island westward of
Troas, A 38, Λ 625, N 33, γ 159.
Τενθρηδών, όνος, chief of Magnesians from Thessaly, father of Pro-
thoos, B 756†.
τένοντε, du., pl. τες, τας, masc.,
(τείνω), muscles; neck-muscles, K 456;
with αὐχενίους, γ 450; E 307, muscles
of hip.
τέξεις, εσθαι, see τίκτω.
τέο, τεο = τοῦ, του = τίνος, τινός,
see τίς 1. and 2.
τεοῖο—τεοῦ, tui, see σύ.
τεός, τεῷ, τεόν, τεώ, τεοῖσιν; τεή,
τεῆς, τεῇ, τεήν, τεῇς; τεόν, τεοῖσιν,
tuus, thy, Ω 739, γ 122, α 295, γ 94.
τέρας, τέρατα, άων, άεσσι; τέραα,
(ἀστήρ, see τείρεα), prodigium, por-
tentum, omen or portent found in
some manifestation of nature, e. g.
lightning, thunder, rainbow, hence
Διός, since Zeus sends it, φαίνει, προ-
φαίνει, ἥσι; but it is sent for the en-
lightenment or warning of men, hence
with gen. ἀνθρώπων; the monster
Gorgo is called, E 742, Διὸς τέρας;
Λ 4, πολέμοιο τέρας, Eris holds in her
hands as dread sign of war possibly the
Gorgon's head, possibly the snakes,
with which she is often represented.
τερέτρῳ, α, (τείρω), terebra, borer,
auger, ε 246 and ψ 198.
τέρην, τέρενα, ntr. τέρεν, τέριν(α),
(cognate with τείρω, teres), perh.
shining, gleaming, usually explained
tender, soft, Δ 237, N 180; Ameis
translates, π 332, pearly tear.
τέρμ(α), pl. τέρματ' = τέρματ(α),
ntr., (τέλος, terminus), goal, pillar
round which chariots had to turn at
races, Ψ 309; mark showing how far
a quoit was thrown, θ 193.
τερμιόεντα, όεσσα, (τέρμις), encircled
with a fringe or border, χιτών, τ 242;
ἀσπίς, furnished with tassels or tufts,
Π 803. (See cut No. 93.)
Τερπιάδης, son of Terpis, Phemios,
χ 330†.
τερπι-κέραυνος, ῳ, ον, (τέρπω), delighting in thunder, also sometimes referred to τρέπω, whirling the thunderbolt, Zeus, A 419, v 75.
τέρπειν, prs. and ipf., (often unaugmented both in act. and mid.), mid.
fut. τέρψομαι, aor. τερψάμενος, 2 aor.
subj. ταρπώμεθα δ 295, aor. red. τι-

τεττίγεσσι, τοῖς, cicada, a kind of grasshopper, probably not unlike the *katydid*; the gossiping elders at the gate of Troja are compared with τεττίγεσσιν, Γ 151†.

τετυγμένα, τετυκεῖν, ἐσθαι, οἴμεθα, τέτυξαι, τετύχθαι, see τεύχω.

τετύχηκε, see τυγχάνω.

τεῦ, τευ = τίνος, τινός.

Τευθρᾱντδης, *son of* Teuthras, Axylos, Ζ 13†.

Τεύθρας, αντος, (1) father of Axylos.—(2) a Greek from Magnesia, slain by Hektor, Ε 705†.

Τεῦκρος, son of Telamon, Ν 170, and of Hesione of Salamis, step-brother of Aias, Μ 371, the best archer before Troja, Μ 350, 372, Ζ 31, Θ 322, 273, Ο 484.

Τευτᾱμτδης, αο, *son of* Teutamias, Lethos, Β 843†.

τεύχε(α), ἑων, ε(σ)σι(ν), ntr., *implement of any kind, tackling*, π 326, 360, ο 218, elswh. arma, *equipment, arms*, Φ 301, Σ 137.

τεύχω, τεύχοιμι, ειν, ων, ούσῃ, ουσαι, ipf. ἐτευχε(ν), τεῦχε, 3 du. ἐτεύχετον (v. l. τετεύχετον, Ν 346), mid. τεύχον-τ(ο), fut. act. τεύξω, etc., aor. ἐτευξα, (εν), αν, τεῦξ(ε), ῃ, ειεν, etc., also red. aor. τετυκεῖν, mid. τετύκοντο, τετυκοί-μεθα, ἐσθαι, (τεύχη), execute, *fabricate, work*, of all kinds of handiwork, Σ 373 ; *build*, Ζ 314, Ξ 240 ; *prepare*, food and drink, Λ 624, ο 77; then generally, Α 110, Ν 209, Κ 6 ; θάνατόν τινι, λ 409 ; γάμον, etc., κ 18, Ο 70 ; *raise*, βοήν, κ 118 ; *render*, (ἐλώρια, Α 4), ν 397 ; mid. only of preparation of meals, *prepare* or *have prepared for one's self*, δόρπον, δαῖτα, etc.; pass. and fut. mid. τεύξεσθαι, pf. τετευχώς μ 423, pf. pass. τέτυξαι, τέτυκται, 3 pl. τετεύχαται, τε-τύχθω, τετύχθαι, τετυγμένος, ον, η, plupf. (ἐ)τετύγμην, ξο, κτο, (ἐ)τετεύχα-το, aor. ἐτύχθη, also 3 fut. τετεύξεται, as pass., *be prepared*, δ 392 ; *be wrought of* or *in*, τινός (τινί, τ 563) ; *be ready*, Ξ 53, β 356 ; τετυγμένος, *well-wrought*, Π 225 ; αἰθούσῃσιν, made (furnished) with polished porticoes; well - tilled, ἀγρός ; i n t e g e r, well-balanced, νόος ; esp. freq. in signif. *take place, happen*, f i e r i, θ 544 ; *be, become*, τέτυκται, ο, Ο 207, Π 622, Σ 120, Δ 84, Χ 30 ; θ 546, ἀντί τινος, takes the place of ;

also with πέρι, cf. περιεῖναι, sur-pass, Ρ 279 ; δίκη, was the habit, σ 275.

τέφρη, fem., (t e p e r e), Σ 25, Ψ 251, *ashes.*

τεχνάομαι, fut. τεχνήσομαι, aor. τεχνήσατο, σαιτο, σάμενος (τέχνη), *contrive, device*, Ψ 415 ; λ 613, where μή prepares the way for μηδ', may not he who contrived it, may he never again contrive a second like it. (Od.)

τέχνης, gen., ῃ, ην, ας, fem., (τε-κεῖν, τεύχω), *art, skill*, Γ 61, λ 614 ; (cunning) *device*, δ 455, 529, θ 327.

τεχνήεντες, adv. -ἑντως ε 270, fem. τεχνῆσσαι, for -ήεσσαι ἱστῶν, *skillful* in weaving, η 110.

τεχνῆσαι, better τεχνήσσαι, see τεχνήεντες.

τέῳ, τέων = τινί, τίνων.

τέως [monosyll., κ 348, ο 231, π 370], τεῖος, v. l., Υ 42 ; v. l., Τ 189, αὖθι τ. (τῆος?), so *long*, Ω 658 ; after ἕως, Υ 42 ; ὄφρα, Τ 189 ; *meanwhile*, ο 127, σ 190 ; *some time*, ο 231.

1. τῇ (old imper. for τῆθι or τάθι, parallel form to τείνω), *stretch out the hand here*, freq. with follg. imper. when its force may be given by *there!* Ξ 219, ε 346.

2. τῇ (also written τῇ, orig. old dat.), adv., (1) demonstrative, *here*, δ 847 ; (2) relative, also with περ, *as*, θ 510 ; δ 565 and τῇ ῥα Μ 118, *where.*

τῇδε, see ὅδε.

τήθεα, ntr., *oysters*, Π 747†.

Τηθύς, ύος, daughter of Uranos and of Gaia, wife of Okeanos, mother of river-gods, Ξ 302 ; of all the gods according to Ξ 201†.

τηκεδόνι, τῇ, (τήκω), *decline*, λ 201†.

τήκω, imp. τῆκε ; θυμόν, *consume* not thy soul, τ 264 ; mid. τηκόμενος, ης, ipf. τήκετο, pf. act. τέτηκα, *pine away*, Γ 176 ; *waste one's self away* with longing disease ; *melt*, of snow, τ 207.

τῆλε, *far away*, ρ 312 ; *far*, Κ 153, Σ 395, Υ 482 ; with gen., *far from*, ρ 250, Χ 445 ; ἀπό, Ψ 880, Χ 468, γ 313 ; ἐκ, *from far away from*, Β 863.

τηλεδάπός, ῷ, άων, ῶν, (τῆλε), *distant*, Φ 454 ; *strange, foreign*, Χ 45.

τηλεθάοντας, ὄωσα, αν, αι, ntr. άον, ὄωντα, (θάλλω), *luxuriant-grow-ing, blooming*, of plants, forest, hair ; παῖδες, Χ 423.

τηλε-κλειτοῖο, όν, οἱ, ὦν, ἀ, and κλυτός, α 30, (κλύω, κλεΓίω), wide-renowned, esp. as epithet of Trojan allies, l 233, E 491.

Τηλέ-μαχος, οιο, ον, etc., son of Odysseus and of Penelope, δ 112, α 156; visits, in search of his father, attended by Athena (in form of Nestor), Pylos, γ 1; Sparta, δ 1; returns home, o 1; helps his father in combat with the suitors, χ 92, 267, 284, 294; ἱερὴ ἲς Τ-οιο, periphrasis, β 409; πεπνυμένος, α 213, ω 510; ἰσόθεος φώς, ν 124. (Od. and B 260, Δ 354.)

Τήλεμος, son of Eurymos, seer among the Kyklopes, ι 509.

Τηλέ-πυλος, town of Laistrygones, κ 82, ψ 318.

τηλε-φᾰνής (φαίνομαι), conspicuous far and wide, ω 83†.

Τηλεφῐδης, αο, son of Telephos, Eurypylos, λ 519.

τηλῐκος, ον, of such an age (as), Ω 487, ρ 20.

τηλόθεν (τηλοῦ), from far (away), ζ 312, E 478, ι 273.

τηλόθι (τηλοῦ), far away, Π 233, α 22; with gen., far from, A 30.

τηλόσε (τηλοῦ), to a distance, far away, Δ 455 and X 407, ε 59.

τηλοτάτω, adv., most distant, η 322†.

τηλοῦ, afar, Λ 712; with gen., far from, ν 249, ψ 68.

τηλύ-γετος, ψ, ον, ην, (ἀταλός, τᾶλις, γέγαα?), of tender age, boy or girl; others explain born long ago (τῆλε γεν-), i. e. full grown; fem., Γ 175; elsewh. masc., N 470, δ 11.

τῆμος, adv., tum, then, thereupon, answering to ἦμος, Ψ 228; εὖτε, ν 95.

τῆπερ, see τή 2.

Τηρείης, ὄρος, mountain in Mysia, B 829†.

Τηΰ-γετον, mountain range in Lakonia, extending to Cape Tainaron, ζ 103†.

τηϋσίην, fem. acc., vain, useless, of journey, γ 316 and o 13.

τίεσκον, see τίω.

τίη, also τί ή, (and τί ή), quidn'am, why then, why pray? always in first or third foot follg. fem. caesura (exc. o 326), Λ 407, π 421, Z 145, ρ 375; it occurs in Od. five times, in Il. twenty times; with δέ, Ξ 264; δή, M 310; after ἀλλά, P 97.

τιθαιβώσσουσι, lay up honey, ν 106.

τίθημι, τίθησθα, ησι, 3 pl. τιθεῖσι, inf. τιθήμεναι, part. τιθείς, έντες, ipf. τίθεσαν, fut. θήσω, εις, ει, etc., inf. σέμεναι, aor. ἔθηκα, ας, (εν), ἔθηχ' = ἔθηκε, καν, and θῆκα, κ(εν), καν, and θῆχ' = θῆκε; ἔθεσαν, θέσαν, subj. θείω, ῃς, ῃ, ομεν, and θήῃς, ῃ, θέωμεν, opt. θείην, ης, η, θεῖμεν, θεῖεν, imp. θές, inf. θεῖναι, θέμεν(αι), part. θέντες, θεῖσα; mid. pres. imp. τίθεσθ(ε), part. τιθήμενον, fut. θήσονται, aor. θήκατο, 2 aor. ἐθέμην, ἔθετο, θέτο, ἔθεσθε, θέσθ(ε), ἔθεντο, subj. θῆαι, opt. θεῖτο, imp. θέο, θέσθω, θέσθ(ε), inf. θέσθαι, part. θέμενος, η; also as if from τιθέω, pres. τιθεῖ (v. l. τίθει), ipf. (ἐ)τίθει, (condere, Ger. thun, Eng. do).—I. act., (1) ponere, collocare, set, put, place, lay, θεμείλια, M 29, followed by dat. without prep., or with ἐν, ἐπί, μετά, ἀμφί, ἀνά, ὑπό; by acc. with εἰς, ἀνά, ὑπό; by gen. with ἐπί; ἐν χείρεσσι, place in the hands or arms, A 45, 441; ἐπὶ γούνασι.— (2) metaphorical, put (into one's mind), suggest, bestow, τινὶ ἐν θυμῷ, ἐν στήθεσσι, ἐν φρεσί, in one's heart (ἔπος, μύθου τέλος, etc.) A 55.— (3) propose prizes in games, deposit gifts, statues in temple, etc.; bury, Ψ 83.—(4) make, bring to pass, cause, κακά, etc., Π 263, O 721; ἔριν μετά τισι, γ 136, cf. M 411; σῆμά τινι, give a sign, Θ 171; ἄλγεα, prepare woes for the Achaians, A 2; Π 96, bring light, i. e. rescue; σκέδασιν = σκεδαννύναι; put into a certain condition or state, constitute, make, αἰχμητήν, A 290; ἱέρειαν, ἄλοχον, λίθον, ν 156; with adj., render, Δ 363, Z 432, Φ 172; bury to half its length, X 490, λ 274, ψ 11.—II. mid. (1) put or place for one's self something of one's own, ἄορ, one's sword in its sheath; ἐν φρεσί, put into one's heart, consider by one's self; ἐλέγχεα ταῦτα, hold this as an insult to yourselves, φ 333; αἰδῶ ἐν στήθεσσι, N 121, O 561, 661.—(2) make or prepare for one's self, ἐπιγουνίδα; δαῖτα, δόρπον, I 88; μάχην, ἀγορήν, πόνον, Ω 402; θυμὸν ἄγριον, make one's temper savage, I 629; τινὰ γυναῖκα, take as one's wife.

τιθήνη, ης, ας, fem., (θῆσθαι), nurse, Z 389. (Il.)

τίθησθα, see τίθημι.

Τιθωνός, οῖο, son of Laomedon, carried away by Eos, Υ 237, Λ 1, ε 1.

τίκτω, τΙκτει, ipf. ἔτικτον, ε(ν), τίκτε, fut. τέξεις, aor. (ἔ)τέκον, τέκες, (εν), ομεν; ῃ, ωνι; οι, οιεν; ἔειν; ὤν, οὖσα, mid. fut. τέξεσθαι, aor. τέκεθ' = τέκετ(ο), ἔσθαι, (τέκτων, τεχ-, τευχ-), gignere and parĕre, beget and bring forth, of divinity, man and beast, Τ 413, Ζ 206, Π 34, π 119.

τίλλω, ipf. τΙλλε, ον, mid. τιλλέσθην, οντο, pluck out, hair; mid., pluck out one's hair; τινά, tear one's hair in sorrow for, Ω 711.

τιμάω, τιμᾷ, ῶσι, τίμα, ῶν, ῶσαι, ipf. ἐτίμα, fut. τιμήσουσι, aor. τιμήσῃς, ῃ, ἤσομεν, τίμησον, ἤσαι, ἤσας, fut. mid. τι,ήσεσθαι, aor. ἐτιμήσασθ(ε), τιμήσαντο, pf. pass. τετίμηται, ἡμέσθα, ἦσθαι, (τιμή), honor, τινά, τινι, with or by any thing; pf. pass. τιμῆς, be deemed worthy of honor, Ψ 649; Ι 608, I deem myself to have been (enough) honored by the decree of Zeus.

τῑμή, ῆς, ῇ, ἤν, fem., (τίω), valuation, (1) pena'ty, (ἀπο)τίνειν τινί, pay (back) a penalty to one; ἄρνυσθαι, exact satisfaction for some one, Α 159; then punishment, ξ 70.—(2) honor, dignity, prerogative, ε 335, λ 338, Δ 410.

τῑμήεις, τιμῆς, ἤεντος, α, and τιμήεντα, τιμήεσσα, comp. τιμηέστερος, sup. τιμηέστατον, (τιμή), (1) precious, λ 327, δ 614. — (2) highly honored, σ 161.

τΙμῖος (τιμή), honored, κ 38†.

τΙνάσσων, οντας, ipf. τΙνασσε, aor. ἐτίναξε(ν), τΙνάξῃ, pass. prs. τινάσσεται, ipf. τινάσσετο, aor. 3 pl. τίναχθεν, mid. aor. 3 du. τιναξάσθην, swing, shake, brandish, weapons, etc.; Γ 385, plucked her garment; θρόνον, overthrow; scatter, ε 368; ἐκ, elisi sunt, were dashed out, Π 348; mid., β 151, shook their wings.

τΙνῦται, νσθον, ὑμενος, (τίω), punish, τινά, λώβην, chastise for insolence, ω 326.

τίνειν, ων, fut. τίσω, aor. ἐτῑσ(εν), τίσειαν, τῖσον, τῖσαι, etc., pay a penalty, τιμήν τινι; τί, atone for something with one's life, χ 218; in good signif. pay a debt, discharge obligation, ζωάγρια, ransom; reward, ξ 166; mid. fut. τίσομαι, aor. ἐτισάμην, τίσαιο, 3 pl. τισαίατο, indemnify one's self, ν 15;

exact satisfaction, (1) τινά, from a person, Γ 28, Β 743.—(2) τί, for a thing, Τ 208, ω 470.—(3) τινά τινος, of a person for a thing, γ 206; τινά τι, ο 236.

τίπτε, also τίπτ' (τίφθ' before rough breathing), from τί ποτε, quidnam, why pray? at beginning of verse or after voc.; in fifth foot only in phrase τίπτε δὲ σὲ χρεώ; with αὖτε, Α 202, λ 93; οὕτως, Δ 243; (τόσσον) ὧδε (ι 403), Λ 656; usually with verbs of motion, Ζ 254, Ο 90; in salutation, ε 87, λ 474.

Τίρυνς, νθος, fem., ancient seat of kings of Argos, of Perseus, with Cyclopean walls, Β 559†.

τίς, τέο, τεῦ, τίνα, τίνες, τέων [monosyll., ζ 119], ntr. τί, (quis), who? interrogative pron. τίς δ' οὗτος, ν 380; οἴδεν εἰ (κε), β 332; τίς πόθεν εἰς ἀνδρῶν, who art thou, and from where in the world dost thou come? α 170; ἐς τί, how long? τί μοι ἀρωγῆς, what befalls me in consequence of succor rendered? used with ἄν in expression of a wish, Κ 303; rarely in indirect question, ο 423. τί; like quid? how? why? Δ 371, Κ 159, α 62; wherefore? Λ 606, Υ 87, φ 333.

τίς, τί, indef. pron. enclitic, τεῦ, τέο, τινί τεω τῳ, τινά, τί, τινέ, τινάς, ntr. ἄσσα, τ 218 = some one, something, quidam, quoddam; many a one, every one, τ 265, Β 388, 355; also to indirectly designate a certain person, Α 289; often to be supplied, as suggested by an oblique case, e. g. τινά, suggested by οἱ, α 392; joined with adjs. it makes them less precise, a certain kind of, a real, and has often a sarcastic force, σ 382; ntr. τί, like aliquid, somewhat, in a degree, hence οὔ τι, nequaquam, by no means; οὐδέ τι, and nothing whatever, γ 184.

τΙσις, ιν, fem., (τίω), recompense, β 76; punishment, vengeance, with gen. for τινός (ἐκ τινος, proceeding from, at the hands of).

τΙτά (τίω) ἔργα, vengeance, Ω 213, better ἄντιτα.

τΙταίνετον, ων, ipf. ἐτίταινε, aor. τιτήνας, (τανύω, τείνω), tendo, bend, draw, the bow; stretch out, the arms; τράπεζαν, spread the table; τάλαντα, poise the balances; elsewh. draw chariot, plough; mid. τιταίνοιτο,-όμε-

νος, ἐτιταίνετο, arcum suum tendere; φ 259, string for one's self the
bow; stretch one's self in running, go
at full speed; πτερύγεσσιν, stretching
out their wings.

Τῖτᾰνος, οιο, place (mountain or
town) in Thessaly, B 735†.

Τῖτᾰρήσιος, river in Thessaly rising
in Olympos, later Europos, a branch
of the Peneios, B 751†.

Τιτῆνες, οἱ, Titans, sons of Uranos
and Gaia; cast down from heaven,
which they recovered by the help of
Kronos, who cast them again into
Tartaros, and ruled alone until his son
Zeus, aided by Gaia, overpowered and
shut him up in turn with the Titans,
Ξ 279, ὑποταρτάριοι; οὐρανίωνες, E
898.

τιτρώσκω, see τρώω.

Τῖτυός, son of Gaia, covering in
Hades nine plethra of space with his
prostrate body, while vultures devour
his liver, λ 576–580, η 324.

τῖτύσκεται, ὅμενος, οι, ων, η, αι,
ipf. τιτύσκετο, (τόξον, τυχεῖν), make
ready, πῦρ; ἵππους ὑπ' ὄχεσφι, couple,
put to; usually aim, of weapons (dat.),
ἄντα, straight before one; τινός, at
some one; with φρεσίν, purpose, design; θ 556, speeding thither.

τίφθ' = τίπτε.

τίω, prs. and ipf. act. and mid. [pres.
ῑ exc. I 238, ξ 84, ο 543, Θ 540; ipf. ῑ
exc. N 176, Ο 551, α 432, τ 247, Ψ
705, so also τίεσκον, but τίεσκεν, N
461, τῖεσκετο, Δ 46]. fut. τίσω, aor.
ἔτῖσε, pf. part. τετῑμένος, ον, etc., value,
aestimare, δυωδεκάβοιον, at twelve
steers' worth; ἐν καρὸς αἴσῃ, at a
hair's worth; otherwise always in
signif., honor, magni aestimare,
θεὸν ὥς, etc.

τλήμων, μονα, ες, (τλῆναι), enduring,
patient, θυμόν; impudent, Φ 430.

τλῆναι (ΤΑΛ, ΤΕΛ, tolero), fut.
τλήσομ(αι), 1 aor. ἐτάλασσα, ταλάσσῃς, ῃ, aor. sync. ἔτλην, ης, η = τλῆ,
τλῆμεν, ἔτλητε, ἔτλαν; τλαίην, ης, η,
τλαῖεν, τλῆθι, τλήτω, τλῆτε; pf. τέτλη-
κας, εν, 1 pl. τέτλαμεν, τέτλᾰθι, ἄτω,
αίη, ἄμεν(αι), τετλᾰότι, ες, τετληυῖα,
suffer, undergo, τί; τινά, resist; part.
pf., steadfast, enduring, E 873; 1 aor.
animum inducere, venture upon,
presume, Ο 164, N 829; prevail upon

one's self, have the heart, courage, heart-
lessness, P 166.

Τληπόλεμος, ου, (1) son of Herakles and of Astyochia, fugitive on account of involuntary murder, found
safety in Rhodos, where he became
king, B 653, 657, 661, E 628, 631, 632,
648, 656, 660, 668.—(2) son of Damastor, slain by Patroklos, Π 416.

τλητόν (τλῆναι), enduring, Ω 49†.

τμήγω, aor. pass. 3 pl. τμάγεν,
(τέμνω), discesserunt, they dispersed,
Π 374.

τμήδην, adv., (τέμνω), so as to cut or
graze, H 262†.

Τμῶλος, mountain in Lydia, near
Sardes, B 866, Υ 385.

τό, therefore, Γ 176, M 9, θ 332;
H 239, τό μοι ἐστι, therefore can I —.
τόθι, adv., ibi, there, ο 239†.

I. τοί, nom. plur. masc. from demon-
strat. ὁ and from relat. ὅ.

II. τοί = σοί, tibi; also as unem-
phatic ethical dat., τ 599, see σύ.

III. τοί (from ethical dat. τοί, A
419, π 187), enclitic particle serving
to strengthen an assertion (also in
negative sentences) expressing confidence: I assure you, verily, A 419, 426,
ο 72, π 187 (A 298); expressing emotion: let me tell you, yet verily, B 298,
E 873, X 488, σ 230 (B 361, Γ 65);
expressing conviction, you may be
sure, certainly, no doubt, I 654, N 115,
O 45 (Δ 29, Z 335, α 203); see also
ἤτοι and μέν. (N 267, καί belongs to
ἐμοί; is not καίτοι.)

IV. τοιγάρ (τοί = τῷ), so then, accordingly, always at beginning of a
clause, with reference to an exhortation, with ἐγώ, (a) beginning a speech,
A 76, K 413, α 179; (b) preceding an
action, δ 612, η 28, θ 402; a second
τοί is tibi, α 214.

τοῖος, ου, ον, οι, ους, τοίη. ην, αι,
τοῖον, τοῖ(α), (το-), talis, of such a
kind, such, corresponding to rel. οἷος,
Σ 105, α 257, δ 345, 421, λ 499 (also
to ὁποῖος, ρ 421; to ὅς, β 286; to
ὅπως, π 208); τεύχεσι, such in his
weapons; χεῖρας, in his hands; with
inf., capable, able; with adjs., so really,
so very, just, α 209, cf. λ 135, β 286;
ntr. τοῖον, so, so very, γ 321, X 241,
Ψ 246 (elsewh. only Od.).

τοιόσδε, ουδ(ε), ῃδ(ε), ονδε, άδε, like

τοῖος, talis, *such*, with reference to something near, under one's eyes; corresponds to οἷος, followed by acc. of that in respect to which, ρ 313; ntr. τοιόνδε, *so good, so bad;* with inf., Z 463.

τοιοῦτος, ούτου, οὖτον, οὖτοι, ούτων, τοιαύτη, τοιαῦτα = τοῖος, talis, with stronger demonstrative sense, *of such a kind,* δ 650; 'Αχαιῶν, P 643; tam praestantes, *so excellent,* B 372, Π 847; tam prava, nefaria, *so heinous things,* Ψ 494, χ 315.

τοῖσδεσ(σ)ι, see ὅδε.

τοῖχος, τοίχου, ψ, ον, οι, ων, ους, murus, *wall of a house* or *court,* Π 212, β 342, χ 126; *sides of a ship,* μ 420, O 382.

τοκάδες, fem., (τίκτω), σύες, (swine), *having just brought forth,* ξ 16†.

τοκῆε, du., pl. τοκῆες, ήων, έων, εὖσι(ν), ῆας, (τίκτω), *parents,* α 170; ἐκ — εἶναι, Ω 387; *ancestors,* δ 596, η 54.

τόκος, οιο, ον, masc., (τεκεῖν), (1) partus, *bringing forth, delivery,* T 119, P 5.—(2) proles, *offspring,* O 141; *young,* ο 175.

τολμάω, ipf. ἐτόλμας, α, τόλμων, fut. τολμήσεις, aor. τόλμησεν, σειεν, σαντα, (τλῆναι, tolero), *endure,* with part., ω 162; *be bold,* K 232, E 670; *dare,* Θ 424, M 51.

τολμήεις, ήεντι, (τόλμη), *daring,* K 205; *enduring, steadfast,* ρ 284.

τολύπεύω, ειν, aor. τολύπευσα, σε(ν), prop. *wind up as a ball* (τολύπη), hence *contrive,* δόλους; *achieve, finish,* ω 95, Ω 7.

τομήν, τήν, (τέμνω), *end left after cutting, stump,* A 235†.

τοξάζεαι, 2 sing. prs., inf. εσθαι, opt. οἵμεθ(α), 3 pl. οίατο, fut. άσσεται, aor. opt. άσσαιτο, (τόξον), *shoot with bow at,* τινός, θ 218.

τοξευτῆσι, τοῖς, (τοξεύω), sagittariis, *bowmen, archers,* Ψ 850†.

τοξεύειν (τόξον), sagittas mittere, *shoot,* Ψ 855†.

τόξον, ον, ψ, (α), ων, οισι(ν), ntr., (τιτύσκομαι, root τυκ, τευχ, τεχ-), *bow,* comm. pl. even of a single bow, either as including entire shooting apparatus, Φ 502, (O 709, sagittarum), or as in its nature pl., consisting of two pieces of horn (of the wild goat, Δ

109) fastened to a middle piece (πῆχυς). The string (νευρή) was fastened at one end of the bow, and had to have the loop at its other end slipped over the other pointed tip (κορώνη) before shooting. Cut No. 37 illustrates the method of stringing the bow ([ἐν] τανύειν); cuts Nos. 67, 96, 97, 111, 133 illustrate the method of shooting (τιταίνειν, (ἀν)ἕλκειν). Cuts Nos. 27, 130 represent the case for the bow. Archers were little esteemed (in comparison with πρόμαχοι), see κέραι ἀγλαέ, Λ 385, ροξότα. — τόξων, also artis sagittariae, *archery,* B 718, cf. 827.

τοξοσύνη, τῇ, (τόξον), *archery,* N 314†.

τοξότα, voc., nom. ότης, (τόξον), *archer,* contemptuously, Λ 385†.

τοξο-φόρῳ, τῇ, (φέρω), *bow-bearing,* epithet of Artemis, Φ 483†.

τοπρίν, see πρίν.

τοπρόσθεν, see πρόσθεν.

τοπρῶτον, see πρῶτον.

τορέω? (τετραίνω), ἔτορε, aor., *pierce,* Λ 236†.

τορνόω, mid. aor. τορνώσαντο, subj. τορνώσεται, (τόρνος), *round off,* Ψ 255, ε 249.

τός, τοί, see ὁ and ὅς.

τόσ(σ)ος, σ(σ)ον, τόσσοι, ων, ους, η, ης, ην, ροι, τόσσας, τόσ(σ)ον, τόσ(σα), also τόσ(σ)ονδε, σσηνδε, σσαδε, and τοσ(σ)οῦτον, τοσαῦτ(α), tantus, *so great, so long, so wide,* etc., pl. tot, *so many;* cf. τρὶς τόσοι; ntr. used alone, *so much, so very,* A 64, Θ 421; with ὅσσον, Φ 370; with ἀλλά, ο 405; so also the forms with -δε, X 41; and -οῦτον, Ψ 476.

τοσσάκι, τοσσάχ' before rough breathing, (τόσος), toties, *so often,* corresponding to ὁσσάκι, quoties, as often, Φ 268.

τόσσος, τοσσοῦτον, see τόσ(σ)ος.

τότε, *at that time, then;* τῶν τότε, of those who *then* lived; freq. in apodosis in phrases, καὶ τότε δή, ῥα, ἔπειτα; esp. after protasis with ὅτε, ὁπότε, ἧμος, ἐπεί, εἰ, etc.; τότε μοι χάνοι εὐρεῖα χθών, Δ 182.

τοτέ = τότε, *at another time, anon,* Λ 63; usually in answering clauses, τ. μὲν—τ. δέ, modo—modo, *now—then.* (Od.)

τοῦ=gen. (1) of ὁ.—(2) of ὅς.—(3)
=τίνος; **τοῦ**, encl.=τινός.

τοὔνεκα=τοῦ ἕνεκα, on this account,
therefore, A 291, γ 15.

τοὔνομα=τὸ ὄνομα.

τόφρα, adv., so long, in apodosis following ὄφρα, ἕως, ὅτε, πρίν, εὖτε, with
δέ, Δ 221; up to the time (when), A
509; meanwhile, N 83, μ 166.

τράγους, τούς, goats, ι 239†.

τράπεζα, ης, ῃ, αν, αι, ας, (τετρά-
πεδϳα, four-footed), table, esp. eating-
table; ξεινίη, hospitable board, ξ 158;
guests had, as a rule, each his own
table, α 111, e. g. the suitors use
their tables as shields against Odysseus's arrows; the tables were four-
cornered and low, χ 84.

τράπεζῆες, ῆας, pl. from -εύς, κύνες,
dogs fed from their master's table, Ψ
173, X 69, ρ 309.

τραπείομεν, subj. 2 aor. pass. from
τέρπω.

τράπέουσι, pres., (τρέπω, torcu-
lar), tread, press, η 125†.

τραφέμεν, **τράφεν**, see τρέφω.

τραφερήν, firm earth, Ξ 308 and υ
98.

τρεῖς, tres, three, I 144, δ 409, see
σύντρεις.

τρέμε, ipf., tremebat; ὑπὸ δ' ἔτρε-
με, ον, he trembled in (all) his limbs, K
390.

τρέπω, imp. **τρέπε**, ipf. τρέπε(ν), 1 aor.
(ἔ)τρέψε(ν), opt. ψειε, part. ψας, 2 aor.
(ἔ)τράπε(ν), (torqueo), turn, bend, e. g.
κεφαλὴν πρός τι, ν 29; ὄσσε ἔς τι, N
7; ἀπό τινος, Π 645; πάλιν, retro
flectere, Υ 439, ὄσσε, look away from,
avert; ἵππους, turn about, Θ 432; guide,
νόον; θυμὸν κατὰ πληθύν, turn his
fury against the mass; ὁμόσε, M 24;
with inf., M 32; φύγαδε (ἵππους, Θ
157), betake one's self to flight, Π 657;
τινὰ εἰς εὐνήν, conduct to bed; mid.
pass. pres. **τρέπεται**, 1 aor. τρεψάμε-
νοι, 2 aor. τράπεθ' = (ἐ)τράπετ(ο), τρά-
ποντο, ὠνται, pf. part. τετραμμένος,
ον, οι, αι, imp. τετράφθω, plupf. τέ-
ραπτο, 3 pl. τετράφαθ' = φατο, aor.
pass. τραφθῆναι, turn, direct one's self,
ἰθύς, straight forward; πρὸς (ἰθύ) οἱ,
right toward him, Ξ 403; ἐπὶ οἱ,
toward him, N 542; to something,
ἔς τι; πάλιν τινός, away from one,
Ω 138, Φ 468; ἑκάς τινος, far from:

ἀν' Ἑλλάδα, versari per Grae-
ciam, wander up and down through
Greece; change, χρώς; νόος, with inf.,
δ 260.

τρέφω, **τρέφει**, ipf. ἔτρεφον, ες, ε(ν),
τρέφον, ε, ον, 1 aor. ἔθρεψε, θρέψ(εν), 2
aor. ἔτραφ(ε), τράφ(ε), B 661, Φ 279, du.
ἐτραφέτην, inf. τραφέμεν, transitive only
in Ψ 90; pf. τέτροφε, intr. 1 aor. mid.
θρέψαιο, aor. pass. τράφη (ἐτράφημεν,
Ψ 84, better read τράφομέν περ), 3
pl. τράφεν, A 251, Ψ 348, (τέρπω), feed,
nourish, of animals, X 69; of plants,
let grow, tend, produce, χαίτην, ἀλοι-
φήν, ἄγρια, φάρμακα; curdle, γάλα; of
children, educate, rear; πῆμα γενέσθαι,
with dat., rear to become a curse to
some one, X 421; A 414, θρέψαιο, rear
for one's self; pass. with pf. and 2 aor.
act., thicken, congeal, stick firmly to, ψ
237; wax, grow up, E 555, ξ 201.

τρέχει, aor. iter. θρέξασκον, 2 aor.
ἔδραμον, (ε), run, of living beings; of
auger, revolve, ι 386.

τρέω, **τρεῖ**, εῖτ(ε), εῖν, ipf. τρέε, 1 aor.
ἔτρεσε, σαν, and τρέσσε, σσαν, αι, ἄν-
ρων, (τρέρων, Trasimenus, terror),
in aor., flee, ζ 138; E 256, τρεῖν μ' οὐκ
ἰᾷ Παλλὰς Ἀθήνη; elsewh. tremble, be
afraid, P 332; dread, with acc., Λ 554,
P 663. (Il.)

τρήρωνα, ες, ωσι, (τρεῖν), pavidam,
trembling, only of doves, X 140.

τρητοῖο, οἷσι(ν), from (τιτράω), perforated, of mooring-stones, pierced with
holes for attaching the cable; λεχέεσσι,
perforated with holes for the bed-cords,
Ω 720.

Τρηχίν, ῖνα, town in Thessaly, B
682†.

Τρῆχος, warrior from Aitolia, slain
by Hektor, E 706†.

τρηχύς, ύν, εῖ(α), εἴης, εἴαν, (τετρήχει), asper, rough, (1) rugged, jagged,
λίθος, E 308.—(2) stony, rocky, ἀταρ-
πόν, ἀκτήν, Ἑλικῶνα, Ἰθάκην, ξ 1.

τρίαιναν, τήν, trident, with which
Poseidon stirs up the sea, and agitates
the earth by earthquakes, M 27, δ
506.

τριβέμεναι, inf. pres., aor. τρῖψαι,
pass. pres. τρίβεσθε, (τείρω, tero),
properly rub, hence thresh, which was
done after the Egyptian and Oriental
manner represented in the following
cut; rub around in, or perhaps plunge

into, ι 333; pass., *wear one's self out*, Ψ 735.

τρί-γληνα (γλήνη), epith. of ear-rings, *with three drops* or *pearls* (lit. eyeballs), Ξ 183 and σ 297. (See cut from ancient Greek coin.)

τρι-γλώχῖνι, dat., (γλωχίν, γλῶσσα), *three-barbed*, epith. of arrow, E 393 and Λ 507.

τρί-ετες, ntr. as adv., (Ϝέτος, ἔτος), *three years long*, β 106. (Od.)

τρίζουσαι, pf. τετριγῶτας, υἷα, υἷαι, plupf. τετρίγει, (stridere, strix), *twitter*, B 314; *squeak*, of birds and bats, ω 5, 7, 9; *gibber*, of souls of departed; of wrestlers' backs, *crack*, Ψ 714.

τριήκοντα, triginta, *thirty*, B 516. (B.)

τριηκόσιοι, κοσίοισιν, κόσι(α), trecenti, *three hundred*, ν 390 and Λ 696.

Τρίκ(κ)η, city in Thessaly, on river Peneios, B 729, Δ 202.

τρί-λλιστος (λίτομαι), *thrice-earnestly prayed for*, Θ 488†.

τρί-πλᾰκᾰ, τήν, *threefold*, Σ 480†.

τρι-πλῆ, *thrice over*, A 128†.

τρί-πολον (colere), *thrice ploughed*, Σ 542, ε 127.

τρί-πος X 164, τρί-πους, ποδος, δι, δα, δες, δων, tripus, *tripod*, a three-footed kettle for warming water, Ψ 702; also served for mixing wine in, and, being often beautifully finished, as prize in gymnastic contests. The Delphic tripod is a favorite subject of representation on ancient reliefs, from one of which the above cut is taken.

τρί-πτυχος, *triple, consisting of three layers*; meaning, as applied to τρυφάλεια, q. v., not altogether clear, Λ 353†.

τρίς, ter, *thrice*, A 213, γ 245; in Homer already a sacred number, cf. τρίλλιστος; τρὶς μάκαρες, *thrice-blessed*, ζ 154.

τρισ-καί-δεκᾰ, tredecim, *thirteen*, E 387; -και-δέκατον, τῃ, tertium decimum, K 495.

τρι-στοιχί, *in three rows*, K 473†.

τρί-στοιχοι, *in three rows*, μ 91†.

τρισ-χίλιαι, *three thousand*, Ψ 221†.

τρίτᾰτος, ψ, ον, οισι, η, ῃ, ῃν, tertius, *third*, B 565, O 195, δ 97.

Τριτο-γένεια, epith. of Athena, also as proper name, Θ 39, X 183, Δ 515, γ 378; explained by old commentators as meaning *born at the lake Tritonis*, in Libya.

τρίτος, ψ, ον, ων, η, ης, *third*, M 95; τὸ τρίτον, Γ 225, *for the third time*, elsewh. *in the third place*.

τρί-χα, *threefold, in three parts*; τρ. νυκτὸς ἔην, *a third of the night remained*, 'twas in the third watch, μ 312. (Od.)

τρίχ-άϊκες (θρίξ, άίσσω), *with waving, flowing plume*, τ 177†.

τρίχες, pl. from θρίξ.

τριχθά, *in three parts*, B 668, ι 71.

Τροιζήν, ῆνος, fem., town in Argolis, near the shore of Saronic gulf, B 561†.

Τροίζηνος, son of Keas, father of Euphemos, B 847†.

Τροίη, fem., (1) country of Trojans, Trojan plain, Troad, B 162.—(2) its chief town, otherwise Ἴλιος, A 129. [When the word is used to designate the *Troad*, its first syllable occurs in arsis of 1st foot five times, in thesis of 1st foot ten times, in thesis of 2d foot fifty-three times, of 3d nine times, of 4th ten times ; when designating the *city*, the 1st syllable stands in thesis of 2d foot ten times, of 3d foot four times.]

Τροίηθε(ν), *from Troja*, Ω 492, γ 257.

Τροίηνδ(ε), *to Troja*, Η 390, Ω 764, γ 268.

τρομέω, **τρομέεις**, *έουσι*, ipf. *ἐτρόμεον*, mid. pres. *ἐοίατο*, *ἐεσθαι*, ipf. *τρομέοντο*, *tremble*, Κ 10, Ο 627, *φρένα*, animo pavere ; *τινά*, *τί*, *dread*, π 446, υ 215; so also mid., also with *φρένες*, *θυμῷ*.

τρόμος, masc., (*τρέμω*), *tremor*, Γ 34 ; *shudder*, sickening, ω 49.

τρόπεον, 3 pl. ipf., (*τρέπω*), *were turning about*, Σ 224†.

τροπαί, pl. fem., (*τρόπος*), *ἠελίοιο*, ο 404†, *turning-places*, *tropics* (yet not in our sense of the word), places where the sun at evening turns about his steeds to return during the night to the east, ready to begin with morning a new day.

τρόπις, **τρόπιος**, *ιν*, fem., (*τρόπος*), *keel*, ε 130. (Od.) (See cut under *δρύοχους, a.*)

τροπός, **τροποῖς**, masc., (*τρέπω*), *thongs* or *straps*, by means of which the oars were attached to the thole-pins, *κληῖδες* (see cut No. 35, *d*), so as to play freely about them, δ 782 and θ 53. A later different arrangement is illustrated in the following cut, and in No. 41.

τροφόεντα, *swelling*, v. l. γ 290.

τροφός, *οῦ*, *όν*, fem., (*τρέφω*), *nurse*, ρ 31, τ 15.

τροχάω, part. pres. *τροχόωντα*, (*τρόχος*), *ἅμα*, *running about after me*, ο 451†.

τροχός, **τροχοῦ**, *όν*, (*τρέχω*), *wheel* (also *κύκλος, a*), Ζ 42 ; *potter's wheel*, Σ 600 ; *round cake of wax* or *tallow*, μ 173, φ 178.

τρυγάω, 3 pl. **τρυγόωσιν**, opt. *τρυγόῳεν*, *gather*, *gather the vintage*, η 124, Σ 566.

τρύζητε, subj. pres., *gossip before me, keep dinning into my ears*, Ι 311†.

τρύπανῳ, *τῷ*, ntr., (*τρυπάω*), *auger*, *drill*, used by carpenters in boring wood, and often set in motion by a bow and string, as with us at the present day, ι 385†. (The cut is from an ancient Egyptian representation.)

τρυπῶ (*τρύπη*, *τείρω*), *bore*, ι 384†.

τρυφάλεια, *ης*, *ῃ*, *αν*, *αι*, *ῶν*, (*τρύω*, *φάλος*), *helmet with crest perforated* to conveniently attach the horse-hair

τροφέω, ipf. mid. **τροφέοντο**, *were swelling*, γ 290†.

τρόφι, ntr., corresponding to *τρόφις*, (*τρέφω*), *swollen, huge, κῦμα*, Λ 307†.

plumes, Γ 376. (Cf. cut on following page and No. 20.)

τρύφος, *τό*, (*θρύπτω*), *fragment*, cf. rupes, from rumpo, δ 508†.

τρύχουσι, fut. τρύξοντα, pass. pres. τρυχώμεθα, όμενος, (τρύω), impover-ished, a 288, κ 177; consume, οἶκον, property.

Τρῳαί, Τρῳάς, see Τρῳός.

τρώγειν, feed upon, browse, ζ 90†.

Τρῶες, ωων, ωσί, and εσσι(ν), inhab-itants of Ilios and of the plain of Troas, Τρώων πόλις = Ἴλιος; but Α 164, πτο-λίεθρον, one of the Trojan cities.

Τρωιάς, άδος, see Τρώιος.

Τρωικός, κόν, esp. πεδίον, the plain of Troja, between Ilios and the sea, Ρ 724, Κ 11.

Τρωίλος, son of Priamos and He-kabe, Ω 257†.

τρώκτης, αι, masc., (τρώγω?), de-ceiver, knave, ξ 289 and ο 415.

Τρῳός, adj., (1) from Τρώς, belong-ing to Tros, son of Erichthonios, Π 393, Ψ 291.—(2) from Τρῶες, belong-ing to the Trojans, Trojan, fem. Τρῳαί, ῇσιν, Ρ 127, Ε 461; but freq. Τρῳαί, Γ 384, Χ 430, 57, Ζ 380, δ 259 = Τρῳ-άδες, Trojan women, Ζ 442, Ι 139, Ω 704; gen. also Τρωϊάδων, Σ 122; exc. ν 263, where it is adj. to ἠίδος.

τρωπάω, τρωπῶσα, (τρέπω), φωνήν, change her note, τ 521; mid. τρωπᾶσθαι and -ῶντο, ipf., turn one's self, πάλιν, back, about; φόβονδε = φεύγειν.

Τρώς, ωός, (1) Tros, son of Erich-thonios, father of Ilos, Assarakos, Ganymedes, Ε 265 sq., Υ 230 sq.—(2) son of Alastor, slain by Achilleus, Υ 463.

τρώσεσθαι, τρώσῃς, see τρώω.

τρωτός, verbal adjective from τρώω, vulnerable, Φ 568†.

τρωχάω, only τρωχῶσι, ipf. τρώ-χων, (τρέχω), run, Χ 163, ζ 318.

τρώω, τρώει, (τορέω), sting, madden, φ 293; aor. subj. τρώσῃ, ητι, wound, fut. mid. τρώσεσθαι, to be wounded.

τυγχάνω, ipf. τύγχανε, fut. τεύξῃ εσθαι, aor. ἔτυχες, τύχε, ωμι, ῃς, ῃσι, ῃ, οιμι, οις, ὤν and 1 aor. ἐτύχησε(ν), τύχησε, ήσας, pf. τετύχηκε, κώς, (τυκ, τύξον, τεκ, τέχνη), (1) τινός, hit, (a) with weapon or missile; freq. τυχών, ήσας, with βάλλειν, οὖτα, νύξε, where the acc. is in each case to be construed with finite verb; δῶκε, φ 13; also κατά with acc.; (b) general sense, happen, chance, Θ 430; (c) τινός, come upon, chance upon some person or thing, and hence gain, obtain, ο 158.—(2) happen to be, be by chance, Λ 116, μ 106; τετυχηκώς, happening to be, lying, Ρ 748, κ 88; often with part. which in English becomes the principal verb, while the form of τυγχάνω is rendered by an adverb, by chance, just, etc.; ἐτύχησε βαλών, he had just hit him, Ο 581; impers., contingit, fall to one's share, Λ 684.

Τυδεΐδης, son of Τυδεύς, ῆος, έος, acc. ῆ, Tydeus is son of Oineus, Ε 813; king in Kalydon in Aitolia, father of Diomedes, Ε 163, Ζ 96; fugitive on ac-count of his uncle's murder, he finds asylum in Argos with Adrestos, whose daughter Deipyle he marries; joins Polyneikes in the expedition against Thebes, where he is slain by Melanip-pos, Δ 393.

τυκτόν, ῷ, ἤν, ῷσι, (τεύχω), manu factus, well-made, well-wrought; δάπεδον, well-trodden; κακόν, a born plague.

τύμβῳ, ον, masc., (tumulus), funeral mound, piled up in conical form over the urn containing the ash-es of the deceased, and sometimes of enormous size, e. g. that of Aisyntes, identified with the mound now called Udschek Tepe, and 284 feet high, Δ 177, Η 336.

τυμβο-χόης, της, (χέω), the throwing up of a mound = funeral mound, Φ 323† (better so read than τυμβοχοῆ-σ(αι), for there is no analogy for the elision of αι).

Τυνδάρεος, Tyndareos, banished from Sparta, harbored in Aitolia by

Thestios, whose daughter Leda he weds, by Herakles he is reinstated in Sparta. —His children: Klytaimnestra, ω 199; Kastor and Polydeukes, λ 298 sq. (Helena, daughter of Zeus.)

τύνη = σύ.

τύπῇσι, ταῖς, (τύπτω), ictibus, blow, stroke, E 887†.

τύπτω, τύπτετε, ουσι, ε, ων, ipf. τύπτον, aor. τύψ(εν), ῃ, ον, ας, pass. prs. τυπτομένων, pf. τετυμμένω, aor. ἐτύπην, τυπείης, εἰς, strike, cut, thrust, wound, τινά, (on any part, τί, λαιμόν, or κατὰ γαστέρα), σχεδίην, in hand-to-hand encounter; fig. τὸν ἄχος κατὰ φρένα τύψε βαθεῖαν, sorrow struck deep into his soul, Τ 125; τύπη, with acc. ὅσσα, quot vulnera accepit. Freq. ἅλα τύπτον ἐρετμοῖς, they were beating (in time) the sea with their oars (see cut under ἰστίον, and No. 41); Ψ 754, trod in his (Ajax's) footsteps; λαίλαπι, lashing with the tempest.

τῦρός, τυροῦ, ῷ, όν, du. ώ, pl. ῶν,

masc., cheese, δ 88; αἴγειος, cheese of goat's milk, Λ 639.

Τυρώ, Tyro, daughter of Salmoneus, wife of Kretheus, β 120, λ 235; mother of Pelias and Neleus by Poseidon.

τυτθός, όν, ά, little, small, young, Χ 480 and α 435, little boy; with διατμήξας and κεάσαιμι, hew or split up small; ntr. as adv., a little, local with ὀπίσσω, μετόπισθεν, ἐδεύησεν, it lacked lütt'e, ι 540; modal: ἔτισεν, φθέγγεσθαι, low; temporal only Τ 335.

τυφλόν, blind, Ζ 139†.

Τυφωεύς, έος, έι Β 782, Typhoeus, a monster under whose form the operations of subterranean fire are symbolized.

τυχήσας, see τυγχάνω.

Τύχιος (τεύχω), from Hylai in Boiotia, Η 220†, the maker of Ajax's shield.

τῶ (τῷ), (1) then, α 239, γ 258, θ 467. — (2) therefore, θ 226, 548, ν 248, 331, ξ 67, π 445, σ 141, τ 259, Φ 190.

τώς = οὕτως, thus, Β 330, Γ 415, τ 234.

Υ.

Ὑάδες (ὕω), Hyades, seven stars in the head of the Bull, whose rising marks the beginning of the rainy season, Σ 486†. The popular etymology of the word derived it from ὗς, and the Romans taking up this derivation called them Suculae, Piglings.

ὑακινθίνῳ, hyacinthine-colored = dark-colored, black, ζ 231 and ψ 158. [ῠ]

ὑάκινθον, masc., Ξ 348†, hyacinth, not the same as ours, possibly the larkspur.

Ὑάμ-πολις, town on the river Kephisos in Phokis, Β 521†.

ὑβ-βάλλειν, see ὑπο-βάλλω.

ὑβρίζεις, ων, οντες, (ὕβρις), be insolent or arrogant, α 227; trans. τινά, insult, outrage, υ 370, Λ 695; λώβην, perpetrate wantonly, υ 170.

ὕβρις, ιος, ει, ιν, fem., (ὑπέρ), superbia, inso'ence, a:rogance, Α 203, 214, violence. (Od.)

ὑβρισταί, άων, ῇσι, masc., (ὑβρίζω), overbearing, violent, wicked persons, Ν 633. (Od.)

ὑγιής (vegetus), healthful, salutary, useful, Θ 524†.

ὑγρόν, ήν, ά, moist; also of ὕδωρ, δ 458, liquid; ἔλαιον, limpid, ζ 79; κέλευθα, watery ways = the sea; ὑγρήν, subst. the waters, opp. τραφερήν, Ξ 308, α 97, δ 709, ε 45; ntr. ἀέντες, humide flantes, blowing moist or rainy, ε 478.

ὑδᾰτο-τρεφέων, gen. pl. from -ής, (τρέφω), growing by the water, ρ 208†.

Ὕδη, town on Mount Tmolos in Lydia, later Sardes? Υ 385†. [ῠ]

ὑδραίνομαι, aor. part. **ὑδρηνᾰμένη,** (ὕδωρ), bathe, wash one's self, δ 750. (Od.)

ὑδρεύοντο, ipf., (ὕδωρ), were wont to draw water, ὅθεν, η 131; act. ὑδρευούσῃ, κ 105.

ὑδρηλοί (ὕδωρ), irrigui, moist, well-watered, λειμῶνες, meadows, ι 133†.

ὕδρου, του, (ὕδωρ), hydrae, water-snake, B 723†.

ὕδωρ, ατος, ι, τ(α), ntr., (udus, unda), water, ἁλμυρόν, salt water; μέλαν, of water of springs, rivers, and sea, when the surface is rippled, and thus, the reflection of the sun's rays being hindered, it assumes a dark color, δ 359; ὑγρόν, flowing, liquid; αἰενάοντα, never failing; ὑ. καὶ γαῖα γένοισθε, H 99, = become dust and ashes. [ῠ, in arsi ῡ.]

ὑετόν, τόν, (ὕω), shower, imbrem, M 133†.

υἱός (Gothic sunus, Ger. sohn), declined from three stems, ΥΙΟ-, οὗ, ᾧ, όν, έ, ὦν, οἷσι; ΥΙ-, gen. υἷος, υἱῖ, υἷα, du. υἷε; υἷες, υἱάσι, υἷας; ΥΙΕΥ-, gen. υἱέος, ἑϊ, ἑα, ἱες, ἑας, εἷς E 464, son, in pl. υἷες Ἀχαιῶν = Ἀχαιοί. [υἱός, όν, έ, in thesi often to be pronounced ἱῠός, όν, έ, Δ 473; voc. υἱέ with lengthened ε, Δ 338.]

υἱωνός, οἷο, οἱ, masc., (υἱός), grandson, B 666, ω 514.

ὑλαγμόν, τόν, (ὑλάω), barking, howling, Φ 575†. [ῠ]

Ὑλᾰκίδης, Κάστωρ, name invented for himself by Odysseus, ξ 204†.

ὑλᾰκόμωροι (ὑλάω), loud - barking, ξ 29 and π 4. [ῠ]

ὑλάκτει, εον, ipf., (ὑλακτέω, ὑλάω), bark, bay, Σ 586; κραδίη (growled with wrath), υ 13, 16. [ῠ]

ὑλάω, ὑλάει, ουσι, ipf. ὕλαον = ὑλάοντο, (ululare), bark, bay; τινά, bark at, π 5. (Od.) [ῠ]

ὕλη, ης, ῃ, ην, (for σύλη, solum, saltus?), (1) silva, wood, ι 234; felled timber, wood for burning; clump of trees, grove, ε 63; forest, freq.; foliage, ξ 353.—(2) stuff of which any thing is made, raw material (willow withes), ε 257. [ῠ]

Ὕλη, town in Boiotia, E 708, H 221, B 500.

ὑλήεις, εντι, τα = ὑλήενθ', ἥεσσα, ης, ῃ, αν, (ὕλη), wooded, α 186; as comm. gender, α 246.

Ὕλλος, branch of the Hermos in Lydia, Υ 392†.

ὑλο-τόμοι, ους, (τομή), cutting or felling wood, axe, Ψ 114; woodmen, Ψ 123. [ῠ]

ὑμεῖς, εἰων, ὑμέων, with synizesis; ὑμῖν, ὕμιν, (ὑμίν), ὑμέας dissyll., parallel forms ὕμμες, ὕμμ(ιν), acc. ὕμμε, vos, vestri, etc. [ῠ]

ὑμέναιος, wedding song, bridal song, πολύς, varied, Σ 493†. [ῠ]

ὑμέτερος, ου, ον, ων, οισι(ν), ους; ης, ῃ, ῃσι, ον, (Ψ 86, ὁνδε, to your house), vester, your, yours, etc., also joined with αὐτῶν, ipsorum, yourselves; ἑκάστου, of each one of you, P 226. [ῠ]

ὕμμε, ες, ι, see ὑμεῖς.

ὕμνον, τόν, (ὑφή), strain, melody, θ 429†.

ὑμός, only the forms, ὑμή, N 815; ὑμήν, E 489; ὑμά, α 375, your. [ῠ]

ὑπ-αγω, ε, ipf., also in tmesi, Ψ 300; as also aor., Ψ 294, ἤγαγεν, bring or lead under; ζυγόν, under the yoke, also with simple verb, yoke, put to; Λ 163, ἐκ—, withdraw.

ὑπ-αείδω, only ipf. ὑπὸ ἄειδεν, and aor. ἄεισεν, accompany with voice, Σ 570; sang under his hand, as he drew and let go of the bow-string, φ 411.

ὑπαί, see ὑπό.

ὕπαιθα, adv., out from under, sidewise, O 520; τινός, sidewise away, at one's side, Σ 421. [ῠ]

ὑπ-αΐξει, fut., (from ἀΐσσω), φρῖχ' = φρίκα, shall dart up under the surface-ripple, Φ 126; aor. part. ἀΐξας βωμοῦ, shooting out from under the altar, B 310.

ὑπ-ακούει, aor. ἄκουσεν, σαι, give ear to, ξ 485; reply, κ 83, δ 283; Θ 4, ὑπὸ ἄκουον, auscultabant; π 10, ποδῶν ὕπο, (proceeding) from the feet I hear a noise = I hear footsteps.

ὑπ-αλευάμενος, aor. part., (ἀλεύω) evitans, avoiding, evading, o 275†.

ὑπ-ἄλυξις, ιν, fem., (ἀλύσκω), escape, X 270 and ψ 287.

ὑπ-ἀλύσκω, aor. ὑπάλυξε(ν), ύξαι, ας, (ἀλεύω), escape, avoid, Κῆρας; in tmesi, N 395, ψ 332; χρείως, evade (the payment) of his debt, θ 355.

ὑπ-αντίἄσας, part. aor., (ἀντιάω), obviam factus, having placed himself (before him) for his defense, Z 17†.

ὕπαρ, ntr., actuality, real appearance, τ 547 and υ 90. [ῠ]

ὑπ-άρχω, aor. subj. ὑπάρξῃ, (so right requires), if one have once made a beginning, ω 286†.

ὑπ-ασπίδια (ἀσπίς), ntr. pl., used as

adv. = ὑπ ἀσπίδι, *under shelter of the shield*, προποδίζων, Ν 158; προβιβῶντος, Π 609.

ὕπᾰτος, ον, ε, ῳ, sup., in form from ὑπό, in meaning more nearly allied to ὑπέρ, cf. summus for sup-mus, κρειόντων, *highest, most exalted*, of rulers; μήστωρα, *sovereign counsellor*; θεῶν, of Zeus; πυρῇ, *on the top of the pyre*, Ψ 165.

ὑπ-έασι, see ὕπ-ειμι.

ὑπ-ὲ(δ)δεισαν, see ὑπο-δείδω.

ὑπ-έδεκτο, see ὑπο-δέχομαι.

ὑπ-εθερμάνθη, see ὑπο-θερμαίνω.

ὑπ-είκω, ὑπο-ϝείκειν, imp. ὑπόεικε, opt. εἴκοι, in tmesi, ipf. -εικον, fut. εἴξω, ομεν in Δ 62 may be aor. subj., aor. -ειξε, fut. mid. -είξομαι, εαι; everywhere with ϝ, ὑπο-ϝ-, exc. ὑπείξομαι μ 117, (Ger. weichen, Eng. weak), cedere, *retire, withdraw* from—, τινός; τῷ, π 42, for, before him; χεῖρας, *escape*, elsewh. τινί, *yield*, Δ 62, Υ 266; with part. *make way for;* with dat. of advantage, Ψ 602; Ο 211, influenced by dread.

ὕπ-ειμι, 3 pl. ὑπ-έασι, ipf. ὑπῆσαν, in tmesi, ὑπὸ ῆεν α 131, (εἰμί), *be under*, ποσίν, a footstool *was below*, for his feet; πολλοῖσι, many *had under them* sucking foals, Λ 681.

ὑπείρ and ὑπειρ-, see ὑπέρ and ὑπερ-.

Ὑπείρ-οχος, a Trojan, slain by Odysseus, Λ 335†.

Ὑπειρ-οχίδης, *son of Hypeirochos*, Itymoneus, Λ 673†.

Ὑπείρων, ονα, a Trojan, slain by Diomedes, Ε 144†.

ὑπ-έκ, before vowels ὑπέξ, adv., *out from under*, freq. with gen., Ν 89, Ρ 581, Σ 232.

ὑπ-εκ-προ-θέει, θέων, οντα, (θέω), praecurrere, *run on before;* τυτθόν, paullo, *a little;* τόσσον, *as much;* with acc., *outruns*, Ι 506.

ὑπ-εκ-προ-έλῦσαν, aor. from λύω, *loose from under* (the yoke), *put out*, ἀπήνης, ζ 88†.

ὑπ-εκ-προ-ρέει, *flows forth from* the depth below, ζ 87†.

ὑπ-εκ-προ-φύγοιμι, ών, aor., (φεύγω), fuga evadere, *escape by flight*, υ 43; Χάρυβδιν, μ 113.

ὑπεκσαόω, aor. ὑπ-εξ-εσάωσε, (σαόω), *save from under, rescue*, Ψ 292†.

ὑπέκ-φερον γ 496, and ὑπ-εξ-έφερον, ε, *raise slightly*, Θ 268; τινὰ πολέμοιο, *carry out secretly;* γ 496, *bear forward;* tmesi, Ο 628, φέρονται, pass.

ὑπ-έκ-φύγον, ες, ε(ν), ῳ, οι, οιμεν, έειν, (φεύγω), also ὑπ-εξ-έφῦγον, εν (φεύγω), *escape secretly, come safely forth from*, τι, Π 687; tmesis, τινός, (Il.), Ν 89.

ὑπ-εμνήμυκε, see ὑπ-ημύω.

ὑπ-ένερθε(ν), opp. καθ-ύπερθεν, adv., *beneath*, Δ 186; *below*, Ν 30; *in the lower world*, Γ 278; with gen., *underneath*, Β 150.

ὑπέξ, see ὑπ-έκ.

ὑπ-εξ-ἀγάγοι, and in tmesi, ἀγάγωμεν, Υ 300; *bring safely forth, rescue*, σ 147.

ὑπ-εξ-ἀλέασθαι, aor. inf., (ἀλεύω), *avoid, shun*, χεῖρας, Ο 180†.

ὑπ-εξ-ἀνᾰ-δύς, aor. part., (-δύομαι), *emerging from under* the sea, ἁλός, Ν 352†.

ὑπέρ, ὑπείρ, following its word ὕπερ, super, *over*, (ὑπό), I. with gen., (1) local: *over, across*, Ο 382, οὐδοῦ; supra, *above;* γαίης, κεφαλῆς, *at his head*, Β 20; *beyond*, τάφροιο.—(2) in derived sense, *for, in defense of*, ῥέζειν, τι, Η 449; with verbs of praying, *by, for the sake of*, per, Ω 466; like περί, de, *concerning*, ζ 524.—II. with acc., (1) local: *over, beyond*, Ε 851; 339, *along* the surface of the hand.—(2) *beyond*, and hence *in opposition to, against*, αἶσαν, μοῖραν, θεών, invito fato, deo, α 34.

ὑπερ-ᾱῆ, dat. from -αής, (ἄημι), *loud-roaring*, Λ 297†.

ὑπερ-άλλομαι, aor. -ᾶλτο, ἅλμενον, (salio), *spring over*, αὐλῆς, Ε 138; στίχας, Υ 327.

ὑπερ-βαίνω, aor. βῆ, 3 pl. βᾶσαν, subj. βήῃ, aor. ἐβήσετο, tmesis, ν 63; transcendere, *step over*, ψ 88; Ι 501, *transgress*.

ὑπερ-βάλλω, aor. βάλε, ἐειν, Ψ 637; ipf. ὑπειρ-έβαλλον, *cast beyond;* σήματα, all the marks; ἄκρον, *over the crest* of the hill; gen. only Ψ 847, τινὰ δουρί, *excel in throwing the spear*.

ὑπέρ-βασαν, 3 pl. aor. from -βαίνω.

ὑπερ-βᾰσίη, ῳ, ην, αι, ας, (βαίνω), *transgression, violence*, Γ 107, Π 18.

ὑπερ-βήῃ, aor. subj. from -βαίνω.

ὑπέρ-βῐος, ον, (βία), superbus,

lawless, wanton, α 368, ὕβριν ; θυμός, *abrupt*, ο 212 ; ntr., *insolently*, π 315.

ὑπερ-δέᾰ for δεέα, from δεής, [synizesis *ĕjā*], (δέομαι), having *very scanty* forces, P 330†.

Ὑπέρεια, fem., (1) former abode of Phaiakes, near the island of the Kyklopes, ζ 4.—(2) spring in Pelasgian Argos, Z 457, B 734.

ὑπ-ερείπω, aor. ἤρῐπε, *sank under* him, Ψ 691†.

ὑπ-έρεπτε, ipf., (ἐρέπτω), κονίην ποδοῖιν, *was washing away* the sand *under* his feet, Φ 271†.

ὑπερ-έσχεθον, aor. from -έχω.

ὑπερ-έχω, ipf., (ὑπείρ-), ἐχε(ν), ον, aor. ἐσχε(θε), τε, σχῃ, σχοι, *hold up, above*, τί ; ἠφαίστοιο, over the fire, χεῖρά(ς) τινι and τινος, *protect*, Δ 249, I 420 ; Γ 210, *overtopped* by his broad shoulders those who stood by ; *rise*, of sun and stars.

ὑπέρας, τάς, (ὑπέρ), *braces* attached to the yards, by which the sails are shifted, ε 260†. (See cuts Nos. 40, 48.)

ὑπερ-ηνορέων, ηνορέοντος, τες, των, τας, (ἠνορέη), *tyrannical, oppressive*, esp. of the suitors of Penelope ; *overbearing*, Δ 176, N 258. (Od.)

Ὑπερ-ήνωρ, ορος, son of Panthoos, slain by Menelaos, Ξ 516, P 24. [ῠ]

Ὑπερησίη, fem., town in Achaia, B 573, ο 254. [ῠ]

ὑπερη-φάνέοντες, pl. part., (φαίνω), superbi, *exulting, arrogant*, A 694†.

ὑπερθε(ν), adv., (ὑπέρ), *from above*, Υ 62 ; *above*, B 218, M 55.

ὑπερ-θρώσκω, fut. θορέονται, aor. θορον, *spring over*, τι, Θ 179, I 476.

ὑπέρ-θῡμος, οιο, ου, ον, οι, οισι, ους, (θυμός), *high-spirited, high-hearted*, of heroes, Trojans, giants, E 376, O 135, Z 111, η 59.

ὑπερ-θύριον, ntr., (θύρη), *lintel of a door*, opp. οὐδός, η 90†.

ὑπερ-ίημι, fut. ἥσει, *will throw beyond* (this mark), θ 198†.

ὑπερ-ικταίνοντο, ipf., *stumbled from haste*, ψ 3†.

Ὑπερῑονίδης, αο μ 176, and Ὑπερίων, ονος, epith. of Helios, Θ 480, T 398, α 8, μ 176.

ὑπερ-κᾰτᾰ-βαίνω, fut. βήσεται, with gen., *leap over, surmount*, O 382 ; τεῖχος, N 50.

ὑπερ-κύδαντας, acc. pl., (κῦδος), *of high renown*, Δ 66, 71.

ὑπερ-μενέοντες (μένος), *haughty*, τ 62†.

ὑπερ-μενής, μενεῖ, έα, έων, (μένος), *high-spirited* (or *courageous?*), Κρονίωνι, Διί, βασιλήων, Θ 236 ; ἐπικούρων, P 362.

ὑπέρ-μορον has often been considered as adj., better separated, ὑπὲρ μόρον, *against fate*, more than is appointed by fate ; in B 155, really adj. used as adv. = ὑπὲρ μόρον.

ὑπερ-οπλίῃσι, ταῖς, (ὑπέροπλος), *presumption, arrogance*, A 205†.

ὑπερ-οπλίσσαιτο, opt. aor. from -οπλίζομαι, *vanquish by force of arms*, ρ 268†.

ὑπέρ-οπλον, ntr., (ὅπλον or πέλω?), *arrogantly*, εἰπεῖν, O 185 and P 170.

(ὑπερ-) ὑπείρ-οχον, (ἔχω), *eminent*, Z 208. (Il.)

ὑπερ-πέτομαι, aor. πτατο, *flew over*, N 408 ; θ 192, *flew past* (the marks of all).

ὑπ-ερράγη, aor. from ὑπο-ρρήγνυμι.

ὑπέρ-σχῃ, οι, see ὑπερ-έχω.

ὑπέρτᾰτος, sup. from ὑπέρ, *on the top, aloft*, M 381 and Ψ 451.

ὑπερτερίη, τῇ, (ὑπέρτερος), *upper part, awning, wagon - cover*, ζ 70† (others interpret as meaning *basket, crate*).

ὑπέρτερος, ον, α, comp. from ὑπέρ, *outer* (flesh), i. e. about the bone, opp. σπλάγχνα, γ 65 (Od.) ; *better, higher, more excellent* (Il.), Λ 786.

ὑπερ-φίᾰλος, ον, οι, ων, οισι(ν), ους, adv. ως, (ὑπερ-φυής), *overgrown*, cf. ferox, i. e. *mighty, courageous*, E 881 ; also in bad signif., *arrogant, insolent*; adv. *exceedingly, excessively*, N 293 ; insolenter, δ 663.

ὑπ-έρχομαι, aor. ἤλυθε, ἤλθετε, ἔλθῃ, subire, *go under, enter*, with acc., ε 476 ; incessit, *steal upon, seize upon*, Τρῶας (γυῖα) τρόμος, H 215.

ὑπ-ερώησαν, *started back*, Θ 122. (Il.)

ὑπερ-ῴην, τήν, (cf. παρ-ειή), oris, *palate*, X 495†.

ὑπερ-ῷον, ίῳ, ῷα, and ὑπερῷα, ntr., *upper chamber* over the women's apartment, occupied during day and night by women and daughters of the house (not by servants), B 514, ρ 101 ;

ὑπερωϊοθεν, *from the upper chamber, α* 328.

ὑπ-έστην, see ὑφ-ίστημι, mid.

ὑπ-έχω, aor. ἔσχεθε, *held out under* (the hand of him who offered the lot), H 188 ; ὑποσχών, supponens, *putting under*, i. e. *getting with foal*, E 269.

ὑπ - ημύω, pf. ἐμνήμῦκε, *is* utterly (πάντα) *bowed down*, X 491†.

ὑπ-ήνεικαν, aor. from ὑπο-φέρω.

ὑπ-ηνῴτῃ, τῷ, (ὑπήνη), *getting a beard*, κ 279 and Ω 348.

ὑπ-ηοῖοι, οἴη, (ἠώς), *toward morning*, matutini, adj., = adv., Θ 530, δ 656.

ὑπ-ισχνέομαι, see ὑπ-ίσχομαι.

ὑπ-ίσχομαι, εται, όμεναι, ipf. ἔσχεο, ετο, ὄσχωμαι, ηται, ωνται, εο, ἔσθαι, ὄμενος, οι, (ἔχω), *take upon one's self, undertake, μέγα ἔργον ; promise*, τινί τι; with inf., Z 93, 274; often also with fut. inf., X 114 ; θυγατέρα, *betroth, vow,* with acc. and inf., θ 347 ; B 112, I 19, the part. may be read as elided dat.

ὕπνος, οιο, ου, ῳ, ον, masc., (sopor, somnus), *sleep,* relaxing the limbs, ambrosial, B 19 ; νήδυμος, *fast, deep sleep*; ἡδέι, Δ 131 ; μαλακῷ, K 2 ; ὕπνον ἀωτεῖς, K 159 ; poured over the eyes of mortals ; lies upon the eyelids, K 187. Personified, Ὕπνος, *Sleep*, the brother of death, Ξ 231 ; his sway extends over gods and men, Ξ 233.

ὑπνώοντας, part., τούς, (ὑπνόω), dormientes, *sleeping*, Ω 344, ε 48.

ὑπό, ancient locative ὑπαί, K 376 and freq., (ὕπαιθα, sub), I. adv. (1) local : *below, beneath*, Υ 37, E 74, Φ 270, H 6, Φ 364, Λ 635, α 131 ; *down,* A 434, Γ 217, X 491.—(2) causal : *there-under, there-by*, θ 380, T 362 sq.—II. prep. A. with acc. (1) of motion, *to* (a position) *under,* with verbs of motion, Δ 279, λ 155, 253, X 144, 195, Ω 274, *below,* around the end of the bolt ; *under* (without idea of motion), in locating wounds, etc., E 67, N 388, 652 (the gen. in like signif., H 12, Λ 578, N 412, etc.) ; *near by, before,* Ἴλιον, B 216 ; Τροίην, δ 146.—(2) of extension *under,* χ 362, β 181, T 259, η 130, Γ 371, X 307, *down under* his thigh ; also of extension in time, *during,* Λ 202, X 102.—B. with dat., local : (1) of rest,

under, B 866, 307, ξ 533 ; sub muris, Φ 277, Ψ 81, Σ 244 (usually with gen. with λύειν, Θ 543, δ 39); of position with reference to parts of body, Ξ 236, θ 522, Ψ 265, ο 469.—(2) motion (properly locative of aim), esp. with τιθέναι, πελάζω, ἐρείδω, κλίνω, Ξ 240, B 44.—(3) instrumental, causal : *under, by,* B 784, Γ 13 ; χερσί (δαμείς, etc., B 860, Ψ 675), ω 97, O 289, N 816 ; δουρί, Δ 479, E 653 ; σκήπτρῳ, Z 159 ; τινί, N 668, ρ 252, Π 490; flee *before,* E 93 ; with τίκτειν, *by* some one ; λαίλαπι, etc., Π 384, δ 295, λ 135, δ 402, *under* the breath ; χ 445, *under* the sway of the suitors ; η 68, *in subjection to* their husbands.—C. with gen., (1) of situation, *under,* Θ 14, Π 375, A 501, ὑπ' ἀνθερεῶνος, taking hold *under* the chin ; also with verbs of wounding specifying the part, Δ 106, N 412, 671, 177.—(2) *under,* i. e. *forth from under, out from under,* Θ 543, δ 39, η 5, P 224, 235; flee *before,* Φ 22, 553, θ 149, N 153. — (3) causal : B 465, Ξ 285, Φ 318, B 268 ; *through,* ι 66, Z 134, κ 78; with verbs of moving, calling, under the hands, at the shout, Π 277, Γ 61, Z 73, Υ 498, N 27, Γ 128, N 334 ; with part., Δ 423, M 74, cf. Π 591; for the attendant circumstance, *under,* amid, Σ 492; *for,* ὑπὸ δείους, K 376, O 4, β 110, ω 146. [Often with accent thrown back, by anastrophe, when following its word.]

ὑπο-βάλλω, inf. ὑβ-βάλλειν, ipf. ὑπ-έβαλλε, *lay underneath,* κ 353 ; *interrupt,* T 80.

ὑπο-βλήδην, adv., (ὑποβάλλω), interpellando, *interrupting,* A 292†.

ὑπό-βρυχα, acc., (βρέχω), θῆκε κῦμα, the wave buried him *under water,* ε 319†.

ὑπὸ δαῖον, ipf., (δαίω, δαῖς), *kindle under,* Σ 347.

ὑπο-δάμνημι, mid. 2 sing. prs. δάμνᾰσαι, *thou subjectest thyself,* γ 214 and π 95.

ὑπο-δέγμενος, see ὑπο-δέχομαι.

ὑπο-δείδω (from δϳειδω), aor. -έδεισαν, imp. δείσατε, part. σας, ασα, αντες, pf. δείδια, plupf. ἐδείδισαν. *fear, shrink under,* κ 296; τινά, Σ 199, X 282 ; τι, Ψ 446, β 66.

ὑπο-δεξίη, fem., (δέχομαι), *hospitable welcome,* I 73†.

ὑπο-δέχομαι, fem. δέξομαι, εαι, aor. ἐδέξατο, aor. sync. 2 sing. -έδεξο, 3 sing. ἔδεκτο, inf. δέχθαι, part. δέγμενος, receive, I 480, so freq. with πρόφρων, gladly, οἴκῳ; κόλπῳ, in her bosom (of Thetis as personifying the sea); βίας, receive in silence, endure; promise, β 387.

ὑπὸ δέω, aor. ἐδήσατο, always in tmesi, ποσσὶ ... πέδιλα, bound the sandals under his feet, B 44.

ὑποδήματα, τά, (ὑποδέω), that which is bound underneath (the foot), sandal, of simplest form, o 369, σ 361.

ὑπο-δμηθεῖσα, see -δάμνημι.

ὑπο-δμώς (δάμνημι), underling, δ 386†.

ὑπό-δρα (δράκων), askance, fiercely, grimly, ἰδών, B 245, θ 165; δεινά, O 13.

ὑπο-δράω, -δρώωσι, ministrant, wait upon, o 333†.

ὑπο-δρηστῆρες, οἱ, (ὑπο-δράω), attendants, o 330†.

ὑπο-δύομαι, fut. δύσεαι, aor. ἐδύσετο and -έδυ, δῦσα, δύντε, tmesis, ἔδυσαν, ἐδύσετο, plunge under, τί, Σ 145; slip into, θάμνους; subire, go under to carry, take on one's shoulders; πᾶσιν γόος, grief penetrated all; with gen., emergere sub, emerge from, θάμνων; κακῶν, escape from misfortune.

ὑπό-εικε, etc., see ὑπ-είκω.

ὑπο-ζεύγνυμι, fut. ζεύξω, put under the yoke, harness, o 81†.

ὑπο-θερμαίνω, acr. pass. ἐθερμάνθη, was warmed, Π 330 and Υ 476.

Ὑπο-θῆβαι, town in Boiotia, B 505†.

ὑποθημοσύνῃσι, ταῖς, (τίθημι), suggestion, counsels, O 412 and π 233.

ὑπο-θωρήσσω, ipf. mid. -εθωρήσσοντο, (θώρηξ), were arming themselves, Σ 513†.

ὑπὸ ἔκαμψαν, aor. from κάμπτω, prep. belong. to γλώχινι, bent under (itself) the end of the yoke-strap, Ω 274†.

ὑπὸ κεῖται, lies below; ὑπό is adv., Φ 364†.

ὑπὸ κεκάδοντο, see -χάζομαι.

ὑπὸ κινέω, aor. κινήσαντος, not a compound; Ζεφύρου ὕπο, under the impulse of the soft-blowing Zephyros, Δ 423†.

ὑπο-κλίνω, aor. pass. ἐκλίνθη σχοίνω, he lay down in the rushes, ε 463†.

ὑπο-κλονέεσθαι (κλονέω) Ἀχιλῆι, to crowd themselves together in flight before, Φ 556†.

ὑπο-κλοπέοιτο (κλοπέω, κλώψ), conceal one's self under any thing, χ 382†.

ὑπο-κρίνονται, aor. κρίναιτο, imp. κρίναι, inf. ασθαι, answer, τινί, H 407; interpret, ὄνειρον, ὧδε, M 228, cf. o 170, τ 535, F 150.

ὑπο-κρύπτω, aor. pass. -εκρύφθη, be hidden in spray, O 626†.

ὑπό-κυκλον, with wheels (κύκλα) underneath, wheeled, δ 131†.

ὑπο-κύομαι, aor. part. κῦσαμένη, having conceived, Z 26; so also of animals, mares, Υ 225.

ὑπὸ ἔλλαβε, with τρόμος, not a compound; ὑπό, adv., underneath, i. e. in his limbs, or causal, from, at the sight.

ὑπο-λείπω, ipf. ἔλειπον, leave over, π 50; mid. ἐλείπετο, fut. λείψομαι, remain, αὐτοῦ, ρ 276.

ὑπο-λευκαίνονται, pass., (λευκός), subalbescunt, chaff heaps whiten, or perh. better as two words, grow white below, i. e. on the ground, E 502†.

ὑπ᾽ ὀλίζονες, not a compound; ὑπό, adv., close by them were the soldiers, on a smaller scale, Σ 519†.

ὑπο-λύω, ipf. ἔλυον Ψ 513, aor. ἔλυσα, σε, (also in tmesi), aor. mid. ἐλύσαο, 2 aor. ἔλυντο, loose from under, unyoke, δ 39; make limbs sink under one, γυῖα, Π 805; γούνατα, O 291; make fail, μένος, Z 27; paralyze by a (deadly) wound, freq. = slay in battle; secretly set free, A 401.

ὑπο-μένω, aor. ἔμεινα, ε(ι), αν, αι, remain, with inf., for one to know him, α 410; ἐρωὴν, sustain; τινά (Il.), withstand, E 498, P 25.

ὑπο-μιμνήσκω, fut. part. μνήσουσα, aor. ἐμνησεν, τινά τινος, to remind, o 3; put in mind of, α 321†.

ὑπο-μνάομαι, ipf. ἐμνάασθε, γυναῖκα, have wooed illicitly, χ 38†.

ὑπο-νήϊον, lying under Mount Νήϊον, γ 81†.

ὑπο-πεπτηῶτες, see -πτήσσω.

ὑπο-περκάζουσιν (περκνός), begin to turn, grow dark, of grapes, η 126†.

ὑπο-πλακίη, situated under Mount Πλάκος, Θήβη, Z 397†.

ὑπὸ πετάννυμι, aor. part. πετάσσας, spreading out underneath, α 130†.

ὑπο-πτήσσω, pf. part. πεπτηῶτες, having crouched down timidly under and hidden themselves amid the leaves, πετάλοις, B 312†.

ὑπ-όρνυμι, 2 aor. ὦρορε Μοῦσα, in so moving strains did the muse begin, ω 62; but 1 aor. ὦρσε, Ψ 108, excited; 2 aor. mid. ὦρτο, a desire to weep was roused, π 215.

ὑπο-ρρήγνυμι, aor. ρραγη (for Fρά-γη), the limitless ether is cleft in twain, οὐρανόθεν αἰθήρ, Π 300 = Θ 558.

ὑπό-ρρηνον (Fρήν), having a lamb under her, K 216†.

ὑπο-σσείουσι (σείω, σFι), whirl around, (laying hold) below, ι 385†; in Ξ 285, ὕπο belongs to ποδῶν, under their feet.

ὑπο-σταίη, στάς, see ὑφ-ίστημι.

ὑπο-σταχύοιτο (στάχυς), wax gradually like the ears of corn, increase, υ 212†.

ὑπο-στεναχίζω, ipf. ἐστενάχιζε, Διί, groaned under Zeus, B 781†.

ὑπο-στορέννυμι, aor. στορέσαι, spread out under, υ 139; ὑπὸ ἔστρωτο, mid. he had spread out under him his shield.

ὑπο-στρέφω, ipf. ἔστρεφε, aor. subj. στρέψωσι, opt. ειας, part. ας, fut. mid. ψεσθαι, aor. part. στρεφθείς, turn about, E 581, 505; turn in flight, M 71, Λ 446; pass. turn, return, σ 23, Λ 567.

ὑπο-σχέθω, see ὑπ-έχω.

ὑπο-σχέσθαι, see ὑπ-ίσχομαι,

ὑπο-σχεσίῃσι, ταῖς, N 369, elsewh.

ὑπό-σχεσις, ιν, B 349, 286, (ὑπίσχομαι), promise.

ὑπο-τάνυσσαν, aor., placed underneath (lengthwise, τανύω), A 486†.

ὑπο-ταρβήσαντες, aor. part. (ταρβέω, terror), τούς, shrinking before them, P 533†.

ὑπο-ταρταρίους, those below in Tartaros, Ξ 279†.

ὑπο-τίθημι, aor. θῆκε in tmesis, fut. mid. θήσομαι, εαι, εται, ὄμεθα, aor. θέσθαι, imp. θεν, place under, attach, Σ 375; mid. suggest, βουλήν, ἔργον, ἔπος; counsel, εὖ, πυκινῶς, prudently, Φ 293.

ὑπὸ (ἔ)τρέμε, his limbs trembled beneath (him), K 390, λ 527.

ὑπο-τρέχω, aor. ἔδραμε, ran up underneath (his weapon), ran up to and

prostrated himself before, Φ 68 and κ 323.

ὑπο-τρέω, aor. ἔτρεσας, σαν, σαι, take to flight, P 275; τινά, flee before one, P 587.

ὑπο-τρομέουσι, ipf. iter. τρομέεσκον, (τρέμω), tremble before, X 241, Υ 28; τρομέει ὑπό (adv.), K 95.

ὑπό-τροπος, ον, (τρέπω), redux, returning, back again, Z 367, υ 332.

ὑπ-ουρἀνιον, ἰων, (οὐρανός), under the heaven, P 675; far and wide under the whole heaven, ι 264.

ὑπο-φαίνω, aor. -έφηνε—θρῆνυν τραπέζης, bring a footstool into view from under the table, ρ 409†.

ὑπο-φέρω, aor. 3 pl. ἤνεικαν, bore me away, E 885†.

ὑπο-φεύγειν, subterfugere, escape by flight, X 200; aor. φυγὼν ὕπο, escaping, Φ 57.

ὑπο-φῆται, οἱ, (φημί), interpretes, declarers of the divine will, Π 235†.

ὑπο-φθάνω, aor. part. -φθάς, mid. φθάμενος, η, be or get beforehand, anticipate, H 144; τινά, ο 171.

ὑπο-χάζομαι, red. aor. κεκάδοντο, ἀνδρός, retired before the hero, Δ 497.

ὑπο - χείριος, under my hands, ο 448†.

ὑπο-χέω, aor. ἔχενε, spread (strew) under(neath), ξ 49, Λ 843; χεῦεν ὕπο, π 47.

ὑπο-χώρει, ipf., aor. χώρησαν, tmesis, Δ 505, retire, retreat, X 96.

ὑπ-όψιος (ὄψις), despised (by the rest), ἄλλων, Γ 42.

ὕπτιος, ον, ον, (ὑπό), resupinus, back, on his back, ι 371, Δ 108.

ὑπ-ώπια, τά, (ὤψ), vultu, in countenance, M 463†.

ὑπ-ωρείας, τάς, (ὄρος), foot of a mountain, skirts of a mountain range, Υ 218†.

ὑπ-ώρορε, see ὑπ-όρνυμι.

ὑπ-ωρόφιοι (ὀροφή), under the (same) roof, table companions, Ι 640†.

Ὑρίη, fem., town in Boiotia, on the Euripos, B 496†.

Ὑρμίνη, fem., harbor town in northern Elis, B 616†.

Ὑρτᾰκίδης, son of Hyrtakos, Asios, B 837 sq., M 96, 110, 163.

Ὑρτᾰκος, ον, a Trojan, husband of Arisbe, N 759 and 771.

Ὑρτίος, son of Gyrtios, a Mysian, slain by Aias, Ξ 511†.

ῦς, ὑός, ὑν, ὑες, ὑεσσι(ν), ὑας. fem., (σῦς), sus, *swine;* alternating with σῦς, according to the requirements of the verse, ξ 419, ν 405, Κ 264.

ὑσμίνη, ης, ᾳ, ην, ἷναι, ἵνας, also dat. sing. ὑσμῖνι Β. 863, *in the conflict,* and ὑσμίνηνδ' Β 477. *into the battle;* λ 417, 612, a c i e s, *pitched combat;* δηιοτῆτος, hostile combat. (Il.)

ὑστάτῃσι (ὕστατος), *last, hindmost,* Ο 634; ntr. ὑστάτιον, *at last.*

ὕστᾰτος, ον, οι, ον, α, sup., (ὕστερος), *last, hindmost,* Β 281; ὕστατον, as adv., *last,* with πύμᾰτον, Χ 203, *at the very last;* also esp., in fourth foot, ὕστατα, with πύματα, δ 685.

ὕστερος, ον, α π 319, comp., (ὕστατος), p o s t e r i o r, *succeeding,* usually of time, *after;* γένει, n a t u m i n o r, *younger;* σεῦ, *after thee;* ntr., *afterward, hereafter,* Κ 450, Υ 127.

ὑφαίνει, etc., prs., (subj. ῃσι, opt. οι), and ipf., iter. ὑφαίνεσκε(ν), ον, aor. ὕφηνεν, ω, ον, ας, ασα; parallel form ὑφάω, prs. **ὑφόωσι, η** 105, *weave,* ἱστόν, at the loom (which stood upright, like the Roman loom represented in the cut, or like the Egyptian loom in cut

No. 63); also in general, *weave garments,* ν 108; fig. δόλον, ους, d o l u m, insidias s t r u e r e, *spin, devise* a plot, ι 422; μῆτιν, c o n s i l i u m t e x e r e, *contrive* a plan, δ 678.

ὑπὸ ἤρεον, *were taking away from under,* Β 154; elsewh. ὑπό is simple adv., e. g. ω 450, ὑπὸ χλωρὸν δέος ᾕρει, *seized* them *below =* in their limbs, or *by reason of what they saw.*

ὑφαντήν (ὑφαίνω), *woven,* ν 136 and π 231.

ὑφάσματα, τά, (ὑφαίνω), t e l a s, *thing woven,* web, γ 274†.

ὑφάω, see ὑφαίνω.

ὕφ-ελκε, ipf., (ἕλκω), ποδοῖιν, *sought to drag away* by laying hold *below* at the feet, Ξ 477†.

ὑφ-ηνίοχος, masc., (ἡνίοχος), *charioteer* as subject to (ὑπὸ) the warrior in the chariot, Ζ 19†.

ὕφ-ίημι, fut. **ἥσει,** aor. **ἧκεν,** (part. ὑφέντες Α 434, better with Aristarchos ἀφέντες), s u p p o n e r e, *put* or *place under,* ι 309, θρῆνυν.

ὑφ-ίσταμαι, aor. ὑπ-**έστην, ης, η, ημεν,** ἔσταν, opt. σταίη, imp. στῆτω, part. στάς, *take upon one's self,* Φ 273; *promise,* τινί τι, ὑπόσχεσιν, with inf., Ι 445, Τ 195, Ψ 20, κ 483; in Β 286, Ε 715, case ἐκπέρσαντ' (ι ? α ?) is doubtful; Ι 160, μοι, let him *submit* to me.

ὑ-φορβός, όν, οἱ, masc., (ὗς, φέρβω), *swine-herd,* with ἀνέρες, ξ 410. (Od.) [ῠ]

ὑφόωσι, see ὑφαίνω.

ὑψ-ἀγόρην, η, masc., (ὕψι, ἀγορεύω), *big talker, boaster,* β 85, α 385. (Od.)

ὑψ-ερεφές, ntr., and -**ηρεφέος,** Ι 582, ές, έα, with synizesis δ 757, (ἐρέφω), *high-roofed.*

ὑψηλός, οῦ, οῖο, ῷ, όν, οί, ῶν, οἶσι(ν), ούς, ή, ῆς, ῇ, ήν, αἱ, άων, ῆσι, άς, όν, ά (ὕψος), *high, lofty,* of situation, *high-dwelling,* Β 855.

Ὑψ-ήνωρ, ορος. (1) son of Dolopion, slain by Eurypylos, Ε 76. — (2) son of Hippasos, slain by Deiphobos, Ν 411.

ὑψ-ηρεφές, etc., see ὑψ-ερεφές.

ὑψ-ηχέες, έας, (ἠχέω), *high-neighing* (with head raised on high), Ε 772 and Ψ 27.

ὕψι, adv., (old locative), (1) *on high,* ἐπ᾽ εὐνάων ὁρμίζειν, Ξ 77, make fast the ships *floating in deep water, on the high sea* (ὕψι), to the anchor-stones; βιβάς, striding along with high, i. e. long steps. — (2) *up, aloft,* Π 374, Ρ 723, Ν 140.

ὑψι-βρεμέτης (βρέμω), a l t e t o n a n s, *thundering aloft, high-thundering,* Α 354.

ὑψί-ζὕγος (ζυγόν), lit. *on high rower's bench, high at the helm, high-ruling,* Δ 166. (Il.)

ὑψῐ-κάρηνοι (κάρη), *with lofty head* or *peak*, M 132†.

ὑψί-κερων, τόν, (κέρας), *with lofty antlers*, κ 158†.

ὑψῐ-κόμοιο, οισιν, ους, (κόμη), *with lofty foliage*, Ξ 398, μ 357.

ὑψῐ-πετήεις, X 308, and -πέτης, N 822, (πίτομαι), *high-flying*.

ὑψῐ-πέτηλον, α, (πέτηλον), *with lofty foliage*, N 437, λ 588.

Ὑψῐ-πύλη, wife of Iason, mother of Euneos, H 469†.

ὑψί-πῦλον (πύλη), *high-gated*, referring to the gates in the towers, Τροίη, Π 698; and Θήβη, Z 416. (Il.)

ὑψόθεν, adv., (ὕψος), *from on high*, Λ 53; ἐκρέμω, thou wast hanging (swinging) *aloft*, Ὀ 18.

ὑψόθῐ, adv., (ὕψος), *high, on high*, K 16, T 376. (Il.)

ὑψ-ορόφοιο, ον, (ὀροφή), *with lofty covering, high-roofed*, Ω 192, 317.

ὑψόσε, adv., (ὕψος), *upward, aloft*; at beginning of verse, or in fifth foot exc. Φ 269, 302.

ὑψοῦ, adv., (ὕψος), *aloft, on high*, A 486; ἐν νοτίῳ τήν γ᾽ ὥρμισαν, they moored the ship, letting her ride *far out* in the roadstead, δ 785.

ὕω, ipf. ὗε, Ζεύς —, *sent rain*; pass. ὑόμενος, *drenched with rain*, ζ 131.

Φ.

φάανθεν, 3 pl. aor. part. from φαίνω.

φάάντατος, sup., (positive would be φάϜας [cf. ἄτλας, γίγας], from φαίνω), *most brilliant*, ν 93†.

φάγον = ἔφαγον, see ἐσθίω.

φάε, aor., ξ 502, for φάϜε (φάϜος, φάος), splendebat, *appeared*, fut. πεφήσεται, P 155, shall have appeared.

φάεα, see φάος.

Φαέθουσα, daughter of Helios and Neaira, "new moon," μ 132†; φαέθων, masc. of foregoing (φαϜος, see φάε), splendens, *radiant*, Helios, Λ 735.

Φαέθων, horse of Eos, ψ 246; acc. Φαέθονθ᾽ = οντα.

φαεινός, οῦ, ῷ, όν, ώ, ῶν, ούς; ή, ῆς, ῇ, ήν, αί, άς, (for φαϜεσ-ινύς), comp.-εινότερον, *gleaming, shining, radiant*, Γ 419, M 151.

φαείνω, subj., ῃ, οιεν, φάεινε, ων, (φαεινός), *shine*, of the sun, μ 383, 385; *giving light*, σ 343.

φάεσί-μβροτος, ον, (φύϜος, μόρ-ος, mortalis), *bringing light to mortals*, sun, κ 138; Eos, Ω 785.

Φαίαξ, see Φαίηκες.

φαιδιμόεντες (φαίδιμος), *illustrious*, of Epeians, N 686†.

φαίδιμος, ῳ, ον, (α), (φαϜιδ-, φάος), *shining, gleaming*, of limbs, candentes umeri, λ 128; usually of persons, *illustrious*, Aias, Hektor, υἱός, Z 144.

Φαίδιμος, king of the Sidonians, δ 617, ο 117.

Φαίδρη, wife of Theseus, λ 321.†

Φαίηκες, dat. ἥκεσσιν and ηξιν η 62, favored inhabitants of the fabulous Scheria, enjoying continual dolce far niente, θ 244 sqq. In earlier times their home was near the Kyklopes; they escort all those whom they receive as guests on swift ships, themselves possessing intelligence, to their desired haven, ε 34, ζ 4, θ 244 sqq.

φαινέσκετο and -ομένηφιν, see φαίνω.

Φαίνοψ, οπος, son of Asios from Abydos, father of Xanthos and Thoon, P 583, E 152.

φαίνω, etc., pres. inf. -έμεν, imp. φαῖν(ε), ipf. φαῖνε, aor. ἔφηνε, φήνωσι, ειε, φῆναι, (φάος), *give light, shine, make appear* (τινί, intr. *give light*, η 102), τέρατα, σήματα, μηροὺς; *show, ὁδόν*; γύνον, ἄκοιτιν, *appoint; display*, ἀρετάς; *make heard, utter*, ἀοιδήν, ἀεικείας; part. pf. μῦθον πεφασμένον (cf. θ 499), *report which has gone abroad; φαίνο-*

μαι, intr. pres., ipf., iter. φαινίσκετο, fut. φανεῖσθαι, 2 aor. (ἐ)φάνη, iter. φάνεσκε λ 587, 3 pl. φάνεν, subj. φανῄ = ἡῃ, opt. εἴη, imp. ηθι, ητω, inf. ἤμεναι =ῆναι, part., εἰς, ἐντα, εῖσα, 1 aor. pass. φαάνθη, 3 pl. φάανθεν, pf. pass. 3 sing. πέφανται, part. see above, shine, πυρά, ὄσσε, Ἠώς; be visible, appear, μάχη; was unprotected at the throat, X 324; offer one's self, appear, K 236, ω 448; σμερδαλέος, τοῖος, πῶς; Δ 278, it appears to him blacker than pitch as it advances over the sea.

Φαῖστος, son of Boros, from Tarne in Maionia, slain by Idomeneus. E 43†.

Φαιστός, city in Kreta near Gortys, B 648, γ 296.

φαλαγγηδόν, adv., (φάλαγξ), in companies, in columns, O 360.

φάλαγξ, **φάλαγγα**, fem., pl. ες, γξιν, ας, line of battle, column, Z 6, Λ 90.

φάλαρ(α), τά, (φάλος), burnished, gleaming plates of metal, rising above the helmet, Π 106†.

φᾰληριόωντα, part. ntr. pl. from -ιάω, (φάλαρος, α), brightly shining, gleaming, N 799†.

Φάλκης, a Trojan chief, N 791; Ξ 513, slain by Antilochos.

φᾰλον, τόν, pl. -οισι, (φάε), (1) metal ridge or crest, extending over the helmet from back to front, and furnished with a socket to receive and support the plume (see cut No. 128).—(2) in narrower signification the rounded boss, in which the φάλος terminated (see cut No. 20), Z 9, N 132.

φάν, see φημί.

φάνεν, εσκε, ἡῃ, ἤμεναι, see φαίνω.

φάος (from φάϜως), and φόως, dat. φάει, acc. φάος, φόως, pl. φάεα, (φάε), light, opp. ἀχλύς; ἠελίοιο, φόωσδε, to the light of day; ἐν φάει, by daylight; fig. lumina, eyes, π 15; γλυκερὸν φ., mi ocelle, light of my eyes, π 23; deliverance, victory, etc., Z 6.

φᾰρέτρη, ης, ην, fem., (φέρω), quiver, Λ 45, φ 11. (Cf. cut, and Nos. 96, 97, 111.)

Φᾰρις, ιος, town in Lakonike, south of Amyklai, B 582†.

φάρμᾰκον, (α), ntr., medicinal herbs, δ 230; in general, remedies, Δ 191, Λ 741;

magic drug, potion, κ 392; poisonous draught, poisonous drug, X 94, α 261, β 329, ἀνδροφόνον.

φαρμάσσων, part., skillfully handling, tempering, ι 393†.

φᾶρος, εἴ, ε(α), ntr., (φέρω), large piece of cloth, a shroud, Σ 353; mantle, cloak, B 43, γ 467; likewise of women, ε 230.

Φᾶρος, small island at mouth of Nile, δ 355†.

φάρυγξ, **φάρῠγος**, fem., throat, ι 373, τ 480.

φάσγᾰνον, ου, ῳ, α, (σφάζω), sword, E 81, π 295.

φάσθαι, see φημί.

φάσκω, ipf. iter. **ἔφασκον**, ες, εν, εθ' = ετε, and φάσκ' = φάσκ(εν), (φημί), declared, λ 306; promise, with inf. fut., ε 135; think, N 100, χ 35.

φασσοφόνῳ, dat., (φάσσα, palumbes, φόνος), dove-slayer; ἴρηκι, pigeonhawk, O 238†.

φάτις, ιν, fem., (φημί), fama, report, reputation, ἐσθλή, ζ 29; ἀνδρῶν ἠδὲ γυναικῶν, among men and women; with objective gen., ψ 362, tidings (of the slaughter) of the suitors.

φάτνῃ, τῇ, (πατέομαι), crib, manger, E 271.

Φαυσιάδης, son of Phausios, Apisaon, Λ 578†.

Φεαί, town in Elis, ο 297†.

φέβωμαι, ὡμεθα, εσθαι, ipf. (ἐ)φέβοντο, fugari, fugere, flee, Λ 121, χ 299; flee from, E 232. (11.)

Φειά, town on the river Jardanos, in northern Elis, H 135.

Φείδας, an Athenian chief, N 691†.

Φείδ-ιππος, son of Thessalos, B 678†.

φείδομαι, **φειδόμενος**, and φείσατ(ο), aor. red. πεφιδοίμην, οιτο, έσθαι, fut. red. πεφιδήσεται, spare, with gen., ι 277, Υ 464.

φειδώ, fem., sparing, thrift, π 315; H 409, one must not fail in the case of the dead to—.

φειδωλή, fem., (φείδομαι), sparing, grudging use, δούρων, X 244†.

Φείδων, king of the Thesprotians, ξ 316, τ 287.

Φεν- and **φα-**, roots of the follg. verbal forms, (φόνος), aor. red. **ἔπεφνον**, ες, (εν), ομεν, ετε, and πέφνε(ν), subj. ῃς, ῃ, inf. έμεν, part. πεφνόντα, pass. pf. **πέφατ(αι)**, 3 pl. νται, inf. άσθαι, 3 fut., πεφήσεαι, σεται, slay, θάνατος, λ 135.

Φένεος, town in Arkadia, B 605†.

Φεραί, ῶν, ῇς, important town in Thessaly, residence of Eumelos, δ 798 ; situated on lake Boibeis, B 711.

Φέρε-κλος, son of Harmonides, builder of the ship in which Paris carried away Helen, slain by Meriones, E 59†.

Φέρης, ητος, son of Kretheus and Tyro, father of Admetos, λ 259†.

φέριστον, ε, οι, bravest, best, esp. freq. in voc., Z 123, ι 269.

Φέρουσα, a Nereid, Σ 43†.

φέρτατος, (ε), οι, = φέριστος, sup. to **φέρτερος**, ον, οι, η, αί, praestantissimus and -ior, pre-eminent, both forms with πολύ, (sup. also with μέγα), χερσίν τε βίηφί τε, βίῃ; comp. with inf., it is better, A 169, μ 109.

φέρτε = φέρετε, imp. from φέρω.

φέρτρῳ, τῷ, ntr., (φέρω), litter, bier for the dead, Σ 236†.

φέρω, subj. **φέρῃσι** τ 111, imp. φέρτε, inf. φερέμεν, ipf. iter. φέρεσκον, κεν, fut. οἴσω, ων, mid. fut. οἴσεται, σόμενος, etc., 2 aor. imp. οἶσε, σέτω, σετε, inf. σέμεν(αι), from stem ενεκ-, 1 aor. ἤνεικεν, καν, and ἔνεικας, ε(ν), αμεν, ατε, αν, subj. ἐνείκω, γ, opt. κοι, imp. κατε, inf. ἐνεῖκαι, and opt. εἴκαι, part. ἐνείκας, 2 aor. (ἤνεγκεν, v. l. χ 493), inf. ἐνεικέμεν, I. act., (1) ferre, bear, carry, τί, with dat. instr. or with ἐν-; γαστρί, in the womb; also of the earth, yield; bring, (θεόν, adducere), δῶρα, τεύχεα, μῦθον, ἀγγελίην, ἔπεα, ῥ 565 ; φόως, rescue; ἦρα, χάριν, gratify ; κακόν, ά; φόνον, δηϊοτῆτα, ἄλγεα.—(2) vehere, carry away, convey, τινά, τί, subj. horses, draught animals, ἅρμα, πέδιλα, α 97 ; drive, πόντονδε, etc., freq. of winds; scatter, πῦρ, κονίην; snatch away, sweep away ; carry off as plunder, esp. with ἄγειν. The part. φέρων serves often to give vividness to the narrative, A 13. The inf. (also pass.) often follows the principal verb to denote purpose, Π 671, Λ 798, or result, ε 343, μ 442.—II. pass. ferri, be borne, either intentionally, charge, rush upon, O 743 ; ἰθύς, straight forward, Υ 172; or, more commonly, involuntarily, be borne, swept, hurried along, A 592. —III. mid. sibi (au)ferre, carry off

for one's self, bear away, esp. of victory, μέγα κράτος, N 486, and prizes, τὰ πρῶτα.

φεύγω, pres., inf. -έμεν(αι), ipf. (ἐ)φεῦγ(ε), and iter. φεύγεσκεν, fut. ξομαι, εσθ(ε), ονται, εσθαι, aor. ἔφυγες, and φύγον, ε(ν), iter. φύγεσκε, subj. γ(σι), opt. οιμι, etc., inf. ἔειν = εῖν, part.; pf. πεφεύγοι, ότες, also **πεφυζότες** Φ 6, X 1, and πεφυγμένος, ον (with ἔμμεναι, εἶναι, γενέσθαι), (fuga), fugere, flee, A 173, Ω 356, γ 166, ω 54 ; flee from, Λ 327, ὑπό τινος, ἐκ-; flee one's country for crime, go into exile, ν 259, π 424 ; πατρίδα, ο 228 ; avoid, τινά, μ 157, A 60 ; escape, τινά, τί, ζ 170, μ 260, κ 131; ποῖόν σε ἔπος φύγεν ἔρκος ὀδόντων, what a word has slipped past the fence of thy teeth! has escaped thee! πεφυγμένος, τί, Z 488 ; ἀέθλων, α 18, escaped from toils.

φῆ = ἔφη, from φημί.

φή, sicut, just as, like, B 144.

Φηγεύς, son of Dares, priest of Hephaistos in Ilios, slain by Diomedes, E 11, 15.

φήγινος, adj., (φηγός), faginus, of oak-wood, oaken, E 838†.

φηγῷ, όν, fem., (fāgus), kind of oak with edible acorns ; an ancient tree of this species was one of the landmarks on the Trojan plain, H 22, I 354. (Il.)

φήμη, ην, fem., (φάναι), fama, ominous or prophetic voice or word, omen, ν 100, β 35.

φημί (φα, φαίνω, fari), enclitic throughout pres. exc. 2 sing. **φής**, φησί, φαμέν, φατέ, φασί(ν), subj. φῇ-(σιν), and φήῃ, opt. φαίην, ης, η, φαῖμεν; φάς, φάντες, ipf. (ἐ)φῆν, (ἔ)φῆσθα, (ἔ)φῆς η 239, (ἔ)φῆ ω 470, (ἐ)φάμεν, 3 pl. (ἔ)φά(σα)ν, no inf., fut. φήσει; mid. = in signif. act. pres. imp. φάο, inf. φάσθαι, part. φάμενος, η, ipf. (ἐ)φάμην, (ἔ)φάτο, 3 pl. (ἔ)φάντο, declare, make known, opp. κεύθειν, cf. φ 194; ἔπος τ' ἔφατ', raise the voice so as to make audible, uttered the word, spoke aloud, Γ 398, Z 253, β 302 ; ἔπος, δ 370 ; φάτο μῦθον, as close of verse, Φ 393 ; report, deliver, τί, Σ 17 ; ο 377, speak out one's mind ; ἴσον ἐμοὶ φάσθαι, fancy himself equal to me; mid. (exc. E 184, dico, mean), think, δ 664, χ 31, 35 ; tradition says, ζ 42 ; with οὐ, negare, deny, ο 213; ὡς φάτο, ὡς ἔφαθ', freq. as conventional phrase where it is not strictly necessary to the sense, ν 54; when the inf. follows with same subj. as the principal verb its subj. is in nom., Α 397 (exc. θ 221, where it is acc.); when the subj. changes, we find acc. with inf.; yet the subj. acc. must sometimes be supplied, Δ 351, 375, α 168, δ 638; likewise sometimes also the inf., I 329, Ξ 126, εἶναι.

Φήμιος, bard in Ithaka, α 154, 337, ρ 263, χ 331; son of Terpios.

φῆμῑς, ιν, fem., fama, rumor, common talk (ο 468, δήμοιο, place of popular discussion, assembly), Κ 207.

φῆν = ἔφην, see φημί.

φήναι, ειε, opt. aor. from φαίνω.

φήνη, αι, fem., sea-eagle, γ 372 and π 217.

φήρ, **φηρσίν**, τοῖς, feris, wild beasts, Α 268; but **φῆρας**, of Centaurs, Β 743, λαχνήεντες, hairy, shaggy.

Φηραί and Φηρῇ, Ε 543, town afterward in Messenia, but by Homer placed in domain of Lakonike, I 151, 293, γ 488, ο 186.

Φηρητιάδης, αο, son of Pheres = Eumelos, Β 763 and Ψ 376.

φής, **φῆς** = ἔφης, **φῆσθα** = ἔφησθα, see φημί.

φθάν, see φθάνω.

φθάνει, fut. φθήσονται, aor. ἔφθης, η, and φθῆ, 3 pl. φθάν, subj. φθῇ(σιν), φθήῃ, φθέωμεν, ἕωσιν [pronounce φθῖώ-μεν, ἶῶσι, π 383, ω 437], opt. φθαίη, no inf., φθάμενος, aor. mid. part. ο 171, come before, λ 58; overtake, anticipate, τινά, Φ 262; with part. may be translated sooner, before, π 383; so also with ἤ, e. g. λ 58, πεζὸς ἐών, thou art come sooner on foot, than— Α 51, with gen. of comparison, they were much (μέγα) sooner arranged than the horsemen; so also part. φθάμενος, before, sooner, Ε 119, τ 449; also with πρίν, Π 322, τοῦ ἔφθη πρὶν οὐτάσαι, hit him on the shoulder before—.

φθέγγομαι, subj. **φθεγγώμεθα**, imp. εο, part. ομένον, ipf. (ἐ)φθέγγοντο, aor. φθέγξατ(ο), subj. φθέγξομ(αι), part. ξάμενος, ον, η, utter a sound, cry or call out, Λ 603, κ 228; Κ 457 = χ 329, while his shout still resounded; ὀλίγῃ ὀπί = τυτθόν, speaking softly; καλεῦν-τες, they called aloud.

φθείρουσι, destroy, ruin, ρ 246; pass. φθείρεσθ(ε), ruin seize ye, Φ 128.

Φθειρῶν also **Φθερῶν**, ὄρος, mountain in Karia, Β 868.

φθέωμεν, ἕωσιν, see φθάνω.

φθῆ, φθήῃ, φθῆσιν, see φθάνω.

Φθίη, dat. Φθίηφι Τ 323, (1) Phthia, chief city of Myrmidons, residence of Peleus, Β 683.—(2) region about Phthia, making up with Ἑλλάς the realm of Achilleus, I 395, λ 496.

Φθίηνδε, to Phthia, Α 169, Τ 330.

φθίμενος, see φθίνω.

φθῑνύθει, ουσι(ν), subj. ω; ipf. φθί-νυθον and iter. φθινύθεσκε, waste, consume; κῆρ, one's heart = pine away (μιν ὀδυρόμενοι, κ 485, whose grief breaks my heart); intrans. waste away, θ 530; perire, Ζ 327.

φθίνω (parallel form **φθίω**, subj. **φθίης** β 368, ipf. ἔφθιεν Σ 446), **φθίνουσι**, έτω, οντος, όντων, pass. mid. fut. φθίσονται, εσθ(αι), pf. ἔφθῖται, plupf. φθίμην, 3 pl. φθίαθ' = ατο, 2 aor. sync. ἔφθῖτ(ο), subj. ωμαι, ὁμε-σθα, opt. ἱμην, ῖτ(ο), inf. ἱσθαι, part. ἱμε-νος, ου, οιο, οισι, aor. pass. 3 pl. ἔφθῖ-θεν, (1) trans. only fut. φθίσει, ειν, aor. 3 pl. φθίσαν, subj. ωμεν, inf. ἱσαι, consume, destroy, slay, Π 461, ν 67, π 428.—(2) intrans. (all other forms), waste away, decay, wane, dwindle; κακὸν οἶτον, die a wretched death; μηνός, ὤν, wane, approach the end, ξ 162, κ 470.

Φθίοι, ων, inhabitants of Phthia, Ν 686, 693, 699.

φθισ-ήνορα, man-consuming, πόλεμον, Β 833. (Il.)

φθῑσί-μβροτος, ον, (βροτός,) which consumes mortals, life-destroying, μάχη, Ν 339; αἰγίδα, χ 297.

φθογγῆς, ήν, fem., (φθέγγομαι,) voice, Β 791, Π 508.

φθόγγῳ, ον, masc., (φθέγγομαι,) voice; φθόγγῳ, σ 198, aloud, i. e. talking.

φθονέω, έεις, ἔοιμι, ἔειν, ἔουσ(α), (φθίνω,) grudge, deny, refuse, τινί τινος, ζ 68; with inf., λ 381, τ 348; acc. and inf., α 346, σ 16.

φι(ν), vestige of several old case endings, applied to the stem-vowel of the various declensions, I. ηφι and ῆφι (but ἐσχαρόφι), II. όφι, III. εσφι (but ναῦφι), of persons only in two words, (ἐκ)θεόφι and αὐτόφι: serves (1) as simple gen. only Φ 295, μ 45; with verbs, Λ 350, Π 762 ; with ἐπί, Τ 255, and διά.—(2) as simple dat., B 363 ; with ἀτάλαντος, Γ 110; with verbs, Ν 700, ρ 4.—(3) as ablat., θ 279, ε 152, also with ἀπό, ἐκ, ὑπό, πρόσθε.—(4) as instrumental case, δακρυόφι πίμπλαντο, Ρ 696, Λ 699 ; ἶφι = Ϝῖφι, vi. —(5) as locative, παλάμηφιν ἀρήρει, and with ἐν, ἐπί, παρά, ἀμφί, πρός, ε 433 ; ὑπό, Τ 404.—(6) of doubtful classification, Μ 114, Ζ 510, Ο 267, Χ 107.

φιάλη, ῃ, ην, fem., large basin or bowl, Ψ 270; urn, Ψ 243.

φῖλαι, φίλατο, see φιλέω.

φιλέω, φιλεῖ and ἐει, inf. φιλεῖν only ο 74, part. εὖντας, ipf. (ἐ)φίλει, elsewh. in pres. and ipf. always uncontracted, subj. ἐῃσι, opt. ἐοι and οίη, inf. ἠμεναι, ipf. iter. φιλέεσκε, fut. inf. ησέμεν, aor. ἐφίλησα, ε, αν, and φίλησα, σ(ε) ; pass. 3 pl. aor. (ἐ)φίληθεν Β 668, and likewise fut. of mid. φιλήσεαι, diligere and amare, love, hold dear, cherish, τινὰ πέρι κῆρι, exceedingly in heart; ἐκ θυμοῦ, heartily ; σχέτλια ἔργα ; τινὰ παντοίην φιλότητα, bestow every mark of affection upon one; ἐφίληθεν ἐκ Διός, were loved by Zeus ; also receive as guest, welcome, ε 135; παρ' ἄμμι φιλήσεαι, acceptus gratusque nobis eris, thou shalt be kindly welcomed by us; mid. aor. (ἐ)φίλατο, imp. φίλαι περὶ πάντων, above all others, Υ 304.

φῖλ-ηρέτμοισι(ν), dat. pl., (ἐρετμόν), fond of the oar, Taphians and Phaiakians, α 181, ε 386. (Od.)

Φῖλ-ητορίδης, son of Philετor, Demuchos, Υ 457†.

Φῖλ-οίτιος, faithful herdsman of Odysseus, υ 185, 254, φ 240, 388 ; slays Peisandros, χ 268, and Ktesippos, χ 286.

φιλο-κέρτομε, voc., (κέρτομος). fond of jeering or mocking, contemptuous, χ 287†.

φῖλο-κτεἄνώτατε, voc., (κτέανον), most greedy of others' possessions, Α 122†.

Φῖλο-κτήτης, αο, son of Poias, from Meliboia in Thessaly, γ 190, θ 219, Β 718, 725.

φῖλο-μμειδής (from σμειδής, Old Ger. smielen, Eng. smile), laughter-loving, Aphrodite, Γ 424, θ 362. (Il.)

Φῖλο-μηλείδης, αο, king in Lesbos, who challenged all strangers to wrestle with him, δ 343 and ρ 134.

φῖλό-ξεινοι, loving guest-friends, hospitable, ζ 121. (Od.)

φῖλο-παίγμονος, gen. from -μων, (παίζω), fond of play, cheering, gay, ψ 134†.

φῖλο-πτολέμων, οισι(ν), fond of war, warlike, bellicosorum, Π 65. (Il.)

φῖλος, η, ον, etc., comp. φιλίων τ 351 and ω 268, and φίλτερος, ον, οι, sup. φίλτατος, ον, ε, (φίλταθ' = ατε), οι, η, αι, suus, one's own, εἵματα, αἰῶνος, and esp. of parts of body, χεῖρες; pl. sui, one's own, servants, relatives, cf. necessarii, "one's dear ones," δ 475 ; then, after one's mind, acceptable, pleasing, τινί ἐστι, (εἴη, γένοιτο, ἔπλετο); with inf., Δ 372, cf. Α 107 ; in general, dear, in direct address φίλος, α 301, and φίλε τέκνον, β 363 ; friendly, μήδεα, φίλα φρονεῖν τινι, εἰδέναι, be kind'y disposed. [φῖλε at beginning of verse, Δ 155.]

φῖλότης, ότητος, τι, τ(α), fem., (φίλος), (1) friendship, τιθέναι, establish ; ἕταμον with ὅρκια, establish a treaty, and hallow with sacrifice the alliance. —(2) hospitium, pledge of friendship, hospitable entertainment, ο 537, 55.—(3) amores, sexual love or intercourse, esp. with ὁμωθῆναι, μίσγεσθαι, μιγάζοντο, be united in, enjoy in common the pleasures of love, Ν 636, θ 267.

φῖλοτήσια (φιλότης), ἔργα, love's delights, λ 246†.

φῖλο-φροσύνη, fem., (-φρων), kindliness, friendly temper, I 256†.

φῖλο-ψευδής (ψεῦδος). friend of lies, false, Μ 164†.

φίλτατος, τερος, see φίλος.

φίλως, gladly, Δ 347, τ 461.

-φιν, see φι(ν).

φιτρῶν, ούς, masc., (φιτυρος, φῖτυ), trunk, block, log, Μ 29, μ 11. (Il.)

φλεγέθω, ουσι, οντι, pass. opt. 3 pl. φλεγεθοίατο, (φλέγω), blaze, glow, Φ 358, Σ 211; consume, burn up, Ρ 738, Ψ 197.

φλεγμά, τό, (φλέγω), flame, blaze, Φ 337†.

Φλέγυες or αι, robber tribe in Thessaly, Ν 302†.

φλέγω, φλέγει, (flagrare), singe,

consume, Φ 13; ipf. pass. φλέγετο, blazed.

φλέψ, φλέβα, τήν, (fluo), main artery, N 546†.

φλïῇσι, ταῖς, postibus, door-posts, ρ 221†.

φλόγεα, ntr. pl., (φλόξ), fulgentia, flaming, gleaming, E 745 and Θ 389.

φλοιόν, τόν, (liber), bark, A 237†.

φλοίσβου and οιο, gen., (φλύζω), roar of battle, E 322. (Il.)

φλόξ, γός, γί, γ(α), fem., (φλέγω), flamma, flame, blaze, Θ 135.

φοβέω, φοβεῖ, εἶτε, έουσι, aor. φόβησα, ἐφόβησας, (ἐ)φόβησε(ν), ῆσαι, fugare, put to flight, τινά; pass. pres. φοβεῖται, έονται, έεσθαι, εὐμενος, ipf. φοβέοντο, aor. 3 pl. (ἐ)φόβηθεν, θείς, (exc. π 163 only Il.), pf. πεφοβημένος, οι, plupf. 3 pl. πεφοβήατο, flee, ὑπό τινος and ὑπό τινι; fut. mid. φοβήσομαί τινα, flee from, X 250.

φόβος, οιο, ου, ον, masc., (φέβομαι), fuga, flight, κρυόεντος, chilling, dreadful; μήστωρα, exciter of flight, M 39; πρὸ φόβοιο, for fear; Αἴαντι ἐν -ῶρσεν, excited in Ajax (the thought of) flight; the horrors of flight, E 739. φόβονδ(ε), to flight; τρωπᾶσθαι, turn to flight; ἔχε ἵππους, ἀγορεύειν, counsel to flight, guide the horses to flight, E 252; abstained from flight, ω 57. (Il.)—Φόβος, attendant of Ares, O 119; son of Ares, N 299, Δ 440, Λ 37.

Φοῖβος (φοÅjος from φάÅος), Phoebus, the god of light; Ἀπόλλων Υ 68, preceding, elsewh. follg., freq. omitted; ἀκερσεκόμης, Υ 39; ἄνακτος, I 560; ἀφήτορος, I 405; ἑκάεργος, I 564; χρυσαόρου, E 509; ῄε, O 365; φίλε, O 221; δεινός, Π 788.

φοινήεντα (φόνος), blood-red, δράκοντα, M 202 and 220.

Φοίνικες, dwellers in Φοινίκη δ 83, ξ 291, described as traders, skillful in navigation, and artful, ο 415, 419; famous alike for artistic skill and for piracy, ξ 288, Ψ 744, ν 272, ο 473; their chief city, Sidon.

φοινικόεντα, εσσαν, εσσαι [by synizesis = ουσσ], (φοῖνιξ), purple, red, K 133, Ψ 717.

φοινικο-πάρῃους (παρειά), purple or red cheeked, with bows painted purple or red, λ 124 and ψ 271.

Φοῖνιξ, ικος, (1) father of Europa, Ξ 321.—(2) son of Amyntor, elder friend and adviser of Achilleus, to whose father he, under his own father's curse, had fled; Peleus constituted him lord of the Dolopes and educator of his son, whom he accompanied to Troja, I 223, 427, 432, 621, 659, 690; διίφιλος, I 168; ἀντίθεον, Ψ 360.

φοῖνιξ, (1) φοίνīκος, fem., date-palm, ζ 163†.—(2) φοίνικι, purpura, purple, the invention of which was ascribed to the Phoenikians.—(3) adj., rufus, gleaming with purple; Z 219, φαεινός, red or bay (horse), blood-bay (?), Ψ 454†.

φοίνιον (φόνος), (blood) red, Σ 97†.

Φοίνισσα (from Φοινικία) γυνή, a Phoenikian woman, ο 417.

φοινόν = φόνιον, red, Π 159†.

φοιτάω, φοιτᾷ, ῶσ(ι), ῶντε, ipf. (ἐ)φοίτων, (ἐ)φοίτα, 3 du. φοιτήτην, 3 pl. (ἐ)φοίτων, aor. φοιτήσασα, frequentare, obire, ambulare, trepidare, go hurriedly about, roam, Ω 533, E 528, O 686, ἔνθα καὶ ἔνθα κατὰ στρατόν, huc illuc per castra; παντόσε, M 266.

φολκός (falx, falcones), bow-legged, B 217†.

φονεύς, φονῆος, ῆας, masc., (φόνος), murderer, homicide, Σ 335, ω 434.

φονῆσιν, ταῖς, (φεν-), caedes, massacre, murder, K 521; rending, O 633.

φόνος, οιο, ου, ῳ, ον, οι, masc., (φεν-), caedes, murder, with κῆρα, B 352; ἀνδροκτασίαι τε; τεύχειν, prepare, E 652, δ 771; φυτεύει, β 165; μερμηρίζει, devises; φέρει, P 757; means of death, Π 144, Τ 391; = caesi, the slain, K 298; blood, gore, Ω 610, χ 376; αἵματος, reeking blood, of mangled beasts, Π 162.

φοξός (φώγειν), sharp-pointed, head low in front, sharp behind, a sugar-loaf head, B 219†.

Φόρβας, αντος, (1) king of Lesbos, father of Diomedes, I 665.—(2) rich Trojan, father of Ilioneus, Ξ 490.

φορβῆς, τῆς, (φέρβω, herba), forage, fodder, E 202 and Λ 562.

φορεύς, pl. φορῆες, οἱ, (φέρω), carrier of grapes in wine-harvest, vintager Σ 566†.

φορέω, φορέεις, etc., prs. always uncontracted, subj. έῃσι, inf. έειν, exc. opt.

φορήμεναι   324   φρήν

οἴη, inf. ἦναι, ἥμεναι, ipf. reg. uncontracted exc. (ἐ)φόρει, (ἐ)φόρεον [in χ 456 pronounce -ευν], iter. φορέεσκε(ν), aor. φόρησεν, mid. ipf. φορέοντο, (φέρω), portare and gestare, *bear, carry,* β 390, O 530, T 11; ρ 245, ἀγλαΐας ἅς φορέεις, scatter to the wind the pomp, vanities, which *thou displayest;* v e h e r e, B 770, K 323, Θ 528.

φορήμεναι, φορῆναι, see φορέω.

Φόρκῡνος λιμήν, harbor or inlet of *Phorkys* in Ithaka, ν 96†.

Φόρκυς, υν, (1) Phrygian chief, son of Phainops, slain by Aias, B 862, P 218, 312, 318.—(2) Φόρκυς, ὗνος, old man of the sea, father of Thoosa, α 72, ν 96, 345.

φόρμιγξ, ιγγος, ι, α, ες, fem., (fremo, Ger. b r u m m e), a kind of *lute* or *lyre;* it had a cross-piece, ζυγόν; pegs, κόλλοπες; was held by the ἀοιδός (exceptionally also by heroes, Achilleus, I 186; by Apollo, Ω 63), and served to accompany the strain or recitative, A 603, θ 67, 99. In form substantially like the κίθαρις in cut.

φορμίζων, *touching* or *playing the lyre,* Σ 605; also said of one who plays on the κίθαρις. (Od.)

φορτίδος, τῆς, (φόρτος), n a v i s o n e r a r i a, *ship of burden,* ε 250 and ι 323. (See cut.)

φόρτου, ον, masc., (φέρω), o n u s, *freight, cargo,* θ 163 and ξ 296.

φορύνετο, ipf. pass. φορύνω, (πορφύρ-ω). *was defiled,* χ 21†.

φορύξας, part. aor. from φορύσσω, (πορ-φύρ-ω), *having defiled* (thee) with much blood, σ 336†.

φόως, φόωσδε, see φάος.

φραδής, only **φραδέος** (φράζω), νόον ἔργα τέτυκται, l u c i d a (p r u d e n t i) m e n t e o p u s e s t, now is the need of a *clear* (*prudent*) mind, Ω 354†.

φράδμων (φραδής), *observing,* Π 638†.

φράζω (for φραδjω), aor. **φράσε,** red. πέφραδον (ἐ)πέφραδι(ν), πεφράδοι, δέμεν and δέειν; mid. pr. φράζεαι, subj. ὤμε(σ)θ(α), imp. φράζεο and ζευ, inf. ζεσθαι, ipf. iter. ζεσθαι, φραζέσκετο, fut. φράσομαι, σσομαι, σσεται, σσόμεθ(α), aor. (ἐ)φρασάμην, ἐφράσαθ᾽ = (ἐ)φράσ-(σ)ατ(ο), (ἐ)φράσ(σ)αντ(ο), subj. φράσεται, imp. φράσαι, pass. aor. ἐφράσθης, (φραδής), *make clear, point out, show,* Ξ 500; θ 68, *showed* him how to take it with his hands, i. e. *guided* his hands to the instrument; *command, direct,* K 127, Ψ 138; μῦθον, *make known* the matter: mid. (1) *perceive, distinguish,* (νοεῖν, s e n t i r e), Ψ 450; ἰσάντα, ὀφθαλμοῖσι, τινά, with part.; χ 129, *look to* this approach.—(2) *make clear to one's self, consider, ponder,* A 83, ο 167, π 237, 257; with dependent clause introduced by εἰ, ὅπως, with fut. or with subj. and κεν, ὥς κεν; μή, v i d e r e n e, *take care lest.*—(3) *devise,* τινί τι, λ 624, nor was he able to devise a harder task; also, *plan for any one, design,* Ψ 126; of Zeus, *decree.*

φράσσω, aor. 3 sing. **φράξε,** part. ξαντες, mid. aor. φράξαντο, aor. pass. φραχθέντες, (f a r c i o), ε 256, *he calked* it from end to end with willow withes (in the cracks between the planks); M 263, *having fenced around* the wall with their ox-hide shields; δόρυ δουρί, *joining* spear *close* to spear (so as to make a fence); O 566, *they surrounded* their ships with a brazen guard (guard of men clothed in brass).

φρέαρ, pl. **φρείατα,** ntr., *well,* Φ 197†.

φρήν K 45, φρενός, ί ζ 65, α, ένες, ῶν, εσί(ν), ένας, (1) only pl., praecordia, *midriff* or *diaphragm* separating the heart and lungs from the remaining inwards, Π 481, K 10, ι 301; hence the nearly synonymous expressions: κραδίη, ἦτορ, θυμὸς ἐνὶ φρεσίν, φρένες ἀμφὶ μέλαιναι, (dark on both sides, wrapped in gloom). The meaning of the word φρήν in Homer stands midway between its literal and its figurative sense; it means *the heart and the parts about the heart,* and signifies (2) *the seat of thought, will, feeling; mind, soul, heart, consciousness,* κ 493;

even *life*, Ψ 104; θεῖναι ἐν φρεσίν, suggest, Α 55; μετὰ and ἐνὶ φρεσίν, Δ 245; *discretion*, ἐσθλαί, ἀγαθῇσι, γ 266; βλάπτειν, blind, injure one's *understanding*; ἑλεῖν, ἐξέλετο, rob; *mind as will*, ἐτράπετο; often of *feelings* and *passions*, also φρένα as cognate acc., Υ 23; *sing.* used in reference to several persons, θ 131; κατὰ φρένα καὶ κατὰ θυμόν, in *mind* and heart.

φρήτρη, ας, ηφιν as dat. fem., (φράτηρ), gens, *clan*, Β 363. (Il.)

φρίξ, φρῑκός, ί, φρῑχ' = φρῖκα, *ruffling, agitation*; esp. of surface of water; Η 63, *a ripple* spreads over the sea.

φρίσσει, ουσι, aor. ἔφριξεν, ξας, pf. πεφρίκασι, υῖαι, horrere, *bristle*, Δ 282, Η 62; *shudder at*, with acc., Λ 383, Ω 775; νῶτον, λοφιήν, are accs. of respect, bristle on the back, on the crest.

φρονέω, έεις, subj. ἔῃσι, ipf. φρόνεον, etc., prs. and ipf. always uncontracted, (φρήν), *have consciousness* (Χ 59, *live*); *think*, Ζ 79; *reflect*, ὧδε δέ οἱ φρονέοντι; *understand, consider*, π 136, τί, ὀπίδα; *deem*, Γ 98, Ι 608; ἤ περ, just as, ἅ τε περ, the very things which; *intend*, Ρ 286, χ 51; τὰ φρονέων ἵνα, *with this intention* that, Ε 564; πυκινά, *have wise thoughts; ἴσόν τινι, imagine one's self* the equal of; ἀγαθά, have noble thoughts (α 43, and Ψ 305, εἰς ἀγ., advise for one's good); φίλα, kindly; κακά, having hostile disposition, Χ 264; ἀταλά, gay; μέγα φρονέων, proud, bold, Π 258; ὅσσον, quantopere superbiunt, Ρ 23; εὖ, intelligent, well-disposed, η 74; κακῶς, mean badly, σ 168; ἐφημέρια, thinking only of matters of a day, base-minded, φ 85.

Φρόνιος, ίοιο, father of Noemon, β 386 and δ 630.

φρόνις, **φρόνιν**, τήν, (φρένες), *knowledge, counsel*; δ 258, much information.

Φρόντις, ιδος, wife of Panthoos, mother of Euphorbos and Polydamas, Ρ 40†.

Φρόντις, ιος, son of Onetor, pilot of Menelaos, γ 282†.

Φρύγες, ας, Κ 431, Β 862, Γ 185; *Phrygians*, inhabitants of **Φρυγίη**, Γ 401, Π 719, Σ 291, a district in Asia Minor, lying partly on the Hellespon-

tos (καθύπερθε, Ω 545), partly on the river Sangarios. Greek art is indebted to the Phrygian costume for the pointed cap, which is an attribute of skilled artisans like Hephaistos, and of shrewd wanderers like Odysseus: the cut, from a Greek relief, represents a Phrygian archer.

φῦ = ἔφυ from φύομαι.

φύγᾰδ(ε), to *flight*, in fugam, Θ 157. (Il.)

φυγή, ῇ, fuga, *flight*, χ 306 and κ 117.

φυγο-πτόλεμος, *cowardly*, ξ 213†.

φύζα, αν, fem., (for φυγja, fugio), flight, *consternation*, Ι 2; panic, ἐμβάλλειν.

φυζᾰκῑνῇς, ταῖς, *shy, timid*, Ν 102†.

φυήν, τήν, (φύομαι), naturā, *growth*, (in) bodily form, stature, Β 58, θ 134.

φυκιόεντι, dat. from ὀεις, *full of seaweed, weedy*, Ψ 693†.

φῦκος, ntr., fucus, *sea-weed, seagrass*, Ι 7†.

φυκτά, verbal adj. from φεύγω, only in phrase οὐκέτι—πέλονται, there is no longer *a chance of escape*, non iam effugium est, Π 128, θ 299.

φυλᾰκή, ῆς, αἱ, άς, fem., (φυλάσσω), vigilatio, excubiae, *watch, guard*, Η 371; φυλακὰς ἔχον, keep guard; *outposts*, Κ 416.

Φυλάκη, town in Phthiotis on northern slope of Mount Othrys, in domain of Protesilaos, λ 290, ο 236, Β 695, 700, Ν 696, Ο 335.

Φυλᾰκίδης, *son of Phylakos*, Iphiklos, Β 705, Ν 698.

φυλάκους, τούς, (φυλάσσω), *guards*, Ω 566†.

Φύλᾰκος, (1) father of Iphiklos, ο 231.—(2) Trojan, slain by Leitos, Ζ 35†.

φῠλακτῆρες, οἱ, nom. -κτήρ, (φυλάσ-σω), c u s t o d e s, *guards*, I 66. (Il.)

φῠλαξ, pl. φῠλᾰκες, ων, εσσι(ν), ας, (φυλάσσω), c u s t o d e s, v i g i l i a e, *guards, outposts*, 1 477. (Il.)

Φύλας, αντος, father of Polymele, king of Thesprotian Ephyra, Π 181 and 191.

φῠλάσσω, pres. (imp. φύλασσε, inf. σσέμεναι), and ipf. (ἐφύλασσεν and φύ-λασσε), fut. ξω, εις, ων, aor. φύλαξε, subj. ξομεν, mid. φυλάσσονται, σσομέ-νοισι, v i g i l a r e, *keep watch, νύκτα, per noctem ; watch over, στρατόν ;* pass., K 309 ; δῶμα, " *keep*," i. e. *not quit* the house; χόλον, *treasure up*, cf. β 350 ; *keep* faith, ὅρκια ; *watch for, νόστον τινά ;* mid. *νύκτα, watch for one's self ;* πεφυλαγμένος εἶναι, *be on thy guard.*

Φῠλείδης, εω and αο, *son of Phyleus,* Meges, E 72, O 519, 528, Π 313.

Φῠλεύς, έος, ῆα, son of Augeias of Elis, banished by his father because, appointed arbiter in the dispute be-tween him and Herakles, he decided in favor of the latter, B 628, K 110, 175, O 530, Ψ 637.

φῠλίης, ῆς, *wild olive-tree,* ε 477†.

φύλλον (φύλιον, f o l i u m), pl. φύλλα, ων, οισι(ν), ntr., *leaves,* Z 146, ε 483.

Φῠλο-μέδουσα, wife of Areithoos, H 10†.

φῦλον, φῦλ(α), οις, ntr., (φύομαι), *nation, people,* Πελασγῶν, Γιγάντων ; *tribe, clan, family,* B 362 ; *class, species, host, swarm,* θεῶν, ἀνθρώπων, etc., μυίας, T 30.

φύλοπις, ίδος, ιδα λ 314, and ιν, fem., (φῦλον), *combat, din of battle, πο-λέμοιο,* λ 314 ; also joined with *πόλε-μος, ἔργον, νεῖκος φυλόπιδος,* angry combat, Υ 141 ; ἔστηκε, the combat arose, Σ 171.

Φῠλώ, οῦς, maid of Helene, δ 125 and 133.

φύξηλιν, acc., (φύξις), *cowardly,* P 143†.

φύξῑμον, ntr., (φύξις), *chance of escape,* ε 359†.

φύξιν, τήν, (φυγεῖν), *flight,* K 311, 398, 447.

φύρω, ipf. ἔφῡρον, fut. φύρσω, *moist-n, wet, δάκρυσιν, αἵματος ;* pass. pf.

πεφυρμένον (η), αἵματι, δάκρυσιν, ρ 103, σ 173.

φύσας, τάς, (πτύω), *bellows,* Σ 412. (Σ)

φυσάω, φῠσῶντες, pres. part., ipf. ἐφύσων, b'οιο, Σ 470 and Ψ 218.

φυσιόωντας, τούς, part. from -ιάω, (φῦσα), *panting,* Δ 227 and Π 506.

φῠσί-ζοος (ζωή), *producing life, life-giving, αἶα,* Γ 243.

φύσιν, τήν, (φύομαι), n a t u r a m, *quality, property,* κ 303†.

φῠτᾰλῐής, τῆς, (φυτόν), *plantation ; vineyard* or *orchard,* Z 195. (Il.)

φῠτεύει, ουσι, ων, ipf. φύτευεν, aor. ἐφύτευσαν, subj. φυτεύσω, inf. εὖσαι, (φυτόν), *plant, σ* 359 ; metaph. *devise, plan,* β 165, δ 668, O 134.

φῠτόν, ὤν, ntr., (φύω), *plant, tree,* coll. ω 227 ; ω 242, *plants.*

φύω, φύει, ipf. φύεν, fut. φύσει, aor. ἔφῡσε, (fui), *bring forth, produce,* φύλ-λα, Z 148, A 235, ποιήν, τρίχας ; but pres. mid. φύονται, ipf. φύοντο, aor. ἐφῦν, ἔφυ = φῦ, φύντες, pf. πεφύκᾱσι = πεφύᾱσι, subj. πεφύκῃ, part. πεφυῶ-τας, υυῖα, plupf. πεφύκει, *grow,* of plants, Δ 484, Ξ 288, ψ 190 ; ἐξ ὁμόθεν, from one stem ; of horns, Δ 109 ; see also ἐμφύομαι ; only in Z 149, φύει = φύεται.

Φωκεῖς, ήων, *dwellers in* Phokis, B 517, 525, O 516, P 307.

φῶκαι, άων, φσι, ας, fem., *seals,* δ 404.

φωνέω, aor. (ἐ)φώνησε, ήσας, άσης, (φωνή), *raise the voice ; φωνήσας, rais-ing his voice* = *aloud*, with *προσηύδα, προσέφη, ἀπαμείβετο ;* B 182, ὕπα de-pends upon ξυνήκε, not so ω 535 ; elsewh. *speak aloud.*

φωνή, ῇ, ήν, ῇσιν, fem., (φάος, φά-ναι), *voice, cry,* P 696 ; of trumpet, Σ 219 ; *outcry,* P 111 ; also of beasts and birds, μ 86.

φωρῐᾱμῶν, οἶσιν, gen. and dat. pl. masc., (φωρέω), *chest, coffer, box,* Ω 228 and ο 104.

φῶς, φωτός, ntr., see φάος.

φώς, φωτός, ί, (α), ε, ες, ὤν, ας, masc., (φύω), *man,* freq. as appositive with ἰσόθεος, α 324, δ 247 ; differing from ἀνήρ, as having reference more to the exterior, yet alternating with it, P 98 ; Ἡρακλῆα, φ 26.

X.

χάδε, ἕειν, see χανδάνω.

χάζομαι, opt. χαζώμε(σ)θ(α), imp. ζεο, ipf. ἐχάζετο, χάζετ(ο), οντ(ο), fut. χάσσονται, aor. χάσσατ(ο), ασθαι, ἀμενος, pf. κεκάδοντο, usually with ὑπό Δ 497, cedere, give way, withdraw before, ἄψ, ὀπίσω, with gen., also with preps. ἐκ, ὑπό; Π 736, nor did he long retire before Hektor; elsewh. rest from, abandon, with gen. μάχης, δουρός. Here is also classed red. aor. κεκαδών, Λ 334, θυμοῦ, depriving of life.

χαίνω, aor. opt. χάνοι, part. χανών, pf. part. κεχηνότα, (hiare), yawn, γαῖα, χθών, may the earth yawn for me, i. e. engulf me; part. with open mouth, πρὸς κῦμα, μ 350, opening my mouth to the wave.

χαίρω, etc., pres., ipf. (ἐ)χαῖρε(ν), χαῖρον, iter. χαίρεσκεν, κον, fut. χαιρήσειν, aor. ἐχάρη, ημεν, ησαν, and χάρη, είη, ἐντες, pf. part. κεχάρηότα; mid. aor. χήρατο, also red. fut. κεχαρησέμεν, mid. fut. κεχαρήσεται, aor. κεχάροντο, οιτο, 3 pl. οἴατο, (gratus), rejoice, ψ 32; (ἐν) θυμῷ, φρεσίν, νόῳ; φρένα, Z 481; χαίοων, joyful, δ 93, τ 461, each bidding the other a hearty farewell; also with ntr. subj., ἦτορ, κῆρ χαίρει; μέγα, greatly, exceedingly, constr. absolute, or with dat., ι 356, β 249; with part. agreeing with dat., Ε 682; with part. agreeing with subj., Γ 76; with οὕνεκα, ὅτι = quod. Χαῖρε, as salutation at meeting, hail, welcome, α 123, θ 408, 413, or at parting, ε 205; λ 248, because of our embrace; οὐ χαιρήσει, shall repent, Υ 363.

χαίτη, ην, αι, άων, ας, fem., flowing hair, Κ 15, Ξ 175, Ψ 141; juba, mane, Z 509, Ψ 282, 284.

χάλαζα, ῃ, αν, fem., grando, hail, Κ 6, Ο 170. (Od.)

χαλεπαίνει, οι, ε, ειν, ων, ipf. χαλέπαινε, aor. subj. χαλεπήνῃ, inf. ἦναι, (χαλεπός), be vexed, angry, τινί, π 114, Ξ 256, Υ 133; ἐπὶ ῥηθέντι δικαίῳ, at what has been justly said; rage, of wind and storm, Ξ 399; storm, ε 485.

χαλεπός, οῖο, ῷ, ῷ, όν, οί. ῶν, οῖσι, οὐς;

ἡ, ῆς, ἥν, αἱ, ά, comp. ὥτερον, adv. ὥς, bad, dangerous, serious, χαλεπόν ἐστι, with (acc. and) inf., difficile est, it is hard or difficult; also pers. construction, Φ 482; Τ 80, for it is annoying even to one skilled (in speaking); grievous, severe; κεραυνός, sharp stroke of lightning; ὀνείδη, harsh insults; of persons, angry.

χαλέπτει, pres., (χαλεπός), irascitur, be angry with, ὃ 423†.

χάλινούς, τούς, bit of bridle, Τ 393†.

χάλι-φρονέοντα, part. from -έω, (-φρων), thoughtless, indiscreet, ψ 13†.

χάλι-φροσύναι, αἱ, (-φρων) = levitas animi, thoughtlessness, π 310†.

χαλί-φρων (χαλάω, φρήν), thoughtless, δ 371 and τ 530.

χαλκεο-θωρήκων, gen. pl., with breastplate of bronze, Δ 448 and Ο 62.

χάλκεος, εῳ, εον, εοι, εα, and χάλκειον, ῳ, ων, η, ῃ, ας, (χαλκός), of copper or bronze, κύκλα, wheels; Ἄρης, clad in bronze; αὐγή, gleam of bronze; fig. brazen voice, ὄψ; ὕπνος = death, Λ 241; ἦτορ, heart of brass.

χαλκεο-φώνῳ, τῷ, (φωνή), with voice of brass or bronze, loud and clear, Ε 785†.

χαλκεύς, ῆἑς, masc., (χαλκός), faber, coppersmith, worker in bronze, also with ἀνήρ, ι 391, Δ 187; worker in metals, ι 391; goldsmith, γ 432.

χάλκευον, ipf., (χαλκεύς), fabricabar, I wrought, Σ 400†.

χαλκεῶνα, τόν, (χαλκεύς), forge, θ 273†.

χαλκήϊον, ια, (χαλκεύς), smith's house, forge, σ 328; smith's tools, γ 433.

χαλκ-ήρης, εος, εἴ, ε(α), .εσιν, εας, (ἀρηρώς), fitted or furnished with bronze = brazen-shod, of weapons and armor in general, Ο 544 (yet not of breastplate), Γ 316, Ο 535, Τ 53, Δ 469, Σ 534, Ν 650, Ρ 268.

χαλκίδα, τήν = κύμινδιν, Ξ 291†.

Χαλκίς, ίδος, fem., (1) town in Euboia on the strait Euripos, Β 537.—(2) town in Aitolia at mouth of the Euenos, ο 295.

χαλκο-βᾰρής, ές, (βάρος), heavy with brass, of ponderous brass, O 465; also fem. from βαρύς, -βάρεια, Λ 96, χ 259.

χαλκο-βᾰτές (βάτος), with bronze threshold, ν 4.

χαλκο - γλώχῑνος, gen., (γλωχίν), with bronze point, X 225†.

χαλκο-κνήμῑδες (κνημίς), with greaves of bronze, H 41†.

χαλκο-κορυστῇ, ήν, (κορύσσω), having bronze armor, brazen-clad, E 699. (Il.)

χαλκο-πάρῃον, gen., (παρειά), with side-pieces (lit. cheeks) of bronze, of helmet, ω 523. (Il.)

χαλκό-ποδ(ε), du., (πούς), with hoofs of bronze, Θ 41 and N 23.

χαλκός, οῖο, and οῦ, and όφι, ῷ, όν, aes, copper or bronze, which consists of copper and tin (brass, an alloy of copper and zinc, was not known to the ancients), Z 48, φ 10; utensils of bronze of every sort, cf. ahenum, Σ 349; knife, hook, axe, weapons and armor in general, exc. shield and breastplate, φ 434 = with sword and spear; αἴθοπι, νώροπι, νηλέϊ, τανᾱηκέϊ, ἀτειρής; ἐπελήλατο, was riveted upon it; bronze (and gold) utensils served also as presents and ransom, X 50, 340.

χαλκο-τύπους (τύπτω), inflicted with weapons of bronze, T 25†.

χαλκο-χῑτωνες, ων, ας, (χιτών), with coat of bronze, brass-clad, A 371.

Χαλκωδοντῐάδης, son of Chalkodon, king of the Abantes in Euboia, Elephenor, B 541†.

Χάλκων, ωνος, a Myrmidon, the father of Bathykles, Π 595†.

χᾰμάδις, adv., (χαμαί), to the ground, Z 147, O 714, δ 114.

χᾰμᾶζε, adv., (χαμαί), to the ground, down, Γ 29; to or into the earth, Θ 134, φ 136.

χᾰμαί (old locative from χαμα, humi), on the ground, E 442; = χαμᾶζε, with πέσε, βάλλω, χύντο, Δ 482, E 588, Φ 181.

χᾰμαι-ευναί, pl., (εὐνή), making their beds on the ground, Π 235†.

χᾰ:ᾰι-ευνᾰδες, pl. fem., (εὐνάζω), σύες, = foreg., lying on the ground, κ 243 and ξ 15.

χανδάνω, ipf. ἐχάνδᾰνον, χάνδανε, fut. χείσεται, aor. ἐχᾰδε, χᾰδε, έειν,

pf. part. κεχᾰνδότα, plupf. κεχάνδει, (prehendo), contain, hold, ὅσον κεφαλὴ χάδε φωτός, he gave as loud a shout as the head of a man (could) contain (cf. Π 76), i. e. shouted as loud as he could, Λ 462.

χανδόν, adv., (χανδάνω), hiantis instar, greedily, φ 294†.

χάνοι, see χαίνω.

χᾰράδρης, gen., pl. αι, (χαράσσω), gully, ravine, mountain torrent, Δ 454 and Π 390.

χᾰρείη, χάρη, see χαίρω.

χαρίεις, χᾰρίεν, εντ(α), εσσαν, comp. ιέστερον, sup. ιέστατος, η, (χάρις), graceful, charming, lovely, A 39; θ 167, winning gifts.

χᾰρίζεαι, εο, εσθαι, όμενος, η, ipf. χαρίζετο, aor. χαρίσαιτο, σασθαι, (χάρις), show favor, gratify, τινί; court favor by lies, ξ 387; ν 15, it is hard for a single person to win for himself gratitude for a gift, i. e. it is too much to expect that one person single-handed should make a gift and look to gratitude alone for the recompense; τί, bestow abundantly, Λ 134; and esp. παρεόντων, α 140, giving freely of her store; pass. plupf. κεχάριστο, was dear to her; pf. part. κεχαρισμένος, ε, α = χαρίεις, pleasing, welcome; ntr. pl., μοι—θείης, thou couldst gratify me.

χάρις, ῑν, ιστν, fem., (χαίρω), gratia, (1) love, favor, φέρειν τινί, confer upon one.—(2) gratitude, ἀρέσθαι, earn; Τρώεσσι, from the Trojans, ἐνεργίων, for benefits; οὔ τις ἦεν, one had no thanks; Ψ 650, may the gods grant thee in return for these things a soul-satisfying recompense; ἰδέω, would thank thee, χάριν Ἕκτορος, for Hektor's sake.—(3) grace, charms, κάλλεϊ καὶ χάρισι στίλβων, shining in beauty and grace; also of things, words, and actions, o 320.

Χάρις, properly the same word as foreg. personified as wife of Hephaistos, Σ 382; pl. Χάριτες, ων, εσσι, the Graces, handmaids of Aphrodite, E 338, Ξ 267, P 51, ζ 18, σ 194.

χάρμα, ατα 185, ntr., (χαίρω), gaudium, joy, τ 471; as appositive, ζ 185; source of malignant joy, Z 82.

χάρμης, ῃ, fem., (χάρμα?), joy in battle, desire for the fray, eagerness for combat, χ 73, N 82; Δ 509, do not yield *in fury* to the Argives; also of animals, Π 823; also = *battle*, προκαλέσσατο, χάρμῃ, he had challenged to battle.

χᾰρ-οποί, *with sparkling eyes,* λ 611†.

Χάροπος, king of Syme, father of Nireus, B 672†.

Χάροψ, οπα, son of Hippasos, brother of Sokos, wounded by Odysseus, Λ 426†.

Χάρυβδις, ιος, ιν, (χάραδρα), fem., *Charybdis,* personification of the whirlpool opposite the "howling" Σκύλλα, μ 113, ψ 327; δεινήν, δῖα, μ 104, 235.

χᾰτέουσ(ιν), and part. έουσι, έουσα, (χάσκω, κῆτος), i n h i a r e, γ 48, θεῶν, *have need of;* elsewh. desire, demand, o 376, I 518.

χᾰτίζεις, ει, ων, (χατέω), with gen., (1) *have need of,* Σ 392, P 221, sc. αὐτῆς; elsewh. (2) *desire, beg,* χ 351.

χειῇ, τῇ, (χάσκω, hio), *hole,* X 93 and 95.

χεῖλος, χείλει, εα, εσ(σ)ι(ν) (χειῇ), *lip,* X 495, ὀδὰξ ἐν χείλεσι φύντες, biting their *lips,* α 381; *border* of the ditch, M 52, cf. δ 132, o 116.

χεῖμα, ατος, ntr., h i e m s, *winter,* η 118, λ 190; *cold,* ξ 487. (Od.)

χειμά-ρροος (from σροος. ῥέω), -ρρῳ, E 88; -ρροι, ους, *swollen* (lit. flowing) *with* (water from melting) *snow,* ποταμός, N 138.

χειμερίῳ, ον, ῃ, αι, ῃσιν, (χεῖμα), *wintry,* Γ 222; ὕδωρ, *snow-water,* Ψ 420.

χειμών, ῶνος, *storm, rain,* Γ 4, P 549, δ 566.

χείρ, χειρός, (ί), (α), (ε), ες, ῶν, εσσ(ιν), ας, also χερί, χερσί(ν) (χερ-, radical meaning "grasp," old Latin h i r), m a n u s, *hand, hand and arm,* Z 81, α 238; *fist,* στιβαρῇσιν, μ 174; ἀνέχειν, raise, in prayer, ν 355; τινί, pray to, Γ 318; pl. freq. in conventional use = sing., ν 225; 288, κατέρεξε, stroked him with the hand; ἐν χερσὶ τίθει, laid in his hands or arms, intrusted, of present or prize, A 441, γ 51; coupled with πόδες, χ 477; pl. fig. = *strength, might,* υ 237, Z 502, coupled with μένος, δύναμις, βίη; ἐπιφέρειν, ἐφιέναι, ἰάλλειν τινί, attack; (εἰς) χεῖρας ἱκέσθαι, *fall into the power.*

χειρῖδας, τάς, (χείρ), *loose* or *false sleeves,* bound over the hands instead of gloves, ω 230†.

χειρότερος, οισιν, (χέρης), = follg., Υ 436 and O 513.

χείρων, ονος, ι, α, ες, (χέρης), de- terior, *inferior, worse,* O 641, λ 621, P 149, φ 325.

Χείρων, *Cheiron,* the centaur, skilled in healing and prophetic arts, intructor of Asklepios and Achilleus, δικαιότα- τος Κενταύρων, Λ 832, Δ 219, Π 143, T 390.

χείσεται, see χανδάνω.

χεῖσθαι, see χέω.

χελιδών, χελιδόνι, h i r u n d i n i, *swallow,* φ 411 and χ 240.

χέρᾰδος, τό, *gravel, pebbles,* Φ 319†.

χέρειον, see χερείων.

χερειότερος, ον, (χέρης), see follg., B 248, M 270.

χερείων, ονος, ι, α, (χέρης), de- terior, *inferior, worse;* δέμας, in figure; φυήν, in size; οὔ τι χέρειον, 'tis not ill, with inf., ρ 176; τὰ χερείονα, ill counsels, A 576.

χέρης; χέρηι, χέρηα, χέρηες, ntr. χέρεια, (χείρ, i. e. under one's hand, subject), *humble, low, base,* A 80, Ξ 382; with gen. has force of comparative, Δ 400.

χερμάδιον, ῳ, α, οισι(ν), ntr., (χείρ), *loose stone,* of such a size as to fit the hand and be easily thrown, E 302, Π 774.

χερνῆτις, fem., (χείρ), *living by hand labor, woman who spins for daily hire,* M 433†.

χέρ-νῐβον (χείρ, νίπτω), *wash-basin,* Ω 304†.

χερ-νίπτομαι only aor. -νίψαντο, *washed their hands,* A 449†.

χέρ-νιψ, acc. νῐβα, *water for washing the hands,* α 136. (Od.)

Χερσι-δάμας, son of Priamos, slain by Odysseus, Λ 423†.

χέρσονδε, *on the dry land,* Φ 238†.

χέρσον, ῳ, ον, fem., *land, shore,* Δ 425, ζ 95.

χεῦαι, αν, ε, see χέω.

χεῦμα, τό, (χέω), *that which is poured out, casting,* Ψ 561†.

χέω, I. act. pres. and ipf. χέε(ν), χέον, mid. χέοντ(ο), etc., only uncontracted forms, exc. χεῖσθαι κ 518, fut. χεύω, aor. ἔχεεν, εαν, (ἔ)χεῦ(εν), χεύαμεν, (ἔ)χεῦαν, subj. χεύομεν, ωσι, imp. χεῦον, ἄντων, inf. χεῦαι, part. χεύας, αντες, ἄντων, aor. mid. (ἔ)χεύατο.— II. pass. pf. κέχυνται, plupf. κέχυτ(ο), (ἐ)κέχυντο, aor. χυθείη ; with pass. signif., aor. sync. (ἐ)χύτο, (ἔ)χυντο, χυμένη, (χεϝω). I. fundo, *pour, scatter* ; Ζεύς ὕδωρ, *it rains* ; Μ 281, *pours down* snow ; σῆμα, *raise* a monument; τύμβον, funeral mound ; χθονί, *throw down, scatter* on the earth ; ἔραζε, *let fall* on the ground; αὐτμένα, *breathe forth* ; φωνήν, *let resound*; mid. χοήν, *pour out* a libation, elscwh. with reflexive signif. ; *strew upon one's* head, *throw one's arms around, they shower their missiles forth.*—II. pass. fundi, *flow, be strewn* ; πάλιν χύτο, *flowed back, lie spread out* ; with ἐκ, effundi ; ἐμέ, *threw themselves* upon me, κ 415; ἀμφί τινι, *embrace.*

χηλός (χάσκω), χηλοῖο, οῦ, ᾧ, όν, οἱ, οἶσιν, fem., *chest*, φ 51, Π 228.

χημεῖς = καὶ ἡμεῖς, Β 238.

χήν, χήν(α), ες, ῶν, ας, masc. and fem., (χαίνω? Ger. Gans), anser, *goose*, ο 174, Β 460.

χηραμόν, τόν, (χάσκω), *hole* or *crevice in a rock*, Φ 495†.

χήρατο, aor. from χαίρω.

χηρεύει (χήρη), *is deprived of, goes without*, ἀνδρῶν, hominibus, ι 124†.

χήρη, ην, αι, (χαίνω), *bereaved, widowed*, Β 289 ; with gen. σοῦ, Ζ 408.

χήρωσας, ε, aor., (χήρη), *thou hast bereft*, Ρ 36 ; *make desolate*, Ε 642.

χηρωσταί, οἱ, (χηρόω), *surviving relatives, heirs of one who dies childless*, Ε 158.

χήτεϊ, ει, ntr., nom. χῆτος, (χατέω), *from lack* (of), τινός, π 35. (Il.)

χθᾰμᾰλή, αί, comp. -ώτερον, sup. -ώτατον, (χαμαί), humilis, *low-lying, low*, λ 194, μ 101, Ν 683.

χθιζός, όν, ά, (χθές), hesternus Α 424, ntr. = heri, *yesterday*, Τ 195; χθιζά τε καὶ πρωΐζ', it was (only) *yesterday* and day before yesterday when the ships of the Achaians were gathered in Aulis, = it was recently (verses 305–307 are parenthetical), Β 303.

χθών, ονός, ί, α, humus, tellus, *ground, earth* ; ἐπὶ χθονί, *upon the earth* ; ἐπὶ χθόνα, *to the ground* ; *the region*, ν 352.

χίλι(α), *thousand*, Η 471, Θ 562. (Il.)

χίμαιρα (χίμαρος), *she-goat*, Ζ 181†.

Χίμαιρα, fem., *Chimaera*, fire-spouting monster ; its fore part a lion, its middle a goat, its hinder part a snake, sent as a plague upon Lykia, but slain by Bellerophon (the cut is from an Etruscan bronze statue of large size in the museum at Florence), Ζ 179 sqq., Π 328.

Χίος, οιο, *island* on the Ionian coast of Asia Minor, γ 170, 172.

χιτών, χιτῶνος, νι, ι'(α), νες, νων, ῶσι, νας, (word of Semitic origin; Heb. ketonet, Eng. cotton), *bodyjacket, tunic*, Σ 595 ; like a shirt, but without sleeves, of woolen, white, worn by men and women next the body, and confined about the middle by a girdle, ξ 72 ; the cut represents Achilleus (clothed in the χιτών) taking leave of Peleus (cf. also Nos. 59, 78) ; there were also long tunics, see ἑλκεχίτωνες; of soldiers, *coat of mail, cuirass*, Β 416, Λ 100 (cf. cuts Nos. 12, 17, 85, 93); λάϊνον, sarcastic expression for *death by stoning*, Γ 57.

χιών, όνος, όνι, fem., *snow*, ζ 44, M 278.

χλαίνης, η, αν, αι, άων, a piece of coarse, shaggy woollen cloth, double or single, διπλῆ, δίπλακα, ἀπλοΐδας, freq. of purple color; cloak, mantle, X 498, ξ 460, 478, 480, 488, 500, 504, 516, 520, 529 ; it served also as covering in sleep, being in fact a sort of blanket, υ 4, 95, γ 349, δ 50.

χλούνην, τύν, (ἐν χλόῃ εὐνήν ἔχοντα, etymology of ancients), making its bed or lair in the grass, epith. of wild boar, σῦν, I 539†.

χλωρηΐς, fem., (χλωρός), pale green, yellow green, epith. of nightingale as dwelling in fresh foliage, τ 518†.

Χλῶρις, ιδος, daughter of Amphion, king in Orchomenos, wife of Neleus, mother of Nestor, Chromios, Periklymenos, and of Pero, λ 281†.

χλωρός, όν, οἱ, άς, (χλοΓερός), flavum, greenish yellow, μέλι ; δέος, pale fear, H 479, λ 43, O 4 ; elsewh. fresh, verdant, ι 379, 320.

χνόος, ὁ, (κνάω, κόνις), foam, ἁλός, ζ 226†.

χοάνοισιν, ntr., (χέω), melting-pits, Σ 470†.

χοήν, άς, (χέω), libation, drink-offering, esp. in sacrifices for the dead, κ 518 and λ 26.

χοῖνιξ, χοίνικος, fem., measure for grain, = a soldier's daily ration, about one quart; ἅπτεσθαί τινος, taste of my bread, τ 28†.

χοίρε(α), ntr., (χοῖρος), κρέα, of swine, swine-flesh, pork, ξ 81†.

χοῖρος, χοίρων, masc., porcus, hog, ξ 73†.

χολάδες, fem., (χορδή, haru-spex), bowels, intestines, Δ 526 and Φ 181.

χόλος, οιο, ου, ῳ, ον, (fel), gall Π 203, elsewh. wrath, τινός, as subj. or obj. gen. one's wrath or wrath against one; τινί, out of regard to any one, with μεθέμεν, λήσεσθαι; X 94, rage.

χολόω (χόλος), act. fut. χολωσέμεν, aor. ἐχόλωσεν, σατε, σῃς ; mid. pass. pres. χολοῦμαι, οὗται, fut. ὤσεαι, pf. κεχόλωται, ὦσθαι, ωμένος, etc., plupf. κεχόλωτο, ωτο, 3 pl. ὤατο, 3 fut. κεχολώσομαι, σεαι, σεται, aor. (ἐ)χολώσατο, χολώσαιτο, σάμενος, etc., aor. pass. (ἐ)χολώθη, χολωθῇς, θείς, I. provoke, enrage, A 78, Σ 111, θ 205,

σ 20.—II. mid. pass. be angry, θυμῷ ἐνὶ φρεσί, κηρόθι, θυμόν, φρένα, ἦτορ, in mind, heart; τινί, at or with a person ; τινός, because of (also with ἐκ, εἵνεκα, ἀμφ' ἀστραγάλοισι), I 523, N 203, P 710.

χολωτοῖσι, dat. pl., (χολόω), angry, wrathful, ἐπέεσσιν, Δ 241, χ 26.

χορδήν, τήν, (χολάδες), chordam, string of gut, φ 407†.

χοροι-τύπίῃσιν, ταῖς, (τύπτω), tripudio, choral dance, Ω 261†.

χοροῖο, ῳ, ὁν, (ὀνδε, to the dance), οἱ, masc., choral dance, (1) dancing-place, Σ 590, μ 318.—(2) dance, χορῷ καλή, beauteous in the dance, Π 180.

χόρτῳ, οισιν, masc., (hortus), enclosure, Λ 774 and Ω 640.

χραίσμε(ε), aor., = ἔχραισμε, ῃ(σι), ωσιν, εῖν, fut. ἤσει, ἠσέμεν, 1 aor. χραίσμῃσι, ἦσαι, (χρήσιμος), always with negative, be useful to, τινί; with reference to—, τί; hence help, aid, and ward off any thing, A 566, 589, Λ 117, 120, Φ 193.

χράομαι (χρέος), part. χρεώμενος, trisyll., Ψ 834, according to his need; pf. κεχρημένος, ῳ, ον, with gen. desiring, Τ 262 (πρόφασιν, as a pretext); as adj. needy, ρ 347; plupf. φρεσὶ γὰρ κέχρητ' ἀγαθῇσιν, she had good sense, right feelings.

χραύσῃ, aor. subj. from χραύω (χράfω, χρώς), scratch, graze, wound slightly, E 138†; here belongs also aor. ἔχράε, ἀετ(ε), fall upon, assail, τινά; with inf. of purpose, Φ 369, φ 69 ; but with τοι, οἱ δαίμων, the god has handled (thee), him) hardly.

χράω, part. χρείων, delivering an oracle, θ 79 ; mid. fut. χρησόμενος, ον, ους, to have an oracle given to one, for the purpose of receiving the divine response, to consult with, θ 81, λ 165, κ 492.

χρεῖος, see χρέος.

χρείων, see χράω.

χρειώ, see χράω.

χρειώς, see χρέος.

χρεμέτίζον, ipf., neigh, whinny, M 51†.

χρέος θ 353, λ 479, χρείως· θ 355, also v. l. χρεῖος, τό, want ; Τειρεσίαο κατά = to consult with Teiresias ; elsewh. affair, business, need, β 45, α 409 ; debt, ὀφείλειν, owe; payment of debt, θ 353;

ἀποστήσωνται, recompensent, recover for themselves (pay back) the
debt of yesterday, N 745 (v. l. ἀποτί-
σωνται, see themselves repaid for).

χρεώ, subst. fem., [monosyll., short,
Λ 606], (χρέος, χράομαι), want, need,
ἐστίν, γίγνεται, cf. opus est, ι 136, Φ
322, δ 634, cf. Α 341, Ι 197 ; with inf.,
Ψ 308 ; τινά, α 225, Κ 85 ; with acc.
and inf., Σ 406, δ 707, Φ 322 ; τινά
τινος, Ι 75, 607, Κ 43, δ 634 ; parallel
form **χρειώ** ἱκάνει, εται, ἵκει, necessity
arises; τινά (τόσον, so sharply), τινός ;
shall he have any need of a tomb, Φ
322.

χρεώμενος, see χράομαι.

χρή, subst. = χρεώ, sc. ἵκει, ἐστίν,
opus est, (there is) need, ι 50 ; with
inf., Δ 57, Π 631, γ 209, ω 324 ; with
pers. acc. and inf., Η 331, Ψ 644, ζ 27,
ω 407, cf. Α 216, κ 490 ; οὐδέ τι (σὲ)
χρή, with inf. (to be supplied, Π 721,
Υ 133, τ 500), or expressed, Ψ 478, α
296, τ 118 ; τινά τινος, Η 109, α 124,
χ 377.

χρηίζεις, ζων, οντι, οντα, pres., (χρή),
need, τινός, ρ 558, Λ 834.

χρῆμᾰτ(α), ασι, ntr., (χράομαι), what
one has for need or use, possessions, property, β 78, ξ 285, π 315. (Od.)

χρίμπτω, aor. pass. **χριμφθείς**,
(scrimp? χρίω?), πέλας, approaching very near, κ 516†.

χρίω, ipf. **χρῖον**, εν, aor. ἔχρισε(ν),
χρῖσεν, σαν, σον, σαι, ἐλαίῳ, smear
with oil, anoint, δ 252; also bodies of
dead, Ψ 186 ; ἀμβροσίῃ, Π 670 ; mid.
χρίεται, εσθαι, fut. χρίσομαι, aor. σάμε-
ναι, anoint one's self, ἐλαίῳ, κάλλεϊ;
ἰοὺς φαρμάκῳ, smear one's arrows with
juice of poisonous plants, α 262.

χροιῇ, τῇ, (χρώς), prop. surface, skin
= body, Ξ 164†.

χρόμᾰδος, masc., (χρεμετίζω), grinding, Ψ 688†.

Χρόμιος, οιο, (1) son of Priamos,
slain by Diomedes, Ε 160.—(2) son
of Neleus, λ 286, Δ 295.—(3) a Lykian, slain by Odysseus, Ε 677.—(4) a
Trojan, slain by Teukros, Θ 275.—(5)
chief of Mysians, Ρ 218, 494, 534.

Χρόμις, ιος, = Χρομίος (5), Β 858.

χρόνιον, acc., (χρόνος), after a long
time, ἐλθόντα, ρ 112†.

χρόνον, τόν, (χερ-, χραίνω?), time,
πολύν, δηρόν, long time ; τόσον, so long,

Ω 670, ὀλίγον ; ἕνα χ., once for all ; ἐπὶ,
for a time, μ 407.

χροός, οΐ, όα, see χρώς.

χρῡσ-άμπῠκας, acc., (ἄμπυξ), with
frontlet of gold, of horses, Ε 358.
(Il.)

χρῡσ-άορου, ον, (ἄορ), with sword of
gold, Apollo, Ε 509 and Ο 256.

χρύσεος, ου, ῳ, ον, οι, οισ(ιν) ; ἰη,
η, ην, αι, ῳσιν ; εον, εα, and parallel
form **χρύσειον**, ω, οι, οις ; η, ῳ, ην, αι,
ῳς, ας ; (α), (χρυσός), aureus, golden,
adorned with gold ; esp. of all which
the gods wear or possess, Ἀφροδίτη,
δ 14, adorned with gold (see cut No.
2) ; golden = golden yellow, ἔθειραι, νέ-
φεα.

Χρύση, Chryse, a harbor town in
Troas, with temple of Apollo, Α 37,
100, 390, 431, 451.

Χρῡσηίς, ίδος, Chryseis, daughter of
Chryses, Α 111, 143, 182, 310, 369,
439. (Her proper name was Astynome.)

χρῡσ-ηλάκᾰτος, ου, ῳ, (ἠλακάτη),
with golden arrows, Artemis, δ 122.

χρῡσ-ήνιος (ἠνις), gleaming with gold,
Ζ 205 and Θ 285.

Χρύσης, αο, voc. η, Chryses, the
priest of Apollon Smintheus at Chryse:
his daughter Astynome had fallen as
booty to Agamemnon ; upon his re-
fusal to release her on ransom to her
father, he induces Apollo, in answer to
his prayers, to send a pestilence upon
the Greek camp, which compels Agamemnon to yield up the maiden, Α 11,
370, 442, 450.

Χρῡσό-θεμις, daughter of Agamemnon and of Klytaimnestra, Ι 145 and
287.

χρῡσό-θρονος, ου, ον, (θρόνος), on
throne of gold, golden-throned (cf. Aphrodite in cut No. 2) ; epithet of Eos,
Hera, Artemis, Α 611, ε 123.

χρῡσο-πεδίλου (πέδιλον), golden-
sandalled [λ 604].

χρῡσό-πτερον (πτερόν), with wings
of gold, Θ 398 and Λ 185.

χρῡσό-ρραπις, voc. ι, (ϝραπ-), bearing a golden rod, of Hermes with his
magic staff, κ 277, 331, ε 87.

χρῡσός, οῖο, οῦ, ῳ, όν, gold, un-
wrought and wrought ; τάλαντον, a
pound ; collective = utensils of gold,
ο 207.

χρῦσο-χόον, τόν, (χέω), goldsmith, γ 425†.

χρώς, ωτός, ῶτ(α), and χροός, gen., οἱ, όα, (χραFος, σκραυ-), properly sur-face, esp. surface of the body, skin, N 191, τ 204, δ 750, φ 412; then, color of the skin, complexion, τρέπεται, changes; body, yet always with refer-ence to the skin, καλός, περὶ χροΐ, λ 191, χ 113.

χυμένη, χύτο, see χέω.

χύσις, ιν, fem., (χέω), heap, ε 483, 487, τ 443.

χυτλώσαιτο, aor. opt. mid. from χυτλόω, (χύτλος), bathe and anoint one's self, ζ 80†.

χῠτή, ήν, (χέω), heaped up, γαῖα, sepulchral mound, Z 464, γ 258.

χωλεύων (χωλός), limping, Σ 411, 417, Υ 37.

χωλός, όν, αί, claudus, lame, ἕτερον πόδα, in one foot, B 217.

χώεται, εο, όμενος, οιο, etc., ipf. χώετο, aor. (ἐ)χώσατο, subj. σεται, part. σάμενος, η, (χέω), confundi, be in agitation, κῆρ, (κατὰ) θυμόν, φρεσίν, in heart, in mind; terrified, A 380; esp. irâ suffundi, be wroth, at some one, τινί; because of something, τινός; also with ὅτι, θ 238.

χωρέω (χῶρος), fut. χωρήσουσι, aor. χώρησεν, (ἐ)χώρησαν, σειεν, σαντ(α), σαντες, give place, withdraw, τινί, before some one, N 324; τινός, from some-thing, M 406, Π 726; ἀπό, N 724; τόσσον, so far, Π 592; πάλιν, back.

χώρη, ης, ῃ, ας, (χῶρος), place, Ψ 849, π 352; space, Ψ 521, θ 573, regions, countries.

χωρίς, adv., (χῆρος), separately, apart, by one's self, H 470, ι 221 sq.

χῶρος, ου, ῳ, ον, (χερ-, Ger. fassen), space, plot, Γ 315, 344, Θ 491, where in fact a space (of the ground) was visi-ble among the corpses; spot, region, N 473, Φ 262.

Ψ.

ψάμᾰθος, οιο, ου, ῳ, ον, οι, οισι(ν), fem., (ψάμμος), sand, in stream, on strand, sand hills of the sea-shore, δ 426; as simile for a countless multi-tude, B 800.

ψάμμῳ, fem., (sabulo), sand, μ 243†.

ψᾰρῶν, gen., acc. ψῆρας, masc., starlings, meadow-larks, P 755 and Π 583.

ψαύουσι, ipf. ψαῦον, 1 aor. subj. ψαύσῃ, (ψαFω), touch, graze, with gen. ἐπισσώτρου; N 132, Π 216, the hel-mets touched with their crests the crests of the others when they (their wearers) nodded.

ψεδνή (ψάω), rubbed off, thin, sparse, B 219†.

ψευδ-άγγελος (ψεῦδος), reporting lies, false messenger, O 159†.

ψευδέσσιν, τοῖς, nom. sing. ψευδής, to liars, Δ 235†.

ψεῦδος, εα, εσσι(ν), ntr., falsehood, lie, οὔτι ψ., in no respect as falsehood,

= with perfect truth, I 115; τ 203, he spoke relating many fables resembling facts.

ψεύδονται, imp. ε(ο), part. όμενα, fut. σομαι, 1 aor. σάμενοι, η, (ψεῦδος), mentiri, lie; ὅρκια, break the treaty; K 534, am I about (against my will) to speak a falsehood or the truth? do I deceive myself or— ?

ψευστήσεις, fut. from -έω, (ψεύστης), thou wilt (tho' thou know'st it not) lie, thou deceivest thyself, T 107†.

ψεῦσται, οἱ, (ψεύδομαι), frauda-tores, liars, deceivers, Ω 261†.

ψηλαφόων, part. from -άω, feel about, grope, χερσί, ι 416†.

ψῆρας, see ψαρῶν.

ψηφῖδες, αἱ, (ψῆφος), pebbles, Φ 260†.

ψιάδας, τάς, guttas, drops, Π 459†.

ψῖλόν, ήν, (ψάω), worn smooth and bare, ν 437; ἄροσις, bare grain fields; i. e. without tree or shrub; τήν (νῆα), μ 421, dismantled, without sides.

ψολόεντι, α, (ψόλος, Ger. schwül), smouldering, sulphurous, of thunderbolt, ψ 330 and ω 539.

Ψύρίη, fem., small island between Lesbos and Chios, γ 171†.

ψυχή, ῆς, ῇ, ήν, αί, έων, άς, fem., (ψύχω), anima, properly breath of life, life, X 161, I 322, γ 74, regarded as escaping, like a material substance, at the moment of death from the mouth, the word is also used in the same sense of the life of beasts, ξ 426; then in derived sense, είδωλον, the soul of the departed in the lower world, disembodied, and so without φρένες, yet retaining the outward appearance

which it had in life, described λ 207, σκιῇ είκελον (είδωλον), and yet as ψυχή, 205. ψυχή has not in Homer its later common signif. of the soul as the nobler, immortal part of man, but denotes the spirit only as opposed to the body.

ψῦχος, ψύχεος, ntr., (ψύχω), cold, coolness, κ 555†.

ψυχρῷ, όν, ή, ῇ, αί, (ψῦχος), frigidus, cold, Τ 358, Ο 171.

ψύχω, aor. part. ψύξᾶσα, (πτύω, spuo), blow, breathe; ἤκα, softly, Υ 440†.

ψωμοί, masc., (ψάω), morsels, gobbets of human flesh, ι 374†.

Ω.

ὦ, sign of voc., may stand between adj. and subst., δ 206; merged by synizesis with following vowel, ρ 375.

ὤ, interjection expressive of astonishment and of grief, heu, vae, oh! alas! ὤ μοι ἐγὼ δειλός, ε 299; ὤ πόποι, ν 209.

'Ωγυγίη, mythical island of Kalypso, α 85, ζ 172, η 244, 254, μ 448, ψ 333. The ancients identified it with Gaudes, now Gozzo, a small island near Malta.

ὧδε, adv. from ὅδε, sic, in this wise, so, thus, (1) referring to what is directly before the thoughts, Ω 398, β 28, ι 447, δ 141, Γ 300; to such a degree, γ 125, Ε 897; with imp. it may be translated come; α 182, just, this moment, cf. δ 159; referring to what has just happened or come to one's knowledge, β 185, Λ 656; to what in a wider sense of the term may be regarded as present, Β 258, ρ 587; so surely as, Σ 464; φ 196, so, right before your eyes; so, by emphasizing one alternative, negativing all others, ζ 39, Δ 308; with following explanatory clause, ὡς, Θ 523, γ 221; adeo, Κ 70, Μ 346.— (2) referring to what follows, π 117, Α 181, Ω 661, Θ 415; ὧδε δέ τις είπεσκεν, δ 769, Β 271; ὧδε γὰρ ἐξερέω, π

440, Α 212; ὧδε δέ (μοι φρονέοντι) δοάσσατο κέρδιον εἶναι, κ 153, Ν 458, Π 652, ε 474; έρξαι, ε 342; ξυνίει, ζ 289; ἐπιτέλλομαι, Λ 765.

ὤδεε, see οἰδέω.

ὠδίνων, ουσαν, part., (αὖ, δίνη?), writhe, ὀδύνῃσι, with pain; be in travail, Λ 269.

ὠδῖνᾰς, τάς, (ὠδίς, ὠδίνω), labor-pains, Λ 271†.

ὠδύσαο, ατο, see ὀδύσσομαι.

ὠθεῖ, ipf. ὤθει, iter. ὤθεσκε, aor. ἔωσε, ὦσα, ας, (εν), αν, ῃ, αιμεν, αι, iter. ὤσασκε, 1 aor. mid. ὤσατ(ο), ἀμεθ(α), αντο, αιτ(ο), αισθε, ασθαι, (Fοθίω), thrust, push, shove, ἰθὺς τάφροιο, straight toward the ditch; λ 596, was rolling the stone aloft; παρέξ, thrust off to one side = off from land; mid., Π 592, protruserunt, thrust themselves = press forward; τινά, drive before them, force back, pursue.

ὤίετο, ὠισθείς, see ὀίω.

ὦκ(α), adv. from ὠκύς, quickly, Λ 354, Α 447.

'Ωκαλέη, village in Boiotia near Haliartos, Β 501†.

'Ωκεανός, οῖο, (1) mighty stream encompassing the earth and sea (Milton's "ocean stream"); the constellations exc. the Great Bear, ε 275, sink below and emerge from its waters as they set and rise; the Pygmies dwell at its southern border; just this side of its western limit is Elysion; while with its opposite bank begins the lower world, the grove of Persephoncia, the chasm into which the waters plunge, κ 511 sqq., and here is the entrance to the dwelling of Aides.—(2) as person, the river-god *Okeanos*, husband of Tethys, father of all the streams and fountains, and indeed of all the gods, δ 568, κ 139, ᾱ 311, 201. (In the adjoining cut, from a representation of the shield of Achilleus, the outer rim, No. 5, indicates the ocean stream.)

ὤκιστος, α, see ὠκύς.
ὤκτειρε, see οἰκτείρω.
ὠκύᾰλος, ον, *swift-sailing* (ship), Ο 705, μ 182.
'Ωκύᾰλος, a Phaiakian, θ 111†.
ὠκύ-μορος, ῳ, α, ων, sup. ὤτατος, Α 505, (μόρος, mors), *quickly dying, doomed to a speedy death*, Σ 95, Α 417; *ioi, quickly slaying*, χ 75.
ὠκύ-πέτᾱ, du., (πέτομαι, -πέτης), *swift-flying*, Ν 24 and Θ 42.
ὠκύ-ποροι, ων, οισι(ν), (πόρος), *swift-sailing, fast-going*, ε 176, δ 708, Α 421.
ὠκύ-ποδες, ων, εσσι, (πούς), *swift-footed*, horses, Ε 296, σ 263.
ὠκύ-πτερος (πτερόν), *swift-winged*, Ν 62†.
ὠκύ-ρόῳ, for -ρρόῳ, (ῥέω), *swift-flowing*, Ε 598 and Η 133.
ὠκύς, ἔι, ὔν, ὕν, ἔες, ἔας, ἔα; εἶαι, ειάων, εἶγσ(ιν), ἔας; ὕ, ἔα, superl. ὠκύτατον, θ 331; ὤκιστος, ntr. α, as adv., *very quickly, at once*, χ 77, 133, (ocior), *swift, quick, fleet*, of men, animals, and

things; πόδας, fleet of foot, swift-footed; adj. in predicate = adv., *quickly*, μ 374, Ψ 880.
Ὠλενίη πέτρη, *Olenian* rock, peak of Mount Skollis, on the borders of Elis, Β 617, Λ 757.
'Ὤλενος, fem., town in Aitolia, on Mount Arakynthos, Β 639†.
ὠλεσί-καρποι (ὄλλυμι), *dropping their fruits*, of willows, which lose their fruit before ripening, κ 510†.
ὤλκα (for ἄϝλοκα, from ϝέλκω, ἔλκω), sulcus, *furrow*, Ν 707 and σ 375.
ὠμηστής, αί, ·ῃσιν, (ὠμός, ἐσθίω), *eating raw flesh* (cf. crudelis), of animals; *savage, brutal*, ἀνήρ, Ω 207.
ὠμο-γέρων (ὠμός, cf. cruda senectus), *fresh, vigorous old man*, Ψ 791†.
ὠμο-θετεῖτο, ipf., -θέτησαν, aor., (ὠμά, θεῖναι), *place* (as offering to the gods) *raw pieces of flesh upon the* μηρία, already wrapped in the caul = *consecrate flesh*, Α 461; ξ 427, mid. *have flesh consecrated*.
ὦμος, οιο, ου, ῳ, ον, ω, οιιν, οι, ων, οισ(ιν), ους, umerus, *shoulder*, Ο 474, β 3.
ὠμόν, acc. masc., ntr. ῳ̃, ά, (amarus), *raw, uncooked; opp.* ὀπταλέα, μ̔ 396; ὠμὸν βεβρώθοις, couldst eat *alive*; ὠμά, *devour raw*; γῆραι, immaturo, in *premature* old age, ο 357.
ὠμο-φάγοι, οισ(ιν), *eating raw flesh*, epith. of wild beasts, Ε 782, Η 256. (11.)
ὤμωξαν, εν, see οἰμώζω.
ὤνατο, see ὄνομαι.
ὤνησας, σε, see ὀνίνημι.
ὠνητή, verbal adj., (ὠνέομαι), *bought* = *slave*-mother, ξ 202†.
ὦνον, τόν, (ϝωνον, venum), *purchase-money*; ὀδαίων, hurry forward the delivery of the goods given in exchange for your freight, i. e. the return freight, ο 445.
ὠνοσάμην, see ὄνομαι.
ὤνο-χόει, see οἰνο-χοέω.
ὦξε, see οἴγνυμι.
ὤρεσσιν, see ὄαρ.
ὤρετο, see ὄρνυμι.
ὤρη, ῃ, ην, αι, ας, (Ger. Jahr, Eng. year), (1) *season, seasons*, Horae, Β 471, Ζ 148, ε 485; περὶ δ᾽ ἔτραπον,

turned about (to begin the new year); ἐπήλυθον, drew near, κ 469, both expressions representing the seasons under the figure of maidens in the choral dance, receding and approaching with measured step ; εἴαρος or εἰαρινή, v e r n a, *spring-time;* also used alone = *Spring,* B 468.—(2) generally, *the fitting time* (καιρός), ἐν, εἰς, in tempore, ad tempus; with gen. κοίτοιο, γάμου, etc., with inf., λ 373, φ 428, with acc. and inf., λ 330.—(3) personified, the *Hours,* door-keepers of Olympos and goddesses of the seasons, πολυγηθέες, Φ 450, E 749, Θ 393, 433.

Ὠρεί-θυια, a Nereid, Σ 48†.

ὥρια, τά, (ὥρη), *in their season,* ι 131†.

ὥριστος, from ὁ ἄριστος.

Ὠρίων, ωνος, (ὄαρ), *Orion,* the mighty and beautiful hunter, λ 310, Σ 486 ; continues the chase in the lower world, λ 572 ; beloved of Eos, ε 121 ; as constellation, Σ 488, ε 274.

ὥρορε, see ὄρνυμι.

Ὦρος, a Greek, slain by Hektor, Λ 303†.

ὦρσε, το, ὠρώρει, see ὄρνυμι.

1. ὡς, prep., with acc., *to,* ὡς τὸν ὁμοῖον, ρ 218†.

2. ὡς (old abl. of pron. ἰος, orig. ἰωτ, thence ἰως, then ὡς; in anastrophe ὧς; lengthens, by position, a preceding vowel followed by a single consonant, e. g. θεὸς ὥς, σῦες ὥς, thirty-seven examples, μ 396, δ 413, Δ 482, E 78), *as,* A. Adv. of manner : quomodo, quam, ut, *just as, as,* before single words, where a verb may be easily supplied, e. g. ὡς τὸ πάρος πέρ, θ 31, τ 340; pleonastically with ἐοικώς, Ψ 430 ; especially freq. in relat. sentence, (1) modal : e. g. ἐκέλευ(σ)εν, χ 190 ; ἂν ἐγὼ Fείπω πειθώμεθα, μ 213 ; *of what sort,* I 528; also with κέ, with opt., ψ 60 (hence the transition to B., see below).—(2) comparative : corresponding to τώς, ὡς, οὕτω, τόσσον, ξ 441; in comparisons or similes, (a) with ind. pres. and aor. ; (b) with subj. pres. and aor., I 323, E 161, X 93, ε 369, θ 523, B 475 ; so esp. ὡς ὅτε, which always (exc. Λ 325, Δ 130, O 606, 624, Π 642) precedes the principal sentence; the principal clause follg. with ὥς

thirty-one times, B 147, E 599 (τοῖοι, Δ 141); protasis begins with ὡς ὅτ' ἄν ten times, K 5, Λ 269, ε 394, χ 468 ; shortened to ὡς ὅτε = velut (see ὡς εἰ), *just like,* λ 368 ; with fut. after opt., to give assurance of the desired result; *so sure as,* ι 525 (cf. B. 3).—(3) exclamatory : *how!* π 364, ω 194.—B. Conjunction, (1) temporal : *as, when,* quom, always of facts, with indic., Ψ 871, when (while) he (Teukros) was (still) shooting.—(2) explanatory, after τόγε, γ 346, = ὅτι οὕτως, *that, because, for,* Δ 157, β 233, ρ 243.—(3) final : *that, in order that,* Λ 32, ν 402, β 816 ; the transition from the relative to the final use of ὡς is illustrated by follg. examples, cf. quâ ratione, (a) ὡς, with opt. and κέν, ψ 135, ω 582, β 53 ; and ἄν, ν 402, ο 538 ; more freq. (b) with subj., A 559 ; with imp. or inf. used as imp. in principal sentence, B 363, ρ 75 (κέν, B 385, A 32, Z 143, τ 319, τ 321, χ 117, T 151 ; with ἄν, π 169); with principal verb in subj., Z 259 (κέν, I 112, Ω 76, α 87; ἄν, δ 672); with principal verb to be supplied in opt., Θ 513; principal verb fut. indic. (κέν, β 816, 868, ε 144, α 205) ; pres., H 294 (κέν, Φ 459); pret., A 559, Ω 337 (ἄν, ω 360, π 84); expressing actual purpose with subj., Θ 182, Π 83.—(4) expressing a wish, *oh that!* with opt., Σ 107, X 286, α 47 ; with κέν, Z 281; μή, ο 359.

1. ὥς = ὡς, *as,* when it receives the accent by anastrophe, see ὡς 2.

2. ὥς (ὧς after οὐδ' and καί), adv., *thus,* καὶ ὥς, even so, nevertheless ; οὐδ' ὥς, ne sic quidem, not even so, in no wise, (1) ὥς, at beginning of sentence, always (exc. π 28, 64) in arsi, ἔφατο, φάτο, ν 54 ; φαμένη, εἰπών, φωνήσας, ὥς ἔφαθ', οἱ δ' ἄρα τοῦ μ. μ., ο 220 ; ὥς ἔφαθ', οἱ δ' ἄρα πάντες ἀκήν ἐγ., π 893 ; ὥς οἱ μὲν τοιαῦτα πρὸς ἀλλήλ. ἀγ., θ 333.— (2) correlative, ὅπως, ο 112; ὥς, talis, *such,* Δ 319, Λ 762, κ 416 ; *thus,* A 512 ; *then,* Ξ 294, T 16, Υ 424.— (3) explanatory, *so then,* Δ 157 ; resumptive, *thus as you think, this being the case,* τ 85, 300, ι 84 ; *thus for instance,* ε 121. For ὥς δ' αὔτως, ζ 166, see αὔτως.

ὡς, εἰ, ὡσεί, never separated by intervening word, *as if,* qua si, ι 314;

also with part., E 374, and without verb, *like, just as, η* 36.

ὥς περ, ὥσπερ, often separated, *just as, even as; ὡς ἔσεταί περ,* just as it shall come to pass, A 211, τ 312; ὥς περ (v. l. ὅς περ) *ἂν εἴη,* just as I would that it might come to pass.

ὥς τε, ὥστε (adv. from ὅς τε), *like as, just as,* Γ 23, 381, a 227, 308 ; also in sentences containing a comparison, with ind. or subj., B 475 ; explanatory, freq. followed by inf. of result, I 42, ρ 21; *as it were* (of girls), ζ 122.

ὠτειλῆς, ἥν, ἰων, άς, fem., (οὐτᾶν), *wound,* τ 456, Σ 351.

Ὦτος, (1) son of Poseidon and of Iphimedeia, a giant, λ 308, E 385.— (2) of Kyllene, chief of the Epeians, slain by Polydamas, O 518.

ὠτώεντα, τόν, nom. -ώεις, (ὦτα), *with ears* or *handles,* Ψ 264 and 513.

ωὑτός = ὁ αὐτός, E 396†.

ὤφελλον, ὤφελες, see ὀφείλω.

ὠχρήσαντα, part. aor. from ὠχράω, (ὠχρος), *having become pale,* λ 529†.

ὠχρος, masc., p a l l o r, *paleness,* Γ 35†.

ὤψ, only εἰς ὦπα, *in the eye, full in the face,* ἰδέσθαι ; *in face, in person,* ἔοικεν, Γ 158.

Ὤψ, Ὤπος, son of Peisenor, father of Eurykleia, a 429, β 347, υ 148.

PLATE I.

PLATE II.

PLATE III.

HOUSE OF ODYSSEUS.

(After L. Gerlach.)

A πρόθυρον.

B αὐλῆς αἴθουσα, δ 678, π 342.

C αὐλή, δ 625.

D αἴθουσα.

E E πρόδομος, ο 5, υ 1.

F μέγαρον.

G Women's apartment; overhead the ὑπερώιον.

a Treasure-chamber.

b Chamber of Odysseus and Penelope.

c Chamber of Eurykleia, β 348.

d Seats of the king and queen.

e e Post of Odysseus as beggar.

f f ξεστοὶ λίθοι.

g Ζεὺς ἑρκεῖος.

h ὀρσοθύρη.

i λαύρη.

k θόλος.

l κλῖμαξ.

m ῥῶγες.

n στόμα λαύρης, } χ 137.

o αὐλῆς καλὰ θύρετρα,

p cf. χ 459 sq.

q ρ 297.

r καλαὶ μεσόδμαι, τ 37, υ 354.

s s Wicket barriers.

t πρόθυρον, σ 10, 33, 102.

u Sleeping-apartment of Odysseus, ψ 190.

PLATE IV.

FIG. 2.—MAST-BOX.

μεσόδμη, mast-box (drawn on a larger scale), β 424, cf. τ 37.

FIG. 1.—RIGGING OF HOMERIC SHIP.

A. Mast (ἱστός).
B. Sail (ἱστίον).
C.C. Forestays (πρότονοι, β 425).
C'. Backstay (ἐπίτονος, μ 423).
D. Yard (ἐπίκριον, ε 254).

E.E. Halliards (κάλοι, ε 260; cf. β 426).
F.F. Braces (ὑπέραι, ε 260).
G.G. Sheets (πόδες, ε 260).
H. Mast-crutch (ἱστοδόκη, Α 434).

PLATE V.

PRESENT ASPECT OF THE TROJAN PLAIN.

The prevalent opinion of antiquity located Homer's Troy on the hill *Hissarlik*, about three miles south of the Hellespont. The only important dissent from this view, among the ancients, was on the part of Demetrios of Skepsis, who was followed by Strabo, and who located Ilios at Ἰλιέων κώμη, some three miles east of Hissarlik, in the valley of the Simoeis.

Toward the close of the last century, the French traveller Le Chevalier visited the Troad, and boldly declared that he had identified the site of the ancient city on the height *Ballyk*, behind the village *Bunarbaschi*. Le Chevalier's view was announced with great positiveness, and has been generally received by modern scholars, e. g., Welcker, E. Curtius, Stark, Tozer, and the geographers Spratt, Kiepert, and Field-Marshal Von Moltke. In 1864 the Austrian Consul in Syra, Von Hahn, an eager partisan of Le Chevalier's theory, undertook excavations at *Ballyk*, which were prosecuted for several months, but without success.

The results of Schliemann's recent excavations at *Hissarlik* are familiar to all, and his discoveries go far to establish the fact that upon the hill *Hissarlik* the metropolis of the Trojan Plain, in prehistoric as well as in more recent times, must have stood. Among those who have advocated the claims of this site may be mentioned Gladstone, Grote, Eckenbrecker, Keller, Christ, Steitz, Büchner, and the writer of the article *Ilium* in Smith's Dictionary of Ancient Geography.